Children's Thinking

Sixth Edition

Sara Miller McCune founded SAGE Publishing in 1965 to support the dissemination of usable knowledge and educate a global community. SAGE publishes more than 1000 journals and over 800 new books each year, spanning a wide range of subject areas. Our growing selection of library products includes archives, data, case studies and video. SAGE remains majority owned by our founder and after her lifetime will become owned by a charitable trust that secures the company's continued independence.

Los Angeles | London | New Delhi | Singapore | Washington DC | Melbourne

Children's Thinking

*Cognitive Development and
Individual Differences*

Sixth Edition

David F. Bjorklund
Florida Atlantic University, Boca Raton

Kayla B. Causey
California State University, Fullerton

Los Angeles | London | New Delhi
Singapore | Washington DC | Melbourne

FOR INFORMATION:

SAGE Publications, Inc.
2455 Teller Road
Thousand Oaks, California 91320
E-mail: order@sagepub.com

SAGE Publications Ltd.
1 Oliver's Yard
55 City Road
London, EC1Y 1SP
United Kingdom

SAGE Publications India Pvt. Ltd.
B 1/I 1 Mohan Cooperative Industrial Area
Mathura Road, New Delhi 110 044
India

SAGE Publications Asia-Pacific Pte. Ltd.
3 Church Street
#10-04 Samsung Hub
Singapore 049483

Acquisitions Editor: Lara Parra
Editorial Assistant: Zachary Valladon
eLearning Editor: Morgan Shannon
Production Editor: Tracy Buyan
Copy Editor: Mark Bast
Typesetter: Hurix Systems Pvt. Ltd.
Proofreader: Bonnie Moore
Indexer: Mary Mortensen
Cover Designer: Janet Kiesel
Marketing Manager: Katherine Hepburn

Copyright © 2018 by SAGE Publications, Inc.

All rights reserved. No part of this book may be reproduced or utilized in any form or by any means, electronic or mechanical, including photocopying, recording, or by any information storage and retrieval system, without permission in writing from the publisher.

Printed in the United States of America

Library of Congress Cataloging-in-Publication Data

Names: Bjorklund, David F., 1949– author. | Causey, Kayla B.

Title: Children's thinking : cognitive development and individual differences /David F. Bjorklund, Florida Atlantic University, Boca Raton, Florida, Kayla B. Causey, Cal State University, Fullerton.

Description: Sixth Edition. | Thousand Oaks : SAGE Publications, [2018] | Revised edition of Children's thinking, c2012. | Includes bibliographical references and index.

Identifiers: LCCN 2016040644 | ISBN 9781506334356 (pbk. : alk. paper)

Subjects: LCSH: Cognition in children. | Individual differences in children.

Classification: LCC BF723.C5 B48 2017 | DDC 155.4/13—dc23 LC record available at https://lccn.loc.gov/2016040644

This book is printed on acid-free paper.

17 18 19 20 21 10 9 8 7 6 5 4 3 2 1

CONTENTS

PREFACE

There has been both continuity and change in the 6th edition of *Children's Thinking*. Concerning continuity, we continue to see cognitive development as a dynamic field. Theories and research findings from a variety of areas combine to produce a picture of a developing child who is born prepared to make some sense of the world but whose mind is also shaped by forces in the physical and social environment. This theme, of the continuous transaction between an embodied child embedded in a social world, continues to serve as the focus of the 6th edition. Throughout this book we attempt to present cognitive development not as a series of separate accomplishments (e.g., memory, language, theory of mind, executive function) but as a process that involves the dynamic interaction between an active organism with a changing environment. As such, we strive to integrate biological (e.g., genetics, brain functioning) with sociocultural and evolutionary factors to describe and explain human cognitive development.

In addition, as in past editions, we emphasize not only the typical patterns of change in thinking observed over time (cognitive development) but also individual differences in children's thinking in infancy, childhood, and adolescence. Moreover, children use their developing cognition to solve real-world problems, and many of those problems are related to acquiring the skills necessary for success in a highly technological world.

Research and theory in cognitive development should do more than inform researchers: They should also provide insights, both for parents and teachers, in how best to deal with children. Although this new edition is in no way a "how to" book for educating children, as in previous editions, we describe research that has implications for education, making it useful for students training to be teachers as well as psychologists.

Concerning changes, there are two big ones and many smaller ones. The big changes include a new publisher, SAGE, that recognizes the importance of a book like this for the field of developmental psychology, and a new coauthor, Kayla Causey. Kayla is a lecturer in the Departments of Environmental Studies and Psychology at California State University, Fullerton. Trained as a cognitive developmentalist and well versed in the latest statistical techniques, theories, and methodologies of cognitive development, she brings a fresh perspective and lively pen to the book, especially important for a discipline that is being influenced by innovations in related fields, such as neuroscience and quantitative analyses.

Somewhat smaller changes in the book include the integration of several contemporary themes in cognitive development, including the neoconstructivist approach, the Goldilocks effect, Bayesian probabilistic reasoning, "hot" and "cold" executive functioning, perceptual narrowing, and causal representation, among others. We also expanded discussion of sociocultural perspectives in several key areas, including gender cognition, language, and the effects of media on the development of attention.

This edition also extends a trend begun in earlier editions of including more research from developmental cognitive neuroscience. There has been a "biologizing" of cognitive development in recent years, and this is most reflected in research looking at how the brains of infants and children change over time and are associated with different patterns of cognitive functioning. We firmly believe that *mind* is a state of brain, and, although knowing what's happening in the brain will not, by itself, tell us what we, as psychologists, need to know, it is an essential ingredient in understanding cognitive development. However, having a developmental theory of the brain does not obviate having a developmental theory of the mind. Our job is to develop an understanding of how children's thinking changes over time and how such changes affect children's functioning in their world. Knowing something about the biology of thinking can help us achieve this goal, although it is not the goal itself. We were careful not to make this book about developmental cognitive neuroscience but to keep the focus on cognitive development, with neuroscience research supporting, rather than replacing, the psychological perspective.

Related to this biologizing of development is an increased interest in evolutionary thinking—how selective pressures in our ancient past may influence how children develop and function today. We have been proponents of the field of evolutionary developmental psychology and believe that such a perspective has much to offer the discipline of cognitive development. This perspective is outlined in Chapter 2, "Biological Bases of Cognitive Development," and found, where appropriate, in various chapters in the book.

Several pedagogical features from the earlier editions have been retained in the 6th edition.

These include a glossary that has all the key terms at the end of the book and the *Key Terms and Concepts* and *Suggested Readings* sections at the end of each chapter. As in the 5th edition, we provide a *Scholarly Works* category and *Reading for Personal Interest* category in the *Suggested Readings* section, the latter including books, articles, and websites suitable for an educated lay audience. Each suggested reading is followed by a brief paragraph explaining why a particular entry is worth perusing.

Other pedagogical features are new to the 6th edition. Long end-of-chapter summaries were replaced with more concise *Section Reviews* following each major section within the chapter. The 6th edition also features *Ask Yourself . . .* questions, consecutively numbered after each *Section Review*, to engage students in reflection and critical thinking. Instructors may find it helpful to assign these questions to students as a "reading check." Boxes were omitted, with most of the information integrated within the text. Feedback we received from students and some instructors suggested that boxed material was the most likely to be skipped material in a chapter. Although textbook writers and instructors often see boxes as an opportunity to include some interesting information related to a topic, students are more apt to see them as an opportunity to reduce their reading with little fear of missing "anything important." We decided that if it's important enough to put in the book, it's important enough to be integrated in the text.

As in previous editions, the 6th edition provides up-to-date research and theory on cognitive development appropriate for graduate and upper-level undergraduate students. Although the total number of references cited in the book remains about the same as in the previous edition, approximately 30% of all references are new to the 6th edition. We aimed to make the book reader-friendly and accessible throughout, reducing discussion of some topics while adding topics that may be of greater interest to a broader range of students. Each chapter starts with a vignette illustrating some concept or phenomenon discussed in the chapter, easing students into the chapter.

The general organization of the book remains unchanged from the 5th edition—13 chapters, all with the same titles as found in the previous edition. However, continuity at the chapter level belies some substantial changes in the content of many chapters. Several chapters have been reorganized, and, throughout each chapter, recent groundbreaking research is summarized to demonstrate and support important concepts and theories in the field. The following provides specific chapter-by-chapter changes to the 6th edition.

CHAPTER-BY-CHAPTER EXAMINATION OF CHANGES BETWEEN 5TH AND 6TH EDITIONS

All chapters in the 6th edition have been substantially revised. There are many new tables and figures, sometimes replacing older research discussed in previous editions, sometimes presenting new phenomena. Here we discuss what we see as major organizational changes (and stabilities) between the 5th and 6th editions of *Children's Thinking*.

Chapter 1. Introduction to Cognitive Development

Chapter 1 has been streamlined to provide a more reader-friendly introduction to the field of cognitive development. We retained all major sections from the previous edition (*Basic Concepts of Cognitive Development, Six Truths of Cognitive Development*, and *Goals of Cognitive Developmentalists*) but reduced coverage of some topics that are discussed in more detail elsewhere in the book (for example, *What Does It Mean to Say Something Is Innate?* and *Dynamic Systems Approaches to Development*). This chapter now provides what we believe is a comprehensible introduction to the major concepts and issues of cognitive development, giving students the background to understand what is to come, without bogging them down in details that will make more sense to them as they read further in the book.

Chapter 2. Biological Bases of Cognitive Development

The organization of this chapter remains essentially the same between the 5th and 6th editions. The opening section *Evolution and Cognitive Development* discusses evolutionary theory and features an expanded section on evolutionary developmental psychology, including some of the material omitted from Chapter 1 of the previous edition (e.g., a discussion of the various types of constraints on development) and a new section, *Evolved Probabilistic Cognitive Mechanisms*. The remaining major sections—*Models of Gene-Environment Interaction, Development of the Brain*, and *Developmental Biology and Cognitive Development*—are the same in both editions, although they have been substantially updated. For example, we modified the discussion of recovery of function from brain damage to discuss the early plasticity versus early vulnerability perspectives, included a section on interactive specialization models of brain development, and eliminated sections on neural Darwinism and the evolution of the human brain.

Chapter 3. Social Construction of Mind: Sociocultural Perspectives on Cognitive Development

We made both substantial additions to and deletions from this chapter. As in the previous edition, we begin the chapter with an overview of the sociocultural perspective on cognitive development, giving special attention to Vygotsky's theory and related research. We replaced the two previous major chapter headings, *Implications for Education* and *Sociocultural Theory of Cognitive Development*, with two new ones: *Cognitive Artifacts That Support and Extend Thinking: Tools of Intellectual Adaptation* and *Social Origins of Early Cognitive Competencies*. These changes reflect mostly a reorganization of information, intended to provide an easier-to-follow organization, as well as the inclusion of new topics (for example, WEIRD—Western, educated, industrialized, rich, and democratic—societies; children as digital natives). The chapter is slightly shorter than in the 5th edition, in part because issues related to the sociocultural perspective of cognitive development are found increasingly in other chapters of the 6th edition.

Chapter 4. Infant Perception and Cognition

This chapter maintains much of the organization of the previous edition, providing an introduction to methods used to study infant cognition as well as a review of the literature on perceptual and cognitive abilities during infancy. We discuss the development of many of these capacities through childhood in later chapters, and so this chapter remains focused on those abilities that are present at birth and/or come online within the first year of life. We added a section on perceptual

narrowing, incorporated discussions of Bayesian learning and the neoconstructivist (or rational constructivist) approach, and omitted the former sections *Intersensory Redundancy Hypothesis* and *Category Learning*, making reference to this latter topic in the section *Habituation/Dishabituation Paradigm*.

Chapter 5. Thinking in Symbols: Development of Representation

This chapter is longer in the 6th edition, reflecting the continued interest in the important topic of the development of representation among developmental scientists. However, the basic organization of the chapter remains unchanged from the 5th edition (*Learning to Use Symbols, Piaget's Theory, Everyday Expressions of the Symbolic Function, Fuzzy-Trace Theory*, and *The Symbolic Species*), with the exception of the addition of a new major section, *Causal Representation*. We also added or expanded coverage of some hot topics in the development of representation, including the role of symbolic play in cognitive development and young children's difficulty distinguishing real objects from their symbolic representation, as reflected by their "scale errors," their ability to hold multiple representations in mind, and by the ease with which imaginary objects or events can be brought to mind.

Chapter 6. Development of Folk Knowledge

The general organization of Chapter 6 remains the same as the 5th edition. We begin with an overview of the *theory theory* approach to cognitive development, followed by major sections devoted to folk psychology, folk biology, and folk physics. We incorporated the neoconstructivist perspective introduced earlier in the text and included description of some relevant findings in brain imaging. We largely omitted the discussion on children's intuitive theories of the afterlife in the folk psychology section but added research describing children's theories about *prelife*, as well as a brief discussion of second-order theory of mind. We added a section on tool innovation under the folk physics section, as well as information regarding the role of executive function in children's understanding of time. We updated research on cross-cultural comparisons in multiple sections.

Chapter 7. Learning to Think on Their Own: Executive Function, Strategies, and Problem Solving

The major headings for Chapter 7 are the same in the 6th edition as in the 5th edition: *Assumptions of Information-Processing Approaches*, *Development of Basic-Level Processes: Executive Function*, *Development of Strategies*, and *Learning to Solve Problems*. We expanded coverage of executive function, reflecting the increasing importance of this area of research in cognitive development, and added two subsections: *Executive Function, Self-Control, and "Hot" EF* and *Executive Functioning and Brain Development*.

Chapter 8. Memory Development

Most of the topics examined in this chapter in the 5th edition are also examined in the current edition, as reflected by the same major headings in the two editions: *Representation of Knowledge*, *Memory Development in Infancy*, *Infantile Amnesia*, *Implicit Memory*, *Development of*

Event Memory, *Children as Eyewitnesses*, and *Remembering to Remember*. While expanding coverage of research on these central topics—including developmental neuroscience studies—we omitted the section *Consistency and Stability of Memory*, believing it to be a bit esoteric for most readers, and expanded discussion of the development of prospective memory in the *Remembering to Remember* section.

Chapter 9. Language Development

The organization of Chapter 9 is the same in the 6th edition as in the 5th edition: *What Is Language?*, *Describing Children's Language Development*, *Some Theoretical Perspectives of Language Development*, *Bilingualism and Second-Language Learning*, *Sex Differences in Language Acquisition*, and *Language and Thought*, with each major section updated to reflect the most current thinking in the field. One major deletion is the previous discussion on language learning in chimpanzees (*Is Language Unique to Humans? Can Apes "Talk"?*). Although especially interesting for many people, this research topic is only tangentially related to children's language development. A major addition to this edition is a new subsection titled *Effects of Socioeconomic Status on Language Development*, focusing especially on the 30-million-word gap between the number of words children from high-income versus low-income families hear by their 3rd birthdays and its consequences.

Chapter 10. Social Cognition

Most of the same topics covered in this chapter in the 6th edition were also covered in the 5th edition (social learning, social cognitive theory, social information processing, the development of a concept of self, and cognitive bases of gender identity), although the organization has changed a bit. We incorporated discussion of most aspects of Bandura's social cognitive theory under the *Social Learning* main heading, with self-efficacy now discussed in the section *Development of a Concept of Self*. The subsection *Age Differences in Social Learning* was substantially expanded, including new research on overimitation. We deleted the former section *Social Learning in Chimpanzees*, although some research discussed in this former section, as well as more recent research, was integrated in other subsections in the chapter. We deleted the section *Gender Knowledge and Sex-Typed Behavior: Possible Predispositions*, replacing it with the section *Gender Cognition in Transgender Children*.

Chapter 11. Schooling and Cognitive Development

The same general topics are covered in the 6th as in the 5th edition of this chapter, but the organization has changed some, with some substantial additions to and deletions from the chapter. With respect to the major section *Development of Reading Skills*, we merged the former section *Emergent Literacy* with *Overview of Learning to Read*, adding a subsection titled *Stages of Learning to Read*. We reorganized the section *Cognitive Development and Reading*, including new subsections titled *Letter Knowledge* and *Rapid Automatized Naming (RAN)*, along with subsections titled *Phonemic Awareness*, *Working Memory*, and *Phonological Recoding*. We deleted the former section *How to Teach Children to Read*. We also reorganized the major section *Children's Number and Arithmetic Concepts*. The first major subsection is new, presenting Siegler and

Lortie-Forgues's integrative theory of numerical development, followed by sections titled *Development of Conceptual and Procedural Mathematical Knowledge* and *Variations in Developing Mathematical Proficiency: Math Disabilities, Cultural Differences, and Sex Differences*. We deleted the former section *What Do Mathematically Gifted Females Do?* Coverage in the major section *Schooling and Cognitive Development* is much as it was in the 5th edition, although we moved the subsection *Costs and Benefits of Academic Preschools* to the section *Evolutionary Educational Psychology*. This latter section was modified quite a bit, including an expanded section contrasting discovery learning and direct instruction and the addition of a subsection titled *"Educational" DVDs and Videos for Infants*, in which we discuss the video-deficit effect reported in young children, all framed by evolutionary educational theory.

Chapter 12. Approaches to the Study of Intelligence

We cover most of the same topics in the 6th edition as in the 5th edition: *Psychometric Approach to the Study of Intelligence*, *Information-Processing Approaches to the Study of Intelligence*, *Sternberg's Theory of Successful Intelligence*, and *Gardner's Theory of Multiple Intelligences*. We made a number of minor deletions and a comparable number of additions, mostly updating research findings.

Chapter 13. Origins, Modification, and Stability of Intellectual Differences

We cover the same major topics in this chapter in the 6th edition as we did in the 5th edition:

Transactional Approach to the Study of Intelligence, *Behavioral Genetics and the Heritability of Intelligence*, *Experience and Intelligence*, and *Stability of Intelligence*, with most additions expanding important topics but also with some significant deletions. The deletions include the discussion of prenatal factors influencing estimates of heritability, the section *How Seriously Should We Take Heritability Studies of IQ?*, and the discussion of the Becker and Gersten (1982) research on the results of Project Follow Through.

ACKNOWLEDGMENTS

Anyone who writes a book such as this does so with much help from many people. David Bjorklund would like to express his greatest gratitude to his wife, Barbara, who provided constructive criticism on many chapters, while working on a textbook of her own—all in addition to being a supportive and understanding spouse. Kayla Causey thanks her husband, Aaron Goetz, for encouraging her to pursue this textbook. Despite his own substantial professional obligations, he always finds time to be an enthusiastic sounding board and capable parent to their son, Simon, providing her the time (and quiet) needed to write. Kayla would also like to acknowledge Simon for the anecdotes he provides and the theoretical questions he poses, just by being himself. He's an excellent pilot subject too. There is perhaps no greater joy to a cognitive developmentalist than observing what she already knows (and to a larger extent, what she's yet to understand) in the behavior of her own child.

We would like to thank our editor, Lara Parra, for her willingness to take on this project, as well as the many other specialty editors and support people at SAGE for making this book possible. We want to thank our students and colleagues for their many discussions with us over the years on issues central to this book, especially Carlos Hernández Blasi, Marc Lindberg, Wolfgang Schneider, Patrick Douglas Sellers II, Karin Machluf, and Martha Hubertz. Finally, we would like to thank the conscientious professional reviewers for their consistently constructive comments:

Cristina Atance, University of Ottawa

Vivian M. Ciaramitaro, University of Massachusetts Boston

Renee A. Countryman, Austin College

Maya M. Khanna, Creighton University

James R. May, Oklahoma State University

Elizabeth P. Pungello, University of North Carolina at Chapel Hill

Roman Taraban, Texas Tech University

Monica Tsethlikai, Arizona State University

One of the benefits of writing a textbook is how much you learn in the process. We hope that this book conveys the excitement we felt in discovering some of these new findings in the field of cognitive development. The book is not just about "what's new," however, but about the field as a whole, including classic studies from earlier decades. Although we have often focused on the new, we have attempted not to forget the tried and true research that still informs us about the nature of children's thinking today. And we have tried to make connections among different levels of analysis—macroprocesses and microprocesses, biology and environment, cognitive development and individual differences—to provide a synthesis of the field of cognitive development. And we enjoyed (almost) every minute while doing it.

David F. Bjorklund
Jupiter, Florida

Kayla B. Causey
Perris, California

1 INTRODUCTION TO COGNITIVE DEVELOPMENT

No one can remember what 4-year-old Jason did to get his father so upset, but whatever it was, his father wanted no more of it.

"Jason, I want you to go over to that corner and just *think* about this for a while," his father yelled.

Instead of following his father's orders, Jason stood where he was, not defiantly, but with a confused look and quivering lips, as if he were trying to say something but was afraid to.

"What's the matter now?" his father asked, his irritation showing.

"But Daddy," Jason said, "I don't know *how* to think."

Jason did know how to think, of course. He just didn't know that he did. In fact, Jason had been "thinking" all his life, although in a very different way when he was an infant, and his current thinking would not be anything like the mental gymnastics he'd be capable of in just a few years.

Intelligence is our species' most important tool for survival. Evolution has provided other animals with greater speed, coats of fur, camouflage, or antlers to help them adapt to challenging and often changing environments. Human evolution has been different. It has provided us with powers of discovery and invention by which we change the environment or develop techniques for coping with environments we cannot change. Although we are not the only thinkers in the animal kingdom, no other species has our powers of intellect. How we think and the technological and cultural innovations afforded by our intellect separate us from all other animals.

This remarkable intelligence does not arise fully formed in the infant, however. We require substantial experience to master the cognitive feats that typify adult thinking, and we spend the better part of 2 decades developing an adult nervous system. Little in the way of complex thought patterns is built into the human brain, ready to go at birth, although biology obviously predisposes us to develop the ability for complex thought. Our mental prowess develops gradually over childhood, changing in quality as it does.

In this first chapter, we introduce the topic of *cognitive development*—how thinking changes over time. In addition to describing developmental differences in cognition, scientists who study children's thinking are also concerned with the mechanisms that underlie cognition and its development. How do biological (genetic) factors interact with experiences in the physical and social world to yield a particular pattern of development? How do children of different ages represent their world? Does a 3-year-old understand the world in much the same way as a 10-year-old, or are these children qualitatively different thinkers? Once a pattern of intellectual competence is established, does it remain stable over time? Will the bright preschooler become the gifted teenager, or is it pointless to make predictions about adult intelligence from our observations of children? These and other issues are introduced in this chapter, but they are not answered until later in the book. Before delving too deeply into these issues, however, we need to define some basic terms (see Table 1.1). These definitions are followed by a look at some issues that define the field of cognitive development and have been the focus of controversy during the last century.

TABLE 1.1   **Basic concepts in cognitive development.**

Cognition

The processes or faculties by which knowledge is acquired and manipulated. Cognition is usually thought of as being mental. That is, cognition is a reflection of a mind. It is not directly observable but must be inferred.

Development

Changes in structure or function over time. Structure refers to some substrate of the organism, such as nervous tissue, muscle, or limbs, or—in cognitive psychology—the mental knowledge that underlies intelligence. Function denotes actions related to a structure and can include actions external to the structure being studied, such as neurochemical or hormonal secretions and other exogenous factors that can best be described as "experience"— that is, external sources of stimulation. Development is characteristic of the species and has its basis in biology. Its general course, therefore, is relatively predictable. Development progresses as a result of a bidirectional, or reciprocal, relationship between structure and function and can be expressed as structure function.

Developmental function

The species-typical form that cognition takes over time.

Individual differences

Differences in patterns of intellectual aptitudes among people of a given age.

Source: © Cengage Learning.

BASIC CONCEPTS IN COGNITIVE DEVELOPMENT

Cognition

Cognition refers to the processes or faculties by which knowledge is acquired and manipulated. Cognition is usually thought of as being mental. That is, cognition is a reflection of a mind. It is not directly observable. We cannot see the process whereby an 8-month-old discovers that a Mickey Mouse doll continues to exist even though it is hidden under a blanket out of her sight, nor can we directly assess the steps a 7-year-old takes to compute the answer to the problem $15 - 9 = ?$. Although we cannot see or directly measure what underlies children's performance on these and other tasks, we can infer what is going on in their heads by assessing certain aspects of their behavior. That is, cognition is never measured directly. It is inferred from the behaviors we can observe.

What psychologists can observe and quantify are things such as the number of words children remember from a list of 20, the number of seconds it takes to identify well-known pictures or words, or the amount of time a 6-month-old spends looking at a picture of a familiar face relative to that of an unfamiliar one. For the most part, cognitive developmental psychologists are not really interested in these overt, countable behaviors; what they *are* interested in are the processes or skills that underlie them. What mental operations does a 6-year-old engage in that are different from those performed by a 4-year-old or an 8-year-old? How does speed in identifying words reflect how information is stored in the minds of children of different ages? What kind of mental picture has the infant formed of the familiar face of his mother that allows him to tell her face apart from all other faces? How

are such mental pictures created? How are they modified?

This is not to say that cognitive psychologists are unconcerned with socially important phenomena, such as reading, mathematics, or communicating effectively; many are, and they have developed research programs aimed at improving these and other intellectual skills so critical for children's success in a high-tech society. But, for the most part, the behaviors themselves are seen as secondary. What is important and what needs to be understood are the mechanisms that underlie performance. By discovering the mental factors that govern intelligent behavior, we can better understand behavior and its development, which in turn can help us better understand children and foster their development.

Cognition includes not only our conscious and deliberate attempts at solving problems but also the unconscious and nondeliberate processes involved in routine daily tasks. We are not aware of the mental activity that occurs when we recognize a familiar tune on the radio or even when we read the back of a cereal box. Yet much in the way of cognitive processing is happening during these tasks. For most of us, reading has become nearly automatic. We can't drive by a billboard without reading it. It is something we just do without giving it any "thought." But the processes involved in reading are complex, even in the well-practiced adult.

Cognition involves mental activity of all types, including activity geared toward acquiring, understanding, and modifying information. Cognition includes such activities as developing a plan for solving a problem, executing that plan, evaluating the success of the plan, and making modifications as needed. These can be thought of as higher-order processes of cognition, which are often available to consciousness (that is, we are aware that we're doing them). Cognition also involves the initial detection, perception, and encoding of a sensory stimulus (that is, deciding how to define a physical stimulus so it can be thought about) and the classification of what kind of thing it is ("Is this a letter, a word, a picture of something familiar?"). These can be thought of as basic processes of cognition, which occur outside of consciousness (we experience the product but are generally unaware of the process).

Cognition, then, reflects knowledge and what one does with it, and the main point of this book is that cognition develops.

Development

Change Over Time

At its most basic, **development** (or **ontogeny**) refers to changes in structure or function over time within an individual. **Structure** refers to some substrate of the organism, such as nervous tissue, muscle, or limbs, or—in cognitive psychology—the mental knowledge that underlies intelligence. When speaking of cognitive development, we use *structure* to mean some hypothetical mental construct, faculty, or ability that frames knowledge and changes with age. For example, children's knowledge of terms such as *dog*, *lion*, and *zebra* could be construed as existing in some sort of mental structure (think of it as a mental dictionary), with the meanings of these words changing over time. Or we could hypothesize some form of mental organization that permits children to place objects in serial arrays according to height, shortest to tallest.

In contrast to structure, **function** denotes actions related to a structure. These include actions external to the structure being studied, such as neurochemical or hormonal secretions, and other factors external to the individual that can best be described as "experience"—that is, external sources of stimulation. Function can also be internal to the structure itself—for example, the exercise of a muscle, the firing of a nerve cell, or the activation of a cognitive process, such as retrieving from memory the name of your first-grade teacher or computing the answer to the problem $26 + 17 = ?$. With respect to cognitive development, function refers to some action by the child, such as retrieving the definition of a word from memory, making comparisons between two stimuli, or adding two numbers to arrive at a third.

Development is characteristic of the species and has its basis in biology. Its general course, therefore, is relatively predictable. By viewing development as a biological concept that is generally predictable across all members of the species, we do not mean to imply that experience and culture do not also play a role in development. During the last several decades, developmental psychologists have become increasingly aware that a child's development cannot be described or understood outside of the context in which it occurs, and we address this issue later in this and other chapters, especially Chapter 3.

Structure, Function, and Development

Development is usually conceived as a bidirectional, or reciprocal, relationship between structure and function, in which the activity of the structure itself and stimulation from the environment can contribute to changes in the structure, which in turn contribute to changes in how that structure operates. Function does more than just maintain a structure (that is, prevent it from wasting away); function is necessary for proper development to occur. Function is limited, of course, to the actions that structures are capable of performing. This bidirectional relationship between structure and function can be expressed as structure $\leftrightarrow$ function.

The **bidirectionality of structure and function** (or **structure ↔ function**) can perhaps be most easily illustrated with work in embryology. Chick embryos, for example, display spontaneous movement before muscle and skeletal development is complete. Such movement obviously stems from the maturation of the underlying structures—in this case, bones, muscle, and nervous tissue. When embryonic chicks are given a drug to temporarily paralyze them for as little as 1 to 2 days, deformations of the joints of the legs, toes, and neck develop, which in turn affect the subsequent movement of the limbs (Drachman & Coulombre, 1962). The spontaneous activity of moving the legs provides critical feedback to the genes, which in normal circumstances leads to a properly developed skeleton (Müller, 2003). In other words, the spontaneous activity (function) of the skeletal structures is necessary for the proper development and functioning of the joints (structure). Development proceeds as a result of the interaction of genes with events and agents external to the genes, including functioning of the body itself, all in feedback loops that, when all goes right, produces a species-typical body.

Let us provide an example of the bidirectional relationship between structure and function at the behavioral level. Individual differences in activity level are found in newborns and are believed to be biologically based (Phillips, King, & DuBois, 1978). A highly active toddler will make it difficult for her parents to confine her to a playpen, resulting in a child who has a greater number of experiences outside of her playpen than a less-active child has. These experiences will presumably affect the child's developing intellect (structure), which in turn will affect that child's actions (function). Thus, inherent characteristics of the child (biological structures) influence her behavior, the experiences

she has, and the reactions of others to her—all of which influence the development of the child's underlying cognitive/behavioral structures, and so on.

The *functioning* of mental structures promotes changes in the structures themselves. This view is most clearly reflected in the work of Swiss psychologist Jean Piaget. He believed that the activity of the child (or of the child's cognitive structures) is a necessary condition for development to occur. That is, for structures to change, they must be active. The structure's contact with the external world is responsible, to a large extent, for its development. Such a viewpoint makes children important contributors to their own development. Intellectual growth is the result of an active interaction between acting and thinking children and their world, not simply the environment shaping children's intellect or genes dictating a particular level of cognitive ability. (More is said of Piaget's theory throughout this book, especially in Chapter 5.)

We think it is fair to say that all developmental psychologists agree there is a reciprocal, bidirectional influence between structures (be they physical, such as neurons, or abstract, such as cognitive structures) and the activity of those structures (that is, the child's behavior). There is still much room for debate concerning *how* various subsystems of the child (neuronal, behavioral, social) interact to produce development, but developmental psychologists agree that development must be viewed as a two-way street. Development is *not* simply the result of the unfolding of genetic sequences unperturbed by variations in environment (structure function), nor is it the product of "experience" on an infinitely pliable child (function structure). The concept of the bidirectionality of structure and function is central to developmental psychology and is a theme throughout this book. A more in-depth discussion of bidirectional models of development, along with more examples, is provided later in this chapter and in Chapter 2 during a discussion of the *developmental systems approach*.

Developmental Function and Individual Differences

We examine two aspects of cognitive development in this book: developmental function, or cognitive development, and individual differences. In the present context, developmental function refers to the form that cognition takes over time—to age-related differences in thinking. What are the mental abilities of infants? What is a 2-year-old's understanding of numbers, words, and family relations? What about that of a 4- or 6-year-old? How do school-age children and adolescents conceptualize cause and effect? How do they evaluate the relative worth of two products in the grocery store? People concerned with developmental function are usually interested in universals—what is generally true about the course and causes of development for all members of the species. Assessments of developmental function, then, are typically based on averages, with individual variations among children being seen as irrelevant.

We all know that at some level, however, this variation *is* important. Our impressive intellectual skills are not uniform among members of the species. Some people at every age make decisions more quickly, perceive relations among events more keenly, or think more deeply than others. How can these differences best be described and conceptualized? What is the nature of these differences? Once differences have been established, to what extent can they be modified? Will differences observed in infancy and early childhood remain stable, or are some intellectual

differences limited to a particular time during development?

Substantial variability in cognitive functioning also occurs *within* any given child. A particular 4-year-old will often show a wide range of behaviors on very similar tasks, depending on the context that child is in. Increasingly, developmental psychologists have come to realize the significance of individual differences and variability in cognitive performance among and within people of a given age and to see these variations as providing interesting and important information about developmental outcomes.

Individual differences have developmental histories, making the relationship between developmental function and individual differences a dynamic one. That is, individual differences do not simply constitute genetic or "innate" characteristics of a child. They emerge as children develop, often showing different manifestations at different times in development. Several chapters in this book are devoted exclusively to examining individual differences. In other chapters, individual differences in intellectual abilities are discussed in conjunction with the developmental function of those same abilities.

Adaptive Nature of Cognitive Immaturity

We usually think of development as something progressive—going from simple to more complex structures or behaviors, with children getting "better" or more "complete" over time. This is a wholly reasonable point of view, but such a perspective can cause us to interpret early or immature forms of cognition as merely less effective and incomplete versions of the adult model. Although this might generally be true, it is not always the case. Early or immature forms of development can serve some function of their own, adapting the infant or young child to his or her particular environment (Oppenheim, 1981). For example, young infants' relatively poor perceptual abilities protect their nervous systems from sensory overload (Turkewitz & Kenny, 1982); preschool children's tendencies to overestimate their physical and cognitive skills causes them to persist (and, thus, to improve) at difficult tasks (Shin, Bjorklund, & Beck, 2007); and infants' slow information processing seems to prevent them from establishing intellectual habits early in life that would be detrimental later on, when their life conditions are considerably different (Bjorklund & Green, 1992). The point we want to make here is that infants' and young children's cognitive and perceptual abilities might, in fact, be well suited for their particular time in life rather than incomplete versions of the more sophisticated abilities they will one day possess (Bjorklund, 1997b, 2007b; Bjorklund, Periss, & Causey, 2009). In other words, what adults often consider to be immature and ineffective styles of thought might sometimes have an adaptive value for the young child at that particular point in development and should not be viewed solely as "deficiencies."

Consider the case of learning. Learning is good, of course, but is early learning always beneficial? Might providing an infant with too much stimulation or learning tasks too soon in development have a negative effect? There is little research on this issue. In one study, Harry Harlow (1959) began giving infant monkeys training on a discrimination-learning task at different ages, ranging from 60 to 366 days. For example, monkeys were to choose which of several stimuli that varied in several dimensions (size, shape, color, and so on) was associated with a reward. Beginning at 120 days of age, monkeys were given a more complicated learning task. Monkeys' performance on these more complicated problems is shown in Figure 1.1 as a function of

the age at which they began training. Chance performance for these problems was 50%. As can be seen, monkeys who began training early in life (at 60 and 90 days) seldom solved more than 60% of the problems and soon fell behind the monkeys who began training later (at 120 and 150 days of age). That is, despite having more experience with the problems, the early trained monkeys performed more poorly than the later-trained monkeys. Harlow (1959) concluded, "There is a tendency to think of learning or training as intrinsically good and necessarily valuable to the organism. It is entirely possible, however, that training can be either helpful or harmful, depending upon the nature of the training and the organism's stage of development" (p. 472).

Might this relate to our species as well? In one of the few such experiments with humans, Hanus Papousek (1977) conditioned infants to turn their heads to a buzzer or a bell. Training

FIGURE I.1 **Discrimination learning set performance.** Discrimination learning set performance for monkeys as a function of age at which testing was begun.

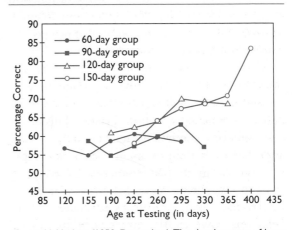

Source: H. Harlow (1959, December). The development of learning in the Rhesus monkey. *American Scientist*, 459–479. Reprinted with permission.

began either at birth or at 31 or 44 days of age. Infants who began training at birth took many more trials (814) and days (128) before they learned the task than did infants who began later (278 and 224 trials and 71 and 72 days for the 31- and 44-day-old infants, respectively), causing Papousek to write that "beginning too early with difficult learning tasks, at a time when the organism is not able to master them, results in prolongation of the learning process."

Infants need stimulation—interesting objects and, especially, responsive people to speak to and interact with. However, if stimulation is excessive, then it can distract infants and young children from other tasks and may replace activities, such as social interaction, that are vital to their development. We are in no way advocating a "hands-off" policy on educating infants and young children. We are advocating a recognition that infants' limited cognitive abilities may afford them some benefits. We have more to say about "educating" infants in Chapter 11 where we discuss the pros and cons of educational DVDs and videos for infants.

Children's immature cognition can be seen as having an integrity and, possibly, a function of its own rather than being seen only as something that must be overcome. Such a perspective can have important consequences not only for how we view development but also for education and remediation. Expecting children who are developmentally delayed or have learning deficits to master "age-appropriate" skills might be counterproductive, even if possible. Young and delayed children's immature cognition might suit them for mastering certain skills. Attempting to "educate" them beyond their present cognitive abilities could result in advanced surface behavior; however, the general effectiveness of that behavior might be minimally, or even detrimentally, influenced despite considerable effort expended (Bjorklund & Schwartz, 1996; J. F. Goodman, 1992).

Section Review

Cognitive development involves changes in children's knowledge and thinking over time.

Cognition

- *Cognition* refers to the processes or faculties by which knowledge is acquired and manipulated.
- Cognition reflects knowledge and what one does with it, and cognition develops.

Development

- *Development* (or *ontogeny*) refers to changes in structure or function over time within an individual.
- *Structure* refers to some substrate of the organism, such as nervous tissue, muscle, or limbs, or—in cognitive psychology—the mental knowledge that underlies intelligence.
- *Function* denotes actions related to a structure, including actions external to the structure being studied, such as neurochemical or hormonal secretions, and other factors external to the individual that can best be described as "experience."
- The *bidirectionality of structure and function* (or structure ↔ function) refers to the bidirectional, or reciprocal, relationship between structure and function, in which the activity of the structure itself and stimulation from the environment can contribute to changes in the structure, which in turn contribute to changes in how that structure operates.
- *Developmental function* refers to the form that cognition takes over time (that is, to age-related differences in thinking).
- Individual differences in cognitive function exist both between children and within the same child for different tasks.

- Some aspects of infants' and young children's immature cognition may be adaptive in their own right and not viewed as handicaps that must be overcome.

Ask Yourself . . .

1. What is cognition? What does it mean to study the *developmental function* of cognition?
2. What is the bidirectional relationship between structure and function during development?
3. What is meant by individual differences in cognitive development?
4. What are some examples of cognitive immaturity that are adaptive?

SIX TRUTHS OF COGNITIVE DEVELOPMENT

The field of cognitive development encompasses a broad range of topics. Moreover, cognitive developmentalists can be a contentious lot, disagreeing on the best way to conceptualize how thought changes from infancy to adulthood. Nonetheless, we believe there are some truths that typify the study of cognitive development—actually generalizations that we think most developmentalists believe are true about cognitive development and around which controversy and differences of opinion swirl. In the following sections, we examine six truths:

1. Cognitive development proceeds as a result of the dynamic and reciprocal transaction of internal and external factors;
2. Cognitive development is constructed within a social context;

3. Cognitive development involves both stability and plasticity over time;
4. Cognitive development involves changes in the way information is represented;
5. Children develop increasing intentional control over their behavior and cognition; and
6. Cognitive development involves changes in both domain-general and domain-specific abilities.

Cognitive Development Proceeds as a Result of the Dynamic and Reciprocal Transaction of Internal and External Factors

This truth follows from the way we define development as the result of the bidirectional relationship between structure and function over time. In essence, this is modern developmental science's answer to the classic nature/nurture issue, which has been the granddaddy of controversies for developmental psychology over its history. How do we explain how biological factors, in particular genetics, interact with environmental factors, especially learning and the broader effects of culture, to produce human beings? At the extremes are two philosophical camps. Proponents of nativism hold, essentially, that human intellectual abilities are innate. The opposing philosophical position is empiricism, which holds that nature provides only species-general learning mechanisms, with cognition arising as a result of experience. As stated, each of these two extreme positions is clearly wrong. In fact, as far as developmental psychologists are concerned, there is no nature/nurture dichotomy. Biological factors are inseparable from experiential factors, with the two continuously interacting. This makes it impossible to identify any purely biological or experiential effects. It is often convenient, however, to speak of biological and experiential factors, and when psychologists do, there is always the implicit assumption of the bidirectional interaction of these factors, as discussed earlier in this chapter (that is, structure ↔ function).

At one level, it is trivial to state that biology and experience interact. There is really no other alternative. It's *how* they interact to yield a particular pattern of development that is significant. For example, one currently popular view holds that children's genetic constitutions influence how they experience the environment. A sickly and lethargic child seeks and receives less attention from others than a more active, healthy child does, resulting in slower or less advanced levels of cognitive development. A child who processes language easily might be more apt to take advantage of the reading material that surrounds him than will a child whose inherent talents lie in other areas, such as the ability to comprehend spatial relations. Environment is thus seen as very important from this perspective, but one's biology influences which environments are most likely to be experienced and, possibly, how those experiences will be interpreted. These issues are discussed in greater detail in the chapters devoted to individual differences, particularly Chapter 13, in which the heritability of intelligence and the role of experience in individual differences in intelligence is explored.

What Does It Mean to Say Something Is Innate?

In defining nativism we used the term *innate*. This term can be contentious, and many developmental psychologists would prefer not to see it used at all. The primary reason for many developmental psychologists' discomfort with the concept of innateness is that this term implies **genetic determinism**—the idea that one's genes *determine* one's behavior—which is the antithesis of a truly developmental (that is, bidirectional) perspective. If, in contrast, by innate we simply mean based in genetics, then surely just about every human behavior can be deemed innate at some level, and the term is meaningless. If, however, we mean that a specific type of behavior or knowledge (of grammar, for example) is determined by genetics, with little or no input needed from the environment, then the term has a more specific meaning, but again, it is still not very useful, for, as we'll see more clearly in our discussions in Chapter 2, all genetic effects are mediated by environment, broadly defined.

Some people equate innateness with instinct. The problem here is that instinct is not easily defined. This is made clear by Patrick Bateson (2002), who wrote:

> Apart from its colloquial uses, the term instinct has at least nine scientific meanings: present at birth (or at a particular stage of development), not learned, developed before it can be used, unchanged once developed, shared by all members of the species (or at least of the same sex and age), organized into a distinct behavioral system (such as foraging), served by a distinct neural module, adapted during evolution, and differences among individuals that are due to their possession of different genes. One does not necessarily imply another even though people often assume, without evidence, that it does. (p. 2212)

Many developmental psychologists are just as uncomfortable (or more so) with the term *instinct* as they are with the term *innate*, and for the same reason—its association with genetic determinism. And, as Bateson's quote illustrates, it is not always clear which definition of instinct one is talking about.

Yet some behaviors, or aspects of cognition, do seem to have a strong biological basis and to typify all (or nearly all) members of a species at some time in their development. Rather than referring to such behaviors as being "innate" or as "instincts," we refer to them as *species-typical behaviors*, or *species-typical patterns of cognition*. These are more descriptive terms and do not carry with them any implications about genetic determinism.

Nature/Nurture and Developmental Contextualism

During the past decades, we have noticed two shifts in emphasis in the field of cognitive development that at first glance might seem contradictory. The first is a greater emphasis given to the role of context (including cultural context) in development. The second is a greater acknowledgment of the role of biological factors in development. In a field where nature and nurture have traditionally occupied opposite scientific, philosophical, and often political poles, seeing an increasing emphasis on both seems a contradiction, perhaps reflecting a field composed of mutual antagonists, each taking an extreme perspective to counterbalance the other (much like the U.S. Congress seems to function in recent years). This is not the case, however. The current perspective on the dynamic transaction of nature and nurture is one in which biological and environmental factors not only can peacefully coexist but also are intricately intertwined (Goldhaber, 2012; Gottlieb, 2007).

Let us provide one brief illustration of how biology and environment are viewed as separate, interacting components of a larger system. Richard Lerner (1991, 2006) has been a proponent of the **developmental contextual model**. The basic contention of this model is that all parts of the organism (such as genes, cells, tissues, and organs), as well as the whole organism itself, interact dynamically with "the contexts within which the organism is embedded" (Lerner, 1991, p. 27). This means that one must always consider the organism context as a unit and that there are multiple levels of the organism and multiple levels of the context. Figure 1.2 graphically presents the developmental contextual model, showing the many bidirectional influences between children, who are born with biological propensities and dispositions, and the contexts in which they find themselves. Perhaps more than anything else, this figure demonstrates the complexity of development. Of equal importance, however, it demonstrates the interactions that occur between the many levels of life, from genes and hormones to family and culture, and the fact that cultural effects cannot be meaningfully separated from their biological influences, and vice versa. The dynamic nature of development, which results from the interaction of a child at many different levels (genetic, hormonal, physical environment, social environment, self-produced activity, and so on), is a theme that runs through most contemporary theories of development.

Cognitive Development Is Constructed Within a Social Context

As we've presented the developmental contextual model, it should be clear that the social environment plays a central role in determining a child's development. A child's biology interacts with a child's social environment to influence a child's developmental trajectory. However, the social environment is not simply the place, so to speak, where development occurs. The culture in which children grow up also shapes, or constructs, their intellects.

We are a social species, and human development can only be properly understood when the influences of social relations and the broader social/cultural environment are considered. Development always occurs within a social

FIGURE 1.2 **A developmental contextual model of person-context interaction.**

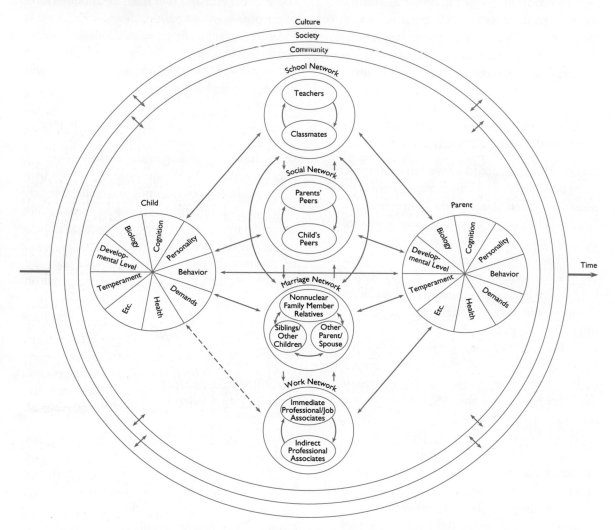

Source: R. M. Lerner. (1991). Changing organism-context relations as the basic process of development: A developmental contextual perspective. *Developmental Psychology, 27,* 27–32. Copyright © 1991 American Psychological Association. Reprinted with permission.

context, culturally shaped and historically conditioned, although the specific details of a child's social environment can vary widely. From this perspective, one's culture not only tells children *what* to think but also *how* to think (Gauvain & Perez, 2015; Rogoff, 2003; Vygotsky, 1978).

Sociocultural Perspectives

Several sociocultural perspectives on cognitive development have emerged over recent decades (Bronfenbrenner & Morris, 2006; Cole, 2006; Rogoff, 2003; see Chapter 3), stemming in large part from the rediscovery of the work of Soviet psychologist Lev Vygotsky (1978). Writing in the 1920s and 1930s, Vygotsky proposed a socio-cultural view, emphasizing that development was guided by adults interacting with children, with the cultural context determining largely how, where, and when these interactions would take place. There are many cultural universals, with children around the world being reared in socially structured, language-using groups. Thus, some aspects of development are also universal. But many aspects of culture, such as the available technology and how and when children are expected to learn the survival skills of their society (for example, formal schooling versus no formal schooling), vary greatly. Such differences can have considerable influence on how cognition develops. But how do different cultures construct different experiences for their children to learn, and what consequences does this have for *how* they learn?

Some researchers have noted that children living in traditional societies are more attentive to what adults do and, thus, develop a keener ability to learn through observation than children from schooled societies such as ours (Lancy, 2015; Morelli, Rogoff, & Angelillo, 2003). These types of cultural experiences affect how children learn. For example, in one study, 6- to 10-year-olds observed a woman creating origami figures and were later asked to make figures of their own (Mejia-Arauz, Rogoff, & Paradise, 2005). Some of the children were of traditional Mexican heritage whose mothers had only basic schooling (on average, a seventh-grade education), and others were of Mexican or European background whose mothers had a high school education or more. The children of the more educated mothers were more likely to request information from the "Origami Lady" than the children with the traditional Mexican heritage. These findings are consistent with the observations that these "traditional" children pay more attention to the actions of the adults and

learn more through observation rather than seeking instructions from adults or learning through verbal instructions (see Cole, 2006; Lancy, 2015).

Integrating Approaches

An approach that takes an even longer view of historical influences on development that we think is important for understanding children is *evolutionary theory*, which helps us better understand *why* children and adolescents behave as they do. We believe that a better understanding of the "whys" of development will help us to better understand the "hows" and the "whats" of development, as well as help us to apply knowledge of child development to everyday problems. Theodosius Dobzhansky (1964) famously said, "Nothing in biology makes sense except in the light of evolution" (p. 449). Many psychologists make the same argument for psychology, particularly for understanding the development of infants, children, and adolescents. In fact, anthropologist Melvin Konner (2010) has written that nothing in childhood makes sense except in the light of evolution. The principles of evolutionary developmental psychology are reviewed in Chapter 2.

Developmental contextual, sociocultural, and evolutionary models of development also represent three levels of analysis (see Figure 1.3). Developmental contextual models examine the development of psychological processes over an individual's lifetime, beginning before birth. Sociocultural models also look at the immediate causes of behavior but, in addition, take into account the impact of humans' 10,000-year cultural history on development. Evolutionary theory takes a truly long view of human history, examining the role that natural selection has played in shaping human development, particularly since the emergence of humans about 2 million years ago. We do not view these three approaches as

FIGURE 1.3 **Levels of analysis of developmental phenomena.**

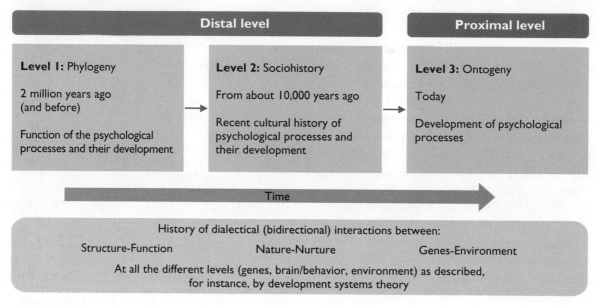

Distal level		Proximal level
Level 1: Phylogeny	**Level 2:** Sociohistory	**Level 3:** Ontogeny
2 million years ago (and before)	From about 10,000 years ago	Today
Function of the psychological processes and their development	Recent cultural history of psychological processes and their development	Development of psychological processes

Time

History of dialectical (bidirectional) interactions between:

Structure-Function   Nature-Nurture   Genes-Environment

At all the different levels (genes, brain/behavior, environment) as described, for instance, by development systems theory

Source: Bjorklund, D. F., & Hernández Blasi, C. (2012). *Child and adolescent development: An integrative approach.* Belmont, CA: Cengage.

competing perspectives of development but as reflecting three different, but compatible, levels of analyses, each of which is important to properly understand development. Because we believe that all of cognitive development (or at least most of it) can benefit from being examined through the lens of these three perspectives, you will find reference to them throughout the book.

Cognitive Development Involves Both Stability and Plasticity Over Time

Cognitive development is about change over time. Yet, once a level of cognitive competence is established, to what extent will it remain constant? Will a precocious infant become a bright 3-year-old and, later, a talented adult? Or is it just as likely that a below-average 5-year-old will become an above-average high school student, or a sluggish infant a whiz-kid computer jock? Once patterns have been established, what does it take to change them? Can they be modified by later experience? How plastic, or pliable, is the human intellect?

The stability and plasticity of cognition are related. **Stability** refers to the degree to which children maintain their same relative rank order over time in comparison with their peers in some aspect of cognition. Does the high-IQ 3-year-old maintain her position in the intellectual pecking order at age 8 or 18? **Plasticity** concerns the extent to which children can be shaped by experience. More specifically with respect to cognition, once a pattern of cognitive ability is established, to what extent can it be altered? Is our cognitive system highly flexible, capable of being bent and rebent, or, once a cognitive pattern has been forged, is it relatively resistant to change?

For the better part of the 20th century, psychologists believed that individual differences in intelligence, for example, were relatively stable over time and not likely to be strongly modified by subsequent environments. These views were held both by people who believed that such differences were mainly inherited and by those who believed such differences were mainly a function of environment, but for different reasons. People on the "nature" side assumed that intelligence was primarily an expression of one's genes and that this expression would be constant over one's lifetime. People on the other side of the fence emphasized the role of early experience in shaping intelligence. Experience was the important component affecting levels of intelligence, with experiences during the early years of life being most critical.

Jerome Kagan (1976) referred to this latter view as the *tape recorder model* of development. Every experience was seen as being recorded for posterity, without the opportunity to rewrite or erase something once it has been recorded. Evidence for this view was found in studies of children reared in nonstimulating institutions (Spitz, 1945). Infants receiving little in the way of social or physical stimulation showed signs of intellectual impairment as early as 3 or 4 months of age. Not only did these deleterious effects become exacerbated the longer children remained institutionalized, they were maintained long after children left the institutions (W. Dennis, 1973). The finding of long-term consequences of early experience was consistent with Freudian theory, which held that experiences during the oral and anal stages of development (from birth to about 2 years) have important effects on adult personality. (This also seems to be the opinion shared by the media and general public.)

Evidence for the permanence of the effects of early experience was also found in the animal literature. For example, Harry Harlow and his colleagues (1965) demonstrated in a series of classic studies that isolating infant rhesus monkeys from their mothers (and other monkeys) adversely affected their later social and sexual behaviors. Without steady interaction with other monkeys during infancy, young monkeys grew up lacking many of the social skills that facilitate important adaptive exchanges, such as mating, cooperation with others, and play. Furthermore, their maladaptive behaviors apparently remained stable over the life of the animals.

Exceptions were found, however, and many began to believe that these exceptions were actually the rule. In one classic study, for instance, infants believed to be intellectually impaired were moved from their overcrowded and understaffed orphanage to an institution for the intellectually impaired (Skeels, 1966). There they received lavish attention by women inmates, and within the course of several years, these children demonstrated normal levels of intelligence. Figure 1.4 shows the average IQs of these children both before they were placed in the institution for the intellectually impaired and approximately 2.5 years later. Also shown are the IQ scores of "control" children, who remained in the same orphanage the experimental children were removed from and who were tested about 4 years later. As you can see, the transferred children showed a substantial increase in IQ (27.5 points), whereas the control children showed a comparable decline (26.2 points). More recent research on the reversibility of intellectual impairment as a result of institutionalization is presented in Chapter 13. In other work, isolated monkeys were placed in therapy sessions with younger, immature monkeys on a daily basis over a 6-month period. By the end of therapy, these isolates were behaving in a reasonably normal fashion and became integrated into a laboratory monkey troop (Suomi & Harlow, 1972). Each of these studies demonstrates plasticity by a young organism and resilience concerning the negative effects of early environments.

Kagan (1976) proposed that one reason to expect resilience is that development does not proceed as a tape recorder. Rather, development is transformational, with relatively drastic

FIGURE I.4 **Average IQ scores before placement and 2.5 years after completion of program for children in the experimental and control groups.**

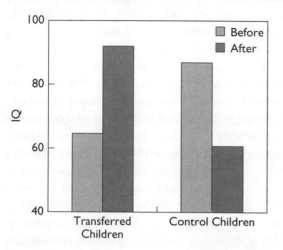

Source: Adapted from data presented in Skeels, H. M. (1966). *Adult status of children with contrasting early life experiences. Monographs of the Society for Research in Child Development, 31* (Serial No. 105).

changes occurring between adjacent stages, or phases. During these times, the "tapes" are changed. Alternatively, methods of representing and interpreting the world change so that the codes of the earlier tapes may be "lost" to the child. The tapes of our infancy might still reside in our heads, but we've lost the ability to play them or, maybe, the ability to understand the code in which they were written. In this view, plasticity should be the rule rather than the exception, especially for the experiences of infancy and early childhood.

One important thing to remember here is that, yes, stimulation and experience are important in the early years of life, but so is later experience. Although early intellectual stimulation is important to get children off to a good start, later experiences are necessary to maintain that positive beginning. And although most children who start

life in nonstimulating circumstances remain there, enhancements in intellectual skills are apt to occur for such children if their environments change for the better. This does not mean that there is infinite plasticity in cognitive development but merely that early experience is not necessarily destiny (just as biology is not) and that change is as much a characteristic of human cognition as is stability.

Cognitive Development Involves Changes in the Way Information Is Represented

One key issue that all theories of cognitive development must address concerns age differences in how children represent experience. Most psychologists believe that there is more than one way to represent a thing, and children of different ages seem to use different ways to represent their worlds. Adults, as well, use a variety of techniques to represent knowledge. While providing directions to your house to someone over the phone, for instance, you must convey the route to your home verbally, through a language code. But how is it represented in your head? What is the nature of the **representation**—that is, the mental encoding of information? You might think of the route you take by generating visual images of the buildings and landmarks you pass and then convert those into words. Or perhaps you sketch a map and then transform it into words that can be understood by your listener. What the person on the other end of the phone must do is encode the information. At one level, your friend might attend only to the sounds of the words you speak, encoding the acoustic properties of your utterances. If she does, she will probably be late for dinner. More likely, she will attend to the semantic, or meaning, features of the words. Once a basic meaning has been derived, however, she might convert the message to a mental (or perhaps a physical) map, realizing that she will be better able to find your house if the relevant information is in the form of a visual image. (Or she may just put your address into Google Maps and have Siri give her directions as she drives.)

How children represent knowledge and how they encode events in their world changes developmentally. Traditional theories have proposed that infants and toddlers much younger than 18 months are limited to knowing the world only through raw perception and through their actions on things, with little or no use of symbols. Let us provide an example from the area of memory development. Most people's earliest memories date back to their 4th and possibly their 3rd birthdays. Few people, including 6- and 7-year-old children, are able to recall anything from their earliest years of life, a phenomenon known as *infantile amnesia*. There have been a number of hypotheses about the origins of infantile amnesia, many of which we examine in Chapter 8. One prominent hypothesis is that there are differences in the way experiences are represented between infancy and later in childhood. Infants represent events in terms of sensations and action patterns, whereas preschool and older children (and adults) represent and recall information using language. Support for this position comes from research by Gabrielle Simcock and Harlene Hayne (2002), who showed children ranging in age from 27 to 39 months sequences of actions and interviewed them 6 and 12 months later, both for their verbal and nonverbal memory of the events. Despite having the verbal ability to describe their previous experience, none of the children did so spontaneously. To the extent that children did talk about these prior events, they did so only if they had the vocabulary to describe the event *at the time of the experience*. That is, children who were more verbally sophisticated at the time of initial testing tended to verbally recall some aspects of the event, but children were seemingly not able to translate earlier preverbal experiences into language. According to Simcock and Hayne (2002), "Children's verbal reports were frozen in time, reflecting their verbal skill at the time of encoding, rather than at the time of test" (p. 229).

Most cognitive developmentalists agree that there are age differences in how children represent their world and that these differences are central to age differences in thinking. Researchers disagree, however, about the nature of these differences. Can children of all ages use all types of symbols, and do they simply use them with different frequencies? Or does representation develop in a stage-like manner, with the more advanced forms of symbol use being unavailable to younger children? We believe most researchers today think that children, beginning in infancy, have multiple ways of representing information, although their ability to mentally represent people, objects, and events increases in sophistication over infancy and childhood. Research and theory pertinent to these and other issues related to changes in representation are central to the study of cognitive development, and they are discussed in the pages ahead.

Children Develop Increasing Intentional Control Over Their Behavior and Cognition

Much cognitive developmental (and educational) research is concerned with how children solve problems. And much of what interests cognitive developmental psychologists is how children go about finding solutions to complex problems that might have multiple paths to a solution. For example, how do children solve a puzzle, how do they go about remembering a grocery list, or how do they study for a history exam? Problem solving begins in infancy, but the problems children face, and their solutions, become more complicated with age.

One central concern of cognitive developmentalists has been the degree to which children of different ages can intentionally guide their problem solving. Much research on this topic has addressed the use of strategies. Strategies are usually defined as deliberate, goal-directed mental operations aimed at solving a problem (Harnishfeger & Bjorklund, 1990a; Pressley & Hilden, 2006). We use strategies intentionally to help us achieve a specified goal. Strategies can be seen in the behavior of infants. Six-month-olds alter how hard they swing at mobiles over their cribs to yield slightly different movements from the inanimate objects. Eighteen-month-old toddlers will deliberately stack boxes one on top of another so that they can reach the kitchen shelf and the chocolate chip cookies. These strategies are no less willful than the rhyming mnemonic the sixth-grader uses to remember how many days are in each month or the plan the 15-year-old uses as he plays all his trump cards first in a game of bridge. Yet strategies do change with development, and children seem increasingly able to carry out successful strategies as they grow older. So, one key research question in cognitive development concerns changes in the strategies children use and the situations in which they use them.

Although children around the world increasingly display goal-directed problem-solving behavior, this is especially evident for children from technologically advanced societies in which formal schooling is necessary to become a successful adult. Much of what children learn in school can be acquired only (or best) by deliberate study. This contrasts with how children in cultures without formal schooling often learn complicated tasks. In all cultures, much of what children learn about their world they acquire incidentally, without specific intention and, sometimes, even without specific awareness. This type of learning

and development is important also, and recent research, particularly in the area of memory development, has recognized this (see Chapter 8).

Many factors are involved in the development of strategic cognition, one of them being how much knowledge children have of the information they are asked to process. For example, when children are asked to remember sets of categorically related words—such as different examples of fruits, clothing, and mammals—they are more likely to use a memory strategy (for instance, remembering all the items from the same category together in clusters) and to remember more of the words if they are *typical* of their category (Schneider, 1986; Schwenck, Bjorklund, & Schneider, 2009). Typical items for the category clothing, for example, would include words such as *shirt*, *dress*, and *pants*, whereas atypical clothing items would include *hat*, *socks*, and *belt*. The latter are all common words and would be well known to children, but they are less typical of what we think of as clothes. How the role of knowledge base influences children's cognition has been a much-studied topic in cognitive development (Pressley & Hilden, 2006; Schneider, 2015).

Becoming a strategic learner involves learning to regulate one's thought and behavior. This involves a set of basic-level cognitive abilities, referred to as executive function. Executive function refers to the processes involved in regulating attention and in determining what to do with information just gathered or retrieved from long-term memory. It plays a central role in planning and behaving flexibly, particularly when dealing with novel information. Among the basic cognitive abilities that comprise executive function are (a) *working memory*, the structures and processes used for temporarily storing and manipulating information; (b) inhibiting responding and resisting interference; and (c) cognitive flexibility, the ability to switch between different sets of rules or different tasks. Thus, becoming a "self-directed thinker" (see Chapter 7) involves an understanding of the development of both lower-level cognitive processes (for example, executive function) and higher-level cognitive processes (for example, strategies).

Cognitive Development Involves Changes in Both Domain-General and Domain-Specific Abilities

Theories that postulate cognitive development results from increases in domain-general abilities assume that at any point in time, a child's thinking is influenced by a single set of factors, with these factors affecting all aspects of cognition. In contrast to domain-general accounts of cognitive development are theories that postulate that development unfolds as the result of changes in domain-specific abilities. This position hypothesizes a certain degree of modularity in brain functions, meaning that certain areas of the brain are dedicated to performing specific cognitive tasks (such as processing language). According to these theories, knowing a child's ability for one aspect of cognition might tell us nothing about his or her level of cognitive ability for other aspects of thinking because different cognitive domains are controlled by different mind/brain functions. At the extreme, domain-specific theories propose that different areas of the brain affect different aspects of cognition, with these areas being unaffected by what goes on in other areas of the brain.

Robbie Case (1992) put the controversy between domain-general and domain-specific theorists succinctly: "Is the mind better thought of as a general, all-purpose computing device, whose particular forte is general problem solving? Or is it better thought of as a modular device, each of whose modules has evolved to serve a unique biological function that it performs in its own unique and specialized way?" (p. 3). As we'll see in Chapters 5 and 7, the predominant theories of cognitive development throughout the 20th century were domain-general ones. Moreover, when talking of individual differences in intelligence, such as those measured by IQ tests, those differences have usually been thought of as being domain general in nature (see Chapters 12 and 13). Domain-specific theories arose primarily because of the failure of the domain-general theories to account for the unevenness of cognitive function that is frequently observed in development.

Modularity implies inflexibility, in that the individual is constrained by biology to process certain information in certain ways. This can be good, increasing the likelihood that complex information will be properly processed and understood. In discussing the benefits of constraints for infants, Annette Karmiloff-Smith (1992) states, "They enable the infant to accept as input only those data which it is initially able to compute in specific ways. The domain specificity of processing provides the infant with a limited yet organized (nonchaotic) system from the outset" (pp. 11–13). But the hallmark of human cognition is flexibility. Our species has come to dominate the globe, for better or worse, because we are able to solve problems that biology could not have imagined and have developed technological systems that expand our intellectual powers (such as writing, mathematics, and computers). Such cognition could not be achieved by a totally encapsulated mind/brain, and of course, no serious domain-specific theorist proposes this degree of modularity. What we must keep in mind is the certainty that both domain-general and domain-specific abilities exist, and we must be cautious of claims that postulate otherwise.

Section Review

Six Truths of Cognitive Development

1. Cognitive development proceeds as a result of the dynamic and reciprocal transaction of internal and external factors.
   - *Nativism* (a belief that all intellectual abilities are innate, and proposing a type of *genetic determinism*) and *empiricism* (a belief that all intellectual abilities are a result of experience) have been rejected as adequate explanations for cognitive development.
   - Biological and environmental factors are seen as interacting in bidirectional relationships, with children playing critical roles in their own development, as reflected by *developmental contextual models*.

2. Cognitive development is constructed within a social context.
   - Contemporary theorists view the social environment as being particularly important for cognitive development, as reflected by *sociocultural perspectives*.
   - Some theorists further argue that developmental contextual and sociocultural models of development should be integrated with evolutionary theory to produce a coherent understanding of psychological development.

3. Cognitive development involves both stability and plasticity over time.
   - *Stability* refers to the degree to which children maintain their same rank order relative to their peers over time.
   - *Plasticity* refers to the extent to which individuals can be shaped by the environment.
   - Although for most of the 20th century it was believed that intelligence is relatively stable over time and that experiences later in life cannot greatly affect patterns of intelligence established earlier, more recent research suggests that human intelligence can be substantially modified under certain circumstances.

4. Cognitive development involves changes in the way information is represented.
   - Most researchers today believe that children, beginning in infancy, have multiple ways of representing information, although their ability to mentally represent people, objects, and events increases in sophistication over infancy and childhood.

5. Children develop increasing intentional control over their behavior and cognition.
   - *Strategies* are deliberate, goal-directed mental operations aimed at solving a problem.
   - Strategies are especially important for children from technologically advanced societies in which formal schooling is necessary to become a successful adult.
   - Strategic cognition is influenced by a host of factors, including how much knowledge a child has, and also by a child's levels of *executive function*, referring to processes involved in regulating attention and in determining what to do with information just gathered or retrieved from long-term memory.

6. Cognitive development involves changes in both domain-general and domain-specific abilities.
   - Most traditional approaches to cognitive development have posited *domain-general abilities*.
   - Recent research has shown that many aspects of cognition and its development are *domain-specific* in nature, with some forms of cognition being *modular*.

Ask Yourself . . .

5. What does it mean to say something is innate?
6. What is meant by an integrative approach to development, and what are the three levels of analysis proposed in this textbook?

7. Why is an integrative approach to development important?
8. What does stability in cognitive development refer to? How is this related to plasticity in cognitive development?
9. What do cognitive psychologists mean when they talk about representations?
10. What is strategic cognition, and what factors are important in its development?
11. What is modularity? How does it relate to domain-specific and domain-general abilities?

GOALS OF COGNITIVE DEVELOPMENTALISTS

Although we believe the topics discussed in the previous section reflect the major issues in the study of cognitive development, what underlies all of these issues, as we mentioned in the opening pages of this chapter, is a search for the mechanisms responsible for change. We can observe changes in how children represent their world and see evidence of enhanced intentional, goal-directed behavior with age, but as scientists, we very much want to know the causes of these changes, and much of the research in the remainder of this book addresses this issue. Thus, description of change is not enough, although it is a necessary start.

Another goal for many cognitive developmentalists is to produce research that can be applied to real-world contexts. For example, issues about the stability and plasticity of intelligence have direct applications to the remediation of intellectual impairment and to some learning disabilities. Understanding how children learn to use strategies of arithmetic, memory, and reading, for example, are directly pertinent to children's acquisition of modern culture's most important technological skills (see Chapter 11). Research on factors that influence children's recollection of experienced or witnessed events has immediate relevance to the courtroom, where children have increasingly been called to testify (see Chapter 8). Understanding the typical development of both basic (and unconscious) cognitive processes as well as forms of higher-order (and conscious) cognition provides insight into the causes of some learning disabilities, whether in math and reading (see Chapter 11) or, perhaps, as a result of attention deficit hyperactivity disorder (ADHD) (see Chapter 7). And although extensions to the schoolhouse or clinic may be the most obvious applications of cognitive development research and theory, we believe perhaps the greatest application is to an appreciation of children in general, particularly when they are your own.

KEY TERMS AND CONCEPTS

bidirectionality of structure and function (structure ↔ function)
cognition
development (ontogeny)
developmental contextual model
developmental function

domain-general abilities
domain-specific abilities
empiricism
executive function
function
genetic determinism
individual differences
modularity

nativism
plasticity (of cognition and behavior)
representation
sociocultural perspectives
stability
strategies
structure

SUGGESTED READINGS

Scholarly Works

Bjorklund, D. F. (2013). Cognitive development: An overview. In P. D. Zelazo (Ed.), *Oxford handbook of developmental psychology* (pp. 447–476). Oxford, UK: Oxford University Press. This introductory article for an entire section devoted to cognitive development briefly reviews the major areas of research interest in the field.

Goldhaber, D. (2012). *The nature-nurture debates: Bridging the gap.* New York: Cambridge University Press. This is a scholarly yet highly readable account of the perennial nature-nurture debate. Goldhaber concludes that it is only through an integration of modern evolutionary and developmental theories that we will attain a true understanding of human nature.

Lerner, R. M. (2006). Developmental science, developmental systems, and contemporary theories of human development. In R. M. Lerner (Series Eds.) & W. F. Overton & P. C. M. Molenaar (Vol. Eds.), *Handbook of child psychology and developmental science: Vol. 1. Theoretical models of human development* (6th ed., pp. 1–17). New York: Wiley. This is a relatively lengthy and thorough examination of contemporary theorizing on developmental psychology, focusing on developmental contextual models.

Reading for Personal Interest

Bjorklund, D. F. (2007b). *Why youth is not wasted on the young: Immaturity in human development.* Oxford, UK: Blackwell. This book, written for a general audience, takes an explicitly Darwinian view of childhood, including the potentially adaptive role of cognitive immaturity.

Rutter, M. (2006). *Genes and behavior: Nature-nurture interplay explained.* Malden, MA: Blackwell. This book provides a highly readable account of research in behavioral genetics, written by one of the leaders of the field who also knows a thing or two about development. We were tempted to include this in the category *Scholarly Works* because it is so thorough, but it is written so it can be understood by the educated layperson.

2 | BIOLOGICAL BASES OF COGNITIVE DEVELOPMENT

Half of the first term had expired, and Tyler's first-grade teacher requested a conference with his parents. The teacher said that Tyler was a bright, creative, and likeable boy, but he was having some problems concentrating and staying on task. He would often blurt out answers to questions or say things that were not on topic, sometimes about one of his favorite TV shows. He was easily distracted and sometimes acted impulsively with the other children. After discussing some things his parents could do at home to help Tyler stay on task, and proposing that he likely did not have attention deficit hyperactivity disorder, the teacher asked the parents in what month Tyler was born. Tyler's father's first thought was, *Uh oh, we've got a teacher who believes in astrology. What's next, Tarot cards?* But when they answered July, the teacher said, "I thought as much. He's a summer child, one of the youngest children in class, and a boy. His brain isn't as mature as most of the other children's. He'll catch up. He's a bright boy."

This experienced first-grade teacher may not have known that it was the slow-developing frontal cortex of Tyler's brain that was primarily responsible for his control problems or that psychologists refer to processing that involves staying on task, resisting interference, and planning as *executive function*. But this teacher had seen enough to know that "summer children," especially boys, were apt to get off to a slow start in first grade.

As we mentioned in Chapter 1, developmental psychology has become increasingly biological over the past few decades. For some time now, we've been including lectures on the biological basis of cognitive development in our undergraduate classes, discussing brain development and the evolution of mental abilities. This has not always been so. For much of the 20th century, social and behavioral scientists interested in cognition gave only lip service, at best, to biology. The mind might emanate from the brain, but understanding the brain was not seen as a prerequisite to understanding the mind. In fact, there existed in the social and behavioral sciences what can be called *biophobia* and an implicit belief that acknowledging biology was akin to rejecting the influence of environment or culture on behavior, something at odds with the central theme of the social sciences (see Tooby & Cosmides, 1992). The study of cognition was essentially isolated from the study of the brain.

Things have clearly changed. The field of cognitive science takes as a given the close connection between mind and brain. As philosopher John Searle (1992) stated, "Mental phenomena are caused by neurophysiological processes in the brain and are themselves features of the brain. . . . Mental events and processes are as much part of our biological natural history as digestion, mitosis, or enzyme secretion" (p. 1). Moreover, cognitive scientists are concerned not only with immediate biological causes (for example, how the brain affects behavior) but also with factors that influenced the evolution of human cognition.

Looking at the biological basis of cognition and its development does not mean that one ignores the psychological level. Biology and psychology provide different levels of analysis. Much as psychology and anthropology present different pictures of human behavior (one at the level of the individual and the other at the level of the culture), so too do biology and psychology. Moreover, just as concepts in biology must be consistent with the known facts of chemistry, concepts in psychology must be consistent with the known facts of biology. Thus, proposing theories of the mind that are inconsistent with what we know about physiology or evolution cannot lead to a productive theory of cognition (see Cosmides, Tooby, & Barkow, 1992).

Psychology, however, cannot be reduced to biology. Knowing how nerve cells function will not tell us all we need to know about how we think. Developing a theory of the brain is important, of course, but it is not enough. Having a theory of the brain does not obviate having a theory of the mind. Cognitive psychology is not just something to do until the biologists get better at their trade. Developmental psychologists should not blindly accept everything that biologists propose, but they should be mindful of the biological causes of cognitive development and formulate theories and design experiments accordingly (Bjorklund, 1997a).

In this chapter, we first describe evolutionary theory and how such Darwinian ideas can contribute to an understanding of the developing modern child. In the next section, we examine several developmental theories that take biology seriously, particularly the relation between genetic/biologic factors and environmental/experiential factors. We then provide a brief overview of brain development. In this chapter, as in later chapters, we comment on the relation between the brain and cognitive development. Although no one ever doubted that the brain was the seat of cognition, only recently, with the emergence of the field of developmental cognitive neuroscience, have brain-cognition relations in development been taken seriously (see M. H. Johnson & de Haan, 2011; Markant & Thomas, 2013). Developmental cognitive neuroscience takes data from a variety of sources—molecular biology, cell biology, artificial intelligence, evolutionary theory, as well as conventional cognitive development—to create a picture of how the mind/brain develops. As will be made clear soon, contemporary biologically based theories of development do not hold that "biology is destiny" but, rather, deal with the classic nature/nurture controversy by explaining how genes and environments interact to produce a particular pattern of development.

Because most research in cognitive development over the last century essentially ignored biological causation, most of what is covered in the rest of the book is at the psychological rather than the biological level. However, we firmly believe that we will develop an understanding of cognitive development only by taking biology seriously, and reference to biological factors is made throughout the remainder of the book.

EVOLUTION AND COGNITIVE DEVELOPMENT

What is the adaptive value of particular cognitive abilities? How might cognitive abilities have a different adaptive value at different times in development? In what contexts should certain cognitive abilities develop? How do some evolved human characteristics, such as bipedality or prolonged immaturity, affect the development of cognition? Developmentalists ask these questions relating to evolution.

Evolutionary Theory

When biologists speak of evolution, they (usually) mean the process of change in gene frequencies within populations over many generations that, in time, produces new species. Modern evolutionary theory had its beginnings in the ideas of Charles Darwin, whose 1859 book *On the Origin of Species* represents one of the grandest ideas of science. The book made an immediate impact on the scientific community and is considered by many today to be one of the most important books ever written. The crux of the theory is that many more members of a species are born in each generation than will survive, and these members of the species all have different combinations of inherited traits (that is, there is substantial *variation* among members of a species). Conditions in the environment for that particular generation cause some members of that species to survive and reproduce whereas others do not, a process that Darwin referred to as natural selection. The inherited traits of the survivors will be passed on to the next generation of that species, whereas the traits of the nonsurvivors will not. Over the course of many generations, the predominant traits of a species will change by this mechanism. The major principle of Darwin's theory is *reproductive fitness*, which basically refers to the likelihood that an individual will become a parent and a grandparent.

Darwin's theory has gone through some substantial modifications during the last century or so, the most significant being the inclusion of modern genetic theory into formulations of evolution. Among scientists today, the *fact* of evolution is not questioned, although some lively debates center on the *mechanisms* of evolution (see S. J. Gould, 2002). Despite controversies, evolutionary theory is the backbone of modern biology, and because human cognition and behavior are rooted in biology, evolutionary theory should be the backbone of modern psychology.

One thing that evolutionary theory provides is a framework for interpreting all aspects of behavior and development. It does this, in part, by providing not only an explanation for *how* a particular mechanism came about (through natural selection) but also a possible explanation of *why* this mechanism evolved. In my early training, I (DB) was taught not to ask "why" questions. Scientists, I was told, ask "how" questions—for example, "How do children come to appreciate that other people have perceptions and ideas other than their own?" rather than *why* do they develop this ability. Evolutionary theory provides answers to both the "how" and the "why" questions. The "how" is through natural selection over evolutionary time, in that children who could not learn to see the perspectives of another person did not grow up to have children of their own. Of course, this is not a sufficient answer to how this ability develops in individual children, but it does provide a mechanism for how it developed in the species. The "why" suggests that this ability was likely important for survival, or that it was *adaptive*. Children who could understand the perspective of another were able to anticipate other people's actions and act accordingly. Such *adaptationist* reasoning must be used cautiously, of course. Not all aspects of present-day life were necessarily adaptive for our ancient ancestors. Some aspects might have been neutral, some associated with other adaptive characteristics, and others just not sufficiently maladaptive to result in extinction. But having a theory that provides a framework for asking why a particular behavior or pattern of development is present can help us develop a better understanding of human nature and to ask better "how" questions.

It is important to understand that what might have been adaptive for our ancestors 10,000, 100,000, or 1 million years ago might not be adaptive for us today. Our preference for sweets and fat is a good case in point. Although these foods would have been rare and much valued sources of energy for our ancient ancestors, they are easily available to people from postindustrial cultures today and are largely responsible for our high incidence of heart disease (Nesse & Williams, 1994). Many cognitive mechanisms can be seen in a similar light. Alternatively, many of the technological problems we must solve as modern humans are only centuries old at most, and no specific mechanisms have evolved to solve them.

Evolutionary Developmental Psychology

Evolutionary theory is currently influencing cognitive development through the field of **evolutionary developmental psychology** (Bjorklund & Ellis, 2014; Bjorklund, Hernández Blasi, & Ellis, 2016; Bjorklund & Pellegrini, 2002). Evolutionary psychologists have suggested that cognitive psychology is the missing link in the evolution of human behavior. Leda Cosmides and John Tooby (1987) proposed that information-processing mechanisms evolved and that "these mechanisms in interaction with environmental input generate manifest behavior. The causal link between evolution and behavior is made through psychological mechanisms" (p. 277). According to Cosmides and Tooby, adaptive behavior is predicated on adaptive thought. Natural selection operates on the cognitive level—information-processing programs evolved to solve real-world problems. How do I tell friend from foe? When do I fight, and when do I flee?

From this viewpoint, it becomes fruitful to ask what kind of cognitive operations an organism must have "if it is to extract and process information about its environment in a way that will lead to adaptive behavior" (Cosmides & Tooby, 1987, p. 285). From an evolutionary perspective, we must ask what is the purpose of a behavior and the cognitive operations that underlie that behavior, and what problem was it designed to solve.

It is also important to remember that cognitive processes *develop* and that the problems infants and children face are different from the problems adults face. Researchers can fruitfully ask how children's cognitions are adapted to the cultural contexts in which they find themselves rather than to the contexts experienced by adults (Bjorklund, 2007b; Turkewitz & Kenny, 1982). For example, what type of information should helpless infants be attentive to? Might some information that is of vital importance to them be less important to older children and adults, and vice versa?

Most mainstream evolutionary psychologists assume that what evolved are domain-specific mechanisms designed by natural selection to deal with specific aspects of the physical or social environment, such as face recognition or the processing of certain types of social relationships. However, natural selection has also influenced the evolution of domain-general mechanisms (for example, executive function, ability to inhibit thoughts and actions), and a number of developmental psychologists believe that these should also be examined from an evolutionary perspective (Bjorklund & Kipp, 2002; Geary, 2005).

Implicit in the idea that there are domain-specific mechanisms is that there are *constraints* on learning (R. Gelman & Williams, 1998; Spelke & Kinzler, 2007). Constraints imply restrictions, and restrictions are usually thought of as being bad. Human cognition is exceptional for its flexibility, not for its restrictiveness. But constraints, from this perspective, *enable* learning rather than hamper it. Jeffrey Elman and his colleagues (1996) have specified three general types of constraints—*architectural*, *chronotopic*, and *representational*—and we think this taxonomy helps articulate the ways that cognitive developmentalists consider biology to constrain psychological development.

Architectural constraints refer to ways in which the architecture of the brain is organized at birth. For example, some neurons are excitatory and others inhibitory, or neurons can differ in the amount of activation required for them to fire. At a somewhat higher level, neurons in a particular area of the brain might be more or less densely packed or have many or few connections with other local neurons. And at a higher level yet, different areas of the brain are connected with other areas of the brain, affecting the global organization of the organ. Because certain neurons/areas of the brain can only process certain types of information and pass it along to certain other areas of the brain, architectural constraints limit the type of and manner in which information can be processed. Thus, architectural constraints imply limits on what is processed as development progresses.

Chronotopic constraints refer to limitations on the developmental timing of events. For example, certain areas of the brain might develop before others. This would mean that early-developing areas would likely come to have different processing responsibilities than would later-developing areas. Similarly, some areas of the brain might be most receptive to certain types of experiences (to "learning") at specified times, making it imperative that certain experiences (exposure to patterned light or language, for example) occur during this *sensitive period* of development (S. C. Thomas & Johnson, 2008). For example, children around the world acquire language in about the same way and at about the same time. If, however, for some reason children are not exposed to language until later in life, their level of language proficiency is greatly reduced. The human brain appears to be prepared to make sense of language, thus making it easy for children to acquire the language that they hear around them. But such neural readiness is constrained by time. Wait too long, and the ability to acquire a fully articulated language is lost. The issue of developmental timing (and sensitive periods) is discussed with relation to language in Chapter 9.

Representational constraints are a more controversial type of constraint and refer to representations that are hardwired into the brain so that some types of "knowledge" are innate. This type of innateness corresponds to what most people think of when they talk about innate concepts. For example, several theorists have proposed that infants come into the world with (or develop very early in life) some basic ideas about the nature of objects (their solidity, for example), mathematics (simple concepts of numerosity), or grammar (see Pinker, 1997; Spelke & Kinzler, 2007; and Chapters 4, 6, and 9 of this book). Children enter a world of sights, sounds, objects, language, and other people. If all types of learning were truly equiprobable, children would be overwhelmed by the stimulation that bombards them from every direction. Instead, the argument goes, infants and young children are constrained to process certain information in "core domains" (such as the nature of objects, language) in certain ways, and this leads to

faster and more efficient processing of information within specific domains.

Evolved Probabilistic Cognitive Mechanisms

From this perspective, humans are "prepared" by natural selection to process some information more readily than others (language, for example). *But prepared is not preformed* (Bjorklund, 2003). Instead, these constraints are the products of structured gene × environment × development interactions that emerge in each generation and are influenced by prenatal as well as postnatal environments. Consistent with this idea, David Bjorklund, Bruce Ellis, and Justin Rosenberg (2007) proposed the concept of evolved probabilistic cognitive mechanisms:

> information-processing mechanisms that have evolved to solve recurrent problems faced by ancestral populations; however, they are expressed in a probabilistic fashion in each individual in a generation, based on the continuous and bidirectional interaction over time at all levels of organization, from the genetic through the cultural. These mechanisms are universal, in that they will develop in a species-typical manner when an individual experiences a species-typical environment over the course of ontogeny. (p. 22)

As an example of how evolved probabilistic cognitive mechanisms may work, consider the phenomenon of *prepared fear*. Monkeys raised in a laboratory show no fear of snakes. However, such monkeys are more likely to react fearfully after watching another monkey respond with fright to a snake than to a rabbit or a flower (Cook & Mineka, 1989), suggesting they are prepared to make fearful associations to snakes rather than having an innate fear of them. Something similar seems to happen with human infants and children. For instance, Vanessa LoBue and Judy DeLoache reported that 3- and 5-year-old children (LoBue & DeLoache, 2008, 2010) and 8- to 14-month-old infants (LoBue & DeLoache, 2010) more readily identified snakes or spiders among pictures of flowers or mushrooms than the reverse (something also found for adults; Öhman, Flykt, & Esteves, 2001). Yet children do not seem to have an innate fear of snakes but rather show a tendency to associate them with fearful responses. DeLoache and LoBue (2009) demonstrated this in studies in which 7- to 9-month-old infants and 14- to 16-month-old toddlers watched brief videos of snakes and other animals (for example, giraffes, rhinoceroses). The children initially showed no fear of the snakes. However, when the video clips were paired with either a happy or fearful voice, the toddlers looked longer at the snakes when they heard the fearful voice than when they heard the happy voice (see Figure 2.1). There was no difference in looking time to the two voices when they saw videos of other animals. This pattern of data suggests that, like monkeys, infants are not born with a fear of snakes. Rather they apparently possess perceptual biases to be attentive to certain classes of stimuli and to associate them with fearful voices, consistent with the idea of evolved probabilistic cognitive mechanisms (see Bjorklund, 2015).

Structure of the Mind

One way of thinking about how the mind is structured has been presented by David Geary

FIGURE 2.1 **Infants looked significantly longer at the snakes when listening to a frightened-sounding voice than when listening to a happy voice.** Looking times to the other animals did not differ significantly for the happy and frightened voices.

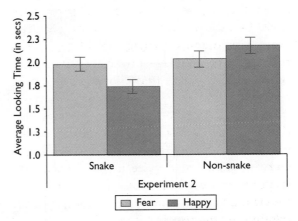

Source: DeLoache, J. S., & LoBue, V. (2009). The narrow fellow in the grass: Human infants associate snakes and fear. *Developmental Science, 12*, 201–207 (Experiment 2, p. 205).

(2005), who proposes that what evolved is a set of hierarchically organized domain-specific modules that develop as children engage their physical and social worlds. Geary's model is shown in Figure 2.2. As can be seen, there are two overarching domains—social (folk psychology) and ecological—with each tapping into a limited pool of domain-general central executive resources and each consisting of more-specific domains (self, individual, and group for social and biological and physical for ecological). Geary acknowledges that this list of domains is not complete (for example, there is no numerical domain listed here, which Geary believes exists), and one could argue about the organization of some of these domains. For example, should language be organized within the social domain, or is it best conceptualized as a separate domain? Nonetheless, Geary's organization reflects one

FIGURE 2.2 **Geary proposed that the mind is hierarchically organized into domains, with lower-level modules, designed to process less-complex information, serving as building blocks for higher-level more complex and flexible modules.** Within the social domain of folk psychology, domains are further organized into those dealing with (a) self-knowledge, (b) individuals, and (c) groups. Within the ecological domain, Geary proposes two subdomains, one dealing with the biological world and the other the physical world.

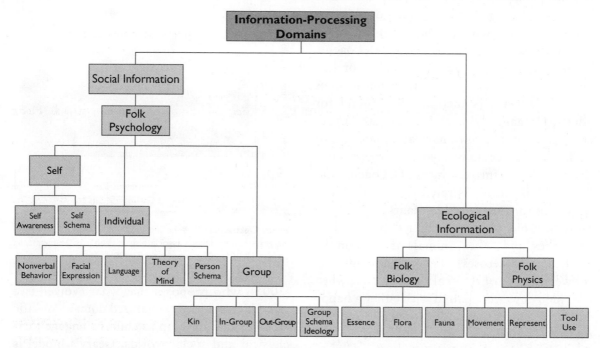

Source: Geary, D. C. (2005). *The origin of mind: Evolution of brain, cognition, and general intelligence.* Washington, DC: American Psychological Association.

that is consistent with the dominant perspective of evolutionary psychologists (Buss, 2009; Tooby & Cosmides, 2005), and it captures much of the developmental data.

Despite the belief that many evolutionarily influenced cognitive abilities are domain-specific in nature, one should not lose track of the fact that human cognition is amazingly flexible. This implies that what evolved in *Homo sapiens* are not highly specific approaches to problems but genes and cognitive mechanisms that are sensitive to different environments and that yield different outcomes (phenotypes) in different contexts that are (or would

have been, in ancient environments) adaptive to local conditions. Such mechanisms become more specific and finely tuned during development, primarily as a result of experience. And humans, more than any other mammal, have time to gather the experience that will be necessary to function optimally as an adult. In fact, evolutionary developmental psychologists have emphasized the importance of our species' extended childhood for cognitive development (Bjorklund & Pellegrini, 2002; Flinn & Ward, 2005). Humans spend a greater proportion of their life spans as juveniles than any other primate species. There are great dangers

TABLE 2.1 **Some distinctions between biologically primary and biologically secondary abilities.** Language is a good example of a biologically primary ability, whereas reading is a good example of a biologically secondary ability.

Biologically Primary Abilities

- Have undergone selection pressure and evolved to deal with problems faced by our ancestors
- Are acquired universally
- Are acquired by children in all but the most deprived of environments
- Children are intrinsically motivated to exercise biologically primary abilities and do so spontaneously
- Most children attain "expert" level of proficiency

Biologically Secondary Abilities

- Do not have an evolutionary history but are built on biologically primary abilities
- Are culturally dependent, reflecting the cognitive skills that are important in a particular culture (such as reading in literate cultures)
- Children are not intrinsically motivated to exercise them and must often be pressured by adults to acquire these skills
- Tedious practice is sometimes necessary to master biologically secondary abilities

Source: Adapted from Geary, D. C. (1995). Reflections of evolution and culture in children's cognition: Implications for mathematical development and instruction. *American Psychologist, 50,* 24–37.

associated with delaying reproduction, however, so there must be some substantial benefits to survival for this prolonged period of immaturity to have been selected. Although there is no single answer to the question of why humans have such an extended juvenile period, one reason proposed by many evolutionary developmental psychologists is that the long period of youth is necessary for children to master the complexities of human societies and technologies (Bjorklund, Periss, & Causey, 2009; Kaplan et al., 2000). This perspective argues that because of the variety of social and physical environments in which people live (both presently and in our evolutionary past), human cognition must be flexible, adapted not to a highly specific environment but to a broad range of potential environments, reflecting the diversity of social groups around the globe and throughout our species' history. To do this requires a long period of apprenticeship as well as a large brain capable of flexible learning and cognition.

Biologically Primary and Biologically Secondary Abilities

Another insight relevant to cognitive development and to education derived from evolutionary psychology is the idea that much of what we teach children in school is "unnatural," in that it involves tasks never encountered by our ancestors. For example, although our species has apparently been using language for tens of thousands of years, reading is a skill that goes back only a few thousand years, and only during the past century have a majority of people on the planet become literate. Geary (1995, 2007) refers to cognitive abilities that were selected over the course of evolution, such as language, as **biologically primary abilities**. Skills that build on these primary abilities but are principally cultural inventions, such as reading, are considered **biologically secondary abilities**. Biologically primary abilities are acquired universally, and children typically have high motivation to perform tasks involving them. Biologically secondary abilities, in contrast, are culturally determined, and tedious repetition and external pressure are often necessary for their mastery. It is little wonder that reading, a supposed "language art," and higher mathematics give many children substantial difficulty. (See Table 2.1 for a summary of the characteristics of biological primary and secondary abilities.)

It is important to emphasize here that an evolutionary account of development is *not* one of biological determinism. That is, although evolution works through changing frequencies of genes within the population, natural selection requires a dynamic interaction between organisms and their environments. Organisms choose environments, the very act of which modifies those environments. Environments in turn affect the organism by "selecting" some behaviors that "match" those environments over others. Because of this dynamic interaction between organisms and environments, we must evaluate these interactions if we want to understand adaptation and cognitive development. Thus, this position rejects any simple notion of biological determinism (for example, "genes cause behavior") on cognitive development, intelligence, or the educability of children.

Although not every cognitive developmental psychologist adopts the specific evolutionary position presented here, we think it's fair to say that virtually all cognitive developmentalists are Darwinians, and most also believe that infants enter the world prepared by natural selection to make sense of a structured world. Nora Newcombe (2011) has proposed that humans, beginning in infancy, have substantial learning capabilities and a strong capacity for probabilistic reasoning that interact with "expected" environments (that is, environments that most members of a species can expect to experience) to produce species-typical patterns of cognitive development. She refers to this approach

as **neuroconstructivism**, and it is consistent with both the evolutionary developmental psychological approach presented here and the developmental systems approach discussed in the next section.

Section Review

Developmental psychology has become increasingly concerned about biological causes of cognition.

Evolution and Cognitive Development

- Darwin's idea of variation and *natural selection* remains the cornerstone for theories of *evolution*.
- *Evolutionary developmental psychologists* believe that both domain-specific and domain-general mechanisms have been modified over time as a result of natural selection.
- *Evolved probabilistic cognitive mechanisms* emerged to solve recurrent problems faced by ancestral populations; they are expressed in a probabilistic fashion in each individual in a generation, based on the continuous and bidirectional interaction over time at all levels of organization, from the genetic through the cultural.
- Three types of constraints have been proposed: *architectural*, referring to innate characteristics of neurons and their connections with other groups of neurons; *chronotopic*, referring to maturational (timing) constraints; and *representational*, referring to innate representations.
- Geary proposed that the mind is hierarchically organized, with two overarching domains evolved to deal with social information (folk knowledge) and ecological information (folk biology and folk physics).
- *Biologically primary abilities* such as language have been selected for in evolution and are acquired universally by children in all but the most deprived environment; children are intrinsically motivated to execute them,

and most children attain "expert" level of proficiency.

- *Biologically secondary abilities* such as reading do not have an evolutionary history but are built on biologically primary abilities; they are culturally dependent, children are not intrinsically motivated to execute them, and tedious practice is sometimes necessary for their mastery.

- Virtually all cognitive developmentalists are Darwinians, believing that inherited and evolved learning abilities interact with a structured environment to produce species-typical patterns of cognitive growth, an approach known as *neuroconstructivism*.

Ask Yourself . . .

1. What are the basic principles of an evolutionary approach to human development? How does this relate to a neuroconstructionist approach?

2. In what ways might *architectural*, *chronotopic*, and *representational* constraints influence development?

3. How is *prepared fear* an example of an evolved probabilistic cognitive mechanism? Can you think of another possible example?

4. How are biologically primary abilities different from biologically secondary abilities? Provide examples of each.

MODELS OF GENE-ENVIRONMENT INTERACTION

All self-respecting developmentalists believe that development is the result of an interaction between genetic/biologic factors and environmental/experiential factors. There is really no other alternative. Some theorists are more explicit about the nature of the interaction than others, however, and in this section we examine two approaches that look at gene-environment interactions and their consequences for development. Each approach posits that the child is an active agent in his or her own development, that development proceeds through the bidirectional effect of structure and function, and that the context in which development occurs is as important as the genes the individual inherits. The two approaches are the *developmental systems approach* (or *developmental contextualism*), as advocated by Gilbert Gottlieb (2000, 2007; Gottlieb, Wahlsten, & Lickliter, 2006) and others (see Lerner, 2006; Lickliter & Honeycutt, 2015), and a theory based on research in behavioral genetics, the *genotype → environment theory*, as presented by Sandra Scarr and Kathleen McCartney (1983; Scarr, 1992, 1993).

There are some important distinctions between the two approaches, centering mainly around the degree to which outside experience, influenced by one's genes, modifies the organism versus the degree to which a biological organism shapes its own development through epigenetic processes. Although debate between theorists in these two camps can be vigorous (see D. S. Moore, 2013; Scarr, 1993), the difference between the two approaches can be seen as a matter of degree. And the critical point for our purposes is that these two models take the transaction of biological and environmental factors seriously, making it clear that we need to give more than lip service to the interaction of the multiple factors that produce development.

Developmental Systems Approach

Concept of Epigenesis

The **developmental systems approach**, so called because it views development as occurring within a system of interacting levels, is centered around the concept of epigenesis: "Individual development is characterized by an increase in novelty and complexity of organization over time—the sequential emergence of new structural and functional properties and competencies—at all levels of analysis as a consequence of horizontal and vertical coactions among its parts, including organism-environment coactions" (Gottlieb et al., 2006, p. 211). (In biology, *epigenetics* also refers to the complex biochemical system that regulates gene expression; see Meaney, 2013; D. S. Moore, 2015.) Epigenesis involves the action of genes, of course, but also the action of RNA, ribosomes, proteins, neurotransmitters, neurons, and so on, all in interaction with the environment, broadly defined. Central to the concept of epigenesis is the activity of the organism itself in influencing its own development; the organism's unique experiences can influence the activation of genes and lead to long-term alterations in the transcription of DNA (such as changes in the way that information contained in DNA about a protein sequence is translated by RNA during protein synthesis). Along similar lines, Gottlieb (1991a) states that epigenesis reflects a bidirectional relationship between all levels of biological and experiential variables, such that genetic activity both influences and is influenced by structural maturation, which is bidirectionally related to function and activity. This relationship can be expressed as follows:

genetic activity (DNA ↔ RNA ↔ proteins) ↔ structural maturation ↔ function, activity

The point here is that functioning at any level influences functioning at adjacent levels. For example, genes clearly direct the production of

proteins, which in turn determine the formation of structures, such as muscle or nerve cells. But activity of these and surrounding cells can turn on or off a particular gene, causing the cessation or commencement of genetic activity. Moreover, experience in the form of self-produced activity or stimulation from external sources can alter the development of sets of cells.

From this perspective, there are no simple genetic or experiential causes of behavior; all development is the product of epigenesis, with complex interactions occurring among multiple levels (LaFreniere & MacDonald, 2013). Some compelling evidence for this claim comes from research involving twins. Identical twins have identical DNA. Yet, as Mario Fraga and colleagues (2005) have shown, as twins age and undergo unique experiences, say differences in diet or tobacco use, they accumulate epigenetic differences. In their study, younger pairs of twins showed fewer markers of epigenetic differences than did older twins. These findings indicate that as even genetically identical individuals develop, their individual experiences can affect them at the cellular level. These cellular changes, in turn, can affect the expression of genes and behaviors, leading to further differences in experience. Such interactive effects lead to a cascade of changes across the life span, making it nearly impossible to distinguish environmental from genetic influences. This bidirectional approach to development is expressed in Figure 2.3. This figure suggests that we can never understand development merely by looking for genetic effects or for environmental effects; to understand development, we must look at the organism-context relationship (Lickliter, 2013). Mark Johnson (1998), in his review of the neural basis of cognitive development, made this point especially clear: "Since it has become evident that genes interact with their environment at all levels, including the molecular, there is no aspect of development that can be said to be strictly 'genetic,' that is, exclusively a product of information contained in the genes" (p. 4).

According to the developmental systems approach, new structures and functions emerge during development by means of self-organization through the bidirectional interactions of elements at various levels of organization (that is, genes, RNA, neurons, overt behavior, and so on). As Gottlieb (1991a) stated, "The cause of development—what makes development happen—is the relationship between the . . . components, not the components themselves. Genes in themselves cannot cause development any more than stimulation in itself can cause development" (pp. 7–8).

If the relations expressed in Figure 2.3 approximate reality, there should be substantial plasticity in development. Yet it is undeniable that development is constrained by one's genes. Because our parents were humans, we develop in a way that a chimpanzee embryo can never develop, and vice versa. However, environments

FIGURE 2.3 **A simplified schematic of the developmental systems approach, showing a hierarchy of four mutually interacting components.**

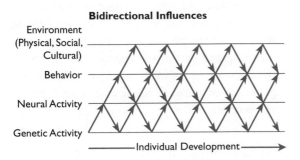

Source: Gottlieb, G. (1992). *Individual development and evolution: The genesis of novel behavior.* New York: Oxford University Press. Used by permission of Oxford University Press, Inc.

also constrain development. Genes will be expressed differently in different environments, yielding different patterns of development.

An example of how the effects of genes vary in different environments was provided in a study by Avshalom Caspi and his colleagues (2007), who examined the relationship among adult IQ, whether a person was breast-fed or bottle-fed, and specific versions of a gene associated with processing fatty acid. Previous research had documented a relationship between breast-feeding and later IQ, with children, adolescents, and adults who were breast-fed as babies having higher IQs than those who were bottle-fed (Mortensen et al., 2002). One explanation for this effect is that breast milk provides fatty acids (not found in cow's milk) that foster brain development early in life. Caspi and his colleagues (2007) identified a gene on chromosome 11 involved in processing fatty acids, as well as two variants of that gene. Recall from your basic biology class that we get one gene for a characteristic from our mother and one from our father and that the genes, or alleles, can vary somewhat (like having one gene for brown eyes and one for blue eyes). Children who had two combinations of the alleles (called CC and CG) *and* who were breast-fed as infants had significantly higher IQs (approximately 104) relative to children who had the same set of alleles but were not breast-fed (approximately 97). In contrast, children with a third version of the genes (called GG) showed no effect on IQ from being either breast-fed or bottle-fed (both groups had IQs of approximately 100; see Figure 2.4). Thus, the benefits of breast-feeding for subsequent IQ are influenced by a particular combination of alleles for a gene that influences how a person processes fatty acid. This study shows that even genes clearly associated with known specific

FIGURE 2.4 **Relation between breast-feeding and IQ for children with different versions of a gene for processing fatty acids.**

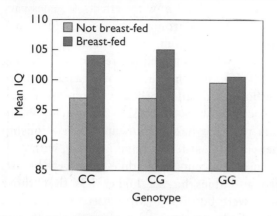

Source: Caspi et al. (2007). Moderation of breastfeeding effects on the IQ by genetic variation in fatty acid metabolism. *Proceedings of the National Academy of Science, 104,* 18860–18865.

biochemical and behavior outcomes (here, high IQ) are expressed differently in different environments (here, breast-fed versus bottle-fed).

If there is so much plasticity in development, however, why do almost all members of a species (human or otherwise) develop in a species-typical pattern? The answer is that a child (or a puppy or a duckling) inherits not only species-typical genes but also a species-typical environment. For example, ducks begin life in eggs, usually surrounded by other eggs, with their mother staying close by before they hatch. These ducks are able to hear and vocalize before hatching, and it turns out that these experiences contribute to an important aspect of posthatching behavior. Under normal conditions, when baby ducks, shortly after hatching, are put into a large container and hear the maternal call of two species of birds—their own and another—they invariably approach the call from their own species. They seem "instinctively" to know what their own species sounds like and to move toward that

sound, something that makes good sense in the wild. However, when experimental procedures are performed so that the embryonic duck in the egg does not hear its mother or any of its siblings and its own vocal chords are temporarily prevented from functioning so that it can produce no sound itself, the duck fails after hatching to show the species-typical pattern of approaching the call of its own species (see Gottlieb, 1991b). In other words, prehatching experience, including hearing its own self-produced vocalizations, plays a major role in posthatching species-typical behavior. The reason that nearly all ducks approach the species-typical call after hatching is that nearly all ducks inherit not only the genetic disposition to make such a selection but also the species-typical environment that provides the necessary experiences for such a pattern to develop. Viewing development from this perspective provides a new meaning for the term *instinctive.* A behavior or function that is inborn in almost all members of the species might be instinctive, but if so, we must consider both the species-typical genes and the species-typical environment as factors contributing to that behavior.

Results such as these indicate that behaviors (here, related to infant-mother attachment) found in almost all normal members of a species are influenced by often-subtle characteristics of the environment. Psychological mechanisms at the human level can be viewed similarly. Strong species-universal biases may exist for certain behaviors, but how any particular behavior or mechanism is expressed will depend on the experiences of the individual at certain times in development.

Developmental Timing

As any comedian will tell you, timing is everything. In the developmental systems approach, the timing of a particular event can influence substantially what effect that event will have on development.

As we described briefly earlier, perhaps the concept most central to the issue of the timing of development is that of the **sensitive period.** The sensitive period (sometimes referred to as the *critical period*) for a specific skill or ability is the time in development (usually early in life) when it is most easily acquired. If a requisite experience occurs outside of this sensitive period (either too early or too late), the target skill will not be readily acquired—or possibly not acquired at all. Although the organism is most sensitive to a particular event at a particular time, similar or perhaps more intense experiences later in life can still have considerable influence on development. Figure 2.5 depicts the idea that a behavior is most easily acquired during a sensitive period.

Researchers have suggested that many aspects of human cognitive development can be described as sensitive periods (see Maurer & Lewis, 2013), with language being perhaps the clearest example (Lenneberg, 1967; Newport, 1991). Both a first and a second language are acquired more easily when learned in early childhood. Although adolescents and adults can learn a second language, it is usually only with great difficulty, and they rarely attain the facility in that language as when it is learned during childhood. More is said about a critical period for language acquisition in Chapter 9.

Examples of the significance of timing of perceptual experience come from research by Robert Lickliter (1990) involving auditory and visual stimulation of bobwhite quail. Like ducks, bobwhite quail approach the maternal call of their own species shortly after hatching. As demonstrated earlier by Gottlieb, this phenomenon has been attributed to auditory experiences the

FIGURE 2.5 **Some cognitive abilities, such as language, might be most easily acquired during a critical period in (usually early) development.**

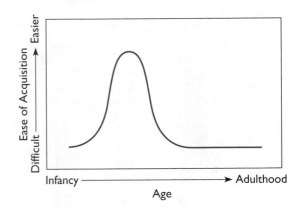

Source: © Cengage Learning.

birds have before hatching. But, Lickliter reasoned, this is caused not just by the *presence* of auditory experiences before hatching but also by the *absence* of other sensory experiences, following an argument originally made by Gerald Turkewitz and Patricia Kenny (1982), who noted that the sensory systems in infants of many species function poorly at birth. Such inefficient functioning is actually adaptive, however, in that it protects the infant from sensory overload, permitting it to deal with small bits of simplified stimuli, which in turn makes it easier for the immature being to make sense of its world. Also, poor functioning in one sensory system (vision, for example) might permit an earlier developing sensory system (hearing, for example) to develop without undue competition for neural resources.

This is exactly the logic that Lickliter adopted for his study with bobwhite quail. In all vertebrates, hearing develops before vision (Gottlieb, 1971). Lickliter argued that the slower development of vision in bobwhite quail allows the

FIGURE 2.6 **Percentage of bobwhite quail chicks that approached the bobwhite maternal call, the chicken maternal call, or showed no preference as a function of whether they received premature visual stimulation.**

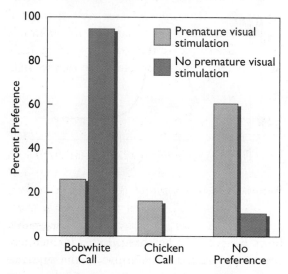

Source: Adapted from Lickliter, R. (1990). Premature visual stimulation accelerates intersensory functioning in bobwhite quail neonates. *Developmental Psychobiology, 23,* 15–27.

auditory system to develop without competition from the visual system. If so, what would happen if quail were given extra visual experience before hatching? One possibility is that it might hinder important aspects of auditory development, such as showing a preference for the maternal call.

Lickliter (1990) developed a procedure whereby he removed part of the eggshell and provided visual experience to bobwhite quail 2 to 3 days before hatching. Control quail had the end of the egg opened but received no visual experience. This ensured that the behavior of the experimental birds would not be caused by removing part of the eggshell per se but by the additional visual experience the chicks received. Lickliter then examined those birds with an auditory preference test in which the birds were placed in an oval container having speakers at opposite ends. From one speaker came the maternal call of a bobwhite quail, and from the other speaker came the maternal call of a chicken. The researchers observed which speaker, if either, the chicks approached.

The results of this experiment are shown in Figure 2.6. The control birds demonstrated the species-typical pattern when tested, with nearly all the birds showing a preference for the maternal call of their own species (that is, approaching the speaker from which the bobwhite quail call came). This was not the case for the birds that had the extra visual experience, however. A majority of these birds showed no preference or approached the speaker producing the maternal call of a chicken! We should note that these animals also displayed greater visual discrimination abilities. That is, the prehatching visual experience resulted in enhanced visual abilities, but at the expense of auditory abilities, which are important in the chick's development of attachment.

This and other studies (see Bjorklund, 1997b) clearly demonstrate that the timing of perceptual experience is critically important and that earlier experience is not always better experience. This is worth remembering for human infants. Might their sensory limitations actually be adaptive, and might extra stimulation in one modality interfere with development in other modalities? Recall our discussion in Chapter 1 on the adaptive nature of cognitive immaturity and the demonstration that providing an infant with too much stimulation or "learning tasks" too soon in development might have a negative effect.

Although almost no research has been conducted with human infants on the topic of sensory overstimulation, researchers have speculated that some of the deficits experienced by premature infants are caused by exposure to too much sensory information too soon. Neonatologist Heidelise Als (1995) suggested the early sensory stimulation that premature infants experience might adversely affect brain development by requiring these infants to process perceptual stimulation that they would not normally deal with for several more weeks (see also Lickliter, 2000). As in the research with quail chicks, "premature" stimulation might result in enhanced performance later in life in some domains but at the expense of functioning in others, which often leads to forms of learning disabilities. And in fact, Als notes that these deficits are often accompanied by accelerated development or enhanced abilities in other areas, such as in mathematics. This idea is provocative, although still speculative. But it is consistent with the idea that the timing of developmentally sensitive periods in the brain is correlated with the species-typical timing of perceptual experiences. According to Bjorklund and his colleagues (2007),

> When animals receive stimulation from one modality earlier than "expected" (i.e., when neural development and sensory experiences are uncoupled), it interferes with this choreographed dance between gene-influenced neural maturation and perceptual experience. This change in the gene-environment relation (in this case, a change in *timing* of different perceptual experiences) causes a species-atypical pattern of development. (p. 13)

More generally, the differential timing of maturation in various areas of the brain influences how the brain becomes organized. For example, Jeffrey Elman and his colleagues (1996) proposed that early developing brain regions effectively serve as filters for later-developing areas. The type and manner in which these early developing areas can process information determines, in a very real sense, the type and way in which later-developing areas can process information. From this perspective, it is the *timing of events* (the chronotopic constraints we described earlier) rather than "knowledge" (or representational constraints) that is inherited, and this timing is largely responsible for the species-typical patterns of brain and cognitive development that we see.

Genotype → Environment Theory

Related to the developmental systems approach are several theories that stem from the field of **behavioral genetics**, which studies genetic effects on behavior and complex psychological characteristics such as intelligence and personality (Plomin et al., 2012; Rutter, 2006). These theories have attracted much attention among mainstream developmentalists, in part because they use human behavioral outcomes such as personality or IQ scores as data rather than generalizing results from ducks, rats, or bobwhite quail to humans. This is also a reason for the substantial controversy the approach has produced (see D. S. Moore, 2013).

Academic psychologists have long been reluctant to accept a strong influence of genetics on human behavior. The argument against a genetic influence on behavior goes something like this: If we are what our genes determine us to be, then there is little hope of modifying the human spirit or human behavior through environmental intervention. If genes affect not only blood type and eye color but also behavior, personality, and intelligence, then biology truly is destiny.

Yet biology rarely dictates anything in an absolute way. As illustrated by Figure 2.3, all genetic effects are moderated by environmental ones. Even the genes for eye color must be expressed in a developing embryo, which is exposed to uncountable environmental factors as a result of its own development. The fact that genes influence behavior does not mean that environment plays only an inconsequential role. To deny the significant role of genetics in behavior is to place one's head in the sand, but to proclaim that genetics determines our personalities, intellects, and behavior is to seriously misinterpret reality.

Genotype → Environment Effects

One of the most influential theories from behavioral genetics with respect to cognitive development is Sandra Scarr and Kathleen McCartney's (1983) genotype → environment theory. Basically, Scarr and McCartney propose that one's genotype (one's actual genetic constitution) influences which environments one encounters and the type of experiences one has. Their basic contention is that *genes drive experience*. One's genetic makeup determines how one organizes one's world. Thus, environment does play a significant role in shaping intellect, but a person's inherited characteristics largely determine what those experiences are and how they are perceived.

Figure 2.7 presents a schematic of Scarr and McCartney's model of behavioral development. A child's phenotype (his or her observed characteristics) is influenced both by the child's genotype and by his or her rearing environment. The child's genotype is determined by the genotype of his or her parents. The parents' genotype also influences the environment; the parents' genetic characteristics affect the types of environments they feel most comfortable in. But in this model, the child's genotype also has an impact on the environment, which affects the child's development. Thus, characteristics of the child, as well as the rearing environment and genetic contributions of the parents, influence the course of development.

FIGURE 2.7 **Scarr and McCartney's model of behavioral development.**

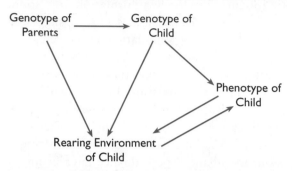

Source: Adapted from Scarr, S., & McCartney, K. (1983). How people make their own environments: A theory of genotype-environment effects. *Child Development, 54,* 424–435. Copyright © 1983 The Society for Research in Child Development, Inc. Adapted with permission.

Scarr and McCartney posit three types of genotype → environment effects that vary in influence over time (see Table 2.2). They are *passive, evocative,* and *active*. Passive effects occur when genetically related parents provide the rearing environment of the child. When biological parents rear a child, the effects of genetics and environment cannot be separated because the people who provide the genetic constitution for a child also provide the environment. The influence of passive effects is proposed to decline with age.

Evocative effects occur when the child elicits responses from others that are influenced by his or her genotype. For example, an irritable child is responded to differently than a well-tempered child is, and the type of attention received by an infant who likes to cuddle is different from that received by an infant who does not want to be held. During early childhood, an attentive and cooperative child receives more positive interactions from parents and teachers than an uncooperative, distractible child does. Evocative effects presumably remain constant throughout development.

TABLE 2.2 **Three types of genotype →
environment effects in Scarr & McCartney's
genotype → environment model.**

Passive:	Biological parents provide both genes and environment for child. Passive effects *decrease* with age.
Evocative:	Temperamental characteristics of child evoke responses from others. Evocative effects remain *constant* with age.
Active:	Children seek out environments consistent with their genotypes. Active effects *increase* with age.

Active effects occur when one's genotype influences the type of environments one chooses to experience. A person actively selects an environment in which he or she feels comfortable. For example, children interested in competitive sports would probably seek out other like-minded children to play with who would be very different from the type of people sport-phobic children would seek. Accordingly, people with different genotypes choose to interact in different environments and, thus, have different experiences that influence their development. Active effects increase with age as children become increasingly independent of their parents and able to select their own environments.

How does Scarr and McCartney's model relate to cognitive development? For one thing, this model suggests that parents' environmental influence on children should be greatest during the early childhood years and decrease with age as active genotype → environment effects increase. Evidence for this position comes from an adoption study by Scarr and Richard Weinberg (1978). They reported that the average correlations of the IQs of samples of adopted siblings (that is, genetically unrelated children living together) measured in early childhood ranged from 0.25 to 0.39. This indicates a moderate level of similarity between the IQs of biologically unrelated children growing up together, a reflection of an environmental influence on IQ. However, the correlation of the IQs for adopted siblings measured late in adolescence was 0! This means that knowing the IQ of one child would not help you predict, to any degree, the IQ of his or her adopted sibling. The predictive power is zero. These results reflect the fact that the longer these genetically unrelated siblings lived together, the less alike in IQ scores they became. Similar findings of reduced correlations of IQs with age have been reported for dizygotic (nonidentical) twins. Correlations of the IQs of dizygotic twins computed during the preschool years ranged from 0.60 to 0.75 but were reduced to 0.55 when measured later in childhood (Matheny et al., 1981). In fact, siblings in general become less alike in most respects the older they get (McCartney, Harris, & Bernieri, 1990; Sundet, Eriksen, & Tambs, 2008). Following Scarr and McCartney's model, passive genotype → environment effects, as reflected by the type of environments that parents provide for their children, decrease with age, and active genotype → environment effects increase. Why? Because as they get older, children are increasingly able to select environments that suit their particular needs, and such selection is determined primarily by one's genotype.

But then, do genes *cause* intelligence? Interestingly, Scarr and McCartney's theory ends up giving the environment a substantial role in directing development. Genotype causes a child to choose certain environments that are compatible with the child's genetic constitution, and the experiences in these environments shape the child's cognition (and other important psychological characteristics). From this perspective, one's genes serve to select "appropriate" environments, but experience is actually responsible for crafting the intellect. The heritability of intelligence is discussed in greater detail in Chapter 13.

Scarr and McCartney's model illustrates how genetic and environmental factors might interact to produce different patterns and levels of intelligence. Particularly attractive about this model is its consideration of developmental effects. Genetic and environmental effects are viewed not as constants but as dynamic factors that have different effects on intelligence at different points in time. This theory in effect postulates a transaction between developmental function and individual differences. As children become more autonomous with age, the influence of genetic and environmental factors on individual differences changes.

Section Review

Differences in models of gene-environment interaction center mainly around the degree to which outside experience, influenced by one's genes, modifies the organism versus the degree to which a biological organism shapes its own development through epigenetic processes.

Developmental Systems Approach

- The *developmental systems approach* centers around the concept of *epigenesis*, a bidirectional relationship between all levels of biological and experiential variables such that genetic activity both influences and is influenced by structural maturation, which is bidirectionally related to function and activity.
- Organisms inherit not only a species-typical genome but also a species-typical environment, and species-typical experiences early in life can greatly influence the course of development.
- Many early perceptual and cognitive abilities are governed by *sensitive periods*, those times in development when certain skills or abilities are most easily acquired.

Genotype → Environment Theory

- Scarr and McCartney's *genotype → environment theory* is based chiefly on research in *behavioral genetics* and proposes that genes drive experience.
- Three kinds of genotype → environment effects are proposed: passive, which occur when biological parents rear the child; evocative, which occur when characteristics of the child elicit responses from others; and active, which occur when children select environments in which they choose to interact.
- Passive effects decrease in influence over time, whereas evocative effects remain constant, and active effects increase.
- Data supporting this theory show that parents' environmental influence on their children's intelligence is greatest during the early years and wanes as the children approach adolescence.

Ask Yourself . . .

5. How is the concept of epigenesis incorporated into modern cognitive developmental psychology?
6. What are some of the ways researchers have shown that the timing of perceptual experience can affect development?
7. What are the three types of genotype → environment effects?

DEVELOPMENT OF THE BRAIN

The human brain is perhaps the most marvelous thing in the universe. Unlike the brains of any other species, ours provides us with self-awareness and a behavioral flexibility that has allowed humans to create culture and to adapt to a limitless diversity of environments. Other animal brains are quite impressive, but only the human brain has led to language, mathematics, physics, and art.

Differences in thinking between humans and other mammals are, of course, directly related to differences in their brains. But the human brain does not have any special structures that other mammals don't have. The major differences between human brains and those of other mammals are in the greater amount of area that is devoted to the cerebral cortex and the extended period of postnatal growth.

At birth, the human brain weighs about 350 grams—25% of its eventual adult weight of about 1,400 grams. Compare this to overall body weight. At birth, an infant weighs only about 5% of what he or she will weigh as an adult. Stated another way, the brain accounts for about 10% of the overall body weight of a newborn but for only about 2% of the overall body weight of an adult. By 6 months, the brain weighs 50% of what it will in adulthood; at 2 years, about 75%; at 5 years, 90%; and at 10 years, 95% (Lenroot & Giedd, 2007; Tanner, 1978). In contrast, total body weight is about 20% of eventual adult weight at 2 years and only 50% at 10 years. So the brain, which grows rapidly before birth, continues its rapid development postnatally. The rapid postnatal growth of the brain and head relative to the body in general is depicted in Figure 2.8. From this perspective, babies are brainy creatures indeed. But from another point of view, the brain of a newborn is grossly underdeveloped. Although the brain works effectively enough to direct basic physiological functions (for example, breathing, wake/sleep cycles), it cannot control coordinated movement, and it cannot perform the mental operations so characteristic of our species. Despite its size, the infant brain is far from the organ it will become.

The human brain, directly or indirectly, is responsible for controlling all aspects of behavior, from respiration and digestion to our most advanced forms of cognition. Our concern here is with the portion of the brain most associated with thought—the neocortex, or cerebral cortex. The neocortex is the most recent structure to appear in evolutionary time, associated primarily with mammals and having its greatest manifestation in primates and, especially, humans (MacLean, 1990). Other areas of the brain—such as the limbic system, which is the seat of emotion—are also important and significantly influence human behavior, but the neocortex—particularly the *frontal lobes* (sometimes referred to as the prefrontal lobes) of the neocortex—provides the characteristics that we most associate with humanness. We discuss briefly certain aspects of the neocortex and its development later in this section.

FIGURE 2.8 Growth curves for the brain and head and the body in general.

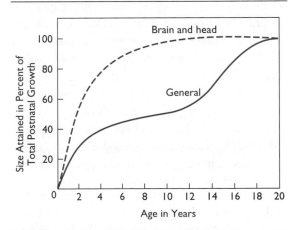

Source: Adapted from Scammon, R. E. (1930). The measurement of the body in childhood. In J. A. Harris, C. M. Jackson, D. G. Paterson, & R. E. Scammon (Eds.), *The measurement of man* (pp. 173–215). Minneapolis: University of Minnesota Press.

Our knowledge of brain development and its relation to cognition has increased substantially during the past several decades, primarily because of new technologies that permit the imaging of brain activities (de Haan, 2015; Lenroot & Giedd, 2007; Markant & Thomas, 2013). These neuroimaging techniques include, among others, *high-density event-related potentials*, which are a form of electroencephalography (EEG) that permits the detailed recording of brain activity when people solve cognitive tasks or are presented with specific stimuli; *positron emission tomography* (PET) and *single-photon emission computed tomography* (SPECT), in which radioactive materials are injected into participants and changes in radioactivity are used to reflect glucose consumption in specific areas of the brain; and *functional magnetic resonance imaging* (fMRI), which is a noninvasive technique that measures blood flow to the brain while people perform cognitive tasks. There are, of course, limits to such methods, but these and related new technologies promise that a new understanding of the relation between brain and cognitive development will soon be upon us.

We begin our discussion of the development of the brain by examining the basic building block of the brain—the neuron. We then examine how the brain gets "hooked up," the relation between brain development and behavior, and the role of experience in brain development and plasticity. This is not the last chapter in which brain development and the relation between children's brains and cognition is examined; many chapters devote space to this topic, for research in developmental cognitive neuroscience has expanded over the past decade.

Neuronal Development

The brain, and the nervous system in general, is a communication system. Electrical and chemical signals are transmitted from one **neuron**, or specialized nerve cell, to another. A recent estimate put the number of neurons in the mature human brain at 86 billion (Azevedo et al., 2009; Herculano-Houze, 2012). Unlike most other cells in the human body, neurons are not compressed together but are separated.

Figure 2.9 presents a drawing of a neuron. The main part of the neuron is the cell body, which contains the nucleus. Extending from the cell body are many projections, one of which is called the **axon**, a long fiber that carries messages away from the cell body to other cells. The other, more numerous fibers are called **dendrites**, which receive messages from other cells and transfer them to the cell body.

Dendrites do not actually come in physical contact with other dendrites (or with dendrite-like branches on axons, called *axon terminals*) when receiving messages. Rather, there are small spaces between dendrites, called **synapses**, through which messages are passed. The result is many billions of connections (synapses) among neurons. Electrical messages flowing down the axon of one cell cause the release of certain chemicals, called **neurotransmitters** (including *neuromodulators* that have an indirect effect on synaptic transmission), into the synapse. Neurotransmitters, which include dopamine, acetylcholine, and serotonin, move across the space between the cells and are "read" at the axon terminals of the adjacent cell, which convert the message back to an electrical signal and pass it on to its cell body. Conditions at the synapse (amount and type of neurotransmitters available) affect the transmission of the messages among neurons.

Fully developed axons are covered by sheaths of **myelin**, a fatty substance produced by supportive brain cells called *glial cells*. Like the plastic cover of an electric wire, myelin protects and insulates axons, speeding the rate at which

FIGURE 2.9 Primary structures of the neuron.

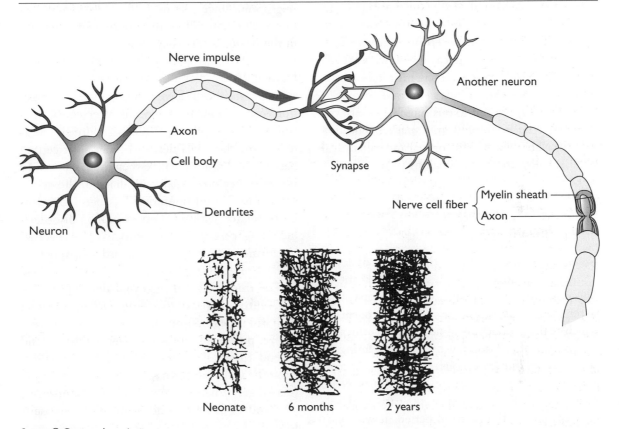

Source: © Cengage Learning.

nervous impulses can be sent and reducing inter-ference from other neurons. Compared with unmyelinated fibers, myelinated nerve fibers fire more rapidly, have lower thresholds of sensitiv-ity to stimulation, and have greater functional specificity, meaning that there is less "leakage" of electrical impulse so that only the target set of neurons are likely to get activated.

Myelination increases throughout childhood and adolescence, not being complete until some-time during the third decade of life or beyond. Myelination proceeds at different rates for differ-ent areas of the brain. For example, myelination begins prenatally for the sensory system, with most sensory structures being completely myelin-ated within the first year. This corresponds to the well-developed sensory abilities of human infants and the adultlike sensory capacities they possess long before they can speak. Myelination of the motor areas follows closely, with most of these brain structures being completely myelinated before the second year. Again, this corresponds to the development of motor abilities in young children, most of whom are walking before their second birthdays. The frontal cortex, the so-called "thinking" part of the brain, is the last to become fully myelinated, not being complete until early adulthood (Giedd et al., 1999; Stiles et al., 2015).

When brains are stained with a chemical so that scientists can get a better look at their structure, myelinated areas appear white, whereas cell bodies and dendrites appear slightly pink or gray. This is a source of the terms *white matter*, reflecting mainly myelinated axons mostly beneath the surface of the brain, and *gray matter*, reflecting mostly cell bodies in both cortical and subcortical (that is, below the cortex) regions.

Proliferation, Migration, and Differentiation

Neurons go through at least three stages of development (Lenroot & Giedd, 2007; Markant & Thomas, 2013; Stiles et al., 2015). The first stage is referred to as proliferation, or neurogenesis, which is the production of new neurons through the process of cell division by mitosis. During its peak, several hundred thousand neurons are generated *each minute* (C. A. Nelson, Thomas, & de Haan, 2006). Proliferation occurs early in development, during the prenatal period. It was once believed that the seventh month after conception essentially marked the end of neuron production. However, subsequent research in both laboratory animals (E. Gould et al., 1999) and humans (P. S. Eriksson et al., 1998) indicated that new neurons are produced in adults at least in some areas of the brain, specifically the hippocampus, a structure that has been implicated in the formation of new memories. New neurons are also produced throughout life in the olfactory bulbs, involved in the sense of smell, and there is some speculation that neurogenesis might occur after birth in several other brain areas (see C. A. Nelson et al., 2006). In general, unlike other cells of the body, new neurons are typically not produced after birth. So with a handful of exceptions, a person has all the neurons he or she will ever have at birth.

The second stage in neuronal development is migration. Once produced, the cells migrate, or move, to what will be their permanent position in the brain, where they collect with other cells to form the major parts of the brain (Bronner & Hatten, 2012). Not all cells migrate at the same time, but most cells have arrived at the final position in the brain by 7 months after conception (C. A. Nelson et al., 2006). Obviously, it is important that cells destined to be in a certain part of the brain be where they are supposed to be. Mistakes do occasionally happen, however, and faulty neural migration has been found to be associated with a variety of human disorders, including cerebral palsy, epilepsy, intellectual impairment, and learning disorders (Aylward, 1997; Volpe, 2000).

The third stage in neuronal development is differentiation (or *cytodifferentiation*). Once at their final destination, neurons begin to grow in size, produce more and longer dendrites, and extend their axons farther and farther away from the cell body. Synapses are created during this stage. When an axon meets an appropriate dendrite from another neuron, a synapse is formed.

It is important to point out that differentiation does not stop at birth. In fact, most neuronal differentiation, particularly myelination (discussed earlier) and synaptogenesis (discussed next), takes place *after* birth (see Lenroot & Giedd, 2007; C. A. Nelson et al., 2006).

Synaptogenesis and Selective Cell Death

The process of synapse formation, or synaptogenesis, is rapid during the early years of life when the brain is first becoming organized. Synaptogenesis continues throughout life as the brain changes in response to new information, although the rate at which new synapses are formed is never as great as it is during those prenatal and early postnatal months when the brain is growing most rapidly. Synapse formation is perhaps more rapid in the months immediately following birth, but the peak of synapse formation varies for different parts of the brain. For example, a burst of synapse formation in the visual cortex begins at about 3 or 4 months of age and peaks between 4 and 12 months. At this time, the visual cortex has about 50% *more* synapses than there are in the adult brain. A similar pattern is found in the prefrontal cortex (the "thinking" part of the brain), but the peak number of synapses is not attained until about 24 months of age (P. R. Huttenlocher, 1994).

At this point, the infant brain has many more synapses and neurons than it needs, and a process of cell and synaptic pruning begins in earnest (Oppenheim, Milligan, & von Bartheld, 2012; Tapia & Lichtman,

2012). (The pruning actually begins late during the prenatal period in a process known as selective cell death, or apoptosis.) Cell death and synaptic pruning occur at different rates for different parts of the brain. For example, the adult density of synapses for the visual cortex is attained from 2 to 4 years of age; in contrast, children continue to have more neurons and synapses in the prefrontal areas into their teen years than adults do (Giedd et al., 1999; Spear, 2007; Stiles et al., 2015; see Figure 2.10). Thus, by their middle to late teens, adolescents have fewer, but stronger and more effective, neuronal connections than they did as children. Interestingly, the pattern of changes in cortical thickness (gray matter, mostly neurons) observed over childhood and adolescence varies with age and with level of IQ, with this difference being especially pronounced in the frontal regions (Shaw et al., 2006). The researchers reported a

FIGURE 2.10 **Age differences in synapse production and pruning in the frontal and visual cortex.** The number of synapses show sharp increases early in development but then experience "pruning," as the brain gets sculpted to its eventual adult form. Note the particularly sharp decline in synapses in the prefrontal cortex during adolescence.

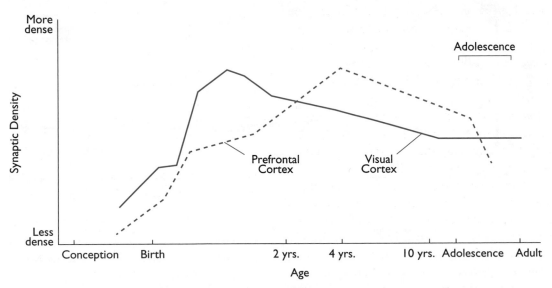

Source: Huttenlocher, P. R., & Dabholkar, A. S. (1997). Regional differences in synaptogenesis in human cerebral cortex. *Journal of Comparative Neurology, 387,* 167–178.

negative correlation between cortical thickness and IQ in early childhood, such that children with higher IQs had thinner cortices than children with lower IQs. This pattern was reversed in late childhood and adolescence. Moreover, children with exceptionally high IQs showed an early acceleration of cortical growth followed by an accelerated thinning in early adolescence. This pattern of cortical thickness for children of average, high, and superior intelligence is illustrated in Figure 2.11.

Rises and Declines in Neural Development

The pattern just described for synaptogenesis is one of rapid development (that is, synapse creation) followed by a decline in the number of synapses (and neurons). Other aspects of brain development show a similar rise and decline over childhood. For example, the basic metabolism of the brain (the rate at which it uses energy) increases sharply after the first year of life and peaks at about 150% of the adult rate from ages 4 to 5 (Chugani, Phelps, & Mazziotta, 1987). Evidence for this comes from studies using PET scans, which measure the amount of glucose uptake in the resting brain. After age 5 or so, the rate of glucose consumption slows down, reaching adult levels at about age 9. Thus, not only do infants and children have more neurons and synapses than adults, but their brains are also working harder (or at least using more calories) than those of adults.

FIGURE 2.11 **Rate of change in cortical thickness for children of average, high, and superior intelligence.** The rate of change for the cluster of cortical points in the right superior and medial frontal gyrus, which showed a significant trajectory difference between children of average, high, and superior intelligence. Positive values indicate increasing cortical thickness, negative values indicate cortical thinning.

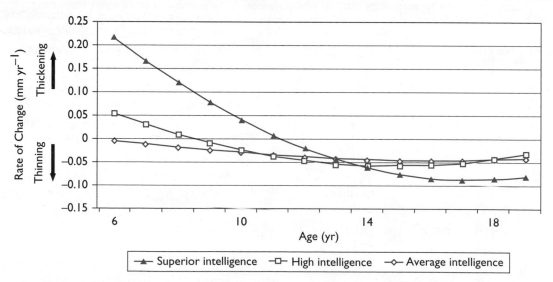

Source: Shaw et al. (2006, March 30). Intellectual ability and cortical development in children and adolescents. *Nature, 440,* 676–679 (p. 677).

In addition to changes in the actual structure of the neurons, developmental changes occur in the presence of various neurotransmitters—chemicals found in the synapses that promote the electrical/chemical communication between cells. Several of these neurotransmitters show increases followed by decreases over infancy and childhood, similar to the changes seen in synapses (M. H. Johnson, 1998; Levitt, 2003).

What function might there be in this rise and fall in several aspects of brain development? One proposal is that the hypermetabolism seen during the preschool years might be necessary for the rapid learning that occurs during this time (Elman et al., 1996)—think of how children's language development proceeds from uttering only single words around 10 months to speaking in long paragraphs by age 3 or 4. Preschool children also have more neurons and synapses than older children and, we think it's fair to say, more to learn that is truly "new." These elevated levels of synapses and neurotransmitters also surely afford greater plasticity should brain damage occur. And although it may seem that slowing down the processes of synaptic pruning and cell death would afford children some advantages (more neurons and synapses can presumably do more learning), the failure to display such losses has been linked to intellectual impairment, schizophrenia, and other developmental disorders (Feinberg, 1982/1983; Margolis, Chuang, & Post, 1994).

A brief description of the major features of neuron development is presented in Table 2.3.

TABLE 2.3   **A brief description of major features in neuronal development.**

Developmental Event	Timeline	Brief Description
Proliferation (neurogenesis)	First 20 weeks after conception	Neurons are born from neural stem cells. This peaks in the third or fourth month of gestation.
Neural migration	6–24 weeks after conception	Neurons move, or migrate, to their "adult" location in the brain.
Differentiation/synaptogenesis	3rd trimester through adolescence	Neurons extent their dendrites and axonal terminals, forming synapses with other neurons.
Postnatal neurogenesis	Birth–adulthood	New neurons develop in some parts of the brain, including the dentate gyrus of the hippocampus and the olfactory bulb.
Myelination	3rd trimester to adulthood	Neurons become coated by a fatty tissue that results in faster transmission of nervous signals and a reduction of interference.
Selective cell death (apoptosis)	3rd trimester to adulthood	Neurons die.
Synaptic pruning	Infancy through adulthood	The number of synapses per neuron is greatest between 4 and 8 months of life and decreases with age.

How Do Young Brains Get Hooked Up?

We have described briefly the process of synaptogenesis and related development of neurons, such as myelination. But how do brains actually get wired? That is, what mechanisms are responsible for building a brain that eventually will be able to recognize faces, solve arithmetic problems, talk, and read? Perhaps the position accepted implicitly by most brain scientists throughout most of the 20th century was that the brain becomes specialized, and complex cognition thus arises, through intrinsic genetic and biochemical mechanisms. In other words, genes dictate the formation, migration, and differentiation of neurons, with experience serving only to "fine-tune" the brain. Few developmental neuroscientists believe this today, however, arguing instead that brain development involves an extended process that is greatly influenced by postnatal experience (Fox, Levitt, & Nelson, 2010; C. A. Nelson et al., 2006).

It has become increasingly clear to those who study brain development that a reciprocal relationship exists between brain and behavioral development. To quote developmental neuroscientist Joan Stiles (2009), "Behavioral development is inextricably linked to brain development and vice versa. They are absolutely interdependent, exerting bidirectional influences that are essential for the normal development of the child" (p. 199). With respect to the survival of neurons and the process of synaptogenesis, William Greenough and his associates (Black et al., 1998; Greenough, Black, & Wallace, 1987) proposed that specific experiences produce neural activity that in turn determines which of the excess synapses will survive (see also M. H. Johnson & de Haan, 2011; C. A. Nelson, 2001). The nervous system of animals (including humans) has been prepared by natural selection to expect certain types of stimulation, such as a three-dimensional world consisting of moving objects. We say "expected" in that these are the types of stimulation that virtually all of humans' ancestors experienced, that is, they are species-typical. Greenough and his colleagues referred to the processes whereby synapses are formed and maintained when an organism has species-typical experiences as experience-expectant processes (or experience-expectant synaptogenesis); as a result, functions will develop for all members of a species, given a species-typical environment. Early experience of merely viewing a normal world, for example, is sufficient for the visual nervous system to develop properly. Those neurons and connections that receive the species-expected experience live and become organized with other activated neurons, and those that do not receive such activation die. Thus, although the infant comes into the world prepared and "prewired" both for certain experiences and to develop certain abilities, these abilities are substantially influenced by experience. What is hardwired seems to be a susceptibility to certain environmental experiences rather than the circuitry for detailed behaviors themselves, a form of architectural constraints we discussed earlier.

Examples of experience-expectant processes can be seen in research that restricts the species-typical perceptual experiences of an animal. For instance, cats or rats reared in total darkness or in the absence of patterned light later have difficulty making simple visual discriminations. That is, because they were not exposed to visual stimulation early in life, when later provided with visual experience they act as if they cannot see, or at least do not see normally (Crabtree & Riesen, 1979). In humans, cataract patients who suddenly gain sight via surgery have difficulty making simple visual discriminations. For example, for several weeks after surgery, they can tell the difference between a square and a triangle only by counting the corners (Senden, 1960). Visual abilities for both animals and humans improve with time, but the longer the period of deprivation, the less reversible are the effects (Crabtree & Riesen, 1979; Timney, Mitchell, & Cynader, 1980).

The behavioral effects of sensory deprivation are reflected in changes at the neuronal level. For example, when a kitten's eyes first open, about half of the neurons in the visual cortex respond selectively to direction of movement or orientation of a stimulus (that is, firing only when an object in their visual field moves in a certain direction or is in a particular orientation, such as diagonal lines or straight lines). Usually, after several weeks of normal visual experience, all the cells in the visual cortex become sensitive to the orientation of a stimulus or to direction of movement. But when kittens are prevented from seeing any patterns (that is, when they experience only homogeneous light without any objects to see), the cells of the visual cortex make fewer connections with other cells and gradually lose their sensitivity to orientation. Experience (or lack of experience) changes the structure and organization of the young brain, even for something as basic as vision. As with behavior, recovery of normal neuronal structure and responsivity following exposure to pattern light occurs, although the amount or degree of recovery declines with longer periods of deprivation (Blakemore & Van Sluyters, 1975; Cynader, Berman, & Hein, 1976).

One cannot do these kinds of experiments with children, of course, but research by Daphne Maurer and her colleagues with infants born having cataracts over their eyes, including some infants who had their cataracts removed shortly after birth, is informative (Le Grand et al., 2001; Maurer, Mondloch, & Lewis, 2007; see Maurer &

Lewis, 2013 for a review). Maurer and her colleagues reported that infants who had their cataracts removed and new lenses placed in their eyes within several months of birth displayed a generally typical pattern of visual development. The longer the delay in removing the cataracts, however, the poorer vision was. Moreover, even for those infants who had their cataracts removed early and developed normal vision, some aspects of *face* processing were impaired (Le Grand et al., 2001). This finding suggests that there may be different sensitive periods for the brain areas associated with visual acuity and those associated with processing faces. It also points to the importance of identifying and correcting visual problems early to minimize their long-term effects.

Greenough and his colleagues (1987) proposed a second process of synapse development, which they called experience-dependent processes (or experience-dependent synaptogenesis). In this case, connections among neurons are made that reflect the unique experiences of an individual rather than the experiences that all members of a species can expect to have. In both cases, the overproduction of neurons enables an individual to make connections (and, thus, store information) that reflect his or her particular environment. When certain experiences are not had—when the world does not cause certain neurons to be activated and synapses to join—the neurons die.

Bennett Bertenthal and Joseph Campos (1987) relate the ideas of Greenough and his colleagues to the old nature/nurture issue and the question of whether infants come into the world fully prepared by biology or as blank slates. Bertenthal and Campos write, "What determines the survival of synaptic connections is the principle of use: Those synapses activated by sensory or motor experience survive; the remainder are lost through disuse. For

Greenough et al., then, experience does not create tracings on a blank tablet; rather experience erases some of them" (p. 560).

The message here is that early brain development is not exclusively under genetic control, consistent with the developmental systems approach discussed earlier. Certainly, genes influence what the basic structure of the brain will be. But experiences play an important role in shaping the precise circuitry of the brain. From electrical and chemical activities of the growing nerve cells before birth to the information obtained through the senses after birth, the brain becomes organized by information it receives and by its own activation as much as or more so than by the instructions emanating from the genes.

Development of the Neocortex

When most people think of the brain, they think of what's on the surface, a convoluted series of lobes. This is the **neocortex, or cerebral cortex,** which is a multilayered sheet of neurons, only 3 to 4 millimeters thick, that surrounds the rest of the brain. Figure 2.12 provides a lateral view of the brain; except for the cerebellum and the

FIGURE 2.12 **A lateral view of the left side of the human brain showing the major structures.** All but the cerebellum and the spinal cord are part of the neocortex.

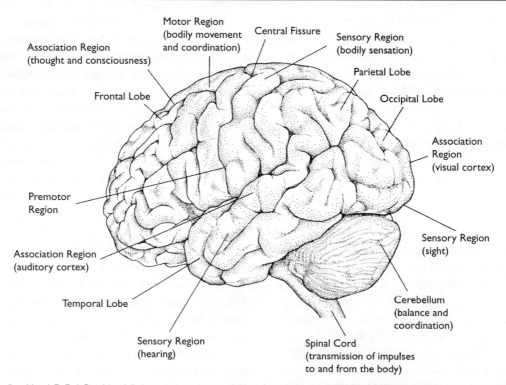

Source: Bjorklund, D. F., & Bjorklund, B. R. (1992). *Looking at children: An introduction to child development* (p. 129). Belmont, CA: Wadsworth.

spinal cord, all of the structures shown are part of the neocortex. Of course, there is much more to the brain than the neocortex, but because the neocortex is the part of the brain primarily associated with thinking, it is the only major part of the brain that we discuss in this chapter.

The neocortex consists of two approximately equal halves, or hemispheres, connected by a thick mass of nerves called the **corpus callosum**. The neocortex can be further divided into regions. Some primary areas, such as the various sensory regions, receive information directly from the senses. Other primary areas, such as the motor regions, send instructions directly to muscles. Secondary areas consist of regions that integrate information and have many connections with other areas of the brain. These are the association (or thought) regions, which are responsible for our more complex mental functioning.

Let us provide a research example of the connection between development of the prefrontal lobes of the neocortex and cognitive development. Development of the prefrontal lobes in humans is rapid between birth and about 2 years of age. As we mentioned, the prefrontal lobes are proposed to be involved in many acts of "higher" cognition, but one important function of the prefrontal lobes appears to be in the inhibition of responses (Fuster, 1989; see Carlson, Zelazo, & Faja, 2013). For example, for some tasks, children must *not* execute a previously acquired response (that is, they must inhibit that response) so that they can make a new response. One such task is Piaget's A-not-B object permanence task. (See Chapter 4 for a more in-depth discussion of object permanence.) On this task, infants watch as a toy is hidden in one of two wells. The infants are then distracted for a delay period, after which they are allowed to retrieve the toy. Over trials, the hiding place is changed to Well B following a

series of correct retrievals from Well A. Piaget reported that infants younger than 12 months have great difficulty performing this task and typically look for the hidden object at the A location, where they were successful previously.

Adele Diamond (1985) tested 25 infants in the A-not-B task, beginning at about 7 months of age and continuing until 12 months. She reported that the delay between hiding and searching that was necessary to produce the A-not-B error increased with age at a rate of about 2 seconds per month. That is, 7.5-month-old infants would search for the hidden object at the erroneous A position following only a 2-second delay. By 12 months of age, infants made the error only if approximately 10 seconds transpired between the hiding of the object and the beginning of the search.

Although such research suggests that memory might be a factor in infants' performance, Diamond believed that the more important factor is infants' ability to *inhibit* prepotent responses in solving the A-not-B task. Substantial research with adults (Luna et al., 2001), older children (Barkley, 1997), and infants (M. A. Bell, Wolfe, & Adkins, 2007) points to the frontal lobes as the locus of inhibitory control, and Diamond (1991) proposed that during the first year, infants' prefrontal lobes develop gradually, which results in their becoming increasingly able to inhibit their behavioral responses. Despite "knowing" that the object was hidden at Location B, young infants cannot stop themselves from executing a response that has been correct in the immediate past. They have learned a response, and before they can learn a new one, they must inhibit the old one. This ability develops over the first year, with girls showing faster progress than boys, suggesting more rapid maturational development of the prefrontal cortex in girls through this age period (Diamond, 1985).

Support for Diamond's claim comes from a study showing significant relations between performance on the A-not-B task and scores on a task of inhibitory ability in 9-month-olds (Holmboe et al., 2008) and from neuroimaging studies that show connections between infants' performance on A-not-B tasks and frontal lobe activity (Baird et al., 2002; M. A. Bell & Fox, 1992). For example, Martha Bell and Nathan Fox (1992) recorded EEG activity from the frontal lobes of 7- to 12-month-old infants performing the A-not-B task. Consistent with Diamond's hypothesis, they reported systematic changes in EEG patterns as a function of age and length of delay.

Age-related changes in brain structure and function associated with changes in cognition and behavior are not only observed in infancy and early childhood but also later in life. It will likely not surprise you to learn that major changes in brain organization occur in adolescence, a time of substantial change in behavior and thinking. Although some, such as Piaget (see Chapter 5), have noted the advent of adultlike cognitive abilities, a more common description of adolescent thought and behavior centers around a new self-centeredness, emotional instability, increases in risk-taking, and the seeking of novelty (see Spear, 2000). Not surprisingly, these behavioral changes are also associated with changes in the brain. For example, changes occur in the distribution of various neurotransmitters, with some decreasing substantially in both the frontal cortex and the limbic system, an area of the brain associated with emotion. Amount of gray matter in the adolescent brain actually decreases relative to childhood, while white matter increases (mainly due to increased myelination in the

frontal cortex), and different areas of the brain become increasingly connected (E. L. Dennis et al., 2013). Moreover, the amygdala and other structures in the limbic system reach adult levels before the prefrontal lobes (Mills et al., 2014). This produces what some researchers refer to as a mismatch in maturation (Giedd, 2015; Mills et al., 2014), which may be responsible in part for the sensation-seeking, risky behaviors and sometimes poor decision making often seen in adolescents.

These changes, which to varying degrees are also characteristic of other adolescent mammals, are likely adaptive, in that the emerging adult must seek independence from his or her parents, experiment with new environments, and establish a place in his or her social group (Sercombe, 2014). That there is a species-typical pattern of brain changes associated with such behavior should not be surprising. But what we have here is only correlation, and the correlation is far from perfect. Although many adolescents experience the storm and strife one might expect from a radical restructuring of the brain, others do not. There is a species-typical pattern of changes in cognition and behavior during adolescence, but there is also much variability. We are convinced that the brain mediates all such behavior; however, we must keep in mind that brain development is a dynamic process, influenced by both internal and external factors, rather than the simple consequence of the "unfolding" of a genetic blueprint.

The Brain's Plasticity

Plasticity, discussed in Chapter 1, refers to the ability to change. To what extent can new synapses be formed and different parts of the brain take over a function intended for another part of the nervous system? Put another way, plasticity also refers to the potential outcomes that are possible for a single neuron, a bundle of neurons, or a larger brain structure. Given certain experiences at certain times during life, how might these cells become organized? Implicit in the theorizing of most developmental neuroscientists is the concept of plasticity.

Neuronal Plasticity

There is apparently little or no plasticity in the production of new neurons, at least in the cerebral cortex. As we noted earlier, new neurons in the hippocampus and olfactory bulb are generated throughout life, but evidence of neurogenesis in the cortex of humans and other mammals is scarce. With few exceptions, a newborn comes into the world with more neurons than he or she will ever need. And from birth on, there is a loss of neurons—a rapid loss during infancy and a gradual decline thereafter.

The picture is different for the formation of new synapses. Contemporary research indicates that new synaptic connections can be formed throughout life (see Greenough et al., 1987; T. J. Shore, 2014). What causes new synapses to form? The simple answer is experience. Perhaps the most convincing evidence of the effects of experience on brain structures comes from studies providing environmental stimulation for laboratory animals, mostly rats and mice. In studies dating back to 1949 (Hebb, 1949), researchers have raised groups of laboratory animals in environments constructed to be enriching or stimulating and then compared their brain development and learning ability with those raised in environments considered to be deprived (Hymovitch, 1952; Turner & Greenough, 1985). Enriched environments usually included animals raised together in large cages that were filled with a variety of objects with which they could interact. Various platforms, toys, and mazes filled some of the cages—not too dissimilar from the cages one might buy for the family gerbil.

These experiments have shown that rats and mice raised in enriched environments are superior at a wide range of complex tasks, such as maze learning. The differences in learning ability between enriched and nonenriched animals are of a general nature, with the most likely explanation for these effects being that "the groups differ in the amount of stored knowledge upon which they can draw in novel situations" (Greenough et al., 1987, p. 547). Concerning changes found in their brains, enriched animals have heavier and thicker neocortexes, larger neurons with more dendrites, and importantly, more synaptic connections. In one study, enriched rats had 20% to 25% more synapses per neuron in their visual cortexes than did rats raised in individual cages (Turner & Greenough, 1985). And these effects are not limited to infant animals; the behavioral and brain benefits of living in a stimulating environment are found even when experienced by older animals (Greenough et al., 1986; C. A. Nelson et al., 2006).

Synaptic plasticity is greatest in infancy. With age and experience, neurons and synapses that were formed prenatally or in infancy die, and with their death, connections that could have formed are now impossible. Thus, experience serves not only to create new connections but also to make other ones impossible or less likely. But even though the plasticity to form new synapses decreases with age, it does not disappear; we retain substantial neural plasticity throughout life (Lillard & Erisir, 2011). What does change is the degree to which experience can change the brain and the intensity of the experience needed to produce change.

We want to make it clear that losing plasticity should not be viewed completely negatively. As a result of genetic programming and experience, neurons become dedicated, or committed to certain functions, effectively eliminating plasticity. This commitment affords greater efficiency of processing, permitting sets of neurons to specialize. For a species such as humans, who have long life spans and must deal with a large diversity of social circumstances, retaining some plasticity into adulthood is necessary. However, much about human life does not change substantially over time and circumstances, and individuals are best served by a nervous system that early in life commits neurons to basic functions.

Recovery of Function From Brain Damage

Perhaps the best-known evidence for the plasticity of the nervous system comes from case studies of people who have experienced brain damage and exhibit deficits in physical or mental functioning. These studies document the process of readjustment these people go through and the differences their ages make to their readjustment.

Before proceeding, we must mention some problems that are inevitable when using brain-damage research to understand brain function. These include the facts that (a) brain damage can rarely be narrowed to one area, (b) brain damage frequently involves complications beyond that of simple lesions, (c) disorders following brain damage might not reveal how the brain functions normally, and (d) lesions in one area of the brain can lead to changes in other areas of the brain (Fuster, 1989). Nevertheless, despite these and other reservations, much can be learned about brain functioning from studying brain damage, especially when viewed in combination with other sources of data.

Research dating back to the middle 1800s has produced mixed results concerning age of brain damage and the likelihood of recovery, with some studies documenting greater recovery of function when brain damage occurs early versus later in life, and others showing just the opposite pattern (see Anderson, Spencer-Smith, & Wood, 2011). Two seemingly contradictory explanations have been offered to explain the relation between age of brain damage and subsequent recovery: *early plasticity* and *early vulnerability*.

The early plasticity view contends that the brains of infants and young children are highly plastic, or flexible, relative to the brains of older children and adults, and as a result they are better able to overcome the adverse effects of brain damage. This perspective is supported by evidence from the most-studied types of brain damage, those associated with insults to areas of the brain associated with language. Since the 19th century, numerous reports have indicated that children who experience brain damage to the language areas of their left hemispheres before they are able to speak are eventually able to attain more advanced levels of language than are older children or adults who experience similar brain damage (Annett, 1973; Woods & Carey, 1979). Likewise, left-hemisphere brain injury for children who can already talk can produce an initial loss of language ability, but in many cases, language is recovered and the child talks again at normal or near-normal levels. Studies conducted on adults have not found the same degree of recovery (see Witelson, 1985). Even in young children, however, full recovery of language is rare, showing that the human brain is not completely plastic, even early in life (Witelson, 1987). Yet the evidence clearly shows that "there is a remarkable functional plasticity for language functions following brain damage in childhood in that the eventual cognitive level reached is often far beyond that observed in cases of adult brain damage, even those having extensive remedial education. These results attest to the operation of marked neural plasticity at least in the immature brain" (Witelson, 1987, p. 676). This pattern is also seen for milder forms of brain injuries, such as concussions. Children tend to recover from the effects of concussion (for example, headaches, memory loss) faster than adolescents and adults do (see Yeats & Taylor, 2005). These patterns of results are consistent with the early plasticity explanation of brain development and the view that if one must have brain damage, have it early, for a young brain is more likely than an older brain to recover normal function. This is the so-called *Kennard effect*, and it is based on the observations of Margaret Kennard, a pioneer in early studies on recovery of function from brain damage (Kolb, 1989).

Other research, however, has shown that the Kennard effect does not hold for all types of brain injuries, with some types of brain damage producing more long-lasting and negative consequences when experienced earlier rather than later in life, supporting the early vulnerability hypothesis. From this perspective, because the brains of infants and young children are becoming increasingly specialized with experience, early damage can alter the typical course of development resulting in serious disruptions of normal neural organization and functioning. Consider the analogy with the effects of teratogens (agents than can adversely affect the development of a fetus) on physical development. Exposure to a drug

such as Thalidomide interferes with the formation of limbs early in prenatal life, before arms and legs have been developed. The drug has no influence on limb development when exposure occurs later in prenatal life, after the limbs have been formed (K. L. Moore & Persaud, 2003). In fact, brain damage that occurs during the prenatal or early postnatal period typically results in permanent neurological impairment (Anderson et al., 2004; Riva & Cazzaniga, 1986), consistent with the early vulnerability perspective.

The early plasticity and early vulnerability views represent extremes of a continuum (see Figure 2.13), and recent research and theory notes that recovery depends on a wider series of variables than previously considered (Anderson et al., 2011; Kolb, 1989). For example, when the focus of damage is to an area of the brain involved with more general cognitive functioning such as attention, executive function, or intelligence as measured by IQ rather

FIGURE 2.13 **The human brain shows both early plasticity and early vulnerability with respect to recovery of function from brain damage.** The age at which an individual experiences a brain insult interacts with a host of other factors to determine the likelihood of recovery.

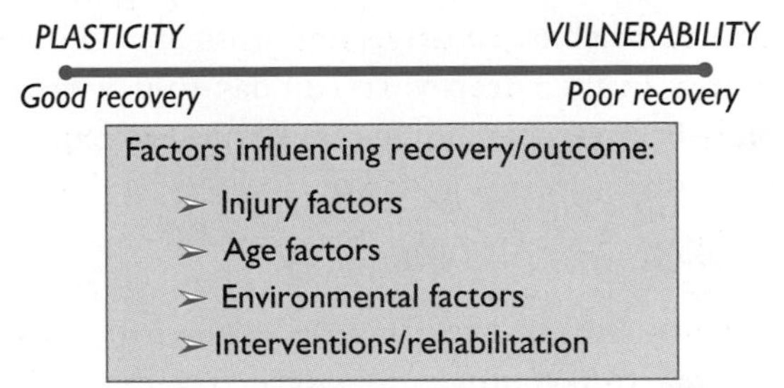

PLASTICITY   *VULNERABILITY*

Good recovery   Poor recovery

Factors influencing recovery/outcome:
➢ Injury factors
➢ Age factors
➢ Environmental factors
➢ Interventions/rehabilitation

Source: Anderson, V., Spencer-Smith, M., & Wood, A. (2011). Do children really recover better? Neurobehavioural plasticity after early brain insult. *Brain, 134,* 2197–2221.

than with a specific cognitive ability such as language, recovery is often greater the later the damage occurs (Anderson et al., 2009; Witelson, 1987). Evidence reviewed by Bryan Kolb and Ian Whishaw (1990) from both animal and human research demonstrates that younger children and animals show more permanent deficits than older children and animals after brain damage to the frontal lobes, which are associated with general processes such as those involved in IQ and executive function. For example, in one study, brain damage before the age of 1 year resulted in lower IQs for children than did similar brain damage that occurred after a child's first birthday (Riva & Cazzaniga, 1986). Another study reported greater reductions in IQ for children who suffered brain damage before the age of 5 than for those who suffered similar injury after age 5 (Kornhuber et al., 1985). In research with rats, Kolb and Whishaw (1981) reported that brain lesions inflicted shortly after birth resulted in a smaller adult brain (approximately 25% smaller) than did lesions inflicted on adult animals (approximately 12% smaller). Also, although infants and young children may demonstrate rapid recovery of cognitive function shortly after brain damage, deficits may appear years later. For example, toddlers with severe brain insults often display substantial recovery of "normal" abilities; however, these same children may show signs of cognitive deficits in their teen years, as day-to-day tasks become more demanding (M. Dennis, 1989).

Slow Growth and Plasticity

As we mentioned in Chapter 1, through most of the 20th century, it was believed that if children suffered severe deprivation for much more than their first year after birth, they were destined to a life of intellectual impairment and psychopathology. Subsequent research with both human and nonhuman-animal participants has clearly shown that this is not true (Beckett et al., 2006; Suomi & Harlow, 1972). When the course of a young child's or young animal's life changes drastically, patterns of development can also be radically altered.

Let us provide one research example for the reversibility of the effects of negative early experience here. We presented some research on plasticity in Chapter 1, and the topic is discussed in greater detail with respect to intelligence in Chapter 13. With the political turmoil in Southeast Asia during the 1970s, many abandoned and sickly children from that part of the world were subsequently adopted by American families. Generally, follow-up interviews of adopted Asian children who were malnourished and socially deprived as infants revealed that their intellectual and social development was either at or above normal by early childhood (E. A. Clark & Hanisee, 1982; Winick, Meyer, & Harris, 1975). In the 1982 study by Audrey Clark and Jeanette Hanisee, for example, 25 adopted Asian children were given a test of verbal intelligence, the Peabody Picture Vocabulary Test (PPVT), and a test of social competence, the Vineland Social Maturity Scale (VSMS). The average age of the children at the time of testing was 44 months, and all the children had been in their adoptive homes for at least 23 months before testing. Before being adopted, most of the children had experienced physical and psychological deprivation. Sixteen of them were reported to have been malnourished sometime during infancy, with many displaying dehydration and muscle weakness. Despite their inauspicious beginnings, the children fared exceptionally well on the tests of verbal and social competencies. The national average on both the PPVT and the VSMS is 100. The adopted children's average scores were 120 on the PPVT and 137 on the VSMS. These children, impoverished and malnourished as infants, showed no residual signs of their early deprivation within 2 years of having been placed in upper-middle-class homes.

This plasticity of behavior and intelligence is attributed, in part, to the slow growth of the brain. As we noted earlier in this chapter, although the human brain is large relative to the rest of the body at birth, it continues to grow well into early adulthood. This prolonged immaturity provides humans the time necessary to master the complexities of social life. But it also provides the opportunity to change behavior and to acquire novel patterns later in life. Seen in this light, the extended immaturity of the human nervous system provides opportunities for resilience, behavioral flexibility, and plasticity unsurpassed by any other species (see Bjorklund & Pellegrini, 2002).

An immature brain means a slow and inefficient brain. Partly because of the extent of myelination and partly because of a paucity of experience, young children process information more slowly than older children do (see Kail, 1991). This slower speed of processing translates directly into less-efficient processing (Case, 1985) and means that more of younger children's processing is effortful in nature, in that it uses substantial portions of their limited mental resources (Hasher & Zacks, 1979; see Chapter 7). In contrast, more of older children's and adults' cognitive processing is automatic, in that it can be done quickly, without conscious awareness, and requires little or none of one's limited mental capacity. In other words, young children must work harder mentally to obtain the same results that older children can achieve more easily.

This inefficiency has its drawbacks, of course. You can't teach much of a complex nature to young children, you can't expect them to gain as much from experiences as older children do, and you can't rely on them to make many important decisions on their own. Despite the obvious disadvantages of a slow and inefficient brain, it also has its benefits. According to Bjorklund and Green (1992),

> Because little in the way of cognitive processing can be automatized early, presumably because of children's incomplete myelination, they are better prepared to adapt, cognitively, to later environments. If experiences early in life yielded automization, the child would lose the flexibility necessary for adult life. Processes automatized in response to the demands of early childhood may be useless and likely detrimental for coping with the very different cognitive demands faced by adults. Cognitive flexibility in the species is maintained by an immature nervous system that gradually permits the automization of more mental operations, increasing the likelihood that lessons learned as a young child will not interfere with the qualitatively different tasks required of the adult. (pp. 49–50)

This should not be seen as implying that the effects of early social or physical deprivation can always be reversed. As you'll see in later chapters, early experiences (or lack of them) can have relatively permanent, negative consequences. The experiences of infancy and toddlerhood establish patterns of behavior that can potentially influence the accomplishments of later years, particularly when those experiences are stable over childhood. But the inefficiency of the young brain does offer children some protection from the perils of an early damaging environment.

Interactive Specialization

Many of the ideas we have described so far in this chapter are incorporated into interactive specialization models of brain development (see M. H. Johnson & de Haan, 2011), including probabilistic epigenesis, architectural constraints, neural plasticity, and experience-expectant and experience-dependent synaptogenesis. Interactive specialization models provide a framework for understanding how brain functioning becomes both localized and specialized as the result of domain-general mechanisms. These models posit that cortical development is a self-organizing process, a bidirectional interaction between brain structure and psychological function. Consider, for instance, that the temporal lobe of the left hemisphere is specialized for language processing in the brain of most adults. Proponents of interactive specialization models argue that this localization is the result of learning and experience that leads to *entrenchment*. As we experience the same type of information throughout development (for instance, language), our neural networks become tuned to process this information more efficiently. As a result, these networks become less able to learn new types of information (for instance, a second language or visuospatial processing). Previous learning and entrenchment then affect the scope of later plasticity. This loss of plasticity is not all bad, however, with the upside being an increase in the specialization and efficiency of neural networks. As different brain regions interact and compete for neural resources during the entrenchment process, networks are "recruited" and become more localized.

The interactive specialization argument relies on some architectural constraints to account for the similarities across individuals' brains, for instance, that the ears, and therefore hearing, are connected to the temporal cortex. The temporal cortex then "recruits" neural networks as they are becoming more specialized to process language. Otherwise, the same plasticity that accounts for recovery after brain damage is the same plasticity that accounts for brain specialization across development (Pennington, 2015). This developmental process depends on both experience-expectant and experience-dependent synaptogenesis, as we have described, ensuring that experience will create and strengthen some synapses while weakening or eliminating others. As a result, neural networks learn the regularities that exist in the world.

These models generate some testable predictions. For example, we should expect to see changes in cortical activation for specific tasks or stimuli as the neural networks responsible for processing said stimuli become more "tightly wired" and localized across development (M. H. Johnson, 2000). Some evidence has already been found to support this prediction, namely that younger infants show larger areas of brain activation during word learning (Neville, 1991) and face processing (de Haan, Oliver, & Johnson, 1998) than older ones, suggesting that perhaps more pathways are activated before experience with these types of stimuli leads to the specialization of one or more of these pathways.

DEVELOPMENTAL BIOLOGY AND COGNITIVE DEVELOPMENT

As the field of cognitive psychology evolved into cognitive science, people interested in mental functioning became increasingly aware of the need to coordinate the psychological level of explanation with the biological level. A similar realization is occurring now in the field of cognitive development. For example, nearly 2 decades ago, James Byrnes and Nathan Fox (1998) reviewed some of the new neuroscience techniques and research findings from the developmental neurosciences and concluded that we are on the threshold of a new revolution, equivalent to the cognitive revolution. Since then, the discipline of *developmental cognitive neuroscience* has emerged, which focuses on the study of normal cognitive and neurological development (M. H. Johnson & de Haan, 2011; Marshall, 2015). Perhaps its greatest contribution is elucidating the neurological mechanisms that underlie behavioral observations made earlier by psychologists. Admittedly, the presentation in this chapter is cursory, but we believe that it provides a foundation for the proper understanding of the ontogeny of human thought. Throughout the remainder of this book, we include contemporary neuroscience research in discussing a variety of aspects of cognitive development, from social cognition to executive function and memory, and we hope that this chapter will have served as an adequate introduction for placing this new brain-based research into perspective.

By acknowledging the importance of biological factors to cognitive development, we do not mean to suggest that the future of the field lies in biology. But having an idea of both the neural and evolutionary causes of behavior and development will help the psychologist ask better research questions and achieve a better understanding of development. For example, knowledge of the developmental relationship between brain and behavior has important implications not only for theories of cognitive development but also for societal practices. How pliable is human intelligence? When, in development, can children most benefit from certain educational experiences? Is earlier always better, or are certain sensitive periods for particular experiences distributed throughout development?

The study of cognition, including its development, has gone through substantial changes since its beginnings in the 1950s. We cannot be certain what the future will hold, but it seems certain that part of the new paradigm will pay closer attention to the biological bases of cognition and cognitive development.

Section Review

New *neuroimaging techniques*, such as high-density event-related potentials, PET, SPECT, and fMRI, are providing new knowledge about brain functioning and development.

Neuronal Development

- The nervous system consists of *neurons*, which transport chemical and electrical signals. Neurons consist of a cell body; *axons*, long fibers that carry messages away from the cell body to other cells; and *dendrites*, more numerous fibers that receive messages from other cells and transfer them to the cell body.
- Electrical messages are transmitted through *synapses*, facilitated by various *neurotransmitters*.
- Neurons go through at least three stages of development: *proliferation* (*neurogenesis*), *migration*, and *differentiation*.
- Synapse formation (*synaptogenesis*) is rapid during prenatal development and during the early months of postnatal life.
- A complementary process to synaptogenesis, *selective cell death*, or *apoptosis*, also occurs, with many neurons dying.

- *Myelin* is a fatty substance that surrounds axons, promoting faster transmission of electrical signals. Different areas of the brain begin and end the process of *myelination* at different times, and degree of myelination is related to certain sensory, motor, and intellectual levels of development.

How Do Young Brains Get Hooked Up?

- Some neural connections are made by all members of a species given typical experiences (*experience-expectant processes*), whereas other connections are made because of the unique experiences of an individual (*experience-dependent processes*).
- Neurons live (and form synapses with other neurons) or die as a function of use.
- Evidence suggests that areas of infants' brains are only weakly specialized for processing certain information (for example, language) but become more domain-specific in nature as a result of experience.

Development of the Neocortex and Plasticity

- The *neocortex* (or *cerebral cortex*) is divided into two hemispheres that are connected by the *corpus callosum*.
- Neuronal *plasticity* has been most clearly demonstrated in studies with animals, including those reared in deprived or enriched environments.
- With age, the plasticity needed to form new synapses declines, but it does not disappear.
- Examination of the recovery of function after brain damage shows that the early plasticity and early vulnerability explanations

represent ends of a continuum and that the degree of recovery of function from brain damage depends not only on the age at which the insult occurs but on a host of other interacting factors, including the area of the brain and cognitive abilities affected, the extent of the injury, and the experiences (including rehabilitation) of the individual following brain damage.

- Humans' prolonged immaturity contributes to our behavioral plasticity and to children's abilities to overcome the effects of deleterious early environments.
- *Interactive specialization* models propose that specialization and localization in the adult brain are the result of self-organizing, domain-general mechanisms operating on experience during development.

Ask Yourself . . .

8. What are the two types of signals that neurons transmit? What is the function of the axon, dendrites, and synapses during these processes?
9. Describe the three stages of neuronal development.
10. How are *synaptogenesis* and *apoptosis* complementary processes? What is their developmental function?
11. According to Greenough and colleagues, what are two ways in which experience influences neuronal development?
12. How does the development of the prefrontal cortex from birth to 2 years influence cognition and behavior?
13. What are some of the costs and benefits of early neuronal plasticity?
14. What do interactive specialization models propose about brain development?

KEY TERMS AND CONCEPTS

architectural constraints
axon
behavioral genetics
biologically primary abilities
biologically secondary
   abilities
chronotopic constraints
corpus callosum
dendrites
developmental cognitive
   neuroscience
developmental systems
   approach
differentiation (of neurons)
epigenesis
evolution

evolutionary developmental
   psychology
evolved probabilistic
   cognitive mechanisms
experience-dependent
   processes (or experience-
   dependent synaptogenesis)
experience-expectant
   processes (or experience-
   expectant synaptogenesis)
genotype → environment
   theory
interactive specialization
migration (of neurons)
myelin
myelination

natural selection
neocortex (or cerebral
   cortex)
neuroconstructivism
neurogenesis
neuroimaging techniques
neuron
neurotransmitters
plasticity (of the brain)
proliferation (of neurons)
representational constraints
selective cell death
   (or apoptosis)
sensitive period
synapses
synaptogenesis

SUGGESTED READINGS

Scholarly Works

Anderson, V., Spencer-Smith, M., & Wood, A. (2011). Do children really recover better? Neurobehavioural plasticity after early brain insult. *Brain, 134,* 2197–2221. This article provides an up-to-date review of research and theory related to recovery of function from brain damage as a function of age. It provides a brief overview of normal brain development and then discusses the early plasticity versus early vulnerability models of recovery of function from brain damage.

Bjorklund, D. F., & Ellis, B. J. (2014). Children, childhood, and development in evolutionary perspective. *Developmental Review, 34,* 225–264. This article presents the basic tenets of evolutionary developmental psychology, including a review of research of some cognitive adaptations of infancy and childhood, such as infant memory, play, tool use, and social learning.

Gottlieb, G. (2007). Probabilistic epigenesis. *Developmental Science, 10,* 1–11. This short article concisely presents the basic ideas of the developmental systems approach. Gottlieb was a major proponent of this perspective, and interested readers may want to refer to his 1997 book, *Synthesizing nature-nurture: Prenatal roots of instinctive behavior* (Erlbaum).

Markant, J. C., & Thomas, K. M. (2013). Postnatal brain development. In P. D. Zelazo (Ed.), *Oxford handbook of developmental psychology, Vol. 1* (pp. 129–163). Oxford, UK: Oxford University Press. This chapter provides an excellent review of several aspects of brain development from infancy through adolescence.

Scarr, S. (1993). Biological and cultural diversity: The legacy of Darwin for development. *Child Development, 64,* 1333–1353. Scarr presents a relatively detailed account of her genotype → environment theory, emphasizing the importance of an evolutionary theory to developmental psychologists. This paper is a response to critics of her theory (by Baumrind and by Jackson, same issue), and Scarr is careful to be precise about her theorizing.

Reading for Personal Interest

Blumberg, M. (2007). *Basic instinct: The genesis of behavior*. New York: Basic Books. In this short book, developmental neuroscientist Mark Blumberg applies developmental systems theory to take on the notion of instincts. In the process, he challenges theorizing in behavioral genetics and evolutionary psychology.

Klingberg, T. (2013). The learning brain: Memory and brain development in children. Oxford, UK: Oxford University Press. Swedish cognitive neuroscientist Torkel Klingberg makes research in cognitive developmental neuroscience accessible to a general audience and shows how these research findings can be used to improve education and better understand children and their developing brains.

Moore, D. S. (2015). *The developing genome: An introduction to behavioral epigenetics*. New York: Oxford University Press. Epigenetics is one of the hottest topics in the biological sciences, and it will soon be a hot topic in the behavioral sciences. David Moore's engaging style, eloquent prose, use of clear examples, and grasp of the relevance of epigenetics for behavior and development make this complicated topic accessible for the nonbiologist.

O'Connor, A. (2008, March 11). The claim: Identical twins have identical DNA. *New York Times*. This article describes the age-based accumulation of epigenetic changes in identical twins that can arise from differences in experiences throughout development.

3 SOCIAL CONSTRUCTION OF MIND

Sociocultural Perspectives on Cognitive Development

After impatiently helping her father finish an online purchase, complete with sighs and rolling eyes, 13-year-old Ashleigh listened as her dad began the spiel she had heard, in one form or another, many times:

> When I was a kid, we didn't have iPhones, MP3 players, or "the cloud," and there was nothing like Facebook or Instagram. I remember when Pong was the latest and greatest in video games! Most of the kids I went to school with didn't even have computers in their homes. It's no wonder why I can't keep up with you and your brother on all this Internet stuff. And your grandparents, for them computers were something that NASA had, not something that sits on your desk, or even in your pocket! I give them credit for trying, but I'm not surprised that they haven't made the jump to the

The advent of the Internet and related technologies has changed the way that people think.

DOONESBURY © 2014 G. B. Trudeau. Reprinted with permission of UNIVERSAL UCLICK. All rights reserved.

high-tech world yet. So be patient with me, and especially your grandparents. We just can't think like you do!

To some extent, Ashleigh and her dad grew up in different cultures. The tools Ashleigh is growing up with for communication, for problem solving, and even for recreation are very different from those her father knew as a child, and those of her grandparents were more different still. Ashleigh is a girl growing up in 21st-century America, and our culture has experienced a substantial technological change over the last two generations. In the distant past, cultures changed slowly, so the experiences of people in one generation were not so different from the experiences of people in previous (or future) generations. One question is central to this chapter: Can one's culture influence how one learns to think? And if so, how do the technologies, institutions, and values of a culture influence cognitive development? Will Ashleigh become a different type of thinker than her father and grandparents because of the technological differences in their cultures?

In the opening chapter, we stated that there were two obvious trends in cognitive development during the past several decades. The first trend was an increased emphasis on the biological basis of development. The second was an increased emphasis on the social construction of cognition—the perspective that how children learn to think is governed largely by the culture in which they grow up. We want to emphasize that these should not be viewed as contradictory positions, with some scientists believing that cognitive development is best described by biology and others that it is best described by the culture. Rather, children's brains (obviously a part of their biology) develop in social contexts, and one cannot truly understand cognitive development without an appreciation of children's biology, their social environment, and, importantly, the interaction of the two.

ROLE OF CULTURE IN COGNITIVE DEVELOPMENT

Advocates of the sociocultural perspective of development believe that how we develop—and particularly how we learn to think—is a function of the social and cultural environment in which we are reared.

Cognitive Development Is Inseparable From Its Cultural Context

The overriding theme of this chapter is that cognitive development is inseparable from its cultural context. The traditional dichotomy of the nature/nurture debate pitted culture *against* biology: How much of a child's development is governed by biology versus how much is shaped by culture? Contemporary theorists see the relation between biology and culture quite differently. Culture is considered to be as much a part of human nature as our big brains. *Homo sapiens* evolved a unique suite of physical and intellectual abilities, and these influenced how we fed ourselves, defended against predators, reared our children, and interacted with other members of our species, which in turn "created" culture. The effects of culture then influenced our behavior and served as pressures for natural selection and subsequent biological evolution (Cole, 2006; Rogoff, 2003). In the words of Henry Plotkin (2001), "Biology and culture relate to each other as a two-way street of causation" (p. 93). Or, as

Michael Cole (2006) wrote, "Culture is, quite literally, a phylogenetic property of human beings" (p. 659).

Culture is transmitted to children by their parents and other members of society. Within the adult-child interchanges of daily life, children's intellectual processes are developed to handle the tasks and problems pertinent to their particular surroundings. Parents might not be conscious of their instructional techniques, but cultural practices of child-rearing are usually well suited for the type of life children can expect to face as adults. Sociocultural theory addresses how children come to understand and function in their social world. From the sociocultural perspective, how children understand their physical world "is embedded within knowledge of the sociocultural world . . . and it is the latter that enables and guides the former" (K. Nelson, 1996, p. 5). This should not be taken to mean that scientists with a sociocultural perspective give biology short shrift in influencing cognitive development. Most do not, but they realize that neurologically influenced, species-typical cognitive abilities emerge in species-typical social environments. This is captured in Mary Gauvain's (2001) statement that "cognitive development is an active, constructive process that involves beings who are evolutionarily predisposed to live and learn in social context with other 'like-minded' beings. They are like-minded in terms of both the neurological system available and the social requirements that are in place" (p. 63).

Sociocultural theorists assume children's brains evolved to develop in a social context. There are universal aspects to cognitive development, much as Piaget and others have proposed, but typical human cognition only arises in a species-typical environment, and for humans this means a social environment, starting with a responsive mother and continuing with interactions with other conspecifics (members of one's own species) over the course of childhood. Individual differences in how children come to think will be determined, in large part, by the practices, values, and intellectual tools their culture provides, but the foundation upon which culture-specific ways of thinking develop is universal to the species.

A sociocultural approach that examines the development of cognition across a variety of cultures is essential for determining the universal features of the human mind. If a way of thinking or a pattern of development is truly characteristic of the species, it should be observed in all cultures, although perhaps expressed somewhat differently. This becomes especially important when one considers that most cognitive development research is performed with children from what Joseph Henrich and his colleagues (2010) called WEIRD (Western, educated, industrialized, rich, and democratic) societies. Much of the world, and our species for most of our history, lives under very different conditions. Restricting our knowledge of development based on data from children from WEIRD societies limits what we can say about any characteristics we may uncover (Lancy, 2015; Sternberg, 2014). Is it truly universal, or might it be limited only to developed societies?

Vygotsky's Sociocultural Theory

The current interest in sociocultural perspectives in contemporary developmental psychology can be traced to the rediscovery of the ideas of Russian psychologist Lev Vygotsky (1962, 1978). Vygotsky, writing in the 1920s and 1930s, emphasized that development is guided by adults interacting with children, with the cultural context determining largely how, where, and when these interactions take place. Vygotsky proposed that cognitive development occurs in situations where a child's problem solving is guided by an adult. For Vygotsky and his contemporary followers, cognitive development progresses by the members of one generation collaborating with the members of another. In other words, children's development is embedded within a culture and proceeds as they are guided through life in collaboration with others. Elaborating on this perspective, Barbara Rogoff (1998) views development as a process of *transformation of participation*:

> Evaluation of development focuses on how individuals participate in and contribute to ongoing activity rather than on "outcome" and individuals' possessions of concepts and skills. Evaluation of development examines the ways people transform their participation, analyzing how they coordinate with others in shared endeavors, with attention to the purposes and dynamic nature of the activity itself and its meaning in the community. The investigation of people's actual involvement and changing goals in activities becomes the basis of understanding development rather than simply the surface to try to get past. (p. 18)

From this perspective, it is clear why Vygotsky and modern sociocultural theorists propose that it is impossible to evaluate the individual without also considering other significant people and institutions in the community.

Vygotsky proposed that we should evaluate development from the perspective of four interrelated levels in interaction with children's environments—ontogenetic, microgenetic, phylogenetic, and sociohistorical. Ontogenetic development (or *ontogeny*), which refers to

development of the individual over his or her lifetime, is the topic of this book and the level of analysis for nearly all developmental psychologists. Microgenetic development refers to changes that occur over relatively brief periods of time, such as the changes one may see in a child solving addition problems every week for 11 consecutive weeks (Siegler & Jenkins, 1989). This is obviously a finer-grained analysis than that afforded by the traditional ontogenetic level. Phylogenetic development (or *phylogeny*) refers to changes over evolutionary time (thousands and even millions of years). Here, Vygotsky anticipated the current evolutionary psychology perspective, believing that an understanding of the species' history can provide insight regarding child development. Finally, sociohistorical development refers to the changes that have occurred, usually across prior generations, in one's culture and the values, norms, and technologies that such a history has generated. For example, children growing up in Western nations today have received a legacy of literacy, computers, and a legal and human rights tradition that influences their development in ways that children growing up in other cultures without literacy, computers, or Western values can't even imagine (and vice versa).

Vygotsky's claim that multiple aspects of a child's endowment (genetic, cultural) must be viewed in interaction makes his theory reminiscent of the developmental systems approach discussed in the previous chapter (see Gauvain, 2013). Vygotsky stressed the need to understand how changing organisms develop in changing environments. Focusing only on the individual or only on the environment could not provide an adequate explanation of development (Hernández Blasi, 1996). However, what modern-day researchers have emphasized most about Vygotsky's ideas is his belief that development can only be meaningfully studied in the social and cultural context in which it occurs.

Section Review

Sociocultural psychologists believe that how children learn to think is primarily a function of the social and cultural environment in which they are reared.

Cognitive Development Is Inseparable From Its Cultural Context

- *Sociocultural perspectives* of cognitive development hold that a child's cognition is constructed by the social environment.
- Most cognitive developmental research is conducted in *WEIRD* (Western, educated, industrialized, rich, and democratic) *societies*, limiting what can be said about cognitive universals.

Vygotsky's Sociocultural Theory

- Contemporary sociocultural theories are based on the ideas of psychologist Lev Vygotsky.
- Vygotsky proposed that development should be evaluated from the perspective of four interrelated levels in interaction with children's environments—*ontogenetic*, *microgenetic*, *phylogenetic*, and *sociohistorical*.

Ask Yourself . . .

1. What is the sociocultural perspective of cognitive development? How does this approach relate to the nature/nurture issue discussed earlier in the text?
2. Why is it important to consider culture to understand human development?
3. What are the main assumptions of Vygotsky's sociocultural theory of development?

COGNITIVE ARTIFACTS THAT SUPPORT AND EXTEND THINKING: TOOLS OF INTELLECTUAL ADAPTATION

Vygotsky claimed that infants are born with a few *elementary mental functions*—attention, sensation, perception, and memory—that are eventually transformed by the culture into new and more sophisticated mental processes he called *higher mental functions*. Take memory, for example. Young children's early memory capabilities are limited by biological constraints to the images and impressions they can produce. However, each culture provides its children with **tools of intellectual adaptation**, which are methods of thinking and problem solving that children internalize from their interactions with more competent members of society and that permit children to use their basic mental functions more adaptively. Thus, children in information-age societies might learn to remember more efficiently by taking written or typed notes, whereas their age-mates in preliterate societies might have learned other memory strategies, such as representing each object they must remember by tying a knot in a string or reminding themselves to perform a chore by tying a string around their fingers. Such socially transmitted memory strategies and other cultural tools teach children how to use their minds—in short, the culture teaches children *how* to think. And because each culture also transmits specific beliefs and values, it teaches children *what* to think as well.

Tools of intellectual adaptation, or *cognitive artifacts* (Hunt, 2012), come in two types: *physical*, or *material*, *artifacts* include computers, maps, and written documents, and *symbolic*, or *mental*, *artifacts* include ways of thinking and reasoning. Table 3.1 provides some examples of physical and mental artifacts important to

TABLE 3.1 **An incomplete list of the cognitive artifacts central to modern society.**

Physical Cognitive Artifacts	Mental Cognitive Artifacts
Written documents	Literacy
Maps	Mathematics
Printing	Law
Telecommunication	Logic
Computers and electronics	Scientific reasoning
Global positioning via satellites	Formal systems of finance and banking

Source: Hunt, E. (2012). What makes nations intelligent? *Perspectives on Psychological Science, 7,* 284–306 (p. 285).

Note: Cognitive artifacts are listed in their historical order of origin.

modern culture (Hunt, 2012). Much of human biological and cultural evolution can be measured by evidence of cognitive artifacts from the fossil and archeological record (for example, improvements in stone tools from *Homo habilis* to modern *Homo sapiens*, metal tools, alphabets, and numerical systems). In fact, Earl Hunt (2012) proposed that modern societies can be evaluated in terms of national intelligence, or general cognitive abilities, based on the extent to which their citizens master modern cognitive artifacts such as literacy and numeracy.

Language Names and Numeracy

A subtle difference in cultural tools of intellectual adaptation that can make a noticeable difference on children's cognitive task performance can be found in how a language names its numbers. Today, most cultures in the world use a system with the concept of zero, negative numbers, and the possibility to enumerate quantities from one to infinity. Some cultures, however, have a more limited way of expressing quantities (for example, only having number words for *one*, *two*, and *many*), and this influences their ability to perform basic arithmetic operations. For instance, adult speakers of two Amazonia languages (Pirahã and Mundurukú) have no number words for quantities larger than five (Gordon, 2004; Pica et al., 2004). As a result, they perform arithmetic tasks involving small quantities easily, but they perform poorly on tasks involving larger quantities. Pirahã children who learn Portuguese, however, are able to perform arithmetic calculations with larger quantities, bolstering the interpretation that the language's ability to represent numbers is responsible for the pattern of numerical thinking in these cultures (Gordon, 2004).

Even more subtle differences in the *number names* that a language uses can affect children's mathematics. For example, in all languages, the first 10 digits must be learned by rote. After that, however, some languages take advantage of the base-10 number system and name numbers accordingly. English does this beginning at 20 (*twenty-one*, *twenty-two*, and so on). However, the teen numbers in English are not so easily represented. Rather, 11 and 12 also must be memorized. Not until 13 does a base-10 system begin (three + ten = thirteen), and even then, several of the number names do not correspond to the formula digit + 10. *Fourteen, sixteen, seventeen, eighteen,* and *nineteen* do, but the number names for *thirteen* and *fifteen* are not as straightforward (that is, they are not expressed as *threeteen* and *fiveteen*). Moreover, for the teen numbers, the digit unit is stated first (*fourteen, sixteen*), whereas the decade unit is stated first for the numbers 20 through 99 (*twenty-one, thirty-four*). Thus, the number system becomes very regular in English beginning with the 20s.

Other languages, such as Chinese, have a more systematic number-naming system. In Chinese, as in English, the first 10 digits must be memorized. From this point, however, the Chinese number-naming system follows a base-10 logic, with the name for 11 translating as *ten one*, the name for 12 translating as *ten two*, and so on. The Chinese and English languages are similar beginning at 20, and both use the base-10 logic once the hundreds are reached.

Kevin Miller and his colleagues (1995) reasoned that differences in the number-naming systems between English and Chinese might be associated with early mathematical competence, specifically counting. They tested 3- through 5-year-old children in Champaign-Urbana, Illinois, and in Beijing, China. They asked each child to count as high as possible. Differences between the Chinese and American sample are shown by age in Figure 3.1. As you can see, no cultural differences were observed for the 3-year-olds, but the Chinese children began to show an advantage by age 4. This advantage was even larger at age 5. Further analyses indicated that cultural differences were limited to the teens decade. Although almost all children could count to 10 (94% of the American children and 92% of the Chinese children), only 48% of the American children could count to 20, compared with 74% of the Chinese children. Once children could count to 20, no cultural differences were noted for counting to 100. These findings indicate how differences in the number-naming system of a language can contribute to early differences in a cognitive skill. This early difference in a tool of intellectual adaptation might contribute to later differences in mathematical abilities found between Chinese and American children (see Chapter 11).

Other differences in how a language expresses its numbers can also influence children's

FIGURE 3.1 **Median level of counting (highest number reached) by age for Chinese and U.S. preschoolers.** Because of the way numbers are named in Chinese versus English, Chinese-speaking children learn to count to 20 before English-speaking children.

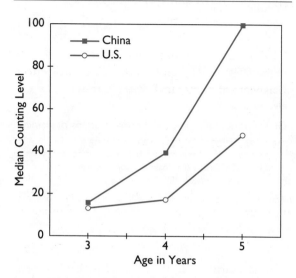

Source: Miller, K. F., Smith, C. M., Zhu, J., & Zhang, H. (1995). Preschool origins of cross-national differences in mathematical competence. *Psychological Science, 6,* 56–60. Reprinted with permission.

development of basic arithmetic abilities. For example, expressing numbers from 21 to 99, English states the decade number first (47 is stated *forty-seven*), but some languages invert the ones and tens decade. For example, in German, 47 is said *siebenundvierzig,* literally "seven and forty," and so on. As a result of this inversion, German-speaking children have problems when learning how to convert spoken numbers (for instance, *fünfundzwanzig,* or "five and twenty") to numerals, with many children inverting the order of the numerals (for example, writing "52" instead of "25") (Zuber et al., 2009). In related research (Göbel et al., 2014), German children also had more difficulty than Italian children on addition problems that involved a "carrying" operation (for example, for the problem 27 + 19, adding 7 plus 9 in the right-hand column involves writing "6" and carrying the "1" to add to the left-hand column), again presumably because of how two-digit numbers are articulated (but see Vasilyeva et al., 2015, for evidence that some differences in how languages express their numbers have little effect on aspects of numeracy).

Age of Digital Natives

The relevance of tools of intellectual adaptation to cognitive functioning is not limited to subtle differences between languages or to comparisons between high-tech and stone-age cultures. It can be seen both within and between modern societies today. The 20th century saw the invention of many new tools of intellectual adaptation, but perhaps the one that will have the most profound impact is the personal computer. Like it or not, there is a global economy, and information is a valuable commodity. To a great extent, access to computers and related electronic devices—and the ability to use them easily—differentiates those cultures that will experience economic boom versus economic bust in the 21st century. Even within a culture, such as mainstream America, access to technology discriminates among those who will reap the greatest benefits that an information-age society has to offer. Being computer literate affects not only what jobs we have and, thus, our income, but it also influences how one learns, how (and what) one remembers, and how one solves problems—just as reading and writing did centuries before. In a sense, we are in the midst of a natural experiment, one in which a new tool of intellectual adaptation has been introduced, and we

should not be surprised if, in decades to come, we are a different-thinking people than we were before the computer revolution.

Most college students today, and certainly nearly all who will follow them, are *digital natives*, people who grew up with digital media and who take these media for granted. As illustrated by the story that opened this chapter, most members of Ashleigh's parents' and grandparents' generation have learned to use the new media, but it rarely comes easy to them. For people who did not grow up with it, using the new media is like using a second language, whereas for most people under 30 today, it is like using a first language. So it should not be surprising that such a near-universal change in how people gather information and communicate has had (and will continue to have) a significant impact on cognitive development.

Moreover, access to digital media varies not only between generations and between developed and developing cultures but also within a culture. For example, in a 2012 survey of American homes, 80% of White and 83% of Asian adults 25 years and older used the Internet compared to 68% for Black and 64% for Latino adults (U.S. Census Bureau, 2014). Smaller ethnic differences were found for using smartphones (45%, 53%, 45%, and 46% for White, Asian, Black, and Hispanic adults 25 years and older, respectively). Most American teenagers use computers and other electronic devices as a source of entertainment. For example, a survey of 12- to 17-year-old American teenagers reported that 97% played video games of some sort (Lenhart et al., 2008). This phenomenon is not limited to the United States. In a five-country survey (Brazil, Germany, Japan, the United Kingdom, and the United States) of the media habits of millennials (people born between 1984 and 1995), 75% stated that they view the computer as more of an entertainment device than their TV (Deloitte, 2009).

In 2012 developmental neuroscientist Jay Giedd wrote, "The way adolescents of today learn, play, and interact has changed more in the past 15 years than in the previous 570 since Gutenberg's popularization of the printing press" (p. 101). Giedd continued with the observation that the brains of children and adolescents evolved to be plastic—to change to the demands of the environment. However, human brains did not evolve for reading—made possible for millions by Gutenberg's press—nor tweeting or playing *Angry Birds*, made possible by the digital revolution. Yet brains obviously develop to be able to do these things, and we should not be surprised that they change in structure and function in the process.

Sociohistorical Influences

Vygotsky also emphasized the importance of a culture's history in shaping cognitive development. For example, different cultures use different writing systems, and these systems can have consequences not only for how children learn to read and write but also for how they think. For instance, in one set of studies, researchers examined the cognitive abilities of Greek and Chinese children (Demetriou et al., 2005; Kazi et al., 2012). Although no differences were found in measures of general intelligence between the two groups, the Chinese children outperformed the Greek children on all measures involving visual/spatial processing. Why might Chinese children excel in this one area of cognitive ability? The researchers proposed that the Chinese children's extensive practice with their logographic writing system (pictorial symbols), in contrast to the phonetic system used by Greek children, was

responsible for their greater spatial abilities. This is reminiscent of the counting advantage that Chinese-speaking children have relative to English-speaking children because of the way their language names the teen numbers (K. F. Miller et al., 1995).

Differences in thinking are even more substantial between literate cultures, which may also have books, newspapers, and computers, and illiterate cultures where reading and writing are not practiced. The differences in cognitive development are similar to what you might expect to find between western Europeans today and 600 years ago, before the printing press, personal computers, smartphones, compulsory education, and laws limiting child labor. Genetic differences between people living in information-age societies and people living in hunter-gatherer cultures today are negligible, as are the genetic differences between Europeans of the early 21st century and those of the early 15th century. But because of differences in the tools of intellectual adaptation provided by different cultures at different historical times, and in the values and institutions of these cultures, children learn to think differently.

As we mentioned previously, sociocultural influences not only reflect differences between modern cultures and those hundreds of years ago, they represent dynamic forces at work today (Greenfield, 2009). For example, drastic changes in the economy such as the world financial crisis beginning in 2008, a natural disaster such as Hurricane Sandy in 2012, or an influx of immigrants to a community can affect people and, thus, children's development in significant ways, influencing how the local community is structured, what educational and economic opportunities are available, and how people interact with one another. In many parts of the developing world, children have their feet in two cultures, one traditional and the other modern, and their exposure to modern culture, including formal schooling, has been shown to affect important aspects of their cognitive development (Gauvain & Munroe, 2009).

Malcolm Gladwell (2008), in his best-selling book *Outliers*, shows not only how a culture's history can influence a child's development and, thus, adult accomplishments but also that such influences can extend back many generations and over different continents. Did one's ancestors make a living as independent farmers tending rice paddies, which required planning and persistent labor, or did they make a living as serfs growing potatoes, which required planting in the spring and harvesting in the fall, with little attention necessary in between? Are you a descendent of farmers, whose crops were relatively immune to theft, or of ranchers, whose livelihood could be rustled from under one's nose? Were people born in a time of economic plenty or hardship? Exceptional people (the "outliers" in the title of his book), Gladwell asserts, are not simply the product of hard work and native intelligence. They are the result of the practices of their culture at a particular time in history. Although Gladwell never mentions Vygotsky or sociocultural theory, his book illustrates the importance of sociohistorical influences on development.

Vygotsky claimed that human cognition, even when carried out in isolation, is inherently sociocultural because it is affected by the beliefs, values, and tools of intellectual adaptation transmitted to individuals by their culture. And because these values and intellectual tools can vary substantially from culture to culture and even within a culture over time, Vygotsky believed that neither the course nor the content of intellectual growth was as universal as Piaget and others had assumed.

Section Review

Each culture transmits beliefs, values, and preferred methods of thinking or problem solving—its *tools of intellectual adaptation*—to each successive generation.

Cognitive Artifacts

- Tools of intellectual adaptation, or cognitive artifacts, come in two types: physical, or material, artifacts that include computers, maps, and written documents, and symbolic, or mental, artifacts that include ways of thinking and reasoning.
- The way a language names its numbers can influence children's numerical and arithmetic development.
- Differences in access to and familiarity with modern electronic technology influences how children from Western cultures learn to think.

A Culture's History Plays an Important Role in Shaping Cognitive Development

- The different writing systems developed in Western versus Chinese cultures are associated with differences in spatial cognition.

Ask Yourself . . .

4. What are two types of cognitive artifacts? Name some examples of each in your environment.
5. How does a child's language affect his or her numerical development?
6. What are sociohistorical influences, and why are they important to consider when studying human development?
7. What does it mean to say someone is a digital native? How might this influence his or her cognitive development?
8. How does spatial cognition differ across individuals from Chinese versus Western cultures? How is this related to the different writing systems of these two cultures?

SOCIAL ORIGINS OF EARLY COGNITIVE COMPETENCIES

Vygotsky viewed young children as curious explorers who are actively involved in learning and discovering new principles. However, he placed little emphasis on *self-initiated* discovery, choosing instead to stress the importance of *social* contributions to cognitive growth. For example, Vygotsky believed that higher psychological processes (those involving self-awareness) have a social origin, developing first on the social plane and only later becoming internalized and developing on the psychological plane (Wertsch & Tulviste, 1992). Vygotsky referred to this dual nature of cognitive development as the general genetic law of cultural development. According to Vygotsky (1981), "Any function in the child's cultural development appears twice, or on two planes. First it appears on the social plane, and then on the psychological plane. First it appears between people as an interpsychological category, and then within the child as an intrapsychological category. This is equally true with regard to voluntary attention, logical memory, the formation of concepts, and the development of volition" (p. 163). According to James Wertsch and Peeter Tulviste (1992), cognitive processes such as memory are not understood as characteristics of individuals but, rather, as functions that can be carried out either between people or internally. Such processes can be viewed as *socially constituted cognitive activity* (Gauvain, 2001), which is "individual thinking that has embedded within it the contributions of the social world" (p. 41). Children learn to use the symbols or the representational tools of the social community, regardless of whether they are sharing a memory with another person, for example, or contemplating a problem in their head.

Studying Children in Natural Settings

Following this logic, Vygotsky believed that to understand cognitive development, psychologists should not focus on individuals as they execute some context-independent process, as Western psychologists have traditionally done. Rather, psychologists should examine individuals as they participate in culturally valued activities.

It is not always practical, of course, to assess children's thinking in naturalistic settings, and even when it is, the loss of experimental control can limit greatly what one can say about the mechanisms underlying cognition. However, to the extent that children's thinking is applied to solve real-world problems (and what else is cognition for, and why else would we want to know about it?), an understanding of cognitive development requires that one appreciate the "larger social and cultural context that provides meaning and purpose" for children's cognitions (Gauvain, 2001, p. 28).

According to Vygotsky, many of the truly important discoveries that children make occur within the context of cooperative, or collaborative, *dialogues* between a skillful tutor, who might model the activity and transmit verbal instructions, and a novice pupil, who first seeks to understand the tutor's instruction and eventually internalizes this information, using it to regulate his or her own performance. The nature of that dialogue may differ, however, as a function of culture. For example, as we mentioned in Chapter 1, children in traditional cultures are often more attentive to what adults *do* rather than to what they *say*. For instance, in one study, researchers observed 2- to 3-year-old children from each of four communities: Two of the communities were from the United States (the middle-class towns of West Newton, Massachusetts, and Sugarhouse, Utah), and two were from more traditional communities (the Efe, foragers from the Democratic Republic of the Congo, and an indigenous Mayan group from San Pedro, Guatemala) (Morelli et al., 2003). These communities vary in a number of ways, of course, but one was the extent to which children were exposed to the day-to-day lives of adults. In Western cultures such as ours, beginning in the preschool years, children are often segregated from adults and receive much culturally important information and instruction in school rather than "on the job." In contrast, in the Efe and San Pedro cultures, children are in close contact with adults during most of the day and observe and interact with adults while they perform important cultural activities. However, unlike in Western cultures, little direct teaching is involved. In fact, adults in traditional societies rarely directly instruct their children (Lancy, 2015, 2016; Lancy & Grove, 2010).

One important finding of the study by Morelli and her colleagues was the extent to which children in these communities observed adults at work. As can be seen from Figure 3.2, the Efe and San Pedro children frequently watched adults at work, whereas children from the middle-class American communities did so much less often. Also, the Efe and San Pedro children were more apt to emulate adult work in their play than the American children were. In contrast, the American children were more likely to be involved in specialized, child-focused activities, including lessons, play with at least one adult, scholastic play with an adult, and conversation with an adult on a child-related topic.

Let us provide an illustration from an everyday task in our own culture. Imagine Miguel, a 4-year-old, is trying to put together a jigsaw puzzle. His early attempts get him nowhere. His mother notices his difficulties, sits down beside

FIGURE 3.2 **Children in different cultures can have drastically different experiences that will affect what they learn and how they think.** Children in more traditional cultures (Efe and San Pedro) observe adults at work and imitate work in their play more than children in middle-class communities, who engage more in child-focused activities.

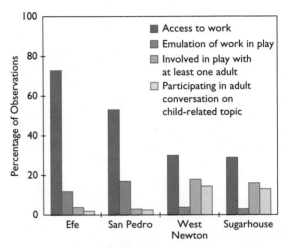

Source: Adapted from Morelli, G. A., Rogoff, B., & Angelillo, C. (2003). Cultural variation in young children's access to work or involvement in specialized child-focused activities. *International Journal of Behavioral Development, 27*, 264–274.

him, and offers some assistance. She first suggests that Miguel look for the corner pieces, selecting one herself and then showing Miguel. Next, she suggests that Miguel look for other edge pieces, starting with those that match the patterns and colors of one of the corner pieces. Miguel selects several pieces, tries to put them together, and on his third attempt finds a piece that fits. Miguel continues to look for other pieces but soon becomes frustrated. His mother then selects two pieces, places them close together, and says, "See if these two fit." Miguel puts them together, smiles, and continues to look for other pieces. Miguel's mother gives him a few words of encouragement and continues to help when he runs into trouble. But Miguel is getting the hang of it, and his mother's assistance is needed less and less. This kind of social interaction, claimed Vygotsky, fosters cognitive growth.

Zone of Proximal Development

How does the kind of social interaction just illustrated by Miguel and his mother foster cognitive growth? First, Miguel and his mother are operating in what Vygotsky called the zone of proximal development—defined as the difference between a child's "actual developmental level as determined by independent problem solving" and his or her level of "potential development as determined through problem solving under adult guidance or in collaboration with more capable peers" (Vygotsky, 1978, p. 86). This is the zone in which sensitive instruction should be aimed and in which new cognitive growth can be expected to occur. Miguel obviously becomes a more competent puzzle solver with his mother's help than without it. More important, he will internalize the problem-solving techniques that his mother uses in collaboration with him and will ultimately use them on his own, rising to a new level of independent mastery. In other words, children can best learn to solve problems at a level between their current ability and their ability when assisted by an adult, and within this zone, adults can do the most effective teaching. One important thing to remember here is that the skills of the child continue to develop, requiring that adults modify their reactions to children. Thus, the sociocultural approach is by necessity dynamic—ever changing—with both adults and children progressing as a result of their repeated transactions.

Related to the concept of the zone of proximal development is the concept of **scaffolding** (D. Wood, Bruner, & Ross, 1976). Scaffolding occurs when experts are sensitive to the abilities of a novice and respond contingently to the novice's responses in a learning situation so that the novice gradually increases his or her understanding of a problem. Scaffolding will be most effective when done within the zone of proximal development. The behavior of Miguel's mother in the earlier example reflected scaffolding and working in the zone of proximal development.

Evidence of scaffolding can be seen in a study in which mothers were instructed to teach their 5-year-old children how to play a board game involving the use of dice to compute moves (Bjorklund, Hubertz, & Reubens, 2004). In this research, kindergarten children and their mothers played a board game of Chutes and Ladders, with the spinner being replaced by a pair of dice. Children had to compute their moves by adding the numbers on the two dice. To what extent did mothers help their children add or attempt to teach their children arithmetic strategies in the process of playing the game? Mothers' behavior often varied with the competence of their children. For children who were using fact retrieval and mental arithmetic spontaneously (that is, children who did not have to count out loud or on their fingers to arrive at an answer), mothers usually provided little support or advice because little or none was needed. In contrast, mothers of less arithmetically competent children often prompted their 5-year-olds to count the dots on the dice, modeled or instructed the use of simple addition strategies (for example, counting all the dots on the dice), and often re-represented the problem by holding up their fingers to correspond to the dots on the dice. Some mothers used these overt procedures more during the early trials and gradually lessened their use of specific prompts and instructions as their children took more responsibility for solving the problem on their own. In other words, these mothers were working in the zone of proximal development to teach their children simple arithmetic strategies in the context of a social game.

There was variability in the degree of scaffolding shown by different mothers, of course. Let us provide one example from this research of a particularly effective mother. On her first move, 5-year-old Yolanda threw the dice, then just stared at them and said nothing, and then looked at her mother. Her mother asked, "How many is that?" Yolanda shrugged her shoulders, and her mother said, "Count them." Yolanda shrugged again, and her mother then pointed to the dots on the first die while saying, "One, two, three," then to the dots on the second die while saying "four, five. You have five. Now you count them." Yolanda complied, pointing to each dot as she counted out loud, and moved her piece on the board. The mother then threw the dice and asked Yolanda, "How many do I have?" Yolanda shrugged her shoulders, and her mother counted the dots on the dice out loud and then said, "You count them," which Yolanda did. The next five turns went very much the same, with Yolanda professing not to know what to do and her mother modeling counting and then directing Yolanda to count the dots on the dice. On the sixth move, Yolanda counted the dots on the dice immediately after her mother's request (no shrug and no modeling of counting by her mother) and even did the same on her mother's turn. Her mother then hesitated on the next several turns before asking Yolanda how many dots she had. Eventually, Yolanda threw the dice and counted the dots herself spontaneously, without any prodding from her mother, and continued to do so on both her and her mother's turns throughout most of the game. The mother corrected Yolanda when she made mistakes counting, but she became less directive

as Yolanda took more of the responsibility for the game herself.

Contrast the behavior of Yolanda's mother with that of Darrell's mother. Darrell would roll the dice and begin counting each dot on the dice, starting with the die closest to him ("one, two, three") and then continuing to count the dots on the second die ("four, five, six, seven, eight"). While he was counting, his mother would interrupt and instruct him to count from the larger number, a more sophisticated strategy. For example, when the child rolled a six and a five and started counting the dots, the mother would interrupt him by saying, "No, Darrell, start counting from the six here," pointing at the six and saying, "You know this is six." The child would start over counting each dot on the dice, asking his mother to stop telling him what to do. This continued throughout the game, with Darrell's mom rolling the dice during her turn and modeling retrieval of arithmetic facts (for example, "six plus four is ten"), which was apparently beyond this child's capability to execute on his own. Darrell usually ignored his mother's demonstrations and instructions and, as a result, showed no improvement in his use of arithmetic strategies over the course of the sessions.

Playing board games is not the only thing that parents in developed cultures do that may facilitate children's understanding of numbers and perhaps arithmetic. Parents also cook, play card games, and shop with children, for example, each providing opportunities for conveying something of the importance of numeracy to young children (LeFevre et al., 2009; Vandermaas-Peeler et al., 2012). And apparently children do learn a few things about numbers when interacting in daily activities with their parents. For example, Jo-Anne LeFevre and her colleagues (2009; Skwarchuk, Sowinski, & LeFevre, 2014) reported that children who more frequently engaged in quantitative activities (such as board and card games involving numbers) with their parents as preschoolers subsequently had higher mathematic skills in kindergarten, first, and second grades than children who engaged in fewer such activities.

We have been careful not to use the word *competence* in describing children's problem-solving abilities. In Vygotsky's sociocultural perspective, learning and development are the result of interacting in specific, culturally defined tasks that have specific rules. Unlike other theories of cognitive development (for example, Piaget's), competence is not an absolute level beyond which a child cannot exceed but, rather, is task specific. A child can show a high level of ability on one highly practiced task but be much less adept on a very similar and perhaps even objectively less-demanding task. A child's level of intellectual functioning is always evaluated by performance on specific tasks or in specific, culturally determined situations.

Apprenticeship in Thinking and Guided Participation

Adults' interactions with children vary depending on their culture. Although child-rearing in all cultures can take advantage of the zone of proximal development, what is taught will depend on what roles the child is eventually expected to play in society. Barbara Rogoff (1990, 2003; Rogoff et al., 1993) has viewed the transaction between children and adults as reflecting an *apprenticeship in thinking*, with novice children improving their "skills and understanding through participation with more skilled partners in culturally organized activities" (1990, p. 39). All the responsibility for the apprenticeship is not placed on the adults, however. Children might actively place themselves in positions to learn, prompting

adults to increase the level of instruction as children become increasingly skilled.

Rogoff developed the concept of guided participation to extend Vygotsky's idea of the zone of proximal development. The zone of proximal development has typically been applied to situations where there is explicit instruction between an older, more skilled teacher and a younger, less knowledgeable learner. Rogoff uses the term *guided participation* to refer to adult-child interactions not only during explicit instruction but also during the more routine activities and communication of everyday life. Guided participation is "the process and system of involvement of individuals with others, as they communicate and engage in shared activities" (Rogoff et al., 1993, p. 6). Guided participation focuses on day-to-day activities in children's lives, such as doing chores, watching television, and eavesdropping on adult conversations. Rogoff believes that children's cognitions are shaped during such mundane activities as much as or more so than in more formal educational settings.

The idea of an apprenticeship or guided participation might seem reasonable in cultures where children are integrated early into the daily activities of adult life, such as among the agrarian Mayans of Guatemala and Mexico or the !Kung of Africa, whose hunting and gathering lifestyles have remained virtually unchanged for thousands of years. But this idea is not as easily grasped for a culture such as our own. Many school-age children might not see their parents in action at their jobs—or even know what their parents do for a living. Moreover, children are generally excluded from adult activities, being segregated from adults for much of the day. Other children around the world, for example, sleep in the same room or even the same bed as their parents throughout childhood, and babies never leave home unless they are strapped to their mothers' backs.

Shared Remembering

Many aspects of cognitive development in information-age cultures have been shifted from parents to professional educators, whose job is to teach important cultural knowledge and skills to children. Yet much learning certainly transpires between parent and child in these postindustrial societies, particularly during the preschool years; in many ways, these transactions are designed to prepare children for the schooling that will follow. For example, formal education in North America, Europe, and much of Asia involves children responding to adults' questions when the adults already know the answers. It also involves learning and discussing things that have no immediate relevance—knowledge for knowledge's sake. Such context-independent learning, foreign to many cultures, is fostered during infancy and early childhood in our own culture. For example, as discussed in Chapter 8, parents frequently prompt their young children to name objects or to recall recent events. Take, for instance, the following exchange between 19-month-old Brittany and her mother:

Mother: "Brittany, what's at the park?"

Brittany: "Babysing."

Mother: "That's right, the baby swing. And what else?"

Brittany: [Shrugs.]

Mother: "A slide?"

Brittany: [Smiling, nods yes.]

Mother: "And what else is at the park?"

Brittany: [Shrugs.]

Mother: "A see . . ."

Brittany: "See-saw!"

Mother: "That's right, a see-saw."

This type of exchange is not at all unusual for a mother and a child from mainstream America, and it is a good example of Vygotsky's zone of proximal development. Brittany, in this case, is learning to recall specific objects with her mother's help, but she is also learning the importance of remembering information out of context (mother and daughter are in their living room at the time, miles from the park). Brittany is learning that she can be called on to state facts to her mother that her mother already knows. And she is learning that she can depend on her mother to help provide answers when she is unable to generate them herself. Table 3.2, from Gauvain (2001, p. 111), provides a list of some of the functions that such "shared remembering" between parent and child can have on memory development.

In the United States and most of the developed world, parents include their young children as conversational partners. Although the quantity and quality of the language environment children are exposed to does influence their language development (Hoff, 2013), children around the world acquire language at about the same time, even in cultures where children are "seen and not heard." But children who are not included as conversational partners by adults might not be prepared for the type of language interaction used in school. These children might become proficient users of language in their own community yet be perceived as language deficient in school (Rogoff, 1990).

This is illustrated through research by Lisa Schröder and her colleagues (2013), who examined conversations between mothers and their 3-year-old children from both Western (Germany and Greece) and non-Western (rural Cameroon and India) cultures. The conversations of mothers from Western countries were longer, involved more elaborate reminiscing, and focused more on children's personal judgments and preferences

TABLE 3.2 Some functions of shared remembering in children's memory development.

- Children learn about memory process, for example, strategies.
- Children learn ways of remembering and communicating memories with others, for example, narrative structure.
- Children learn about themselves, which contributes to the development of the self-concept.
- Children learn about their own social and cultural history.
- Children learn values important to the family and the community, that is, what is worth remembering.
- Promotes social solidarity

Source: Gauvain, M. (2001). *The social context of cognitive development* (p. 111). New York: Guilford.

(termed "autonomous talk") than the conversations of mothers from non-Western countries. In contrast, the conversations of the mothers from the non-Western countries were more repetitive and used fewer evaluations than the conversations of mothers from the Western countries. Schröder and her colleagues argued that the way mothers and children interact during conversations is consistent with differences in socialization between the cultures, with mothers from Western cultures encouraging children to develop an autonomous sense of self, independent of other people, whereas mothers from the non-Western cultures encourage children to be more obedient, socially responsible, and respectful to authority (Keller, 2012).

Reading and Talking to Children

Another school-related skill that might be associated with parent-child conversations is reading. We know that reading to children is an important predictor of children's later reading ability (see Chapter 11). There are substantial differences in how frequently preschool children are read to (see M. J. Adams, Treiman, & Pressley, 1998), and differences in how children are read to can have important implications for later language, and possibly reading, development. For example, Grover Whitehurst and his colleagues (1988) trained parents of 2- and 3-year-old children in a technique

of *interactive story reading*. Instead of just reading to the children, parents were told to stop every so often and to ask open-ended questions (such as "What is Eeyore doing?") and were encouraged to expand on their children's responses, suggest alternative possibilities, and make the questions progressively more challenging as children's understanding increased. A control group of parents was simply asked to read to their children. Analysis of recordings of the sessions indicated that the parents in the two groups did read to their children equally often and that parents in the experimental group followed the interactive story reading instructions. After 1 month of such reading, children in the experimental group were 8.5 months more advanced on a measure of verbal expression than were children in the control group, despite the fact that the two groups were equal at the beginning of the study. Subsequent research produced similar effects, reporting enhanced expressive language for low-income and at-risk preschool children as a result of interactive story reading (Brannon et al., 2013; Mol & Neuman, 2014; Valdez-Menchaca & Whitehurst, 1992). The effect, it seems, is quite robust, and it demonstrates that the way in which parents or teachers read to young children—taking into consideration children's understanding of the task and encouraging their active participation—facilitates their subsequent language development and prepares them for life in a literate society.

When most parents read picture books with their young children they are actually using a scaffolding strategy. Parents are more directive when children are younger and become less so as their children's language skills improve (DeLoache & DeMendoza, 1987). Parents establish a book-reading routine in which they may ask questions, point out and label pictures, provide feedback, and make categorical distinctions, such as saying, "This is a dog and this is a bird; birds fly and make their nests in trees." They often elaborate about the stories' plots and the details depicted in the book (Simcock & DeLoache, 2006; Symons et al., 2005).

Let us provide an example of a joint-reading interaction between a parent and a 4-year-old child, whom we'll call Rose, and her mother (adapted from Tudge, Putnam, & Valsiner, 1996, pp. 215–216).

For her regular bedtime story, Rose chose *Mike Mulligan and His Steam Shovel* for her mother to read. (The text of the story is placed in quotation marks.)

Mother: "Mike Mulligan and His Steam Shovel." [She turns the page.]

Rose: "To Mike."

Mother: Good. "Mike Mulligan had a steam shovel. A beautiful red steam shovel. Her name was . . .? [Mother pauses.] What was her name?

Rose: "Marianne."

Mother: Marianne. "Mike Mulligan was very proud of Marianne."

Mother: "It was Mike Mulligan and Marianne and some others who cut through the high mountains so that trains could go through. It was Mike Mulligan and Marianne and some others who lowered the hills and straightened the curves to make the long highways for the automobiles."

Rose: [Pointing to the picture.] And the holes for um er for the er um cars.

Mother: Yep, there are some holes for the cars to go through. "It was Mike Mulligan and Marianne and some others who smoothed out the ground and filled the holes to make the landing fields for the airplanes." Rose, look at this airport. What do you think is strange about that airport?

[Rose looks at the picture.]

Mother: Have you ever been to an airport that looked like that?

[Rose shakes her head, indicating no.]

Mother: What's different about that airport? Why does it look different from the airports we've been to?

Rose: Got houses.

Mother: It's got houses, but that wasn't what I was thinking of. But that's true. I was thinking that the airports that we've been to, the airplane landing is a long rectangular-shaped road called a landing strip, a runway. Is that what this one looks like?

[Rose shakes her head no.]

Mother: No. What's different about this one?

Rose: Don't know.

Mother: It's round! Have you ever seen . . . been to an airport where the airplane landed on a round road?

Rose: No.

Mother: [Laughs.] Pretty strange. Oooh, look at that. "Then along came new gasoline shovels, and the new electric shovels and the new diesel motor shovels and took all the jobs away from the steam shovels. Mike Mulligan and Marianne were . . ." [Pauses and looks down at Rose.]

Rose: ". . . very sad."

Mother: Why were they sad?

Rose: Because they um, because, because um all the um gasoline shovels and all the [looks at mother] . . . shovels and all the mo . . . the motor shovels took all the jobs away from her.

Mother: Aaaah [sad]. That's right. "All the other steam shovels were sold for . . ." [Pauses.]

Rose: ". . . junk."

Mother: ". . . or just left out in old gravel pits to rust away."

As this passage illustrates, Rose and her mother are working toward the same goal (joint reading of the story) and seem to be jointly attending to the task. The two partners are also generally responsive to one another. This is obviously a familiar routine for mother and child, and each knows what to expect of the other. The two are not sharing the load equally, however. The mother takes the lead in most of the exchanges. Although we have a dyadic (two-way) interaction, the relations are not symmetrical. In this case, the mother is doing most of the work, but that might change over time as Rose's reading improves. Note also that although the mother is contributing more to the interaction, Rose is not a passive participant. She selected the book, responded appropriately when her mother requested, and interjected her own comments at times. The mother seems to be providing adequate scaffolding for her daughter. When the context was clear, she requested that her daughter fill in parts of the text, but she read most of the text for Rose.

Is it just reading to children that prepares them for life in a literate society, or might talking to children also be related to later reading skills? Apparently, the latter is the case, but not all types of talking are equally effective at fostering later reading ability. Elaine Reese (1995) recorded conversations between mothers and their preschool children and related aspects of these conversations to children's understanding of print at 70 months of age. Most children were just beginning kindergarten, so few were actually reading. Children's understanding of print and prereading skills were assessed by their familiarity with letters and their ability to identify simple words (such as *cat* and *no*), a test of vocabulary, their knowledge about how books are read (front to back, with sentences running from left to right), and their ability both to comprehend and to produce coherent stories. Reese reported that mothers' conversations with their children about past events, especially when including elaborations of those events and associations with other events, was a good predictor of children's subsequent print skills (see the discussion of emergent literacy in Chapter 11). Reese proposed that mothers provide scaffolding by increasingly involving their children in collaborative conversations. According to Reese (1995), "A tentative conclusion that can be drawn from this study is that children who participate to a greater degree in early adult-child conversations may be honing different abilities from those children who allow the adult to direct the interaction" (p. 402). In related research, Monique Sénéchal and Jo-Anne LeFevre

(2002) assessed shared, or interactive, storybook reading at home and reported that it was positively related to the development of some receptive language skills, including listening comprehension and vocabulary, which in turn were related to children's reading level in the third grade.

Playing With More Skilled Partners

Play is another area in which parents and older siblings guide children's development. One particularly important type of play for our purposes is *symbolic play*. (The development of symbolic play is discussed in Chapter 5.) Symbolic play is essentially pretending and can be solitary (for example, the child pretending that her chair is a car) or cooperative (for example, a child pretending that she's the driver of the car and her mother is a passenger). Symbolic play has been viewed by many as requiring mental representation and as an indication of children's general cognitive development (Piaget, 1962). According to Marc Bornstein and his colleagues (1996), "In symbolic play, young children advance upon their cognitions about people, objects, and actions and in this way construct increasingly sophisticated representations of the world" (p. 2923).

But how do parents, or more expert siblings and peers, contribute to children's symbolic play development? It seems that young children are more likely to engage in symbolic play when they are playing with someone else rather than when they are playing alone and that mothers in particular bring out high levels of symbolic play in their children (Bornstein et al., 1996; Youngblade & Dunn, 1995). Consistent with Vygotsky's idea of a zone of proximal development and Rogoff's idea of guided participation, young children who interact with a more skilled partner who structures the situation appropriately for them advance in their skills faster than when such support is

not provided. Evidence for this comes from a study in which mothers and their 21-month-old children were videotaped during play sessions (Damast, Tamis-LeMonda, & Bornstein, 1996). Many mothers adjusted their level of play to that of their children or to slightly above the level their child was displaying. And mothers who knew more about play development were more likely to increase the level of play with their children than were less-knowledgeable mothers and, thus, provided appropriately challenging play interactions. Other research with 2- and 3-year-old children indicated that children were much more apt to look at an adult immediately after performing a symbolic action in play rather than an instrumental action, reflecting, according to the authors, the essential social nature of symbolic play (Striano, Tomasello, & Rochat, 2001).

Why might it be important to facilitate symbolic play? Children learn about people, objects, and actions through symbolic play, and research indicates that such play might be related to other aspects of cognitive development (see Pellegrini, 2013b). For example, researchers reported that the greater the level of representation preschool children show in their play, as reflected by role-playing or transforming one object to represent another, the better their subsequent early writing ability (Pellegrini & Glada, 1991). Other researchers have found a relationship between the amount of cooperative social play in which preschoolers engage (often with a sibling or parent) and later understanding of other people's feelings and beliefs (Astington & Jenkins, 1995; Youngblade & Dunn, 1995). An understanding that other people have thoughts, feelings, and beliefs other than one's own reflects what has been called a *theory of mind* and is discussed in Chapter 6. Developing an advanced theory of mind is necessary if children are to succeed in any society, and it appears that the guided participation afforded by parents, siblings, and other more expert partners during symbolic play contributes to this development.

Socialization of Attention

Research has documented cultural differences in aspects of selective attention. For example, some have proposed that Westerners are socialized to focus their attention on key features of objects, whereas East Asians are socialized to divide their attention between objects and events in their environments (Duffy & Kitayama, 2007). This is related to hypothesized differences in holistic (Asian) versus analytic (North American) styles of reasoning that have been proposed to characterize the two cultures (Nisbett et al., 2001; Varnum et al., 2010). For instance, it is hypothesized that Asians see the world in a more holistic way, being especially sensitive to relationships among objects within the current context, whereas Westerners are more apt to take an analytic perspective, focusing on individual "target" items. This is illustrated in a study in which Japanese and American adults were shown stimuli similar to those presented in Figure 3.3 (Kitayama et al., 2003). In this study, participants were shown a box with a line drawn in it and, in a smaller box, had to reproduce either the absolute length of the line (bottom left in Figure 3.3) or the relative length of the line (bottom right in Figure 3.3). Consistent with the divided-versus-focused-attention hypothesis, the American adults were more accurate performing the absolute task, whereas the Japanese adults were more accurate performing the relative task.

When does this cultural pattern develop? By 6 years of age, both Japanese and American children display the same pattern as adults in their culture do (Duffy et al., 2009; Vasilyeva, Duffy, & Huttenlocher, 2007). However, 4- and 5-year-old children in both America and Japan make more

FIGURE 3.3 **The frame-line test.** Children are asked to draw the line in the boxes at the bottom that is either the same absolute length as the line in the top box (absolute task) or the same relative length (relative task). Beginning at age 6, Americans perform better on the absolute task and Japanese perform better on the relative task. However, 4- and 5-year-old children in both America and Japan make more errors on the absolute task.

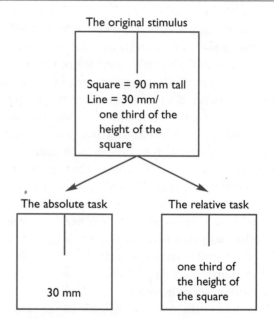

Source: Kitayama, S., Duffy, S., Kawamura, T., & Larsen, J. T. (2003). Perceiving an object and its context in different cultures: A cultural look at new look. *Psychological Science, 14,* 201–206.

errors on the absolute tasks (Duffy et al., 2009). This and other research (Duffy, Huttenlocher, & Levine, 2005) suggest that both American and Japanese young children initially have an easier time dealing with relative information. However, depending on cultural practices, sometime around 6 years of age some children (in this case, Americans) become socialized to *focus* their attention, whereas others (in this case, Japanese) become socialized to *divide* their attention. A similar interpretation has been proposed for the development of analogical reasoning, with Asian preschool children performing better on complex problems dealing with relations among objects than Western (American) children (Richland et al., 2010).

Cultural Influences on Guided Participation

Although the process of guided participation may be universal, how it is carried out varies as a function of how children are perceived and treated in a culture. Rogoff and her colleagues (1993) proposed that different parent-child interactions (that is, differences in the nature of guided participation) occur in different cultures. They made contrasts between two general types of cultures: (1) cultures such as ours, where beginning in the preschool years children are often segregated from adults and receive much culturally important information and instruction outside of the context of skilled activity (that is, in school); and (2) cultures where children are in close contact most of the day with adults and both observe and interact with adults while they perform culturally important activities. Rogoff and her associates observed 14 families with toddlers in each of four communities: two where culturally important information is transmitted mainly out of context, through formal schooling (Salt Lake City, Utah, and Keçiören, a middle-class community in Turkey) and two where culturally important information is transmitted mainly in context (the Mayan town of San Pedro, Guatemala, and Dhol-Ki-Patti, a tribal village in India). Rogoff and her colleagues observed toddlers and their caregivers while doing routine activities (for example, feeding, dressing); while playing social games

(for example, peek-a-boo, finger games); and while playing with novel objects (for example, a clear glass jar with a small doll inside, an embroidery hoop, a jumping jack [a marionette that kicks its legs when its bottom string is pulled and the top string is held]). Following are examples of guided participation in each of the four communities.[1]

Salt Lake City. A 21-month-old boy and his mother, exploring a glass jar that contains a peewee doll.

Sandy's mother held the jar up and chirped excitedly, "What is it? What's inside?" and then pointed to the peewee doll inside. "Is that a little person?" When Sandy pulled down on the jar, she [his mother] suggested, "Can you take the lid off?"

Sandy inspected the round knob on top and said, "Da ball."

"Da ball, yeah," his mother confirmed. "Pull the lid," she encouraged, and demonstrated pulling on the knob. "Can you pull?" Sandy put his hand on hers, and they pulled the lid off together triumphantly. "What's inside?" asked his mother, and took the peewee out. "Who is that?"

Sandy reached for the lid, and his mother provided running commentary. "OK, you put the lid back on." And when Sandy exclaimed "Oh!" his mother repeated "Oh!" after him. When Sandy lost interest, his mother asked with mock disappointment, "Oh, you don't want to play anymore?" and suggested, "We could make him play peek-a-boo."

When Sandy took the peewee out, she [his mother] asked, "Where did she go?" and sang, "There, she's all gone," as she covered the peewee with her hands, "Aaall gone." (p. 81)

---

[1] From "Guided participation in cultural activity by toddlers and caregivers," by B. Rogoff, J. Mistry, A. Goncu, C. Moiser, 1993, *Monographs of the Society for Research in Child Development, 58* (Serial No. 236, No. 8). Copyright © 1993 The Society for Research in Child Development, Inc., reprinted with permission.

Keçiören, Turkey. A 14-month-old girl and her mother, playing with an embroidery hoop.

A mother introduced a game in which she and her 14-month-old daughter, Lamia, took turns putting the embroidery hoop on each other's head and then dropping it on the floor. The mother created a sense of pretend excitement by saying, "Ay ay ay . . . ," each time they dropped the hoop. This was followed by joint laughter. The game became explicitly pretend when the mother put the hoop on Lamia's head, making the girl look like a bug with the handles of the hoop sticking out like antennas. The older brother chipped in, saying, "Lamia is a bug, Lamia became a bug." "What kind of a bug?" asked the mother in a coquettish way. "A lady bug," the mother and brother said simultaneously. (p. 136)

Dhol-Ki-Patti, India. An 18-month-old girl and her mother, playing with a jumping jack [a wooden doll that does "jumping jacks" when a child pulls on a string].

Roopa was not holding the top and bottom strings taut enough to cause the jumping jack to jump, so her mother took Roopa's hand in her own, grasped the bottom string with both hands, and pulled on the string twice, saying, "Pull here, pull here," as she demonstrated. She then released her hold of Roopa's hand to enable Roopa to do it on her own.

But the jumping jack fell to the ground because Roopa was not holding it tight. The mother, quick to help, lifted the jumping jack as Roopa reached for it. Twice again, she pulled on the bottom string with her left hand, repeating, "Pull it here." Then she released her hold, letting Roopa take the object. She held her hands close to (but not touching) Roopa's, ready to help if necessary. (p. 114)

San Pedro, Guatemala. A 19-month-old boy and his mother, playing with a jumping jack.

The mother used a firm manner of placing the child's hands on the strings to mark the importance of holding firmly onto them, positioning the jumping-jack toy in a position that indicated to the child to hold the bottom string lower, and tapping the child gently on the arm, indicating not to pull the string so hard. (p. 71)

Although toddlers and caregivers in all communities interacted in ways permitting all participants to develop an understanding of the task at hand, important differences were found between the middle-class and more traditional communities. Parents in Salt Lake City and Keçiören placed a greater emphasis on verbal than on nonverbal instruction, with the adults providing a good deal of structure to foster children's involvement in learning, including praise and other techniques to motivate the children. The middle-class parents also frequently instructed their children in specific tasks. In contrast, parents in the Mayan and Indian villages used more explicit nonverbal communication and rarely directly instructed their children in a particular task. As we noted earlier, adults in traditional cultures rarely engage in direct teaching with children (Lancy, 2015; Lancy & Grove, 2010). In these communities, children are rarely segregated from adults; because children are around adults most of the day, they can observe competent adult behavior and interact with adults while they perform the important tasks of their society. Rogoff and her colleagues reported that observation skills are more important and better developed in the traditional communities than in the middle-class communities, with children in traditional communities being better at attending to relevant adult behavior. The acquisition of mature, culturally appropriate behaviors via observation has been termed legitimate peripheral participation (Lave & Wenger, 1991), and although adults seemingly play a less active role than in guided participation, it is nonetheless an important component of an apprenticeship in thinking.

The findings of Rogoff and her colleagues make it clear that there is no single path to becoming an effective member of society but that, depending on the demands of one's particular community, different forms of guided participation are apt to be used. One form is not necessarily better than another. It depends on how a competent adult in a society is supposed to behave.

Section Review

Vygotsky placed little emphasis on self-initiated discovery, choosing instead to stress the importance of social contributions to cognitive growth.

- According to Vygotsky's *general genetic law of cultural development*, cognitive function occurs on two planes, first on the social (between individuals) and only later on the individual (internalized by the child).

Studying Children in Natural Settings

- Children acquire cultural beliefs and problem-solving strategies in the context of collaborative dialogues with more skillful partners in everyday tasks.
- Children in different cultures acquire information from adults differently, with adults in traditional societies rarely directly instructing children.

Zone of Proximal Development

- Learning is most effectively done working within the *zone of proximal development*, defined as the difference between a child's "actual developmental level as determined by independent problem solving" and his or her level of "potential development as determined through problem solving under adult guidance or in collaboration with more capable peers" (Vygotsky, 1978, p. 86).

- Related to the concept of the zone of proximal development is *scaffolding*, which occurs when experts are sensitive to the abilities of a novice and respond contingently to the novice's responses in a learning situation.

Apprenticeship in Thinking and Guided Participation

- *Guided participation* refers to adult-child interactions not only during explicit instruction but also during the more routine activities and communication of everyday life.
- Different cultures prepare their children for adult life differently. For example, in modern Western societies, parents talk to children extensively and prepare them for the types of tasks they will encounter in schools.
- In more traditional societies, adults are less likely to use language and more likely to demonstrate certain abilities to their children.
- Children acquire important cultural behaviors by working alongside and simply observing more skilled members of the community, a process termed *legitimate peripheral participation*.

Ask Yourself . . .

9. What are some perspectives on how cognition is socially constructed?
10. What questions can we try to address by studying children in natural settings?
11. How is *scaffolding* related to the *zone of proximal development*?
12. How does *shared remembering* influence the cognitive development of children from different cultures?
13. In what ways do parents influence their child's cognitive development through reading and other conversation?
14. What are some cultural differences in the effects of *guided participation*?

SOCIOCULTURAL THEORY AND COGNITIVE DEVELOPMENT

The focus of sociocultural theory is unabashedly the social environment. But one need not reject any idea of looking at biological factors to adopt a sociocultural perspective. Contemporary sociocultural theorists clearly view development as occurring in a system of interacting levels (Gauvain & Perez, 2015; Rogoff, 2003), including the child and his or her behavior; people interacting with the child; other people in the immediate environment; and the school, the family, and the community. However, there is also the recognition that children's brains evolved to fit with children's environments, and those environments just happen to be essentially social in nature (M. H. Johnson, 2010; J. G. Miller & Kinsbourne, 2012).

We think it is easy to espouse belief in the idea that development is the result of multiple levels of causation, each interacting in a bidirectional way. But it is more difficult to practice such a belief. We don't doubt that some researchers taking a sociocultural approach *do* view any mention of biological causation as unnecessary, and we believe some people who focus more on biological causation see the environment as nothing much more than a place for the genes to express themselves. These researchers, however, are in the minority. And at times, it is certainly convenient to talk about a pattern of development or a characteristic of a child as being primarily environmental or biological in origin, even though we know that *all* characteristics are the product of a complex interaction of bidirectional effects at multiple levels of organization. There are surely some spirited debates ahead for developmental scientists concerning *how* biological and sociocultural mechanisms interact to produce a developing child. But there should not be any debates concerning *if* they do. In our opinion, and in those of probably most leading developmental scientists, one cannot look at human development independently of culture. Humans' social, emotional, and cognitive abilities evolved for life in a human group. And such a perspective is not at odds with other, more biologically oriented models of development. Rather, models describing how the specific social environment in which a child lives influences development must be integrated with theories such as those presented in Chapter 2 on the biological bases of development. Only by studying children, with their genetic and congenital characteristics, in dynamic interaction with their environment, including the larger culture, can we attain a complete understanding of development.

KEY TERMS AND CONCEPTS

general genetic law of
    cultural development
guided participation
legitimate peripheral
    participation

microgenetic development
ontogenetic development
phylogenetic development
scaffolding
sociocultural perspective

sociohistorical development
tools of intellectual
    adaptation
WEIRD societies
zone of proximal development

SUGGESTED READINGS

Scholarly Works

Gauvain, M., & Perez, S. (2015). Cognitive development in cultural context. In R. Lerner (Series Ed.) & L. Liben & U. Müller (Vol. Eds.), *Handbook of child psychology and developmental science: Vol. 2. Cognitive processes* (7th ed., pp. 854–896). New York: Wiley. This article by Mary Gauvain and Susan Perez presents a modern version of the sociocultural perspective and how it is integrated with evolutionary and developmental contextual viewpoints.

Lancy, D. F. (2015). *The anthropology of childhood* (2nd ed.). Cambridge, UK: Cambridge University Press. David Lancy provides a thorough review of children and childhood in cultures throughout the world and makes clear that children in most cultures have very different experiences from children in WEIRD (Western, educated, industrial, rich, developed) cultures such as our own. Yet this book is not just about children's lives in exotic societies but has much to say about children and childhood in our own culture.

Miller, K. F., Smith, C. M., Zhu, J., & Zhang, H. (1995). Preschool origins of cross-national differences in mathematical competence. *Psychological Science, 6,* 56–60. This paper presents a good example of a study examining how cultural differences in tools of intellectual adaptation (in this case, how different languages represent numbers) can influence children's cognitive performance. It demonstrates how subtle differences between two cultures can have unexpected intellectual differences.

Reading for Personal Interest

Carr, N. (2008, July/August). Is Google making us stupid? *The Atlantic.* In this essay, published in *The Atlantic* magazine, Carr discusses the impacts of online reading, computers, and of course Google, among other things, on thinking and cognition. He references research on the brain's plasticity in his discussion of how technology shapes the way we think. Although he never uses the term *tools of intellectual adaptation*, he discusses examples of cognitive artifacts, such as the clock, and how such cultural instruments influence action and thought. The article can be retrieved online here: www.theatlantic.com/magazine/archive/2008/07/is-google-making-us-stupid/306868.

Gauvain, M. (2001). *The social context of cognitive development.* New York: Guilford. This book, although over a decade old, presents an authoritative yet highly readable account of research and theory from the sociocultural perspective. The first set of chapters discusses mainly theory, whereas the second set of chapters presents sociocultural research in areas of higher mental functions, including the acquisition of knowledge, memory, problem solving, and planning.

Gladwell, M. (2008). *Outliers: The story of success.* New York: Little, Brown. Popular writer Malcolm Gladwell explains how success is as much a function of a person's cultural heritage and time in history as it is of natural intelligence or hard work. Although never mentioning Vygotsky or the sociocultural approach to development, Gladwell's book provides many examples of how a child's social surroundings and cultural traditions interact with other aspects of their personalities and intellects to produce successful people from Bill Gates to the Beatles to professional hockey players.

Harari, Y. N. (2015). *Sapiens: A brief history of humankind.* New York: Harper. Historian Yuval Noah Harari presents a history of *Homo sapiens* from proto-humans to modern times and examines the many factors that have influenced our species development, including the reciprocal relationship between human thought and human culture.

4 INFANT PERCEPTION AND COGNITION

IN THIS CHAPTER

Audrey tells of an unusual preference in her healthy 9-pound newborn daughter Michelle. For the first several weeks of life, Michelle would nurse only from one breast, despite the fact that Audrey expressed milk equally well from both. Michelle's preference was the left breast, the one over her mother's beating heart, a sound Michelle had heard from the time her auditory system began to function several months after conception. Michelle would nurse from the left breast only and inevitably fall asleep, presumably being soothed not only by the milk she was consuming but also by the familiar sound she was hearing.

If you ask most people what newborn babies do, the answer you'll likely get is, "Sleep, eat, cry, and soil their diapers." This is true enough, but newborns are also making sense of their world. They are perceiving (hearing, seeing, smelling) and learning about events that surround them, and have been for some time prior to birth. Not all that many years ago, well-informed people believed that infants enter the world unable to perceive sights and sounds. When I (DB) was teaching my first child development class as a graduate student in the early 1970s, I stated that newborns can see, meaning that they can tell the difference between two visual displays. A middle-age woman informed me that I was wrong, that newborns cannot see. She had had four children, and her obstetrician and pediatrician had both told her that babies were functionally blind at birth and learned to see during their first month of life. Newborns are far from mental giants, but they do enter the world able to perceive information with all their senses. Furthermore, babies have some perceptual biases. Some sights, sounds, and smells are inherently more pleasing to them than others, and they learn to prefer additional sensations during the first weeks of life.

But infants, even newborns, do more than perceive their world. As the example of Michelle suggests, they are also learning, something that most people call cognition. Even among experts, it's not always easy to know where perception ends and cognition begins (see, for example, L. B. Cohen & Cashon, 2006, for a review). Perception is usually defined as involving the organization of the sensations (for example, sights, sounds, smells), whereas cognition deals more with what we do with those perceived sensations (for example, classifying items or events into categories, solving problems, memorizing). In this chapter, we first examine the developing perceptual abilities in infants and then look at some basic cognitive abilities, focusing on aspects of what has been called *core knowledge*—specifically, infants' understanding of object representation and babies' abilities to make sense of quantitative information. Other topics related to infant cognition are examined in later chapters.

BASIC PERCEPTUAL ABILITIES OF YOUNG INFANTS

The study of infant perception has been one of the most successful endeavors in the field of cognitive development over the past half century (see S. P. Johnson & Hannon, 2015). What infants perceive and know was once thought to be beyond the limits of science. However, the development of often simple techniques—using behaviors that infants, even newborns, can control themselves to peek into their minds—has permitted developmental psychologists to get a relatively clear picture of what infants perceive and how their perceptions change over time.

Most research on infant perceptual development has concerned audition (hearing) and vision. This is partly because of the importance of these two senses for human information processing and because vision in particular shows substantial development during the first year of life. The development of audition and vision are discussed in separate sections later in this chapter.

Research on other senses has also been conducted, of course. For example, it was once believed that newborns were relatively insensitive to pain. More recent research, however, clearly demonstrates that they do, indeed, perceive pain (Delevati & Bergamasco, 1999), and some evidence indicates that, for extremely low birth weight (ELBW) infants (below 1,000 grams, or about 2.2 pounds), their response to pain is affected by repeated painful episodes, which are often necessary for preterm infants (Grunau et al., 2001). When tested at 8 months of age, the number of invasive procedures ELBW infants had from birth was associated with reduced facial and heart-rate reactions to pain (blood collection). Yet other studies report that children who were exposed to more pain as preterm infants experience increased sensitivity to pain in childhood and adolescence, compared to their full-term peers. Fortunately, these threshold differences do not seem to persist into adulthood; adults' self-reports indicate there is no increased prevalence of pain syndromes for those born at extremely low birth weight (see Grunau, 2013, for a review). Newborns also respond to another skin sense, that of touch, or tactile stimulation. Actually, research with both animals and human preterm infants indicates that tactile stimulation is important in ameliorating pain responses in particular and promoting normal growth and development in general. For instance, very small preterm infants who receive extra tactile stimulation gain more weight, spend more time awake,

and display more advanced cognitive and motor skills than do normally treated preterm babies (see Honda et al., 2013; Schanberg & Field, 1987). This research has led to an increased prevalence of skin-to-skin care, also known as kangaroo care, in neonatal intensive care units and newborn nurseries (see Johnston et al., 2014).

The chemical senses (olfaction and taste) tend to develop early and are quite well developed shortly after (and even before) birth. In fact, a pregnant woman's diet can influence taste preferences in her newborn. This was illustrated by a study in which some women consumed anise-flavored food during pregnancy whereas others did not. At birth and 4 days later, infants born to anise-consuming mothers showed a preference for anise odor, whereas those born to non-anise-consuming mothers displayed aversion or neutral responses to anise (Schaal, Marlier, & Soussignan, 2000). Young infants can also tell the difference among a wide range of odors early in life (Steiner, 1979), and they develop preferences for certain odors within the first week. In a study by Aidan Macfarlane (1975), for example, 6-day-old nursing babies were able to discriminate the odor of their mothers from those of other women. In this study, mothers wore breast pads in their bras between nursings. Two breast pads—one from the baby's mother and the other from another woman—were placed on either side of an infant's head. Although no differences in infants' behaviors were seen in this situation at 2 days of age, by 6 days of age babies were turning to their own mother's pad more often than to the pad of another woman. That is, not only can babies discriminate odors, they quickly learn to make associations with odors and to modify their behavior accordingly. In subsequent work using a procedure similar to that of Macfarlane, researchers found that infants develop a preference for the odor of milk versus amniotic fluid (which they had been living in for 9 months) by 4 days of age (Marlier, Schaal, & Soussignan, 1998) and that bottle-fed, 2-week-old infants preferred the breast odor of a lactating female to that of a nonlactating female (Makin & Porter, 1989).

Section Review

- From birth, infants actively use their perceptual systems to acquire information from their surroundings.
- By 1 week of age, babies can discriminate their mothers from other women by smell and by the sound of their voices.
- Infants also experience pain at birth and respond to tactile stimulation.
- Olfaction and taste are well developed at birth and affected by maternal diet.

Ask Yourself . . .

1. How have changes in our knowledge of infants' perceptual abilities influenced neonatal practice?

METHODOLOGIES USED TO ASSESS INFANT PERCEPTION

How can a psychologist tell if an infant can see or hear something? That is, how can we determine if an infant can tell the difference between a bull's-eye pattern and a checkerboard pattern, for example, or between the mother's voice and that of another woman? This basic problem hampered serious investigation of infants' perceptual abilities for years, but the solution is really quite simple. What one must do is find some

behavior that an infant can control and then use that behavior as an entry into what babies can perceive. For example, the Macfarlane (1975) study just presented took advantage of babies' abilities to turn their heads in one direction or another to determine if they could discriminate and develop a preference for certain odors. Such measures are considered implicit measures of infant cognition because they are thought to capture aspects of cognition that are unconscious and cannot be expressed directly or verbally. As we'll discuss, these aspects include implicit memory, such as familiarity. In contrast, explicit measures require that the participant report on the contents of his or her cognition or behave in observable ways that are directly related to the task at hand. Because infants lack sophisticated verbal ability and behavioral control, many of the techniques we discuss next are considered implicit measures of cognitive functioning. The distinction is important to introduce however because, as you'll see, the responses of infants (and the conclusions drawn about their cognitive abilities as a result) often differ based on whether implicit or explicit measures are used.

"This Sucks": Using Infant Sucking to Provide Insight Into Infant Perception

Another behavior that very young infants can control is sucking. How might researchers use this behavior to tell if babies can discriminate between two different auditory signals? Anthony DeCasper and Melanie Spence (1986) used infants' ability to regulate their sucking to examine whether infants were learning something about the outside world while still in utero. DeCasper and Spence asked pregnant women to read aloud one of three passages twice a day during the last 6 weeks of their pregnancies. Shortly after birth, the neonates were tested for which passage, if any, would have more reinforcing value. Headphones were placed over the babies' ears, and various passages were played to the infants. Nonnutritive sucking (that is, sucking on a pacifier) was assessed as a function of which passage was being played. First, a baseline sucking rate was determined for each baby (that is, how rapidly the infant sucked on a nipple when no passage was being played). Then, babies were trained such that changes in their rate of sucking determined whether they heard a familiar passage (the one their mothers had read during pregnancy) or a novel passage (one their mothers had not read). Some infants heard the familiar passage when they increased their sucking rate, whereas the contingency was reversed for other infants. The general finding was that the familiar passage was more reinforcing than the novel passage; infants were more likely to alter their sucking rate to hear the familiar passage than to hear the novel passage. Furthermore, the reinforcing value of the passage was independent of who recited it, an infant's mother or another woman. These results present unambiguous evidence of prenatal conditioning to auditory patterns. The infants were able to discern the auditory characteristics (the rhythm and sound pattern) of these often-repeated passages, and the researchers were able to determine this by associating the various passages with changes in a behavior that infants could control themselves (sucking rate).

Visual Preference Paradigm

The simplest (and first) technique to test infants' *visual* discrimination abilities was developed by Robert Fantz (1958, 1961). He placed alert babies in a looking chamber. Series of visual stimuli were placed in front of infants' eyes, and an observer peeking through a hole in the chamber above the infant recorded which stimuli the baby looked at the most. If groups of infants spent significantly more time gazing at one pattern than at another, it could be assumed that they can differentiate between the two patterns and prefer to look at one relative to the other. If they couldn't tell the difference between the paired stimuli, there would be no difference in their looking behavior. Using this **visual preference paradigm**, Fantz was able to show that babies younger than 1 week can tell the difference between stimuli such as a schematic face, a bull's-eye pattern, and an unpatterned disk (see Figure 4.1).

FIGURE 4.1 **Infants' visual attention to different patterns.** Infants look longer at faces and patterns with more information.

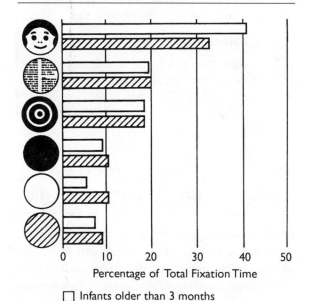

Source: Fantz, R. L. (1961). The origin of form perception. *Scientific American, 204,* 66–72. Copyright © 1961 Scientific American, Inc. All rights reserved. Reprinted with permission.

We use the term *preference* not to reflect a conscious liking for one thing over another—for alternative rock versus country music, for example—but only to indicate that an infant looks at one object more than another. *Preference*, as used here, is synonymous with *perceptual bias* and merely reveals that infants are not responding randomly.

If infants failed to show a preference (or perceptual bias) between two items, however, this would not necessarily mean that they could not tell them apart. Perhaps both are equally interesting. But if infants have no preference for one stimulus over another, how can you tell if they can discriminate between them? One technique is the habituation/dishabituation paradigm, which we now describe.

Habituation/Dishabituation Paradigm

A somewhat more complicated procedure is often used to evaluate infants' perception, memory, and concepts, and this is the *habituation/dishabituation paradigm*. **Habituation** refers to the decrease in response as a result of repeated presentation of a stimulus. The first day on the job in a noisy factory, for example, produces increased levels of physiological stress (for example, elevated heart rate and blood pressure). After a week in this environment, however, levels of stress decline, even though the noise remains. This is habituation. **Dishabituation** (sometimes referred to as *release from habituation*) occurs when, following habituation, a new stimulus is presented that increases the level of responding. If we switch from Factory A to Factory B, for instance, levels of physiological stress rise, even though the new factory is no louder than the old one was. The noises are different, however, which causes an increase in responding, or a release from habituation.

How does this phenomenon relate to infant perception? The amount of time babies look at visual stimuli (or orient to auditory stimuli) is analogous to the worker's physiological reactions to loud noise. The longer infants are exposed to a visual stimulus, the less time they spend looking at it. Habituation is said to occur when an infant's looking time is significantly less than it was initially (often defined as when visual fixation to the stimulus is 50% of what it was on the early trials). At that point, a new stimulus is presented. If attention (that is, looking time) increases from the level of immediately before, dishabituation is said to occur. A typical habituation/dishabituation curve is shown in Figure 4.2.

What does such a pattern mean? First, it demonstrates that infants can discriminate between the two stimuli. Babies might not prefer one to the other, but that they respond to the new

FIGURE 4.2 **An example of results from a habituation/dishabituation experiment on infant visual attention.** The amount of looking time decreases with repeated presentation of the same stimulus (habituation) but increases with the presentation of a new stimulus (dishabituation).

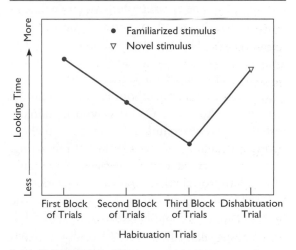

Source: © Cengage Learning.

stimulus with increased attention indicates they can tell the difference between the two. This paradigm is very useful in determining infants' discrimination abilities when researchers are using stimuli for which babies might not have a decided bias. Habituation and dishabituation also indicate memory. Infants are making a discrimination between one stimulus that is physically present and another that is present only in memory. They are not choosing between two stimuli that are before them but between one stimulus that is in front of their eyes and another that is only represented in their minds.

Using this procedure, evidence of habituation/dishabituation (and, thus, of rudimentary memory) has been found in newborns for vision (S. Friedman, 1972) and haptic perception (identifying an object by active touch) (Streri, Lhote, & Dutilleul, 2000). Moreover, fetuses as young as 30 weeks habituate and later dishabituate (as demonstrated by their movement) to vibrations delivered via sound waves through the mother's abdomen (Dirix et al., 2009; Sandman et al., 1997). In one of the first studies to demonstrate habituation/dishabituation in newborns, Steven Friedman (1972) habituated 1- to 3-day-old infants to one visual pattern and then, immediately after habituation, showed the babies a novel pattern. These neonates displayed the classic increase in responding to the new stimulus, indicative of memory (be it ever so brief).

One word of caution about Friedman's results is in order, however. Of 90 newborns initially tested, 50 were excluded for reasons such as crying and falling asleep. Of the 40 remaining, only 29 displayed dishabituation. Thus, only 32% of the original sample demonstrated the habituation/dishabituation phenomenon. The high dropout rate challenges the generalizability of Friedman's (and others') findings. What Friedman's results do indicate, however, is that

visual memory is within the capability of many human newborns, although the possibility exists that many infants do not possess such memory until several weeks after birth. (Dropout rates have been lower in some more recent studies. For example, of the 34 newborns tested by Alan Slater et al. [1991], only 10 [29%] were excluded for fussiness and related problems.)

Not only can the habituation/dishabituation paradigm be used to show discrimination and memory but also concept formation. This is done by varying the stimuli presented during habituation trials. Rather than habituating infants to a picture of the face of a single individual (Sally), for example, pictures of different individuals can be presented (Sally, Maria, Barbara, and Teresa). In both the single- and multiple-face cases, looking time declines with repeated exposure (that is, habituation). In the former case, infants are habituated to a specific stimulus (Sally), and in the latter case, infants are habituated to a category of stimuli (women's faces). After habituation has occurred, a new female face can be presented (Elizabeth). Infants who were habituated to a single face should recognize this new face as a novel stimulus and increase their attention to it (that is, show dishabituation). In contrast, infants who were habituated to women's faces in general should recognize it as just another example of a woman's face and continue to habituate. That is, even though they have never seen this face before, they should categorize it as familiar and direct relatively little of their attention to it.

The procedure and results just described are similar to those reported by Leslie Cohen and Mark Strauss (1979) for a group of 30-week-old infants. Cohen and Strauss interpreted their findings as evidence that such infants can abstract "appropriate conceptual categories regarding the human face" (p. 422). By continuing to habituate to the new stimulus, infants are, in effect, telling us that although the face is perceptually different from anything they have seen before, it is similar in general form to what they already know. They are telling us that they have acquired a category for female faces. Using these and similar techniques, research during the past 40 years has shown that infants as young as 3 months can organize objects into perceptual categories during relatively brief experimental sessions (Eimas & Quinn, 1994; Younger & Gottlieb, 1988).

These are not the only methods to assess infant perception. But these methodologies have been used for more than 40 years to evaluate what babies can perceive and what they know, and most of the research reviewed in this chapter involves variants of these well-developed techniques.

presentation of a stimulus. *Dishabituation*, or release from habituation, occurs when looking time increases with the presentation of a new stimulus. Habituation and dishabituation to visual stimuli are found for some newborns and reflect both discrimination and memory.

Ask Yourself . . .

2. What are the basic visual and auditory abilities in newborns? How do these abilities develop over infancy?
3. What are the differences in *implicit* and *explicit measures* of cognition and perception?
4. How can we know what babies perceive and what they are thinking about? What are some of the more frequently used methods to assess infant perception and cognition?

Section Review

From birth, infants actively use their perceptual systems to acquire information from their surroundings. By 1 week of age, babies can discriminate their mothers from other women by smell and by the sound of their voices. A number of implicit measures have been used to assess infants' perceptual abilities.

- Infants will alter their sucking rate to different stimuli, indicating their ability to discriminate.
- Researchers measure the amount of time infants spend looking at two stimuli in a *visual preference paradigm*. If infants spend more time looking at one stimulus than another, researchers can infer that infants can discriminate between the stimuli and prefer to look at one versus the other.
- *Habituation* occurs when infants' looking time diminishes as a result of repeated

DEVELOPMENT OF VISUAL PERCEPTION

When can infants begin to make sense of their visual world? When, for example, can they discriminate between two visual stimuli or form visual concepts? We, like our primate cousins, are a visual species. Survival during our prehistoric past would have been unlikely for a visually impaired child. Vision gives us information about both near and distant objects that touch and hearing cannot easily provide. Spatial cognition is an important higher-order skill (see Chapter 6), and such thinking is based on vision. Perhaps because of the importance of vision to the species, or perhaps because we're better at thinking about ways of testing vision, visual perception has been the most studied sense in psychology, both in children and in adults.

Vision in the Newborn

Newborns can perceive light, as demonstrated by the pupillary reflex (constriction of the pupil to bright light and dilation to low levels of illumination). However, **accommodation**, or focusing, of the lens is relatively poor at birth, regardless of the distance an object is from an infant's eyes, and most of what newborns look at they see unclearly (Tondel & Candy, 2008). Development of the muscles of the lens is rapid, however, and under favorable stimulus conditions, accommodation is adultlike by as early as 3 months of age.

Newborns will visually track a moving object, but their eyes will not necessarily move in harmony. **Convergence** refers to both eyes looking at the same object, an ability apparently not possessed by newborns (Wickelgren, 1967). Convergence and **coordination** (both eyes following a moving stimulus in a coordinated fashion) improve during the first months of life and are adultlike by 6 months of age (Aslin & Jackson, 1979).

Studies attempting to determine the *acuity*, or the ability to see clearly, of infants have yielded varied results, depending on the technique used. Acuity improves substantially during the first year of life, but it is very poor at birth (Kellman & Banks, 1998). To assess visual acuity in infants, babies are shown high-contrast patterns of various sizes, such as the pattern of stripes shown in Figure 4.3. If they look at the striped pattern longer than at a plain gray one, we infer that they can "see" the lines. When they show no preference for any one pattern, we assume that they cannot tell the difference between them. With normal acuity for adults being 20/20 (that is, one can see at a distance of 20 feet what a person with "normal" vision can see at 20 feet), estimates of newborn acuity range from 20/400 to 20/600 (Slater, 1995), making

the neonate legally blind in most states. Acuity improves substantially during the first year of life, although it does not reach adult levels until 6 years of age (Skoczenski & Norcia, 2002).

An important reason for newborns' poor vision is the underdeveloped state of their foveas, the area of the retina where there is the highest concentration of cones (color-perceiving cells that provide the clearest vision). Although the fovea of a newborn is larger than that of an adult, individual cells are arranged differently, cells vary in size and shape, and cones are more widely distributed in the foveas of newborns relative to adults. This makes the cones of newborns much less sensitive to light than those of an adult—by some estimates, by a difference of 350 to 1 (Kellman & Banks, 1998). However, recent research has demonstrated that, when

FIGURE 4.3 **If infants look at a striped pattern like this one longer than at a plain gray one, we know that they can "see" the lines.** When they can no longer tell the difference between the gray pattern and the striped pattern, it reflects the narrowest width of stripes that an infant can discriminate, and this is used to determine the infant's visual acuity.

Source: © Cengage Learning.

supplemented in infant formulas, omega-3 long-chain polyunsaturated fatty acids (LCPUFAs) like those found in fish oil supplements and other "healthy fat" foods, lead to significant improvement in visual acuity by as early as 2 months of age (Qawasmi, Landeros-Weisenberger, & Bloch, 2013).

Do newborns see the world in color, the way adults do? Although newborns might not be color-blind, they apparently do not perceive much in the way of color. When differences in brightness are controlled, infants fail to discriminate among a wide range of colors until about 8 weeks of age (Allen, Banks, & Schefrin, 1988). Research has shown newborns can likely discriminate between the colors red and white but cannot differentiate blue, green, and yellow from white (R. J. Adams, Courage, & Mercer, 1994). In general, newborns seem to process color information the same *way* adults do, but their color vision itself is extremely poor (R. J. Adams & Courage, 1998). However, by about 4 months of age, their color perception has improved greatly and is similar to that of adults (Franklin, Pilling, & Davies, 2005; Ozturk et al., 2013).

The research just cited indicates that newborns can discriminate differences in intensity of light, can track a moving object, and likely can see differences between contrasting colors (see Photo 4.1). Can they tell the difference, however, between a checkerboard pattern and a bull's-eye pattern? In the earlier section on methodology, we described a simple procedure developed by Fantz (1958) in which infants are shown two pictures and the time they look at the various stimuli is noted. If the chosen stimuli are sufficiently different, even very young infants will show a bias for one over the other, demonstrating by their differential looking time that they can tell the difference between the two. Because of the relatively poor acuity of young infants'

PHOTO 4.1 Young infants' attention is attracted by high contrast.

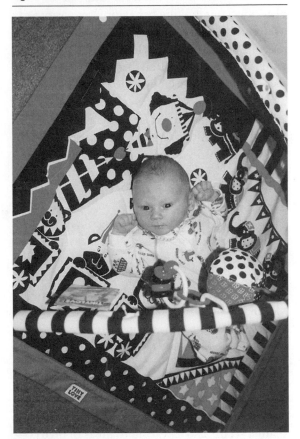

Source: Barbara Bjorklund.

vision, however, stimuli must be reasonably discrepant before discriminations can be made, but newborns do make such discriminations (Slater, 1995).

Development of Visual Preferences

What a baby, or anyone else for that matter, chooses to look at depends on a variety of physical stimulus characteristics as well as psychological characteristics. Physical characteristics, such as movement, amount of contour or contrast, complexity, symmetry, and curvature of the stimulus, affect our looking behavior from a very early age. Familiarity and novelty, which determine the psychological significance of a stimulus for us, also affect the visual biases of infants, but these psychological factors increasingly influence infants' attention from 2 to 4 months of age. Until this time, babies' visual attention is affected chiefly (but not exclusively) by physical stimulus features.

Physical Stimulus Characteristics

Movement is a potent stimulus characteristic influencing infants' visual attention. Everything else being equal, babies look more at a moving stimulus than at a comparable stimulus that is stationary. In an experiment by Marshall Haith (1966), newborns sucked on a nipple while watching a light display. On some trials, the light moved, tracing the outline of a triangle. Babies decreased their sucking on these trials relative to those when the light did not move, indicating increased attention to the moving light.

Infants are also attracted to areas of high contrast, as reflected by the outline, or contour, of an object. In a pioneering study, Philip Salapatek and William Kessen (1966) assessed the visual scanning of newborns. Infants less than 1 week of age were placed in a modified looking chamber with a white triangle painted on a black background situated before their eyes. The infants' eye movements were recorded and then contrasted with those that occurred when the triangle was not visible. Examples of the scanning patterns of the newborns when the triangle was present are shown in Figure 4.4. As can be seen, the infants' visual fixations were centered near the vertices of the triangles, the areas of most

contrast. Subsequent research indicated substantial individual variability in newborn scanning, with many infants during the first 6 weeks of life showing no systematic visual attention to stimulus contours; much of this variation has been attributed to differences in infant neurological maturity at birth (Bronson, 1990). By about 2 months, however, infants in the Bronson (1990) study were able to consistently direct their attention toward stimulus contours. Work by Salapatek and his colleagues (Maurer & Salapatek, 1976; Salapatek, 1975) indicated that infants at 1 month of age direct their attention primarily to the outside of a figure and spend little time inspecting internal features. Salapatek referred to this tendency as the externality effect. By 2 months, however, most of infants' fixations are on internal stimulus features. An example of scanning patterns of 1- and 2-month-olds is shown in Figure 4.5.

FIGURE 4.4 **Examples of scanning patterns of newborns.**

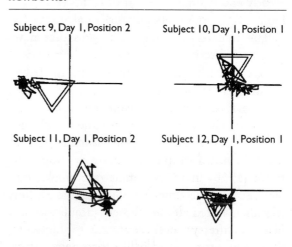

Subject 9, Day 1, Position 2

Subject 10, Day 1, Position 1

Subject 11, Day 1, Position 2

Subject 12, Day 1, Position 1

Source: Salapatek, P., & Kessen, W. (1966). Visual scanning of triangles by the human newborn. *Journal of Experimental Child Psychology, 3,* 155–167. Copyright © 1966 Academic Press. Reprinted with permission from Elsevier.

FIGURE 4.5 **Examples of visual scanning of faces by 1- and 2-month-old infants.** One-month-old infants explore the contour of faces, called the *externality effect*, whereas 2-month-olds spend more time looking at the internal features of faces.

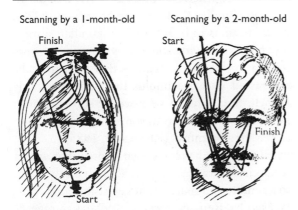

Scanning by a 1-month-old   Scanning by a 2-month-old

Source: Adapted from Shaffer, D. R. (1993). *Social and personality development* (3rd ed.). Pacific Grove, CA: Brooks/Cole.

Infants' bias for and processing of symmetrical forms have been shown for vertical stimuli. Although there seems to be no bias for *vertical symmetry* until the latter part of the first year, infants as young as 4 months process vertically symmetrical stimuli (stimuli that are the same on the left and right sides) more efficiently than they do vertically asymmetrical or horizontal stimuli (Bornstein, Ferdinandsen, & Gross, 1981). Efficiency of visual processing in these studies was measured by rates of visual habituation. Four-month-old infants acquired information about vertically symmetrical stimuli more effectively than they acquired information about asymmetrical or horizontal information, as reflected by their faster rates of habituation (that is, they looked at the symmetrical stimuli less on later trials than they looked at the asymmetrical or horizontal stimuli). According to Marc Bornstein and his colleagues (1981), "The results . . . support the view that verticality has a special status

in early perceptual development. . . . Whether innate, early maturing, or based on experience, the special quality of verticality generally may derive from the importance of the vertically symmetrical body and face" (p. 85).

Infants also have a bias to attend to "top-heavy" stimuli, with more information in the upper portion of a stimulus than the lower portion, as is typically the case with faces (Macchi Cassia, Turatin, & Simion, 2004; Turati et al., 2002). This explains, in part, infants' greater attention to upright versus inverted faces.

Another physical stimulus feature of importance is that of curvature, or *curvilinearity*. Some of Fantz's original work demonstrated infants' biases for curved stimuli, such as a bull's-eye pattern, over linear (that is, straight-line) stimuli of comparable contour (Fantz, 1958). Holly Ruff and Herbert Birch (1974) similarly observed a bias for curvilinear stimuli in 3- and 4-month-old infants, but they also found a bias for concentric stimuli (see Figure 4.6). This bias for curvature was reported even in a sample of newborns (Fantz & Miranda, 1975), although only when the stimuli differed in their outer perimeter (recall the externality effect).

The recent innovation of a head-mounted eye tracker has allowed researchers to glimpse the visual biases of mobile infants on the go. Using this technology, John Franchak and his colleagues (Franchak et al., 2011) found that 14-month-old infants' visual exploration is opportunistic during free play. For instance, they reported that infants did not often look at their mothers' faces following her infant-directed utterances, unless the mother was sitting at infants' eye level. Infants did spend a significant amount of time gazing toward their own hand movements during manual actions and crawling, but gazing at obstacles was less common during leg movements. These findings suggest that in

FIGURE 4.6 **Examples of stimuli used to assess infants' preferences for curvature.** All other things being equal, infants prefer curvilinear and concentric stimuli.

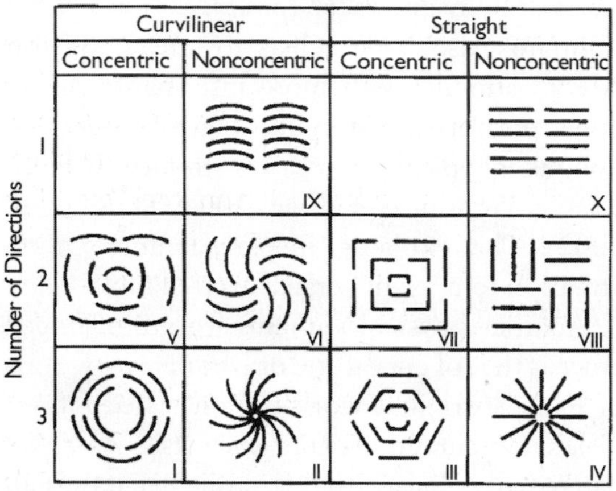

Source: Huff, H. A., & Birch, H. G. (1974). Infant visual fixation: The effect of concentricity, curvilinearity, and number of directions. *Journal of Experimental Child Psychology, 17,* 460–473. Copyright © 1974 Academic Press. Reprinted with permission from Elsevier.

naturalistic settings, infants prefer to look at relevant areas in the environment to meet changing task demands. It also reminds us that we cannot ignore the interplay between physical constraints and infants' preferences in shaping social interactions. Future studies using this technology will surely yield additional insights as to the ways infants filter the visual input during everyday interactions.

Psychological Stimulus Characteristics

Movement, contour, complexity, symmetry, and curvature continue to affect the attention of people throughout life. Beginning sometime around 2 to 4 months, however, the psychological characteristics of a stimulus—that is, the stimulus's familiarity or novelty—exert an increasing influence on whether and for how long it will be attended to. The fact that a stimulus's familiarity or novelty influences infants' attention implies some sort of memory for the stimulus event, as we discussed when interpreting the result of dishabituation studies (L. B. Cohen & Strauss, 1979). For a stimulus to be regarded as familiar, it must be contrasted with some previous mental representation of that stimulus—that is, it must be contrasted with a stimulus that was previously known. Similarly, to be novel, a stimulus must be slightly different from something that the perceiver already knows (Rheingold, 1985).

However, it has long been known that, under some circumstances, infants actually show a bias to attend to familiar, not novel, stimuli (Bahrick, Hernandez-Reif, & Pickens, 1997; Courage & Howe, 2001). In general, a bias for familiarity typifies younger infants but also holds for older infants in the early phases of visual processing. For example, Susan Rose and her colleagues (1982; see Experiment 2 in that study) showed that groups of 3.5- and 6.5-month-old infants initially showed a bias for familiarity, followed by no preference, and eventually, a bias for novelty (see also Courage & Howe, 1998, for similar results with 3-month-olds). Other research has found that whereas 3-month-old infants preferred to look at faces from their own race (a bias toward familiarity), 9-month-old infants had a preference to look at faces from other races (a bias toward novelty) (S. Liu et al., 2015). In a similar vein, Richard Bogartz and his colleagues (Bogartz & Shinskey, 1998; Bogartz, Shinskey, & Speaker, 1997) proposed that infants prefer to look at familiar stimuli when processing is in its early stages, based on Eleanor Gibson's (1991) differentiation theory, which posits that infants' perception becomes increasingly specific with time, as the sense of familiarity allows them to distinguish one stimulus from another. It takes time to create and store memory representations, and the brain is limited on how much information it can collect in a single exposure to a novel stimulus, so infants should prefer attending to familiar stimuli while memory representations are still being formed. Once a stable memory representation has been formed, an infant's preference should switch to a novel stimulus (see also Bahrick et al., 1997).

Richard Aslin and his colleagues (Aslin, 2014; Kidd, Piantadosi, & Aslin, 2012; see also Kidd, Piantadosi, & Aslin, 2014) have described the novelty-familiarity conundrum as the Goldilocks effect, whereby infants take an active role in sampling their environment, looking longer at stimuli that are neither too simple nor too complex (see also Kagan, 1971). Consistent with Gibson and Bogartz, Aslin argues that infants' tendency to maintain fixation on events of intermediate familiarity, as demonstrated by their own work (which we describe later) and that of others (McCall, Kennedy, & Appelbaum, 1977), "appears to be based on [infants'] implicit sense that some patterns of information are more or less informative than others and therefore worthy of further sustained attention" (Aslin, 2014, p. 12).

Development of Face Processing

Infants, like older children and adults, like faces. Some of the earliest work in infant visual preferences revealed that babies of 4 months and older demonstrate a preference for the human face over other nonface-like stimuli (Fantz, 1961). Infants' preferences for physical features, such as curvilinearity and vertical symmetry, may largely account for babies' more general bias to attend to faces.

Might a bias to attend to faces be present shortly after birth? Such a bias would not be surprising, for no single visual stimulus likely is of greater importance to a human infant than that of the face of another member of his or her own species. Human infants are highly dependent on their parents for support and protection for a far longer time than other mammals are, and human infants' survival is made more likely by the strong social attachment they establish with their parents. Given this, it makes sense from an evolutionary perspective for infants to be oriented to the most social of stimuli, the human face.

Research following Fantz's pioneering work pushed back the age at which infants show a preference for face-like stimuli to the newborn period. For example, Mark Johnson and his colleagues demonstrated that newborns can distinguish between face-like and nonface-like stimuli (M. H. Johnson, Dziurawiec, et al., 1991; Morton & Johnson, 1991). These studies did not use a visual preference paradigm, however. Rather, they showed infants different head-shaped stimuli, moving each stimulus across the babies' line of visual regard. Investigators measured the extent to which the infants followed each moving stimulus (a) with their eyes and (b) by turning their heads. Using these measures, other researchers have reported significantly greater eye or head movement to face-like stimuli than to nonface-like stimuli for infants ranging in age from several minutes to 5 weeks. (Figure 4.7, from M. H. Johnson, Dziurawiec, et al., 1991, presents the results of one such study.) Subsequent research using related methodologies has found special attention for face-like stimuli for newborns (Easterbrook et al., 1999; Mondloch et al., 1999).

Such evidence suggests that infants are born with some notion of "faceness" and will attend to such stimuli more than they will to others.

FIGURE 4.7 Newborn eye and head turns in following different stimuli.

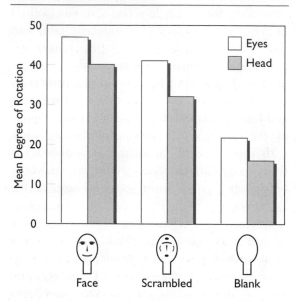

Source: Johnson, M. H., Dziurawiec, S., Ellis, H. D., & Morton, J. (1991). Newborns' preferential tracking of faces and its subsequent decline. *Cognition, 40,* 1–19. Copyright © 1991 Elsevier Science Publishing Co., Inc. Reprinted with permission.

Based on the results of their own studies plus those of others, Morton and Johnson (1991) concluded that "it can now be accepted with some degree of confidence that neonates find slowly moving faces with high-contrast definition particularly attractive stimuli" (p. 172). These researchers went on to caution, however, that this does not mean newborns understand the conceptual meaning of a face, merely that they are biased to visually track face-like rather than nonface-like patterns.

Morton and Johnson (1991) developed a two-process theory for infant face preference. An initial process is accessed primarily through subcortical pathways, and this controls newborns' tracking of faces. This system is responsible for human newborns' preference for the human face, but because of limited sensory capabilities, infants are not able to learn about the features of faces until about 8 weeks of age. Beginning around that time, this system loses its influence over infants' attention to faces, and the second process, which is under the control of cortical circuits, begins to take over. The functioning of this system depends on cortical maturation and experience with faces during the first 2 months of life, as infants begin to build a representation, or **schema**, that enables them "to discriminate the human face from other stimuli and especially from faces of other species" (Morton & Johnson, 1991, p. 178). A schema is not an exact copy of a stimulus but "a representation of an event that preserves the temporal and spatial arrangement of its distinctive elements without necessarily being isomorphic with the event" (Kagan, 1971, p. 6). This face-processing specialization is corroborated by some neuropsychological studies that, through measuring scalp-recorded brain electric potentials (event-related potentials, ERPs) (Halit, de Haan, & Johnson, 2003) or performing positron emission tomography (PET) scans (Tzourio-Mazoyer et al., 2002), suggested that the first signs of cortical specialization for faces can be observed in 2- to-3-month-olds.

More recently, researchers have begun to investigate at what age infants detect and attend to faces within complex visual displays (Di Giorgio et al., 2012; Frank, Amso, & Johnson, 2014). Much of this research is based on L. B. Cohen's (1972) proposal that infant attention develops as two separate processes: an attention-getting process and an attention-holding process. In these experiments, infants and adults are shown a series of dynamic (that is, moving) or static visual displays featuring a target face among a half dozen or so distractor objects. Eye-tracking devices are attached to the subjects to determine how quickly and how often they orient toward faces (that is, Cohen's attention-getting process) and how long faces retain their attention (that is, the attention-holding process). Using this method, Elisa Di Giorgio and her colleagues (2012) showed that adults made more initial fixations (were faster) to orient toward faces than 3- and 6-month-old infants. However, 6-month-olds performed similarly to adults in how frequently they looked at faces and for how long. Three-month-olds did not look longer or more often at faces compared with other objects. Other studies confirm that 3-month-olds do not prefer faces in either dynamic displays or static stimulus arrays but that children 6 months and older show a clear face preference (Gliga et al., 2009; Gluckman & Johnson, 2013).

How do we reconcile 3-month-olds' apparent lack of interest in faces in these visual-search paradigms with infants' bias for faces in the preferential looking task? One interpretation may be that young babies have a weak ability to inhibit attention toward salient background information. Therefore, in preferential looking tasks, where the context in which stimuli are displayed is simple (a face and a nonface stimulus), 3-month-olds demonstrate a bias for faces because the amount of distracting stimuli is limited. In contrast, when faces are embedded in complex displays, infants may find it difficult to inhibit attention to distracting background stimuli, failing to promptly detect and privilege the face stimulus (Di Giorgio et al., 2012). Attentional control develops throughout the first year of life and is undoubtedly not mature at 3 months of age (M. H. Johnson, Posner, & Rothbart, 1991).

Michael Frank and colleagues (2009) proposed another possible interpretation, one consistent with the Goldilocks effect introduced earlier. They have shown that 3-month-olds' visual search patterns are best predicted by the salient low-level characteristics of the stimuli presented rather than by any particular type of stimuli, such as a face (see also Easterbrook et al., 1999). Therefore, it could be that it is harder for younger babies to detect a complex visual stimulus composed of different features, such as a human face, among other complex and novel visual stimuli as distractors. Consistent with this proposal, Frank et al. (2014) found a relationship between infants' attentional abilities in general and their attention to faces in particular; infants showing weaker attentional abilities looked less at faces, and this correlation was strongest in 3-month-old participants, mediating (partially accounting for) the relationship between age and face looking. Taken together, these findings suggest that even though neonates may often look at face-like images over other visual stimuli in forced-choice paradigms, infants' attention to faces in complex displays that more closely resemble the input in "the real world" increases considerably over the first year.

Some evidence suggests, however, that even newborns might be able to make discriminations among individual faces, looking longer at faces of their mothers than at those of other women, for example (Bushnell, Sai, & Mullin, 1989). In related research, Gail Walton and her colleagues (1992) reported that 12- to 36-hour-old infants would vary their rate of sucking more to see a picture of their mother's face than that of another woman. This suggests not only that newborns can tell the difference between faces and nonfaces but also that they learn a preference for their mothers' faces shortly after birth. This early developing ability to prefer familiar faces may be evolutionarily quite old. Similar patterns have been reported for an infant gibbon (a lesser ape), which displayed a preference for looking at faces in general, and at familiar faces specifically, by 4 weeks of age (Myowa-Yamakoshi & Tomonaga, 2001).

In addition to preferring familiar faces, another quality seems to drive infants' perception—specifically, infants show a bias toward faces that adults classify as being attractive. For example, Judith Langlois and her colleagues (1987) asked college men and women to judge the attractiveness of adult Caucasian women from photographs. From these ratings, photographs of eight attractive and eight less attractive faces were selected, although the distribution of attractiveness was relatively normal (that is, there were no extremely attractive or unattractive faces). The photographs were selected so that all women had neutral expressions, had medium to dark hair, and did not wear glasses. In one part of the study, 2- to 3-month-old and 6- to 8-month-old infants were shown pairs of faces from the selected photographs that varied in attractiveness (one more attractive and one less attractive), and their looking time was measured. Both the younger and older infants spent significantly more time looking at the more attractive faces than at the less attractive faces, with approximately two thirds of the infants showing a bias for the more attractive faces. Furthermore, the bias for the more attractive faces was unrelated to how attractive an infant's mother was judged to be. More recent research has shown that this bias toward attractive faces is found even in newborns (Slater et al., 1998). Other research has shown that this bias extends across sex, race, and age of the modeled face: Six-month-olds consistently show a bias for attractive faces of both men and women, of both Black and White adult females, and of 3-month-old infants, despite the fact that the infants had little or no experience with some of these classes of faces (Langlois et al., 1991).

One possible explanation for these findings is that attractive faces have more of the physical stimulus characteristics that draw infant attention than do unattractive faces. For example, attractive faces might be more curvilinear, concentric, and vertically symmetrical than unattractive faces (see earlier discussion). From this perspective, infants' bias for faces is simply a by-product of their bias for many of the physical features that happen to be characteristic of faces. Facial symmetry may be the most important factor here, for it is perhaps the single most potent determinate of attractiveness in adults (Gangestad & Thornhill, 1997). Likewise, a recent study independently manipulated the symmetry, averageness, and sexual dimorphism (how feminine or masculine a face is) of pictures of adult faces and found that infants between 12 and 24 months old looked longer at symmetrical than asymmetrical faces as well as feminine faces (Griffey & Little, 2014). Evolutionary psychologists have indicated that symmetry is a sign of physical health (Gangestad & Thornhill, 1997) and of psychological health (Shackelford & Larsen, 1997), making it possible that a preference for facial symmetry when selecting mates may have been selected for in evolution. Although mate selection is not on the minds of infants, the bias may be a general one, which is weak early in life but becomes stronger with experience. However, evidence suggesting that the bias for attractive faces involves more than just symmetry comes from work with newborns, who displayed a bias for (that is, looked longer at) upright attractive faces versus less attractive faces but not for the same faces when presented upside down (Slater et al., 2000). Moreover, infants also show a preference for more attractive faces versus less attractive faces of cats and tigers (as judged by an independent sample of adults), suggesting that this preference is not specific to human faces (Quinn et al., 2008).

The face is a complicated stimulus with many defining features, but one that has attracted much attention (from both infants and researchers) is the eyes. For example, newborns prefer to look at faces with eyes opened (Batki et al., 2000), and mutual gaze (eye contact between two people) plays a critical role in social interaction. Research has shown that even newborns are sensitive to eye gaze and are more attentive to faces that are gazing at them than to faces with eyes averted (Farroni et al., 2002). For instance, Teresa Farroni and her colleagues (2002) sat infants between 24 and 120 hours old in front of two photographs of the same female face. One face had a direct gaze, whereas the other face had its eyes averted to either the right (for about half of the babies) or to the left (for the other half). Figure 4.8 shows an example of the type of faces babies saw. A flashing light attracted infants' attention, and then the two pictures were presented, side by side. Farroni and her colleagues reported that the newborns

were more likely to orient toward the gazing face and spent significantly more time looking at the face with the direct gaze than at the picture with the averted eyes. A follow-up experiment with 4-month-olds demonstrated that infants showed enhanced neural processing, as indicated by patterns of brain activity (event-related potentials from EEGs) when they viewed faces looking directly at them as opposed to looking at faces with averted gazes. Farroni and her colleagues (2002) concluded that infants' preference for direct gaze "is probably a result of a fast and approximate analysis of the visual input, dedicated to find socially relevant stimuli for further processing" (p. 9604).

Other research has shown that even newborns pay special attention to the eyes. For example, researchers showed newborns right-side-up and upside-down faces that were partially occluded, so that some faces showed the eyes whereas the eyes were hidden for others (Gava et al., 2008; see Figure 4.9). When babies could see the eyes, they looked longer at the right-side-up versus the upside-down faces, a pattern also shown by older infants and adults. They showed no preference, however, for either the right-side-up or upside-down face when the eyes were covered.

Research from a variety of perspectives using a variety of methodologies has illustrated that infants, from birth, are oriented toward faces, or face-like stimuli. This makes sense from an evolutionary perspective; it is also consistent with the speculation of Fantz (1961), who wrote more than 50 years ago that infants' preferences for face-like patterns may "play an important role in the development of behavior by focusing attention to stimuli that will later have adaptive significance" (p. 72).

FIGURE 4.8 **Newborns are attracted by eye movements, particularly by mutual gaze (like the face figure on the left).**

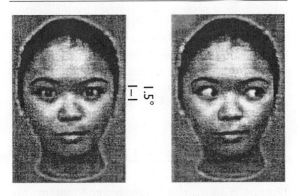

1.5°

Source: Drawings adapted from Farroni, T., Csibra, G., Simion, F., & Johnson, M. H. (2002). Eye contact detection in humans from birth. *Proceedings of the National Academy of Science, 99,* 9602–9605.

FIGURE 4.9 **Using a visual preference paradigm, Gava et al. (2008) found that newborns who could see the eyes of a person showed a stronger preference toward the right-side-up (versus the upside-down) face, as is typically found in research using faces without occlusions.** In contrast, newborns showed *no* preference for either the upside-down or right-side-up faces in the condition in which the eyes were covered.

Eyes Visible

Eyes Covered

Source: Gava, L., Valenza, E., Turati, C., & de Schonen, S. (2008). Effect of partial occlusion on newborns' face preference and recognition. *Developmental Science, 11,* 563–574.

Section Review

Vision is not well developed at birth, although the abilities of *convergence, coordination,* and *accommodation* of the lens improve rapidly during the first 6 months. From birth, infants look longer at some stimuli than at others, indicating they can discriminate between the stimuli and have preferences, or perceptual biases.

- During the first month of life, infants tend to direct their attention to the outside of a figure, which is referred to as the *externality effect.*
- Among the physical characteristics of a stimulus that attracts infants' visual attention are movement, contour and contrast, certain levels of complexity, vertical symmetry, and curvature.
- Beginning around 2 months of age, infants' attention is increasingly influenced by psychological factors, such as the familiarity or novelty of a stimulus.
- Infants form long-term sensory representations, or *schemas.* Gibson proposed the differentiation theory to explain infants' preferences for novel stimuli, stating that stimuli that are moderately discrepant from a previously acquired schema are most likely to be attended to. Aslin has described a similar phenomenon as the Goldilocks effect.
- Starting at a young age, infants develop a bias toward attending to the human face and look longer at attractive compared to less attractive faces. The eyes in particular are important in processing faces.

Ask Yourself . . .

5. What visual preferences, or perceptual biases, have been found in infancy? How are these preferences explained from an evolutionary perspective?
6. How have *differentiation theory* and the *Goldilocks effect* been used to explain infants' biases toward novel and familiar stimuli?
7. What are the major milestones in the development of face processing?

AUDITORY DEVELOMENT

Hearing is functional before birth, so infants are born with some auditory experience, notably the voice of their mother but also the sounds one would hear when living inside the body of another person (the heartbeat, for instance). Despite this early experience, newborns are often described as being a bit "hard of hearing" (Trehub & Schellenberg, 1995). Their audition improves substantially over the first year of life, but their hearing will not be adultlike until about 10 years of age (Saffran, Werker, & Werner, 2006). To hear a sound clearly, newborns require that sound to be about 15 decibels louder than adults need. (A decibel is a measure of sound intensity. For example, a typical conversation is about 60 decibels, a train about 90 decibels, and conversation in a library about 30 decibels.) At birth, babies are relatively good at localizing the source of a sound, as reflected, for example, by turning their heads toward a sound, and this ability improves markedly by the end of the first year (S. P. Johnson, Hannon, & Amso, 2005; Morrongiello et al., 1994).

As with vision, infants enter the world with some auditory biases. For example, infants appear to be more sensitive to high-frequency than to low-frequency tones (Saffran et al., 2006), and this might explain their preference for the voices of women (Jusczyk, 1997). As with smell, infants less than 1 week old have been shown to recognize their mothers' voices (DeCasper & Fifer, 1980). For example, Anthony DeCasper and William Fifer (1980) measured the rate at which 1- to 3-day-old infants sucked on a pacifier. They then conditioned the babies to alter their sucking rate (faster for half of the babies and slower for the other half) to the tape-recorded voices of their mothers and of an unfamiliar woman. DeCasper and Fifer reported that these young infants varied their sucking rates to hear their mothers' voices, indicating not only that they could discriminate the voices of their mothers from those of other women but that they also acquired a distinct preference for the voices of their mothers in a matter of days.

We noted earlier that infants who heard stories being read to them by their mothers during the last 6 weeks of pregnancy were able to discriminate between that story and another and preferred the one their mother had read to them (DeCasper & Spence, 1986). The findings of DeCasper and his colleagues indicate not only that the auditory system in newborns is working well but also that babies are learning some things about the outside world while still in utero. Moreover, subsequent research following the same design as that of DeCasper and Spence has found changes in heart rate to familiar and novel passages among third-trimester fetuses, unambiguously indicating that learning occurs before birth (DeCasper et al., 1994).

We'd like to revisit the *Goldilocks effect* and how it applies to auditory processing in infants (for a review, see Aslin, 2014). As with visual perception, a substantial amount of research indicates that infants actively allocate attention to auditory information that is sufficiently novel from—but also sufficiently related to—their existing knowledge (e.g., Gerken, Balcomb, & Minton, 2011; Spence, 1996). In one recent study, Celeste Kidd, Steven Piantadosi, and Richard Aslin (2014) exposed 7- to 8-month-old infants to sound sequences that were designed to vary in terms of how predictable they were. For instance, some events in the sequence were highly predictable (for instance, a *flute note* continues to occur after 20 consecutive *flute note* sounds) and some were less predictable (a *train whistle* occurs after 10 consecutive *flute notes*, for instance). In addition, some sequences contained more of these predictable events than others. Kidd and her colleagues measured the point at which infants terminated their attention while listening to each of these sequences. Based on their manipulation of these stimuli, the researchers developed a model that predicts, on an event-by-event basis, what infants should expect and how they might update their expectations based on experience with the auditory stimuli. For instance, as shown in Figure 4.10, at the beginning of a trial, infants have no reason to expect anything other than that all sounds will be presented equally. However, as a sequence progresses and they detect patterns in the sounds being played, they may alter their expectations to accommodate these patterns. The Goldilocks hypothesis holds that infants should terminate their attention to sound events that are expected but should continue allocating attention to events that have only moderate probability. Likewise, if an event is completely unexpected (exposure to a *door closing* sound, or Sound C in Figure 4.10), infants may perceive this as overly complex and terminate their attention at this point.

Kidd et al. (2014) used two types of models to determine the predictability or complexity of each event in the auditory sequence. The *nontransitional* model treated each event as statistically independent, whereas the *transitional* model tracked the probability that one type of event (for example, a train whistle) follows another type of event (for example, a flute note). The results of Kidd et al. demonstrated that infants adopted the Goldilocks pattern; infants were 1.15 times more likely to terminate attention to sounds in the sequences that were very low or very high in complexity (that is, very predictable or very surprising). Interestingly, this pattern was best approximated by the transitional model, suggesting that attention to auditory stimuli relies more heavily on temporal order and sequence than absolute probability. Tracking the transitional probabilities of auditory stimuli may be important for developing expectations about the auditory world, particularly in language learning, where word meaning is based on sequences of sounds rather than single events.

FIGURE 4.10 **Schematic showing an example sound sequence used by Kidd et al. (2014) and how the infant may combine heard sounds with prior expectations to form new probabilistic expectations about upcoming events (that is, the *updated belief*).** The degree of complexity of the next sound is based on these updated beliefs, and the Goldilocks hypothesis predicts that infants will stop allocating attention at the point when the sequence becomes overly simple (that is, provides no new information) or overly complex (that is, is unexpected).

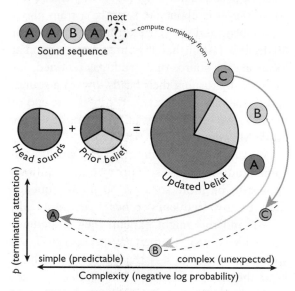

Source: Kidd, C., Piantadosi, S. T., & Aslin, R. N. (2014). The Goldilocks effect in infant auditory attention. *Child Development, 85*(5), 1795–1804.

Speech Perception

One particularly interesting aspect of infant auditory perception is the extent to which it is attuned to language. For example, at birth, babies prefer to listen to language relative to comparably complex nonlanguage sounds. This suggests that infants begin life with a bias for listening to speech, thus giving them a leg up on acquiring language (Vouloumanos & Werker, 2007). In fact, recent research has shown that the amount of time infants spend listening to speech versus nonspeech in a preferential listening procedure predicts expressive vocabulary at 18 months (Vouloumanos & Curtin, 2014).

The basic units of speech are called **phonemes**, and evidence indicates that infants come into the world with the ability to perceive most, if not all, of the phonemes found in all human languages (see Aslin, Jusczyk, & Pisoni, 1998; Tsao, Liu, & Kuhl, 2004), suggesting substantial biological preparation for infants to learn language. This phenomenon caused Patricia Kuhl (2007) to describe young infants as "citizens of the world," in that they seem equally ready and able to acquire any of the world's 6,000 or so languages.

Like colors, phonemes (such as *ba* and *pa*) can be arranged on continua, with gradual changes between them. For example, there is a range of sounds that we hear as *pa* and another range that we hear as *ba*. Despite this continuum, we categorize phonemes into distinct groups. For example, we tend to hear either a *pa* sound or a *ba* sound, and not some hybrid of the two of them. And most of us agree on the point at which *ba* ends and *pa* begins, just like we agree on the division between orange and red. The gradual changes in phonemes (and in colors) are considered to be physical, and the dichotomies we perceive are considered to be perceptual.

In a classic study, Peter Eimas and his colleagues (1971) presented 1-month-old infants with one physical example of the *ba/pa* continuum until they had decreased the rate at which they sucked on a pacifier (habituation). The researchers then replaced the phoneme with another example along the *ba/pa* continuum. If the infants perceive the new sound as being from the same phonemic category as the

previous sound (both *ba*, for instance), then they should continue to habituate (that is, decrease their sucking). This is because even though the sound is physically different from the one they heard before, it is just another example of the sound they had just heard repeatedly (that is, just another *ba*). If, however, they recognize this new sound as being from a different phonemic category (a *pa* rather than a *ba*, for example), they should increase their sucking rate (dishabituation). Using this technique, Eimas and his colleagues found that very young infants, like their parents and older siblings who already possess language, can categorize phonemes. They hear either *ba* or *pa*, and the dividing line they make between the two is the same as older members of their species make.

Other studies have used reinforcement techniques to assess infants' abilities to discriminate among phonemes. For example, G. Cameron Marean, Lynne Werner, and Patricia Kuhl (1992) used the activation of a mechanical toy to reinforce 2-, 3-, and 6-month-old infants for turning their heads when they heard a change from one vowel sound to another (either *a* to *i* or vice versa). This technique showed that even 2-month-olds were able to make the discrimination, despite changes in other auditory characteristics (that is, in the voice of the individual speaking).

Speech perception is more than the ability to detect phonemes, of course. It involves the discrimination of individual words. And perhaps the word that infants hear most frequently is their own name. Denise Mandel, Peter Jusczyk, and David Pisoni (1995) asked at what age can infants recognize the sound of their own name? They used a reinforcement technique (infants turned their heads to hear a name spoken, either their own or one of three other names) to test this. Infants at 4.5 months of age spent more time listening to their own names than to other names, regardless of whether the other names had the same stress pattern as their own (for example, *Johnny* versus *Abby*) or a different stress pattern (for example, *Johnny* versus *Elaine*). These findings indicate that infants are able to recognize frequently heard sound patterns at least by 4.5 months of age. In Chapter 9, we discuss research on how infants learn to parse out other words from the speech stream.

Music Perception

Although humans are especially prepared to process language, we also seem to be well prepared to process music. For example, some evidence indicates that infants can imitate the pitch, loudness, melodic contour, and rhythm of their mothers' songs. Other research shows that song (even when performed by an untrained singer) is just as effective at eliciting 11-month-old infants' attention as speech (Costa-Giomi & Ilari, 2014). Moreover, there are specific types of brain damage that affect musical abilities, suggesting that the ability to perceive and produce music is rooted in evolution and biology (see Gardner, 1983).

Many aspects of music perception appear to be adultlike very early in infancy (see Trehub, 2003, for a review). For example, babies seem to respond to changes in melody, rhythmic pattern, and redundancy much the same way that adults do and appear able to distinguish "good" from "bad" melodies (see Schellenberg & Trehub, 1999; Trehub, Trainor, & Unyk, 1993). Examples of telling the difference between "good" (regular or natural) musical patterns and "bad" (irregular or unnatural) musical patterns are particularly impressive given the diversity of human musical systems. Carol Krumhansl

and Peter Jusczyk (1990) demonstrated this by having 4.5- and 6-month-old infants listen to segments of Mozart minuets. Some of the segments had pauses inserted at the end of each musical phrase (natural), whereas other segments had pauses inserted in the middle of phrases (unnatural). Infants learned to control which music they heard—natural or unnatural—by turning their heads in the direction of the speaker playing the music they preferred. Overall, infants spent more time listening to the natural than to the unnatural versions. Of the 6-month-olds, 22 of 24 showed this pattern; of the 4.5-month-olds, 20 of 24 showed this pattern. Other research has found that infants as young as 6 months prefer tones related by simple ratios (what most adults consider to be consonant, or pleasant sounding) over dissonant sounds (as found in atonal music) (Schellenberg & Trehub, 1996; Virtala et al., 2013). Newborns also seem to know the difference between major (happy-sounding) and minor (sad-sounding) chords, as indicated by event-related potential readings (Virtala et al., 2013). Other research has shown that by 4 months of age, infants display a preference for the music of their own culture relative to that of another culture (Soley & Hannon, 2010). Given these infants' lack of musical experience, the results of these experiments suggest that music appreciation might not require a college class to attain and, in fact, might be a basic characteristic of the human nervous system.

Some of the most compelling evidence that musical perception is inherent to the newborn comes from research using functional MRI (fMRI) to measure brain activity of 1- to 3-day-old newborns as they listen to Western tonal music (Perani et al., 2010). In adults, the right hemisphere shows a specialization for processing musical sequences. When neonates listened to Western tonal music, they showed activation of the primary and higher auditory cortex in the right hemisphere as well. When altered excerpts of these sequences were played, which included changes in the tonal key or continued dissonance, activation reduced in infants' right auditory cortex and emerged in the left inferior frontal auditory cortex and limbic structures. These findings suggest that the hemispheric specialization for music observed in adults is the result of neurobiological constraints present in neonates. In addition, this neural architecture is sensitive to changes in tonal key and differences in consonance and dissonance in the first postnatal hours.

Numerous hypotheses have been advanced about the evolutionary origins of music, dating back at least to Darwin (1871). One hypothesis is that music played a social function, stemming from early humans' ability to synchronize body movements to an external beat. In support of this idea, Sebastian Kirschner and Michael Tomasello (2009) reported that 2.5-year-old children were better able to synchronize their body movements to a beat in a social situation (a person drumming to create the beat) versus a nonsocial situation (with the drumming done by a machine). Another proposal for the origins of music looks to early mother-infant interaction. The lullabies that mothers around the world sing to their babies are performed in an expressive and highly ritualized manner (see Masataka, 1999; Trainor, 1996) and serve to regulate infants' attention and emotion (see Trehub, 2003). In fact, although infants are highly attentive to infant-directed speech—the sing-songy and expressive style that mothers around the world use when talking to their babies (see Chapter 9)—they are even more attentive to their mothers' singing (Trehub & Nakata, 2001–2002).

Section Review

Infants begin learning about the world via auditory input while still in the womb. They are born with a preference for high-pitch voices and speech, as well as music.

- As with visual information, young infants learn auditory patterns and develop expectations based on these experiences. Based on these expectations, infants attend to auditory information that is neither too simple nor too complex, and this is referred to as the Goldilocks effect.
- Young infants can discriminate among *phonemes* and categorize language sounds much as adults do, and they appear to be biologically prepared to perceive music.

Ask Yourself . . .

8. What are the major milestones in the development of speech processing and music? What does the development of these abilities have in common with face processing, if anything?

COMBINING SENSES

Although we often think of each sense as being distinct from all others, as adults we do a great deal of coordinating information between senses. We direct our vision to a loud noise, and we can identify our slippers by touch alone when we are awakened in the middle of the night by a barking dog outside our window. In fact, the environment for adults is "intrinsically multimodal" (Bahrick, Lickliter, & Flom, 2004). To what extent is such sensory integration available to infants, and how can we interpret such integration when we observe it?

Intersensory Integration

Intersensory integration refers to the coordination of information from two or more sensory modalities. At one level, intersensory integration is present at birth. Newborns move their heads and eyes in the direction of a sound, as if they wish to see what all the noise is about. In a series of experiments examining the effects of sound on visual scanning in newborns, Morton Mendelson and Marshall Haith (1976) found that the presence of sound increased infants' visual attentiveness. The researchers suggested that this response to sound increases the likelihood that infants will discover something to look at.

Elizabeth Spelke (1976) provided an interesting demonstration of intersensory integration in infants. Spelke showed 4-month-old infants two films on side-by-side screens. On one screen was a film of a woman playing peek-a-boo; on the other screen was a hand holding a stick and striking a block of wood. A single sound track was played, corresponding either to the peek-a-boo or the drumming. The babies figured out which sound track went with which screen, devoting more looking time to the screen that matched the sound. That is, these 4-month-old infants realized that certain sound sequences go with certain visual displays, and they visually attended to those displays that provided such a match (see also Bahrick, 2002).

In somewhat related work, Lorraine Bahrick and John Watson (1985) investigated the ability of 5-month-olds to integrate proprioceptive (relating to perception of body movements) and visual information. The babies were seated in infant seats equipped with a type of tray that prevented them from seeing their legs. Two video screens were placed in front of the infants. One screen displayed the infant's own legs; that is, the picture was transmitted live. The other screen displayed a film of the legs of another infant (or in one experiment, the same infant's legs from a session recorded earlier). Thus, for one display (the contingent display), the movement of infants' legs was contemporaneous with their actual movement, whereas for the other display (the noncontingent display), the movement of legs was independent of the infants' current activity. Bahrick and Watson reasoned that if infants are able to integrate proprioception (as reflected by their own leg movements) and vision, they should be able to discriminate between the two films and spend more time looking at one than at the other. This was their finding. In three experiments, 5-month-olds spent, on average, 67% of their time looking at the noncontingent display. Presumably, the lack of contingency between their leg movements and those seen on the video produced some discrepancy, and this resulted in increased attention to the noncontingent display. In another experiment, Bahrick and Watson (1985) tested 3-month-olds and found no overall preference for either the contingent or the noncontingent display. They concluded that proprioceptive-visual integration is well established by 5 months and that the ability to detect the congruency between one's movements and their visual representation plays a fundamental role in an infant's perception of self, possibly underlying the development of visual self-recognition (discussed in Chapter 10). Other researchers, using a similar design that varied the spatial orientation of the images that infants saw, report that even 3-month-olds can detect the congruence between their actual leg movements and a video image of those movements (Rochat & Morgan, 1995), suggesting that this might be an early developing ability (for further review, see Zwicker, Moore, & Povinelli, 2012).

Is intersensory integration present at birth? Although research clearly indicates that intersensory abilities improve with age (see Lewkowicz & Lickliter, 2013, for a review), even newborns are capable of recognizing the equivalence between stimuli in two different modalities (a bright light and loud sound, for instance; Lewkowicz & Turkewitz, 1980) and prove capable of matching monkey vocalizations with facial gestures (Lewkowicz, Leo, & Simion, 2010). Yet this does not mean that such abilities are innate, at least not in the way that term is typically used. The developmental systems approach, introduced in Chapter 2, argues that all traits develop as a result of the bidirectional interaction between different levels of organization within the organism and that normal prenatal experiences are crucial in determining species-typical patterns of development. Such arguments are also applied to intersensory integration in infants (Lewkowicz & Lickliter, 2013). Perceptual experience begins before birth, and the specific experiences a fetus or an embryo receives can alter its development, including the ability to integrate information between senses. For example, we discussed in Chapter 2 research by Robert Lickliter (1990) in which exposure to light before hatching augmented bobwhite quails' subsequent visual abilities but was detrimental to some important auditory skills (identifying their species' call). Although space limitations prevent us from discussing these ideas in any detail, what's important to keep in mind when seemingly advanced abilities are observed in very young infants is that these skills are not preformed and functioning without the benefit of prior experience. Rather, such skills are constructed from the interaction of genes and environment, broadly defined, which begins prenatally and continues throughout life.

Intersensory Matching

A seemingly more complex intermodal feat concerns intersensory matching (or cross-modal matching). In intersensory matching, a child must be able to recognize an object initially inspected in one modality (touch, for example) through another modality (vision, for example). Susan Rose and her colleagues (1981) showed that 6-month-old babies can perform visual-tactual integration. The infants were presented an object (either through touch alone or vision alone) for 60 seconds (familiarization phase) and later presented a small set of objects through the alternative mode (transfer phase). The researchers reported that the infants spent more time during the transfer phase exploring the novel objects (by manipulating or gazing at them) than exploring the familiar ones. That is, the babies showed dishabituation by examining the novel stimuli more than the familiar stimuli, even though familiarization was done in a different sensory modality. Other studies using similar methods have demonstrated intersensory matching for 4- to 6-month-old infants (Streri & Spelke, 1989).

Substantial research has been done examining infants' developing ability to integrate sound patterns to the face patterns and movements that produce them. For instance, 4- to 5-month-old infants can associate lips movements congruent with the speech they are hearing (Spelke & Cortelyou, 1981) or with the utterance of specific phonemes, like *i* and *a* (Kuhl & Meltzoff, 1982). This early developing ability to associate auditory and visual information becomes more specific with experience. For instance, although 9-month-old infants can interconnect females' voices and faces, they can't reliably associate male voices and faces until about 18 months (Poulin-Dubois et al., 1994). This superiority of matching the voices and faces of females likely results from babies having more experience interacting with women than with men (Ramsey-Rennels & Langlois, 2006).

Section Review

- *Intersensory integration* refers to the coordination of information from two or more sensory modalities and may be present at birth or shortly thereafter.
- *Intersensory (or cross-modal) matching* refers to the ability to recognize a stimulus initially inspected in one modality (vision, for example) through another modality (touch, for example).

Ask Yourself . . .

9. What are the major milestones in the development of intersensory integration? How do we know that experience is important for normal development to occur?

PERCEPTUAL NARROWING

An infant is born a "citizen of the world," not knowing the particular culture, language, or perhaps even primate taxa in which he or she will develop. As such, newborns' perceptual abilities are broadly tuned to a wide variety of stimuli. However, there is growing evidence that perception narrows across many domains within the first year, including those related to facial and speech perception. This phenomenon, referred to as **perceptual narrowing,** is the process by which infants use environmental experience to become specialists in perceiving stimuli relevant to their species and culture. As a result, however, infants become relatively less effective at perceiving some things with which they have less experience (Lewkowicz & Ghazanfar, 2009; Pascalis et al., 2014). This developmental process is the result of neuroplasticity, discussed in Chapter 2. Human infants are born with the ability to process a wide variety of stimuli; however, as neural pathways are more consistently used they are strengthened (and those used less frequently are weakened), resulting in a more selective perception of information that is socioculturally relevant.

Perceptual Narrowing for Facial Discrimination

Earlier in this chapter, we discussed research that showed babies initially have a weak bias to attend to faces, which becomes stronger with age and experience. For example, from about 3 to 9 months, infants process upright faces more efficiently than inverted faces, revealing what appears to be an early developing appreciation of what the proper orientation of faces is "supposed" to be (Bhatt et al., 2005; de Haan, Oliver, & Johnson, 1998). By 9 months, perception has further narrowed such that, like adults, 9-month-olds show this bias only for human faces, whereas 6-month-olds show it for both human and monkey faces (Pascalis, de Haan, & Nelson, 2002). This pattern suggests that the brains of infants are biased to process right-side-up faces, perhaps the most important stimulus in the world of a young animal highly dependent on care from others. However, the fact that 6-month-olds do not give special privilege to human faces suggests that brain processing of faces becomes more specialized with age and experience. According to Olivier Pascalis and his colleagues (2002), "The ability to perceive faces narrows with development, due in large measure to the cortical specialization that occurs with experience viewing faces. In this view, the sensitivity of the face recognition system to differences in identity among the faces of one's own species will increase with age and with experience in processing those faces" (p. 1321).

As we noted elsewhere in the text, it takes time and experience for this special status for faces to develop. This can be seen in how infants process male versus female faces. For instance, 3- and 4-month-old infants can discriminate more easily between female than between male faces, and they generally prefer to look at female faces, with the exception of when the father is an infant's primary caretaker (Quinn et al., 2002; see also Rennels et al., 2016). Infants' increasing specialization at making distinctions between the faces of men and women and between different species (for example, monkeys versus humans; see de Haan et al., 1998) clearly illustrates the importance of experience in processing this most important of social stimuli (Ramsey-Rennels & Langlois, 2006; Turati, 2004). Still not convinced that experience is important in shaping these specializations? Consider that the ability to continue discriminating monkey faces is preserved in 9-month-old humans who were repeatedly exposed to monkey faces starting at 6 months (Pascalis et al., 2005; see also Fair et al., 2012).

Infants not only become "specialized" in discriminating among faces of different species and between men and women, they also develop an increasing ability to discriminate between faces of their own race relative to those of other races. This is termed the **other-race effect**. For instance, infants are shown faces from a particular ethnic group until they habituate; later, they are shown photos of people from their own ethnic group and others (for example, Caucasian versus Asian). In studies by David Kelly and his colleagues (2007, 2009) with both British and Chinese infants, 3-month-olds showed no other-race effect. They were equally skilled at recognizing faces from all ethnicities tested (Caucasian, Chinese, and African, as well as Middle Eastern for the British infants). However, by 6 months of age, infants could only recognize faces from their own race plus one other (Chinese and Caucasian), and by 9 months, infants were only able to recognize faces in their own race (Chinese or Caucasian). This phenomenon is not an indication of implicit racism in infancy; rather, it reflects the role of familiarity in shaping infants' perceptual abilities (see Anzures et al., 2013). However, infants retain the neural plasticity to modify their face-discrimination abilities. For example, in one study 8- and 10-month-old Caucasian infants were exposed to photographs of Asian female faces for 3 weeks and were later able to discriminate among Asian as well as Caucasian faces (Anzures et al., 2012).

Overall, infants' abilities to process faces is initially very general. Early on, they make no distinction among faces from different species, races, or genders. This changes with experience. In the process, infants lose some plasticity—the ability to process all "face" information equally. In general, the consensus among researchers seems to be that there are dedicated and complex areas of the brain for processing faces, and these areas develop as a result of experience over infancy and childhood (Pascalis & Kelly, 2009).

Perceptual Narrowing in Speech Perception

Just as infants' preference for faces becomes species-specific over time, so does their preference for speech narrow within the first 3 months of life. As we described earlier, human neonates prefer listening to speech compared to many nonspeech sounds, suggesting that humans are born with a bias for speech. However, as Athena Vouloumanos and colleagues (2010) demonstrated, this preference is not specific to human vocalizations at birth and minimally includes speech and monkey vocalizations. Vouloumanos and her colleagues (2010) presented thirty neonates and sixteen 3-month-olds with nonsense speech and rhesus monkey vocalizations. Neonates showed no preference for speech over rhesus vocalizations but showed a preference for both these sounds over synthetic sounds. In contrast, 3-month-olds preferred speech to rhesus vocalizations. These findings parallel results on infant face perception and suggest that a species-specific preference for speech develops across the first 3 months.

How else might infants' speech perception narrow early on? If, as we described earlier, infants can discriminate basic phonemes shortly after birth, how is it they acquire the language sounds peculiar to their mother tongue? English-speaking adults have a difficult time discriminating phonetic contrasts that occur in Czech but not in English, for example. Yet babies from English-speaking homes have little difficulty with these contrasts, suggesting that they were born with the ability (Trehub, 1976). Other studies have similarly shown that infants can make discriminations among speech sounds that are not found in their mother tongues and that their parents cannot make (Kuhl et al., 2006; Saffran et al., 2006). Before about 6 months of age, infants can discriminate all consonant contrasts in native and nonnative languages, but by 10 to 12 months, perception becomes more adultlike, with infants losing the ability to discriminate nonnative contrasts but maintaining the distinction between those that are native. For example, Rebecca Eilers and her colleagues (1979) reported that 6- to 8-month-old infants

from English-speaking homes were unable to discriminate some phonetic contrasts that are found in Spanish but not in English. Babies from homes where Spanish was spoken, however, had no trouble with such contrasts. This change in infants' sensitivity may develop earlier, as young as 6 months, for vowels (Kuhl et al., 1992). What these and other data suggest is that babies can make some sound discriminations that adult speakers of their language communities cannot make; with time, babies lose the ability to make these contrasts because they rarely hear them.

At the same time that infants are losing their abilities to discriminate among "foreign" phonemes, they are becoming more sensitive to the speech regularities in the language they hear every day. For instance, they are able to make increasingly fine discriminations between the phonemes in their mother tongue (Kuhl et al., 2006). They also become increasingly able to recognize the stress patterns of their language (such as the first syllable of two-syllable words stressed in English, as in *table* and *carpet*), to identify some typical phoneme combinations and syllables that occur more often in their language, and to pay attention to the pauses between words (Aslin, Saffran, & Newport, 1998).

Other research has shown that young infants are able to differentiate sentences uttered in their native language versus those in a foreign language on the basis of vision alone, but as with sound discrimination, they lose this ability over time (Weikum et al., 2007). For instance, 4-, 6-, and 8-month-old infants watched silent video clips of a woman speaking sentences either in the infants' native language (English) or in a foreign language (French). After infants' looking time to the videos decreased (that is, after habituating), some were shown videos of a woman speaking the other language (for instance, French if infants had been habituated to English). The 4- and 6-month-old infants increased their looking time to the new video, indicating that they could tell the difference between sentences spoken in their native versus a nonnative language by vision alone—that is, just by watching the lips of the speaker. However, 8-month-old infants continued to habituate, indicating that they could not discriminate between the two languages on the basis of vision alone. Other research has shown hearing babies similarly lose the ability to discriminate signs in American Sign Language from 12 to 14 months of age (Baker Palmer et al., 2012). These findings indicate that with experience, infants lose some of their ability to discriminate between languages on the basis of vision alone, much as they lose the ability to discriminate between sounds in nonnative languages. As children become more experienced with their native tongue, they lose some perceptual plasticity, becoming specialists in their own language.

Why should children lose this seemingly valuable ability? The flexibility to learn the sounds (or lip movements) of any possible human language would seemingly provide a great adaptive advantage, of course, but keeping this flexibility beyond a certain age likely was not adaptive in practice. Once our ancestors learned one language, there was likely little need (or opportunity) to become proficient in another. Thus, it makes more sense for the brain to dedicate neurons to processing the sounds it hears early in life. The alternative would give individuals more flexibility but likely less proficiency in perceiving or producing any one language. Infants exposed to more than one language are an interesting exception to this general rule. For instance, bilingual children are able to discriminate among a broader range of phonemes than monolingual children (see Bosch & Sebastián-Gallés, 2001; MacWhinney, 2015).

Perceptual Narrowing and Music

As you might be expecting by now, infants' perception of music follows a similar trajectory as speech and facial perception; newborns can discriminate musical structures that elude their parents. By the end of the first year, however, these abilities decline to the cultural-specific structures. For example, in one study, infants and adults were played a series of notes based on Western scales and Javanese pelog scales (Lynch et al., 1990). The formal description of these two musical systems is beyond the scope of this book (and our expertise); suffice it to say that the underlying scales differ considerably (to listen to some pelog music, Google "pelog music YouTube"). Adults and 6.5-month-old infants heard well-tuned or out-of-tune patterns of both types of music and were asked to distinguish between the two. The infants, of course, weren't asked to "tell" the difference; an operant-conditioning paradigm was used in which infants were rewarded for turning their heads toward out-of-tune series. The adults, who merely raised their hands for an out-of-tune series, were better able to distinguish between in-tune and out-of-tune patterns in the Western music than in the Javanese music, reflecting the influence of experience on their musical perception. (The adults were American, and all were familiar with the Western but not the Javanese system.) The infants, however, were equally good at distinguishing the out-of-tune series for both the Western and Javanese patterns, "suggesting that infants may be born with an equipotentiality for the perception of scales from a variety of cultures" (Lynch et al., 1990, p. 275). That is, just as children are capable of and biologically prepared for acquiring any human language, they seem also to be prepared for acquiring any system of music.

Perceptual Narrowing Within Intersensory Integration

We described that infants' abilities to discriminate between different phonemes in all the world's languages and to differentiate between faces from other races decline with age and experience. Something similar seems to be happening for intersensory perception. For instance, 2-month-old infants will look longer at a human face that corresponds to a sound (for instance, seeing a face saying *ee* and hearing the sound *ee*) than at a face that does not correspond to a sound (for instance, a face saying *ee* and the sound *ah*), and this ability improves with age (Patterson & Werker, 2003). How general is this ability, and do children always get better at it with age? In one study, 4-, 6-, 8-, and 10-month-old infants watched the face of a monkey as it made one of two sounds, a coo or a grunt (see Photo 4.2, from Lewkowicz & Ghazanfar, 2006). Sometimes the infants heard a sound that corresponded with the face (for example, the coo face with the coo sound), and other times the sound and the face were mismatched (for example, the coo face with the grunt sound). The 4- and 6-monthold infants looked significantly longer at the faces that matched the sounds, but the 8- and 10-month-old infants did not. A later study found that even newborns looked significantly

PHOTO 4.2   The face of a monkey making a grunt sound (A) and making a coo sound (B). Both 4- and 6-month-old infants looked longer at the face making the sound, but older infants did not.

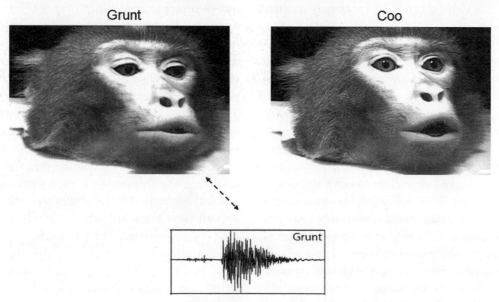

Source: Lewkowicz, D. J., & Ghazanfar, A. A. (2006). The decline of cross-species intersensory perception in human infants. *Proceedings of the National Academy of Sciences, 103,* 6771–6774.

longer at the faces that matched the sounds (Lewkowicz et al., 2010). Much like unimodal perception of language sounds, intersensory perception also shows a narrowing of ability with age and experience. What begins as a general ability to match sounds and faces becomes specialized to the types of faces (humans) and sounds (native language) that one hears (for similar results see Pons et al., 2009; Weikum et al., 2007).

Perceptual Narrowing as an Evolved Social-Cognitive Mechanism

Perceptual narrowing has been documented for infant and young children's processing of language, gestures (sign language), face processing, and music, as well as intersensory processing of vision and speech. Olivier Pascalis and his colleagues (2014) have proposed that this pattern of perceptual narrowing reflects an evolved mechanism that serves to foster social communication. The mechanism, they proposed, is not specific to any single cognitive ability but is common to several early developing forms of communication. Humans' highly social nature requires that infants learn to identify and communicate effectively with others—not just other members of their own species but other members of their particular social group. Through interactions with their mothers and others during their first year of life, infants become increasingly skilled at recognizing faces, speech sounds, gestures, and even the music characteristic of their social group, while losing the ability to process faces, sounds, and gestures from other social groups. The social and survival value of the rapid development of such communication skills appear obvious.

Section Review

Human infants are born with the ability to process a wide variety of stimuli. *Perceptual narrowing* is a process by which infants become tuned to sociocultural relevant information as a result of experiences during the first year of life. As perception becomes specialized, infants lose the ability to distinguish stimuli with which they have less experience. This developmental process is the result of neuroplasticity.

- Over the first year, face processing becomes increasingly specialized, and infants develop an increasing ability to discriminate between faces of their own race and experience a decreasing ability to discriminate between faces of other races, termed the *other-race effect*.
- By 9 months of age, infants lose the ability to discriminate phonemes that do not correspond to meaningful differences in their own language and become more sensitive to the speech regularities in the language they hear every day.
- Similar narrowing is observed for music perception and intersensory perception within the first year of life.
- This process is based on experience. With continued exposure to stimuli, infants maintain the ability to discriminate.
- Perceptual narrowing may be an evolved mechanism that serves to foster social communication.

Ask Yourself . . .

10. What is meant by perceptual narrowing, and what are some evolutionary explanations for its development?
11. How does the perception of speech and faces narrow across development? Are there parallels between these processes?
12. How does experience influence perceptual narrowing?

HOW DO WE KNOW WHAT BABIES KNOW? THE VIOLATION-OF-EXPECTATION METHOD

Despite how much we have learned about infant perceptual development, we need to be cautious and not attribute too much "intelligence" to babies based on sucking rate or looking time (Haith, 1993; Hood, 2004). As evidenced by the research on perceptual narrowing that we've just discussed, one should not view an infant's perceptual skills as fully developed the first time one sees them. Like most aspects of development, perceptual development is context dependent, and an infant's response can vary substantially from one time or situation to the next. This becomes even more important when we go beyond perception and examine infant *cognitive* development.

As we mentioned earlier in this chapter, it is not always easy to tell when perception ends and cognition begins. Many of the feats we described in the previous sections on perception, such as discriminating between different faces, can be quite complex and perhaps better deserve the label *cognition* than *perception*. In this section, we look at what many consider to be some lower-level cognitive abilities, including infants' understanding of objects, understanding of quantities, and abilities to form categories. Other higher-level forms of infant cognition, such as understanding social relations, memory, and problem solving, are discussed in later chapters. Before examining specific aspects of infant cognition, however, we first look at the most frequently used method for assessing aspects of infants' cognition—the violation-of-expectation method.

In the violation-of-expectation method, an infant's reaction to an unexpected event is used to infer what he or she knows. This method uses infants' looking behavior, much as in the preference-for-novelty and habituation/dishabituation procedures, to assess infants' reaction to unexpected events. The logic is simple: If infants see an event that deviates from what they expect—in other words, that violates their expectation—they should look longer at that event than at an "expected" event.

Let us provide an example from a study by Andréa Aguiar and Renée Baillargeon (1999) on the development of infants' understanding of objects. In this study, 2.5-month-old infants watched as a toy mouse disappeared behind one screen on the right side of a display and then reappeared seconds later from behind another screen on the left side of the display without appearing in the gap between the two screens (Aguiar & Baillargeon, 1999; see Figure 4.11). Infants looked longer at the magically appearing mouse than at the "expected" event (the mouse traveling through the gap between the two screens), suggesting that they were puzzled about how the mouse could have made the trip from one side of the display to the other without passing through the middle. As you can see, the violation-of-expectation method does more than simply inform researchers that infants can tell the difference between two stimuli, and variants of this method have been frequently used to provide insights into the infant mind (see Aslin, 2007; Baillargeon, 2008; and discussion later in this chapter).

As we warned for measures of infant perception, we must be cautious and not attribute too much in the way of sophisticated cognition based on how long infants look at one event versus another. But when the looking behavior of groups of infants systematically varies between expected and unexpected events, a researcher can be confident that something is going on in

FIGURE 4.11 **An example of an "impossible" occlusion event.** A toy mouse disappears behind a first screen and appears later behind a second screen, without appearing in the gap between them. Infants as young as 2.5 months of age seem to realize that objects cannot disappear at one point and then magically appear at another.

 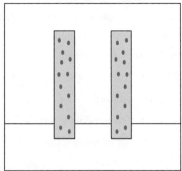 

Source: Adapted from Baillargeon, R. (2004). Infants' physical world. *Current Directions in Psychological Science,* 13(3), 89–94 (p. 90).

the minds of babies to produce such reliable results. It's the job of the psychologist to determine what exactly that something is.

CORE KNOWLEDGE

Infants are obviously not born as blank slates—beings with no biases simply waiting for experience to mold their minds. As we saw in the previous sections, babies enter the world, or develop shortly thereafter, with things they are biased to look at and listen to, and they are better at processing some types of information (faces, for instance) than others. Elizabeth Spelke and her colleagues (Spelke, 2000; Spelke & Kinzler, 2007), among others (for example, Baillargeon, 2008; R. Gelman & Williams, 1998), argue that babies possess core knowledge about several different domains from birth. They argue that infants are born with a small set of distinct systems of knowledge that have been shaped by natural selection over evolutionary time and upon which new and flexible skills and belief systems (such as reading,

arithmetic, navigating by maps, reasoning about other people's thoughts) are later built.

Spelke and her colleagues argue that strong evidence indicates the existence of at least three core-knowledge systems in infancy (see Table 4.1): (1) object representation, (2) knowledge of people and their actions, and (3) an ability to represent numbers, or quantities. David Geary (2005, 2007) has made a similar proposal, arguing that infants are born with a small set of *skeletal competencies* specialized to process information relating to the physical world (*folk physics*), the biological world (*folk biology*), and people (*folk psychology*; recall our discussion of Geary's theory in Chapter 2). These skeletal abilities become fleshed out with time and experience, allowing children to deal effectively with a wide range of objects, events, and relationships as they develop. Infants thus enter the world prepared to learn and understand some things better than others, but such biases are modified, in a species-typical way, as a result of experience.

Core-knowledge systems are inferred not only by evidence from experiments with infants but also from research with nonhuman animals and

TABLE 4.1 **According to the core-knowledge systems perspective, human infants are endowed with at least three core-knowledge systems to represent and make inferences about relevant aspects of their surrounding environment.**

Core-knowledge system 1: Inanimate objects and their mechanical interactions

1. *Cohesion* (objects have boundaries and their components are connected to each other)
2. *Continuity* (objects move along unobstructed paths and cannot be in the same place)
3. *Contact* (one object must contact another to make it move)
4. *Number limitation* (infants cannot represent more than about three objects at a time)

Core-knowledge system 2: Persons and their actions

1. *Goal directness* (intentional human actions are directed to goals)
2. *Efficiency* (goals are achieved through the use of effective means)
3. *Contingency* (means are not applied rigidly but adjusted to the conditions found)
4. *Reciprocity* (such as turn taking in conversation)
5. *Gaze direction* (the direction of a gaze is used to interpret social and nonsocial actions)

Core-knowledge system 3: Numbers representation

1. *Abstractness* (number representations are abstract: they apply to different entities or things, from different sensory modalities, for example, a set of objects or set of sounds)
2. *Comparability and combinability* (number representations are comparable and can be combined by addition and subtraction operations)

Source: Adapted from information in Spelke, E. S., & Kinzler, K. D. (2007). Core knowledge. *Developmental Science, 10,* 89–96.

with people from traditional cultures. For example, in some cases, evidence suggests that humans share some core abilities, such as aspects of object representation (see Dore & Dumas, 1987), basic arithmetic abilities (see discussion later in this chapter), and understanding of social partners (see Chapters 6 and 10), with other animals. However, some abilities, such as shared attention (for example, mother and infant sharing information and attention about a third object) may be unique to *Homo sapiens* (Tomasello, 2000; see Chapter 6). Evidence that humans share early developing abilities with other species, especially taxa closely related to humans, is central to a core-knowledge perspective; if we observe at least hints of these core competencies in our primate relatives, it suggests we may have also shared them with our last common ancestor and that these abilities have a long phylogenetic history. In other words, these comparative findings lend weight to the argument that humans are born prepared to process information within these core-knowledge systems as a result of millions of years of natural selection.

In this chapter, we examine some research motivated by the core-knowledge approach with respect to object representation and understanding of numbers. Research looking at infants' and children's folk psychology is explored in Chapters 6 and 10.

Object Representation

A basic question in infant spatial cognition concerns what they know about the nature of objects, for example, the extent to which they understand that physical objects follow the basic Newtonian laws of physics—must everything that goes up eventually come down? Infants have to recognize at least three features related to objects: (1) *object constancy*, (2) *object cohesion and continuity*, and (3) *object permanence*. Object constancy refers to the fact that an object does not change size or shape depending on how one views it. It may *look* different from a different angle, but it's still the same size and shape. Object cohesion and continuity refers to the fact that individual objects are seen as cohesive wholes with distinct boundaries. Object permanence refers to the fact that objects are permanent in time and space, whether we are perceiving them or not; that is, objects continue to exist even if they are out of our sight. In the following sections, we discuss the development of each of these aspects of object representation.

Object Constancy

Perhaps the most basic form of spatial cognition concerns infants' understanding of the constancy of physical objects in time and space. **Object constancy** refers to the knowledge that an object remains the same despite changes in how it is viewed. Consider a table, for instance. When we see the table at a certain distance, it makes a specific impression on the retinas of our eyes. As we move away from the table, that image on the back of our eyes gets smaller, but we continue to perceive the table as maintaining a constant size and shape. We don't act as if the table is changing before our eyes; although the literal sensation

changes, we maintain a perceptual constancy in our minds.

This would seem to be a very basic form of spatial cognition, and in fact, it is possessed to varying degrees even by newborns. Imagine, for example, that newborns are habituated to an object of a particular size. During test trials, the infant is then shown one of two objects: the same object presented at a different distance so as to project a different-sized retinal image or a new object of a different size but presented at a distance so that the retinal image it projects is the same size as the retinal image projected by the original habituated object (see Figure 4.12). If infants perceive size constancy, meaning they understand that the object remains the same even

FIGURE 4.12 **Size constancy experiment.** After becoming used to looking at a small cube at different distances (habituation to changes in retinal image), infants are presented a second larger but more distant cube (same retinal image for both cubes). If infants pay more attention to the larger than to the smaller cube, researchers conclude that they are distinguishing the cubes on the basis of their actual, not their retinal, size. That is, infants are demonstrating size constancy.

Source: Adapted from Slater, A. M., Mattock, A., Brown, E., & Bremner, G. J. (1991). Form perception at birth: Cohen and Younger (1984) revisited. *Journal of Experimental Child Psychology, 51*, 395–406.

though the retinal image changes across space and orientation, then they should continue to habituate to the same object at a different distance, even though the actual retinal image is different. If they do *not* possess size constancy, however, they should dishabituate to the same object at a different distance and continue to (erroneously) habituate to the new object that produces the same retinal image. In one such study (Slater, Mattock, & Brown, 1990), newborns showed the former pattern, displaying a degree of size and shape constancy that, although not quite adultlike, indicates that human infants are well-prepared at birth for making sense of physical objects.

Despite this precocious ability, older children sometimes reveal what appears to be a surprising ignorance of size and shape constancy. For example, I (DB) recall sitting with 4-year-old Brendan, looking at planes flying overhead. "How do they get so small?" he asked. "Huh?" was probably my response, and he went on to wonder how big planes like he sees at the airport can get so tiny when they go up in the air. He seemed not to have realized that the plane stays the same size despite the vastly changing retinal image it projects as it soars away. Brendan is not unique in his confusion, for we have heard other people describe their children's mystification of the "amazing shrinking abilities" of airplanes. ("When do we get small?" asked one preschool child of her mother on her first airplane trip. This child figured out that if the plane gets smaller, then so, too, must the people inside it.) What we seem to have here is a discrepancy between the *implicit* knowledge of the infant, assessed by looking-time or operant-conditioning procedures, and the *explicit*, verbalizable knowledge of the older child. Granted, in most of children's everyday experiences, they behave as if objects maintain their size and shape despite changes

in retinal image. Yet for extraordinary events—extraordinary in that they were unlikely to be experienced by our ancestors hundreds of thousands or even millions of years ago, such as large, rapidly moving, flying objects—the appearance of a change in size seemingly overpowers children's intuitive knowledge of object constancy, reflecting a disconnect between what they know implicitly (without conscious awareness) and what they know explicitly (with conscious awareness).

Object Cohesion and Continuity

Another form of basic spatial cognition in infancy concerns the Gestalt concept of continuation. As mentioned earlier, object cohesion and continuity refers to the fact that individual objects are seen as cohesive wholes with distinctive boundaries. For example, Figure 4.13 shows a solid rectangle with

FIGURE 4.13 Example of the Gestalt concept of continuation. An important acquisition in visual perception is identifying objects that appear connected, or together, visually as independent objects. A widely used stimuli has been this rectangle with two broken rods. Typically, adults infer that the rectangle is overlapped over a solid bar behind it. Four-month-old infants (and even 2-month-old infants, in some cases) infer the same, but only if both rods exhibit a continuous same-speed movement.

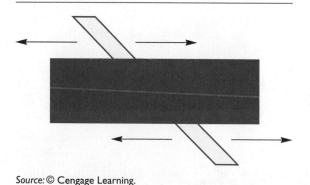

Source: © Cengage Learning.

bars extending from its top and bottom. Adults infer that the rectangle is occluding a solid bar. Although no solid bar is actually seen, we "fill in the gaps" or form an expectation of what is behind the box. Will infants make the same inference? How can one tell? One way is by repeatedly showing infants the stimulus until their attention to it decreases (habituation) and then showing them a picture of a solid bar in the same orientation as the partial bars in the original stimulus. If the infants increase their attention to the complete rod, they would be treating it as if it were novel, indicating that they had perceived the original rod as a disjointed object. If, however, when shown the solid bar they show little interest in it (that is, they continue to habituate), they would be treating it like an "old" stimulus, one they've gotten tired of looking at. But it is not literally the "same old thing." It is a different physical stimulus. If they treat it like an old stimulus, it would be because they have inferred that the rectangle in the original stimulus was occluding a solid bar.

When doing experiments like this, how do babies respond? Infants at 4 months of age treat the solid bar as if it were an old stimulus (that is, they continue to habituate), but only for moving stimuli (as shown by the arrows in Figure 4.13) or displays in which the rod parts underwent apparent motion (sometimes referred to as *phi* motion; Valenza & Bulf, 2011), not for stationary stimuli (S. P. Johnson & Aslin, 1996; Kellman & Spelke, 1983). Elizabeth Spelke (1985) speculated that this is an indication that infants are born with the notion of the persistence, coherence, and unity of objects. They "know," at some level, that objects are continuous in space. However, subsequent research indicated that 2-month-old (S. P. Johnson & Aslin, 1995) and 4-month-old (Eizenman & Bertenthal, 1998) infants will show evidence of inferring object unity in some, but not in other, situations

and that newborns *increase* their attention to the solid bar (Slater et al., 1990), suggesting that babies are likely *not* born with this knowledge.

Spelke and her colleagues have conducted other studies consistent with the interpretation that infants as young as 2.5 months of age have a knowledge of the solidity and continuity of objects (the fact that a moving object continues on its path) (see Spelke & Kinzler, 2007). More recently, Renée Baillargeon and her colleagues have investigated young infants' understanding of support (an object must be supported or it falls) (Baillargeon, Kotovsky, & Needham, 1995), collisions (an object that is hit by another object moves) (Baillargeon et al., 1995), and containment (a larger object cannot fit into a smaller object) (Aguiar & Baillargeon, 1998).

We discussed infants' understanding that objects must travel through space to get from Point A to Point B earlier in this chapter when describing the violation-of-expectation method. As you may recall, infants as young as 2.5 months of age looked longer at an event in which an object somehow moved behind one barrier and appeared seconds later from behind another without traversing the area in between (Aguiar & Baillargeon, 1999). The concept of collision seems to develop about the same time. For example, 2.5-month-old infants increased their looking time when a toy bug on wheels remained stationary after being hit by a cylinder rolling down a ramp or, conversely, when the bug moved in the absence of contact (Kotovsky & Baillargeon, 2000; S. Wang, Kaufman, & Baillargeon, 2003). Based on looking time, infants behave as if they understand that objects are solid and move only when contacted by some outside force.

Another interesting expectation of infants is that objects require support—that an object cannot remain suspended in midair or it will

FIGURE 4.14 **Example of possible and impossible events for object support.** Although 3-month-old infants were not surprised by the impossible event, by 4.5 months of age infants begin to understand that the *amount* of contact between the box and the platform is important.

Possible Event

Impossible Event

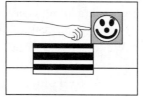 

Source: Baillargeon, R. (1994). How do infants learn about the physical world? *Current Directions in Psychological Science, 3,* 133–140. Reprinted with permission.

fall—and this, too, develops gradually over infancy. Baillargeon and her colleagues (1995) showed infants possible and impossible events reflecting the idea of support (see Figure 4.14). A gloved hand would push a box that sat atop a platform from left to right. In the possible event, the box stopped while firmly situated on the platform. In the impossible event, the box was pushed until only 15% of it rested on the platform. How did babies react to the impossible event? If they understand that objects need to be supported lest they fall, they should show surprise and increase looking time when observing the impossible event. The youngest infants (3-month-olds) weren't surprised. As long as the box maintained some contact with the platform, they acted as if they expected it to

remain on the platform and not fall. Beginning about 4.5 months of age, the amount of contact between the box and the platform became important, and by 6.5 months, infants expected that the box would fall unless a significant portion of it is in contact with the platform.

Other studies indicate that infants' understanding of object cohesion and continuity continues to develop over the first year. For example, Figure 4.15 presents three ways in which Baillargeon and her colleagues have tested infants' understanding of the role of height in object continuity. The first is in an occlusion experiment. A tall object is placed behind and, thus, is occluded by a shorter object, as shown in the top row of Figure 4.15. This is impossible, of course, and 4.5-month-old infants act surprised when this happens (Baillargeon & DeVos, 1991). Now consider nearly the same situation, but instead of the taller object being placed *behind* the shorter object, it is placed *within* it, a containment event, as shown in the second row of Figure 4.15. Now infants do not show surprise until about 7.5 months (Hespos & Baillargeon, 2001), and it is not until 12 months that they show surprise when a shorter object covers a taller object (S. Wang, Baillargeon, & Paterson, 2005), as seen in the bottom row of Figure 4.15. This pattern reflects what Piaget referred to as *horizontal décalage* (see Chapter 5), in which an ability—in this case understanding the physical relationship between short and tall objects—develops at different rates in different contexts.

As we have seen, infants' knowledge of objects seems to be dominated by an expectation that inanimate objects behave in continuous (in the sense of being permanent and solid entities) and cohesive (as a bounded whole) ways, that contact is necessary for an inanimate object to move, and that objects must be supported or they will fall. Some of these expectations seem to develop

FIGURE 4.15 **Three ways of assessing infants' understanding of the role of height in object continuity.** Depending on how infants are tested (that is, by an occlusion event, a containment event, or a covering event), they display an understanding of the role of height in object continuity at different ages.

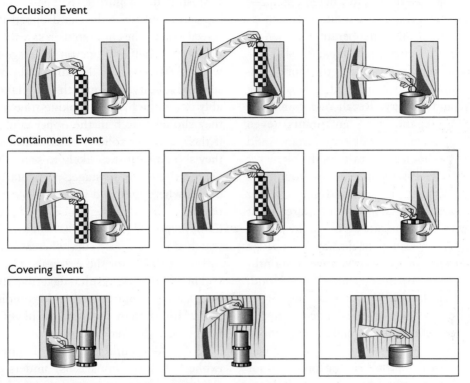

Occlusion Event

Containment Event

Covering Event

Source: Baillargeon, R. (2008). Innate ideas revisited: For a principle of persistence in infants' physical reasoning. *Perspectives on Psychological Science, 3,* 2–13.

earlier than others, and the range of contexts in which infants will show this knowledge increases with age and experience. Baillargeon (2008) proposed that infants possess an innate idea she called the principle of persistence, defined as "objects not only exist continuously and remain cohesive, they also retain their individual properties. According to this principle, no object can undergo a spontaneous or uncaused change in the course of an event" (p. 3). The principles of continuity and cohesion would be derivations of this more general principle. This does not mean that experience is unnecessary, however.

For Baillargeon and her colleagues, when infants watch a physical event for the first time, their representation of it is initially impoverished, so that they may be attentive to only some violations of persistence. For example, they attend to the fact that an object cannot disappear at one location and appear at another without traversing the area in between but do not yet demonstrate expectations about the height or color of the objects. With increasing experience, their representations become enriched, and infants will demonstrate sensitivity to a broader range of violations of persistence (for example, they will notice when the color or height of an object has unexpectedly changed). However, infants can develop a sensitivity to these secondary characteristics of objects—their color, height, shape— earlier under certain task conditions, such as when their attention is deliberately drawn to these features (T. Wilcox & Chapa, 2004).

There is an interesting aside to the work demonstrating infants' often-substantial knowledge of support and solidity. Recall our comments about the discrepancy between infants' (even newborns') appreciation of object constancy and that of the preschooler ("How does the plane get so small?"). This discrepancy is also found for an understanding of support and solidity. For example, in search tasks, in which children must find an object hidden in one of several locations, 2-year-olds generally fail to display knowledge of these concepts, unlike their younger 6-month-old counterparts (Berthier et al., 2000; Hood, Carey, & Prasada, 2000). For example, Bruce Hood and his colleagues (2000) showed groups of 2- and 2.5-year-old children a ball being dropped onto a stage behind a screen. The screen was removed to reveal the ball resting on the floor of the stage (Experiment 1). After the children witnessed this event three times, the experimenter placed a cup on the floor of the stage, a shelf over the cup, and then a second cup on that shelf. This is illustrated in Figure 4.16. The screen was then replaced, and the ball was dropped behind the screen again. The children then saw the two cups, one on the shelf and one on the stage floor, and were asked to retrieve the ball. If they possessed a sense of solidity, as 6-month-old infants presumably do on the basis of looking-time procedures, they should search in the upper cup. However, if their sense of solidity is not fully developed, they should be just as likely to search in the cup on the floor of the stage, particularly because that is where they had successfully retrieved the ball three times before. Hood and his colleagues (2000) reported that only 40% of the 2-year-olds searched in the upper cup, whereas this percentage rose to 93% for the 2.5-year-olds.

This perplexing result, suggestive that infants have a more sophisticated understanding of spatial relations than 2-year-olds, likely is caused by the very different nature of the tasks (Keen, 2003). Older children must demonstrate an explicit (that is, conscious) understanding of solidity and support in the search tasks, whereas

FIGURE 4.16 **The apparatus used in a study by Hood et al. with 2- and 2.5-year-old children.** Children watched as a ball was dropped behind the screen and saw that it rested on the floor. A shelf and two cups were then added to the stage, and the ball was dropped again behind the screen. Children were then asked to retrieve the ball.

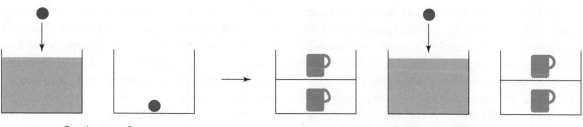

Familiarize x 3   Introduce Shelf + Cups, Then Search

Source: Hood, B., Carey, S., & Prasada, S. (2000). Predicting the outcomes of physical events: Two-year-olds fail to reveal knowledge of solidity and support. *Child Development, 71,* 1540–1554. Adapted with permission of the Society for Research in Child Development.

the looking-time tasks used with infants require only implicit (that is, out-of-conscious awareness) knowledge. As such, postulating that infants who look longer at an impossible than at a possible event have the same type of knowledge as older children have for the phenomenon under question (here, support) is likely unwarranted. What young infants appear to possess, or to develop early, is implicit knowledge, which likely cannot be used as flexibly as explicit knowledge can.

Object Permanence

If a tree falls in the middle of the forest and no one is there to hear it, is there any noise? Young infants (presuming, of course, that they could communicate their response to us) would answer this perennial philosophical question very easily. Their answer would be no, for there can be no noise unless someone is there to perceive it. But the young infant would go on to say that there is also no tree and no forest. Nothing exists unless it is directly perceived or, more precisely, unless it is personally perceived by them.

This hypothetical philosophical discussion illustrates infants' concept of **object permanence** or, more appropriately, the lack of object permanence. For infants who lack object permanence, out of sight is literally out of mind. Object permanence is obviously a cognitive skill necessary for normal intellectual functioning in all human cultures. The concept of object permanence was introduced by Jean Piaget (1954), and in this section we first describe Piaget's account of object permanence. We then examine newer research, some of which challenges the interpretation, if not the findings, of Piaget.

Piaget's account of object permanence. Piaget believed that between birth and 4 months, infants understand objects only as extensions of their own actions. Objects have no reality for babies independent of their perceptions or actions upon them. For example, a 2- or 3-month-old follows his mother with his eyes, but when she leaves his visual field, he continues to gaze at the point where he lost sight of her, not anticipating her reappearance at another location. Piaget saw the first semblance of object permanence at about 4 months. At this age, infants now attempt to retrieve an object that "disappears," but only if the object is still partially visible. For example, babies at this stage fetch a toy that has been partially covered by a cloth, apparently realizing that the entire toy exists under the cloth even though they can see only a portion of it. They do not search, however, for a toy that is completely hidden, even if the hiding occurred right before their eyes. An exception to this behavior seems to be that late in this substage, infants search for a completely hidden object if they are moving in that direction when the object is hidden. So, for example, a 6-month-old infant playing with a favorite toy does not attempt to retrieve that toy when her father places it under a blanket while she is watching. She does retrieve it, however, if she is reaching for the toy in front of her as Dad places the blanket over it. Beginning at about 8 months, infants can retrieve a completely hidden object. However, object permanence is not yet complete, for if an object is hidden in one location and then later moved to a second, all while the child is watching, the infant searches at the first location and often acts quite surprised not to find the desired object. This is the **A-not-B object permanence task,** which we discussed briefly in Chapter 2.

Let us provide a real-life example of the A-not-B object permanence task. At approximately 10 months, my (DB) daughter Heidi was seated in her high chair, having just completed lunch. She was banging her spoon on the tray of the chair when it fell to the floor to her right. She leaned to the right, saw the spoon on the floor, and vocalized to me; I retrieved it for her. She began playing with the spoon again, and it fell to the right a second time. She again leaned to the right, saw the spoon on the floor, and vocalized until I returned it to her. Again, she played with the spoon, and again, it fell to the floor, but this time to her left. After hearing the clang of the spoon hitting the floor, Heidi leaned to the right to search for the spoon, and she continued her search for several seconds before looking at me with a puzzled expression. Heidi had been watching the spoon at the time it fell. Thus, when it fell the third time, she had both visual and auditory cues to tell her where it must be. But she searched where she had found the vanished object before. She trusted her past experience with the fallen spoon more than her perceptions. You see, up until this last event, Heidi's behavior of searching to the right was always reinforced by the retrieval of her spoon. This pattern of reinforcement seemed to override her perceptual reasoning, leading her to persist in the reinforced behavior of searching to the right.

Beginning around 12 months, infants can solve problems like the one just described. What they cannot yet do, however, is solve what Piaget called *invisible displacements*. In invisible displacements, an object is hidden in one container and then hidden under another container out of the vision of the observer. An example from Piaget (1954) will help clarify this task:

> Jacqueline is sitting on a green rug playing with a potato which interests her very much (it is a new object for her). She says "po-terre" [pomme de terre] and amuses herself by putting it into an empty box and taking it out again. . . . I then take the potato and put it in the box while Jacqueline watches. Then I place the box under the rug and turn it upside down, thus leaving the object hidden by the rug without letting the child see my maneuver, and I bring out the empty box. I say to Jacqueline, who has not stopped looking at the rug and who has realized that I was doing something under it: "Give papa the potato." She searches for the object in the box, looks at me, again looks at the box minutely, looks at the rug, etc., but it does not occur to her to raise the rug in order to find the potato underneath. During the five subsequent attempts the reaction is uniformly negative. . . . Each time Jacqueline looks in the box, then looks at everything around her including the rug, but does not search under it. (p. 68)

According to Piaget, to solve invisible displacement problems, that is, to track their "chain of custody," children must be able to mentally represent objects, something that is not found, according to Piaget, until about 18 months.

Piaget's basic observations of the development of object permanence have been replicated in both large- and small-scales studies, using variants of the procedures he described (Kopp, Sigman, & Parmelee, 1974; Uzgiris & Hunt, 1975). However, researchers using some of the new techniques developed to study infant cognition believe that babies possess knowledge of the permanency of objects at earlier ages than Piaget proposed.

A new look at object permanence. Evidence of object permanence in young infants is probably best exemplified by Baillargeon's work (Baillargeon, 1987; Baillargeon & DeVos, 1991) using the violation-of-expectation method, much as was done in her work on understanding support. In Baillargeon's (1987) initial experiment, infants 3.5 and 4.5 months of age were habituated to a moving screen (see Figure 4.17). The screen was rotated 180 degrees, starting from being flat in a box with its leading edge facing

FIGURE 4.17 **The habituation and test (dishabituation) events shown to infants in the experimental and control conditions in the object permanence experiment by Baillargeon.**

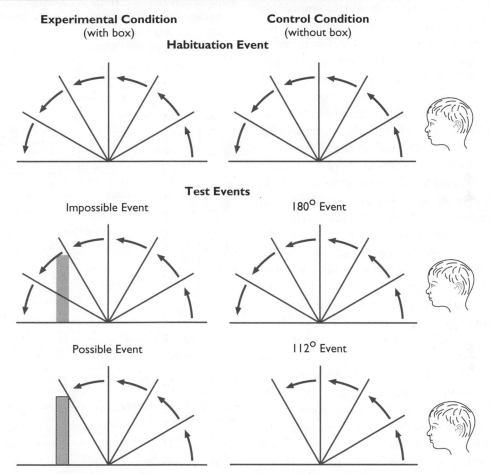

Source: Baillargeon, R. (1987). Object permanence in 3½- and 4½-month-old infants. *Developmental Psychology, 23,* 655–664. Copyright © 1987 American Psychological Association. Reprinted with permission.

the infant and rising continuously through an arc until it rested in the box with its leading edge farthest away from the infant. Once habituated to this event, infants in the experimental group were shown a colorful wooden block with a clown face painted on it, placed to the rear of the flat screen. In the impossible-event condition, the screen was rotated upward (exactly as in the habituation trials), which in the process obscured the wooden block from the infant's sight. When the screen reached 90 degrees, the wooden block was removed, out of the view of the infant. The screen then continued its downward rotation until it lay flat. After this, the screen was rotated upward again, and the wooden block was replaced, again unbeknownst to the infant, so that it reappeared once more when the screen was being rotated toward the infant. From the infant's perspective, such a series of events (the continuous movement of the screen, despite the presence of an obstacle) should be impossible and violate the infant's expectation of what should happen. If the wooden object were real in space and time, the screen should have stopped when it reached it. This, in fact, is what infants did see on some trials (the possible event), with the screen stopping at the point where it should have, given that there was an object on the other side. If the infants believed that the wooden block continued to exist, they should have shown surprise or increased looking time at the impossible event relative to the possible event. Infants in the control condition saw the same sequence of screen movements but were never shown the wooden block. Thus, these infants had no reason to express surprise. Infants in all conditions received four test trials.

The results of this experiment for the 4.5-month-old infants are graphed in Figure 4.18. As you can see, the infants in the experimental condition looked significantly longer at the impossible event than at the possible event. For the experimental infants, there was apparently nothing surprising about the possible event, but they knew that something was amiss when the screen failed to stop. No differences in looking time were found for the infants in the control condition. Similar findings were reported for 3.5-month-old infants (see Experiments 2 and 3 in Baillargeon, 1987; Baillargeon & DeVos, 1991). Other studies using this (Baillargeon & DeVos, 1991) and similar (Baillargeon, 2004) methods have produced similar results.

The most straightforward interpretation of these results is that the infants believed the block continued to exist even though it was out of their sight and were surprised when the screen failed to stop. Their performance in the impossible-event condition reflects not only a knowledge

FIGURE 4.18 **Looking times of infants in the experimental and control conditions during habituation and test trials in Baillargeon's experiment.** Note the increased looking time for the infants in the experimental condition during the test trials for the impossible event.

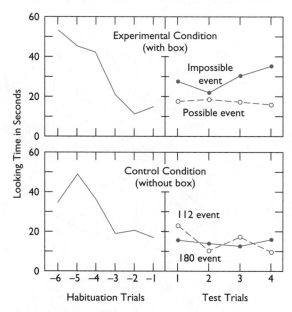

Source: Baillargeon, R. (1987). Object permanence in 3½- and 4½-month-old infants. *Developmental Psychology, 23,* 655–664. Copyright © 1987 American Psychological Association. Reprinted with permission.

of the permanence of objects but also a knowledge that one solid object cannot pass through another (see the earlier discussion of solidity). This does not necessarily mean that Piaget was wrong but that infants' understanding of the permanence of objects varies with the type of task used to assess it.

Other research using looking-time measures has shown that 5-month-olds code the spatial location of hidden objects. In a study by Nora Newcombe and her colleagues (1999), for instance, babies watched as an object was buried in a sandbox. After a 10-second delay, the object was dug out. This was repeated four times. On the fifth occasion, instead of digging up the object at the location where it had been hidden, the experimenter dug out the object from a different location (as near as 6 inches from where the first had been hidden). Babies looked significantly longer at these "trick" trials than at the previous trials, suggesting that they had coded the specific location of the objects. During a final experiment in this same study, infants were not surprised (that is, did not look longer) when a *different object* was retrieved from the sand. This finding suggests that spatiotemporal characteristics may play a central role in defining objects to young infants, with shape and color being unimportant.

One very interesting aspect of the findings of this study by Newcombe and her colleagues is that toddlers usually fail an analogous hiding task. In this task, toddlers watch as an object is hidden in a sandbox, then move to the opposite end of the box and are asked to retrieve the object. Not until 21 months of age can children solve this problem reliably (Newcombe et al., 1998), calling into question what, exactly, are the skills involved in solving these simple spatial tasks (Newcombe, 2002). Maybe the act of moving around the sandbox makes the task too demanding of children's limited mental resources or disrupts their memory, accounting for the discrepancy. It is also possible that the difference between the implicit and explicit natures of the two tasks is responsible for the different findings. Children may possess an understanding of spatial relations at first only implicitly (Bremner & Mareschal, 2004; Newcombe, 2002), with explicit understanding, as reflected by an overt search task, being displayed only later in development. Recall that a similar interpretation was made for differences between infants' and 2-year-olds' understanding of support (Hood et al., 2000).

Richard Aslin might agree, stating that infants' performance in the habituation/dishabituation task is further evidence of the *Goldilocks effect*, as we described earlier. When the same object appears in an unexpected spot, this amount of complexity is "just right," leading infants to look longer at this type of event. In other words, it appears to infants there may be something to learn about the pattern of this particular object's disappearance and reappearance in this instance. However, when a completely different object appears in a completely different location, infants may disengage because this is now too complex. That is, now two dimensions have changed—the object and the location. It's likely that the violation-of-expectation method assesses perceptual knowledge, whereas the reaching task assesses self-aware thought, the ability to combine an old habit (finding the object) with a new cognitive update (looking under something). This is not to say that one method is better than the other but that the meaning of "infants possess object permanence" may differ depending on how object permanence is measured.

Other research has questioned Piaget's results for the A-not-B task. As you may recall from Chapter 2, infants as young as 7.5 months of age will sometimes reach correctly on the B trials if the delay between hiding the object and searching for it is very brief (Diamond, 1985). As the delay increases, infants are more likely to look where the toy was previously hidden (that is, at the A location). This has caused some people to propose that memory or inhibition is involved in solving this task. It is not so much that infants fail to understand that objects have permanence in time and space but that they forget the object's location or do not have the neurological maturation to inhibit a previously reinforced behavior (reaching to the correct A location) (Diamond, 1991).

Even when using Piaget's reaching paradigm, differences in infants' tendencies to successfully retrieve a hidden object are affected by some simple task variables, such as the number of times infants retrieve the object at the A location before it is switched to the B location in the A-not-B task (Marcovitch, Zelazo, & Schmuckler, 2002) or the familiarity of the objects being hidden. For example, in one study, 7.5-month-old infants were tested in the classic Piagetian object permanence tasks (retrieve an object hidden under a cloth) for either familiarized clay objects they had seen and reached for many times or novel objects (Shinskey & Munakata, 2005). Infants were tested for their preference when the items were *uncovered* and their understanding of object permanence when the items were covered. The results are shown in Figure 4.19. When the familiar and novel objects were visible, the infants almost always reached for the novel items, showing a classic novelty bias. However, when the objects were hidden, they were more likely to reach for the familiar item. Infants had a stronger mental representation for the familiar objects and, as a result, showed greater sensitivity for the continued existence of the familiar objects when hidden. In other words, they displayed evidence of object permanence for the familiar objects but not for the novel objects, suggesting that infants' understanding of the permanence of objects, counter to Piaget, gradually develops as infants acquire stronger mental representations of objects through experience.

Early Number Concepts

A second proposed core-knowledge system is an understanding of quantities and numbers. Researchers have proposed that human infants share with other animals a nonsymbolic system

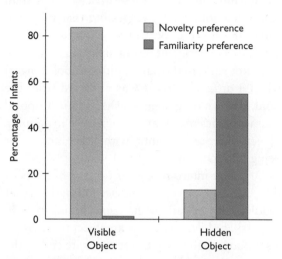

FIGURE 4.19 **Infants at 7.5 months of age reach more for novel versus familiar objects when the objects are in plain sight.** When objects are covered as infants watch, however, they are more apt to reach for the familiar object. This indicates that infants' familiarity with objects affects their understanding for the permanence of the objects.

Source: Shinskey, J. L., & Munakata, Y. (2005). Familiarity breeds searching: Infants reverse their novelty preferences when reaching for hidden objects. *Psychological Science, 16*, 596–600.

for thinking about quantities in an imprecise and intuitive way, referred to as the *approximate number system (ANS)* (Feigenson, Libertus, & Halberda, 2013). This system is universal and continues to operate throughout the life span, but it is supplemented by explicit culturally invented systems for dealing with exact numbers (biologically secondary abilities), to which it is linked. We discuss the development of ANS in children and its connection with more advanced forms of mathematical cognition in Chapter 11. Here, we discuss two aspects of ANS in infancy: (1) numerosity and (2) ordinality (and see Geary, 1995, 2005). **Numerosity** refers to the ability to determine quickly the number of items in a set without counting, whereas **ordinality** refers to a basic understanding of *more than* and *less than*—for instance, that the number of items in one array is more (or less) than the number of items in another array. To do this, one does not necessarily have to understand the concept of *two* or *three*. Rather, infants display numerosity and ordinality by consistently being able to differentiate between two arrays with different numbers of items in them.

Numerosity

Very young infants can detect differences in numerosity—that is, they can tell the difference between two arrays that differ in the number of objects they contain (van Loosbroek & Smitsman, 1990). In research with slightly older infants, 10- and 12-month-olds watched as different numbers of graham crackers were placed inside two boxes (Feigenson, Carey, & Hauser, 2002). The boxes were then separated, and infants could crawl to retrieve the crackers from whichever box they pleased. Infants consistently crawled to the box that contained the larger number of crackers when the boxes contained one versus two and two versus three crackers, but they responded indiscriminately when the larger quantity was four or greater (for example, three versus four, two versus four, and three versus six).

This pattern of results with 10- to 12-month-old infants is similar to one reported for a group of rhesus monkeys (Hauser, Carey, & Hauser, 2000). In that study, researchers placed pieces of apples, one at a time, into one of two containers as the monkeys watched. The researchers then stepped back and watched to see which container the monkeys, living wild on an uninhabited island but accustomed to the human researchers, would approach first. Much like

the human babies, the monkeys approached the box with the larger number of apple pieces in it for contrasts of zero versus one, one versus two, two versus three, and three versus four (the latter contrast being one the babies failed). When the number of apple pieces in a box exceeded four, the animals responded randomly. These findings suggest that both human infants within their first year of life and adult rhesus monkeys develop a natural understanding of *more than* and *less than*, at least for small quantities, making this ability evolutionarily old and not unique to humans.

No one claims that infants really "know" arithmetic the way that a first-grade child knows how to add and subtract small quantities. But some provocative evidence indicates that even 5-month-old babies' concept of numerosity allows them to keep track of small changes in quantities, a behavior that looks like an understanding of how to add and subtract.

This is best illustrated in the study by Karen Wynn (1992). Wynn used the violation-of-expectation method to determine if 5-month-old infants could "add" and "subtract" small quantities. Wynn (1992) sat 5-month-old infants in front of a display. Infants were then shown a sequence of events that involved the addition or subtraction of elements. Two of these sequences are shown in Figure 4.20. One sequence (the possible outcome) led to the conclusion that 1 + 1 = 2; the other sequence (the impossible outcome) led to the conclusion that 1 + 1 = 1. Infants sat in front of a stage and watched as one object was placed on it (Step 1 in Figure 4.20). A screen was then raised, hiding the object (Step 2 in Figure 4.20). The infant then watched as a second object was placed behind the screen (Steps 3 and 4 in Figure 4.20). The screen was then lowered, revealing either two objects (the possible outcome) or one object (the impossible outcome). If infants have some primitive concept of addition, they should be surprised and, thus, spend more time looking at the impossible outcome. This was exactly what occurred, both for the addition problem shown in Figure 4.20 and for a simple subtraction problem (2 – 1 = 1).

How can these results best be interpreted? On the surface, at least, infants seem not to be making only a perceptual discrimination between two arrays (that is, telling the difference between an array with one item in it and another with two). Rather, when they watch as one item is added to another behind a screen, they expect to see two items when the screen is dropped. This seems to require some rudimentary ideas about addition. They must infer that the second object was added to the first, without actually seeing that this was done (recall that the screen occluded their vision).

Others have replicated these results (Simon, Hespos, & Rochat, 1995), and research using methods much like those used with human babies has shown that 3- and 4-day-old chickens show similar quantitative abilities (Rugani et al., 2009), suggesting that such basic computation is not unique to humans. However, the interpretation of these findings is not without debate (Clearfield & Westfahl, 2006; D. S. Moore & Cocas, 2006). For example, some researchers suggest that babies are not responding to *number* but to the total amount of *substance* present (Mix, Huttenlocher, & Levine, 2002). In other words, infants are not doing primitive (and unconscious) addition and subtraction. They are responding to changes in the amount of "stuff" that is present in the various arrays. For example, rather than reflecting infants' abstract understanding of integers (that is, there should be "1" or "2" objects behind the screen), performance on such tasks may be based on

FIGURE 4.20 **Sequence of events for the 1 + 1 = 2 (possible) outcome and the 1 + 1 = 1 (impossible) outcome from the experiment by Wynn (1992).**

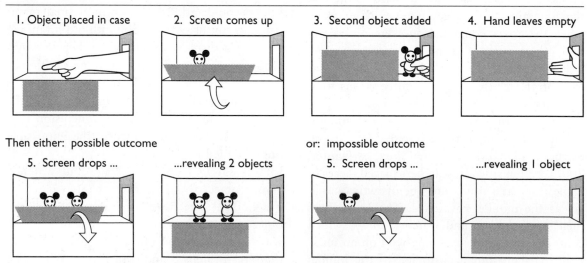

Source: Wynn, K. (1992). Addition and subtraction by human infants. *Nature, 358*, 749–750. Copyright © 1992 Macmillan Magazines Ltd. Reprinted with permission from *Nature*.

representations of the actual objects (for example, ♥ versus ♥ ♥), suggesting that decisions are based more on perceptual than on conceptual relations). Susan Carey (2009; see also Mandler, 2000; Mou & vanMarle, 2014) refers to this system of representation as parallel individuation and the explicit symbols as individual files. She points out that infants' performance on this task and others that seem to tap into an infant's knowledge of number is not affected by the ratio of the comparisons in the way that ordinality tasks are, as we describe shortly. Instead, performance on the task seems constrained by how many individual files an infant can represent in working memory. Much like the graham cracker study described earlier, infants seem limited to represent only three, maybe four, individual items in a set at a time.

Ordinality

Other research indicates that 6-month-old infants can tell the difference between quantities larger than four but that the *ratio* of the larger and smaller quantities must be large, indicating that reasoning about ordinality conforms to Weber's law, used to describe the perceptual discriminability of many sensory stimuli. For example, using preferential-looking methods, 6-month-olds can tell the differences between large arrays of dots on a computer screen when the larger quantity is twice as numerous as the smaller quantity, such as 8 versus 16 or 16 versus 32. However, 6-month-olds fail to discriminate between arrays with smaller ratios, such as 8 versus 12 or 16 versus 24 (Cordes & Brannon, 2009; Xu, Spelke, & Goddard, 2005). The critical ratio (often referred to as the Weber ratio) for discrimination gets progressively finer with age, most drastically during the first year. A variety of factors influence infants' abilities to discriminate different quantities of objects in arrays, including the density of the items in arrays (spaced out or packed together) and the size of the items (large items versus small items), making any definitive statements about what underlies these early abilities difficult. Many of these variables are controlled for in the studies referenced earlier by equating for these factors across habituation and test stimuli. As such, these results seem to represent more than infants' simple differences in visual perception. In addition, infants' quantity judgments are not limited to visual arrays. For example, 6-month-old infants can also distinguish between two sequences of 8 and 16 sounds (Lipton & Spelke, 2000) as well as between sequences of events (for example, a puppet jumping up and down four versus eight times) (J. N. Wood & Spelke, 2005).

This line of work is provocative and, regardless of interpretation, suggests substantially greater quantitative knowledge in young infants than was previously believed. However, it does not mean that infants and toddlers should be able to learn complicated mathematics given the proper instructions. The nature of their numerical competencies might not be fully known, but it seems relatively certain that it is not equivalent to the abilities found in children only a few years older.

Newborn Statisticians?

More recently, researchers have begun to ask to what extent infants can make inferences about the environment based on very limited experience. Six- to 12-month-old infants are sensitive to probabilistic relations when making inferences from samples to populations, and vice versa (Denison, Reed, & Xu, 2013). When 6- and 8-month-old infants were shown a box of ping-pong balls—four of which were red and one of which was white—and an experimenter closed her eyes and randomly drew out a handful of balls, infants' looking times suggested they found a sample of four red balls and one white ball more probable than a sample of one red ball and four white balls. That is, they looked longer at the improbable, or unexpected, event (one red ball and four white balls). Six-month-olds, but not 4.5-month-olds, extrapolated these probabilities from a larger population of ping-pong balls as well, expecting only one white ball and four red balls to be drawn from a population of, say, 100 balls in which 80 were red and 20 were white.

Arguments Against Core Knowledge

We think it's fair to say that research over the past 30 years or so using the "new" infant technologies has demonstrated that babies have far more cognitive abilities than we once thought. However, not everyone believes that systematic changes in looking time reflect complex underlying cognitive abilities. These arguments are based on insights from computer modeling, dynamic systems theory, and Bayesian networks. For example, Richard Bogartz and his colleagues (Bogartz & Shinskey, 1998; Bogartz et al., 1997; see also Spencer et al., 2009) have argued that it is not necessary to attribute innate knowledge of physical objects to account for the findings of studies that use infants' looking behavior as an indication of what they know. Bogartz and his colleagues (1997) "assume that young infants cannot reason, draw inferences, or have beliefs" (p. 411) and "that the infant does not enter the world with [knowledge of objects] nor does it acquire such knowledge of physical laws in the first 6 months of life" (p. 412).

How, then, can one explain the data if there are no innate conceptual constraints? Bogartz and his colleagues suggest that infants come into the world with a set of mechanisms for processing perceptual information and that infants acquire knowledge of objects through perceptual experience. The nature of perceptual processing produces looking patterns that Baillargeon, Spelke, and others interpret as innate knowledge. According to Bogartz and his colleagues (1997), however, infants' perceptual processing "consists of analysis of the immediate representations of events, the construction in associative memory of the transformations of these immediate representations, abstraction of their forms, and the comparison of immediate perceptual representations to the representations stored in memory" (p. 411). All this processing takes time. In habituation/dishabituation tasks, infants look at familiar stimuli because it takes time to store memory representations. Novel events (that is, impossible events in the studies described earlier) take even more time because initial encoding of the stimuli needs to be done. Infants show a preference for looking at the novel (impossible) event over the familiar (habituated and possible) event simply because more processing is required to make sense of the former than the latter. There is no need to postulate innate knowledge of physical laws, only laws about how infant perception and memory work.

Another currently popular approach is Bayesian statistical inference, a mathematical probability theory that accounts for learning as a process by which prior knowledge is compared to currently observed evidence. For example, recall the work of Richard Aslin and colleagues that we described earlier in this chapter on the Goldilocks effect. This research demonstrated how infants develop expectations about the world based on the patterns that emerge in their environment. As they experience matches and mismatches between these expectations and what they perceive, they maintain or modify their expectations accordingly.

Specifically, when infants encounter mismatches, or unexpected information, looking longer at it provides them the opportunity to learn from the event and update their future expectations with this knowledge. There are several examples of infants seeming to compute probabilities, some of which we've already described, to reason about events in simple and complex patterns, tones, phonemes, words, colored shapes, and human actions (for a review, see S. P. Johnson & Hannon, 2015). The critical point about Bayesian inference models, then, is that they provide a principled explanation for how new evidence is combined with prior beliefs during the learning process.

To make the concept more concrete, we elaborate on just one example of 12-month-olds' reasoning about objects moving out of a container with an occluded opening (Téglás et al., 2011). In this study, infants viewed movies of four objects, blue or red circles or squares, bounced randomly inside a circular container with an opening on the bottom (see Figure 4.21). After several seconds, an occluder covered the container from view for a period of 0 to 2 seconds before one object visibly exited through the bottom opening while the occluder was still in place. At this point, the occluder faded out. Researchers monitored infants' looking time to assess how surprised infants were to see the object exit. Across 12 kinds of movies, three factors were manipulated that could be used to predict which object should exit first: the number of each type of object (in a configuration of three blue circles and one red square, it is more probable that a blue circle will exit first); their physical arrangement (objects near the bottom should be more likely to exit first); and the duration of the occlusion (the objects' locations before occlusion are most predictive of which object will exit first when the duration of occlusion is short). To form correct expectations, infants must be able to integrate these

FIGURE 4.21 **An example of the stimuli used by Téglás et al. (2011) to demonstrate that 12-month-old infants are capable of combining experience related to physical arrangement, duration of occlusion, and the number of objects with more abstract principles of object motion to make probabilistic inferences.**

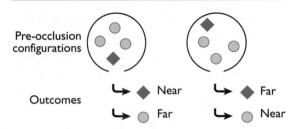

Source: Téglás, E., et al. (2011). Pure reasoning in 12-month-old infants as probabilistic inference. *Science, 332*(6033), 1054–1059.

three factors as well as some abstract knowledge about how objects move. In other words, they must hold prior beliefs that objects are unlikely to pass through walls and tend to move only short distances over brief periods of time and longer distances over longer durations. The results confirmed just that; 12-month-olds were capable of combining prior knowledge with current information to develop appropriate expectations. After a short occlusion, infants' looking times reflected that their expectations were based on only the physical distance of each object. However, when occlusion duration increased to 1 second, infants' looking times reflected that they considered both the number of objects of each type and their last-seen distance to the exit. Finally, when the occlusion was longer than 2 seconds, infants appeared to disregard the preocclusion distance of objects from the exit and based their expectations on the number of each object type. These findings suggest that infants are capable of combining experience related to physical arrangement, duration of occlusion, and the number of objects with more abstract principles of object motion to make probabilistic inferences (see also Denison & Xu, 2010).

There has been much debate about the nature of infant cognition. Some researchers propose that infants are born with "core knowledge" for important aspects of their world that develop rapidly with experience (for example, Spelke & Kinzler, 2007), and still others propose that infants' and toddlers' cognitive skills are constructed via more domain-general mechanisms (for example, Newcombe, 2010; Spencer et al., 2009). We concur that infants possess perceptual systems that are tuned to a richly structured and predictable world and interact with developing attention and learning mechanisms. Together, these systems aid infants in discovering and making computational inferences about their environment. As Nora Newcombe (2010) states, Piaget's fundamental ideas seem "now to have been absolutely right: that a biologically prepared mind interacts in biologically evolved ways with an expectable environment that nevertheless includes significant variation" (p. vi).

Section Review

Core knowledge refers to the idea that infants possess a small set of domain-specific systems of knowledge that have been shaped by natural selection and upon which new and flexible skills are built. There are at least three core-knowledge systems in infancy: object representation, knowledge of people and their actions, and an ability to represent numbers, or quantities.

Early Object and Number Representation

- From birth, infants seem to have a rudimentary understanding of *object constancy*, the knowledge that an object remains the same despite changes in how it is viewed.

- Infants' understanding of *object cohesion and continuity* (understanding that objects have boundaries) develops over the first year, as reflected by experiments using the violation-of-expectation method.

- Baillargeon proposed that infants possess at birth the *principle of persistence* (knowledge that objects remain cohesive and cannot undergo a spontaneous or uncaused change in the course of an event).

- *Object permanence* refers to the belief that objects exist independent of one's perceptions or actions. Piaget was the first to describe the development of object permanence and proposed that infants cannot retrieve a hidden object until about 8 months, cannot solve the *A-not-B task* until about 12 months, and cannot understand invisible displacements until about 18 months.

- By using variations of the violation-of-expectation method, researchers have demonstrated evidence of object permanence earlier than Piaget had proposed.

- Using variations of the *violation-of-expectation method*, researchers have also demonstrated evidence for simple quantitative abilities in infants. Among these are *numerosity* (the ability to determine quickly the number of items in a set without counting) and *ordinality* (a basic understanding of *more than* and *less than* relationships).

Newborns as Statisticians

- Infants seem capable of developing expectations about the probability that an event will occur based on their experiences.

Arguments Against Core Knowledge

- Some researchers argue that it is not necessary to postulate core knowledge or innate conceptual constraints; rather, infants are born with a set of mechanisms for processing perceptual information and acquire knowledge of objects through perceptual experience.

Ask Yourself . . .

13. What is meant by the core-knowledge approach to infant cognition? What are the main findings regarding infants' understanding of objects, people, and quantitative relations?

14. What is object permanence? Describe two ways in which it has been measured. How might our interpretation of infants' understanding of object permanence differ based on the findings of Piaget's task and Baillargeon's task?

15. What kind of statistics do infants seem able to do?

16. Are infants born as "blank slates"? What does modern research in infant perception and cognition contribute to this issue?

WHAT IS INFANT COGNITION MADE OF?

There is little debate that cognition and behavior change drastically over infancy. Brain growth is more rapid during the first 2 years than at any other time in postnatal life. Cognitive differences between the 10-month-old and the 2-year-old are dramatic, obvious to anyone who takes the time to look. Yet increasing evidence indicates that the huge changes in overt behavior that are apparent to all might be masking much smaller changes in underlying competencies. Infants seem to know a lot about their physical world from birth or shortly thereafter, and they may even be able to do simple computations.

Not everyone believes that the new research findings truly reflect advanced symbolic functioning or innate knowledge, of any type. For example, Kurt Fischer and Thomas Bidell (1991) argued that any particular infant skill should not be viewed in isolation but in the context of overall development. Rather than asking, for instance, when infants "really" have object permanence, Fischer and Bidell (1991) suggest that developmental researchers ask more fruitful questions, including these: "What is the developmental sequence of object knowledge from earliest infancy through early childhood? How is the development of this sequence related to developments in other domains? How is it constrained by the nature of perceptual and sensorimotor processes, which are partly regulated by the genome, and by environmental inputs? How are such constraints evident at various points in developmental sequences?" (pp. 223–224). These are similar to the arguments Marshall Haith (1993) made regarding infant perceptual abilities.

There is much excitement in infant research these days. Regardless of which interpretation one prefers, we think most researchers would agree that infants have far greater conceptual abilities than was previously believed, and every year, we learn something else that infants know or can do. We should not lose sight, however, of what infants cannot do. There is no evidence, for example, that infants can be taught arithmetic, reading, or chemistry. Infancy is still a special time, and the infant mind remains far different from the mind that resides in the 3-year-old child. Remembering the limits of infant cognition is sometimes difficult when we look at all the things infants can do, but it is a thought we shouldn't lose.

KEY TERMS AND CONCEPTS

accommodation (of the lens)
A-not-B object permanence
    task
Bayesian statistical inference
convergence (of the eyes)
coordination (of the eyes)
core knowledge
differentiation theory
dishabituation
explicit measures
externality effect

Goldilocks effect
habituation
implicit measures
intersensory integration
intersensory matching
    (or cross-modal matching)
numerosity
object cohesion and
    continuity
object constancy
object permanence

ordinality
other-race effect
perceptual narrowing
phonemes
principle of persistence
schema
violation-of-expectation
    method
visual preference paradigm

SUGGESTED READINGS

Scholarly Works

Baillargeon, R. (2008). Innate ideas revisited: For a principle of persistence in infants' physical reasoning. *Perspectives on Psychological Science, 3*, 2–13. This article reviews research by Reneé Baillargeon and her colleagues on object representation in infants using the violation-of-expectation method. She proposes the principle of persistence, in which babies seem to know coming into the world something about the continuity of objects.

Kelly, D. J., et al. (2007). The other-race effect develops during infancy. *Psychological Science, 18*, 1084–1089. These leading researchers in the field of face processing in infants present findings demonstrating the other-race effect in infancy. The article also provides a good example of how researchers test hypotheses regarding how infants process complicated information.

Spelke, E. S., & Kinzler, K. D. (2007). Core knowledge. *Developmental Science, 10*, 89–96. Elizabeth Spelke and Katherine Kinzler present evidence for the core-knowledge perspective of infant cognition, listing five areas in which core knowledge is proposed to exist.

Xu, F., & Kushnir, T. (2013). Infants are rational constructivist learners. *Current Directions in Psychological Sciences, 22*(1), 28–32. This article describes empirical evidence that infants are best characterized as rational constructivist learners. The authors describe the new approach against the background of nativism and empiricism, arguing that the new rational constructivism perspective blends elements of both while adopting probabilistic models of cognition.

Reading for Personal Interest

Dobbs, D. (2005). Big answers from little people. *Scientific American Mind, 16*(3), 38–43. This article, written for the layperson, examines the latest research into infants' cognitive abilities, focusing on the work of Elizabeth Spelke, Harvard developmental psychologist and advocate of the core-knowledge approach.

Rochat, P. (2004). *The infant's world.* Cambridge, MA: Harvard University Press. Philippe Rochat examines the development of infant social cognition, taking an ecological perspective somewhat different from the core-knowledge perspective as advocated by Elizabeth Spelke and her colleagues.

5 | THINKING IN SYMBOLS

Development of Representation

Three-year-old Nicholas sometimes spent the night with his grandparents, who would take him to preschool the following morning. Nicholas especially liked to ride with his grandfather because he drove a somewhat battered, stick-shift Chevy, which Nicholas called "Papa's car." Nicholas's grandmother, however, only drove cars with automatic transmissions. Thus, she was unable to take Nicholas to school in Papa's car. One morning when Grandma was about to drive Nicholas to school, he said,

"Grandma, dress up like a man this morning. Put on Papa's shirt and wear his hat." When asked why he wanted her to do that, he responded, "Then you can take me to school in Papa's car." Nicholas had a problem and attempted to solve it by changing his grandmother's appearance, which he believed would temporarily transform her into a man and give her the ability to drive a stick-shift car.

What's going on here? Does little Nicholas really think that clothes, quite literally, make the man? His thinking may reflect many things, but one is his ability to represent reality. We noted in Chapter 1 that one of the major issues in cognitive development concerns changes in the way children represent information. **Representation** refers to the mental coding of information, and as we also noted in previous chapters, children can represent information in a variety of forms. We discussed some aspects of representation in infancy in Chapter 4. Most, but not all, of the focus in this chapter is on slightly older children, as we examine different aspects of children's developing abilities to symbolically represent their worlds.

We start by examining what it means to use symbols—specifically to use one object to represent another. We then look at the theory of Swiss psychologist Jean Piaget, who brought to light many of the phenomena of symbolic functioning that psychologists are researching today and who made the study of the development of representation a central issue of our field. We next examine two expressions of symbolic functioning in children and how they change with age: symbolic play and distinguishing between fantasy and reality. We conclude by looking at two very different types of approaches to the development of representational abilities and their relationship to thinking: Alison Gopnik's theory of causal maps and Charles Brainerd and Valerie Reyna's fuzzy-trace theory.

LEARNING TO USE SYMBOLS

In everyday parlance, the term *symbol* usually refers to external referents for objects and events. For example, a picture or a photograph of an object is a stand-in for the real thing—it is a concrete yet symbolic representation of an object that

is not physically present. Likewise, scale models, such as a miniature room complete with doll-sized furniture, can serve as a symbolic representation of a larger, real room. Similarly, some things are not exactly what they seem. The ubiquitous refrigerator magnet attests to this. Cookies, candy bars, and many other "real" things are, in actuality, only magnets that look like something else. At a more abstract level, the letters and numbers so central to our technological culture are not what they seem to be but, rather, are symbols necessary for reading and computation. Judy DeLoache (2010; DeLoache & Marzolf, 1992) has referred to the knowledge that an entity can stand for something other than itself as **representational insight**. When can children understand and effectively use external forms of representation, such as pictures and models, and what does this tell us about their representational development?

In this section, we examine two areas of research related to young children's use of external symbols. The first is the research of DeLoache and her colleagues regarding children's abilities to use pictures and scale models as representations for the real things. The second is research examining children's abilities to distinguish the differences between the appearance and the reality of objects.

Young Children's Interpretation of Pictures and Models

How do children come to understand that pictures and models are symbols for other things? Judy DeLoache and her colleagues have investigated this question, and their studies have produced some interesting and, at first look, counterintuitive findings (DeLoache, 2010; DeLoache & Marzolf, 1992). In DeLoache's studies, 2- and 3-year-old children are asked to find a toy hidden in a room. Before searching for the object, they are shown a picture or scale model of the room, with the location of the hidden object made obvious in the picture or model. For example, children are shown a scale model of a room, and they watch as the experimenter hides a miniature toy behind a miniature chair in the model. The miniature toy and the model chair correspond to a large toy and a real chair in the adjoining real room. Children are then asked to find the toy in the room (Retrieval 1). After searching for the toy in the room, they return to the model and are asked to find where the miniature toy was hidden (Retrieval 2). If children cannot find the large toy in the room (Retrieval 1) but can find the miniature toy in the scale model (Retrieval 2), then their failure to find the large toy cannot be because they forgot where the miniature toy was hidden. A better interpretation would be that the children cannot use the model in a symbolic fashion.

The results of one such experiment with 2.5- and 3-year-old children are graphed in Figure 5.1 (DeLoache, 1987). As can be seen, 3-year-olds performed comparably in both retrieval tasks, indicating that they remembered where the miniature toy was hidden and used the information from the scale model to find the large toy in the real room. The younger children showed good memory for where the miniature toy was hidden (Retrieval 2 in the figure) but performed very poorly when trying to find the large toy in the real room (Retrieval 1 in the figure). This pattern of results suggests that 2.5-year-old children failed to recognize that the scale model was a symbolic representation of the large room. Recalling DeLoache's definition of representational insight as realizing that one entity can stand for another, it appears that, on the scale-model task, 3-year-olds possess representational insight whereas 2.5-year-old children do not.

A similar pattern of results was found when *pictures* of a room were used, with an experimenter pointing to the location in a picture where the toy was hidden (DeLoache, 1987, 1991; Jowkar-Baniani & Schmuckler, 2013). The primary difference between the picture and scale-model experiments was that the picture task was solved by 2.5-year-old children but not by 2-year-olds. Thus, when pictures are used as symbols, 2.5-year-olds demonstrate representational insight. Such competence is not achieved until 3 years of age, however, when a scale model is used.

Why should children perform better when using pictures as opposed to a scale model? If we had been asked to make a prediction of which task would be easier, our guess would have been exactly the reverse. The model, being a more

FIGURE 5.1 **The number of errorless retrievals (correctly locating the hidden toy) for 2.5-year-olds (younger) and 3-year-olds (older) on a model task.** Retrieval 1 involved locating the real toy in the real room; Retrieval 2 involved locating the miniature toy in the model.

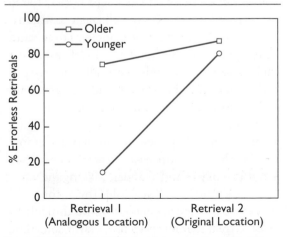

Source: DeLoache, J. S. (1987). Rapid change in the symbolic functioning of very young children. *Science, 238,* 1556–1557. Copyright © 1987 American Association for the Advancement of Science. Reprinted with permission.

concrete stimulus, is more like the real room, and it would seem that less symbolic sophistication would be required to use it to guide behavior. In fact, when young children are given toy objects versus pictures of objects to use in memory and simple problem-solving tasks, they usually perform better with the objects, not the pictures (Daehler, Lonardo, & Bukatko, 1979). Such was not the case with DeLoache's study, of course, and she proposed that one reason for the pattern of results was related to children's difficulty in thinking about an entity in two different ways at the same time, or what she refers to as dual representation (or dual orientation). A model, she argues, is an object worthy of attention all by itself. A picture, by contrast, is itself uninteresting, with its primary purpose being to represent something else. (In fact, even 9-month-olds can match two-dimensional pictures to actual three-dimensional objects; see Jowkar-Baniani & Schmuckler, 2011.) When models are made less interesting and less concrete, or when pictures are made more salient, performance should change.

This is exactly what DeLoache (1991) found. When models were viewed through a window, 2.5-year-olds' performance increased substantially relative to the standard model task. Likewise, when 3-year-olds were allowed to play with the model before the hiding task, their performance significantly *decreased*. Making the model *less* salient for the 2.5-year-olds (by requiring that they view it through a window) enabled them to more easily represent the model as both an object and a model. Making the model *more* salient for the 3-year-olds (by encouraging them to play with it) made it more difficult for them to treat it as a representation for something else, and their performance deteriorated. A similar result was found when pictures were made more salient (DeLoache, 1991), whereas other

studies have shown that under favorable conditions, even 2-year-olds can appreciate that a picture can relate both to something else and be an object itself (Jowkar-Baniani & Schmuckler, 2013; Preissler & Bloom, 2007).

If dual representation is the key here, as DeLoache proposes, what would happen if young children had to use a model to find a hidden toy *without* dual representation? How can this be done? DeLoache, Kevin Miller, and Karl Rosengren (1997) convinced children that a "shrinking machine" (an oscilloscope with flashing lights and computer-generated sounds) could actually shrink a room, something that the 2.5-year-old children easily believed. The children were then given the hiding test as in previous research. First, a toy was hidden in the large room. Then, the room was "shrunk," and the children searched for the toy in the miniaturized model. Their performance this time was exceptional. Whereas children who were given the standard (no shrinking room) instructions successfully found the toy on only 19% of all trials (about what one would expect by chance), children who searched in the shrunken (model) room were correct nearly 80% of the time. Why the difference? DeLoache and her colleagues reasoned that the children believed *the miniaturized room was the same room as the larger room*; it was not a model and, thus, not a symbol. In this case, as far as the children were concerned, dual representation was not necessary.

The ability to use one object to represent another is the essence of what we mean when we refer to symbol use. At a very basic level, we see this ability in very young children, most easily perhaps in symbolic play. For example, an 18-month-old might hold a shoe to her ear and pretend that it's a phone, or a 20-month-old might place a napkin on his head and parade around the living room drawing attention to his "hat." In these cases, one object is being used as a symbol for another. But this is not quite what DeLoache means when she refers to representational insight. It is not enough to use an object as a symbol; one must know that the object can be both a symbol (for example, a representation of a room) and an object (for example, a model) at the same time. DeLoache and Donald Marzolf (1992) make this point nicely, stating, "Young children are capable of responding to a single entity either concretely, as an object itself, or abstractly, as a representation of something else. It is very difficult for them to do both at once, that is, to achieve dual representation" (p. 328).

Subsequent research has documented the development of dual representation for children's understanding of one common symbolic entity—pictures. DeLoache and her colleagues (1998) presented pictures of objects to children ages 9 to 19 months in the United States and the Ivory Coast. The youngest children in both countries initially touched the pictures as if they were real objects, sometimes even trying to pick them off the page. By 19 months of age, however, children in both countries realized that the pictures represented something else; they now pointed at the depicted objects rather than try to manipulate them. DeLoache and her colleagues propose that infants' initial uncertainty about pictures causes them to explore the pictures, which gradually results in their acquisition of the concept of *picture* and the understanding that they represent something else. Later research has indicated that, under some contexts, infants as young as 15 months old understand that pictures are representations of objects (Ganea et al., 2009).

Young children's difficulty distinguishing real objects from their symbolic representation is also seen in what DeLoache, David Uttal, and Karl Rosengren (2004) have called scale errors. Scale errors occur when children attempt to use a miniature object, such as a toy car, as if it were a real one, in this case by attempting to fit into it. Watching a toddler trying to squeeze her foot into a toy shoe or her entire body into a toy truck can be amusing, but its frequency among young children suggests that it is another reflection of toddlers' poorly developed representational insight (Casler et al., 2011; DeLoache et al., 2013). For example, in DeLoache et al.'s original study, nearly half of 18- to 30-month-old children made at least one scale error.

Appearance/Reality Distinction

Adults know very well that things are not always what they seem to be. We realize that the appearance of an object does not necessarily correspond to its reality. This is not knowledge we are born with but knowledge that has a developmental history. The appearance/reality distinction refers to the knowledge that the appearance of an object does not necessarily correspond to its reality. This is illustrated in a pioneering study by Rheta De Vries (1969). In this study, De Vries first familiarized 3- to 6-year-old children with a trained cat named Maynard. In one condition, after the children petted Maynard, the cat was fitted with a realistic dog mask. (We did mention that he was a trained cat.) Although the children did not actually see the mask being placed on Maynard, the cat's body and tail remained in full view of the children during the transformation. They were then asked questions about the identity of the animal. What kind of animal is it now? Would this animal eat dog food or cat food? Does it bark or meow? In general, 3-year-olds frequently believed that the mask had actually changed the identity of the animal, turning the cat into a dog, whereas most 5- and 6-year-olds believed that changes in the appearance of the animal had not altered its identity. De Vries referred to this type of qualitative constancy as *generic identity*.

In addition to her research on changing the appearance of animals, De Vries also interviewed children regarding their beliefs about people wearing masks and about the constancy of gender as a result of certain irrelevant changes (for example, boys wearing dresses). Again, she reported that 3-year-olds tended to believe that changes in appearance result in changes in identity. This can account for young children's sometimes puzzling responses to costumes worn both by others and by themselves. For instance, as my (KC) son, Simon, approached his third Halloween at age 2, I asked him what he would like to be. His reply was consistently, "I want to be Simon." Despite my attempts to clarify and reword the question ("I know you want to be Simon, but what do you want to dress up as for Halloween?"), he was persistent that he only wanted to be himself. It is also not uncommon at Halloween for 2- and 3-year-old children to be excited about wearing a costume, only to become distressed when the masks are placed over their faces or when they look at themselves in the mirror. Wearing a SpongeBob SquarePants outfit is one thing, but wearing the mask is another story. Not all transformations of personal identity are upsetting, however, as evidenced by the number of scraped elbows and knees on children who wear their Superman underwear, tie capes around their necks, and jump from tables and fences, convinced that they can fly. These children's behaviors are consistent with the belief that a significant change in appearance results in a change in identity. The story that opened this chapter reflects a young boy's wish to change his grandmother into a man, temporarily, so she can drive him to school in "Papa's car."

In related research, John Flavell and his colleagues extensively investigated young children's knowledge about the distinction between appearance and reality (Flavell, Green, & Flavell, 1986). In some experiments, children were presented with a realistic-looking fake rock made of sponge, or they watched as white milk was poured into a red glass. The children were then asked two questions. The first concerned what the objects looked like, "how they look to your eyes right now." The second concerned the actual identity of the objects, "how they really and truly are." Somewhat surprisingly, Flavell and his colleagues reported that most 3-year-olds could not solve these seemingly simple problems. Children stated, for example, that the milk looked red and "really and truly" was red, or they would say that the fake rock was, indeed, a sponge and looked like a sponge. In general, when children erred, they did so by giving the same answer to both questions. Subsequent research that simplified the task or provided training to young children generally failed to find any enhancement in performance for 3-year-olds (Deák, Ray, & Brenneman, 2003; Flavell et al., 1986), causing Flavell and his colleagues (1986) to conclude that 3-year-olds "truly did not understand [the appearance/reality distinction], even minimally" (p. 23).

Flavell and his colleagues (1986) speculated about the factors that can mediate children's development of the appearance/reality distinction. One likely candidate is *dual encoding*. Three-year-olds' inability to differentiate between the appearance of an object and its actual identity might stem, in part, from their difficulty with representing an object in more than one form at a time. Young children might focus on only one aspect of a stimulus (its visual appearance or its actual identity) and give the same answer, based on either appearance or reality, regardless of the question asked. Thus, on the one hand, if the visual change in color is more salient to a child, the object *looks* red and *is* red. If, on the other hand, the identity of the object is more salient, it *is called* a sponge and therefore *looks like* a sponge. Flavell argued that young children cannot act on multiple representations of an object simultaneously. However, others (Deák, 2006; Siegal, 1997) have proposed that the challenge for young children is not in upholding multiple representations, per se. Instead, young children, who are still developing language, struggle with the linguistic demands of Flavell's tasks. Whereas the appearance of an object is encoded visually, actual identity is usually coded verbally when participants are told what the object *really* is. In fact, when researchers use nonverbal tasks to require participants to distinguish between appearance and reality, children younger than 3 years (Moll & Tomasello, 2012) and even great apes (Karg et al., 2014) perform quite well. For instance, Trix Cacchione and colleagues (Cacchione, Schaub, & Rakoczy, 2013) demonstrated that even 14-month-old infants seem capable of representing two identities of one object simultaneously. These researchers presented infants with a plush toy rabbit. To half of the participants, they demonstrated that the rabbit could be changed into a carrot by turning it inside out. The other half of participants did not see this transformation. This rabbit was then put into an opaque box. The experimenter surreptitiously changed the rabbit to a carrot prior to asking the infant to search the box. Infants who had not been informed that the rabbit could transform persisted in searching the box after retrieving a carrot, presumably expecting that a rabbit should still be in the box. In contrast, infants who had observed the rabbit transform into a carrot earlier in the session seemed unsurprised to find a carrot instead of a rabbit when searching the box (that is, on average they reached into the box fewer times than naive infants after retrieving the carrot). These findings suggest that infants are

capable of representing the dual identity of an object (for instance, that a toy rabbit can also be a toy carrot) when provided with this information visually. With increasing age, children become more adept at representing the linguistic and visual forms of objects, but not until later childhood or early adolescence can they "think about notions of 'looks like,' 'really and truly,' 'looks different from the way it really and truly is,' and so on in the abstract, metaconceptual way that older subjects can" (Flavell et al., 1986, p. 59).

The findings and interpretation of Flavell and his colleagues are similar to those DeLoache (1987; DeLoache & Marzolf, 1992) reported with respect to dual representation for pictures and models. Together, these findings suggest that a dual-representational ability does not emerge at a single time and affect thinking across all tasks. Rather, this ability appears to develop gradually from infancy to 5 years, being found early (14 months) in some circumstances (visual transformations), a little later (2.5 to 3 years) in other contexts (using pictures and models as symbols, respectively), and later yet (4 to 5 years) in still other situations (making the appearance/reality distinction).

Section Review

Representation refers to the mental coding of information.

Young Children's Interpretation of Pictures and Models

- The knowledge that an entity can stand for something other than itself has been referred to as *representational insight*. Whereas children as young as 2.5 years show representational insight when pictures are used, they do not show representational insight with models until age 3.

- *Dual representation* (or *dual orientation*), the ability to think about an entity in two different ways at the same time, is required before children can show representational insight.

Appearance/Reality Distinction

- Young children also have a difficult time distinguishing between an object's appearance and its actual identity (*appearance/reality distinction*).
- Young children's dual representational abilities develop gradually over the preschool years, being expressed in some contexts earlier than in others.
- Toddlers frequently make *scale errors* when they attempt to use miniature objects, like model cars, as though they were real ones.

Ask Yourself . . .

1. What is required for children to gain representational insight? How does the representational insight of children vary across ages and situations?
2. What does dual encoding have to do with the development of the appearance/reality distinction?

PIAGET'S THEORY

Jean Piaget (1896–1980) has had a greater impact on the field of cognitive development than any other person in the brief history of our science. The self-proclaimed experimental philosopher formulated a grand theory of intelligence that made children themselves, rather than their environment or their genetic constitution, the primary force in the development of thought. Piaget changed the way we look at children. Following Piaget, we no longer view the child as an incomplete adult. Piaget taught us that children's thinking, at any age, reflects a unique way of interpreting the world

(for example, changes in appearance can produce changes in reality). Development is more than the simple acquisition of skills and knowledge. The 4-year-old is not just a smaller model of the 12-year-old who merely lacks the experience and knowledge of his older peer. Rather, in addition to quantitative differences in what these two children know (that is, differences in amount, degree, or speed), there are qualitative differences in how they know it (that is, differences in form, or type). Because of Piaget's work, it is difficult today for us to conceive of the child as a passive organism, shaped and molded by environmental pressures. At any given developmental level, children are seekers of stimulation who act on their environment as much as their environment acts on them.

Many cognitive developmentalists hold great reverence for Piaget's theory because of the impact it has had on the field of developmental psychology (see Barrouillet, 2015; Brainerd, 1996). Although the number of active researchers today who are strict adherents of Piaget's theory is relatively small (many would describe themselves as neo-Piagetians), familiarity with Piaget's theory is essential for understanding cognitive development as it is studied today.

Some Assumptions of Piaget's Theory

Piaget was a stage theorist. He believed that cognition develops in a series of discrete stages, with children's thinking at any particular stage being qualitatively different from that which preceded it and that which will follow it. In other words, Piaget did not view cognitive development as the gradual accretion of knowledge or skills. Rather, he viewed cognitive development as a series of transformations, with children's thinking going through abrupt changes over relatively brief periods. Despite his belief in the discontinuous nature of changes in children's thinking, Piaget did believe that the *functions* underlying cognitive development are continuous. New abilities do not just pop up but emerge from earlier abilities. Given this underlying continuity, Piaget hypothesized transition, or preparatory, phases between stages—brief times when a child can have one foot in each of two qualitatively different cognitive worlds.

Piaget also believed that the mechanisms of cognitive development are domain general. Children come into the world with a general, species-typical nervous system—a nervous system that is not specially prepared to acquire any one type of information more than another. Thus, all intellectual accomplishments of infancy, for example, are governed by a general developmental function. Infants' mastery of early language, knowledge of objects, imitation abilities, and problem-solving skills are all interrelated and are the products of changes in a single cognitive system.

Piaget viewed children as being *intrinsically active*. They are not passive creatures, waiting to be stimulated by their surroundings before they behave. Rather, they are active initiators and seekers of stimulation. Intrinsic activity in children can be viewed as curiosity. Children are not content with what they already know, and they seek to know more. Although a child can be enticed to acquire certain information through external rewards, such exogenous reinforcements are not necessary to motivate learning and development. The motivation for development is within the child, whom Piaget made not only the focus of development but also its major perpetrator. Children are the movers and shakers of their own experiences and, thus, are primarily responsible for their own development. Environmental and genetic sources play a role in influencing development as well, of course, and Piaget most explicitly believed that development is the result of an interaction between a biologically prepared child and his or her environment. Nevertheless, unlike most of his contemporaries, Piaget placed his emphasis squarely on the child.

Related to the concept of intrinsic activity is Piaget's belief that cognition is a *constructive* process. According to Piaget, our current state of knowledge guides our processing, substantially influencing how (and what) new information is acquired. This concept is also reflected by Bayesian mathematical models, which we introduced in Chapter 4. In other words, the world is not out there for everyone to perceive in exactly the same manner. Knowing is an active, constructive process—an interaction between the environment and the active individual who updates and informs expectations based on experiences.

If reality is a construction, however, then children at different developmental levels must surely construct different realities. The same event experienced by a 2-, a 7-, and a 14-year-old will be interpreted very differently by each. This is true not only because of differences in the amount of knowledge possessed by these children (that is, quantitative differences) but also because of differences in how each child can process information (that is, qualitative differences). For a 6-month-old whose rattle is hidden by a blanket, reality is that the rattle no longer exists; a 3-year-old boy believes that wearing girls' clothes or playing girls' games transforms him temporarily into a girl; and a 6-year-old is convinced that a baloney-and-cheese sandwich cut into quarters provides more to eat than when it is cut into halves. An older child or adult believes none of this, but for Piaget, reality is not an absolute. It is a construction based on our past experiences and our current cognitive structures.

But how do children "construct" the world in their minds? Piaget proposed that infants initially come to "know" objects by physically acting on them. He referred to organized and sequential series of actions as *action schemes*, as, for example, when an infant voluntarily grasps things with her hands (grasping scheme) or sucks everything that comes in contact with her mouth (sucking scheme). A scheme (sometimes referred to as *schema*) is the basic unit of knowledge for Piaget. Later in development, children internalize these actions so they can "think without hands"—that is, mentally manipulate the things they perceive (like we do, for example, when thinking of the different possible arrangements for furniture in a living room). Piaget called these internalized actions operations, or *operational schemes*. Operations are organized and follow a system of logical rules. According to Piaget, the nature of schemes varies over development. Roughly speaking, they correspond to the four stages in the development of thought described later in this chapter.

Functional Invariants

Piaget used the term functional invariants to describe two processes that characterize all biological systems (including intelligence) and operate throughout the life span: *organization* and *adaptation.*

Organization. Organization refers to the fact that intellectual operations are integrated with one another in a hierarchical nature. Through the process of organization, every intellectual operation is related to all other acts of intelligence. Thus, one scheme does not exist independently of other schemes but is coordinated with them. Similarly, organization is the tendency to integrate schemes into higher-order systems. For example, a week-old infant has one scheme for sucking and another for hand and

arm movements. It doesn't take long, however, for these two schemes to become coordinated, resulting in a thumb-sucking scheme. Thumb sucking is not innate but represents the organization of two initially independent schemes into an integrated, higher-order scheme (even if these schemes become coordinated before birth).

Adaptation. Adaptation is the organism's tendency to adjust its schemes to environmental demands. Piaget defined two aspects of adaptation: assimilation and accommodation. Basically, assimilation is the incorporation of new information into already-existing schemes. Assimilation is not a passive process; it often requires that children modify or distort environmental input (hence, one source of cognitive errors) so that they can incorporate it into their current schemes.

Complementary to assimilation is the process of accommodation, in which a current scheme is changed to incorporate new information. Accommodation occurs when children are confronted with information that cannot be interpreted by current cognitive schemes. Accommodation is obviously an active process, resulting in the modification of existing schemes as a result of the interaction of those schemes with the environment.

As a simple example of assimilation and accommodation, consider the grasp of an infant. Babies will reflexively grasp objects placed in the palms of their hands. This grasping scheme can be applied to a variety of objects that fit easily into the infant's hand. So grasping the handle of a rattle, Daddy's finger, or the railing of a crib all involve (primarily) assimilation. The infant is incorporating information into an existing scheme. If the same infant is presented with a small ball, some small modifications in hand movements are required if the infant is to "know" this new object and successfully apply the grasping scheme to it. These modifications constitute (primarily) accommodation, permitting the infant to incorporate new data by slightly changing current schemes.

Piaget stressed that every act of intelligence involves both assimilation and accommodation. However, some actions involve a predominance of one over the other. For example, Piaget proposed that play is the purest form of assimilation, with children modifying the information in the environment to fit their make-believe actions. Conversely, Piaget proposed that there is a relative predominance of accommodation in imitation, with children adjusting their schemes to match those of a model.

For Piaget, children enter the world possessing the functional invariants of organization and adaptation, with little else, if anything, prespecified. Thus, counter to neonativists or core-knowledge theorists (see Chapter 4), children are not specifically "prepared" to process some information more readily than others; rather, they actively construct knowledge, chiefly through the mechanisms of assimilation and accommodation.

Equilibration

Piaget stated that at least four major factors contribute to development: (1) maturation, or the gradual unfolding of genetic plans; (2) the physical environment, or the child's actions on objects in his or her world; (3) social transmission, or the knowledge abstracted from people in the environment; and (4) equilibration, a concept unique to Piagetian theory.

Equilibration refers to the organism's attempt to keep its cognitive schemes in balance. This concept explains the motivation for development; it is meant to answer the questions "Why should we develop at all?" and "Why do cognitive schemes change?" When a child encounters some information that does not match his or her current schemes, an imbalance, or disequilibrium, results. The child experiences cognitive incongruity, with the new information not quite fitting his or her current state of knowledge. States of disequilibrium are intrinsically dissatisfying, and the child attempts to reinstate equilibrium.

How is this equilibration achieved? According to Piaget, equilibration is achieved by altering one's cognitive schemes. That is, given the disconfirming information, accommodation can occur, with the child slightly modifying current schemes to match the environmental data. As a result, a new and more stable scheme develops. This new scheme is more stable because fewer intrusions will set it into a state of disequilibrium than the immediately previous scheme was vulnerable to.

Discrepant information, however, is not always dealt with in such a way as to produce cognitive change (that is, by accommodation). If new information is too discrepant from a child's current schemes, for example, accommodation becomes impossible, and assimilation becomes unlikely. The alternative is to ignore (that is, not act on) the information, thus returning the schemes to their original state. For instance, a first-grader given algebra problems to solve will likely remain in a state of disequilibrium only briefly, realizing very soon that he or she hasn't the foggiest idea what these symbols mean, and will go on to something else.

Another alternative is to distort the new information by assimilation, making it compatible with the old schemes. In this case, no qualitative change in the schemes occurs, only a possible broadening of the original schemes. Nevertheless, the environmental intrusion is dealt with effectively, although it might not appear that way to an outsider. For example, the same algebra problem given to a 9-year-old will likely be recognized as a math problem, and the child might apply his or her basic arithmetic schemes to derive an answer. Such an answer will probably be wrong, but distorting an algebra problem to an arithmetic one can re-establish a temporary equilibrium. The equilibration process is schematically represented in Figure 5.2.

Let us provide one more example of how the equilibration process might work. The Elf on the Shelf has become a holiday guest in many households in recent years, based on a storybook describing a magical toy elf who appears around the holidays, monitors children's behaviors, and reports to Santa on a nightly basis who has been "naughty or nice." Parents, of course, are in on the trick and move the elf to a new location around the house each night to maintain the appearance that the elf has left to "visit Santa" and returned by the following day. For many 3-year-olds, the concept of a magical elf is entirely new. The child may not even have a scheme for elves, much less the kinds of magic they can or cannot do. This new information produces cognitive incongruity, or a state of disequilibrium. At this point, the child can distort somewhat the characteristics of the elf in her mind and assimilate it into her toy doll scheme. She also has the option of ignoring the elf altogether. Her third option is to modify her current elf scheme or create a new scheme altogether by accommodating this new information and changing slightly her knowledge of elves. Much to my (KC) own disappointment, my 3-year-old son Simon began the holiday season with our elf (named Nomis) by simply ignoring him. Despite our best efforts, he was neither amazed nor amused when Nomis moved to different rooms overnight, left notes, or rearranged toys. For about the first week, I would start the morning

by saying, "Oh my goodness, Simon! Look at where Nomis is today! Look at what he's done!" Simon would just stare momentarily, unreactive, and then change the subject or say, "Oh yeah." Soon enough, however, as we read more of the storybook that explains Nomis as a magical elf, and as my son experienced more of Nomis's antics, his scheme of the magical elf began to emerge. He was excited to discover Nomis each morning and asked questions like, "Did Nomis fly or climb to the mantle?" and "Why can't Nomis talk to us?" With each answer, his schema adjusted slightly to accommodate this new information.

Accommodation—and, thus, the attainment of more stable schemes—is most apt to occur when the new information is only slightly discrepant from current schemes. Information that exactly matches current schemes can be assimilated into those schemes, and information that is too different from what a child already knows is likely to be either distorted or ignored. These concepts should remind you of the *Goldilocks effect* that we described with respect to infants' learning in Chapter 4. Recall that infants' pattern of looking times across a variety of tasks often constitute a U-shaped curve; stimuli that are similar to what infants have already experienced, or are "expected," seem to not warrant further attention, or are habituated to, resulting in relatively short looking times. Likewise, stimuli that are too unexpected are not attended to. Richard Aslin (2014) described this as the "Goldilocks effect," with infants spending the most time looking at information of moderate complexity. If we combine these ideas with Piaget's theory, we could interpret this pattern as indicating that very familiar or similar stimuli are easily assimilated into existing schemas, and therefore infants need not spend time looking at such information. Similarly,

FIGURE 5.2 **A schematic representation of the equilibration model.** Although Piaget specified that equilibration involves accommodation (Option C), Options A and B reflect ways in which children may achieve temporary states of stability.

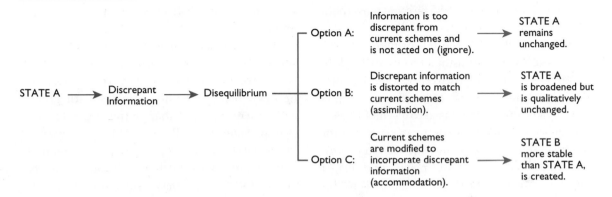

Source: © Cengage Learning.

when the stimulus is so different that it cannot be assimilated or accommodated easily, infants ignore it, as reflected in relatively shorter looking times. Of course, if the stimulus is "just right" in novelty, Piaget would argue that infants should attempt to make sense of it by either assimilating the information to an existing scheme or accommodating it to develop a more stable scheme. Doing so, however, takes time, as reflected by infants' relatively longer looking times for information of moderate complexity. Regardless of whether we wish to think of children as seeking out information that is "just right" or as resolving disequilibrium, it is clear that children remain active operators on their environments.

Stages of Development

Piaget divided cognitive development into four major stages, or periods: (1) sensorimotor, (2) preoperations, (3) concrete operations, and (4) formal operations. A brief description of the major characteristics of children's thinking during each of these stages is provided in Table 5.1. Piaget insisted that the order in which children progress through these stages is invariant and culturally universal; stages cannot be skipped. This assumption of the invariant order of stages is a direct consequence of Piaget's belief that development is *epigenetic* in nature—that it proceeds gradually, with later developments being based on earlier developments (see discussion of epigenesis in Chapter 2). So, from a Piagetian perspective, a precocious 8-year-old who has mastered analytic geometry acquired these skills by going through the same sequence of stages as his adolescent peers, but he went through those stages at a faster rate.

Sensorimotor Stage

The first major stage in Piaget's theory is the sensorimotor stage, or sensorimotor period, which lasts from birth to approximately 2 years of age (Piaget, 1952, 1954, 1962). In this period, children's intelligence is limited to their own actions. During their first 18 months or so, children develop some complex problem-solving skills, but they do this without the benefit of mental representation. They know the world only by their direct actions (both sensory and motoric) on it.

Movement through the sensorimotor period can be described in terms of a cognitive developmental "trip" in two basic dimensions. The first dimension is in terms of representation. Infants progress from an action-based to a symbol-based intelligence—in other words, from sensorimotor to representational thought. The second dimension is in terms of personal perspective. Piaget described infants at birth as being unable to differentiate themselves from the external world; all the world is one, with themselves at the center. By the time children are 2 years old, they realize they are independent from the objects they act on and that objects exist in time and space even when they are not interacting with them (object permanence, discussed in Chapter 4). In general, over the course of the first 2 years of life, infants move from cognition centered on their own bodies and actions to cognition that displaces them in time and space from the things they think about.

Piaget's basic description of development through the sensorimotor period has been replicated using variants of the procedures he described and almost always with greater experimental control than in the original studies (Kopp, Sigman, & Parmelee, 1974; Uzgiris & Hunt, 1975). However, as we saw in Chapter 4, subsequent research has demonstrated that young infants may have substantially greater cognitive abilities than Piaget proposed.

Piaget divided the sensorimotor stage into six substages. As with Piaget's theory in general, infants progress through these increasingly complex substages in an invariant sequence, with the successful accomplishments of earlier substages forming the basis for the

TABLE 5.1 **Characteristics of major periods in Piaget's theory.**

Period and Approximate Age Range	Major Characteristics
Sensorimotor: birth to 2 years	Intelligence is limited to the infant's own actions on the environment. Cognition progresses from the exercise of reflexes (for example, sucking, visual orienting) to the beginning of symbolic functioning.
Preoperations: 2 to 7 years	Intelligence is symbolic, expressed via language, imagery, and other modes, permitting children to mentally represent and compare objects out of immediate perception. Thought is intuitive rather than logical and is egocentric, in that children have a difficult time taking the perspective of another.
Concrete operations: 7 to 11 years	Intelligence is symbolic and logical. (For example, if A is greater than B and B is greater than C, then A must be greater than C.) Thought is less egocentric. Children's thinking is limited to concrete phenomena and their own past experiences, that is, thinking is not abstract.
Formal operations: 11 to 16 years	Children are able to make and test hypotheses: possibility dominates reality. Children are able to introspect about their own thought processes and, generally, can think abstractly.

accomplishments of later substages. Central to each substage is children's problem-solving skills, particularly the extent to which they display intentionality, or **goal-directed behavior**, and this is the focus of our description of Piaget's sensorimotor substages. A brief description of the major characteristics of children's intelligence at each sensorimotor substage is presented in Table 5.2.

Substage 1: Basic reflexes. In the first substage of basic reflexes (birth to 1 month), infants apply the set of action patterns, or reflexes, they were born with to interpret their experiences. Piaget used the term reflex broadly, so that infant reflexes include not only obvious behaviors, such as sucking and grasping, but also more subtle behaviors, such as eye movements, orientation to sound, and vocalization. If an object "fits" an infant's reflex, he or she applies that reflex to the object and assimilates it to existing schemes. However, accommodation also occurs during the first weeks of life. For example, Piaget (1952) made careful observations of his son, Laurent, who was adjusting to nursing. Piaget noted how Laurent would suck his hand or a quilt even when not hungry, the reflex being released by almost anything that touched his lips. Piaget also observed that Laurent's ability to locate the nipple and nurse successfully improved gradually over the first 3 weeks of life, as he learned to apply his sucking reflex selectively to the nipple (rather than to the skin surrounding the nipple) when hungry.

Substage 2: Primary circular reactions. Piaget called the second substage primary circular reactions (1 to 4 months). According to Piaget, primary circular reactions are the first class of repetitive actions, and they are based on hereditary reflexes. Piaget discussed these

first circular reactions primarily with regard to sucking, vision, hearing, vocalizations, and grasping. For example, Piaget detailed how Laurent, between 1 month 1 day and 1 month 21 days, acquired the ability to suck his thumb. The initial contact between Laurent's hand and his mouth was by chance. That is, babies don't start out thinking, Gee, I'd like to suck my thumb. I wonder how I should go about doing it? Rather, in the process of random activity or activity directed toward a biological outcome (for example, nursing), reflexes are fortuitously activated. Once Laurent's thumb or fingers were in his mouth, sucking occurred. And Laurent repeatedly attempted to re-create the experience, gradually coordinating his arm, hand, and finger movements with his mouth until he had established the ability to suck his thumb whenever (presumably) he pleased.

Substage 3: Secondary circular reactions. This is followed by the stage of secondary circular reactions (4 to 8 months) and the first acquired adaptations of new (that is, not reflexive) behaviors. With no intention beforehand, babies cause something interesting to happen and then attempt to re-create the interesting event. A major difference between primary and secondary circular reactions is that for the former, the interesting events are based on reflexes and, thus, are necessarily centered on the infant's body. In contrast, for secondary circular reactions, interesting events are found in the external world. This is especially true of visual events, although Piaget also discussed secondary circular reactions for other schemes, particularly grasping and hearing.

Let me (DB) provide an observation of my own. My daughter, Heidi, at 4 months of age, was lying in her playpen. She did not seem particularly interested in any of the toys

TABLE 5.2 **Characteristics of the sensorimotor substages in Piaget's theory.**

Substage and Approximate Age Range	Major Characteristics
Substage 1 (basic reflexes): birth to 1 month	Cognition is limited to inherited reflex patterns.
Substage 2 (primary circular reactions): 1 to 4 months	Infant acquires first adaptations, extends basic reflexes: reflex is activated by chance (for example, thumb comes in contact with lips, activating sucking reflex); infant attempts to reproduce reflex, resulting in acquisition of new, noninherited behavior (thumb sucking) that can be activated at the infant's discretion; initial occurrence of behavior is by chance, so need follows action.
Substage 3 (secondary circular reactions): 4 to 8 months	By chance, infant causes interesting event in environment to occur (for example, infant kicks mattress, causing mobile over crib to move) and tries to re-create event: beginning of control of objects and events external to infant; as in previous stage, initial occurrence of interesting event is by chance so need follows action.
Substage 4 (coordination of secondary circular reactions): 8 to 12 months	Infant uses two previously acquired schemes in coordination with each other to achieve a goal; first sign of need preceding action, or goal-directed behavior, is exhibited.
Substage 5 (tertiary circular reactions): 12 to 18 months	Infant discovers new means through active experimentation and develops new techniques to solve problems; goal-directed behavior is exhibited, but entire problem-solving process is conducted by overt trial and error: intelligence is still limited to child's actions on objects.
Substage 6 (mental combinations): 18 to 24 months	Infant shows first signs of symbolic functioning; infant is able to represent events in environment in terms of symbols (for example, language, imagery); problem solving can now be covert.

that surrounded her, although she was awake, alert, and active. Strung over her head was a "crib gym," a complex mobile with parts that spin when they are hit. I had spun the objects for her on several occasions, and when I did, Heidi seemed to like it. But today was to be different. While flailing her arms and legs, she hit the mobile, causing it to spin. She happened to be looking at the mobile, and its movement caught her attention. She suddenly stopped and stared intently at the moving object over her head. It ceased moving, and she began to shake her arms and legs, to squirm, and finally, to cry. Again she hit

the mobile, and again, she froze and quieted, staring straight ahead at the wonderful event she had caused.

Substage 4: Coordination of secondary circular reactions. Beginning around 8 months of age, infants enter Substage 4, the coordination of secondary circular reactions (8 to 12 months). A major change in intentionality is found in Substage 4, in that the need now precedes the act. That is, we have for the first time goal-directed behavior and the beginning of the differentiation between means and ends (that is, cause and effect). This means/ends separation is first accomplished by the coordination of two previously acquired secondary schemes to obtain a specific goal. Piaget suggested that one of the simplest coordinations is that of removing an obstacle to retrieve a visible object. Piaget (1952) provided a lengthy description of experiments in which he placed obstacles, such as his hand, between his son, Laurent, and some desired object. Laurent acquired the ability to brush aside his father's hand to obtain the desired goal. That is, Laurent was able to use one well-established scheme (striking) so that another scheme (reaching, grasping, and retrieving an object) could be activated.

Substage 5: Tertiary circular reactions. Between 12 and 18 months of age, infants enter Substage 5 and develop tertiary circular reactions. Infants in this substage are not restricted to applying previously acquired and consolidated schemes to achieve a goal. Rather, when faced with a problem, children can now make subtle alterations in their existing schemes that are directly related to obtaining a solution to their conundrum. This, Piaget stated, reflects a process of active experimentation.

Along with their new intellectual tools come increasing locomotive abilities. By 12 months of age, most babies can get around well, be it on two limbs or four, and this combination of increased locomotor and cognitive skills results in a child who is apt to be into everything. Children of this age often show a peak in curiosity. They want to know what makes things tick and, more importantly, how *they* can make them tick. They are explorers and adventurers. Is it possible to unravel the toilet paper, getting it all into the toilet without breaking the paper? How does one get into the bathroom sink? Isn't it interesting how by turning one knob the music becomes so much

louder? Adults are often perplexed about why 15-month-olds find dog food and kitty litter so fascinating, why they are so interested in electric sockets and wastebaskets, and why they insist on climbing out of their high chairs and manipulating and mouthing everything on the kitchen table.

Although children during this substage are wonderful problem solvers, their intelligence, according to Piaget, is still basically limited to physical actions on objects. They know objects by acting on them and cannot yet make mental comparisons or represent objects and events symbolically. These children solve problems by a trial-and-error process, with all their trials available for public examination. So, for example, if a 15-month-old wants to see if her brother's tricycle fits beneath the coffee table, she will have to do it by physically attempting to place it there. It makes no difference that the tricycle rises a foot above the table. She cannot simply examine the two objects and discern that one is too big to fit under the other. She can learn this, however, by attempting it, although it may take several such tries before she concludes what, to an adult, is obvious.

Substage 6: Invention of new means through mental combinations. In the final substage of the sensorimotor period, invention of new means through mental combinations (18 to 24 months), children show the first glimmer of mental (symbolic) representation—of being able to think about objects without having to directly act on them. With the advent of mental representation, the process of children's problem solving is no longer totally in the open. Trial-and-error procedures can occur covertly in the head, producing what appears to be sudden comprehension or insight. New means can be invented through mental combinations.

What develops at this time, according to Piaget, is the *symbolic function*, which is expressed by language, deferred imitation (imitating a model after a significant delay), gestures, symbolic play, and mental imagery. These varied mental abilities arise alongside the more action-based forms of intelligence during the latter part of the second year. During this substage, the cognitions of the sensorimotor stage begin to be internalized as representational thought, setting the stage for a revolutionary change in the nature of human intelligence.

Development of Operations

With the advent of symbols, children's thinking becomes uniquely human. We might not be the only thinking species, and other species may occasionally use symbols (Lyn & Savage-Rumbaugh, 2013; Savage-Rumbaugh et al., 1993), but the intellectual prowess that language, imagery, and deferred imitation provide us makes humans different from any other creature on the planet. In comparing the intellectual abilities of a 12-month-old infant, a 3-year-old child, and a 21-year-old adult, most would agree that, despite their vast age difference, the 3-year-old and the 21-year-old are more alike, cognitively speaking, than the 12-month-old and the 3-year-old. But no one would mistake a 3-year-old and 21-year-old as intellectual equals. Both the young child and the adult possess and use symbols, but there are many differences in their cognitions.

The three stages that follow the sensorimotor period are all similar in that children have symbolic (that is, mental representational) abilities, but they differ in how children are able to use these symbols for thought (Piaget & Inhelder, 1969). Piaget labeled these three stages preoperations, describing children's thinking between the ages of 2 and 7 years, concrete operations, occurring between the ages of 7 and 11 years, and formal operations, characterizing the advent of adult thinking and beginning about 11 years of age (see Table 5.1). As the names denote, each stage is characterized by operations (or in the case of preoperations, the lack of them). Most of Piaget's work beyond the period of infancy dealt, in one way or another, with the development of operations.

As we mentioned previously, operations are particular types of cognitive schemes, and they describe general ways that children act on their world. Piaget specified four characteristics of operations. First, they are mental; thus, they require the use of symbols. Second, operations derive from action, so operations can be thought of as internalized actions. For example, children will first count on their fingers or physically line up red checkers with an equal number of black checkers, discovering through action that the one-to-one correspondence between red and black checkers remains the same no matter where they start counting or how they arrange the pieces. Third, operations exist in an organized system. Piaget believed that all cognitive operations are integrated with all other operations, so a child's cognition at any particular time should be relatively even, or homogeneous. And fourth, operations follow a system of rules, the most critical of which is that of reversibility, the knowledge that an operation can be reversed or that, for any operation, another operation can compensate for the effects of the first. For example, in arithmetic, subtraction is the inverse of addition. If 5 plus 2 equals 7, then 7 minus 2 must equal 5. Such a rule would seem to be obviously critical in children's learning basic arithmetic. This brings to mind the 5-year-old who proudly announced to his mother that he had learned at school that 3 plus 2 equals 5. After praising him for his new knowledge, his mother asked him how much 2 plus 3 equaled, and the child answered that he didn't know; he hadn't learned that one yet. Reversibility is also reflected in the knowledge that a change in one dimension can be compensated by a change in another dimension. For example, if water is poured from a short, fat glass into a tall, thin glass, the increased height of the water level in the second glass is compensated by a decrease in the breadth of the water.

The following subsections give a general account of Piaget's description of the thought of preoperational, concrete operational, and formal operational children. Many other topics relating to the development of operations in Piaget's theory are discussed in later chapters.

Transition from preoperational to concrete operational thought. Piaget described preoperational thought, although based on symbols, as lacking the logical characteristics of concrete operations. By this, Piaget meant that operations do not generate contradictions. In contrast to concrete operational children, preoperational children are greatly influenced by the appearance of things, and their thought is said to be intuitive. Thus, young children are less affected by what, according to logic, must be and are more affected by what, according to appearance, seems to be.

Perhaps giving an example is the easiest way to explain the distinction between preoperational and concrete operational thought. Conservation, the realization that an entity remains the same despite changes in its form, is the sine qua non of concrete operations. For Piaget, conservation is not just a convenient task to illustrate cognitive differences among children; it represents the basis for all rational thinking (Piaget, 1932/1965). The concept of conservation can apply to any substance that can be quantified, and conservation has been

studied with respect to length, number, mass, weight, area, and volume. In general, Piaget's conservation tasks take the following form:

$$A = B$$
$$B \rightarrow B'$$
$$A\,?\,B'$$

In words, the equivalence between A and B is first established (for example, two balls of clay). Object B is then transformed while children watch (for example, rolling one ball of clay into a sausage). The children are then asked to judge the equivalence of the transformed object with the initial, unchanged object and to provide a justification for their decision. Basically, children must realize that the quantitative relation between the two objects remains the same despite changes in the appearance of one. You may recognize this as a form of the appearance/reality distinction discussed earlier. The question here is whether children realize that, despite changes in appearance, the actual amount of substance remains the same.

Piaget's conservation-of-liquid task is illustrated in Figure 5.3. A child is presented with two identical glasses containing equal amounts of water. A third glass is introduced that is taller and thinner than the original two containers. The water in one of the original glasses is then poured into the third, taller glass while the child watches. The water level in the new glass is, of course, higher than the water level in the original glass because of the newer glass's narrower width. The child is then asked if the two glasses have the same amount of water in them and to justify his or her answer.

Most 5-year-old children answer by saying no, the amounts of liquid are not the same anymore—there is more water in the new, taller glass. Ask them why this is so, and they will point out the difference in the height of the water. They will ignore the fact that the shorter glass is wider, and if this is pointed out to them, they will either dismiss it as insignificant or, in some cases, actually change their minds and tell you that there is more water in the shorter glass because it is so fat. They will admit that the water in the two glasses was the same to begin with, and they do not think that anyone is playing a trick on them. The difference in appearance between the water levels in the two glasses is too great for them to believe that the same amount of water is contained in both.

In contrast, most 8-year-olds given the same problem tell you that the two glasses still contain the same amount of water. When pressed to explain why, they say that all you did was pour the water from one glass to the other and that you could just as easily pour it back to confirm equivalence (reversibility). If you ask them "Why do they look so different then?" they will likely comment that although the water level is much higher in the tall, skinny glass, it is much wider in the short, fat glass and that the difference in height is made up by the difference in width. Children's responses to such questions are important, for in conservation problems, it is not sufficient just to provide the correct answer to demonstrate concrete operations; a justification that involves the concept of reversibility is also necessary.

This example demonstrates the intuitive thinking of the preoperational child. There really seems to be more water in the tall, skinny glass. In fact, most objective adults would probably concur, although we know that this cannot be so. The young child's intuitive approach to the problem leads to some contradictions, however. What happens when the water in the tall glass is returned to its original container? Most preoperational children will tell you that the amount of water in the two glasses is now the same as it was to begin with. The contradiction, however, is one of objective fact; there is no apparent contradiction to the child. Some cognitive discrepancy (disequilibrium) may be experienced by slightly older and cognitively more advanced children, who realize that something is not quite right but can't figure out exactly what it is. For Piaget, these children

FIGURE 5.3 **Piaget's conservation-of-liquid problem.**

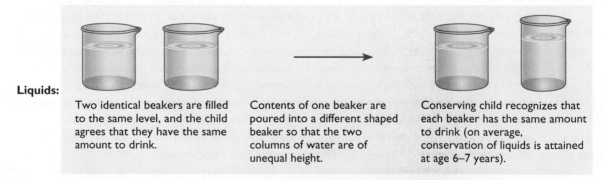

Liquids:

Two identical beakers are filled to the same level, and the child agrees that they have the same amount to drink.

Contents of one beaker are poured into a different shaped beaker so that the two columns of water are of unequal height.

Conserving child recognizes that each beaker has the same amount to drink (on average, conservation of liquids is attained at age 6–7 years).

Source: © Cengage Learning.

are in a transition phase between preoperations and concrete operations. Their cognitive structures are thrown into states of disequilibrium, and within a short time they will make the accommodations necessary to achieve conservation. No such disequilibrium is experienced by younger children; they assimilate the information to their preoperative schemes.

With a few mainly laboratory-based exceptions, conservation is not something that children are taught. The notion of conservation develops gradually, and once it is acquired, most children assume they always thought that way. Ask most 8-year-old conservers if they ever in their lives thought the glass with the higher water level had more water, and they will answer no—and often give you a funny look as

well. After all, why would an adult even ask such a question?

An operational knowledge of conservation does not develop simultaneously for all properties of material; conservation develops for some properties before others. Piaget referred to this phenomenon as *horizontal décalage*. When children acquire the concept of conservation for one property, they do not realize that the same general principle applies to other properties. Piaget claimed that the order in which conservation is acquired for different properties is constant across children. Thus, conservation of number is acquired before conservation of mass, and both of these are acquired before conservation of weight, which precedes the conservation of volume. Other researchers have generally confirmed this

TABLE 5.3 **Several Piagetian tasks that preoperational children "fail" and concrete operational children "pass."** Note, however, that subsequent research found that, under certain stimulus or training conditions, preoperational children could "solve" many of these tasks.

Conservation. The ability to realize that changes in the physical appearance of things have no influence on changes in their substantial, real properties, like number, length, area, mass, liquid weight, or volume. Children are first able to conserve number, followed by conservation of mass, and these are acquired before conservation of weight, which precedes the conservation of volume.

Multiple classification. The ability to classify objects simultaneously on two dimensions (size and shape, for instance). Preoperational children can classify objects on a single dimension (size or shape) but not both simultaneously. Concrete operational children realize that a woman can be both a mother and a daughter at the same time, something that preoperational children have a difficult time doing.

Class inclusion. The knowledge that a class must always be smaller than any more inclusive class in which it is contained. In a typical class-inclusion problem, children are given several examples from two subordinate categories of a single superordinate category (for example, seven pictures of dogs and three pictures of cats). They are then asked whether there are more dogs or more animals. Although preschool children can easily make correct numerical judgments when comparing two subordinate sets (for example, dogs versus cats), correct responses on class-inclusion problems are not found reliably until late childhood or early adolescence (see Winer, 1980).

Seriation. The ability to order objects according to the quantitative dimension of a certain trait, such as size. For example, concrete operational children can order a pair of scissors, a pen, and a paper clip by length.

Transitive inference. Ability to infer quantitative relationship between three or more elements. For example, if a concrete operational child is told that a pair of scissors is longer than a pen, and a pen is longer than a paper clip, he or she can infer that the pair of scissors is longer than the paper clip (that is, if A > B and B > C, therefore A > C). There is no need to actually check the difference in length between A and C.

pattern of development (for example, Brainerd & Brainerd, 1972; Uzgiris, 1964).

Conservation is only one of the many phenomena described by Piaget that concrete operational children "pass" and preoperational children "fail." Table 5.3 summarizes several other phenomena Piaget investigated that differentiate preoperational from concrete operational children.

Piaget's description of children's performance on conservation tasks illustrates the importance of the concept of reversibility, discussed earlier. Preoperational children, stated Piaget, are unable to apply the rules of reversibility to arrive at correct solutions to conservation problems. Preoperational and concrete operational children differ in ways other than reversibility, however. Generally, Piaget described preoperational children as being more influenced by their immediate perceptions and more egocentric, all relative to concrete operational children. These factors are discussed briefly in the following subsections.

Perceptual centration versus decentration. Preoperational children's perception is said to be centered in that they attend to and make judgments based on the most salient aspect of their perceptual fields, which Piaget referred to as perceptual centration. They are highly attentive to particular portions of a perceptual array and often are unable to integrate various parts into a whole. In the conservation-of-liquid problem discussed earlier, their attention is directed only to the difference in heights of the water levels, and they are unable (according to Piaget) to coordinate the two dimensions of height and width simultaneously. In contrast, concrete operational children's perception is said to be decentered in that they can divorce themselves from specific aspects of a perceptual array and attend to and make decisions based on the entire perceptual field, which Piaget referred to as perceptual decentration. Unlike their younger peers, they can consider two dimensions at once, partly because they are not so highly focused on one dimension that differences in the other escape their awareness.

Perceptual centration is not limited to young children's performance on laboratory tasks but is reflected in their everyday thinking. For example, Piaget (1929/1969) noted that preoperational children often use height as a means of estimating age. Take, for example, the 5-year-old who told her 35-year-old, 4-foot-11-inch mother that she was the "youngest mommy in the whole neighborhood." In actuality, she was the shortest mommy in the whole neighborhood and, if truth be known, one of the oldest among her daughter's friends.

Consider another example of young children interpreting age on the basis of height. As a young graduate student, I (DB) was finishing a day of testing at a kindergarten when I ran into the mother of one of the children. We talked for a while about the project, and then she said she was surprised to see that I was so young. She had questioned her son about me, and he had told her that I was older than his mother and much older than his teacher. In reality, I was 22 years old at the time, the child's mother looked to be in her early 30s, and his teacher was a woman nearing retirement. How could a 5-year-old child be so far off? The answer is that I am about 6 feet tall, the boy's mother was about 5 feet 3 inches, and his teacher was a petite woman, likely no more than 5 feet tall. To this child's mind (and eyes), I was a good "foot older" than his teacher.

Egocentricity. In general, Piaget described preoperational children as being more egocentric than older, concrete operational children. Piaget used the term egocentricity to describe young children's intellectual perspective. Young children interpret the world through preoperative eyes and generally assume that others see the world as they do. Their cognition is centered around themselves, and they have a difficult time putting themselves in someone else's shoes. Preoperational children are, of course, less egocentric than sensorimotor children, who know objects and events only by direct action on them. Yet young, preoperational children are more self-centered in cognitive perspective than concrete operational children.

According to Piaget, this egocentric perspective permeates young children's entire cognitive life, influencing their perceptions, their language, and their social interactions. For example, 6-year-old Jamal assumes that all children in the first grade have older siblings and can never be the eldest child in their family. Jamal himself is in first grade and has an older brother; therefore, all first-graders, if they have siblings at all, must have older siblings. Or consider, for example, my (DB) encounter with a neighbor child, Maurice, when I, and he, were about 6. Maurice asked about the ages of my parents. I told him I wasn't sure about their ages, but I knew that my mother was older than my father. Maurice quite emphatically told me that that was impossible. "Daddies are *always* older than mommies. It's the law." That evening, I talked to my parents and was told that my mother was, indeed, a few months older than my father and that this was perfectly legal in the state of Massachusetts. Maurice's assertions were related to the structure of his own family. His father was about 15 years older than his mother, so Maurice assumed that *all* fathers must be older than *all* mothers. There is also the fact that my father was nearly a foot taller than my mother, so Maurice's egocentrically based belief in age differences between mothers and fathers may

have been further influenced by his centering on the difference in height between my parents.

Like most other aspects of preoperational thought, the young child's egocentricity is viewed as ineffective—and in most situations, it is. However, there might be some adaptive advantage to a young child's egocentricity (Bjorklund, 1997b; Bjorklund & Green, 1992). From a global perspective, young children should be self-centered and less concerned with the thoughts, feelings, and behaviors of others. They are universal novices and need to learn the complicated ways of their culture, making a self-centered perspective for young children likely to be beneficial from a Darwinian point of view. For instance, research with both adults and children has shown that when information is related to oneself (for example, when one is asked to determine how words on a list or events in a story relate to you), it is remembered better than when no self-referencing is done (Ross, Anderson, & Campbell, 2011). Young children's tendencies to relate new information to themselves might thus give them a learning advantage, making egocentricity beneficial and not detrimental for the young child (see Bjorklund & Sellers, 2014).

Transition from concrete to formal operational thought. Children in the concrete operational stage are impressive thinkers. Compared to preoperational children, they can reverse thought (as reflected by their answers to conservation problems), can decenter their perception, and are less egocentric. Given a set of data, they can arrive at an answer (generally) free of contradictions. They can solve reasonably complex problems as long as the general form of the problem and of the solution are previously known to them. Their thought is directed to the objects and events in their immediate experience, and thinking about things suffices to get most people, of any age, through most of the routine tasks of everyday life.

Most of us also recognize, however, that a change takes place in early adolescence. Children are no longer tied to thinking about concrete objects. Their thoughts can roam to discover or invent objects, events, and relations independent of their previous experiences. Their thinking is no longer restricted to things but can be applied to itself. As one Piagetian scholar put it, "Concrete operations consist of thought thinking about the environment, but formal operations consist of thought thinking about itself" (Brainerd, 1978, p. 215).

The benchmark of formal operations is what Piaget referred to as **hypothetico-deductive reasoning** (Inhelder & Piaget, 1958). Deductive reasoning, which entails going from the general to the specific, is not in itself a formal operational process. Concrete operational children can arrive at a correct conclusion if they are provided with the proper evidence. However, their reasoning is confined to events and objects with which they are already familiar. Concrete operations are so named because children's thinking is limited to tangible facts and objects; it does not include hypotheses. Formal operational children, on the other hand, are not restricted to thinking about previously acquired facts but can generate hypotheses—for these children, what is possible is more important than what is real.

Thinking during the formal operational period can be done solely on the basis of symbols, with no need for referents in real life. Although this might bring to mind a person whose head is perpetually in the clouds and who cannot carry on a conversation without getting into metaphysics, this was not Piaget's intention. Rather, we have a person who is not tied to facts in his or her thinking but can postulate *what might be* as well as *what is*. The formal operational thinker can generate ideas of things not yet experienced, accounting for the novel (to the child) and often-grand ideas adolescents generate concerning morality, ethics, justice, government, and religion. Adolescents are entering, cognitively, the adult arena and ponder many of the weighty issues of the day without having had to experience directly the things they think about. The theories of most adolescents are naive because of their limited knowledge, but Piaget believed these children are flexing their mental muscles, using their newly acquired symbolic skills to deal with ideas rather than with things.

Hypothetical thinking is also critical for most forms of mathematics beyond arithmetic. If $2x + 5 = 15$, what does x equal? The problem does not deal with concrete entities, such as apples or oranges, but with numbers and letters. Mathematics in general is based on hypotheses and not necessarily in reality. Let y be 22, or let it be 7, or -12, or 45 degrees, or the cosine of angle AB. Once provided with a premise, formal operational thinkers can go on to solve the problem. They don't ask, "Is y *really* 22?" It is an arbitrary, hypothetical problem—and one that can be answered only if it is approached abstractly, using a symbol system that does not require concrete referents.

In addition to developing deductive reasoning abilities, formal operational children are able to think inductively, Piaget theorized, going from specific observations to broad generalizations. **Inductive reasoning** is the type of thinking that characterizes scientists, in which hypotheses are generated and then systematically tested in experiments. By controlling for extraneous or potentially confounding factors, experiments lead to conclusions about nature. Bärbel Inhelder and Piaget (1958) used a series of tasks to assess scientific reasoning, one of which, the *pendulum problem*, we discuss briefly.

In the pendulum problem, children are given a rod from which strings of different lengths can be suspended. Objects of varying weight can be attached to the strings. The children are shown how the pendulum operates (one places a weighted string on the rod and swings it) and are asked to determine the factors responsible for the speed with which the pendulum swings (the rate of oscillation) (see Figure 5.4). The children are told that in addition to varying the length of the string and the weight of the object attached to it, they can drop the object from varying heights (for example, high versus low) and alter the force of the push they give the object when initially propelling it. Thus, in attempting to solve the problem of the oscillating pendulum, the children can consider four possible factors (string length, weight of object, height of release, and force of push), with several levels within each factor (for example, three lengths of string, four weights of objects). The children are given the opportunity to experiment with the apparatus before providing an answer to the question of which factors are responsible for the pendulum's rate of oscillations. (The correct answer is the length of the string—short strings swing faster than long strings, regardless of all other factors.)

How might a scientist go about solving this problem? The first step is to generate a hypothesis. It doesn't matter if the hypothesis is correct or not, merely that it be testable and yield noncontradictory conclusions. This initial step is within the ability of concrete operational children. The next step is what separates the concrete from the formal operational thinkers—the testing of one's hypothesis. The trick is to vary a single factor while holding the others constant. For example, a child might examine the rate of oscillation for the 100-gram weight in combination with all the other factors (that is, short string, high release, easy push; short string, high release, hard push; short string, low release, short push; and so on). This can then be done for other weights, until the child has tested all of the various combinations.

Concrete operational children often get off to a good start on this problem, but they rarely arrive at the correct answer. Their observations are generally accurate (which is not the case for preoperational children), but they usually fail to isolate relevant variables and will arrive at a conclusion before exhaustively testing their hypotheses. For example,

FIGURE 5.4 **The pendulum problem.** Children are to determine what factors or combination of factors are responsible for the rate at which the pendulum oscillates.

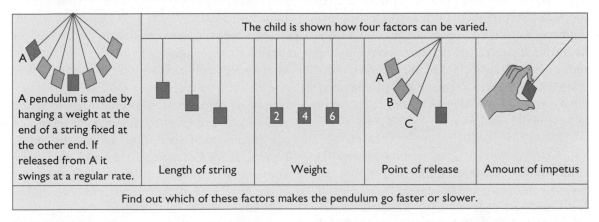

Source: © Cengage Learning.

children might observe that the pendulum swings fast with a short string and a heavy weight and then conclude that both string length and weight are jointly responsible for the rate of oscillation. According to Inhelder and Piaget (1958), it is not until the formal operational stage that children can test their hypotheses correctly and arrive at the only possible, logical conclusion. More is said about scientific reasoning in Chapter 7.

A further formal operational characteristic involves the ability to examine the contents of one's thought, or to *think about thinking*. Concrete operational thinkers have available to them some powerful problem-solving skills. But according to Piaget, they are not able to reflect on the content of their thinking to arrive at new insights. Concrete operational children gain knowledge from the outside world but cannot learn anything new by contemplating what they already know. In contrast, formal operational children can acquire new information as a result of internal reflection. Piaget (1971) used the term reflective abstraction to refer to "a rearrangement, by means of thought, of some matter previously presented to the subject in a rough or immediate form" (p. 320). In other words, formal operational children can reflect on knowledge they already possess and, without needing additional information from the external environment, arrive at a previously unknown truth. Reflective abstraction is thinking about thinking, and it might allow a child to apply more readily information that he or she knows to new situations or to discover alternative cognitive routes to solving old problems.

Egocentricity in adolescence. One interesting observation Piaget made about adolescents that ties their cognition to that of much younger children concerns egocentricity, which is usually associated with preoperational thought. Piaget,

however, defined egocentrism broadly, as an inability to decenter, and proposed that adolescents demonstrate their own form of centration.

Piaget stated that adolescents are concerned about their future in society, and often with how they might transform society, but many of the grand social and political ideas of adolescents conflict with the beliefs or attitudes of others (particularly people in authority). Adolescents also might believe that these abstract ideas are unique to them, making them impatient with the "stodgy and simple-minded" ideas of their elders. This view changes as the adolescent approaches adulthood, with adults demonstrating a better ability to reflect on their own motivations and the motivations of others. Many of us can identify with Mark Twain, who (supposedly) professed to be impressed by how much his father had learned between Twain's 14th and 21st birthdays.

Adolescence is a time when young people are trying to leave childhood behind and adopt adult roles, an attempt that often results in extreme self-consciousness. Adolescents' self-centered perspectives result in the mistaken belief that other people are as concerned with their feelings and behavior as they are, which only enhances their self-consciousness. David Elkind (1967; Elkind & Bowen, 1979) hypothesized that adolescents feel they are constantly "on stage" or playing to an imaginary audience. This hypothesis has been confirmed in several studies, where adolescents' responses to potentially embarrassing situations and their tendencies to reveal aspects of themselves to others were related to age and formal operational abilities (Elkind & Bowen, 1979; Galanaki, 2012). Although there are some discrepancies in the findings, the effect of the imaginary audience seems to peak during early adolescence and to decline as formal operational skills increase.

Elkind also proposed that the egocentrism of adolescence leads to what he called the personal fable, a belief in one's uniqueness and invulnerability. This is reflected in the often-reckless behavior of adolescents and the belief that bad things happen only to other people (for example, "I won't get pregnant," or "I can get off the tracks before the train gets here") (Vartanian, 2000).

In one study, Smita Banerjee and colleagues (2015) explored how imaginary audience and personal fable ideations influence modern adolescents' attitudes and intentions toward indoor tanning. Although it is widely held that indoor tanning increases risk of skin cancer, many adolescents persist in their patronage of tanning parlors. Consistent with Elkind, Banerjee and colleagues (2015) proposed that adolescents who perceive an imaginary audience of admiring (or critical) peers are more self-conscious and motivated to appear attractive, leading to appearance-enhancing behaviors, such as indoor tanning. They also considered that adolescents who believe in their own personal fables should be more likely to associate with peers who engage in risk-taking, as this reinforces their perception of reduced susceptibility. These researchers measured the extent to which male and female adolescents had developed *personal fables* by asking them to report on perceptions of their own vulnerability, uniqueness, and omnipotence (feeling capable of anything). To assess the perception they were being viewed by an imaginary audience, the adolescents were asked to report, for instance, how often they would feel embarrassed at not being invited to a party. They also reported how many of their peers used tanning beds and whether they intended to use tanning beds themselves. The results indicated that there was a direct relationship between an adolescent's attitudes and intentions toward tanning salons and his or her imaginary audience ideations. This relationship was strongest for those whose peers also used tanning beds. In other words, adolescents who felt more strongly that they were always "onstage" before an audience of peers were more motivated to use indoor tanning and seemed to be more strongly influenced by the behavior of their peers in terms of their own attitudes and intentions toward tanning. Similarly, the extent to which adolescent participants felt invulnerable predicted their association with friends who used tanning beds as well as their own intentions to engage in indoor tanning. What do these findings tell us about egocentricity and risk-taking during adolescence?

The risk-taking and narcissistic behavior that springs from adolescents' egocentricity clearly has its drawbacks, but it might also have some adaptive value, just as preschool children's egocentricity might (Hill & Lapsley, 2011). For example, teenage egocentricity ensures that adolescents will experiment with new ideas and generally behave more independently (Bjorklund & Green, 1992). Many of these experiences will be beneficial to adult functioning and might hasten entry into adult life. Many parents do not welcome such independence, of course, for the negative consequences of much adolescent risk-taking are real, but for most adolescents, their egocentricity might be adaptive in the long run. Moreover, their sense of psychological invulnerability ("I won't get my feelings hurt," "I don't care what other people think") seems to promote positive coping and adjustment mechanisms (Hill, Duggan, & Lapsley, 2012).

Piaget saw adolescence as a time of great intellectual awakening rather than a time of emotional storm and strife. But few scientists today believe that Piaget's picture of adolescent (and adult) intelligence as reasonable, systematic, and logical is correct. Adults in general are not nearly as logical in their thinking as Piaget would have us be. We take mental shortcuts, make estimations, and arrive at conclusions before exhausting all possibilities. In fact, formal operational thinking does not seem to be typically used by adults in daily life (Capon & Kuhn, 1979), and it is rare in cultures where formal schooling is not the norm (Cole, 1990; Dasen, 1977). Moreover, among educated people from developed cultures, formal operational abilities may be used in some contexts but not others. For instance, when college students were given a series of formal operational problems to solve, they tended to perform best when the problems were in their area of expertise—physics majors on physics problems (the pendulum problem), political science majors on political problems, and English majors on literary problems (De Lisi & Staudt, 1980; see Figure 5.5). Piaget's description of

formal operations may reflect the best adults can do, but it fails to capture how grown-ups deal with real-world problems on a daily basis. To quote Peter Wason and Philip Johnson-Laird (1972), "At best, we can all think like logicians: At worst, logicians all think like us" (p. 245). Even with its shortcomings, however, Piaget's account of adolescent thought captures some of the uniqueness of adolescence and has provided insight to psychologists, educators, and parents about the teenage mind.

Culture and Symbolic Development

The description Piaget and others have provided of cognitive development is intended to be universal: Children across the globe develop the use of symbolic representation at about the same time and in the same manner. Culture, however, does matter. As we noted in Chapter 3 when discussing sociocultural perspectives of development, the culture that a child grows up in not only limits *what* that child thinks about but also *how* the child thinks. How might culture influence thinking as studied by Piaget?

Although Piaget argued that the developmental sequence for attaining the various accomplishments of concrete operations is universal, there are individual differences in the rate at which conservation and other concrete operational abilities are achieved. Cultural differences in the rate of attaining conservation have been repeatedly observed, with most studies finding a slower rate of development for nonschooled children relative to schooled children (Dasen, 1977). Yet these cultural differences in the rate of development might be attributed less to differences in the actual competence of these children than to cultural differences in the nature of the tasks and how they are administered. For example, in

FIGURE 5.5 **Percentage of college students displaying formal thought.** College students performed best on formal-operational problems in their area of expertise—physics majors on physics problems, political science majors on political science problems, and English majors on literary problems.

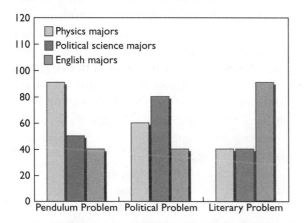

Source: De Lisi, R., & Staudt, J. (1980). Individual differences in college students' performance on formal operations tasks. *Journal of Applied Developmental Psychology, 1, 163–174.*

many studies, children from traditional cultures were tested either through interpreters or in their second or third language (see Nyiti, 1982). This contrasts sharply with the way that American or European children are tested and makes it difficult to interpret differences in performance found between these groups.

For example, in a study of conservation, Raphael Nyiti (1982) compared two cultural groups of Canadian children: Europeans (White and English speaking) and Micmacs (a First Nations people of eastern Canada). The Micmac children attended school, where they learned English, but they spoke their native language (Micmac) at home. Both the European and Micmac children were given a series of conservation tasks, following standard Piagetian procedures. The European children were all tested in English. The Micmac children were divided into two groups, with half being tested in English by a European and the other half being tested in Micmac by a Micmac. No difference was found in how the European and Micmac children performed the tasks when tested in their "home" language—European children in English and Micmac children in Micmac. When the Micmac children were tested in English by a European examiner, however, they gave much shorter and less complete answers, and they were significantly less likely to be classified as conservers than their European counterparts. These results bolster Piaget's contention that certain aspects of cognitive development are universal and that concepts such as conservation develop on a predictable schedule in all cultures. This truism can be overlooked, however, if one is not mindful of the cultural context in which performance is assessed.

Cultural differences have also been found in the attainment of formal operations, with adults from nonschooled cultures often failing to display formal operational thinking, at least as measured by Piaget. People who lack formal schooling might not have had sufficient exposure to the kinds of thinking that stress logic, mathematics, and science—experiences that Piaget believed help children to reason at the formal level (Cole, 1990; Dasen, 1977). Indeed, Steven Tulkin and Melvin Konner (1973) found that preliterate Bushman hunters who fail Piaget's problems often do reason at the formal level on at least one task—tracking prey. Clearly, this is an activity of great importance to them that requires the systematic testing of inferences and hypotheses.

Consider children's classification abilities. In the 1930s, Russian neuropsychologist Alexander Luria (1976) evaluated the cognitive styles of inhabitants from a remote area in the former Soviet Union (Uzbekistan) and reported that, unlike Westerners, most of the adults he studied did not develop a conceptual, or taxonomic, way of classifying objects. Rather, they used a more functional approach, one perhaps better suited for their ecology. Consider the following example from Rakmat, a 38-year-old illiterate peasant (Luria, 1976):

He is shown drawings of the following: *hammer-saw-log-hatchet.*

"They're all alike. I think all of them have to be here. See, if you're going to saw, you need a saw, and if you have to split something you need a hatchet. So they're all needed here."

We tried to explain the task by another, simpler example: "Look, here you have three adults and one child. Now clearly the child doesn't belong in this group."

"Oh, but the boy must stay with the others! All three of them are working, you see, and if they have to keep running out to fetch things, they'll never get the job done, but the boy can do the running for them. . . . The boy will learn; that'll be better, then they'll be able to work well together." (p. 55)

Subject is then shown drawing of: *bird-rifle-dagger-bullet.*

"The swallow doesn't fit here. . . . No . . . this is a rifle. It's loaded with a bullet and kills the swallow. Then you have to cut the bird up with the dagger, since there's no other way to do it. . . . What I said about the swallow before is wrong! All these things go together." (pp. 56–57)

When we look at the way illiterate Uzbekistani peasants classify objects, we might feel tempted to evaluate them as being less cognitively advanced than the classifications used by Western people. (In fact, a functional type of classification is typical of many 5-year-old children in Western societies.) However, this would be a mistake, for these differences in classification style are, in fact, well suited to the local environment.

Culture certainly counts in shaping children's thinking. However, children across the globe possess the same set of symbolic abilities, and these abilities develop in much the same fashion. What seems to differ is how children in different cultures express their symbolic abilities, not the abilities themselves.

State of Piaget's Theory Today

Piaget is a giant in the field of human development. As one scholar quoted by Harry Beilin (1992) put it, "Assessing the impact of Piaget on developmental psychology is like assessing the impact of Shakespeare on English literature or Aristotle on philosophy—impossible" (p. 191). But what does Piaget's theory, initially formulated nearly a century ago, tell us about development today? Table 5.4 lists some of the major contributions that Piaget made to the field of cognitive development.

The list is based, in part, on an assessment of Piaget's contributions made by several prominent researchers, written in honor of the centennial of Piaget's birth (see papers in Brainerd, 1996).

Piaget's theory has undergone more scrutiny than any other theory in cognitive development, and nearly 50 years of intense investigation (some would say 50 years of Piaget bashing) has shown that Piaget's theory is not the final word. For example, children often display greater abilities than Piaget proposed. For instance, we saw in Chapter 4 that infants display what appear to be glimmers of representational thought much earlier than Piaget proposed (Spelke & Kinzler, 2007). And we'll see later in this chapter that children may be capable of concrete operations and reasoning about cause and effect relationships much earlier than Piaget proposed (A. Gopnik et al., 2004). In later chapters, we explore at least rudimentary evidence that infants, in their first year of life, show deferred imitation, a landmark measure of the symbolic function for Piaget (P. J. Bauer, 2007), and represent other people as intentional agents (Tomasello & Carpenter, 2007).

Perhaps most research has focused on Piaget's underestimation of the representational abilities of preschool children. This is illustrated by studies examining preoperational children's egocentricity. For instance, preschool children can identify and empathize with the emotions of others (Hoffman, 1975), can take the visual perspective of another person (Borke, 1975), and can realize that they possess knowledge that others do not share (see discussion of the development of theory of mind in Chapter 6). In fact, research during the last 4 decades has indicated that Piaget underestimated the perspective-taking abilities of young children and that egocentricity is far from an all-or-none matter.

Other researchers have shown that children who do not spontaneously solve problems in a

TABLE 5.4 **Contributions of Piaget to the study of cognitive development.**

1. Piaget founded the field of cognitive development as we know it. The study of children's thinking has focused on high-level cognitive tasks, very different from the emphasis on basic-level and mainly unconscious cognition that has characterized the study of adult cognition. Because of Piaget, cognitive development is a unique field to itself and not simply the application of ideas and methods developed in the study of adult cognition to children.

2. The child is an active, self-motivated agent, playing an important role in his or her own development. This might seem obvious to anyone today who has seriously considered the nature of cognitive development, but it was an innovation of Piaget and counter to the dominant perspective of his time.

3. Piaget's equilibration model was one of the first attempts to explain, rather than just describe, the process of development. Despite the many years since Piaget originally formulated this model, only recently have psychologists taken seriously the challenge to explain, rather than just describe, developmental transitions.

4. Piaget introduced many interesting and useful concepts to cognitive development, including *scheme*, *object permanence*, *egocentrism*, *centration*, *decentration*, and *conservation*, among many others. Accompanying these concepts were many experimental tasks used to assess them, many of which are still used by psychologists today.

5. Piaget provided a highly memorable description of cognitive development that gave a relatively accurate picture of how children of different ages think. Piaget's description of development still captures much of the richness and uniqueness of children's thinking. Children can, under certain circumstances, be trained or biased to think in a more advanced way, but such training is usually limited and rarely transforms the child into a totally different type of thinker. In other words, Piaget's description of intellectual development has ecological validity in that it depicts well the day-to-day functioning of most children.

6. Piaget's influence extended beyond the field of cognitive development to other areas of development (social, emotional) and, importantly, to education.

7. Piaget made more important empirical discoveries, on a wider range of topics, than any other developmental psychologist, and he is not likely to be displaced from this lofty seat of honor soon.

8. Finally, Piaget asked important questions and drew literally thousands of researchers to the study of cognitive development. And as often happens when heuristic theories such as Piaget's are repeatedly scrutinized, some of his research led to new insights.

Source: This list is based, in part, on an assessment of Piaget's contributions made by several prominent researchers, written in honor of the centennial of Piaget's birth. (See Brainerd, C. F. [1996]. Piaget: A centennial celebration. *Psychological Science, 7,* 191–195.)

concrete operational way can be trained to do so. For example, although scientists have replicated the stages involved in the acquisition of conservation proposed by Piaget (Brainerd & Brainerd, 1972), many have demonstrated that children as young as 4 years of age can be trained to conserve by way of a variety of techniques, at least in the laboratory (Brainerd & Allen, 1971; R. Gelman, 1969). Other researchers have successfully trained concrete operational children to perform formal operational tasks (Adey & Shayer, 1992; C. A. Stone & Day, 1978).

In still other situations, research has shown that Piaget's account of formal operations greatly overestimates how adults actually think (Capon & Kuhn, 1979; De Lisi & Staudt, 1980). For example, Noel Capon and Deanna Kuhn (1979) investigated whether adults tend to use formal operational abilities in a practical task. These researchers interviewed 50 women in a supermarket and asked them to judge which of two sizes of the same product was the better buy. For example, one task involved two bottles of garlic powder: a smaller bottle containing 1.25 ounces (35 grams) selling for 41 cents and a larger bottle containing 2.37 ounces (67 grams) selling for 77 cents. The women were provided with pencil and paper to use if they wished and were asked to justify their explanations. The most direct way to arrive at the correct answer is to compute the price per unit of weight for each product and then compare the two. This involves reasoning about proportions, which Inhelder and Piaget (1958) said was a scheme characteristic of formal operations. Fewer than 30% of the women used a proportional reasoning strategy, however, and at least 50% of the women used a strategy that yielded inconclusive evidence at best and was just as likely to be wrong as to be right. For instance, some women used a subtraction strategy, saying, for example, "With the bigger one you get 32 more grams for 36 more cents," concluding that the bigger one was thus the better buy. Others merely relied on their past experiences, making statements such as "The big one must be cheaper" without providing any justification for the statement. In general, formal operational reasoning was not observed for a majority of these women. This does not mean that these adults would not have displayed formal reasoning under some other conditions, but it does suggest that formal operations are not typical of adult thought in general.

Researchers have also questioned Piaget's stage account of development. Children are not as even, or homogeneous, in their cognitive abilities as Piaget's stage theory suggests. For example, a particular child may display a highly egocentric attitude in one situation but show impressive perspective-taking skills in another. The success of training studies mentioned earlier, for example, indicates that, in some contexts, children can acquire a skill that would otherwise have to wait for several years, or can show advanced cognitive abilities in one context (knowledge of the win-loss percentage of favorite NASCAR drivers, for example) but not in a related context (long-division problems in school). As an aside, we know of no studies that have taught children to conserve on a laboratory task and then examined the transfer of this ability to everyday life. Will a 4-year-old child who has been taught to conserve liquid or mass be fooled when her sandwich is cut into four pieces instead of two at lunch? Cognitive development is more heterogeneous, or variable, both across and within stages than Piaget proposed, and his whole notion of underlying cognitive structures as the basis for cognitive development has been seriously questioned.

Such findings challenge Piaget's notion of stages of development that represent qualitatively unique forms of thinking, with transitions between stages reflecting discontinuities in development (see Brainerd, 1978). As John Flavell (1978) wrote, "However much we may wish it otherwise, human cognitive growth may simply be too contingent, multiform, and heterogeneous—too variegated in developmental mechanisms, routes, and rates—to be accurately characterized by any single stage theory of the Piagetian kind" (p. 187).

Yet homogeneity of cognitive function is a relative thing. Although most researchers concur that cognitive development is not as uniform as Piaget proposed, most children's thinking most of the time can be described as being well integrated and relatively consistent. For example, Robbie

Case (1992) acknowledged that children's thinking is more heterogeneous, or uneven, than proposed by Piaget and is likely governed by many domain-specific mechanisms; nonetheless, he argued that some important aspects of cognition are likely under the influence of a domain-general mechanism, much as proposed by Piaget, and are relatively unfluctuating. In sum, Piaget's account of development does not fully capture what actually occurs, but it does provide a reasonable picture of the behavior of most children most of the time and a good jumping-off point for further investigation.

Section Review

Jean Piaget's theory of intellectual development has had a profound impact on how we view children, their thinking, and their development. Piaget believed that *schemes* are systematic patterns of actions or mental operations that underlie intelligence, and he viewed children as being intrinsically active and, thus, largely responsible for their own development. Piaget also believed that cognition is a constructive process and that our current state of knowledge influences how we perceive and process new information.

Some Assumptions of Piaget's Theory

- Piaget described the *functional invariants* of *organization* and *adaptation* as processes that are characteristic of all biological systems (including intelligence) and that operate throughout the life span.
- Organization is an organism's tendency to integrate structures into higher-order systems or structures.
- Adaptation is the process of adjustment the organism goes through in response to the environment. This process has two complementary components: *Assimilation* is the structuring of environmental input to fit a child's current schemes, and *accommodation* is the structuring of the child's schemes to match environmental data.
- Piaget proposed *equilibration* as a mechanism for development. When confronted with information that cannot be assimilated into existing structures, one enters a state of cognitive incongruity, or disequilibrium. When disequilibrium is resolved by accommodation, a new, more stable scheme results.

Stages of Development

- Piaget postulated four major stages, or periods, of cognitive development. These are the *sensorimotor* (from birth to about 2 years), *preoperations* (between 2 and 7 years), *concrete operations* (between 7 and 11 years), and *formal operations* (between 11 and 16 years).
- During the sensorimotor period children's thinking is limited to their own actions on objects. Piaget also described six substages during the sensorimotor period.
- During the earliest substages of the sensorimotor period, cognition is limited to inherited reflexes and simple extensions of these reflexes. *Goal-directed behavior* is seen first in Substage 4. Infants become capable of mentally representing environmental events in the final substage of the sensorimotor period.
- Sometime from 18 to 24 months, children begin to use symbols, exemplified by language, imagery, symbolic play, and deferred imitation. From this point on, development consists of the acquisition of operations.
- Piaget proposed four characteristics of *operations*: (1) They are mental, (2) they are derived from action, (3) they integrate with one another, and (4) they can be reversed.
- Piaget considered the thought of preoperational children to be intuitive, in contrast

with the logical thought of concrete operational children.

- Differences between preoperational and concrete operational children are displayed on many tasks, the most critical of which is *conservation*. Conservation represents the cognitive constancy of quantitative relations and refers to the knowledge that the quantity of a substance remains the same despite a perceptual transformation of that substance.
- The thought of preoperational children lacks *reversibility*, the knowledge that an operation can be reversed or that, for any operation, another operation can compensate for the effects of the first.
- Piaget described the perception of preoperational children as being *centered* on the most salient aspects of a perceptual array, in contrast with the *decentered* perception of concrete operational children.
- Preoperational children are said to be *egocentric*, in that they have a difficult time seeing the perspective (visual, communicative, or social) of another.
- The major factor in the transition from concrete to formal operations is the advent of *hypothetico-deductive reasoning*, in which thinking can be done solely in terms of symbols, without need for referents in real life. The child can think about what is possible as well as what is real.
- Piaget described the formal operational child as being able to think like a scientist, or to use *inductive reasoning*. Formal operational children are able to think about thinking, or to reflect on the outcome of their own thought (*reflective abstraction*).
- Adolescents display a form of egocentrism reflected in their feeling as if they are constantly "onstage" or playing to an *imaginary audience* as well as a belief in their uniqueness and invulnerability, which Elkind referred to as the *personal fable*.

Culture and Symbolic Development and State of Piaget's Theory Today

- Although Piaget believed his stages of development were universal, cultural differences can influence rate of development.
- Although Piaget's account of the development of operations has generated tremendous interest for more than 8 decades, research investigating his account has frequently been critical. Piaget often underestimated the cognitive competencies of children, and numerous studies have demonstrated that children can be easily trained to display both concrete and formal operational abilities. Young children can display sophisticated cognitive processing in certain situations and, in general, are less homogeneous in cognitive functioning than Piaget proposed.

Ask Yourself . . .

3. What are the critical concepts necessary to understand Piaget's description of cognitive development? Provide examples.
4. What are the most distinctive characteristics of thinking at each of Piaget's four major stages of cognitive development?
5. What are some major milestones during the sensorimotor stage?
6. What are operations, according to Piaget?
7. How does the conservation task demonstrate the differences in thinking between preoperational and concrete operational children?
8. How does an egocentric child think and behave? At what stage do children begin to transition away from being egocentric?
9. What are some major milestones in the transition from concrete to formal operations?
10. In what ways does egocentrism re-emerge in adolescence?

11. How does culture influence stagelike development? Provide examples.
12. What are the major contributions and criticisms of Piaget's theory of cognitive development?

EVERYDAY EXPRESSIONS OF THE SYMBOLIC FUNCTION

In this section, we provide a more detailed look at two aspects of the symbolic function that reflect not just what children say and do when being interviewed by psychologists but also how their developing symbolic abilities are expressed in their daily activities: symbolic play and distinguishing between fantasy and reality.

Symbolic Play

Play is usually seen as a "purposeless" activity, in that it is done voluntarily and without any obvious immediate function (Rubin, Fein, & Vandenberg, 1983). Children play for the sake of playing. Yet most people who have given the topic serious thought believe that play does, in fact, serve a number of functions (see Pellegrini, 2013b).

Symbolic play (or **fantasy play**), also called *pretend* or *make-believe play*, includes an "as if" orientation to objects, actions, and peers that advances during early childhood as a result of children's growing abilities to use symbols to represent something other than itself (Carlson, White, & Davis-Unger, 2014; Lillard, 2015). At its simplest, symbolic play involves substituting one thing for another in a playful setting. The simplest forms of symbolic play are first seen late in the second year of life, usually from 15 to 18 months of age, consistent with Piaget's (1962) observations. In fact, the absence of symbolic play at 18 months predicts a later diagnosis of autism (Baron-Cohen, Allen, & Gillberg, 1992). At this time, children substitute perceptually similar objects for the real thing. For instance, a banana may be used as a telephone, or children may take an empty teacup, put it to their lips, and make drinking noises. For older children, the physical similarity between the objects they use in play and the real things diminishes. For instance, a 3-year-old child may take a baby bottle and comb her doll's hair with it (R. Kelly et al., 2011; Ungerer et al., 1981).

Although symbolic play can be solitary (for example, a child pretending he is driving a car or making a phone call), most such play, especially for children beyond 3 years of age, is social (for example, playing "doctor," "school," or "store" with other children) (Power, 2000). As we noted in Chapter 3, mothers in particular promote symbolic play in their preschool children (Lillard, 2015). One social form of symbolic play that is not seen until about 3 years of age is called **sociodramatic play**, in which children take on different roles and follow a story line as if they were in a theatrical performance. For example, children may play "school," taking turns as the teacher and the student and follow a script that involves what children think goes on at school. Sociodramatic play requires more than using one object as a substitute for another; children must also be able to represent the actions and thoughts of other people (if I'm a pretend teacher, you're a pretend student).

Symbolic play is virtually nonexistent until about 15 months of age, emerges around age 3, peaks from 5 to 7 years, and decreases thereafter (Lillard et al., 2013; Power, 2000). In contrast to language development (which we discuss more in Chapter 9), in play, production tends to precede comprehension. In other words, children are able to produce pretend actions and represent pretend objects at a younger age than they can understand or comprehend what someone else is pretending to do (Hopkins, Smith, & Lillard, 2013). When measured during preschool or in children's homes, symbolic play accounts for between 10% and 33% of children's waking time, making it one of the most frequent behaviors in which children of this age engage (Fein, 1981; Haight & Miller, 1993). Part of the decline in symbolic play during the school years may involve parents and, especially, teachers discouraging such play, as well as the increase in other types of playful activities, such as games (Lillard, 2011). Yet older children continue to engage in symbolic play from time to time, such as building LEGO "monsters" and other characters and inventing make-believe scenarios in which they interact, and many people claim to still pretend as adults (E. D. Smith & Lillard, 2012).

There are sex differences in the content or themes of symbolic play. For instance, girls are more apt to engage in various types of play parenting and in play involving relationships and families than are boys. In contrast, the themes of boys' symbolic play are more likely to involve aggression, power, and dominance, frequently finding their expression in rough-and-tumble play (often involving superheroes). Such play may serve to prepare both girls and boys for roles they would have played in traditional environments. Girls' symbolic play also tends to be more complicated, as reflected by the use of language, and to last longer than that of boys (Pellegrini & Bjorklund, 2004).

Symbolic and sociodramatic play are strongly influenced by culture (Gaskins, Haight, & Lancy, 2007). In all cultures, children's symbolic play is based on the materials they have available (various toys, or cardboard boxes that can be used as spaceships for children in contemporary society, for instance) and on the activities and roles of adults in their culture that they can emulate during play. For example, children from traditional cultures are more likely to include real or toy tools and imitation of real adult work in their symbolic play than children from developed countries. This is because children from hunter-gatherer or horticultural societies are more likely to observe adults at work on a daily basis than are children in schooled cultures (see Chapter 3). In some traditional societies, children are given toy tools, often made by their parents, to use in play. For instance, among the Parakanas of the Amazon rainforest, mothers give their daughters small baskets, and fathers give their sons toy bows and arrows, both tools that adults use and that children then use in their play. Four- to 6-year-old Parakana girls make small baskets with palm leaves, imitating their mothers' activities, although the baskets are not strong enough to be useful. By 8 years of age, however, most girls are making functional baskets (Gosso et al., 2005).

Contemporary researchers see symbolic play not only as an expression of the symbolic function, as Piaget did, but as serving a crucial role in promoting cognitive development. For example, according to Laura Berk and her colleagues (2006), symbolic play stimulates children's brains to focus on learning. This is supported by research that finds that children who engage in more symbolic play display higher levels of language development, perspective taking, and executive-function abilities (Berk et al., 2006; Pierucci et al., 2014). We discussed executive functions briefly in Chapter 1 and examine its development more thoroughly in Chapter 7. Executive function refers to the processes involved in regulating attention and in determining what to do with information just gathered or retrieved from long-term memory, and individual differences in executive function measured during the preschool years predict academic, social, and emotional competencies later in life (e.g., Berk & Meyers, 2013; Carlson & White, 2013). Although most of this research is correlational in nature, one study experimentally manipulated 3- to 5-year-old children's fantasy play experiences and reported that children who participated in a fantasy pretend-play intervention showed greater improvements in executive function than children in a nonimaginative play intervention (Thibodeau et al., 2016). According to Clancy Blair and Adele Diamond (2008), "During social pretend play, children must hold their own role and those of others in mind (working memory), inhibit acting out of character (employ inhibitory control), and flexibly adjust to twists and turns in the evolving plot (mental flexibility); all three of the core executive functions thus get exercise" (p. 907). In fact, Mark Nielsen (2012) proposed that fantasy play, in addition to imitation, is a critical feature of human childhood and played a central role in the evolution of human intelligence. According to Nielsen (2012), "By pretending children thus develop a capacity to generate and reason with novel suppositions and imaginary scenarios, and in so doing may get to practice the creative process that underpins innovation in adulthood" (p. 176).

Distinguishing Between Fantasy and Reality

Related to fantasy play is children's ability to distinguish what they imagine from what they experience. In other words, do children realize that thinking or imagining something is distinct from actually doing or experiencing something? Does pretending make it real? At one level, even young children clearly know the difference between imagining and doing. For example, although dreams can seem quite real to people of any age, apparently even 3- and 4-year-olds know the difference between dreams and reality, although many 3-year-olds seem to believe that the same dream is experienced by different people (Woolley & Wellman, 1992) and that dreams are highly controllable (Woolley & Boerger, 2002). Children seem to make these distinctions categorically. They seem to maintain separate schemes for different pretend worlds and games, knowing, for instance, that Mickey Mouse does not interact with Spider-Man (Skolnick & Bloom, 2006; Skolnick Weisberg & Bloom, 2009). Occasionally this categorization scheme leads to errors in the fantasy-reality distinction. For example, 3- to 8-year-old children are more apt than adults to state that fantasy characters (for example, anthropomorphized animals such as a smiling ant) are real, although it takes children longer to make such decisions about fantasy stimuli relative to "real" stimuli, reflective of their uncertainty about how to think about fantasy items (Martarelli & Mast, 2013). In other situations, however, young children reject factual information as real because it is presented in a make-believe context. For instance, Marie-Louise Mares and Gayathri Sivakumar (2014) reported that after viewing *Dora the Explorer*, 3-year-olds were above chance in claiming that Spanish words are "just pretend" and "made up for the show." In their study, 4-year-olds were at chance, and only among 5-year-olds did a majority of participants say that the words were real.

Yet the ability to make the distinction between imagined and experienced events is far from complete by age 5. For example, in research evaluating developmental differences in **source monitoring**—the awareness of the origins of one's memories, knowledge, or beliefs—children and adults are asked to perform certain actions (for instance, "touch your nose") or to imagine performing certain actions (for instance, "imagine touching your nose") (Foley & Ratner, 1998). The ability to distinguish imagined from real actions improves during the preschool years (Sussman, 2001) and with experience (Subbotsky & Slater, 2011), but even 6- and 7-year-olds have greater difficulty making such distinctions than older children or adults do (Foley & Ratner, 1998). When children make errors in studies such as these, they usually claim that they had performed an action they had actually only imagined.

Related to distinguishing real from imagined events is the distinction between real and imaginary characters. Young children are more apt to believe in fantasy figures such as superheroes, monsters, Santa Claus, and the Tooth Fairy than are older children, especially when adults heartily promote their existence (Harris, 2012; Principe & Smith, 2008).

Young children's tenuous grasp of the distinction between fantasy and reality is seen in experiments by Paul Harris and his colleagues (1991). These researchers demonstrated that 4- and 6-year-olds could easily distinguish between real and imagined objects. For example, when asked to imagine that there was either a bunny or a monster in a box on a table in front of them, few children had any difficulty with the task. Most stated quite clearly that the bunny or the monster was pretend and not real, but this knowledge was tenuous for many of the children. For example, after asking children to imagine a bunny or a monster in the box, the experimenter said she had to leave the room for a few minutes. Of the twelve 4-year-olds who had imagined a monster in the box, four became frightened and wouldn't let the experimenter leave, whereas no child who was asked to imagine a bunny became frightened. When the experimenter returned and questioned the children, nearly half of both the 4- and 6-year-olds admitted to wondering whether there was, indeed, a monster or a bunny in the box. That is, although nearly all of the children admitted that the bunny or the monster was make-believe at the beginning of the experiment, many had second thoughts at the end. Perhaps imagining really did make it so.

Harris and his colleagues (1991) view this contradiction between children's beginning and final beliefs as a reflection of the uncertain state of young children's knowledge of fantasy versus reality. These results help explain why young children are often frightened by imagining bogeymen in the closet or monsters under the bed. Jacqueline Woolley (1997) has suggested that when children feel intense fear of an imaginary agent, the feeling is very real to them, and this makes it difficult for them to discount the reality of the imaginary entity. Children's difficulty inhibiting the intense emotion allows the emotion to interfere with the cognitive processes that would lead to them to evaluate whether the imaginary being actually exists. Tamar Zisenwine and colleagues (2013) proposed that children's inability to distinguish fantasy from reality is also influenced by the ease with which imaginary objects or events are brought to mind. This proposal is based on the availability heuristic hypothesis (Tversky & Kahneman, 1973), which states that information that is more easily brought to mind tends to be judged as more common and probable. Applied to children's ability to discern fantasy from reality, Zisenwine and her colleagues (2013) argue that when children visualize frightening stimuli, it becomes accessible and is perceived as real as a result.

Let us provide an anecdote to illustrate young children's uncertainty about what is real and what is fantasy. Five-year-old Jeffrey was very impressed with the Disney movie *The Lion King*. He knew the cartoon was fiction, of course, and was quite aware that lions and hyenas can't actually talk. He was especially impressed with the character of Simba, the young lion cub and star of the movie. "Simba was so sad when his father died," he said. "Boy, what a good actor he is. He *really* looked sad." Jeffrey knew that this was fiction and that the characters were not real. But he still got confused. As children grow older, they make a clearer distinction between fantasy and reality, which might make playing pretend less enjoyable and could account for the decline in pretending in middle childhood (E. D. Smith & Lillard, 2012).

It's not just cartoon characters and possible monsters or bunnies in boxes that young children attribute life qualities to but also "people" in their daily lives. At about the same time that children begin to engage in sociodramatic play, many create imaginary friends. By 3 or 4 years of age, children endow these invisible agents (usually make-believe children but sometimes talking animals or beings from another planet) with personalities, feelings, ideas, and motivations of their own (Taylor, 1999). Having imaginary friends is quite common. In one study, 65% of children up to age 7 had had an imaginary friend sometime in their lives (Taylor, Batty, & Itier, 2004). There may even be some cognitive advantage to having imaginary friends. One study found that 5-year-old children with imaginary friends tell more detailed stories than children without such friends (Trionfi & Reese, 2009).

Believing in fantasy beings requires a relatively sophisticated cognitive system. For example, Woolley and her colleagues introduced 3- to 5-year-old children to a new fantasy character, the Candy Witch (Woolley, Boerger, & Markman, 2004). The Candy Witch comes on Halloween night into children's homes and replaces candy she finds under children's pillows with a toy. Children were shown a doll representing the Candy Witch but were not told anything about whether she was real. The parents of some of the children exchanged a toy for candy after their children were asleep. When these children who had actually been visited by the Candy Witch (much as they are visited by the Tooth Fairy) were later interviewed, older preschoolers (average age of 5.3 years) were more likely to express belief in the Candy Witch than younger preschoolers (average age of 3.7 years). In other words, it was the older and presumably more cognitively advanced children, not the younger children, who were more likely to believe in the Candy Witch.

In another study by Jesse Bering and Becky Parker (2006), three groups of children (ages 3 to 4 years, 5 to 6 years, and 7 to 9 years) were asked to perform a task in which they had to guess in which of two boxes a prize was hidden. Children could place a hand on either box, and whichever box their hand was on at the end of each trial, they would get whatever was in the box (the prize or nothing). Some children were shown a picture of Princess Alice—an invisible princess who was in the room and wanted to help them win the prize. They were told, "Princess Alice will tell you when you pick the *wrong* box." Other children were told nothing about Princess Alice. During two of the trials, "unexpected" events happened: a picture of Princess Alice fell from the wall or a table lamp flashed on and off in rapid succession. Bering and Parker were interested in whether children would view these unexpected events as messages from Princess Alice and move their hand from one box to the next.

Figure 5.6 presents the percentage of trials on which children moved their hands in response to the unexpected event (percentage of receptive trials). As you can see, the two younger groups of children in the experimental (Princess Alice) condition were no more likely to move their hand on the critical trials than were children in the control group, who knew nothing of Princess Alice. Only the 7- to 9-year-old children in the Princess Alice condition moved their hands significantly more on these receptive trials than did children in the control group. Children were later asked what they thought the unexpected events meant. The youngest children usually stated some physical cause for the event (for instance, "The picture fell because it wasn't sticking very well"). The 5- and 6-year-olds most often attributed the unexpected events to Princess Alice but said it had nothing to do with helping them win the prize (for example, "Princess Alice did it because she wanted to"). Only the older children attributed the unexpected events to Princess Alice doing something to communicate to the child (for instance, "Princess Alice did it because I chose the wrong box"). Thus, similar to the findings in the study about children's belief in the Candy Witch, only the older children attributed intention to Princess Alice, suggesting that mature, not immature, cognition is associated with how imaginary (and supernatural) agents behave.

How different are children from adults regarding magical thinking? Woolley (Woolley & Ghossainy, 2013) thinks not too much. Children may be more likely to attribute unfamiliar events to magic and to believe that "just wishing" can make something come true. But such thinking does not disappear at adolescence or adulthood. In fact, skepticism appears to decline with age (Vaden & Woolley, 2011). The belief systems of most cultures include supernatural beings who intervene in the physical world on a regular basis and who can be asked to intervene on people's behalf, and many adults are highly superstitious.

FIGURE 5.6 **Only older children in the experimental condition who were told that "Princess Alice wants to help you win the prize" were more likely to move their hand from one box to the other (that is, make a receptive response) than children in the control condition who did not hear the story about Princess Alice.**

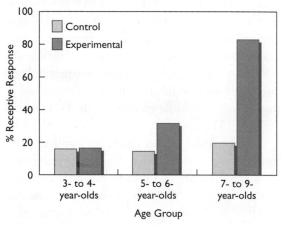

Source: Bering, J. M., & Parker, B. D. (2006). Children's attributions of intentions to an invisible agent. *Developmental Psychology, 42,* 253–262.

They believe that blowing on dice before a roll will produce a good outcome, knocking on wood will prevent a bad one, and breaking a mirror will result in bad luck. Belief in the paranormal approaches 50% among American adults, including faith healing, demonic possession, and astrology. Thus, the tendency to provide a magical explanation for phenomena about which we have no known physical explanation is not unique to children. One likely reason for children's greater tendency to believe in fantasy, however, is knowledge. Older children and adults know more about how the physical world works, and they also know the domains in their culture where belief in supernatural explanations is accepted (for example, religion) and where it is not (for example, Criss Angel's illusions).

Section Review

Children use their symbolic abilities in everyday interactions with family members and peers.

Symbolic Play

- *Symbolic play*, or *fantasy play*, involves an "as if" orientation to objects, actions, and peers. *Sociodramatic play* is first seen at about 3 years of age and involves children playing roles, usually with parents or peers.
- Symbolic play is based on the materials children have available and on the activities and roles of adults in their culture. In cultures that lack industry, play tends to develop into work as children grow into adults.
- Engaging in fantasy play may enhance other aspects of children's cognitive development, including executive functions.

Distinguishing Between Fantasy and Reality

- Although 3- and 4-year-old children can distinguish between imagined and experienced events, this distinction is tenuous, with preschoolers often thinking that make-believe objects can become real by imagining them as real.
- Young children also often show *source-monitoring* errors, confusing whether they had imagined or experienced an event.
- Most children have *imaginary friends* sometime during childhood and believe in fantasy characters, such as Santa Claus or the Easter Bunny. Although belief in such fantasy characters decreases with age, a certain level of cognitive development is required for such a belief in the first place.

Ask Yourself . . .

13. When and how is symbolic play exhibited by children? How is symbolic play affected by culture?

14. When are children able to distinguish real from imagined events, and how can we know this? What are some caveats? To what extent is it correct to state that the belief in fantasy characters represents immature cognition?

CAUSAL REPRESENTATION

One of the tasks charged to children during development is to determine the causal structure of the world. That is, how does one thing lead to the next? What are the cause and effect relationships between our actions and the objects upon which we act? What about the way two or more objects interact to influence one another? Mental representations of causality allow us to make predictions about the world and intervene when we deem it necessary to change the course of events. These representations are also important for helping us make inferences about the actions and behaviors of others—what beliefs and/or desires caused that individual to behave in that way? This is the fundamental representation involved in *theory of mind*, a topic that we discuss in more detail in Chapter 6. For now, we focus on children's ability to form causal representations of the observable, nonmental world.

Constructing Causal Maps

Alison Gopnik and her colleagues (Gopnik et al., 2004) have made the case that children represent causal knowledge and causal learning as *causal maps*. Gopnik proposes that children develop causal maps based on two types of observations: (1) their observations of patterns of correlation among events and (2) their observations of the effects of intervention, or direct manipulations on objects. Like scientists, children use the information gathered from their observations to develop predictions about the world. They then test these predictions against additional observations and make adjustments to their "theory" as needed. This idea that children have intuitive theories about the world that change in ways similar to scientific theory is referred to as *theory theory*, a concept we return to in Chapter 6.

This hypothesis is contrasted with three other views of children's learning. The first is the possibility that children do not learn any new causal relations but instead are born with a few innate *core-knowledge* capacities. For instance, in Chapter 4 we discussed the concept of *collision* and described how 2.5-month-old infants increased their looking time when a toy bug on wheels remained stationary after being hit by a cylinder rolling down a ramp (Kotovsky & Baillargeon, 2000; S. Wang, Kaufman, & Baillargeon, 2003). Based on looking time, young infants behave as if they understand that objects *cause* other objects to move when they make contact. This early competence is argued to represent core-knowledge concepts. Another alternative hypothesis is that children rely on operant and classical conditioning mechanisms to associate events but do not actually infer anything genuine about the causal relationship between events. In other words, children learn that events occur together but not necessarily that one event causes another. A third hypothesis is that children use trial and error or imitative learning to understand the causal connection between their own actions or others' actions and their consequences.

Gopnik and her colleagues have conducted many studies to rule out these alternative explanations and in doing so have provided empirical evidence that children's representations and causal inferences rely on much more powerful learning mechanisms than can be explained by the alternatives. For instance, in one task using the *blicket detector*, children are shown a square wooden and plastic box that lights up and plays music when certain specific objects (blocks, called *blickets*) are placed on top of it. Blickets, then, are objects that *cause* the box to light up and play music (in fact, an out-of-sight experimenter really causes the sound and lights to activate by pressing a button on a remote). Using this task, Gopnik and her team present children with different patterns of evidence about the blocks and the detector to discover what kinds of causal inferences children make. For instance, in one study, 3- and 4-year-old children were presented with the blicket detector and told that it was a "blicket machine" and that "blickets make the machine go" (A. Gopnik et al., 2001). Children were then given one of two tasks. Examples of these tasks are presented in Figure 5.7. In the one-cause task, the experimenter first activated the machine by placing one object on it (a wooden cube, for example). Next, the experimenter put a different kind of object on the machine (for instance, a cylinder), which did not activate it. Then both objects were placed on the machine at the same time, twice in a row, and the machine activated both times. Children were then asked whether each object was a blicket. Gopnik argued that children should be tracking *causal dependence* (how often does one object's actions cause a change in another object) and *causal independence* (how often does the same action *not* cause a change). She expected that children would combine these patterns with their own preexisting knowledge about cause and effect relationships to reason that the first object (the cube) was a blicket. In fact, almost all children (96%) said the first object (the cube) was a blicket, and only 41% said the second object (the cylinder) was a blicket.

However, it is still possible for children to solve this task by simply picking the object that made the machine activate more frequently. To rule out this possibility A. Gopnik et al. (2001) designed a second task, the two-cause task. In this task, one object (or wooden cube, to continue the previous example) was placed on the machine by itself three times, and the machine activated each time. Then the other object (the cylinder) was placed on the machine three times, with the machine not activating the first time but activating the next two times. At this point, children were then asked whether each object was a blicket. Gopnik and colleagues reasoned that

if children were deciding based on frequencies alone or simply picking the object that activated the machine first, then they might say that only the first object, the wooden cube, was the blicket. In contrast, however, children were equally likely to say that the cube and the cylinder was a blicket (97% and 81.5%, respectively). These findings provided preliminary evidence that children were able to represent, based on their observations of causal independence and dependence, which objects "caused" the machine to activate.

FIGURE 5.7 **In the one-cause condition, children see the cube activate the blicket detector, whereas the cylinder has no effect.** Children correctly reason that the cube is a blicket and the cylinder is not. In the two-cause condition, the cube activates the machine three times, whereas the cylinder activates the machine only two out of three times. Children reason that both objects are blickets.

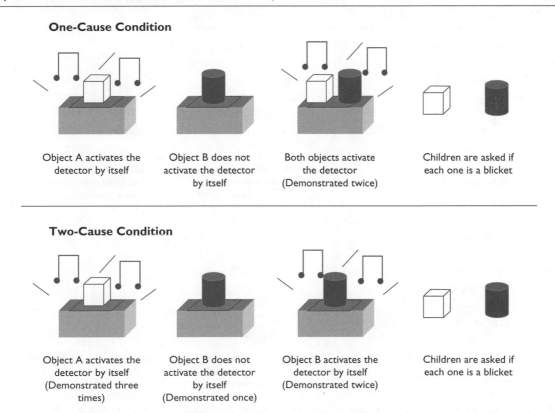

One-Cause Condition

Object A activates the detector by itself

Object B does not activate the detector by itself

Both objects activate the detector (Demonstrated twice)

Children are asked if each one is a blicket

Two-Cause Condition

Object A activates the detector by itself (Demonstrated three times)

Object B does not activate the detector by itself (Demonstrated once)

Object B activates the detector by itself (Demonstrated twice)

Children are asked if each one is a blicket

Source: Gopnik, A., Sobel, D. M., Schulz, L., & Glymour, C. (2001). Causal learning mechanisms in very young children: Two, three, and four-year-olds infer causal relations from patterns of variation and covariation. *Developmental Psychology, 37,* 620–629 (experiment 1).

Gopnik went a step further, reasoning that if children really thought that the blickets made the machine go, then children should be able to use the blickets themselves to cause the machine to activate. Moreover, if this information is represented mentally as a causal map, then children should be able to reason backward that removing a blicket will make the machine stop, even if they have never seen this event. In fact, A. Gopnik et al. (2001) found just that. The blicket task was modified so that children did not see that removing the block made the machine stop (see Figure 5.8). In the one-cause task, children watched as an experimenter placed one block, the cylinder, on the machine and nothing happened. Then the experimenter removed the cylinder and placed the other block, the cube, on the machine, and the machine activated. After a few moments, the cylinder was placed on the machine next to the cube, and the machine remained activated. At

FIGURE 5.8 **In the one-cause condition, the cylinder is placed on the machine, and the machine does not activate.** The cube is then used to activate the machine and the cylinder is placed next to the cube. Children correctly reason that removing the cube will deactivate the machine. In the two-cause condition, children view the cylinder activate the detector. When the cylinder is removed, the detector is deactivated. Children then view the cube activate the machine, and the cylinder is placed next to the cube. Children correctly reason that both objects must be removed to make the machine deactivate.

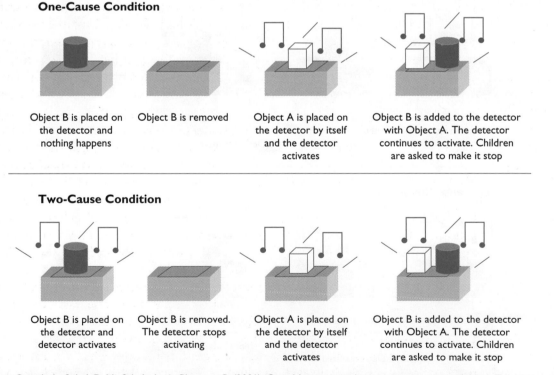

One-Cause Condition

Object B is placed on the detector and nothing happens

Object B is removed

Object A is placed on the detector by itself and the detector activates

Object B is added to the detector with Object A. The detector continues to activate. Children are asked to make it stop

Two-Cause Condition

Object B is placed on the detector and detector activates

Object B is removed. The detector stops activating

Object A is placed on the detector by itself and the detector activates

Object B is added to the detector with Object A. The detector continues to activate. Children are asked to make it stop

Source: Gopnik, A., Sobel, D. M., Schulz, L., & Glymour, C. (2001). Causal learning mechanisms in very young children: Two, three, and four-year-olds infer causal relations from patterns of variation and covariation. *Developmental Psychology, 37,* 620–629.

this point, children were asked, "Can you make it stop?" In the modified two-cause task, children watched the same sequence of events, except that the cylinder *did* activate the machine when it was placed on it, and so children who were reasoning causally should remove both blocks. As predicted, participants removed the cube alone more often in the one-cause task than the two-cause task yet removed both objects more often in the two-cause task than in the one-cause task.

The results ruled out several alternative hypotheses about children's casual learning. Because children did not activate the machine themselves, they could not have solved the tasks through trial and error or operant conditioning. Additionally, because children never saw the removal of the objects in the "make it stop" experiments, classical conditioning or imitative learning cannot explain their responses. And because both objects made contact with the machine, children should not have been able to solve the task by relying on core-knowledge representations of everyday physics. Instead, these results imply that children, as young as 30 months, formed a mental representation of the causal connection between the blicket and the blicket machine and were able to reflect on this representation to make inferences about how to "undo" the cause-effect relationship and deactivate the machine. These mental representations allow children to engage in a kind of *counterfactual reasoning* to consider alternative situations such as, "What would happen if the cube were not on the machine?"

Role of Play in Causal Learning

Alison Gopnik, Daphna Buchsbaum, and colleagues have also shown that children's ability to form causal representations is strongly related to their pretend play (Buchsbaum et al., 2012).

These researchers argued that "pretend play provides an opportunity to practice and perfect the skills of reasoning from, and learning about, a causal model, just as play fighting or hunting allows animals to perfect complex motor skills" (p. 2205). Pretend play, counterfactual reasoning, and reasoning about the potential effects of one's actions all involve the same cognitive processes. One has to consider events that have not occurred and distinguish those events from reality to consider what could occur or would have occurred.

In one study, Buchsbaum and her team (2012) adapted the blicket task, described earlier, to explore the relationship between 3- and 4-year-olds' pretend play and causal reasoning. In this study, the blicket machine was called the Birthday machine, and it played "Happy Birthday" when activated by a blicket-like object, called a zando. The researchers told children that it was a stuffed monkey's birthday and that they would be singing "Happy Birthday" to Monkey as a surprise, using the Birthday machine. As in the blicket task, children were taught that only the zando would make the Birthday machine work. They then watched as zando and non-zando objects activated or did not activate the machine, respectively, and then they were asked to indicate which object was the zando. The experimenter followed up a correct choice by asking a counterfactual question, "If this one were not a zando, what would happen if we put it on top of the machine?" Over 80% of children answered correctly that the object would not activate the machine if it were not a zando (69% of children reasoned correctly about counterfactual statements regarding both the zando and non-zando). Next, a confederate entered the room and said that she needed to borrow the machine. The experimenter then expressed that the experimenter and child should pretend that another white wooden box was a Birthday machine and that two other blocks were each a zando and non-zando. After confirming that the child understood which was which, the experimenter pulled the stuffed monkey out from hiding and asked the child what they should pretend in order to make the *pretend* Birthday machine play music. Once the child placed a block on the machine, the experimenter asked, "What are we pretending now?" to determine whether the child understood the pretend causal structure. The experimenter than suggested the child try the other block and repeated the procedure. After the child had tried both blocks, the experimenter reversed the pretend roles of the blocks, indicating that the original pretend zando was now the non-zando and vice versa. Then the experimenter repeated the series of questions asking, "*Now* what should we do to pretend to make the machine play?" In this pretend phase, over half of children were successful in choosing to use the pretend zando block to cause music to play in both the original and reversal conditions. These children also said that the pretend zando was having the pretend effect of playing music, consistent with what would be the outcome in the real world. A strong, positive correlation emerged between children's performance in the pretend phase and their performance during the counterfactual phase of the experiment. Those children who reasoned correctly about the effect of the zando if it were not a zando were more likely to maintain correct causal structure in the pretend scenario, acting upon a pretend causal relationship to bring about a pretend effect. A follow-up study showed that this correlation held up regardless of children's age or performance on other cognitive tasks, indicating that children who apply appropriate causal constraints in their pretend play also do better in *counterfactual* reasoning in the real world.

Buchsbaum and colleagues (2012) argued that these results suggest that one of the important functions of symbolic play across an extended period of childhood may be to allow children to explore, test, and deploy causal models that enable

counterfactual inferences ("What if this were not a stick but a *sword*?") in a broad and flexible way. Buchsbaum et al. (2012) analogized the human strategy of play to the economic strategy

> whereby companies invest in research divisions that are not immediately profitable, but that allow for flexibility and retooling in light of changing conditions. Investment in extended childhood [and play], with its many opportunities for free exploration and causal learning, may have allowed human beings to turn from simply making the same ecological widgets to developing our staggeringly wide variety of strategies for adaptive success. (p. 2210)

Section Review

Alison Gopnik has proposed that children track the causal dependence and causal independence of events and combine this information with previous knowledge to form causal representations of the world.

- These causal representations are referred to as causal maps.
- Research using the blicket task shows that children, as young as 30 months, can form a mental representation of the causal connection between objects and engage in counterfactual reasoning.
- Children who apply appropriate causal constraints in their pretend play also do better in counterfactual reasoning in the real world.

Ask Yourself . . .

15. How do children form causal representations of the world?
16. What is counterfactual reasoning? When do children demonstrate it, and how do we know?
17. How does pretend play relate to children's causal representation?

FUZZY-TRACE THEORY

Theories like Piaget's emphasize that the quality of children's mental representation changes with age. But as important as Piaget's theory has been to understanding children's thinking, as we saw earlier in this chapter, cognitive development just doesn't work this way, at least not exclusively. New forms of thinking do not necessarily replace (or emerge from) earlier forms. Older children and adults sometimes still solve problems using the same type of illogical, intuitive thinking that characterizes preschoolers. They do it, however, with more "processing power" than preschoolers do (such as enhanced working memory and faster speed of processing) and with greater logical abilities. Collectively, theories that propose multiple (usually two general) "ways of knowing" people use to solve problems are referred to as *dual-processing theories* (Barrouillet, 2011; Klaczynski, 2009).

One influential dual-processing theory of cognitive development is **fuzzy-trace theory**. Charles Brainerd and Valerie Reyna (1993, 2015) proposed the metaphor of *intuitionism*, in which people prefer to think, reason, and remember by processing inexact, "fuzzy" memory representations rather than by working logically from exact, verbatim representations. In a nutshell, according to Brainerd and Reyna (1993), most cognition is intuitive, in that it is based on "fuzzy representations (senses, patterns, gists) in combination with construction rules that operate on those representations" (p. 50).

Fuzzy-trace theory makes several basic assumptions about aspects of cognitive processing as well as about how these aspects of processing vary with development. We first mention each of the assumptions, outlined in Table 5.5, and then discuss how they relate to cognitive development.

Assumptions of Fuzzy-Trace Theory

At the core of fuzzy-trace theory is the idea that memory representations (or memory traces) exist on a continuum from literal, verbatim representations to fuzzy, imprecise, gistlike traces. Take, for example, a transitive-inference problem in which children are shown a series of sticks that vary in length. Stick A is 20 centimeters long, Stick B is 20.5 centimeters long, and Stick C is 21 centimeters long. Children are shown each of two adjacent pairs of sticks (A and B; B and C) and asked to judge which item of each pair is longer. They then are asked to decide whether Stick A or Stick C is longer, without having seen these two particular sticks together and without being allowed to make a visual comparison of their lengths. Verbatim traces would correspond to the actual lengths of the sticks (expressed, perhaps, in the form of visual images). Fuzzy or gistlike traces would be of a less exact form, such as "C is long, B is not long and not short, A is short," or "The sticks get taller to my right." Either of these forms of representation can be used to solve the problem. Fuzzy-trace theory poses such questions as these: Which representation is cognitively easier? Which representations do people actually use? And, important for us, what develops?

An important assumption in fuzzy-trace theory is the idea that gist can exist at several levels for the same information (for example, "A is short, C is long" and "The sticks get taller to my right") and that a single event will be represented in memory by a number of different traces, from exact **verbatim traces** to a variety of inexact

TABLE 5.5 Assumptions of fuzzy-trace theory and their relation to cognitive development.*

---

1. *Gist extraction and the fuzzy-to-verbatim continua*

   Basic assumption: People extract fuzzy, gistlike information from the stimuli and events they experience, following the reduction-to-essence rule. Traces for an event exist on a fuzzy-to-verbatim continuum. At one extreme are fuzzy traces that are vague, degenerated representations that maintain only the sense or pattern of recently encoded information. At the other extreme are verbatim traces, which are elaborated, exact representations of the recently encoded information.

   Age differences: Young children's memory is specialized for encoding and processing verbatim information; with age, their ability to extract gist improves.

2. *Fuzzy-processing preference (intuition)*

   Basic assumption: People prefer to reason, think, and remember intuitively, processing fuzzy rather than verbatim traces.

   Age differences: There is a shift in the reliance on verbatim and gist traces, sometime during the elementary school years, with children becoming increasingly facile at processing gist traces. Processing of verbatim traces declines in efficiency during adolescence.

3. *Output interference*

   Basic assumption: As people make responses, output interference occurs and interferes with subsequent processing.

   Age differences: Young children are more sensitive to the effects of output interference than are older children or adults.

---

*A fourth assumption of fuzzy-trace theory is that short-term memory is reconstructive. However, because the theory predicts few developmental differences in reconstructive processes, this aspect of the theory is not discussed here.

fuzzy traces. Moreover, these various traces are independent of one another. That is, gist traces are not simply the result of the deterioration of verbatim traces.

A central assumption of fuzzy-trace theory is that people of all ages prefer to use fuzzy traces when solving problems, although this preference does vary with age (see *Developmental Differences* section). Brainerd and Reyna refer to this as the *reduction-to-essence rule*. Fuzzy traces cannot always be used to solve a problem, but according to Brainerd and Reyna (1990), "it is a natural habit of mind to process traces that are as near to the fuzzy ends of fuzzy-to-verbatim continua as possible" (p. 9). In other words, there is a bias in human cognition toward thinking and solving problems intuitively rather than logically.

Fuzzy traces and verbatim traces differ in important ways. First, relative to verbatim traces, fuzzy traces are more easily accessed and generally require less effort to use. Also, verbatim traces are more susceptible to interference and forgetting than are fuzzy traces. For example, when a shopper is comparing the prices of shirts at two stores, he or she will quickly forget the exact prices of the shirts. More resistant to forgetting, however, will be the less-precise information that the shirt at Old Navy was cheaper than the comparable shirt at Macy's. If your problem is to decide which shirt is the better buy, you can rely on the degraded, fuzzy knowledge of the relative prices of the two shirts. If, however, you are required to write a check for one of the shirts, you will need the verbatim information, and in that case, it would be helpful if you wrote the exact price down, for it is unlikely that you will have remembered it.

A final assumption of fuzzy-trace theory has to do with the role of *output interference* and how it varies with development. Brainerd and Reyna (1990) hold that the act of making responses produces output interference that hinders subsequent performance. According to Brainerd and Reyna, output interference occurs in two forms: *scheduling effects* and *feedback effects*. Scheduling effects are caused by the serial nature of response systems. Although people can perform several cognitive operations simultaneously (that is, in parallel), responses are made serially (that is, one at a time). This leads to a parallel-to-serial bottleneck at output, or response competition, with the various possible responses competing for priority of execution. Once a response is made, Brainerd and Reyna (1990) propose, irrelevant feedback is generated "that reverberates through the systems, degrading performance as it goes . . . [and] introducing noise into working memory" (p. 29).

Developmental Differences

How does processing of fuzzy traces and verbatim traces vary with development? Fuzzy-trace theory makes specific predictions, some of which have been confirmed by research. First, there are age differences in gist extraction. Early in life, children are biased toward storing and retrieving verbatim traces. They do extract gist, of course, but relative to older children and adults, young children are biased toward the verbatim end of the continuum. A verbatim → gist shift occurs sometime during the early elementary school years, with children now showing a gist bias. Thus, the memory system for processing verbatim information should develop earlier than the system for processing fuzzy, gistlike information. Moreover, the memory system used for processing verbatim information should decline relatively early in development, likely during adolescence or young adulthood.

Evidence from a variety of sources supports the idea that preschool and early school-age children are more biased toward encoding and remembering verbatim traces, whereas older children, like adults, are more prone toward encoding and remembering gist traces (Brainerd & Gordon, 1994; Odegard et al., 2009). For example, in research by Brainerd and Gordon (1994), preschool and second-grade children were given simple numerical problems. In one problem, children were given the following background information: "Farmer Brown owns many animals. He owns 3 dogs, 5 sheep, 7 chickens, 9 horses, and 11 cows." They were then asked a series of questions, some requiring verbatim knowledge for their correct answer, such as "How many cows does Farmer Brown own, 11 or 9?" and others requiring only gist information, such as "Which of Farmer Brown's animals are the most, cows or horses?" (called global) and "Does Farmer Brown have more cows or more horses?" (called pairwise). The results of this experiment are shown in Figure 5.9. Brainerd and Gordon found that preschool children were better at remembering the verbatim numbers than the numerical gist, whereas the reverse was true for second-graders.

Note that the theory does *not* say that young children are better at processing or remembering verbatim traces than older children are; the ability to deal with *both* verbatim and fuzzy traces improves with age. Young children merely start with a bias toward processing verbatim relative to gist traces, and this tendency shifts with age. Children become increasingly biased toward processing at the fuzzy end of the continuum, but the overall processing effectiveness for both types of traces improves.

Age differences have been also found in sensitivity to output interference, with younger children being more adversely affected than older children. Support for this contention has come from studies of selective attention (for example, Ridderinkhof, van der Molen, & Band, 1997), including research that has used developmental differences in evoked brain potentials on tasks involving interference (Ridderinkhof & van der Molen, 1995). One reason for young children's greater interference sensitivity is their reliance on verbatim traces, which are more susceptible to interference than fuzzy traces are.

FIGURE 5.9 **Proportion of correct recognition responses for verbatim, global, and pairwise problems for preschool and second-grade children.** As you can see, preschool children were better at remembering the verbatim numbers than the numerical gist, whereas the reverse was true for second-graders.

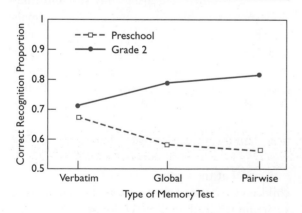

Source: Brainerd, C. J., & Gordon, L. L. (1994). Development of verbatim and gist memory for numbers. *Developmental Psychology, 30,* 163–177. Copyright © 1994 by the American Psychological Association. Reprinted with permission.

Section Review

Brainerd and Reyna's *fuzzy-trace theory* suggests intuitionism as a metaphor for cognition.

- Fuzzy-trace theory assumes that memory representations exist on a continuum from *verbatim traces* to *fuzzy traces* (or gistlike traces).
- People generally prefer to think with fuzzy traces rather than verbatim traces, following the reduction-to-essence rule, but this preference develops over time, with young children showing more of a verbatim bias than older children.
- Processing of verbatim traces is relatively good in young children but declines in efficiency during adolescence. Fuzzy-trace theory assumes that output interference, resulting from scheduling effects and feedback effects, causes deterioration of performance and that younger children are more susceptible to the effects of output interference than older children or adults are.

Ask Yourself . . .

18. What are the critical concepts of fuzzy-trace theory?
19. How does this theory distinguish between different types of mental representations, and how does processing of these representations change with age?

THE SYMBOLIC SPECIES

Humans are a symbolic species—perhaps *the* symbolic species. How people come to mentally represent their experiences has been of great concern to psychologists, as has how such representational abilities develop. Piaget contended that children lack symbolic ability until late in their second year of life and that their mental world changes in a stagelike fashion over early childhood (preoperational thought), the elementary school years (concrete operational thought), and into adolescence and adulthood (formal operational thought). As we saw in Chapter 4 on infant perception and cognition, many scientists now believe that infants, perhaps even newborns, are not totally devoid of symbolic abilities. However, as much of the research reviewed in this chapter indicates, children seem to have available to them at any one time multiple ways of representing experiences. There does not seem to be a time when children "have" versus "don't have" a particular symbolic skill. Rather, such ways of knowing develop over infancy and childhood, and their expression is influenced not only by their inherited mental architecture but also by aspects of the task and context in which they are "thinking." Young children are able to treat pictures as symbols before models, but depending on context, this too can change. College students can solve formal operation tasks best in their area(s) of expertise (for example, English majors for literary problems). In many ways, human symbolic functioning and its development, perhaps more than any other single factor, make us the species that we are. We should not be surprised that figuring out how such ability develops is complicated.

KEY TERMS AND CONCEPTS

accommodation
adaptation
appearance/reality
    distinction
assimilation
centration
concrete operations
conservation
decentration
dual representation (or
    dual orientation)
egocentricity
equilibration

formal operations
functional invariants
fuzzy traces
fuzzy-trace theory
goal-directed behavior
hypothetico-deductive
    reasoning
imaginary audience
imaginary friends
inductive reasoning
operations
organization
personal fable

preoperations
reflective abstraction
representation
representational insight
reversibility
scale errors
scheme
sensorimotor stage
sociodramatic play
source monitoring
symbolic play
    (or fantasy play)
verbatim traces

SUGGESTED READINGS

Scholarly Works

Brainerd, C. J. (1996). Piaget: A centennial celebration. *Psychological Science, 7,* 191–195. This is the introductory article to a special issue of *Psychological Science* devoted to commemorating the centennial of Piaget's birth. Piaget's many contributions are summarized in the articles written by prominent cognitive developmental psychologists, documenting that Piaget's influence and legacy live on.

DeLoache, J. S. (1995). Early understanding and use of symbols: The model model. *Current*

Directions in Psychological Science, 4, 109–113. Judy DeLoache provides a brief and easily comprehensible account of her research and theory about preschool children's developing understanding of symbols.

Lane, J. D., & Harris, P. L. (2014). **Confronting, representing, and believing counterintuitive concepts: Navigating the natural and the supernatural.** *Perspectives on Psychological Science,* 9(2), 144–160. Jonathon Lane and Paul Harris describe how children and adults come to believe a variety of concepts that defy their firsthand perception and intuitions of the world. They make the case that the same processes that underlie mental representation of the natural world also underlie representation of the supernatural world—namely God and the afterlife.

Piaget, J. (1952). *The origins of intelligence in children.* **New York: Norton.** This is Piaget's first book in his series of three on infant cognition, and it presents many of the central concepts of his theory of sensorimotor intelligence. It was the first book by Piaget I (DB) ever read, perhaps accounting for my fondness toward it.

Reading for Personal Interest

Bering, J. (2012). *The belief instinct: The psychology of souls, destiny, and the meaning of life.* **New York: Norton.** Jessie Bering deconstructs the way that belief manifests in the human brain and describes how our belief in supernatural entities is the result of our theory of mind and predisposition to represent causal structure in the world.

Gopnik, A. (2009). *The philosophical baby: What children's minds tell us about truth, love, and the meaning of life.* **New York: Farrer, Straus, and Giroux.** In this delightfully written book, developmental psychologist Alison Gopnik examines how babies and young children form and test theories, how they use their imagination, and what it's like to be a baby.

Paley, V. G. (2004). *A child's work: The importance of fantasy play.* **Chicago: University of Chicago Press.** In this book, well-known preschool educator and researcher Vivian Gussin Paley tells us about the importance of storytelling and fantasy play in children's development in contemporary societies, describing their positive effects on children's academic and social development.

6 | DEVELOPMENT OF FOLK KNOWLEDGE

IN THIS CHAPTER

ight-year-old Mitchell sat beside the tree stump in his backyard, watching the ants and other insects crawling in and out of the rotten log. From time to time, he would poke a stick into the log or flake off some loose pieces of wood to see where the crawly bugs were going and what else resided inside the dead tree. Eventually, he went to his house, returned with a jar, and placed some wood, ants, and what he assumed were ant eggs into it, then punched holes in the top. He put the jar on top of his dresser, where for more than a week he examined it every morning when he awoke and every night before he went to bed. For his birthday, he asked his parents for an ant farm.

Kids have a fascination with animals and the natural world. Although this is most easily seen in children's love of pets like cats and dogs and in their fascination with petting zoos, for some youngsters it extends to other creatures, such as ants living in dead trees. Recently, psychologists have recognized that children may possess an early and intuitive understanding of the biological world and acquire biological facts relatively easily.

However, it's not just biology that children seem to have a propensity to learn about but also physics and psychology. In this chapter, we discuss the evidence that children possess or acquire very easily naive or intuitive notions about how the psychological, biological, or physical world works. These intuitive theories are often referred to as the domains of folk psychology, folk biology, and folk physics—or collectively, folk knowledge (Geary, 2005). Folk knowledge reflects how people naturally come to understand aspects of their world and is differentiated from scientific knowledge. For example, children perceive the Earth as a flat surface, with people standing on top of it, and not as the globe with people on both the northern and southern hemispheres, held to the ground by gravity that science informs us it is.

We encountered the concept of folk knowledge earlier in this book, initially in Chapter 2, when discussing David Geary's (2005) model for the structure of the mind and, in Chapter 4, when discussing core-knowledge theories (Spelke & Kinzler, 2007). As you may recall, Geary argued that the mind consists of hierarchically organized modules within the social (psychological), physical, and biological domains. Children are born with *skeletal competencies* within these domains, which become fleshed out with experience. In other words, natural selection has biased children to process information within these broad domains of knowledge, with experience shaping the eventual form of a child's mind. Similarly, core-knowledge theorists argue that infants possess knowledge about aspects of their physical and social environments from birth or shortly thereafter and upon which new and flexible skills and belief systems are built.

As both Geary and core-knowledge theorists recognize, however, folk knowledge is not complete in infancy but develops over childhood. In this chapter, we look at the development of children's intuitive psychology, biology, and physics (that is, their folk knowledge) past infancy. Much of this research has been done following a particular theoretical perspective called theory theory, and we start the chapter with an overview of this approach. We then examine three aspects of the development of folk knowledge, beginning with folk psychology (children's understanding of other people, including their mental lives). Next, we examine the development of folk biology (children's understanding of plants, animals, and biological processes). In a final section, we look at the development of folk physics (children's knowledge of the physical world, such as physical objects and their movement). Much of Piaget's research on conservation, for example, can be seen as reflecting children's developing, naive theories of physics (how does the physical world "behave"?). This is an extension of infants' understanding of objects, discussed in some detail in Chapter 4.

THEORY THEORIES OF COGNITIVE DEVELOPMENT

Many developmental psychologists view infants and children as theorists just like themselves. They propose that these youngsters are like scientists, having sets of intuitive theories that they modify over the course of childhood until their understanding of the world is like that of adults in their culture. Children test theories about how different aspects of the world work, and when their experiences contradict their existing theories, they eventually change those theories (that is, they make a conceptual change) and, as a result, develop a more reliable mental map to navigate in the real world.

Many *theory theorists* see themselves as the inheritors of Piaget's tradition. They see cognitive development as being a constructive process, much as Piaget did, with mechanisms of change not so dissimilar from those hypothesized by Piaget. First, they argue that children's theories have a distinctive structure involving coherent, abstract representations of the world similar to the *schemas* described by Piaget. These representations are like hypotheses about objects or people, for instance. As such, they allow for predictions about what may happen in the future and influence a child's interpretations of his or her present and past experiences. Second, children's theories have dynamic features, reflecting the interaction between hypotheses and data, similar to Piaget's ideas of *accommodation* and *assimilation*.

Advocates of theory theories propose that the process of cognitive development is similar, or perhaps even identical, to the process of scientific discovery. An initial theory is tested (experimentation), and when the old theory can't explain the new data, the theory is revised. Children use these theories to predict, interpret, and explain the world, just as scientists do.

Theory theories have much in common with the core-knowledge theories discussed in Chapter 4 (Spelke & Kinzler, 2007), in that each assumes children possess rudimentary ideas about how a specific segment of their world works, yet each also assumes that these naive theories are modified by experience (A. Gopnik & Wellman, 2012). They tend to differ in terms of the degree to which knowledge is viewed as being innate versus constructed (*a la* Piaget) by experience. At the extreme, core-knowledge (or neonativist) theorists propose that cognitive processes that Piaget claimed undergo gradual, constructivist development are actually innate and await only the requisite motor or sensory skills for their demonstration. Theory theorists (or neoconstructivists) rarely take this strong perspective, proposing

instead that children are *rational constructivists*, who revise their initial theories in favor of better ones, based on their experiences and observations (A. Gopnik, 2011). We discussed this probabilistic view as it applies to representations of causal maps in Chapter 5. However, as these research disciplines mature, the distinction between the various theories on this point seems to be diminishing (see Newcombe, 2011). Both approaches adopt an evolutionary perspective, arguing that infants and children have been prepared by natural selection to make sense of their world, with infants and children's initial, naive theories changing with experience. Infants' and children's cognition is *constrained*, in that they are not able to process all information equally well, but they are especially able to make sense of "expectable input," particularly information in *core domains* (for example, psychological, biological, and physical information).

Section Review

- Children possess naive, or intuitive, notions about how the psychological (*folk psychology*), biological (*folk biology*), and physical (*folk physics*) worlds work, collectively known as *folk knowledge*.
- *Theory theories* extend Piaget's ideas, assuming that children possess some rudimentary naive theories to represent and reason about the principal domains of knowledge and that these theories are evaluated in a probabilistic way based on experience.

Ask Yourself . . .

1. How does theory theory differ from the nativist/core-knowledge perspective? In what ways are these theories similar? To what extent does each derive from Piagetian theory?

FOLK PSYCHOLOGY: DEVELOPING A THEORY OF MIND

The topic of children's **theory of mind** has become immensely popular. In general, the term *theory of mind* is used to refer to children's developing concepts of mental activity. A theory of mind is more than just a collection of concepts, however. *Theory* implies some coherent framework for organizing facts and making predictions. Having a theory of mind implies recognizing different categories of mind, such as dreams, memories, imagination, beliefs, and so on, and having some causal-explanatory framework to account for the actions of other people (that is, to explain why someone behaves as he or she does). For example, Henry Wellman (1990) believes that adults' theory of mind is based on **belief-desire reasoning**. Basically, we explain and predict what

people do based on what we understand their desires and beliefs to be—that is, by referring to their wants, wishes, hopes, and goals (their desires) and to their knowledge, ideas, opinions, and suppositions (their beliefs). Such belief-desire reasoning is depicted in Figure 6.1. Essentially, this is what researchers mean when they talk about children developing a theory of mind: To what extent do children have a coherent explanatory "theory" to understand, predict, and explain behavior?

Developmental differences in theory of mind are reflections of developmental differences in how children represent the world—in this case, the mental world. In fact, some of the research reviewed in Chapter 5 examining children's ability to distinguish between appearance and reality (Flavell, Green, & Flavell, 1986) or between imagining and experiencing (Harris et al., 1991) could properly be classified as theory-of-mind research (see Flavell & Miller, 1998).

FIGURE 6.1 **Children's perception of the world affects their knowledge, or beliefs, and their emotions influence their wants and desires.** Beliefs and desires, in turn, motivate one's actions. Children learn that such belief-desire reasoning not only describes their own behavior but also that of other people.

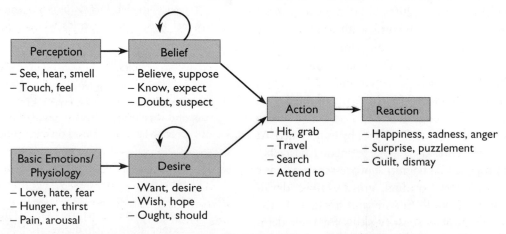

Source: Wellman, H. M. (1990). *The child's theory of mind.* Cambridge, MA: MIT Press. Copyright © 1990 Massachusetts Institute of Technology Press. Reprinted with permission.

The aspect of theory of mind that has spawned the most research, however, concerns children's abilities to "read the minds" of others (Perner, 1991; Wellman, Cross, & Watson, 2001). What we really mean is, to what extent do young children understand that the perceptions, knowledge, and thoughts of others may differ from their own? Children's representation of others and of themselves as thinkers is vitally important to our species' way of life. Adults make inferences about the minds of others all the time (although not always necessarily correctly). For instance, imagine you and a friend are walking in a downtown area when you pass by a cupcake shop. Your friend stops in his tracks, eyes the cupcakes through the window, and starts licking his lips. You likely infer that he wants a cupcake based on his behavior. Cooperation, competition, and social interaction in general would be radically different if we did not develop a theory of mind and the ability to "read" others' minds. We believe that one reason for the popularity of this topic is its significance for understanding the human condition. "Mind reading," however, is a relatively advanced aspect of theory of mind and is based on more basic social-cognitive abilities, which we examine in the following section.

Basic Social-Cognitive Skills Underlying Theory of Mind

What are the most elementary social-cognitive abilities required for a theory of mind? The best candidates we believe are (a) viewing oneself and other individuals as **intentional agents**—that is, as individuals who do things on purpose or *cause* things to happen in an effort to achieve some goal (see Bandura, 2006; Tomasello & Carpenter, 2007)—and (b) the ability to take the perspective of another, which is to understand what the intentions of other people are (Machluf & Bjorklund, 2015).

Infants are not born with this knowledge; it develops over the first several years of life, beginning in infancy with **shared attention** (sometimes called *joint attention*) (Tomasello, 2009; Tomasello & Carpenter, 2007). Shared attention refers to the *triadic interaction* between two social partners (for example, an infant and her mother) and a third object (which can sometimes be another person). For instance, a mother may point or gaze at the family dog while catching her infant's attention, drawing the baby into a social relationship that extends beyond the mother-infant dyad. Although mothers (and fathers) may engage in this type of behavior from the earliest days of a baby's life, it takes infants a while to catch on, although they do seem to be oriented to social interactions from birth. For instance, neonates orient to the human face and quickly learn to seek their mothers' faces (Feldman & Eidelman, 2004).

Shared attention, however, is typically not seen in babies until about 9 months of age, when they will gaze in the direction adults are looking or pointing, engage in repetitive interaction with an adult and an object, imitate an adult's actions, and point or hold up objects to another person (see M. Carpenter, Nagell, & Tomasello, 1998; Tomasello, 2014). Pointing out distant objects is a form of *referential communication* and indicates the pointer understands that he or she sees something the observer does not. These abilities increase over the next year. For example, 12-month-olds will point to alert others about events they are not aware of (Liszkowski, Carpenter, & Tomasello, 2007), and from 12 to 18 months of age, infants use the eye gaze of others to achieve shared attention (Brooks & Meltzoff, 2002) and point to objects to direct an adult's attention to something that adult is searching for (Liszkowski et al., 2007). From 18 to 24 months of age, toddlers use eye gaze along with other directional cues, such as pointing and head orientation, for word learning and social referencing (Poulin-Dubois & Forbes, 2002). These findings indicate that beginning about 9 months of age, infants view other people as intentional agents, with this knowledge increasing over the next year or so (see Tomasello, 2009; Tomasello, Carpenter, & Liszkowski, 2007). Beate Sodian and Susanne Kristen-Antonow (2015) provide evidence consistent with the position that joint attention and referential communication are necessary skills in the development of more advanced forms of theory of mind. In their short-term longitudinal study, they assessed infants on a series of social-cognitive tasks from 12 to 50 months. They reported that 12-month-old infants' declarative pointing—intended to convey information about a target object and thus a form of referential communication—predicted children's performance on theory-of-mind tasks (false belief, discussed shortly) at 50 months.

Is there other evidence, independent of shared attention, that indicates more directly that infants and toddlers view others as intentional agents? Research on imitation indicates that babies are more likely to copy the behavior of a model when the model engages in the action on purpose as opposed to accidentally. (More is said about the development of imitation in Chapter 10.) For example, in research by Malinda Carpenter and her colleagues (M. Carpenter, Akhtar, & Tomasello, 1998), 14- to 18-month-old infants watched adults perform complex behavior sequences, some of which appeared to be intentional, as reflected by the model's vocal behavior, and others of which, based on what the models said, were

Knowing that someone else has thoughts and being able to infer those thoughts have important social and intellectual implications.

" I KNOW WHAT I THINK , BUT WHAT'S IMPORTANT IS WHAT MY MOM THINKS I THINK ! "

Source: Dennis the Menace® used by permission of Hank Ketcham and Copyright © 1990 by North America Syndicate.

accidental. When the infants were later given the chance to imitate the model, they reproduced twice as many intentional as accidental behaviors. One study even suggests that infants understand and selectively imitate a model's goal as young as 7 months (Hamlin, Hallinan, & Woodward, 2008). In other research, Andrew Meltzoff (1995) had 18-month-old infants watch as an adult performed actions on objects both successfully and unsuccessfully. For one task, a model picked up a dumbbell-shaped object and made deliberate movements to remove the wooden cube at the ends of the dumbbell (successful condition). In the unsuccessful condition, toddlers watched as the model pulled on the ends of the dumbbell, but her hand slipped off the cubes, which stayed on the dumbbell. When the infants were later given the dumbbell, those who had watched both the successful and the unsuccessful demonstrations removed the ends of the dumbbell significantly more often than those infants in control conditions (who did not see a demonstration of the dumbbell). They seemed to understand what the model in the unsuccessful condition *intended* to do, and they imitated her behavior to achieve an inferred (but not witnessed) goal.

Eighteen-month-old infants also discriminate between intentional and unintentional actions of another person when deciding whether to render help. In a study by Felix Warneken and Michael Tomasello (2006), 18-month-old infants sat across a table from an adult who performed a series of tasks. The adult had difficulty performing the tasks, but in some cases it was obvious that the adult was trying to achieve a specific outcome (the intentional condition). For instance, in one task, the adult accidentally dropped a marker on the floor and reached unsuccessfully to retrieve it. In a control condition, the adult deliberately threw the marker on the floor. In another task, the adult attempted to place a book on a stack of other books, but it slipped and fell beside the stack. This was contrasted with a control condition, in which the person simply placed the book beside the stack. In 6 of 10 tasks, children helped the adult (for example, retrieved the marker, placed the book on top of the stack) more in the experimental than in the control condition, reflecting not only an understanding of another person's intention but a willingness to help (a form of altruistic behavior).

You may find it difficult to get too excited about infants and young children's abilities to share attention and attribute intention to others. These hardly appear to be high-level cognitive accomplishments. Yet nearly all forms of complex human social interaction start with the understanding that the people we are dealing with are intentional agents—that they do things on purpose and that they see us the same way. Treating others as intentional agents is a necessary, but not sufficient, condition for mind reading.

Development of Mind Reading

When and how do children come to appreciate that other people have beliefs and desires, often different from their own, that motivate their behavior? To assess this question, researchers have developed tasks in which children must predict what another person will do or state, or what another person thinks, in an effort to determine what young children know about the minds of others.

False Belief

The most frequently used tool to assess children's theory of mind is the false-belief task, first developed for use with chimpanzees (Premack & Woodruff, 1978). In a standard false-belief task (first used with children by H. Wimmer & Perner, 1983), children watch as candy (or some other treat) is hidden in a special location (in a cupboard, for example). Another person—for example, a puppet named Maxi—is present when the treat is hidden but then leaves the room. While Maxi is out of the room, the treat is moved from the cupboard to another container. When Maxi returns, will he know where the treat is hidden? The results of studies using variants of this standard task are relatively straightforward. Most 4-year-old children can solve the problem, stating that Maxi will look where the candy was originally hidden. Three-year-olds, in contrast, generally cannot solve the problem, stating that Maxi will look for the candy in the new hiding place, apparently not realizing that Maxi is not privy to the new information (Wellman et al., 2001). This pattern has been reported across the globe (Sabbagh et al., 2006; Tardif & Wellman, 2000), even among the children of Baka Pygmies living in the rain forests of Cameroon (Avis & Harris, 1991), although the timetable for passing false-belief tasks has been found to vary for children in different cultures (see, for examples, Mayer & Träuble, 2013; Shahaeian et al., 2011; Slaughter & Perez-Zapata, 2014; Wellman, 2011).

Why do 3-year-olds fail false-belief tasks? For one thing, they seem not to remember what they originally believed before any switch was made (A. Gopnik & Slaughter, 1991; Zelazo & Boseovski, 2001). For example, in a modification of the false-belief task, called the Smarties task, developed by G.-Juergen Hogrefe, Heinz Wimmer, and Josef Perner (1986), children are shown a box of Smarties (a type of candy in a distinctive box, with which British children are highly familiar) and asked what they think is in the box. Naturally, they say, "Smarties." The box is then opened, revealing not candy but pencils. Children are then asked what they originally thought (that is, what they believed was in the box before being shown the contents) and to predict what another child (who is not privy to the trick) will think is in the box. The first question assesses children's memory for their initial belief, whereas the second question assesses their ability to understand false belief. The correct answer to both of these questions,

of course, is "Smarties," but most 3-year-olds say "pencils" to both questions—that is, they seem to forget their initial belief. Alison Gopnik and Virginia Slaughter (1991) found that this memory deficit is not a general one but is specific to beliefs (referred to as *representational change*). Three-year-olds have little difficulty remembering their past images, perceptions, or pretenses, but they have particular difficulty remembering their past beliefs.

If young children's problem with false-belief tasks is not one of general memory, what can account for their poor performance? Josef Perner (1991), among others, has proposed that 3-year-old children lack the conceptual structures necessary to solve problems dealing with beliefs. In other words, they have a *representational deficit* and do not possess a true theory of mind. One possibility along these lines, originally proposed by Heinz Wimmer and Perner (1983), is that young children have difficulty with contradictory evidence. They cannot deal with two representations of a single object simultaneously (the candy in Location 1 and in Location 2). This is similar to the *dual-encoding hypothesis* (or *dual-representation hypothesis*) John Flavell and Judy DeLoache proposed to explain representational differences between younger and older preschoolers discussed in Chapter 5. Basically, this position argues that young children will fail in situations where they must consider two different beliefs or representations for one target.

Support for this position comes from a study by Alison Gopnik and Janet Astington (1988), in which they assessed 3-, 4-, and 5-year-old children's performance on a series of tasks, each requiring the children to deal with contradictory evidence: false belief, appearance/reality distinction (Flavell et al., 1986), and representational change (remembering their past beliefs). The results of this study are graphed in Figure 6.2.

As you can see, performance on each of the three tasks varied with age, consistent with the idea that a single, domain-general mechanism underlies preschool children's representational abilities. This interpretation has received support from more recent research that showed that preschool children's performance on theory-of-mind tasks is associated with a variety of symbolic abilities (as reflected in language, pretend play, and understanding representations; Lillard & Kavanaugh, 2014).

FIGURE 6.2 **Scores on false-belief, appearance-reality, and representational change questions for 3-, 4-, and 5-year-olds.** Note the similar pattern of developmental change for each task.

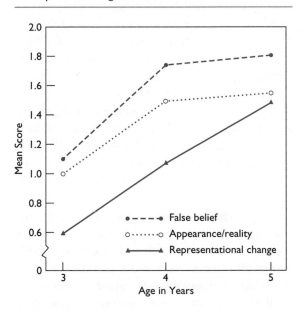

Source: Gopnik, A., & Astington, J. W. (1988). Children's understanding of the representational change and its relation to the understanding of false belief and the appearance-reality distinction. *Child Development, 59,* 26–37. Copyright © 1988 The Society for Research in Child Development. Reprinted with permission.

Related to this interpretation is the idea that young children have a general lack of *executive function* (Carlson, Claxton, & Moses, 2015; R. T. Devine & Hughes, 2014; Perner & Lang, 2000). Executive function refers to the basic cognitive abilities involved in planning, executing, and inhibiting actions, which we discuss in greater detail in Chapter 7. From this perspective, rather than seeing young children's failure to solve false-belief tasks as a representational deficit, their failure results from an inability to regulate their own behavior. In other words, before children can display advanced levels of theory of mind, they must first develop some requisite, lower-level information-processing skills. Emma Flynn and her colleagues (2004) provided support for this hypothesis in a study in which 3-year-old children were tested on a battery of false-belief and executive-function tasks once every 4 weeks for six phases (24 weeks in all). They reported that most children performed well on the executive-function tasks *before* they performed well on the false-belief tasks. That is, having good executive control preceded and was necessary for successful performance on false-belief tasks. Executive function and measures of theory of mind continue to be related into middle childhood (R. T. Devine et al., 2016).

Of the various components of executive function related to theory of mind, inhibition mechanisms have received the most attention (Bjorklund & Kipp, 2002; Perner & Lang, 2000), and brain-imaging studies have established substantial neural overlap for both processes in specific prefrontal regions of the brain (Rothmayr et al., 2011). Cognitive inhibition refers to the ability to inhibit certain thoughts and behaviors at specified times. With respect to theory of mind, many tasks require children to inhibit a prepotent response if they are to "pass" the task. For example, Joan Peskin (1992) showed preschool children a series of stickers, some more attractive than others. She then introduced "Mean Monkey," a hand puppet controlled by the experimenter, who played a game with the children. Mean Monkey would ask the children which of the stickers they really wanted and which of the stickers they did not want; he then selected the children's favorite sticker, leaving them with the least desirable ones. By 4 years of age, children understood the dynamics of the interchange and quickly learned to tell Mean Monkey the opposite of their true desires. Younger children rarely caught on, however, and played most of the game telling Mean Monkey the truth and not getting the stickers they wanted. Similarly, in research by James Russell and his colleagues (1991), 3-year-old children were shown a series of windows, some of which had treats in them. To get the treat, the children had to select the nontreat window. Children had a difficult time doing this, and they repeatedly failed to get a treat, seemingly being unable to inhibit their "pick-the-treat" response.

What can we learn from these individual differences in 3- and 4-year-olds' performance on these tasks? In one study, David Liu and colleagues (2009) tested preschoolers on over two-dozen false-belief tasks. A close examination of the data revealed that not only did all children produce a mix of correct and incorrect answers, but they also provided a mix of explanations as to why Maxi, for instance, might be looking in the wrong place. Some reasoned that Maxi must not want his toy anymore, others said that Maxi doesn't know where it is, whereas others provided actual evidence of false-belief understanding, stating that Maxi "thinks his toy is there." Alison Gopnik and Henry Wellman (2012) interpret this variability as evidence that children are "sampling from a range of hypotheses" (p. 1098). Recall our discussion in Chapter 4 that infants and children might use Bayesian-like statistics to make probabilistic inferences about the world. According to this view, children's intuitive concepts of others' minds change as they continue to put forth "hypotheses," or explanations, and find evidence for or against these. As the evidence accumulates in favor of some explanations, for instance that others possess false beliefs, these explanations become more probable. And as a result, they are more likely to be sampled and confirmed in the future. In turn, other explanations become less probable (for instance, that Maxi doesn't want his toy anymore), and over time children test these less probable hypotheses less frequently. The development of theory of mind is much more continuous then, in contrast to Piaget's proposal that children develop in a stagelike fashion, with qualitative changes in thinking.

Do other factors contribute to individual differences in children's attainment of theory of mind? Research has found a host of factors that predict children's performance on these tasks, among them quality of attachment, parenting styles, and parent-child communication (Pavarini, de Hollanda Souza, & Hawk, 2013); language skills (Milligan, Astington, & Dack, 2007); and parental warmth and the extent to which parents use mental-state talk (that is, talking about what they and their children are thinking) (Lundy, 2013; Taumoepeau & Ruffman, 2008).

One interesting finding is that 3- and 4-year-old children's performance on false-belief tasks is related to family size (Jenkins & Astington, 1996; Perner, Ruffman, & Leekam, 1994). Children from larger families perform false-belief tasks better than do children from smaller families. Why should there be a relation between family size and theory-of-mind reasoning? One explanation has to do with the role of siblings. The type of interaction provided by siblings facilitates developing a sophisticated theory of mind. Jennifer Jenkins and Janet Astington (1996) showed that family size is particularly important for children with low linguistic skills. Apparently, having siblings can compensate for delayed language development in influencing performance on false-belief tasks. Subsequent research indicates that it is only having *older*, not younger, siblings that has a facilitative effect on theory-of-mind reasoning (Ruffman et al., 1998). Ted Ruffman and colleagues (1998) believe that having older siblings stimulates pretend play, which helps younger children represent counterfactual states of affairs, a necessary skill for solving false-belief tasks.

Although siblings may be important, they are not necessarily more effective tutors than adults. Charlie Lewis and his colleagues (1996) administered a series of theory-of-mind tests to 3- and 4-year-old children and found that the number of adults children interact with daily is the best single predictor of a child's performance on theory-of-mind tasks.

Denise Cummins (1998) suggested an alternative explanation based on dominance theory. Siblings are always competing for resources, with older siblings typically having the advantage because of their greater size and mental abilities. Younger children would be motivated to develop whatever latent talents they have to aid them in their social competition with their older siblings, and developing an understanding of the mind of one's chief competitor sooner rather than later would certainly be to the younger child's advantage. A similar argument can be made for interacting with older peers.

Despite the impressive demonstrations that most 3-year-old children cannot solve false-belief tasks, evidence that 3-year-olds do solve other tasks that seemingly require an understanding of other minds challenges the strong version of the representational-deficit hypothesis (see A. J. Caron, 2009). In one particularly interesting study, Wendy Clements and Josef Perner (1994) evaluated children's *implicit* understanding of false belief. In this study, children ranging in age from 2 years 5 months to 4 years 6 months were told a story about a mouse named Sam, who had placed a piece of cheese in a specific location (Location A) so that he could get it later when he was hungry. While Sam was sleeping, a mouse named Katie found the cheese and moved it to another place (Location B). When Sam woke up, he said, "I feel very hungry now. I'll go get the cheese." Children were then asked, "I wonder where he's going to look?" The answer most older children should give is Location A, where he originally hid it, whereas most younger children should say Location B, reflecting their lack of understanding of false belief. This is the standard, or *explicit*, false-belief task, and this was the pattern of results that Clements and Perner (1994) found. However, Clements and Perner also recorded where children *looked*, at Location A or Location B. This is an *implicit task*, requiring no verbal response and, presumably, no conscious awareness. Now all but the youngest children showed high levels of correct responding (that is, they looked at Location A). Figure 6.3 shows the average explicit and implicit understanding scores, based on children's performance on the tasks in this experiment. This finding has been replicated (Clements, Rustin, & McCallum, 2000; Garnham & Ruffman, 2001), and other studies, using looking time, spontaneous response tasks, and the violation-of-expectation paradigm, have suggested that infants as young as 7 months may have an implicit understanding of false belief (for a review, see Baillargeon, Scott, & Bian, 2016). In fact, an EEG experiment revealed that 6-month-old infants showed motor activation in the sensorimotor cortex when viewing an agent who falsely believed a box contained a ball, but they showed no motor activation when the agent falsely believed the box contained no ball. This suggests infants do more than *expect* what others believe, they actually *anticipate* others' behaviors based on this belief—for instance, that an agent would search for a ball when she falsely believed it was present but not when she falsely believed it was absent (Southgate & Vernetti, 2014). Others have shown that 3-year-olds successfully pass nonverbal versions of false-belief tasks and argued that verbal tasks disrupt children's effort to track a protagonist's perspective over the course of events (Rubio-Fernández & Geurts, 2012). Another study found that 18-month-olds' performance in an anticipatory-looking task, like that described by Clements and Perner (1994), was related to children's performance at 4 years old in tasks requiring children to predict another's behavior based on an understanding of false beliefs (Sodian, Kristen, & Licata, 2015). What these findings suggest is that by about 3 years of age, and perhaps younger, children have a well-developed *implicit*, or intuitive, understanding of false belief that exceeds their explicit (verbalizable) knowledge. However, much debate remains about how to interpret these findings. Some researchers argue these findings indicate that, before their second birthday, children understand the mental states of others and that toddlers "realize that others act on the basis of their beliefs and that these beliefs are representations that may or may not mirror reality" (Onishi & Baillargeon, 2005, p. 4). In contrast, others argue that infants' and toddlers' performance on these tasks can be explained by impressive statistical learning skills (see discussion of statistical learning and Bayesian statistical inference in infants in Chapter 4) and biases to attend to faces and motion (Ruffman, 2014).

Deception

Another research area that has produced compelling evidence that young children have knowledge of the beliefs of other people concerns *deception*. Perhaps the consummate political skill, deception

FIGURE 6.3 **Average implicit and explicit understanding scores on false-belief tasks by age.** Although most children much under 4 years of age could not correctly say where Sam the mouse would look to find the piece of cheese he had hidden earlier (explicit false-belief task), 3-year-old children *looked* in the proper location (implicit false-belief task), suggesting that they may have greater knowledge of false beliefs than they can verbalize.

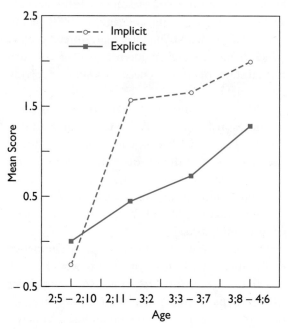

Source: Clements, W. A., & Perner, J. (1994). Implicit understanding of belief. *Cognitive Development, 9,* 377–395.

is useful in love, war, and poker games. In fact, some theorists have speculated that early hominins' abilities to deceive may have contributed significantly to the evolution of intelligence in our species (Bjorklund & Harnishfeger, 1995; Humphrey, 1976). But deception also reflects knowledge of other minds. However, if children are so self-centered in perspective that they assume that if they know something (for example, where an apple is hidden) then other people must know it too, they will see trying to deceive as fruitless. Deception is only reasonable when a person (the deceiver) knows something that another person (the deceived) doesn't know; only then can attempts be made to mislead or conceal information.

Despite young children's inability to solve explicit false-belief tasks, when preschoolers play tricks on others, they sometimes seem to be aware of what the other person does and doesn't know. Observations by many parents would suggest that 2- and 3-year-old children frequently practice (sometimes successfully, sometimes not) deception. For example, 3-year-old Tamara had gotten into her mother's makeup and spilled powder over the top of the bureau. She found a handkerchief and covered up the offending mess, acting as if nothing had happened. In this case, the ruse did not work. Kate Sullivan and Ellen Winner (1993) relate an example of more successful deception by a 2-year-old. The child pretended to cry when his aunt said that she could not come over to play with him. When she relented, the child turned to his mother and said, "I tricked her. I made her think I was sad so she would come" (p. 160).

These observations have been supported by empirical science. For example, Michael Chandler, Anna Fritz, and Suzanne Hala (1989; see also Hala, Chandler, & Fritz, 1991) assessed deception in hide-and-seek tasks in children ranging in age from 2.5 to 4 years. In these studies, children were introduced to a hiding task involving several containers placed on a white surface made of a washable oilcloth material (see Figure 6.4). A puppet hid various pieces of "treasure," making footprints on the cloth from the start box to the container in which the treasure was hidden. A sponge was available that could be used to wipe up the puppet's footprints. After ensuring that the children understood the basics of the game, one of two experimenters (El) left the room, and the remaining experimenter explained to the child that he or she should help the puppet hide the treasure so that El wouldn't be able to find it. The hide-and-seek game went on for several

trials, with the sponge being taken away on later trials so that the puppet's footprints could not be wiped off. If children didn't think of it themselves on these later trials, they were shown how false tracks could be made (that is, tracks leading to the wrong container). The question of interest was the extent to which children would use a variety of deception strategies to make it difficult for El to find the treasure.

Several types of deception were scored. The simplest involved withholding information—for example, by making sure that El was out of earshot before commenting on the hiding strategy they would use. Another involved destroying evidence by wiping away the tracks, leaving no sign of the path that the puppet took in hiding the treasure. A third involved openly lying—for example, telling El to look in an incorrect container. A fourth involved leaving a false trail of footprints leading

FIGURE 6.4 **Illustration of the hide-and-seek game used in research by Chandler and colleagues (1989).** The puppet would hide a "treasure" in one of the four containers, leaving footprints tracing her path.

Source: Chandler, M., Fritz, A. S., & Hala, S. (1989). Small-scale deceit: Deception as a marker of two-, three-, and four-year-olds' early theories of mind. *Child Development, 60,* 1263–1277. Copyright © 1989 The Society for Research in Child Development. Reprinted with permission.

to an incorrect container. The most sophisticated deceptive strategy involved a combination of both destroying the correct trail and laying a false one.

Table 6.1 shows the percentage of 2-, 3-, and 4-year-olds who used the various deceptive strategies. As can be seen, children of all ages used deception, with no age differences between the three groups. Chandler and his colleagues (1989) concluded that these findings "leave little room for doubt that even children as young as 2.5 are already capable of engaging in a variety of well-crafted deceptive practices, best interpreted as strategies aimed at instilling false beliefs in others" (p. 1274).

In a related study (Hala & Chandler, 1996), 3-year-olds were asked to play a trick on a person (Lisa) by moving some biscuits from their distinctive jar to a hiding place so that Lisa would be fooled. When later asked where Lisa will look for the biscuits and where she will think the biscuits are, children who helped plan the deception performed quite well. In contrast, children who merely observed the experimenter planning the deception or other children who planned a nondeception themselves (for example, moving the biscuits to a new location but not trying to deceive Lisa) did not perform so well. Rather, they were more likely to

perform this false-belief task erroneously, stating that Lisa would look for the biscuits in the new hiding place. In other words, when they planned to deceive someone, they were later able to take the perspective of that person; when they were not actively involved in the deceit, however, they performed egocentrically, stating that the unsuspecting person would look for the biscuits where the children knew them to be.

In other research, K. Sullivan and Winner (1993) reported that 3-year-old children can solve the Smarties false-belief task (discussed earlier) but only when they are asked to actively trick another person. When the same task is used without the trick instructions, 3-year-olds perform poorly. Sullivan and Winner interpreted these findings as indicating that 3-year-olds can understand false belief when it is embedded within a deceptive context. Subsequent research has similarly shown that 3-year-olds are able to use deception successfully under some situations (Carlson, Moses, & Hix, 1998).

Unfortunately, the picture is not as simple as the research by Chandler and his colleagues and by Sullivan and Winner suggests, with more than a little room for doubt, at least according to some researchers. Most other studies report little evidence that children much under 4 years

TABLE 6.1 **Percentage of 2-, 3-, and 4-year-olds using various deceptive strategies.**

Deceptive Strategy	2-Year-Olds	3-Year-Olds	4-Year-Olds
Withholding evidence	80%	90%	100%
Destroying evidence	50	60	80
Lying	30	60	55
Producing false trails without destroying evidence	20	35	20
Destroying evidence and producing false trails	50	25	50

Source: Chandler, M., Fritz, A. S., & Hala, S. (1989). Small-scale deceit: Deception as a marker of two-, three-, and four-year-olds' early theories of mind. *Child Development, 60,* 1263–1277.

of age use deception in a way that reflects mind reading (Peskin, 1992; Sodian et al., 1991). For example, Beate Sodian and her colleagues (1991) reported that 3-year-olds were just as likely to use a deceptive strategy whether they were asked to mislead a competitor or to help a collaborator (although Hala et al., 1991, reported evidence that 3-year-olds can use a deceptive strategy selectively). Subtle differences in the way the deception tasks are performed seem to make a big difference in whether children younger than 4 years use deception selectively or not.

Related to deception is lying. Perhaps not surprisingly, children's tendencies to tell lies (and the effectiveness of those lies) increase over the preschool years and are related to their improved executive function and theory-of-mind skills (Talwar & Crossman, 2011).

What can we make of the often-contradictory evidence concerning young children's theory of mind? There is actually much that the various researchers agree on. Three-year-olds seem to have a limited knowledge of other minds. In some circumstances, particularly involving deception or when implicit tasks are used, even 2.5-year-old children seem to be aware that they have knowledge not possessed by others. But young children's theory of mind, or belief-desire reasoning, is tenuous at best.

The findings we've discussed here suggest substantial continuity in early folk psychology. Indeed, Renee Baillargeon and colleagues (2016) have made the argument that we should forego the term *theory of mind* when referring to infants' ability to infer others' mental states and instead use the broader term *psychological reasoning*. Doing so underscores the similarities between the development of infants' folk theories across multiple domains, including psychology, physics, biology, and other core knowledge. It also frees us from the assumption that acquiring a theory of mind is some endpoint in psychological development, whereby an explicit form of knowledge replaces more implicit, intuitive forms. Intuitive psychological reasoning persists throughout the life span, just as theory testing does, and we are only at the beginnings of our understanding of its link to explicit psychological reasoning.

Theory of Mind, Evolved Modules, and Autism

Some theorists have proposed that theory of mind evolved during the course of human evolution and is the basis of our social intelligence (Baron-Cohen, 1995; Leslie, 1994). The social complexity of human groups demands attention to the actions of fellow members, and having an idea of the beliefs and desires of others would provide a tremendous political advantage for anyone trying to predict the actions of other members of a group or of rival groups. Consistent with the premises of evolutionary psychology (see Chapter 2), many of the cognitive and brain mechanisms underlying theory of mind have been proposed to be domain specific and modular in nature rather than resulting from some domain-general ability. Thus, the theory goes, our ancestors developed specific skills relating to mind reading, and these skills are relatively independent of more general cognitive abilities. One modular-type account of theory of mind was presented by Simon Baron-Cohen (1995, 2005), who proposed two complementary systems of interacting modules involved in mind reading that develop during infancy and early childhood: (1) the *mindreading system* and (2) the *empathizing system* (see Table 6.2).

TABLE 6.2 **A description of Baron-Cohen's mindreading and empathizing systems of theory of mind.**

The Mindreading System

Intentionality Detector (ID)	Interprets moving objects as having some volition or intention. Develops by 9 months.
Eye-Direction Detector (EDD)	Detects the presence of eyes or eye-like stimuli, determines whether the eyes are looking toward it or toward something else, and infers that if an organism's eyes are looking at something, then that organism sees that thing. Develops by 9 months.
Shared-Attention Mechanism (SAM)	Involves triadic (three-way) interactions or representations, such as those that babies and their parents engage in during joint-attention episodes. Develops from 9 to 18 months.
Theory of Mind Module (ToMM)	Roughly equivalent to the belief-desire reasoning and reflected by passing false-belief tasks. Develops from 24 to 48 months.

The Empathizing System

The Emotion Detector (TED)	Represents affective, or emotional, states between two people. Develops by 9 months.
The Empathizing SyStem (TESS)	Permits an empathic reaction of another person's emotions and assumes that there is an associated drive to help other people. Develops by 14 months.

Source: Adapted from Baron-Cohen, S. (2005). The empathizing system: A revision of the 1994 model of the mindreading system. In B. J. Ellis & D. F. Bjorklund (Eds.), *Origins of the social mind: Evolutionary psychology and child development* (pp. 468–492). New York: Guilford.

The Mindreading System

The earliest developing module in the mindreading system is the *Intentionality Detector (ID)*, which interprets moving objects as having some volition or intention. For example, an object that is moving toward an individual might be perceived as an agent with some intention toward that individual (for instance, it wants to harm me, to be near me). All animals that have nervous systems likely possess this very primitive skill, as do human infants by 9 months of age, if not younger. For example, in one study, 12-month-old infants watched a computer screen that depicted a ball repeatedly jumping over a barrier to land beside a ball on the other side (Csibra et al., 2003; Gergely et al.,

1995). When adults see something like this, they attribute it to the ball "wanting" to jump the barrier to join the other ball. Infants apparently see this similarly. When the barrier was removed, the babies increased their looking time when the ball continued to jump, apparently surprised that it didn't just move straight across the screen to achieve its "intention" of getting to the other side.

The second module is the *Eye-Direction Detector (EDD)*, which has three related functions: (1) It detects the presence of eyes or eye-like stimuli, (2) it determines whether the eyes are looking toward it or toward something else, and (3) it infers that if an organism's eyes are looking at something, then that organism sees that thing. In other words, this module is responsible for our belief that knowledge is gained through the eyes (both ours and the eyes of others). According to Baron-Cohen (1995), this module also develops between birth and 9 months of age.

The third module in Baron-Cohen's mindreading system is the *Shared-Attention Mechanism (SAM)*. Whereas ID and EDD involve only two objects/individuals (that is, dyadic interactions/representations), SAM involves triadic (three-way) interactions/representations. These are the interactions that babies and their parents engage in during shared-attention episodes, and as noted previously, these abilities develop from about 9 to 18 months of age (Tomasello, 2009).

The final module, the *Theory-of-Mind Module (ToMM)*, is roughly equivalent to the belief-desire reasoning described earlier and is reflected by passing false-belief tasks. As we've seen in the research discussed in this section, this develops from the ages of about 24 to 48 months.

The Empathizing System

More recently, Baron-Cohen (2005) updated his model, proposing that the mindreading system is accompanied in development by the empathizing system. In addition to ID and EDD, Baron-Cohen proposed a new, early developing mechanism, *The Emotion Detector (TED)*. According to Baron-Cohen, infants from an early age are sensitive to the emotions of others. The emotion detector can represent affective, or emotional, states between two people. For instance, an infant can represent the idea that "Mother is happy" or "Father is angry at me." Within their first 6 months of life, infants can detect another's emotional state through facial expressions or vocalizations, with infant-directed speech (see Chapter 9) being a particularly effective means by which infants pick up on the emotions of their mothers (or others). TED permits infants to detect the

basic, or primary, emotions—for example, joy, anger, and sadness.

Beginning around 9 months, emotional information derived from TED can be converted into a triadic representation by SAM (just as information derived from EDD can be converted into a triadic representation). So, for example, infants who months before could represent the idea that "Mother is sad" can now represent the idea that "I'm sad that Mother is sad," or "Mother is sad that I am sad."

Beginning around 14 months of age, more than 2 years before the development of ToMM, *The Empathizing SyStem (TESS)* comes online. TESS permits an empathic reaction to another person's emotions and assumes that there is an associated drive to help other people. Baron-Cohen (2005, p. 473) illustrates the distinction between TESS and ToMM by using the following example: "I see you are in pain" requires ToMM. A child must use facial cues (perhaps) to infer the state of mind (in this case, pain) of another individual. In contrast, "I am devastated that you are in pain" requires TESS. The reactions of another individual trigger an empathic response and may cause children to act appropriately (for example, consoling the hurt person). This type of empathy is a secondary, or self-conscious, emotion, typically emerging late in the second year of life (M. Lewis, 1993). Baron-Cohen places the initial emergence of empathy as reflected by TESS a bit earlier, but all agree that the expression of empathy develops much earlier than theory of mind, as reflected by false-belief reasoning.

Baron-Cohen's proposal is that his various modules are specific to theory of mind and that they evolved to deal with the types of problems that are posed by having to cooperate and compete with other people. In other words, theory of mind is not a reflection of general intelligence. It is a set of mechanisms shaped by natural selection to handle the problems of living in a complex social world.

Mindblindness

Baron-Cohen's primary source of evidence for his model is that the more advanced forms of mind reading (SAM and ToMM) and empathizing (TESS) are typically absent or significantly delayed in children with autism spectrum disorder (ASD), which is characterized by severe social and communication disabilities. Baron-Cohen (1995) claims that the primary deficit of these children is an inability to read minds, or what he calls mindblindness. Evidence for this comes from studies in which children with ASD are presented with false-belief and other theory-of-mind tasks and consistently fail them, despite performing well on other, nonsocial tasks. This is in contrast to children with intellectual impairment, such as Down syndrome, who perform the theory-of-mind tasks easily, despite often doing poorly on other tasks that assess more general intelligence (Baron-Cohen, Leslie, & Frith, 1985). Most children with ASD are able to perform well on the simpler tasks requiring ID, EDD, or TED modules, but they fail tasks involving SAM and, especially, ToMM and TESS. An example of this can be demonstrated using the very simple stimuli depicted in Figure 6.5, in a task known as the Charlie task (Baron-Cohen, 1995). When children are shown the picture of Charlie and asked, "Which candy is Charlie looking at?," both ASD and typically developing children identify the correct candy (in this case, the top left one). Answering this question requires EDD. However, when asked, "Which candy does Charlie *want*?," children with ASD are unable to answer correctly, whereas typically developing children can correctly infer Charlie's desires from Charlie's gaze. This question requires more than EDD, it also requires SAM and ToMM.

However, it is not just the more advanced forms of theory-of-mind abilities that children with ASD lack. For example, 3- and 4-year-old children with

FIGURE 6.5 **Illustration of the Charlie task.** Typically developing and ASD children can correctly indicate where Charlie is looking (at the top left candy), but ASD children cannot answer the question, "Which candy does Charlie want?" whereas typically developing children 4 years and older are able to infer Charlie's desires from his gaze.

Source: Ward, J. (2015). *The student's guide to cognitive neuroscience* (3rd ed., p. 316). New York: Psychology Press.

ASD perform significantly worse than typically developing children in social orientation, shared attention, attending to the distress of another, and attending to faces (Dawson et al., 2004; Hobson et al., 2006; Kikuchi et al., 2009). According to Baron-Cohen (2005) children with autism are unable to understand other people's different feelings and beliefs, and as a result, the world consisting of humans must be a confusing and frightening one, even for those children who are functioning at a relatively high intellectual level.

Extending Theory of Mind

As we've seen from our discussion so far, theory of mind seems to be based on two underlying abilities. The first is the tendency to view the actions of others as intentional, executed on purpose to achieve specific goals (that is, to view other individuals as *intentional agents*). The second is *perspective taking*, specifically being able to read the minds of other people. Might these aspects of theory of mind be extended to nonsocial phenomena?

Finalism, Promiscuous Teleology, and Artificialism

Some researchers have suggested that such intentional reasoning causes children to interpret natural phenomena as being caused or created by someone with a purpose in mind (Bering, 2012; E. M. Evans, 2001; Kelemen, 2004). For example, 4- and 5-year-old children will say that mountains are "for climbing," clouds are "for raining," and pointy rocks are "so animals could scratch on them when they get itchy," and school-age children will say things such as "the sand was grainy so that animals could easily bury their eggs in it" (Kelemen, 1999a, 1999b). Piaget termed such thinking finalism. Deborah Kelemen (2004) goes a step further, referring to such thinking as promiscuous teleology. Teleology refers to the tendency to reason about events and objects in terms of purpose—what they are "for." Young children, claims Kelemen, see purpose everywhere, and this is a product of their sophisticated social cognition, interpreting people's actions in terms of intentions.

Closely related to finalism is artificialism, the belief that everything that exists was constructed by people (or God) for specific purposes, much as artifacts (for example, tools, tables, automobiles) are constructed. According to Piaget (1929/1969), artificialism "consists in regarding things as the product of human creation, rather than in attributing creative activity to the things themselves" (p. 253). An example of this would be a preschool-age child who, upon being asked where the rain comes from, answers that the rainmaker in the sky pushes the button to make the rain fall down. We know that young children, and even infants, have some understanding about physical causality and that they understand people make artifacts but not natural objects (S. A. Gelman & Kremer, 1991). Despite this knowledge, children still seem to view objects and events as existing for a purpose and to believe that natural phenomena are created intentionally, although not necessarily by humans; supernatural agents may be involved (Kelemen, 2004). Such a perspective may help explain how children understand the natural world and their belief in supernatural beings.

Children as Intuitive Theists

All cultures have religion and a belief in some supernatural beings or powers. There have been a number of explanations for the universality of religion, including the idea that God is innate (although one's conception of a deity varies radically among cultures), that religion serves to combat our fear of death, and that religion serves a social function, bringing people together and providing rules to live by. An alternative view now developing among a set of scientists is that religion (or at least belief in supernatural agents) is a by-product of our developing social-cognitive system (Atran & Henrich, 2010; Bering, 2012; P. Bloom, 2004; Gervais, 2013).

What aspects of children's developing social cognition may be extended to the belief in the supernatural? Kelemen (2004) proposes that children's beliefs that things occur "for a reason" and their endowment of fantasy creatures with opinions, desires, and knowledge (see the discussion of children's belief in fantasy beings in Chapter 5) makes them prone to cultural beliefs of the supernatural, particularly to the idea of God or gods. Kelemen refers to children as *intuitive theists*. They believe in the existence of supernatural beings, attribute belief-desire reasoning to such characters, and assume that everything happens for a reason. Children do not come into the world with a concept of God, but their social-cognitive system develops over the preschool years to make it likely that they will acquire the supernatural beliefs of their culture. Kelemen (2004) argues that "children make sense of the world in a manner superficially approximating adult theism, by forming a working hypothesis that natural phenomena derive from a nonhuman 'somebody' who designed them for a purpose—an intuition that may be elaborated by a particular religious culture but derives primarily from cognitive predispositions and artifact knowledge" (p. 297). From this perspective, children generalize what they know about how people make decisions (that is, based on belief-desire reasoning) to explain natural objects and events (the weather, good fortune, the Rocky Mountains).

Paul Bloom (2004) has made similar arguments, proposing that children (and adults, for that matter) are intuitive Cartesians, easily making a distinction between body and soul, following 18th-century French philosopher Rene Descartes. Descartes proposed that nonhuman animals were "beast-machines," or automata without minds or souls. Humans, by contrast, have both bodies and minds/souls. Despite modern science's demonstration that the mind is the product of the physical brain, Bloom claims that the mind-body distinction feels "right" to all of us. Bloom proposes that this separation originates in children's distinction between social beings who intentionally make things happen and physical objects that do not do things themselves but obey the laws of nature (for example, unsupported objects will fall). With the development of theory of mind, children come to understand that what people do is based on what they think—their unseen (and unseeable) desires and knowledge—and this serves to solidify the distinction between

body and soul. With this distinction, children can easily grasp the death of the body—pets die, people die, and their bodies cease to function. However, children (or adults, for that matter) have no experience, other than perhaps sleep, with the cessation of the mind, and so they find it difficult to conceive of the mind not working. This natural mind-body dualism makes the belief in the continuation of the mind/soul after death a reasonable thing.

Final Reflections on Theory of Mind

The centrality of theory of mind to human social functioning seems incontrovertible. Although the beginnings of theory of mind are seen in the first year of life, the ability to read minds develops over the preschool years and into childhood. By age 7, children perform what are known as second-order theory-of-mind tasks, which require the ability to infer what one person thinks about another person's thoughts (Perner & Wimmer, 1985). For instance, recall the false-belief task with Maxi that we described earlier. Imagine that children observe that another puppet—Maxi's mother—is the one who instructs Maxi to put the treat in the cupboard and then is also the one to move the treat from the cupboard to another container when Maxi is out of the room. As we described, when children reason that Maxi will think the treat is still in the cupboard, that is, that Maxi possesses a *false belief*, they are passing a first-order theory-of-mind task. Imagine now that children are asked about Maxi's mother's beliefs, specifically, where she thinks Maxi thinks the treat is. The correct answer is that she should think that Maxi thinks that the treat is in the cupboard. (Is your head spinning yet?) Arriving at the correct answer here may not seem particularly difficult considering a child who can pass the first-order task. All the child must do is recognize that the mother's view of the situation is the same as the child's own and then project the child's understanding on to her. However, the situation becomes more difficult if Maxi's mom is presented as having a false belief, for instance, if Maxi re-enters the room and unbeknownst to his mother finds the treat in the new location. Now children must attribute a second false belief to the mother, and this appears more challenging for children prior to age 7 (Perner & Wimmer, 1985).

Unlike with first-order false-belief tasks, children can pass verbal versions of second-order tasks before they can pass nonverbal versions, suggesting that language supports reasoning about the beliefs of others (Hollebrandse, van Hout, & Hendriks, 2011). Executive functioning is also related (see S. A. Miller, 2009). The ability to track and anticipate the thoughts and behaviors of others continues to improve with age, of course, as older children and adolescents perform what are known as third- and fourth-order theory-of-mind tasks (for example, "Shelia knows that Daphne knows that I was lying when I told Karl that Makayla likes him") (see S. A. Miller, 2009).

Section Review

- *Theory of mind* refers to children's developing concepts of mental activity, including the understanding that people's behavior is motivated by what they know, or believe, and by what they want, or desire (*belief-desire reasoning*).
- The beginnings of theory of mind are seen in infants viewing other people as *intentional agents* (beings who are goal directed). *Shared attention*, which is reflected in gaze following, pointing, and other forms of triadic interaction, is seen as early as 9 months and continues to improve over the next year, reflecting infants' increasing abilities to take the perspective of others.
- Concerning children as mind readers, 3-year-olds usually fail *false-belief tasks*. One explanation for young children's poor performance on false-belief tasks is that they have a representational deficit. Other explanations look at children's executive function or their reasoning about true-belief tasks.
- Children with autism are particularly deficient in mind-reading skills and have been described as having *mindblindness*.
- Preoperational children have a tendency toward *finalism*, believing that natural objects and events must have a specifiable cause, with some people describing such thinking as *promiscuous teleology*.
- Preoperational children also display *artificialism*, the belief that everything that exists was constructed by people (or God) for specific purposes.

Ask Yourself . . .

2. To what extent do young children understand that the perceptions, knowledge, and thoughts of others are different from their own?

3. What are the most elementary social-cognitive abilities required for a theory of mind?

4. What is a false-belief task, and how does it assess children's theory of mind? At what age can children explicitly pass these tasks? At what age can they implicitly pass them?

5. What are the components of Baron-Cohen's mindreading system and empathizing system? What is the function of each? At what age do these components come online in typically developing children?

6. How does the cognition of preoperational children, specifically finalism and artificialism, contribute to their promiscuous teleology?

FOLK BIOLOGY: UNDERSTANDING THE BIOLOGICAL WORLD

The story that opened this chapter—of a boy's fascination with creepy-crawly things living in a rotting log—illustrates some children's interests in the biological world. In fact, most children across the globe are interested in the natural world and, like social relations, seem especially prepared to make sense of it (see Inagaki & Hatano, 2006; P. C. Lee, 2013). Given the central role that animals would have played in the lives of our ancestors—both as predators and prey—it is perhaps not surprising a number of theorists have proposed that natural selection produced mechanisms that made it easy for children to acquire knowledge about those animals (H. C. Barrett, 2005; Geary, 2005).

Is It Alive?

A good place to begin our discussion of children's understanding of the biological world is their ability to distinguish (a) animate from inanimate objects and (b) agents (things that act intentionally, like people and nonhuman animals) from nonagents (things that do not act intentionally, like rocks and trees). Within the first year of life, infants are able to distinguish between animate and inanimate objects based on self-propelled movement (Schlottmann & Ray, 2010). For example, newborns will preferentially look at light displays that depict biological motion (Bardi, Regolin, & Simion, 2011, 2014). To assess this, infants watch a human figure walking with 10 to 12 light patches at the joints, as well as other displays with randomly moving patterns of light (see Figure 6.6). Infants from birth usually look longer at light patterns generated by a walking person than at randomly generated patterns,

although they do not seem to recognize the same walking figure if it is presented upside down (see middle panel in Figure 6.6; Bertenthal, Proffitt, & Cutting, 1984). However, although they spend more time looking at displays showing biological motion, they do not seem to treat it as a person until about 9 months (Bertenthal, 1996), and by 12 months infants will follow the gaze of a point-light human figure, indicating that such displays convey sufficient information for babies to treat them as intentional agents (Yoon & Johnson, 2009). And it will be several more years before they understand that animate beings cause things to happen, whereas inanimate objects do not. Relatedly, the lack of spontaneous movement seems to be the major reason children have a difficult time identifying plants as living things. It is not until about 7 to 9 years of age before children agree that plants are alive (Opfer & Gelman, 2001), although the intuitive conception of living things based on an object's mobility persists into adolescence (Babai, Sekal, & Stavy, 2010).

Once young children get it into their minds, however, that living things can have thoughts and feelings and can act intentionally, they tend to generalize such beliefs to inanimate objects. Piaget (1929/1969) was one of the first people to describe this form of "magical thinking" in children and referred to it as animism. More recently, this way of thinking and behaving is referred to as anthropomorphism. Children attribute human properties, like hopes, feelings, and thoughts, to inanimate things ("The wind came and blew on me because I was hot"). I (DB) recall as a not-too-young elementary school student having mixed feelings about getting a new baseball glove, not wanting to "hurt the feelings" of my old, trusty glove, or being careful to use all the ink in a favorite pen so not to "disappoint" the unused ink. I knew very well that baseball gloves and ink were inanimate and had no thoughts or emotions, and

FIGURE 6.6 **Biological motion.** Three- to five-month-old babies look longer at the first panel of moving lights, that is, the one depicting biological (here, specifically human) motion, than to the other patterns of moving lights.

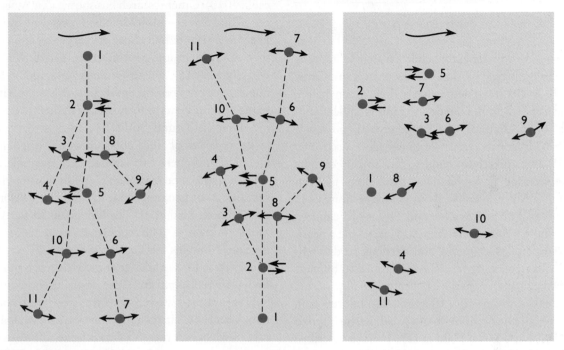

Source: Bertenthal, B. I., Proffitt, D. R., & Cutting, J. E. (1984). Infant sensitivity to figural coherence in biomechanical motions. *Journal of Experimental Child Psychology, 37*, 213–230.

I remember, even then, believing how silly such thinking was. But I could not avoid my intuitions of attributing intentions and emotions to some of the inanimate objects that I was particularly fond of (see Bjorklund, 2007a).

Anthropomorphism doesn't totally disappear with the advent of concrete operations, either. William Looft and Wayne Bartz (1969) summarized research examining animistic thinking in adults and reported that from 50% to 75% of adults tested displayed some anthropomorphic thinking. For example, some college students stated that the sun is alive "because it gives off heat" or that a lighted match was alive because "it has a flame which indicates life." Looft and Bartz believed that the anthropomorphism shown by adults was qualitatively different from that shown by children; nonetheless, the high frequency of adults, even those with college educations, who attribute life characteristics to inanimate objects indicates that this tendency extends beyond early childhood. This, along with newer research (for example, R. F. Goldberg & Thompson-Schill, 2009, who show that even biologists display some remnant of anthropomorphic thinking), suggests that adults retain some of the same biases about living things as children do. Although adults come to learn the scientific way of thinking about the world, these concepts come to mask rather than replace their initial intuition (see Shtulman & Valcarcel, 2012).

What Young Children Know and Don't Know About Biology

Susan Carey and her colleagues (Carey, 1985, 1999; Slaughter, Jaakkola, & Carey, 1999) were pioneers in investigating children's understanding of the biological world and how it develops. Carey (1985, 1999) argued that children much before the age of 7 do not have an organized understanding of the natural world but, instead, possess a series of isolated pieces of knowledge. According to Carey, preschool children fail to differentiate between folk biology and folk psychology, generalizing what they know about people to animals in general. For instance, 4- and 5-year-old children attribute human properties, such as having a heart, having bones, thinking, and sleeping, to different species depending on their similarities to humans (Carey, 1985). A major conceptual change occurs sometime from 7 to 10 years, as children gain more knowledge about biology. Similarly, Kayoko Inagaki and Gyoo Hatano (1991) have described young children's animistic beliefs as reflecting an egocentric tendency to explain things in terms of what is familiar to them, such as human behavior. However, experience and culture play a role here. When preschool children have more day-to-day experiences with living things, they are less apt to characterize other animals in terms of what they know about people. For example, young rural European Americans who have more interactions with the natural world are less apt to attribute human characteristics to other animals, unlike their urban counterparts. These experiences certainly interact with culture, however, as shown by the behavior of rural children from a Native American tribe. The rural Menominee tribe adopts an animal-based clan system and tells an origin story of how humans evolved from the bear. In contrast to the behavior of rural European American children, 4- to 5-year-old Menominee children

more readily generalize human properties (than dog properties) to bears and other animals (Medin et al., 2010). Other research has shown that American 3- and 5-year-old children with pets were more likely to attribute biological properties to animals than children without pets (Geerdts, Van de Walle, & LoBue, 2015). These findings underscore the importance of experience and children's sensitivity to the belief systems of their culture in their reasoning about the natural world.

By 3 years of age, children easily attribute intention and agency to animals. For example, a majority of 3-year-old Shuar children from the rain forests of Ecuador made appropriate attributions to both predator ("The lion wants to eat the zebra") and prey ("The zebra wants to escape from the lion") animals (H. C. Barrett, 2004). This rose to over 80% for 4- and 5-year-old children. Similar findings were found for German children, whose only exposure to wild animals was from television, books, and zoos. In fact, in many ways the biological knowledge of preschoolers is quite impressive. For example, Inagaki and Hatano (1993, 2002) reported that 4- and 5-year-old children understand that eye color, one's heartbeat, and breathing are not under voluntary control and that children who are poorly nourished are susceptible to illness. Other research has shown that 4- and 5-year-old children understand that dead animals cannot exhibit living functions, such as moving, but that, in contrast, sleeping animals can act once they awaken (H. C. Barrett & Behne, 2005). Preschool children's distinction between living and nonliving is reflected in the different questions they ask when trying to discover the identity (category membership, "Is it a bear?") and location ("Where does it live?") of animals as opposed to artifacts (functions, "What does it do?") (Greif et al., 2006). They can also understand some complex biological phenomena, such as contamination (for example, if a cockroach is in a glass of orange juice, the juice should not be drunk, even if the cockroach is removed; see Siegal & Share, 1990) and reproduction (that babies grow inside their mothers and that seeds of a certain species of plant produce a new plant of the same species; see Hickling & Gelman, 1994; Springer, 1999). Children's understanding that certain organs, like the heart, are important for maintaining life increases from ages 4 to 6, and some research shows that boys are more likely than girls to conceptualize life as an important function of a body part (Schroeder et al., 2010). We have more to say about children's

understanding about where babies come from in the next section.

Young children's understanding of biological life is far from that of adults, however (see Siegal, 2008). For instance, it is not until children are about 7 years old that they understand that some traits are linked to one's biological family whereas others are not (for example, beliefs). Four-year-old children in both Western and non-Western cultures initially believe, for example, that the inheritance of some physical traits, such as eye color,

TABLE 6.3 **Development of children's thinking about reproduction.**

Level	Piagetian Stage	Ages	Name	Description	Example
1.	Preoperational	3–7	Geographer	Babies have always existed in completed form; need to be acquired (bought, found, ordered, delivered).	Mommy got me at the hospital.
2.	Preoperational	4–8	Manufacturer	Babies haven't always existed in completed form; need to be assembled.	Mommy made me out of blood and bones she had left over from my brother.
3.	Transitional	5–10	In-betweens	Babies need two parents in special relationship, sexual intercourse, sperm egg; process is unclear.	Doctor put a seed in Mommy, and Daddy put some stuff in to make the seed grow.
4.	Concrete	7–12	Reporters	Know the basic facts but don't speculate on why; only accuracy counts.	Daddy puts sperm in Mommy and the baby starts growing. (Why?) I guess it loosens up the egg or something.
5.	Transitional	10–13	Theoreticians	Know basic facts and basic why's; don't understand that eggs and sperm can join to produce a third entity.	Baby is in the egg, and the sperm makes it start growing.
6.	Formal operations	14–adult	Putting it all together	Know that two distinct entities, sperm and ovum, can become one qualitatively different entity, the embryo.	The male injects sperm into the female's womb and fertilizes the egg and it grows into a fetus, and nine months later a baby is born.

Source: Adapted from Bernstein, A. C. (1978). *Flight of the stork.* New York: Delacorte Press.

depends on environmental factors, such as the family children are living with, regardless of whether children live with their biological or adoptive parents (Astuti, 2001; Astuti, Solomon, & Carey, 2004). In other research, children in preschool through second grade believe that you are more apt to catch a cold from a stranger than from a relative or friend (Raman & Gelman, 2008). Other studies have demonstrated that young children often think that dead people retain some biological properties of life, like eating and breathing (Bering & Bjorklund, 2004; Slaughter et al., 1999). Although young children show quite a sophisticated understanding for some aspects of biological life, others take a while to develop.

Where Do Babies Come From?

Most parents have stories they tell about awkward moments when their children ask, "Where do babies come from?" Although anecdotes abound about children's understanding—and misunderstanding—of reproduction, there is relatively little research on the topic. Exceptions to this are studies by Anne Bernstein and Philip Cowan (1975) and by Ronald and Juliette Goldman (1982), who examined children's understanding of "where babies come from" from an explicitly Piagetian perspective. Both investigations reported several well-defined levels of understanding that followed Piaget's stages of cognitive development. Table 6.3 presents Bernstein and Cowan's description of the stages children pass through while learning the origin of babies.

At Level 1, many children think that babies have always existed and were somehow given to their mothers. Parents in generations past have supported this type of thinking by telling

children, for example, that the stork brings babies. At Level 2, children think that babies are somehow "made," but they do not understand the process. Consider 4-year-old Carlos, who had been pondering the process whereby his new baby sister came into the world. Out of the blue one afternoon, he stated that his mother had gone to the paint store, drew a picture of a baby, and then she "popped" out of his mother's tummy. Children in Level 3 realize the importance of mothers and fathers to produce a baby, but they are unclear about the process. For example, 8-year-old Christopher was confused how his divorced mother could be pregnant. Didn't she have to be married to get pregnant? The presence of her live-in boyfriend did not seem to make a difference. Children at this stage understand that a special relationship between a man and a woman is needed for reproduction, but they do not understand the nature of that relationship. Children seem to understand the basic facts of reproduction between 7 and 11 years of age (Level 4), but it takes them some time to fully understand the biology of the process. For example, many preadolescents in Level 5 often believe that babies exist in the egg fully formed, waiting for the sperm to initiate growth. (This is also how most educated people several centuries ago, before the advent of modern biological science, thought about reproduction.)

A. C. Bernstein and Cowan (1975) concluded that children do not wait to be told about reproduction but construct their own notions about where babies come from. Consistent with Piagetian theory (see Chapter 5), these self-constructed ideas reflect the children's present cognitive structures. More extensive research (S. L. Caron & Ahlgrim, 2012) has basically replicated the findings of A. C. Bernstein and Cowan but has also found national differences in the attainment of knowledge of reproduction. For example, children from Sweden and the Netherlands had the most advanced understanding of where babies come from, well ahead of Australian (Goldman & Goldman, 1982) and English children, with North American children being the slowest. Subsequent research has confirmed that preschool children know little about procreation and also have little knowledge of adult sexual behavior (Volbert, 2000).

What do children think about *prelife*—their mental and bodily states during the time prior to conception? Natalie Emmons and Deborah Keleman (2014, 2015) investigated this question in two groups of 5- to 12-year-old children; one group was made up of urban Ecuadorians, the other rural indigenous Shuar. Each child was shown drawings of a young woman, a pregnant woman, and a baby and instructed to imagine that the pictures were of themselves and their mom. The experimenter pointed to the drawing of the young woman and described to each child that this was "your mom before she was pregnant with you, that is, before you were in your mom's belly" (Emmons & Keleman, 2014, p. 1621). Children were then asked 12 yes or no questions about their mental and bodily functions during the time, such as "Could you feel happy?" (emotional), "Could your eyes work?" (biological), "Could you be thirsty?" (psychobiological), "Could you watch something?" (perceptual), "Could you want anything?" (desire), and "Could you think things?" (epistemic). Children from both cultures viewed themselves as emotional beings who desired things before their mothers were pregnant with them but not beings who could function in other biological or perceptual ways—they

couldn't "see" or "feel hungry," for instance. This bias decreased with age, with half of 11- to 12-year-olds indicating all 12 of their prelife capacities were nonfunctioning. These findings are consistent with afterlife research demonstrating that children are inclined to reason that mental function, but not bodily function, persists after death (Bering & Bjorklund, 2004; Bering, Hernández Blasi, & Bjorklund, 2005). Taken together, this line of research suggests children have a robust belief in the enduring functionality of emotions and desires, even in the absence of biological existence.

Section Review

- Children in all cultures are interested in animals and biological life.
- Movement is a key component in whether children think something is alive.
- With increasing age, children make clearer distinctions between animate and inanimate objects, although some aspects of *animism* and *anthropomorphism* persist in adults.
- Children's understanding of folk biology becomes more adultlike with age and is affected by culture and children's experience with animals.
- Children's knowledge about reproduction follows a developmental course similar to that suggested by Piaget.

Ask Yourself . . .

7. At what age do children begin to have an organized understanding of the biological world? What are some examples of how their understanding changes?
8. How does children's understanding of reproduction differ across each Piagetian stage?

FOLK PHYSICS: UNDERSTANDING THE PHYSICAL WORLD

According to theory theorists and others (Geary, 2005), children are not only specially prepared to make sense of their social and biological world but also their physical world. For example, we saw in Chapter 4 that infants develop early an understanding of objects, culminating in the attainment of object permanence. Core-knowledge theorists, however, argue that children's understanding of objects in space continues to develop, and this is often studied under the term *spatial cognition*. Children are not only biased to *perceive* the physical world but also to *act* upon it. For example, David Geary (2005), among others (see Bjorklund & Gardiner, 2011; P. K. Smith, 2005), proposed that children are biased to interact with objects, often through what is called object-oriented play, to learn properties of those objects that can later be used as tools. Children also develop an understanding

of how events unfold over time, an important component in how people interact with their social and physical environments. In this section, we examine three aspects of children's developing folk physics: (1) spatial cognition, (2) object play and tool use, and (3) understanding time.

Development of Spatial Cognition

Spatial cognition refers to processing information with respect to spatial relations. Most animals, including humans, need to navigate their environment (find their way home after roaming in the backyard), judge the distances between different objects (and oneself), and regulate one's action in time and space (knowing when to execute a jump over a log, lest you end up tripping on it). This is why most experts in psychology think that the ability to deal with spatial information must have deep evolutionary roots (see Haun et al., 2010). Basically, spatial cognition involves coding information about the environment (where something is in relation to you

TABLE 6.4 **Ten spatial skills that young children exhibit and develop.** This listing does not pretend to be exhaustive.

- Geometric sensitivity (mostly to angles, distances, and handedness/sense)
- Dead reckoning or inertial navigation (that is, coming back to a starting point)
- Voluntary or conscious navigation (that is, orient/reorient in a physical space)
- Use of beacons/landmarks to represent spatial information
- Perspective taking (that is, to "read" others' spatial perspective)
- Mental rotation (that is, exploring objects by mentally moving them)
- Building "cognitive maps" about physical environments
- Making spatial inferences (that is, applying logical thinking to space)
- Communicating linguistically spatial information to others
- Using real maps and models and understanding graphs and diagrams

Source: Based partially on Newcombe & Huttenlocher (2006).

or how something might look from a different orientation). Table 6.4 lists 10 spatial skills that develop through childhood and adolescence that children seem prepared to acquire.

Spatial cognition shows substantial improvements during the preschool years and into the school years (Vasilyeva & Lourenco, 2012). Spatial cognition is sometimes divided into three broad categories: (1) *spatial orientation*, (2) *spatial visualization*, and (3) *object and location memory*. Spatial orientation refers to how people understand the placement of objects in space with themselves as the reference point. Spatial-orientation tasks include those in which participants are asked to distinguish geographic directions in an unfamiliar locale or to draw their way from Point A to Point B on a map. In contrast, spatial visualization is tested using tasks that involve visual operations, such as mentally rotating a figure or adjusting a tilted object to bring it to an upright position. Object and location memory is tested by having participants remember objects and their location from a spatial array. Both developmental and sex differences have been reported in each of these areas.

Spatial Orientation

Aspects of children's spatial-orientation abilities are relatively well developed during the preschool years. For instance, in one study, toddlers watched as an object was hidden in a room, were disoriented, and then were asked to find the hidden object. Most were able to find the object if it was hidden in a distinctive location, such as a corner in both rectangular- and triangular-shaped rooms (J. Huttenlocher & Vasileya, 2003). Even 5-month-old infants code distances about a hidden object in a

3-foot-long sandbox (Newcombe, Huttenlocher, & Learmonth, 1999). In other research, 1- to 2-year-old children were able to successfully trace their paths back to the appropriate place in a sandbox where a toy was previously hidden after they had been distracted and brought to a different place by a route where no landmarks were available (Newcombe et al., 1998). This is called *dead reckoning*, or inertial navigation, the ability to come back to an initial starting point.

Spatial orientation increases with age as the tasks become more demanding. This is reflected by children's ability to form *cognitive maps* of large areas. In one study, 5-, 7-, and 10-year-old children walked repeatedly through a large model town consisting of buildings, streets, railroad tracks, and trees. After the walks, the children were asked to re-create the layout from memory. Performance increased with age (Herman & Siegel, 1978). Similar age changes in cognitive maps have been reported between 3- and 5.5-year-old children, although the spatial representations were not that sophisticated for either group (Herman, Shiraki, & Miller, 1985).

The use of real maps also develops over the school years (Hirsh & Sandberg, 2013; Liben, 2009). Preschoolers have a difficult time using maps, even if they are very simple and depict a familiar environment (Liben & Yekel, 1996). The ability to deal with maps improves by the ages of 4 to 6 (J. Huttenlocher et al., 2008), but it is not adultlike until about the age of 10 (Uttal, Fisher, & Taylor, 2006). However, even younger children can use maps effectively under certain conditions. For instance, Andrea Frick and Nora Newcombe (2012) found individual variability in 3-year-olds' success at locating objects in a two-dimensional spatial layout using a map. However, they improved when landmarks were provided or circular maps were used, as opposed to rectangular maps (children found orienting the rectangular map more confusing than the circular map; see also Shusterman, Lee, & Spelke, 2008).

In any case, remember that maps (like models, diagrams, or graphs) are not just devices to assess spatial skills in children but also a way to promote them. In this sense, maps can be seen as a *tool of intellectual adaptation* that a culture provides its members to think about important aspects of their environments (Vygotsky, 1978; see Chapter 2). The relation between maps and spatial development is thus reciprocal: Children's developing spatial skills influences their ability to use maps, but the very process of using maps influences spatial cognition (Uttal, 2000). According to Uttal (2000), "Maps provide a cognitive tool that helps children extend their reasoning about space in a new way. Over time, children can internalize the tool and think about space in maplike ways, even if they are not looking at a map at the time" (p. 249). Tentative evidence for Uttal's position was found in an experiment in which 4- to 7-year-old children were asked to learn which of six animals went with each of six rooms in a life-sized playhouse (Uttal & Wellman, 1989). One group of children was given a simple map, with each room represented by a box that contained a picture of the animal. A control group of children was shown a series of flash cards, with the picture of one animal on each of six cards. Children in both groups learned perfectly the six animals that went with the playhouse. They then were walked through the playhouse and asked to anticipate which animal would be found in each room. Although both groups of children had, as mentioned, learned the list of animals

perfectly, the children in the map group performed significantly better than the children in the control group. Why did the children in the map group do so well? Uttal and Wellman (1989) argued that the experience with the map changed the way those children represented space, allowing them to more easily see spatial relationships among elements. Thus, the development of spatial cognition is influenced not only by endogenous (internal, or maturational) factors but also by children's experience in the real world. In this case, a cultural invention (maps) not only permits children (and adults) to apply their spatial skills to solve problems but also influences how those skills develop.

FIGURE 6.7 **A mental rotation task.** Are the two figures in each pair alike or different? The task assesses the ability to mentally rotate visual information and is a task on which average differences between males and females are large. Males typically outperform females on this task.

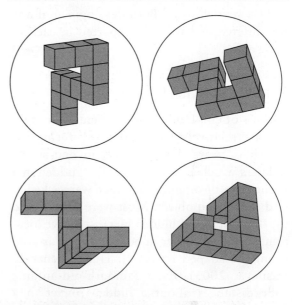

Source: © Cengage Learning.

Spatial Visualization

In contrast to spatial-orientation tasks, *spatial-visualization tasks* involve visual/mental operations, such as mentally rotating a figure or adjusting a tilted object to bring it to an upright position. One type of spatial-visualization task that shows substantial improvement over development is **mental rotation** (see Figure 6.7), in which a person must mentally rotate a visual stimulus to determine if it matches another stimulus (see Halpern, 1992). Both 4- and 5-year-old children are able to mentally rotate simple stimuli (see Newcombe & Huttenlocher, 2006), but even adults have difficulty mentally rotating more complex stimuli, such as the ones shown in Figure 6.7.

A relatively simple test of spatial visualization is Piaget and Inhelder's (1967) water-level problem (see Figure 6.8). Children are shown a tipped bottle, then asked to imagine the bottle half full and to draw a line depicting the water level. The correct solution to this is to draw a line parallel to the ground, horizontal across the bottle. However, most preschool children

draw a line parallel to the bottom of the bottle. This is a seemingly simple task that Piaget and Inhelder found was mastered by most children by the time they reached concrete operations, around 7 years of age. Other researchers, however, have reported that many adolescents and young adults continue to have difficulty with the concept (see Kalichman, 1988; Vasta & Liben, 1996), with females making more errors than males.

Object and Location Memory

Another early developing spatial ability is object and location memory (Plumert & Hund, 2001; Schumann-Hengsteler, 1992). Consider the board game Concentration (or Memory), in which players must find matches to cards placed facedown on a table by turning over two cards on each turn. During the early stages of such games, when strategies are less important (older children and adults use strategies more effectively than younger children; see Chapter 7), 5-year-olds perform as well as, and sometimes better than, adults (Baker-Ward & Ornstein, 1988). Five-year-old children's object and location memory performance is especially impressive, given their generally limited memory abilities (Schneider, 2015; see Chapter 8).

Sex Differences in Spatial Cognition and Evolutionary Hypotheses

Although the job of developmentalists is to describe and explain age-related changes in functioning, sometimes reliable individual differences are also found that pique researchers' attention as much as, or even more than, developmental difference. This has been the case for spatial cognition. In fact, some of

FIGURE 6.8 **Piaget and Inhelder's (1967) water-level task.** Children are to draw the water line in each bottle to represent how it would look if it were half filled with water. Although Piaget and Inhelder reported that most children draw the line correctly by age 7 or so, other researchers report that even adolescents and adults have difficulty with this problem.

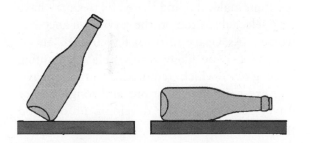

our culture's most familiar gender stereotypes relate to spatial cognition. Women, for example, are alleged to have difficulty using maps, especially when one must turn the map (that is, mentally rotate it) to find where one is and where one wants to go. And men are supposed victims of the "Where's the mayonnaise, Honey?" syndrome, in which they stare into a crowded refrigerator searching futilely for the mayonnaise, which their wives find with little difficulty. Do these stereotypes have any basis in reality? Like all stereotypes, they do not describe the abilities of *all* men or *all* women (or perhaps even most of them), but does the research literature suggest at least a general trend in these directions?

In general, the answer is yes, with many of the gender differences being found early and persisting into adulthood (see Halpern, 2012). In fact, several theorists have proposed that some sex differences in spatial cognition may have been selected for over the course of human evolution. For example, David Geary (2007, 2010b) proposed that there has been selection pressure on human males to develop spatial abilities, primarily for the purpose of navigation, which is important in hunting and for eye-hand coordination, which is important in tool and weapon use. Sex differences favoring males in map reading and mentally rotating figures (see Figure 6.7) have been found in the preschool years (Anooshian & Young, 1981; Levine et al., 1999), with sex differences in mental rotation favoring males being observed even in infancy (D. S. Moore & Johnson, 2009).

Although gender differences in spatial cognition have been consistently found, the absolute magnitude of those differences is small. One way of evaluating the size of such differences is to conduct a *meta-analysis*—a statistical technique that allows an investigator to evaluate the magnitude of a significant effect across a large number of studies. Janet Hyde (1981) performed such an analysis, reanalyzing the findings of spatial cognition studies initially reviewed by Eleanor Maccoby and Carol Jacklin in 1974. Hyde reported that differences in spatial ability attributed to the gender of the child accounted for less than 5% of the difference in performance. Other meta-analyses have reported similar findings. For example, Marcia Linn and Anne Petersen (1985) reported that only between 1% and 5% of differences in spatial abilities can be attributed to gender, depending on the particular task. One exception Linn and Petersen noted was mental rotation, in which males of all ages performed better than females did. Robert Rosenthal and Donald Rubin (1982) similarly reported small differences between the sexes in their meta-analysis and that the size of the effect diminished across the years, with females showing a substantial gain in cognitive performance (relative to males) in recent years. One exception to this trend is, again, mental rotation, which has shown no diminution in the gender difference over time (Masters & Soares, 1993). Moreover, sex differences in mental rotation, favoring boys, were found to be primarily responsible for sex differences in science and technology test scores among middle-school children (Ganley, Vasilyeva, & Dulaney, 2014).

Not all sex differences in spatial cognition favor males, however. Females typically show greater performance in object and location memory than males do, and these abilities may have been selected to promote the survival of ancestral women. As Geary (2010b) has argued, ancestral males were likely responsible for hunting large game, which required accurate throwing, eye-hand coordination, and long-distance travel—and, thus, the development of good spatial-orientation skills. Ancestral women, in

FIGURE 6.9A **The initial stimulus array shown to participants in a test of object and location memory.**

FIGURE 6.9B **The stimulus array with objects added.** Participants were to cross out all items not found in the original array. One hypothesis for this sex difference is that females evolved spatial skills for detecting small perceptual differences, important in food gathering.

Source: Silverman, I., & Eals, M. (1992). Sex differences in spatial abilities: Evolutionary theory and data. In J. H. Barkow, L. Cosmides, & J. Tooby (Eds.), *The adapted mind: Evolutionary psychology and the generation of culture* (pp. 537 [a], 538 [b]). New York: Oxford. Copyright © 1992 by Oxford University Press. Used by permission of Oxford University Press.

contrast, likely stayed near camp, where they tended to children and gathered food, the latter requiring fine-motor capabilities and the recognition of small perceptual differences (to tell the difference between poisonous and edible berries, for instance). Different evolutionary pressures should have led to different patterns of spatial abilities in males and females.

Females' superior performance on object and location memory tasks is illustrated in studies in which people are shown an array containing many objects (see Figure 6.9a) and, after studying it for a short while, are shown a larger array (see Figure 6.9b). Their task is to identify only objects that were in the initial array. Females of all ages tested performed better than males on this task (Silverman & Eals, 1992).

How can these gender differences in spatial ability be explained? Myriad factors have been proposed to explain these differences, including differential experience for males and females, genetics, prenatal hormones, and evolutionary accounts. For example, boys typically engage in more spatial activities, including object-oriented play (see discussion to follow), and these differences may be related to sex differences in spatial cognition (Connor & Serbin, 1977). Research examining the differential-experience hypothesis has shown that spatial abilities in women are related to personality measures of masculinity (D. I. Miller & Halpern, 2014). One reason for the relationship between masculine personality characteristics and spatial abilities might have to do with the types of activities in which girls engage. For example, Nora Newcombe and her colleagues (1983) found that differences in spatial experience accounted for observed differences in spatial performance. They created a list of everyday activities that might occur

TABLE 6.5 **Examples of masculine, neutral, and feminine activities.**

Masculine	Neutral	Feminine
touch football	bowling	figure skating
baseball	softball	field hockey
basketball	advanced tennis	gymnastics
darts	table tennis	ballet
hunting	diving	disco dancing
skateboarding	drawing	embroidery
shooting pool	sculpting	knitting
car repair	photography	baton twirling
electrical circuitry	navigating in a car	tailoring
sketching house plans	marching in a band	touch typing

Source: Adapted from Newcombe, N., Bandura, M. M., & Taylor, D. C. (1983). Sex differences in spatial ability and spatial activities. *Sex Roles, 9,* 377–386.

in a population of high school and college students. In the first part of the study, college students were asked to classify the activities as masculine, feminine, or neutral. The raters typically selected those tasks judged to have high spatial content as masculine and as having more male participants (see Table 6.5). Subsequently, the researchers found small but significant gender differences among college students on a psychometric test with strong spatial components. Newcombe and her colleagues also reported a significant correlation between spatial activities and aptitude scores, particularly for females; that is, the more spatial activities one engages in, the greater one's spatial ability is likely to be.

Not surprisingly, the most sophisticated explanations of sex differences in spatial abilities consider interactions of biological and experiential factors during development. For example, Diane Halpern (2012) developed a model designed to explain sex differences in cognitive abilities; this model is illustrated in Figure 6.10. Halpern argues that to understand sex differences on academic and cognitive tasks, one must examine how information is acquired, stored, selected, retrieved, and used, each of which can vary depending on a variety of personal and contextual factors. Halpern argues that we cannot specify how much of average differences between males and females on any task is the result of nature or nurture. Rather, the relation between nature and nurture is dynamic, interacting and varying over time. What children learn alters their brains. This in turn affects their ability to acquire and perform specific skills, which leads children to select new experiences, which will change the structure of their brains. According to Halpern (2004), "Differences in the interests of females and males both derive from differences in the areas in which they have achieved success and lead to further differential success in these areas because of differential knowledge and experience. Learning is both a biological and an environmental variable, and biology and environment are as inseparable as conjoined twins who share a common heart" (p. 138).

Even infants are able to process objects in space as they relate to them. These abilities, however, should not be thought of as inborn; they develop with experience. Indeed, a recent meta-analysis indicated that training and experience can improve spatial skills in both males and females (Uttal et al., 2013). Over the preschool and early school years, children learn to form and use cognitive maps of their surroundings and to use real maps to help them navigate. During this same time, children become

FIGURE 6.10 **A psychobiosocial model that can be used as a framework for understanding cognitive sex differences.** It replaces the older idea that nature and nurture are separate influences and instead indicates that biological and psychosocial variables exert mutual influences on each other (graphically represented as a circle).

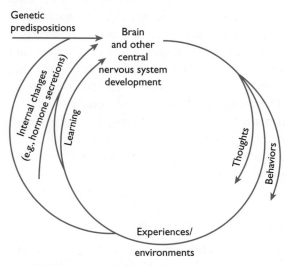

Source: Halpern, D. F. (2000). *Sex differences in cognitive abilities* (3rd ed., p. 18). Mahwah, NJ: Erlbaum. Copyright © 2000 by Lawrence Erlbaum Associates.

increasingly skilled at spatial visualization, such as mentally rotating an object, and at object and location memory, the latter of which seems to be particularly well developed even in 5-year-olds. Reliable sex differences are also found for various forms of spatial cognition, with males generally showing higher levels of performance on spatial-orientation and spatial-visualization tasks and females performing better on object and location as well as memory tasks. Like many other aspects of development, children seem prepared to make sense of spatial information. However, the way they engage their environment (for example, differences in play styles between boys and girls) interacts with their intuitive notions of space, producing ever-increasing spatial-cognitive abilities.

Object-Oriented Play and Tool Use

Just as infants and young children seem oriented to attend to people, they also seem biased to explore and play with objects and to use objects as tools (Bjorklund & Gardiner, 2011; Geary, 2005). In this section, we first explore briefly the development of *object-oriented play,* followed by a more in-depth look at the development of *tool use,* and then conclude by examining the relation between the two.

Development of Object-Oriented Play

In Chapter 5, we defined play as a "purposeless" activity, in that it is done voluntarily and without any obvious immediate function. Yet, as we mentioned then, most researchers see different types of play as having some functions important for children's development (see Pellegrini, 2013b). Although object-oriented play (or object play) has been viewed differently by different authors, it is usually defined as the active manipulation of objects, such as banging them and throwing them, but also as the use of objects to build something (Bjorklund & Gardiner, 2011; Pellegrini, 2016).

Object play is differentiated from *exploration,* which involves gaining information about an object by manipulating it, possibly with visual inspection (Belsky & Most, 1981). Particularly in infancy, however, it can be difficult to know when exploration ends and object play begins. It seems safe to say that nearly all interaction with objects in infants before 9 months of age can be considered exploration but that most of an infant's interaction with objects from 12 months onward can be better described as play (Belsky & Most, 1981), with boys engaging in both object exploration and object play more than girls (Bornstein et al., 1996).

Much object play in infants and toddlers involves making noise—for instance, by banging or shaking objects (S. Goldberg & Lewis, 1969; Morgante & Keen, 2008). Such perceptually contingent play gives way to more sophisticated forms of object play, such as building things, or constructive play, with boys usually engaging in such play more than girls (Caldera et al., 1999; Gredlein & Bjorklund, 2005). Other research has shown that girls exposed to high levels of androgen prenatally (congenital adrenal hyperplasia) engage in more object-oriented play than unaffected girls (Berenbaum & Hines, 1992), suggesting a biological origin, at least in part, for this sex difference. Because object play is sometimes confused with exploration, and because some researchers exclude constructive play (for example, children building a fort with boxes or a house with LEGOs) from their definition of object play, it is difficult to get an accurate measure of how frequently children engage in it. However, a fair estimate would seem to be that preschool children devote about 10% to 15% of all behaviors to object play (Pellegrini & Gustafson, 2005). As with other forms of play, object play is typically low in frequency during the early preschool years, peaks in childhood, and declines in early adolescence (see Pellegrini, 2013a). Similar frequencies and patterns of developmental change have been observed for children from hunter-gatherer and other traditional cultures (Bakeman et al., 1990; Bock, 2005).

What function might object play serve for children? One prominent hypothesis is that through object play, children discover *affordances* of objects (functional relationships between objects and the environment) and how objects can be used as *tools* (Bjorklund & Gardiner, 2011; Geary, 2005; P. K. Smith, 2005). Humans are one of only a handful of species that uses tools to any significant degree. In fact, it was not long ago that anthropologists considered tool use to be a defining feature of *Homo sapiens*. We now know that many other species use tools to solve problems and that chimpanzees, like humans, actually make tools (for example, the sticks used in termite fishing) (for a review see Seed & Byrne, 2010). However, no other species constructs and uses tools to the extent that humans do, and tool use begins early in life.

Learning to Use Tools

By the time children are 3 or 4 years old, they are using, on a regular basis, many of the tools a culture offers, such as forks, spoons, chopsticks, pencils, hammers, or scissors. As such, the origins of tool use must be sought in infancy and the preschool years. How is it that children come to use objects (that is, tools) to solve problems? What factors are involved in early tool use, and how might they relate to cognitive functioning both in infancy and in later childhood?

Jeffrey Lockman (2000) has argued that children's eventual use of tools to solve problems may have its origins in infants' manipulation of their physical world. According to Lockman, "The origins of tool use in humans can be found during much of the first year of life, in the perception-action routines that infants repeatedly display as they explore their environments" (p. 137). From this perspective, tool use develops continuously over infancy and early childhood, and it should be thought of as a gradual process of discovery (often through play and exploration) rather than as resulting from the emergence of new representational skills. It develops from infants and young children's interactions with objects in the real world (for example, seeing what objects "do," hitting two objects together), often to obtain some perceptual outcome, such as noise. In the process, children learn how objects relate together, and they learn, often through trial and error, how best to manipulate one object (a spoon, for example) in relation to other objects (various types of food, for instance) to achieve specific goals (getting food to one's mouth) (see Bjorklund & Gardiner, 2011).

Development of tool use in young children. According to Piaget (1954), the first signs of tool use in infants are seen around their first birthdays. However, subsequent research has indicated that infants are able to use tools earlier than Piaget proposed. Most tool-use research with infants and young children has used a variant of the *lure-retrieval task*, first developed by Köhler (1925) for use with chimpanzees, in which a desired object is placed out of the child's reach and a number of potential tools are available to use to retrieve the object. Infants as young as 9 and 10 months of age are able to use tools to solve lure-retrieval problems, although performance is influenced by features such as physical proximity (performance is greater when the tool is close to the target item) and perceptual similarity (performance is greater when the tool and lure are of contrasting colors and textures) (Bates, Carlson-Luden, & Bretherton, 1980).

In a study with slightly older children by Zhe Chen and Robert Siegler (2000), 1.5- and 2.5-year-old children were shown an

FIGURE 6.11 **Example of the lure-retrieval task used by Z. Chen and Siegler (2000).** The child needed to choose the appropriate tool (here, the rake) to retrieve that toy (here, the turtle).

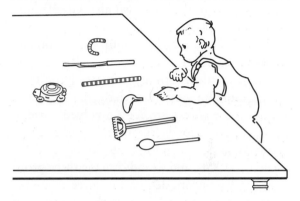

Source: Chen, Z., & Siegler, R. S. (2000). Across the great divide: Bridging the gap between understanding of toddlers' and older children's thinking. *Monographs of the Society for Research in Child Development, 65*(2) (Serial no. 261). Reprinted with permission of the Society for Research in Child Development.

out-of-reach toy and a group of toy tools, only one of which could be used to get the toy. The setup for their experiments is shown in Figure 6.11. As can be seen from the figure, only one tool, the rake, was both long enough and had the appropriate shape to retrieve the toy. Children sat with their parents, and for three consecutive trials, an experimenter urged them to get the toy. If they did not retrieve the toy after these trials, some children were given hints about using the tool (hint condition), whereas others saw the experimenter retrieve the toy with the appropriate tool (model condition). Children were then given a second (and third) set of trials using different tools and toys. Chen and Siegler found that older children (about 30 months) were more likely to use the tools to retrieve the toy before any instruction (hint or model) than younger children (about 21 months), but even these children retrieved the toy successfully only 15% of the time. Following the hint or modeling, however, even the youngest group of children used the tool to retrieve the toys (see also Gredlein & Bjorklund, 2005).

Z. Chen and Siegler (2000) also examined the types of strategies children used to get the toy. The *forward strategy* involved the children leaning forward to reach the toy with their hands, the *indirect strategy* involved turning to their parent for help, and the *tool strategy* involved using one of the tools. In Figure 6.12, the letters (A, B, and C) indicate the three problems, and numbers denote the three trials for each problem. As can be seen, the incidence of tool use increased over the problems, although children continued to use the forward strategy on the same trials in which they used the tool strategy. Thus, these young children, although not spontaneously using tools to retrieve the out-of-reach toy initially, could do so easily after receiving a simple hint or demonstration, and they generalized their newfound skill to a similar, but new, task.

One interesting finding in the Z. Chen and Siegler (2000) study was that boys were more likely than girls to choose a tool-use strategy. This difference was particularly large initially, but it was greatly reduced (though not eliminated) when hints were given. Although not all studies find sex differences in tool use, when such differences are found, they usually favor boys (T. M. Barrett, Davis, & Needham, 2007; Bates et al., 1980; Gredlein & Bjorklund, 2005).

Design Stance

When a person sees someone use a tool to achieve a goal, he or she assumes that that

FIGURE 6.12 **Percentage of children who used each strategy on the pretraining trials of the Z. Chen and Siegler (2000) study.**

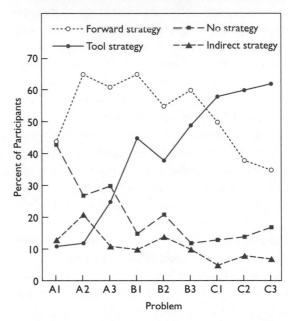

Source: Chen, Z., & Siegler, R. S. (2000). Across the great divide: Bridging the gap between understanding of toddlers' and older children's thinking. *Monographs of the Society for Research in Child Development, 65*(2) (Serial no. 261). Reprinted with permission of the Society for Research in Child Development.

tool was designed for that intended purpose. This is referred to as the **design stance** (Dennett, 1990). Thus, pencils were made for writing, hammers were made for hammering, and objects that resemble pencils and hammers were likely made for writing and hammering, respectively. As a result, selecting tools becomes very efficient, although it sometimes results in **functional fixedness**, the tendency not to identify alternative uses for familiar objects (German & Johnson, 2002). Children as young as 3 years tend to believe that an object designed for one purpose (catching bugs, for instance) is, indeed, only a "bug catcher," even though it can be successfully used for another function (collecting raindrops, for example) (German & Johnson, 2002).

Research has shown that even 12-montholds have learned that some tools are special-purpose objects. For example, by 1 year of age, children already have extensive experience with spoons. In one study (T. M. Barrett et al., 2007), 12- and 18-month-old infants saw a box with a light display and a small hole on its side (see Figure 6.13). The experimenter then grasped the round end of either a spoon or a novel spoonlike object and inserted the object's straight end into the box, turning on the light. Infants were then given the opportunity to turn the light on themselves ("Now it's your turn"). When the familiar spoon was used, infants grasped the round end less than 25% of the time, failing to insert the tool into the box and turn on the light. In contrast, when they used the novel tool, they succeeded about 60% of the time, with most grasping the tool by the round end and inserting the straight end into the box.

FIGURE 6.13 **The light box and the spoon and novel tool used in the study by T. M. Barrett and colleagues (2007).** Twelve- and 18-month-old children used the novel tool to turn on the light but displayed functional fixedness with the spoon, failing to use it in a novel way.

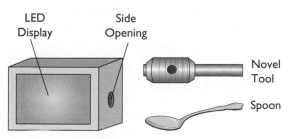

LED Display   Side Opening   Novel Tool   Spoon

Source: Barrett, T. M., Davis, E. F., & Needham, A. (2007). Learning about tools in infancy. Developmental Psychology, 43, 352–368 (p. 354).

That is, even 12-month-old infants had formed a category of *spoon* and knew how they should interact with it (hold it by the straight end). In this case, it resulted in less flexible problem solving on a novel task, but like their older peers, they had learned how an important cultural tool was usually used and behaved accordingly.

Young children will apparently treat a novel tool as having a "special function" after only limited exposure. For example, in one study, 2- and 3-year-old children were shown a box with a slot in it and two similar objects (see Figure 6.14), both of which could fit into the slot (see Experiment 2 in Casler & Kelemen, 2005). An adult then took one of the objects (Tool i in Figure 6.14) and placed it in the slot of the box, which turned on a light. The children were told that they could do the task themselves if they wanted, and the experimenter handed them both of the tools. The adult even inserted the alternative object (Tool ii) into a case similar to the slot on the box (although the light did not turn on). The adult also commented about the similarity of the bottoms of the two objects ("Hey, I noticed something. These look really different, but at the bottom, they're exactly the same size. Wow! See that?"). Children were later given both tools (sometimes of different colors) and asked to select one to (a) turn the light on in the box (the original task) or (b) crush a cracker. To turn on the light, the children consistently chose the same tool that the adult had demonstrated, even when it was a different color. In contrast, they consistently used the alternate tool to crush the cracker, even though the original tool would have worked equally well.

What these results reflect is that young children do not select a tool based solely on its properties to solve a problem but on their past

FIGURE 6.14 **The box and two tools in the study by Casler and Kelemen (2005).** Two- and 3-year-old children who watched an experimenter insert Tool i to turn on a light were reluctant to use it for another purpose (crushing a cracker).

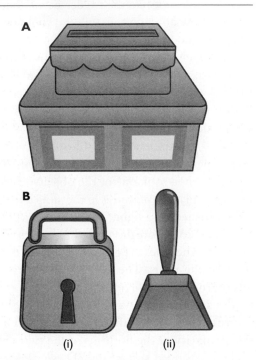

A

B

(i)   (ii)

Source: Casler, K., & Kelemen, D. (2005). Young children's rapid learning about artifacts. *Developmental Science, 8,* 472–480.

history with a tool. From a single demonstration by an adult, children acquired a tool category for an object and acted as if the tool was invented for that purpose. This reflects a primitive form of the design stance that older children and adults have toward tools, and it seems to be based on young children's belief that other people's behavior is based on intention (that is, they perform actions for a reason) (Tomasello, 2009; see the discussion of treating people as intentional agents earlier in this chapter). As a result, they quickly learn that a

tool has a specific function. According to Krista Casler and Deborah Kelemen (2005), "Young children exhibit rapid learning for artifact function, already possessing an early foundation to some of our most remarkable capacities as tool manufacturers and users" (p. 479). These findings are consistent with David Geary's (2005) proposal that tool use is part of children's intuitive notions of physics. An ability to understand how objects can be used to affect other objects and change the environment underlies tool use in humans and develops as children interact with their world.

The design stance may be unique to humans (Ruiz & Santos, 2013). For example, although chimpanzees have been observed to use tools in the wild, they (along with bonobos and gorillas) seem not to realize that a tool that someone freely chose to use to solve a task was more likely to be effective in achieving a goal than a tool someone was obliged to use (Buttelmann et al., 2008). In contrast, 14-month-old infants were more likely to select the tool that was freely chosen by a model to solve a task, a reflection of the design stance. Interestingly, orangutans performed more like children than the other great apes on this task, suggesting that hints of the design stance can be found in the great apes. This is especially interesting in that orangutans are less likely to use tools in the wild than gorillas, bonobos, or chimpanzees.

Relationship Between Tool Use and Object-Oriented Play

Many factors influence children's tool use, and one is children's tendencies to interact or play with objects. Some researchers have proposed that object-oriented play should enhance problem solving by creating a flexible cognitive set whereby children learn that materials can be used in a variety of ways, which will help them develop generalized approaches for solving problems (Bruner, 1972; Cheyne & Rubin, 1983). Based on research with preschool children, Peter Smith (1982, 2005) speculated that object-oriented play, often done as part of sociodramatic play (see Chapter 5), encourages children to understand that objects can be used in a variety of ways to solve problems. According to Smith (1982), object exploration and play may help prepare children to use tools "over and above what could be learnt through observation, imitation, and goal-directed practice" (p. 151).

For example, in some studies, children must select a properly shaped tool in order to retrieve a toy (for instance, a rakelike object long enough to reach a toy placed out of a child's reach, as described earlier). Children who are given the opportunity to play with the objects beforehand are more likely to later use the objects as tools to retrieve the toy than children who did not play with them and are just as good or better at the task as children who are given specific instructions (Cheyne & Rubin, 1983; P. K. Smith & Dutton, 1979). In related research, the amount of object-oriented play 3-year-old children engaged in on a separate task with different objects predicted their later performance on a toy-retrieval task (Gredlein & Bjorklund, 2005). Boys were more apt to engage in object-oriented play than girls, and boys were more likely to use a tool to solve a lure-retrieval task than girls. Similar to the findings of Z. Chen and Siegler (2000) discussed earlier, the sex difference in using tools to solve the problem was greatly reduced when girls were given hints, indicating that girls were as capable of solving the problems as boys: They were just less likely to spontaneously use a tool than the boys were. When examining the relation between object-oriented play and tool-use scores, there were no significant effects for girls. In contrast, the amount of object-oriented play was significantly correlated with tool-use scores for boys ($r = 0.59$). These findings are consistent with arguments made by Geary (2005, 2010b) and others (Bjorklund & Pellegrini, 2002; Pellegrini & Bjorklund, 2004) that sex differences in early behavior interact with inherent, but still developing, folk-physics systems, yielding differential behavioral competencies in males and females. According to Geary (2010b), the relation between object play and tool use is consistent with the idea that "the early skeletal structure of folk domains is enhanced during children's self-initiated social and play activities" (p. 316). Moreover, also consistent with evolutionary theory, there are sex differences in some aspects of children's folk physics. Geary (2010b) continues: "In this case, sex differences in some folk physical abilities . . . may be accompanied by early sex differences in sensitivity to corresponding forms of information (e.g., attending to objects and implicitly framing them as potential tools)" (p. 316).

Tool Innovation

As we've pointed out, children seem especially prepared to learn to use tools—developing the design stance early and learning with very few observations how a tool is used from watching others. Given this precocious propensity for tool use, it's a bit surprising that children have a difficult time with *tool innovation*—making tools to solve specific problems. Several studies have presented preschool children with simple tasks and opportunities to modify items to use as tools, only to find that children generally have no clue about how to solve the problem

(Beck et al., 2011; Chappell et al., 2013; Cutting et al., 2014). In these experiments, preschool-age children are shown stickers that are out of reach (usually in a clear plastic bottle) along with an unbent pipe cleaner. To retrieve the sticker, children must bend the pipe cleaner, making a hook. In these studies, children rarely spontaneously bent the pipe cleaner, and even when they were shown the properties of the pipe cleaner (it can be easily bent) and given practice bending them, many children continued to fail to make a tool that could be used to retrieve the sticker. In one study, many 5- and 6-year-old children, but fewer 4- to 5-year-olds, did successfully make a tool and retrieved the sticker, but only after watching an adult demonstrate the pipe cleaner's properties, including the formation of a hook at the end of the pipe cleaner.

Why do children have such difficulty with tool innovation? Mark Nielsen and his colleagues (2014) speculated that perhaps children from developed countries have little need in their lives to develop tools and that tool innovation would be found in children from traditional cultures, who seem to show some innovation in creating toys from found objects in their surroundings. Nielsen et al. used a variant of the pipe cleaner task discussed earlier with 3- to 5-year-old children living in Bushman communities in South Africa. Their performance was compared to Western children of the same age from Brisbane, Australia. Counter to their predictions, neither the Bushman nor the Western children performed well on the tool-innovation task: 3% of the Western children and no Bushman children solved the problem.

What's the reason for young children's poor performance in constructing new tools? Nicola Cutting and her colleagues (2014) speculated that tool-innovation tasks are ill-structured and require children to retrieve information (for example, pipe cleaners can be bent) from memory and to recognize that this information can be used to solve the problem. In other words, although children may be prepared to learn to use tools (the design stance), a certain level of basic cognitive ability is needed before they can easily create tools.

Children seem to use tools to solve problems soon after the first glimmers to goal-directed behavior. Children's effective use of tools increases with age and is influenced by a host of factors, possibly even their tendencies to engage in object-oriented play (Gredlein & Bjorklund, 2005). Once children learn about tools, however, they seem to become part of their basic toolkit of problem-solving skills—and an essential component of human cognition. However, creating tools apparently requires additional cognitive abilities not yet available to most preschool children.

Children's Understanding of Time

A topic that can fall through the cracks when examining children's folk physics is their understanding of *time*. Typically, when we speak of understanding the physical world, we think of perceiving or acting on solid "stuff," something that time is not. However, if it was good enough for Einstein, it should be good enough for us. In fact, it was Albert Einstein's question in 1928 about the origins and relations of the speed, time, and movement concepts in children that prompted Piaget (1946) to first investigate the topic. In this section, we examine briefly some of the research literature on children's developing understanding of time.

Perceiving and understanding time is both a very basic and a very complex thing. At its most basic, the understanding that events follow one another in time is almost self-evident and, as we will see, within the grasp of young infants. On the other hand, understanding concepts such as past and future, and knowing when future events, such as one's birthday, will occur relative to other future events, such as Halloween, for example, take many years to master (see McCormack, 2015, for a review).

Understanding Temporal Order and Causality

Let's start with the "easy" concepts. Consider a sequence of different objects (a circle, A; a triangle, B; a square, C; and a diamond, D) falling from the top to the bottom of a computer screen in a particular order, ABCD, each making a distinctive sound when it hits bottom (see Figure 6.15). When 4- and 8-month-old infants watch such a display for a while, their attention wanes (that is, they habituate). When they are then shown the same objects falling in a different temporal sequence (circle, diamond, triangle, and square, or ADBC), their attention increases, demonstrating that they recognize something has changed (Lewkowicz, 2004). What has changed is not the objects or what they do but the temporal order in which they fall. Two-month-old babies are also sensitive to the order in which words in a sentence are spoken (for example, "cats would jump benches" to "cats jump wood benches") (Mandel, Kemler Nelson, & Jusczyk, 1996), indicating that babies from their first months of life have some rudimentary notion of time.

Infants' understanding of temporal sequencing, as in "Event A comes before Event B," is further illustrated by research in **causal perception**. For example, when adults watch a

FIGURE 6.15 **After 4- and 8-month-old infants were habituated to one sequence of falling objects (circle, triangle, square, diamond) they were shown a different sequence of falling objects in the test phase (circle, diamond, triangle, square).** Infants' attention increased during the test phase, indicating that they recognized that the temporal order of the falling objects had changed.

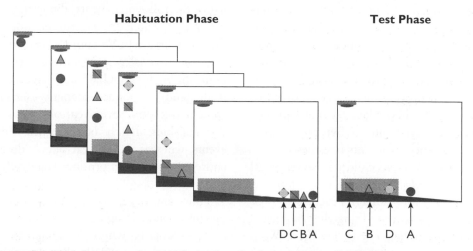

Source: Lewkowicz, D. J. (2004). Perception of serial order in infants. *Developmental Science, 7,* 175–184.

computer screen and see a moving shape collide with a stationary shape, they expect the stationary shape to move. The first shape is seen as an intentional agent, hitting and launching the other (Michotte, 1963). Infants behave similarly, interpreting events of moving and colliding shapes much as adults do, making movement an important clue to agency (Leslie & Keeble, 1987; Oakes, 1994). For example, 2.5-month-old infants act surprised when a toy bug on wheels remains stationary after being hit by a cylinder rolling down a ramp or, alternatively, if the bug moves in the absence of the cylinder contacting it (Kotovsky & Baillargeon, 1994, 2000; S. Wang, Kaufman, & Baillargeon, 2003).

Yesterday, Today, and Tomorrow

In many ways, children are truly living in the moment as creatures of the here and now. As they grow, children have a lot to learn about time, particularly as we use it to organize our everyday lives. Some things happen at about the same time and in the same order every day: We wake up in the morning, have breakfast, go to school or work, have lunch, have dinner, and go to bed. We understand concepts such as yesterday, today, and tomorrow, and we understand that Tuesday comes after Monday, June comes before October, and Halloween comes before Thanksgiving. These are all recurring events—things that happen every day, week, month, or year—and we are able to place ourselves in time along these various continua. When can children understand sequences of events like these?

Even 2- and 3-year-old children use temporal terms such as *yesterday*, *last night*, and *tomorrow*, but they frequently use such terms incorrectly. For instance, they refer to everything that happened in the past as occurring "yesterday" (see W. J. Friedman, 2008). By 4 years of age, children have

a relatively firm grasp on concepts such as before and after, being able to state, for example, that an event that happened 1 week ago did, indeed, occur more recently than one that happened 7 weeks ago (W. J. Friedman, 1991). However, preschool children still have a difficult time judging the recency of important future (and past) events, such as determining which will occur sooner, their birthday or Valentine's Day (W. J. Friedman, Gardner, & Zubin, 1995). Around age 7, children become better at overtly estimating how long things will take (see Droit-Volet, 2013, for a review).

How can one tell what children know about the timing of future events? In one study, William Friedman (2000) showed 4-, 7-, and 10-year-old children a road map with various features marked on it. Some were marked very close to where the child sat, representing events that would happen soon in the future, and some were marked farther away, representing events that would happen in the more distant future (see Figure 6.16). Children were then given a series of future events and asked to show on the road map where each belonged. Testing was done in October, a few weeks before Halloween. Children were asked about the timing of the following events: dinnertime, Saturday (when they watch cartoons in the morning), Halloween, Christmas, Valentine's Day, and summer. The 4-year-olds' responses were generally random, although about half of the youngest children in the study responded properly that Halloween was coming soon. Seven-year-olds did a better job, distinguishing mainly between near and distant events, whereas the 10-year-old children used the entire road map and produced generally accurate judgments.

Four- and 5-year-olds are not totally incompetent when judging the timing of events, however, especially when dealing with recurrent events that happen daily. For example, 4- and

FIGURE 6.16 **Children pointed to various points on the road map to designate when an event would happen—points nearest to them on the path for events that would happen soon, such as dinnertime, and points farther down the path for events that would happen later in time, such as Valentine's Day.** Four-year-olds generally did not differentiate the timing of events, whereas 10-year-olds performed much as adults would.

Source: Friedman, W. J. (2000). The development of children's knowledge of the times of future events. *Child Development, 71,* 913–932.

5-year-olds can distinguish between events that happen during the course of a day (for example, waking up, eating breakfast, eating lunch), but events occurring at longer intervals (for example, days of the week or seasons of the year) still give them trouble (see W. J. Friedman, 2008). For instance, although most 6- and 7-year-old children can recite in correct order the days of the week, and many can do the same for the months of the year, they have difficulty thinking about days of the week in relation to one another (for example, "If this is Saturday and you go backward in time, which will you come to first, Thursday or Tuesday?"). It's not until

midadolescence that children can solve problems such as these (W. J. Friedman, 1986).

Time, of course, is a complicated concept but one that most of us have a reasonable grasp of by adulthood (although understanding the time-space continuum of modern physics remains beyond most of us). Even infants have an understanding of some aspects of time—for example, simple causality (events that happen first cause events that happen second) and duration (see Droit-Volet, 2013). However, it takes children years to fully grasp time as adults do, with even something as fundamental as the language one speaks influencing its rate of development.

What aspects of cognition are responsible for children's developing understanding of time? Most agree that there is not a single brain region responsible for time judgments. Rather, a variety of neural networks are involved and to varying degrees depending on the type of task. Time judgments seem to be the result of a few interacting processes: (a) some kind of internal system, like a pulse, that represents the passage of time; (b) memory processes capable of storing duration or seriation; (c) attention to relevant information (the timing of events, the onset and offset of durations, for instance); and (d) decision processes. We discuss these executive functions in greater detail in Chapter 7. These abilities develop across childhood, along with frontal brain regions, and seem to contribute to children's understanding and reasoning about timing (Droit-Volet, 2013).

Final Reflections on Children's Understanding of the Physical World

A true understanding of the physical world requires an understanding of both the main facts involved about a topic and the causal links among them. This is how scientists usually operate. Some of these facts and causes are easier to understand than others, and infants and young children seem to have a better grasp of many of these concepts than scientists once believed (as some core-knowledge and theory-theory theorists have pointed out). Others require more time, cognitive effort, and cultural instruction (for example, understanding time). It's worth noting that children's and adults' thinking about many aspects of reality are often not so different from one another. Modern science is only about 500 years old, and knowledge provided by telescopes, moon trips, microscopes, and other technologies was not available when our psychological structures were shaped by natural selection. When, as parents or teachers, we feel pleased seeing our children overcome their temporary erroneous explanations about why the sun is not out, how mountains and lakes are formed, or where babies come from, we should not forget that scientific explanations about those phenomena are historically quite recent. Forms of "magical thinking" about reality have pervaded throughout human history, and they still seem to operate today when facing the unknown.

Section Summary

- *Spatial cognition* develops over childhood, with age differences being found on tasks of *spatial orientation*, which measure how people understand the placement of objects in space with themselves as the reference point, and on tasks of *spatial visualization*, which deal with the mental manipulation of visual stimuli, such as performing tasks involving *mental rotation*.
- Sex differences favoring males are found on tasks of spatial orientation and spatial visualization, whereas females usually perform better on tasks assessing *object and location memory*.

- Infants and young children explore objects and engage in *object-oriented play* (or *object play*), with boys usually engaging in such play more than girls.
- Even young children adopt the *design stance*, assuming tools are designed for an intended function. Higher levels of tool use are sometimes found for boys than for girls.
- Even infants have a rudimentary understanding of time, as reflected, for example, by research on *causal perception*, in which one object is seen as launching another when it hits the second object.
- Children's understanding of the relationship among past, present, and future events continues to develop into adolescence.

Ask Yourself . . .

9. How does children's spatial orientation improve and change with age? How do maps serve as a tool of intellectual adaptation, helping children improve their spatial skills?
10. How is spatial visualization similar to and different from spatial orientation?
11. What are some proposed explanations for sex differences in mental rotation tasks? How does performance on these tasks change across development?
12. What is a real-life example of an object and location memory task? How would you predict a 5-year-old would perform on this task? What about an 8-year-old? An adult?
13. What is the difference between object play and exploration? How does object play help children learn about tools?
14. What did Z. Chen and Siegler (2000) demonstrate about the development of children's tool use?
15. Why are very young children less prone to *functional fixedness* compared to older children?
16. How does children's understanding of time develop?

KEY TERMS AND CONCEPTS

animism
anthropomorphism
artificialism
belief-desire reasoning
causal perception
design stance
false-belief task
finalism
folk biology
folk knowledge

folk physics
folk psychology
functional fixedness
intentional agents
mental rotation
mindblindness
object and location memory
object-oriented play (or
 object play)
promiscuous teleology

shared attention
spatial cognition
spatial orientation
spatial visualization
theory of mind
theory theory

SUGGESTED READINGS

Scholarly Works

Geary, D. C. (2005). *The origin of mind: Evolution of brain, cognition, and general intelligence.* Washington, DC: American Psychological Association. This is Geary's magnum opus (at least to date) concerning his theory about the evolution and development of human cognition. It covers, among other topics, evolutionary theory and his views about the development of folk psychology, folk biology, and folk physics.

Kelemen, D. (2004). Are children "intuitive theists"? Reasoning about purpose and design in nature. *Psychological Science, 15,* 295–301. This paper presents the argument that young children's tendencies to see purpose in all things makes them susceptible to cultural beliefs of the supernatural, particularly to the idea of God or gods.

Newcombe, N. S., & Huttenlocher, J. (2006). Development of spatial cognition. In W. Damon & R. Lerner (Series Eds.) & D. Kuhn & R. S. Siegler (Vol. Eds.), *Handbook of child psychology, Vol. 2: Cognition, perception, and language* (6th ed., pp. 734–776). New York: Wiley. This chapter presents a state-of-the-art review of research on the development of spatial cognition by two prominent researchers in the field.

Reading for Personal Interest

Baron-Cohen, S., Lombardo, M., Tager-Flusberg, H., & Cohen, D. (Eds.). (2013). *Understanding other minds: Perspectives from developmental social neuroscience.* Oxford, UK: Oxford University Press. This volume has become a classic text on autism and theory of mind. This latest edition includes important updates from neuroimaging studies and research in genetics and hormones.

Siegal, M. (2008). *Marvelous minds: The discovery of what children know.* Oxford, UK: Oxford University Press. Developmental psychologist Michael Siegal presents a clear and comprehensive review of research over the last several decades of children's developing understanding of people, biology, and the physical world.

Tomasello, M. (2014). *A natural history of human thinking.* Cambridge, MA: Harvard University Press. Primatologist and comparative psychologist Michael Tomasello reviews 20 years of research on great ape cognition and describes the shared intentionality hypothesis of complex forms of thinking. This books provides a thorough review of the mind-reading abilities (or lack thereof) in other great apes and how they are similar to and different from our own.

7 LEARNING TO THINK ON THEIR OWN

Executive Function, Strategies, and Problem Solving

IN THIS CHAPTER

Four-year-old Benjamin was a talkative child, and unlike many other preschoolers, he almost always had plenty to say when his parents asked him, "So what did you do in preschool today?" On this occasion, Benjamin was excitedly telling his parents about the pet iguana that one of his classmates had brought in for show-and-tell when, without warning, he started talking about a character on one of his favorite TV shows. Within a few seconds, Benjamin paused and then said, "Oops, I just interrupted myself." He couldn't keep the distracting thought about the TV show from intruding on his story about his day at school.

Benjamin may be more talkative than most 4-year-olds, but he is very much like his peers when it comes to being distracted and getting off task. He is not easily able to keep intruding thoughts from his mind (and mouth), and this shortcoming makes it difficult for him to successfully control his thought and behavior to solve problems effectively. As we mentioned in Chapter 1, one of the major issues in cognitive development is how children gain control over their own cognition—how they intentionally regulate their actions and thoughts.

In this chapter, we examine how children come to learn to think on their own. Most of the research and theorizing on this topic can trace its roots to *information-processing theories* of cognitive development. Information-processing theories use the computer as a model for how the mind works and changes with age. From this perspective, cognitive development can be seen as reflecting changes in *hardware* (such as the capacity of memory systems and the speed with which information is processed through the systems), *software* (such as children's access to and ability to use strategies), or both. After reviewing briefly some assumptions of information-processing approaches to cognitive development, we examine the development of *executive function*—a set of lower-level cognitive processes associated with planning and self-regulation. We then look at the development of strategies and, finally, the development of problem solving, including both analogical and scientific reasoning.

ASSUMPTIONS OF INFORMATION-PROCESSING APPROACHES

There is no single information-processing theory of cognition or cognitive development. Rather, information-processing theories are built on a set of assumptions concerning how humans acquire, store, and retrieve information. A core assumption of information-processing approaches is that information moves through a system of stores, as reflected in Figure 7.1A. Initially, processing was viewed as occurring serially, with the product of one stage of processing serving as the input for the next stage, and so on, until some final response or decision is made. The initial multi-store models of the sort shown in the figure were first suggested as theories of memory (Atkinson & Shiffrin, 1968). These theories assume that information from the external world is initially represented, perceptually intact, in *sensory registers*. There is a separate sensory register, or *sensory store*, for each sense modality (for example, vision, audition), and these registers can hold large quantities of information—but only for a few seconds. When we direct our attention to this information, it gets passed through to the short-term/working memory (STWM), where capacity is smaller but the representations are more durable. STWM could be considered the *contents of consciousness*. It's whatever we're currently thinking about, and it's where we hold information long enough to evaluate it. We apply strategies for remembering or solving problems in STWM. Its capacity is limited, however, and if something is not done to information once it is in STWM, that information will be lost. But if we apply some cognitive operation to the information in the short-term store, that information is transferred to long-term memory.

FIGURE 7.1A **The flow of information through the memory system according to the standard theory of memory.**

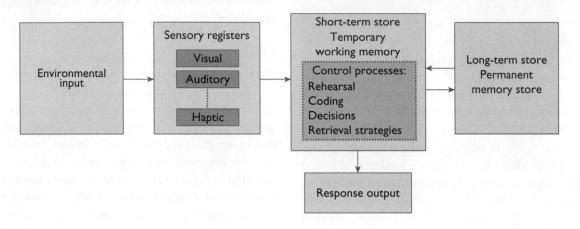

FIGURE 7.1B **A revised model of information processing.**

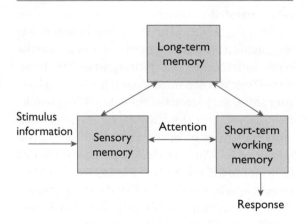

Sources: Figure 7.1A based on Atkinson, R. C., & Shiffrin, R. M. (1968). Human memory: A proposed system and its control processes. In K. W. Spence & J. T. Spence (Eds.), *The psychology of learning and motivation: Advances in research and theory* (Vol. 2, pp. 89–195). New York: Academic. © 1968 by Academic Press, Inc. Figure 7.1B based on Radvansky, G. A., & Ashcraft, M. H. (2016). *Cognition* (6th ed.). Boston: Pearson.

The modern information-processing approach, depicted in Figure 7.1B, recognizes that information is not processed serially but rather that the sensory store, STWM, and long-term memory interact to produce **top-down** and **bottom-up processing.** When the information we perceive and process in sensory memory directs our attention to something we already know or have experienced, stored in long-term memory, this is an example of *bottom-up*, or data-driven, processing. In contrast, if our experiences and information stored in long-term memory direct our attention to some aspects of the world more than others, this is considered *top-down*, or concept-driven, processing. Consider the analogy of putting together a jigsaw puzzle. One option is to look at the cover of the box, which typically shows the completed image of the puzzle, and use that as a guide to place individual pieces in the correct location. This would be an example of top-down processing. You use the "big picture" to guide your interpretation of each little puzzle piece. In contrast, you might put the cover of the box away and begin to connect the puzzle piece by piece, perhaps starting with the corners, then the edge pieces, and then filling in the puzzle from there. Over time, the larger picture will emerge and finding the correct location for individual pieces will become easier. This is an example of bottom-up processing.

Central to information-processing approaches is the idea of limited resource capacity. We can only process so much information at any single time. Theorists have used a variety of metaphors for capacity, including a space metaphor (one has only so much mental space in which to store or operate on information), a time metaphor (one can only perform operations so fast), an attention metaphor (one can only pay attention to so many things at once), and an energy metaphor (one has only so much energy to allocate to the storage or execution of cognitive operations). Some researchers have taken the energy metaphor seriously and shown, for instance, that glucose consumption in areas of the brain associated with cognitive processing is elevated for difficult (that is, for resource-consuming) tasks relative to easier (that is, for less-resource-consuming) tasks (Haier et al., 1988). If you've ever bogged down your computer or tablet by running too many programs at once, you've experienced another metaphor of this limited capacity. As another example, most of us have enough mental space or energy to walk and chew gum at the same time, but add to these operations a nontrivial arithmetic problem, and a change in our rate of gum chewing or walking will be discerned. We have added something else to do, and doing it will interfere with the execution of other operations.

Cognitive theorists also assume that mental processes can be placed on a continuum relative to how much of one's limited capacity each process requires for its execution (Hasher & Zacks, 1979). At one extreme are automatic processes, which require very little attention and none of the short-term store's limited capacity; at the other extreme are effortful processes, which require the use of mental resources for their successful completion. In addition to not requiring any mental effort, truly automatic processes are hypothesized (a) to occur without intention and without conscious awareness; (b) not to interfere with the execution of other processes; (c) not to improve with practice; and (d) not to be influenced by individual differences in intelligence, motivation, and education (Hasher & Zacks, 1979). In contrast, effortful processes, which have also been called strategies or control processes, are hypothesized (a) to be available to consciousness; (b) to interfere with the execution of other effortful processes—that is, to drain mental resources; (c) to improve with practice; and (d) to be influenced by individual differences in intelligence, motivation, and education.

Within this general framework, researchers have investigated age differences in both lower-level or basic processes, such as speed of processing and working memory, and higher-level processes, such as the use of strategies and problem solving. We examine the development of both basic and higher-level processes in this chapter, starting with the processes involved in executive function and moving to an examination of the development of cognitive strategies and, finally, to problem solving, with a special look at the development of analogical and scientific reasoning. Other topics that have been examined mainly from an information-processing perspective are the topics of later chapters, such as memory in Chapter 8. The major emphasis in this chapter is not an evaluation of information-processing theories of cognitive development, however, but how children come to control their own thinking and problem solving—how they become *self-directed thinkers*.

Section Review

- Information-processing approaches to the study of cognition emphasize the flow of information through a *limited resource capacity* processing system—specifically, the sensory registers, the *short-term/working memory*, and the *long-term* store.
- Processing is also described as being either *top-down* (concept driven) or *bottom-up* (data driven).
- Cognitive operations are conceptualized as existing on a continuum, with *automatic*, or effortless, *processes* at one extreme and strategic, or *effortful, processes* at the other.

Ask Yourself . . .

1. How does the modern information-processing approach differ from the traditional version?

DEVELOPMENT OF BASIC-LEVEL PROCESSES: EXECUTIVE FUNCTION

How do children learn to exert control over their problem solving and thinking? Stated another way, how do children acquire the ability to control or regulate their own thought and behavior? Researchers have argued that attaining cognitive self-control requires the development of a set of basic-level abilities. These abilities are collectively referred to as **executive function** (or **executive control**) (Wiebe et al., 2011; Zelazo, 2015).

Executive function (EF) refers to the processes involved in regulating attention and in determining what to do with information just gathered or retrieved from long-term memory. It plays a central role in planning and behaving flexibly, particularly when dealing with new information. It involves a related set of basic information-processing abilities, including (a) working memory, or updating—how much information one can hold in the short-term store and think about at a time; (b) how well one can inhibit responding and resist interference; and (c) cognitive flexibility, or shifting, as reflected by how easily individuals can switch between different sets of rules or different tasks (see Garon, Smith, & Bryson, 2014; Miyake & Friedman, 2012). In addition, each of these abilities is related to how quickly one can process information and to selectively attending to relevant information. Each of these abilities develops over time, and age differences in these functions determine how well children are able to regulate their behavior and thinking.

Individual differences in various measures of EF are related to a host of higher-level cognitive abilities, including reading, mathematics, theory of mind, and IQ, among others (each of which is discussed in later chapters). EF abilities have been shown to have high genetic heritability (for a review, see Miyake & Friedman, 2012) but are also significantly associated with environmental factors, such as exercise (C. L. Davis et al., 2011), patterns of mother-child interactions (Fay-Stammbach, Hawes, & Meredith, 2014; Sarsour et al., 2011), and culture (C. Lewis et al., 2009). Individual differences in EF are considered to be stable over time, that is, one's rank order is fairly consistent across development (Miyake & Friedman, 2012), although some research shows that interventions and training can aid EF development (Diamond & Lee, 2011; Röthlisberger et al., 2012).

Traditionally, EF has been examined "in the lab," using relatively abstract tasks that often fail to take into account motivation or other affective significance. More recently, Phillip Zelazo and Stephanie Carlson (2012) have distinguished "hot EF" from "cool EF" to capture the extent to which EF varies along a continuum, as a function of motivation. In their view, *hot EF* is a top-down control process that we engage when a task is motivationally or emotionally significant. *Cool EF* involves those processes that operate in more neutral or abstract situations.

We'll revisit their distinction throughout this section, as we examine the development of five cognitive abilities associated with EF, beginning with speed of processing and followed by memory span and working memory, various aspects of attention, inhibition and children's abilities *not* to respond, and finally, cognitive flexibility.

Speed of Processing

With respect to overall speed of processing, young children require more time (and, thus, presumably use more of their limited capacity) to execute most cognitive processes than do older children (Dempster, 1981). In a series of studies, Robert Kail (1997; Kail & Ferrer, 2008) reported that the general developmental changes in processing speed are similar across different tasks. In Kail's studies, participants ranging in age from 6 to about 21 years were given a series of reaction-time tasks. For example, in some experiments, participants were presented with a pair of letters in different orientations and were to determine as quickly as possible whether the two letters were identical or mirror images of each other. To do this, participants had to mentally rotate one letter into the same orientation as the other. In a name-retrieval task, the participants were shown pairs of pictures and asked to determine whether they were physically identical or had the same name (for instance, different examples of a banana, one peeled and one unpeeled). Patterns of responses over these two and several other tasks were highly similar, with reaction times becoming faster with age.

Figure 7.2 presents the pattern of reaction times across age for a variety of tasks used in Kail's experiments. Note that despite substantial differences in the task requirements and the length of time it takes to perform the tasks (processing time is measured in milliseconds for some tasks and in seconds for others), all show essentially the same pattern of changes in reaction time across age. This pattern has been confirmed by other researchers (Iida, Miyazaki, & Uchida, 2010; Nettelbeck & Burns, 2010), and some research even showed a similar (though not identical) age trend in reaction time over the first year of life (Rose et al., 2002) and between 22 and 32 months of age (Zelazo, Kearsley, & Stack, 1995).

Kail interpreted these findings as reflecting age-related increases in the amount of processing resources available for the execution of cognitive operations. Kail acknowledged that knowledge influences speed of processing and, thus, levels of performance on cognitive tasks, but he argued that maturationally based factors are primarily responsible for age-related differences in speed and, therefore, efficiency of processing (see Kail & Salthouse, 1994). One maturationally based change likely involves the myelination of nerves in the associative ("thinking") area of the brain. As noted in Chapter 2, myelin is a fatty substance that surrounds nerves and facilitates transmission of nerve impulses. Whereas myelination of most sensory and motor areas of the brain is adultlike within the first several years of life, myelination of the associative area is not complete until the teen years and beyond (see Lenroot & Giedd, 2007).

Memory Span and Working Memory

Central to information-processing models of cognition is the idea that people can hold only so

FIGURE 7.2 **Developmental patterns of speed of processing for five cognitive tasks.** For both simple and complex tasks, children become faster with age.

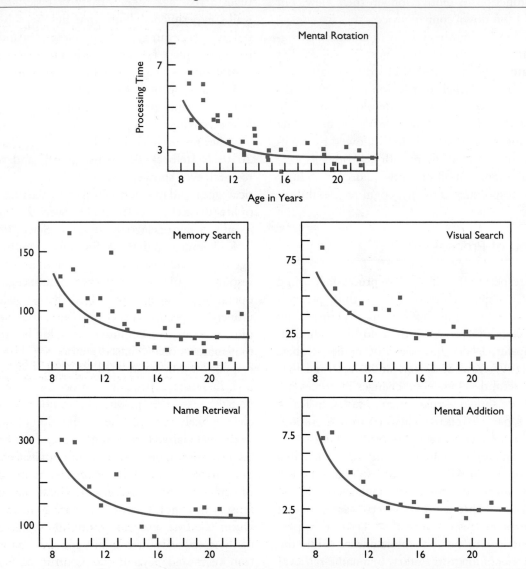

Source: Kail, R.V. (1991). Development of processing speed in childhood and adolescence. In H.W. Reese (Ed.), *Advances in child development and behavior* (Vol. 23, pp. 151–187). San Diego, CA: Academic Press. Copyright © 1991. Reprinted with permission from Elsevier.

much information in the short-term store before it deteriorates. While information is in the short-term store people can process that information, that is, think about it. Two useful concepts that relate to how much information people can hold and process in the short-term store are *memory span* and *working memory*, and we discuss the development of each here.

Age Differences in Memory Span

Traditionally, the capacity of the short-term store has been assessed by tests of memory span that measure the number of (usually) unrelated items that can be recalled in exact order. Presentation of items is done rapidly (usually one per second), so there is minimal time for the application of strategies to aid recall. A child's memory span is considered to be a reflection of the size of the short-term store. When children are presented with randomly ordered items, the number of items they can recall in exact order increases with age (Cowan, 2016; Schneider, Knopf, & Sodian, 2009). The average memory span of 4- and 6.5-month-olds is about one item, of 2-year-olds about two items, of 5-year-olds about four items, of 7-year-olds about five items, and of 9-year-olds about six items. The average memory span of adults is about seven items. Figure 7.3 shows the highly predictable growth of the memory span for digits (digit span) from age 2 years through adulthood.

A better understanding of the developmental differences in the capacity of the short-term store comes from a study by Nelson Cowan and his colleagues (1999) assessing span of apprehension, which refers to the amount of information people can extract from a passively held store such as auditory sensory memory, the first stop for information on its way to STWM, as you recall. For instance, in the critical condition in the study by Cowan and colleagues (1999), first-grade and fourth-grade children and adults heard series of digits over headphones while playing a computer game. They were told to ignore the digits and focus on the game. Occasionally and unexpectedly, however, they were signaled to recall, in exact order, the most recently presented set of digits they had heard. Participants were not explicitly attending to the digits, making it unlikely that they were using any encoding

FIGURE 7.3 **Children's memory span for digits (digit span) shows regular increases with age.** With increasing age, children are able to hold more things in mind (here digits) at once, and this affects their ability to perform more complicated tasks.

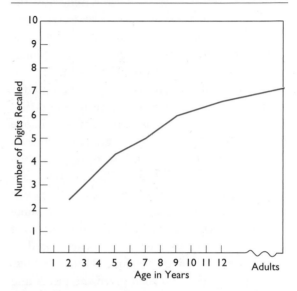

Source: Dempster, F. N. (1981). Memory span: Sources of individual and developmental differences. *Psychological Bulletin, 89,* 63–100. Copyright © 1981 American Psychological Association. Reprinted with permission of the author.

strategies to remember them. Thus, the span of apprehension seems to be a fair assessment of the capacity of the auditory sensory store. Average span of apprehension was about 3.5 digits for adults, about 3 digits for fourth-graders, and about 2.5 digits for first-grade children. Because the sensory store feeds directly into STWM, Cowan and his colleagues concluded that developmental differences in sensory storage is what underlies age differences in the capacity of the short-term storage. In other words, the span of apprehension (about four items for adults) is lower than the average memory span we described earlier (seven items for adults) because factors such as focused attention, knowledge of the to-be-remembered information, and encoding strategies can affect memory span when items are presented slowly enough to be processed in STWM. The underlying difference in the auditory sensory store, as reflected by differences in the span of apprehension, seems to serve as the foundation for age differences on memory span tasks.

Despite these impressive and robust findings, researchers have seriously questioned the idea that the capacity of the sensory store is the only (or even the most important) source of age differences on memory span tasks. For example, in one often-cited study, a group of graduate students at the University of Pittsburgh were given two simple memory tests (Chi, 1978). On one, they were read a series of numbers quickly (about one per second) and were asked to recall them immediately in exact order. On a second test, they were briefly shown chess pieces on a chessboard in game-possible positions (again, about one chess piece per second) and then given the pieces and asked to place them at their previous positions on the board. Their performance on these tasks was compared with that of a group of 10-year-olds. In all fairness, these were not typical 10-year-olds—they were all chess experts, either winners of local tournaments or members of chess clubs. When memory for the chess positions was tested, the children outperformed the adults. This finding is probably not surprising, given the expert status of the children. But the critical question is how they did when remembering the numbers. Does being a chess expert cause one's memory capabilities to improve overall, or was the children's remarkable performance limited to what they knew best? The results supported the latter interpretation. The adults, despite being outdone by the children when memory for chess positions was tested, were superior to the children when the test stimuli were numbers. The results of this experiment can be seen in Figure 7.4 (see also Schneider et al., 1993).

Development of Working Memory

A distinction is made between short-term memory and **working memory**. The former involves only the storage of information held in the short-term system, whereas the latter involves storage capacity plus the ability to transform information held in the short-term system. Digit-span tasks described earlier assess the capacity of short-term memory. An example of a working memory task can be found in the research of Linda Siegel and Ellen Ryan (1989), who gave children sets of incomplete sentences, requiring them to supply the final word (for example, "In the summer, it is very ____"). After being presented with several such sentences, children were asked to recall the final word in each sentence, in order. Such a test requires not only the short-term storage of information but also some mental work dealing with the to-be-remembered information. Similar to the findings reported for digit span, reliable age differences in working memory are found, although working memory span is usually about

FIGURE 7.4 **The average memory span for digits and chess arrays by chess-expert children and college-educated adults.**

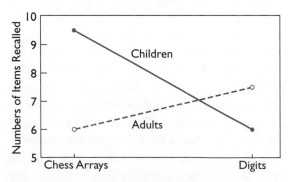

Source: Adapted from Chi, M. T. H. (1978). Knowledge structure and memory development. In R. Siegler (Ed.), *Children's thinking: What develops?* (pp. 73–96). Hillsdale, NJ: Erlbaum. Copyright © 1978 Lawrence Erlbaum Associates, Inc. Reprinted with permission.

two items fewer than a child's memory span (see Case, 1985; Cowan & Alloway, 2009).

Alan Baddeley and Graham Hitch (1974) presented one popular account of working memory and its development. According to their model, working memory consists of a central executive that stores information and two temporary systems, one for coding verbal information, called the articulatory loop, and another for coding visual information, which is referred to as the visuospatial scratch pad. Because relatively little developmental research has been conducted on the visuospatial scratchpad (but see Lourenco & Frick, 2014, for a review), discussion here focuses on the articulatory loop. Figure 7.5 presents a simplified model of the working memory system as Baddeley and Hitch (1974) think of it. According to the theory, age differences in verbal memory span (for example, how many digits or words one can remember) are primarily caused by developmental differences in the articulatory loop. When engaged in a verbal span task, one stores verbal representations, in the form of phonological information, in the articulatory loop. These verbal representations (or memory traces) decay rapidly unless they are maintained in working memory by verbal rehearsal, or mental articulation (saying something over and over again in your head). Although age differences in the rate that information decays in working memory have been reported (see Cowan & Alloway, 2009), most researchers believe that age differences in rehearsal rate are the primary reason for developmental differences in memory span. The faster one rehearses, the more memory traces one can rehearse, the more information that can be kept active in working memory, and the more one can remember.

Baddeley and Hitch assume that the articulatory loop involves a literal subvocalization process, with people saying the items to themselves.

FIGURE 7.5 **A simplified version of Baddeley and Hitch's working memory model.**

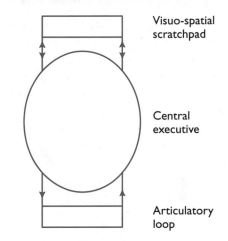

Visuo-spatial scratchpad

Central executive

Articulatory loop

Source: Baddeley, A. D. (1983). Working memory. *Philosophical Transactions of the Royal Society, B302*, 311–324. Reprinted with permission of the Royal Society.

One factor that influences rehearsal rate is word length. Longer words (that is, those with more syllables) require more time to say, thus leaving less time to rehearse other words before they decay and are lost from working memory. There is good evidence from the adult literature that such a process (or one very like it) actually occurs (see Baddeley, 1986, for an extensive review). In the developmental literature, research has shown a relationship between the speed with which children can say words and memory span. With age, children are able to read or say words at a faster rate, and memory span increases accordingly (Chuah & Maybery, 1999; Hulme et al., 1984). Figure 7.6 presents data from a study by Charles Hulme and his colleagues (1984) showing a very regular, age-related relationship between speech rate (that is, how fast people can say the words) and the number of words recalled on a word-span task. Older children and adults have a faster rate of speech than younger children do, and their memory spans vary accordingly.

FIGURE 7.6 **The relationship between word length, speech rate, and memory span as a function of age.** As speech rate increases, more words are recalled, with both speech rate and words recalled increasing with age.

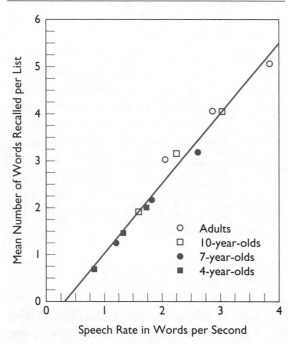

Source: Hulme, C., Thomson, N., Muir, C., & Lawrence, A. (1984). Speech rate and the development of spoken words: The role of rehearsal and item identification processes. *Journal of Experimental Child Psychology, 38,* 241–253. Copyright © 1984 Academic Press. Reprinted with permission.

It is interesting to note that differences in digit span have been found as a function of the language a person speaks. For example, Chinese speakers have considerably longer digit spans than English speakers do; this difference is apparent as early as age 4 and extends into adulthood (C. Chen & Stevenson, 1988; Geary et al., 1993). This cultural effect seems to be caused by differences in the rate with which number words (*one, two,* and so on) in the two languages are spoken. Languages such as Chinese, with relatively short number words that can be articulated quickly, enable longer digit spans than do languages such as English, with relatively long number words that are articulated more slowly (C. Chen & Stevenson, 1988). In fact, in one study with bilingual children, the children had longer digit spans in their *second* language (English) than in their first language (Welsh). This counterintuitive finding was because number words can be articulated more rapidly in English than in Welsh (N. C. Ellis & Hennelley, 1980). Thus, the greater digit spans of Chinese children relative to American children, for example, seem not to be the result of some inherent cognitive or educational superiority for the Chinese children but, rather, the result of the language they speak. From a Vygotskian perspective (see Chapter 3), the number words in a language are a tool of intellectual adaptation, provided by the culture, that influences cognition.

Learning How Not to Respond: Inhibition and Resistance to Interference

To this point, the cognitive processes we have discussed all involve some process of activation. Children must *encode* information, *hold* it in short-term store, *rehearse* it in the articulatory loop, and do it all as fast as possible if performance is to be optimal. There should be no surprise here, for thinking is nothing if not an active process, and one important point of cognitive development would seem to be that children can do "more" thinking "more effectively" with age. Well enough. But sometimes what one *doesn't* do is as important to effective thinking as what one does do. Sometimes people must inhibit distracting stimuli, thoughts, and action if they expect to get a job done. **Inhibition** refers "to an active suppression process, such as the removal of task-irrelevant information from working memory" (Harnish-feger, 1995, p. 188). Of course, not doing something is actually a very active process itself. For instance, consider how much more difficult it is to inhibit that urge to snack on chocolate cake in the evening, when you're tired, compared to earlier in the day. As adults, our ability to resist temptation and inhibit our thoughts and behavior depletes with our energy levels because of the amount of effort doing so requires (Baumeister et al., 1998). Similarly, alcohol lowers inhibitions because it is a depressant and acts on the prefrontal cortex, weakening our ability to actively inhibit behaviors we might otherwise not engage in. Indeed, research has indicated that stress, lack of sleep, loneliness, or lack of exercise impair EF (see Diamond, 2013, for a review). Yet we are still better at it than young children. Many of children's cognitive errors and everyday "problem" behaviors come from things they do despite instructions otherwise (for example, "I didn't mean to talk about poo at the table, it was an accident"). The basic idea at its simplest is that, with age, children become increasingly able to inhibit prepotent (primary) and often inappropriate mental or behavioral responses from both internal and external sources and that these improved skills permit the more efficient execution of other cognitive operations.

Related to the concept of inhibition is **resistance to interference**, which refers to "susceptibility to performance decrements under conditions of multiple distracting stimuli" (Harnishfeger, 1995, pp. 188–189). Resistance to interference, for example, is shown on dual tasks, when performing one task (chewing gum or watching television) interferes with performance on a second task (walking or doing one's homework). Inhibition and resistance to interference have often been treated as reflecting the same underlying mechanisms, which is likely true, but the two concepts, although highly related, are not synonymous. Nevertheless, they do seem to have a similar neurological locus and to follow the same developmental function. As such, we discuss them in this section as reflecting a single set of processes.

Inhibition and resistance to interference are central components of *attention*. In everyday parlance, we use the term interchangeably with *concentration*. When we tell a child to pay attention, we usually want that child to concentrate on the task at hand and not let his or her mind wander to other things. Having difficulty keeping unwanted thoughts out of mind (inhibition) or from being distracted from external stimuli (resistance to interference) are thus impediments to paying attention.

Developmental Differences

Inhibition abilities develop over infancy, early childhood, and into adolescence and are assessed by a variety of simple tests. For example, in the *day-night task*, children must say *day* each time they see a picture of the moon and *night* each time they see a picture of the sun, which is very difficult for preschoolers, presumably because they cannot inhibit the response to say the highly associated word with its corresponding picture (for example, *day* with the sun). Young children's difficulties are eliminated when they are requested to pair unrelated words (for example, *dog* and *pig*) with the pictures (Diamond, Kirkham, & Amso, 2002). Preschoolers also have difficulty in the *tapping task*, in which they must tap once each time the examiner taps twice, and tap twice each time the examiner taps once; in the *opposites task*, where they point to one of two pictures an interviewer did *not* point to (Baker, Friedman, & Leslie, 2010); and in playing *Simon Says*, where they must perform an action only when Simon says so (for example, "Simon says, touch your nose"). Simplifying the Simon Says game helps, but young children still make many more inhibitory errors than older children do (Diamond & Taylor, 1996; Sabbagh et al., 2006).

Children also have a difficult time inhibiting their speech. For example, when kindergarten children were to name out loud only certain pictures on a page (for example, animals) but not say the names of distractor items (for example, people), the children showed no evidence of inhibiting their responses. They mentioned the distractor items as frequently on trials when they were told not to mention them as on trials when they were told to mention them (Kipp & Pope, 1997).

Changes in inhibitory processes over childhood have been related to a number of cognitive tasks. For example, children's ability to selectively forget information is affected by their ability to keep the to-be-forgotten information out of mind. Older children are better able to execute

these inhibitory processes than are younger children (Harnishfeger & Pope, 1996; Wilson & Kipp, 1998). Age differences in selective attention can be explained by young children's difficulty ignoring task-irrelevant stimuli. Although task instructions make it clear that they are to attend only to the central stimuli and ignore peripheral stimuli, they have a difficult time doing so (see Ridderinkhof, van der Molen, & Band, 1997). And young children's difficulty in inhibiting some behaviors (such as pointing to where an object is hidden) has been linked to the ability to deceive others and in the development of theory of mind (Carlson, Moses, & Hix, 1998; see Chapter 6).

As we mentioned, inhibition and resistance to interference are related to the concept of attention, specifically selective attention, the ability to focus only on chosen stimuli and not be distracted by other "noise" in the environment. Young children are notorious for their relatively poor selective attention abilities, focusing their attention disproportionately on aspects of a situation that

Young children often have a difficult time not saying whatever is on their minds.

Source: © Baby Blue Partnership. Reprinted with special permission of King Features Syndicate.

are irrelevant to the task at hand. They are easily distracted and spend much time off task. Cognitive neuroscientists have used changes in evoked-response brain-potential patterns and heart rate to reveal that beginning around 7 months, infants are capable of "deciding" to focus on a stimulus, as opposed to having their attention passively captured (Colombo, 2002). These abilities improve with age, as children are increasingly able to stay on task and select appropriate information to attend to (Lane & Pearson, 1982). Yet even 5-year-old children are easily distracted by extraneous information in their environments. For example, one study reported that kindergarten children who were in classrooms with many displays on the walls and throughout the classroom showed fewer learning gains than children in less-distracting classrooms (A. V. Fisher, Godwin, & Seltman, 2014).

Inhibition and Attention Deficit Hyperactivity Disorder

In recent decades, the phenomenon of attention deficit hyperactivity disorder (ADHD) has gained substantial attention, with children (and adults) who have this disorder displaying hyperactivity, impulsiveness, and great difficulty sustaining attention. The incidence of ADHD in the United States is estimated to be between 5% and 11% of the childhood population; it is more common in boys than in girls, with between about a third to half of all childhood cases of ADHD persisting into adulthood (see Barbaresi et al., 2013). Children with ADHD are more likely to experience school problems, including poor academic performance, grade retention, suspensions, and expulsions, than are children without ADHD, and they are also at greater risk for delinquency, substance abuse, and troubled social relationships in adulthood (see Barkley, 1997).

Russell Barkley (1997) proposed that the principal cause of ADHD is deficits in behavioral inhibition. Behavioral inhibition, claims Barkley, influences working memory, self-regulation of emotion, internalization of speech (critical in directing problem solving and reflecting upon one's behavior), and what Barkley calls *reconstitution*, which involves the "creation of novel, complex goal-directed behaviors" (p. 72). Given the importance of these abilities for cognition and successful day-to-day functioning, children with deficits in behavioral inhibition would be especially disadvantaged.

There is ample support for Barkley's contention that children with ADHD show deficits in these areas (see Barkley, 2014, for a review). For example, relative to non-ADHD controls, children with ADHD

- Do more poorly on working memory tasks (Martinussen et al., 2005).
- Are less proficient at imitating lengthy sequences of actions (Mariani & Barkley, 1997).
- Have a poorer sense of time (Quartier, Zimmerman, & Nashat, 2010).
- Demonstrate greater variability in reaction time (Castellanos et al., 2005).
- Are more adversely affected by delay (Sonuga-Barke, 2002).
- Are more likely to be described as irritable, hostile, and excitable (see Barkley, 1990).
- Have greater problems with emotional regulation (Sjöwall et al., 2013).
- Perform more poorly on comprehension tasks (Papaeliou, Maniadaki, & Kakouros, 2012).
- Are less likely to use strategies on memory tasks (August, 1987).

Some have speculated that many youngsters diagnosed with ADHD may merely be highly active children within the "normal range" of functioning but who have a difficult time adjusting to the "sit still and listen" regime of school (Panksepp, 1998). Others have suggested that high activity levels and frequent switching of attention may actually be beneficial in some environments and were adaptive to our hunter-gatherer ancestors (P. S. Jensen et al., 1997). For example, the benefits of having individuals in a group who constantly scanned the horizon for signs of predators or prey would seem to be obvious. One must be cautious, however, in taking these arguments too far. As Sam Goldstein and Barkley (1998) comment, it is unlikely that any person with a true case of ADHD would be at an advantage in any environment, modern or ancient. But one must keep in mind that schools are a recent invention for our species. Although sometimes interfering with ideal educational practices, "normal" levels of activity and playful behavior (especially as displayed by preadolescent boys) may not, in and of themselves, be signs of pathology.

Cognitive Flexibility

Cognitive flexibility refers to the ability to shift between sets of rules or tasks. Philip Zelazo and his colleagues (Zelazo, 2015; Zelazo et al., 2003) have argued that the development of EF involves the increasing ability to formulate and maintain rules, as illustrated on simplified "shifting tasks" in which children must change from following one criterion to another (see Hanania & Smith, 2010 for a review). Such shifting is seen in the *dimensional card sorting task*, developed by Zelazo and his colleagues (Zelazo, 2006; Zelazo, Frye, & Rapus, 1996). In this task, children are shown sets of cards that vary on two dimensions. Figure 7.7 provides an example of the cards used in these experiments. Children are shown two target cards, a yellow car and a green flower, for

FIGURE 7.7 Dimensional card sorting task.
Children are to sort cards initially by one dimension (color) and later by a second dimension (shape). Children much younger than 4 years of age have difficulty on the switch trials and usually continue to sort by the original dimension.

Source: Zelazo, P. D., Frye, D., & Rapus, T. (1996). An age-related dissociation between knowing rules and using them. *Cognitive Development, 11*, 37–63. Copyright © 1996, reprinted with permission from Elsevier.

instance. When playing the *color game*, they are told that all the yellow cards go in one pile (with the yellow car) and all the green cards go in the other pile (with the green flower). Children then are given a series of test cards (for instance, yellow flowers and green cars) and asked to sort them by color. Most 3-year-olds do this easily. Then, children are told they are going to play a new game, the *shape game*. (For half the children, the shape game is played first, and for the other half, the color game is played first.) In the shape game, children are to place cars in one box (with the yellow car) and flowers in the other box (with the green flower). These are called *switch trials*, because the rules have been switched (from sorting on the basis of color to shape, or vice versa). Now, most 3-year-old children fail, particularly on trials where the rules conflict, such as green cars or yellow flowers. They continue to sort the cards according to the original dimension. Yet when asked what the new rule is, most can easily and correctly tell the experimenter. That is, 3-year-olds can verbalize the rule but cannot execute the problem. By 4 years of age, however, most children do fine on both tasks.

Executive Function, Self-Control, and "Hot" EF

As we'll see in subsequent chapters, EF is related to performance on many cognitive tasks, including the important academic tasks of reading and arithmetic. Components of EF are also related to *self-control*, which involves "actions aligned with valued, longer-term goals in the face of conflicting impulses to seek immediate gratification" (Duckworth & Steinberg, 2015, p. 32). Whereas executive functions related to reading and mathematics are examples of *cool EF*, most tasks involving self-control are examples of *hot EF*.

Perhaps the best-known research example of self-control is the *resistance to temptation* study performed originally more than 40 years ago by Walter Mischel and his colleagues (1972). In the original study, 4-year-old children sat at a table on which was placed a bell and two treats (marshmallows were used in the original study). An experimenter told children they would receive a treat, but first he had to leave the room for a while. The children were told "if you wait until I come back by myself then you can have this one [two marshmallows]. If you don't want to wait you can ring the bell and bring me back any time you want to. But if you ring the bell then you can't have this one [two marshmallows], but you can have that one [one marshmallow]" (Shoda, Mischel, & Peake, 1990, p. 980). Some children waited for up to 15 minutes, but most rang the bell, or in other studies

ate a single marshmallow after some delay rather than waiting to get two. The special significance of this study is that the researchers interviewed many of the child participants as teenagers (Eigsti et al., 2006; Shoda et al., 1990) and again when they were in their early 30s (Ayduk et al., 2000, 2008; Schlam et al., 2013). The longer 4-year-old children waited before ringing the bell or eating the single treat the higher were their school grades and SAT scores and the better were they able to deal with stress and to concentrate as adolescents. As adults, self-control at 4 years of age was positively related to body mass index, sense of self-worth, and general psychological adjustment. Other researchers have reported similar findings. For example, 4-year-old children with lower levels of self-control show higher levels of behavior problems 2 years later than children with better self-control (Sawyer et al., 2015). In other longitudinal research, Michael Daly and his colleagues (2015) reported that low levels of self-control in childhood predicted persistent unemployment in adulthood. And in a 30-year longitudinal study of more than 1,000 participants from New Zealand (Moffitt et al., 2011), childhood measures of self-control predicted important adult outcomes, including physical health, personal finances, substance dependence, and criminal behavior. The cognitive mechanisms involved in self-control, a "hot" form of EF, may be similar to those involved in "cool" EF tasks, but they predict important psychological outcomes beyond those typically measured by cognitive developmental or education psychologists.

Executive Functioning and Brain Development

EF consists of components that are related to one another and are associated with age-related changes in different areas of the *prefrontal cortex* (J. R. Best & Miller, 2010; Zelazo & Carlson, 2012). The frontal lobes of the neocortex have many projections to other areas of the brain, including the limbic system (the "emotional" part of the brain). The prefrontal cortex is one of the last areas of the brain to reach full maturity. Development of the frontal lobes in humans is rapid between birth and about 2 years of age. Another less pronounced growth spurt occurs between about 4 and 7 years. Additional changes occur over adolescence into adulthood, with neural circuits associated with hot EF developing more slowly than those for cool EF, which may contribute to risk-taking behavior in adolescence (Prencipe et al., 2011).

Much evidence for the role of the frontal lobes in executive function in humans comes from cases of brain damage. Humans with frontal lobe damage have difficulty with planning and concentration. Frontal lobe dysfunction has been implicated in some psychiatric syndromes, such as obsessive-compulsive disorder (Malloy, 1987). One test that demonstrates the difficulty frontal-lobe patients have with executive function is the Wisconsin Card Sorting Test (WCST). The WCST consists of cards on which are depicted different objects (such as squares, stars, and circles) that vary in color and number (see Figure 7.8). The participant's task is to sort the cards into specified categories (that is, according to color, number, or shape), which is reinforced by the examiner. Without specifically informing the participant, the examiner then switches reinforcement to another category. (This is similar in form to the dimensional card sorting task described earlier in the chapter.) For example, the initial category may be number, in which case participants would be reinforced for sorting all the target cards with four items on them under the cue card consisting of four circles, all the cards with three items on

them under the cue card with the three crosses, and so on, regardless of the color or shape of the items on the cards. The examiner may then switch from number to shape, so that all target cards are now to be placed with the cue card consisting of the same shape (stars with stars, triangles with triangles, and so on), with color and number being irrelevant. Participants are corrected after a mistake, so they should presumably be able to learn a new classification scheme after only a few trials. People without brain damage do exactly this. However, patients with lesions in the frontal lobes do poorly on this task, often finding it difficult to make a new response (Milner, 1964). This reflects an inability to inhibit a previously acquired response and a lack of cognitive flexibility. Based on these and related findings, it has become clear that the frontal lobes play a central role in the selection and regulation of behavior by inhibiting previous responses and fostering resistance to interference from extraneous stimuli (see Dempster, 1993; Luria, 1973).

Both executive function and the prefrontal lobe take time to develop. We saw in Chapter 2 that infants' performance on A-not-B object permanence tasks was related to the ability to inhibit responses and development of the prefrontal lobes (M. A. Bell, Wolfe, & Adkins, 2007; Holmboe et al., 2008). During childhood, age differences are found in performance on the WCST, with young children performing much the way that adults with frontal lesions do (Chelune & Baer, 1986). Research using structural magnetic resonance imaging (MRI) shows ongoing structural development within the prefrontal cortex and increased myelination in the prefrontal cortex and between the prefrontal cortex and other areas of the brain responsible for emotional regulation and response monitoring (the amygdala, for instance) throughout the teen years (Liston et al., 2006; Sowell et al.,

FIGURE 7.8 **The Wisconsin Card Sorting Test.**

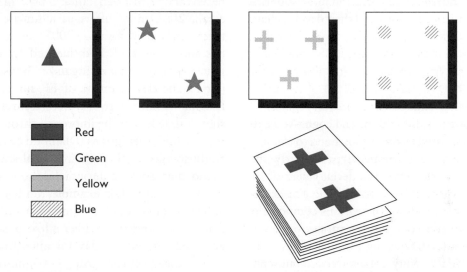

Red

Green

Yellow

Blue

Source: Milner, B. (1964). Some effects of frontal lobectomy in man. In J. M. Warren & K. Akert (Eds.), *The frontal granular cortex and behavior.* New York: McGraw-Hill.

2002). These studies suggest an increased efficiency along the neural circuits that subserve EF.

In one study, Beatriz Luna and her colleagues (2001) gave participants between the ages of 8 and 30 years tasks that assessed inhibition abilities. They reported that adultlike abilities to inhibit inappropriate responses developed gradually and were correlated with patterns of brain activity. Using fMRI techniques, Luna and her colleagues found that the prefrontal cortex was more active on these inhibition tasks in adolescents than in either children or adults. Thus, age-related changes in task performance were not related to underlying brain activation in a straightforward, linear way. Task performance increased gradually with age, whereas brain activation in the frontal cortex on this task increased sharply between childhood and adolescence, only to decrease again in adulthood. This sensitive period of cortical development in adolescence has prompted some brain scientists

to suggest that drinking alcohol to excess can have the most deleterious effects during late adolescence and early adulthood (Volkow, 2007).

Developmental lags in the frontal cortex are associated with the incidence of ADHD. For example, in one study, development of the frontal cortex of 7- to 13-year-old children with ADHD lagged about 3 years behind those of children without ADHD, whereas development of their motor areas developed slightly earlier (Shaw et al., 2007). This uneven pattern of brain development may account for the increased fidgeting and restlessness seen in children with ADHD.

It should not be surprising that brain and cognitive development are closely related. The brain, quite obviously, is the source of our thought. The relation between prefrontal cortex development and various components of executive function has been especially well documented, both in adults and over the course of development. These discoveries not only tell us about the brain but also provide insights into the types of cognitive mechanisms that underlie both basic and more sophisticated cognitive operations and their development.

Final Thoughts on Executive Function

Developmental changes in speed of processing, working memory, inhibition, and cognitive flexibility are all related to one another and to changes in neurological development, particularly the frontal cortex. However, the development of EF seems not to proceed in a straight line. For example, the degree to which the various components of EF are related to one another varies over development. In adults, working memory, inhibition, and cognitive flexibility are interrelated but separate and distinct components of EF (Miyake & Friedman, 2012). A similar three-factor structure is also found for adolescents (K. Lee, Bull, & Ho, 2013), but analyses with younger children typically find two related factors (K. Lee et al., 2013; Monette, Bigras, & Lafrenière, 2015), or only a single interrelated factor (Hughes et al., 2010). The details of these analyses need not concern us, but they show that not only do the individual components of EF change over time (consistently improving with age), but the relations among the various components of EF, as reflected by the different cognitive tasks used to assess EF, also vary over age. From another view, hot EF seems to develop more gradually and later than cool EF, which improves early, in middle to late childhood (Prencipe et al., 2011). EF is not quite the same thing for 5-year-olds as it is for 15-year-olds.

As we noted earlier, EF is highly heritable, and individual differences in executive function are relatively stable over time (that is, children who are high in EF at one time in development are apt to be high in EF later in development). However, this does not mean EF cannot be changed by experience. We saw in earlier chapters that EF can be enhanced through fantasy play (Thibodeau et al., 2016) and differs as a function of culture (Duffy & Kitayama, 2007). Some research has shown that EF is influenced by parenting practices (living in a disorganized household can impair the development of EF skills; Vernon-Feagans et al., 2016). Other researchers have shown that EF can be improved through educational training programs (Diamond & Lee, 2011; Röthlisberger et al., 2012). Several studies have found that exercise during childhood can positively affect EF. For example, Catherine Davis and colleagues (2011) assigned 7- to 11-year-old children at random to either a low-dose exercise group (20 minutes a day for about 3 months), a high-dose exercise group (40 minutes a day for about 3 months), or a control group (no exercise). The groups documented a dose-specific response, meaning that those children in the high-dose group showed greater gains in EF following completion of the exercise program than did those children in low-dose groups or control groups. But even the low-dose group had greater EF gains than controls. The researchers also documented increased prefrontal cortex activity during EF tasks, following completion of the exercise program. These patterns were even observed in their small subsample of children with ADHD. The authors interpreted their findings as indicating that movement and exercise lead to neural stimulation and cognitive changes. They hypothesized that "aerobic exercise increases growth factors . . . leading to increased capillary blood supply to the cortex and growth of new neurons and synapses, resulting in better learning and performance" (C. L. Davis et al., 2011, p. 96).

Developing control over one's thoughts, emotions, and behavior is essential to the performance of most, if not all, higher-level cognitive tasks. Some have speculated that the evolution of executive function was an important component in the emergence of the modern human mind (Causey & Bjorklund, 2011; Geary, 2005). Inhibiting inappropriate behavior, resisting distraction, and controlling one's actions in general are critical to effective functioning in any social group, as well as for activities such as constructing tools, hunting, and preparing meals, among many others. These abilities are better developed in humans than in other primates, and in older children than in younger children, and may be a key to understanding both human cognitive development and human evolution.

Section Review

- *Executive function (EF)*, or *executive control*, refers to the processes involved in regulating attention and in determining what to do with information just gathered or retrieved from long-term memory.
- EF involves a related set of basic information-processing abilities, including *working memory* (or updating), inhibition, and *cognitive flexibility* (or shifting), each of which develops with age.
- Speed of processing increases with age and is related to performance on many more complex cognitive tasks.
- Working memory involves the storage capacity of the short-term store plus the ability to transform information held in the short-term system. *Span of apprehension* refers to the amount of information people can attend to at a single time and is several items fewer than *memory span*.
- According to one popular model, working memory consists of a central executive, which stores information, and two temporary systems, one for coding verbal information, called the *articulatory loop*, and another for coding visual information, referred to as the *visuospatial scratch pad*.

- *Inhibition* refers to an active suppression process, such as the removal of task-irrelevant information from working memory. *Resistance to interference* refers to susceptibility to performance decrements under conditions of multiple distracting stimuli. Both inhibition and resistance to interference are related to the concept of *selective attention*, the ability to focus only on chosen stimuli and not be distracted by other noise in the environment.
- *Attention deficit hyperactivity disorder (ADHD)* is a common childhood disorder associated with deficient executive control.
- Self-control is related to EF, and measures of self-control in childhood predict important outcomes later in life, including school grades, employment, and physical and psychological health.
- The prefrontal cortex is the area of the brain that supports executive functioning.
- The structure of EF changes over childhood, and EF can be affected by environmental factors, as well as through training.

Ask Yourself . . .

2. What is meant by executive function, and what are the specific cognitive skills that comprise it?
3. How do the various components of executive function develop, and what are the consequences it has for other forms of psychological functioning?
4. How does speed of processing relate to working memory? What underlies the development of working memory capacity?
5. What is the evidence that STWM is constrained by sensory storage capacity?
6. Why might measures of self-control in childhood predict important physical, social, and psychological outcomes in adults?
7. What is known about the relationship between brain development and executive functioning?

DEVELOPMENT OF STRATEGIES

Strategies are relevant to most aspects of cognitive development. For example, in memory development, commonly used strategies include rehearsing information and grouping to-be-remembered items by conceptual categories (for example, remembering all the outfielders on a baseball team in one group and all the pitchers in another). In mathematics, simple strategies of addition include counting on one's fingers and mental counting (for instance, for the problem 3 + 2 = ?, mentally starting with 3 and counting up two to arrive at 5). Strategies can be much more complicated and involve an evaluation component, a form of *metacognition*—knowledge about one's own cognition and factors that influence thinking. For example, in reading, one must occasionally determine how well one understands recently read information. In all cases, strategies are used to achieve some cognitive goal (for example, remembering, adding, comprehending).

Strategies are usually defined as deliberate, goal-directed mental operations aimed at solving a problem. Strategies are usually viewed as being deliberately implemented, nonobligatory (one does not have to use them to perform a task), mentally effortful, and potentially available to consciousness (Harnishfeger & Bjorklund, 1990a; Pressley & Hilden, 2006). To some extent, strategies lie at the heart of what it means to be a self-directed learner or to think on one's own. Children use strategies to achieve goals that they cannot achieve without thinking. A 2-year-old stares at the place where a favorite toy is hidden so that she can find it again after a time-out; a 6-year-old counts on his fingers, holding up one finger for each item counted, to determine how many cookies he has;

and a 10-year-old memorizes a simple rhyme so she can remember the number of days in each month ("Thirty days has September, April, June, and November"). These are all deliberate strategies, effortful cognitive operations used to solve some problem. Children discover many strategies themselves while trying to come up with answers to everyday problems, and parents or teachers explicitly teach other strategies to them. The frequency and effectiveness of strategy use change with age, as children become increasingly able to direct their own learning and problem solving.

Increases in Strategy Use, Improvements in Performance

For most cognitively effortful tasks, older children are more likely to use strategies, select more effective and efficient strategies, and perform better on tasks than younger children. Younger children can often be taught strategies that they do not use spontaneously and, as a result, improve their performance (Schwenck, Bjorklund, & Schneider, 2007; see Bjorklund, Dukes, & Brown, 2009; Ornstein & Light, 2010). For example, simply telling young children to repeat, or rehearse, words that they are asked to remember results in children remembering more words (Ornstein, Naus, & Stone, 1977). This phenomenon has been termed a **production deficiency** (Flavell, 1970). That is, although children do not *produce* strategies spontaneously, they can be trained or prompted to use them and enhance their performance as a result. However, the performance of trained younger children rarely reaches the levels of the performance of older children who use strategies spontaneously, and young children frequently fail to generalize a trained strategy to new tasks, often resorting to their nonstrategic ways (see Bjorklund, Dukes, & Brown, 2009, for examples with respect to memory strategies).

If young children are not using strategies (unless we train them), then what are they doing? The answer is, basically, they are still being strategic. Preschool children, who do not spontaneously conserve liquid (see Chapter 5) or organize sets of pictures according to familiar categories (such as animals, tools, and vegetables), nevertheless do things to help them perform tasks (see Ornstein & Light, 2010, and Wellman, 1988, for reviews). These strategies often result in incorrect answers, but they are strategies nonetheless.

For instance, Judy DeLoache, Ann Brown, and their colleagues engaged children in a hide-and-seek game in which a toy (a stuffed animal, for example) was hidden in one of several locations in a child's home. Following delays of several minutes, the child was asked to retrieve the toy. DeLoache and Brown reported that children as young as 18 months engaged in strategic behavior during the delay periods, including looking or pointing at the hiding location and repeating the name of the toy (DeLoache & Brown, 1983; DeLoache, Cassidy, & Brown, 1985). These results, and others like them (M. Cohen, 1996), make it clear that production deficiencies are relative. Even very young children use strategies, although the strategies that they use tend to be simple and to increase in efficiency with age.

Following these findings, it seems clear that preschool children engage in some planning that warrants being called strategic. Still, their strategies lack the effectiveness of the procedures used by older children and often may not aid task performance at all. However, Henry Wellman (1988) asserted that preschoolers' strategies are every bit as goal-directed and performance-influencing as the strategies of older children and that they are used in a wide range of situations. Subsequent findings support Wellman's interpretation (see Bjorklund, Dukes, & Brown, 2009). However, we must be careful not to attribute too much in

the way of strategic competence to the preschool child, for cognitive skills are clearly more effective and more easily observed in older children.

Utilization Deficiencies

Sometimes children will use a strategy, either spontaneously or as a result of training, but their performance will not improve. For example, in one set of studies, 3- and 4-year-old children were shown a miniature room containing toy animals and furniture (Blumberg & Torenberg, 2005; Blumberg, Torenberg, & Randall, 2005). Children were told that one set of items was special (for example, "It's very important that the animals get fed regularly"), and the children's job was to help the experimenter take care of these special things. They were then told to remove all of the objects from the room, and later, they were asked to put them back in the room where they had been placed before. A simple strategy for achieving this goal would be to remove the items according to category membership (that is, take out the "special" objects one after the other), something that 70% of the preschoolers did. However, using this strategy did not help them put the items back in their proper place. In other words, although children used a strategy, it did not help them achieve their goal.

Using a strategy that does not improve performance is called a **utilization deficiency** (P. H. Miller, 1990; P. H. Miller & Seier, 1994) and is something that is frequently observed in children's strategy use. Utilization deficiencies are not limited to preschool children; they are also seen in the behavior of older children as well (see Bjorklund, Dukes, & Brown, 2009; P. H. Miller, 1990). For example, Patricia Miller and Wendy Seier (1994) reported strong or partial evidence of utilization deficiencies in more than

90% of all experiments examining children's spontaneous use of memory strategies. Similarly, utilization deficiencies were found in more than 50% of memory training studies conducted during a 30-year period (Bjorklund et al., 1997).

Let us provide an example of a utilization deficiency in research by Patricia Miller and her colleagues, which involved children's use of a selective-attention strategy (DeMarie-Dreblow & Miller, 1988; P. H. Miller et al., 1986). In this research, children (usually from 3 to 8 years of age) are shown a series of boxes with doors on top arranged into two rows of six columns (see Photo 7.1). On half of the doors are pictures of cages, meaning that those boxes contain pictures of animals. On the remaining doors are pictures of houses, meaning that those boxes contain pictures of household objects. Children are told to remember the location of one group of objects, either the animals or the household objects. They are also told that they can open any doors they wish during a study period. Children's strategies can be examined by looking at the doors they choose to open during this study period.

The most efficient strategy, of course, is to open only those doors that have a drawing of the relevant category. In a series of experiments, Patricia Miller and her colleagues found a developmental sequence in strategy use. In the first phase, preschoolers show no selective strategy, usually opening all the doors on the top first and then all the doors on the bottom, regardless of what picture is on the door or what category they're instructed to remember. In the second phase, children use the selective strategy, but only partially: They still open many irrelevant doors. In the third phase, children use the most efficient strategy (that is, open mainly the relevant doors), but the strategy does not help them

remember the locations of the items. This third phase constitutes a utilization deficiency. Not until the fourth phase, usually late in the preschool years, are children able to use the strategy and to benefit from its use.

If strategies are so important to children's cognitive performance, why should they sometimes *not* benefit from them? And when strategies don't do the children any good, why do they bother using them? There is surely no single reason for utilization deficiencies. But perhaps the factor that is most responsible for utilization deficiencies, especially in young children, is lack of mental resources. By definition, strategies are effortful to use, and children who use a strategy may not have enough mental resources left over to devote to solving the problem at hand (Bjorklund & Harnishfeger, 1987; P. H. Miller et al., 1991). Other factors that are likely involved include children's lack of awareness that the strategy is not helping them. That is, children may possess poor metacognition and fail to realize that all the extra effort they are putting in isn't resulting in any benefit (Ringel & Springer, 1980). In fact, young children frequently overestimate their physical and cognitive abilities, thinking they are performing better than they actually are. This may not always be such a bad thing, however. Children who practice strategies eventually get good at them, and their task performance does, indeed, improve (Shin, Bjorklund, & Beck, 2007). That is, utilization deficiencies are often short-lived (Bjorklund, Coyle, & Gaultney, 1992). If young children realized how poorly they were doing, they might stop using the strategy and, although saving themselves some effort in the short term, hinder their overall effectiveness in the long term. Finally, children may use a new strategy just for the sake of novelty (Siegler, 1996). Although from an adult perspective the number-one reason

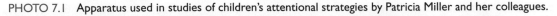

PHOTO 7.1 Apparatus used in studies of children's attentional strategies by Patricia Miller and her colleagues.

Courtesy of Patricia Miller

to use a strategy is to improve task performance (that's what strategies are for, after all), this may not reflect the child's point of view. Trying something new may be a goal unto itself, and the fact that it does not improve performance may be relatively unimportant to children.

How Do Children's Strategies Develop?

For any given task, children have a variety of strategic options available to them. Although psychologists may study a single strategy at a time, in actuality children use multiple strategies to solve a single problem—and sometimes even several strategies at a single time. Evidence for multiple and variable strategy use has been found everywhere it has been looked for, including arithmetic (Alibali, 1999), scientific reasoning (Schauble, 1990), memory (Schwenck et al., 2007), spelling (Rittle-Johnson & Siegler, 1999), and conservation (Church & Goldin-Meadow, 1986), among others (see Siegler, 2006).

Robert Siegler's (1996, 2006) adaptive strategy choice model best exemplifies this perspective of multiple and variable strategy use. Basically, Siegler proposes that, in cognitive development, children generate a wide variety of strategies to solve problems. Depending on the nature of the task and the goals of the child, certain strategies are selected and used frequently, whereas others that are less effective are used less often and eventually decrease in frequency.

The technique Siegler and his colleagues used to assess children's multiple strategy use has been referred to as the *microgenetic method*, which involves looking at developmental change within individuals over short time intervals—usually days or weeks (see Siegler, 2000; van der Ven et al., 2012).

Basically, Siegler sees multiple strategies existing within a child's cognitive repertoire at any one time, with these strategies competing against one another. Early in development, or when a child is first learning a new task, relatively simple strategies will "win" most of the time.

With practice and maturation, the child will use other more effortful but more effective strategies more frequently. Thus, Siegler believes that development does not occur in a steplike fashion but, rather, as a series of overlapping waves, with the pattern of those waves changing over time. Figure 7.9 presents Siegler's wave approach to cognitive development. Multiple strategies are available to children at every age, but which strategies are used most frequently changes with age.

Perhaps the single most investigated topic using the microgenetic method and following Siegler's adaptive strategy choice model is simple arithmetic. For example, in learning to add, children frequently use a strategy that involves counting out loud both addends, called the *sum strategy* (for example, for 5 + 3 = ?, saying "1, 2, 3, 4, 5 [pause], 6, 7, 8"). A more sophisticated strategy, called the *min strategy*, begins with a child identifying the larger addend (in this case, 5) and counting up from there

(for example, saying "5 [pause], 6, 7, 8"). A still more sophisticated strategy, known as *fact retrieval*, is "just knowing" the answer—retrieving it directly from long-term memory without having to count at all (for example, simply saying "8" to the question "How much is 5 + 3?"). When looking at group data, one gets the impression that children progress from using the sum strategy to using the min strategy to using fact retrieval. Yet closer examination reveals that individual children use a variety of these strategies at any one time, and the frequencies with which these strategies are used vary with age. (More is said of children's arithmetic strategies in Chapter 11.)

Children's multiple strategy use can be seen in more naturalistic settings as well. For example, in one study, kindergarten children computed moves on a board game (Chutes and Ladders) by throwing a pair of dice (Bjorklund & Rosenblum, 2002). Children used a variety of strategies to compute their moves. Moreover, these strategies were not random but varied with the numbers on the dice. For example, children used fact retrieval for most doubles (for example, 6 + 6, 5 + 5), the min strategy when the difference between the two addends was large and the smaller number was (usually) a 1 or 2 (for example, 5 + 1, 6 + 2), and the sum strategy for all others (for example, 4 + 2, 5 + 3). Thus, not only do children use multiple and variable strategies on a task, they are highly sensitive to factors within the testing context (here, the particular combination of numbers they were asked to add) when choosing which strategy to use.

Other examples of children's multiple strategy use come from experiments assessing memory development. For example, Kate McGilly and Siegler (1990) gave children in kindergarten, second grade, and fourth grade a serial-recall task

FIGURE 7.9 **Siegler's strategy choice model of development.** Change in strategy use is seen as a series of overlapping waves, with different strategies being used more frequently at different ages.

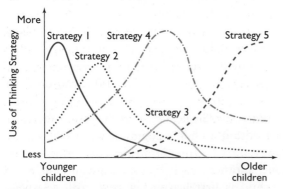

Source: Adapted from Siegler, R. S. (1996). *Emerging minds: The process of change in children's thinking.* New York: Oxford University Press.

(remember a list of digits in exact order). McGilly and Siegler observed the strategies the children used and later questioned the children about their strategy use. They reported that the children used a variety of strategies on these tasks (single word rehearsal, repeated rehearsal), with any given child using a combination of strategies over repeated trials. That is, multiple strategy use was the rule rather than the exception (see also Coyle & Bjorklund, 1997; Schwenck, Bjorklund, & Schneider, 2009).

Siegler believes that age differences in how strategies are selected and used reflect an important way of viewing cognitive development that differs from conventional Piagetian and information-processing models. Perhaps the most important message from Siegler's work is that children use strategies *selectively* and *adaptively* and that at any point in time and for any given task, children have a variety of strategies available to them. The issue facing cognitive developmental psychologists is not whether children are being strategic. Rather, we are seeking to discover what strategies and combination of strategies children of different ages use and how the simpler strategies used by young children develop into the more sophisticated and effective strategies used by older children and adults.

Development of Memory Strategies

Children's strategies have been investigated for a wide range of topics. To provide an example of strategy development for a particular content, in this section we describe the development of **memory strategies** (or **mnemonics**). Developmental researchers have studied a variety of memory strategies, and here we review briefly the two most investigated: **rehearsal**, in which a child repeats the target information, and **organization**, in which the child combines different items into categories, themes, or other units.

Rehearsal

In a pioneering study by John Flavell and his colleagues (Flavell, Beach, & Chinsky, 1966), children in kindergarten and the second and fifth grades were shown a set of pictures that they were asked to remember. Following the presentation, a 15-second delay allowed the children to prepare for the recall test. An experimenter, who was trained to identify lip movements corresponding to the words the children were trying to remember, watched the children's mouths. Flavell and his associates reported age-related increases in recall with corresponding increases in the amount of rehearsal. Eighty-five percent of the fifth-graders displayed evidence of some spontaneous rehearsal, whereas only 10% of the kindergarten children did so. Furthermore, within a grade level, children who rehearsed more recalled more, on average, than did children who rehearsed less. These findings led the researchers to conclude that rehearsal is a powerful mnemonic that increases with age, with the frequency of rehearsal (the absolute number of times one rehearses) determining memory performance.

Later research by Peter Ornstein, Mary Naus, and Charles Liberty (1975) questioned Flavell's frequency interpretation. These researchers used an *overt rehearsal procedure* with children in the third, sixth, and eighth grades. In this procedure, children are presented with a series of words to recall, with several seconds between each successive word. During this interval, the children are told they must repeat the most recently presented word at least once and, if they wish, that they may practice any other words they like. Thus, rehearsal is made obligatory (they must rehearse at least one word once during each interval), and the experimenters can determine exactly what the children are doing. Using this procedure, the researchers found no differences in the frequency of rehearsal across the three grade levels. Despite this equivalence in quantity of rehearsal, age differences in recall persisted—a perplexing finding given the interpretation of the earlier study by Flavell and his colleagues. However, Ornstein and his associates did report differences in the quality, or *style*, of rehearsal.

Typical rehearsal protocols for a third- and an eighth-grade child are shown in Table 7.1. The number of words actually rehearsed is similar for the two children, but the style of rehearsing is very different. The younger child includes only one or, at best, two unique words per rehearsal set. (A rehearsal set refers to the words repeated during the interstimulus interval.) The researchers referred to this method as a passive rehearsal style. In contrast, the older child includes several different words per rehearsal set, a style labeled active rehearsal (or cumulative rehearsal). The child repeats the most recently presented word and then rehearses it with as many other different words as possible. From these and other data, Ornstein and his colleagues (1975) asserted that the important developmental changes are in style rather than frequency of rehearsal. A main feature of rehearsal seems to be the sequence in which items are rehearsed. For instance, one study assessed the rehearsal and recall sequences of children ages 8 to 10 years. Children tended to rehearse items with other neighboring items, in the same order as they were presented in the original list (what the authors called the contiguity effect). This was also the case during recall—sequences tended to be recalled in the same order as they were presented. The older the children were, the more pronounced was the effect, as well as the link between contiguity at rehearsal

TABLE 7.1 Typical rehearsal protocols for an eighth-grade child and a third-grade child.
Note the use of cumulative rehearsal by eighth-graders and the more passive rehearsal style by third-graders.

| | Rehearsal sets | |
Word presented	Eighth-grade child	Third-grade child
1. Yard	Yard, yard, yard	Yard, yard, yard, yard, yard,
2. Cat	Cat, yard, yard, cat	Cat, cat, cat, cat, yard
3. Man	Man, cat, yard, man, yard, cat	Man, man, man man, man
4. Desk	Desk, man, yard, cat, man, desk, cat, yard	Desk, desk, desk, desk

Source: Ornstein, P. A., Naus, M. J., & Liberty, C. (1975). Rehearsal and organizational processes in children's memory. *Child Development, 46,* 818–830. Copyright © The Society for Research in Child Development, Inc. Reprinted with permission.

and recall performance. These results point to the main mechanism of rehearsal in facilitating recall as the strengthening of associations between items in a list based on the order they're presented, and this mechanism improves with age (Lehmann & Hasselhorn, 2012).

A causal relationship between differences in the frequency and style of rehearsal and age differences in memory performance has been demonstrated in training studies. Preteen-age children trained to use a cumulative rehearsal strategy display elevated levels of recall (B. C. Cox et al., 1989; Ornstein, Naus, & Stone, 1977). Thus, young children can be trained to use a rehearsal strategy, resulting in increases in memory performance (although age differences are rarely eliminated). What differs in development is children's inclination to implement a strategy rather than their ability to use it (that is, a *production deficiency*). This general pattern is not unique to rehearsal but, as you will see, typifies other strategies as well.

Organization

At a very basic level, rehearsing information in the temporal order it was presented, as in the study we described in the previous section, is a way of maintaining organization. However, another reason that active rehearsal benefits memory might be that *conceptual* relations are noticed among items that are rehearsed together (Ornstein & Naus, 1978). *Organization* in memory refers to the structure discovered or imposed on a set of items that is used to guide subsequent performance. In attempting to remember what groceries one must buy at the store, for example, we benefit by organizing the information by categories (dairy products, meats, vegetables) or meals (food necessary for pot roast, food necessary for Saturday's barbecue).

In a typical study of organization and recall, children are given a randomized list of items that can be divided into categories (several instances of furniture, tools, and occupations, for example). Children are sometimes given the opportunity to sort items into groups before recall (a *sort-recall* task). Will children sort categorically similar items together? And when they recall the items, will they remember different ones from the same category together, even though they were not originally presented together? Recalling items from the same category together is referred to as *clustering*, and adults who display high levels of clustering in their recall typically remember more than adults who display lower levels of clustering. Developmentally, levels of sorting, clustering, and recall usually increase with age (see Bjorklund, Dukes, & Brown, 2009; Schneider, 2015). In fact, preschool children's clustering is often at chance levels (see Salatas & Flavell, 1976; Schwenck et al., 2009). Older children are more likely to group

items by meaning and, as a result, realize higher levels of recall (D. L. Best & Ornstein, 1986; Hasselhorn, 1992). Yet when the instructions are modified, stressing to children that they should make their groups on the basis of meaning, even preschoolers comply and demonstrate enhanced levels of memory performance (Lange & Jackson, 1974; Sodian, Schneider, & Perlmutter, 1986).

Other experiments that more explicitly train children to use an organizational strategy have also yielded positive results. Young children, under certain instructional conditions, use an organizational strategy and display elevated levels of memory performance (Lange & Pierce, 1992; Schwenck et al., 2007). In other words, young children are capable of organizing information for recall, but they generally fail to do so spontaneously. As with rehearsal, training children to use an organizational strategy rarely eliminates age differences, and under most conditions, young children fail to generalize the strategy to new situations or new sets of materials (D. Cox & Waters, 1986).

Longitudinal Assessment of Memory Strategy Development

The impression one gets when looking at the memory strategy literature is that children show regular and gradual changes in strategy use (rehearsal or organization) with time. Most data looking at age-related changes in strategy use, however, are cross-sectional in nature, with different children of different ages being tested to assess developmental changes. Although cross-sectional studies have many benefits (their economy in time, effort, and expense being the foremost values), they cannot adequately test developmental hypotheses. Only longitudinal studies can do this, and unfortunately, there have been very few longitudinal studies of basic strategic processes.

Two exceptions are the Munich Longitudinal Study on the Genesis of Individual Competencies (LOGIC) (Schneider & Bullock, 2009; Sodian & Schneider, 1999; Weinert & Schneider, 1992), which followed participants from age 4 to 18 years and evaluated performance on sort-recall tasks every other year as part of their assessments, and the Wurzburg Longitudinal Memory Study (Schneider et al., 2004; Schneider, Kron-Sperl, & Hunnerkopf, 2009), which followed children ages 6 to 9 years at intervals as short as 6 months. Wolfgang Schneider and his colleagues reported that relatively few children displayed gradual change in memory strategy development. Figure 7.10 presents the patterns of strategy change in the LOGIC and the Wurzburg longitudinal studies (from Schneider, Kron-Sperl, & Hunnerkopf, 2009). A few children in each study were strategic from the beginning, and a few others never developed strategic proficiency. However, most children in both studies showed significant improvement in strategy use over time, with more children in both studies (but especially with older children in the LOGIC study) demonstrating "jumps" rather than gradual increases. These findings indicate that, despite the impression of gradual change in strategic functioning obtained from cross-sectional studies, most children actually display a relatively abrupt change from astrategic to strategic memory functioning, with the change happening at different ages for different children.

Even the 6-month interval used in the Wurzburg Longitudinal Memory Study, however, may cause a researcher to interpret a relatively gradual change as a true discontinuity. This was addressed in a microgenetic study, in which 8- to 12-year-old children performed a series of sort-recall tasks over 11 consecutive weeks (Schlagmuller & Schneider, 2002). Changes in organizational strategies were assessed weekly.

FIGURE 7.10 Patterns of strategy change in the LOGIC and the Wurzburg longitudinal studies. As can be seen, most children showed abrupt jumps from being nonstrategic to being strategic.

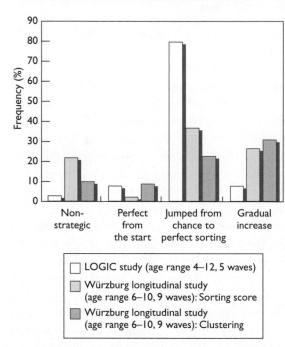

Source: Schneider, W., Kron-Sperl, V., & Hunnerkopf, M. (2009). The development of young children's memory strategies: Evidence from the Wurzburg Longitudinal Memory Study. *European Journal of Developmental Psychology, 6,* 70–99.

The researchers reported that children made the transition from astrategic to strategic functioning quickly, not gradually, and that once children started to use an organizational strategy, they continued to do so and also showed corresponding improvements in their recall.

Factors That Influence Children's Strategy Use and Effectiveness

A number of factors contribute to both developmental and individual differences in children's tendencies to use and benefit from strategies. Three important ones that we discuss here are (a) *mental capacity*, (b) *knowledge base*, and (c) *metacognition*.

Mental Capacity

By definition, strategies are effortful cognitive operations, and one factor that affects whether children will use strategies and their effectiveness if used is limited mental capacity. That is, strategy use has a cost in mental effort, and young children exert so much of their limited resources executing the strategy that they do not retain sufficient mental capacity to perform other aspects of the task efficiently (Case, 1985; Cowan, 2014).

This is seen in research showing a relation between strategy use and working memory (Lehmann & Hasselhorn, 2007; van der Ven et al., 2012), as well as in *dual-task experiments* that are based on the simple idea that it is difficult to do two things at once (Guttentag, 1984; P. H. Miller et al., 1991). Katherine Kipp Harnishfeger and I (DB) demonstrated this possibility in a dual-task memory experiment (Bjorklund & Harnishfeger, 1987). Third- and seventh-grade children were instructed in the use of an organizational memory strategy (remembering all the words from a category together). In addition, the children were required to tap an index finger on the space bar of a computer as fast as they could. Their tapping rates during the memory training were compared with their rates during a baseline period when no memory task was given and during a free-recall memory task for which no training instructions had been provided. Decreases in tapping rate during the memory tasks were used as an indication of how much mental effort the children were expending on the tasks. The more slowly the children tapped (relative to when they were performing no memory

task), the greater the mental effort required to perform the memory task was presumed to be. That is, the more mental effort required for the memory task, the more interference (as measured by the decreased tapping rate) there should be on the secondary task (tapping).

Both the third- and seventh-graders showed increased interference relative to the free-recall task as a result of the training (see Table 7.2). Furthermore, both groups later used the strategy that they had been shown during training. This use was indicated by increased clustering scores in recall, with children remembering

TABLE 7.2 **Mean recall, clustering, and percentage interference scores for free recall (baseline) and trained recall for third- and seventh-grade children.** Both the third- and seventh-grade children transferred the trained strategy, as reflected by significant increases in clustering, and experienced significant increases in interference. However, only the seventh-graders showed an increase in recall as a result of training.

	Free Recall	Trained Recall
Third Grade		
Interference	17.31%	21.29%*
Clustering (ARC)	0.14	0.53*
Mean recall	4.60	5.07
Seventh Grade		
Interference	18.07%	23.53%*
Clustering (ARC)	0.09	0.80*
Mean recall	5.89	7.73*

Source: Bjorklund, D. F., & Harnishfeger, K. K. (1987). Developmental differences in the mental effort requirements for the use of an organizational strategy in free recall. *Journal of Experimental Child Psychology, 44,* 109–125 (Experiment 2).

Note: Cluster scores range from 0, meaning no clustering beyond what would be expected by chance, to 1, meaning perfect clustering.

*Significant difference between trained-recall and free-recall trial.

words from the same category together. Only the seventh-grade children, however, showed a corresponding improvement in the number of words they remembered relative to the free-recall task. The third-graders remembered no more words during training than they did when no memory instructions had been given, despite the fact that they used the strategy and expended greater amounts of mental effort. We interpreted these results as indicating that the third-graders used too much of their limited mental capacity in executing the strategy to have enough left over for other aspects of the memory task, such as retrieving specific words. Strategies are supposed to provide greater efficiency in processing, and had the third-grade children mastered the strategy to a greater degree, their memory performance would probably have improved. Nevertheless, under the conditions of this experiment, their memory performance did not improve. Similar findings and interpretations have been reported for other strategies, including rehearsal (Guttentag, 1984), simple attentional strategies (P. H. Miller et al., 1991), and a more complex elaboration memory strategy (Rohwer & Litrowink, 1983; see also Bjorklund, Dukes, & Brown, 2009).

Strategies are effortful. Young children process information less efficiently than older children do, making them less likely to use a strategy spontaneously and less likely to benefit from the imposition of a strategy. Cognitive processing becomes more efficient with age, allowing children to execute more strategies and to use them with greater effectiveness.

Knowledge Base

We discussed earlier the role that children's **knowledge base** could have on their memory performance. For example, the research with chess-expert children by Chi (1978) demonstrated that when someone knows a lot about a specific topic, memory span for information *in one's area of expertise*, but not beyond it, is significantly enhanced. Perhaps the relationship between knowledge and processing is most easily seen with respect to strategies. According to Daniel Kee (1994), "Most researchers acknowledge that strategic processing is dependent on the availability and accessibility of relevant knowledge" (p. 9). The primary reason hypothesized for this relationship is that having a detailed, or elaborated, knowledge base results in faster processing for domain-specific information, which in turn results in more efficient processing and greater availability of mental resources. The relationship between knowledge and strategy use has been demonstrated for a variety of domains, including mathematics (Ashcraft, 1990), reading (Daneman & Green, 1986), text comprehension (Schneider, Körkel, & Weinert, 1989), problem solving (Chi, Feltovich, & Glaser, 1981), communication (Furman & Walden, 1990), memory (Ornstein, Baker-Ward, & Naus, 1988), and forming inferences (Barnes, Dennis, & Haefele-Kalvaitis, 1996), among others.

The role of knowledge base on children's memory strategies is perhaps most easily illustrated on sort-recall tasks, in which children are given lists of words or pictures from different categories to remember. Children's knowledge of relations among the to-be-remembered items can then be manipulated so that some items are typical of their categories (for example, *pants, dress, sweater* for clothing) whereas others are equally familiar but atypical of their category (for example, *belt, shoes, necklace* for clothing). Children are more likely to use one or more strategies and to remember more items when recalling the more typical and categorically integrated sets of items than the atypical items (D. L. Best, 1993; Schwenck et al., 2007, 2009). In general, as children's world knowledge increases with age, so does their strategic performance.

But *how* does knowing a lot (or a little) about the task materials influence performance? This will vary with the nature of the task, but knowledge should influence task performance in some general ways. One theory (Bjorklund, 1987b) proposed three ways, some of which are directly related to strategies, in which knowledge may enhance children's performance: (1) by increasing the accessibility of specific items (item-specific effects), (2) by the relatively effortless activation of relations among sets of items (nonstrategic organization), and (3) by facilitating the use of deliberate strategies. *Item-specific effects* are most easily observed when children are asked to recall sets of unrelated items (for example, *apple, army, clock, day, dress, flower, hammer, snow*). Recall typically improves with age, but there are no corresponding improvements in measures of organization (Ornstein, Hale, & Morgan, 1977). One interpretation of these findings is that individual items are more richly represented in the long-term memories of older children than in those of younger children, resulting in greater ease of retrieval (Chechile & Richman, 1982; Ghatala, 1984).

Nonstrategic organization occurs when children have highly developed knowledge of relations among sets of to-be-remembered items and the retrieval of one item acts to automatically activate the retrieval of related items without the need of implementing a deliberate (that is, effortful) strategy. For instance, highly associated words (for example, *dog* and *cat, hand* and *glove, mouse* and *cheese*) are processed faster and are more likely to be remembered together by young children than are nonassociated words that are categorically related (for example,

dog and *lion, cheese* and *milk, hand* and *head*) (Bjorklund & Jacobs, 1985; Schneider, 1986). In other studies, age differences in recall have been eliminated or greatly reduced when children have detailed knowledge about the information they are asked to remember (Bjorklund & Zeman, 1982; Lindberg, 1980). For example, Barbara Zeman and I (Bjorklund & Zeman, 1982) asked children in the first, third, and fifth grades to recall the names of their current classmates. Age differences in class recall were small and were significantly less than age differences found for lists of categorically related words (see Figure 7.11). Furthermore, children's recall of their classmates'

FIGURE 7.11 **The average recall and clustering on class- and word-recall tasks by children in first, third, and fifth grades.**

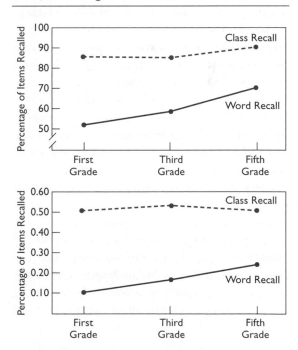

Source: Bjorklund, D. F., & Zeman, B. R. (1982). Children's organization and metamemory awareness in their recall of familiar information. *Child Development, 53,* 799–810. The Society for Research in Child Development, Inc.

names was not random but was highly organized (by seating arrangement, reading groups, sex, and so on). Yet when queried about their use of strategies, most of the children in all grades were unaware of using any special technique to remember the names. We proposed that the classmates' names represented a well-established knowledge base, with relations among names being activated with relatively little effort. Thus, a strategy was not necessary for successful retrieval. In other words, although the outcome of the children's recall appeared to be strategic (highly organized retrieval), the processes underlying their performance were not. Rather, they represented the relatively automatic activation and retrieval of relations among items in memory.

Another interpretation for our findings is that the elaborated knowledge base the children had for their classmates' names allowed them to use memory strategies efficiently. In fact, we proposed this possibility for the oldest children, who might have identified categorical relations in their recall while retrieving names on the basis of the relatively automatic activation of long-term memory relations and then continued to use this fortuitously discovered strategy for the remainder of their recall ("Hey, all those kids sit in the same row. I think I'll remember the rest of the kids by where they sit"). Peter Ornstein and his colleagues have championed this position—namely, that an elaborated knowledge base for sets of items allows the effective use of mnemonics (Folds et al., 1990; Ornstein et al., 1988). Ornstein and his colleagues proposed that the use of memory strategies is facilitated by the automatic execution of certain parts of a task, even in very young children. Later in development, when children have a more sophisticated knowledge base and more experience, entire problem-solving routines can become automated.

Although knowledge typically is positively correlated with memory performance (that is, the more one knows about a topic, the better one remembers), there is at least one interesting exception. In what is known as the Deese/Roediger-McDermott (DRM) paradigm (named after the researchers who developed it), participants are given a list of words all related to a single concept. For example, the words on the list might include *butter*, *food*, *eat*, *sandwich*, *jam*, *milk*, *flour*, *jelly*, *dough*, *crust*, *slice*, *wine*, *loaf*, and *toast*. You've probably figured out that what's missing here is the word *bread*, associated with each of the words on the list. When adults are given such a list and later asked to recall the items, they frequently remember *bread* or, when given a recognition list, erroneously select *bread* as being on the list (see Brainerd, Reyna, & Ceci, 2008). What's interesting is that children are generally *less* apt to make such mistakes, thus making fewer false responses than adults (see Brainerd et al., 2008; Brainerd, Reyna, & Zember, 2011).

What can account for this developmental reversal in accurate memory performance? One explanation involves the ease with which children can identify and activate semantic relations among category members. The better-elaborated knowledge base of older children and adults causes them to spontaneously activate the word *bread* when they hear or read *butter*, *sandwich*, and *jam*. Younger children, because of their less-elaborated knowledge base, are less apt to automatically activate such relations (M. C. Wimmer & Howe, 2010) or to identify category relations among items (Bjorklund, 1980) and, thus, are less likely to falsely remember *bread* when presented with a long list of its associates. So, although increasing knowledge base usually is positively associated with their strategic and nonstrategic memory performance, it can sometimes be a double-edge sword, resulting in increased false memories, at least in DRM-type tasks.

The relationship among knowledge, strategies, and task performance is a complicated one and centrally important to cognitive development. What is important to remember is that what and how much one knows influences both what and how well one thinks. With age, children acquire more knowledge and, simply as a result of these quantitative increases, process information differently. Because knowledge affects processing, children (and adults) think differently about topics on which they have detailed knowledge versus those on which they have less knowledge.

Metacognition

Earlier, we defined **metacognition** as the knowledge of one's cognitive abilities. Every type of cognition has a corresponding type of metacognition—that is, metamemory, meta-attention, meta-comprehension, and so on. Someone with high metacognitive awareness should be aware of the cognitive operation he or she is engaged in and perhaps how successful his or her attempts are at solving a particular problem. Strategies as we defined them earlier in the chapter almost require a degree of metacognitive awareness. If strategies are available to consciousness, it implies that children know (that is, are self-aware) of using them. At one level, this is true, but much room for variability remains. Children differ greatly in the degree to which they know what strategies they have available in their cognitive arsenal, their relative effectiveness, when they are needed and when they are not, and in monitoring task performance. These various factors can influence strategy use and effectiveness and, not surprisingly, they each develop.

Children with higher levels of metacognition usually (but not always) display higher levels of cognition, and young children are generally more out of touch with their cognitive abilities than older children are. This is especially true when it comes to using strategies (Clerc, Miller, & Cosnefroy, 2014), as has been found for a host of cognitive domains, including scientific reasoning and critical thinking (Kuhn, Amsel, & O'Loughlm, 1988; Magno, 2010), mathematics (Schneider & Artelt, 2010), attention (P. H. Miller & Weiss, 1982), and memory (DeMarie et al., 2004), among others.

Metacognition can be divided into two types: *declarative* and *procedural* (Schneider & Lockl, 2002). **Declarative metacognition** refers to the explicit, conscious, and factual knowledge a person has about the characteristics of the task he or she is performing, one's own weak and strong points with respect to performing the task, and the possible strategies that could be used on the task. For example, for simple addition problems, are children aware of their own abilities to add and subtract numbers? Do they realize that computing sums may be easier if they use some external aids, such as their fingers or pips on a pair of dice, rather than doing the computation in their heads? Do they know that they can derive an answer to the problem by counting all the numbers (for example, for the problem 3 + 2 = ?, saying, "1, 2, 3, . . . 4, 5"), by counting from the larger number (for example, saying "3 . . . 4, 5"), or in some cases, just knowing the answer ("5!")? In contrast to declarative metacognition is **procedural metacognition**, which refers to the knowledge about when strategies are necessary ("Do I need to do something special to remember this telephone number?") as well as to monitoring how well one is performing on a task (see Schneider, 2015). In the following subsections, we describe research into two types of metacognition—meta-attention and metamemory—and their relation to strategy use and development.

Meta-attention. Meta-attention refers to children's knowledge of their attentional abilities. As noted earlier in this chapter, young children often attend as much (or more) to task-irrelevant stimuli as to task relevant ones. Might such performance be attributed (or at least related) to deficits in meta-attention? Well, yes and no. Even though 4-year-olds generally cannot overcome distractions when performing selective-attention tasks, they are apparently aware that distractions are a problem, for they realize that two stories will be harder to understand if the storytellers speak simultaneously rather than taking turns (Pillow, 1988). In contrast, 3-year-olds would just as soon listen to stories told simultaneously as to have the storytellers take turns. In other research, Patricia Miller and Michael Weiss (1982) asked 5-, 7-, and 9-year-olds to answer a series of questions about factors known to affect performance on an incidental-learning task in which they must attend to relevant stimuli and ignore irrelevant stimuli. Although knowledge about attentional processes generally increased with age, even the 5-year-olds realized that one should at least *look first* at task-relevant stimuli and then *label* these objects as an aid to remembering them. The 7- and 10-year-olds further understood that one must *attend selectively* to task-relevant stimuli and *ignore* irrelevant information to do well on these problems.

At other times, however, young children seem unaware that paying attention is something special. In one study, John Flavell and his colleagues (Flavell, Green, & Flavell, 1995) asked 4-, 6-, and 8-year-old children a series of questions about attention. For example, if a woman were examining a set of decorative pins so that she can select one as a gift, what would be on her mind? Would she be focusing just on the pins,

or might she have other things on her mind as well? Whereas almost all 8-year-olds and most 6-year-olds were aware that the woman would be thinking primarily about the pins and not likely thinking about other things, few 4-year-olds had this insight. It's as if they did not realize what is involved in selective attention. By 8 years of age, however, children's understanding of attentional focus was about as good as that of adults.

Do children benefit from constant reminders to pay attention? Some research indicates that indeed they do. For instance, Kathleen Kannass and colleagues (Kannass, Colombo, & Wyss, 2010) examined 3- and 4-year-olds' attention and cognitive performance on a problem-solving task (for example, a puzzle or building blocks) while a television show was playing in the background (a distractor). For some children, the background program was in a foreign language and consisted of continuous presentation of random 5-second segments of a children's TV show (in other words, an incomprehensible distractor). For other children, the distractor program was in English and played in the normal sequence (a comprehensible distractor). In addition, some children received frequent instruction to stay on task, some received moderate instruction, and others received no instruction. Results indicated that when the distractor was comprehensible, frequent instruction to pay attention was the most effective in increasing attention to the primary task (measured as total looking time and average look length at the task). Any amount of instruction improved performance when the distractor was incomprehensible. Four-year-olds showed better resistance to interference from the comprehensible distractor than did 3-year-olds, but 3-year-olds were just as resistant when the task was incomprehensible. And how well children performed on the problem-solving tasks was directly related to their ability to sustain attention. That is, as children spent more time looking at the primary task, their performance improved, and as they spent more time looking at the distractor program, their performance declined. These findings indicate that children as young as 3 are able to use explicit task instructions to guide their attention, and these reminders may be particularly beneficial in the preschool years when children's meta-attention is lacking.

Metamemory. As another example, consider metamemory (see Schneider, 2015; Waters & Kunnman, 2009, for reviews). In a pioneering study of children's metamemory abilities, Mary Anne Kreutzer, Catherine Leonard, and John Flavell (1975) asked children in kindergarten and the first, third, and fifth grades a series of questions about memory. For example, the children were asked if they ever forget things, if it would be easier to remember a phone number immediately after being told the number or after getting a drink of water, and if learning pairs of opposites (for example, boy/girl) would be easier or harder than learning pairs of unrelated words (for example, Mary/walk)—all of which are forms of declarative metacognition. Some kindergarten children asserted that they never forget things, and fewer than 50% believed that hearing the phone number immediately would yield more accurate recall. About half of the kindergarten and first-grade children believed that the arbitrary pairs would be just as easy (or even easier) to learn as the opposites.

Let us relate an anecdote about how young children can be out of touch with their memory performance. I (DB) was conducting a memory test with a 5-year-old boy. I showed him 16 pictures of familiar objects from four categories (fruit, tools, body parts, and animals), which he had 2 minutes to study. After the

2 minutes, I asked him a few questions as a simple distraction task ("How old are you? When's your birthday?"), and then I asked him to remember as many of those pictures as he could, out loud, in any order that he wanted. The child did not hesitate and quickly said, "Cow, hammer, screwdriver, apple," then just as quickly stopped and sat quietly, waiting for me to say something. After sitting silently for about 10 seconds, I asked, "Can you remember any more of the pictures?" He looked incredulously at me and said, "You mean there were *more* pictures?" This child had told me all he could remember of the list, and as far as he was concerned, his recall was perfect. His ability to monitor his performance (procedural metamemory) would (one hopes) improve considerably in the years to come.

More specifically with respect to strategies, are children aware that strategies are necessary to perform a task well and of the relation between using strategies and task performance (procedural metacognition)? Not surprisingly, young children are often unaware of simple strategies they can use to solve problems, or at least they are not conscious that such techniques can be useful when they are given a specific task. For example, children who are aware of the connection between strategies such as rehearsal and organization and memory performance often remember more information than do children who do not possess such awareness (Justice et al., 1997). Furthermore, young children who have been taught a strategy are often unaware that using it facilitated their memory performance. This is illustrated in an experiment by Barbara Ringel and Carla Springer (1980). They trained first-, third-, and fifth-grade children to use an organizational memory strategy. The children were given pictures and instructed to sort them into groups by meaning and to use the groupings to help them remember the pictures. Each group of children showed improved memory performance after training (relative to an earlier baseline phase). The children were then given a third memory task to assess transfer of training. After completing the training but before beginning the transfer list, some of the children were provided with explicit feedback concerning their improved performance on the task, whereas others were not. The fifth-grade children transferred the organizational strategy to the new task under all conditions, whereas Ringel and Springer found no evidence of significant transfer for any group of first-graders. For the third-grade children, however, feedback made a difference. Those third-graders who had received feedback concerning their memory performance transferred the organizational strategy to a new set of pictures. Third-graders receiving no feedback did not; for the most part, they reverted to a nonstrategic style characteristic of their pretraining behavior. In other words, knowing how well they were doing influenced the third-graders' generalization of a strategy. The older children, apparently being better able to assess their own progress, did not require such explicit feedback to transfer the strategy, and the younger children either were unable to transfer the strategy or, at best, needed more intensive instructions before generalization would take place. Other researchers have emphasized the role of metamemory in the effectiveness of strategy use and transfer, demonstrating that training in memory monitoring or other aspects of metamemory is responsible for the effectiveness and maintenance of strategy training (Ghatala et al., 1986; Melot, 1998). Indeed, one longitudinal study of first- and second-graders demonstrated that the acquisition of metamemory preceded strategic sophistication over time, making clear that metamemory is important for the development of mnemonic strategies (Grammer et al., 2011).

We will have more to say about metacognition with respect to specific types of cognition in other chapters in the book. For now,

it's important to keep in mind that possessing and using strategies are not enough to ensure competent performance. Being aware of when to use strategies, of which ones to use, and of how effective the strategies you're using really are will all influence task performance.

Transactions Among Capacity, Knowledge, and Metacognition

Metacognition is obviously an important component in children's cognitive development. However, research findings suggest that metacognitive competence is as much a consequence as it is a cause of competent cognitive behavior, with the two being intimately entwined, and that this relationship varies as a function of age and task variables. For example, children who are experts in a domain will perform better in that domain than will less-expert children (Schneider, Bjorklund, & Maier-Brückner, 1996). However, expert children's cognitive performance will be greatest when they also have substantial metacognitive knowledge (Schneider, Schlagmuller, & Vise, 1998).

Darlene DeMarie and her colleagues have investigated how mental capacity, knowledge base, and metamemory transact to produce changes in children's memory performance (DeMarie & Ferron, 2003; DeMarie et al., 2004). Children 5 to 11 years of age were administered a series of strategic memory tasks, measures of memory capacity (for example, working memory), and metamemory assessments. DeMarie et al. (2004) then performed a series of analyses, evaluating different theoretical models of memory development. The model that best fit the developmental data is shown in Figure 7.12. DeMarie and colleagues concluded that capacity and metamemory interact over age to produce patterns of strategic memory performance, and that (a) both strategy production (that is, whether children produce a

FIGURE 7.12 **A model of children's memory development.** Mental capacity and metamemory interact over age to produce patterns of strategic memory performance.

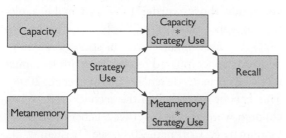

Source: DeMarie, D., Miller, P. H., Ferron, J., & Cunningham, W. R. (2004). Path analysis tests of theoretical models of children's memory performance. *Journal of Cognition and Development, 5,* 461–492.

strategy or not) and strategy efficiency (that is, how much a strategy helps in enhancing recall) are important factors in memory development; (b) multiple strategy use must be considered; and (c) metamemory plays a significant role in predicting multiple strategy use and strategy effectiveness. They further speculated that different factors have greater impact at different times in development. For example, individual differences in capacity may be more important in influencing memory strategies for young children (Woody-Dorning & Miller, 2001), whereas individual differences in metamemory may be more important for older children.

Culture and Strategies in the Classroom

Cultures clearly differ in the extent to which they support and encourage particular strategic activities (Kurtz, 1990; Mistry, 1997). For example, the memory strategies of rehearsal and organization are especially helpful to children from Western industrialized societies, where school

activities involve a great deal of rote memorization and list learning. Yet these same strategies might not be so useful to unschooled children from nonindustrialized societies, where the most important memory tasks might involve recalling the location of objects (for example, water, game animals) in a natural setting or remembering instructions passed along in the context of proverbs or stories.

For example, in list-learning experiments, Western children rely heavily on strategies acquired at school and clearly outperform their unschooled peers from nonindustrialized societies (Cole & Scribner, 1977; Rogoff & Waddell, 1982). The picture is much different, however, when the memory task is embedded in a meaningful and structured context. When tests are structured so that people must recall organized prose (as in a story) or items from spatially organized arrays (as in familiar scenes), few cultural differences in memory performance are found (see Rogoff, 1990).

There are also differences in strategy use between children in different schooled cultures. For example, in studies comparing German and American second- and third-grade children, German children were found to use more memory strategies than American children (Carr et al., 1989; Kurtz et al., 1990). The reason for these cultural differences can be traced to the behaviors and attitudes of children's parents and teachers. German parents buy their children more games that require strategic thinking, give them more direct strategy training, and check their homework more than American parents do. Similarly, German teachers provide more direct strategy instruction than American teachers (Carr et al., 1989; Kurtz et al., 1990).

We'd like to think that all (or nearly all) aspects of cognitive development have some practical utility, but this seems to be especially the case for strategies. Many aspects of cognition develop because of children's normal, day-to-day interaction with their environment. Change happens when no one (including the child) is watching. Many strategies are less apt to be acquired spontaneously. Although children often discover strategies on their own in the process of performing a task (Siegler & Jenkins, 1989), many important cognitive strategies are explicitly taught in school (Moely et al., 1992; Pressley & Woloshyn, 1995) or sometimes by parents (Güler et al., 2010; Larkpna et al., 2008). As such, knowledge of how strategies develop and factors that influence their use can be of great practical value for the educator or parent of a school-age child.

But how much explicit strategy instruction do children get in school? This, of course, will vary from school to school and from teacher to teacher, but it may surprise you to learn that strategy instruction is rarely on the top of most teachers' to-do list. In a classroom observational study, Barbara Moely and her colleagues (1992) reported that teachers in kindergarten through sixth grade taught a wide range of strategies that varied with the age of the child and the nature of the task. These included rote learning for simple and repetitive tasks, imagery, and self-checking, among others. Despite the diversity of strategies taught, Moely and colleagues reported that the absolute frequency of strategy instruction was low. For example, specific strategy instruction was observed on an average of fewer than 3% of the teacher observations, with teachers providing some general instruction about how to deal with a task strategically in 9.5% of the observations. In fact, 10% of the teachers observed in this study provided no strategy instruction at all. Thus, strategy instruction in school varies with the teacher, the task, and the age of the children, with teachers generally providing children with instruction that is age appropriate (that is, neither too simple nor too complicated for them to understand).

In other research, first-grade children with teachers who used a mnemonic orientation in their classroom and related it to children's strategic memory behavior (for example, "How did you study those words?"; "If you make a picture in your mind, it will help you to remember") displayed higher levels of strategic memory performance compared to children with less mnemonically oriented teachers (Coffman et al., 2008). This benefit extended to the second grade when children were taught by other teachers (Ornstein, Grammar, & Coffman, 2009; see Ornstein et al., 2010).

Strategy instruction is more likely to occur for some subjects than for others and, especially, for children just beginning to tackle a new challenge. For example, teachers (and parents) often give children specific instruction in simple arithmetic strategies—teaching them, for instance, how to use the min strategy ("Start with the bigger number, 6, and then count from there, 7, 8, 9")—and provide quite explicit directions about how to decode letters and printed words into spoken sounds and language (Moely, Santulli, & Obach, 1995; Pressley & Woloshyn, 1995). In a study of preschoolers and their teachers, the amount of "math talk" that teachers did (much of which could be considered pointing out simple strategies) was related to children's growth of mathematical knowledge over the school year (Klibanoff et al., 2006). Strategy instruction occurs less frequently for higher-level cognitive tasks, such as reading comprehension, yet researchers have investigated such strategies with known positive effects of instruction on children's performance (Gaultney, 1995; Mastropieri & Scruggs, 1991).

The goal of strategy instruction is to make children into effective learners. Michael Pressley and his colleagues (Pressley, Borkowski, & Schneider, 1989) proposed three stages in which knowledge is acquired via instruction:

TABLE 7.3   General model of how to teach strategies.

- Teach a few strategies at a time, intensively and extensively, as part of the ongoing curriculum; in the beginning, teach only one at a time, until students are familiar with the idea of strategy use.
- Model and explain each new strategy.
- Model again and re-explain strategies in ways that are sensitive to aspects of strategy use that are not well understood. (Students are constructing their understanding of the strategy, refining the understanding a little bit at a time.)
- Explain to students where and when to use strategies, although students will also discover some such metacognitive information as they use strategies.
- Provide plenty of practice, using strategies for as many appropriate tasks as possible. Such practice increases proficient execution of the strategy, knowledge of how to adapt it, and knowledge of when to use it.
- Encourage students to monitor how they are doing when they are using strategies.
- Encourage continued use of and generalization of strategies, for example, by reminding students throughout the school day about when they could apply strategies they are learning about.
- Increase students' motivation to use strategies by heightening student awareness that they are acquiring valuable skills that are at the heart of competent functioning with learning tasks.
- Emphasize reflective processing rather than speedy processing; do all possible to eliminate high anxiety in students; encourage students to shield themselves from distraction so they can attend to the academic task.

Source: Pressley, M., & Woloshyn, V. (1995). *Cognitive strategy instruction that really improves children's academic performance* (2nd ed.). Cambridge, MA: Brookline Books.

1. Children are taught by teachers or parents to use a strategy, and with practice, they come to learn the attributes and advantages of the strategy (specific strategy knowledge).
2. Teachers demonstrate similarities and differences of various strategies within a domain (for example, rehearsal versus organization for memory), allowing children to make comparisons among strategies (relational knowledge).
3. Children come to recognize the general usefulness of being strategic, leading to general strategy knowledge.

Although methods of instruction will vary depending on the age of the child and the specific strategy that is being taught, Michael Pressley and Vera Woloshyn (1995) provide a general model for how to teach strategies (see Table 7.3). As a result, children learn to attribute their academic successes to the effort they spend using a strategy,

and they also gain higher-order skills, such as selecting and monitoring strategies appropriate for the task (*metacognitive acquisition procedures*).

Section Review

- *Strategies* are deliberately implemented, nonobligatory operations that are potentially available to consciousness and are used to improve task performance.
- Children who fail to use a strategy spontaneously can often be trained to use one and, thus, improve task performance, a phenomenon called a *production deficiency*.
- Although both strategy use and task performance typically increase with age, children frequently display a *utilization deficiency*, using a strategy without experiencing any benefit from its use.
- Siegler's *adaptive strategy choice model* proposes that children have a variety of strategies

available to them at any one time and that these strategies "compete" for use, with strategies changing in frequency over time.

- Two frequently studied *memory strategies*, or *mnemonics*, are *rehearsal* and *organization*. Younger children frequently engage in *passive rehearsal*, repeating only one unique word at a time, whereas older children are more apt to engage in *active*, or *cumulative*, *rehearsal*, repeating many different words in the same rehearsal set. Organization in recall is reflected by children sorting or remembering related items together.

- Many factors influence children's strategy use, including mental capacity; *knowledge base*, or how much children know about the problems they are trying to solve; and *metacognition*, or an awareness of one's cognitive abilities.

- *Declarative metacognition* refers to explicit, conscious, factual knowledge about person or task variables.

- *Procedural metacognition* refers to knowledge about when strategies are necessary as well as to monitoring one's progress on a task.

- Metacognitive knowledge increases with age, as reflected by studies of *meta-attention* and *metamemory*.

- Strategies are particularly important to children in schooled societies, and classroom teachers instruct children in the use of a variety of different strategies. The absolute level of strategy instruction in school is often low and varies with subject, and children who receive more strategy instruction tend to show more strategic behavior.

Ask Yourself . . .

8. What are cognitive strategies, why are they important for development, and how do they generally change over childhood?

9. What does Siegler's adaptive strategy choice model add to psychologists' understanding of strategy development?

10. How do the various memory strategies children typically use change over childhood?

11. What three major factors influence the memory strategies that children use?

LEARNING TO SOLVE PROBLEMS

Life is full of problems that we seek to solve. Problems and their attempted solutions start early. Infants will strive to retrieve a fallen toy, overcoming obstacles along the way. The problems we face (and their solutions) become more complicated as we get older, but they all have certain things in common. We say that someone is solving a problem when there is a specific goal in mind that cannot be attained immediately because of the presence of one or more obstacles. We solve problems by learning rules or by using (and sometimes discovering) one or more strategies. Sometimes a problem takes several attempts before it is solved, and we must be able to evaluate our progress toward the goal, if for no other reason than to know when the problem has been solved. Thus, the four basic requirements of problem solving are (1) goals, (2) obstacles, (3) strategies for overcoming the obstacles, and (4) an evaluation of the results (DeLoache, Miller, & Pierroutsakos, 1998).

Much of what we have covered in this book to this point can be considered as being in the realm of problem solving. The classic Piagetian tasks of retrieving covered objects and conservation, for example, are problem-solving tasks. Arithmetic problems, which are discussed in Chapter 11, are clearly problem-solving tasks. In this section, we describe children's general problem-solving abilities beginning in infancy, and we conclude by looking at a special type of problem solving: reasoning.

Development of Problem Solving

When do children first solve problems? Based on the definition of what constitutes problem solving (having a goal, obstacles to that goal, strategies, and evaluation of results), infants cannot be said to solve problems until they demonstrate some sense of goal-directed behavior. Recall from our discussion of Piaget's theory of sensorimotor development (see Chapter 5), goal-directed behavior requires that need precedes action. That is, infants do not discover an interesting outcome fortuitously (for example, hitting a mobile with their arm) but, rather, first seek to achieve a specific goal (move a mobile) and then act accordingly. This is also the beginning of cause and effect (means-end) thinking. Infants must realize that they must do something quite specific (make physical contact with the mobile) before the mobile will move.

Piaget proposed that infants are not able to accomplish this until about 8 months of age. At this time, they can use one behavior *strategically* in the service of another (for example, push aside a cloth to retrieve a toy hidden underneath). Thus, following from Piaget's classic work, we can say that problem solving begins at least during the latter part of the first year of life.

Peter Willatts (1990) performed some interesting experiments demonstrating means-end problem solving in infants. In one study, 6-, 7-, and 8-month-old infants were placed on a table. In front of the infants was a long cloth with a toy placed on it, out of the infants' reach. Here's a goal (get the toy) and an obstacle (the toy is out of reach). The solution is to strategically use one behavior (pull the cloth toward them) to achieve the goal (get the toy). How did the infants do? The 6-month-olds often retrieved the toy, but their behavior was not always intentional. Instead of pulling the cloth toward them and fixing their attention on the toy, these youngest infants often simply played with the cloth, looked away from the toy, and after a while, the toy finally was in their reach. By 8 months of age, infants were much less apt to play with the cloth. They grabbed the cloth and immediately began pulling it to bring the toy closer to them. They kept their fixation on the toy and quickly and efficiently brought the toy within their grasp, often holding out a hand in anticipation of the toy's arrival. The 7-month-olds fell between the 6- and 8-month-olds.

In other research, Zhe Chen, Rebecca Sanchez, and Tammy Campbell (1997) assessed means-end problem solving in 1-year-old infants. The basic task involved placing a desirable toy out of reach of the infant, with a barrier between the baby and the toy. Two strings, one attached to the toy and one not, were also out of the infant's reach, but each string was on a cloth that *was* within reach. To get the toy, the infants had to pull the cloth toward them and then pull the string attached to the toy. There were three similar tasks, although the toy, the barrier, and the color of the cloth varied among the three tasks. These are illustrated in Figure 7.13. If infants did not solve the problem after 100 seconds, their parents modeled the correct solution for them. The primary research question concerned whether, after solving an initial problem with or without parental modeling, the infants would see the similarity with the later problems and be more apt to solve them.

Few children solved the first problem spontaneously (most required help from a parent). However, the percentage of infants solving the problems increased from 29% for the first problem to 43% for the second and to 67% for the third. Infants' problem solving was also rated for efficiency, with higher scores reflecting a greater

FIGURE 7.13 Configuration of the three problems 1-year-old infants solved.

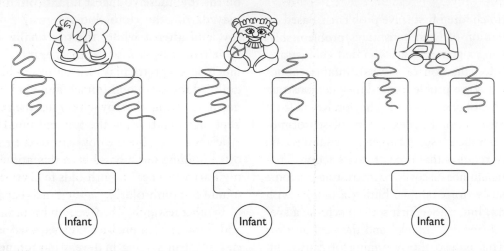

Source: Chen, Z., Sanchez, R. P., & Campbell, T. (1997). From beyond to within their grasp: The rudiments of analogical problem solving in 10- and 13-month-olds. *Developmental Psychology, 33*, 790–801. Copyright © 1997 by the American Psychological Association. Reprinted with permission.

goal-directed approach, as opposed to a trial-and-error approach to the problem. As can be seen in Figure 7.14, efficiency increased steadily over the three problems.

Although means-end problem solving might be within the capacity of infants as young as 7 and 8 months of age, it does not mean that children will display such behavior on more complicated tasks. This is illustrated in an interesting study by Merry Bullock and Paul Lutkenhaus (1988), who asked children between the ages of 15 and 35 months to perform one of several tasks—for example, stacking blocks to copy a house built by an adult. The youngest children (average age, 17 months) showed little specific goal-directed behavior. They did play with the blocks and built something, but there was little evidence that they kept the goal of building a house in mind during their activities. In contrast, most 2-year-olds were able to keep the goal in mind and build the house. These children also did a good job at monitoring

FIGURE 7.14 Infants' problem-solving efficiency scores.

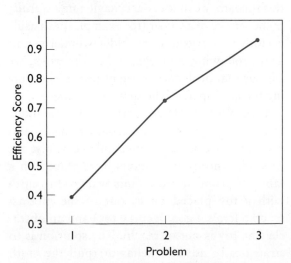

Source: Chen, Z., Sanchez, R. P., & Campbell, T. (1997). From beyond to within their grasp: The rudiments of analogical problem solving in 10- and 13-month-olds. *Developmental Psychology, 33*, 790–801. Copyright © 1997 by the American Psychological Association. Adapted with permission.

their performance (evaluating the results of their behavior). Almost all these children made at least one correction, and 85% of the 2-year-olds stacked all the blocks correctly on at least one trial. The reactions of the children to their problem-solving attempts also revealed their evaluations of their behavior toward achieving their goal. Only about a third (36%) of the 17-month-olds showed some clear sign of emotion with their performance (smiling or frowning), whereas 90% of the older children (32-month-olds) did so.

The tasks children need to solve get more complicated as they grow older, so their problem-solving abilities must also improve. One factor found to have a significant impact on problem solving is knowledge. The more one knows about a particular topic or the more familiar one is with the context, the more sophisticated problem solving will be. Let us provide an example for learning the rules behind a computer game. Stephen Ceci (1996) proposed that context influences how people approach and solve problems. Ceci defined context as the way in which a problem is represented in long-term memory; that is, it consists of what a person knows about a task, including the reason for performing it. Ceci reported an experiment in which 10-year-old children were asked to predict where on a computer screen an object would land by using a joystick to mark on the screen the next position of the object. The object varied in size (big or small), color (dark or light), and shape (square, circle, or triangle), producing 12 combinations of features (two sizes × two colors × three shapes). A simple algorithm was written so that (a) squares would move upward, circles downward, and triangles would stay horizontal; (b) dark figures would move to the right and light figures to the left; and (c) large objects would move diagonally from lower left to upper right, whereas small objects would move in the opposite direction. For example, a large, light square would move upward, leftward, and from the lower left to the upper right.

Figuring out how the object would move (that is, where it would be on the next trial) seems like it would be a difficult task for children (as well as for adults), and it was. The children were given 15 sessions with the task, with 50 trials per session. Some children were simply asked to predict where the object would move on each trial. Other children were told that this was a video game, the purpose of which was to capture flying animals; for these children, the three shapes were changed to a butterfly, a bee, and a bird. These children were told to use the joystick to place the butterfly net so that they could capture the prey on each trial. The rule by which the target moved on each trial was identical in both conditions.

The results of this study are graphed in Figure 7.15. As can be seen, the two groups started out similarly, performing poorly over the first five sessions. However, the children in the video-game context then took off, performing at levels approaching 90% by the ninth session. In comparison, the children given the laboratory context continued to perform poorly, never really improving on the task over the 15 sessions. Discovering the algorithm depended on the mental context in which the problem was presented. The rules were the same for all children, but the context, a form of knowledge, influenced greatly children's problem-solving performance.

Reasoning

Reasoning is a special type of problem solving. Reasoning usually requires that one make an inference—that is, to reason, one must go beyond the information given. It is not enough to figure out the rules of some game. That's problem solving,

FIGURE 7.15 **Children's mean proportion of accurate predictions of the position of a moving object in a video game versus laboratory context.**

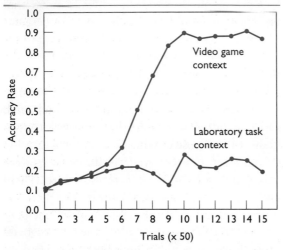

Source: Ceci, S. J. (1996). *On intelligence . . . more or less: A bioecological treatise on intellectual development* (2nd ed., p. 39). Englewood Cliffs, NJ: Prentice Hall. Reprinted by permission of Prentice Hall.

but not necessarily reasoning. In reasoning, one must take the evidence presented and arrive at a new conclusion based on that evidence. The result is often new knowledge (DeLoache et al., 1998).

In cognitive development, we might contrast reasoning with folk knowledge, discussed in Chapter 6. Whereas folk knowledge operates on domain-specific problems and is heuristic in nature, reasoning involves more logical, analytic processing and tends to be a domain-general form of cognition (J. St. B. T. Evans, 2012). We use some forms of reasoning in our everyday lives, and we are so accustomed to thinking this way that we are often unaware of it. Other types of reasoning are more formalized. Most of us do not engage in these forms regularly, so when we do, we are certainly conscious of it. In the following sections, we discuss the development of two types of reasoning: analogical reasoning and scientific reasoning.

Analogical Reasoning

Analogical reasoning involves using something you already know to help you understand something you don't know yet. Analogical reasoning involves relational mapping—the application of what one knows about one set of elements (the relation of A to B) to relations about different elements (the relation of C to D). Classic analogical reasoning problems are stated A:B :: C:?. For example, *dog* is to *puppy* as *cat* is to ?. The answer here, of course, is *kitten*. By knowing the relation between the first two elements in the problem (a *puppy* is a baby *dog*), one can use that knowledge to complete the analogy for a new item (*cat*). Analogies are thus based on *similarity relations*. One must understand the similarity between dogs and cats and puppies and kittens if one is to solve the previous analogy.

How basic is analogical reasoning to cognitive development? How well adults are able to solve analogies is related to general intelligence as measured by IQ tests (Sternberg, 1985), and one advantage gifted children have over nongifted children is in their ability to solve analogies (Muir-Broaddus, 1995). Children with greater executive-function skills in early elementary school perform better on analogy tasks at age 15, suggesting that "strong executive-functioning resources during early childhood are related to long-term gains in fundamental reasoning skills" (Richland & Burchinal, 2013, p. 87). This suggests that it is a complex skill that is influenced by a variety of other cognitive abilities and does not peak early in life. According to Piagetian theory (Inhelder & Piaget, 1958), analogical reasoning is a sophisticated ability that is not seen until adolescence, although others have proposed that analogical thinking serves as the basis for other reasoning and problem-solving tasks (Halford, 1993) and might be present at birth (Goswami, 1996).

The first study to demonstrate analogical reasoning in young children using a traditional A:B :: C:? task was performed by Keith Holyoak, Ellen Junn, and Dorrit Billman (1984). In their study, preschool and kindergarten children had to move some gumballs in one bowl on a table to another out-of-reach bowl, without leaving their chair. The children had various objects available to them that they could use to solve the problem, including scissors, an aluminum cane, tape, string, and a sheet of paper. Before solving the problem, children heard a story about a genie who had a similar problem. The genie's problem was to move some jewels from one bottle within his reach to another bottle, out of his reach. One way in which he solved this problem was to roll his magic carpet into a tube and pass the jewels down the tube into the second bottle. Another solution that other children heard was to use his magic staff to pull the second bottle closer to him. After hearing the stories, children were told to think of as many ways as they could to solve *their* problem—to get the gumballs from one bowl to another. About half of the preschool and kindergarten children solved the magic staff problem, and the remainder did so after a hint. That is, these 4.5- to 6-year-old children were able to reason by analogy. However, they were less successful with the magic carpet analogy, suggesting that young children's performance on analogical-reasoning tasks is highly dependent on the similarity between objects. Holyoak and his colleagues argued that the magic staff and the aluminum cane were more perceptually similar to one another than were the magic carpet and the sheet of paper, making the former analogy easier to use for these young children than the latter. But the basic finding that preschool children could use the similarity in one story to solve an analogous problem suggests that such reasoning is well within the capability of these children, counter to the traditional Piagetian position.

Not all similarity is perceptual, however. Sometimes the similarity between objects is *relational*. This is illustrated in a study by Usha Goswami and Ann Brown (1990), who showed 4-, 5-, and 9-year-old children sets of pictures of the A:B :: C:? type. Children were given four alternatives and had to choose which of the four best completed the analogy. An example of a problem used in this study is shown in Figure 7.16. In this problem, children must discover the relation between bird and nest (a bird lives in a nest) and find the proper match for dog (here, dog house). Chance performance on this task was 25%, and children of all ages performed greater than expected by chance (59%, 66%, and 94% correct for the 4-, 5-, and 9-year-olds, respectively). Note that children were not solving the problem based on *perceptual similarity*. The bird and dog look nothing alike, nor do the nest and the dog house. To solve this problem, they must do so on the basis of *relational similarity*—the relation between the A and B terms (*bird* and *nest*) is used to find the best match for the C term (*dog*).

Children might not have been using analogical reasoning to solve this problem, however. Maybe they were simply selecting the item that "went best with" the dog. This apparently was not the case. Children in a control group were given exactly this directive—pick the one that "goes best" with the C term (in this case, *dog*). When asked to do this, children were no more likely to select the analogical choice (dog house) than select a highly associated choice (bone). Thus, children's performance on the analogical-reasoning task cannot be attributed to responding on the basis of strictly associative or thematic relations; rather, it reflects the use of true analogical reasoning.

That at least some young children were solving these problems using true analogical reasoning was reflected by the type of errors they made.

FIGURE 7.16 **Example of problems used by Goswami and Brown (1990).** Children must select from the set of pictures in the bottom row (pictures D through G) the one that best completes the visual analogy on the top row. (The correct answer is D).

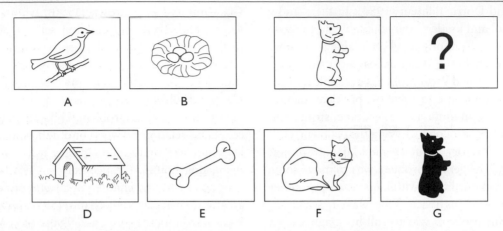

Source: Goswami, U., & Brown, A. L. (1990). Higher-order structure and relational reasoning: Contrasting analogical and thematic relations. *Cognition, 36,* 207–226. Reprinted with permission of Elsevier Science.

For example, Goswami (1996) reported a 4-year-old child, Lucas, who, after seeing the *bird:nest :: dog:?* problem, figured out what the answer should be without seeing the alternatives. However, what he figured was wrong. "Lucas first told us that the correct solution was *puppy.* He argued, quite logically, 'Bird lays eggs in her nest . . . dog—dogs lay babies, and the babies are— umm—and the name of the babies is puppy'" (Goswami, 1996, p. 102). Lucas quickly changed his mind when he saw that a puppy was not among the alternatives, rethought the problem, and identified the "lives in" relation. However, his first idea was also relational. He had simply identified a type of relation (*type of offspring*) different than that identified by the experimenters. Successful analogical reasoning requires identifying the "right" relation. However, there can be many different relations existing between sets of items, and outside of the laboratory or classroom, there might not be clear-cut "right" and "wrong" answers.

Factors Affecting Children's Analogical Reasoning

Many factors influence children's success on any given task. For example, Graeme Halford (1993) proposed that analogical reasoning develops in a stagelike fashion reminiscent of Piaget, based on the availability of mental resources, and others have assumed that age-related differences in various aspects of executive function greatly influence children's ability to solve analogical reasoning problems (Richland, Morrison, & Holyoke, 2006; Thibaut, French, & Vezneva, 2010). A child's ability to symbolically represent concepts and relations will also affect whether and how a child will use analogical reasoning (see DeLoache et al., 1998).

Analogical reasoning and relational shift. Related to how children represent a problem are the types of relations they identify and base their reasoning on. For example, although the research of

Goswami and Brown (1990) indicates that young children *can* use analogies based on relational similarity, this does not mean that they do so easily, especially when they can form analogies based on perceptual similarity. Dedre Gentner (1989) argued that a **relational shift** occurs in the development of analogical reasoning, in which young children are more likely to focus on perceptual similarity whereas older children and adults focus more on relational similarity in solving problems. For example, infants and young children are more influenced by the surface similarity of objects, such as an object's shape. Older children, on the other hand, are more tuned to the underlying relation between sets of objects. For example, the better performance of the preschool children for the magic staff versus the magic carpet analogy in the study by Holyoak and his colleagues (1984) was attributed to the greater perceptual similarity between the magic staff and the aluminum cane available to solve the gumball problem than between the magic carpet and the sheet of paper. When there is a conflict between perceptual similarity and relational similarity, young children's ability to use relational similarity is hindered (see Goswami, 1996).

Knowledge. One factor that affects whether children will use relational similarity to solve an analogical-reasoning problem is knowledge, or familiarity. How familiar are children with the underlying relations used to make the analogy? Remember, the function of analogical reasoning is to use something you know to help you understand something you don't know. From this perspective, analogical reasoning can only make sense if a child is familiar with the base relation. You might get a better understanding of the human nervous system, for example, if you see it as analogous to electrical circuits. But if you know nothing about electrical circuits,

this won't help you understand the nervous system at all, no matter how well developed your analogical-reasoning abilities are. It is fair to say that all major theorists acknowledge the importance of knowledge and familiarity on the development of analogical reasoning, although they might disagree on the exact role that knowledge plays in such development (see DeLoache et al., 1998; Goswami, 1996).

The role of familiarity is illustrated in a study by Goswami (1995) that used a familiar children's story as the basis for analogical reasoning. Goswami used the familiar story of *Goldilocks and the Three Bears* ("The Daddy Bear has all the big things, the Mummy Bear has all the medium-sized things, and the Baby Bear has all the tiny things") to help children make *transitive mappings*. A transitive relation involves at least three objects varying in some dimension, such as length. If Object A is longer than Object B, and Object B is longer than Object C, then Object A must be longer than Object C (that is, A > B > C). Can young children use the transitive relation on one dimension as a basis for mapping transitive relations on another dimension? Or, stated somewhat differently, can children map the transitive relation from one dimension (the Daddy, Mummy, and Baby bears) to another (size, for instance)?

In Goswami's study, 3- and 4-year-old children were asked to use the relations in the Goldilocks story (Daddy Bear > Mummy Bear > Baby Bear) to classify objects that differed in quantity (a lot versus a medium amount versus a little of pizza, candy, or lemonade) or to rank order (three levels) certain phenomena on the basis of loudness (of footsteps), pitch (of voices), temperature (of porridge), saltiness (of porridge), width (of beds), or height (of mirrors). Four-year-olds generally performed well on all these tasks, using the Three Bears analogy to map onto other dimensions.

Three-year-olds did less well, although they performed above chance levels on most tasks, indicating that they, too, could use the familiar (perhaps less familiar to them than to the 4-year-olds) story as a basis for making analogical relations.

Metacognition. To what extent is explicit awareness of the relations between entities on analogical-reasoning tasks important in solving problems? That analogical relations can be explicit to young children was illustrated by the previously discussed example of 4-year-old Lucas, who generated an analogical relation (albeit an incorrect one) for the bird:nest :: *dog* ? problem before seeing the alternatives. Successful training of analogical reasoning is often best accomplished when children receive explicit instruction about the rationale behind the training (A. L. Brown & Kane, 1988), similar to what has been found in the training of memory strategies, as discussed earlier in this chapter. This suggests, not at all surprisingly, that knowing what one is doing (that is, having metacognitive knowledge) facilitates analogical reasoning.

One set of studies relevant to metacognitive knowledge was done by Ann Brown, Mary Kane, and their colleagues (A. L. Brown & Kane, 1988; A. L. Brown, Kane, & Long, 1989), who assessed children's *learning to learn* on a series of analogical-reasoning tasks. Learning to learn refers to improvements in performance on new tasks as a result of performance on earlier tasks, during which time children learn a general rule or approach to problems. That is, participants learn a general set of rules that they can apply to new tasks so that performance on later tasks is enhanced relative to performance on earlier tasks.

In Brown and Kane's studies, preschool children were given a series of problems similar to the magic carpet story used by Holyoak and his colleagues (1984). For example, some children were first given the genie problem. If they did

not solve it, they were told about how rolling the carpet could be used to transport the jewels. They were then given a second similar problem (the Easter Bunny needing to transport eggs by using a rolled-up blanket) and then a third (a farmer transporting cherries using a rolled-up rug). Children who received this series of problems and were given the solution to a problem when they failed showed a large learning-to-learn effect. For the rolling solution, 46% of the children used analogical reasoning to solve the second problem, and 98% of the children did so for the third task. The control group, who received the three sets of rolling problems but did not receive the hints, showed only 20% transfer on the second problem and 39% on the third.

Does a learning-to-learn effect have to involve metacognition? Not necessarily. But some of the children's comments suggested that their improved performance on the later problems was the result of their awareness of analogical reasoning strategies. For example, one 4-year-old child in the A. L. Brown and Kane (1988) study, after solving two rolling problems, said at the beginning of the third problem: "And all you need to do is get this thing rolled up? I betcha!" (p. 517). A. L. Brown and Kane (1988) commented that children had developed a mind-set to look for analogies, expecting to extract some general rule to solve problems and to be able to use knowledge they acquired in one context elsewhere.

Scientific Reasoning

Scientific reasoning involves generating hypotheses about how something in the world works and then systematically testing those hypotheses. Basically, one uses scientific reasoning by identifying the factors that can affect a particular phenomenon (for instance, the rate at which a pendulum oscillates, as in the example provided in Chapter 5) and then exhaustively varying one factor at a time while holding the other factors constant. As you will recall, Piaget proposed that scientific reasoning is not found until adolescence (Inhelder & Piaget, 1958). Subsequent research has not always supported Piaget's theories, but it is generally agreed that scientific reasoning is a late-developing ability that is not easily demonstrated by many adults (Bullock, Sodian, & Koerber, 2009; Kuhn et al., 1988).

Let us provide an example from research by Deanna Kuhn and her colleagues (1988), who presented hypothetical information about the relation between certain foods and the likelihood of catching colds to sixth- and ninth-grade students and to adults of varying educational backgrounds. Participants were first interviewed to determine which foods they thought might be associated with colds. Then, over several trials, they were given a series of foods (for example, oranges, baked potatoes, cereal, Coca-Cola), each associated with an outcome (cold or no cold). Some foods were always associated with getting a cold (baked potatoes, for instance), some were always associated with not getting colds (cereal, for instance), and others were independent of getting colds (that is, sometimes they were associated with getting colds and sometimes not). At least one outcome was consistent with a participant's initial opinion about the healthiness of a food, and at least one outcome was inconsistent with it.

Scientific reasoning involves hypotheses, but what is most crucial about the scientific method is that it involves *evidence*. Maybe you have grown up believing that eating chicken soup will make you healthy, but science requires that evidence, when available, be used to provide an answer. Initial responses of the participants on these questions were usually based on prior beliefs, but as more evidence accumulated, most adults increased their decisions based on that evidence.

The adolescents, however, were much less apt to consider evidence in their decisions and, instead, relied more frequently on extra-experimental beliefs (for example, "The juice makes a difference because my mother says orange juice is better for you"). In fact, 30% of the sixth-graders never made a single spontaneous evidenced-based response. Yet when asked how they knew one food did, or did not, have an effect, most participants of all ages were able to provide an evidenced-based answer, although children were still less likely to do so than adults. This indicates that reasoning from evidence is something that sixth-graders can do but that they tend not to do it spontaneously. It's also worth noting that the adults did not perform perfectly on these problems, either. Only the most highly educated adults (philosophy graduate students) consistently solved these problems using the evidence that was presented.

Scientific reasoning can improve with practice. Several researchers have given participants of varying ages sets of scientific problems to solve over repeated testing sessions (Kuhn, Pease, & Wirkala, 2009; Schauble, 1996). In these studies, participants' performance improved over sessions and generalized to different scientific problems (for example, from determining what factors affect the speed of a car to determining what factors influence school achievement). Although participants of all ages showed improvements over sessions, preadolescent children showed fewer gains than adults.

There is evidence that elementary school children can be trained to use scientific reasoning with explicit instruction and then transfer such strategies to new tasks. Zhe Chen and David Klahr (1999) trained second-, third- and fourth-grade children to use the control of variables strategy (CVS), which essentially involves setting up experiments so that contrasts are made between experimental conditions one at a time. This is essential in being able to assess properly a scientific hypothesis. Children received explicit instruction in how to use the CVS as well as implicit training via the use of probes, in which children were asked systematic questions about factors in the experiments as they were conducting them. Children performed hands-on experiments—for example, testing factors that influence how far a ball will travel down an inclined plane (such as degree of the slope, surface of the ramp, length of the ramp, and type of ball). To assess transfer of training, children were given new problems 1 and 2 days after training.

Figure 7.17 presents the percentages of correct CVS usage for the condition in which children received both direct training and probes for second-, third-, and fourth-grade children. The exploration phase in the figure can be considered a baseline, whereas the assessment phase reflects children's performance on the training trials. As can be seen, all groups of children improved as a result of training, although the improvement for the second-graders was only marginally significant. Perhaps more critically, both the third- and fourth-grade children continued their high level of CVS use on the 1- and 2-day transfer tests. These results indicate that elementary school children can, indeed, learn to use scientific reasoning to solve problems and then generalize them to new tasks. However, when some of the third- and fourth-grade children were tested 7 months later, only the fourth-graders showed any long-term benefits of training, indicating that the instruction given to the younger children was not sufficient to have lasting effects.

Why do children, adolescents, and many adults perform so poorly on scientific reasoning problems? Kuhn and her colleagues (1988) argued that

FIGURE 7.17 **Percentage of correct control of variables strategy (CVS) usage by phase and grade for children receiving both explicit training and probes.**

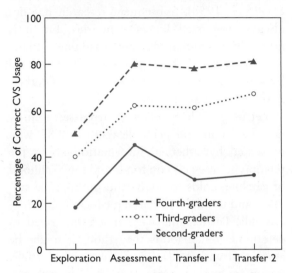

Source: Chen, Z., & Klahr, D. (1999). All other things being equal: Acquisition and transfer of the control of variables strategy. *Child Development, 70,* 1098–1120. Reprinted with permission of the Society for Research in Child Development.

scientific reasoning involves thinking *about* theories rather than just working with them. In other words, scientific reasoning requires a high level of metacognition. It requires integrating theories (or hypotheses) with data (or evidence). When the two agree, there is little problem. When hypotheses and evidence are in conflict, however, problems occur. Kuhn (1989) speculated that children (and many adults) take one of two extreme approaches to theory-data conflicts: *Theory-bound children* distort the data to fit the theory, whereas *data-bound children* focus not on the global theory to explain their results but on isolated patterns of results (to avoid conflict with the theory).

Although poor metacognition might be the overarching reason for peoples' difficulties with scientific reasoning, it is not the only one.

Children and adolescents often do not conduct effective experiments. They frequently fail to vary one factor systematically, or they come to a decision before all possible factors have been tested. Children (and, to a lesser extent, adults) have a positive-results bias. They put more weight on results that produce good outcomes (for example, good academic performance, good health) than on results that yield negative outcomes.

Adolescents' preexisting beliefs also strongly influence their scientific reasoning. Outcomes consistent with their prior beliefs are quickly and uncritically accepted, whereas evidence counter to their beliefs is regarded more critically (Klaczynski, 2000; Klaczynski & Narasimham, 1998). Croker and Buchanan (2011) found an interesting interaction between biases for positive results and the belief consistency effect discovered by Klaczynski (2000). Four- to 8-year-olds (but not 10-year-olds) were more likely to use CVS in belief-*consistent* conditions than in belief-inconsistent conditions when the purpose of the experiment was to explain good outcomes (oral health). However, this pattern reversed when bad outcomes (poor oral health) were the focus—now, all age groups in the study were more likely to use CVS in belief-*inconsistent* conditions than in belief-consistent conditions. The influence of outcome on the use of CVS, even in older children, may reflect their view that the purpose of science is to produce positive effects rather than to explain or understand truths. Of course, this outcome-based view may compromise their inferences.

In general, the big picture of scientific reasoning painted by Inhelder and Piaget (1958) nearly 60 years ago has not changed drastically. Scientific reasoning is rarely found in children. What the new research indicates, however, is that scientific reasoning is only occasionally found in adolescents and adults without specific training.

Given these findings, it makes good sense for university-level psychology students to have a course in research methods, in which the logic of experimental design is made explicit. College students are clearly capable of such thinking, but we should not be surprised that it does not come spontaneously or easily to them.

Section Review

- *Problem solving* involves a goal, obstacles to that goal, strategies for overcoming the obstacles, and an evaluation of the results.
- Infants show signs of *goal-directed behavior* and problem solving in the latter part of the first year. Problem solving improves over the preschool years and is influenced by how much knowledge the problem solver has about the task to be solved or the context in which the task is embedded.
- *Reasoning* is a special type of problem solving that requires one to make an inference. *Analogical reasoning* involves *relational mapping*—the application of what one knows about one set of elements to relations about different elements.
- There appears to be a *relational shift* in the development of analogical reasoning, in which young children are more likely to focus on perceptual similarity whereas older children and adults focus more on relational similarity in solving problems. Other factors that influence children's success at analogical reasoning are knowledge for the relations on which the analogy is based and metacognition.
- *Scientific reasoning* involves generating hypotheses about how something in the world works and then systematically testing those hypotheses. Scientific reasoning is a late-developing ability, in part because of the metacognitive difficulty involved in reasoning about theories.

Ask Yourself...

12. What is the evidence that infants engage in means-end problem solving?
13. How is reasoning different from folk knowledge?
14. How does analogical reasoning develop? How does the development of perceptual reasoning differ from relational reasoning?
15. What factors influence the development of analogical reasoning, and how?
16. What effect does training have on the development of scientific reasoning and the CVS?
17. What are some factors that limit children and adults' scientific reasoning?

KEY TERMS AND CONCEPTS

active rehearsal (or cumulative rehearsal)
adaptive strategy choice model
analogical reasoning
articulatory loop
attention deficit hyperactivity disorder (ADHD)
automatic processes
bottom-up processing
cognitive flexibility
declarative metacognition
effortful processes
executive function (or executive control)

goal-directed behavior
inhibition
knowledge base
limited resource capacity
long-term memory
memory span
memory strategies (or mnemonics)
meta-attention
metacognition
metamemory
organization
passive rehearsal
problem solving
procedural metacognition
production deficiency

reasoning
rehearsal
relational mapping
relational shift
resistance to interference
scientific reasoning
selective attention
short-term/working memory (STWM)
span of apprehension
strategies
top-down processing
utilization deficiency
visuospatial scratch pad
working memory

SUGGESTED READINGS

Scholarly Works

Best, J. R., & Miller, P. H. (2010). A developmental perspective on executive function. *Child development*, *81*(6), 1641–1660. This article provides a critical analysis of executive function development from childhood through adolescence.

Bjorklund, D. F., Dukes, C., & Brown, R. D. (2009). The development of memory strategies. In M. L. Courage & N. Cowan (Eds.), *The development of memory in infancy and childhood* (pp. 145–175). New York: Psychology Press. This chapter presents an up-to-date review of research in memory strategy development.

Meltzer, L. (Ed.). (2011). *Executive function in education: From theory to practice*. New York: Guilford Press. This edited volume covers a variety of applied topics related to executive function development.

Ricco, R. B. (2015). The development of reasoning. In R. Lerner (Series Ed.) & L. Liben & U. Muller (Vol. Eds.), *Handbook of child psychology and developmental science: Vol. 2. Cognitive processes* (7th ed., pp. 519–570). Hoboken, NJ: Wiley. This chapter offers a contemporary and comprehensive review of research on reasoning during child and adolescent development.

Siegler, R. S. (2000). The rebirth of learning. *Child Development, 71*, 26–35. This short paper presents some of the basic ideas of Siegler's adaptive strategy choice model, including how to use the micro-genetic method to study children's learning.

Zelazo, P. D., Carlson, S. M., & Kesek, A. (2008). The development of executive function in childhood. In C. A. Nelson & M. Luciana (Eds.), *Handbook of cognitive developmental neuroscience* (2nd ed., pp. 553–574). Cambridge, MA: MIT Press. This article presents a state-of-the-art review of thinking about the development of executive function in childhood, including a discussion of correlated changes in brain development.

Reading for Personal Interest

Thornton, S. (1998). *Children solving problems.* Cambridge, MA: Harvard University Press. This relatively old book from the *Developing Child* series still offers an accessible and interesting summary of some post-Piagetian research findings on cognitive development as well as a readable account of why problem solving should be at the foundation of cognitive development research.

8 | MEMORY DEVELOPMENT

Although rare, some people have one or more vivid memories from infancy or early childhood. One of us (DB), for example, recalls a memory stemming from the first year of life. My memory is of me as a sick baby. I had the croup (something like bronchitis). When I recall this memory, I can feel the congestion in my chest, hear the vaporizer whir, smell the Vicks VapoRub, and see the living room of my grandparents' house while looking through the bars of my crib. The memory is like a multisensory snapshot. I have no story to tell, only the recall of an instant of my life as a sickly baby. My mistake was relating this vibrant and personally poignant memory to my mother. She listened carefully and then told me that I had never had the croup; my younger brother Dick had the croup as a toddler. I was about 4 years old at the time. My "memory" was a reconstruction—and of an event I had only *observed*, not one I had actually *experienced*. Most memories of infancy, it seems, are like mine—reconstructions of events that never happened or, perhaps, that happened to someone else, but what one is remembering is the retelling of that event by other people.

It's hard to overestimate the significance of memory for our lives. Our memories define for us what we've done, who and what we know, and even who we are. Nearly all acts of cognition involve memory. A 4-month-old looks longer at a new picture than at one he has seen repeatedly, a 3-year-old recounts her class field trip to a bakery, a 7-year-old lists for her mother the names of all her classmates in preparing to send Valentine's Day cards, and a high school sophomore attempts to remember everything his father asked him to get at the corner store. Each of these diverse activities involves memory. The 4-month-old can recognize a new stimulus only if he has some notion that it is different from a previously experienced but currently unseen one. The memory requirements for the three older children are more demanding, but all involve retrieving from memory some previously stored information.

Memory is not a unitary phenomenon. Information must be encoded and possibly related with other information known to the individual. What knowledge already resides in memory influences the ease with which new information is stored and later retrieved.

Memory development is one of the oldest, continuously researched topics in the field of cognitive development. But how it is researched, and the theoretical focus of the researchers, is much different today than it was 30 years ago. In the previous chapter, we discussed that how much children remember is influenced by developmental differences in basic information-processing abilities of encoding, storage, and retrieval and by the strategies they use to intentionally learn information. Today, however, there is an increasing awareness that memory is used *for* specific purposes and *in* specific social contexts (Ornstein & Light, 2010). It is not enough merely to assess children's memory behavior in one context, particularly a context devoid of social meaning. How and what children remember depends on a host of dynamically interacting factors that vary over time. Despite the wealth of information we have about children's memory today, we are just beginning to develop an appreciation for the factors and contexts that influence children's memory performance and the development of those abilities.

In this chapter, we examine research and theory dealing with the development of memory in children. We open the chapter with a brief examination of the different ways knowledge can be represented in memory. We then examine memory development in infancy, followed by a look at children's implicit memory. Children's memories for events—specifically, autobiographical memories—are discussed next. We also review research on children as eyewitnesses and the factors that influence their suggestibility. This is followed by a brief look at the development of "remembering to remember," or prospective memory. Throughout the chapter we describe social-cultural influences on memory, as well as the adaptive nature of memory, from an evolutionary perspective.

REPRESENTATION OF KNOWLEDGE

As we saw in Chapters 5 and 6, how people represent information changes with age, and this is a central issue in cognitive psychology. We take it for granted that knowledge is represented somehow in our brains and that we can access it whenever we want. But knowledge is not quite so simple. Is everything we know represented in such a way that we can easily (and consciously) retrieve it on demand? Might there be some things we know that affect our thoughts and behavior that are difficult or impossible to bring to consciousness? And if so, how do these things develop?

Endel Tulving (1987, 2005) proposed that information in long-term memory can be represented in one of two general ways: declarative memory and nondeclarative memory. Declarative memory refers to facts and events and comes in two types: episodic memory and semantic memory. Episodic memory—literally, memory for episodes, such as what you had for breakfast this morning, the gist of a conversation you had with your mother last night, and the Christmas visit to your grandparents when you were 5 years old—can be consciously retrieved. Such memory is sometimes called explicit memory, which refers to the fact that it is available to conscious awareness and can be directly (explicitly) assessed by tests of recall or recognition memory.

Semantic memory refers to our knowledge of language, rules, and concepts. So, for instance, the meaning of the term *democracy* or the rules for multiplication are examples of semantic memory. For instance, the definition for the word *perfunctory* is part of my (KC) semantic memory, but my recollections of the events surrounding my learning the word (preparing for comprehensive exams in graduate school) are part of my episodic memory.

The second general type of memory has been termed nondeclarative memory (or procedural memory). Nondeclarative memory refers to knowledge of procedures that are unconscious. For example, some have argued that the learning and memory observed in classical and operant conditioning are unconscious, as are many familiar routines once they have become well practiced (tying one's shoe, for example). Such memory is sometimes called *implicit memory*, which refers to the fact it is unavailable to conscious awareness ("memory without awareness") and can be assessed only indirectly (that

is, you just can't ask someone to remember something he or she knows only implicitly).

Consider the classic case of amnesia, where a person walks into a police station and announces to the desk sergeant that he has no idea who he is or how he got there—the perfect beginning of a mystery novel. Now consider a person who knows very well who she is and can carry on a conversation just fine, but 5 minutes after meeting you, she has forgotten who you are and anything you talked about. Yet were you to meet with her every day and teach her how to tie a complicated knot, after a week of practice she would be able to tie the knot expertly without having any awareness of doing it before. These are both forms of amnesia (*retrograde amnesia* in the first case and *anterograde amnesia* in the second), but different memory systems are involved. In the first case, the person has lost his personal history. He remembers nothing about "the self." In the second case, the person's sense of self and personal history is intact. However, she can learn no new information other than some procedures (tying knots), and she will have no recollection of having ever learned them. In both cases, people keep their knowledge of their language, multiplication tables, and basic facts of the world. For example, if they were American citizens, they would likely know the current president and who the first U.S. president was. The example of the person with retrograde amnesia who forgot who he was displays a deficit in a form of *explicit/declarative memory*—specifically, *episodic memory*. The example of the person with anterograde amnesia displays access to past episodic memories but an inability to form new ones (usually because of damage to the hippocampus), although she can form new procedural memories. The existence of these *dissociations*—instances where one form of memory is impaired while others remain intact—provides evidence for independent memory systems that serve specific

FIGURE 8.1 **Classification of different types of memory.** The human memory system can be divided into two general types of memory: explicit, or declarative, which is available to consciousness, and implicit, or nondeclarative, which is not available to consciousness, with both types able to be divided further. Age differences are greater in explicit than implicit memory.

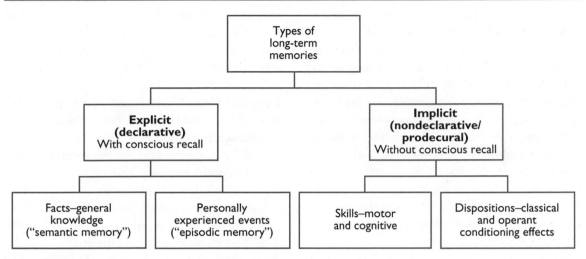

Source: © Cengage Learning.

functions. Figure 8.1 shows the various components of the explicit and implicit memory systems.

In addition to tapping different types of memories, different areas of the brain are involved in declarative and nondeclarative memories (Schacter, 1992). This supports the argument that memory is not a single phenomenon (that is, domain general) but, rather, is a set of domain-specific mental operations that may show different patterns of developmental function.

MEMORY DEVELOPMENT IN INFANCY

Babies obviously remember things. The questions of interest are when and under what conditions infants demonstrate memory and how long these memories last. For example, research

Section Review

- Memory is multifaceted, involves a host of other cognitive operations, and is involved in all complex forms of thinking.
- *Declarative (explicit) memory*, which includes *episodic* and *semantic memory*, is proposed to be available to consciousness and is often contrasted with *nondeclarative (procedural or implicit) memory*, which is unavailable to consciousness.

Ask Yourself . . .

1. When you ride a bike, what type of memory are you using?
2. Think about some movies you've seen that depict different types of memory loss or amnesia (*The Vow*, for instance, or *Finding Nemo* or *Memento*). What types of amnesia are depicted? What form of memory is impaired, and what remains intact?

examining infants' search behavior, as reflected by object permanence tasks (see Chapter 4), indicates changes in memory with age during the first ycar (Diamond, 1985). Recall Adele Diamond's findings that the amount of delay necessary to yield the A-not-B error increased with each successive month between 7 and 12 months of age. Although Diamond proposed that developmental differences in the ability to inhibit a prepotent response were partly responsible for this effect, she also acknowledged that such results reflect age changes in memory during this 6-month period (Diamond, Cruttenden, & Neiderman, 1994).

Preference for Novelty as an Indication of Memory

The bulk of research assessing infant memory, particularly in the early days of such research, used variants of the habituation/dishabituation paradigm discussed in previous chapters. To review, infants' attention declines as a result of repeated presentation of a stimulus (habituation) but returns to its previously high levels when a new stimulus is presented (dishabituation). Such a finding not only indicates that infants can discriminate between the two stimuli but also implicates memory, in that the discrimination is being made between one stimulus that is physically present and another that is present only memorially. In a related procedure, infants are familiarized with a stimulus and later shown two stimuli: the original, familiarized stimulus and a novel one. As in the habituation/dishabituation paradigm, preference (or longer looking times) for the novel stimulus is (usually) taken as evidence of memory for the original. Using these preference-for-novelty paradigms, memory for visual stimuli has been found for some newborns. Basic visual memory is an early developing ability—certainly within the capacity of most infants during their first months of life.

Perhaps the most influential work demonstrating memory in infants using the preference-for-novelty paradigm is that of Joseph Fagan (1973, 1974). One study showed that 5- and 6-month-old babies formed visual memories following brief exposures (5 to 10 seconds) and that these memories lasted as long as 2 weeks (Fagan, 1974). Fagan's procedures have been widely used by researchers, and later work suggested a relationship between individual differences in preference for novelty during infancy and childhood memory and intelligence. This research is examined in Chapter 13.

Subsequent research has shown that even 1-month-old infants demonstrate relatively long-lived memories. For example, in one study, the mothers of 1- and 2-month-old infants read their babies one of two nursery rhymes over the course of 2 weeks. Infants were then brought into the laboratory, and their preferences for the familiar versus a novel nursery rhyme were tested. This was done by permitting infants to choose hearing either the familiar or a novel nursery rhyme by modifying their sucking on a pacifier (for example, increase sucking rate to hear one rhyme, decrease sucking rate to hear the other). After a 3-day delay between the time infants last heard their mothers read the familiar nursery rhyme and being tested in the lab, even 1-month-old babies showed a preference for the familiar rhyme, indicating memory for the auditory event (Spence, 1996).

It's worth noting here that infants' preference in Melanie Spence's (1996) study was for the familiar stimulus, not for the novel one. To demonstrate memory, all that is required is that infants show a decided bias for one stimulus over the other. As we noted in earlier chapters, infants' preferences for novel versus familiar objects/events varies as a function of their age and stage of learning in a task, among other factors (Bogartz & Shinskey, 1998). For example, Mary Courage and Mark Howe (2001) showed 3.5-month-old infants a stimulus for 30 seconds and then tested their preference for the old (familiar) versus a new (novel) stimulus after delays of 1 minute, 1 day, and 1 month. The researchers reported a bias for the novel stimulus after the 1-minute delay, no bias after the 1-day delay, and a bias for the familiar stimulus after the 1-month delay (see Figure 8.2). Following the theorizing of Lorraine Bahrick and Jeffrey Pickens (1995), Courage and Howe (2001) interpreted these findings as indicating that infants' attention to novel versus familiar stimuli varies as a function of the strength of the familiar information in long-term memory at the time of testing. Infants will attend more to novel stimuli when memory traces are strong (after the 1-day delay) and attend more to familiar stimuli when the memory traces are weak (after the 1-month delay). Null effects (that is, neither a preference for the novel nor a preference for the familiar stimuli) reflect a transition phase in which both stimuli compete equally for attention. Richard Aslin and colleagues have since characterized this phenomenon as the *Goldilocks effect*, which we introduced in Chapter 4 (and see Kidd et al., 2012). According to their interpretation, infants are implicitly motivated to maintain intermediate rates of stimulation and encoding. In this way, they avoid wasting cognitive resources on overly simply or overly complex events. When the stimulus is still familiar, they will attend to the relatively novel stimulus, but after some time and forgetting, they will return their attention to the familiar stimulus, strengthening the fading memory trace as a result.

FIGURE 8.2 **Mean proportion of total looking time infants directed to the novel stimulus during the 1-minute, 1-day, and 1-month delays.** Chance is 0.5. mean looking time significantly greater than chance reflects a preference for novelty. Mean looking time significantly less than expected by chance reflects a preference for familiarity.

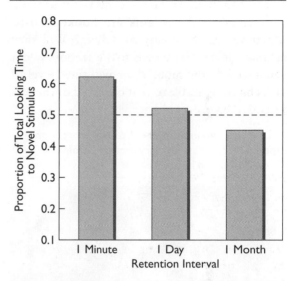

Source: Courage, M. L., & Howe, M. L. (2001). Long-term retention in 3.5-month-olds: Familiarization time and individual differences in attentional style. *Journal of Experimental Child Psychology, 79,* 271–293. © 2001 Elsevier. Reprinted with permission.

Kicking Up Their Heels

Other research by Carolyn Rovee-Collier and her colleagues has used conditioning techniques, demonstrating retention over relatively long periods for very young infants (see Rovee-Collier & Cuevas, 2009, for a review). In their **conjugate-reinforcement procedure**, a ribbon is tied to an infant's ankle and connected to a mobile that is suspended over the crib (see Photo 8.1). Infants quickly learn that the mobile moves when they kick their feet, and they soon make repeated kicks, controlling the movement of the mobile overhead. In a typical experiment, for the first 3 minutes the ribbon is not connected to the mobile, so kicks do not cause it to move (baseline nonreinforcement period). This is followed by a 9-minute reinforcement period in which the ribbon and mobile are connected, and infants quickly learn to kick to make the mobile move. What will happen when the infants are hooked up to the apparatus hours or days later? Will they resume kicking (even when the ribbon is not connected to the mobile), or will their level of kicks be comparable to that observed during the 3-minute baseline? If the kicking rate is high on these delayed trials, it reflects memory; if it is low, it reflects forgetting.

Rovee-Collier and her colleagues have used this procedure successfully with infants as young as 2 months of age. For example, Margaret Sullivan, Carolyn Rovee-Collier, and Derek Tynes (1979) varied the delayed memory test between 48 and 336 hours (2 weeks) with 3-month-old infants. The researchers reported no forgetting by these young infants for as much as 8 days, and some babies displayed memory for the full 2-week interval. In related work, infants as young as 8 weeks demonstrated retention of conditioned responses during a 2-week period, although evidence of memory was obtained only under optimal conditions (distributing training over several sessions) (Vander Linde, Morrongiello, & Rovee-Collier, 1985). These results indicate that young infants can remember events over long intervals, although these skills do improve over the first several months of life.

Subsequent research by Rovee-Collier and her colleagues focused on the role of context in infants' memories. How similar must the learning environment and testing environment be for babies to show retention? This was assessed by a study in which different aspects of the learning environment (in this case, the playpens in which the infants were tested) were changed between the time of learning and the time of testing (Rovee-Collier et al., 1992). Six-month-old infants were tested using the conjugate-reinforcement procedure described earlier, but the testing situation was made very distinctive. Infants sat in an infant seat that was placed in a playpen. The sides of the playpen were draped with a distinctive cloth (for example, yellow liner with green felt squares). Some infants were tested 24 hours later with the same cloth, whereas others were placed in the playpen that

PHOTO 8.1   An infant connected to a mobile in an experiment to assess memory used by Carolyn Rovee-Collier and her colleagues.

Thanks to Carolyn Rovee-Collier

was draped with a blue liner and vertical red felt stripes. The results of this experiment are presented in Figure 8.3 (expressed as kicking rate during testing relative to kicking rate during baseline). As you can see, infants in the *no change* condition demonstrated significantly better retention of the learned behavior than infants in the *context change* condition, indicating the important role that context plays in reinstating infants' memories.

Rovee-Collier et al. (1992) performed six other experiments, varying different aspects of the context. They concluded that infants do not respond to the context as a whole but, rather, seem to process individual components of a context. For instance, changes in visual patterns (for example, stripes versus squares) or reversal of the foreground and background (for example, yellow liner with green squares versus green liner with yellow squares) disrupted memory,

but changes in color did not (for other examples, see Bhatt, Rovee-Collier, & Shyi, 1994; Fagen et al., 1997). Rovee-Collier and Gary Shyi (1992) speculated that infants' reliance on specific aspects of a context prevents them from retrieving memories in "inappropriate" situations. This may be especially important for infants with poor inhibitory abilities, who would be apt to retrieve previously acquired memories (actions) in a wide range of often-inappropriate situations unless there were some potent constraints (such as context specificity) on the memory system. The role of inhibitory factors in infant cognition has been addressed by several researchers, most notably Adele Diamond, and some of this work is discussed in Chapter 2.

Rovee-Collier and her colleagues have also used conjugate-reinforcement procedures to assess age-related changes in long-term memory in infants. For example, in addition to the mobile task, they developed the *train task*, which uses the same logic as the mobile task but is appropriate to use with older babies. In the train task, infants sit in front of a display that includes a miniature train set. They can learn to move the train around the set by pressing a lever in front of them, and retention is tested as it is in the mobile task, with infants sitting in front of the display after a delay and the rate with which they press the lever (when it is now not connected to the train) being measured. With these two comparable tasks, it is now possible to ask how long memories last for infants of different ages. Figure 8.4 presents the maximum number of weeks that infants from 2 to 18 months of age demonstrated retention on the mobile and train tasks. As can be seen, the duration of infants' memories showed gradual but steady increases with age, reflecting a continuously developing memory system.

FIGURE 8.3 **Mean baseline ratios for 6-month-old infants in a no-change (control) condition and a context-change condition.** The higher ratio for infants in the no-change condition reflects greater retention of the behaviors that were learned 24 hours earlier.

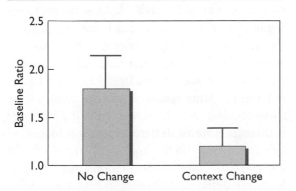

Source: Adapted from Rovee-Collier, C., Schechter, A., Shyi, C.-W. G., & Shields, P. (1992). Perceptual identification of contextual attributes and infant memory retrieval. *Developmental Psychology, 28,* 307–318.

FIGURE 8.4 **Maximum duration of retention from 2 to 18 months of age.** Filled circles show retention on the mobile task, and open circles show retention on the train task. Six-month-olds were trained and tested on both tasks.

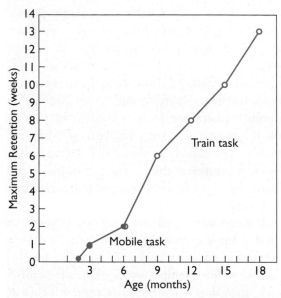

Source: Rovee-Collier, C. (1999). The development of infant memory. *Current Directions in Psychological Science, 8,* 80–85.

Deferred Imitation as a Measure of Memory

Another task that has been used to assess infants' long-term memory is deferred imitation, which refers to imitating a model after a significant delay. In most deferred-imitation experiments, infants watch as an experimenter demonstrates some novel behavior with an unfamiliar object. At some later time, they are given the object. If they display the novel behavior more than a control group of infants who had not previously been shown the object, it implies that the study group formed a long-term memory for the action. The results of

this research are quite striking, showing that infants form long-term memories for these novel actions that can last as long as 1 year (see P. J. Bauer, 2002, 2007). These results suggest that preverbal infants and toddlers do represent events in their long-term memories and, under the right conditions, can access those memories months later.

At what age do infants display deferred imitation? Although results vary with the specific task used, infants as young as 9 months old will imitate simple actions up to 5 weeks later, and 6-month-olds have been shown to imitate simple behaviors after a 24-hour delay and remember events for up to 8 weeks (see Rovee-Collier & Giles, 2010, for a review).

Once infants observe an action, how long do those memories last? The answer depends primarily on the age of the infant, with older infants being able to remember more complicated sets of behaviors over longer periods of time. For example, Patricia Bauer and her colleagues (P. J. Bauer, 2002, 2007; P. J. Bauer et al., 2000, 2001) showed infants a series of three-step sequences. For example, the researcher placed a bar across two posts, hung a plate from the bar, and then struck the plate with a mallet (see Photo 8.2). After delays ranging from 1 to 12 months, the babies were given the objects, and their imitation was measured. About half of the 9-month-olds imitated the simpler two-sequence actions after a 1-month delay, but these infants required at least three exposures to the events to achieve this level of performance. Rate of deferred imitation increased substantially for 13-, 16-, and 20-month-old infants, with older infants demonstrating higher levels of deferred imitation during each delay interval than younger infants did (P. J. Bauer et al., 2000). Figure 8.5 shows results of long-term retention as a function of age of infant

PHOTO 8.2   Bauer's three-step sequence as shown by the gong task. Infants watched as a model performed a three-step sequence: placing the bar across two posts, hanging a plate on the bar, and striking the plate with a mallet. Infants were later given the opportunity to reproduce the sequence, demonstrating evidence of deferred imitation, and thus memory.

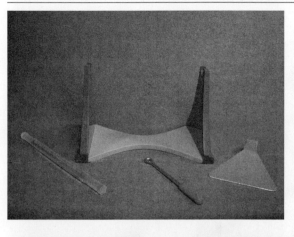
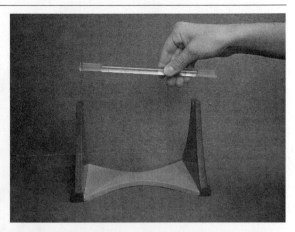

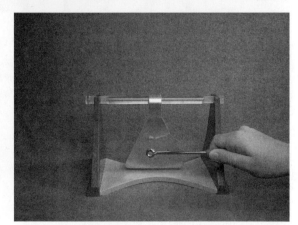

Thanks to Patricia Bauer

and length of delay from this study. These findings are similar in form to those Rovee-Collier and colleagues reported using the conjugate-reinforcement procedures. They illustrate that infants are able to form long-term memories early in life and that the ability to retain these memories increases gradually during the first 2 years.

Is deferred imitation a type of explicit, declarative, memory? Recall from earlier in this chapter that *explicit* memory is contrasted with *implicit* memory. The former represents a deliberate attempt to remember and is potentially available to conscious awareness, whereas the latter is often referred to as memory without awareness. Most researchers who have investigated

FIGURE 8.5 Percentage of 13-, 16-, and 20-month-old infants displaying deferred imitation of three-step sequences as a function of length of delay.

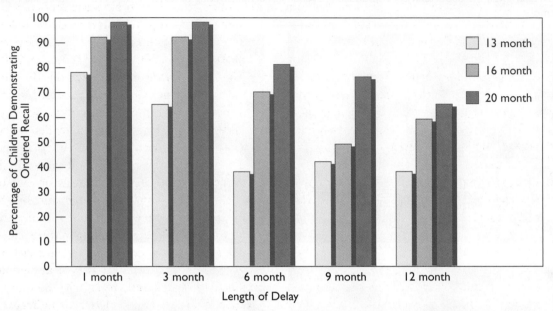

Sources: Data from Bauer, P. J., Wenner, J. A., Dropik, P. L., & Wewerka, S. S. (2000). Parameters of remembering and forgetting in the transition from infancy to early childhood. *Monographs of the Society for Research in Child Development, 65*(4) (Serial No. 263). Figure from Bauer, P. J. (2002). Long-term recall memory: Behavioral and neuro-developmental changes in the first 2 years of life. *Current Directions in Psychological Science, 11,* 137–141.

deferred imitation in older infants believe it to be a form of nonverbal explicit memory (P. J. Bauer, Larkina, & Deocampo, 2011; Hayne, 2007). If so, it would be using the same type of representational system as that used by older children on verbal memory tasks.

How can one tell the difference between explicit and implicit memory in preverbal children? Perhaps one can't definitively, but support for this distinction comes from a study of adults with anterograde amnesia, like the woman we described earlier who learned to tie complicated knots but had no recollection of doing so. People with anterograde amnesia are unable to acquire new declarative memories (memory with awareness) but perform well on implicit memory tasks (memory without awareness). So how do they perform on deferred-imitation tasks? Just like they do on declarative memory tasks—they fail them (McDonough et al., 1995). These findings suggest that deferred-imitation tasks tap the same memory system as do declarative tasks used with older children and adults (for example, "Tell me what you had for breakfast this morning") and "that the neurological systems underlying long-term recall are present, in at least rudimentary form, by the beginning of the second year of life" (Schneider & Bjorklund, 1998, p. 474).

Neurological Basis of Infant Memory

The pattern of deferred imitation shown by infants ages 9 months to approximately 2 years is consistent with what is known about brain development during this time (see Bachevalier, 2014; P. J. Bauer, 2009). Long-term memory requires the integration of brain activity from multiple sites, including the hippocampus and the prefrontal cortex and structures within the temporal lobe. Most parts of the hippocampus develop early and are adultlike before birth, although the **dentate gyrus** (part of the hippocampus), which plays an important role in episodic memory, continues to develop after birth and into adulthood (Aimone & Gage, 2011; Richmond & Nelson, 2007). In fact, one layer of the dentate gyrus includes at birth only about 70% of the number of cells that it will have in adulthood (Seress, 2001), meaning that about 30% of the neurons in this layer will be generated after birth. As we saw in Chapter 2, it was once believed that no new neurons were generated after birth. However, we now know that neurogenesis continues throughout life in the hippocampus, particularly in the dentate gyrus. Once neurons are generated, synapses between neurons need to be formed, and this reaches its peak in the dentate gyrus during the fourth or fifth month after birth. Synapses are then pruned to adult levels by about 10 months.

The early developing hippocampus presumably underlies the deferred imitation of simple actions by 6-month-olds (Collie & Hayne, 1999), but other brain areas must mature before infants can retain more complicated information for longer periods.

The frontal cortex is important in the encoding and retrieval of declarative memories, and this develops more slowly than the hippocampus (Monk, Webb, & Nelson, 2001). For instance, synaptic density reaches its peak in the frontal cortex between 15 and 24 months after birth, and significant pruning takes place during childhood (P. Huttenlocher, 1979). Not until the second year of life do these and other systems (hippocampus, prefrontal lobe, temporal lobe)

begin to coalesce, with development continuing well into the third year. The relatively gradual development of these brain structures correlates with the relatively gradual improvement in long-term retention of infants during this same period (P. J. Bauer et al., 2000; Liston & Kagan, 2002).

The *neuromaturational model* of memory development, as we've discussed so far, is sometimes interpreted as a transition from implicit to explicit memory, controlled by two different neuroanatomical memory systems that mature at different rates. An alternative ecological model holds that the basic memory process does not change ontogenetically (but is emergent, and quite continuous, as depicted in Figure 8.4). Rather, what immature infants versus adults select to encode for learning does. Rovee-Collier and Giles (2010) has argued that the lack of long-term, declarative memory in infancy is not a memory deficit or indicator of immaturity but represents *"rapid forgetting . . . an evolutionarily selected survival-related strategy* that facilitates young infants' adaptation to their rapidly changing niche and enables them to shed the excessive number of recent, rapidly formed associations that are potentially useless, irrelevant, or inappropriate" (p. 203). She describes the first 9 months of life as a period of "exuberant learning," when synaptic pruning occurs, marking a developmental change in what young infants need to learn and remember around 10 months, as they transition to a period of perceptual tuning (a phenomenon we discussed in Chapter 4). At this point, infants have acquired more stable associations between stimuli in the world. As these associations begin to crystallize, infants have a firmer knowledge base onto which they can attach new information, aiding in the retention of long-term, declarative memory. Although the question remains open, the findings we've described so far make it apparent that the memory systems that support implicit and explicit memory are both present from early in infancy.

Understanding the nature of infants' long-term memory is important for our appreciation of the effects of early experience (P. H. Miller, 2014). For instance, some evidence of the relation between brain and memory development in infancy comes from studies of premature infants. For example, Michelle de Haan and her colleagues (2000) administered deferred-imitation tasks to three groups of 19-month-old children. One group of babies was born full term. Another group of infants had been born premature, after 35 to 37 weeks of gestation, but were physiologically healthy. A third group had been born premature after 27 to 34 weeks and were physiologically immature. The three groups of infants showed comparable levels of immediate imitation; however, they differed on deferred-imitation tasks, with the preterm infants, especially those who were physiologically immature, having significantly lower levels of memory. These results suggest that the declarative memory system of these preterm infants was adversely affected by depriving them of the last several weeks of their prenatal environment.

Other research indicates that the memory abilities (and their underlying brain structures; see Kolb et al., 2012) of infants are impaired as a result of living in deprived environments. For example, the deferred-imitation abilities of 20-month-old infants, some of whom had been adopted about 8 months earlier from a Romanian orphanage, where they had experienced extreme deprivation, were impaired relative to typically developing children (Kroupina et al., 2010). Toddlers who had spent their first year or so in conditions of extreme deprivation showed immediate imitation similar to

that of home-reared children but displayed significantly poorer levels of deferred imitation. As we noted in Chapter 2, postnatal experience plays a critical role in getting the brain "hooked up" properly, and when infants receive less-than-optimal experiences during their first year of life, their brains and memories suffer.

Indeed, Rovee-Collier has made the argument that even though younger infants forget more rapidly, how long they can retain information is determined by their experience, not their level of maturation. She views long-term memory as an emergent process, whereby infants' retention is affected by the number and strength of associations between the target memory and other events, as well as the frequency and rate at which the infant is repeatedly exposed to the target information. Rovee-Collier and Cuevas (2009) have argued that younger infants forget more rapidly, not because they are neurologically less mature but because they have less experience and thus fewer associations to which the memory can be linked.

Section Review

- Infants display memory in habituation/dishabituation and *preference-for-novelty paradigms* shortly after birth. Conditioning techniques, particularly *conjugate reinforcement procedures*, have been used to demonstrate memory in infants as young as 3 months for periods as long as 2 weeks, with infants' memories in these situations being greatly influenced by context effects.
- *Deferred-imitation* tasks have shown that older infants can retain information over

relatively long periods, with infants' long-term memory for actions increasing gradually over the first 2 years of life. Maturation of an area of the hippocampus, the *dentate gyrus*, as well as of the frontal cortex, is associated with infants' ability to display deferred imitation.

Ask Yourself . . .

3. How do researchers use infants' preference for novelty to assess newborns' memory?
4. What role does context play in infants' memories? How have researchers assessed this?
5. What is a deferred-imitation task? How do we know it is a measure of explicit memory?

INFANTILE AMNESIA

The results of Rovee-Collier, P. J. Bauer, and their colleagues indicate that infants do, indeed, form long-term memories. This finding, on the surface, contradicts the phenomenon of infantile amnesia—the seeming inability of adults to recall specific events or episodes from early childhood. Such amnesia is bothersome not only to researchers but also to some parents. For example, my wife and I (DB) used to write a column for a parenting magazine and would occasionally get letters from concerned parents. One letter came from a woman who was worried because her 10-year-old son could remember very little from his preschool days. She said that she and her husband had always tried to be good parents but thought her son's inability to remember things from early childhood was an indication that either they hadn't done a very good job after all or, worse yet, they had done a truly terrible job and her son was repressing this painful period of his

life. We wrote back to the woman, assuring her that her son's inability to remember events much before his fourth birthday is quite normal and that just because her child can't remember his experiences from this age doesn't mean that they didn't have an impact on him.

It is not just memories from infancy that escape us. For the most part, we are unable to remember much of anything before the age of 3.5 or 4 years (P. J. Bauer, 2014). Most of us have a few memories for events that happened between the ages of about 3 and 6 years, but these memories are very few in comparison with what we can remember from after this time (Pillemer & White, 1989). What we lack specifically are autobiographical memories, which refer to personal and long-lasting memories and are the basis for one's personal life history (K. Nelson, 1996). If children younger than 2 can form explicit memories, why are they unable to retain those memories as autobiographical episodes that they can recall later in life?

JoNell Usher and Ulric Neisser (1993) studied this lack of memory for the early years by questioning college students about experiences they had had early in life—experiences such as the birth of a younger sibling, a stay in the hospital, a family move, or the death of a family member. To assess recall, a series of questions was asked about each event the person had experienced (Who told you your mother was going to the hospital to give birth? What were you doing when she left? Where were you when you first saw the new baby?). The percentage of questions college students could answer increased substantially the older the person was when he or she had experienced the event. Usher and Neisser concluded that the earliest age of *any* meaningful recall was about 2 years for the birth of a sibling or a hospitalization and 3 years for the death of a family member or a family move.

Most people cannot remember anything from the first few years of their lives, but this does not mean that this information is being repressed.

CALVIN & HOBBES

Source: CALVIN AND HOBBES © Watterson. Reprinted with permission of UNIVERSAL PRESS SYNDICATE. All rights reserved.

A more recent series of longitudinal studies conducted by Carol Peterson and colleagues involved asking children 4 to 13 years old about their earliest three memories (Peterson, Grant, & Boland, 2005). Two years later, researchers followed up with these children (Peterson, Warren, & Short, 2011). They found that, as children aged, so did their earliest childhood memory. That is, older children had later ages of first memory than did younger ones, and there was an overall shift of about 1 year for the earliest provided memories from the time of the first interview to the second. There was also some inconsistency in children's earliest memories from one time to the next, particularly in the youngest age groups (former 4- to 7-year-olds). However, in the oldest group, almost one quarter of children recalled at least two of the same three memories during both interviews. Thus, children's recollection of early childhood memories seems to become more stable with age.

These findings are consistent with others (for examples, Scarf et al., 2013; Tustin & Hayne, 2010) showing that young children form episodic memories but fail to recall them over long delays. Thus, it seems that we should not overlook the role that forgetting plays in childhood amnesia. Of course, many people do claim to have memories from infancy or even from birth (or before). But are these memories to be trusted? The story that opened this chapter (a sick baby looking out the bars of his crib) is an example of how a vivid memory from infancy can be a reconstruction of an event and not the recollection of an event that actually happened to the "rememberer." Are all early memories like this? And, perhaps more to the point, does the inability to retrieve memories from infancy contradict the new research findings of long-term retention in early infancy?

Why Can't We Remember Events From Infancy and Early Childhood?

Sigmund Freud (1963) was the first to speculate on the reason for infantile amnesia, proposing that the events of infancy and early childhood are rife with sexual overtones toward one's mother and are just generally so traumatic that they are actively repressed. We protect our adult egos, claimed Freud, by preventing these disturbing memories from rising to consciousness.

Few scientists today agree with Freud's interpretation. To the contrary, research shows that we are *more* likely to remember events from early childhood that are enhanced by emotion, as well as those more chronologically, thematically, and contextually coherent (Peterson et al., 2014). Other more cognitively based interpretations propose the possibility that (a) information is not stored for long-term retention before about 2 years of age, and (b) information is encoded differently by infants and toddlers than by older children and adults (see P. J. Bauer, 2007; Howe, Courage, & Rooksby, 2009; Rovee-Collier & Giles, 2010). The first possibility seems unlikely; as we've seen, research using the deferred-imitation procedure (P. J. Bauer, 2007; Meltzoff, 1995), discussed earlier in this chapter, has shown that infants from 6 to 16 months of age can encode and retain a simple experience for as long as 1 year.

The second alternative, that information is encoded differently during the early and later years of life, is consistent with observations made by Jean Piaget and others that the nature of representation changes from infancy to early childhood and then again (although less drastically) somewhere from age 5 to age 7. The minds that resided in our heads when we were infants are no longer there, replaced by minds that process symbols, especially verbal ones. We reconstruct memories through adult schemes and representations, which are not suitable for events encoded in infancy and early childhood. For example, the memories tested in infancy all involve recall of action patterns, whereas the recall assessed in childhood and adulthood involves verbal recall,

using language. Perhaps the inability to convert motor memories into verbal ones prevents children from recalling events from infancy.

Evidence for this latter interpretation has been accumulating over the past 2 decades or so (Hayne & Simcock, 2009; Simcock & Hayne, 2002). For example, Gabrielle Simcock and Harlene Hayne (2002) showed children ranging in age from 27 to 39 months sequences of actions and then interviewed them 6 and 12 months later for their verbal and nonverbal memory of the events. Despite having the verbal ability to describe their previous experience, none of the children did so spontaneously. To the extent that children did talk about these prior events, they did so only if they had the vocabulary to describe the event *at the time of the experience*. That is, children who were more verbally sophisticated at the time of initial testing tended to verbally recall some aspects of the event, but children were seemingly not able to translate earlier preverbal experiences into language. According to Simcock and Hayne (2002), "Children's verbal reports were frozen in time, reflecting their verbal skill at the time of encoding, rather than at the time of test" (p. 229; see also a review by Reese, 2014).

Such an interpretation can account for our inability to retrieve memories from infancy, but 3- and 4-year-old children are clearly verbal and would presumably represent information in a symbolic form similar to the way adults do. The fact that 3- and 4-year-old children can recount verbally events that happened many months or even years ago suggests that this interpretation cannot be the entire answer (Fivush & Hamond, 1990).

A number of alternative explanations for infantile amnesia have been proposed. For example, several authors have suggested that for autobiographical memories to be laid down and later retrieved, there needs to be a sense of self (the *auto* in autobiographical) (Fivush, 2011; Howe, 2014). Research has shown that the sense of self develops gradually during the preschool years (see discussion of the development of self-concept in Chapter 10) and that, although young children have memories, the experiences of early childhood occurred when the sense of self was poorly developed, thus providing no anchor for such events. Unless events can be related to the self, they cannot be retrieved later.

Another alternative is that infantile amnesia is merely a consequence of the child's developing information-processing system (Leichtman & Ceci, 1993). Following the tenets of fuzzy-trace theory (Brainerd & Reyna, 2014; see discussion in Chapter 5), Michelle Leichtman and Stephen Ceci (1993) proposed a developmental shift in how events are represented, with young children encoding events primarily in terms of verbatim (precise) memory traces and older children relying more on gist (less precise) traces. Verbatim traces are more susceptible to forgetting than gist traces are. Thus, the heavy reliance on the highly forgettable verbatim traces makes memories from infancy and early childhood unavailable. Gist traces become increasingly available by the early school years, about the time when more memories can be retrieved.

Recent neurocognitive research also points to changes in hippocampal neurogenesis as important (Akers et al., 2014). Recall that rates of hippocampal neurogenesis are high early in life and decline with age, as we described earlier. These high rates of neurogenesis and subsequent pruning may result in our inability to access hippocampus-dependent episodic memories later in life. In fact, when neurogenesis was experimentally reduced in mice at an early developmental stage, their hippocampus-dependent memories persisted. But when neurogenesis was increased at a later stage of development, mice demonstrated an increase in forgetting. These results are interesting, but they do not account for the large and somewhat exclusive loss of autobiographical memories, yet not other forms of declarative memory, as we transition from infancy to childhood. Thus, shifts in encoding, representation of the self, and language, as we describe next, provide additional explanation for infantile amnesia.

Other theorists have proposed changes in language and how language is used as explanations for the phenomenon of infantile amnesia (Fivush & Hamond, 1990; K. Nelson, 1993, 1996). This was illustrated in Simcock and Hayne's (2002) research, which showed that 2- and 3-year-old children were not able to translate a preverbal memory into language 6 months later. But language is not fully developed by 3 years of age, and other language-related changes may further influence children's ability to remember events from their past. Young children, in trying to understand and predict their world, are attentive to routines and embed novel events in terms of these routines (for example, what happens at breakfast, what happens on a trip to the grocery store). Such memories, ensconced as they are in routines, are not very distinctive and, thus, are not easily retrieved later on. Even when events *are* distinctive, however, young children do not necessarily know how to organize them in a memorable form. As we'll discuss in more detail later in this chapter, children "learn" to remember through interactions with adults. Adults provide the cues and structure for children to form narratives—stories for embedding events and, later, for remembering them. Only after being guided by adults can children learn to code memories and realize that language can be used to share memories with others.

Katherine Nelson (1993) makes this point especially clear:

> The claim here is that the initial functional significance of autobiographical memory is that of sharing memory with other people, a function that language makes possible. Memories become valued in their own right—not because they predict the future and guide present action, but because they are shareable with others and thus serve a social solidarity function. I suggest that this is a universal human function, although one with variable, culturally specific rules. In this respect, it is analogous to human language itself, uniquely and universally human but culturally—and individually—variable. (p. 12)

Research examining the earliest memories of people from different cultures lends some support for Nelson's ideas. For instance, in a series of studies, White North Americans reported earlier memories than Asians, in most cases by about half a year (Peterson, Wang, & Hou, 2009; Q. Wang, 2006, 2014). In addition, American adults' earliest memories were more likely to include emotions and less likely to involve family activities than were the childhood memories of Chinese adults (Q. Wang, 2001). These patterns are correlated with cultural differences in parent-child interaction. For example, compared to Korean mothers, American mothers talk about past events more with their 3-year-old children (Mullen & Yi, 1995) and also have earlier memories than Korean adults (Mullen, 1994). (Gender also seems to have an effect, with women tending to have memories from earlier in life than men; see Fivush & Zaman, 2014.)

K. Nelson's (1993) claim suggests that infantile amnesia might not be so significant in its own right, as Freud believed, but, instead, reflects an important transition in human cognition. This transition is based on everyday adult-child interaction and the developing language system, and it transforms the child into an individual who has a personal past that can be shared with others. This does not preclude the possibility that changes in the self-system (Howe, 2014) or in the information-processing system (Leichtman & Ceci, 1993) also play an important role. Our guess is that they do. The most recent research suggests that infantile amnesia reflects important changes occurring during early childhood—changes that permit autobiographical memory and that truly separate our species from all others. However, even later-developing skills, such as perspective taking and abstract reasoning, may be important for helping us organize life experiences along a timeline (Habermas & Bluck, 2000). Some research shows that it is not until age 12 that children begin to link single events together (Habermas & de Silveira, 2008), although others have shown that even 8-year-olds can nominate "chapters" or stages of life that describe their history, and the number and complexity of these periods increases with age (Reese et al., 2010).

Infantile Amnesia and Hypnotic Age Regression

Are memories from infancy and early childhood really gone, or are they just not retrievable by our conscious minds? What about hypnosis? Don't psychologists often use hypnosis to help people remember forgotten or repressed memories, and doesn't that sometimes include remembering events from one's early childhood? But are memories recalled using hypnosis reliable, and are these memories even real? In general, people under hypnosis often do recall more details about an event than do people not under hypnosis, but many of these details turn out to be false (Erdelyi, 1994).

In hypnotic age regression, adults are hypnotized and "brought back" to an earlier age. In doing so, will the adults now truly think like they did as children, and will they remember events from their childhood better than nonhypnotized people? Michael Nash (1987) reviewed more than 60 years of this literature, and his answer is a definitive no. For example, in research during which adults are regressed to the preschool years and then given Piagetian tasks such as conservation (see Chapter 5), they act more like adults who are asked to *pretend* to solve the problem like a 4-year-old would than like an actual 4-year-old child. In one study, adults were regressed to 3 years of age and asked to identify objects such as dolls, blankets, or teddy bears that were of particular importance and comfort to them at that time (Nash et al., 1986). The parents of both hypnotized and control participants were contacted to confirm the subjects' recollections. The hypnotized people were substantially *less* accurate in identifying favorite objects from their early childhoods than were the controls. The reports of the hypnotized participants matched those of their parents just 21% of the time, whereas the hit rate for the controls was 70%.

People who experience age regression might have the feeling of recalling a real memory. However, how confident one is in the veracity of a memory, unfortunately, does not always predict the truth of the memory. There is no evidence that hypnotic age regression can succeed in retrieving repressed, or simply forgotten, memories from childhood, despite many people's claims to the contrary.

Section Review

- *Infantile amnesia* refers to the inability to recall information from infancy and early childhood. Current theories about the reason for infantile amnesia focus on the development of self-concept, developmental differences in how information is encoded, and changes in children's use of language to communicate their memories to others.
- The use of hypnotic age regression is not successful in retrieving memories from infancy.

Ask Yourself . . .

6. How does the emergence of autobiographical memory correspond to other measures of self-awareness, such as mirror self-recognition and metacognition?
7. What are some explanations for infantile amnesia? What evidence is there to support these theories?

IMPLICIT MEMORY

The memory infants show in the preference-for-novelty task or in Rovee-Collier's conditioning experiments does not seem to require conscious awareness. Typically, conscious awareness has been a prerequisite for explicit, or declarative, memory, with the unconscious memories of infants typically being classified as a form of **implicit memory**. (See, however, Howe, 2000, and Rovee-Collier & Giles, 2010, for arguments against this distinction.) Implicit memory is "memory without awareness" (see Schacter, 1992), and it is not limited to preverbal infants and toddlers but occurs also in older children and adults.

The distinction between implicit and explicit memory has more than heuristic value, for the two types of memories seem to be governed by different brain systems, as revealed by research on people with brain damage (Schacter, 1992; Schacter, Norman, & Koutstaal, 2000). For instance, as we mentioned previously, the hippocampus is involved in transferring new explicit information from the short-term store (the location of immediate awareness) to the long-term store. People with damage to the hippocampus can acquire a new skill as a result of repeated practice, but they will have no awareness of ever learning such skills. For example, Brenda Milner (1964) reported the case of H.M., a patient with hippocampal brain damage. H.M. was given a mirror-drawing task over several days, in which he had to trace figures while watching his hand in a mirror. H.M.'s performance was quite poor initially but improved after several days of practice, despite the fact that he had no recollection of ever performing the task before. The enhancement of performance as a result of practice is a reflection of intact implicit (procedural) memory, whereas H.M.'s failure to recall previously performing the task is a reflection of a lack of explicit memory.

There has been less developmental research on implicit memory compared to explicit memory, but what research has been done presents a consistent picture. Although substantial age differences are found on tests of declarative memorization, few age differences are found when implicit memory is tested (see Finn et al., 2016; Lloyd & Miller, 2014). For instance, Riccardo Russo and colleagues (1995) adapted a perceptual priming task to assess the implicit memory of children. Children first viewed pictures of classmates and were asked to make decisions about the portrayed expressions and gender. After a delay, they were shown another series of pictures, half of which had been presented in the earlier phase and half of which had not.

In this second phase, children were tasked with responding whether they knew the person pictured. Regardless of age, 5-, 8-, and 11-year-olds showed implicit priming effects; they were faster to respond that they recognized previously presented faces than those of faces they knew that had not been presented earlier in the experiment. To rule out the influence of explicit, declarative memory, Russo and colleagues excluded from their analysis those responses to pictures that participants could explicitly recall having seen during the first phase of the study, instead focusing only on those responses to pictures that children did not remember seeing earlier (even though they indeed had). These findings provide strong evidence for similar priming effects (implicit memory) across age groups when the influence of explicit memory is controlled for. A similar finding was reproduced in 4-, 5-, and 10-year-olds (Hayes & Hennessy, 1996). In other words, although children exhibited substantial age differences in explicit memory, no developmental differences were found in implicit memory.

Another interesting study of implicit memory again involved showing 9- and 10-year-olds pictures of preschool children, including some who had been their classmates 4 and 5 years earlier (Newcombe & Fox, 1994). Children were asked to determine whether each picture they were shown was that of a former classmate (an explicit recognition memory task); changes in the electrical conductance of their skin were also recorded. Greater changes in skin conductance for former classmates' pictures relative to pictures of unfamiliar children was used as a reflection of implicit recognition memory (that is, requiring no conscious awareness). Not surprisingly, children's performance was relatively poor on both the explicit and implicit tasks (although greater than expected by chance, indicating some memory of both the explicit and implicit types). However, no difference in skin conductance was found between children who performed well on the explicit task and those who performed poorly. This suggests that even the children whose performance on the explicit memory task was no greater than chance still recognized, implicitly, as many of their former classmates as those children who had performed better. This pattern of data indicates that some children remembered (implicitly) more than they knew (explicitly). A similar pattern of findings was demonstrated in the event-related potentials (ERPs, a measure of brain response as the direct result of exposure to a stimulus) of 6-month-old infants when viewing previously experienced stimuli. The ERPs recorded when they viewed repeated faces showed greater negativity (in other words, a stronger response) than when they viewed new faces, suggesting that infants were sensitive to the previously experienced stimuli (Webb & Nelson, 2001).

These findings suggest that implicit memory is an early developing ability. Performance on implicit memory tasks is associated with the basal ganglia, neocortex (priming), striatum (skill learning), and cerebellum (conditioning; see Toth, 2000, for a review), which develop earlier than areas of the brain associated with declarative memory (see Lukowski & Bauer, 2014). Many believe that nondeclarative, implicit memory is an evolutionarily older memory system in contrast with explicit, declarative memory (see Bjorklund & Sellers, 2014).

Some theorists have speculated that implicit memory is under the control of automatic rather than effortful processes (Jacoby, 1991) and, following the theorizing of Lynn Hasher and Rose Zacks (1979), the evidence suggests that these processes show little development across childhood, supporting the *developmental invariance* hypothesis (Schneider, 2015). Indeed, Nora Newcombe and colleagues (2000) suggest that we may retain much in the way of implicit memories from infancy that can affect our behavior much later in life.

It is worth noting, as Lloyd and Miller (2014) have, that implicit memory is a broad umbrella term, used by memory researchers to describe a variety of aspects of nondeclarative memory, from operant and classical conditioning, to perceptual and conceptual priming, and procedural memory, to name a few, each of which is linked to different brain areas. As neuroscience advances, it is likely that we will develop more detailed distinctions between the different forms of implicit memory and their development (Lloyd & Miller, 2014).

Section Review

- In contrast to explicit memory, few age differences are observed for *implicit memory*, when there is no conscious intention to remember something.

Ask Yourself...

8. What do we know about the development of implicit memory? How does it differ from the development of explicit memory?

DEVELOPMENT OF EVENT MEMORY

Much of what we remember is for *events*, things that happen to us during the course of everyday life. Unlike implicit memory, event memory is explicit. We are aware that we are remembering. For most aspects of event memory, however, we did not specifically *try* to remember the event when we experienced it. In other words, for most event memories, the encoding of the event was unintentional. Because we did not intend to learn new information, our unintentional memory is not influenced by the use of deliberate encoding strategies, which accounts for much of the age differences observed on intentional memory tasks. (See discussion of strategic memory in Chapter 7.) Rather, memory representations can be laid down involuntarily as part of ongoing activity, and several researchers have speculated that, in some cases, such naturalistic learning could actually produce higher levels of memory performance than would more deliberate memorization attempts, especially for young children (Istomina, 1975; Piaget & Inhelder, 1973).

The issue at hand is when and how children remember the experiences of their everyday lives. How are these memories organized? How long do they last? And how is it that children acquire them?

A young child must master many aspects of memory if he or she is to remember important events. First, an event must be attended to and perceived. Then, the child must make some sense of that event so that it can be represented in his or her mind and recalled later on. If a child doesn't attend to the important aspects of an event or cannot make sense of what he or she experienced, there is really nothing to remember. One important thing to realize is that young children pay attention to different aspects of events than adults do, and they do not necessarily know which aspects of an event are important and which are trivial. For example, as adults, we know that the purpose of a baseball game is to watch the players on the field play ball. We automatically pay less attention to the field maintenance staff, the players on the bench, and most of the other spectators. However, young children don't always select the "right" things to pay attention to. At a baseball game, they might spend more time watching the hot dog vendors, the batboys, and the second-base umpire. What they remember of the game will thus be very different than what an older child or adult remembers.

It is also worth noting that event memory is *constructive* in nature. Event memory does not involve the verbatim recall of a list of facts or the memorization of lines, like an actor in a play (although children, and adults, do retain some specific, or verbatim, aspects of events; see Brainerd & Reyna, 2014). Rather, we recall the gist of the message, and in the process, we transform what was actually said or done. That is, we interpret our experiences as a function of what we already know about the world, and our memory for events is colored by previous knowledge (see our discussion of top-down processing in Chapter 7 and Bartlett, 1932). Memory, in general, is not like a tape recorder. True, we sometimes do retain verbatim information and use that information to construct stories. But the tales we tell about our lives are best thought of as constructions, based on our actual experiences, our background knowledge of the things we are trying to remember, our information-processing abilities, and the social context in which the remembering is being done.

Script-Based Memory

What is it that young children remember? One thing they tend to remember well is recurring events—what typically happens on a day-to-day basis (Hudson & Mayhew, 2009). Katherine Nelson and her colleagues have demonstrated that preschool children tend to organize events in terms of **scripts**, which are a form of schematic organization with real-world events organized in terms of their causal and temporal characteristics (K. Nelson, 1993, 1996; see also Fivush, 2008). For example, a fast-food restaurant script might involve driving to the restaurant, entering the restaurant, standing in line, ordering, paying the cashier, taking the food to the table, eating, and then throwing away the trash before leaving. Children learn what usually happens in a situation, such as what happens during snack time at school, a birthday party, or breakfast, and they remember novel information in the context of these familiar events.

Substantial research demonstrates that even very young children organize information temporally in a scriptlike fashion (see P. J. Bauer, 2007; Fivush, Kuebli, & Clubb, 1992) and that such schematic organization for events doesn't change appreciably into adulthood (for reviews of this literature, see Fivush & Hudson, 1990; K. Nelson, 1996). Perhaps even more impressive is evidence that even preverbal infants use temporal order to remember events. For example, Patricia Bauer and Jean Mandler (1989, 1992) tested infants ranging in age from 11.5 to 20 months on imitation tasks. The toddlers were shown a sequence of events (for example, putting a ball in a cup, inverting a smaller cup on top of the larger one, and shaking the cups) and, later, given the opportunity to interact with the materials again. Bauer and Mandler reported that the children reenacted the sequence of events in the same temporal order they had been shown. This finding argues for the existence of a script-style memory organization long before children are able to talk.

Young children's tendencies to organize information following familiar scripts seem to result in their tendency *not* to remember much in the way of specific (that is, nonscript) information. For example, Robyn Fivush and Nina

Hamond (1990) asked 2.5-year-old children specific questions about recent special events, such as a trip to the beach, a camping trip, or a ride on an airplane. Rather than recalling the novel aspects of these special events, the children were more apt to focus on what adults would consider routine information. Take, for instance, the following conversation reported by Fivush and Hamond (1990) between an adult and a child about a camping trip. The child first recalled sleeping outside, which is unusual, but then remembered very routine things:

Interviewer: You slept outside in a tent? Wow, that sounds like a lot of fun.

Child: And then we waked up and eat dinner. First we eat dinner, then go to bed, and then wake up and eat breakfast.

Interviewer: What else did you do when you went camping? What did you do when you got up, after breakfast?

Child: Umm, in the night, and went to sleep. (p. 231)

It seems strange that a child would talk about such routine tasks as waking up, eating, and going to bed when so many new and exciting things must have happened on the camping trip. But the younger the child, the more he or she might need to embed novel events into familiar routines. According to Fivush and Hamond, everything is new to 2-year-olds, and they are in the process of learning about their surroundings.

Why should young children's memory be so tied to recurring events? One way to answer this question is to ask what the function of memory is for young children. Katherine Nelson (1996, 2005) has taken such a functional view, arguing that memory has an adaptive value of permitting children to predict the likelihood of events in the future. Basically, by remembering the likelihood of an event's occurrence in the past, one can predict its likelihood of occurring in the future. From this perspective, some events (recurring ones) are more likely to be remembered than are others (single events). According to K. Nelson (1996),

> Memory for a single, one-time occurrence of some event, if the event were not traumatic or life-threatening, would not be especially useful, given its low probability. Thus, a memory system might be optimally designed to retain information about frequent and recurrent events—and to discard information about unrepeated events—and to integrate new information about variations in recurrent events into a general knowledge system. (p. 174)

K. Nelson's ideas are related to *theory-theory* concepts discussed in Chapters 4 and 5, specifically the *Goldilocks effect*, *Bayesian statistical learning*, and *causal representation*. Nelson makes the point that memory for routine events allows infants to anticipate events and to take a part in (and, possibly, control of) these events. There is no such payoff for a novel event; thus, it makes sense to forget it.

Children do, however, eventually remember specific events, not just some generalized event memory. In fact, although 2- and 3-year-old children may rely heavily on scripts, they have been shown to remember specific information for extended periods (Hamond & Fivush, 1991; Howe, 2000). Hamond and Fivush (1991) presented research that demonstrates how long memories for specific events can last for young children. They interviewed 3- and 4-year-old children 6 or 18 months after they had gone to Disney World. All children recalled a great deal of information about their trip, even after 18 months. The older children recalled more details and required fewer prompts (cues) to generate recall than did the younger children, and children who talked more about the trip with their parents recalled more information about the trip. Nevertheless, recall for this single, special event was quite good, even though it did not fall nicely into a familiar routine.

Role of Parents in "Teaching" Children to Remember

Children begin to talk about past events not long after they acquire their first words, and their recollection skills develop rapidly from 2 to 4 years of age (K. Nelson, 2014). Parents play an important role in this development, as Hamond and Fivush's research demonstrated. In effect, parents "teach" children how to remember (Fivush, 2014). As it turns out, parents, especially mothers (but also sometimes fathers), and their children spend a good deal of time reminiscing about the past, and individual differences in how this is done are related to how well children remember past events. This suggests that parents can play an important role in children's early remembering, a point that has been made by several theorists (Fivush, 2014; Haden & Ornstein, 2009) and that is consistent with the theorizing of Lev Vygotsky (1978) and the sociocultural perspective discussed in Chapter 3 (see the discussion of shared remembering; Gauvain, 2001). For example, Judith Hudson (1990) argued that children learn how to remember by interacting with their parents, that "remembering can be viewed as an activity that is at first jointly carried out by parent and child and then later performed by the child alone" (p. 172). In most families, Hudson proposed, parents begin talking with young children about things that happened in the past. They ask questions such as "Where did we go this morning?," "What did we see at the zoo?," "Who went with us?," and "What else did we see?" From these interchanges, children learn that the important facts to remember about events are the whos, whats, whens, and wheres of their experiences. Through these conversations with their parents, they are learning to notice the important details of their experiences and to store their memories in an organized way so that they can be easily retrieved when needed. Parents also often discuss future events with children (for example, an upcoming trip to Disney World), and when they do, particularly when they include photographs of what they may see, children later remember more about the event (Salmon et al., 2008).

In studying these interchanges between parents and preschoolers, Hudson found that parents do more than just ask the right questions. They also give the right answers when the child can't remember, showing children how the conversation should go. Young children generally show low levels of free recall when remembering an event, but they can remember much more when specific cues are presented. In fact, Fivush and Hamond (1990) stated that "young children recall as much information as older children do, but they need more memory questions in order to do so" (p. 244). By asking repeated questions to children, adults are structuring the conversation, showing children how "remembering" is done. Moreover, by providing the missing information, children also learn that their parents will help them out when they can't seem to retrieve the information called for.

A good example of this was a conversation I (DB) overheard while riding on the Metro in Washington, D.C. A young mother and her 19-month-old daughter, Tanya, were returning home after a trip to the zoo.

Mother: Tanya, what did we see at the zoo?

Tanya: Elphunts.

Mother: That's right! We saw elephants. What else?

Tanya: [shrugs and looks at her mother]

Mother: Panda bear? Did we see a panda bear?

Tanya: [smiles and nods her head]

Mother: Can you say *panda bear*?

Tanya: Panda bear.

Mother: Good! Elephants and panda bears. What else?

Tanya: Elphunts.

Mother: That's right, elephants. And also a gorilla.

Tanya: Go-rilla!

Hilary Ratner (1984) illustrated the importance of these parent-child conversations. She observed 2- and 3-year-old children interacting with their parents at home and recorded the number of times the mother asked the child about past events. She then tested the children's memory abilities. The children who showed better memory abilities at that time, and also a year later, were those whose mothers had asked them many questions about past events. Other research has shown that mothers who provide their preschool children with more evaluations of their memory performance, and who use more elaborative language when talking about memory with their children, have children who remember past events better than do children with less elaborative mothers (Fivush, Haden, & Reese, 2006; McDonnell et al., 2016). That is, after making a statement about some previous event (for example, "Then we ate the cake"), *elaborative* mothers are more likely to provide comments that confirm or negate a child's statement (such as "That's right," "Yes," or "No") than less elaborative mothers are. Other research has even shown that preschool children whose mothers used more elaborative language in talking with them about past events had earlier memories as adolescents than did children with less elaborative mothers (Jack et al., 2009).

In other research, mothers and their young children engaged in three novel events, one when children were 30 months, a second at 36 months, and a third at 42 months (Haden et al., 2001; Hedrick et al., 2009). For example, in one study (Haden et al., 2001), children were tested for their memory of each event at 1 day and at 3 weeks following each episode. The events were carried out in children's homes and involved the investigator setting up props and asking the mother and child to carry out an elaborate make-believe activity. For example, for the camping event, the mother and child first loaded supplies in a backpack, hiked to a fishing pond, caught a fish with a fishing rod and net, and then moved to their campsite, where they found sleeping bags, pots, pans, and utensils, which they used to cook and eat their food. The frequency with which mothers and children jointly carried out these activities, and the degree to which language was involved during the execution of the task, were observed and related to children's subsequent memory performance. First, and not surprisingly, children's overall memory performance increased with age and was greater for the 1-day delay than the 3-week delay. Most pertinent for our discussion here was the relation between mother-child activities during the event and children's later recollections. Features of the events (for example, putting food in the backpack) that were jointly handled and talked about by the mother and child were better remembered than were features that were handled and talked about only by the mother or that were jointly handled by the mother and child but not discussed. This result clearly points out the important role of joint activity guided by the mother, including the use of language, in fostering young children's event memory.

The results of recent research point to the interactive role of parents and children in the process of "learning" how to remember. Thus, remembering becomes a cultural phenomenon, consistent with the ideas of Vygotsky and others who propose a sociocultural perspective of development (see Chapter 3; Fivush, 2014). Parents teach children how to construct narratives (that is, create stories) in which to embed the important things that happen to them. This in turn allows children to share their experiences with others. This is a practice that may vary somewhat, however, between cultures (Schröder et al., 2013). For example, Mary Mullen and Soonhyung Yi (1995) examined how frequently Korean and American mothers talked to their 3-year-old children about past events and reported that the American mothers talked about the past with their young children nearly 3 times as often as the Korean mothers did. This is consistent with reports that American children talk about past events more than Korean children do (Han, Leichtman, & Wang, 1998) and that American adults report earlier childhood memories than Korean adults (Mullen, 1994). This suggests that early language experience contributes to the onset of autobiographical memory, consistent with the argument made by Katherine Nelson (1996, 2005).

It is also worth noting that there are differences in the event memories reported by girls and boys. When asked to remember information about earlier experienced events, girls tend to remember more information than boys do (Reese, Haden, & Fivush, 1996), but not always (see K. D. Lewis, 1999). For example, in a study by Elaine Reese, Catherine Haden, and Robin Fivush (1996), children ages 40 to 70 months participated in several sessions during which their mothers, fathers, or an experimenter asked them to recollect about salient events that had occurred in the recent past. Regardless of who interviewed the children (that is, their mothers, fathers, or the experimenter), girls remembered more details about past events than boys did. These gender differences were related to ways in which parents conversed with their sons and daughters about the past. Both mothers and fathers tended to be more elaborative with daughters than sons when engaged in parent-child reminiscing, and girls generally received more evaluations of their memory responses than boys. These findings suggest that the roots of females' greater event memory lie early in development and might result, in part, because of the way parents talk to boys and girls during attempts at remembering, with daughters being encouraged to embellish their memories more than sons are. Other research indicates that mothers talk to their male and female preschool children about different topics. For example, Dorothy Flannagan, Lynne Baker-Ward, and Loranel Graham (1995) reported that in their conversations about school, mothers talked to their sons more about learning and instruction, whereas they tended to talk to their daughters more about social interactions. Thus, there are differences both in how parents talk to boys and girls about remembering events and in what they are asked to remember, both of which seemingly affect what and how well children remember.

It's hard to minimize the significance of autobiographical memory and to think that there may have been a time in our lives when it didn't exist. Our recollections about what we've experienced in the past define for us who we are and how we interact with others. But autobiographical memory develops over the course of infancy and early childhood. In fact, Alison Gopnik (2009) proposed that although 2- and 3-year-old children can remember specific events, a reflection of episodic memory, they lack true autobiographical memory. According to Gopnik, "They do not experience their lives as a single timeline stretching back into the past and forward into the future. They don't send themselves backward and forward along this timeline as adults do. . . . Instead, the memories, images, and thoughts pop in and out of consciousness as they are cued by present events, or by other memories, images, and thoughts" (pp. 153–154).

Section Review

- Young children's *event memory* is based on *scripts*, a form of schematic organization with real-world events organized by their causal and temporal characteristics.
- Children's early memories are for general routines and not for specific *autobiographical* experiences.
- Parents "teach" children how to remember by interacting with them and providing the structure for putting their experiences into narratives.

Ask Yourself . . .

9. What do we mean when we say that event memory is constructive in nature?
10. What evidence is there for the social-cultural perspective of event memory?
11. How do children remember and organize events in memory?

CHILDREN AS EYEWITNESSES

One topic in event memory that has attracted substantial research attention concerns the reliability of children as eyewitnesses. How reliable is children's testimony? How much do they remember, and for how long? How suggestible are children? Can a persuasive interviewer make children report things that didn't really happen, and can faulty interviewing techniques actually result in children believing they were victims of (or witnesses to) a crime when they were not? These are questions not only for the justice system but also for psychologists because they deal with the nature of children's developing memory systems and the construction of a particular kind of event memory.

In the following sections, we review research and theory into children as eyewitnesses and the degree to which their testimonies and their memories are subject to change. In the first section, we review age differences in children's eyewitness reports when no one is trying to change their minds. That is, what do children remember, and what factors influence their memory, when they are asked to report what they witnessed or experienced? In the second section, we examine the large literature on age differences in suggestibility. How susceptible are children to suggestion, and to what extent will they change their answers or their memory representations as a result of suggestive questioning?

First, however, let us provide a general framework for making sense of this research literature. Children's eyewitness testimony and suggestibility, like event memory in general, are influenced by a host of interacting factors. Which factors are most important? Can we specify how the various factors will interact to predict performance? And can we be confident enough in our conclusions to inform the legal system? Marc Lindberg (1991;

Lindberg, Keiffer, & Thomas, 2000) has suggested three major categories of factors that we should consider in evaluating studies of children's eyewitness memory and suggestibility (see Figure 8.6). The first category in Lindberg's scheme is *memory processes*, and these concern the different memory operations of encoding, storage, and retrieval. *Encoding* refers to children's representation of an event and how children respond to information they receive before the event. For example, how are children influenced by being told that someone they are about to meet is a "bad boy" or prone to breaking things? *Storage* refers to information provided to participants after witnessing an event. This may be in the form of suggestive questions (for example, "He spilled chocolate milk over the book, didn't he?") or postevent information, which includes any experiences that intervene between witnessing an event and recollecting it. *Retrieval* refers to manipulations at the time of testing. For instance, how is memory tested? With open-ended, free-recall questions (for example, "Tell me everything you can remember about what happened at the park last week"), cued-recall questions (such as "Tell me what color was the boy's T-shirt"), or recognition (for instance, "Look at these pictures. Was one of these the boy who took the bike?")? How are these questions posed?

Lindberg refers to the second category of his taxonomy as *focus of the study*, by which he means the type of information that is being assessed. For example, is the interviewer concerned with psychologically and legally central (or focal) information (who did what to whom, which is critical in determining innocence or guilt in court), or is peripheral (incidental) information (for example, "What color pants was the man wearing?" or "How tall was the girl?") also important? Similarly, is the memory for gist information or for details, or verbatim information (as

FIGURE 8.6 **Three major interacting classes of variables in interpreting children's eyewitness memory and suggestibility.**

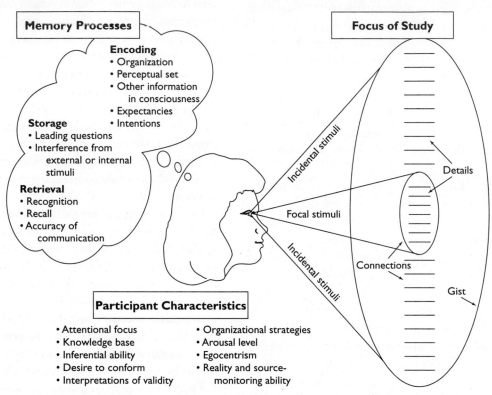

Source: Lindberg, M. A. (1991). An interactive approach to assessing the suggestibility and testimony of eyewitnesses. In J. Doris (Ed.), *The suggestibility of children's recollections: Implications for eyewitness testimony* (pp. 47–55). Copyright © 1991 by the American Psychological Association. Reprinted with permission.

in fuzzy-trace theory's description of memory traces; see Brainerd & Reyna, 2014)?

And, finally, one must consider *participant factors*. Here, developmental level and the associated social, emotional, and cognitive skills of children are important. Also of potential importance are personality characteristics of the participants, their level of stress at the time of the event (or at the time of retrieval), their past experiences with a situation, and their more general knowledge of the things they witness. No single study will include all relevant factors from this taxonomy, but it is worthwhile to keep these categories in mind if for no other reason than to remember that understanding children's eyewitness memory is not child's play.

Age Differences in Children's Eyewitness Memories

Although there is much variability in methods from study to study, most investigations of children's eyewitness memory begin by showing children a video of some event, having them observe some activity in their school, or involving them personally in an activity. Usually, children are not told that they will be asked to remember what they view. Later, often minutes after the event but in some cases days or weeks later, children are asked what they remembered (for example, "Tell me what happened in the video you saw" or "Tell me what happened in your classroom yesterday morning"). This is essentially a request for free recall. Typically, children will then be asked some more specific recall questions (for example, "What was the girl in the video wearing?" or "What did the man who came into your class yesterday morning do?"), which constitute cued recall. Often, children will be asked some recognition memory questions (for example, "Was the girl wearing a white T-shirt?" or "Did the man play with the teddy bear?"). In some studies, the same or similar questions may be repeated, and in others, questions are often intentionally suggestive, sometimes directing children to a "correct" answer (such as "Did the man play nicely with the teddy bear?") and sometimes leading to an "incorrect" answer (such as "Did the man rip the book?"). There are, of course, many variations, depending on the purpose of the study, but in most cases, children's memories for specific events are probed, often with the purpose of seeing how likely children are to change their answers or to be swayed by leading questions posed by an interviewer (see Brainerd & Reyna, 2014; Bruck, Ceci, & Principe, 2006).

How Much Do Children Remember, and How Accurate Are They?

First, how much do children of different ages remember shortly after witnessing an event? When examining immediate (that is, within the same experimental session) free recall, substantial age differences are found (Ornstein, Gordon, &

Larus, 1992; Poole & White, 1995). How much is remembered differs from study to study, but preschool children typically recall only a small proportion of information from an event in answer to free-recall questions. Although young children remember very little information, what they do recall is highly accurate and central to the event—if there are no suggestions or coaching (G. S. Goodman, Aman, & Hirschman, 1987; Poole & White, 1995). For example, in a video involving a boy and a girl in a park, with the boy stealing a bike, young children typically recall the bike theft but are much less apt than older children or adults to mention in their free recall descriptions of the participants, characteristics of the bicycle, or things about the setting (Cassel & Bjorklund, 1995; Cassel, Roebers, & Bjorklund, 1996). Thus, young children's free recall is typically low, accurate, and about central aspects of an event.

When children are provided general cues (for example, "Tell me what the girl looked like"), they recall more information, as you would expect. However, in addition to remembering more *correct* facts, they also tend to remember some *incorrect* "facts" as well, reducing the overall accuracy of their recall (Bjorklund et al., 1998; Lindberg et al, 2000).

When children do falsely remember information to cues, does this actually change their memory representations? Will these children, when interviewed later, remember this misinformation again? The answer seems to depend on several factors, including the amount of time between the initial and later interviews. With delays of only several weeks or less, children seem *not* to recall their earlier false memories (Cassel & Bjorklund, 1995). But when delays are longer (Poole, 1995) or when children are merely asked to recognize rather than to recall information (Brainerd & Reyna, 1996), these false memories not only tend to persist, they might even be *more* resistant to forgetting than true memories (Brainerd & Mojardin, 1999).

These counterintuitive findings have been interpreted in terms of fuzzy-trace theory (Brainerd & Reyna, 2014; see also Chapter 5). According to fuzzy-trace theory, correct recognition is based on literal, or verbatim, memory traces, which are more susceptible to forgetting than are less-exact fuzzy, or gist, traces. In contrast, false recognition must be based on gist traces because there are no verbatim traces for false memories. Gist traces are more resistant to forgetting than verbatim traces are, so the gist-based false memories become more likely to be remembered over long delays than the more easily forgettable, verbatim-based true memories.

How Long Do Memories Last?

Although most studies have not assessed the long-term recollections of children, several have investigated children's memories of specific events for periods ranging from several weeks to 2 years (Flin et al., 1992; Salmon & Pipe, 1997). This is important for the legal system, given that children are sometimes asked in forensic interviews to remember events they witnessed weeks, months, or even years earlier (Paz-Alonso et al., 2009; Pipe & Salmon, 2009). Although the results of these studies are not always consistent, a picture emerges of greater age differences in the accuracy of recall with increasing delays. *Accuracy*, as used here, does not refer to how much was remembered but, rather, to the ratio of incorrect-to-correct information remembered. Children who recall very little, for example, but correctly recall what they do remember, have perfect accuracy. In contrast, a child who recalls a substantial amount of both correct (accurate) and incorrect (inaccurate) information might demonstrate more recall but less accuracy.

First, with delays of about 1 month or less, children of all ages and adults remember about the same proportion of accurate and inaccurate information as they did originally (Baker-Ward et al., 1993; Cassel & Bjorklund, 1995). Age differences in recall accuracy are found with longer delays, however. For example, Rhona Flin and her colleagues (1992) reported that both 6-year-olds and adults recalled as much correct information after a 5-month delay as they had originally but that recall by the 6-year-olds was less accurate than recall by the adults. Thus, the ratio of incorrect-to-correct recall became higher for the children than for the adults during the 5-month period. The conclusion from this and similar studies is that age differences in accuracy are found, but only when memory is assessed after extended delays. Fuzzy-trace theory (Brainerd & Reyna, 2014; see also Chapter 5) explains these findings by the greater rate of decay of verbatim (exact) traces relative to gist traces. Verbatim traces, favored by younger children, deteriorate more rapidly than the gist, or fuzzy, traces favored by older children, resulting in greater loss of information over delays and corresponding increases in erroneous recall. These are the same arguments that have been used to explain the phenomenon of infantile amnesia (see earlier discussion). The verbatim traces favored by infants and young children are especially susceptible to deterioration, making it highly unlikely that these memories would be available years after their original encoding (Leichtman & Ceci, 1993).

Factors Influencing Children's Eyewitness Memory

A host of factors other than age and length of delay have been found to influence the amount and accuracy of children's eyewitness memories. For instance, children with high IQs show higher levels of eyewitness recall than do their peers with lower IQs (Roebers & Schneider, 2001); children given incentives to be accurate in their recall are, indeed, more accurate than children not given incentives (Roebers, Moga, & Schneider, 2001); intermediate levels of stress (when experiencing the event) seem to facilitate recall of an event relative to overly high or low levels of stress (Bahrick et al., 1998); children having emotionally supportive mothers who discuss upcoming medical procedures with them recall less inaccurate information about the procedure than children having less sympathetic or talkative mothers (G. S. Goodman et al., 1994; 1997); and children whose parents score as more avoidant are less accurate after experiencing higher distress levels during a medical procedure, whereas children's parents who are less avoidant are more accurate after experiencing higher distress (Chae et al., 2014). Two sets of factors that have substantial influences on children's eyewitness reports are children's background knowledge for the event (Ornstein et al., 2006) and the characteristics of the interview (Ceci, Bruck, & Battin, 2000), each of which we discuss in greater detail next.

Role of knowledge. We saw in Chapter 7 that knowledge has a potent role in children's working memory and strategic memory, so we should not be surprised that it also plays an important role in eyewitness memory (Elischberger, 2005; Ornstein & Greenhoot, 2000). Indeed, some researchers (see Howe, Wimmer, Gagnon, & Plumpton, 2009) have proposed an alternative approach to fuzzy-trace theory in explaining children's false memories, the associative activation theory, arguing that age differences in knowledge base and automatic processing are the most important factor underlying false-memory production. For example, children's recollections of stressful and invasive medical procedures are related to their knowledge of the procedures; children who know more about the procedure remember more accurate information (Clubb et al., 1993; Ornstein et al., 2006) and recall less inaccurate information (G. S. Goodman et al., 1994). Yet although knowing a lot about an event (that is, how actions in an event are supposed to go) is usually associated with increased memory accuracy, knowledge can be a double-edged sword. For example, in a study of 4- and 6-year-old children's recall of a mock physical examination, Peter Ornstein and his colleagues (1998) included some typical, script-consistent features in the exam (for example, the doctor listened to the children's hearts with a stethoscope and looked into their ears), but they also included some atypical, unexpected features (for example, the doctor measured children's head circumference and used alcohol to wipe their belly buttons). In addition, some expected features were omitted from the exams (for example, measuring blood pressure and looking in children's mouths). Children were interviewed about the exam both immediately and after a 12-week delay. They were first asked open-ended questions (for example, "Tell me what happened during your checkup" and "Tell me what the doctor did to check you"), followed by increasingly specific questions (for instance, "Did the doctor check any parts of your face?" and "Did the doctor check your eyes?"). In addition to questions about what really did happen during the exam, children were also asked specific questions about things that did not happen. For example, children for whom the doctor did not check their ears would be asked, "Did the doctor look into your ears?" Some of the questions referred to events that are likely to occur in an exam, such as looking into children's ears, whereas others were for events that were unlikely to occur (for example, "Did the doctor give you some stitches?").

How did the children do? The results for the 12-week assessment of this study are shown in Figures 8.7 and 8.8. The first figure reports the percentage of correct responses for the 4- and 6-year-old children for the present-typical and present-atypical features (that is, aspects of the exam that children actually experienced) for the open-ended questions and for the specific questions. As can be seen, children of both ages recalled more typical features correctly than atypical features, for both types of questions. This reflects the positive effects of knowledge base. This was not the first medical exam for any of the children, and they presumably had a script for what usually happens in such an exam. As a result, features that are typically found in medical exams, based on children's past experiences, were more likely to be remembered than atypical features. But there was a negative side to knowledge, and this is reflected in the results displayed in Figure 8.8. Correct denials (the dark portion of the bars in Figure 8.8) refer to children correctly stating that an event did not happen ("Did the doctor give you stitches?" "No."). As can be seen, children were more likely to correctly reject these nonevents for the atypical features. False alarms (the light portion of the bars

FIGURE 8.7 **Percentage of present-typical and present-atypical features recalled correctly in response to open-ended and specific questions for 4- and 6-year-old children, 12-week assessment.**

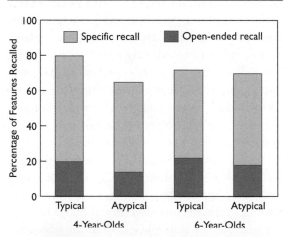

Sources: Ornstein, P. A., & Greenhoot, A. F. (2000). Remembering the distant past: Implications of research on children's memory for the recovered memory debate. In D. F. Bjorklund (Ed.), *False-memory creation in children and adults: Theory, research, and implications.* Mahwah, NJ: Erlbaum. © 2000 Lawrence Erlbaum Associates, Inc. Based on data in Ornstein, P. A., Merritt, K. A., Baker-Ward, L., Furtado, E., Gordon, B. N., & Principe, G. F. (1998). Children's knowledge, expectation, and long-term retention. *Applied Cognitive Psychology, 12,* 387–405.

FIGURE 8.8 **Percentage of absent-typical and absent-atypical features to which children responded with correct denials and false alarms for 4- and 6-year-old children, 12-week assessment.**

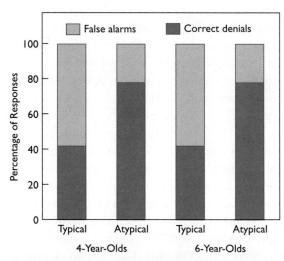

Sources: Ornstein, P. A., & Greenhoot, A. F. (2000). Remembering the distant past: Implications of research on children's memory for the recovered memory debate. In D. F. Bjorklund (Ed.), *False-memory creation in children and adults: Theory, research, and implications.* Mahwah, NJ: Erlbaum. © 2000 Lawrence Erlbaum Associates, Inc. Based on data in Ornstein, P. A., Merritt, K. A., Baker-Ward, L., Furtado, E., Gordon, B. N., & Principe, G. F. (1998). Children's knowledge, expectation, and long-term retention. *Applied Cognitive Psychology, 12,* 387–405.

in Figure 8.8) refer to children *incorrectly* agreeing that an event happened when it did not ("Did the doctor look into your ears?" "Yes."). Here, both the 4- and 6-year-old children were more likely to erroneously say that these events did, indeed, happen when they were typical rather than atypical features of a physical exam. Knowing what usually happens caused children to falsely remember what did happen, at least when their memory was tested 12 weeks after the event.

A similar finding was produced by Henry Otgaar and colleagues (2010) with slightly older children, 7 to 11 years old. Regardless of age, children developed more false memories after listening to false narratives describing events about which they had a lot of knowledge (for example, getting their fingers caught in a mousetrap) versus little knowledge (for example, receiving a rectal enema). These studies provide convincing evidence that script knowledge boosts children's false memories.

Characteristics of the interview. Not surprisingly, how children are interviewed can greatly affect what they remember and the accuracy of their recollections (D. A. Brown & Lamb, 2015; Bruck et al., 2006). The type of questions asked, for example, influences what children remember. Young children tend to recall relatively little to open-ended, free-recall questions ("Tell me everything that happened when the man came into your classroom"), but what they do recall tends to be highly accurate. Children recall more when given neutral cues, but the accuracy of their recall declines (that is, they also recall more false information).

Interviewer characteristics, such as whether the interviewer is warm and supportive or high status (for example, a police officer), influences the accuracy of children's memory, as does the use of any special recall-facilitating technique or props. For example, many forensic interviews make use of anatomically correct dolls when questioning children who are suspected of being victims of sexual abuse. Does the use of such dolls increase the accuracy of children's reports? Maggie Bruck and her colleagues (1995) interviewed 3-year-old children following a routine medical exam (these children were *not* suspected child-abuse victims). Half of the children received a genital exam by the doctor, and half did not. Immediately after the examination, children were shown an anatomically correct doll and were asked, with the interviewer pointing to the genital area of the doll, "Did the doctor touch you here?" Only about half of the children who did receive the genital exam answered correctly, whereas about half of those who did not receive a genital exam also said yes. When simply asked to "show on the doll" how the doctor had touched their genitals or buttocks, only 25% of the children who had received the genital exam responded correctly, and 50% of the children who were not given such an exam falsely showed anal or genital touching. Similar results have been reported by other researchers (see Poole & Bruck, 2012). Other research indicates that interviewers who use dolls and other objects to aid recall ask fewer open-ended questions and are less likely to stay on topic than interviewers who do not use such objects (Melinder et al., 2010). Findings such as these call into question the use of anatomically correct dolls, at least with young children, indicating that the dolls themselves may cause children to "make accusations" of abuse when no abuse occurred.

How warm or supportive an interviewer is can also influence the accuracy of children's recollections. For instance, children remember more correct information, and less incorrect information, when they are questioned by a warm and supportive interviewer (Bush et al., 2014; Quas, Bauer, & Boyce, 2004). In one study, 4- to 6-year-old children who had high levels of stress showed increased levels of recall accuracy when they were questioned by an emotionally supportive interviewer but reduced levels of accuracy when questioned by a nonsupportive interviewer (Quas et al., 2004).

Age Differences in Suggestibility

Perhaps the single most investigated area of eyewitness testimony in both the adult and child literatures concerns suggestibility (for a review, see Ceci, Hritz, & Royer, 2016). To what extent are children susceptible to suggestion? Research has shown that people of all ages report more inaccurate information when misleading questions are posed (that is, questions suggesting incorrect "facts"). The questions for developmentalists, and for the legal profession, include are children more suggestible than adults, what factors influence their suggestibility, and how can we maximize memory accuracy and minimize suggestibility?

The general consensus regarding the question of whether children are more suggestible than adults seems to be yes. In an extensive review of the early literature, Stephen Ceci and Maggie Bruck (1993) concluded, "There do appear to be significant age differences in suggestibility, with preschool children being disproportionately more vulnerable to suggestion than either school-age children or adults" (p. 431). Most investigators looking for age differences in suggestibility have found it, although in varying degrees and sometimes only under certain circumstances (Ackil & Zaragoza, 1995; Bruck et al., 1995).

How Do Children Respond to Misleading Questions?

Let us provide an example from research that asked children different types of suggestive

(leading) questions. William Cassel and I (DB) (1995) showed groups of 6- and 8-year-old children and college adults a brief video of a boy and a girl in a park, with the boy eventually taking the girl's bike without permission. Participants were interviewed 15 minutes after viewing the video and then again 1 week and 1 month later. During these later interviews, participants were given either sets of misleading questions, suggesting things that did not happen (for example, "The girl said it was okay for the boy to take her bike, didn't she?"), or positive-leading questions, suggesting things that did, indeed, happen (for example, "The girl told the boy not to take the bike, didn't she?"). Figures 8.9 and 8.10 present some of the results for the 1-week interview. As can be seen, the 6- and 8-year-olds tended to follow the lead of the interviewer, agreeing both with the misleading questions (see Figure 8.9), thus getting

FIGURE 8.9 **Percentage of correct and incorrect responses by age to misleading questions.**

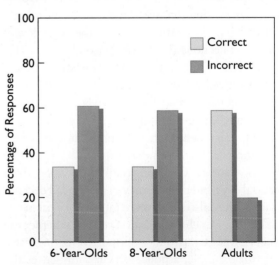

Source: Based on data from Cassel, W. S., & Bjorklund, D. F. (1995). Developmental patterns of eyewitness memory and suggestibility: An ecologically based short-term longitudinal study. *Law & Human Behavior, 19*, 507–532.

more wrong than the adults did, and with the positive-leading questions (see Figure 8.10), thus getting more right than the adults did. In fact, as can be seen in Figure 8.9, both the 6- and 8-year-olds had more incorrect than correct responses to the misleading questions, whereas the reverse was true for the adults.

In the 1-month interview, participants were first asked sets of leading questions by one examiner suggesting one interpretation (either misleading or positive leading) and then immediately thereafter were asked a second set of questions by a second examiner, asking for the *opposite* interpretation (misleading if positive leading had been asked first, and vice versa). How would children respond to the same question they had just been asked, but with an opposite spin? The answer is that children often changed their answers. For example, when asked about the color of the bike,

FIGURE 8.10 **Percentage of correct and incorrect responses by age to positive-leading questions.**

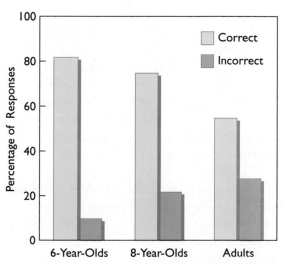

Source: Based on data from Cassel, W. S., & Bjorklund, D. F. (1995). Developmental patterns of eyewitness memory and suggestibility: An ecologically based short-term longitudinal study. *Law & Human Behavior, 19*, 507–532.

71% of the 6-year-olds who had agreed with the suggestion of the first interviewer later changed their answers to comply with the suggestion of the second interviewer. The corresponding percentages for the 8-year-old children and adults were 53% and 35%, respectively. For the more critical central question—that is, whether the girl had given the boy permission to take her bike—42% of the 6-year-old children changed their answers in response to the second interviewer, whereas only 7% of 8-year-olds and 12% of adults did so. These results make it clear that younger children are highly susceptible to the suggestion of an adult interviewer, modifying their answers, it seems, to suit the desires of whomever is interviewing them.

Yet despite the ease with which young children can be led to give answers consistent with the suggestion of any adult, are their memories actually changed as well? Research that has asked children misleading questions over repeated interviews indicates that such repetition will, indeed, cause some children to report the incorrect information in later tests of free recall and recognition, particularly information that is peripheral, or incidental, to the event. Such findings indicate that suggestive questioning changes not only children's answers but also their memories. However, in many other cases, children who follow the lead of an interviewer fail to incorporate that misinformation, especially information that is central to the event, in their subsequent free recall of the event, suggesting that it is far easier to change children's answers with such questions than it is to change their minds (see Bjorklund, Brown, & Bjorklund, 2002).

In an early investigation, Gail Goodman and Allison Clarke-Stewart (1991) illustrated the extent to which young children's reports of a witnessed event can be swayed and the extent to which they will stick to their interpretation.

Preschool children watched a man, posing as a janitor, who either cleaned and arranged some toys, including a doll, or played with the toys in a somewhat rough and inappropriately suggestive manner. About an hour later, the janitor's "boss" interviewed the children about what they had seen. Of primary concern here is the situation in which children watched the janitor merely cleaning the toys, although it was suggested to them that he had actually been playing with the toys improperly instead of doing his job. If a child in this situation initially did not agree with the interviewer's suggestion, subsequent leading questions were asked, with each question becoming increasingly stronger in its suggestion (that is, more explicitly suggesting misbehavior). Two thirds of these children eventually followed the interviewers' suggestions, even though the suggestions did not correspond to what they had seen. Moreover, when the children were questioned by their parents at the end of the session, all stuck with the story that they had given the interviewer. In sum, when suggestions and accusations were strong and persistent, young children were easily led and did not alter their newfound interpretations when later questioned by their parents.

In other research, Leichtman and Ceci (1995) assessed the effects of negative stereotyping and suggestion on preschool children's recollections of an event that happened at their school. An unfamiliar person, Sam Stone, came into children's classrooms, talked to the teacher, sat with the children during the reading of a story, made a comment about the story ("I know that story; it's one of my favorites!"), walked around the classroom, and finally left the room, waving good-bye to the children. Children in the *stereotype* condition were given information about Sam Stone before his visit that depicted him as accident prone and irresponsible ("That Sam Stone is always getting into accidents and breaking things!"). Children in the *suggestion* condition were interviewed several times after Sam Stone's visit and given misinformation about the visit ("Sam ripped a book and soiled a teddy bear when he visited"). Children in the *stereotype-plus-suggestion* condition received both the negative stereotype before Sam Stone's visit and the misinformation afterward, and children in the *control* condition received neither the stereotyped information nor the misinformation about Sam.

Ten weeks after the visit, the children were given an open-ended interview about what happened the day Sam Stone visited the classroom. Leichtman and Ceci (1995) reported that, relative to children in the control condition, children who had been given the stereotypes made a modest number of false statements about Sam in the interview and that children in the suggestion condition made a substantial number of false reports. The highest levels of false reports about Sam's visit, however, came from children who had received both the stereotyped information before and the misinformation after the visit: 46% of 3- and 4-year-old children and 30% of 5-and 6-year-old children said that Sam had either ripped a book, soiled a teddy bear, or both. The percentage of erroneous responses increased to 72% and 44% for the younger and older preschoolers, respectively, when children were asked specific follow-up questions concerning whether Sam had ripped a book or soiled a teddy bear.

Why are younger children often more susceptible to the effects of misinformation and suggestion than older children are? One explanation comes from fuzzy-trace theory, as discussed earlier (Brainerd & Reyna, 2014). Because verbatim traces deteriorate rapidly, they may not be available when postevent information is provided or when suggestive questions are asked.

Thus, the erroneous information has an excellent chance of being incorporated with "real" memories and becoming indistinguishable from them. Similarly, it would seem that young children's elevated rates of erroneous information to unbiased cues (that is, questions that ask for more information but do not attempt to bias a child's answer one way or the other) might be the result of their greater reliance on verbatim traces.

Many factors influence suggestibility in children. For example, social factors, such as a desire to comply with adult requests, surely play a role in children's greater suggestibility (Bjorklund et al., 1998). Children are more likely to comply with the suggestion of a high-status versus a low-status person (Ceci, Ross, & Toglia, 1987). Children's background knowledge for the witnessed event also influences their performance (Ornstein et al., 2006), as does the number of times an event is experienced (Powell et al., 1999). Much research has investigated how other aspects of children's cognitive development influence suggestibility. For example, developmental and individual differences in working memory and inhibitory control are related to suggestibility in children (Ruffman et al., 2001). Preschool children who perform better on theory-of-mind tasks tend to be less suggestible than are children with poorer theory-of-mind abilities (Welch, 1999), and children and adults with better metacognitive skills are more accurate in suggestive interviews than are their less-metacognitively sophisticated peers (Roebers, 2002).

One topic that has received considerable attention is that of **source monitoring**, which refers to being aware of the source of information one knows or remembers. For example, did a particular experience happen to them, to a friend, or did they see it on TV? This can be particularly important in cases of eyewitness testimony. *Was the information that the boy stole the bike something I saw or something someone told me?* Research has shown that preschool and early school-age children often have difficulty monitoring the source of their memories (see discussion in Chapter 5). For example, children sometimes have difficulty determining whether they actually performed an act or just imagined it (Foley, Santini, & Sopasakis, 1989), and they often incorrectly remember that an action carried out by another person during a joint activity was actually performed by them (Ackil & Zaragoza, 1995; Foley, Ratner, & Gentes, 2010). When young children make errors in such situations, they are much more likely to attribute an action to themselves that someone else actually did than vice versa. Findings such as these have caused some researchers to propose that young children's increased susceptibility to suggestion might be caused largely by their difficulty in monitoring the source of what they know (Ceci & Bruck, 1995). Some research supports these speculations, showing that 6-year-olds who are poor at source monitoring are more prone to the effects of suggestion (Mazzoni, 1998). Moreover, children who are given some source-monitoring training (for example, training in distinguishing between events they experienced directly versus events they heard about in a previous interview) make fewer false statements to misleading questions (Thierry & Spence, 2002), although some researchers have found this effect only for older (7- and 8-year-old) children and not for preschoolers (Poole & Lindsay, 2002).

Another reason contributing to young children's suggestibility might be their beliefs that their memory is invulnerable to suggestion, or poor *metamemory*. For example, Julia O'Sullivan, Mark Howe, and Tammy Marche (1996) interviewed preschool, first-grade, and third-grade children about factors that might influence their memories. Although children of all ages believed that central aspects of a story would be more likely to be remembered than peripheral details, only the third-grade children believed that their memories would be susceptible to suggestion. The preschool and first-grade children were confident that suggestion from a parent or sibling would not affect their recollection of an event.

False-Memory Creation

How easy is it to create a false memory in a person? Asking children misleading questions about an event they have seen can cause children to confuse the source of the information, thinking that the misinformation was actually something they experienced and not just something they heard someone else say (Ackil & Zaragoza, 1995). But how easy is it to actually get children, or adults, to believe an event happened to them that never really did?

Elizabeth Loftus and her colleagues first investigated this with adults (Loftus & Pickrell, 1995). College students were interviewed about four events that had supposedly happened to them in childhood (based on reports of parents and older siblings). One event, being lost in a mall at age 5, never actually occurred. The students were asked to write as much about each event as they could remember. They remembered, on average, 68% of the true events; they also "remembered" 25% of the false events, sometimes vividly.

It seems that preschool children are even more susceptible to creating false memories than are adults. Ceci and his colleagues (1994) used a similar technique to that used by Loftus and Pickrell (1995) and interviewed children throughout an 11-week period about events that might have happened to them. For example, children were asked if they remember ever getting their finger caught in a mousetrap. The percentage of false reports (that is, recalling something about the

event) for the 3- and 4-year-old children and for the 5- and 6-year-old children in this study over the 11-week period is shown in Figure 8.11. Although few children admitted to experiencing these false events in the initial interviews, by the conclusion of the study more than 50% of the 3- and 4-year-old children and about 40% of 5- to 6-year-olds assented that these events did, indeed, happen—and often provided substantial detail about the events. Moreover, many children continued to believe that these events actually happened even after being told by the interviewers and their parents that the events were just made up. It seems that false memories

FIGURE 8.11 **Percentage of false reports over sessions for 3- and 4-year-olds and 5- and 6-year-olds.**

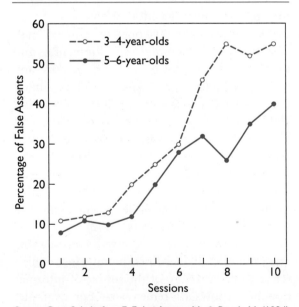

Source: Ceci, S. J., Loftus, E. F., Leichtman, M., & Bruck, M. (1994). The role of source misattributions in the creation of false beliefs among preschoolers. *International Journal of Clinical and Experimental Hypnosis, 62,* 304–320. © 1994 by SAGE Publications, Inc. Reprinted by permission.

of plausible but extraordinary events are relatively easy to put into young children's minds.

Other research has examined how *rumors* may influence children's memory of events. For example, in research by Gabrielle Principe and her colleagues (Principe et al., 2006, 2010, 2012), preschool children witnessed a magic show by Magic Mumfrey, during which, toward the end of the show, Mumfrey tried to pull a rabbit out of his hat but failed. After the show, some children heard an unfamiliar adult tell their teacher that she knew why the trick failed: The rabbit had escaped and was in the classroom eating carrots. Other children didn't hear the rumor from an adult but were classmates of the children who did, and they heard the rumor as they interacted with children in their classroom. Finally, some children saw the show but were not exposed to any rumor. One week later, children were interviewed about the show. A majority of children in both rumor conditions reported that the rabbit had gotten loose in the classroom, and many of these children actually professed seeing the runaway bunny. Five- and six-year-old children who were warned that there was a false rumor going around about what had happened in the school made fewer such claims when they heard the rumor from their classmates, although such a warning did not affect 3- to 4-year-old children's reports. Moreover, children who said they saw the rabbit in the classroom provided more vivid descriptions of the (non)event than children who did not, suggesting that the implanted rumor produced a true false memory, complete with perceptual details, and was not simply the result of children wanting to conform with what other children had witnessed (Principe et al., 2010).

Henry Otgaar and colleagues (Otgaar et al., 2012) were further interested in the question of whether children's implanted memories represent real memory traces or just compliance. They presented 8-year-olds with a narrative about a true (first day at school) and false event (hot air balloon ride). Across two interviews, the majority of children developed at least a partial false memory of the balloon ride. To analyze whether the false memories were guided by children's compliance with the experimenter or actual memory traces, the researchers examined how quickly children responded yes or no to statements that were either consistent or inconsistent with the true and false events. On some trials, children were instructed to tell the truth, and on other trials they were instructed to lie. So, for example, when instructed to tell the truth, a yes response to a statement consistent with the real narrative would be correct. When instructed to lie, a no response would be correct. The manipulation becomes a bit more complicated when we look at the false event. For children who correctly rejected the false narrative as never occurring, a yes response would be the correct response for the statement, "I have been on a hot air balloon ride" when instructed to lie. However, for children who indicate they have a false memory of the balloon ride, the expected response when instructed to lie would be no.

The researchers first looked at response times to the true events (school-related trials) and found that children took longer to respond when they had to lie versus when they had to tell the truth. Next, they compared these response times to those of children with false memories who were responding to statements about the false event (hot air balloon ride). The rationale was that if children's false memories were caused by faulty memory traces, then denying that the false event took place would actually feel like a lie. These trials should then demonstrate elevated response times and error rates relative to trials in which they have to confirm that the event took place. However, if implanted false memories are based on compliance (in other words, they never believed the ride took place, but they said it did to please the experimenter), then the pattern should be the opposite: Denying that the false event occurred would be a truthful response, and response times should be relatively quick. The pattern of results confirmed that false memories were indeed treated like true memories, with children taking longer when they had to "lie" about these events, suggesting they were based in actual faulty memory traces, not just a desire to conform.

Final Thoughts on Children as Eyewitnesses

Children do not have perfect memories, making them less than ideal witnesses. Of course, adults' memories are also fallible, so how different are children from adults when it comes to providing reliable testimony? As we've seen, young children's spontaneous recall is typically sparse, but it also tends to be accurate and about psychologically and legally central aspects of an event. They are also more prone to suggestion than adults, at least in most contexts (but see Brainerd & Reyna, 2012, for important exceptions). Since the 1980s, when issues about the accuracy of children's testimony became of increasing interest to the legal community (Ceci & Bruck, 1995), developmental psychologists have investigated children's event memories for forensically relevant information and have discovered important things about the emotional, social, and cognitive factors that influence children's reports and memories.

However, most of the investigations described in this section were laboratory studies. Because children's testimony may have significant legal consequences, it is important to do research in the real world, developing paradigms where researchers have some control over the situation but where children remember "real" events that may have legal implications, which some researchers have done. For example, researchers have assessed children's recollections of events surrounding natural disasters (Ackil, Van Abbema, & Bauer, 2003; Bahrick et al., 1998). Other real-life research paradigms involve assessing children's recollections of invasive medical procedures—some traumatic (such as trips to the emergency room) and others not (such as well-child pediatric exams). In general, older children remember more than younger children, and prior knowledge of the exam procedure is positively related to amount of initial (but not delayed) recall of the events (see Peterson, 2012). Other studies attempt to construct forensic interviews similar to those that abused children would experience (D. A. Brown & Lamb, 2015; Pipe & Salmon, 2009). Such studies afford control of variables that are difficult, if not impossible, to control in real life. However, there is always the question of the ecological validity of the studies. How do we know that children who experience child abuse behave in the same way? This is where field studies, interviewing children who are suspected victims of child abuse, become important (D. A. Brown & Lamb, 2015). Of course, field studies lack control of important factors, and one does not know for certain what children actually experienced. But the combination of laboratory and field studies can provide greater insight into the reliability and accuracy of children as witnesses.

This research has made significant contributions to the legal system, affecting how children are interviewed by police officers, social workers, and lawyers (Bruck et al., 2006; Howe, 2013) and the development of a number of protocols to help those in the legal profession get the most accurate information possible when interviewing children. For example, the National

TABLE 8.1   **Sequence of phases recommended by the NICHD guidelines.**

1. Introduction of parties and their roles
2. The "truth and lie ceremony" (warning the child of the necessity to tell the truth)
3. Rapport building
4. Description of a recent salient event
5. First narrative account of the allegation
6. Narrative accounts of the last incident (if the child reports multiple incidents)
7. Cue question (for example, "You said something about a barn. Tell me about that")
8. Paired direct-open questions about the last incident
9. Narrative account of first incident
10. Cue questions
11. Paired direct-open questions about the first incident
12. Narrative accounts of another incident that the child remembers
13. Cue questions
14. Paired direct-open questions about this incident
15. If necessary, leading questions about forensically important details not mentioned by the child
16. Invitation for any other information the child wants to mention

Source: Adapted from Poole, D. A., & Lamb, M. E. (1998). *Investigative interviews of children: A guide of helping professionals* (pp. 98–99). Washington, DC: American Psychological Association.

Institute of Child Health and Human Development (NICHD) protocol incorporates research findings from both laboratory and field settings (Lamb, Sternberg, & Esplin, 1998), and an outline of the protocol is presented in Table 8.1.

We may never know with 100% certainty the veracity of a child's recollections (or that of an adult, for that matter), but developmental science has made great leaps in understanding children's memory and factors that affect its accuracy.

- The accuracy of children's event memory is influenced by a host of factors, including their knowledge for the event they experienced and the characteristics of the interview, such as the use of an anatomically correct doll.
- Young children are generally more susceptible to misleading questions (suggestions) and misinformation than are older children and can easily be caused to form false memories.
- Many factors influence children's suggestibility, including deficits in *source monitoring*, with children confusing the source of information they know or remember.

Section Review

- Age differences are found in the amount of information children remember, but what young children do recall tends to be accurate and for central components of an event.

Ask Yourself . . .

12. What are the major age differences found in children's eyewitness testimony?
13. How suggestible are children? What factors affect the accuracy of their memories?

REMEMBERING TO REMEMBER

To this point, our discussion of memory has focused on what is called *retrospective memory*, or remembering something that happened in the past. But another type of memory, one that we engage in every day, is prospective memory, or remembering to do something in the future (Einstein & McDaniel, 2005). For example, if you need to pick up a bottle of wine tonight on your way home from school or work for that special dinner and remember to do so, you are demonstrating good prospective memory. If you neglect to do so, you are displaying a failure of prospective memory (and, perhaps, a less successful evening than you had hoped for). Prospective memory involves what some people refer to as *mental time travel*—anticipating the future and planning for it (Suddendorf & Corballis, 2007; Tulving, 2005). This requires a sophisticated cognition/memory system.

Researchers have paid less attention to the development of prospective memory relative to retrospective memory, but this is gradually changing (see Mahy, Moses, & Kliegel, 2014, for a review). One of the first studies to examine prospective memory in young children was performed by Susan Somerville and her colleagues (1983), who asked the parents of 2-, 3-, and 4-year-old children to remind them to perform some task in the future, some of which were of low interest to the children (for example, "Remind me to buy milk when we go to the store tomorrow") and others of which were of high interest (for instance, buying candy at the store). Figure 8.12 shows the performance of the children for the high- and low-interest tasks for short (5 minutes or less) and longer (for example, from morning to afternoon) delays.

As you can see, even the 2-year-olds were very good at reminding their parents when the task was one of high interest and over short delays. Performance for all children dropped sharply, however, for the low-interest and long-delay tasks. In fact, none of the 2-year-olds spontaneously remembered to remind their parents about a low-interest task over a long delay. Children improved when given a clue ("Was there something you were supposed to remind me to do?"), increasing their performance by about a third, on average. These results suggest that motivation plays an important role in when children display prospective memory, as does the length of time they have to wait.

More recent research using controlled laboratory experiments has shown that 2-year-olds

FIGURE 8.12 **Proportion of children who reminded their parents to perform some task for 2-, 3-, and 4-year-old children for high- and low-interest tasks over short and long delays.**

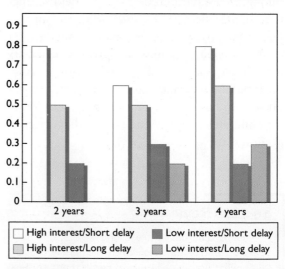

Source: Adapted from Somerville, S. C., Wellman, H. M., & Cultice, J. C. (1983). Young children's deliberate reminding. *Journal of Genetic Psychology, 143*, 87–96.

rarely perform as well as Somerville's youngsters did (Kliegel & Jager, 2007) and that prospective memory continues to improve over the preschool (Quon & Atance, 2010) and school years (R. E. Smith, Bayen, & Martin, 2010; Yang, Chan, & Shum, 2011).

Many factors influence age differences in prospective memory performance, including the type of task. Somerville's tasks involved *event-based* prospective memory, a type that researchers distinguish from *time-based* prospective memory. Whereas event-based tasks require us to remember to do something after some specific circumstances occur (for instance, being at the store), time-based tasks require that we act at a particular point in time or after the passage of a specific duration (for instance, attending a meeting at 2:00). Children's performance on these tasks varies as a function of age, with children remembering event-based tasks at a younger age than time-based tasks, but the general trend is improvement across development. For instance, in one study, 7- to 12-year-old children played a computer game called CyberCruiser, a time-based task, in which they used a joystick to maneuver around obstacles. They also had to occasionally check the fuel gauge to make sure they did not run out of gas and to fill up when they had less than a quarter of a tank. Perhaps not surprisingly, younger children ran out of gas more often than older children (Kerns, 2000).

Like performance on some retrospective memory tasks (Lehmann & Hasselhorn, 2007), children's performance on prospective memory tasks is influenced by individual differences in executive function (Causey, 2010; Causey & Bjorklund, 2014; Mahy & Moses, 2011). For example, in the study by Kimberly Kerns (2000) described in the previous paragraph, the author reported a moderate but significant negative correlation ($r = -0.29$) between executive-function measures and the number of times children ran out of gas. Subsequent research reported significant relations between measures of strategic time monitoring (checking a clock to indicate the passage of every 5 minutes while watching a film), prospective memory success (Voigt et al., 2015), and metacognition (Causey, 2010). Other research has shown that executive function predicts 3-year-olds' performance on a low-interest event-based prospective memory task ("Remind me to remove the sign on the door when we leave") but not for high-interest tasks ("Remind me to get you a prize when we finish") (Causey & Bjorklund, 2014). These patterns of findings suggest that the relation between executive function and prospective memory is complex and highly task dependent.

Prospective memory involves a host of cognitive skills, among them a symbolic system that can represent the self in the future, which is the essence of episodic memory, and executive function (Causey & Bjorklund, 2014; Ford et al., 2012). In fact, some people have referred to this type of memory as *episodic future thought* (Atance, 2015; Nigro et al., 2014). Relatedly, self-awareness in the form of metacognition seems important in ensuring children implement relevant strategies (like clock checking) to succeed in prospective memory tasks (Causey, 2010; Mahy & Moses, 2011). Apparently, under some limited conditions with delays of 5 minutes or less, this is something that 2-year-old children can do. However, the tendency to travel through time and to remember to do something in the future develops with age, as children's representational abilities, memories, and executive functions improve.

Section Review

- Developmental differences are found in *prospective memory*, which refers to remembering to do something in the future.
- Researchers distinguish between event-based and time-based prospective memory.
- Age differences in performance on these tasks are influenced by many extrinsic and intrinsic factors, including task type, motivation, executive function, representational ability, and metacognition.

Ask Yourself . . .

14. How are time-based tasks different from event-based tasks? How might children's strategies differ across each type?
15. How is the development of prospective memory influenced by executive function? What about representational ability? Metacognition?

KEY TERMS AND CONCEPTS

autobiographical memories
conjugate-reinforcement
  procedure
declarative memory
deferred imitation
dentate gyrus
episodic memory

event memory
explicit memory
implicit memory
infantile amnesia
nondeclarative memory
preference-for-novelty
  paradigms

procedural memory
prospective memory
scripts
semantic memory
source monitoring

SUGGESTED READINGS

Scholarly Works

Bauer, P., & Fivush, R. (2014). *The Wiley handbook on the development of children's memory.* New York: Wiley. This two-volume edited handbook includes up-to-date reviews written by leading researchers in the field, reviewing specific topics in children's memory development.

Brainerd, C. J., & Reyna, V. F. (2005). *The science of false memory.* Oxford, UK: Oxford University Press. This book, by the originators of the fuzzy-trace theory, provides a detailed look at the research and theory pertinent to false-memory creation in general, including research on children as eyewitnesses and the extent to which they remember falsely or can be misled. The book also provides an excellent account of fuzzy-trace theory. A concise summary of this work can be found in Brainerd, C. J., & Reyna, V. F. (2002). Fuzzy-trace theory and false memory. *Current Directions in Psychological Science, 11,* 164–169.

Principe, G. F., Ceci, S. J., & Bruck, M. (2014). *Children's memory: Psychology and the law.* New York: Wiley. This book presents the latest research and theory on children's eyewitness memory and suggestibility, including children's recollections of traumatic events and autobiographical memory.

Schneider, W. (2015). *Memory development from early childhood through emerging adulthood.*

Cham, Switzerland: Springer International. This book, by one of the leading researchers in children's memory, provides an up-to-date review of research and theory on memory development.

Reading for Personal Interest

Lamb, M. E., Hershkowitz, I., Orbach, Y., & Esplin, P. W. (2008). *Tell me what happened: Structured investigative interviews of children victims and witnesses.* **West Sussex, UK: Wiley.** Child forensic science is one of the fields in which cognitive development research has had a great practical impact. This book, written by leading researchers in the field, provides a recent summary of how professionals (for example, psychologists, police officers, social workers) should approach children suspected of abuse and child witnesses to obtain reliable accounts of what happened.

9 LANGUAGE DEVELOPMENT

"Up, Daddy," 2-year-old Darius called to his father, who turned around and put out his arms to pick up his son. But Darius immediately protested, pointing to the candy dish his mother recently placed on a high shelf out of his reach and saying, "No, Daddy! Up!" Seeing this, his father said, "No, Darius, no candy right now." Darius whined, "Please, Daddy" and then again pointed to the out-of-reach dish and said, "Up!"

Darius can barely string more than two words together at a time and has few verbs in his limited vocabulary. Yet by speaking just one or two words at a time, along with pertinent gestures and a social context shared with a familiar person,

Darius is able to get his message across, even if he doesn't always get what he wants. Darius is at the early stages of learning language, something that he will master in a very short time and that, perhaps more than any other single ability, will distinguish him from all other animals.

Children around the globe acquire language without formal instruction. Language belongs to the class of abilities that are too important to be relegated to our conscious awareness and free will (Spelke & Newport, 1998). Some scientists believe that the evolution of language made human thought possible (Bickerton, 1990; K. Nelson, 1996). Although a few nonhuman primates have shown simple language abilities (see Savage-Rumbaugh et al., 1993) none has approached the level found in all normal humans. And despite the universality of language (that is, all groups of people possess it and develop it at about the same age), the language people learn depends on what is spoken around them. Language is thus strongly influenced both by humans' general biological inheritance and by the uniqueness of the environments in which they grow up.

In this chapter, we examine some of the fascinating and often controversial research and theory related to language development. We first consider what characteristics a communication system has to have to be considered language. We then provide a brief sketch of children's developing language abilities, from cooing and babbling to communicative competence. Next, we investigate some of the major theoretical perspectives of language development, particularly the contrast between *nativist theories*, which hold that the mechanisms and structures underlying language acquisition (specifically, the acquisition of syntax, or grammar) are largely innate, and *social-interactionist theories*, which hold that the social environment plays a substantial role in language development. We then examine the development of bilingualism, followed by a brief look at sex differences in language development and, finally, a look at the developmental relationship between language and thought.

WHAT IS LANGUAGE?

Perhaps the first thing to realize is that language is a special form of communication, qualitatively different from the ways in which other animals send messages back and forth to one another. Language is also multilayered. One level involves the actual speech sounds. Then there is a layer where these sounds are combined in different ways to form different words with different meanings. At another level, there are rules for how these words can be combined into sentences. Then of course, there is the understanding of how to use all of these layers of language in social interaction. And each of these different layers of language develops.

At its most basic level, language refers to the systematic and conventional use of sounds, signs, or written symbols for the intention of communication or self-expression (Hoff, 2014). Although other animals have communication systems, they differ from humans in at least three important ways (Tomasello, 2006): Human language is *symbolic*, *grammatical*, and although all biologically typical people acquire language, *the particular language children learn to speak varies with culture*.

By symbolic, psychologists mean that the sounds of spoken language, or the hand movements of sign language, *represent* something independent of the actual sounds or movements. Moreover, the meaning of any pattern of sound is arbitrary. A word is not necessarily related to the concept it represents. In English, for example, we refer to man's best friend as a *dog* and to the purring and usually more independent domesticated pet as a *cat*. The words themselves are arbitrary. The exception in English would be onomatopoeia, referring to those words that are derived from an actual sound with which they are associated, such as *buzz* or *zap*. For all other words, if we wished, we could agree to reverse the names. For instance, the word *bad*, when used in the right context with the proper pronunciation, has come to have a positive, not a negative, connotation. Moreover, because it is symbolic, language can displace the speaker in time and place, referring to events that happened in the past, that will happen in the future, and that happen in locations that may be miles away from the speaker (that is, language allows mental time travel; see Chapter 8).

By grammatical, psychologists mean that language has a system of rules that permits a speaker to produce and understand sentences that have never been uttered before. A language does not have a set number of sentences that all speakers memorize. Rather, speakers can generate an infinite number of sentences—and, thus, meanings—using a finite number of words. There are two aspects of grammar that concern us here: morphology and syntax. *Morphology* refers to the structure of words and to a system of rules for combining units of meaning into words (for instance, adding *ed* to verbs to make them past tense). *Syntax* refers to rules governing how words are ordered into meaningful phrases and sentences.

Finally, there are many different languages with different vocabularies and rules. Currently, the world is estimated to have about 7,000 languages, many with only a handful of speakers, whereas some languages, such as English, Spanish, and Mandarin Chinese, are spoken by many hundreds of millions of people. This means that although language may be rooted in human biology, experience with a specific language is required. That all biologically normal members of our species acquire language in much the same way, regardless of the specific language they speak, is evidence that language is rooted in biology. Language fits the description of a biologically primary ability (Geary, 1995; see Chapter 2) that develops in all normal members of the species without the need of special instruction or motivation.

As a communication system, language serves many functions. Linguist Michael Halliday (1973) identified seven functions of language that motivate children to use language to attain a variety of goals. Those functions and some examples are presented in Table 9.1.

Section Review

- Human language has three important components: (1) It is symbolic, (2) it is grammatical, and (3) the particular language children learn to speak varies with culture.
- Children's language development can be described in terms of several dimensions, including phonology, semantics, grammar, and pragmatics.

Ask Yourself . . .

1. What are some (different) examples of the seven functions of language described in Table 9.1?
2. How does language fit the definition of a biologically primary ability?

TABLE 9.1 **Seven functions of language according to M. A. K. Halliday.**

Instrumental: Using language to express needs (for example, "More milk")

Regulatory: Using language to tell others what to do (for example, "Get me juice")

Interactional: Using language to make contact with others and form relationships (for example, "I love you, Mommy")

Personal: Using language to express feelings, opinions, and individual identity (for example, "I'm a good boy")

Heuristic: Using language to gain knowledge about the environment (for example, "What's that?")

Imaginative: Using language to tell stories and jokes and to create an imaginary environment

Representational: Using language to convey facts and information

Source: Halliday, M. A. K. (1973). *Explorations in the functions of language.* London: Edward Arnold.

DESCRIBING CHILDREN'S LANGUAGE DEVELOPMENT

There are at least five aspects of language: (1) *phonology*, (2) *morphology*, (3) *syntax*, (4) *semantics*, and (5) *pragmatics*, and they all develop over time. Figure 9.1 presents a schematic overview of some of the major developmental milestones for each of these aspects of language over the preschool years. In this section, we look at the five aspects of language just mentioned and provide a brief description of children's development for each aspect.

Phonological Development

Phonology refers to the sounds of a language. Our unique anatomy permits us to make a wide range of sounds that can be combined into sequences of words. Age-related changes occur in the

FIGURE 9.1 **Major milestones in early language development.** *Lexicon* refers to the words that a child knows (semantics), and *communication* refers to a child's ability to use language in social situations (pragmatics).

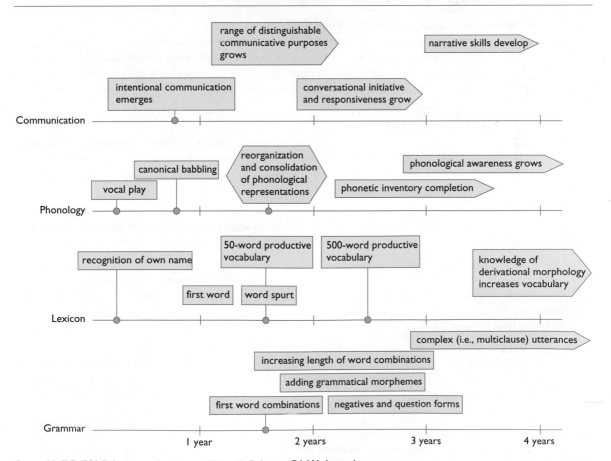

Source: Hoff, E. (2014). *Language development* (5th ed.). Belmont, CA: Wadsworth.

tongue, mouth, and position of the larynx in the throat, and these physical differences mean that the sounds infants and children are able to produce change over time (Stoel-Gammon & Menn, 1997).

Infants begin cooing and laughing at 2 to 4 months, and these vocalizations increase until 9 to 12 months, when they decline and one-word utterances begin (see Table 9.2). Sounds made during babbling vary widely, including both sounds heard in the baby's native language and sounds that are not. Over the course of the first year, babies' babbles come to resemble the sounds they hear around them (for instance, Chinese babies babble in "Chinese" and Spanish babies in "Spanish"), indicating that babbling development is based, at least partially, on children reproducing sounds that they hear. Some evidence consistent with this is that deaf children do not engage in true babbling, although they pass successfully through the earlier stages of speech production (Petitto, 2000). This evidence is important because it points out that speech production before 6 months of age (that is,

TABLE 9.2 **Developmental stages of infants' babbling.**

Stage 1: *Reflexive crying and vegetative sounds (0 to 8 weeks)*
Infants in stage 1 cry as a reaction to a distressed state and make various vegetative sounds associated with feeding and breathing, such as burps, coughs, and sneezes. The vocal tract of these young infants closely resembles that of nonhuman primates; their tongue fills their oral cavity and their larynx is high in their neck (which permits them to breathe and swallow simultaneously). This leaves little room for making different sounds. As the infant's head and neck grow, a greater variety of sounds become possible.

Stage 2: *Cooing and laughter (8 to 20 weeks)*
Infants at this age begin to make pleasant noises, especially during social interactions. These are mostly vowel sounds such as "oooh" and are termed cooing because they resemble the sounds made by pigeons. A few of the sounds will also contain some consonants such as g and k. Crying decreases and takes distinct forms that convey meaning to caregivers—discomfort, call, and request. Sustained laughter appears.

Stage 3: *Vocal play (16 to 30 weeks)*
This is a transition between cooing and true babbling. Infants begin to utter single syllables with prolonged vowel or consonant sounds.

Stage 4: *Reduplicated babbling (25 to 50 weeks)*
True babbling sounds appear, such as "bababa" and "nanana." Consonant-vowel patterns are repeated, and playful variations of pitch disappear. This type of vocalization is not just a response to caregiver's social interaction, but often occurs when no one is present. Deaf infants, although going through the first three stages, do not engage in true babbling at this time (Oller & Eilers, 1988).

Stage 5: *Jargon (9 to 18 months)*
Babbling consists of many nonrepeated consonant-vowel patterns. Jargon babbling is strings of sound filled with a variety of intonations and rhythms to sound like meaningful speech. Infants at this stage often sound as if they are carrying on their end of a conversation, with their intonations sometimes sounding as if they reflect questions or explanations, but their "words" are only babble sounds.

Sources: Stark, R. (1978). Features of infant sounds: The emergence of cooing. *Journal of Child Language, 5,* 1–12; Stoel-Gammon, C., & Menn, L. (1997). Phonological development: Learning sounds and sound patterns. In J. Berko Gleason (Ed.), *The development of language* (4th ed.). Boston: Allyn & Bacon.

before true babbling begins) is driven primarily by endogenous (internal) forces rather than by the language environment. However, even deaf babies in the latter part of the first year babble, but they do so with their hands. For instance, deaf infants exposed to American Sign Language from early in life begin "babbling" with their hands around 8 months, following patterns identical to those of hearing infants (Petitto, 2000).

It has been suggested that babbling plays a more important role in language development than just a poor attempt at spoken words (Sachs, 1977). Babbling might serve as a way to relate socially with family members long before the cognitive system is able to appreciate the intricacies of language. In addition, evidence suggests that although the *sounds* of babbling don't gradually approximate speech, the *intonation* of babbling does. By now, many of us have probably seen the viral video of twin infants seeming to "talk" to one another in nonsense sounds. (If you haven't, check out the link at the end of the chapter.) This is one example of how infants begin to "converse" in many ways that do not involve words but that do involve the conventions of speech. Infants develop the ability to take turns (Snow & Ferguson, 1977), match the speaker's tone of voice, pause between strings of syllables, end phrases with upward or downward inflections (Tonkova-Yompol'skaya, 1969), and match the pitch of adults speaking to them— higher for mother, lower for father (Lieberman, 1967).

The variety of sounds children can make increases from about 18 months to 8 or 9 years of age. For instance, 2-year-olds can produce between 10 and 20 consonants. Preschool and early school-age children often drop the unstressed syllables of words (*spaghetti* is pronounced as *getti*), repeat consonants (*Daddy* is pronounced as *dada*), and oversimplify complex consonants (*blanket* is pronounced as *bankee*). Children can pronounce most vowels and consonants in their language by 4 to 6 years, but they often have trouble with *fricatives* such as *z* and *s* (as in *zone*, *song*, *this*), the *l* (as in *lamb*), and the *r* (as in *rope*). By 6 to 9 years of age, children can pronounce all the sounds of their language correctly about 75% of the time (Kent, 2005).

Speech perception (as opposed to production) was discussed in Chapter 4. To reiterate briefly, very young infants can perceive *phonemes*, the basic sound units of language, and they categorize them much as adults do (Eimas et al., 1971). Young infants can also discriminate between the sounds of many different languages, something that their parents cannot do (see Saffran, Werker, & Werner, 2006). Over time, however, infants lose the ability to tell the difference between sounds that are not found in their mother tongue. As we mentioned in Chapter 4, this phenomenon is referred to as *perceptual narrowing* and is the process by which infants use experience (in this case, hearing language) to become specialists in perceiving stimuli relevant to their species and culture. As a result, however, infants become relatively less effective at perceiving some things with which they have less experience. Such perceptual narrowing suggests that infants' auditory systems are prepared to make sense of *any* language or human speech, although their perception is modified over childhood as a function of what language sounds they hear.

Speech perception skills are not complete by the end of infancy, however. An important aspect of speech perception related to reading is phonemic awareness, which refers to the knowledge that words consist of separable sounds. Preschool children first become aware of syllables, followed by the sounds at the beginning of words (for example, *dog* begins with a *d* sound and *cat* with a *k* sound), rhymes, and eventually, the identification of individual phonemes (Hoff, 2014). Phonemic awareness is important in proficient reading (see Chapter 11), and some believe improvement in phonemic awareness is influenced by learning to read.

Morphological Development

Morphology refers to the structure of something—in the case of language, the structure of words. Counter to what you might think, the word is *not* the smallest unit of meaning in a language. In English, for example, we add sounds to words to make them past tense (add *ed*), to express the present progressive (add *ing*), or to make a word plural (add *s*), and these word endings are also units of meaning. The smallest unit of meaning in a language is called a **morpheme**, and these occur as two types. **Free morphemes** can stand alone as words, such as *fire*, *run*, or *sad*. In contrast, **bound morphemes** cannot stand alone but, rather, convey meaning by changing the free morpheme they are attached to. These include the rules for making nouns plural (add an *s*), for making a verb past tense (add an *ed*), as well as prefixes (*un*likable) and suffixes (like*ness*). The average number of morphemes a child uses in a sentence, or the **mean length of utterance (MLU)**, is one indication of young children's linguistic development. MLU is measured by recording a child's speech during a period and then computing the average number of morphemes (both free and bound).

Roger Brown (1973) identified many of the morphemes used in children's early language and analyzed the speech of three unacquainted children (Adam, Eve, and Sarah) to determine the order in which these morphemes appear in development. He found 14 morphemes that occurred in almost the same order for the three children in his sample (see Table 9.3). Later research by Jill and Peter de Villiers (1973) extended these findings to 21 other preschoolers and found a high correlation between their sample and Brown's.

As can be seen from Table 9.3, many of the morphemes children learn are word endings. Once children learn these rules, they tend to apply them, even when it is not correct. For example, 2- and 3-year-olds learn that adding *ed* to a verb makes it past tense and *s* to a noun makes it plural. Although this may be generally true, there are many irregular verbs and nouns (especially in English), and although words such as *goed* (or *wented*), *drinked*, *runned*, *feets* (or *footes*), and *mices* follow the rules, they are incorrect. Children make these kinds of mistakes even when they have previously used the proper irregular word forms (for example, *went*, *drank*, *ran*, *feet*, and *mice*). This phenomenon is referred to as **overregularization** and usually begins around 20 months of age. Children continue to overregularize words throughout the preschool years, although beginning around age 3, they are increasingly likely to use the irregular forms of verbs and nouns properly (Marcus, 1995; Marcus et al., 1992). With overregularization, children have learned a rule for regular words and generalize it to irregular words. Apparently, the acquisition of a rule and its generalization to all situations, if even erroneously, is more important in early language acquisition than is being understood. This phenomenon is not limited to children learning English; it has been found in a wide variety of languages, suggesting that children around the world approach the problem of language acquisition in a similar way (Slobin, 1970).

TABLE 9.3 **Mean order of acquisition of 14 morphemes for three children.**

Children start using the present progressive (verb + *ing*) when their *mean length of utterance* is about 2.5 morphemes. They do not start using contractions of the verb *to be* ("the dog's big"; "I'm going") until their mean length of utterance is about 4.0 morphemes.

Morpheme	Example
1. Present progressive (verb + *ing*)	I sing*ing*, he walk*ing*
2. Preposition *in*	*in* chair, *in* car
3. Preposition *on*	*on* table, *on* head
4. Plural (noun + *s*)	apples, shoes
5. Past tense, irregular verbs	*went, saw, ran*
6. Possessives (noun + *'s*)	Eve's, hers
7. Use of *to be* (uncontracted)	The dog *is* big, I *am* tired
8. Articles *a* and *the*	*the* man, *a* toy
9. Past tense, regular verbs (verb + *ed*)	talk*ed*, throw*ed*
10. Third-person regular verbs (adding *s* to verb)	he runs, she swims
11. Third-person irregular verbs	he *does*, she *has*
12. Auxiliary verb, not contracted	I *am* going, he *is* drinking
13. The verb *to be* contracted	the dog's big, I'm scared, they're here
14. The verb *to be* contracted and used as an auxiliary	I'm going, she's running

Source: Adapted from Brown, R. (1973). *A first language: The early stages.* Cambridge, MA: Harvard University Press.

How can you know whether children understand the morphological rules of their language? One technique that has been quite successful is the "wug test" (Berko, 1958; see Figure 9.2). Children are shown a series of unfamiliar objects (for example, "This is a *wug*") or pictures of people performing unfamiliar actions (for example, "This is a woman who knows how to rick"). For the wug example, children are then shown two of these objects and told, "Now there are two of them. There are two _____." If children know the regular rules for making plurals, they will say "wugs." When shown a picture of a woman who knows how to rick and asked what she did yesterday, children who know the rules will say that "she ricked," and if they know the rules for the present progressive, they will say that currently "she is ricking" (Marcus et al., 1992).

Syntactic Development

Syntax is the knowledge of sentence structure, or grammatical rules—rules for how words are combined into sentences and how sentences are transformed into other sentences. Competent speakers of a language can use the same set of words to create very different meanings by applying basic grammatical rules. For example, the sentence "The man drove the car" can be made negative ("The man didn't drive the car"), transformed to pose a question ("Did the man drive the car?"), or expressed in the passive voice ("The car was driven by the man"). If you followed these simple transformations of these English sentences, it means that you know the underlying structure, or syntax, of English. You might not be able to pass a freshman test of English grammar, and these

FIGURE 9.2 **Two examples from the wug test.**

This is a wug.

Now there is another one.
There are two of them.
There are two _____.

This is a woman who can rick.
She is ricking. She also did it yesterday.
What did she do yesterday?
Yesterday she _____.

Source: Adapted from Berko, J. (1958). The child's learning of English morphology. *Word, 14,* 150–177.

rules might not be part of your explicit (declarative) knowledge, but you implicitly know the rules. Few of us can actually state the rules used for transforming an active declarative sentence into a question or to the passive voice, but nonetheless, we are all linguistic experts when it comes to actual performance. Our syntactic expertise is so good that we can even recognize grammatical sentences that contain nonsense words. For example, the sentence "The golup was pudaded under his limnex" is meaningless because *golup, pudaded,* and *limnex* are all meaningless. But because you are an expert at English syntax, you know that the subject of the sentence is *golup* (and that it is animate and masculine), that *pudaded* is a verb (specifically, an action that was done to the golup), and that a *limnex* is something (a noun) possessed by the golup (possibly a body part). Not bad for nonsense.

Although technically you can't have syntax until you have two-word sentences, which usually happens around 18 months, toddlers begin speaking one word at a time and can often convey complicated meaning from such utterances. "MOMMY!" can be a clear cry of distress, whereas "Mommy?" can be the initiation of a light conversation. Add a little hand waving and an empty cup, and "Mommy" becomes a request for a drink refill. And coming from behind a chairback, "Mommy" can be the beginning of a round of peek-a-boo. Take, for example, the toddler who gets his mother's attention by climbing up next to her on the sofa, putting one hand on each of her cheeks, and turning her face toward his as he finally says "Cookie?" These have been termed holophrases (one-word sentences, sometimes referred to as holophrastic speech), and children from language groups all over the world use them to achieve different functions or purposes (Tomasello, 2006).

When children get beyond the two-word phase, they do so mostly by including only those words that convey the most meaning and omitting the little words that make language easy to understand but that are not absolutely necessary for comprehension. For example, a child might say "Daddy give milk me" or "Amy me go Grandma's?" rather than "Give me the milk, Daddy" or "May Amy and I go to Grandma's?" When heard in context, the meanings of these abbreviated sentences are straightforward. Children are economical in their word choice, using only the concrete and high-information words that are most important in conveying meaning. Such speech has been described as telegraphic speech, in that it is accomplished much as telegrams were once written and text messages are written today—including only the high-content words and leaving out all the ifs, ands, and buts.

By about 3 years of age, most children begin to use longer and more complex sentences and to understand that word order is important (see Tomasello, 2006). For instance, between 2 and 3.5 years, children can recognize an improperly worded sentence; within another year, they can recognize incorrect word order even when unfamiliar verbs are used. For example, Nameera Akhtar (1999) presented English-speaking children with sentences including made-up verbs, sometimes in a familiar subject-verb-object order (for instance, "Ernie meeking the car") and sometimes in a less-familiar subject-object-verb order (for example, "Ernie the cow taming") or verb-subject-object order (for example, "Gopping Ernie the cow"). As can be seen in Figure 9.3, even 2-year-olds were able to understand the familiar subject-verb-object sentences, but about half of these young children "corrected" the subject-object-verb or verb-subject-object sentences to make them fit "standard" subject-verb-object order (for example, "Ernie gopping the cow"). By 4 years of age, about 90% of children corrected the unusual adult speech, demonstrating children's increasing sensitivity to the familiar word order as well as, perhaps, their comfort in correcting an adult.

In general, children begin to produce more complicated sentences around the age of 2, when they are able to put four words together in their utterances, with most children using complex sentences by 4 years of age (L. Bloom, 1993). The earliest types of complex sentences involve object complementation (that is, sentences with direct objects: "Look at me hit the ball") and *wh*-embedded clauses (that is, sentences with *wh* words embedded in them: "Do you want to play when we get home?"). The coordination of sentences (using *and* to connect two simple

FIGURE 9.3 **Proportion of matches by children to sentences of different word order.** SVO = subject-verb-object, SOV = subject-object-verb, VSO = verb-subject-object.

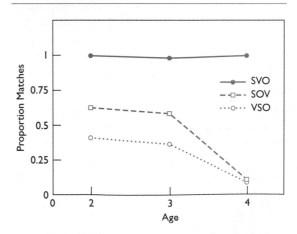

Source: Akhtar, N. (1999). Acquiring basic word order: Evidence for data-driven learning of syntactic structure. *Journal of Child Language, 26,* 339–356.

sentences: "I tripped Justin, and he fell") appears later, around the age of 3. More complex sentences linking a subordinate clause with a main clause using words such as *if*, *because*, *although*, *until*, *while*, and *since* ("I'll go to the park if Jesse goes") are usually mastered by age 4.

One way of assessing syntactic development is to look at common grammatical forms and see how children of different ages use them. Here, we examine briefly young children's development of negatives, questions, and passive sentences.

Negatives

Early in the preschool years, children learn the power of negatives. Actually, many problems during the so-called terrible twos spring from children's new knowledge that they can have thoughts and wishes that don't necessarily reflect those of their parents and that they can express these by using negatives. Early use of negatives involves tacking *n* words onto positive sentences, as in "No drink milk" or "Not bath, Mommy." Children sometimes add the negative to the end of a sentence, as in "Drink milk no."

Following this stage, the negative term is moved inside the sentence next to the main verb—for example, "I no do it" or "She no go." Eventually, children learn to use auxiliaries much as adults do and as reflected in sentences such as "I don't want to do it" and "She can't have it." These later, more sophisticated negatives are also associated with longer sentences (L. Bloom, 1993).

Questions

Questions develop from adding a raised intonation at the end of declarative sentences ("Aaron go outside, Mommy?") to more adultlike forms ("Can I go outside, Mommy?"). Sometime during the third year, the *wh* questions begin: "Where Daddy?" and "What's this?" and the all-too-common "Why?" (Van Valin, 2002).

More significant to developmentalists is the child's growing ability to *answer wh* questions. Different *wh* words refer to different parts of speech—*who*, *what*, and *where* refer to people, objects, and locations and are easily answered by young toddlers. For example, "Where's Mommy?" requires a simple response of "Outside" or "In the kitchen." In contrast, *when*, *which*, *how*, and *why* require more difficult concepts and greater language ability. For example, asking a toddler "When did Daddy go to work?" or "Why did you leave the door open?" could result in great frustration for both the adult asking and child trying to answer it (de Villiers & de Villiers, 1978).

Passive Sentences

Late in the preschool years, around age 5 or 6, children learn about passive sentences. With active sentences, the word order tells the story ("John hit the ball"). Passive sentences take away that cue ("The ball was hit by John"), and young preschoolers get confused (Goodz, 1982). Interestingly, children first learn to interpret passive sentences when the verb refers to some observable event, such as "The horse was kicked by the cow." Later, they learn passive sentences with less observable verbs, such as "Tommy was remembered by the teacher."

Passive sentences are used relatively infrequently in English (Hoff, 2014), and they are not typically produced by English-speaking children until 4 or 5 years of age (Budgwig, 1990). However, with languages that make greater use of passive sentences (Inuktitut, K'ich'e Mayan, Sesotho, and Zulu), children 2 to 3 years of age produce them (see Tomasello, 2006).

Syntactic development does not stop at age 5, of course, but the differences between the grammar used by 6- and 7-year-olds and adults are subtle and minor. For instance, school-age children still must master subject-verb agreement (for example, "They were going" instead of "They was going") and the use of personal pronouns (for example, "He and she went" instead of "Him and her went"). But in general, the basic grammatical structure of school-age children's sentences varies little from that of adults.

Semantic Development

Semantics refers to meaning—specifically, the meaning of language terms. Here, however, meaning refers to more than just a simple definition. For example, children must learn not only that *dog* refers to a four-legged family pet called Spot but also to other perceptually similar creatures, who themselves are members of the larger group of mammals and animals. In this section, we look at the development of children's lexicon (basically, vocabulary development) and how it is that children acquire the meaning of language utterances so readily.

Vocabulary Development

Perhaps the simplest indication of children's semantic development is the number of words they know. Children typically say their first words late in the first year of life or shortly thereafter. Early words are sometimes only recognized by family members and usually refer to people in the family (*Mama, Dada*) or important objects. By 6 years of age, most children have a vocabulary of over 10,000 words, which will double by third grade and steadily increase to about 60,000

words by 18 years and 100,000 words by adulthood (Aitchinson, 1994; see Figure 9.4).

Children speak their first words at about 10 to 12 months of age and learn new words at a rate of about 8 to 11 per month. However, at about 18 months of age, or when children have about 50 words in their active vocabulary, the rate at which they learn new words increases substantially, to between 22 and 37 words per month (Benedict, 1979; L. Bloom, 1998). This has been termed the word spurt. Most of the words children learn during this time are nouns, often labels for objects. Some children begin their word spurt shortly after their first birthdays, whereas others don't start until age 2 or later (Mervis & Bertrand, 1994; see Figure 9.4). There has been some debate about whether all children have this word spurt (P. Bloom, 2000; Goldfield & Reznick, 1990), with some research using different methodological procedures suggesting that it might actually be typical for only about 20% of children, with the rest following a more linear, gradual progression of vocabulary development (Ganger & Brent, 2004).

Some research indicates that infants in their second year of life spontaneously look at objects for familiar words (for instance, hearing the word *cup* and then looking at a picture of a cup versus a picture of another object). This ability increases in efficiency from 15 to 20 months of age, and the oldest children are about as fast as adults at doing this (Fernald et al., 1998). In other words, children in the latter part of their second year are getting faster at understanding the words they hear. Other research has shown that even children at 12 to 17 months of age are learning new words at a rapid rate, but for their receptive vocabulary (words they can recognize) rather than for their productive vocabulary (words they can say, or produce) (Schafer

FIGURE 9.4 **Different children show different times of onset of their growth spurt, although most (but not all) children show an abrupt and rapid increase in vocabulary.**

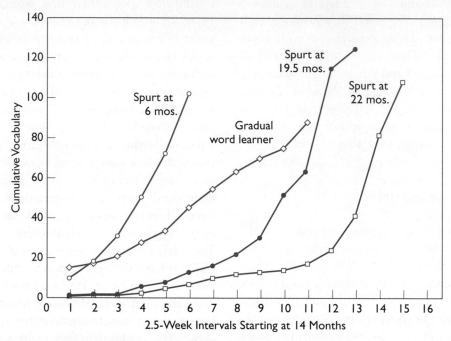

Source: Goldfield, B. A., & Reznick, J. S. (1990). Early lexical acquisition: Rate, content, and the vocabulary spurt. *Journal of Child Language,* 17, 171–184.

& Plunkett, 1998). This all indicates that a toddler's word spurt doesn't appear out of nowhere but has its beginnings in prespeaking processing.

What accounts for children's rapid acquisition of words, specifically nouns, during this time? Some have speculated that children have a set of specific language-processing constraints that kick in at this time to make word learning easy (Carey, 2010; Mervis & Bertrand, 1994). Susan Carey and Elsa Bartlett (1978) labeled the process underlying the word spurt as **fast mapping**. Fast mapping refers to the ability to learn new words based on very little input (that is, with very little exposure). In other words, when encountering a word they don't know, some children are able to guess with surprising accuracy.

Carolyn Mervis and Jacquelyn Bertrand (1994) demonstrated fast mapping by showing children ages 16 to 20 months a set of objects, one of which was unfamiliar to them (for example, a garlic press). They were asked to pick out the items by name, one at a time, and were given a nonsense word for the unfamiliar item (for example, "May I have the bliff?"). Only some of the children were able to learn new words for these unfamiliar items after only a few exposures (the fast mappers). These children were found to have larger vocabularies than the children who did not learn words for these novel items. This latter group of children was seen several months later, after they had gone through their word spurts, and now showed the ability to fast map.

These results indicate that the word spurt is associated with a special processing ability, reflected by fast mapping, in which children map novel words to novel objects for which they do not yet have a name.

Most of the first 50 or so words that children acquire refer to familiar people, toys, and food (K. Nelson, 1974), and this is apparently true across different languages (Caselli et al., 1995). Early words also tend to be those relevant in social interaction (*hello, bye-bye*). Although nouns constitute most of children's first words, verbs begin to increase in frequency following the early noun spurt (K. Nelson, 1973; Snedecker, Geren, & Shafto, 2007).

Constraints on Word Learning

How do children figure out what the words spoken by others refer to? When a child sees a white, long-eared object hopping across the lawn and her father points and says "See the rabbit," how does the child know what he is referring to? Is it the animal itself, the color of the animal, the long ears, the act of hopping, or perhaps the phenomenon of an object moving across one's lawn? There must be a lot of trial-and-error learning in acquiring the meaning of words, of course, yet once children begin their word spurts, they learn words with great speed, suggesting that some **lexical constraints** on word learning exist such that children do not consider all possibilities each time they hear a new word (Markman, 2014).

One proposed lexical constraint is the **whole-object assumption**, in which children, when hearing a word, assume that it refers to the whole object and not to some part of that object. Thus, the child is not likely to think that *rabbit* refers to color, or long ears, or pattern of movement when her father shouts the word. Another proposed constraint is the **taxonomic assumption**, in which children assume that words refer to things that are similar. For example, after associating the word *rabbit* with the white, long-eared creature that hopped across her backyard, a child should assume that the similar-looking, brown animal sitting in the pet store window also goes by the same name. Indeed, it appears that even very young infants are capable of linking speech with categories of objects. In one experiment, 3- to 12-month-old infants viewed a series of images from one object category (e.g., rabbit). For some infants these objects were accompanied by a segment of speech, for others a sequence of sine-wave tones. Next, infants viewed two test images, one from the same category (a new rabbit) and one from a new category (e.g., a fish). Infants should distinguish between the test images if they formed the object category (here, rabbits). By 3 months, infants listening to speech successfully formed categories; those listening to tones failed to form object categories at any age (Ferry, Hespos, & Waxman, 2010). Although musical tones were insufficient to elicit categorization, infants' ability to categorize based on audio input is not entirely restricted to human speech. Indeed, when 3- and 4-month-olds heard lemur calls during object presentation, their categorization mirrors precisely their categorization in response to human speech. However, through the process of perceptual narrowing (described in Chapter 4), the link between categorization and speech has become tuned specifically to human vocalizations by 6 months (Ferry, Hespos, & Waxman, 2013). This suggests an early link between human language and core cognitive processes, including object categorization. Despite differences in 3- and 4-month-olds' exposure to speech (substantial) versus lemur vocalizations (likely none), both signals bestow the same cognitive advantage for categorization.

And finally, the mutual exclusivity assumption holds that different words refer to different things, so that the word *rabbit*, for example, would not overlap with the word *mouse*. For instance, when children are given a novel word and asked to select a referent for that word, they pick the objects they do not already have a word for, realizing, apparently, that the new word is not a synonym for a word they already know but, instead, must refer to a distinct (mutually exclusive) object. For example, in studies by Ellen Markman and Gwyn Wachtel (1988), 3-year-olds who knew the word for *cup*, but not for *tongs*, were asked, "Show me the dax." Eighty percent of children selected the tongs, presumably believing that *dax* referred to the novel object rather than being another word for *cup*. Indeed, this may account for the relationship between the *word spurt* and *fast mapping* that we described. As children's vocabulary increases, the number of objects they can exclude increases as well. Therefore, through a process of elimination, they are more efficient at recognizing new names for new objects.

Children may also get some idea of what a word means by its grammatical form. For instance, in the sentence "Here is a blicket," the use of the determiner *a* indicates that the word *blicket* must be a proper noun or the name of a discrete object or thing, such as a cat, a cookie, or a wink. In contrast, for the sentence "I want some blicket," the use of the adjective *some* indicates that the word *blicket* cannot be a discrete object but is instead a quantity, such as juice, sugar, or peace and quiet (MacWhinney, 2015). This is referred to as syntactic bootstrapping (Gleitman, 1990; Hoff & Naigles, 2002).

In a social species such as ours, however, it would be hard to believe that word learning relied only on these sorts of linguistic constraints, and accordingly, it has been proposed that shared, or joint, attention is an important mechanism that gives rise to word learning (see discussion of the development of shared attention in Chapter 6). For example, children attend to a speaker's gaze and gestures, and they are sensitive to behavioral and emotional cues and to a speaker's intentions when figuring out the referent of an utterance (Baldwin, 1993; Diesendruck & Markson, 2001). Most likely, children use multiple cues, including lexical constraints and social cues, and are also influenced by general mechanisms of memory and attention and conceptual knowledge in deciding what a novel vocal utterance refers to (Callaghan & Corbit, 2015; Hollich, Hirsh-Pasek, & Golinkoff, 2000).

The point most critical for our discussion here is that children are *prepared* to learn words. Whether this preparation comes in the form of lexical constraints or is a by-product of their developing social cognition, children seem *not* to experience language as random noise. Rather, their cognitive systems (or social cognitive systems) are ready to make sense of the connection between things they hear and things they see, making the process of word learning much easier than it would be in the absence of such constraints.

Overextensions and Underextensions

Often, the errors children make in using words provide us with a good indication of their level of semantic development. Researchers who have analyzed these early errors find that one common pattern is to use overextensions—stretching a familiar word beyond its correct meaning (Thompson & Chapman, 1977). For example, children might use the word *doggie* to describe all four-legged creatures, even Daddy when he is on his hands and knees (whether barking or not). Many developmental psychologists argue against the concept of error in children's early language use, pointing out that practices such as use of overextensions result in having adults provide the correct words and, thus, can be very effective learning devices. For example, although children might use the word *doggie* to label a kitten or a horse, they usually perform well when given a set of pictures and asked to choose which one is a doggie (Thompson & Chapman, 1977). By overextending the word *doggie*, however, they often get some expansion or clarification from adults (for example, "That's not a doggie, that's a kitty"), thus receiving more information about language than they would have gotten had they remained silent.

At other times, children will make underextensions—for example, claiming that only their pet Lucy Starbright is a cat and that other felines must go by another name. Underextensions indicate that children's boundary for a category is too restricted. During childhood, children learn to classify words and concepts as adults in their culture do. This process doesn't stop in childhood, however, but continues throughout life. It is likely that none of us has exactly the same meaning for all common concepts used in our native language (K. Nelson, 1996). That speakers of a language are able to make sense of what others say most of the time, however, suggests that most of us have very similar interpretations for the words we use. Both the number of words we know and our understanding of these words change during development. In fact, most changes in language development beyond the age of about 5 years are not in syntax or phonology but in semantics, in the form of vocabulary growth.

Pragmatics

How we actually use language in a social context, or the ability to use language to get things done in the world, is termed pragmatics. *Pragmatics* refers to knowledge about how language can be used and adjusted to fit different circumstances, such as using different tones when speaking to a teacher versus a peer. Knowing the phonology, morphology, syntax, and semantics of language does one little good in communicating unless one can use language appropriately in a social context. For example, although babies are not competent at language use, they are able to communicate to adults when they are hungry, uncomfortable, or unhappy. On the other hand, we all know people who are quite capable of forming proper sentences but who are less adept at truly communicating with people. They find it difficult to express their thoughts properly, explain how to do something, or to refrain from saying things that offend people.

Children must learn a number of conversational principles to become effective communicators (Grice, 1975). Children must learn that messages need to have the right *quantity* of information or be at the proper level of description. For example, a mother might request her son to "put the plates on the table." Such a message is likely to be understood, at the proper level of abstraction. It would be unnecessary and inappropriate for the mother to say, "Open the kitchen cupboard door, remove a dish using two hands, take it into the dining room, and place it at the head of the table where your father usually sits. Repeat the procedure for the place where I usually sit, where your sister usually sits, and where you usually sit." At the other extreme, an instruction to "prepare the table for dinner" might not have enough information in it, especially if the job of putting out silverware usually fell to the boy's sister. Not surprisingly, children are more likely to provide too little rather than too much information when presenting their own messages.

Good messages should have other characteristics, such as being truthful (except for jokes and sarcasm) and relevant to the present context. Also, speakers need to realize the importance of taking turns. Monologues do not make for good conversation.

Beginning early in life, children learn these various conversation principles. For example, toddlers know to watch their listener for signs that they are being understood (J. Wilcox & Webster, 1980). They know that they must be close to their listener to be heard and if they are not close to their listener, that they need to speak louder (Wellman & Lempers, 1977). They also know to clarify their speech when they are being misunderstood (Shwe & Markman, 1997). A responsive listener provides a speaker with nonverbal cues, such as nods, gazes, and smiles, and he or she says "yes" and "uh huh" at appropriate times to make it clear that the message is being understood. These skills increase with age, but even 2-year-olds use many of these tactics when listening to an adult (L. C. Miller, Lechner, & Rugs, 1985). Children also learn that, depending on the context, sometimes a question is not really a question. For example, when a father says "How many times do I have to tell you to leave that alone?" and "Why do you insist on carrying that blanket everywhere?," children learn that the question is a rhetorical one and does not require a serious answer. Children learn from the speaker's tone of voice that these are really statements because even young preschoolers seldom mistake them for real questions (de Villiers & de Villiers, 1978). The reverse is also true: Sometimes questions can be hidden in statements, such as asking a babysitter for a bedtime extension by stating, "Mommy always lets me watch *The Simpsons*" (Reeder, 1981).

Speech Registers: The Case of Black English

One aspect of pragmatics involves using different styles of speech in different situations. For example, children use one style of speech when at home or with their friends and another, more formal style when in school. These different styles are referred to as **speech registers** (Warren & McCloskey, 1997).

When the speech registers, or codes, children use at home and the ones they are expected to use in school differ considerably, there is the potential for educational difficulties. Usually, children from middle-class families speak a "standard" version of the language that is similar to the more formal style used in school. In contrast, children from less affluent homes often speak a nonstandard version of the language that is often appreciably different from the one used in school (see, for example, B. Bernstein, 1971). In the United States, this distinction between social (or home) language and school language among native speakers is often more obvious for children whose home language is described as **Black English** (or sometimes *Ebonics*, or *African American Vernacular English*) (Green, 2002; Rickford, 1999).

Black English is familiar to most Americans, but the term can be somewhat misleading. Although it is used mostly by African Americans, not all African Americans speak it, and many non–African Americans do. Black English has some special rules of pronunciation and syntax (see Table 9.4), the most obvious to many speakers of standard English being the use of the verb *to be*. Unlike standard English, this verb is often not conjugated (for example, "We be" or "She be" rather than "We are" or "She is"), and it sometimes is dropped from a sentence entirely. For instance, the verb *to be* can be left out if the sentence refers to a one-time or unusual occurrence of an event, as in the sentence "He playing tennis" for a person who doesn't usually play tennis. But if the sentence refers to a recurrent event, the verb *to be* is included in the sentence. So, for example, "He be playing tennis" describes a person who regularly plays tennis and is playing tennis at this moment (Warren & McCloskey, 1997). Black English is *not* a simplified or inferior linguistic form of standard English. For the most part, the two share common vocabulary and syntax, both are syntactically complex, and both are used to express complicated ideas and emotions (Green, 2002; Heath, 1989).

Despite the linguistic legitimacy and complexity of Black English, it is not the language of the schools, nor of the mainstream American marketplace. This means that teachers, who usually speak standard English, will often not understand children who speak Black English, and vice versa. Such children can have a difficult time reading text or comprehending directions expressed in standard English. As a result, they might be unjustly classified as less bright than children who speak standard English. For instance, the language abilities of

TABLE 9.4 **Sample differences between standard and Black English.**

Pronunciation and word forms

Consonant Substitutions:	/d/ for initial /th/	"Dey" for "They"
	/f/ or /t/ for final /th/	"toof" for "tooth"
	/v/ for medial /th/	"muvver" for "mother"
Consonant Deletions:	medial /r/	"doing" for "during"
	medial /l/	"hep" for "help"
	final consonants	"doe" for "door"
Syllable Contractions:		"spoze" for "suppose"
Stress on First Syllable in (some) Bisyllabic Words:		"Po'-lice" for "Police"
Hypercorrection:		"Pickted" for "picked"
		"2 childrens" for "2 children"

Sentence structure	**BE**	**SE**
Multiple Negation:	"I ain't done nothing"	"I have not done anything"
Aspect:	"He be crazy"	"He's (usually) crazy"
	"He crazy"	"He's crazy (right now)"

Nonmarking or nonmatching of verb with subject

	"She do all the work"	"She does all the work"
	"Two girl wearing hats"	"Two girls wearing hats"
Double Subjects:	"My daddy, he works..."	"My daddy works..."
Perfective *Done*:	"You done lost your mind"	"You have (already) lost your mind"

Source: From Warren, A. R., & McCloskey, L. A. (1997). Language in social contexts. In J. Berko Gleason (Ed.), *The development of language* (4th ed.). Boston: Allyn & Bacon.

children who speak Black English are often underestimated when they are tested using standard English (Adler, 1990; Wheldall & Joseph, 1986).

There has been substantial debate over how best to instruct children whose home language is Black English. Should they be taught using Black English, the dialect they know best, or should they be taught using standard English—the dialect, or register, of the marketplace? Some studies have shown the more familiar 5- to 8-year-old African American children are with standard English, the better their reading achievement is, making the link between speech register and school success clear (Charity, Scarborough, & Griffin, 2004). Most young speakers of Black English do learn some aspects of standard English and use it in school (DeStefano, 1972). For example, in one study, the classroom speech of 8- to 11-year-old African American children contained more components of standard English than did their speech out of school, indicating that elementary school children are able to switch between social (Black English) and school (standard English) registers (DeStefano, 1972). Yet many African American adolescents tend to *increase* their use of Black English compared with standard English, as use of Black English becomes an important part of their social identity in this period (Delpit, 1990; Delpit & Dowdy, 2002).

The debate about how to educate children whose home language register is different from the language register used by teachers is a controversial one, involving social and political aspects as well as linguistics and educational ones, and no simple answer can—or will—be offered here. But one important thing to remember is that Black English, or any other dialect, is not a linguistically inferior language relative to standard English, just as modern English is neither inferior nor superior to the Elizabethan English used by Shakespeare. One must also keep in mind that, despite Black English's linguistic equivalence to standard English, its use can hinder educability and the opportunity to partake fully in the American economy. Black English is more than just a different language register; it is also a different dialect with some different syntactic and phonological rules compared with standard English. One's language also identifies its user as a member of a social group, and children and adolescents might be reluctant to give up their language style merely for the sake of doing well in school. Ideally, children would master both dialects, just as children might ideally acquire a second language, and have the flexibility to switch between them as the context demands. In such a situation, different dialects would then truly become different registers, to be used when and where appropriate.

Communicative Competence

Although children may have acquired the basic structure of language and know enough words to make most of their wants and feelings known by age 5 or 6, their ability to communicate effectively continues to increase with age. All types of language knowledge (phonology, morphology, syntax, semantics, and pragmatics) are combined in a package called communicative competence (Hymes, 1972). Generally, as children—or, indeed, adults—participate in varied contexts, they become communicatively more competent.

Despite the seeming communicative sophistication of many preschoolers, effective communication between adult and child, or between child and child, is variable. Many messages within the grammatical competence of a child are simply not understood. Also, young children often have difficulty in conveying exactly the right message and are frequently unaware that their message was inadequate. To some extent, their difficulties in communicating effectively can be attributed to other aspects of their cognitive development, in particular to a tendency to assume that other people understand the world exactly as they do. In fact, communication problems are very common among adults and sometimes require therapeutic assistance, such as learning how to be more assertive in one's speech, claiming one's rights in an appropriate manner, or speaking up appropriately when one disagrees with another person.

Early language development in general, and development of conversational skills in particular, does not take place only in the context of adult-child conversations but often in the context of other children, particularly siblings. Firstborn children usually surpass later-born children in both the early development of vocabulary and grammar but not in the development of conversational skills (Hoff, 2014). In fact, later-born children tend to be better than firstborn children in the production of personal pronouns (*I, you*) (Oshima-Takane, Goodz, & Deverensky, 1996). Although reasons for these differences are far from clear, firstborn children's vocabulary and grammar advantages likely stem from getting more of their mothers' exclusive attention. Later-born children, in contrast, seem to take advantage of the richer and more varied speech they hear and of social interactions with both their parents and their older siblings (Hoff, 2014). For example, it has been suggested that later-born children's advantage over firstborns regarding the use of personal pronouns might result from the fact that they are overly exposed to a type of speech between firstborns and mothers that includes more personal pronouns than the speech they each address to them (Oshima-Takane & Robbins, 2003).

Communication and Egocentrism

For years, research and theory in communicative development followed the interpretation of Jean Piaget (1955), who proposed that young children's speech is *egocentric* and *presocial*. In social situations, young children attempt to communicate with others, but their egocentric view of the world often results in speech that does not get the message across to a listener. This failure often does not bother preschool children, however, because in many cases, they are unaware that the message is not being comprehended. Such egocentric speech can be observed in young children in a variety of contexts. Listen to the phone conversation of a 4-year-old. When the voice on the other end of the receiver asked Alese, "What are you wearing today?," Alese responded, "This," while looking down and pointing at her dress. This apparently is not an atypical phone conversation for a preschooler (see Warren & Tate, 1992, for other examples). The conversation of two 5-year-old boys playing together in a sandbox can be interesting. "I drive my truck over here, and then I drive beside your plane and I fill it up with stuff," says one child. In the meantime, the other is saying, "My plane's coming in for a landing. I drop bombs on your truck and crash into it. Boom!" Such a conversation would not be taking place if each child were alone. However, what one child says has little to do with the comments of the other. The two boys are talking *with* each other but not necessarily *to* each other. Piaget labeled such egocentric exchanges collective monologues.

Metacommunication

Do children have any idea that they are sometimes not being understood or that the message they are receiving from someone else is unclear? Research by Carole Beal and John Flavell (1982) indicated that children 5 years of age and younger seem to recognize an inadequate or ambiguous message but seldom act on their uncertainty, behaving as if the message had been understood loud and clear. When kindergarten children were provided with ambiguous instructions for making a block building, for instance, they often looked puzzled and hesitated in selecting the appropriate block. Yet when their building was completed, these children said that it was just like the model (which it was not) and that the instructions had been adequate for reproducing the model (which they had not). Beal and Flavell (1982) found that children's poor performance on these tasks could not be attributed to memory or attentional failures. Rather, their problems were a result of metacognitive deficits; they had "a poor understanding of message quality and its role in determining the success or failure of a communication" (Beal & Flavell, 1982, p. 48).

Another **metacommunication** skill involves children's abilities to monitor their own speech. Again, young children tend to display deficits in this area of metacommunication (for reviews, see Shatz, 1983, and Whitehurst & Sonnenschein, 1985); their speech includes a greater incidence of omissions and ambiguities and requires greater contextual support to be comprehended than does the speech of older children.

One way of assessing children's self-monitoring abilities is to examine the frequency with which they correct their speech by repeating, by including new information, by telling the listener to forget the last thing that was said until later, and so forth. Mary Ann Evans (1985) studied such *verbal repairs* in the speech of kindergarten and second-grade children during classroom show-and-tell sessions. Evans reported that the incidence of verbal repairs was significantly greater for the second-grade

children than for the kindergartners, occurring for 19% of all the utterances by the older children compared with only 7% by the younger. The following is an example of a story by a second-grade girl that includes several verbal repairs:

> We went to—uh me and Don went to Aunt Judy's. And . . . and uh my brother came down on Fri—Friday night, Uh there was a acc—came on the train, And there was an accident. And they thought uh . . . that uh . . . the—there was an accident with a—a van, And they thought—there was pig's blood in it. And they thought there was somebody hurt. But it was the pig. (M. A. Evans, 1985, p. 370)

Evans proposed that the high incidence of self-repairs for the second-grade children relative to the kindergartners reflected an increased ability by the older children to monitor their speech. Evans suggested that as communication skills increase from this point through childhood, the ability to plan and organize one's thoughts improves, resulting in a reduction of verbal repairs into adolescence (see also Sabin et al., 1979). Thus, the incidence of verbal repairs is low in young children's speech because of poor self-monitoring skills, increases during middle childhood as children become increasingly aware of the effectiveness of their speech in conveying a message, and then decreases as other skills, such as planning, improve.

The verbal repairs discussed earlier were made during a monologue, but conversation involves two or more people. One important metacommunication skill that develops over childhood is sensitivity to other people, often reflected in linguistic turn taking. Some researchers have suggested that such turn taking may stem from parent-infant interactions, such as when parents and babies take turns making cooing or babbling sounds (see Snow & Ferguson, 1977). Piaget described such interchanges as *mutual imitation*, with infants imitating adults who are imitating them. The parents are the real imitators here, of course, but the result is bouts of turn taking, with one partner making a sound and the other copying it, until one of them (usually the parent) tires of the routine. Other examples of preverbal turn taking are games such as peek-a-boo (Bruner, 1983) and exchanges during feeding, with the infant learning to take turns with Mom or Dad (it's Mom's turn to put the spoon to my mouth, my turn to eat it and then request more) (see Kaye, 1982). Not surprisingly, children whose mothers are more responsive to their vocalizations speak their first words earlier and have larger vocabularies than children whose mothers are less responsive (Nicely, Tamis-LeMonda, & Bornstein, 1999).

Despite the ample evidence of young children's poor communication skills, preschoolers' language is not as egocentric as Piaget and other early researchers believed. In fact, several researchers have reported clearly nonegocentric use of language in the communication attempts of young children. For example, in M. A. Evans's (1985) study of speech repairs cited earlier, many 5-year-olds displayed at least limited self-monitoring abilities. In other research, Marilyn Shatz and Rochel Gelman (1973) observed the speech of 4-year-old children when they talked to adults, to other 4-year-olds, or to 2-year-olds. Shatz and Gelman found that these children modified their speech to the 2-year-olds, using different tones of voice and shorter sentences, much as adults do. Other research has demonstrated that preschool children show greater metacommunicative competence when the messages are embedded in familiar scripts, such as a trip to the grocery store (Furman & Walden,

1990). Findings such as these, among others (Nadig & Sedivy, 2002; Warren-Leubecker & Bohannon, 1989), suggest that young children have substantial metacommunication skills. As with many newly acquired skills, however, communication abilities seem to develop first in highly specific, familiar situations and are easily disrupted. With age, children display their communication skills in increasingly diverse contexts, generalizing what they know to new and unfamiliar settings.

Section Review

- Phonology refers to the sounds of language and is first reflected in infants' babbling, which varies initially as a function of physical anatomy and later as a function of the language infants hear. *Phonemic awareness* becomes important later in learning to read.
- Morphology refers to the structure of language, specifically words. *Morphemes* (both *free* and *bound*) are the smallest unit of meaning in a language. Children learn rules and *overregularize* irregular words to fit these rules (forming words such as *goed* and *mouses*). The average number of morphemes used in a sentence, or the *mean length of utterance (MLU)*, is one indication of the language complexity of a preschool child. Children use single words, referred to as *holophrases* (or *holophrastic speech*), to convey complex meaning, and early sentences are *telegraphic*, including only high-content words.
- Syntactic development progresses quickly during the preschool years and is reflected by regular, age-related changes in forming negatives, asking questions, and using the passive voice.
- The *lexicon* refers to a mental dictionary, or all the words in a child's vocabulary.
- Semantic development refers to the development of word meaning. Around 18

months of age, children experience a *word spurt*, in which the rate of new word learning (mostly nouns) increases rapidly. Children's *receptive vocabulary* (words they can understand) is greater than their *productive vocabulary* (words they can speak). This has been attributed to *fast mapping*, in which children are able to learn novel words with minimal input. Researchers have proposed the existence of *lexical constraints* to make word learning easier. These include the *whole-word assumption*, the *taxonomic assumption*, the *mutual exclusivity assumption*, and *syntactic bootstrapping*. Infants and young children also likely make use of social cues from speakers, such as gazes, to help them identify the referents to words. Early in development, children often make *overextensions* (applying a word beyond its correct meaning, such as calling all four-legged animals *dog*), but children also sometimes make *underextensions* (incorrectly restricting the use of a term).

- *Pragmatics* refers to knowledge about how language can be used and adjusted to fit different circumstances. Even young children are aware of some basic aspects of pragmatics, although substantial improvements occur with age. *Speech registers* refer to a distinct style of speaking that is used only in specific contexts (for instance, when talking to children, when talking in school). As an example, *Black English*—a dialect of American English used mostly (but not exclusively) by members of the African American community—is characterized by some special rules of pronunciation and syntax.

- *Communicative competence* refers to the various types of language knowledge (*phonology*, *morphology*, *syntax*, *semantics*, and *pragmatics*) combined in a package to yield effective communication. Preschool children often display poor communication and *metacommunication* skills, being less aware of factors that influence comprehension of messages than older children are, and they sometimes speak in *collective monologues* (speaking *with* but not necessarily *to* one another).

Ask Yourself . . .

3. What are the functions of language that motivate children?
4. How does human language differ from the communication systems of other animals?
5. How do infants progress through the stages of phonological development?
6. When do children tend to overregularize morphemes, and what does this tell us about language acquisition?
7. At which age do children demonstrate various aspects of syntax?
8. What is fast mapping, and how might it relate to word learning and the word spurt?
9. What are overextensions and underextensions? What might they tell us about children's understanding of words?
10. What are the pragmatics of language? How might they vary across speech registers? Provide an example.

SOME THEORETICAL PERSPECTIVES OF LANGUAGE DEVELOPMENT

The question central to language acquisition has been the acquisition of syntax. How is it that children make sense of the jumble of sounds that surrounds them to eventually discover the underlying rules of language? Although each of the world's 7,000-plus languages might have some unique features to them, they also all have some things in common with one another. That is, they all possess, at some "deep level," some common aspects of syntax (see MacWhinney, 2015; Pinker, 1994). In this section, we do not intend to cover the intricacies of theories of syntax development in great detail but merely to describe some of the major points of the dominant perspectives so that the reader can get a general idea of how children approach the seemingly complicated task of learning to talk (see Hoff, 2014; MacWhinney, 2015; Tomasello, 2006).

In very general terms, three major types of theories have been postulated to account for language acquisition: (1) behavioral theories, (2) nativist theories, and (3) social-interactionist theories. Behavioral theories were popular in the early and middle part of the last century and proposed, basically, that children learn language like they learn any other complex behavior, through the principles of classical and operant conditioning (Skinner, 1957). Behaviorists emphasized the role of parents as models of, and reinforcers for, language. The behaviorists actually paid relatively little attention to children, who for generations had been producing perfectly understandable original sentences and phrases they could not have possibly learned through conditioning and imitation, such as "all-gone, sticky" to announce that their hands have been washed.

Many claims of the behaviorists have not stood the test of time. For example, although words can be learned through conditioning principles in the laboratory, little evidence suggests that parents use such structured techniques at home; yet almost all children are fluent in their native language before they reach school age. Other research has shown that parents seldom comment to children about the grammatical correctness of their spoken messages, only the meaningfulness of them (R. Brown & Hanlon, 1970), and although new words are obviously learned by imitation, new grammatical forms (such as plurals or the past tense) are typically not imitated until children are able to produce them spontaneously

(L. Bloom, Hood, & Lightbown, 1974). In addition, although 2- and 3-year-old children hear between 5,000 and 7,000 utterances each day, more than 20% of those utterances are incomplete sentence fragments, and only about 15% are in the subject-verb-object form that is standard for English (Cameron-Faulkner, Lieven, & Tomasello, 2003). All this makes it very unlikely that a behavioral theory of language development is adequate. Thus, one way in which children apparently do *not* learn the syntax of their mother tongue is through the conventional rules of classical and operant conditioning.

More recent research, however, has discovered that infants seemingly use a domain-general mechanism of **statistical learning** to discern what is a word and what is not, consistent with some claims of the behavioral position (Aslin, Saffran, & Newport, 1998; Saffran, Aslin, & Newport, 1996). In this context, statistical learning refers to infants essentially keeping track of how often different syllables follow one another and then using this information to determine which sound sequences are meaningful (that is, are words) and which are not. As adults, it might seem obvious how infants segment fluid speech into words. Surely it is because of the breaks, or pauses, between words. However, as Jenny Saffran, Richard Aslin, and Elissa Newport (1996) have shown, there are indeed more pauses *within* words than between words. For example, the phrase "pretty baby" consists of two words, but when spoken, the syllables run together. Figure 9.5 shows a spectrogram of a person's fluent speech when pronouncing part of the sentence "Where is the break between the words?" Note how the pauses offer no reliable cue to word boundary. (If you still don't believe this, listen to speakers of a foreign language and see if you can be certain where one word ends and

FIGURE 9.5 **A spectrogram from the sentence "Where is the break between the words?" taken from fluent spoken speech.**

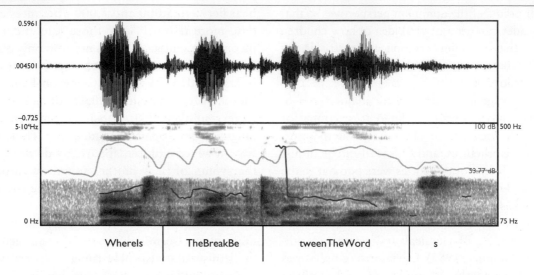

WhereIs | TheBreakBe | tweenTheWord | s

another begins.) If infants can't rely on breaks between words, how do they figure out which sound sequences constitute a word? (Why "pretty baby" and not "pre tyba by"?) The answer is statistical learning. The syllable *pre* precedes *ty* not just in "pretty baby" but also in "pretty boy," "pretty good," and "pretty much a lot of things." Similarly, the syllable *ba* precedes *by* in a variety of utterances, such as "Mama's baby," "happy baby," and "crybaby." In contrast, infants rarely hear the syllable *pre* followed by the syllable *ba* or *by*. Because of the frequency with which infants hear certain syllables uttered in close proximity to one another, they learn that *pretty* is likely one word and *baby* another.

This is certainly a nice idea, but how does one test it? Saffran et al. (1996) used a preference-for-novelty paradigm (see Chapter 4) in which 8-month-old babies heard a series of nonsense words, such as *golabupabikututibubabupugolabu*,

repeatedly over a 2-minute period. If infants engage in statistical learning, they should come to recognize that *gol* is always followed by *abu*, that *ku* is always followed by *tu*, and so on. To test this, after the initial 2-minute exposure, the infants were given a tape consisting of the same syllables but in different orders as well as a tape identical to the one they had heard during the first 2-minute period. Infants preferred to listen to the novel tape, with the same sounds in different orders, indicating that they recognized it was different from the original tape, thus providing evidence for statistical learning of language sounds. Moreover, subsequent research demonstrated that infants' statistical learning is not limited to language sounds but also is found for tones (Saffran et al., 1999). This suggests that statistical learning is a domain-general ability and not one specific to learning language.

Despite evidence of a domain-general language-learning mechanism, most contemporary researchers believe that traditional behavioral accounts of language acquisition are not adequate to account for learning syntax. What are the alternatives? Proponents of nativist theories propose that children are biologically prepared to learn language and do so with special, innate learning mechanisms, not through some domain-general set of learning devices as proposed by the behaviorists. As Steven Pinker (1994) put it, children are born with a *language instinct*. In contrast, proponents of social-interactionist theories blend aspects of the behavioral and nativists perspectives, granting that humans are specially prepared to acquire language but holding that aspects of the environment, especially parents, also might be specially prepared to foster language acquisition, although not to the extent that Skinner and his behaviorist colleagues once believed. For instance, proponents of these theories criticize the findings of Saffran et al. (1996) and Aslin, Saffran, and Newport (1998) by arguing that the pseudolanguage presented to infants was highly simplified compared to natural language. Infants are unlikely to hear the same four words uttered repeatedly for 2 minutes in a natural language learning situation, after all. Therefore, statistical learning may not be sufficient to account for infants' word segmentation in the real world. Indeed, in a slightly modified version of the original experiment, Elizabeth Johnson and Peter Jusczyk (2003) presented infants with pseudowords of varying length and found that this added complexity hindered infants from learning to segment words. That is, infants showed no preference for the novel tape after 2 minutes of familiarization with the original string of nonsense syllables. Johnson and Jusczyk (2003) concluded "that

infants' statistical learning capabilities might be of limited use in a natural language setting" (p. 5) given that "the process of word segmentation in the real world is undoubtedly much more complex than simply tracking the conditional probabilities between syllables" (p. 7).

In the following sections, we outline some of the theory and data associated with nativist and social-interactionist theories of language acquisition. This account is admittedly a cursory one, and readers who would like to pursue some of the ideas mentioned are encouraged to seek out some of the suggested readings at the end of the chapter.

Nativist Perspectives on Language Development

Contemporary nativist perspectives on language development can trace their beginnings to the work of Noam Chomsky (1957). In 1959, Chomsky wrote, in his review of B. F. Skinner's (1957) book *Verbal Behavior*, "I can find no support whatsoever for the doctrine . . . that slow and careful shaping of verbal behavior through differential reinforcement is an absolute necessity" (p. 42). Chomsky's ideas were as radical in one direction as Skinner's were in the other. Instead of viewing language as something that is taught, produced by the child's environment, Chomsky insisted that language is something innate, produced by the child's biology. Chomsky believed that language, as we commonly use the term, is only one part of this process—the surface structure. Infants hear language being spoken around them and end up being able to speak it themselves within a few years. No simple rules of learning or conditioning account adequately for this acquisition, however, because the language children hear is too complicated, and often too ambiguous, for them to discern the rules. Chomsky suggested that another mechanism is necessary to explain why children have the ability to sample the surface structure of the language being spoken around them and then produce it fully and fluently by the age of 3, even creating sentences that they could not have heard before.

Chomsky believed that a second structure of language exists, the **deep structure**, which refers to the underlying meaning of language. This is a more gut-level understanding of language, a "species-specific characteristic . . . latent in the nervous system until kindled by actual language use" (Sacks, 1989, p. 81). According to Chomsky, all human languages share this deep structure, and it is an innate concept in humans, much like the concepts of time and space.

Chomsky believed that humans possess a mental organ, much like a heart or liver, that is dedicated to language use and is located in the brain. This innate neural device (the **language acquisition device**, or **LAD**) imposes order on incoming stimuli. This is not a totally novel concept. As Chomsky points out, a similar function has been found for the visual cortex; it orders incoming visual stimuli into meaningful patterns before passing them on to higher levels of the brain.

Chomsky's ideas about the innateness of language derive from linguistic theory. Other support for the nativism school of thought is less specifically linguistic in nature. For example, more than 40 years ago, Eric Lenneberg (1967) argued that language is a special human ability (that is, not just a result of learning) that has a strong biological basis. Lenneberg noted several characteristics of language as support for this contention, among them the following.

1. *Language is species specific.* Humans are the only species to possess it. Apes can be taught simple sign language comparable with that of a 2-year-old child (Savage-Rumbaugh et al., 1993), and other species certainly do communicate complicated ideas (such as bees' ability to communicate the location of pollen-rich flowers). However, at least as human linguists define it, only humans possess language.

2. *Language is species uniform.* All normal members of the species possess language. Moreover, the complexity of a language is not related to the complexity of a culture's technology. That is, the language of "primitive" people is no more or no less complicated, on average, than is the language of people from information-age societies (Pinker, 1994).

3. *Language is difficult to retard.* Except for children raised in closets or in other severely deprived situations, nearly all children learn to speak. This is true even for many severely intellectually impaired children, whose language is often far in excess of their more general intellectual abilities.

4. *Language develops in a regular sequence.* Children around the world acquire language in about the same way at about the same time. This is similar to the universal sequence of motor development.

5. *There are specific anatomical structures for language.* The structure of the mouth and throat is unique to our species and especially suited for the task of speaking. Equally critical, areas in the brain are dedicated to different aspects of language, and damage to specific areas of the brain can result in very specific types of *aphasia*, or language disability.

6. *There are language disabilities that are genetically based.* Specific language disorders run in families, suggesting that there is a genetic basis for these disorders, with some apparently being controlled by

a dominant gene. For instance, mutations of the FOXP2 gene in humans cause severe speech and language disorders, as was discovered during investigations of the KE family, half of whom suffered a speech and language disorder (M. Gopnik & Crago, 1991).

All this is well and good, but how does it give us a better picture of how children actually learn to talk? What it does is place language in the realm of an important, species-uniform skill that was likely selected in human evolution for its survival value. But saying that language is based in biology doesn't, by itself, tell us a whole lot. We need to look at more specific theories and research to get a better picture of how children acquire language. We do this briefly in the next two sections. First, we examine the neurological basis of brain development. We then look at evidence for universal grammar that all children begin life with and modify until it resembles the language spoken around them. Finally, we review research suggesting that there is a critical period for language—a time when the child is biologically prepared to learn language.

Language and Brain Development

Since the 19th century, scientists have known that certain areas of the brain are associated with aspects of language functioning. Specific areas of the left hemisphere (in right-handed people) are associated with specific language functions, and damage to these areas produces specific language impairment. For example, damage to **Wernicke's area**, located in the temporal lobe, results in problems comprehending speech, although the ability to produce speech is not usually affected. Damage to **Broca's area**, located in the frontal lobes, usually results in problems with speech production. As we mentioned in Chapter 2,

when these areas are damaged in infancy or early in childhood, recovery of language function is often good, and much better than when damage occurs later in life, especially after adolescence (Stiles et al., 2012).

Advances in neuroimaging technologies have permitted scientists to examine how the brain operates when it processes language and, important from our perspective, to look at the neurological basis of language development. For example, Figure 9.6 (from Sakai, 2005) presents two views of the left hemisphere in an adult. Figure 9.6A identifies areas of the brain associated with phonology, semantics, syntax, and sentence comprehension. Other areas of the brain are also involved in language processing, but the areas identified here are domain-specific areas, as hypothesized by nativist theorists, specialized for particular types of language processing. Figure 9.6B shows what Kuniyoshi Sakai (2005) has termed the **grammar center**. The frontal lobe has areas that are specifically related to processing grammatical information. Although these areas are also involved in other types of processing, they appear to represent a domain-specific neural system dedicated to syntactic processing. For instance, Ryuichiro Hashimoto and Sakai (2002) reported that activation of the grammar center was found only when people made syntactic decisions (for example, is a sentence grammatical?); activation was not found during tasks involving verbal short-term memory (for example, recalling a list of words in exact order). This and related work led Sakai (2005) to conclude that "the human left frontal cortex is thus uniquely specialized in the syntactic processes of sentence comprehension, without any counterparts in other animals" (p. 817).

Do children or infants display this same neurological specialization for language? Perhaps

FIGURE 9.6 **Two views of the left hemisphere.** Figure A shows possible networks for various language functions. Figure B shows the grammar center and other areas involved in language, as proposed by Sakai (2005).

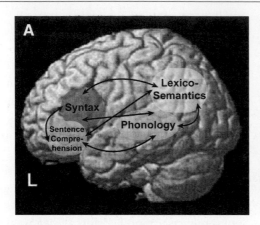
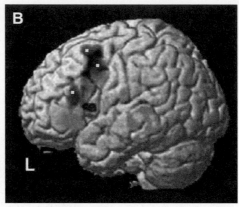

Source: Sakai, K. L. (2005). Language acquisition and brain development. *Science, 310*, 815–919.

not surprisingly, there has been much less neuro-imaging research with children than with adults, making it difficult to provide any definitive answer to the question of when such hemispheric specialization begins. However, research has shown that even the hemispheres of newborns are different, or *lateralized*. For example, neonates show greater electrical activation to language in the left than in the right hemisphere, whereas music and other nonlanguage sounds show the opposite pattern (Molfese & Molfese, 1980, 1985). More recent research has shown that children's brains are especially sensitive to language and that different parts of the brain, in addition to those used to process language in adults' brains, are involved in language learning (specifically, the frontal cerebella and occipital regions) (Redcay, Haist, & Courchesne, 2008).

Evidence also indicates that different areas of the brain are involved when a second language is learned in childhood versus in adolescence or adulthood (Kim et al., 1997; Wartenburger et al., 2003). For example, in one study (Wartenburger et al., 2003), brain images were taken of "early"

and "late" adult bilinguals while they spoke in either their first or second language. For people who had learned their second language during childhood, the same areas of their brains lit up regardless of whether they were using their first or second language. In contrast, different parts of the brains of the late bilinguals were activated when using their first versus their second language (see Figure 9.7). Both the early and late bilinguals in this study reported comparable fluency in their second languages, so differences in language ability between these two groups is not likely to be the cause of this effect. Rather, these results suggest that different parts of the brain and, thus, likely different cognitive processes are involved when a second language is learned early in childhood rather than later.

Scientists have long known that the brain is the source of our language facility and that developmental differences in children's language skills are associated with age-related differences in brain functioning. New technologies are giving us a glimpse of the brain-language relationship during development (see Bialystok, Craik, &

FIGURE 9.7 **Bilingual speakers made grammatical judgments in their second language.** For adults who were highly proficient in both languages (A), different parts of the brain were involved in making grammatical judgments for those who learned their second language late (LAHP; late acquisition, high proficiency) versus those who learned their second language early (EAHP; early acquisition, high proficiency). When considering people only who learned their second language late (B), different areas of the brain were involved for people with high- (LAHP; late acquisition, high proficiency) versus low-language proficiency (LALP; late acquisition; low proficiency) in their second language (B).

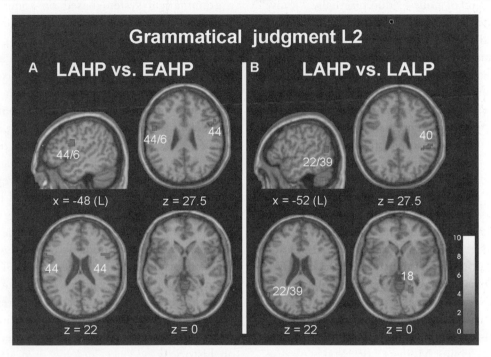

Source: Wartenburger, I., Heekereb, H. R., Abutalebi, J., Cappa, S. F., Villringer, A., & Perani, D. (2003). Early setting of grammatical processing in the bilingual brain. *Neuron, 37*, 159–170.

Luk, 2012), which will give us greater insight into language acquisition and how we can intervene when children (and adults) have language impairments.

Universal Grammar and Language Development

Following the nativist ideas of Chomsky, most linguistic theorists today believe that children around the world acquire language so easily because they possess at birth a mental organ specially designed to perform the job of learning language. In addition to this mental organ (the language acquisition device), infants also have at birth some primitive knowledge about the structure, or syntax, of language. This is referred to as **universal grammar**, which consists of the basic grammatical rules that typify all languages. Having this theory of syntax in their heads from the beginning of life, children do not have to learn all the rules of their language. Rather, they have to examine the language that surrounds them, see how it fits with the universal grammar that resides in their brains, and make the appropriate modifications so that their innate theory of syntax comes to match the theory that people around them use.

Children, of course, don't actually "know" any language (universal or otherwise) at birth, but, the theory goes, they have a set of *principles* and *parameters* that guide their interpretation of speech. Parameters, as used here, refers to aspects of a grammar that vary across languages. For example, although all languages have subjects, some languages require that proper sentences state the subject (as in the English, "I love you"), whereas in other languages, the subject can be expressed as part of the verb, eliminating the necessity of stating the subject (as in the Spanish, "Te amo"). This is a parameter, and children must learn whether their language requires the subject to be explicitly stated (as in English) or not (as in Spanish). One piece of evidence for universal grammar is that English-speaking children's early sentences often resemble those of languages that don't require an explicit subject. This is reflected in children's statements such as "Helping Mommy" or "Make a house" (L. Bloom, Lightbown, & Hood, 1975).

The many similarities across languages argue for a universal grammar. For example, all languages have extensive vocabularies divided into part-of-speech categories that include nouns and verbs; words are organized into phrases that follow a similar underlying rule system (called the X-bar system); all permit movement of grammatical categories, such as the subject-auxiliary inversion used to transform declarative sentences in English into questions (for example, "You are going" transformed to "Are you going?"); and all use word prefixes or suffixes for verbs and nouns (for example, adding the *ed* to make a

verb past tense) (see Hoff, 2014; Pinker, 1994). The similar way and rate that children around the world acquire many of the same grammatical forms is further evidence for a universal grammar.

One source of evidence that children create a grammatical system based on some universal principles comes from pidgins and creoles (Calvin & Bickerton, 2000). When a group of people with a variety of native languages are taken from their homes and transported to a foreign land where they are not given the opportunity to participate in the majority culture or to learn the language of their new homeland, they develop a communication system termed a *pidgin*. Pidgins combine several languages at a rudimentary level and are used to convey necessary information within the group and between the group and its hosts. Word order is often highly variable, and there is little in the way of a grammatical system. (Derek Bickerton [1990] proposed that pidgins might be similar in form to the protolanguage spoken by our ancient ancestors.) In the hands (or mouths) of children, however, pidgins can quickly transform into true languages. Bickerton (1990) documented (based on historical evidence and his own studies of Hawaii creole) how the children of pidgin speakers take the remnants of their parents' language and create a fully developed language in only one generation—a language termed a *creole*. Thus, rather than acquiring language in the typical sense, these children *create* a language. Although there might not be an easy interpretation of this phenomenon, the creation of a creole by children suggests that they possess an intuitive grammar and use it to "correct" the fragmented pidgin spoken by their parents and convert it into a true (and new) language.

Evidence consistent with this hypothesis comes from a study of several cohorts of children creating Nicaraguan Sign Language (*Idioma de Señas de Nicaragua*) (Senghas & Coppola, 2001; Senghas Kita, & Ozyürek, 2004). Deaf education in Nicaragua began only in the 1970s, with deaf children before this time having little contact with one another. There was also no recognized form of Nicaraguan Sign Language for children to be taught. Such a language began to emerge in the 1980s, however, in the Managua school for the deaf and was well developed by the late 1990s. Ann Senghas and Marie Coppola (2001) tested deaf Nicaraguan signers who had first been exposed to Nicaraguan Sign Language as early as 1978 (Cohort 1) or as late as 1990 (Cohort 2) and examined changes in early linguistic structures of the newly emerged sign language. They found that Nicaraguan Sign Language was systematically modified from one cohort of children to the next, with children aged 10 years and younger generating most of the changes. In other words, sequences of children created a new sign language from the incomplete forms used by their predecessors.

The evidence of children "inventing" language suggests that they have been especially prepared by natural selection to make sense of vocal and gestural information for the purpose of communicating. Given that language today is acquired most easily by children, it is likely that language first evolved through the mouths of babes. The physician and science writer M. Lewis Thomas (1993) proposed that our ancient adult ancestors likely used gestures and a few words to express themselves but that it was children who discovered how to put them together into sentences while playing with other children.

Language has many important functions for adults, of course, but it may have had some particularly important functions for ancestral children. For example, John Locke and Barry Bogin (2006; see also Locke, 2009) proposed that language improved communication between young children and their parents at a time when children are particularly in need of assistance—from the ages of about 3 to 7, when children are no longer nursing and can get around their environment relatively well but are still highly dependent on adults for support. Facility with language also may have been particularly important in adolescence, being related to same-sex competition and courtship. These ideas must remain speculative, for we may never know with certainty the adaptive roles that language played for our ancestors. However, we think we can be confident that the greatest adaptive pressures for evolving language were placed on children, not on adults, and that it was the structure and functioning of children's brains that afforded the invention of language and its many advantages.

Is There a Critical Period for Learning Language?

Almost without exception, adults learn things more easily than children do. This is hardly surprising, and this truism is apparent in our school system. Children first starting school are not expected to master complicated material. In fact, some schools of thought argue that expecting too much in the way of intellectual mastery from young children is not only foolish but also emotionally harmful (Elkind, 1987). Young children just don't have the mental capacity to acquire and understand information that an older child or adult has.

One major exception to this, however, is language development. Children are better than adults at acquiring both first and second languages. The cognitive system of the child is seemingly not less efficient in any respect than the adult's when it comes to language learning; in fact, it is well suited to the demands, making immaturity highly adaptive for the important human ability of acquiring language. This has suggested to many that there is a *critical period*, or *sensitive period*, for learning language—that children must be exposed to language early in life if they are ever to master it.

Lenneberg (1967) was the first vocal proponent of a critical period for language acquisition. With age, the nervous system loses its flexibility, so by puberty, the organization of the brain is relatively fixed, making language learning difficult.

In support of Lenneberg's claim, John Locke (1993) proposed four types of evidence for a sensitive period for language acquisition. The first involves people who were socially deprived or isolated during infancy and early childhood, who typically demonstrate only a tenuous mastery of language (particularly syntax) (Curtiss, 1977).

The second and largest body of evidence for a sensitive period comes from studies involving second-language learning, with eventual proficiency in the foreign tongue being related to the age of first exposure. For example, Jacqueline Johnson and Elissa Newport (1989) tested 46 native Chinese or Korean speakers who had immigrated to the United States and learned English as a second language. These people had arrived in the United States at ages ranging from 3 to 39 years and had lived in the United States for between 3 and 26 years when they were tested (all were educated adults). Johnson and Newport reported that their subjects' proficiency in English was related to the age at which they arrived in the United States, not to the number of years they had been speaking the language or to years of formal instruction. Figure 9.8 graphs average scores on a test of grammatical competency (having people determine whether a sentence is properly grammatical) as a function of age of arrival in the United States. As you can see, people who learned their second language early in childhood showed greater proficiency as adults than did people who learned their second language later in childhood. In fact, people who arrived in the United States between the ages of 3 and 7 years had grammatical proficiency comparable with that of native speakers. Grammatical proficiency decreased gradually the older people were when they immigrated to the United States and were first exposed to English (see also Hakuta, Bialystok, & Wiley, 2003). Although it might not be surprising that one maintains an accent when the second language is not learned until the teen years, these data demonstrate that the same holds true for syntax.

A third source of evidence for a sensitive period comes from deaf children who are not exposed to any formal language, spoken or signed, until late in childhood or adolescence.

FIGURE 9.8 **Relationship between age at arrival in the United States and total number of correct answers on a test of English grammar** (data from J. S. Johnson & Newport, 1989, as reported in Newport, 1991).

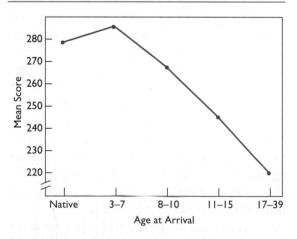

Source: Johnson, J. S., & Newport, E. L. (1989). Critical period effects in second language learning: The influence of maturational state on the acquisition of English as a second language. *Cognitive Psychology, 21,* 60–99. Copyright © 1989 Academic Press. Reprinted with permission.

Newport (1990) performed studies with such a population, evaluating their proficiency in American Sign Language as a function of when they were first exposed to it. The logic here is similar to that in the J. S. Johnson and Newport study (1989), except in this study, American Sign Language is people's first language, not their second. Newport (1990) reported results similar to those she found for second-language learning: Grammatical proficiency is related to age of first exposure to sign language, not to the number of years one has been using the language.

The fourth type of evidence concerns recovery of language function after specific brain damage. We discussed some of this research in Chapter 2. Basically, when the language areas of the left hemisphere are damaged early in life, much plasticity is observed, with other areas of the brain taking over the language function of the destroyed area. This plasticity is reduced with age (see Anderson, Spencer-Smith, & Wood, 2011; Witelson, 1987).

Although much remains to be learned about the nature of language acquisition, it is clear that the cognitive system of the young child is especially suited to language learning—both of a first and a second language. This ability is gradually lost over childhood, and although adults are able to acquire a second language, they rarely attain the same proficiency as achieved when language is acquired in childhood.

But why is language learning easier early in life compared with later? There has been much speculation over the years, with recent data providing evidence permitting researchers to go beyond interesting speculation to real (if still preliminary) theories. One theory proposes that young children acquire language so easily not so much because of their advanced cognitive abilities for processing language but, somewhat counterintuitively, because of their cognitive limitations.

This is called the less-is-more hypothesis. When it comes to cognitive abilities, we naturally think that more is better, but with respect to language development, that may not always be the case. For example, Elisa Newport (1991) proposed that the cognitive limitations of infants and young children simplify the corpus (the body of language they process), thus making the complicated syntactical system of any human language easier to learn. Newport's **less-is-more hypothesis** is based on the ideas of Gerald Turkewitz and Patricia Kenny (1982), who proposed that perceptual limitations in infancy are adaptive, in that they allow one sensory system to develop (hearing, for example) without having to compete for neural resources with another, usually later-developing system (vision, for example). (See Turkewitz and Kenny's ideas of the advantage of perceptual immaturity in infancy, along with some research examples, in Chapter 2.) The principal application of these ideas to language acquisition is that children's limited information-processing abilities reduce the complexity of what they must master, resulting in easier initial acquisition. With success and time, maturationally paced abilities gradually increase, as does language learning.

Newport (1991) observed that children in the early stages of language learning start out slowly—more slowly, in fact, than adults do when learning a second language. This is partly because children perceive and store only component parts of complex stimuli. Their speech starts with single morphemes (usually a single syllable), and they gradually increase the syntactic complexity and the number of units they can control. This is true not only in spontaneous speech but also in imitation. As a result, children are able to extract only limited pieces of the speech stream. Newport claims that because of their limited cognitive abilities, the simplified language that they deal with makes the job of learning language easier. Adults, in contrast, begin learning a second language faster than children do, producing more complex words and sentences. This is because adults more readily perceive and remember the whole, complex stimulus. But the advantage is short-lived. Adults extract more of the language input but are then faced with a more difficult problem of analyzing everything all at once. As a result, adult learners often fail to analyze aspects of language they have acquired in a rote-like fashion, limiting the eventual proficiency they are apt to attain.

Newport (1991) presented the result of a simulation in which a computer program was given aspects of language to "learn." The language-learning mechanism of the computer program was constant, but the size of the input filter was varied, which effectively limited how much the computer program could keep in memory at any one time. This is essentially equivalent to varying the size of a child's short-term store. In the simulation, the input filter became less restricted over repeated trials, similar to the effect that maturation has on the size of the short-term store in developing children (Dempster, 1981). Newport reported that the restricted filter did result in the loss of data for morphology (the smallest units of word meanings, including word endings that denote pluralization and verb tense), making initial learning worse than when a less restricted input filter was used. However, there was greater loss at the whole-word level than at the morphology level (indicating that prefixes and suffixes were often retained). Importantly, the restricted filter resulted in an improvement in the signal-to-noise ratio (that is, the ratio of relevant linguistic information to irrelevant background information). There was also greater loss of data from accidental co-occurrences than from systematic co-occurrences

of form and meaning. This means that with the less restricted filter (reflecting a larger short-term store), many language-irrelevant associations were retained, which impeded rather than facilitated language learning. Newport (1991) concluded, "Overall, then, a learning mechanism with a restricted input filter more successfully acquired a morphology; the same learning mechanism with a less restricted filter, or with no filter at all, entertains too many alternative analyses and cannot uniquely determine which is the better one" (p. 127). Jeffrey Elman (1994) reached a similar conclusion, using a very different connectionist type of computer simulation. Elman used the metaphor of the importance of starting small to describe his findings and suggested that the critical period for language acquisition involves the developmental delay of certain abilities rather than the loss of some language-specific capabilities. Preliminary empirical support for the importance-of-starting-small position comes from evidence that adults learn an artificial grammar faster when presented with smaller units of the language (Kersten & Earles, 2001).

Social-Interactionist Perspectives of Language Development

Most contemporary theorists who adhere to a social-interactionist perspective believe that the nativists have much of the story right. There is an overwhelming (though not unanimous) belief that humans are specially prepared to acquire language, that something akin to universal grammar exists, and that there is a critical period for language. Despite this near consensus, some theorists see the social environment as playing a more important role than some of the more vocal proponents of the nativist camp believe.

As Michael Tomasello (2006) stated, one of the problems in studying language is "that quite often the study of language acquisition has been cut off from the study of children's other cognitive and social skills" (p. 292).

This interactive perspective is well illustrated in the theorizing of Jerome Bruner (1983). He rejected the idea that language is encountered willy-nilly by the child and that the innate LAD abstracts rules from this shower of spoken language. Instead, Bruner believes that language is carefully presented to children by the people around them. Not only is the content selected for the child's current abilities, but the presentation is executed to provide the best possible chance of learning. Others concur, arguing that language has fewer true universals than the nativists propose and that the similarities in language and language acquisition around the world result from the constraints of human cognition and cultural-historical factors (N. Evans & Levinson, 2009). Language is viewed as a powerful social-cognitive tool, used to manipulate other people's attention. It is based on more primitive social processes, such as shared attention, which makes language possible. In this section, we first examine some of the underlying social-cognitive abilities that may make language possible, focusing on infants seeing others as intentional agents. We then look at the role of gestures in early language acquisition and, finally, review research on the role of child-directed speech and how the way adults talk to infants and young children might contribute to language acquisition.

Emergence of Communicative Intentions

By the time toddlers put their first two-word sentence together around 18 months of age, they have been communicating with their parents for some time. Early communication is sometimes vocal (coos, babbles, cries, and holophrastic phrases) and sometimes physical (gestures). As we described in Chapter 6, beginning around 9 months, babies engage in *shared attention*, sharing experiences with other social beings. For example, an infant, while looking at his mother, may vocalize and simultaneously point to the kitty that has gotten into a flowerbed. Behavior like this implies that the infant sees his mother as an *intentional agent*, someone whose actions are based on what she knows and what she wants and who acts deliberately to achieve her goals.

The connection between seeing others as intentional agents and language acquisition may not seem immediately obvious. However, advocates of the social-interactionist perspective argue that shared-attention activities between children and their mothers (and others) provide the context for effective communication in which language will emerge (see Tomasello, 2005, 2006). Parents begin treating their infants as intentional agents, pointing out objects and events to them, before they actually are, and beginning around 9 months of age, babies start to catch on and even initiate such interactions. There is often much language from the parents in these exchanges. For instance, a toddler, while gazing at her mother's eyes, may point to an object on a shelf. Mom in turn may focus on the object, perhaps identifying it ("Oh, those are Mommy's glasses"), explaining something about them ("I need those to read" or "They're not a toy"), asking the child to name them ("Can you say *glasses*?"), or having it lead to other interactions ("Yes, those are Mommy's reading glasses. Do you want to read one of your books?").

Children who engage in shared-attention activities early tend to begin talking early. For example, Malinda Carpenter and her colleagues (Carpenter, Akhtar, & Tomasello, 1998) followed infants from 9 to 15 months of age, observing the social interaction between the infants and their mothers. They found that infants of mothers who engaged them in more shared-attention events and who used language that made some reference to objects that the infants were holding developed better communication skills than infants of less-sharing mothers.

Gestures and Language Development

One prevalent component of shared attention between parents and their infants and toddlers is pointing (as well as gesturing in general). Whereas a more verbal child would use language, infants often use pointing to request things (for example, pointing to a doll with a plaintive look on her face as if to say, "Please hand me my doll"). Some researchers have argued that, by 12 months of age, infants understand that the pointing of others has a specific communication intent (Krehm, Onishi, & Vouloumanos, 2004) and they deliberately use pointing to influence how other people behave and think (Tomasello, Carpenter, & Liszkowski, 2007) and that pointing and gestures more generally serve as a prelinguistic form of communication and predict children's later language development (for a review, see Goldin-Meadow, 2015; Goldin-Meadow & Cook, 2012). Jana Iverson and Susan Goldin-Meadow (2005) named this the *gesture-facilitation hypothesis*. In support of the idea that gestures point the way to language, children who produce word-plus-gesture combinations (for example, say *play* plus pointing to a toy) produce their first two-word utterances sooner than children who don't produce such combinations (Iverson & Goldin-Meadow, 2005). In addition, the more children used gestures at 14 months of age, the larger their vocabularies were at 54 months (M. L. Rowe & Goldin-Meadow, 2009). Of particular interest is the finding that

more affluent parents were more likely to use gestures with their young children than less affluent parents, which in turn affected the gesturing and communication skills of their children, accounting for some of the differences in vocabulary size between children from higher- and lower-socioeconomic-status families (M. L. Rowe & Goldin-Meadow, 2009). We discuss other effects of socioeconomic status on language development shortly.

How do pointing and gestures make language learning easier for children? Susan Goldin-Meadow (2009) suggests at least two possibilities. First, gestures could cause parents to say words and sentences that children need to expand their speaking abilities. For instance, a child may point to a bottle and be told "milk," or she may point to an object in a particular context, say *hat*, and be told "Yes, that's grandpa's hat." In this example, a child's word plus gesture becomes translated by an adult as a complete sentence. Second, children who use gestures tend to perform better on a host of cognitive tasks, and this may also be true for language learning (Goldin-Meadow, 2015). For example, encouraging school-age children to use gestures while solving math problems increases their chances of getting the problems right (Goldin-Meadow, Cook, & Mitchell, 2009).

Treating other people as intentional beings does not *cause* children to develop language, of course. Instead, shared attention and seeing others as intentional beings serve as the social-cognitive foundation for language development. However, a social-interactionist perspective also recognizes that parents present language to children not in a random way but, instead, in a form that is packaged just for them (Bruner, 1983). It is not only *what* adults say to children that is carefully selected but also *how* they say it that facilitates the process of language learning.

Child-Directed Speech

Anyone who has listened to adults, especially mothers, talking to babies knows that this is a special type of speech that is *not* used when talking to other adults. In everyday parlance, this is "baby talk" ("Hi, big girl! How is my baby today? Huh? How is Mama's little angel? Did we just go for a walk? Did you and Mommy just walk around the block? We did, didn't we? Did you see the kitty? Huh? Did we see the little kitty?").

The speech that mothers and others use with infants and young children is special. It is simpler and more redundant than the speech they use with their older children. Such speech was originally termed motherese (Snow, 1972), and subsequent research has revealed additional properties, showing that mothers typically talk to their young children using high-pitched tones, exaggerated modulations, simplified forms of adult words, many questions, and many repetitions (see Hoff, 2014). It is done spontaneously and is found in caregivers around the world (Fernald, 1992; Kuhl et al., 1997). In fact, for many people, it is difficult *not* to speak in these exaggerated ways to young children. When it was recognized that fathers and 4-year-old children use motherese, the new term became child-directed speech (or infant-directed speech when directed specifically to infants). This special form of speech has been characterized as some innate language-transmittal mechanism found in adults—the counterpart to Chomsky's language acquisition device. Bruner (1983) proposed that adults have a device in their brains that responds to infants and young children by automatically altering speech to a more understandable form, and he even suggested an appropriate name, language acquisition support system, or LASS.

Prosodic features of child-directed speech. Beginning in the late 1970s and early 1980s, a new phase of research focused on the prosodic features of speech, or prosody, referring to the ups and downs of the tones and the rhythms of the sounds we make. Instead of counting repetitions or comparing words used in infant-directed (I-D) speech versus adult-directed (A-D) speech, researchers used instruments to measure the acoustic features of different types of speech. I-D speech, compared with A-D speech, was found to have a higher mean frequency, a wider range of frequencies, and a greater incidence of rising frequency contours. In other words, when mothers talk to infants, they use higher tones of voice in general, more high and low tones, and more tones that move from low to high (Fernald & Mazzie, 1991).

In a study of French, Italian, German, Japanese, British, and American families, Anne Fernald and her colleagues (1989) demonstrated typical I-D speech versus A-D speech differences for both mothers and fathers. These same general prosodic features were found for Fijian, Latvian, Comanche, Mandarin Chinese, Japanese, Sinhala, Russian, Thai, and Swedish mothers (see Broesch & Bryant, 2015; Fernald, 1992; C. Fisher & Tokura, 1996; Kitamura et al., 2002; Kuhl et al., 1997). Not all cultures use the same exaggerated style of I-D speech as American mothers (and fathers) frequently do, but as the previous list of cultures suggests, some aspects of I-D speech might be universal (Fernald, 1992; Kuhl et al., 1997).

Why do people use I-D speech when talking to babies? One reason seems to be that this is the way babies "want" to be spoken to (Vouloumanos & Waxman, 2014). They are more attentive to adults who speak to them using I-D rather than A-D speech. For example, 4-month-old infants who have been conditioned to turn their heads to one side or the other to select which of two audio tapes they will listen to will turn their heads to hear I-D speech rather than A-D speech. There is even evidence that 1-month-old infants show a preference for I-D speech (Cooper & Aslin, 1990, 1994).

One interesting study examined mothers of deaf infants signing to their babies and to their deaf friends (Masataka, 1996). Similar to the findings for spoken language, these mothers signed more slowly and used more repetitions and greater exaggerations of movements to their deaf infants than to their deaf adult friends. Moreover, like hearing babies, the deaf infants paid greater attention and made more affective responses to I-D signing than to A-D signing. In a follow-up study, Nobuo Masataka (1998) demonstrated that *hearing* babies who had never been exposed to sign language were also more responsive to the greater exaggerations found in I-D sign language than to A-D sign language, suggesting that this effect is not modality specific (see also O'Neill et al., 2005).

Other studies have shown that when I-D speech styles are used, young infants can discriminate between words that have very slight differences in sounds (D. S. Moore, Spence, & Katz, 1997). For example, research has shown that 1- to 4-month-old infants can discriminate among three-syllable sequences (such as "ma*ra*na" versus "ma*la*na") if the words are spoken using the exaggerated style of I-D speech (Karzon, 1985). In these examples, the middle syllables would be accented in I-D speech ("ma-*ra*-na" and "ma-*la*-na"), which would not be the case in normal adult-to-adult speech (see Trehub, Trainor, & Unyk, 1993). Babies at this age cannot tell the difference between the two words when they are spoken in normal A-D speech.

The results of these and other studies suggest that babies are born ready to process certain types of language, and it is no coincidence that the sing-songy type of speech babies best understand is the same kind of speech that adults and children seem compelled to produce in the presence of an infant. Research has clearly shown that infant-directed speech supports social interactions between infants and their caregivers, promoting language development (Golinkoff et al., 2015).

Role of child-directed speech. Earlier theories about child-directed speech centered on mothers' roles as teachers of language for their children (Hoff-Ginsburg, 1985). Individual differences in how mothers converse with their 1- and 2-year-old children has been related to early aspects of language development (see Hoff, 2000). For example, the more a mother used expansions (that is, expanding a statement that a child made), repetitions, and questions, all of which are frequent in child-directed speech, the better her child's language development overall.

Infant-directed speech also seems to serve other types of development at much earlier ages. Daniel Stern and his colleagues (1983) showed that the prosodic features of mothers' I-D speech peak when the infant is 4 months old, almost half a year before the infant shows any sign of understanding specific words. This has led to the alternative interpretation that I-D speech plays a role not only in syntactic development but also in fundamental cognitive and social capacities, including pattern extraction, categorization, the identification of potential communicative partners, and insight into others' minds (for a review, see Vouloumanos & Waxman, 2014).

For instance, Fernald (1992) suggested that by using specific tones, the mother regulates the infant's emotions, behavior, and attention and conveys her own emotional state to her infant. Fernald divided I-D speech into four acoustical patterns, all of which are used by British, American, German, French, and Italian mothers when talking to their 12-month-old infants. These patterns convey the mother's approval, express prohibition, ask for attention, and provide comfort to the infant. Such nonverbal communication is important in developing secure mother-infant attachment, and according to Locke (1994), "Spoken language piggybacks on this open channel, taking advantage of mother-infant attachment by embedding new information in the same stream of cues" (p. 441). Although children do not need a secure attachment to develop language, evidence suggests that maltreated toddlers have significant delays in language acquisition (Cicchetti, 1989). Fernald's claim is that the evolutionary origins of language may stem from mothers attempting to regulate the emotions of their infants, something that I-D speech continues to do today (see also Trainor, Austin, & Desjardins, 2000). Consistent with Fernald's argument, there is evidence that rhesus-monkey mothers use special vocalizations with their infants that serve to attract and engage their attention, much as human mothers do (Whitham et al., 2007).

In the previous section examining the critical period for language acquisition, we emphasized the importance of starting small. Children's limited information-processing abilities might constrain the amount of information they can process, which in turn might make the task of acquiring language easier. But if young children acquire language best by starting small, this is apparently accomplished not only because of their limited cognitive abilities but also because of the help of adults (Bjorklund & Schwartz, 1996). Adults around the world talk to children using highly repetitive and greatly simplified child-directed speech. As children's language competencies increase, so too does the complexity of language addressed to them. Thus, in the early phases of language acquisition, children receive a highly simplified language corpus. As Richard

Schwartz and I (DB) wrote, "Such modified language, accompanied with young children's limited information-processing abilities, results in children receiving a much reduced body of linguistic evidence from which to extract the phonological, syntactic, and semantic rules of their mother tongue" (Bjorklund & Schwartz, 1996, p. 26). We should also note the large variation in the amount of speech adults in different cultures direct toward infants (Lancy, 2015), yet children from cultures that address little speech directly to children still acquire language pretty much on schedule, making it unlikely that child-directed speech is necessary for language acquisition.

The significance of using simplified child-directed speech for language acquisition is illustrated by anecdotal evidence that simply being exposed to A-D speech is not sufficient to learn a first or second language. For example, a hearing child of deaf parents who was confined to his home because of poor health learned sign language from his parents but could neither speak nor understand spoken English by the age of 3, despite frequently watching television (Moskowitz, 1978). In another example, Dutch children who regularly watched (and frequently preferred) German television often failed to understand the programs and did not achieve appreciable control of the German language (reported in Snow et al., 1976). Not only does watching and listening to television provide no opportunity for social (and language) interaction, but the language heard on television consists almost totally of A-D speech and not the modified (and simplified) child-directed speech that children typically receive from adults.

Research examining the role that child-directed speech plays in development makes it clear that although infants might be biologically prepared to acquire their mother tongue, language development is embedded within the social-emotional context of the family.

Effects of Socioeconomic Status on Language Development

We noted earlier that socioeconomic status (SES) relates to child gestures at 14 months, which is related to later child vocabulary (M. L. Rowe & Goldin-Meadow, 2009), and we've also described the importance of parents' speech in explaining variation in children's linguistic skills (for a thorough review of the effects of SES, see Bornstein & Bradley, 2014; Hoff, 2013). Other research shows that disparities in vocabulary and language processing are evident before children's second birthdays (Fernald, Marchman, & Weisleder, 2013). For instance, in one study, English-learning infants ($n = 48$) were followed longitudinally from 18 to 24 months, using real-time measures of spoken language processing. By 18 months, there was a significant difference in vocabulary and language processing efficiency between infants from higher- and lower-SES families. By age 2, there was a 6-month gap between SES groups in processing skills critical to language development.

Betty Hart and Todd Risley (1995, 2003) conducted a longitudinal study of 42 families from various socioeconomic backgrounds to assess the ways in which daily exchanges between a parent and child shape language and vocabulary development. One key finding was that children derive between 86% and 98% of their vocabulary from their parents' vocabularies by age 3. This underscores the influence of parents' linguistic input during language acquisition. Importantly, then, is the finding that the amount of input parents provided varied substantially by SES. Figure 9.9 presents children's vocabulary growth (9.9A) and the estimated number of words a child hears during the first four years of life (9.9B) as a function of SES. Children from low-income households heard about 616 words per hour, nearly half what children from working-class families heard (around 1,251 words per hour). Children from higher-income professional families heard roughly 2,153 words per hour. Thus, SES was significantly related to how much language exposure children have to draw from. The authors extrapolated these results to determine how many words a child heard by his or her third birthday and discovered a 30 million word difference between children from high-income and low-income families. This disparity was dubbed the thirty million word gap and sparked increased calls for universal preschools and research on how the word gap factors into achievement gaps observed later in school.

However, as we described, research has shown that preschool may not be an early enough intervention. Others have argued that the quantity of words is not as important as the quality. As part of a 4-year longitudinal study of language learning in children (for a full review, see Goldin-Meadow et al., 2014), Janellen Huttenlocher and colleagues (2010) analyzed video tapes of 47 typically developing families, concentrating on the period when children begin to acquire complex syntax (26–46 months). Their sample included children who came from homes that varied in SES and who thus likely received differing amounts and types of linguistic input. Rather than counting words, Huttenlocher and her team analyzed the *variety*, or different types, of words, phrases, and clauses produced by parents and children. Their findings revealed that parents and children both displayed large individual differences in the diversity of their speech, and more diverse parent speech predicted more diverse child speech. They also found an interesting reciprocal relation between parent and child vocabulary, showing that parent speech predicted later child speech but also that earlier child speech predicted later parent speech. However, in the case of syntax, it was only parents who were influencing children, not vice versa. J. Huttenlocher et al.

FIGURE 9.9 **These figures depict aspects of the 30 million word gap.** Figure 9.9A shows the differences in children's vocabulary between 10 and 36 months, as a function of SES. Children from higher SES households demonstrated much larger vocabularies than children from middle/lower SES households and those from households on welfare. Figure 9.9B depicts the extrapolated data estimating the number of words a child hears during the first 4 years of life. As shown, there are substantial differences based on income group.

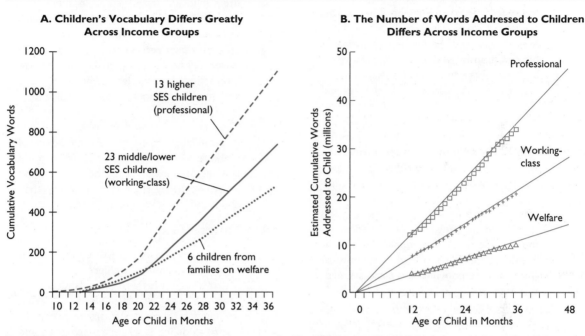

A. Children's Vocabulary Differs Greatly Across Income Groups

B. The Number of Words Addressed to Children Differs Across Income Groups

Source: Hart, B., & Risley, T. R. (2003, Spring). The early catastrophe: The 30 million word gap by age 3. *American Educator,* pp. 4–9.

(2010) also found effects of SES on child speech; children from lower-SES families had less diverse speech than children from families of higher SES. Next, they examined whether this relationship could be accounted for in some way by differences in parent speech. Indeed, it could. When the diversity of parents' speech was considered, the relationship between SES and children's speech became weaker. Huttenlocher and her team also examined *the quantity* of talk parents addressed to their children, as well as the *quality* of this talk. They found that parents of lower SES spoke less to their child than parents of higher SES but that the quality of speech was not influenced by SES. In fact, 14- to

18-month-old children of parents who provided higher-*quality* linguistic experiences had better vocabulary 3 years later. The bottom line from these studies, taken together, is that parents around the world provide children with an environment that promotes communication, motivates language development, and acts as a model for language (Hoff, 2006). Some aspects of parent language input matter for particular features of a child's language acquisition, and some aspects of input vary by SES whereas others do not. Nevertheless, language development cannot be properly understood unless it is viewed as part of the broader human developmental perspective (see Locke, 1993; Tomasello, 2005).

Section Review

- Behavioral theories of language acquisition have generally been discredited, although evidence suggests that infants engage in *statistical learning* to determine which sound sequences are words.
- *Nativist theories* follow the theorizing of Noam Chomsky, who proposed language has both a *surface structure* and a *deep structure*, that children are born with a *language acquisition device (LAD)*, and that exposure to speech is all that is needed for language acquisition.
- *Broca's area* refers to the part of the frontal lobe responsible for language production, whereas *Wernicke's area* refers to the part of the temporal lobe associated with language comprehension.
- Nativist theories argue that the brain is specialized for language, as evidenced by the identification of a *grammar center* in the frontal lobe, and propose an innate *universal grammar* that contains the basic syntactic structure of all human languages.
- Both a first and a second language are learned more easily by younger than by older children, suggesting a critical period for language learning.
- Some support for the nativist position comes from children creating *creoles* from *pidgins* after only one generation.
- Newport's *less-is-more hypothesis* suggests that young children's cognitive limitations actually make it easier for them to acquire a first or second language compared with older children or adults.
- *Social-interactionist theories* explain the interplay among language, cognitive, and social development. Young infants are responsive to human speech and are especially responsive to *infant-directed* (or *child-directed*) *speech*, formerly called *motherese*, which includes a distinctive type of prosody, or rhythm. Bruner suggested that adults have an innate device, which he called the *language acquisition support system*, or *LASS*, that causes them to respond to infants and young children with child-directed speech.
- Parents' use of language has large effects on their children's language development. Several studies have documented differences in vocabulary and language processing efficiency between infants from higher- and lower-SES families. The quality of language interactions seems less affected by SES and may be important to later linguistic abilities.
- The *thirty million word gap* refers to differences in language exposure as a function of a child's SES. Children from high-income families are projected to hear 30 million more words by their third birthday than children from low-income families.

Ask Yourself . . .

11. In what key ways do the three theories of language development differ?
12. What evidence is there that infants acquire language using statistical learning? What evidence is there against this proposal?
13. What evidence is there that children and infants have a neurological specialization for language?
14. How does the concept of universal grammar relate to pidgins and creoles?
15. What is the sensitive period for language development? What evidence supports its existence?
16. How does the less-is-more hypothesis account for language acquisition?
17. In what ways do infants engage in early communication? How does the use of gesture facilitate language development?
18. What are the features of infant-directed speech? What role does it play in language acquisition?
19. What do we know about the relationship between SES and language development? How early do we see these effects?

BILINGUALISM AND SECOND-LANGUAGE LEARNING

Bilingualism—being fluent in two languages—is becoming increasingly common and has long been the norm in some parts of the world. For instance, about 20% of children in the United States do not speak English as a first language, with this figure soaring to between 33% and 43% for some states, such as California, New Mexico, and Texas (Ryan, 2013). In some European countries, such as Switzerland and Luxembourg, it is typical for people to speak three or four languages.

There has been a long debate about the benefits and detriments of bilingualism. Should children be taught a second language early, when they are "primed" to learn language, or will learning a second language before they have mastered their first have long-term negative effects? This question has attracted the attention of psychologists as well as educators, and despite some intense debate (see V. C. M. Gathercole, 2013; Paap, Johnson, & Sawi, 2015), the conclusion seems to be that bilingualism has both costs and benefits (see Bialystok & Craik, 2010).

There are different ways to become bilingual, and there are different types of bilingualism. For example, in **simultaneous bilingualism**, children are exposed from birth to two languages. By contrast, in **sequential bilingualism**, children learn a second language *after* mastering their first. Simultaneous bilinguals generally acquire the two languages separately and show relatively little interference from either language (see de Houwer, 1995; Hakuta & García, 1989). Children who are learning two languages at the same time do make some temporary mistakes, such as when they apply a rule from one language to their speech in another. For example, in Spanish, the adjective comes after the noun ("flor roja") whereas in English the order is reversed ("red flower"). It would not be unusual to hear a Spanish/English-speaking child say "flower red" or "roja flor" as he or she learns the two languages together. Moreover, simultaneous bilingual children often have smaller vocabularies in both languages and a slight delay in syntactic development compared with monolingual children, but by the age of 8 or so, there are typically no differences between them and monolingual children (V. C. M. Gathercole, 2013). Bilinguals of all ages are also slower than monolinguals at retrieving individual words from their long-term memories (Bialystok, Craik, & Luk, 2008).

Learning two languages, either simultaneously or sequentially, requires more effort than learning one (Díaz, 1983; Pearson et al., 1997). But even with the greater effort and, for sequential bilinguals, the developmental lag in vocabulary and syntactic development, there are many benefits. Bilinguals are better at automatically processing sound in general (such as music and fundamental frequencies; Krizman et al., 2012) and can recognize a wider range of phonemes than monolinguals (Bosch & Sebastián-Gallés, 2001; MacWhinney, 2015). They often develop a greater sensitivity toward the cultural values and the speakers of both the languages they have mastered (Pérez, 2004; Snow & Yusun Kang, 2006). Bilingual children and adults display higher levels of metalinguistic awareness than monolingual children, which has been linked to greater proficiency in reading and writing.

One interesting area in which bilinguals seem to have an advantage is in terms of executive function, particularly on tasks that demand flexible thinking (Bialystok, 2011; Bialystok &

Feng, 2011; A. Prior & MacWhinney, 2010). Bilinguals must manage two languages at the same time, ensuring that one does not interfere with the other one, and this requires significant attentional control. As a result, simultaneous bilingual children display enhanced levels of executive control (see Chapter 7; Bialystok, 2011; Bialystok & Craik, 2010; Crivello et al., 2016), and such bilingualism postpones the deterioration of executive function in the elderly (Bialystok et al., 2014; Woumans et al., 2015). Perhaps related to their greater executive control, 3-year-old bilingual children have been shown to perform better on theory-of-mind tasks compared to monolingual children (Kovács, 2009).

Interestingly, even preverbal infants growing up in bilingual versus monolingual homes show some executive-function advantage (Kovács & Mehler, 2009; L. Singh et al., 2015). For example, in a series of three studies by Ágnes Melinda Kovács and Jacques Mehler (2009), 7-month-old infants from bilingual and monolingual homes learned to associate either a verbal nonsense word or a visual cue (for instance, ♦♦♣) with the appearance of a reward (dancing puppets) at a specific location (to their left or right). Both groups of infants learned these associations quickly, after which the rules were changed so that infants now had to look toward the *opposite* side than had been previously rewarded. This requires inhibiting a previously rewarded behavior, an important component in executive function. Infants from bilingual homes showed increased performance on these postswitch trials with experience (that is, they increasingly looked in the right direction with practice), unlike the infants from monolingual homes, whose performance never improved with experience. The authors of this study argued that even before children can speak, having to process information from two languages results in enhancements of executive function.

Bilingual children, however, are a large and diverse group, and a number of factors affect the acquisition of a second language, making it difficult to draw too many definite conclusions. For instance, the age when a child is exposed to a second language influences eventual proficiency. As discussed earlier in this chapter, when learning the second language is begun during the preschool years, pronunciation and complex grammatical forms are mastered more easily than if learning the second language is begun later (J. S. Johnson & Newport, 1989). How similar the two languages are may also affect the ease of learning the second language. For example, English-speaking children learning Japanese may experience more difficulty than English-speaking children learning German, because Japanese and English are linguistically more different than German and English (Bialystok & Hakuta, 1994; Snow & Yusun Kang, 2006).

How well children have mastered the first language before starting on the second seems also to be important in the eventual proficiency of a second language. When young children arrive in a country and are exposed to a new language for the first time, their initial exposure to the second language is often in school. Such a scenario presents the possibility of semilingualism, or the lack of mastery of both languages. This can influence cognitive development, school achievement, and social adjustment (Argynbayev, Kabylbekova, & Yaylaci, 2014; Ovando, 2003). However, when children master their first language and the second language is as highly valued as the first in social contexts, as is the case in Canada with French and English, this negative impact is greatly minimized or absent (Genesee, 2003; Turnbull, Hart, & Lapkin, 2003).

Section Review

- *Bilingualism* refers to people who speak two languages.
- *Simultaneous bilingualism* refers to children who are exposed to two languages from birth, whereas *sequential bilingualism* refers to children who learn a second language after mastering the first. For sequential bilinguals, there is generally a developmental lag of 3 to 5 years before children become proficient in their second language.
- When children immigrate to a country in which the dominant language is different from their native language, there is the possibility of developing *semilingualism*, which refers to the lack of mastery of both languages.

Ask Yourself . . .

20. In what ways do simultaneous bilinguals and sequential bilinguals differ?
21. Why might bilinguals have better executive-function abilities?
22. When does semilingualism occur? How can it be prevented?

SEX DIFFERENCES IN LANGUAGE ACQUISITION

There is a persistent belief that females are better than males at language and language-related skills. For example, girls and women are believed to be better readers than boys and men, with this difference appearing early and lasting into adulthood. Research pertinent to this question is examined in Chapter 11. Here, we review research concerning possible sex differences in the acquisition of a first language.

Some researchers have reported faster rates of language acquisition for girls (M. Eriksson et al., 2012; Galsworthy et al., 2000). Other studies have failed to observe any significant sex differences (McCarthy, 1954), and some find a difference favoring young girls for spontaneous speech but not on standardized tests (Morisset, Barnard, & Booth, 1995). In related research, Michael Lewis and his colleagues reported greater vocalization by infant girls than by infant boys. For example, 3-month-old girls were found to vocalize more than boys in response to their mother's invitation to talk (M. Lewis & Freedle, 1973), and infant girls between the ages 3 to 13 months vocalized more in response to facial stimuli than did boys of the same age (M. Lewis, 1969). In a meta-analysis summarizing the effects reported in more than 30 studies looking at differences in how mothers talked with their sons and their daughters, Campbell Leaper, Kristin Anderson, and Paul Sanders (1998) reported moderate sex differences, with mothers talking more and using more supportive speech with their daughters than with their sons. Other research has shown that mothers talk about different things with their sons than with their daughters. For example, examining the emotion talk of women to their 2-, 3-, and 4-year-old children, mothers were more apt to explain emotions to boys rather than just label them, but they showed no difference in the use of explanations and labels with their daughters (Cervantes & Callanan, 1998). Of equal interest, even the youngest girls in this study talked about emotions quite frequently and as often as older girls. In contrast, emotion talk was less frequent for the youngest boys but increased with age.

Others have proposed that the sex differences sometimes found in language acquisition are related to cultural factors. In Greece, for example, where boys are often valued more than girls, there is evidence that boys rather than girls are more vocally responsive (Hofstede & Hofstede, 2001; Roe et al., 1985). Perhaps the sex differences favoring girls in the United States can be attributed to different ways in which girls and boys are spoken to rather than to endogenous factors. Recall from Chapter 8 on memory development that parents use a more elaborative conversation style with their daughters than with their sons when prompting them to remember past events (Reese, Haden, & Fivush, 1996). Such differences are related to sex differences in event memory (girls' event memory being better than boys') and are consistent with the hypothesis that differences in cultural practices are responsible, in part, for sex differences in rate of language acquisition (Roe et al., 1985).

Some sex differences in early language that are *not* related to differences in how parents talk to boys and girls, however, are also found. Catherine Haden, Rochel Haine, and Robyn Fivush (1997) reported that girls 40 to 70 months of age produced longer and more structured narratives than did boys of the same age; however, unlike with other aspects of language presented to boys and girls, these authors found no differences in how parents used narratives to talk about past experiences with their sons and daughters. These results indicate that girls are more advanced in their narrative production than boys are and that a simple socialization explanation cannot adequately account for these differences. Similarly, in a behavior-genetics study examining more than 3,000 pairs of 2-year-old twins (Galsworthy et al., 2000), sex differences favoring girls in verbal ability were found (although they accounted for only 3% of the variance). Interestingly, the heritability of verbal ability was higher for the boys than for the girls. In other research, 18- and 24-month-old girls had significantly larger vocabularies than boys did, and this difference was related to exposure to fetal testosterone—that is, the greater exposure to testosterone (a male hormone) prenatally, the smaller a child's vocabulary tended to be (Lutchmaya, Baron-Cohen, & Raggatt, 2002). Another hypothesis is that boys are more variable than girls in verbal abilities (see Arden & Plomin, 2006), which might lead to a lower mean performance in measured language skills among boys compared to girls and could account for an overrepresentation of boys in the lower percentiles of tests for language delay. Marten Eriksson and colleagues (2012) examined this hypothesis and others by comparing the early use of gestures, as well as receptive and expressive vocabularies, for 13,783 infants and toddlers from 10 different non–English speaking language communities. They found that girls are generally ahead of boys in the use of communicative gestures, word production, and word combination and that this gap widens until age 2. Importantly, the differences between boys and girls did not vary across language communities, despite observed variation in the social and linguistic environments of the 10 languages (including their valuation of masculinity and distribution of gender roles). These findings provide further evidence that sex difference in at least some aspects of language development were not related to general cultural differences in the ways boys and girls were raised or spoken to. In addition, boys were not found to be more variable in their linguistic development than girls prior to the age of 2, disproving the greater male variability hypothesis. These findings suggest that some sex differences in language may be due to more robust factors than sociocultural differences.

As of this writing, the question of sex differences in language acquisition is unanswered.

Research suggests that girls might be more vocal than boys early in infancy and that this difference leads to a subsequent advantage in learning a first language. However, other research suggests that whatever small advantage in language acquisition girls do hold is a function of cultural practices, with boys in some cultures displaying the typical "feminine" pattern of faster language acquisition we've come to expect in our own.

Section Review

- Sex differences in language acquisition favoring girls have occasionally been found.
- Some evidence suggests that different cultural practices regarding how boys and girls are treated play an important role in possible sex differences in language acquisition, whereas other evidence fails to confirm cultural differences.

Ask Yourself . . .

23. Given the evidence, what do you think accounts for the sex differences in children's language abilities?

LANGUAGE AND THOUGHT

Although most laypeople would agree that language is not only a system of communication but also an important vehicle for thought, most theorists of language would likely disagree. Language is used to *express* thought, both to others and to ourselves, but it is not thought itself (Pinker, 1994). For example, we frequently have a difficult time putting thoughts into words. We often have an image in our head, or understand a problem (perhaps a math problem) intuitively, but have a difficult time expressing it. It was once

believed that deaf children who had not been taught sign language were intellectually impaired because they lacked language. What these children truly lacked, however, was a way to communicate their knowledge and intelligence, and when tested in ways that overcame their communication difficulties, they showed typical rates of cognitive development in terms of Piaget's stages (Furth, 1964). Researchers also have demonstrated that 12-month-old infants use pointing to communicate about absent entities, something that is usually handled by language (that is, talking about something that is not in one's immediate perception). Chimpanzees do not use pointing in this way (nor language, of course), suggesting that young children's underlying cognitive abilities, and not language, are what allows them to communicate about absent entities (Liszkowski et al., 2009).

Some developmental psychologists have taken a different perspective. For example, theorists such as Bruner (1966) have argued that children's thinking is transformed in early childhood when they develop the ability to use language as a conceptual tool; moreover, the use of language in social situations facilitates this transformation. When a child begins to use language to communicate ideas and thoughts (in other words, mental representations) to other people, his or her language is in turn structuring these mental representations. This perspective is probably best represented by the work of Katherine Nelson (1993, 1996) and was discussed with respect to the development of autobiographical memory in Chapter 8.

Along similar lines, Soviet psychologist Lev Vygotsky (1962) proposed that the relationship between language and thought changes across development. Vygotsky believed that thought and speech are initially independent. In development, however, thought and speech merge, with thought becoming verbal and speech rational. This developmental relationship between language and thought, particularly during the stages in which the two cross, has attracted the interest of psychologists.

Vygotsky was particularly interested in the role of egocentric speech in affecting children's thought. Egocentric speech, also known as private speech, can be thought of as speech for self. This overt language is carried out with apparent satisfaction even though it does not function to communicate. Anyone who has spent much time around 4-year-olds is likely to have experienced their tendency to talk about anything and everything, regardless of whether anyone is really listening. Private speech can be observed both when children are alone and in social settings. Vygotsky believed that private speech plays a specific role in affecting children's thought and problem solving. Language can guide children's behavior (and, thus, their thought), but young children cannot yet use language covertly, in their heads. To benefit from the self-regulatory function of language, young children must essentially talk to themselves, using their speech to guide thought and behavior. With development, the self-regulatory function of language changes so that children can direct their behavior using inner speech. In other words, private speech serves as a cognitive self-guidance system and then goes "underground" as covert verbal thought. (Vygotsky contrasted his position with that of Piaget, 1955, who believed that private speech plays no functional role in cognitive development but is merely symptomatic of ongoing mental activity.)

Several studies have assessed aspects of Vygotsky's theory of private speech, and most generally find support for his ideas (Kohlberg, Yaeger, & Hjertholm, 1968; Lidstone, Meins, and Fernyhough, 2011; see Diaz & Berk, 2014,

Young children have a difficult time keeping their thoughts to themselves.

DENNIS THE MENACE

"I'M GONNA HAVE TO STOP THINKIN' OUT LOUD."

Source: *Dennis the Menace* used by permission of Hank Ketcham and © 1986 by North America Syndicate.

for a review). In fact, adolescents and adults still sometimes talk to themselves when facing a difficult task, but it is questionable whether such speech actually helps their performance (Alderson-Day & Fernyhough, 2015; R. Duncan & Tarulli, 2009).

Other research has shown that school-age children use private speech to help them solve a host of school-type tasks, such as addition and subtraction problems (Berk, 1986). For example, Laura Berk (1986) observed first- and third-grade children during daily math periods for 4 months. Various forms of private speech were recorded (for example, task-irrelevant, self-stimulating speech; task-relevant, externalized speech; and task-relevant, external manifestations of inner speech, such as lip movements), as were other aspects of their overt behavior (movement, pointing to objects to help them add) and measures of their task performance (daily math papers and achievement and IQ tests). Berk reported high levels of private speech in this sample of children that changed with age. The self-guidance function of private speech varied with age and eventually gave way to covert, inner speech. Most of the children's task-relevant, externalized speech was used to guide their problem solving, with third-graders using more internalized forms of speech (for example, inaudible mutterings, lip and tongue movements) to facilitate their performance. The total amount of private speech was positively related to intelligence at Grade 1 but not at Grade 3. This indicates that brighter children not only begin to use private speech to guide their problem solving earlier than less bright children but also stop sooner, as thought goes underground in the form of inner speech (see also Berk & Landau, 1993; Kohlberg et al., 1968).

Also consistent with Vygotsky's claims, children rely more heavily on private speech when facing difficult rather than easy tasks and when deciding how to proceed after making errors (Berk, 1992), and their performance often improves after turning to self-instruction (Behrend, Rosengren, & Perlmutter, 1989; Berk & Spuhl, 1995). Moreover, private speech does eventually go underground, progressing from words and phrases to whispers and mutterings and then to inner speech (Bivens & Berk, 1990). In related research, children who are asked to generate explicit explanations for problems they are solving (for example, "7 + 2 - 2 = 7, because you add 2 and take it away, so you don't really have to add and subtract all the numbers, you just know that it's 7") perform better on a variety of academic-type tasks than children who are not prompted to provide such self-directed speech (Rittle-Johnson, 2006; Siegler, 2002). In fact, when children are prevented from using private and inner speech, they perform more poorly on tasks that require planning (Lidstone, Meins, & Fernyhough, 2010). Although the use of private speech on problem-solving tasks persists into adolescence, such speech is not associated with improved task performance for these older children (Winsler, 2003).

The debate about the relationship between language and thought extends far beyond the role of private speech in children's problem solving (see Winsler, Fernyhough, & Montero, 2009). However, the developmental association between the two can be informative. For instance, telling a young reader to "Read quietly to yourself!" may not be worthwhile because beginning readers may not be able to read quietly in their heads. In fact, some researchers have suggested that preschool children do not believe that inner speech is possible, believing instead that a person cannot "talk to himself" and think at the same time. When preschool children are prompted to use inner speech (for example, "Silently think about how your name sounds"), they are just as likely to say that they had a *picture* of their name in their heads while thinking as to say that they said their names in their heads (Flavell et al., 1997). Although it seems unlikely that preschool children never engage in inner speech, it is difficult to know when the monologue that seems to run constantly through people's minds begins. However, it appears that the inner life of young children is not as (linguistically) rich as that of adults.

Although some general discrepancies from Vygotsky's theory have been reported, the existing research suggests that there is, indeed, a developmental relationship between language and thought, along the lines that Vygotsky and his colleagues hypothesized.

Section Review

- Vygotsky proposed that *egocentric* (or *private*) *speech* has a special role in guiding children's thinking and behavior.
- Young children's private speech serves as a *cognitive self-guidance system* and is eventually replaced by covert verbal thought, or *inner speech*. Recent research provides support for Vygotsky's theory.

Ask Yourself . . .

24. How does egocentric speech guide children's thinking and behavior?

KEY TERMS AND CONCEPTS

bilingualism
Black English
bound morphemes
Broca's area
child-directed speech
cognitive self-guidance system
collective monologues
communicative competence
creoles
deep structure
egocentric speech
fast mapping
free morphemes
grammar center
holophrases (or holophrastic speech)
infant-directed speech
inner speech
language acquisition device (LAD)

language acquisition support system (LASS)
less-is-more hypothesis
lexical constraints
lexicon
mean length of utterance (MLU)
metacommunication
morpheme
morphology
motherese
mutual exclusivity assumption
nativist theories
overextensions
overregularization
phonemic awareness
phonology
pidgins
pragmatics
private speech

productive vocabulary
receptive vocabulary
semantics
semilingualism
sequential bilingualism
simultaneous bilingualism
social-interactionist theories
speech registers
statistical learning
surface structure
syntactic bootstrapping
syntax
taxonomic assumption
telegraphic speech
thirty million word gap
underextensions
universal grammar
Wernicke's area
whole-object assumption
word spurt

SUGGESTED READINGS

Scholarly Works

Hoff, E. (2014). *Language development* (5th ed.). Belmont, CA: Wadsworth. This textbook presents an overview of all aspects of language development, from linguistic theory to brain development.

Senghas, A., & Coppola, M. (2001). Children creating language: How Nicaraguan Sign Language acquired a spatial grammar. *Psychological Science, 12,* 323–326. This is a report of a research project looking at children's spontaneous invention of a sign language. In addition to providing fodder for debates about the nature of language development, it is an excellent demonstration of a naturalistic experiment.

Seyfarth, R. M., Cheney, D. L., & Marler, P. (1980). **Monkey responses to three different alarm calls: Evidence of predator classification and semantic communication.** *Science, 210*(4471), 801–803. This short, classic paper describes the use of three different alarm calls by wild vervet monkeys to differentiate three distinct species of predators. The authors discuss the development of this naming and its relevance to the evolution and development of human language.

Tomasello, M. (2005). *Constructing a language: A usage-based theory of language acquisition.* **Cambridge, MA: Harvard University Press.** Michael Tomasello presents a social-constructivist approach to language as a contrast to the nativist approach advocated by people such as Noam Chomsky and Steven Pinker.

Reading for Personal Interest

Karmiloff, K., & Karmiloff-Smith, K. (2002). *Pathways to language: From fetus to adolescent.* **Cambridge, MA: Harvard University Press.** This is a comprehensive, well-grounded, and easy-to-read book about the state of the art in children's language development. The book is part of *The Developmental Child Series*, addressed to a general audience.

Pinker, S. (1994). *The language instinct: How the mind creates language.* **New York: Morrow.** This popular book (but *not* a book of pop psychology) presents the nativist position of language acquisition perhaps more clearly and thoroughly than any other source. Whether you agree with Pinker's arguments or not, it provides an excellent look at the issues and data dealing with the child's acquisition of language.

Pinker, S. (2007). *The stuff of thought: Language as a window into human nature.* **New York: Penguin Group.** This is a very readable book that examines how our words offer insight to our underlying nature. Here, Pinker covers metaphors, swearing, pop songs, jokes, and the pragmatic side of language. Throughout the book he refers to research on children's developing language skills. He also critically reviews theories of language and thought.

Talking Twin Boys. Part 2 (https://www.youtube.com/watch?v=_JmA2ClUvUY). This is the video of twin infants we referred to earlier in the chapter. As you can observe, although the sound of these infants' babbling does not approximate speech, their intonation does. Their gestures are also very communicative. This is one example of how infants begin to "converse" in many ways that do not involve words but that do involve the conventions of speech.

10 | SOCIAL COGNITION

A 4-year-old boy eating at an Italian restaurant with his parents and another couple noticed that his father and the other gentleman had ordered pizza, whereas his mother had ordered lasagna. In the car on the way home, the child announced that he had figured it out: "Men eat pizza and women don't."

What is this child thinking? What does eating pizza have to do with being a man or a woman, and why is this topic even important to this child? It is important because being male or female is a distinction made by people in all societies, and it is one that is acquired over the course of childhood. It is an example of social cognition—thinking about one's own thoughts, feelings, motives, and behaviors as well as those of other people (Olson & Dweck, 2009).

As cognitive psychologists, we tend to believe that most aspects of human behavior are a function of one's cognitions. We find this especially easy to believe for the social behavior of children, who can only be as social as their level of cognitive functioning will permit. One cannot expect children to behave in a socially appropriate way if they cannot understand the social relationships among individuals and the ramifications of behaving in one way rather than another.

Many of a child's day-to-day activities involve interactions with people. These interactions require thought. Children must make evaluations of social situations and must understand their relationships with other people in a particular context. This requires an appreciation of who they are as social beings and who their fellow interactants are. It involves anticipating the thoughts and feelings of others and the execution of social "strategies." These strategies can be aimed at facilitating the formation of relationships, such as mother-infant attachment or playground friendships, or the successful completion of some cooperative task, such as jumping rope or playing baseball.

There are few narrow topics in cognitive development. Research into memory, perception, and language involves many subtopics, with numerous facets to each. The number of topics subsumed under the rubric of social cognition, however, is even greater. Any thinking involved in any social setting or about any social phenomenon is a potential area of inquiry. And there is not necessarily a hard line drawn between social and nonsocial cognition. For example, much of the research we reviewed on theory of mind in Chapter 6 could just as easily have been included in a chapter on social cognition.

Social cognition represents *folk psychology*, people's intuitive understanding of themselves and other people, as we discussed in Chapter 6. Recall that David Geary (2005) proposed that children are born with *skeletal competencies* within the domain of folk psychology and that these competencies become fleshed out with experience. He also proposed that folk psychology was organized in a hierarchy, with three major subgroups, or domains (self, individual, group), each having more specific components. For example, the *self* subgroup includes a component dealing with self-awareness; the *individual* subgroup has components for reading facial expressions, language, and theory of mind; and the *group* subgroup has components for relating to kin and for making distinctions between in-groups versus out-groups. Although we do not follow Geary's model rigidly here, our focus in this chapter is on how children come

to be functional social beings in their culture, based on the development of their intuitive folk psychologies.

As a specific example of children being "prepared" by natural selection to deal with social situations (that is, of children possessing skeletal competencies, to use Geary's term), consider the proposal of evolutionary psychologists Leda Cosmides and John Tooby (1992). They claimed that one important form of social reasoning involves social exchanges—or "the art of the deal," as Donald Trump might call it. We make social contracts all the time. They are central to normal functioning in everyday life. Some of these contracts are formal, as when we agree to make monthly payments to someone who sells us his car, and some are informal, as when we lend someone our notes for a class she missed and expect that she will reciprocate if the need arises. Sometimes the deals we make "work," but other times they do not. We get cheated when a person defaults on the car payment (or neglects to tell us about the series of accidents the car had been in) or refuses to share her notes when we miss a class. Cosmides and Tooby (1992) found that adults were particularly sensitive in identifying when rules were broken in a social contract, much more so than when the same rules were presented in a nonsocial or abstract way.

Forming such contracts and avoiding social cheaters involves complicated cognition and is beyond the abilities of young children. However, social-contract problems reflect a form of *deontic reasoning*, which is reasoning about what one may, should, or ought to do, and this type of reasoning has been found in young children (Cummins, 1996, 2013; Keller et al., 2004). For instance, in one study (see Experiment 4 in Harris & Nuñez, 1996), 3- and 4-year-old children were told a series of short stories, some of which involved breaking a rule and some of which had the same content but without breaking any rule. For instance, in the deontic condition (or *prescriptive* condition, to use the authors' term), children were told, "One day Carol wants to do some painting. Her Mum says if she does some painting she should put her apron on." In contrast, children in the descriptive condition were told, "One day Carol wants to do some painting. Carol says that if she does some painting she always puts her apron on." Children were then shown four drawings: (1) Carol painting with her apron, (2) Carol painting without her apron, (3) Carol not painting with her apron, and (4) Carol not painting without her apron. Children in the deontic conditions were then told, "Show me the picture where Carol is doing something naughty and not doing what her mum said." Children in the descriptive condition were told, "Show me the picture where Carol is doing something different and not doing what her mum said." Both the 3- and 4-year-old children were correct more often in the deontic, or "naughty," condition (72% and 83% for the 3- and 4-year-olds, respectively) than in the descriptive (no-social-rule-breaking) condition (40% for both the 3- and 4-year-olds). Like adults, young children reasoned correctly about a problem in which a social contract was being broken but not about a problem in which no such social obligation was mentioned (see also Dack & Astington, 2011; Kalish & Lawson, 2008).

Is this ability innate? Probably not. Rather, children are biased from early in life to be sensitive to feedback related to social contracts/exchanges, which facilitates the development of deontic reasoning. In other words, children seem specially prepared for developing "the art of the deal," particularly for recognizing when someone is breaking a social rule. These biases, along with children's abilities to see other people as intentional agents and to take the perspective of others (discussed in Chapter 6), increase the chance that they will not only survive but also thrive in a complex social world.

We will not attempt to provide a representative review of the topics in developmental social cognition. Rather, we have selected several topics to examine, in varying degrees of detail, hoping to provide a flavor of developmental social cognition, how the research is done, and how it relates to nonsocial cognitive development. In the sections to follow, we first define and describe various forms of social learning and their development. We then review Kenneth Dodge's social information processing model. We follow this with an examination of research on the cognitive bases for the development of self and of gender identification.

SOCIAL LEARNING

"Two-year-old Shayne and his father walked hand-in-hand from the car to the supermarket. As they approached the automatic door, Shayne raced into the store and stepped onto the scale in the lobby. Once on the scale, he stood very still, his arms to his side and his head pointed upward, staring at the face of the scale. After a few moments he looked at his father, smiled, and stepped down. His father then repeated the same routine" (Bjorklund & Hernández Blasi, 2012, p. 290).

If this were the only observation one had, you may think that Shayne's dad is copying his young son's behavior. In actuality, it's the other way around. Shayne's dad routinely checks to see how his latest diet-and-exercise regime is going by stepping on the grocery-store scale, and Shayne has learned this routine and mimics it perfectly.

Young Shayne likely has no idea of the purpose behind his actions; but he is a social creature. Copying the repeated behavior of an important person in his life just seems to make sense.

At its most basic, **social learning** refers to acquiring information from other individuals. A narrower definition of social learning refers to "situations in which one individual comes to behave similarly to others" (Boesch & Tomasello, 1998, p. 598). We cannot emphasize enough the significance of social learning in everyday functioning and the emergence of the modern human mind. Although humans are not the only animals that acquire information through social learning, we do this better than any other species on the planet. The ability to learn from others permitted our ancestors to pass knowledge from one generation to another with great fidelity. Like all other animals, ancient humans learned through their own experiences. But by excelling at social learning, each individual no longer had to depend on trial and error to acquire new knowledge. Rather, each generation could begin where the last one left off, which is a tremendous advantage and results in the rapid accumulation of cultural knowledge (Dunbar, 2014; Tomasello, 2014). Of course, teaching is perhaps the most sophisticated form of social learning, but as we noted in Chapter 3, direct teaching by adults is rare in traditional cultures and was likely rare for our ancestors (Lancy, 2015).

A number of scholars have proposed the *social brain hypothesis* to account for the evolution of human intelligence and our species' eventual ecological dominance (R. D. Alexander, 1989; Bjorklund, Causey, & Periss, 2010; Dunbar, 2014). Basically, the hypothesis is that humans evolved the ability to better learn from other members of their species, which resulted in enhanced skills at both competing and cooperating with one another as well as the rapid acquisition and transmission of material culture. Some versions of the social brain hypothesis hold that our species' advanced form of social cognition resulted from the confluence of a big brain, living in socially complex groups, and an extended juvenile period (Bjorklund & Bering, 2003). Human social environments are complicated and vary from culture to culture. People need not only a large brain to figure out such environments but also a long time to do so. An extended childhood may also be necessary to acquire some important nonsocial skills, such as tool use (Kaplan et al., 2000); however, the ability to learn how to use tools is greatly afforded by social learning. In support of the social brain hypothesis, there is a significant relationship between brain size and social complexity among primates (correlation between neocortex size and group size = 0.76; see Dunbar, 1992, 2014), and primate species with larger brains have, on average, the longest juvenile periods and live in the most socially complex groups (Joffe, 1997).

The important point for our purposes is that social learning develops. More specifically, social learning involves many basic cognitive abilities that develop over early childhood, including shared attention and theory of mind, which were discussed in Chapter 6 in the section on folk psychology. In this section, we examine various forms of social learning and their development.

Bandura's Social Cognitive Theory

Through most of the 20th century, when developmental psychologists talked about social learning, they did so with Albert Bandura's **social learning theory** in mind, which Bandura later renamed **social cognitive theory** to reflect a more mentalistic approach (Bandura, 1986, 1989). Initial formulations of social learning theory were based on extensions of models of classical and operant conditioning, popular throughout most of the 20th century in American psychology. It became apparent, however, that explicit reinforcement was not necessary for children (and adults) to learn about their social world. Rather, people learn much about their world simply by watching.

Factors Involved in Observational Learning

Bandura proposed five capabilities that contribute to children's learning about their social world and their place in it, each of which develops (see Table 10.1): (1) symbolization, (2) forethought, (3) self-regulation, (4) self-reflection, and (5) vicarious learning. The first capability, symbolization, means that we can think about our social behavior in words and images. This is necessary for us to be aware of various aspects of our actions. The capability of forethought means that we are able to anticipate the consequences of our actions and the actions of others. This future-time perspective motivates behavior. Self-regulation involves adopting standards of acceptable behavior for ourselves. These include aspirational standards (hoped-for levels of accomplishment) as well as social and moral standards. A capacity for self-reflection allows us to analyze our thoughts and actions. The final capability, vicarious learning, is the cornerstone of social cognitive theory. Children do not need to receive specific reinforcement for their behavior to learn; rather, they learn much social behavior merely by observing others. This places observational learning at the center of Bandura's theory.

Bandura proposed four subprocesses that govern observational learning: (1) attentional processes, (2) retention processes, (3) production processes, and (4) motivational processes. Information must be attended to, coded in memory,

stored, and retrieved, and the behavior must be performed at the appropriate time. Each of these processes changes with age, and a failure in any one process (retention, for example) rules out successful observational learning. Children do not need to physically imitate a model to have learned from observing the model. Children might have learned all they need to know from observing but never have the motivation to produce the behavior.

Following Bandura's theory, after children have attended to a model and formed a mental representation of the behavior, they must convert that representation to action. Yet children observe some things that they do not have the motoric ability to reproduce. For example, a 5-year-old boy may have watched and mentally practiced the behaviors involved in driving a car, but because of his short arms and legs (among other things),

TABLE 10.1 **Capabilities involved in Bandura's social cognitive theory and the four subprocesses of observational learning.**

Key Cognitive Capabilities

Symbolization: The ability to think about social behavior in words and images

Forethought: The ability to anticipate the consequences of our actions and the actions of others

Self-regulation: The ability to adopt standards of acceptable behavior for ourselves

Self-reflection: The ability to analyze our thoughts and actions

Vicarious learning: The ability to learn new behavior and the consequences of one's actions by observing others

Subprocesses of Observational Learning

Attentional processes

Retention processes

Production processes

Motivational processes

he is physically unable to produce the behaviors he has observed. Despite such obvious shortcomings, young children frequently overestimate their imitative abilities. They have watched a behavior being performed and believe that seeing is knowing. (More than one parent has been shocked to see his or her young child behind the wheel of a moving car.) During a study in which mothers recorded the imitative attempts of their preschoolers, children overestimated their imitative abilities 55.5% of the time—stating that they were capable of imitating a behavior when they were not. Cases of underestimation were rare, occurring on only 4.7% of the observations (Bjorklund, Gaultney, & Green, 1993). As this study reminds us, young children have great confidence in their own abilities. To improve observational learning, children must learn to monitor and compare their actions with their symbolic representations and to correct mismatches. As these production processes improve with age, the difference between what children know and what they can produce declines (Bandura, 1989).

Forms of Social Learning

Following Bandura's theory, most child developmentalists who studied social learning assumed that, if children acquire some behavior by observation, the mechanism of that learning is imitation. However, imitation is only one rather sophisticated form of social learning. In fact, behaviors that may *appear* to have been acquired through imitation could have actually been acquired through various less-sophisticated forms, including local enhancement, emulation, and mimicry.

Table 10.2 presents these mechanisms by which social learning can occur. Most of these mechanisms have been identified by comparative

TABLE 10.2 **Forms of social learning.**

Local enhancement. An individual notices activity at a particular location, moves to that location, and, in a process of trial and error, discovers a useful behavior. *Example:* One chimpanzee notices another chimpanzee cracking nuts with stones at a location, moves to that location, and, in a process of trial and error, learns to crack nuts with stones, although using other techniques than the ones observed.

Mimicry. The duplication of a behavior without any understanding of the goal of that behavior. *Example:* A 2-year-old child steps on a scale, looks at the scale face, and steps off, just like Dad does.

Emulation. One individual observes another interacting with an object to achieve a specific goal. The first individual then interacts with the object attempting to attain the same end but does not duplicate the same behavior as the model to achieve that goal. *Example:* A child watches someone sifting sand through her fingers to get seashells, then tosses sand in the air to find seashells.

Imitative learning. Reproduction of observed behavior to achieve a specific goal. May require an understanding of the goal that the model had in mind, as well as the reproduction of important components of the observed behavior. *Example:* A child watches an adult open a latch and push a button to open a box to get a piece of candy and repeats the same actions with the same result.

Teaching (instructed learning). Actor A modifies his or her behavior only in the presence of another, Actor B, without attaining any immediate benefits. As a result of Actor A encouraging or discouraging B's behavior, B acquires a new skill. To be done effectively, teaching requires that both the instructor and student take the perspective of the other. *Example:* An adult shows a child how to make actions to open a box, perhaps making slow and deliberate motions, molding the child's fingers, and the child, not the adult, gets the candy inside.

(animal) psychologists to explain the behavior of their subjects, but the list is equally applicable to human children (see Want & Harris, 2001). Local enhancement (or stimulus enhancement) occurs when an individual notices activity at a particular location (for instance, some chimpanzees cracking nuts at a spot that has plentiful stones), moves to that location, and in a process of trial and error, discovers a useful behavior (for instance, cracking nuts with stones, although perhaps using other techniques than the ones observed). Other mechanisms include mimicry, which is the duplication of a behavior without any understanding of the goal of that behavior. The behavior of 2-year-old Shayne in the story that opened this section is an example of mimicry. Shayne would step on the scale, look up at the face of the scale, and then step off, just like his father did, despite not having any understanding of the purpose of such actions. More cognitively sophisticated processes include emulation (sometimes called *goal emulation*), true imitation (or imitative learning) (Tomasello, 2000), and teaching (or instructed learning) (Tomasello, 2016; Tomasello, Kruger, & Ratner, 1993).

Emulation refers to understanding the goal of a model and engaging in similar behavior to achieve that goal without necessarily reproducing the exact actions of the model (Horner & Whiten, 2005; Tomasello, 2000). For example, Simon may observe June sifting sand through her fingers to search for seashells. Simon may then start searching through sand with his hands but by tossing handfuls of sand that separates sand from the shells. Unlike in mimicry (or imitative learning), Simon does not reproduce the behaviors of the model (in this case, June) but, rather, through a trial-and-error process, achieves the desired goal he had observed June attain by using different behaviors.

In contrast to emulation, imitative learning is defined as "reproducing an observed outcome using the same action the model used with an understanding of the intention behind the actions" (Nielsen, 2012, p. 172). Imitative learning thus requires that the observer take the perspective of the model, understand the model's goal, and reproduce important portions of the model's behavior in an effort to reach that goal. Imitative learning involves an understanding of the causal relationship between the model's behavior and the outcome, or goal.

If imitative learning were the most sophisticated form of learning, then human culture and cognition would be much less complex than we know it to be. A more sophisticated form of cultural learning, requiring more sophisticated perspective taking, is instructed learning, or teaching, with a more accomplished person instructing a less accomplished person. According to Michael Tomasello and his colleagues (1993), not all cases of instruction qualify as instructed learning. Specifically, instructed learning requires that "children learn about the adult, specifically, about the adult's understanding of the task and how that compares with their own understanding" (Tomasello et al., 1993, p. 499). Following instructed learning, as opposed to learning from instruction, children will reproduce the instructed behavior in the appropriate context to regulate their own behavior. That is, as in imitative learning, children must understand the purpose of the behavior—the adult's purpose when he or she initially taught the behavior. Children must internalize the adult's instruction, not just repeat a behavior on demand. Thus, a child who is taught to bounce a ball off the wall and into the wastebasket has learned a complicated trick. However, it is a trick that can be acquired by a monkey, and it is not the same as learning that putting a ball in a basket in certain situations is a goal to a game. Each is learning through instruction, but only the latter is instructed learning. According to Tomasello et al. (1993), "To learn from an instructor culturally—to understand the instruction from something resembling the instructor's point of view—requires that children be able to understand a mental perspective that differs from their own, and then to relate that point of view to their own in an explicit fashion" (p. 500).

The more advanced forms of social learning, such as emulation, imitative learning, and teaching, are not the mindless matching behavior of an unsophisticated organism, as in mimicry, but reflect rather sophisticated cognitive processing. These underlying abilities develop over infancy and early childhood. In the following section, we examine the development of social learning in children, starting with neonatal imitation.

Age Differences in Social Learning

Neonatal Imitation

Social learning is supported by social interaction, which begins in the first hours of life. Forty years ago, Andrew Meltzoff and Moore (1977) reported that infants within their first days of life will copy the facial expressions of an adult, a phenomenon known as neonatal imitation. Photo 10.1 shows examples of the facial gestures modeled to infants in this experiment and responses by infants. Following each demonstration, the model continued to look at the newborn but made no facial gestures. The researchers videotaped the infants' faces during this time and later compared the expressions of the babies to those of the model. Did infants make more tongue protrusions when they had just seen the model stick out his tongue at them, or were infants' expressions simply random—that is, not related to what they had just

seen? Meltzoff and Moore reported that infants' facial gestures were selective: They opened their mouths more often when the model had displayed mouth opening, and they stuck out their tongues more often when the model had demonstrated tongue protrusion. Other researchers have similarly reported imitation of tongue protrusions and other facial gestures in infants during the first 2 months of life (Meltzoff & Moore, 1992; Nagy & Molnar, 2004), with several researchers reporting imitation of facial (Field et al., 1982; Vinter, 1986) and hand gestures (Nagy, Pal, & Orvos, 2014) in newborns.

The effect is somewhat elusive, however, and several experimenters have failed to replicate early imitation using procedures similar to those Meltzoff and Moore used (Anisfeld et al., 2001; Oostenbroek et al., 2016). Other researchers have reported that the most frequently assessed gesture of tongue protrusion is elicited by flashing stimuli (Jones, 1996; Legerstee, 1991), music (Jones, 2006), or a looming black pen or small ball (Jacobson, 1979), causing Susan Jones (2009) to propose that neonatal imitation is young infants' response to interesting or arousing stimuli rather than reflecting true imitation. Janine Oostenbroek and her colleagues (2016) recently reported that infants tested at 1, 3, 6, and 9 weeks showed no selective copying of facial gestures, being just as likely, for example, to display tongue protrusion in response to observing a model opening her mouth as to sticking out her tongue. Moreover, imitation of facial gestures actually declines during the first year of life. For the most-studied facial gesture of tongue protrusion, the majority of investigators who have examined infants of different ages report a peak in imitation sometime during the first 2 months, followed by a decline within weeks to chance values (Abravanel & Sigafoos, 1984; Jacobson, 1979). This is, indeed, perplexing, in

PHOTO 10.1   Neonatal imitation in humans (a) and monkeys (b, c). Photographs of 2- to 3-day-old infants imitating (1) tongue protrusion, (2) mouth opening, and (3) lip protrusion as demonstrated by an adult experimenter. Newborn rhesus monkeys will also imitate facial expressions.

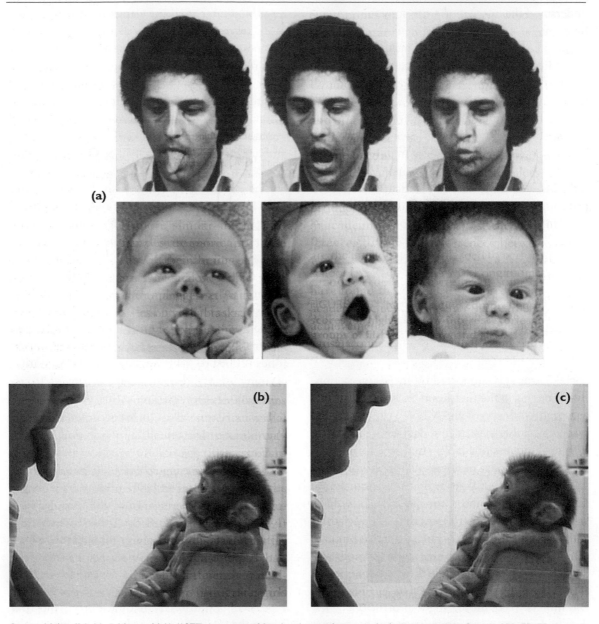

Sources: Meltzoff, A. N., & Moore, M. K. (1977). Imitation of facial and manual gestures by human neonates. *Science, 198,* 75–78. Gross, L. (2006). Evolution of neonatal imitation. *PLoS Biol, 4*(9), e311. doi:10.1371/journal.pbio.0040311

that we have what appears to be a sophisticated cognitive phenomenon that actually decreases in frequency over a very brief period.

How can neonatal imitation be explained? Meltzoff and Moore (1977, 1985) have suggested that modeling effects during early infancy could be attributed to (a) learning; (b) selective imitation, guided by the integration of information from one sensory modality (vision) with information from another (proprioception derived from self-initiated movements); or (c) an *innate releasing mechanism*, where reflex-like responses are elicited by a specific set of stimuli.

According to Meltzoff and Moore, the first possibility, learning, is an unlikely candidate to explain early imitation. The most compelling reason for rejecting a learning or reinforcement interpretation is that infants who are only hours old will match certain facial expressions to those of an adult (Field et al., 1982; Vinter, 1986). It is unlikely that such young infants would have had sufficient experience to "learn" these responses.

The second alternative, selective imitation, is the one Meltzoff and Moore favor. They propose that the matching behavior observed in the early weeks of life is true imitation. Newborns are able to coordinate information from two senses. They can visually observe a stimulus, store an abstract representation of that stimulus, and compare it shortly thereafter with a proprioceptive representation (that is, their own movements). This position holds that newborns possess the ability to integrate information from two senses—in other words, they possess intermodal integration (see Chapter 4). Meltzoff and Moore (1985) referred to this as **active intermodal mapping**. If one accepts this interpretation, it advances the ability to coordinate two sensory modalities to a period many months earlier than that suggested by Piaget.

Yet babies are not learning anything new during these episodes; the behaviors they are copying are already within their behavioral repertoire. Richard Byrne (2005) described such matching behavior as *social mirroring*, in which one member of a dyad (the newborn) copies the behavior of the other (the caregiver) to stay "in tune" with one another, serving to foster and consolidate the social interaction. This social-mirroring interpretation is supported by research showing that newborns both imitate an adult and provoke imitation from an adult, with different patterns of heart-rate changes accompanying imitation (decreasing heart rate) and provocations (increasing heart rate) (Nagy, 2006; Nagy & Molnar, 2004). This suggests that neonatal imitation may serve a different role than the imitative responses seen later in infancy, one better described by Meltzoff and Moore's third alternative explanation. Rather than reflecting active intermodal mapping and true imitation, the newborn's matching behavior may reflect an **innate releasing mechanism** (or **fixed-action pattern**), which refers to inherited sets of behaviors elicited by specific sets of stimuli without prior environmental experience (Tinbergen, 1951). Such mechanisms would serve an adaptive role for the young infant and disappear when they are no longer needed.

What adaptive function might neonatal imitation play? One interpretation is that such responses play a specific role in survival of the infant at that time and that time only, and that they disappear when they are no longer needed (Bjorklund, 1987a). R. W. Oppenheim (1981) referred to such phenomena as **ontogenetic adaptations**. He argued that the young organism lives in a very different world from the adult and requires different behavioral or neurological organization to cope with life. Such organization might not be the basis for later development but, rather, might be present only for survival at that time and in that specific environment. Sandra Jacobson (1979), for example, suggested that tongue protrusions might be functional in early nursing, and others have argued that the neonatal imitation might play a role in fostering early social interaction (Bjorklund, 1987a; Byrne, 2005). The matching of adult facial gestures by the infant might help maintain social interaction between the two, with these reflexes declining when infants are better able to intentionally direct their gaze and control their head and mouth movements in response to social stimulation, somewhere from the second to fourth months of life (Cairns, 1979). In a similar vein, Maria Legerstee (1991) suggested that early imitation serves as a form of prelinguistic communication (see also Nagy et al., 2014). Mikael Heimann (1989) provided tentative support for these positions, documenting a relationship between imitation in newborns and mother-infant social interactions at 3 months of age (specifically, infants who showed high levels of neonatal imitation had more social interactions with their mothers 3 months later).

One reason for favoring the social as opposed to the symbolic interpretation of neonatal imitation is that, as we mentioned earlier, these behaviors decline to chance values over the first 2 months (Abravanel & Sigafoos, 1984). Another reason is that neonatal imitation is also observed in chimpanzees (Bard, 2007; Myowa-Yamakoshi et al., 2004) and monkeys (Ferrari et al., 2006) (see Photo 10.1), and it is questionable whether mother-reared chimpanzees or monkeys ever develop the cognitive abilities that a symbolic interpretation of neonatal imitation implies. Like with human babies, the incidence of neonatal imitation declines in chimpanzees around 2 months of age (Myowa-Yamakoshi et al., 2004). These behaviors are also more frequently seen in

the context of more natural social communication as opposed to more formal (and unnatural) settings, causing some primate researchers to argue for a communicative and/or affiliative function of neonatal primate imitation (Bard, 2007; Ferrari et al., 2006), similar to what has been argued for human infants (Bjorklund, 1987a; Byrne, 2005).

Social Learning in Infancy Beyond the Neonatal Period

Jean Piaget (1962) documented in detail the development of social learning over infancy, and his basic observations have generally been replicated (Kaye & Marcus, 1981). Piaget claimed that the earliest form of social learning is mutual imitation, in which the baby initiates a behavior that is mimicked by the adult, which in turn activates the baby to continue that behavior (Nagy & Molnar, 2004). Piaget's (1962) description of such interaction with his daughter will help illustrate this phenomenon: "I noted a differentiation in the sounds of her laughter. I imitated them. She reacted by reproducing them quite clearly, but only when she had already uttered them immediately before" (p. 10). As in neonatal imitation, infants are learning nothing new; they are merely engaging in social give-and-take with an adult, involving behaviors that they already possess (and, in fact, that they were the first to emit). Infants apparently enjoy these bouts of mother-infant imitation. For example, 3.5-month-old babies smile and vocalize more during and immediately after being imitated by their mothers than they do for nonimitative behaviors (Field, Guy, & Umbel, 1985). A similar facilitating effect on social interaction of being imitated has been reported for rhesus monkey infants (Sclafani et al., 2015).

Mothers and infants continue this reciprocal imitative relationship over the course of infancy. For instance, Elise Frank Masur and Jennifer Rodemaker (1999) observed mothers and their infants during free play or bath time when the babies were 10, 13, 17, and 21 months old. Rates of imitation were about one episode per minute, with mothers imitating infants more than infants imitated mothers. And unlike neonatal imitation or the mutual imitation described by Piaget, infants at these ages are learning many new things through social learning. For example, in a study in which parents were asked to keep diaries of their children's imitative behavior, 12-, 15-, and 18-month-olds learned, on average, one or two new behaviors a day simply by watching (Barr & Hayne, 2003).

Piaget did not observe the first signs of true social learning (that is, in which infants acquire some new behavior) until from 8 to 12 months. At this time, infants are now able to copy bodily movements and sounds that they have not produced before, although the new behaviors must be close to what the infants can already produce if they are to be successful. During this time, infants also begin to reproduce behaviors for which they receive no visual or auditory feedback, such as facial gestures. (These are the same facial gestures newborns will copy but that drop off around 2 months of age.) Piaget referred to these unseen actions as *invisible gestures*. During the next 6 months, infants become increasingly skilled at acquiring new behavior through observation, but according to Piaget, children of this age are limited to imitating a model in the model's presence. They are unable to observe a model and delay imitation for any length of time. More recent research, discussed previously in Chapter 8 in the context of memory development, has shown that infants are capable of *deferred imitation* much earlier than Piaget observed (see P. J. Bauer,

2007). Yet Piaget's overall description of observational learning in infancy has generally been supported, with infants showing no copying of motor behaviors before 6 months of age and then gradually increasing their observational-learning abilities over the next 14 months (Jones, 2007).

Young Children as Imitators and Emulators

Piaget, like most child developmental psychologists, did not differentiate among the forms of social learning but used the term *imitation* to describe all forms of learning by observation. As we noted earlier, social learning can take various forms, with imitative learning being the most cognitively sophisticated. In fact, when looking closely at observational learning in infants and young children, the picture gets quite complicated (see Want & Harris, 2001).

For example, toddlers 2 years of age and younger frequently engage in emulation, seemingly understanding the goal of the model but using alternative behaviors to achieve that goal (McGuigan & Whiten, 2009; Nielsen, 2006). Such emulation is even seen as young as 14 months of age. For example, Gyorgy Gergely and his colleagues (2002) replicated an earlier experiment by Andrew Meltzoff (1988) in which 14-month-old babies would imitate an adult by using their heads to press a button to turn on a light. This is a novel action (one would usually use one's hand), and it indicates that the babies were reproducing the exact behaviors of the model they had witnessed to achieve a goal. Gergely and his colleagues hypothesized that infants may have believed the model did not use her hands when she could have because using her head may have provided some advantage in turning on the light. In their study, 14-month-old infants watched as a model turned on the light with her head either (a) with her hands free, as in the earlier Meltzoff study, or (b) with her hands wrapped in a blanket (that is, her hands were occupied and thus not available to turn on the light). Figure 10.1 presents the percentage of infants in the hands-free versus hands-occupied conditions who turned on the light using their head (reflective of imitation) versus using their hands (reflective of emulation). As you can see, most of the infants in the hands-free condition used their head to turn on the light, just as Meltzoff had found. But the pattern was reversed in the hands-occupied condition. Now most of the infants (79%) used their hands to turn on the light. That is, when there was a reason why the model did not use her hands (they were wrapped in a blanket), the babies focused on the goal (turn on the light), not on the means (use your head), and they used their hands as the most efficient way to turn on the light. When no such reason was available, they copied the model's behavior exactly, reflective of imitative learning or perhaps mimicry. Gergely and his colleagues referred to this behavior as *rational imitation*. Other researchers have similarly shown that young children's social learning is flexible, with children 12 to 26 months of age displaying both imitative learning (focusing on the means as well as the ends of a model) and emulation (focusing only on the ends), depending on the context (M. Carpenter, Call, & Tomasello, 2005; Nielsen, 2006).

However, children soon develop a tendency to copy faithfully the actions of a model, even if those actions are unnecessary. For instance, several researchers have noted that preschoolers will faithfully reproduce the actions of a model even when those actions are irrelevant to attaining a goal (Gardiner, Greif, & Bjorklund, 2011; Hoehl et al., 2014; Nielsen, Moore, & Mohamedally,

2015). This was illustrated by a study in which an experimenter, using a rake to retrieve an out-of-reach object, displayed one of two sets of actions to 2-year-old children (Nagell, Olguin, & Tomasello, 1993). The children copied the actions of the adults even when a more effective way of solving the problem was possible. In contrast, chimpanzees given the same task achieved the goal not by copying the often-inefficient behaviors of the model (that is, by mimicry or imitative learning) but by using often more straightforward and effective actions to attain the goal (that is, by emulation) (see also Horner & Whiten, 2005, for other examples of chimpanzees using emulation rather than imitative learning). Similarly, in a study by Derek Lyons and his colleagues (2007), preschool children watched adults perform a series of actions on

FIGURE 10.1 **Percentage of infants who used their hands or head to turn on the light as a function of whether the model had her hands free or occupied.**

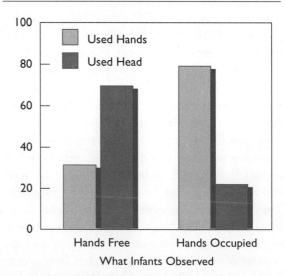

Source: Gergely, G., Bekkering, H., & Kiraly, I. (2002). Rational imitation in preverbal infants. *Nature, 415,* 755.

a puzzle box to retrieve a toy that had been locked inside. Some of the actions were seemingly irrelevant to opening the object, but even when being warned to avoid "silly," unnecessary actions, the children copied them anyway. Such **overimitation** is not limited to actions on artifacts but is also observed for verbal behavior (for example, mispronouncing known words when a model does; Subiaul et al., 2016). Nor is it limited to children from Western culture but has also been observed in Kalahari Bushman 2- to 6-year-old children (Nielsen, Mushin, Tomaselli, & Whiten, 2014; Nielsen & Tomaselli, 2010). Also, there is no evidence that chimpanzees engage in overimitation (Nielsen, 2012).

This and similar research suggest that, unlike chimpanzees, young children are motivated to copy the actions of others to maintain a social interaction or to be part of a group (Howard et al., 2015; Over & Carpenter, 2013). Consistent with this, 2-year-olds are more likely to mimic the actions of a live, socially responsive person than a person in a video, and they are more likely to copy the behavior of a person they could communicate with via a closed-circuit TV system than the behavior of a person on a videotape who could not provide feedback (Nielsen, Simcock, & Jenkins, 2008). Two- and 3-year-old children also learn about the uses of tools during simple problem-solving tasks more readily by watching a model than by actually manipulating the materials themselves (Gardiner et al., 2012).

It is easy to see how overimitation can be viewed as being maladaptive, given that it involves irrelevant and time-consuming actions. Such an approach may cause a child to focus too much attention on a model's behavior and less on the ultimate goal of the performance. However, Mark Nielsen (2012) proposed that "directly replicating others also affords the rapid acquisition of a vast array of skills that have been developed and passed on over multiple generations, avoiding the potential pitfalls and false end-points that can come from individual learning" (p. 171). Such imitation also may be adaptive in acquiring cultural information that is critical to children's social group (Nielsen, Mushin, Tomaselli, & Whiten, 2014). Children identify types of social interactions that they believe are especially important for living in richly symbolic environments (Froese & Leavens, 2014) and learn those techniques through exact imitation. This is referred to as the *normative account*. Children understand that some actions are relevant and others are irrelevant for completing a task, but they believe all of the actions are important for the "bigger overarching action sequence" (Keupp, Behne, & Rakoczy, 2013, p. 393). In other words, children believe that irrelevant actions must have a greater purpose (Kenward, 2012; Williamson & Marksman, 2006), and knowing how to perform these actions is important because it may "align[n] oneself with one's cultural in-group" (Nielsen, 2012, p. 171). Moreover, the tendency to overimitate does not disappear in early childhood but persists, at least in some contexts, into adulthood (McGuigan, Makinson, & Whiten, 2011).

These findings seem to suggest that young children are blind mimics (or imitators), copying the exact behaviors of a model with regard to the model's intention (that is, why the model is engaging in the behavior in the first place). Yet we know that toddlers are more apt to engage in emulation than in imitation (McGuigan & Whiten, 2009) and that even infants can sometimes "read" the intentions of a model and behave accordingly. Recall the experiments described in Chapter 6, in which infants as young as 7 months old copied behavior based on what they inferred the model's *intentions* were (for example, to remove the ends of a dumbbell) (M. Carpenter, Akhtar, & Tomasello, 1998;

Meltzoff, 1995). These results demonstrate quite clearly that infants can, under some circumstances anyway, display true imitation (imitative learning) and not just mimicry. Older preschool children also do not slavishly copy all actions of a model all the time. Preschoolers are less apt to overimitate a model when they know the goal of a task beforehand (Williamson & Markman, 2006), when the contexts differ between observing the model and executing the task (Keuup et al., 2015), when they have some awareness of the intentions of the model (Gardiner, 2014), when a model speaks a different language than they do (Buttelmann et al., 2013), when the task is performed by a low-status versus a high-status person (McGuigan, 2013), and when the model appeared unknowledgeable or engaged in trial and error (Gardiner & Causey, 2015). In fact, despite children's overall tendency to imitate models, children's social learning becomes increasingly flexible with age as they become more familiar with specific tasks, dropping many irrelevant actions (Nielsen, Mushin, Tomaselli, & Whiten, 2014; Whiten et al., 2009).

Despite the contextual nature of overimitation, its prevalence during the preschool years is compelling and counterintuitive, and a number of researchers believe that it reflects an evolved adaptation (Chudek, Baron, & Birch, 2016; Nielsen, 2012; Whiten et al., 2009). For example, Andrew Whiten and his colleagues (2009) noted that, unlike other species, human children must learn how to use thousands of cultural artifacts, and an economical way to learn about such artifacts (for example, using tools, how to treat a sacred object) is to copy exactly the actions of others. Although some irrelevant actions may be acquired during this process, they can be weeded out as children gain more experience interacting with the artifact. In a similar vein, György Gergely and Gergely Csibra (2005; Csibra & Gergely, 2011) proposed that

children's overimitation is a human adaptation permitting fast and accurate transmission of information between individuals, which they refer to as *natural pedagogy*. They argue that when learning to use objects by watching adults, children apply an *assumption of relevance*, presuming that all actions an adult performs are necessary for achieving a goal. After all, surely the grown-up knows what he or she is doing.

Most of the social-learning research we've reviewed here involves children imitating adults. But children learn a lot from observing one another, of course, and this has been a focus of much research, most of it from the perspective of Bandura's social cognitive theory, discussed earlier. Recent research has examined the fidelity with which children learn specific skills from a child model over several different generations of children (Hooper et al., 2010; Horner et al., 2006). For example, in *diffusion chain* studies, one child is shown how to operate a novel apparatus. For instance, in research by Lydia Hooper and her colleagues (2010), a preschool child was shown one way to operate panpipes, shown in Figure 10.2. There are three possible ways to operate the panpipes using a stick tool to receive a reward. The stick can be (1) inserted through a hole to lift the T-bar (lift method), (2) inserted through a different hole and used to poke the base of the T-bar (poke method), or (3) used to push and then slide the T-bar (push-lift method). A single child was shown the lift method. This child in turn served as a model for another child, who in turn served as a model for another child, and so on for a total of 20 children. Hooper and her colleagues reported that all 20 children learned the lift method. In contrast, only 3 of 16 children learned to operate the panpipes without observing another child (that is, by discovering how to release the reward), and only one of these children used the lift method. These findings make it clear that preschool children are successful social learners and are able to learn a detailed skill from watching one another.

In actuality, of course, children rarely sit down one-on-one, with one child demonstrating a skill to another. In a group setting, several children at a time may play together, with skill transmission being a more complicated affair. This was examined in a study by Andrew Whiten and Emma Flynn (2011), who taught preschool children one of two ways to operate the panpipes (lift or poke), placed the panpipes in the classroom, and watched what happened. Many children played with the panpipes, most after watching the trained child

first successfully operate them, and 83% of children who attempted the task received the reward. Initially, most of the children not only used the method that the trained child had initially used but also stuck with this method over the course of several days. Consistent with the earlier studies, this likely reflects imitation, passing the skill from one child to the next with great fidelity. However, some children in both the lift and poke classrooms discovered other methods to operate the panpipes, and these too spread to different members of the groups. This would seem to reflect a form of emulation, with children understanding the goal of a model but achieving that goal through alternative

FIGURE 10.2 **Panpipes apparatus.** (A) The stick tool inserted under the T-bar for the lift method. (B) The stick tool inserted into the top hole for the poke method. (C) The push-slide method by using the stick tool to push the T-bar back. (D) The panpipes viewed from the child's perspective, inside the clear plastic box with the access holes, with lift being demonstrated.

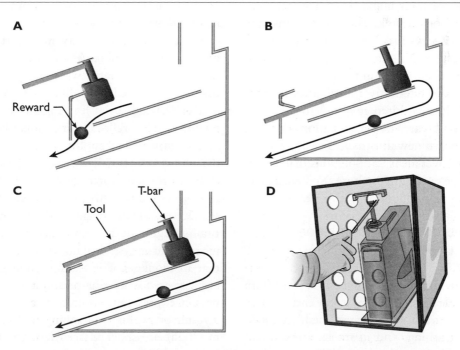

Source: Hooper, L. M., Flynn, E. G., Wood, L. A. N., & Whiten, A. (2010). Observational learning of tool use in children: Investigating cultural spread through diffusion chains and learning mechanisms through ghost displays. *Journal of Experimental Child Psychology, 106*, 82–97.

means. Perhaps not surprisingly, in addition to simply demonstrating the method, many children talked about what they were doing, attempting to teach other children how to operate the panpipes. This research indicates that preschool children have a variety of social-learning abilities available to them and that a skill learned by one child will, indeed, be transmitted to other children, sometimes exactly as initially demonstrated and sometimes with modifications.

We concur with researchers who propose that children are especially adapted to learn from watching others and that children's tendencies to imitate (even overimitate) in some contexts and emulate in others reflect evolved adaptations, perhaps unique to humans and our highly social way of life. We noted in Chapter 5 that Nielsen (2012) proposed that imitation (along with fantasy play) is a critical feature of childhood and was critical in shaping human cognitive evolution. Similarly, Alison Gopnik, Thomas Griffiths, and Christopher Lucas (2015) proposed that humans' extended period of childhood permits children to further explore, to think in more abstract ways, and to consider alternative possibilities to solutions that older children may fail to see. This may lead to a greater use of emulation, allowing children to learn new affordances of objects and to generate novel ideas and solutions that can be applied to the cumulative culture (Nielsen, 2012).

Mirror Neurons: The Foundation of Social Learning?

It seems clear that humans are born to learn from others (or at least learn to do so very early in life). As for all other types of learning, the brain mediates social learning, and in recent years, scientists have begun to probe the neurological basis of social learning and cognition, creating the field of social neuroscience (Decety & Cacioppo, 2010). One phenomenon in social neuroscience of particular relevance for the development of social learning is the discovery of **mirror neurons**. First identified in the frontal lobes of monkeys, mirror neurons responded when a monkey either performed or watched someone else perform a goal-directed act, such as grasping a piece of food (Rizzolatti & Craighero, 2004; Rizzolatti et al., 1996). The neurons did not fire when a monkey watched a hand making grasping movements without something to grasp. In other words, these animals possessed specific neurons that became active when they performed an action *and* when they watched others performing actions the monkey itself could make.

Giacomo Rizzolatti and his colleagues speculated that these neurons might permit monkeys to perform certain behaviors without having to think about them and to comprehend such behaviors without the need of explicit reasoning. Neurons such as these may play an important role in observational learning. A monkey sees an action, and neurons associated with motor areas of the brain are activated, providing a neurological system underlying social learning. More generally, mirror neurons reflect an individual being "able to recognize when another is doing something that the self can do" (Byrne, 2005, p. R499).

It wasn't long after the discovery of mirror neurons in monkeys that neuroscientists began to search for them in humans, and they found them. Brain-imaging studies, however, showed that the mirror-neuron system in humans is different from that in monkeys. For example, mirror neurons are activated when one person observes another person express an emotion, such as disgust as a result of smelling something foul or pain as a result of being shocked (see Rizzolatti, Fogassi, & Gallese, 2005). Also, mirror neurons in humans become active both for goal-directed behavior (for example, grasping a piece of food) and, unlike monkeys, for "meaningless" actions, such as random finger movements. And human mirror neurons, unlike those of monkeys, seem to code for movements *forming* an action, not only for the action itself (see Rizzolatti & Craighero, 2004). This suggests that mirror neurons are important in imitative learning, where the specific behaviors a model performs (the means) are as important as the goal the model attains (the ends). Giovani Buccino and his colleagues (2004) investigated the possible role of mirror neurons in imitative learning by asking people to watch an expert as he played guitar chords. Mirror neurons were activated when participants watched the expert play chords, and these neurons were even more active when they tried to imitate the movements.

Most research on human mirror neurons has been performed with adults, although evidence of mirror neurons in infants and children has been found in several studies. For example, using EEG recordings, evidence of mirror neurons for children as young as 3 years of age has been documented for the observation and execution of hand movements (Fecteau et al., 2004; Lepage & Theoret, 2006). Similarly, fMRI studies suggest that 10- to 14-year-old children have a mirror-neuron system for emotional expressions (Dapretto et al., 2006). Some have speculated that the mirror-neuron system is functioning at birth (Lepage & Theoret, 2007; Pfeifer et al., 2008; Simpson et al., 2014), based mainly on the presence of neonatal imitation, discussed earlier in this chapter. To date, however, there is no solid neurological evidence of a mirror-neuron system in newborns of any species (Lepage & Theoret, 2007), but a 2009 study by Victoria Southgate and her colleagues provided evidence of such a system in 9-month-old infants. The researchers measured EEG recordings of infants when they reached for objects and when they observed someone else reach for the same objects. Southgate and her colleagues reported that, as in adults, watching a grasping action activated the motor portion of infants' brains, although only after the infants had observed the action several times. At that point, the neural activity began *before* they observed the behavior, in anticipation of the action. That is, observing someone perform a behavior they too could perform did not directly activate infants' mirror neurons; instead, activation was determined by their knowledge of the forthcoming action.

V. S. Ramachandran (2000; Ramachandran & Oberman, 2006) proposed that mirror neurons provide the brain-based mechanisms for identifying with others, which is the basis of empathy, perspective taking, imitative learning, and even language (see also Marshall & Meltzoff, 2014; Meltzoff et al., 2009). Mirror neurons fire when people observe another person doing something or even attempting to do something. This may provide the neurological basis for understanding another person's intention. Recall from Chapter 6 our discussion about the important role in folk psychology of infants seeing others as *intentional agents*, individuals who *cause* things to happen and whose behavior is designed to achieve some goal (Tomasello & Carpenter, 2007). Some have speculated that the seeming absence of well-developed theory-of-mind abilities in people with autism spectrum disorder may be associated with defects in the mirror-neuron system (Ramachandran & Oberman, 2006; Williams et al., 2001), and these speculations have been confirmed in research with both children (Dapretto et al., 2006) and adults (Oberman et al., 2005).

Mirror neurons are a hot topic today, but understanding the neurological basis of social learning and its development is still in its infancy. Future research will shed more light on how brain organization and development foster social learning and provide valuable insights into social cognition, the development of social learning, and possibly even the evolution of the human mind. Some have speculated, for example, that changes in the mirror-neuron system over hominid evolution afforded greater social-learning abilities and set the stage for the revolutionary changes in thinking and lifestyle that occurred over relatively brief periods of evolutionary time (Ramachandran & Oberman, 2006; Rizzolatti & Craighero, 2004).

Section Review

Social cognition is cognition about social relations and social phenomena. Many topics can be subsumed under the heading of social cognition.

Bandura's Social Cognitive Theory

- Bandura's *social cognitive theory* is an extension of earlier *social learning theory* and is mainly a theory about how children operate cognitively on their social experiences.
- Bandura postulated five capabilities that contribute to development, all of which change with age: (1) *symbolization*, (2) *forethought*, (3) *self-regulation*, (4) *self-reflection*, and (5) *vicarious learning*.
- Following social cognitive theory, *observational learning* involves four subprocesses, each of which changes with development: (1) attentional processes, (2) retention processes, (3) production processes, and (4) motivational processes.

Forms of Social Learning

- *Social learning* refers to the acquisition of social information and behavior.
- Forms of social learning include *local enhancement* (or *stimulus enhancement*), *mimicry*, *emulation*, *imitative learning*, and *teaching* (or *instructed learning*).
- Whereas both emulation and imitative learning involve the observer understand-

ing the intention of the model, only imitative learning also includes reproducing many of the same actions of the model.

Age Differences in Social Learning

- *Neonatal imitation* has been observed, with Meltzoff and Moore attributing this phenomenon to *active-intermodal* mapping and thus seeing it as a reflection of symbolic functioning.
- Neonatal imitation typically disappears by about 2 months, and some researchers suggest that it reflects an *innate releasing mechanism* (or *fixed-action pattern*) and an *ontogenetic adaptation*, serving a specific function at a particular time in development, rather than a reflection of symbolic ability.
- Even infants display imitative and emulative learning in some contexts, including *mutual imitation*, in which the baby initiates a behavior that is mimicked by the adult.
- Children 2 years and younger are more apt to engage in emulation than imitation, with children 3 years of age and older frequently displaying *overimitation*, copying even irrelevant behaviors of a model.

Mirror Neurons

- *Mirror neurons*, which may play an important role in social learning, have been identified in the brains of monkeys and humans.

Ask Yourself . . .

1. What is social cognition (as opposed to nonsocial cognition)?
2. What are the basic concepts of Bandura's social cognitive theory? How does it differ from operant and classical forms of learning?
3. What is social learning? What are four types of social learning? Provide examples. Why is social learning important for development and evolution?
4. How does imitation develop? What are some explanations for neonatal imitation?

SOCIAL INFORMATION PROCESSING

Social cognitive theorists have adopted many of the tenets of information processing. Social information must be encoded, compared with other pertinent information, and retrieved so that social interactions run smoothly. The more skillfully social information is processed, the more socially competent a child is seen to be. Kenneth Dodge and his colleagues (Crick & Dodge, 1994; Dodge, 1986; Dodge et al., 1986; see also Rubin & Krasnor, 1986) have postulated a theory that describes the mental processes involved in evaluating social information. Dodge's original model of social exchange in children is shown in Figure 10.3.

As can be seen in Figure 10.3, the model has five major units of social interaction. The first unit is the social stimulus, or cue. This is the information that a child must process. For example, a shove by another child, a smile, a scowl, a pout, and an invitation to join a game are all social signals that must be interpreted. The second unit of the model is a child's processing of these cues. A child must make sense of the social cues and decide how to respond. More will be said of this unit shortly. Once a child evaluates the information, he or she must emit some social behavior (Unit 3). Does the 6-year-old enter the playgroup by jumping in the middle of an ongoing game and ask if she can play, or does she just stand to the side, waiting to be asked? This behavior serves as a social stimulus for a child's peers, who make some judgment of the child (Unit 4) and then act themselves (Unit 5). (The model has been reformulated to include a sixth stage between the representation and search processes in which children clarify their goals in the situation [Crick & Dodge, 1994]. The reformulated model refines the theory but does not substantially change it. The basic model has been quite successful in accounting for a wide range of children's social behaviors.)

FIGURE 10.3 Dodge's model of social exchange in children.

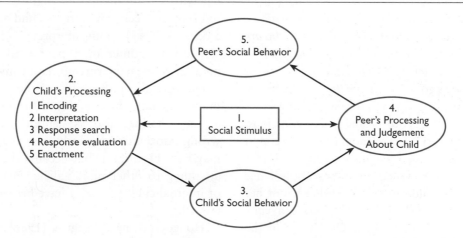

Source: Dodge, K. A., Pettit, G. S., McClaskey, C. L., & Brown, M. M. (1986). Social competence in children. *Monographs of the Society for Research in Child Development, 51* (Serial No. 213). Copyright © 1986 The Society for Research in Child Development, Inc. Reprinted with permission.

Of major concern here is the part of Dodge's theory dealing with social information processing (Unit 2). How do children make sense of social information to select a proper social response? Dodge postulated five sequential steps of information processing necessary for competent social functioning.

Encoding. The child must first encode the social stimulus. This requires that the child be properly attentive and adequately perceive the social signal. The child must know what cues are important to encode. For a child entering an already established group, for example, whether he is greeted by a smile or a frown is an important social cue. Less critical are things such as what the other children are wearing or that Kevin needs a haircut.

Interpretation. Once encoded, the social information must be interpreted. What does this information mean? To determine meaning, children must compare this information with what they already know. What does it mean if the child is greeted by smiles? This will depend on what this child knows about the smiles of others in similar situations. *When I approach a group of kids I know who are already playing a game, smiles are usually a sign of welcome. But when Marvin smiles at me, it usually means he's going to trip me the first chance he gets.* Children develop rules for interpreting social signals. These rules are probably not conscious, and they are executed in a matter of microseconds.

Response search. Once an interpretation has been made, a child must decide what his or her next move is. Children must generate a variety of response alternatives. Do they join the group? If so, by what means? Do they approach the playground bully, walk around him, think of something clever to say, or run away? With

age, children have a greater number of more sophisticated options from which to choose, which should contribute greatly to behaving in a socially competent fashion.

Response evaluation. Once responses have been generated, they must be evaluated. *Does it make sense to approach the bully, hitting him before he hits me, or might one of the other options be wiser?* To what extent can children anticipate the consequences of their behavior, selecting the response alternative that will be most successful in the current situation?

Enactment. Finally, the child must execute the chosen response.

Dodge proposed that these steps are executed in order. However, steps can be skipped, and when they are, socially incompetent behavior will likely result. For example, the first response a child comes up with might not be the ideal response for the situation. If this response is not evaluated and found wanting, the resulting behavior will probably not ingratiate the child to his or her peers. Similarly, a child might make a decision based on misinterpreted information. The quiet manner of a peer while studying may have been interpreted as an invitation to horse around, or the smile of the well-known bully may have been construed erroneously as a peace offering. Also, as mentioned earlier, the wrong information might be encoded. The cues may have been there, but because the child was attending to other more salient environmental or internal cues, they may have been ignored or missed.

Dodge and his colleagues (1986) tested this model with respect to the social skill of peer-group entry—that is, entering an established group of other children. Children in kindergarten and the first and second grades were shown videotapes of two children playing a game and asked a series of questions related to peer-group entry. The questions were selected so that each of the five aspects of Dodge's model of social information processing could be evaluated. After viewing the video, for example, the children were asked to imagine that they wanted to join the group. They were then asked how much the child on the left and how much the child on the right from the video would like to play with them. Answers to these questions reflected the children's interpretation of social cues, or Step 2 of the model. The children were then asked the reasons for their decisions. Answers to this question indicated the children's use of specific cues from the videotapes in making their decisions, or Step 1 of the model (encoding). Next, the children were asked to think of as many ways as possible to join the group, or Step 3 of the model (response search). After this, the children viewed five scenarios consisting of the original video of two children playing followed by the arrival of a third child who attempted to join the group. The new arrival displayed one of five strategies for joining the group (competent, aggressive, self-centered, passive, or authority intervention). After watching these scenarios, the children were asked a series of questions concerning the potential effectiveness of each of the five strategies to assess Step 4 of the model (response evaluation). Finally, the children were asked to pretend that they wished to play with the experimenter and were told to "show me how you would ask me if you could play with me." This corresponded to Step 5 of the model (enactment).

In a separate session, conducted 1 to 2 weeks later, each child was brought into a room in which two other children were already playing and was told to play with these children. Based on videotapes of these sessions and interviews with the children, each child's actual peer-group entry was evaluated.

The most important aspect of the results of this study concerns the prediction of children's peer-group entry (their actual social behavior) as a function of their skills at social information processing. In general, children who scored higher on the assessment of social information processing were rated as more successful at actual peer-group entry. Children who used presented cues (Step 1), who generated competent and nonaggressive strategies in response to a hypothetical entry situation (Step 3), who evaluated incompetent responses negatively (Step 4), and who demonstrated high skill in enactment of responses (Step 5) were relatively likely to perform competently and successfully in actual group entry. Furthermore, Dodge and his colleagues reported that these skills were relatively independent of one another, suggesting that each contributes something unique to social judgment and behavior rather than reflecting different aspects of a single social intelligence. Other researchers have tested the relation between children's competence for each of the five areas of social information processing and subsequent social behavior and, as Dodge and his colleagues (1986), report modest relations (Dodge & Price, 1994; Slaby & Guerra, 1988).

The area in which social information processing theory has been most frequently applied is aggressive behavior (Coie & Dodge, 1998; Dodge, Coie, & Lynam, 2006; Fontaine, 2006). Research has found characteristic ways in which at least some aggressive children encode, interpret, search, evaluate, and enact social behavior. For example, highly aggressive children are less likely to recall relevant social cues from a videotape (Dodge et al., 1995) and are more attentive to potentially aggressive cues (Gouze, 1987) than less aggressive children. Concerning interpretation, highly aggressive children are more likely to interpret an ambiguous situation (for example, a peer spills water on you) as having an aggressive, rather than an accidental, intent (Graham & Hudley, 1994) and also interpret events with clearly benign intentions as hostile (Dodge et al., 1986) more often than less aggressive children. Concerning response search, aggressive children tend to generate more atypical and socially inappropriate responses than less aggressive children do (see Coie & Dodge, 1998), and they have a difficult time inhibiting aggressive responses (Perry, Perry, & Rasmussen, 1986). Aggressive children perceive aggressive responses as socially appropriate and normative (Guerra, Huesmann, & Hanish, 1995), and they believe that they can engage in aggression relatively easily (Perry et al., 1986). Although such a pattern does not reduce in any way the effect of other, more traditionally social factors on aggression, it does point to the conclusion that how children process social information with respect to aggression is related to their own level of aggressive behavior.

The work of Dodge and his colleagues clearly points to the cognitive basis of social behavior. Complex social situations must be evaluated and thought about just as strictly intellectual situations must be contemplated. Theories of nonsocial information processing have routines, such as encoding and retrieval, and structures, such as the short-term store and semantic memory, that are specified with relative precision. Although there is still much debate concerning the particulars of nonsocial information processing, there is also much consensus. The field of social information processing is less advanced, however, because it is more complicated. How can one specify the features of a social stimulus? How is social information represented in long-term memory? How is it retrieved? Can the concepts of the short-term store, schemas, and strategies, which are so useful for explaining nonsocial cognition, be successfully applied to social cognition? Social information

processing theory represents an area of research that will surely lead to a better understanding of the development of children's social lives.

Section Review

Dodge proposed a model that adopts many of the tenets of contemporary information processing approaches to explain children's social functioning.

- Dodge proposed five sequential steps of *social information processing* necessary for competent social behavior: (1) encoding of the social stimulus; (2) interpretation of the social information; (3) response search, in which children generate possible response alternatives; (4) response evaluation, in which children evaluate the potential effectiveness of the various alternatives; and (5) enactment, in which children execute the chosen response.
- Dodge and his colleagues have shown a relationship between the efficacy of children's social information processing and their social behavior, suggesting that how children process social information plays a significant role in their social competence.

Ask Yourself . . .

5. What are the five steps of Dodge's social information processing model?
6. How has this model been used to explain aggressive and other behavior in children?

DEVELOPMENT OF A CONCEPT OF SELF

Few mental concepts are more important to us than the personal sense of self. By self-concept, we mean the way a person defines himself or herself. Some theorists have speculated that a conscious awareness of oneself greatly influences cognitive development, particularly the use of goal-directed strategies. Others have stressed the significance of a sense of self for social and emotional development (Brooks-Gunn & Lewis, 1984; Gallup, 1979). Many believe our well-developed sense of self is what makes humans unique as a species. Some people have even speculated that the development of self-awareness vaulted our hominid ancestors to full human cognition and social organization (R. D. Alexander, 1989). The significance of the concept of self for the developing person and for the species cannot be overstated.

Although self-awareness may seem self-evident to you, there can be—and has been—great debate among philosophers, psychologists, theologians, and people in general about what exactly it entails. It certainly involves an awareness of one's thoughts (that is, reflecting on the contents of one's mind). It requires a psychological sense of self, an ability to distinguish oneself from others and to identify one's actions as intentionally motivated (*I did that for a reason*). Having a sense of self permits us to evaluate the causes of our behavior and, importantly, the behavior of others. That is, by becoming self-aware, we also become "other-aware," and this becomes useful when dealing with other members of our species. In fact, we may actually come to see ourselves as others see us. Charles Cooley (1902) used the term *looking-glass self* to capture the idea that our self-concept is a reflection of how other people see and respond to us or, according to Philippe Rochat (2009), that "self-consciousness stands for the representation we hold of ourselves through the eyes of others" (p. 3).

We discussed in Chapter 8 how children's developing sense of self might play a role in the offset of infantile amnesia and the onset of true autobiographical memory. In this section, we examine the early development of self-awareness. We then look at the development of self-efficacy and how children's perceptions of themselves as effective individuals can influence their actions.

Beginnings of Self-Awareness

How can we know if young children have a concept of self? If they are too young to talk, we cannot ask them and must infer self-awareness from their behavior. Piaget (1952), among others, proposed that infants only gradually come to recognize themselves as distinct from the objects around them, with the distinction becoming fully developed sometime around 18 to 24 months of age (see Chapter 5).

Perhaps one of the earliest indications of a self-concept is infants' ability to differentiate themselves from other people and objects. During the first several months of life, infants should be receiving various forms of proprioceptive, visual, and acoustic feedback from their behavior. This should give them some sense of who they are, at least with respect to other people.

How can one determine this? One technique is to show infants pictures or videos of themselves along with pictures or videos of other infants or objects and assess their looking time (Legerstee, Anderson, & Schaffer, 1998; Rochat & Striano, 2002). If infants "recognize" themselves, they should pay less attention (a novelty effect) or, possibly, more attention (a familiarity effect) to these other stimuli than to images of themselves (see the discussion of preference for novelty/familiarity effects in Chapter 4). If they can't tell the difference between images of themselves and those of other people or objects, there should be no differential attention to any of the stimuli. In experiments using variants of this technique, infants as young as 3 months were able to discriminate between images of themselves and same-aged infants (Legerstee et al.,

1998; Rochat & Striano, 2002), suggesting a primitive form of self-recognition early in infancy. How do infants this young know what they look like? The most likely source of this self-knowledge is mirrors. Infants as young as 2 months old often have daily exposure to their image from mirrors (Bahrick, 1995), and so by 3 months of age, they recognize themselves as a familiar sight.

Still, the ability to differentiate one's self from the environment is a far cry from what we typically mean by a sense of self. Theorists have proposed that two types of self-concept develop in the first 2 years of life. The first, which typifies infants from birth to about 15 or 18 months of age, has been referred to as the *I-self* (M. Lewis, 1991), or the *implicit self* (Case, 1991). The I-self reflects what M. Lewis (1991) termed the "machinery of the self." There is no self-awareness of the I-self. There is a distinction between the self and others and a realization that *I can cause things to happen*. This is contrasted with the *me-self* (M. Lewis, 1991), or the *explicit self* (Case, 1991). The me-self requires a conscious (explicit) awareness of the self or, as Lewis has stated, the "idea of me."

How can one tell if an infant has an explicit self rather than an implicit self? One technique that some people think captures the idea of an explicit self (or the me-self) is *visual self-recognition*. Children prove they have a sense of self by recognizing themselves in a mirror. The procedure involves surreptitiously placing a mark on a child's nose or forehead and then seeing the child's reaction to his or her image in the mirror. Children's behavior in the marked condition is then compared to their behavior when their faces have no marks or to the behavior of other unmarked children. Beginning around 15 months, children show the first signs of self-recognition by touching the mark on their face rather than touching the mirror (M. Lewis & Brooks-Gunn, 1979). Not all studies report mark-directed behavior this early (Schulman & Kaplowitz, 1977), but by 18 to 24 months, this form of self-recognition is found in about 75% of all children tested (Brooks-Gunn & Lewis, 1984; Nielsen, Suddendorf, & Slaughter, 2006). It is also found in great apes—chimpanzees, orangutans, and a few gorillas (Gallup, 1979)—as well as in dolphins (Reiss & Marino, 2001), elephants (Plotnik, de Waal, & Reiss, 2006), and magpies (H. Prior, Schwarz, & Gunturkun, 2008), but not in any other animal tested.

Our culture provides more ways than mirrors for children to identify themselves. For example, when do children show a sense of self in pictures or videos? Daniel Povinelli and his colleagues (Povinelli, Landau, & Perilloux, 1996; Povinelli & Simon, 1998) took Polaroid photos or videotaped preschool children while they played. Without the children knowing it, the experimenters placed large stickers on the children. How would children react when they saw themselves in the photos or on the video with stickers on their heads? Most 2- and younger 3-year-old children did not reach for the sticker on their heads, whereas most older preschoolers did. All children, however, removed the sticker when they looked at themselves in a mirror (Povinelli et al., 1996). These results suggest that children's sense of self develops gradually over the preschool years, as their ability to deal with different modes of representation (mirrors, photos, videos) develops (see also Skouteris, Spataro, & Lazaridis, 2006).

The development of a sense of self, as reflected by self-recognition, has important consequences for emotional, social, and cognitive development. Brooks-Gunn and Lewis (1984) make this clear: "The acquisition of the self by the end of the second year not only facilitates the acquisition of social knowledge, but underlies social competence, peer relations, gender identity, and empathy" (p. 234). The change from a helpless newborn, who seemingly cannot distinguish where he or she ends and the world begins, to a self-conscious child is a remarkable and important change indeed.

Mirror recognition is not the only sign of self-awareness that develops late in the second year. Perhaps the most important indication of a sense of self can be gleaned from children's use of language. Sometime late in the second year or early in the third year, many children begin using the personal pronouns *I, me, my*, and *mine*, thereby indicating a distinction between themselves and others (M. Lewis & Brooks-Gunn, 1979; M. Lewis & Ramsay, 2004). Children also begin to display secondary, or self-conscious, emotions, such as shame, pride, and embarrassment (M. Lewis et al., 1989). As Piaget (1962) observed, this corresponds to the advent of symbolic, or representational, abilities, and self-concept seems to be one important product of the symbolic function. Neuroscience researchers have reported a connection between the onset of these early signs of self-awareness and brain development. For example, the degree of self-representation that 15- to 30-month-old children display, as reflected by mirror self-recognition, use of personal pronouns, inner speech, and pretend play, is related to maturation of a portion of the left hemisphere (M. Lewis & Carmody, 2008).

As was noted in Chapter 8 on memory, the development of a sense of self during the second and third years of life has been proposed as one reason for infantile amnesia—that is, our inability to remember information from infancy and early childhood. What we fail to recall is autobiographical memory, and there can be no such memory (no *auto*) unless there is a sense of self (see Bogdan, 2010; Howe & Courage, 1993).

Development of Self-Efficacy

Related to a sense of self is the concept of self-efficacy. Bandura (1997) defined self-efficacy as the extent to which a person views himself or herself as an effective individual. Self-efficacy develops through experience. Children evaluate the effectiveness of their own actions, compare it with the actions of others, and are told by others how their behavior meets certain standards. Children who believe they are competent (even if they are not) develop feelings of positive self-efficacy. Conversely, when self-efficacy is poor, people tend to behave ineffectually, regardless of their actual abilities. Developing feelings of positive self-efficacy has important consequences for children's social, emotional, and intellectual development (Bandura et al., 1996). One should not, however, think of self-efficacy as a general characteristic of a child. Although it is part of the larger construct of *self-esteem*, self-efficacy (and the related concept of self-worth) is specific to a domain and a task (Harter, Waters, & Whitesell, 1998). A child can have a positive sense of self-efficacy for playing baseball, for example, but a poor sense of self-efficacy for doing long division.

The development of self-efficacy begins early, as infants learn that they can exert some control over their environment. Beginning around 3 or 4 months, babies learn that their actions have consequences—for example, if they kick their feet, the mobile over the crib will move, and if they smile and coo, their parents will smile and talk back to them. Infants who have experienced some control over their environments are better able to learn new behaviors (Finkelstein & Ramey, 1977). Mary Ainsworth and her colleagues (1978) proposed that parents' responsiveness to their infants' attempts to communicate their needs gives the infants some sense of control over their environment and is related to later social and cognitive development.

With the development of language and other symbols, children are able to reflect on their new social and intellectual abilities and evaluate what others tell them about their skills. Initially, the family provides children with feedback on their effectiveness. As children approach school age, their peer group becomes a valuable source of information, and school itself is a potent agent in forming children's self-efficacy. Children learn through daily experience with teachers and peers that they are good at some tasks and not so good at others (Bandura, 1997).

Although children learn self-efficacy through experience, developing a positive sense of self-efficacy is facilitated by a generally optimistic (and unrealistic) opinion of their own abilities. Preschool children think that they can remember more items, communicate more effectively, perform tasks better, imitate a model more accurately, and perform a host of tasks better than they actually can (Bjorklund et al., 1993; Lipko, Dunlosky, & Merriman, 2009; Plumert, 1995).

Most of us can likely recall a time from childhood when we overestimated our abilities. I (DB) have one especially vivid memory that is now over 50 years old:

> The first grade class was getting fidgety. There were a few minutes left before the bell rang, so the teacher decided to fill the time with some entertainment. "Can anyone sing a song for us?" she asked, and several children gave renditions of their favorite tunes. "Can anyone dance?" she asked. I felt that this was my time to shine. "I can tap dance!" I answered. I walked to the front of the room and proceeded to shuffle my feet, trying my best to imitate the dancers I had seen on TV. Well, the result

> *was* entertainment, but strictly comedy. My classmates roared with laughter and even the teacher was unable to hide her amusement. Fortunately, the bell rang soon and the children lined up to go home, so my stint in the spotlight was short lived. (Bjorklund, 2007b, p. 11)

My false belief in my dancing ability is not uncommon, and although this particular event led to some embarrassment without any obvious benefit (other than having a story to tell many years later), young children's beliefs that they know more than they actually do, and that they can do more than they actually can, provide them with positive perceptions of their own skills. This positive sense of self-efficacy might encourage children to attempt things that they would not try if they had a more realistic idea of their abilities. In other words, their cognitive immaturity, as reflected by their unrealistic assessments of their abilities, can actually facilitate development rather than hinder it (Bjorklund & Green, 1992). For example, research has shown, for example, that 8- to 11-year-old children who overestimated their capabilities had better school performance than did less optimistic children (Lopez et al., 1998). These children may not have been quite as good as they thought, but their school performance was better than that of their more accurate peers. In other research, kindergarten, first-grade, and third-grade children who overestimated their memory abilities showed greater subsequent improvement on memory tasks than more accurate children (Shin, Bjorklund, & Beck, 2007).

Children's overly optimistic appraisal of their abilities also poses some problems, however. For example, Jodie Plumert (1995; Plumert & Schwebel, 1997) reported that 6-year-olds who consistently overestimate their physical abilities were more accident-prone than less optimistic children were. In other research, Plumert and her colleagues (Plumert, Kearney, & Cremer, 2004, 2007) asked 10- and 12-year-old children and adults to determine when it was safe to ride their bikes across a busy street. (They did not actually cross streets. Judgments were made on a virtual street.) Plumert and her colleagues reported that the children were less accurate in making safety judgments than the adults. Children took longer to get moving, so the gap between cars that they judged to be safe resulted in more close calls than when adults made judgments.

What is the origin of young children's tendency for overestimation? It does not seem to stem from a general cognitive deficit in evaluating performance. For instance, Deborah Stipek (Stipek, 1984; Stipek & Daniels, 1988) noted that young children can make relatively accurate predictions of how other children are likely to perform on school-like tasks but are overly optimistic in predicting their own future performance. Stipek suggested that this overly optimistic self-perception is the result of wishful thinking, a concept originally introduced by Piaget (1930): Children wish for A's on their report cards; therefore, they expect A's. By the third or fourth grade, however, children's assessments of their own abilities move closer to reality, and they are able to tell the difference between what they wish would happen and what they can reasonably expect to happen. This is a reflection of children's improving metacognition, discussed in Chapter 7. Stipek believes that this tendency to overestimate one's own abilities enhances children's self-efficacy and gives them the confidence to attempt things they would not otherwise try. Stipek (1984) proposed that rather than trying to make young children's self-assessments more accurate, we

should "try harder to design educational environments which maintain their optimism and eagerness" (p. 53).

Section Review

Few mental concepts are more important to us than the personal sense of self.

Beginnings of Self-Awareness

- Researchers make a distinction between the I-self, or the implicit self, and the me-self, or the explicit self.
- A child's *self-concept* begins to develop in infancy, with mirror recognition being observed as early as 15 months for some children.

Development of Self-Efficacy

- *Self-efficacy* is the sense of control people have over their lives, beginning in infancy and developing during childhood.
- Young children tend to overestimate their abilities, which can be attributed in part to *wishful thinking*, in which children fail to differentiate between their wishes and their expectations.

Ask Yourself . . .

7. What is meant by self-concept, self-esteem, and self-efficacy? Provide examples. What do these concepts share in common, and, conversely, how do they differ?
8. What is the difference between the I-self and me-self of self-concept, and how do they develop? What is meant by saying that a sense of self implies a sense of others?
9. What are the major milestones in self-efficacy development, and how does the concept of self-efficacy relate to social-learning theory? How do children's tendencies to overestimate their abilities relate to the development of self-efficacy?

COGNITIVE BASES OF GENDER IDENTITY

Being male or female is a matter of biology. But behaving in a fashion consistent with societal views of masculinity and femininity and identifying oneself with males or females encompasses more than biology. This process of incorporating the roles and values of one's sex is referred to as **gender identification**. Our identification of ourselves as male or female has implications far beyond reproduction. Unlike other demarcations of social standing, such as age, occupation, or marital status, our gender is one characteristic that, for most of us, remains constant throughout development. All societies make distinctions between the sexes, although outside of reproduction, few (if any) universal roles or behaviors delineate the sexes. What is universal is the significance that gender has in defining who an individual is in society and the striving of children around the world to acquire an appropriate gender role.

Many factors contribute to children's gender identification (see Leaper, 2013; Martin & Ruble, 2004; Ruble, Martin, & Berenbaum, 2006). One important factor is their ability to understand gender as a concept and to understand that gender remains stable over time and is consistent over situations. Whether a boy decides to identify with his father is related to what the boy understands about his gender, that of his father, and the continuity of his own gender over time. Children should not be expected to behave as if gender is important if they are not yet aware that differences among males and females exist and that their own gender is constant. Another important factor is children's knowledge of gender stereotypes. What information do they have about how

boys and men and girls and women behave, and what consequences does this knowledge have for their own actions and attitudes? In the following sections, we review research on the development of gender constancy and gender schemas and how these cognitive factors relate to the societally important process of gender identification.

Gender Constancy

One of the first people to postulate a cognitive basis for gender identification was Lawrence Kohlberg (1966). He proposed that children's understanding of gender develops in the same way as their understanding of the physical world. According to Kohlberg, knowledge of gender follows Piaget's model of cognitive development, with children not having a mature notion of gender until the advent of concrete operations, beginning about 7 years of age.

Development of Gender Constancy

Kohlberg proposed that a key cognitive accomplishment in the understanding of gender is that of **gender constancy**—the knowledge that gender remains the same over time and despite changes in physical appearance. Rheta De Vries (1969) conducted one of the first studies to test this aspect of Kohlberg's theory as part of a larger study of the appearance/reality distinction, discussed in Chapter 5. De Vries reported that 3-year-olds believed a person temporarily changes his or her sex when engaging in opposite-sex behavior or when wearing opposite-sex clothing. That is, boys who wear girls' clothes or play girls' games are, for the time being, girls.

The significance of dress in determining gender for young children is illustrated by an observation that L. J. Stone and Church (1973) reported. A new family with a baby had moved into the neighborhood. When a 4-year-old girl was asked whether the baby was a boy or a girl, she responded, "I don't know. It's so hard to tell at that age, especially with their clothes off" (L. J. Stone & Church, 1973, p. 297). Another demonstration of gender being determined by dress came from my (DB) daughter, Heidi, when she was about 3. She declared that I could not wear a pink shirt because if I did, I would be a girl. The major difference between boys and girls, she said, is that girls wear pink and boys do not. Always fashion conscious, she added that both boys and girls could wear blue and yellow. Pink, it seemed, is the critical color.

Following De Vries's study, several researchers investigated the development of gender constancy in greater detail (Ruble, Balaban, & Cooper, 1981; Slaby & Frey, 1975). In a pioneering study, Ronald Slaby and Karin Frey (1975) interviewed children aged 2 to 5.5 years about their beliefs in the constancy of gender. In agreement with Kohlberg's theory, Slaby and Frey reported three components in the development of gender constancy: (1) gender identity, (2) gender stability, and (3) gender consistency. As Slaby and Frey defined the term, **gender identity** refers to the ability to identify oneself as male or female and to accurately identify the gender of others. **Gender stability** refers to the knowledge that gender remains stable over time. Thus, at some point, little boys come to believe that they will become fathers when they grow up, and little girls believe that they will become mothers. The questions these researchers asked made it clear that the children were expressing not just a preference but a necessity; for example, they asked boys: "Could you ever be a mommy when

you grow up?" **Gender consistency** refers to the knowledge that gender remains the same despite changes in behavior or dress. The researchers tested this knowledge with questions such as "If you wore boys' clothes, would you be a girl or a boy?" and "If you played girls' games, would you be a boy or a girl?" These questions might seem trivial to an adult, but answers by preschool children can be quite revealing (for example, "I can't wear girls' clothes, 'cause then I'd be a girl!").

Slaby and Frey (1975) reported an age-related developmental sequence such that gender identity was acquired before gender stability and gender stability was acquired before gender consistency (that is, identity stability consistency). Other researchers have confirmed this three-stage sequence, with gender identity being achieved, on average, by 2.5 years, gender stability by 4 or 5 years, and gender consistency by 6 or 7 years (Eaton & Von Bargen, 1981; Ruble et al., 2007; see Ruble et al., 2006, for a review). This sequence of development is not confined to North America or to industrialized countries; it has also been found in traditional communities in Belize, Kenya, Nepal, and American Samoa (Munroe, Shimmin, & Munroe, 1984).

As with many other aspects of cognition in young children, performance can be helped or hindered by subtle changes in the task. For example, Warren Eaton and Donna Von Bargen (1981) asked preschool children gender-constancy questions pertaining to (a) themselves, (b) a same-sex child, and (c) an opposite-sex child. The children answered the questions relating to themselves at a more advanced level than they did the questions relating to a same-sex child, and the questions relating to a same-sex child were answered at a more advanced level than the questions relating to an opposite-sex child. In other words, young children become confident of the stability and consistency of their own gender before that of the gender of other children, particularly children of the opposite sex. These and other research findings (for example, Szkrybalo & Ruble, 1999) indicate that seemingly subtle differences in how the gender-constancy task is administered can result in dramatic changes in children's responses. These findings also indicate that beliefs about the constancy of gender are not well established until middle childhood but that even preschoolers sometimes believe gender is constant over time and situations. The range of situations in which they believe this, however, is limited and expands with age.

Consequences of Gender Constancy for Gender Identification

Why should knowing that gender is constant over time and over situations affect children's gender identification? For one thing, it makes little sense to learn the behaviors and roles of one gender if you are not certain that your own gender will remain the same.

Several researchers have compared attention to same-sex models for children who score high on tests of gender constancy (knowing that gender is stable or consistent over time) with children who seem unaware of either the consistency or the stability of gender. In an early study by Slaby and Frey (1975), preschool children were shown a 5.5-minute silent video depicting a man and a woman engaging in simple, separate activities. The man was on one side of the screen and the woman on the other. As children watched the film, an observer recorded the amount of time the children spent attending to the male and female models. Slaby and Frey reported that the high-gender-constancy children spent more time looking at the same-sex model than did the low-gender-constancy children and that

this effect was stronger in boys than in girls. That is, the high-gender-constancy boys looked at the male model longer than did the other boys (108.2 seconds versus 63.0 seconds), and the high-gender-constancy girls looked more at the female model than did the other girls (86.8 seconds versus 63.8 seconds).

Other researchers have reported findings similar to those of Slaby and Frey. For example, in one study, 5-year-old boys who scored high on gender constancy spent more time viewing TV programs featuring a greater percentage of men than did boys who scored lower on a test of gender constancy; no such effect was found for girls, however (Luecke-Aleksa et al., 1995).

In other research, Diane Ruble and her colleagues (1981) showed high- and low-gender-constancy children cartoons, complete with commercials of same-sex or opposite-sex children playing with a gender-neutral toy (a movie viewer). Children were later given the opportunity to play with the movie viewer, along with many other toys not shown in the commercial. The results of this study are shown in Figure 10.4. As can be seen, little difference was found between the high- and low-gender-constancy children when viewing a same-sex model. Differences were substantial, however, when the children viewed an opposite-sex model playing with the toy. The low-gender-constancy children showed no differentiation. They actually played with the movie viewer slightly more when they had seen an opposite-sex child in the commercial. Not so for the high-gender-constancy children, however. These children knew that gender remains constant over time and that there are certain things boys do and other, different things that girls do. When these young children thought that a toy was appropriate for an opposite-sex child (as reflected by the commercial), they avoided it. The

FIGURE 10.4 **Average amount of time spent playing with a toy as a function of stage of gender constancy (high versus low) and sex of model in the commercial (same-sex versus opposite-sex).**

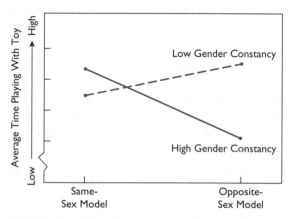

Source: Adapted from Ruble, D. N., Balaban, T., & Cooper, J. (1981). Gender constancy and the effects of sex-typed television toy commercials. *Child Development, 52,* 667–673. Copyright © 1981 The Society for Research in Child Development, Inc. Adapted with permission.

important point here is that this distinction is not made until children have acquired the cognitive sophistication to know that gender is a stable characteristic. In a more recent study, 3- to 6-year-old children who displayed an understanding of gender stability were more likely to wear gender-typed outfits than children with a less-well-developed understanding of gender stability (Halim et al., 2014).

Despite the impressive effects of some of these studies, not everyone looking for the influence of gender constancy of behavior has found it (see Ruble & Martin, 1998; Ruble et al., 2006). One reason some studies fail to find relations between gender constancy and children's behavior may be attributed to overestimating children's knowledge of constancy. For example, some children may display *pseudoconstancy* (Ruble & Martin, 1998; Szkrybalo & Ruble, 1999), revealing

high levels of gender constancy when answering forced-choice questions ("If John wore a dress, would he be a boy or a girl?" "A boy") but illustrating less-secure knowledge when asked to explain their answers ("He's still a boy 'cause he has a boy's face," or "I don't know why"). In general, gender constancy does show regular increases with age and is (often) related to important gender-related behaviors.

Certainly, the process of gender identification involves more than strictly cognitive factors, but it is also very likely that cognitive factors other than gender constancy might be involved in the process as well (see Ruble et al., 2006). For example, recent research has reported that gender constancy is predicted by children's performance on false-belief tasks, a critical measure of preschool children's developing theory of mind (Zmyj & Bischof-Köhler, 2015). In recent years, researchers have emphasized the role of knowledge of gender stereotypes as an important factor, with gender schemas playing a central role as the organizing mechanisms underlying children's gender knowledge.

Gender Schemas

Contemporary cognitive theories of gender identification have been based on the tenets of information processing, particularly the concept of schemas (Bem, 1981; Martin & Halverson, 1981), discussed in Chapter 4. A *schema* is a mentalistic structure consisting of a set of expectations and associations that guide processing with respect to a particular content. According to Diane Ruble and her colleagues (2006), **gender schemas** "are interrelated networks of mental associations representing information about the sexes. Schemas are not passive copies of the environment, but instead they are active constructions, prone to errors and distortions" (p. 908). Carol Martin and Charles Halverson (1981) state that schemas develop primarily from observation. Sex is a salient characteristic in children's worlds, relating both to themselves and to others. Thus, it is used to organize information in place of other, more subtle characteristics of a person or event that older and more knowledgeable children might use. Children use their developing gender schemas to evaluate the appropriateness of some behavior. When children can answer questions such as "Is this OK for boys to do?" positively, they attempt to acquire more information about the activity ("What are the rules of football? How do you throw a pass?").

Martin and Halverson (1987) provide a model of how children might interpret gender-relevant information (see Figure 10.5). Based on observing others, children acquire some idea of sex stereotypes (trucks are for boys, dolls are for girls). Once children have identified themselves as a boy or a girl, they label objects and activities that are for their gender as being "for them," and they incorporate those objects, behaviors, or attitudes into their own-sex schemas. Objects or activities they interpret as being for the other gender are labeled as "not for me" and are avoided, not attended to, or forgotten. Interestingly, American 4- to 8-year-old children viewed adhering to gender roles to be mostly a matter of personal choice, realizing that there may be different gender norms in different cultures, for instance. This effect of gender flexibility was stronger in the older children (Cony-Murray & Turiel, 2012).

Although even infants make distinctions between males and females, they do not seem to have any knowledge of gender stereotypes. This knowledge, however, develops early during the preschool years. Most studies assessing children's knowledge of gender stereotypes use concrete

FIGURE 10.5 **A model of how gender knowledge may be processed beginning in early childhood in agreement with a gender schema theory approach.** Once children identify themselves as boys or girls, they label objects, behaviors, and attitudes as being for one gender or the other, and they incorporate the gender-appropriate ones and avoid the gender-inappropriate ones.

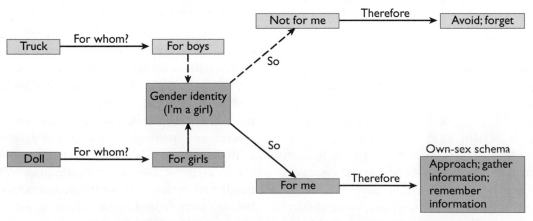

Source: Martin, C. L., & Halverson, C. F. (1987). The roles of cognition in sex role acquisition. In D. B. Carter (Ed.), *Current conceptions of sex roles and sex typing: Theory and research.* New York: Praeger.

objects (for example, a hammer or a doll) or specific activities (for example, playing football or jumping rope) as stimuli (see Ruble et al., 2006). Children are typically shown some objects or pictures of some activities and asked if these objects or activities are usually for girls, for boys, or for both. Not surprisingly, older children generally show greater gender-stereotype knowledge than younger children (for reviews, see Ruble et al., 2006; Signorella, Bigler, & Liben, 1993). Girls are also more likely to say that a toy or activity is appropriate for both sexes, reflecting greater flexibility regarding sex stereotypes in girls than in boys (see Ruble et al., 2006).

Carol Martin and Diane Ruble (2004) proposed that gender stereotyping can be described as involving three phases (see Figure 10.6). The first phase reflects children learning about gender-related characteristics during the first 3 or 4 years of life. The second phase is a period of consolidation, in which gender-related activities are viewed in an inflexible manner, so that children view cross-gender play and activities negatively. Girls and women behave in one way, and boys and men behave in another. Such rigidity of gender stereotypes peaks from 5 to 7 years of age. Children's gender stereotypes become more flexible over the elementary-school years until adolescence, when they become more rigid again. Perhaps not surprisingly, both periods of gender rigidity seem to correspond with milestones in subsequent development of gender identity: the acquisition of gender constancy around 5 to 7 years of age and, in adolescence, awareness of sexual feelings and orientation. Sex-typed behaviors are relatively stable, with children who show the most highly sex-typed behavior from 2.5 to 5 years of age being the most sex-typed at age 8 (Golombok et al., 2008).

This pattern is seen in a study of gender schemas and their relations to sex-stereotypic behavior by Lisa Serbin and Carol Sprafkin (1986). Because sex is a highly salient dimension, Serbin and Sprafkin hypothesized that young children would use gender to classify people and activities to a greater extent than older children would. Older children, whose knowledge of sex roles is greater and whose gender schemas are thus more elaborated, were expected to be more flexible in their classifications, relying less on gender and more on other characteristics of behavior. To assess this hypothesis, 3- to 7-year-old children were administered a gender classification task. In this task, the children were shown photographs of adults engaging in some routine activities. For example, one picture was of a man stirring a pot. The children were then shown three other pictures and were asked to choose the one

FIGURE 10.6 **A model of phase changes in the rigidity of children's gender stereotypes as a function of age.** As children first learn about gender characteristics as preschoolers, they become increasingly rigid in their stereotypes, with rigidity peaking as their gender knowledge becomes consolidated from 5 to 7 years of age. Children become less rigid in their stereotypes until adolescence, when they increase again (not shown in figure).

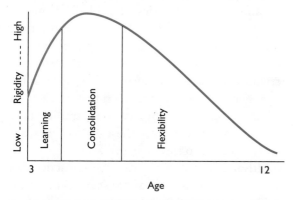

Source: Martin, C. L., & Ruble, D. (2004). Children's search for gender cues. *Current Directions in Psychological Science, 13,* 67–70.

that "went best" with the standard. One picture was of a man reading (same sex, different activity); children who chose this picture as going with the standard would be making a classification based on gender. A second picture was of a woman rolling dough (different sex, similar activity); children choosing this picture would be making their classification on the basis of type of activity. A third picture was of a woman sweeping (different sex, different activity). This third picture was a control picture, and children who chose this alternative would, presumably, be responding randomly. The children were also administered tests of sex typing. For example, they were shown pictures of objects typically associated with males (hammer, shovel, baseball) and others typically associated with females (iron, needle and thread, baby bottle) and were asked who would use each object—boys, girls, or both. When children said that either boys or girls could use the object, they were later asked which sex would use it most. The extent to which children made sex-stereotypic responses was used as an indication of their knowledge of sex stereotypes.

Following the researchers' predictions, children's classifications of activities on the basis of gender declined with age. Three-year-olds chose the same-sex, different-activity picture 57% of the time. This percentage decreased to 20% for the 7-year-olds. Furthermore, children's gender classifications were significantly related to their knowledge of sex stereotypes. Children who knew more about sex stereotypes tended to make *fewer* classifications based on gender. In other words, as children's knowledge of sex roles expands, so do their gender schemas. The better established children's gender schemas are, the more flexible those children become in interpreting gender differences and the more tolerant they become of people engaging in cross-sex activities

(Stoddart & Turiel, 1985). Thus, whereas a 4-year-old might be aghast that his sister's teenage boyfriend wears a dangling earring, the 7-year-old codes it only as an exception to the rule and realizes that it does not alter the maleness of the person (see also Basne et al., 2010).

One primary function of schemas is to organize information, making it more accessible in memory. Several researchers have demonstrated that children remember information that is consistent with their sex stereotypes better than they do information that is inconsistent (P. J. Bauer, 1993; Liben & Signorella, 1993). Perhaps the most impressive demonstration of this is Patricia Bauer's (1993) study with a group of 25-month-old toddlers. In her study, children were shown a series of six activities: two stereotypically masculine activities (for example, building a house), two stereotypically feminine activities (for example, putting a diaper on a baby), and two neutral activities (for example, having a birthday party). Children were then encouraged to imitate each activity, both immediately and following a 2-week delay. The results were similar both for immediate and for delayed imitation: Although no difference was found in successful imitation among the three types of activities for the girls, the boys showed greater imitation of the masculine and neutral activities than of the feminine activities. Moreover, the boys spent more time interacting with the props for the masculine and neutral activities than with those for the feminine activities. These results suggest that, at least for boys, gender schemas are operating as early as 2 years of age, with boys avoiding traditionally feminine activities when these stereotypes are incorporated into their schema.

Although both boys and girls show a decided preference for same-sex toys and activities, and both boys and girls seem to remember and understand same-sex stereotypes better than opposite-sex stereotypes (Liben & Signorella, 1993), these effects generally appear earlier (as in the P. J. Bauer, 1993, study) and are more extreme in boys than in girls. Consistent with these observations, boys show sex-stereotyped toy preferences earlier than girls do (O'Brien & Huston, 1985), and they avoid opposite-sex toys more than girls do (Fagot, Leinbach, & Hagan, 1986). One interpretation of these findings is that young boys are more strongly sex-stereotyped than are young girls (P. J. Bauer, 1993).

There are many levels of gender identification, and even young children who have mastered only the rudiments of gender differences can behave in a more sex-typed fashion than do less knowledgeable children. For example, Beverly Fagot and her colleagues (1986) assessed the relationship between the ability of young children to identify pictures of males and females and their adoption of sex-typed behaviors. Children ages 21 to 40 months were shown pairs of pictures (one of a male, one of a female) and were asked to identify the boys and girls (or men and women). The children were also observed in their preschool classroom to obtain measures of sex-typed behaviors. Differences in aggression, interaction with same-sex peers, and play with sex-stereotyped toys (for example, blocks, trucks, and carpentry tools for boys) were measured. Fagot and her colleagues reasoned that 2- and 3-year-old children with greater knowledge of gender differences (as reflected by their ability to identify males and females) should show greater sex-typed behavior.

The results generally supported the researchers' hypothesis of a relationship between gender knowledge and sex-stereotypic behavior in young children. Children who could correctly apply gender labels to the pictures were more likely to play with same-sex peers, and girls who

performed well on this task showed almost no aggression in the classroom.

In other research, 3-year-old children were shown pairs of photographs of unfamiliar objects with unfamiliar names (for example, *spoodle, blicket*) (Shutts, Banaji, & Spelke, 2010). Each object was paired with a photo of a girl or a boy who expressed a preference for one of the objects (for example, "My name is Mary. I love playing with spoodle; spoodle is my favorite thing to play with" versus "My name is Kevin. I love playing with blicket; blicket is my favorite thing to play with"). Children were then asked which object they would like to play with ("Would you rather play with spoodle like Mary or blicket like Kevin?"). Children in two experiments chose the object associated with their own sex significantly more than by chance. They showed a similar pattern when asked to choose objects preferred by a same-aged child versus an adult. They showed no preference, however, for selecting objects preferred by children of their own race. Shutts and her colleagues (2010) suggested that children encode gender and age categories spontaneously and that these are powerful guides to preferences, more so than race.

Although most of the research cited so far suggests that children's knowledge of gender and gender stereotypes does not become apparent until into the third year of life, this would be an overstatement. Before their first birthdays, infants are able to discriminate between men and women, and by their second birthdays, infants can identify themselves and other children as boys or girls. Table 10.3 (adapted from Martin, Ruble, & Szkrybalo, 2002) provides some of the gender-based knowledge that children demonstrate from 6 months to about 2 years of age. As can be seen, gender has been a salient category in children's lives from very early on, and it should not be surprising that children are quick

TABLE 10.3 **Timeline for early gender development**

Age	Gender-Based Knowledge and Perception
6–8 months	Discriminate between voices of males and females
	Will habituate (reduce looking time) to one category of faces (male or female)
9–11 months	Discriminate between male and female faces
	Associate female faces with female voices
12–14 months	Associate female faces with female voices and male faces with male voices
18–20 months	Associate sex-stereotypic objects with "appropriate" gender (that is, associate male faces with male-stereotypic objects and female faces with female-stereotypic objects)
	Associate verbal labels (*lady, man*) with appropriate faces
24–26 months	Correctly identify pictures of boys and girls
	Imitate gender-related sequences
	Generalize imitation to appropriate gender (for example, using a male doll to imitate a masculine activity)

Source: Martin, C. L., Ruble, D. N., & Szkrybalo, J. (2002). Cognitive theories of early gender development. *Psychological Bulletin, 128,* 903–933.

to associate different behaviors and expectations from males and females, including themselves (once they identify which they are).

Gender Cognition in Transgender Children

In this section, we have described the development of children's gender cognition, from infancy to middle childhood, and how such cognition may influence children's gender-related preferences, beliefs, and behaviors. Gender development involves more than cognition, of course (Eagan & Perry, 2001; Leaper, 2013). Moreover, our account to this point has been one of developmental function, implicitly assuming that all children will eventually develop a mature understanding of what it means to be male or female in a particular culture. However, there can be substantial individual differences in children's gender

identity, with such differences being perhaps most apparent for transgender children. In the United States, the phenomenon of transgender has recently received increased attention, highlighted by the 2015 "coming out" of Caitlyn Jenner (formerly Olympic gold medalist Bruce Jenner). A transgender person is one whose natal, or birth, sex is inconsistent with one's gender identity. This is often expressed as "being a man in a woman's body" or "being a woman in a man's body." Although most of the headlines have been captured by adults who announce their transgender status, there is increasing awareness of transgender children.

One concern about children who feel their birth sex is at odds with their gender identity is that children may be too young to understand the implications of identifying with the opposite sex or they may simply be reporting what they know to be the opposite for their gender and not really identifying with the other gender (Walsh, 2014).

Alternatively, children who express the belief that they were born into the wrong body may only be experiencing a delay in their gender-identity development. For instance, in a study done before *transgender* became a familiar term, Kenneth Zucker and his colleagues (1999) reported that children referred for problems in their gender identity showed more immature levels of gender constancy (gender identity, gender stability, gender consistency) than control children, suggesting to the authors that these children's gender identity reflected a developmental lag.

Although much research has been done with gender-nonconforming children (Byne et al., 2012), little research has been done examining the gender cognition of transgender children. An exception is a recent study that examined both explicit (that is, being consciously aware, as in self-reports) and implicit (that is, without conscious awareness) gender identity in a group of 5- to 12-year-old transgender children. Kristina Olson, Aidan Key, and Nicholas Eaton (2015) reasoned that if transgender children were confused, they may display a discrepancy in their self-reported gender identity (explicit) and their implicit gender identity. Explicit gender identity was measured by (a) *explicit gender preference*, in which children were asked on a series of trials which of two people (one male, one female) they would prefer to be friends with, and (b) *explicit object preference*, in which children were asked to choose which novel object with an unfamiliar name (*flerp, babber*) they would like to play with, the one associated with a female or the one associated with a male. (This is similar to the task described earlier by Shutts et al. [2010].)

For implicit tests of gender identity, children were given two versions of the implicit association test (IAT) (Greenwald, McGhee, & Schwartz, 1998). This test uses the speed with which people make decisions about words or concepts (for example, *good* and *bad*) when they are associated with different social groups (for example, boys and girls). Participants perform a number of reaction-time tasks, responding as quickly as they can. In the critical series of tests, participants see a boy's (or girl's) face and a set of positive words (for example, *puppies, ice cream cone, flowers*) or negative words (for example, *snake, spider, car accident*). For instance, in one block of trials, participants must hit one key when they see a boy's face and a positive word and another key when they see a girl's face and a negative word. Then the relations are switched, and they must hit one key when they see a boy's face and a negative word and a different key when they see a girl's face and a positive word. This test was first developed to assess implicit (unconscious) racial bias in adults; college students typically have faster reaction times when White faces are paired with positive words and Black faces are paired with negative words, revealing an implicit bias for White and against Black faces. This pattern is usually at odds with explicit, self-report measures of racial bias (most college students claim to have none).

Children performed two implicit association tests: (a) *gender-preference IAT*, in which children's reaction times were compared when presented with photos of boys and girls associated with "good" and "bad" words, as described in the preceding paragraph; and (b) *gender-identity IAT*, in which the categories *good* and *bad* were replaced by the categories *me* (*I, mine,* and *myself*) and *not me* (*them, theirs,* and *other*). When children's reaction times are consistent with their sex, scores will be positive (that is, above zero). For the transgender children, reaction-time patterns were computed based both on their gender identity and on their birth sex.

The performance of 32 transgender children, ranging in age from 5 to 12 years, was compared to an age-matched control group of 32 nontransgender (cisgender) children and to 18 cisgender siblings of the transgender children. Patterns for the two implicit and two explicit tasks are shown in Figure 10.7. When children's reactions are consistent with their sex, scores are positive (that is,

FIGURE 10.7 **Patterns for the transgender and control children on implicit and explicit tests of gender identity.** Results of the (a) gender-identity implicit association test (IAT), (b) gender-preference IAT, (c) explicit peer preferences, and (d) explicit object preferences. For each measure, mean scores are shown separately for transgender participants (coded both for their expressed gender and for their birth sex), control participants, and siblings of the transgender participants. Means above zero indicate preference for the same sex or gender, and means below zero indicate preferences for the opposite sex or gender. As you can see, the transgender children showed a clear preference for their expressed gender rather than for their birth gender.

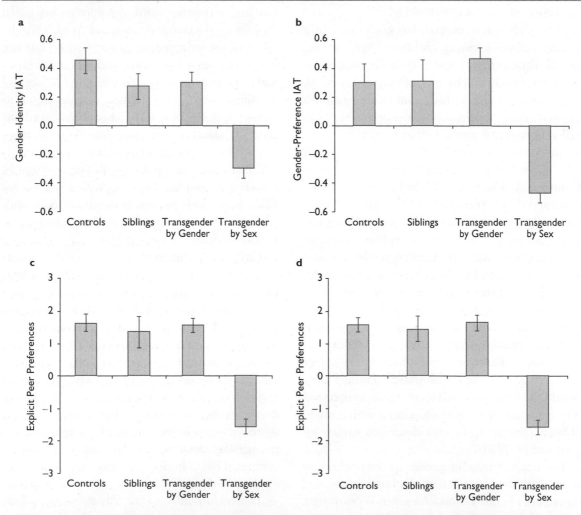

Source: Olson, K. R., Key, A. C., & Eaton, N. R. (2015). Gender cognition in transgender children. *Psychological Science, 26*, 467–474.

above zero). As can be seen, patterns for the control children and the siblings of the transgender children were positive for all tasks, both the implicit (gender-identity IAT, gender-preference IAT) and the explicit (explicit peer preference, explicit object preference) tests. The same consistent pattern was found for the transgender children, but only when viewed from their gender identity. In contrast, the transgender children displayed the opposite pattern to the cisgender children when responses were coded in terms of their birth sex.

Olson and her colleagues (2015) interpreted these findings as reflecting the fact that the transgender children were not confused or displaying a delay in their gender identity. Rather, they showed the age-typical pattern of gender identity, except their decisions—both explicit and implicit—were based on their transgender identity and not on their natal sex.

Children's Theories of Gender

The process of gender identification is a complex one, involving biological dispositions and culture-appropriate experiences. However, it also seems clear that cognitive differences among children contribute substantially to their developing identification with members of their own sex. Controversy does exist concerning how important cognitive factors are in gender identification (in comparison with environmental and biological factors), as well as about which aspects of cognitive development are most important. Moreover, once cognitive factors are given their due, there is the question of how gender knowledge in its various forms influences children's sex roles and behaviors. But there is little question that children's knowledge of gender roles and their understanding of the concept of gender are important for development.

Children realize early that gender is an important dimension and formulate theories concerning exactly what it is that differentiates the sexes. Many of these theories are wrong. For example, a 6-year-old boy, noticing that my (DB) infant daughter had brown hair, just like his, asked if that meant "she will be a boy when she gets older." It's also reflected by the story that opened this chapter, of a 4-year-old boy declaring that he had figured it out: "Men eat pizza and women don't."

Once a child starts mingling with peers, what other children do largely determines what is viewed as appropriate male and female behavior, often independent of the wishes of that child's parents. For example, people we know refused to buy guns for their 3-year-old son and restricted the number of aggressive programs he watched on television. Nevertheless, the boy learned from his preschool peers that gun play is boys' stuff: He ran around the house pointing sticks, spoons, or fingers at people and saying "bang," despite constant reprimands from his parents. He had learned from other 3-year-olds one special thing that boys do and, over his parents' objections, was making it something that he did as well.

Children continually gain knowledge about what differentiates males and females in society, and with this knowledge, they continually devise and test theories about sex differences (as suggested by theory theories of cognitive development; see Chapter 6). Their early theories are simplistic, based on the grossest of characteristics (clothing, for example), and often are not even tangentially related to societal sex stereotypes. However, much like the scientist delving into a new field of inquiry, children discard old theories, try new ones, and eventually acquire the meaning of gender that is implicitly agreed on by members of their society.

Section Review

The process of incorporating the roles and values of one's sex is referred to as *gender identification*.

- Children's knowledge of *gender constancy* develops during the preschool years, with *gender identity* preceding *gender stability*, which in turn precedes *gender consistency*.
- *Gender schemas* are mentalistic structures consisting of a set of associations and expectations related to gender.
- Gender schemas influence how children process information related to gender and are related to their knowledge of sex stereotypes and gender-related behavior.
- *Transgender children* display age-typical patterns of gender identity, except their decisions—both explicit and implicit—are based on their transgender identity and not on their natal sex.
- Implicit understanding of gender identity can be assessed using the *implicit association test (IAT)*.
- As children's knowledge of gender expands, their schemas change, resulting in a more sophisticated use of gender in classifying people and behavior.

Ask Yourself . . .

10. What is meant by the concepts of gender identity, gender constancy, gender consistency, and gender stability? Provide examples. When do these concepts develop, and how do they influence one another?
11. What are gender schemas? How do these relate to social learning?
12. What does the evidence say about transgender children's patterns of gender identity? Are these children "confused"? How is the IAT used in this research?
13. How does knowledge of gender schemas and stereotypes influence children's perceptions of gender and behavior? Do they become more or less rigid with age?

HOW SPECIAL IS SOCIAL COGNITION?

Should social cognition be covered at all in a textbook on cognitive development, or does it more properly belong in books about social development? Our opinion on this issue should be obvious, given the inclusion of this topic in this book. People use the same brains that they do to solve analogical-reasoning problems or to compute the cost per ounce of laundry detergent to figure out what other people are thinking and how they themselves should best behave. Whereas people with faulty mathematical or scientific reasoning abilities will likely get along all right in the world, someone who lacks a well-developed sense of self, shows deficits in social learning, or is ineffective at social information processing is in for a tough time.

We mentioned in the introduction to this chapter that some people believe human intelligence evolved in the form that it has chiefly to deal with other members of our species (R. D. Alexander, 1989). We are far more intelligent than necessary to eke out an existence on the African savannas. In fact, so are chimpanzees. Nicholas Humphrey (1976) suggested that most of humans' technological genius is absent from our daily lives. If alien anthropologists had observed Albert Einstein during a typical day, they would likely infer that he had a humdrum mind. But we do use our superior intelligence every day when dealing with other people. We became the intelligent species not so much to cope with the demands of a hostile physical world but to cooperate and compete with members of our own species.

Like all others, however, this form of cognition develops. Children are born prepared by evolution for a social world, but they do not have the requisite skills necessary to function effectively in that world. Their social intelligence emerges, in part, following a universal timeline, much as Piaget proposed, but also varying as a function of the particular society they are born into. There is much variability among cultures, and children must have the cognitive skills to adapt to the particular environment in which they live. But what is common to all children across the globe is that they are part of a social species, and they develop the intellectual skills necessary to live in such a world.

KEY TERMS AND CONCEPTS

active intermodal mapping
emulation
forethought
gender consistency
gender constancy
gender identification
gender identity
gender schemas
gender stability
imitative learning
implicit association test (IAT)
innate releasing mechanism
    (or fixed-action pattern)

local enhancement (or
    stimulus enhancement)
mimicry
mirror neurons
mutual imitation
neonatal imitation
observational learning
ontogenetic adaptations
overimitation
self-concept
self-efficacy
self-reflection
self-regulation

social cognition
social cognitive theory
social information
    processing
social learning
social learning theory
symbolization
teaching (or instructed
    learning)
transgender children
vicarious learning
wishful thinking

SUGGESTED READINGS

Scholarly Works

Leaper, C. (2013). Gender development during childhood. In P. D. Zelazo (Ed.), *The Oxford handbook of developmental psychology: Vol. 2. Self and other* (pp. 326–377). New York: Oxford University Press. This is a comprehensive review of gender development written by a leading expert in the field.

Nielsen, M. (2012). Imitation, pretend play, and childhood: Essential elements in the evolution of human culture? *Journal of Comparative Psychology, 126,* 170–181. Mark Nielsen proposes that children's developing mental representational abilities as reflected by pretend play and their natural imitative abilities, as reflected by overimitation, were the essential ingredients in the evolution of the modern human mind and that these abilities were afforded by humans' extended period of childhood. This is a provocative paper that reviews much of the literature on the development of children's social learning.

Tomasello, M. (2016). Cultural learning redux. *Child Development, 87,* 643-653. This paper presents a brief summary of Tomasello's ideas on the social origins of human cognition and a discussion of some of the different forms of social learning.

Reading for Personal Interest

Seligman, M. E. P. (with Reivich, K., Jaycox, L., & Gillham, J.). (1995). *The optimistic child.* Boston: Houghton Mifflin. Martin Seligman describes children as being inherently optimistic and provides some ideas for how to promote such optimism and how to turn optimistic kids into optimistic and psychologically healthy adults.

Tomasello, M. (2009). *Why we cooperate.* Cambridge, MA: MIT Press. In this short book, Michael Tomasello provides a concise and highly readable review of his group's research with both children and great apes, all pointing to the importance of social cognition in the development and evolution of human intelligence.

11 SCHOOLING AND COGNITIVE DEVELOPMENT

IN THIS CHAPTER

Eight-year-old Nicholas was reading a book with his grandmother, who was impressed at how well he was reading and told the young boy so. "It's a trick, Grandma," he said, almost conspiratorially. "I'm not really reading. I just see the word and I know it." Nicholas no longer had to sound out words to "know" them, and to him, this wasn't reading, it was a trick. Nicholas had "broken the code." He was no longer learning to read but was on his way to reading to learn.

Reading is perhaps the single most important technological skill in postindustrial cultures. Children learn to read using universal cognitive skills, but it is unheard of for an unschooled child from an illiterate culture to learn to read. Humans did not evolve to read. Unlike language, reading is rarely acquired spontaneously.

Reading is understandably classified in educational circles as a language skill, but it is a very different language skill, acquired in a very different way, from a child's native tongue. Although all neurologically typical children learn to be proficient speakers of their native language, not all learn to be proficient readers, even with instruction.

If reading is the number one technological skill in modern society, mathematical abilities must come in second. Verbal and quantitative skills constitute the two major subtests of the Scholastic Assessment Test (SAT), the Graduate Record Exam (GRE), and even most IQ tests (see Gardner, 1983). Although there is more to verbal and quantitative abilities than reading and mathematics, these are the core abilities. Unlike with reading, basic mathematical skills can be acquired without formal schooling. However, beginning in preschool, children in postindustrial societies receive instruction in simple number concepts and arithmetic, and math constitutes one of the primary subject areas in schools.

In this chapter, we review the development of reading and mathematical abilities. Individual, gender, and cultural differences in these topics have been of great interest to educators and the public at large, and we devote considerable space to these issues. In the latter part of the chapter we look at several issues directly related to cognitive development and schooling. We selected these issues from the many topics we could have included in this chapter primarily because we believe they are related to issues that we have already dealt with in this book or will deal with in the final two chapters: First, how does the effect of schooling influence cognitive development in comparison with the effect of age? Second, what is the effect of schooling on IQ? We conclude the chapter with a brief section on a new way of thinking of the relation between schooling and cognitive development: *evolutionary educational psychology*.

DEVELOPMENT OF READING SKILLS

Overview of Learning to Read

Learning to read involves acquiring a set of skills that are built on preceding skills. Jeanne Chall (1979) proposed five stages in the development of proficient reading, ranging from the prereading skills of the preschool child to the highly skilled reading of the adult.

Stages of Learning to Read

In Stage 0, covering the years before a child enters first grade, children must master the prerequisites of reading, most notably learning to discriminate the letters of the alphabet. By the time children enter school, many can already "read" some words, such as *Pepsi, McDonald's, Pizza Hut*, and perhaps their own names. Many also now recognize some of the letters in their name, especially the first letter (Trieman et al., 2007). Their ability to recognize these symbols, flashed at them from the television and seen repeatedly on the roadside or the dinner table, indicates that they can tell the difference between patterns of letters, even if they are unable to sound out the words. Children's knowledge of letters and single words is generally better than it was several generations ago, partly because of the influence of children's television shows such as *Sesame Street*.

Stage 1 covers children's first year of formal reading instruction. In kindergarten or first grade, children learn phonological recoding skills, used to translate written symbols into sounds and thus words. This is followed in the second and third grades by Stage 2, in which children learn to read fluently. By the end of the third grade, most children have mastered the letter-to-sound correspondence and can read many words and simple sentences. But reading is effortful for these children, in that the process of identifying individual words requires so much of their limited mental resources that they often do not comprehend much of what they read. They are still concentrating on what individual sets of letters mean and are not very skilled at putting the words together to discern the broader meaning of the text.

The change from learning to read to reading to learn begins in Stage 3, usually spanning Grades 4 through 8. Children can now more readily acquire information from written material, and this is reflected by the school curriculum. Children in these grades are expected to learn from the books they read. If children have not mastered the "how to's" of reading by fourth grade, progress in school can be difficult. Stage 4, beginning in the high school years, reflects truly proficient reading, with adolescents becoming increasingly able to comprehend a variety of written material and to draw inferences from what they read.

Not surprisingly, like many other things, children become better readers the more they read. This results in an interesting phenomenon called the **Matthew effect**, in which the difference between good and poor readers increases over time (Stanovich, 1986). The name comes from the New Testament's Book of Matthew, which makes the observation (basically) that the rich get rich and the poor get poorer. ("For to everyone who has, more shall be given, and he will have an abundance; but from the one who does not have, even what he does have shall be taken away," Matthew 25:29, New American Standard Version.) Good readers, because they enjoy and are relatively good at reading, read more and thus become increasingly proficient at reading, whereas poor readers, who are less skilled and enjoy it less, read less and, although they may be improving in an absolute sense, find themselves falling further behind their more skilled peers. And developing reading proficiency early has important implications for later reading and achievement. In fact, the results of a 2011 longitudinal study of nearly 4,000 students revealed that children who had not become proficient readers by the end of third grade were 4 times more likely to drop out of school than proficient readers, with this rate being nearly 6 times greater for children who failed to master basic reading skills by the end of the third grade (Hernandez, 2011).

Emergent Literacy

Although most children learn to read in school, most learn *about* reading in the home. They learn that arbitrary written symbols correspond to spoken language and convey meaning. They learn that writing is used to communicate with others, as a memory reminder (writing down a phone number to call later), and for pleasure. In the United States and many other literate cultures in the world, books are written for the sole purpose of adults to read to children. Parents who share storybooks and picture books with their preschool children are teaching them much about reading and are preparing their children for success in a literate culture. For example, mothers and fathers who read to their children have children with better language, cognitive, and reading abilities (Oliver, Dale, & Plomin, 2005), as do preschoolers who participate in shared reading programs at school (Piasta et al., 2012). Reading child-appropriate picture books to children may be especially important, as such books have a greater diversity of words than is found in conversation with children, providing an important source of vocabulary for preschoolers (Montag, Jones, & Smith, 2015). In fact, the American Academy of Pediatrics (2014) advises that all parents should read age-appropriate books aloud to their children, beginning in infancy, to promote language and preliteracy skills.

Further evidence that reading to young children promotes language and literacy skills is provided by a recent brain-imaging study. John Hutton and his colleagues (2015) imaged the brains of nineteen 3- to 5-year-old children while they listened to age-appropriate stories and related patterns of brain activation to children's history of being read to. Children who were exposed to more language, including being read to, compared to children who were read to less often, showed greater neural activation in the left parietal-temporal-occipital association cortex, an area of the brain associated with language processing, mental imagery, and narrative comprehension. This effect held even after controlling for family income. This result suggests that being read to not only affects the brain while children are hearing a story but also establishes a pattern of neural activation associated with better imagery and understanding, critical in efficient reading.

But most preschool children do not read—not really. They might be able to identify Coca-Cola, Burger King, or Fruit Loops signs when they see them, but this is not really reading. Nevertheless, what children are learning during story times with a parent and in a household where reading is done frequently are skills that set the stage for true reading. The idea that there is a developmental continuum of reading skills, from those of the

preschooler to those of the proficient reader, is referred to as **emergent literacy**. According to Grover Whitehurst and Christopher Lonigan (1998) emergent literacy "consists of the skills, knowledge and attitudes that are presumed to be developmental precursors to conventional forms of reading and writing . . . and the environments that support these developments (for example, shared book reading)" (p. 849). Whitehurst and Lonigan (1998) list nine components of emergent literacy:

1. *Language.* Reading is obviously a language skill, and children need to be versatile with their spoken language before they can be expected to read it. However, skilled (and even early) reading requires more than just proficiency with spoken language. Reading does *not* seem to be simply a reflection of spoken language, with children with advanced language skills becoming children with advanced reading skills.

2. *Conventions of print.* Children exposed to reading in the home know the conventions of print. For example, in English, children learn that reading is done left to right, top to bottom, and front to back.

3. *Knowledge of letters.* Knowledge of letters is critical for reading, and most children can recite their ABCs before entering school and can identify individual letters of the alphabet (although some children think *elemeno* is the name of the letter between *k* and *p*).

4. *Linguistic awareness.* Children must learn to identify not only letters but also linguistic units, such as phonemes, syllables, and words. Perhaps the most important set of linguistic abilities for reading deals with phonological processing, or the discrimination and

making sense of the various sounds of a language.

5. *Phoneme-grapheme correspondence.* Once children have figured out how to segment and discriminate the various sounds of a language, they must learn how these sounds correspond to written letters. Most begin this process during the preschool years, with letter knowledge and phonological sensitivity developing simultaneously and reciprocally.

6. *Emergent reading.* Many children pretend to read. They will take a familiar story book and "read" one page after another, often "just like Daddy does," or will take an unfamiliar book and pretend to read, making up a narrative to go along with the pictures on the pages.

7. *Emergent writing.* Similar to pretend reading, children often pretend to write, making squiggles on a page to "write" their name or a story, or stringing together real letters to produce something they think corresponds to a story, a shopping list, or a note to Mom.

8. *Print motivation.* How interested are children in reading and writing? How important is it for them to figure out what the secret code is that permits adults to make sense of a series of marks on a page? Children who are interested in reading and writing are more likely to notice print, ask questions about print, encourage adults to read to them, and spend more time reading once they are able.

9. *Other cognitive skills.* A host of individual cognitive skills, in addition to those associated with language and linguistic awareness, influence a child's reading ability. Various aspects of memory are important, and some of these will be discussed.

Relations between any specific component of emergent literacy and later reading are sometimes difficult to establish. However, it is clear that families that provide the whole package of emergent literacy skills to their children have children who are better readers, both early in school and later, than do families that provide less of the package (Sénéchal & Jo-Anne LeFevre, 2002, 2014; Whitehurst & Lonigan, 1998). This has been confirmed by longitudinal studies that report significant relations between emergent literacy skills assessed during the preschool years and reading ability in elementary school (Lonigan, Burgess, & Anthony, 2000; Storch & Whitehurst, 2002).

As in other aspects of school performance, differences in reading are frequently found as a function of socioeconomic status (SES) (Schwanenflugel & Knapp, 2016). Children from poverty homes are much more likely to encounter reading problems in school than are children from middle-income homes. The point we want to make here is that these SES differences do not begin in school but in the home in the years before children begin formal reading instruction. Parents from lower-SES families are much less likely to read to their children, have fewer books in the house, and generally do not foster the emergent literacy skills that are so important in learning to read. Reading may be a highly technological skill, but its origins are in everyday family interactions.

Does this mean that children's literacy skills are determined before they enter school? No, but their experiences at home do establish a foundation on which school instruction is based. And the quality of home environments tends to be stable. Children who receive intellectual support for literacy early in life can expect similar support later on. (See Chapter 13 for a discussion of the stability of intelligence.) This implies that children from homes in which emergent literacy is *not* fostered will likely not receive the kind of support during the elementary school years that is associated with proficient reading. It also suggests that if the amount or quality of support in the environment (both home and school) changes for the better, so, too, may children's reading abilities (Lonigan et al., 2013; Schwanenflugel et al., 2010). For example, Anne Hargrave and Monique Sénéchal (2000) reported that preschool children with vocabulary skills more than 1 year behind their peers showed significant gains in vocabulary as a result of small-group (eight children per group) shared book reading. More recent research by Christopher Lonigan and his colleagues (2013) similarly reported improvements in letter knowledge or phonological knowledge as a function of small-group reading interventions for groups of low-income children.

Cognitive Development and Reading

There are a number of cognitive abilities related to skilled reading that develop over the preschool and school years (Hulme & Snowling, 2013). Charles Hulme and Margaret Snowling (2013) examined the cognitive processes underlying early reading skills in alphabetic languages, using evidence from (a) comparisons of children with and without reading disabilities, (b) longitudinal studies examining the early cognitive abilities that predict later reading ability, and (c) training studies that look at the effect that instruction in a particular skill has on improvements in children's reading proficiency. They identified three "cognitive foundation" skills for early reading: letter knowledge, phonemic awareness, and rapid automatized naming. We investigate research on each of these skills briefly in the following

sections, as well as two other cognitive skills that become important in children's later reading, phonological recoding and working memory.

Letter Knowledge

In the previous section on emergent literacy, we noted letter knowledge is critical for reading. A number of studies have reported a connection between letter knowledge and later reading. For example, several studies have found moderate associations between children's letter knowledge at the beginning of first grade and reading ability at the end of the school year (Lervåg, Bråten, & Hulme, 2009; Muter et al., 2004), whereas other research has shown that preschool children given training in letter knowledge improved their pre-literacy skills both immediately following the training and 5 months later (Bowyer-Crane et al., 2008). Hulme and Snowling (2013) proposed that letter knowledge permits children to sound out words on a letter-by-letter basis, as well as establish letter-to-sound (visual-phonological) associations, which permits children to mentally represent a printed word with its pronunciation. Proficient reading does not involve sounding out individual letters but rather recognizing whole words and retrieving meaning directly from long-term memory, but this cannot be done effectively until children master knowledge of individual letters.

Phonemic Awareness

Phonemic awareness is the knowledge that words consist of separable sounds. Such awareness is generally not available to preschool children. In one early study, 4- and 5-year-olds were taught to tap once for each sound in a short word (Liberman et al., 1974). For instance, children would tap twice for *at* and three times for *cat*. Although the children presumably understood the task, their performance was poor, with none of the 4-year-olds (and only a few of the 5-year-olds) performing it accurately. Although this task might seem trivial, it predicts children's early reading achievement quite well (Melby-Lervåg, Lyster, & Hulme, 2012). Other aspects of phonological awareness (such as children's abilities to detect rhymes) also develop slowly during the preschool and early school years and predict reasonably well children's early reading skills (Brunswick, Martin, & Rippon, 2012; Wagner et al., 1997). This is also true in languages other than English (Caravolas et al., 2012), including Chinese, which includes a phonetic component in its characters (McBride-Chang & Wang, 2015).

These findings are only correlational, and perhaps children who read well acquire good phonemic awareness along the way. But there is also evidence of a causal influence of phonemic awareness on reading abilities. For example, some longitudinal studies that measure phonemic awareness well before children learn to read show that children with good phonemic awareness as prereaders become more proficient readers when they start school (Brunswick et al., 2012; Lyytinen et al., 2001). Also, preschool, kindergarten, and first-grade children who receive instruction in phonemic awareness show enhanced early reading ability relative to children not given such instruction (Bowyer-Crane et al., 2008; Cunningham, 1990). Anne Cunningham (1990) states that the results from her training study argue against the idea that phonemic awareness is a consequence of learning to read. Rather, she proposes, as have others (Hulme & Snowling, 2013), phonemic awareness is causally related to reading achievement, even in the early stages of learning to read.

Research has shown that children's sensitivity to rhymes leads to awareness of phonemes, which in turn affects reading and also presumably makes it easier for children to recognize written words that both sound and look alike (for example, *cat* and *hat*) (Bryant et al., 1990). Other research has suggested that it is not children's sensitivity to rhymes, per se, that is the critical component to literacy but rather the ability to segment phonemes (Muter et al., 1998). Valerie Muter and her colleagues tested a group of preschool children (average age, 4 years, 3 months) on rhyming and phonemic segmentation abilities. Tests of rhyming included asking children to identify pictures and then to pick out those that rhyme, and to produce words that rhymed with each of two words (*day* and *bell*). For one test of phonemic segmentation, children were shown a picture of an object (a cat, for instance), the interviewer provided the first two phonemes (*ca*), and children were asked to finish the word (in this case, say *t*). In another test, children were shown a picture and asked to say the word without the first phoneme (for example, "Bus without the /b/ says . . . ," with the correct response being "us"). The researchers reported that reading ability at the end of first grade was significantly related to preschool phonemic segmentation ability but not to rhyming ability.

Rapid Automatized Naming (RAN)

In Chapter 7 we discussed speed of processing with respect to executive functions and working memory. Briefly, we noted that children become faster at processing information with age and that the speed with which they process information is related to how many items they can hold in working memory. The less time it takes children to process a word, for example, the more time they have to work on that word (rehearse it, for instance) before it decays from working memory. With respect to reading, speed of processing has been investigated using **rapid automatized naming (RAN)** tasks. RAN refers to the ability to rapidly name as many familiar items (words, numbers, colors, digits) as possible. Many studies have reported significant relations between RAN and reading fluency for children over a broad age range (Kirby et al., 2010), and between children with and without reading disabilities (Norton & Wolf, 2012), with "faster" children displaying better reading abilities.

George Georgiou and his colleagues (2013) questioned why RAN is related to children's reading fluency. The researchers administered groups of Grade 2 and Grade 6 Greek children a series of speeded tasks and related children's performance to their reading proficiency. Georgiou et al. reported that the RAN tasks that best predicted reading ability were those in which children had to name randomly arranged recurring digits and objects (for example, naming as quickly as possible the digits *2, 4, 5, 7,* and *9,* presented randomly a total of 10 times each on a computer screen). Georgiou and his associates suggested that the reason RAN and reading ability are so highly correlated is because both require serial processing—processing a known set of items sequentially (words in text for reading and items on a computer screen for RAN)—as well as the articulation of specific names. In other words, speed matters, and children who are faster to articulate series of individual items display greater reading fluency than slower children.

Phonological Recoding

The reason that phonological awareness is such a good predictor of early reading is that early reading generally involves sounding out words. This process of **phonological recoding** is the basis of the majority of reading-instruction programs in the United States today (the *phonics* method).

Children are taught the sound of each letter and how to combine these sounds, blending them into words.

The relation between printed and spoken words is referred to as *grapheme-phoneme correspondence,* and how easy it is for children to learn to read is related to how obvious these relationships are in their language. For example, as speakers and readers of English, you are likely aware that the relationship between letters and sounds is often quite variable, and this represents a difficult task for readers. For instance, the playwright George Bernard Shaw commented that, following the rules of English spelling, *ghoti* should be a perfectly acceptable alternative spelling for the word *fish*: *gh* as in *cough, o* as in *women,* and *ti* as in *nation* (go ahead, sound it out). English has what is called a *deep orthography,* meaning the spelling system for converting letters into sounds is irregular, with there being multiple ways in which some letter combinations can be sounded out. Other languages, such as Finnish, German, and Italian, have *shallow orthographies,* with there being a close correspondence between letters and their sounds. For example, Italian uses 25 phonemes, and 33 combinations of letters are used to represent these sounds. In contrast, English uses 40 phonemes, but 1,120 different letter combinations are needed to completely represent these sounds. Because of these differences, languages with shallow orthographies such as Spanish and Italian are relatively easy to learn to read, whereas languages with deep orthographies such as English and Danish are more difficult to learn to read.

The relationship between children's reading ability and the degree to which the written language corresponds to the spoken language (that is, the degree to which a language is orthographically regular) is illustrated in Figure 11.1. This figure presents the percentage of children speaking and reading languages with shallow orthographies (Greek, Finish, and Italian) and languages with deep orthographies (French, Danish, and Scottish English) who correctly read familiar real words and pseudowords (Seymour, Aro, & Erskine, 2003; Ziegler & Goswami, 2005). Pseudoword reading requires children to read a sequence of pronounceable letters that do not make up a word (for example, *joak*, *kake* in English). As you can see, performance was nearly perfect for children reading languages with regular (shallow) orthographies but much lower for children reading languages with irregular (deep) orthographies. The effect of the depth of a language's orthography not only influences children's ability to decode nonsense words but is associated with the rate at which children learn to become proficient readers. For example, Philip Seymour and his colleagues (2003) reported that after 1 year of instruction, children learning Dutch, which has a shallow orthography, were able to read an average of 95% of words correctly, whereas English-speaking children achieved only a 34% accuracy.

The importance of phonological coding to proficient reading can also be seen by looking at children with reading disabilities, often referred to as **dyslexia** (Melby-Lervåg et al., 2012). Children are said to have a reading disability if they have great difficulty in learning to read despite an average intelligence. Stated another way, if a child's reading ability is substantially worse than his or her general intellectual ability would predict, that child is said to have a reading disability, or dyslexia. Perhaps the single best predictor of reading difficulty is phonological processing, including phonological recoding (Melby-Lervåg et al., 2012; S. White et al., 2006). For example, early research by Linda Siegel and her colleagues (Siegel, 1993; Siegel & Ryan, 1988) compared the phonological processing of groups of children

FIGURE 11.1 **Percentage of correct responses of children reading familiar real words and pseudowords for orthographically regular languages (Finish, Greek, and Italian) versus orthographically irregular languages (French, Danish, and Scottish English).**

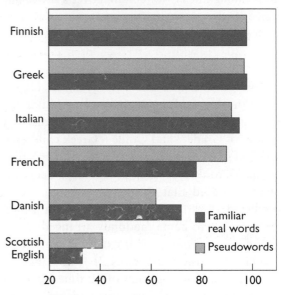

Source: Adapted from data in Seymour, P. H. K., Aro, M., & Erskine, J. M. (2003). Foundations of literacy acquisition in European orthographies. *British Journal of Psychology, 94*, 143–174.

with and without reading disabilities ages 7 to 14 years. As one test of phonological processing, children were asked to read pseudowords. As can be seen in Figure 11.2, older children with reading disabilities were better at pseudoword reading than younger disabled readers were, demonstrating that these skills were developing. However, the performance of 13- and 14-year-old children with reading disability was comparable to that of 7- and 8-year-old nondisabled readers, reflecting a significant delay of this skill. Moreover, longitudinal research suggests that phonological-processing abilities remain relatively stable over childhood (Storch & Whitehurst, 2002; Wagner et al., 1997), making early intervention all the more important.

Research using brain-imaging techniques has supported the interpretation that phonological problems are at the core of many reading disabilities (Shaywitz, Mody, & Shaywitz, 2006; Shaywitz et al., 1998). For example, Sally Shaywitz and her colleagues (1998) gave adults with developmental reading disabilities and non–reading disabled adults a series of reading-related tasks that varied in the amount of phonological processing required to perform each task. Brain activation patterns, as measured by functional MRI (see Chapter 2), were observed between the normal and dyslexic readers. Shaywitz and her colleagues reported different brain-wave patterns for the nondisabled and disabled readers, especially when the tasks required substantial phonological processing. Compared with the nondisabled readers, the normal readers showed underactivation in some portions of the brain (mainly posterior regions) and overactivation in others (mainly anterior regions). Underactive parts of the brain included those areas typically associated with phonological processing and cross-modal integration. In reading, cross-modal integration (see the discussion of cross-modal integration in infancy in Chapter 4) involves the translation of symbols in one modality (in this case vision, as in the letters and words on a page) into another modality (in this case audition, as in the sounds of letters and words). Shaywitz and her colleagues (1998) concluded that the patterns of brain activity of dyslexic readers "provide evidence of an imperfectly functioning system for segmenting words into their phonological constituents . . . and adds neurobiological support for previous cognitive/behavioral data pointing to the critical role of phonological analysis and its impairment in dyslexia" (p. 2640).

Further evidence for the neurological basis of reading disability comes from a study assessing brain activation patterns of dyslexics in Great Britain, France, and Italy (Paulesu et al., 2001). Eraldo Paulesu and his colleagues reported similar patterns of brain activity (PET) while reading for groups of university-level English-, French-, and Italian-speaking dyslexics. Moreover, all three groups showed deficits in tests of phonological short-term memory, pointing, again, to problems in phonological processing as the basis for dyslexia. But there was an interesting catch in this study. Although dyslexics from the three languages did equally poorly in tests of phonological processing, only the English and French speakers

FIGURE 11.2 **Accuracy of pseudoword reading as a function of age for normal and reading-disabled children.** The number of pseudowords correctly read increased with age for both groups of children but was higher at each age for the normal children than for the children with reading disability.

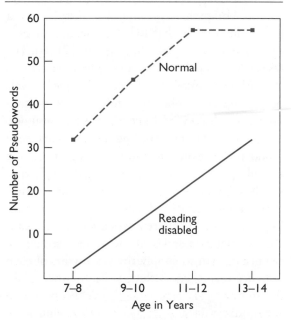

Source: Siegel, L. S. (1993). The cognitive basis of dyslexia. In R. Pasnak & M. L. Howe (Eds.), *Emerging themes in cognitive development: Vol. 2. Competencies* (pp. 33–52). New York: Springer-Verlag. Copyright © 1993 Springer-Verlag New York, Inc. Reprinted with permission.

showed problems in reading. The Italian dyslexic group displayed relatively good reading ability. They had been identified as dyslexic based on impaired reading speed and poor phonological processing, true reading difficulties being rare in Italian university-level adults.

Why should this be so? The reason seems to be related to the specific language people speak, and specifically, the relationship between how a language is spoken and how it is written. As noted earlier, the correspondence between spoken and written Italian is quite close, whereas both English and French have deep orthographies.

What this research indicates is that the neurological basis of dyslexia is universal, likely the result of unknown genetic or prenatal anomalies; however, the likelihood that this particular neurological abnormality will adversely affect reading is a function of how closely the written language of one's culture corresponds to the structure of its spoken language. If you recall from Chapter 3 our discussion of the tools of intellectual adaptation a culture provides to its members, the relationship between the structure of one's spoken and written language is another unexpected (at least to us) way in which one's culture influences one's thought.

Working Memory

Efficient reading involves a series of processes, each of which must be integrated with one another for proper comprehension. Individual words must be identified and related to other words in the sentence. One factor that limits children's comprehension is the amount of information they can hold in working memory at any one time. Over 30 years ago, Meredyth Daneman and her colleagues proposed that it is necessary for information to be retained in working memory for as long as possible so that each newly read word in a passage can be integrated with the words and concepts that preceded it. Younger or less-proficient readers have less available mental capacity to store and maintain information in working memory because it is necessary for them to devote considerable capacity to the processes involved in identifying words and comprehension. Daneman and her colleagues showed that listening span, defined as the number of successive short sentences that can be recalled verbatim, correlates significantly with comprehension for people ranging from preschoolers to college students (Daneman & Blennerhassett, 1984; Daneman & Green, 1986).

More recent research has clearly shown the relationship between memory span and reading ability for children over a broad age range (Pickering, 2006; S. Wang & Gathercole, 2013). The relationship between working memory and reading comprehension was demonstrated in a longitudinal study that followed children ages 8 to 11 years (Cain, Oakhill, & Bryant, 2004). The researchers reported that individual differences in working memory predicted subsequent levels of reading comprehension independent of children's vocabulary and general reading abilities. Moreover, deficits in working memory have been found to be related to the incidence of reading disabilities (S. E. Gathercole et al., 2006; Swanson & Jerman, 2007). For example, in an early study, Linda Siegel and Ellen Ryan (1989) gave 7- to 13-year-old children with and without reading disabilities a series of incomplete sentences, requiring them to supply the final word of each sentence. Sentences included the following: "In the summer it is very _____," "People go to see monkeys in a _____," "With dinner we sometimes eat bread and _____." After being presented two, three, four, or five such sentences, children were asked to repeat the final words, in order, that they had generated for each sentence (presumably *hot*, *zoo*, and *butter* here). The results of the study are graphed in Figure 11.3. As can be seen, working memory improved with age for both the children with and without reading disabilities, but the children with reading disabilities had shorter memory spans than the normal readers at each age level.

Sex Differences in Reading and Verbal Abilities

"Female superiority on verbal tasks has been one of the more solidly established generalizations in the field of gender differences," wrote Eleanor Maccoby and Carol Jacklin (1974, p. 75) in introducing their section on gender differences

FIGURE 11.3 **Performance on a working-memory task as a function of age for children with and without reading disabilities.** Working memory increased with age for both groups of children but was higher at each age for the normal children than for the children with reading disability.

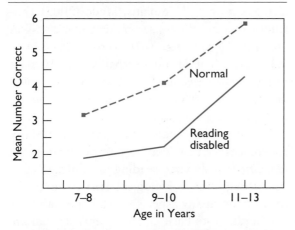

Source: Siegel, L. S. (1993). The cognitive basis of dyslexia. In R. Pasnak & M. L. Howe (Eds.), *Emerging themes in cognitive development: Vol. 2. Competencies* (pp. 33–52). New York: Springer-Verlag. Copyright © 1993 Springer-Verlag New York, Inc. Reprinted with permission.

in verbal ability in their seminal book that set the stage for contemporary investigations of sex differences. In reviewing research on sex differences in verbal abilities more than 20 years after the publication of Maccoby and Jacklin's book, Diane Halpern (1997) concluded that females, on average, perform better than males do on "tasks that require rapid access to and use of phonological and semantic information in long-term memory, [and] production and comprehension of complex prose" (p. 1091). The topic of sex differences in verbal ability has continued to be of interest to contemporary researchers, in part because of the importance reading and verbal ability have for education and economic success in modern society.

One technique that has permitted researchers to better evaluate the extent of sex differences in verbal abilities is meta-analysis. Meta-analysis provides an estimate of *effect size*, which is expressed in terms of how large the average differences between males and females are across various studies, taking into consideration the overall amount of variability. An effect size of 1.0 would mean that the average male-female difference was one standard deviation in magnitude. If this were for IQ, for example, it would be equivalent to saying that the average difference between the sexes was about 15 points, which would be quite substantial. The statistic of effect size is used because it would be meaningless to compute mean performance across the many different studies, which used different measurements and often assessed different verbal tasks. By using the effect-size statistic, differences in performance among different studies can be meaningfully combined.

The first meta-analysis of verbal sex differences was reported by Janet Hyde (1981), who examined 27 studies of verbal ability included in the original Maccoby and Jacklin (1974) review.

Hyde reported an effect size of 0.24 (about one quarter of a standard deviation, favoring females). Since the publication of Hyde's report, several other meta-analytic studies have been published, and they point to similar conclusions. For example, in the most recent meta-analysis, examining sex differences in language achievement based on teacher-assigned grades for 81 samples, Daniel and Susan Voyer (2014) reported an effect size of 0.37, favoring females, slightly greater than one third of a standard deviation. Other studies have reported that the sex differences in verbal abilities favoring females have become smaller in recent decades, especially when assessed via standardized tests (Feingold, 1988). More recent studies typically continue to show a small female advantage on most verbal tests, but the magnitude of the advantage varies with the test, with males actually scoring higher than females on some. For example, since revising the Verbal portion of the Scholastic Assessment Test (SAT) in 1972, males have consistently scored slightly higher than females, from 2 to 13 points, on the Critical Reading portion of the test, from 1972 to 2013. The 2013 SAT results for college-bound high school seniors reported a slight edge for males on the Critical Reading test (499 versus 494), although females showed an advantage on the writing test (493 versus 482), as they have every year since the test was first offered in 2006 (College Board, 2013).

Sex differences in reading and verbal abilities are not limited to the United States but are found worldwide. The results of a 25-nation study assessing the reading/verbal abilities in fourth-grade children in 2001 are presented in Figure 11.4 (from Halpern et al., 2007; based on data reported in Mullis et al., 2003). The length of each line reflects the magnitude of the sex difference, favoring girls, in each country. In every country, females performed significantly

better than males. Similarly, in a 2006 study of sex differences in reading ability among secondary school students in over 40 countries, the average effect size, favoring females, was 0.19 (Lietz, 2006).

Despite the relatively consistent female advantage in verbal abilities, the absolute difference is small. For example, in her original meta-analysis, Hyde (1981) concluded that the gender of the child alone accounted for approximately 1% of the variance in verbal performance. In other words, these findings mean that the difference, although statistically significant, is small in absolute magnitude. To understand the magnitude of these differences, look at the idealized distribution of verbal skills for males and females graphed in Figure 11.5 (expressed as standard scores). You can see substantial overlap of performance between males and females, and the absolute difference in the means is small. Moreover, there is even more variability within the sexes than between them. That is, although there is a substantial and consistent average difference in reading ability between boys and girls, many boys are better readers than many girls. In fact, in a review of meta-analyses of sex differences for all domains, Hyde (2005) concluded that the effect sizes in most meta-analyses are in the close-to-zero (< 0.10) or small (0.11 to 0.35) range. This includes verbal ability. Based on results summarized in Hyde (2005), we computed an average effect size for verbal ability of about 0.10 (favoring females).

There is no single reason for these sex differences, but boys are far more likely to be identified as having reading disabilities than girls, suggesting a biological basis. Moreover, the fact that many aspects of reading disabilities can be traced to basic cognitive abilities that are found early and tend to be stable over childhood suggests that there is a substantial biological component to reading disabilities.

FIGURE 11.4 **Sex differences in reading/verbal abilities in 25 countries.** The longer the line, the greater the sex difference, favoring girls.

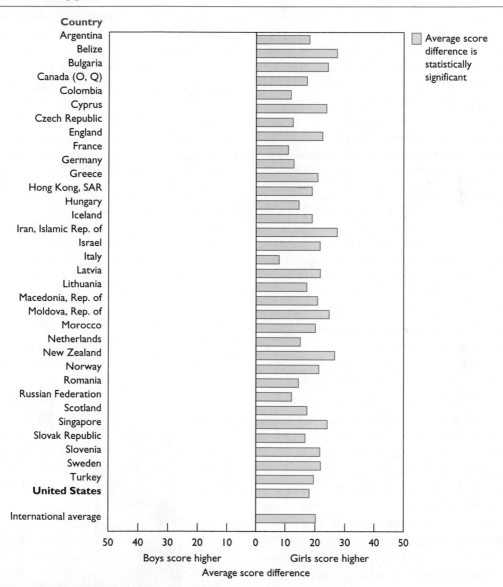

Source: Halpern, D. F., Benbow, C. P., Geary, D. C., Gur, R. C., Hyde, J. S., & Gernsbacher, M. A. (2007). The science of sex differences in science and mathematics. *Psychological Science in the Public Interest, 8*, 1–51.

Sex differences in brain structure or function may be partly responsible for sex differences in reading and verbal abilities. We discussed briefly sex differences in brain development in Chapter 4. Females' brains are more symmetrical than males, in that the proportion of gray

FIGURE 11.5 **Idealized distribution of verbal ability for males and females.**

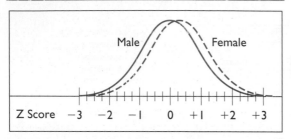

Source: Hyde, J. S. (1981). How large are cognitive gender differences? A meta-analysis using w² and d. *American Psychologist, 36,* 892–901. Copyright © 1981 American Psychological Association. Reprinted with permission.

and white matter is more similar in the two hemispheres. Also, females are more apt to use language-related areas of their brains in solving complex problems than males (see Halpern et al., 2007). This pattern suggests that females should outperform males on verbal tasks, consistent with the findings.

But experiential factors also likely play a role in sex differences in reading ability. Reading and the expression of feelings (both verbal tasks) are viewed as stereotypically female activities and might contribute to girls' superior verbal skills. Also, many of the stories in children's reading books are not inherently interesting to children, and evidence suggests that boys are particularly motivated by the interest level of the reading material (Renninger, 1992). For example, Steven Asher and Richard Markel (1974) reported that fifth-grade boys displayed better comprehension for stories of high interest than for those of low interest. This difference in reading level was much smaller for fifth-grade girls (see Figure 11.6).

Book publishers are aware of the importance of interest in getting boys to read and are publishing books with topics more appealing to boys. The *Harry Potter* series did a lot to get boys (and girls) interested in reading, and recently publishers have come out with boy-oriented books that are not always welcomed into the elementary school classroom. For example, a 2015 list of popular fiction books for boys found on Amazon.com included *Diary of a 6th Grade Ninja, Ninja Farts: Silent but Deadly (The Disgusting Adventures of Milo Snotrocket),* and *Aliens in Underpants Save the World (The Underpants Series).*

The origins of sex differences have long fascinated psychologists. Are differences mainly the result of genes and biology or mainly the product of culture and learning? This led many in academic psychology to use the term *sex differences* to refer to differences between males

FIGURE 11.6 **Mean reading comprehension scores for high- and low-interest stories for groups of fifth-grade boys and girls.**

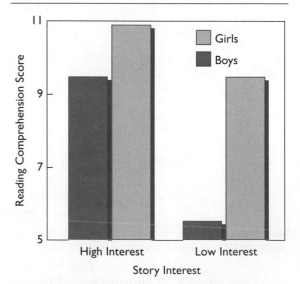

Source: Adapted from Asher, S. R., & Markel, R. A. (1974). Sex differences in comprehension of high- and low-interest reading material. *Journal of Educational Psychology, 66,* 680–687.

and females that were attributed chiefly to biology and *gender differences* to those that were attributed chiefly to learning and culture. Although well meaning, such a distinction perpetuates a false nature-nurture dichotomy—the belief that the contributions of biology and culture (or genes and environment, or biology and learning) can be neatly separated and packaged (Halpern, 2004). For all practical purposes, the terms *sex differences* and *gender differences* are equivalent. (For simplicity sake, we use *sex differences* here, although *gender differences* would have been equally appropriate.) According to Halpern (2004), "Differences in the interests of females and males both derive from differences in the areas in which they have achieved success and lead to further differential success in these areas because of differential knowledge and experience. Learning is both a biological and an environmental variable, and biology and environment are as inseparable as conjoined twins who share a common heart" (p. 138). This does not mean that searching for the origins of sex differences is not useful, only that it is not an either/or matter. Rather, all aspects of psychological functioning interact over time to produce the differences between males and females that we observe.

Section Review

Reading is perhaps the most critical technological skill for people in postindustrial societies.

Overview of Learning to Read

- Chall proposed five stages of learning to read: (1) the prereading skill of letter identification, (2) phonological recoding in the first grade, (3) fluent but effortful reading in Grades 2 and 3, (4) reading to learn in Grades 4 through 8, and (5) proficient reading in high school and beyond.
- Children become better readers the more they read, producing the *Matthew effect*, in which the difference between good and poor readers increases over time.
- *Emergent literacy* refers to the skills, knowledge, and attitudes presumed to be developmental precursors to conventional forms of reading and writing and the environments that support these developments.
- There are at least nine components to emergent literacy: language, knowledge of the conventions of print, knowledge of letters, linguistic awareness, phoneme-grapheme correspondence, emergent reading, emergent writing, print motivation, and other cognitive abilities, such as memory.

Cognitive Development and Reading

- Letter knowledge is critical for reading, with early letter knowledge predicting later reading proficiency.
- *Phonemic awareness* is the knowledge that words consist of separable sounds and is an essential skill for proficient reading in children learning alphabetic languages.
- *Rapid automatized naming (RAN)* refers to the ability to rapidly name as many familiar items (words, numbers, colors, digits) as possible. Many studies have reported significant relations between RAN and reading fluency for children over a broad age range.
- *Phonological recoding* is the process of sounding out words and is the basis of the phonics method of reading instruction. Children with *dyslexia*, or reading disability, generally have poor phonological recoding skills.
- The relation between printed and spoken words is referred to as grapheme-phoneme correspondence, and the ease with which children learn to read printed words is related to how obvious these

relationships are in their language. Learning grapheme-phoneme correspondence is more difficult in languages with deep orthographies, such as English, than in languages with shallow orthographies, such as Spanish.

- Individual differences in working memory are related to children's reading proficiency, with children with dyslexia having deficits in working memory relative to nondisabled readers.

Sex Differences in Reading and Verbal Abilities

- Sex differences on verbal tasks have been assessed using *meta-analysis*, which summarizes the findings of different studies using effect size.
- The magnitude of sex differences in verbal ability has been declining over recent decades.
- More boys than girls are classified as dyslexic.
- Interest is more important for boys' reading than for girls' reading.

Ask Yourself . . .

1. What is the Matthew effect? How does it pose a challenge for educators?
2. What are the components of emergent literacy, and how are these skills related to reading later in school?
3. How does the family/home environment influence reading development?
4. What are the cognitive foundation skills for early reading, and how do they contribute to the development of reading?
5. How does the depth of orthography of a child's language affect his or her reading development? How is it related to the presentation of a learning disability?
6. How is working memory important for reading? What tasks are used to measure the relationship between working memory and reading ability?
7. How have meta-analyses been used to examine sex differences in verbal ability? What have we learned from these studies?
8. What gender differences have often been found in reading and writing, and how do you explain them?

CHILDREN'S NUMBER AND ARITHMETIC CONCEPTS

Although the quintessential symbols of human cognition are probably found in language, a good case can be made for the primacy of numbers. Our tendency to quantify objects and events in our world is ubiquitous. The bulk of the technological advancements made during the past 3 centuries, and particularly in this and the last century, can be attributed to our species' quantitative skills. Although children develop a basic sense of number and mathematical relations without explicit instruction, most people's mathematical abilities are acquired through formal instruction. This is true even of simple arithmetic as well as more complicated mathematics.

Arithmetic is one of education's three *R*s, and thus a discussion of its development clearly belongs in a chapter devoted to schooling and cognition. But, just as language serves as a basis for reading (and writing), there are cognitive primitives that underlie arithmetic and other mathematical skills, and we examine the development of these abilities as well.

We begin this section examining Robert Siegler and Hughes Lortie-Forgues's (2014) *integrative theory of numerical development*, which suggests that mathematical development can be explained by "the continuing growth of understanding of numerical magnitudes"

(p. 144), beginning with intuitive and nonsymbolic representations of numbers through more advanced mathematics including fractions and negative numbers. We follow this with a look at the development of mathematical conceptual and procedural knowledge, focusing primarily on the development of arithmetic strategies. We then look briefly at characteristics of children with math disabilities, followed by an examination of cross-cultural differences in mathematical achievement. We then explore the controversial topic of sex differences in mathematical ability. Do such differences exist? If so, how big are they, and what difference do they make?

Integrative Theory of Numerical Development

Robert Siegler and Hughes Lortie-Forgues (2014), in their integrative theory of numerical development, propose that numerical development involves four major acquisitions: (1) representing with increasing precision nonsymbolic numbers; (2) linking nonsymbolic and symbolic numerical representations; (3) extending the range of numbers that can be accurately represented; and (4) representing numbers other than whole numbers, including fractions, decimals, and negative numbers.

Contemporary theory proposes that the representation of nonsymbolic quantities is performed by the approximate number system (ANS), an intuitive, nonsymbolic system for thinking about quantities (Feigenson, Libertus, & Halberda, 2013; Mussolin et al., 2016), discussed with respect to numerosity, ordinality, and simple arithmetic in Chapter 4 on infant cognitive development. The ability to represent approximate numbers using ANS is sometimes referred to as *number sense* (Feigenson, Dehaene, & Spelke, 2004).

Although as we saw in Chapter 4, even infants within their first year of life can use ANS to make "more than" and "less than" decisions about the numerosity of two sets, this ability develops with age into adulthood. For example, when presented with arrays of black and white dots and asked to determine as quickly as possible without counting whether there are more black dots or more white dots, age differences are found in the magnitude of the ratio needed before accurate discriminations can be made. Figure 11.7 presents arrays of black and white dots and the average ratio needed at five ages before accurate distinctions can be made. (The 6- and 9-month-old infants obviously are not verbally asked to make a decision, but differences in visual attention are used to determine their ability to differentiate the arrays; see Chapter 4.) As you can see, 6-month-olds are able to make accurate assessments only when the ratio of the black to white dots is 2:1. This ratio improves to 3:2 by 9 months of age, to 4:3 by about 3 years of age, and to 6:5 by about 6 years of age. Some adults are able to make accurate discriminations for ratios of 11:10 (from Siegler & Lortie-Forgues, 2014).

Other research has shown that young children's performance on tasks tapping ANS predicts later mathematics achievement, consistent with Siegler and Lortie-Forgues's second acquisition, linking nonsymbolic and symbolic numerical representations. For example, preschoolers who are better able to select the more numerous of two sets of dots (much like those shown in Figure 11.7) have higher math achievement 1 to 2 years later (Chu, vanMarle, & Geary, 2015; Libertus, Feigenson, & Halberda, 2011).

The skills tapped by ANS represent what David Geary has described as biologically primary abilities. Recall from Chapter 2 our discussion of Geary's (1995, 2005) ideas about

FIGURE 11.7 **Development of knowledge of nonsymbolic numerical magnitudes.**

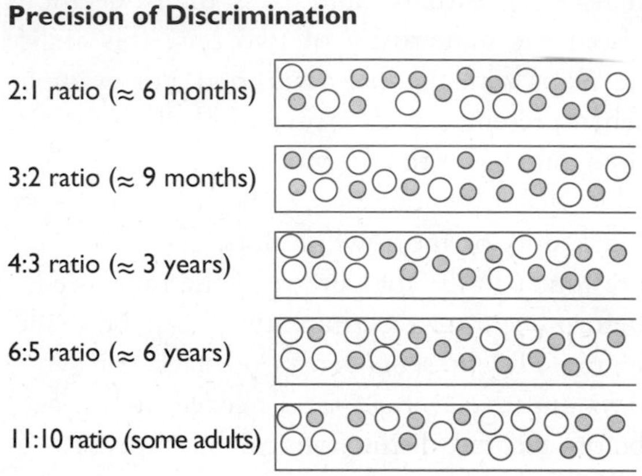

Precision of Discrimination

2:1 ratio (≈ 6 months)

3:2 ratio (≈ 9 months)

4:3 ratio (≈ 3 years)

6:5 ratio (≈ 6 years)

11:10 ratio (some adults)

Source: Siegler, R. S., & Lortie-Forgues, H. (2014). An integrative theory of numerical development. *Child Development Perspectives, 8,* 144–150.

biologically primary and biologically secondary abilities. The former represent basic cognitive abilities that were selected during evolution to solve recurrent problems faced by our ancestors, are universal, and are acquired at about the same time and in about the same way by all typically developing children. In contrast, biologically secondary abilities are built on biologically primary abilities, are specific to a particular culture, and often need tedious repetition and external pressure for their mastery. Siegler and Lortie-Forgues's theory considers both biologically primary and secondary abilities and shows that the two are related.

Siegler and Lortie-Forgues's third acquisition, extending the range of numbers that can be accurately represented, is reflected by children's increasing ability to estimate relative magnitude of symbolic numbers (for example, Arabic numerals) and its association with mathematical performance. One task used for such purposes is the *number line estimation* task, in which children are shown a line with the two end points

identified by whole numbers (for example, 0 and 10 for young children, 0 to 100 for older children) (Siegler & Opfer, 2003). With increasing age, children are better able to accurately place a number on the number line, with individual differences in number line placement being positively associated with math achievement from kindergarten through eighth grade (Booth & Siegler, 2008; Siegler, Thompson, & Schneider, 2011).

Another task that has been used to measure children's understanding of number magnitude is the *symbolic numerical comparison* task, in which children are presented with two Arabic numbers and asked to determine as quickly as possible which is the larger of the two. This is typically done by presenting two numbers on opposite sides of a computer screen and asking children to press one key (*S*, for instance) if the number on the left is numerically larger and a different key (*L*, for instance) if the number on the right is larger. For most school-age children, accuracy is near perfect, but what does differ among children is the speed with which they make their decisions, with older children being faster than younger children. Children who make faster decisions also have higher math achievement. This latter effect has been found across a broad age range (including adults) and for children from diverse cultures (see DeSmedt et al., 2013).

With respect to the ability to represent numbers other than whole numbers, the fourth acquisition in Siegler and Lortie-Forgues's theory, children seem not to acquire an understanding of fractions, decimals, and negative numbers without explicit instruction. Moreover, unlike their understanding of whole numbers, most adults seem not to develop a sophisticated mastery of these concepts (DeWolf et al., 2014). However, like with simpler forms of arithmetic, children's ability to estimate number magnitude using the line estimation task predicts children's later understanding of fractions (Jordan et al., 2013; Vukovic et al., 2014). For example, in one longitudinal study, children's performance on number line estimation tasks and their knowledge of whole-number arithmetic in first grade predicted fraction knowledge in middle school, even after controlling for IQ, SES, and working memory (Bailey et al., 2015).

As the theory's name suggests, Siegler and Lortie-Forgues's integrative theory of numerical development integrates a wide range of numerical cognitions—from discriminating between arrays of dots, a task that can be performed by 6-month-old infants, to understanding fractions and negative numbers. The theory connects unconscious and nonsymbolic processes associated with the approximate number system to the conscious and symbolic processing of whole numbers and fractions.

Development of Conceptual and Procedural Mathematical Knowledge

A distinction can be made between conceptual and procedural mathematical knowledge. *Conceptual knowledge* refers to understanding the principles underlying a particular mathematical operation, such as knowing that each item in an array is associated with one and only one number name when counting or that fractions represent part-whole relations. *Procedural knowledge* refers to the use of basic operations involved in solving a math problem, such as the strategies used in addition and subtraction. In this section we examine the development of some of the basic conceptual and procedural abilities in children's mathematics, including conservation of number, counting, and arithmetic strategies.

Conservation of Number

Piaget (1965) believed that the concept of number is reflected in conservation. **Conservation-of-number** tasks follow the same basic procedures as all of Piaget's conservation problems (see Chapter 5). Children are first shown a set of items—black jelly beans, for instance. The children are then asked to take white jelly beans from a container so that there are an equal number of black and white beans. Once the appropriate number of white beans has been selected (with assistance from the experimenter, if necessary), the beans are arranged in two rows, one black and one white (see Figure 11.8). While the children are watching, the experimenter spreads out the white jelly beans so that the line of white beans extends beyond the line of black beans. The children are then asked if the two rows still have the same number of jelly beans. If they answer no, they are asked which row has more, and why.

As with conservation in general, Piaget proposed three stages in the acquisition of the conservation of number. In Stage 1, children are unable to consistently establish a one-to-one correspondence between the two sets of items. So, for example, Stage-1 children select too few or too many white jelly beans or fail to arrange them in a one-to-one relationship with the black beans. When two equal sets of beans are established and one is modified, children say that the longer, less-dense row now has more beans in it, being unable to ignore the perceptual differences between the two rows. During Stage 2, children can establish an "intuitive one-to-one correspondence" (Piaget, 1965) between the items in the two sets, but judgments of equivalence between the sets do not last long. Once the beans in one row are extended, the children say that there are more in the longer row. Only the Stage-3 child (concrete operations) realizes that the number of

FIGURE 11.8 **A conservation-of-number task.**

"Select from the jar the same number of white jelly beans as there are black jelly beans."

"Are there the same number of black jelly beans as there are white jelly beans?"

The row of white jelly beans is extended while the child watches.

"Are there the same number of white jelly beans as there are black jelly beans now? Which has more? Why?"

beans does not change when one of the rows is elongated and that changes in spatial extension of elements are compensated for by equivalent changes in the density of the elements.

Non-Piagetian research, using variants of Piaget's original task, has generally replicated his observations, illustrating that (a) children are able to form a one-to-one correspondence before they can conserve; (b) young children make their evaluations on the basis of relative length, independent of other factors; (c) slightly older children sometimes consider density but do not coordinate the dimensions of length and density, thus failing to conserve in many situations; and (d) not until 7 or 8 years of age do children

consistently pass conservation-of-number tasks (see Brainerd, 1978).

According to Piaget, the core ability underlying conservation of number, *inversion reversibility*, is necessary if children are to understand addition and subtraction. For example, if 5 + 3 = 8, then, by the logical rule of inversion, 8 − 3 must equal 5. In one experiment, Piaget (1965) showed children an array of eight objects. The array was then modified; for example, it was divided into two equal sets of four objects and was then divided a second time into unequal sets (seven and one, for instance). Do children recognize the equivalence of these two groupings? In other words, do they know that 4 + 4 is the same as 7 + 1? As with conservation of number, Piaget reported three stages in children's early arithmetic abilities. In Stage 1, characterizing 5- and 6-year-olds, the children typically relied on the spatial arrangement of the objects, erroneously asserting that there were different numbers of elements in the two combinations. In Stage 2, the children could correctly solve the task, but only after counting the objects or establishing a spatial one-to-one correspondence between the items. The Stage-3 children (7-year-olds) solved the problem without resorting to physical counting techniques. Without this understanding, according to Piaget, children cannot have a true comprehension of addition, although they can be taught to memorize certain formulas (for example, 2 + 3 = 5, but will they know what 3 + 2 equals?).

Learning to Count

Three-year-old Paul was fascinated by the staircase in a neighbor's home, and, while climbing the stairs and then scooting down them on his backside, he counted them, saying one number word for each step he traversed: "One, two, three, four, five, seven, nine, ten, eleven-teen, twelveteen, fiveteen, seventeen, nineteen, *twenty*." He usually said the last number word with some authority, often stating, "There are 20 of them." Paul used some, but certainly not all, of the number words that adults in his culture use, but he obviously had some things to learn. He also likely did not understand numbers and counting the way he would in just a few years. But he was motivated to count, realizing, at some level, that this is an important thing to do.

By the time children can speak, most give the impression of having some concept of number. The 18-month-old might respond with a loud and definitive "Two!" when asked how many cookies he wants, and the 3-year-old might point at her dolls, saying, "One, two, three, seven, nine, twelveteen, threeteen, seventeen." Each is displaying some knowledge of number, yet neither is using numbers with the same consistency and meaning that a 7- or 8-year-old child can.

How do children's conceptions of numbers develop? One popular non-Piagetian candidate for the precursor of number conservation is counting. Rochel Gelman and C. R. Gallistel (1978) extensively investigated children's early counting and proposed five principles:

1. *The one-one principle.* Each item in an array is associated with one and only one number name (such as *two*).
2. *The stable-order principle.* Number names must be in a stable, repeatable order.
3. *The cardinal principle.* The final number in a series represents the quantity of the set.
4. *The abstraction principle.* The first three principles can be applied to any array or collection of entities, physical (for example, chairs, jelly beans) or

nonphysical (for example, minds in a room, ideas).
5. *The order-irrelevant principle.* The order in which things are counted is irrelevant.

R. Gelman and Gallistel (1978) referred to the first three principles as the "how-to" principles of counting and proposed that children as young as 2.5 years demonstrate knowledge of them under some circumstances. For example, in a counting experiment where 3-, 4-, and 5-year-old children were asked to discern the number of objects in a series of arrays, all groups of children used the one-one principle (that is, one unique number name per object), although performance deteriorated for the youngest children for arrays of six or greater. Let us provide an example of a 4-year-old child's difficulty applying the one-one rule. Brendan and his grandfather were playing a catch game, in which each took a specified number of steps backward before one threw a ball to the other. In playing, Brendan called his numbers aloud, one number per step. This began to break down, however, once the numbers got larger than five. He'd call out "One, two, three, four, five, six, seven, eight, nine," pausing between announcing some of the larger numbers. But although his counting slowed down when he reached six, his stepping didn't. By the time he got to nine he'd taken more than a dozen steps, violating the one-one rule of counting.

R. Gelman and Gallistel (1978) also reported that children who counted items in arrays used the stable-order principle; more than 90% of the 4- and 5-year-olds and 80% of the 3-year-olds used the same list of number words in the same order on all trials. The children sometimes used an idiosyncratic list of number words, as young Paul did on the example that opened this section, but they used this list consistently across arrays of varying size.

Children seem to have mastered the cardinal principle by age 4. For example, Karen Fuson and her colleagues demonstrated that after counting arrays of objects ranging in number from 2 to 19, 3- and 4-year-old children generally gave the last counting word they had spoken in response to the question "How many things are there?" (Fuson et al., 1985). This was true even for children who counted incorrectly, implying that accurate counting is not a requirement for attainment of the cardinal principle. However, many 2- and 3-year-olds seem to have only a tenuous grasp of the cardinality principle. For example, children might correctly count a set of objects, "One, two, three, four, five," but, when asked how many objects are in the set, instead of stating the last number they counted ("five"), they often count again (Fuson, 1988). It's as if the purpose of the first count was independent of determining how many objects were in the set. Most of these children can come up with the correct answer, but that they seemed to think that a second count was necessary suggests that this knowledge is not well established.

In related research, Diane Briars and Robert Siegler (1984) investigated children's knowledge of the counting principles. These researchers asserted that children must induce which features of counting are critical and which are merely optional in enumerating an array, and they speculated that some children might believe that more is required for successful counting than is actually the case. In their experiment, 3-, 4-, and 5-year-old children watched a puppet counting and were asked to determine whether the puppet had counted properly. The puppet demonstrated (sometimes accurately and sometimes inaccurately) five features of counting, one of which was necessary for counting and four of which were optional. The necessary feature was that of word-object correspondence, which encompasses the first two principles of R. Gelman and Gallistel (one-one correspondence and stable order). The four optional features were that (1) adjacent objects were counted consecutively, (2) counting started from the end rather than the middle, (3) counting progressed from left to right, and (4) each object in an array was pointed to exactly once.

Children's knowledge that word-object correspondence was critical in counting increased with age (30%, 90%, and 100% for the 3-, 4-, and 5-year-olds, respectively). However, 60% of the 5-year-olds also viewed other features, such as beginning to count at an end rather than in the middle and pointing to each object only once, as essential. Other research has shown, however, that children as old as 11 years of age continue to believe that the order in which items are counted (for example, left to right or top to bottom) is essential for proper counting (Kamawar et al., 2010). In other words, young children learn the critical features of counting by 4 years of age but infer, from watching others, additional features that are characteristic of, but not necessary for, proper counting. They must not only learn the necessary rules for proper counting but also ignore conventional but unnecessary rules (Rodríguez et al., 2013). Other research has shown that children's mastery of counting principles at the end of kindergarten predicted their level of arithmetic abilities at the end of first grade (Stock, Desoete, & Roeyers, 2009).

Many children refer to their fingers when counting, often touching or lifting each finger with each verbal count, and holding up the number of fingers to correspond to the total sum.

Recent research has shown that preschool children's use of gestures when counting (that is, holding up the number of fingers to represent the total count) is often more accurate than their verbal response (Gunderson et al., 2015), suggesting that children's knowledge of numerical information is expressed first in gestures and only later in language.

In summary, young children do possess a limited knowledge of numbers, relations among numbers, and counting, but they are restricted to dealing with small quantities. As children's knowledge of numbers expands, they refine their numbers concept, discriminating between what is necessary and what is optional in dealing with numbers, and importantly, their ability to deal with large quantities increases and their belief in the invariance of numbers is applied more consistently across a wider range of tasks.

Development of Arithmetic Strategies

Learning to add and subtract. Although Piaget believed that addition and subtraction were based on the ability to conserve number and reversibility (that is, if $5 + 3 = 8$, then $8 - 5$ must equal 3), more recent research has questioned some of Piaget's interpretations and has demonstrated that even preschool children are able to handle simple addition and subtraction problems. They do so by using strategies. Children's earliest arithmetic strategies involve counting out loud, often using their fingers or other objects. We discussed children's counting strategies briefly in Chapter 7. The simplest strategy consists of counting from 1 to the first addend (in $3 + 5 = ?$, the first addend is 3), then counting the second, then counting the two together (for example, "1, 2, 3 . . . 1, 2, 3, 4, 5 . . . 1, 2, 3 . . . 4, 5, 6, 7, 8"; or a bit

more efficiently, "1, 2, 3 . . . 4, 5, 6, 7, 8"). This has been referred to as the **sum strategy**, and although it usually produces the correct answer, it takes a considerable amount of time to execute and is not very effective when large addends are involved (such as $23 + 16 = ?$). A more economical counting strategy has been called the **min strategy** and involves starting with the larger addend and then counting up from there—that is, making the minimum number of counts. For example, given the problem $3 + 2 = ?$, a child would start with the cardinal value of the first number (3) and continue counting from there (4, 5). Preschoolers use a variety of such rules to arrive at correct answers to simple addition and subtraction problems. These rules, however, almost always involve forward counting by ones of concrete objects, including fingers (T. P. Carpenter & Moser, 1982). Table 11.1 presents some of the more frequently used arithmetic strategies.

Sometime during the early school years, children's solutions to simple arithmetic problems become covert. They no longer rely on counting objects or their fingers but perform the calculations in their heads. At this point, knowing precisely what children are doing becomes more difficult because the only evidence of the mental processes underlying performance is the answers they give. However, children's arithmetic strategies can be inferred from how quickly they solve the problems. For example, if children are using the min strategy, their reaction times to solve problems will vary as a function of the second, smaller addend. Thus, for any individual child using the min strategy, arriving at an answer for $5 + 4$ (thinking "5 . . . 6, 7, 8, 9") takes longer than arriving at an answer for $5 + 2$ (thinking "5 . . . 6, 7").

Based on patterns of reaction times to solve simple addition problems, researchers have

TABLE 11.1   Some of the addition strategies children use for the problem "How much is 3 plus 2?"

Sum strategy. This is a counting strategy in which young children count, often on their fingers, each addend (for example, saying, "1, 2 . . . 1, 2, 3 . . . 1, 2, 3, 4, 5"; or a bit more efficiently, "1, 2, 3 . . . 4, 5").

Min strategy. This is a more efficient counting strategy than the sum strategy, in which children count from the larger addend (in this case 3), thus making the minimum number of counts (for example, saying "3 . . . 4, 5"). Slightly older children will use both the sum and min strategy in their head, counting covertly.

Max strategy. This is like the min strategy but counting from the smaller addend (for example, saying, "2 . . . 3, 4, 5").

Finger recognition. Without apparent counting, children hold up five fingers and say "5."

Fact retrieval. This is a noncounting strategy in which children have memorized the answer to a problem (for the problem "How much is 3 plus 2," they "just know" that 2 plus 3 equals 5) and say the answer quickly without counting either out loud or covertly.

Decomposition. Transforming the original problem into two or more simpler problems (for example, saying, "2 and 3 is like 3 plus 3 minus 1").

Guessing. Saying "4" or "8" without apparent counting.

demonstrated that children in the early elementary school years frequently use both the sum and min strategy in their heads (Groen & Resnick, 1977). Sometime during the elementary school years, children begin to use fact retrieval to answer simple arithmetic problems (see Siegler, 2006). When adults are given the problem $7 + 5 = ?$, for example, they need not start at 7 and mentally increase this by 5 to arrive at the answer. Rather, the knowledge that $7 + 5 = 12$ resides in long-term memory, and this fact can be retrieved just like any other fact in memory. Many elementary school–age children eventually will use a decomposition strategy for more difficult problems (Lemaire & Callies, 2009). Decomposition consists of transforming the original problem into two or more simpler problems. If the problem were $13 + 3 = ?$, for example, a child might say, "13 is 10 plus 3; 3 and 3 are 6; 10 and 6 are 16; so the answer is 16."

This shift in development from procedural (that is, counting) to retrieval-based techniques for solving simple arithmetic problems reflects changes in the efficiency of information processing. With age, children solve problems more quickly. This increased speed can be attributed to the fact that processes are becoming more automatic, requiring less of one's limited mental capacity for successful execution. First-graders' use of counting strategies is highly conscious and laborious in contrast with the fact retrieval of older children. However, even 5- and 6-year-olds apparently store and retrieve some arithmetic facts. For small whole-number problems (for example, $2 + 2 = ?$), young children's performance is relatively rapid, indicating fact retrieval (Siegler & Shrager, 1984). With age and experience, more arithmetic facts become stored and can be retrieved with increasing ease, without the need of laborious counting procedures. Although children learn how to multiply later than they learn how to add, much of even third-grade children's multiplication seems to be based on fact retrieval (Koshmider & Ashcraft, 1991), likely as a result of memorizing the multiplication table.

Arithmetic becomes more complex, of course, and as it does, children must rely again on procedural knowledge. When subtraction involves borrowing (as in 92 − 59 = ?) or addition involves carrying (as in 92 + 59 = ?), procedures are at first slow and difficult, but with practice they become more efficient. In general, the development of arithmetic competence can be described as involving an increase in the efficiency of both procedural knowledge and, most important, information retrieval (Geary, 2006). Older children know more facts, can retrieve those facts more easily, and, when necessary, can use arithmetic procedures more efficiently than younger children can.

One factor that appears to be important in successful mental arithmetic is working memory (Cragg & Gilmore, 2014). To arrive at a correct answer to a simple problem such as 7 + 5 = ?, children must hold the two addends in mind and execute the addition operation (either by retrieving the fact or through some counting method). For example, John Adams and Graham Hitch (1997) showed that differences in memory span play a critical role in computation for groups of both English- and German-speaking children (ranging in age from about 7.5 to 11.5 years). Adams and Hitch also found a relation between the speed of adding the digits and both age and memory span, confirming the role of speed of processing in memory span discussed in Chapter 7.

Is children's acquisition of arithmetic strategies stagelike? The impression one might get from this research is of a steady improvement in arithmetic strategy use, with children moving from the sum to the min to the fact-retrieval strategy in a regular, stagelike progression. Such a view is not entirely accurate, however. At any given age, children use a variety of strategies to solve arithmetic problems, although the average sophistication of their strategies increases with age (Siegler, 2006).

Robert Siegler and his colleagues have demonstrated this in several studies. Recall our discussion in Chapter 7 of Siegler's (1996, 2006) *adaptive strategy choice model.* According to this model, strategies develop in a wave-like fashion, with children using multiple strategies; new strategies never fully displace older ones but become more frequent as a result of experience and the development of underlying cognitive capacities. Sometimes one strategy will win the mental competition (the min strategy, for example) and sometimes another strategy will win (fact retrieval, for example). For new problems or problems with which children are less familiar, the older, more familiar, or fallback, strategies often come up as the winners.

For example, Siegler and Eric Jenkins (1989) looked at the acquisition of the min strategy using a short-term longitudinal study (or a microgenetic approach; see Chapter 3). In this study, Siegler and Jenkins examined the development of arithmetic strategies in eight children over an 11-week period. Four- and 5-year-old children were selected who (a) could perform simple addition using counting methods but (b) never used the min strategy. Over 11 weeks, these children were given a series of addition problems to solve.

Siegler and Jenkins reported that all the children used multiple strategies. These included the sum, min, fact-retrieval, and decomposition strategies discussed earlier, plus strategies such as finger recognition (putting up two fingers on one hand and three on the other and saying "five"), shortcut sum (similar to the sum), counting from the first addend (similar to min but counting the larger addend), and guessing.

The percentage of the most frequently used strategies can be seen in Figure 11.9, and there was great variety in strategy use. Moreover, different children used different combinations of the strategies, so that any particular child used a unique mixture of the strategies in his or her solutions. (See similar findings reported for arithmetic and other strategies in Chapter 7.) Also, during the 11 weeks, the children's strategies tended to become more sophisticated, so that the children who started mainly by guessing or using the sum strategy progressed to using the min or fact-retrieval strategy more frequently.

One major aspect of the Siegler and Jenkins study was children's discovery of the min strategy. Remember that none of the children was

FIGURE 11.9 **Percentage use for each arithmetic strategy.**

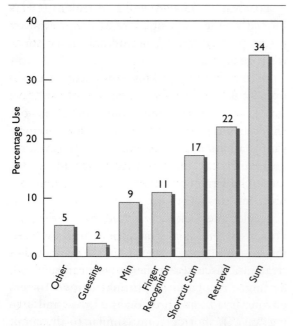

Source: Adapted from Siegler, R. S., & Jenkins, E. (1989). How children discover strategies. Hillsdale, NJ: Erlbaum.

using the min strategy at the beginning of the study. By the 11th week, seven of the eight children were using the min strategy, and six of these children were able to describe how they used it. It is interesting to note that the first time the children used the min strategy, and on the problem immediately before it, they took much longer than average to arrive at a solution. Siegler and Jenkins speculated that the longer times spent on these problems indicated that the children were experiencing conflict, or interference from alternative strategies, and that new strategies require more mental effort than previously established ones. Thus, the children required more time and did some hemming and hawing before arriving at an answer.

Learning arithmetic strategies through games. Children are explicitly taught basic arithmetic in school, yet instruction rarely starts in school; rather, it begins in the home, often in the context of games, usually with a parent or older sibling. Card games such as Go Fish help young children to identify numbers, and games such as War help them learn the cardinal value of numbers (the larger number always wins). Children also play board games, in which they have to move their game piece around a board according to the outcome of a roll of dice or a twirl of a spinner. Sometimes all children have to do is to recognize the number on a single die or that an arrow points to and move their game piece the corresponding number. This is less trivial than it may sound, for children need to learn that each of their counts corresponds to one space on the board. Real arithmetic becomes possible when two dice are used and children must combine their total to arrive at an answer.

In one study, parents and their 5-year-old children played a modified game of Chutes and Ladders, but the spinner that is usually used in this game was replaced by a pair of dice (Bjorklund, Hubertz, & Rubens, 2004). Did parents take the opportunity to teach their children some basic addition, and if they did were they successful? Some children started the game using fact retrieval (that is, they did not count out loud or on their fingers, but just "knew" the answer), and parents usually gave such children little assistance or instruction—they did not need it. Most children, however, used more effortful counting strategies, especially *sum*. For example, if they rolled a 3 and a 4, they would count the pips on the first die ("one, two, three") then count the pips on the second die ("four, five, six, seven") and then move their game piece seven squares. Many parents made an effort to teach their children more effective ways of arriving at an answer. For instance, many demonstrated the *min* strategy on their moves or guided children to use the strategy on the child's turn. ("Look here, this is a 4, you know 4. So start here, say 'four,' and count the other ones, 'five, six, seven.'") Some prompted them to use fact retrieval. ("See, that's 2 and 2. You know what 2 plus 2 is, right? You don't have to count them. You can just say 'four.'") Many parents were working in what Vygotsky described as the *zone of proximal development*, scaffolding their children's behavior.

In other work, 4- and 5-year-old low-income children played a board game with squares on the board having either the numbers 1 to 10 on them or being different colors (Ramani & Siegler, 2008; Siegler & Ramani, 2009). Moves on the game were determined by twirling a spinner that had either numbers or colors to denote children's moves. Children's numerical knowledge (for example, counting, identifying numerals, judging which of two numbers was larger) was measured both before and after playing these games. Roughly 1 hour of playing the game with numbers resulted in significant improvements in children's numerical knowledge, and the gains were still apparent 9 weeks later. There were no corresponding improvements for children who played the color game.

What these studies demonstrate is that young children can learn about numbers, numerical relations, and even arithmetic, all while playing games. The work with low-income children is especially impressive. Low-income children tend to lag behind their middle-class peers in numerical knowledge before ever entering the schoolhouse. The demonstration that playing simple games that merely exposes them to numbers can increase their numerical knowledge may result in easy ways for parents, preschool teachers, or day care workers to enhance low-income children's mathematical understanding. This also reminds us why involving parents in early intervention programs increases their effectiveness by showing parents specific things to do at home.

As for strategy development in general, children's use of arithmetic strategies starts simple but increases in complexity as their basic cognitive abilities improve (for example, working memory, speed of processing, metacognition), as they practice adding numbers, and as they perhaps learn to use their hands to help them discover new strategies. New, more efficient strategies increase in frequency but never fully replace older simpler strategies that children will sometimes use when the newer strategies fail to produce an easy answer (Siegler, 2006). Children are explicitly taught some of these strategies in schools, but they often learn them in less-formal venues, such as playing number and math games with their parents, siblings, or friends.

Variations in Developing Mathematical Proficiency: Math Disabilities, Cultural Differences, and Sex Differences

As with any type of cognition, there are individual as well as developmental differences in children's rate of acquisition or eventual end state of an ability. We've discussed individual differences in mathematical achievement briefly throughout this section, noting, for example, that differences in early numerical abilities are related to later levels of mathematical achievement. However, as with reading, there are also some children who display specific disabilities in math as well as reliable cultural and sex differences, and we examine each of these topics in the following sections.

Math Disabilities

Not all children show regular improvement in mathematical skills over the school years. Although estimates vary depending on how math disability (or *developmental dyscalculia*) is measured, approximately 5% to 10% of school-age children display specific disabilities in mathematics (A. Devine et al., 2013; Hulme & Snowling, 2009). Children with math disabilities have math achievement substantially below their age level, display poor procedural knowledge (for instance, knowledge of the rules of counting; Geary, Brown, & Samaranayake, 1991), and show memory-retrieval deficits. Children with math disability retrieve fewer facts from long-term memory (that is, they use fact retrieval less often), and when they do, they are often wrong (Geary, Hoard, & Bailey, 2012).

There is much debate among scholars about the cognitive deficits of children with math disabilities. In fact, researchers are confident that there is no single cause of math disabilities and

that different children experience difficulties with mathematics for different reasons (Rubinsten & Henik, 2009; Szücs, & Goswami, 2013). For example, a number of researchers have shown that children with math disabilities often have deficient number sense, performing poorly on tasks assessing the approximate number system (ANS), such as the dot-estimation task described earlier (Piazza et al., 2010). Other researchers report that many children with math disabilities display poorer magnitude estimation abilities (De Smedt et al., 2013), consistent with Siegler and Lortie-Forgues's integrative theory of numerical development.

Many children with math disabilities also show deficits in working memory and speed of processing (Geary, 2011; Swanson, 2011). For example, Geary and his colleagues (1991) reported that the digit spans for children with math disability (4.2 words) were about one word less than for nondisabled children (5.3 words). This deficit might be the result of faster decay of information (that is, the memory representations might disappear more quickly in working memory for math-disabled children) or of slower counting speed (recall from Chapter 7 that digit span is related to articulation rate). Because these children make computation errors, they arrive at many incorrect answers, and these answers can become part of their long-term memory representations of arithmetic facts. Unfortunately, the answers are wrong.

The deficits shown by many children with math disabilities are similar to those shown by many reading-disabled children. In fact, there is considerable overlap between the two populations (see Hulme & Snowling, 2009). For example, in a large-scale study of math disabilities, N. A. Badian (1983) reported that 43% of children with math disability were also classified as reading disabled and that 56% of children with reading disability were similarly classified as math disabled. Both math and reading disabilities seem to share a common problem—the inability to retrieve information efficiently from long-term memory. Math facts are proposed to be represented in a semantic network, much as word definitions are. Geary (1993) proposed that a single deficit underlies many math and reading disabilities: "At the cognitive level, this deficit manifests itself as difficulties in the representation and retrieval of semantic information from long-term memory. This would include fact-retrieval problems in simple arithmetic and, for instance, word-recognition and phonological awareness in reading" (p. 356).

Yet many children read just fine but have great difficulty in math, and vice versa. It appears that there is no single cause of math disability (or of reading disability, for that matter) and that some of these disabilities are domain specific. However, the substantial overlap between the reading- and math-disabled populations suggests that some domain-general abilities are involved in these important technological skills, namely working-memory capacity and efficiency of retrieval from semantic memory.

Cultural Differences in Mathematics

Mathematics is truly the universal language (although many would give that distinction to love, we suppose). Regardless of one's native tongue, the rules of mathematics are the same all over the globe. However, most forms of mathematics beyond arithmetic are explicitly taught, at least in our culture. Yet people from traditional cultures still have a need for basic arithmetic and other forms of mathematical problem solving. How do people from non-schooled societies acquire mathematics? How is it similar to and different from what happens

in cultures such as ours where formal schooling is universal?

Differences in mathematical attainment also occur between different information-age cultures. In recent years, this has been brought to the public's attention by reports of substantial differences in mathematics performance between American children and college students and those from other information-age cultures, particularly those in East Asia. How different are Americans from East Asians in mathematical attainment, when do those differences appear, and what factors contribute to them? These issues are discussed in the next section.

Arithmetic in unschooled children. In Chapter 3 we discussed how the language a culture uses can affect arithmetic computation. For example, children (and adults) whose language is limited to words for *one, two,* and *many* perform arithmetic tasks involving small quantities easily but are unable to perform arithmetic calculations with larger quantities (Gordon, 2004), and how languages express their number words can influence early numerical performance (for instance, how quickly children learn to count to 20; K. F. Miller et al., 1995). Given that most forms of mathematics are explicitly taught, one major difference between cultures influencing mathematical development is access to formal schooling. Although nearly all children in developed societies receive formal instruction in basic mathematics in elementary school, many children in developing countries do not, yet nonetheless they develop some semblance of mathematical proficiency.

Research examining the arithmetic ability of nonschooled Brazilian children has shown that they possess a high level of computational skill but only when the problems are tied to real-life situations. For example, Terezinha Carraher, David Carraher, and Analucia Schliemann (1985) gave 9- and 15-year-old unschooled street vendors a series of arithmetic problems to solve. Problems that were imbedded in real-life contexts (for example, "If a large coconut costs 76 cruzeiros, and a small one costs 50, how much do the two cost together?") were solved at a much higher rate than were the same problems presented out of context (for example, "How much is 76 + 50?"). Carraher and her associates reported that the children answered the context-appropriate questions correctly 98% of the time; in contrast, the out-of-context questions were answered correctly only 37% of the time. Reviewing their research on schooled versus nonschooled Brazilian children's mathematical reasoning, Schliemann (1992) stated that these children use mathematics to solve everyday problems where mistakes have real consequences. This is contrasted with school learning, in which children are taught standardized procedures with little or no application. Schliemann (1992) concluded that unschooled street vendors (and unschooled people from other professions, such as brick layers and lottery bookies) develop a flexible arithmetic system and apply it appropriately within their work context; "unschooled people develop at work not only fixed procedures to solve specific problems but a conceptual and flexible understanding of the mathematical models applied to solve problems" (p. 2).

In other research, Steven Guberman (1996) has shown that Brazilian shantytown children frequently use their knowledge of currency to help them to solve school-type arithmetic problems. Also, interviews with children's parents indicated that parents adjusted the complexity of the purchases they asked their children to make depending on the perceived skill of the child. As children grew older and more

arithmetically competent, parents presented them with more difficult real-world problems to solve (such as purchases to make). This is consistent with working within the zone of proximal development, a concept developed by Lev Vygotsky (1978) and discussed in some detail in Chapter 3.

Academic performance by American and Asian schoolchildren. Evidence has been accumulating that American schoolchildren lag behind children from other industrialized countries in their academic knowledge, including mathematics. In fact, American children typically fall in the middle of the pack in most international comparisons of mathematics performance, often scoring much below nations with considerably less wealth (Mullis et al., 2012; Organisation for Economic Co-operation and Development, 2014). Differences favoring the Asian children appear as early as first grade and become larger by the fifth grade (Stevenson & Lee, 1990). More recent research has shown that Chinese sixth-grade children outperform American children in their ability to use fractions and that this difference is based almost entirely on knowledge of fractions procedures—the application of the basic operations of addition, subtraction, multiplication, and division as related to solving problems involving fractions (Bailey et al., 2015).

Differences between Asian and American children are found early, even before the start of formal school. For example, Chinese kindergarten children outperformed American kindergarteners on line-estimation tasks, even though neither the Chinese nor American children had any instruction or exposure to such tasks (Siegler & Mu, 2008). Early differences between Chinese and American children are also found in the use of arithmetic strategies. For instance, Geary and his colleagues reported that Chinese first-grade children used a more sophisticated mix of strategies, including decomposition (Geary et al., 1996; Geary, Fan, & Bow-Thomas, 1992). The Chinese children were also faster at retrieving an answer directly from long-term memory (that is, at fact retrieval) than the American children were. However, this speed advantage was apparently limited to retrieval of arithmetic facts and did not reflect an overall greater speed-of-processing advantage, for the Chinese and American children were equally fast at counting (recall, however, our discussion in Chapter 3 about Chinese preschool children being able to count to 20 before American children could [K. F. Miller et al., 1995]).

One might ask, "So what?" We're talking about the most basic of arithmetic abilities, which American children clearly master by the end of elementary school. But children's early arithmetic accomplishments set the stage for later achievements. Geary and his colleagues (1992) argue that "if the mastery of basic skills facilitates the acquisition of more complex mathematical concepts and procedures, then the results of the current study suggest that Chinese children will have a consistent 3- to 4-year advantage over their American peers in the development of mathematical cognition" (p. 184). Recall the research we presented earlier demonstrating that children's early competence in number magnitude tasks predicted later mathematical proficiency, consistent with Siegler and Lortie-Forgues's integrative theory of numerical development.

What are the origins of these differences? One source of the difference is likely practice. Children who practice elementary computation more frequently are able to retrieve math facts more quickly from long-term memory and have greater opportunities to develop arithmetic strategies than do children who practice them less often (Geary et al., 1992). Harold Stevenson and his colleagues reported that Chinese and Japanese children do indeed spend more time on mathematics, both in and out of the classroom (Fuligni & Stevenson, 1995; Stevenson & Lee, 1990). This pattern of cultural difference begins in preschool (Siegler & Mu, 2008; Zhou et al., 2006). Thus, we have the very commonsense finding of practice makes perfect (or at least makes for enhanced performance), with children who practice arithmetic more frequently (Chinese and Japanese children) performing better than children who practice it less frequently (American children).

But what causes this cultural difference in time invested in mathematics and the overall greater academic performance? Again, the answer is quite commonsensical: parents' attitudes and behavior regarding education and child-rearing. Although American parents tend to believe that their children's academic performance is due to effort, this tendency to emphasize effort and hard work is even more obvious in Japanese and Chinese parents (Ng, Pomerantz, & Lam, 2007).

Because of Japan's cultural traditions, children also spend more time in school and devote a higher percentage of their school time to academic material than do American children. For example, whereas the average school year in Minneapolis is 174 days, it is 230 in Taipei and 243 in Sendai (Stevenson & Lee, 1990). Subsequent research showed that American first-grade children show greater improvements in academic subjects as a result of attending an extended-year schooling program (210–230 days) rather than a school program of conventional length (180 days) (Frazier & Morrison, 1998).

It's worth noting that American children of recent Asian descent perform better in school, on average, than do White or Black native-born Americans (Chen & Stevenson, 1995). A major reason for this difference is the attitudes that Chinese American and Japanese American parents have toward education. For example, Chin-yau Lin and Victoria Fu (1990) compared the child-rearing practices of Caucasian American parents with those of Chinese parents from Taiwan and immigrant Chinese parents living in the United States. Lin and Fu reported that both the immigrant Chinese and the Taiwanese parents rated higher on parental control, encouragement of independence, and emphasis on achievement than Caucasian American parents did. In other research, Chinese American 7- and 8-year-old children spent more time doing homework and taking music lessons, spent less time playing organized sports, and had less free time than comparable European American children (Huntsinger, Jose, & Larson, 1998). The Chinese American parents also used more formal teaching methods for math and reading than did the European American parents. From these findings, we can see how cultural attitudes of Chinese American parents exert an influence on their children's educational attainment, which is likely responsible for the academic edge these children have in American schools.

Sex Differences in Mathematical Ability

When most people think of sex differences in academic abilities, perhaps the first area to come to mind is mathematics, with males generally being better than females. (The other area is verbal abilities, with the common wisdom being that females are generally more verbal than males, as discussed earlier in this chapter.) Such observations date back in the scientific literature to at least 1894, with Havelock Ellis's comments on male superiority on a host of cognitive tasks, and continue

to be much studied today. What is the nature of sex differences in mathematical abilities? When, in development, are they observed? Are they a reflection primarily of biology or of educational opportunities?

Perhaps somewhat surprisingly given the stereotype, on average, girls get better school grades than boys in mathematics at all academic levels (Halpern et al., 2007; Voyer & Voyer, 2014). This is related in large part to girls performing better in all school subjects than boys. In a 2-year longitudinal study examining math performance in children initially in fifth grade, girls displayed greater achievement goals (as reflected, for example, by statements such as "An important reason I do my math work is because I want to improve my skills") and showed less disruptive behavior than boys, both of which were related to learning strategies and grades in math (Kenney-Benson et al., 2006). However, males score higher on standardized math tests than females (Halpern et al., 2007; Hedges & Nowell, 1995), although the absolute magnitude of the sex difference is small and varies in different countries (Else-Quest, Hyde, & Linn, 2010). As an example, Figure 11.10 presents the average SAT mathematics scores for males and females from 1967 to 2003 (from Halpern et al., 2007). As can be seen, the gap between males and females has been from 30 to 40 points for most years, with a decided male advantage. In general, females tend to perform better on familiar material, as reflected by assessments of school learning, whereas males tend to perform better applying mathematical knowledge to new contexts, as reflected by standardized tests.

However, a 2008 report analyzing results of standardized math tests from over 7 million American children in Grades 2 through 11 as part of No Child Left Behind assessments

FIGURE 11.10 **Average SAT mathematics scores for males and females from 1967 to 2003.**

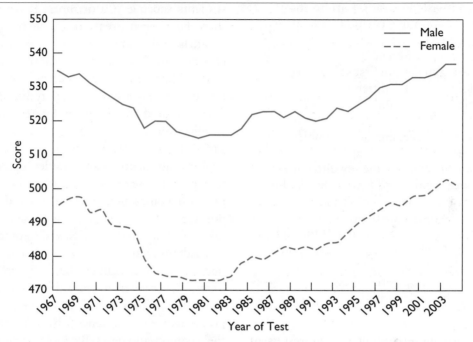

Source: Halpern, D. F., Benbow, C. P., Geary, D. C., Gur, R. C., Hyde, J. S., & Gernsbacher, M. A. (2007). The science of sex differences in science and mathematics. *Psychological Science in the Public Interest, 8,* 1–51.

reported no sex differences in math scores at any grade (Hyde et al., 2008). Males continued to score higher than females on the mathematics portion of the SAT by about 7%, however, suggesting that a small male advantage is still found, although its explanation may not be straightforward. The male-female SAT difference for the Mathematics portion of the 2013 SAT was 32 points (males = 531; females = 499), a difference of about 6% (College Board, 2013).

Similar to what has been done in evaluating sex differences in verbal abilities, researchers have used meta-analysis to evaluate the many studies looking at sex differences in mathematical ability. To reiterate, meta-analysis is a statistical technique that allows an investigator to evaluate the magnitude of a significant effect across a large number of studies. Differences between the sexes across studies are expressed in terms of effect size, with 1.0 corresponding to a difference equivalent to one standard deviation. Hyde (1981) reported the first meta-analysis of sex differences in mathematical ability, but more recent and extensive studies have since been published, each reporting similar results (Hedges & Nowell, 1995; Hyde, Fennema, & Lamon, 1990; see Halpern et al., 2007).

Take, for example, the meta-analysis Hyde and her colleagues (1990) reported, which included 100 studies and the data of 3,175,188 participants. Contrasts were made between elementary schoolchildren for simple arithmetic computation, high school students, college students, and adults. Several main conclusions can be stated:

1. Sex differences are small and often nonsignificant for arithmetic computation in elementary school, and what effect there is favors girls.
2. Significant differences in mathematics favoring males are first seen in high school, with this difference increasing some in college and adulthood (effect sizes = 0.29, 0.41, and 0.59 for high school, college, and adult samples, respectively).
3. The magnitude of the sex differences between males and females has declined since the 1970s (effect sizes: pre-1973 = 0.31; post-1973 = 0.14).
4. Sex differences are greater at the highest ability levels, with males much more likely than females to be represented among the top percentiles of mathematics ability.

Related to this last point are the results of meta-analyses by Alan Feingold (1992) and by Larry Hedges and Amy Nowell (1995) looking at sex differences in *variability*. Both studies reported that males are much more variable than females in their performance. This greater male variability has long been noted (H. Ellis, 1894) and is not limited to mathematics (Hedges & Nowell, 1995). These results suggest that for most of the population, there is much overlap and little real difference in mathematical abilities between males and females.

As just noted, sex differences in mathematics are most apparent at the extremes, particularly at the upper levels of performance. For example, in a study that included SAT scores of nearly 40,000 college-bound adolescents, Camilla Benbow and Julian Stanley (1983) found that the ratio of boys to girls scoring 420 or more on the SAT Math was 1.5:1. In contrast, this boy-to-girl ratio was 4.1:1 for students scoring

600 or more and 13:1 for the small number of students scoring 700 or more. Since that time there have been great strides in opportunities for girls and young women to take more math classes, and according to Julian Stanley, the male-to-female ratio for scoring 700 and over on the SAT Math has been reduced to only 2.8:1 (quoted in Monastersky, 2005). This is a reflection of a more general trend discussed earlier (Hyde et al., 2008).

Although Benbow and Stanley's results point to substantial sex difference at the highest levels of mathematics performance, their data reveal nothing about the sources of these differences, nor about the source of sex differences in the general population. There is also no compelling reason to conclude that SAT scores reflect innate differences in aptitude or capacity. For example, children's and adolescents' academic performance is influenced by the attitudes of their parents and peers. By adolescence math and science are viewed as masculine disciplines, and girls may receive less support from their peers for such activities than boys (Stake & Nickens, 2005).

Cindy Raymond and Camilla Benbow (1986) investigated the connection among parental attitudes, gender typing, and mathematical ability for groups of adolescents scoring high on the quantitative and verbal portions of the SAT. Raymond and Benbow reported that mathematically talented students received greater parental encouragement in mathematics than did verbally talented students and that this pattern did not differ with sex. Related to this, the amount of encouragement in mathematics that children received was comparable for boys and girls, regardless of their area or level of talent (that is, high verbal or high math). Finally, mathematically talented girls were no more sex typed as masculine than were verbally talented girls, and there was no relationship between sex typing and SAT scores. Raymond and Benbow (1986) concluded that parental socialization practices during adolescence could not account for mathematical ability in this group of mathematically talented children.

One interesting sex difference in mathematics performance concerns **stereotype threat**, in which females perform worse on a mathematics test after simply being reminded that math is typically a masculine activity. This effect has been observed in children as young as 5 years (Ambady et al., 2001) and for elementary and middle-school children (Muzzatti & Agnoli, 2007). These findings suggest that females, from an early age, may have the ability to perform as well as males on many mathematics tasks but are highly susceptible to the stereotype threat that identifies excellence in math as a male and not a female thing. Consistent with this interpretation, one study suggests that when first- and second-grade girls have female teachers who demonstrate high levels of math anxiety, they develop the stereotype that boys are better at math than girls and score lower on math achievement tests than boys or than girls who do not have teachers with math anxiety (Beilock et al., 2010).

We also cannot ignore sex differences in brain development. As mentioned in the discussion of sex differences in reading ability, differences between the brains of males and females may, in part, be responsible for sex differences in some cognitive tasks.

One fascinating and educationally important finding is the steady reduction of sex differences in mathematics ability since the 1960s. Why are sex differences in mathematics ability decreasing over time? The answer favored by many is that attitudes and curricula are changing, that gender roles are being viewed more flexibly (Hyde & Linn, 1988), and that girls are taking more mathematics courses than before (Marsh, 1989). Some evidence suggests that this is true. In Herbert Marsh's (1989) assessment of math performance of 14,825 students in the High School and Beyond project, much smaller sex differences in performance were found than in previous studies. This was associated with evidence that the boys and girls in the study had taken, on average, equal numbers of mathematics courses in high school. However, evidence also suggests that test publishers during the past 40 years have been attempting to minimize sex differences in their tests, possibly accounting for the diminished sex differences in performance (Stanley et al., 1992). Whatever the reason, sex differences favoring males in high school mathematics and beyond are still found, but they are relatively small in magnitude and getting smaller. The only exception to this statement concerns performance at the highest levels, where males are disproportionately represented.

Sex differences in mathematical performance are apparently real, but they are not simple. Girls actually get better grades in math than boys at all levels, whereas boys consistently perform better than girls on standardized tests. There seems to be no single reason for this pattern of differences. The gap between the sexes at the highest levels of achievement is declining, a result of increased academic opportunities for girls and young women. But differences in socialization practices and interests are also related to the sex differences we see in mathematics performance. As for nearly all sex differences, biological, cognitive, and psychosocial factors clearly interact over time to produce the pattern. Figure 11.11 shows a representation of the relationships among these various factors on sex differences in mathematics (from Geary, 1994).

FIGURE 11.11 **Relationship among biological, cognitive, and psychosocial influences on the development of sex differences in mathematics.**

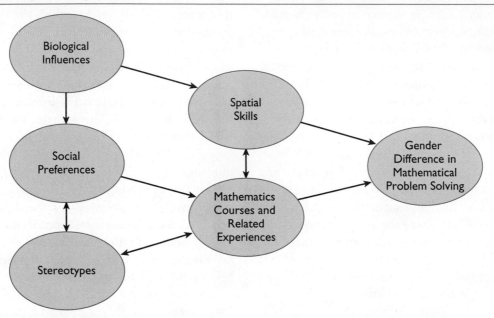

Source: Geary, D. C. (1994). *Children's mathematical development: Research and practical applications.* Washington, DC: American Psychological Association.

Section Review

The ability to process numbers is second only to language as a human symbol system. People's tendency to quantify objects and events in our world is ubiquitous and begins early.

Integrative Theory of Numerical Development

- The theory proposes that numerical development involves four major acquisitions: (1) representing with increasing precision nonsymbolic numbers; (2) linking nonsymbolic and symbolic numerical representations; (3) extending the range of numbers that can be accurately represented; and (4) representing numbers others than whole numbers, including fractions, decimals, and negative numbers.

- The *approximate number system (ANS)* is an intuitive, nonsymbolic system for thinking about quantities.
- Young children's performance on tasks tapping ANS predicts later mathematics achievement.
- On number line estimation tasks participants are asked to place a number at its proper position on a number line. Children's accuracy on such tasks increases with age, as does the magnitude of the numbers they can deal with.
- In symbolic numerical comparison tasks children are presented with two Arabic numbers and asked to determine as quickly as possible which is the larger of the two. The speed with which children make correct judgments increases with age.
- Many children learn to deal with fractions, decimals, and negative numbers, with individual differences in earlier number

magnitude predicting children's later ability to use fractions.

Development of Conceptual and Procedural Mathematical Knowledge

- Children's concept of number has been studied in terms of *conservation of number*, following Piaget.
- Children appear to acquire knowledge of counting gradually during the preschool years, and this knowledge precedes that necessary for conservation of number.
- R. Gelman and Gallistel proposed five principles of counting: one-one principle, stable-order principle, cardinal principle, abstraction principle, and order-irrelevant principle.
- Children acquire knowledge of counting gradually during the preschool years although often continue to believe that some conventional rules (for example, counting left to right) are necessary for accurate counting.
- Early arithmetic is done out loud, often on fingers. Children's early strategies include the *sum strategy*, with children counting all numbers, and the *min strategy*, with children beginning with the larger addend and counting up from there. More sophisticated strategies include retrieving addition and subtraction facts directly from long-term memory (*fact retrieval*) and *decomposition*, in which a problem is decomposed into simpler problems.
- Children use a variety of arithmetic strategies at any one time, including gestures.
- Children can acquire arithmetic strategies and number knowledge by playing math-related games.

Variations in Developing Mathematical Proficiency

- Children with math disabilities (developmental dyscalculia) have math achievement substantially below their age level, display poor procedural knowledge, and show memory-retrieval deficits.

- Children with math disabilities display cognitive deficits in working memory, speed of processing, number magnitude estimation, and tasks assessing the approximate number system.
- The deficits shown by many children with math disabilities are similar to those shown by many reading-disabled children.
- The mathematics performance of unschooled children tends to be good when they are familiar with the test materials and the context of testing is considered.
- Patterns of cognitive abilities vary as a function of culture even in those societies that require formal education, with different values and educational practices affecting children's academic performance.
- Sex differences in mathematics favoring males are not typically found until high school and then increase slightly into college and adulthood.
- The absolute magnitude of these differences is small, however, and has been decreasing during the past 40 years.
- The largest sex differences are found among the most mathematically gifted, with males being disproportionately represented.
- A number of factors have been hypothesized as responsible for sex differences, including *stereotype threat*, in which females perform worse on a mathematics test after simply being reminded that math is typically a masculine activity.

Ask Yourself . . .

9. What is the *integrative theory of numerical development*? According to this theory, what are the stages of math acquisition?
10. How does the approximate number system (ANS) develop, and what does it predict about later mathematical proficiency?
11. What are the number line estimation and symbolic numerical comparison tasks, and how does performance on these tasks

change with age? What do these tasks tell us about individual differences in later math achievement?

12. How do children of different ages perform on a conservation of number task? What does this reflect about their knowledge of counting?

13. What are R. Gelman and Gallistel's five principles of counting? Provide examples of each.

14. How does children's counting and understanding of cardinal numbers change across preschool?

15. What are four arithmetic strategies, and when and how do children apply these strategies? How do children acquire these strategies? What role does working memory play in arithmetic development?

16. What are some ways that games are used to facilitate children's arithmetic abilities?

17. How are math deficits similar to and different from reading deficits?

18. How is the acquisition of arithmetic skills influenced by gender and culture?

SCHOOLING AND COGNITIVE DEVELOPMENT

There should be little question that schooling makes a difference in how a child thinks. In our day-to-day experience, children who attend school are brighter than children who don't, and children in more advanced grades are smarter than children in lower grades. But children in higher grades not only have had more school experience than have children in lower grades, they are also older. Does attending school actually make a difference in cognitive development beyond the effect of age?

Schooling Versus Age Effects on Intelligence

The question of how schooling versus age influences intelligence has been addressed by examining the effects of years of education on intellectual performance while statistically controlling for age (Cahan & Cohen, 1989) or, more frequently, by using the *cut-off method*, in which children who just missed the cut-off date for entering school are compared with children who are close to their age but just made the cut-off date. Thus, the two groups of children are nearly identical in age but differ in that the former group has had 1 more year of education than the latter group (Morrison, Griffith, & Frazier, 1996). For example, Sorel Cahan and Nora Cohen (1989) compared intelligence test scores and school achievement of fourth-, fifth-, and sixth-grade children. They reported significant effects of schooling; children in the higher grade scored better than children their same age in the lower grade. These findings clearly show that IQ and related cognitive skills are strongly associated with schooling. In this study, effects of both age and schooling were reported (that is, older children did better than younger children, and children with 1 more year of school did better than children without the extra year), but the effect of schooling was 2 to 3 times greater than the effect of age.

The results of this line of research may not be surprising. After all, we expect education to produce smarter children. But these findings force us to question the concept of intelligence as measured by IQ tests. IQ tests are age-based. The norms change as a function of age, not grade. (The construction of the logic behind IQ tests is discussed in Chapter 12.) The results of the research cited here indicate that not only should age be considered in computing an IQ score, but so should school experience. Moreover, the idea that some intelligence tests can be "culture fair" (that is, used in any culture without yielding biased results) must be questioned. One of the tests Cahan and Cohen (1989) used was the Ravens' Progressive Matrices Test, a test that has been proposed to produce "an index of intellectual capacity whatever [a person's] nationality or education" (Raven, Court, & Raven, 1975, p. 1). The effect of 1 year's schooling was found to be twice as large as the effect of 1 year of age on the Ravens' test, seriously challenging the fairness of such a test when assessing children from cultures where there is no formal education.

Other researchers, notably Frederick Morrison and his colleagues (1996), have looked at age versus schooling effects for specific cognitive and educational abilities for children just beginning formal education. In Morrison's research, "old kindergarten" children, who just missed the school-entry cut-off date, are compared with "young first-grade" children, with contrasts typically being made at the beginning and end of the school year. Morrison and his colleagues report both schooling and age effects, depending on the particular skill being assessed. For example, 1 year of schooling has a greater effect than 1 year of age on (a) phonological awareness (Morrison et al., 1996); (b) free-recall memory, including simple strategy use (Morrison et al., 1996); (c) accuracy in mental arithmetic (Bisanz, Morrison, & Dunn, 1995); (d) the ability to understand complex sentences with longer subjects (Ferreira & Morrison, 1994); (e) knowledge of the alphabet (Christian et al., 2000); and (f) the ability to use causal structure (that is, connections between different pieces in a story) in recalling stories (Varnhagen, Morrison, & Everall, 1994). However, significant *age* effects have also been found for (a) subsyllabic segmentation (the ability to differentiate between sounds within one-syllable words, for example, for the word *grasp*, being able to segment *gr* from *asp*) (Morrison et al., 1996); (b) conservation of number (Bisanz et al., 1995); (c) the use of simple arithmetic strategies, such as fact retrieval and various counting methods (Bisanz et al., 1995); (d) gist recall of stories (Varnhagen et al., 1994); (e) the ability to understand the use of pronouns in sentences (Ferreira & Morrison, 1994); and (f) vocabulary, cultural knowledge, and general narrative skills (Morrison et al., 1996). Of course, for most academic abilities, significant effects are found for both school experience and age (Morrison, Griffith, & Alberts, 1997). And at least some of these effects are not unique to American schools and children but have been reported for some aspects of arithmetic abilities in Japanese children (Naito & Miura, 2001).

The conclusion to draw from this research is that changes in different cognitive skills follow different developmental paths, reflecting a large degree of domain specificity. Some skills, such as phonemic awareness, free-recall memory, accuracy of mental arithmetic, and the abilities that underlie IQ test performance, are greatly affected by schooling experiences. Presumably, the experiences children have in school have a direct impact on these skills (for example, reading instruction affects phonemic awareness). However, other seemingly closely related skills, such as story recall, use of arithmetic strategies, and vocabulary, are more influenced by the presumably maturational and general (versus schooling-specific) experiences associated with age. According to Morrison and his colleagues (1996), this pattern reflects a substantial degree of specificity in the timing, magnitude, and nature of changes in cognitive abilities.

Effect of Schooling on IQ

The research contrasting the effects of 1 year of schooling versus 1 year of age demonstrates that schooling, indeed, plays a role in cognitive development, at least for some important skills. We suppose that this should not be surprising, given the evidence presented earlier in this and in previous chapters demonstrating substantial differences in mathematics, memory, and classification abilities for children from schooled versus nonschooled cultures. Reading may be particularly important, as reflected by the findings from a longitudinal study of identical twins. Differences in reading ability at age 7 not only predicted differences in reading 9 years later but also differences on scores of tests of general intelligence (Ritchie, Bates, & Plomin, 2015). This is consistent with the idea that reading has a positive influence on general intelligence (Ritchie & Bates, 2013), with these differences becoming magnified over time (recall the Matthew effect).

But the question of a relationship between schooling and intellectual functioning is not a trivial one. For example, to what extent does schooling affect IQ? Cahan and Cohen (1989) found that 1 year of schooling has a substantial effect on IQ, twice the size associated with 1 year of age. That schooling affects IQ indicates that an IQ score is greatly influenced by experiential factors and is not solely under the influence of genetic or other biological factors that are relatively impervious to societal-level effects. The effects of schooling on IQ have been studied for a number of years, and Stephen Ceci (1991, 1996; Ceci & Williams, 1997) has organized and reviewed this literature, making the point that schooling indeed has a powerful impact on IQ.

In addition to citing Cahan and Cohen's (1989) data as evidence for the influence of schooling on IQ, Ceci examined several additional areas of research pertinent to the schooling-IQ question, some of which we mention here.

1. Perhaps the most obvious approach to the question would be to compute correlations between years of education and IQ. When this is done, the correlations tend to be very high, usually higher than 0.60 and often in excess of 0.80. The effects remain large even after controlling for differences in socioeconomic status.

2. There is a small but statistically significant drop in children's IQ over summer vacation. This drop is larger among children from low-income homes, probably because their summer activities have less resemblance to school activities than do those of children from more affluent homes.

3. Children who attend school intermittently, being frequently absent, have lower IQs than do children who attend school regularly. What is typically found in samples of frequently truant children is that IQ scores get lower with age. That is, children lose IQ points as they get older, partly because they increasingly fall behind in school.

4. Children who enter school late show an IQ decrement relative to children who start school on time. In one study, children experienced, on average, a five-point IQ deficit for each year that their schooling was delayed.

5. Just as people who start school late have lower IQs, so, too, do people who drop out of school early.

6. Evidence suggests that the quality and not just the quantity of schooling is important for IQ effects. For example, a classic study of African Americans who migrated from segregated and poor school systems in Georgia to better-

quality systems in Philadelphia between World Wars I and II showed that children gained about one half an IQ point for each year they were enrolled in the Philadelphia schools.

More recently Heiner Rindermann and Stephen Ceci (2010) concluded that international differences in cognitive abilities are not due to genetic differences but to differences in countries' educational systems.

Taken together, the evidence is impressive that attending school influences one's IQ. Again, perhaps this should not be too surprising, in part because IQ tests, although purporting not to assess specific aptitudes, do tap general cultural knowledge (the information and vocabulary subtests on the Wechsler scales, for example, do this), much of which is learned in school. What seems inarguable is that whatever IQ tests measure, it is influenced greatly by the school experience.

Section Review

Schooling is associated with increased cognitive abilities.

- Attending school enhances development of many cognitive skills beyond the effects of age, although age has a greater impact on development of other cognitive abilities.
- Evidence from a variety of sources suggests that schooling influences IQ.

Ask Yourself . . .

19. What is the role of schooling in cognitive development? How do we know that schooling is more influential than age, and what does this indicate about the nature of IQ assessment?

EVOLUTIONARY EDUCATIONAL PSYCHOLOGY

We have highlighted throughout this chapter (in fact, throughout this book) how children's thinking is influenced by evolved psychological biases (Bjorklund, Hernández Blasi, & Ellis, 2016; Geary & Berch, 2016). For example, in Chapter 6 we examined the development of folk physics, folk biology, and folk psychology (see also Chapter 10), and we saw that children are motivated to attend to certain aspects of their physical and social worlds. These aspects proved valuable to our ancestors and help people predict and control important parts of their environments. Although people certainly become aware of some of this knowledge, much of it remains unavailable to consciousness. Moreover, although these processing biases continue to be useful for people today, they sometimes conflict with the demands of modern society. We live in environments that are evolutionarily novel, and children must learn things that could not have been conceived by their ancestors. To do this requires formal education, something that itself is novel for our species.

Humans have always educated their children. The complexity of social groups and the technological skills that even early humans acquired could be not mastered without some form of instruction or sophisticated social learning. For most of our history, cultural knowledge was transmitted by "on the job training" and still is today in traditional cultures and for many occupations even in developed societies. In fact, based on the anthropological literature, David Lancy (2015, 2016) notes that, unlike adults in modern cultures, adults in traditional societies rarely engage in direct teaching. Instead, education in traditional cultures is informal, accomplished chiefly by observations, "through participation with more skilled partners in culturally organized activities" (Rogoff, 1990, p. 39).

Unlike other animals, however, each generation of humans does not start out from square one but begins with the knowledge of the previous generation, permitting the rapid expansion of information over time (Tomasello, 1999). Until relatively recently, humans have been able to transmit this valuable knowledge in social settings, with apprentices learning from masters. But as knowledge has accumulated and culture has moved away from the environments in which we evolved as a species, new skills were required, and these were best learned out of context. In other words, these skills were best learned not on the job but rather in classrooms of one form or another. Formal education—teaching the new technological skills of reading, writing, and arithmetic—has only recently become important for economic success, dating back a few hundred years at most (and it is only within the past 100 years or so that a majority of people in most societies received formal education). Such education is a necessity today, guiding children in the acquisition of many of the explicit cognitive skills discussed earlier in this chapter, and this presents a serious challenge for human educability. Modern children possess the same brains and minds as did their hunter-gatherer peers dating back at least 60,000 years, and perhaps as far back as 300,000 years, yet modern culture necessitates that children learn things unimaginable by their ancient predecessors.

Principles of Evolutionary Educational Psychology

David Geary (1995, 2007, 2010a; Geary & Berch, 2016) has championed the new field of **evolutionary educational psychology**, defined as "the study of how children's evolved cognitive, learning, and motivational biases influence their ability and motivation to learn novel academic abilities and knowledge in school"" (Geary & Berch, 2016, pp. 242–243). Geary proposed six principles of evolutionary educational psychology, which are summarized in Table 11.2.

As we saw in Chapter 6, Geary proposes that children evolved cognitive and motivational systems for dealing with their physical, biological, and social worlds (folk physics, biology, and psychology, respectively). He referred to these as biologically primary systems, and they are mostly implicit in nature (see discussion in Chapter 2 and earlier in this chapter). These systems helped children, and later adults, to predict and control their world. However, despite facilitating peoples' understanding of their physical and social environments, they were not always scientifically accurate. For example, children assume that a container with a higher level of liquid in it contains more of that liquid than a container with a lower level, often ignoring differences in width. This will generally result in correct assessments, in that containers that look like they hold more usually do. This can result in some problems, however, when the contents are poured from a tall, thin container to a shorter, wider container, causing children to assert that the amount of liquid has now changed (this is Piaget's conservation-of-liquid task discussed in Chapter 5). Children's intuitive understanding interferes with logical thinking. A more sophisticated example involves understanding the forces on a thrown ball. Most people believe (and nearly all did before Isaac Newton) that there are two forces acting on a thrown ball: the first impels it forward and dissipates over time. The second pulls the ball downward. This second force, of course, is gravity. The first force also has a name, impetus, but in the context of a

TABLE 11.2 **Principles of evolutionary educational psychology.**

1. Biologically secondary abilities associated with scientific, technological, and academic advances emerged from the biologically primary abilities associated with folk physics, folk biology, and folk psychology. As a society's knowledge increases, the gap between folk knowledge and the skills necessary to acquire the technological skills of society widens.

2. Schools emerged in societies to fill the gap between folk knowledge and needed technological skills.

3. The purpose of schools is to organize the activities of children so they can acquire the biologically secondary abilities that close the gap between folk knowledge and the occupational and social demands of their society.

4. Biologically secondary abilities are built from biologically primary abilities and components of general intelligence, evolved to deal with environmental variation and novelty.

5. Children are inherently motivated to engage in activities that promote their folk knowledge, but this sometimes conflicts with the need to engage in activity that will promote secondary learning (for example, reading), because children are not inherently motivated to engage in biologically secondary abilities.

6. There is a need for direct instruction for children to learn most biologically secondary abilities.

Source: Adapted from Geary, D. C. (2007). Educating the evolved mind: Conceptual foundations for an evolutionary educational psychology. In J. S. Carlson & J. R. Levin (Eds.), *Educating the evolved mind: Conceptual foundations for an evolutionary educational psychology* (pp. 1–99). Charlotte, NC: Information Age Publishing.

thrown ball it does not exist. Once the ball leaves the person's hand, it has no propelling force (that was provided by the thrower), only gravity. Our naive (nonscientific) understanding is sufficient to let us predict where a thrown object is likely to fall, but our underlying theory, despite permitting us to make relatively accurate predictions, is wrong.

Although folk knowledge works well enough most of the time, the accumulation of knowledge over many generations and the development of new technologies results in a gap between folk knowledge and the skills necessary for being successful in one's society. Most of these new skills are in the form of biologically secondary abilities, which are available to consciousness (that is, a form of explicit cognition). It is under these situations that schools become necessary. It is unlikely that most children will learn to read or multiply on their own or acquire the knowledge of biology, government, or world geography without instruction, for example. The job of schools is to organize children's activities

so that they acquire the biologically secondary abilities (built upon biologically primary abilities) deemed important by their culture, such as reading and mathematics.

Geary notes that although children have intrinsic motivation to engage in biologically primary abilities, this is not the case for biologically secondary abilities, which often require tedious practice and external pressure to master some of these skills and the strategies that underlie them. Reading is an obvious example. Based upon the biologically primary abilities of language, few children learn to read spontaneously as they seem to learn how to talk. It is not surprising that many young children fail to see the big picture of the importance of reading and thus have little intrinsic motivation to learn how to read. (Although we have noticed in several families, younger children are motivated to learn to read because they see it as something that an older sibling has mastered.) Children learn to read because teachers and parents make them. Once a certain level of reading ability is acquired, children's motivation to read to learn new information can increase. In fact, reading instruction can likely be facilitated by having children read content related to their biologically primary interests. As Geary (1995) states, "The motivation to read . . . is probably driven by the content of what is being read rather than by the process itself. In fact, the content of many stories and other secondary activities (e.g., video games, television) might reflect evolutionary relevant themes that motivate engagement in these activities (e.g., social relationships, competition)" (p. 28). As we noted earlier in this chapter, boys are more sensitive to the interest level of what they read than girls, showing lower levels of reading comprehension for low-interest stories compared to girls (Renninger, 1992). As a result of less motivation for acquiring biologically secondary skills, explicit instruction (as opposed to discovery learning) is necessary for many children to acquire these skills.

According to Geary and Berch (2016), educators should be sensitive to the type of skills children are acquiring and modify their instruction accordingly. Geary and Berch write: "*We have suggested that structured, explicit, teacher-directed instruction should be most effective when acquiring secondary skills that are remote from supporting primary systems and that take place in a species atypical, classroom context where the goal is oriented toward acquiring knowledge for its own sake*" (2016, p. 240, italics in the original). At other times, however, when the skills children are acquiring are related to biologically primary abilities for which they have intrinsic motivation to learn, explicit, direct instruction may not be necessary and, in fact, may actually hinder learning. Educators have long argued about the pros and cons of direct instruction versus discovery learning, and this is perhaps best reflected in debates about the

best ways to educate preschool children. On the one hand, given how important it is to master evolutionarily novel skills such as reading, mathematics, and managing digital technology, the earlier one can begin to acquire these biologically secondary abilities the better the long-term outcome is apt to be. On the other hand, natural selection has adapted young children so that they learn through observation and play, and explicit, direct instruction may interfere with preschool children's evolved learning styles. In the next two sections we investigate research relevant to this debate about the best way to educate young children, first looking at the costs and benefits of academic preschools and second examining infant and young children's learning through modern visual media.

Costs and Benefits of Academic Preschools

Earlier in this chapter we reviewed evidence clearly showing that schooling has a powerful impact on cognitive development. One year of schooling has a greater impact on some components of cognition than does 1 year of age, and schooling influences IQ. All this, along with evidence that a longer school year likely produces cognitive gains, makes a compelling argument for extended education, at least in postindustrial societies. In fact, some people have looked at the evidence and concluded that intellectual gains could be even greater if formal education were to begin even earlier (Doman, 1984). If starting formal education at 5 is good, surely starting at 4, 3, or even 2 is better.

Evidence indicates that children who attend high-quality child-care programs during the preschool years score higher on measures of cognitive ability during elementary school than do matched groups of children who do not attend preschool programs (Li et al., 2013). Quality preschool education may be especially important for children from high-risk environments, who may not receive adequate preparation for school in their homes (Vandell et al., 2010; see discussion of preschool intervention programs in Chapter 13). But quality child care and preschool education does not necessarily mean *academically oriented* education. In fact, several researchers and educators have seriously questioned the idea of rigorous academic instruction for preschoolers (Elkind, 1987; Reed, Hirsh-Pasek, & Golinkoff, 2012). David Elkind (1987), for example, stated that academic programs for preschoolers amount to *miseducation*. Young children do not have the cognitive capacity to adequately master the academic skills of these programs, and the overall result is unnecessary stress with no long-term benefits.

Research has been done assessing the costs and benefits of formal education during the preschool period. Contrasts are often made between preschool programs that take children's natural propensities for play and activity into consideration (termed **developmentally appropriate programs**) and those that stress formal instruction (termed **direct-instruction programs**). Concerning academic abilities after a year in these programs, some studies find better performance for children attending developmentally appropriate programs (Stipek et al., 1998), some for direct-instruction programs (Stipek et al., 1995), and some find no differences (Hirsh-Pasek, Hyson, & Rescorla, 1990). When long-term effects (greater than 1 year) are assessed, more studies find greater benefits for developmentally appropriate programs (Burts et al., 1993; Marcon, 1999). For instance, in one study children who had attended either a developmentally appropriate or direct-instruction preschool were followed for 6 years (Marcon, 1999). Although there were no differences in academic performance between the two groups of children by the end of third grade, by the end of fourth grade children who had the developmentally appropriate preschool curriculum had higher grades than those who had attended the direct-instruction programs.

Differences between developmentally appropriate and direct-instruction programs are clearer when motivational and psychosocial factors are considered, with most studies finding that children attending developmentally appropriate programs experience less stress, like school better, are more creative, and have less test anxiety than children attending direct-instruction programs (Burts et al., 1993; Stipek et al., 1995, 1998; see Bjorklund, 2007a). For example, in a study by Deborah Stipek and her colleagues (1995), preschool and kindergarten children from a range of households attended either developmentally appropriate or direct-instruction programs. Although children who attended direct-instruction programs showed greater knowledge of letters and reading achievement than children attending developmentally appropriate programs, no differences were found on knowledge of numbers, and children in the developmentally appropriate programs rated themselves as having greater intellectual abilities, were less dependent on adults for permission and approval, expressed greater pride in accomplishment, had higher expectations for success on school-like tasks, chose more challenging math problems to perform, and said they worried less about school than children in the direct-instruction programs. In other words, any academic benefits gained from a teacher-directed program had its costs in terms of motivation.

Most of these effects, although statistically significant, are small in magnitude. Nevertheless, the pattern is clear. In general, there are no long-term benefits of academically oriented preschool programs for middle-class children, and some evidence indicates that such programs might actually be detrimental. The authors of one study proposed two alternative interpretations of this pattern of findings (Hyson, Hirsh-Pasek, & Rescorla, 1990; Rescorla, Hyson, & Hirsh-Pasek, 1991). The first points to the small differences between the schools, so that from a practical perspective the academic orientation of a school likely makes little difference in the long run. The second and stronger interpretation of the data holds that an academic orientation provides no advantage and actually has some small negative consequences. Marion Hyson and her colleagues concluded that whichever interpretation is adopted, there seems to be no defensible reason for encouraging formal academic instruction during the preschool years. Rather, for most children from middle-class homes, cognitive development and creativity can best be fostered in a developmentally appropriate preschool program that considers children's limitations as well as their abilities. In the opinion of these researchers, "it may be developmentally prudent to let children explore the world at their own pace rather than to impose our adult timetables and anxieties on them" (Hyson et al., 1990, p. 421).

We should note that most developmentally appropriate programs involve some explicit teaching, and most direct-instruction programs offer children some playtime. Moreover, children learn through both instruction and play (recall our brief discussion in Chapter 5 that social play may serve to foster the development of executive function in children [Berk & Meyers, 2013]), and programs that afford some opportunities for both activities likely provide the proper balance for effective preschool education. However, although play and instruction may both result in learning, one style may be preferable to the other during the preschool years, depending on what is being learned.

The different benefits to learning of play and instruction for preschool children were illustrated in a study by Elizabeth Bonawitz and her colleagues (2011). Bonawitz et al. proposed that direct instruction, or teaching, facilitates children's acquisition of specific skills or information, but in doing so, it also "limits the range of hypotheses children consider" (Bonawitz et al., 2011, p. 333). In comparison, Bonawitz and her associates hypothesized that learning through play, or *discovery learning*, may result in learning new properties of a stimulus or event, although it may slow or even prevent the learning of specific information or a specific skill. To test their hypotheses, Bonawitz and her colleagues introduced preschool children with a novel toy and taught children in the *pedagogical* condition how to perform a specific set of behaviors to produce a specific outcome (make a squeaking sound). Other children were shown the same behaviors with the same outcome but without specific instructions, and still others were introduced to the new toy without any demonstration. Children were then allowed to play with the toy ("Wow, isn't that cool! I'm going to let you play and see if you can figure out how this toy works"). Children in the pedagogical condition spent more time playing with the squeaker, the one function they were shown, but they played with the toy less and discovered significantly fewer functions of the toy than children in the other conditions.

The instruction done by Bonawitz et al. (2011) took advantage of children's social-learning abilities and reveals that simple instructions can result in fast and effective learning of simple behaviors, exactly the goal of teachers for many skills preschool children need to learn. However, such direct instruction has a downside in that it serves to limit exploration and the discovery of novel properties of artifacts. As Bonawitz et al.

(2011) state, "The decision about how to balance direct instruction and discovery learning largely depends on the lesson to be learned" (p. 329). Moreover, some scholars and educators note that there is a middle ground between free play and direction instruction, *guided play*, which includes the "enjoyable and engaging nature and the child's own agency, but adds a focus of the extrinsic goal of developing children's skills and knowledge" (Toub et al., 2016, p. 121). Teachers who are trained to guide children toward specific goals through play can gain the benefits of the discovery value of free play as well as the fast and effective learning of specific skills provided by direct instruction.

"Educational" DVDs and Videos for Infants

As we noted, modern educational environments would be alien to our forechildren. Ancient children lived in small groups and learned most important skills and knowledge from observing and interacting with other children. The modern classroom would make no sense to them. One aspect of modern environments that differs greatly from ancient environments that may be not so obvious and may influence how children learn is the ubiquity of two-dimensional stimuli.

Until relatively recently, when children looked at people or things, it was three-dimensional objects they saw. Although cave paintings have been around for nearly 40,000 years, and artists have been creating two-dimension renderings of people and things for thousands of years, until the 20th century, most of the world children encountered was 3D in nature, not 2D. Today, photographs, an invention of the 19th century, share children's attention with videos displayed on computers, tablets, and smartphones, all 2D representations.

As we mentioned in Chapter 3, children growing up in developed countries in the 21st century are digital natives, easily mastering what have rapidly become essential technological skills. However, to what extent are young children prepared to make sense of the two-dimensional stimuli used on their various devices? We noted in Chapter 5 that children much younger than 18 months do not have a well-developed understanding that pictures represent real objects but rather treat pictures as worthy entities in their own rights, often attempting to pick them off the page of a book (DeLoache et al., 1998).

Although infants and young children may have evolved in a three-dimensional world, research has clearly shown that they are able to acquire information from two-dimensional stimuli (Barr, 2010, 2013; Moser et al., 2015), particularly when learning experiences are frequently repeated (Linebarger & Vaala, 2010). For instance, infants who watch a televised model perform some novel actions on objects later imitate those actions significantly greater than expected by chance (Barr et al., 2007; Meltzoff, 1988). Yet researchers consistently report a video deficit, such that children much younger than 2 years of age who observe via video a model performing some novel actions remember about half as many actions as children who observe a live model (see Barr, 2010). In fact, Rachel Barr (2013) notes that this deficit is not restricted to videos but is found for other 2D displays as well, including touchscreens (Zack et al., 2009) and picture books (Ganea, Bloom Pickard, & DeLoache, 2008), and refers to the reduced ability to learn from such displays as a *transfer deficit*.

Despite this well-documented deficit, the fact that infants and toddlers *can* learn from video displays has led many parents to attempt to accelerate their children's cognitive development through the use of commercially available DVDs and educational software aimed at enriching infants' intelligence. However, despite parents' beliefs, there is little research evidence to suggest that such video experiences actually facilitate cognitive development (DeLoache et al., 2010; Richert et al., 2010). For example, Judy DeLoache and her colleagues (2010) taught 12- and 18-month-old infants new words over the course of 1 month by either watching a video with parents being encouraged to interact with their children, watching a video without parental interaction, or direct parent teaching. Only the infants who had direct parent teaching showed later learning of words greater than that of infants in a control condition who had not had any instruction. In other research, Michael Robb, Rebekah Richert, and Ellen Wartella (2009) assigned some 12- and 15-month-old infants to watch episodes of *Baby Wordsworth*, a DVD featuring words found around the infants' houses, and others to a no-exposure control group for 6 weeks. The researchers reported no difference in either expressive or receptive language measures between the DVD and the control group.

Some research suggests that frequent viewing of baby DVDs may actually be harmful to children's cognitive development (Courage et al., 2010; F. J. Zimmerman, Christakis, & Meltzoff, 2007), consistent with the American Academy of Pediatrics (2011) recommendation that parents should avoid exposing children under 2 years of age to television, background media, and other video media. For instance, Frederick Zimmerman and his colleagues (2007) reported that the amount of time 8- to 16-month-old infants spent watching baby DVDs such as *Baby Einstein* was *negatively* associated with receptive vocabulary: Each hour children watched baby DVDs/videos was associated with 6 to 8 *fewer* vocabulary

words. Moreover, although infants are often attentive to and seem to enjoy these DVDs, as well as television, it is not until 18 months that the *content* of the video, rather than the physical stimulus qualities of the display, will hold a child's attention (Courage & Setliff, 2010).

Why might young children not benefit from exposure to video and other 2D displays? As we discussed in Chapter 5, young children seem to lack *representational insight*, the ability to use one object to stand for another (DeLoache, 1987). But why may exposure to video actually be detrimental to young children's cognitive functioning? One line of research suggests that media exposure before the age of 2 is related to impaired executive functions, those abilities including working memory, inhibition, and cognitive flexibility used for planning and regulating behavior (see Chapter 7) (Lillard, Li, & Boguszewski, 2015). For example, Jenny Radesky and her colleagues (2014) found that 9-month-olds who were exposed to higher amounts of media had poorer self-regulation (for example, irritability, distractibility, failure to delay gratification, problem shifting focus from one task to another) at 3 years of age, even after controlling for important parental and family factors. In other research, Amy Nathanson and her colleagues (2014) reported that preschool children who had spent a greater number of cumulative hours watching TV had poorer executive functions than children who had viewed fewer hours. Furthermore, those children who began watching television earlier had poorer executive functions than those who began watching TV at a later age. This effect was only found when children watched rapid-pace cartoon shows with atypical sequencing. This latter finding is consistent with studies by Angeline Lillard and her colleagues (Lillard & Peterson, 2011; Lillard, Drell et al., 2015), who reported that viewing just 9 minutes of a fast-pace cartoon show produced reduced levels of executive functioning in groups of 4-year-old children.

As we noted in Chapter 5, it is not until well into the second year of life that children are able to properly understand that these two-dimensional artifacts represent real things (that is, they are symbolic), and thus it should not be surprising that infants and toddlers have a difficult time learning from such representations. Yet children show increasing facility in dealing with symbols, including videos, beginning shortly before their second birthdays. Although research shows that exposing infants and toddlers to visual media has no educational benefits and may even be detrimental, we are reluctant to conclude that occasional exposure to such displays produces any long-term detriment to young children. What may be detrimental, however, is *overexposure* to two-dimensional displays that, although amusing to and attracting the attention of infants and toddlers, rarely teaches them and often distracts them (Bjorklund & Beers, 2016). Although the research is admittedly scant, the evidence is consistent with the position that stimulation in excess of the species norm early in development can have negative consequences (Turkewitz & Kenny, 1982).

Physical Activity

It is not just children's cognitive abilities that are sometimes at odds with the demands of formal schools but also aspects of their physical and social development. For instance, in most American schools, children spend the bulk of their day inside, seated in chairs or at tables and attending to instruction from a teacher. They are usually encouraged to perform "seat work" independently, keeping their hands and eyes to themselves. Schools understandably discourage more vigorous activity, such as rough-and-tumble play, a favorite activity of many elementary school-age boys. However, some have argued that physical activity, often in the form of recess, actually facilitates young children's learning and should be incorporated into the daily curriculum (Pellegrini & Dupuis, 2010).

A number of studies have shown a positive relation between physical activity and academic performance in elementary schoolchildren (Murray & Ramstetter, 2013; A. Singh et al., 2012). For instance, in a series of three studies, Anthony Pellegrini and his colleagues (1995) varied the timing of school recess for kindergarten, second-grade, and fourth-grade children. Some children had recess delayed by 30 minutes for 2 days a week relative to the other days.

Children's attention to seat work was assessed both before and after recess. At each grade, children were significantly more attentive after recess than before, and the effects of delaying recess were significantly greater for the younger than for the older children.

Earlier in Chapter 7 we discussed evidence that increased physical activity is associated with increased executive function (C. L. Davis et al., 2011). Other correlational research further supports this finding. For instance, in one study, one group of 9-year-old children described as physically fit in terms of aerobic capacity (number of laps they could do), muscle strength (doing push-ups and curl-ups), and body mass index and a second group described as less fit were given a test of executive function while their brain activity was monitored (Hillman et al., 2009). The physically fit children had significantly greater executive function abilities—specifically, in terms of allocating their attentional resources—as shown both by performance on the cognitive task and by measures of brain functioning (EEG).

Despite these positive effects, the frequency of recess has been steadily declining in schools in the United States (see Murray & Ramstetter, 2013). This seems not to be the case, however, in many successful school systems in other countries. For instance, elementary schoolchildren in Japan have a 10- to 15-minute break every hour (Murray & Ramstetter, 2013), and children in Finland, which boasts one of the world's best educational systems, provides a 15-minute break for students and teachers every hour (Walker, 2014). That is, despite having what most people believe are more rigorous curricula, these schools recognize the cognitive and behavioral limitations of young children and structure the day to take these limitations into consideration.

One must keep in mind that schools are an evolutionary novelty and that normal levels of activity and playful behavior, especially as shown by preadolescent boys, although sometimes interfering with ideal educational practices, may provide more cognitive benefits than deficits.

Evolutionary thinking as applied to education is not monolithic; in fact, as in other areas of psychology and education, there is often heated debate about how to implement the most effective evolutionarily informed curriculum. For example, although Geary and Berch (2016) argue that direct instruction is likely required for learning biologically secondary abilities, other evolutionary theorists disagree, arguing that children always learn best through the process of discovery learning (Gray, 2013, 2016). Yet we agree with Geary and Berch (2016) who stated that

> there is a value-added to framing educational goals (among others) within an evolutionary context,

and most important they provide direction for future empirical studies. The ultimate, so to speak, benefit of this approach will be in its ability to generate testable hypotheses about instructional approaches and based on these improve the educational outcomes of all children. In other words, evolutionary educational psychology will flourish or flounder based on its contributions to our ability to meet the goals of a universal education. (p. 243)

Section Review

Evolutionary educational psychology applies the concepts of evolutionary psychology to education.

- Geary proposes that children evolved cognitive and motivational mechanisms for dealing with their physical, biological, and social worlds, and an understanding of these mechanisms can facilitate the development of educational systems.
- Although the effects are typically small, middle-class children who attend preschool programs that stress academics (*direct-instruction programs*) demonstrate no long-term gains and have less positive attitudes about school than do children who attend nonacademic preschool programs (*developmentally appropriate programs*).
- Although infants and toddlers can learn from videos, children much younger than 2 years of age learn and remember information better when they view or interact with a live model rather than via video, termed a *video deficit*.
- There is little research evidence to suggest that watching baby DVDs actually facilitates young children's cognitive development, with some research suggesting that frequent viewing of baby DVDs and television may actually be harmful to cognitive development.
- Some research suggests that media exposure before the age of 2 is related to impaired executive functions.

- Physical activity, in the form of recess, may facilitate children's attention to course work and enhance schooling effects.

Ask Yourself . . .

20. What are the basic tenets associated with evolutionary educational psychology? How might these tenets be applied at the elementary, intermediate, secondary, and college levels?
21. What kind of skills might require direct instruction?
22. How do screen time and media exposure influence the cognitive development of children at different ages?

KEY TERMS AND CONCEPTS

approximate number system (ANS)
conservation of number
decomposition
developmentally appropriate programs
direct-instruction programs
dyslexia

emergent literacy
evolutionary educational psychology
fact retrieval
integrative theory of numerical development
Matthew effect
meta-analysis

min strategy
phonemic awareness
phonological recoding
rapid automatized naming (RAN)
stereotype threat
sum strategy
video deficit

SUGGESTED READINGS

Scholarly Works

Geary, D. C., & Berch, D. B. (2016). Evolution and children's cognitive and academic development. In D. C. Geary & D. B. Berch (Eds.), *Evolutionary perspectives on education and child development* (pp. 217–249). New York: Springer. This is the most recent presentation of David Geary's ideas about applying evolutionary psychology to modern education. It is part of a volume edited by Geary and Berch that includes other chapters integrating evolutionary theory with child development and education.

Halpern, D. F., Benbow, C. P., Geary, D. C., Gur, R. C., Hyde, J. S., & Gernsbacher, M. A. (2007). The science of sex differences in science and mathematics. *Psychological Science in the Public Interest, 8,* 1–51. This paper, written by leading researchers in various aspects of sex differences, examines the controversial topic of sex differences in science and mathematics and their possible origins.

Nunes, T., & Bryant, P. (2015). The development of mathematical reasoning. In R. M. Lerner (Series Eds.) & L. Liben & U. M. Müller (Vol. Eds.), *Handbook of child psychology and developmental science: Vol. 2. Cognitive processes* (7th ed., pp. 715–762). New York: Wiley. This chapter reviews research and theory on children's developing mathematical abilities, covering topics of more advanced math as well as the basic number concepts and arithmetic discussed in this chapter.

Schwanenflugel, P. J., & Knapp, N. F. (2016). *The psychology of reading: Theory and applications.* Guilford: New York. This book provides a highly readable and in-depth account of the cognitive and social factors involved in reading, with a strong developmental perspective.

Reading for Personal Interest

Christakis, D. (2015, September). *Dmitri Christakis: Media and children* [Video file]. Retrieved from http://www.npr.org/2015/09/11/439192407/when-it-comes-to-kids-is-all-screen-time-equal. Dimitri Christakis is the director of the Center for Child Health, Behavior, and Development at Seattle Children's Research Institute. He's also a pediatrician at Seattle Children's Hospital and professor in the School of Medicine at University of Washington. In his TED talk, he discusses research on the long-term effects of fast-paced media on attention. With examples of popular children's programs, he draws stark comparisons and describes how parents can make television beneficial for kids.

Golinkoff, R. M., Hirsh-Pasek, K., & Eyer, D. (2004). *Einstein never used flashcards: How our children really learn—and why they need to play more and memorize less.* New York: Rodale Books. This trio of developmental psychologists makes the compelling argument that preschool children learn better when they are not pressured to perform academic-type work. Rather, young children acquire problem-solving, social, and attentional skills best through play.

Sugata, M. (2010, September). *The child-driven education* [Video file]. Retrieved from https://www.ted.com/talks/sugata_mitra_the_child_driven_education. Mitra Sugata is winner of the 2013 TED prize and has given a series of talks on his work with students given unsupervised use of computers and the Internet and how they teach themselves. His ideas are compelling and offer a model for how educators can incorporate modern technology and take advantage of the active nature of children's learning.

Wolf, M. (2007). *Proust and the squid: The story and science of the reading brain.* New York: Harper. Maryann Wolf provides a fascinating account of how our ancestors taught their brains how to read only a few thousand years ago and in the process changed the intellectual evolution of our species.

12 APPROACHES TO THE STUDY OF INTELLIGENCE

"Look at the fingers of your right hand. No two are alike. That's the way children are." This homily, attributed to a retired elementary school teacher, reflects the individuality of children.

In the previous chapters of this book, we focused on different ways in which cognition changes from infancy through adolescence. Although we occasionally discussed individual differences in children's thinking—for example, how children with ADHD display poor executive function, or how children with autism have an underdeveloped theory of mind—for the most part our attention has been on age-related differences in children's thinking. Yet we are all aware that some children think better than other children of the same age. Some kids are smarter than others. When psychologists and educators discuss relatively stable individual differences in cognitive functioning between people, they usually use the term *intelligence*. If Ashley gets better grades in school, follows the complicated story lines of movies and TV dramas more easily, and generally solves everyday problems more effectively than Isabella, then despite the two being the same age, we would typically say that Ashley is more intelligent than Isabella.

For psychologists, however, intelligence is more than just a synonym for *smart*. Rather, it reflects an important characteristic of individuals that can be measured and used to predict people's performance on a host of social and cognitive tasks. In fact, that is why the study of intelligence is important to child development: Children who score high on tests of intelligence tend to perform better in school, acquire important technological skills more easily, and often display better social adjustment than children who score lower on such tests. Scores on intelligence tests can alert parents, teachers, and other people concerned with a child's welfare to potential problems and their amelioration (or to potential areas of giftedness and their amplification).

We should also say a few words about the connotation that the word *intelligence* has for most people. Although our intention is to focus on the psychological definition of the term, it also has significance from a sociological perspective. We all show different patterns of cognitive skills: Some people have better memories than others; some are more distractible, more verbal, or better with numbers than others; and most of us do not hesitate to comment on our cognitive strong and weak points. However, to say someone is of high or low intelligence means a lot more to most people than to say someone has good or poor memory, high or low mathematical ability, or is more or less attentive. In part, this results from how theorists and educators have defined intelligence as a set of intellectual skills that affect nearly all problems one attempts to solve. We value people of high intelligence, believing that they are more effective at a broad range of tasks, are apt to be more interesting to talk to, and are more economically successful. We likewise tend to undervalue people of

low intelligence, thinking they are less skilled at performing the tasks of daily living. One often hears people saying things like people should have to take an IQ test before they have children or before they're allowed to vote. Although we cannot change peoples' connotation for the term, we can alert students to the unconscious bias that most of us have attached to *intelligence*, and we can emphasize that our discussion is limited to the cognitive aspects of the term.

What exactly do psychologists and educators mean when they use the term **intelligence**? Most broadly, it refers to acting or thinking in ways that are goal directed and adaptive. This definition covers a lot of ground, allowing much leeway for theorists to sculpt their own meanings of the concept while still being understood by others. We are in general agreement with Linda Gottfredson's (1997) definition of intelligence as "involving the ability to plan, solve problems, think abstractly, comprehend complex ideas, learn quickly and learn from experience. It is not merely book learning, a narrow academic skill, or test-taking smarts. Rather, it reflects a broader and deeper capability for comprehending our surroundings—'catching on,' 'making sense' of things, or 'figuring out' what to do" (p. 13). Following this definition, intelligence is obviously a multifaceted phenomenon that no single test can likely tap. Several researchers have produced tools that aim to assess some of the multiple aspects of intelligence described in this definition (Sternberg, Ferrari, & Clinkenbeard, 1996; Wexler-Sherman, Gardner, & Feldman, 1988), but the bulk of data, both historically and in contemporary research, has come from the testing, or *psychometric approach*, with IQ tests being the measure most often associated with intelligence. Much of this chapter concentrates on the theory and practice of IQ testing, but alternatives to the testing approach to intelligence are given even more space.

More specifically, we examine information-processing approaches to intelligence, followed by a detailed look at two popular alternative theories: Robert Sternberg's theory of successful intelligence and Howard Gardner's theory of multiple intelligences. In the next chapter, we continue the discussion of intelligence, focusing on the extent to which intelligence is biologically and environmentally influenced and on the stability of intelligence over time.

We should also note that most of this book to this point has been concerned with intelligence but from a developmental rather than a psychometric perspective. Generally, when developmental psychologists speak of intelligence they are referring to age-related changes in thinking and reasoning, much as Piaget did in formulating his theory (see Chapter 5). In contrast, the psychometric approach primarily focuses on the structure of intelligence and differences in the measurement of intelligence between people (J. R. Flynn & Blair, 2013). However, as you'll see, primarily in Chapter 13, the developmental and the psychometric approaches to intelligence can be integrated to provide a more thorough understanding of intelligence and its significance in childhood.

PSYCHOMETRIC APPROACH TO THE STUDY OF INTELLIGENCE

The major approach to the study of individual differences in intelligence since the turn of the 20th century has been the psychometric approach (or the differential approach). Psychometric theories of intelligence have as their basis a belief that intelligence can be described in terms of mental factors and that tests can be constructed that reveal individual differences in those factors that underlie mental performance. Factors are related mental skills that (presumably) affect thinking in a wide range of situations.

Factors of Intelligence

What constitutes a factor is determined by a statistical procedure known as factor analysis. In factor analysis, numerous test items are administered to people, and the resulting data are examined to see which items fit together well. Tests might show, for example, that the pattern of individual differences among people is very similar on vocabulary, reading comprehension, story completion, and verbal analogies. That is, people who score high on one of these tests usually score high on all of them, whereas people who score low on one usually score low on all. In contrast, performance on these test items might not correlate as highly with performance on items that involve rotating three-dimensional figures, solving maze problems, or quickly placing geometric forms in a form board, although these three tests might all correlate highly with one another. What do the first tests (vocabulary, reading comprehension, story completion, and verbal analogies) have in common? It is not difficult to conclude that all involve some aspect of verbal thinking, whereas the second set (three-dimensional rotation, maze learning, and form-board performance) are all basically nonverbal and involve some form of spatial thinking. Accordingly, based on the results of the statistical analysis, an investigator can assume that two factors that account for individual differences among people are verbal ability and spatial thinking.

Patterns of performance are not always clear-cut, however. The extent to which sets of test items correlate with one another is a matter of degree. Only in textbooks do we find perfect data that can be interpreted in only one way. Thus, how one defines mental factors is influenced not only by the data but also by one's theoretical and statistical perspective.

General Intelligence, or g

Determining the number and makeup of factors is a function of the items included on a test (you could not very well have a verbal component if no verbal items were included in your test) and the particular way you perform statistical analyses. Based on variants of the same form of analysis, the number of factors that have been proposed to account for human intelligence has varied considerably. At one extreme is J. P. Guilford's (1988) theory that includes 180 unique intellectual factors. More influential (and older), however, is Charles Spearman's (1927) proposal that intelligence consists of only two kinds of factors. He viewed the most critical kind of factor as a general one, labeled **g** (or **general intelligence**) that influences performance on all intellectual tasks. He saw the other kind of factors as specific ones that are not generalizable and pertinent to only a single task. As such, these highly specific abilities are of little interest to psychologists trying to construct theories to explain individual differences among people. In other words, from Spearman's point of view, intelligence exists on a single dimension and is not some multifaceted phenomenon (that is, there is actually only one factor of intelligence, *g*). Intellectual functioning is relatively homogeneous, or similar, across different tasks performed by a single person—in other words, it is a domain-general ability. Smart people are smart all the time (or most of the time, anyway), and less bright people are consistently so.

Raymond Cattell (1971) provided an expansion of Spearman's original theory by recognizing both a general intellectual factor similar to *g* and two second-order factors that he called **fluid abilities and crystallized abilities**. Basically, Cattell proposed that fluid abilities (or fluid intelligence) are biologically determined and are reflected in memory span, reasoning, and most tests of spatial thinking. In contrast, crystallized abilities are best reflected in tests of verbal comprehension or social relations, skills that depend more highly on cultural context and experience (see Blair, 2006).

One interpretation of the importance of general intelligence is that it evolved as a means of solving problems that are evolutionarily novel (Kanazawa, 2004). Humans, more so than other animals, are able to deal effectively with a wide range of environments, including conditions that were never regularly faced by our ancestors. Our abilities to reason inductively, to see analogies, and to predict and plan for the future all help us to deal with unpredictable events and thus to survive in conditions for which we are not biologically well prepared. The same intelligence that permitted hunter-gatherers to develop new foraging strategies or to develop ways to catch new game allows us to figure out how to operate computers.

The best evidence for the existence of *g* is what has been termed the **positive manifold**, the frequent finding of high correlations among scores on sets of cognitive tests that have little in common with one another in content or types of strategies used (A. R. Jensen, 1998). This is exactly what Spearman proposed earlier in the 20th century, and the finding is still with us.

Research has produced at least one interesting caveat to the positive manifold, suggesting that the extent to which *g* influences performance on various cognitive tests decreases with increasing levels of intelligence (Deary et al., 1996; Tommasi et al., 2015). This is illustrated in a study by Douglas Detterman and Mark Daniel (1989) who found much higher correlations among scores on a variety of cognitive and intelligence tasks for people with low IQs than for people with high IQs. For example, in one study, adults with intellectual impairment (mean IQ = 67.5) and college students (mean IQ = 115.5) were given a battery of nine cognitive tasks (for example, memory, identifying rapidly presented items) and an IQ test. Detterman and Daniel correlated performance on the cognitive tasks with IQ and then examined the correlations of the scores on the nine cognitive tasks with each other. The correlations were considerably higher for the low-IQ group (0.60 for IQ scores and 0.44 for the cognitive tasks) than for the high-IQ group (0.26 for IQ scores and 0.23 for the cognitive tasks), which means that the cognitions of people with high IQs (in this case, college students) are more varied than the cognitions of people with low IQs.

There is no single interpretation of this finding, but Detterman (1987) proposed that intelligence is made up of several independent mechanisms, with each of these being influenced by central (domain-general) processes. According to Detterman (1987), intellectual impairment is caused by a deficit in central processes, which in turn affects all other components in the cognitive system, producing relative homogeneity of cognitive function. When there is no central deficit, however, variability is more apt to be found in different components of intelligence, thus producing lower correlations. In other words, a certain level of domain-general central processing resources must exist for individual components of intelligence to operate adequately. Once that level is achieved, there will be substantial variability in cognitive task performance within a given person. If that level is not achieved, as is the case for the people with intellectual impairment, then no individual component will receive enough in the way of processing resources to function well, resulting in relative homogeneity of cognitive functioning and, thus, high correlations.

Some tentative evidence also suggests that the positive manifold develops. Thomas Price and his colleagues (2000) investigated the degree to which verbal and nonverbal cognitive abilities were related in early childhood. As we've just commented, verbal and nonverbal abilities tend to be highly correlated in later childhood and adulthood, suggesting that they are influenced by some general intellectual factor, such as *g*. However, in a sample of nearly 2,000 same-sex 2-year-old twins, Price and his colleagues reported that, although correlations between verbal abilities within twins were quite high, as were correlations between nonverbal abilities, the cross-correlation (for example, the relationship between verbal ability of Twin 1 and nonverbal ability of Twin 2, and vice versa) were only of moderate magnitude. This suggested to the authors that cognitive abilities are relatively domain-specific in infancy and early childhood and become more domain-general in nature as children get older.

Hierarchical Model of Cognitive Abilities

Most psychometricians today adhere to some form of the **hierarchical model of cognitive abilities** (Carrol, 1993; Deary, 2012, 2013). Basically, this model postulates a series of relatively specific cognitive abilities, specifically verbal, spatial, speed of processing, and memory, as shown in Figure 12.1. These abilities, however, are correlated with one another (recall the positive manifold) and are influenced by a second-order general factor, or *g*. Thus, this model suggests that, depending on how one looks at the data, one can find evidence for either domain generality (*g*) or domain specificity (separate verbal and spatial modules, for example), and both could be correct (Petrill, 1997).

FIGURE 12.1 **Hierarchical model of cognitive abilities.** Intelligence is composed of specific cognitive abilities (e.g., verbal, spatial, speed of processing, memory) that are intercorrelated and influenced by a higher-order general intellectual factor, *g*.

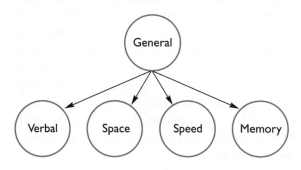

In some interesting research using neural imagining techniques, John Duncan and his colleagues (2000) used PET to examine which parts of the brain were most activated when adults performed a variety of cognitive tasks. These researchers compared verbal, spatial, and perceptual-motor tasks with high-*g* involvement (that is, those that loaded heavily on *g*) with low-*g* tasks (that is, those that did not load heavily on *g*). They found that the high-*g* tasks are associated with activation of a particular area of the brain—specifically, the lateral frontal cortex. More recent research has shown that the thickness of cortical areas of the brains in children 6 to 18 years old were positively associated with performance on a set of cognitive tasks that load heavily on *g*, further pointing to a connection between brain structure and function and intelligence (Karama et al., 2009).

As we'll see when we examine some alternative approaches to intelligence, not everyone agrees with the way psychometricians define or measure intelligence. However, regardless of whether you are a fan of psychometric theory, it has had great influence on generations of children and society in general by way of its best-known product, the IQ test.

IQ Tests

Although mental testing has had a profound influence on psychologists' attempts to conceptualize the nature of intelligence, the greatest impact of mental testing has been the intelligence quotient (IQ) test. Intelligence testing is so widespread in our society that it is virtually impossible for a child to graduate from high school without having been administered at least one IQ test and more than a dozen other tests assessing more specific academic aptitudes.

IQ tests are less the result of psychometric theorizing than they are the instruments that produce the raw data for theory construction. IQ tests were developed at the turn of the 20th century in France by Alfred Binet and Theodore Simon. The original tests—and even modern versions, to a large extent—were not based on explicit theory. Rather, they were constructed to assess school-related abilities and to differentiate among those children who could benefit from standard school instruction and those who would require special education. It would be inappropriate, however, to classify IQ tests as atheoretical. Modern IQ tests are based on certain concepts of what intelligence is (for example, the hierarchical model of cognitive abilities). Nevertheless, pragmatic considerations of which items best differentiate children of a given age are critical in constructing IQ tests, causing some to question their contribution to understanding the underlying mechanisms of intelligence (Sternberg, 1985).

Numerous IQ-type tests are available today. Many are pencil-and-paper tests that can be administered to a group. The standard tests by which most are judged include the Stanford-Binet and the three intelligence scales developed by David Wechsler. These tests have been standardized on large samples and are individually administered by trained examiners using standardized procedures.

The Stanford-Binet was developed in 1916 by Lewis Terman, who made extensive revisions to Binet's original scale. The test has gone through revisions from time to time, the most recent one being in 2003 (Roid, 2003). The latest version of the Stanford-Binet has 10 subtests, organized in a three-level hierarchical model of the structure of intelligence. A general reasoning factor (g) is the most inclusive, followed by five second-level abilities (fluid reasoning, knowledge, quantitative processing, visual/spatial processing, and working memory) and then sets of more specific tasks within each of the second-level abilities.

The Wechsler scales have similarly been revised periodically since their inception in the 1940s. There are three primary Wechsler scales, developed for people of different ages: (1) the Wechsler Preschool and Primary Scale of Intelligence (WPPSI) for children 2 to 7 years old, (2) the Wechsler Intelligence Scale for Children (WISC) for children 6 through 16 years old, and (3) the Wechsler Adult Intelligence Scale (WAIS) for adults. The latest version of the WISC (the WISC-IV; Wechsler, 2004) provides a full-scale IQ based on four separate indexes: Verbal Comprehension, Perceptual Reasoning, Working Memory, and Processing Speed. Table 12.1 lists the subtests for each index and provides brief examples of the types of items on these tests.

There are many other IQ tests, some nonverbal measures of visual reasoning (the Ravens Progressive Matrices; Raven, Raven, & Court, 2003; see Figure 12.2 for an example), and many paper-and-pencil tests that can be administered to groups of people, such as a classroom of students, with only minimal supervision. Enter "IQ test" in Google and you will find several online tests you can take in the comfort of your home. These tests do not have the reliability or validity of the individually administered Stanford-Binet or the Wechsler scales, but the logic in their construction is pretty much the same. Like the gold-standard tests, most of the easily administered tests will give you a score, with 100 being average, that will tell you where you stand with respect to other people who have taken the test. (One teenager we know paid $20 to take one of these tests, scored 141, and announced that he is a genius. Now if he can only pass Algebra II.)

Although the youngest children who can be assessed using the Wechsler or Stanford-Binet scales are early preschoolers, psychometricians have not forgotten infants. Tests to assess infant intelligence have been developed with the same psychometric properties as IQ tests and are called developmental quotient (DQ) tests. Tests such as the Bayley Scales of Infant Development (Bayley, 2005), the Gesell Developmental Schedules (Gesell & Amatruda, 1954), the Neonatal Behavioral Assessment Scale (Brazelton, 1973), and their precursors are based primarily on evaluations of individual differences in sensory and motor abilities (although the newest version of the Bayley scales [2005] includes more cognitive measures). These tests have been well standardized, are reliable (that is, there is high test-retest and intertester agreement), and describe important differences among infants (McCall, Hogarty, & Hurlburt, 1972). For example, items used to compute a DQ at different age levels in the Bayley scales include

1 to 3 months: responds to sound of bell; vocalizes once or twice; displays social smile;
5 to 7 months: smiles at mirror image; turns head after fallen spoon; vocalizes four different syllables;

TABLE 12.1 **Examples of the types of items on each subtest of the WISC-IV.**

Verbal Comprehension Index

Similarities. Children are read two words in pairs similar to the following and are to tell how they are alike: pear-peach, inch-ounce, snow-sand.

Vocabulary. Children are read words and are to tell what each word means, for example, "What is a magazine?" "What does democracy mean?"

Comprehension. Children are asked questions assessing their knowledge of societal conventions and of appropriate behavior in a variety of situations, for example, "What are some reasons we need soldiers?," "What are you supposed to do if you find someone's watch in school?," "Why is it important to have speed limits on roads?"

Information. Children are asked questions assessing their general world knowledge, similar to the following: "How many pennies make a dime?," "What do the lungs do?," "What is the capital of Italy?" This is an optional test, not included in the index total score.

Word Reasoning. Children are given sets of hints and must identify the object that the hints describe. For example, "This has a flat end and a long handle," "You use it to dig holes."

Perceptual Reasoning Index

Block Design. Children are given nine cubes, colored red on two sides, white on two sides, and red and white on two sides. They are shown designs and are to reproduce them using the nine blocks. Bonus points are given for fast response times.

Picture Concepts. Children are shown pictures and must match those that belong together based on common features, for example, things to drink, toys.

Picture Completion. Children are shown black-and-white pictures and are to determine what important part of each picture is missing. This is an optional test, not included in the index total score.

Working Memory Index

Digit Span. Children are read digits at a rate of one per second and are to repeat them back in exact order. This is followed by a test in which children must repeat the numbers in the reverse order from the order the examiner spoke them.

Letter-Number Sequencing. The examiner reads children a sequence of letters and numbers (for example, 7, K, 3, P, 8, D) and asks children to recall the numbers in ascending order (3, 7, 8) and the letters in alphabetical order (D, K, P).

Arithmetic. Children are given arithmetic problems. The easiest involve counting, addition, and subtraction using physical reminders. A child might be shown a picture of nine trees and asked to cover up all but five. More complex problems are read aloud, for example, "Joyce had six dolls and lost two. How many dolls did she have left?" "Three girls had 48 cookies. They divided them equally among themselves. How many cookies did each girl get?" This is an optional test, not included in the index total score.

Processing Speed Index

Coding. Children are shown a key associating simple geometric figures (for instance, a triangle, a square, and a circle) with other symbols (a cross, a vertical line, and so on). Children are to mark the associated symbol below a set of randomly arranged figures as quickly as possible without skipping any. Bonus points are given for fast response times.

Symbol Search. Children are shown a target symbol (for example, $\neq$) and beside it a series of three symbols (for example, $\partial \infty \yen$ or $\yen \partial \neq$). Children must determine if the first (target) symbol is contained in the second (search) set of symbols.

Cancellation. Children are shown arrays of objects and asked to mark each object of a certain type (all the trucks, for example) as quickly as possible. This is an optional test, not included in the index total score.

FIGURE 12.2 **Example of a type of item used on the Ravens Progressive Matrices.** Which of the eight items below the solid line best completes the pattern in the top of the figure?

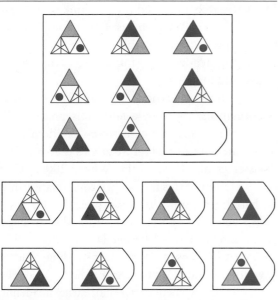

Source: Meo, M., Roberts, M. J., & Marucci, F. S. (2006). Element salience as a predictor of item difficulty for Raven's Progressive Matrices. *Intelligence, 35,* 363.

9 to 12 months: responds to verbal requests; stirs with spoon in imitation; attempts to scribble; and

14 to 17 months: says two words; shows shoes or other clothing; builds a tower of three cubes.

Basically, IQ tests (and DQ tests) are standardized on large samples of people, and items that differentiate among people of a given age are retained whereas items that do not (those that are too easy or too difficult) are eliminated. For each age assessed, the number of test items the average child passes is determined. For example, the number of items passed by 50% of the 8-year-olds in the standardization sample would reflect the number of items an average 8-year-old should be able to pass.

Historically, the relationship between the number of items passed and the age of the child was expressed as a quotient of one's mental age to one's chronological age (thus the term *intelligence quotient*, or *IQ*). A child's mental age corresponds to the number of items he or she passes. If a child passes the number of items equal to the number passed by an average 12-year-old, the child's mental age is 12 years. The child's mental age is then divided by his or her chronological age, and the result is multiplied by 100. Thus, a 10-year-old child with a mental age of 10 years has an IQ of 100 (10/10 × 100). A 10-year-old with the mental age of 9.5 years has an IQ of 95 (9.5/10 × 100), and a 10-year-old with a mental age of 12 has an IQ of 120 (12/10 × 100).

Today, use of the mental age/chronological age quotient to compute an IQ score has been generally abandoned in favor of the deviation IQ. In this method, children's performance is compared with that of children of their own age and not with the performance of older or younger children. Thus, tests can be constructed so that the statistical characteristics of IQ are the same at each age level. Modern tests are constructed so that IQ scores are distributed according to a normal distribution with specified statistical properties. The theoretical distribution of IQ scores for the WISC is shown in Figure 12.3. As can be seen, children with scores of 100 have IQs equal to or greater than 50% of the population. Children with scores of 115 have IQs equal to or greater than approximately 84% of the population. Thus, by knowing a child's IQ score, one knows

FIGURE 12.3 **Theoretical distribution of WISC-IV scores.** The test is constructed so that 50% of all people at a given age will have IQ scores of 100 and below and 50% will have scores of 100 and above.

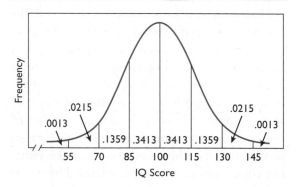

where he or she stands with respect to intelligence relative to his or her agemates. (The IQ score of our genius teenager would put him in the top 1% of all people, if we believe the validity of the test.)

Using the deviation IQ to express intelligence makes developmental contrasts difficult. IQ tests are not constructed to be a mechanism for understanding the development of intelligence. In fact, by using the deviation IQ, we hold developmental differences constant, so that we can make comparisons among agemates in the same way for children of all ages. Although this procedure has advantages for making comparisons of IQ scores for children of similar age, difficulties arise when changes in intelligence over time are of interest.

We think few people would argue that IQ tests are the last word in intelligence—that a score on a test accurately reflects one's true intelligence. Yet we think that most educators and scientists (but not all) who have given the subject serious thought would concur that IQ tests measure some aspect of intelligence, particularly as it relates to academic performance.

What Does IQ Predict?

Does IQ measure anything important? Does it predict how well one will do in school or in life? Many researchers and educators think so, at least to some degree. Research has shown, for example, that IQ predicts reasonably well individual differences in academic performance, occupational status, and longevity.

First, how well does IQ predict academic performance? The simple answer is pretty well. The average correlation between children's IQ scores and current and future grades is about 0.50 (Neisser et al., 1996; S. H. White, 2000). One interpretation of this relatively strong relationship is that the mental abilities tapped by IQ tests reflect general intelligence, or g, and that these are the intellectual skills needed to perform well in school (A. R. Jensen, 1998). Longitudinal studies have found that IQ measures predict subsequent academic achievement better than earlier academic achievement predicts later IQ, suggesting a causal connection between IQ and achievement (Watkins, Lei, & Canivez, 2007). Keep in mind, however, that although the correlation between IQ and academic performance is relatively high, it still only accounts for about 25% of the differences in school performance among children. Clearly, other factors, perhaps some in interaction with IQ, affect how well children do in school (motivation, for example) (Spinath et al., 2006).

How does IQ do in predicting occupational status? Again, pretty well. People with higher-status (and usually higher-paying) jobs have higher IQs than people with lower-status (and usually lower-paying) jobs (Bergman, Ferrer-Wreder, & Žukauskien , 2015; Schmidt & Hunter, 2004; Strenze, 2007). There are many potentially confounding factors for this relationship, with the most obvious being those between IQ and education and between education and occupation.

Nonetheless, even when levels of education are controlled, a significant relationship between IQ and occupational status remains (Neisser et al., 1996). Also, there is a positive correlation of about 0.50 between IQ and job performance for people *within* a profession (among a group of lawyers or accountants, for example). People with higher IQs tend to be rated as better at their jobs than people with lower IQs, although the strength of the correlation depends on the occupation. The average correlation for jobs requiring relatively little judgment and reasoning—such as assembly-line work—is about 0.20 compared to correlations from about 0.50 to 0.60 for jobs requiring a great deal of judgment and reasoning—such as scientist, accountant, and shop manager (Schmidt & Hunter, 2004).

In addition to its association with academic performance and occupational status, childhood IQ is positively related with longevity (Deary et al., 2008; C. L. Hart et al., 2005; Leon et al., 2009). A study in Scotland, for instance, showed that people who scored high on an IQ test given to all 11-year-olds in the nation were significantly more likely to still be alive at age 76 than were those who scored lower on the test (Deary, 2008; Deary & Der, 2005). Also, IQ has been found to be positively related to better physical (Batty et al., 2006) and mental (Deary, Weiss, & Batty, 2010) health, fewer nonintentional and intentional (including suicide) injuries, and a lower incidence of late-onset dementia (Deary et al., 2010). There are no consensually agreed-upon explanations for these relationships. Are genes associated with high IQ also associated with longevity and health? Might these all be related to prenatal environments, with healthier prenatal environments being associated with higher IQ, longevity, and health, or might the effect of IQ be related to education? Perhaps people with higher IQs are more aware of many health hazards, such as smoking and obesity, and choose to lead healthier lives as a result. Support for the latter possibility comes from a study that reported positive correlations between IQ scores and measures of physical fitness and healthy diets and negative correlations between IQ, alcoholism, smoking, obesity, and traffic accidents (Gottfredson & Deary, 2004).

IQ Tests and Minority Children

There has been much controversy about IQ testing of minority children, with critics arguing that the tests and the testing situation do not serve as fair assessments for such children (C. E. Daley & Onwuebuzie, 2011). For example, on average, the IQ scores of African American children are about 10 to 15 points lower than those of European American children (Herrnstein & Murray, 1994), with most of these differences being attributed to differences in general intelligence, or *g* (Frisby & Beaujean, 2015; A. R. Jensen, 1998). Part of the group difference can be attributed to socioeconomic status (SES). Children from lower-SES homes score lower on IQ tests than children from middle-SES homes (Heckman, 2006; von Stumm & Plomin, 2015), and African American children are more likely to live in low-SES homes than European American children (Suzuki & Valencia, 1997). This is clearly illustrated by adoption studies in which African American children born of parents from lower-income homes were adopted by middle-class parents. In one study (Scarr & Weinberg, 1976; Weinberg, Scarr, & Waldman, 1992), the average IQ of the adopted African American children was about 110, or 20 points higher than the average IQ of comparable children being reared in the local African American community. Hispanic children also score lower than European American children on most subtests of IQ tests, for many of the same reasons that

African American children score lower (for example, factors associated with SES, education, and cultural bias). In addition, proficiency in English must also be taken in consideration for children for whom English is not a first language (Thaler & Jones-Forrester, 2012).

Stereotype threat. One source of differences in IQ scores between cultural-minority and European American children is related to stereotype threat (Steele, 1997). We discussed stereotype threat with respect to females' poorer performance on standardized mathematics tests in Chapter 11. People are aware of negative stereotypes for their particular social group, and when the stereotype is activated, they tend to confirm them. For instance, the cultural stereotype for African Americans is that they perform poorly on IQ tests. When groups of African American and European American college students were administered a test of verbal intelligence, performance of the African American students varied, depending on whether they were told it was a test of intelligence (Steele & Aronson, 1995). The African Americans who were told the test was assessing their intelligence scored significantly lower than those who were not told it was an intelligence test. This suggests that the tests may not be measuring people's intelligence per se but their tendency to choke under situations in which a stereotype threat was activated (see, however, Sackett, Hardison, & Cullen, 2004, who caution that the stereotype threat does not eliminate the White/African American difference in IQ).

Voluntary versus involuntary minorities. Not all minority groups perform poorly on IQ tests or in academic performance. John Ogbu (1986; Ogbu & Stern, 2001) suggested that one factor that may influence how minorities view themselves within a culture (and in turn their performance in school and on IQ tests) is related to how they originally obtained their minority status. *Voluntary minorities* include groups such as Chinese and German Americans, who left their home countries in search of a better life and usually view themselves as better off compared to those they left behind. They see themselves as making progress, irrespective of how people in the majority may see them. In contrast, *involuntary minorities* are groups who became minorities through being conquered, colonized, or enslaved, such as Native Americans and African Americans, and who for long periods were, and in many ways still are, treated as if they were a separate, inferior class. Ogbu summarizes research showing that involuntary minorities across the globe perform more poorly in school and score an average of 10 to 15 points lower on IQ tests than people from the dominant majority.

Consider the comparison of the Buraku outcasts of Japan with African Americans in the United States. The Buraku are not racially distinct from other Japanese but, in feudal Japan, performed "dirty" jobs, such as undertakers, butchers, tanners, or executioners, and were relegated to the lowest social order. They were officially emancipated in Japan by a royal degree in 1871, shortly after the emancipation of African Americans during the American Civil War. Much like Blacks in America, the Buraku in Japan score lower on IQ tests and in academic performance than people from the majority culture. However, the IQ/academic achievement gap is eliminated for people of Buraku descent when they immigrate to the United States. They continue to be a minority, but people in the United States are generally not aware of their social status in Japan, and they become a voluntary minority and show enhanced intellectual performance relative to the Buraku living in Japan. According to Ogbu (1986), it is the perception of being an outcast and believing that conventional routes to achievement are unavailable to them that depresses their academic achievement and IQ scores, and not their minority status, per se.

Possible biases in the IQ test. Another possibility for racial and ethnic differences in IQ scores is that the tests are biased as a result of being based on skills and knowledge deemed important by the majority culture but perhaps not the minority one. Children from minority homes might not share the same values or even have access to the same knowledge that middle-class children do, making the test culturally biased. Many believe that intelligence can only be meaningfully assessed within the culture in which a child lives (Laboratory of Comparative Human Cognition, 1983; Miller-Jones, 1989; see discussion of Sternberg's theory later in this chapter). Thus, although IQ tests measure accurately some aspects of intelligence for children from the majority culture, they do not assess intelligence adequately for minority children. For example, IQ differences between minority and majority children are reduced when "culture fair" tests, such as the nonverbal Ravens Progressive Matrices test mentioned earlier, are used (Anastasi, 1988). Moreover, the rigorously standardized nature of IQ tests might be a detriment to minority children because the tests must be administered in a constant format. The examiner cannot provide feedback to a child and, usually, cannot probe a child's answers to determine if he or she has more knowledge than is reflected by an initial response. Minority children might have different expectations of what type of answers the examiner is looking for, and children's competencies will be masked by the requirements of standard test administration (Miller-Jones, 1989).

Dalton Miller-Jones (1989) provided several examples of how a 5-year-old Black child's performance on an IQ test could be underestimated because of the standardized nature of the test:

Tester: "How are wood and coal alike? How are they the same?"

Child: "They're hard."

Tester: "An apple and a peach?"

Child: "They taste good."

Tester: "A ship and an automobile?"

Child: "They're hard."

Tester: "Iron and silver?"

Child: "They're hard." (p. 362)

These answers all earn a score of zero, but does this mean that the child does not know the conceptual relation between iron and silver or between an apple and a peach? By the rules of the test, no feedback can be provided, and the child must guess what type of answer the examiner wants. There is nothing incorrect about the child's answers to these questions, but they do not fit the test makers' conceptions. They also do not likely exhaust this child's knowledge of the relations between these objects, but the test format precludes finding this out.

Other aspects of test administration also influence minority children's performance on IQ tests. The testing situation, for example, with a child sitting quietly across the table from an adult and answering a series of questions, might be more familiar and comfortable to a middle-class child than to a lower-class or minority child. Also, in most testing situations, the examiner is a member of a different ethnic and social class than the minority child, adding further discomfort and novelty to the testing situation.

Not all agree that there is bias against minority children in mental testing (A. R. Jensen, 1998). Despite all the criticism, the tests are cost-efficient and widely (though not universally) accepted by both educational professionals and the public. Yet most would argue that we could do a better job of assessing minority children's intelligence and achievement, and Miller-Jones (1989) makes five recommendations for improving minority assessment:

1. When assessing any area of intelligence, it is important to specify the cognitive processes that might be involved in the task or elicited by the stimuli.
2. Multiple tasks with different materials should be used with the same individual.
3. Tests must be appropriate for the culture from which the child comes.
4. The connection must be validated between the cognitive operations assessed by a test and the attainment of school-related concepts, such as arithmetic and reading.
5. Procedures must be developed that permit an examiner to probe for the reasoning behind a child's answers.

Miller-Jones's advice is sound and applies to nonminority as well as to minority children.

The Pygmalion effect. Teachers also sometimes expect less of minority students in terms of academic performance than they expect of children from the majority culture. Can the expectations of teachers (and perhaps of parents and peers) affect school performance and IQ? The answer seems to be a resounding yes, as illustrated in a classic study by Robert Rosenthal and Lenore Jacobson (1968) titled *Pygmalion in the Classroom*. The title refers to a play by George Bernard Shaw, in which a professor bets that in a short time he can pass off a poor, uneducated flower girl as a proper member of society. (You may know it from the movies as *My Fair Lady*.) The **Pygmalion effect** is a form of *self-fulfilling prophecy*, in which a person internalizes the expectations of an authority figure. In the play, the flower girl internalized the professor's perception of her. In the classroom, children internalize the intellectual expectations teachers have for them (see McGown, Gregory, & Weinstein, 2010).

Rosenthal and Jacobson told elementary school teachers at the beginning of the year that some children in their class were expected to bloom intellectually. In fact, the names of the children were chosen randomly. At the end of the school year, children took an IQ test, and the results were compared to one that had been taken a year earlier. Children identified as bloomers gained significantly more on the IQ tests than the other children, illustrating the effect that teacher expectation can have not only on academic performance but also on IQ scores.

There is nothing magic about the IQ test itself. It does not necessarily measure innate intelligence, nor does it necessarily reflect a constant value that will typify an individual throughout life. However, IQ does predict reasonably well academic performance, occupational status, and even longevity. Yet the psychometric approach, with its emphasis on a single score, is not the only way to think of individual differences in intelligence. Scientists and educators have developed alternative ways of conceptualizing intelligence, and the remainder of this chapter deals with alternative approaches to the study of intelligence—basically, approaches that don't see IQ tests as the only, or the best, or perhaps even a good measure of intelligence.

Section Review

Intelligence is generally understood to reflect goal-directed and adaptive functioning. The primary approach to the study of individual differences in intelligence has been the *psychometric* (or *differential*) *approach*.

Factors of Intelligence

- Intelligence is described in terms of *factors*, or sets of related abilities that can be discerned on tests by the statistical technique of *factor analysis*.
- The most general factor is called *g*, or *general intelligence*, which describes a domain-general mechanism that influences thinking on all tasks.
- Others have divided intelligence into two general factors: *fluid abilities*, which are biologically determined and reflected by tests of memory span, speed of processing, and spatial thinking, and *crystallized abilities*, which are more highly dependent on experience and are reflected in tests of verbal comprehension or social relations.
- The best evidence for the existence of *g* is the *positive manifold*, the fact that a person's performance on a variety of cognitive tasks tend to be similar.
- The *hierarchical model of cognitive abilities* proposes four related sets of cognitive skills (verbal, spatial thinking, speed of processing, and memory) that are all influenced by a general intellectual factor.

IQ Tests

- The impact of the psychometric approach has been most strongly realized in *intelligence quotient* or *IQ tests*, which assess intellectual abilities relative to a normative population.
- Frequently used IQ tests are the *Stanford-Binet* and *Wechsler scales* (WPPSI, WISC, WAIS), both of which are individually administered and highly standardized.
- Infant intelligence has been expressed in terms of *DQ* (*developmental quotient*) *tests*.
- IQs were originally derived based on a ratio between *mental age* and chronological age. Modern tests abandoned the concept of mental age and developed the *deviation IQ*.
- IQ scores predict academic performance, occupational status, health, and longevity relatively well.
- The IQ test has been criticized as being inappropriate for minority children, who may misinterpret the testing situation and illustrate *stereotype threat*, in which minority members perform worse on IQ tests after being reminded of the negative stereotype concerning their groups' performance on such tests.
- Involuntary minority status is particularly likely to reduce a group's IQ.
- Teachers' expectations for their students' academic performance can also influence children's accomplishments and even their IQ scores, which is termed the *Pygmalion effect*.

Ask Yourself . . .

1. What is meant by the psychometric approach to intelligence? What are some of the more important theories proposed from this approach, and what do they suggest about the nature of intelligence?
2. What are three outcomes that IQ tests typically predict relatively well, and what do you believe accounts for this level of predictability?
3. Why might IQ tests not be appropriate for children from minority groups, and what can be done to improve their validity in such cases?

INFORMATION-PROCESSING APPROACHES TO THE STUDY OF INTELLIGENCE

One criticism of the psychometric approach, and of IQ tests specifically, is that test construction is based primarily on pragmatic considerations—which items discriminate reliably among children—and not on theoretical considerations (Sternberg, 1985). The factors that constitute intelligence are determined by statistical analyses and not because of any a priori model of intelligence. As we noted earlier, however, it would be unfair to say that IQ tests are atheoretical. Nevertheless, pragmatic considerations of selecting items that discriminate among children at a given age are still extremely important in choosing which items will be included on the tests. Thus, although IQ tests can assess individual differences in intelligence well, they are less successful at providing insight into the nature of the intelligence that underlies test performance. This is critical not just from the point of view of theory but also for practice. For instance, Douglas Detterman and Lee Ann Thompson (1997) proposed that the key to improving education (particularly special education) is an understanding of the basic cognitive abilities that underlie individual differences in intelligence. With such an understanding, educational interventions can be individualized, and only through such practices will children, especially those whose style of learning differs from that of the majority, reap the benefit of educational research.

Individual differences in cognitive abilities have been extensively studied from the information-processing perspective. In a sense, the same mechanisms used to describe cognitive development from an information-processing perspective can be used to describe individual differences. Thus, for example, differences in how information is encoded, speed of processing, how easily information is categorized, and metacognition are all sources of individual (as well as developmental) differences in thinking and intelligence.

When cognitive psychologists examine individual differences in children's thinking, they often make contrasts between groups known to vary on the basis of IQ, for example, children with and without intellectual impairment or gifted (or advanced learners) and nongifted (or typical learners) children, or between children matched in IQ who differ on the basis of some academic ability, for example, good and poor readers or children with and without learning disabilities. In such studies, researchers attempt to discover the underlying processes responsible for group differences in IQ, task performance, or academic skill. No attempt is made here to assess the origins of intellectual impairment, learning and reading disabilities, or giftedness. The etiologies of these intellectual exceptionalities are interesting and important, but they would require separate chapters (or books) to investigate properly (although we did discuss possible origins of reading and math disabilities in Chapter 11). Rather, in this section, we examine differences in cognitive processing between exceptional and normal children, as well as among children with developmentally typical cognitive abilities, to elucidate the nature of cognition in general and to discover educationally important differences in thinking among these groups of children. We look at a number of aspects of cognitive processing that are implicated in intelligence, classified into two broad categories: basic-level processes, including speed of processing as well as working memory and executive function, and higher-level cognitive abilities, including strategies, knowledge base, and metacognition.

Basic-Level Processes

Basic-level processes include tasks of working memory and memory span (such as the digit-span task, versions of which are included in the Stanford-Binet and Wechsler IQ tests) and laboratory tests designed to measure people's response times as they make presumably simple decisions. These latter tasks include short-term memory scanning, retrieval of familiar words from the long-term store, and simple categorization tasks (see A. R. Jensen, 1998). The basic processes measured by these tasks are presumed to be closely related to neurological functioning and, thus, primarily under the influence of endogenous (and inherited) factors and may be the cognitive abilities underlying general intelligence (Gignac, 2014; Nettelbeck, 2011; Sheppard & Vernon, 2008). Although a number of basic-level processing abilities have been touted as influencing individual differences in intelligence, including, among others, inhibition (McCall & Carriger, 1993), resistance to interference (Dempster, 1993), and the ability to process novelty (Bornstein & Sigman, 1986; Sternberg, 1985), most research has focused on two general mechanisms: (1) speed of processing and (2) working memory and executive function. We discuss research on these two topics here.

Speed of Information Processing

Older children perform most, if not all, aspects of information processing faster than younger children do (see Kail, 1991). Moreover, both children and adults show similar patterns of reaction times across a large variety of tasks (Kail & Salthouse, 1994). Similar differences in speed of retrieval between gifted and nongifted children (Saccuzzo, Johnson, & Guertin, 1994) and between children with and without learning disabilities (Ceci, 1983) have also been observed. The differences in memory performance between children with and without learning disabilities and between good and poor readers attributed to higher-order cognitive abilities (discussed shortly) might be mediated by differences in speed of processing. Some children might require more time to activate relevant concepts used on these memory and problem-solving tasks than other children do, which in turn requires greater expenditure of mental effort. The increased effort associated with the slower retrieval of language terms, for example, might be indirectly responsible for the less strategic approach of these children to the task and, thus, for their overall lower levels of performance.

In addition to distinguishing children with and without learning disabilities and good readers from poor ones, the efficiency of retrieval from long-term memory has been hypothesized to be an important component of individual differences in intelligence in the general population (Coyle et al., 2011; Fry & Hale, 2000; A. R. Jensen, 1998). Most forms of intelligence require retrieving information from memory and acting on that information. Several researchers have reasoned that people who retrieve information quickly and efficiently will display an advantage on cognitive tasks, particularly verbal ones. Earl Hunt and his colleagues (1981) provided support for this position using a variety of experimental tasks. In an early study, Hunt and his colleagues asked adults to verify category statements, such as "A dog is an animal." They found that the time needed to confirm such simple statements correlated significantly with verbal ability.

Several literature reviews of the evidence from both children and adults reported modest correlations (from about −0.30 to −0.50) between speed of responding and intelligence, with faster responding (and, thus, presumably faster information processing) being associated with higher

IQs (Fry & Hale, 2000; A. R. Jensen, 1998). Moreover, speed of information processing correlates significantly both with performance on timed tests, when speed is important, and on nontimed tests, when fast responding is irrelevant (Vernon & Kantor, 1986). This pattern of results, along with the evidence from the developmental literature indicating the role of processing speed in cognitive development (Kail, 1991), suggests that speed of processing is an important component of individual differences in intelligence.

Individual differences in speed of processing are reliable but often small, and they point to important differences in intelligence at a microscopic level. Differences are often in milliseconds, and you may wonder what the significance of a 50-millisecond (that is, 1/20th of a second) difference might be with respect to intelligence. Although such differences are small, they can be important indeed. Perhaps one of the most vital cognitive skills for people in technological societies is reading. Small differences in rate of retrieving the meaning of a word or in integrating letters to form words can, over a very short time, result in substantial differences in reading rate and reading comprehension.

Working Memory and Executive Function

Several researchers have suggested that working memory and executive function may be important components of intelligence (Alloway & Alloway, 2010; Žebec, Demetriou, & Kotrla-Topić, 2015), above and beyond the effects of speed of processing. For example, Linda Miller and Philip Vernon (1996) administered the WISC and batteries of reaction-time and working-memory tasks to children ages 4 to 6 years. Not surprisingly, children became faster with age, and working-memory span increased with age. Also, when general reaction time and memory factors were computed, the two were found to correlate significantly (-0.44; the shorter the reaction time, the greater working memory tended to be). Reaction time was also significantly correlated with IQ at each age (overall correlation = -0.42). The correlation between IQ and working memory, however, was even greater (0.82), and it remained significant even after the effects of reaction time and age were taken into consideration. L. Miller and Vernon (1996) concluded that, for children ages 4 to 6 years, "memory accounts for significant variability in intelligence" (p. 184). Reaction time, in contrast, has a smaller role in intelligence, at least once individual differences in working memory are taken into consideration.

Working memory is a significant component of executive function (see Chapter 7), which recent research suggests plays an important role in almost all areas of thinking. For instance, in addition to correlating significantly with IQ, individual differences in working memory correlate significantly with a host of higher-level cognitive abilities in children, including reading comprehension (Daneman & Green, 1986), writing ability (Neuenschwander et al., 2012), the speed and accuracy of arithmetic computation (Zheng, Swanson, & Marcoulides, 2011), number knowledge in preschoolers (Verdine et al., 2014), and the use of arithmetic (Berg, 2008) and memory (Lehmann & Hasselhorn, 2007) strategies. Also, several studies have shown that children and adults with intellectual impairment have shorter working-memory spans (Henry & MacLean, 2003) and perform more poorly on executive function tasks (Kittler, Krinsky-McHale, & Devenny, 2008) than people without intellectual impairment. Similarly, gifted children have higher levels of executive function than nongifted children do

(Arffa, 2007). In fact, the only psychological measures that have been found to predict school performance better than IQ are those reflecting executive function. For example, in one study, the effects of self-regulation (or self-discipline, to use the authors' term) on children's academic performance accounted for more than twice as much of the differences in school grades as did IQ (Duckworth & Seligman, 2005). In other research, a measure of working memory at age 5 predicted academic performance at age 11 better than IQ measured either at age 5 or at age 11 (Alloway & Alloway, 2010).

Although the relationship among measures of speed or processing, working memory, and executive function and IQ sometimes differ as a function of the age of the children tested (Fry & Hale, 2000; L. Miller & Vernon, 1996), it is clear that basic-level processes and intelligence are strongly interrelated, and as pointed out by Fry and Hale (2000), they have nearly the same developmental function, suggesting a single underlying mechanism.

Higher-Order Cognitive Abilities

Speed of processing, working memory, and executive function are clearly important components of intelligence. Yet other, more macro processes vary among people and contribute to individual differences in intelligence. Chief among these are *strategies*, *knowledge base*, and *metacognition*.

Strategies

Strategies allow people to plan the course of their cognitive operations, to anticipate the consequences of their acts and the acts of others (see Chapter 7). Given this view, it is not surprising that many researchers have proposed that strategies are a central aspect of intelligence (Das, 1984). For example, J. P. Das (1984) wrote, "What qualifies as intelligence may be the ability to plan or structure one's behavior with an end in view. The more efficient and parsimonious the plan is, the more intelligent the resulting behavior" (p. 116).

Differences in strategy implementation have been hypothesized to explain the difference in task performance between children with and without intellectual impairment, children with and without learning disabilities, good and poor readers, and gifted and nongifted children. For example, Richard Bauer (1979) gave 9- and 10-year-old children with and without learning disabilities a series of free-recall tasks. No group differences were found for the last several items on the lists. Recall for these last items was characteristically high and was attributed to children's emptying the contents of their short-term store, without the need of any specific strategy, termed a *recency effect*. In contrast, large group differences were noted in the recall of items from the beginning of the list. Recall of items from the beginning of a list has usually been interpreted as reflecting the use of strategies to recall the information from long-term memory. In other words, the children with learning disabilities differed from the nondisabled children in strategy use but not in nonstrategic functioning. This interpretation was bolstered by the results of two subsequent experiments in which Bauer observed lower levels of categorical clustering (an indication of the memory strategy of organization; see Chapter 7) for the children with learning disabilities. Similar observations have been made for poor readers, who likewise show lower levels of memory performance than do good readers of equal IQ (D. Goldstein, Hasher, & Stein, 1983).

In other research, Jane Gaultney (1998) statistically equated the amount of strategy use on memory tasks between third-, fourth-, and fifth-grade children with and without learning disabilities and found that children without learning disabilities benefited more from comparable strategy use than children with learning disabilities did. That is, even when children with learning disabilities were strategic (sometimes as strategic as nondisabled children), they didn't reap the benefits of the strategy in terms of memory performance compared to the children without learning disabilities. This is a utilization deficiency (see Chapter 7), and Gaultney proposed that the children with learning disabilities exerted more mental effort executing the memory strategies than the nondisabled children did and, as a result, had less mental capacity available for holding items in working memory.

Differences in strategy use have sometimes been found to be a source of differences in task performance between gifted and nongifted children (Coyle et al., 1998; Gaultney, Bjorklund, & Goldstein, 1996). For example, in a series of free-recall experiments, Gaultney and her colleagues (1996) contrasted gifted and nongifted middle-school children for their use of memory strategies and found that gifted children consistently were more likely to be strategic than were their nongifted peers. One interesting finding of their study was that, despite the greater use of strategies by gifted than by nongifted children, it was more important to task performance to be strategic for the nongifted children than for the gifted children. This is illustrated by looking at the average performance of children classified as strategic compared with those classified as nonstrategic for the gifted and nongifted children in this study. Figure 12.4 presents the mean difference in recall between the strategic and nonstrategic children through five trials for the gifted and the nongifted children. The higher the score, the greater advantage to recall there was for being strategic.

FIGURE 12.4 **Mean strategic minus nonstrategic difference in recall for gifted and nongifted children at each trial in the study by Gaultney and colleagues (1996).** The higher the score, the greater the advantage for being strategic.

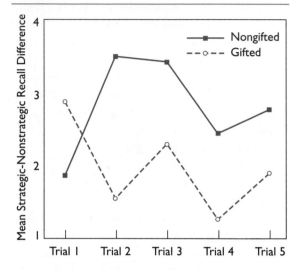

Source: Gaultney, J. F., Bjorklund, D. F., & Goldstein, D. (1996). To be young, gifted, and strategic: Advantages for memory performance. *Journal of Experimental Child Psychology, 61*, 51. Reprinted with permission.

The first thing to note is that all the scores are positive (from a little over 1 word to about 3.5 words remembered per trial). This means that, on average, being strategic was always to a child's advantage. But look at the difference between the gifted and nongifted children. Except for the first trial, it made a greater difference in amount recalled for the nongifted children to be strategic than it did for the gifted children. That is, the difference between nongifted children who used a memory strategy and those who did not was quite large. This difference was much smaller for the gifted children.

Why should being strategic be more important for nongifted than gifted children? Gaultney and her colleagues (1996) proposed that many gifted children did not need strategies to perform reasonably well on this task. When nonstrategic gifted and nongifted children were compared, the gifted children did significantly better. Thus, according to Gaultney and her colleagues, much of the superior performance of the gifted children was mediated by nonstrategic factors, including, perhaps, faster speed of processing and a more elaborated knowledge base.

Interestingly, the tendency of many gifted children to "just know" an answer can sometimes have a negative side effect. For example, Katherine Kipp Harnishfeger and David Bjorklund (1990b) speculated that some gifted children did not need to use deliberate learning and memory strategies during the elementary school years because they were able to apprehend course material in a relatively automatic fashion. When the cognitive demands become more challenging in middle or high school, however, these children might be at a disadvantage relative to their lower IQ but more strategic peers, accounting, in part, for some of the academic difficulties some gifted teenagers encounter. We have seen similar difficulties in some bright students making the transition from high school to college or from junior college to university.

In other research, David Geary and Sam Brown (1991) assessed third- and fourth-grade gifted children, nongifted children, and children with math disability for their selection and use of strategies in solving a series of addition problems. All the children used some combination of strategies to solve the problems, but the gifted children used the most mature mix of strategies, followed by the nongifted children, and, finally, the children with math disability. Geary and Brown concluded that the principal reason for the group differences in strategy use in this experiment was children's long-term memory organization of basic addition facts. The gifted third- and fourth-grade children knew their basic math facts ($9 + 7 = 16$; $6 + 8 = 14$)

better than did the other two groups of children, permitting them to use more efficient strategies. In other words, one of the reasons for gifted children's more effective use of strategies was their greater knowledge base.

Knowledge Base

One factor that seems to make an important contribution to all other factors in terms of cognitive performance is *knowledge base*. What a person knows about the topic he or she is thinking or reasoning about greatly influences cognitive performance.

Just as developmental differences in cognition can be explained, in part, by differences in knowledge base (see Chapter 7), so too can individual differences. For example, some researchers have suggested that memory differences between good and poor readers more likely stem from differences in knowledge base than from differences in strategy use. The semantic memories of poor readers are not as well developed as the semantic memories of good readers, resulting in the inefficient retrieval of word meaning from long-term store and, thus, less effective processing of verbal information (Bjorklund & Bernholtz, 1986; Vellutino & Scanlon, 1985). David Bjorklund and Jean Bernholtz (1986) illustrated this possibility by giving a series of concept and memory tasks to good and poor readers in junior high school (average age = 13 years) who were matched for IQ. In a first experiment, children were asked to select examples from specified natural language categories (for example, birds, clothes, tools) and to rate each item by how typical it was of its category. In general, differences in judged typicality affect the performance of both children and adults on a variety of tasks, and children's judgments become more adultlike with age. Bjorklund and Bernholtz reported that the judgments of the 13-year-old poor readers resembled those of normal 9-year-olds and were less adultlike than were the ratings of the good readers. In other words, differences in the semantic memory organization of good and poor 13-year-old readers were found with respect to category typicality.

In later experiments (see Experiments 3 and 4 in Bjorklund & Bernholtz, 1986), children were given sets of 12 typical and 12 atypical items to recall in any order they wanted. In one experiment, the typicality of the items was based on norms generated by adults (adult-generated lists). In another experiment, the typicality of the items was based on each child's self-generated norms, obtained from the earlier session (self-generated lists). Significant differences in memory performance were observed only for the adult-generated lists. Recall was comparable between the good and poor readers when typical and atypical category items were selected based on each child's own judgments. Furthermore, measures of strategy use in these experiments (based on amount of clustering and latencies between the recall of words) indicated that the good readers were no more strategic than the poor readers were. Rather, their superior memory performance could best be attributed to differences in knowledge base. These results do not mean that there are no strategic differences between good and poor readers. Instead, they indicate that differences in knowledge base contribute significantly to performance differences observed between these two groups of children and might be partly responsible for any apparent differences noted in strategy use.

One study that demonstrates the importance of knowledge base in learning and memory and its relation to IQ is that of Wolfgang Schneider, Joachim Körkel, and Franz Weinert (1989). In that study, German children in Grades 3, 5, and 7 were classified as either soccer experts or soccer novices and also classified as successful or unsuccessful learners based on IQ tests and their grades in school. The children were then presented with a well-organized narrative text about soccer and were later asked to recall it. Amount remembered was computed as the number of idea units children recalled about the story. The patterns of results with respect to expertise and IQ were similar for the children at each of the three grade levels and are summarized in Figure 12.5 (averaged over grade). As would be expected, memory performance was better for the soccer experts than for the soccer novices. However, the researchers reported no difference in performance between the academically successful learners and the unsuccessful ones. That is, being a good learner (and having a high IQ) did not result in better performance by either the expert children or the novice children. Having a detailed knowledge of the subject matter was enough to yield high levels of memory performance. Similarly, having an impoverished knowledge of the subject matter was enough to yield low levels of performance, regardless of a child's level of IQ (see also Recht & Leslie, 1988). Although IQ might be related to academic performance, such as reading comprehension, what seems especially important for intelligent performance is knowledge. Children with substantial knowledge of a subject act smart when dealing with matter from that subject area, independent of their level of IQ.

One reason for expert children's high levels of performance on these tasks, independent of level of intelligence, is the greater motivation that experts may have for performing well with material from their area of expertise. Although this is likely true to some extent, the results of one study of soccer-expert children found no difference in interest in soccer between high- and low-IQ experts, although patterns of performance between the high- and low-IQ children were comparable to that found in other expert/novice studies (Schneider & Bjorklund, 1992). Thus, although motivation may play an important role in overall levels of performance, it seems not to be responsible for the patterns observed for high- and low-aptitude expert and novice children for remembering information from their area of expertise.

This situation is admittedly not typical. In most contexts, successful learners do perform better than unsuccessful learners. One important reason why this is so, however, is that successful learners generally know more about the things they are dealing with than unsuccessful learners do. Successful learners acquire information more readily and, thus, have a more elaborated knowledge base on which to base future learning. The more children know, the more easily they are able to learn and remember new information.

FIGURE 12.5 **Number of idea units remembered about a soccer story for high- and low-aptitude soccer experts and soccer novices.** In this case, being an expert eliminated any effect of academic aptitude (IQ) on performance.

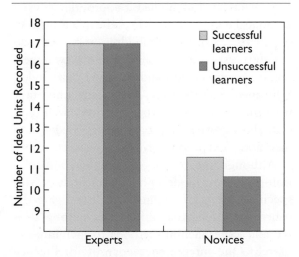

Source: Adapted from data presented in Schneider, W., Körkel, J., & Weinert, F. E. (1989). Domain-specific knowledge and memory performance: A comparison of high- and low-aptitude children. *Journal of Educational Psychology, 81*, 306–312.

A detailed knowledge base does not always eliminate IQ effects, however. Wolfgang Schneider, David Bjorklund, and their colleagues (Schneider & Bjorklund, 1992; Schneider, Bjorklund & Maier-Brückner, 1996) classified high- and low-IQ second- and fourth-grade children as soccer experts and novices and gave them two sort-recall memory tasks. Children were given sets of written words to remember, which they could sort into categories before recalling them (see Chapter 7). On one task, stimuli were sets of soccer-related words in one of four categories (soccer plays, equipment, players, parts of the field); in the second task, sets of words from familiar language categories were used (tools, fruits, mammals, vehicles—the nonsoccer list). As in the earlier study by Schneider and his colleagues (1989) that examined story recall, experts remembered more than novices did from the soccer-related list but not from the nonsoccer-related list. However, the effect of IQ was not eliminated in these studies, with high-IQ children remembering more than low-IQ children on both the soccer and nonsoccer lists, regardless of level of expertise. Schneider and Bjorklund (1992) argued that intelligence played a greater role here than in the story-recall experiment because of the more deliberate encoding strategies used on sort-recall tasks. Expertise can reduce or eliminate the impact of intelligence (as measured by IQ) in some situations, but IQ will have a residual effect when explicit strategies, such as those used in sort-recall tasks, are called for.

Metacognition

One higher-level aspect of cognition that has been postulated as being significant to individual differences in intelligence is metacognition, a person's understanding of his or her own cognitive abilities. Basically, the brighter individuals of any age are those who possess the ability to monitor their task performance and to apply the techniques they possess to solve a problem. John Borkowski and his colleagues suggested that differences in metacognition are a major cause of differences in strategy use and training effectiveness between children with and without intellectual attainment (Borkowski, Reid, & Kurtz, 1984), between reflective and impulsive children (Borkowski et al., 1983), between gifted and nongifted children (Borkowski & Peck, 1986), and among children within the normal range of intelligence (Carr, Borkowski, & Maxwell, 1991).

This is illustrated in a study by Borkowski and Virginia Peck (1986), who instructed gifted and nongifted 7- and 8-year-olds to use an elaboration strategy or a simpler clustering strategy on a memory task. The children were later tested for transfer of the strategy to other memory problems. Elaboration involves creating a relationship between two items so that the presentation of one item elicits the recall of the other. For example, if you wanted to remember the pair of words *banana-coat*, you might form an image of a bunch of bananas hanging in the closet where you usually find your coat, or you might think that a banana peel covers a banana in a way similar to how a coat covers your body. Although forming such relations may seem like a lot of work, the memory performance of both children and adults is facilitated by the use of an elaboration strategy (see Pressley, 1982). For the children who received the clustering instructions (for example, "Try to remember words from the same category together"), training was less explicit than it was for the children who were trained to use the elaboration strategy. Would both the gifted and nongifted children be able to benefit from the training, and would the extent of training affect the transfer of the strategy differently for the two groups of children?

Both the gifted and the nongifted children who were trained in the elaboration strategy learned it. Differences between the groups for this strategy became apparent only during a generalization task, when the children were given different sets of problems to learn. The gifted children were more likely to generalize the strategy they had learned than were the nongifted children, with the extent of generalization being significantly related to scores on a battery of metacognition questions, specifically questions assessing their metamemory (see Chapter 8). For the clustering strategy, differences in training as well as transfer between the two groups of children were noted. The gifted children benefited more from the minimal training than did the nongifted children. This difference was extended to the transfer trials. That is, gifted children required less explicit prompting before they learned a strategy and generalized it to new situations, all relative to the nongifted children. According to Borkowski and Peck (1986), because of their greater metamemory awareness, "gifted children realized the effectiveness of the strategy and applied it appropriately even without the aid of complete and explicit instructions" (p. 193). Gifted children apparently do not always show greater metacognitive awareness relative to nongifted children (J. M. Alexander, Schwanenflugel, & Carr, 1995), but when task performance is challenging, gifted children typically show greater metacognitive knowledge than their nongifted peers do (Kurtz & Weinert, 1989).

Although the picture is complex, information-processing models provide researchers with specific aspects of cognition to investigate the source of intellectual differences among people and experimental methods to facilitate the search. One integrated theory of intelligence that takes individual differences in information processing seriously is Robert Sternberg's theory of successful intelligence, which we turn to now.

Section Review

Information-processing approaches to intelligence provide researchers with well-developed theories and methods for assessing individual differences in intelligence.

Basic-Level Processes

- Differences in speed of processing, working memory, and executive function have been proposed to be the cognitive abilities that underlie general intelligence, or g.
- Individual differences in each of these basic-level processes correlate with IQ, academic performance (for example, reading, writing, mathematics), and performance on other higher-level forms of cognition (for example, memory strategies).

Higher-Order Cognitive Abilities

- Strategy use, knowledge base, and meta-cognition have been suggested as the basis for individual differences in children's thinking.
- Developmental psychologists often use information-processing paradigms to explain differences in the thinking of children of different IQ levels (for example, children with and without intellectual impairment) and children of comparable IQ levels but differential academic abilities (for example, children with and without learning disabilities).

Ask Yourself . . .

4. In what ways have studies assessed differences in the speed of processing, working memory, and executive functioning of gifted and nongifted students? How do these studies contribute to our understanding of general intelligence?
5. How do higher-order cognitive abilities, such as strategy use, knowledge base, and metacognition, contribute to intelligence?

STERNBERG'S THEORY OF SUCCESSFUL INTELLIGENCE

Robert Sternberg's (1985, 2005, 2011, 2014) **theory of successful intelligence** was originally called the *triarchic theory of intelligence* because it includes three subtheories: (1) the contextual, (2) the experiential, and (3) the componential (see Table 12.2). Sternberg defines successful intelligence as "the ability to achieve success in life in terms of one's personal standards, within one's sociocultural context" (Sternberg & the Rainbow Project Collaborators, 2006, p. 323). More specifically, Sternberg (2005) defines successful intelligence as: "1) the ability to achieve one's goals in life, given one's sociocultural context; 2) by capitalizing on strengths and correcting or compensating for weaknesses; 3) in order to adapt to, shape, and select environments; 4) through a combination of analytical, creative, and practical abilities" (p. 189). Success is attained via a balance of three aspects of intelligence: (1) practical skills, (2) creative skills, and (3) analytic skills, each of which is examined in the following sections.

Sternberg's Contextual Subtheory, or Practical Intelligence

The **contextual subtheory** holds that intelligence must be viewed in the context in which it occurs. Intelligent behaviors for the middle-class American schoolchild might not be considered intelligent for the ghetto dropout or the unschooled Guatemalan farm boy. By defining intelligence in terms of real-world environments, Sternberg stresses the importance of the external as well as the internal world to intelligence. Such a definition also avoids the circularity of theories that basically define intelligence

TABLE 12.2 The componential (analytic), experiential (creative), and contextual (practical) subtheories/intelligence in Sternberg's triarchic theory of successful intelligence. Some examples related to a college course in psychology are provided for each subtheory.

Contextual (Practical) subtheory/intelligence. Intelligence must be viewed in the context in which it occurs. This type of intelligence is involved in solving everyday problems, for example, "What would you do about a friend who has a substance-abuse problem," or "What are the implications for Freud's theory of dreaming for your life?" It has three subprocesses:

Adapting. Adjusting one's behavior to obtain a good fit with one's environment.

Selecting. Selecting an environment to obtain a good fit with one's abilities.

Shaping. Modifying the behaviors and reactions of others so that they become more compatible to oneself.

Experiential (Creative) subtheory/intelligence. Examines how people deal with novel information and the extent to which they are able to *automatize* certain processes. For example, "Design a study to test a theory of language acquisition."

Componential (Analytic) subtheory/intelligence. A set of information-processing mechanisms that can be used in any environmental context or culture. This type of intelligence is involved in tasks requiring the analysis of information. For example, "Compare Piaget's theory of cognitive development to Vygotsky's." It has three components:

Metacomponents control, monitor, and evaluate task performance and allocate attentional resources.

Performance components execute strategies assembled by the metacomponents. These include encoding, mental comparison, and retrieval of information.

Knowledge-acquisition components are involved in acquiring new knowledge and selectively acting on newly acquired information.

Source: Adapted from Sternberg, R. J., Ferrari, M., & Clinkenbeard, P. (1996). Identification, instruction, and assessment of gifted children: A construct validation of a triarchic model. *Gifted Child Quarterly, 40,* 129–137 (p. 131).

as a score on an IQ test (or a test of information processing). In other words, intelligence can only be assessed in terms of the real-world problems that children experience, and it must be evaluated within a cultural context (Sternberg, 2004). Because people who are gifted in this subtheory have street-smarts, making an ideal fit between themselves and whatever context they find themselves in, this subtheory is sometimes called **practical intelligence.** People with practical intelligence may also excel in social intelligence. Most real-world contexts where intelligence is useful in solving problems involve other people, and being able to deal effectively with other, sometimes contrary members of one's own society can be a sign of substantial practical intelligence.

Sternberg proposes three processes of intelligence within the contextual subtheory: (1) *adaptation,* (2) *selection,* and (3) *shaping.* Adaptation is adjustment of one's behavior to achieve a good fit with one's environment. For example, how effectively do children recognize that their attempts at joining a playgroup are not successful, and are they able to modify their behavior to become included in the games at recess and make new friends? When adaptation is not possible or is not desirable, a person can select an alternative environment in which he or she can adapt well. Failing to adapt to the whims of a new supervisor, for example, a person can choose to quit her job and select another. Or a child might find it difficult to get along with children in the neighborhood and instead become friendly with other children from school who do not live as close by. If for some reason a new environment cannot be selected, a person can attempt to shape the environment. The employee can try to convince her supervisor to change his ways or may go over his head to bring changes from above, and the child can try to alter the behavior of his neighborhood peers by placating them with his mother's homemade cookies or by inviting one child at a time over to play instead of the entire group.

Although these three processes typify intelligence universally, what is required for adaptation, selection, and shaping will vary among different groups of people, so a single set of behaviors cannot be specified as intelligent for all individuals. Also, what is deemed intelligent at one point in life might not be so judged later. For example, because children have less freedom than adults to select new environments and are often powerless to significantly shape certain aspects of these environments, adapting to their uncomfortable surroundings might be the most intelligent option they have. Thus, whereas the school-phobic adult will select nonacademic environments, the 10-year-old child typically cannot, making adaptation the most intelligent choice.

Basically, the contextual subtheory is one of **cultural relativism**. Intellectual skills that are critical for survival in one culture might not be as important in another. Likewise, important intellectual skills within a culture can undergo some change from one generation to another. For example, arithmetic computation has unquestionably been a vital skill for people in technological societies. Wechsler noted the significance of arithmetic to intelligence in the construction of the WISC and WAIS and in their subsequent revisions: Each has an arithmetic subtest. Yet with the widespread use of calculators, being able to add and subtract numbers quickly and accurately becomes a little less critical to everyday functioning. Although we would not care to say that

arithmetic computation will become unimportant, it will probably be viewed by generations to come as being much less critical to intelligence than it is today, and it will certainly be seen as less important than it was a generation ago.

Sternberg is not the only person to propose a theory of intelligence that is culturally relative (see, for example, Laboratory of Comparative Human Cognition, 1983). Such theories have rightly been criticized, however, for preventing any general conclusions about the universal nature of human intellectual functioning. According to such theories, everything is relative; thus, intelligence can be studied only from the perspective of a particular culture or subculture. Sternberg avoids this problem by combining his contextual subtheory with the experiential (creative) and componential (analytic) subtheories, which propose aspects of intelligence that are universal.

Sternberg's Experiential Subtheory, or Creative Intelligence

The **experiential subtheory** is concerned with how prior knowledge influences performance on certain cognitive tasks. More specifically, the subtheory examines the ability to deal with novelty and the degree to which processing is automatized (that is, made to involve relatively little mental effort). Both skills are highly dependent on experience. A stimulus is novel only to the extent that it differs from what is already familiar (Rheingold, 1985). Similarly, newly acquired processing skills are rarely executed effortlessly; rather, they require substantial expenditure of one's limited mental effort for their deployment. Only when a skill has been exercised frequently does it become automatized. Sternberg proposes that how people respond to novelty and the ease with which they can automatize information processing are important and universal aspects of intelligence. Because Sternberg believes that people who are gifted in the mechanisms of this subtheory are especially able to generate new ideas and solve novel problems, this subtheory is sometimes referred to as creative intelligence.

The importance of such skills is apparent in any occupation. Good scientists must be able to apprehend quickly the relevant factors influencing whatever phenomenon they are concerned with. If scientists are to make major contributions to their field, however, they must also be able to devise clever ways of testing their hypotheses and to appreciate the significance of an unexpected result. These factors are important not only in the ivory tower but also in more worldly occupations. This importance was made apparent to me (DB) by an electrician who installed three ceiling fans in my home after two other electricians had failed. He quickly discerned what approach to take, and after 9 hours of running into more obstacles than I knew existed in my walls and above my ceilings, he finished the task. After I expressed my appreciation for a job well done, the electrician commented: "Any yahoo can lay wire in a straight line. It only takes brains when things don't go as you planned."

The experiential subtheory suggests what tasks are good indicators of intelligence—namely, those that involve dealing with novelty or automatic processing for their successful completion. Many of the laboratory tasks of modern cognitive psychology are good candidates for assessing intelligence because they stress speed of responding, which is a good indicator of the extent to which processing has become automatized. For example, simple letter-identification tasks, in which people must respond as rapidly as possible to signal the presence of a specified letter, measure the degree to which processing for this overlearned code (the alphabet) is automatized. Similarly, word-identification tasks (deciding whether a letter string is a word) and category-identification tasks (deciding whether a word is a member of a specified category) also test automatic processing. More complex laboratory tasks, such as solving analogies or syllogisms, probably assess aspects of both automatic processing and response to novelty. Similarly, many items on psychometric batteries test the same processes as do laboratory tasks and, Sternberg (1985) asserts, are probably better estimators of intelligence than laboratory tasks. Why? Because these items are usually more difficult than the laboratory tasks, involving, on the average, greater degrees of novelty. Examples of psychometric test items that would fit Sternberg's experiential subtheory include picture arrangement ("Put these pictures together so that they make a story"), similarities ("How are television and education alike?"), and comprehension ("Why might it be important that Supreme Court judges be appointed and not elected?").

Sternberg's Componential Subtheory, or Analytic Intelligence

The componential subtheory is Sternberg's information-processing model of cognition. Sternberg (1985, 2014) argues that intelligence has a common core of mental processes that can be used in any environmental context or culture. These include recognizing the existence and defining the nature of a problem, representing information about the problem, devising a strategy for solving the problem, allocating sufficient mental resources to solve the problem, and monitoring and evaluating one's solution to the problem. How does one go about doing all these things? Basically, they require different aspects of information processing. Because a person gifted in information-processing abilities is able to take apart, or analyze, problems and see solutions that are not seen by less-gifted individuals, Sternberg refers to this type of thinking as analytic intelligence.

Briefly, Sternberg proposed three general types of information-processing components: (1) metacomponents, (2) performance components, and (3) knowledge-acquisition components. *Metacomponents* allocate attentional resources and control, monitor, and evaluate task performance. These reflect metacognition. Are people aware about their progress on a task? Do they need to slow down, alter a strategy, or attend more to some aspects of a task or situation than to others? *Performance components* execute strategies assembled by the metacomponents and include encoding the to-be-processed information ("The letters l-i-o-n spell a word I know"), retrieving information ("Lions live in Africa"), and making mental comparison ("A lion is like a cat in some ways"). *Knowledge components* are involved in acquiring new knowledge and in selectively acting on newly acquired information. Individual differences in these three interacting components influence how people process information and, thus, how they solve problems, which is what human intelligence is for.

What causes people to get smarter with age? The simple answer from Sternberg's theory is knowledge. We saw in Chapter 7 that the more a person knows about a particular topic, the more efficiently he or she can process information within that domain. For example, children who know a great deal about dinosaurs can incorporate new information about dinosaurs more effectively than a novice. This involves the knowledge-acquisition components in Sternberg's theory. Dinosaur experts know how to categorize a new species and know many details about the extinct beasts (their diets, habitats, and offensive and defensive weapons). This in turn makes it easier for them to acquire new knowledge, further enhancing processing efficiency (via the performance components in Stenberg's theory). New knowledge also

serves to enhance the metacomponents, leading to greater self-awareness about the topic ("I'm not really sure if triceratops and stegosaurus lived at the same time, come to think about it"), which in turn results in the increased effectiveness of the metacomponents. This interaction of the subcomponents of the componential subtheory is shown in the bottom portion of Figure 12.6.

FIGURE 12.6 Relationship among the various aspects of the triarchic theory of intelligence.

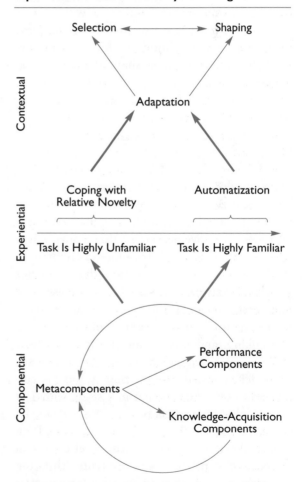

Source: Sternberg, R. J. (1988). *The triarchic mind: A new theory of human intelligence.* New York: Viking. Reprinted with permission of the author.

The various mechanisms of the different sub-theories also interact, as seen in Figure 12.6. The information-processing components are applied differently depending on if the task is a highly familiar one (classifying dinosaurs for our dinosaur expert) or an unfamiliar one (learning how to make chocolate chip cookies). In one setting (classifying dinosaurs), much processing would be automatic, whereas in the other (baking cookies), the novelty of the task would require more deliberate and effortful problem solving. Finally, we must evaluate the context in which these aspects of intelligence are applied (during play, in school, with or without adult help) and how children adapt, select, or shape the contexts in which they live.

Theory of Successful Intelligence Goes to School

If people do, indeed, have different intellectual patterns based around Sternberg's three thinking styles (practical, creative, and analytic), then people who receive instruction that matches their preferred style should learn more easily than do people who receive instruction that does not match their style. To assess this hypothesis, one must first generate a test to assess thinking style, then develop a curriculum tailored to each style of thinking, and finally, adequately assess how much was learned as a result of matched versus mismatched instruction. Sternberg and his colleagues (1996) did just that in a study with 199 gifted high school students.

Gifted high school students attended an intense 4-week summer college-level course in introductory psychology. Students' thinking style was evaluated as practical, creative, analytic, or balanced (that is, similar on all three styles). All students were assigned the same textbook and attended the same morning lecture series. Instruction varied, however, during afternoon sessions, with students receiving instruction that either matched their preferred style (for example, analytic style–analytic instruction) or not (for example, creative style–analytic instruction). Examples of the type of tasks that would exemplify each of the three thinking style types are shown in Table 12.2. Course performance was assessed by multiple-choice exams; homework assignments that evaluated practical, creative, or analytic thinking; and essay exams that asked for practical, creative, or analytic responses.

Children were administered an abbreviated version of the *Sternberg Triarchic Abilities Test (STAT)*. This test assessed the three basic types of thinking styles (practical, creative, and analytic) for three types of content (verbal, quantitative, and figural), resulting in nine subtests. Examples for each thinking style for the verbal content follow.

- *Practical-Verbal.* Students were presented with some everyday problems in the life of an adolescent and asked to come up with a solution (for example, what would you do about a friend who has a substance-abuse problem?).
- *Creative-Verbal.* Students were given verbal analogies preceded by false premises (for example, money falls off trees) and had to solve the analogies as if the false premises were true.
- *Analytic-Verbal.* Students had to figure out the meaning of artificial words from a natural context. Students would see a novel word used in a paragraph and would have to infer the meaning of the word from the context. (Sternberg et al., 1996, p. 131)

Sternberg and his colleagues reported that the three subsections of the STAT (practical, creative, and analytic) were low to moderately correlated with one another. When factor-analytic techniques were applied to the data, nine factors emerged (one for each thinking style × content combination). According to Sternberg and his colleagues (1996), these findings indicate that "clearly, the STAT is not just another measure of Spearman's (1927) g (general ability)" (p. 134). Most psychometric tests load heavily on g likely because of the relatively narrow range of abilities tested—not because it underlies *all* intellectual functioning.

Sternberg and his colleagues next correlated children's STAT scores with their performance in the course and found moderate but significant correlations between scores on each of the three subtests and course performance (correlations ranged from 0.24 to 0.42). More critical, however, was the performance of students whose thinking style matched the instruction they received. The results here were quite consistent: Students who received instruction matched to their thinking style performed significantly better than did mismatched students. Moreover, the same pattern of results was found not just for the homework and essay assessments (some of which would have matched children's thinking style) but for the multiple-choice items as well.

In subsequent research, Sternberg, Bruce Torff, and Elena Grigorenko (1998) designed, based on Sternberg's theory, a social studies curriculum for third-grade children (Study 1) and an introductory psychology curriculum for advanced eighth-grade children (Study 2). Unlike their earlier research (Sternberg et al., 1996), the curriculum in each study involved all three aspects of thinking for all students. Course performance was contrasted among students who had the successful intelligence/triarchic

instructions, those who had special instruction in critical thinking, and those who received a traditional curriculum. The results of the research were consistent across the two studies: Students who received the successful intelligence/triarchic instruction performed better on a variety of dependent measures than did children who received either the critical thinking or traditional curriculum (although those receiving the critical thinking curriculum usually performed better than did those receiving the traditional one). To top it off, third-grade children given the successful intelligence/triarchic instruction enjoyed the course more than the other students did.

Sternberg and his colleagues subsequently developed an assessment device to serve as a college entrance exam (Sternberg & the Rainbow Project Collaborators, 2006). They administered a modified version of the STAT to nearly 1,000 students in their first year of college and evaluated how well it predicted first-year grade-point average (GPA) in comparison to high school grades and scores on the SAT. They reported that the successful intelligence/triarchic measure doubled the amount of variance in college GPA accounted for by the SAT alone. Moreover, the STAT reduced differences among ethnic groups (who generally score lower on standardized tests, such as the SAT) in predicting GPA, making "a compelling case for furthering the study of the measurement of analytic, creative, and practical skills for predicting success in college" (Sternberg & the Rainbow Project Collaborators, 2006, p. 344).

In some sense, Sternberg is arguing for educating "the whole child," instructing children in the use of their analytic intelligence, their creative intelligence, and their practical intelligence, which differs from the one-track emphasis of curricula based on a general ability (g) theory of intelligence.

Section Review

Sternberg's *theory of successful intelligence* (or *triarchic theory of intelligence*) consists of three subtheories: contextual, experiential, and componential, each with a characteristic thinking style (practical, creative, and analytic, respectively).

Contextual Subtheory

- The *contextual subtheory* states that intelligence must be evaluated in the environment in which the individual lives, which by itself reflects a form of *cultural relativism*.
- There are three processes of intelligence within the contextual subtheory: adaptation, selection, and shaping.

Experiential Subtheory

- The *experiential subtheory* proposes that how people deal with novelty and the extent to which they can automatize cognitive functioning are important aspects of intelligence.
- The experiential subtheory suggests what tasks are good indicators of intelligence—namely, those that involve dealing with novelty or automatic processing for their successful completion.

Componential Subtheory

- The *componential subtheory* describes three universal information-processing mechanisms by which knowledge is acquired and manipulated.
- Metacomponents allocate attentional resources and control, monitor, and evaluate task performance.
- Performance components execute strategies assembled by the metacomponents and include encoding the to-be-processed information.
- Knowledge components are involved in acquiring new knowledge and in selectively acting on newly acquired information.

Theory of Successful Intelligence Goes to School

- The theory of successful intelligence is an attempt to go beyond earlier approaches by viewing intelligence from a wider scope, and it has been successfully applied to educational settings.
- Students who receive instruction matched with their preferred style perform better than students who receive instruction mismatched to their style.
- Students who receive a curriculum based on the theory of successful intelligence perform better than students receiving special instruction in critical thinking or standard instruction.

Ask Yourself . . .

6. How does Sternberg's triarchic theory of intelligence differ from Spearman's *g*?
7. What does Sternberg mean when saying that we should educate the whole child?
8. How does Sternberg measure intelligence? What evidence is there to suggest that Sternberg's way of measuring intelligence is more informative than conventional IQ tests?

GARDNER'S THEORY OF MULTIPLE INTELLIGENCES

Howard Gardner (1983, 1993, 1999, 2006) has proposed that intelligence is composed of separate components, or modules, much like the concept of factors used by the psychometric approach. Gardner's theory of multiple intelligences (referred to as *MI* by its practitioners) is different, however, because it relies heavily on neuropsychological evidence for the existence of relatively independent frames of mind. Gardner originally proposed seven such abilities but has since added one more and has speculated about a ninth (K. Davis et al., 2011; Gardner, 1999): (1) linguistic, (2) logical-mathematical, (3) musical, (4) spatial, (5) bodily-kinesthetic, (6) interpersonal, (7) intrapersonal, (8) naturalist, and (possibly) (9) spiritual/existential. Linguistic and logical-mathematical intelligences are highly valued in technological societies such as ours, and people high in these types of intelligence are generally viewed as smart. Musical intelligence is usually associated with the composition or performance of music, and spatial intelligence involves the ability to perceive form, to solve visual problems, and to get around effectively in one's environment. Bodily-kinesthetic intelligence is reflected in control of one's body, as epitomized by athletes of exceptional ability. The two forms of personal intelligence involve knowing how to deal with others (interpersonal) and knowledge of one's self (intrapersonal). Naturalistic intelligence concerns knowledge of the natural world (fauna and flora), and spiritual/existential intelligence deals with issues related to the meaning of life (and death) and other aspects of the ultimate human condition. Gardner has been reluctant to raise the spiritual/existential intelligence to full status, in part because there is little evidence that existential intelligence is associated with particular areas of the brain. Gardner (2006) thus continues "for the time to speak of '8½ intelligences'" (p. 21). Table 12.3 summarizes the various types of intelligences, lists people who excel in each type, and provides the neurological system hypothesized to underlie each intelligence.

Gardner views intelligence not as a single factor that influences thinking and problem solving in all realms but rather as the ability to solve problems or create products that are valued across all forms of human activity. Gardner emphasizes that what one thinks about determines, to a large extent, how one thinks. According to Gardner (2014),

My work on "multiple intelligences" is based on the premise that the content matters, and that forms of pattern recognition in one sector may not be analogous to forms of pattern recognition in another sector. To be perhaps excessively concrete, the fact that I can recognize patterns well in algebra does not have any predictive value for my pattern recognition skills in geography, cooking, manners, or the law. And even if there were a slight positive correlation between pattern recognition across two domains, it would have little explanatory power for what nurtures the pattern recognition skill of a surgeon as compared to the pattern recognition skill of an editor or a master of table tennis. (pp. 56–57)

Gardner's claim is not that these are eight (or nine) different components of a single intelligence but, rather, that these represent eight distinct intelligences, each being independent of the others. And there may be more. Gardner's proposal is for different, domain-specific forms of intelligence—the antithesis of *g*-based theories. For Gardner, each form of intelligence represents a modular, brain-based capacity. Gardner asserts that these various forms of intelligence have different degrees of importance in different cultures and at different times in history. For example, in a hunting society, physical dexterity, an ability to locomote effectively, and an understanding of one's natural surroundings are more important than numerical computation skills. In medieval Europe's apprenticeship system, emphasis was placed on bodily, spatial, and interpersonal abilities, whereas in today's Western society, 400 years later, the emphasis is on linguistic and logical-mathematical skills. Thus, Gardner views the cultural aspects of intelligence to be of utmost importance: Different cultures value different types of intelligence. Moreover, Gardner argues that our society's reliance on IQ tests to classify children by intelligence does a great disservice

TABLE 12.3 **List of multiple intelligences in Gardner's theory:** their definition, people who exemplify them, and their theorized neurological locus.

Intelligence	Definition	People who exemplify this intelligence	Neurological system hypothesized to be associated with this intelligence
Linguistic	Sensitive to meaning and order of words	Maya Angelou (poet) Stephen King (writer) Martin Luther King (civil rights leader and orator)	Left hemisphere, temporal and frontal lobes
Logical-mathematical	Ability to reason logically and recognize patterns and order	Bill Gates (former CEO of Microsoft) Stephen Hawking (physicist) James Watson (biologist)	Left parietal lobe; left hemisphere for verbal naming; right hemisphere for spatial organization; frontal system for planning
Musical	Sensitivity to pitch, melody, rhythm, and tone	Yo Yo Ma (cellist) Mariah Carey (singer) Wolfgang Amadeus Mozart (composer)	Right anterior temporal; frontal lobes
Bodily-kinesthetic	Ability to use one's body skillfully and handle objects adroitly	David Copperfield (magician) LeBron James (basketball player) Debbie Allen (dancer)	Cerebral motor strip; thalamus; basal ganglia; cerebellum
Spatial	Ability to perceive physical environment accurately and to re-create or transform aspects of that environment	Frank Lloyd Wright (architect) Pablo Picasso (painter) Georgia O'Keefe (painter)	Right hemisphere, parietal occipital lobe
Naturalist	Ability to recognize and classify numerous species of flora and fauna	Charles Darwin (biologist) Jane Goodall (primatologist) E. O. Wilson (biologist)	Left parietal lobe (discriminating living from nonliving)
Interpersonal	Ability to understand people and relationships	Barack Obama (politician) Ronald Reagan (politician) Hillary Clinton (politician)	Frontal lobes
Intrapersonal	Access to one's emotional life as a means to understand oneself and others	Oprah Winfrey (talk show host) Bono (singer, philanthropist)	Frontal lobes
Spiritual/existential	Individuals who exhibit the proclivity to pose (and ponder) questions about life, death, and ultimate realities	Albert Einstein (scientist) Socrates (philosopher) Dali Lama (monk)	Hypothesized as specific region in the right temporal lobe

Sources: Adapted from Gardner, H. (1983). Frames of mind: The theory of multiple intelligences. New York: Basic; Gardner, H. (1999). Are there additional intelligences? The case for naturalist, spiritual, and existential intelligences. In J. Kane (Ed.), Education, information and transformation. Englewood Cliffs, NJ: Prentice Hall.

to many of them and to society itself. Because these tests emphasize linguistic and mathematical abilities, children gifted in other areas, such as working with their hands, are often "thrown on society's scrap heap" instead of receiving the education that could enhance their special abilities.

Criteria of an Intelligence

On what basis did Gardner select his list of intelligences? To answer this question, Gardner (1983, 2006) provides a set of criteria that must be met for an ability to be considered an intelligence. Each of these criteria does not have to be met for an ability to be classified as an intelligence, but these are the criteria that Gardner lists (1983) "by which each candidate intelligence can be judged" (p. 66).

Potential Isolation by Brain Damage

Ample evidence indicates that damage to specified areas of the brain can selectively impair language production or comprehension. Similar evidence abounds for mathematical, musical, and spatial abilities. Evidence even suggests that damage to the frontal lobes of the neocortex can leave general intellectual functioning unimpaired but produce a socially tactless individual, affecting interpersonal intelligence. The frontal cortex plays an important role in the inhibition of task-irrelevant and inappropriate responses (see Chapters 2 and 7), and many of those inappropriate responses that are no longer inhibited occur in social situations (Fuster, 1989).

Existence of Savants and Prodigies

An intelligence is reflected by exceptionalities and, thus, can be exhibited by savants and prodigies. *Savants* are people with intellectual impairment but who possess an exceptional talent in a single domain. Savants have been identified for several skills, most notably mathematics and music. For example, neurologist Oliver Sacks (1985), in his book *The Man Who Mistook His Wife for a Hat*, describes John and Michael, 26-year-old twin brothers who had been in institutions since the age of 7, diagnosed at various times as autistic, psychotic, or intellectually impaired. John and Michael were already well known for their extraordinary facility with the calendar, a skill possessed by many savants, being able to provide quickly the day of the week for any date in history (for example, December 9, 1786). Working with these young men, Sacks discovered several other remarkable abilities. For example, the twins would sometimes play a game in which they said numbers to one another and smiled. Sacks (1985) wrote: "John would say a number—a six-figure number. Michael would catch the number, nod, smile and seem to savour it. Then he, in turn, would say another six-figure number, and now it was John who received, and appreciated it richly. They looked, at first, like two connoisseurs wine-tasting, sharing rare tastes, rare appreciations. I sat still, unseen by them, mesmerised, bewildered" (pp. 201–202). Although it took some detective work for Sacks to figure out what the twins were doing, it turned out that the numbers that brought smiles were all, and only, prime numbers.

Savants are perhaps most impressive when it comes to musical ability. There have been numerous newspaper articles and television stories about people with severe intellectual impairment who can play Beethoven piano sonatas after hearing them only once. Although these are impressive abilities, what is customarily lacking in savants is creativity. To our knowledge, there have been no musical savants who also compose great music or who are great improvisers, only those with an outstanding ability to play back accurately what they have heard.

The *prodigy* is on the other side of the coin from the savant. A prodigy is a child with generally normal abilities in all but a small number of areas (usually one). Similar to savants, prodigies are most frequently found in the areas of mathematics and music. Wolfgang Amadeus Mozart was the quintessential musical prodigy. Raised in a musical family, he, while still a preschooler, was playing instruments and composing music at a level few humans ever attain. He was touring the great capitals of Europe by age 8, but aside from his musical prowess, Wolfgang was a normal boy. This is shown in an observation made in 1764 by Daines Barrington (cited in S. J. Gould, 1992), who was impressed by the 8-year-old Mozart's musical skill but who also noted that music seemed to be the only area in which Mozart was exceptional:

> I must own that I could not help suspecting his father imposed with regard to the real age of the boy, though he had not only a most childish appearance, but likewise had all the actions of that stage of life. For example, whilst he was playing to me, a favorite cat came in, upon which he immediately left his harpsichord, nor could we bring him back for a considerable time. He would also sometimes run about the room with a stick between his legs by way of horse. (p. 10)

Why do savants and prodigies indicate multiple intelligences? Gardner believes that such exceptionalities reflect modular, brain-based skills. The savant and the prodigy are only extreme examples of unevenness in abilities, but their existence suggests that the special skills they possess are domain-specific and can be found in lesser degrees of development in the vast normal range of the human population.

Identifiable Core Operation or Set of Operations

Consistent with modern cognitive science, Gardner believes that each intelligence should have associated with it one or more basic information-processing operations, specialized to deal with a particular type of input (language, music, and so on). For example, sensitivity to pitch relations would be a core operation for musical intelligence, and the ability to imitate movements made by others would be central to bodily intelligence.

Distinctive Developmental History, Along With a Definable Set of Expert End-State Performances

An intelligence must develop. Any skill that is present fully formed when it first appears does not qualify as a type of intelligence. Also, it must have an identifiable end state—that is, a level of performance attainable by mature experts. We can certainly specify a developmental course and an expert end state for all of Gardner's intelligences. The gifted writer or speaker serves as the expert for verbal intelligence, as does the mathematician for logical-mathematical intelligence, the professional athlete or dancer for bodily intelligence, the composer or musician for musical intelligence, the visual artist or trail guide for spatial intelligence, perhaps the skilled politician or therapist for interpersonal intelligence, the philosopher for intrapersonal intelligence, the biologist (or possibly the hunter or farmer) for naturalist intelligence, and religious leaders for spiritual/existential intelligence. Some of these intelligences can have different developmental courses, leading to slightly different expert end states, with developmental milestones along the way from immature to mature performance.

Evolutionary History and Evolutionary Plausibility

Why do humans possess these intelligences? Human intelligence is a significant part of the human condition, and it likely played an important role in the evolution of our species. As such, there should be some evolutionary history of an intelligence (and perhaps evidence of antecedents of these abilities in other species) and a plausible evolutionary explanation of how these intelligences may have been selected. We clearly share social skills and social organization with our primate cousins (see Byrne & Whiten, 1988) and spatial and bodily intelligence with most large mammals.

Even abilities that might be unique to humans, such as music (although this is debated), have an evolutionary plausibility. Music is an important part of contemporary humans' lives. We fall in love to music, praise God to music, and go to war to music. (We love Woody Allen's line, directly related to this last point: "Every time I hear Wagner, I get the urge to invade Poland.") Although we find it hard to find phylogenetic antecedents to music (our guess is that it grew out of general vocal communication ability; see Chapter 4), it is easy to see how once the ability evolved, those who had control of music could have an important social (or perhaps sexual) advantage relative to others.

Support From Experimental Psychological Tasks and From Psychometric Findings

Psychologists from both the psychometric and cognitive-experimental approaches have been studying tasks that assess at least some of the eight intelligences, and findings from these literatures should reveal important individual differences. For example, many of both the basic-level tasks (for example, working memory, speed of processing) and higher-order cognitive tasks (for example, use of strategies, metacognition) described in the section *Information-Processing Approaches to the Study of Intelligence* provide information about individual differences in verbal and mathematical intelligences.

Susceptibility to Encoding in a System

One of the hallmarks of human cognitive functioning is that it is based on symbols. Ideally, an intelligence should have its own symbol system. This seems to be true for language, mathematics, and music, and perhaps for spatial and bodily intelligence.

Multiple Intelligences and Education

Gardner argues for the exclusion of intelligence and aptitude tests from our schools because, as currently practiced, they measure only two types of intelligence and ignore other, equally important types. Gardner is not opposed to intellectual assessment in general, however. He advocates the development of measures that would evaluate all types of intelligence. He believes that such assessments should be done early so that intellectual strengths can be discovered and developed through education. Although Gardner believes that each form of intelligence has its origins in biology, he also believes that they are flexible and can be enhanced by education.

Gardner's theory has been perhaps the most widely applied theory of intelligence to education since the advent of the psychometric approach over 100 years ago (Hoerr, 2014). The theory has been applied and evaluated in hundreds, if not thousands, of schools around the world, mostly in kindergarten through 12th grade (see J.-Q. Chen, Moran, & Gardner, 2009; Cuban, 2004; Hoerr, 2004) but also in college and graduate education (J. R. Shore, 2004) and in special populations, such as second-language learners (Haley, 2004) and children with ADHD (Schirduan & Case, 2004).

Table 12.4 presents some of the distinctions between a traditional classroom and one based on multiple intelligences (from Hoerr, 2004). Typically, curricula based on the theory of multiple intelligences give children substantial freedom to explore a range of topics, with many hands-on opportunities. Although textbooks may be used, teachers are more apt to create their own curricula, working with their students and other teachers. Children, rather than the curriculum, are the center of a multiple-intelligences classroom, with individual differences in intellectual abilities being valued.

Gardner's theory has attracted a lot of attention since its inception in 1983. We find that of all the theories of intelligence we discuss in class, Gardner's is usually our students' favorite. But the merits of a theory are not determined by popular vote. Critics have argued that there is little or no scientific evidence to support the theory of multiple intelligences (Allix, 2000; Waterhouse, 2006), although proponents of the theory disagree (J.-Q. Chen, 2004; Gardner & Moran, 2006). In fact, a claim often made against Gardner's theory is that it is not testable—that it is not really a theory but a framework about what is and what is not an intelligence. Yet even here there is room for debate. For example, chess performance would fit many of the criteria set by Gardner to qualify as a candidate for an intelligence: There are chess prodigies, chess has a developmental history with an expert end state, and chess ability perhaps meets other criteria (symbol systems, core set of operations). It does

TABLE 12.4 **Some differences between a traditional classroom and one based on multiple intelligences (MI).**

In a traditional classroom	In a multiple intelligences (MI) classroom
Kids with strong scholastic intelligence are smart, and the other kids aren't.	Everyone has a different profile of intelligence; we are all smart in different ways.
Teachers create a hierarchy of intellect.	Teachers use all students' intelligences to help them learn.
The classroom is curriculum centered.	The classroom is child centered.
Teachers help students acquire information and facts.	Teachers help students create meaning in a constructivist way.
The focus is on the scholastic intelligences, the 3 Rs.	Personal intelligences are valued: Who you are is more important than what you know.
Teachers work from texts.	Teachers create curriculum—lessons, units, themes.
Teachers assess students by paper-and-pencil, "objective" measures.	Teachers create assessment tools—projects, exhibitions, presentations (PEPs)—that incorporate MI.
Teachers close the door and work in isolation.	Teachers work with colleagues in using MI, developing collegiality.

Source: Hoerr, T. (2004). How MI informs teaching at New City School. Teachers College Record, 106, 40–48.

not have a plausible evolutionary explanation, however, and rightly seems not to be an intelligence. Also, Gardner's theory includes abilities that most people have not traditionally considered to be in the realm of intelligence. Musical talent has always been recognized as something special but also usually as something distinct from intelligence. And although athletic ability and bodily control are certainly important human characteristics, they are not typically considered to be mental operations in the way that mathematical computation and verbal comprehension are, which have been at the center of the definition of intelligence.

In many ways, Gardner's theory is an extension of the domain-specific theories of psychometricians such as Guilford. Gardner's considerable contribution has been getting people to look for evidence beyond psychometric testing, placing intelligence in the realm of both biology and culture, where it belongs. Gardner's ideas have been very influential, particularly in educational circles. Gardner might, indeed, find greater independence of intellectual abilities than *g* theorists typically do, and one reason for this might be that Gardner includes a broader range of abilities than conventional psychometric theorists. Thus, part of Gardner's appeal is his broader definition of intelligence. However, this may also be part of the difficulty in evaluating his theory.

The book is not closed on the nature of intelligence. Sternberg and Gardner make it clear that intelligence is a many-splendored thing—that any theorist who proposes intelligence is a single phenomenon that influences all aspects of intellectual functioning equally is just not looking at the data (see also Ceci, 1996). Yet the evidence of the positive manifold and the fact that basic cognitive processes such as individual differences in working memory do predict IQ test performance relatively well, for example, argue that there might be some general, cross-domain mechanisms that influence, to various degrees, most if not all cognitive task performance. We do not plan to provide our own theory of intelligence here. But it is clear to us that intelligence is multifaceted and that intellectual functioning varies considerably as a function of a person's knowledge and the context in which the cognitive operations were acquired and are assessed. Yet certain aspects of information processing also appear to be domain general and will influence task performance to a significant degree in a variety of contexts. Factors such as motivation and practice are critically important, and even at their best, measures of basic information processing cannot account for all, or even most, of the variance in intellectual development. The most tenable position from our point of view is that some aspects of human intelligence are domain general in nature, whereas others are domain specific in nature.

Section Review

Gardner's *theory of multiple intelligences* relies heavily on neuropsychological evidence and postulates eight (and possibly nine) distinct forms of intelligence: linguistic, logical-mathematical, musical, spatial, bodily-kinesthetic, interpersonal, intrapersonal, and naturalistic (and possibly spiritual/existential).

Criteria of an Intelligence

- Gardner lists several criteria of an intelligence, including potential isolation by brain damage, the existence of savants and prodigies, an identifiable set of operations, developmental history, an evolutionary history and plausibility, support from experimental and psychometric tasks, and susceptibility to an encoding system.

Multiple Intelligences and Education

- Like Sternberg's theory, Gardner's theory has frequently been applied to educational settings.
- The theory has been applied widely in schools across the globe, mostly in kindergarten through 12th grade but also in college and graduate education and in special populations.

Ask yourself . . .

9. How does Gardner's theory of intelligence differ from that of Sternberg's and Spearman's? What shortcomings does he see in IQ tests, and what does he propose as an alternative?
10. What examples could you provide of each of Gardner's distinct forms of intelligence? What form(s) of intelligence might a military pilot possess, for instance? An engineer? An architect?
11. Might you propose a form of intelligence that Gardner does not include? How does it measure up to his criteria?
12. How is Gardner's theory applied in educational settings?

KEY TERMS AND CONCEPTS

componential subtheory (or analytic intelligence)
contextual subtheory (or practical intelligence)
crystallized abilities
cultural relativism
developmental quotient (DQ) tests
deviation IQ
experiential subtheory (or creative intelligence)

factor analysis
factors
fluid abilities
g (or general intelligence)
hierarchical model of cognitive abilities
intelligence
intelligence quotient (IQ) tests
mental age
positive manifold

psychometric approach (or differential approach)
Pygmalion effect
Stanford-Binet
stereotype threat
theory of multiple intelligences
theory of successful intelligence (theory of triarchic intelligence)
Wechsler scales

SUGGESTED READINGS

Scholarly Works

Alloway, T. P., & Alloway, R. G. (2010). Investigating the predictive roles of working memory and IQ in academic attainment. *Journal of Experimental Child Psychology, 106*, 20–29. This study reports research demonstrating the important role of working memory on children's academic performance, predicting school abilities better even than IQ.

Blair, C. (2006). How similar are fluid cognition and general intelligence? A developmental neuroscience perspective on fluid cognition as an aspect of human cognitive ability. *Behavioral and Brain Sciences, 29*, 109–160. This article examines the relation between fluid intelligence and g, examines the cognitive mechanisms involved in intelligence (for example, working memory and executive function), and presents a neurological model to account for the findings. This target article is followed by 19 commentaries, reflecting the controversy that surrounds the concept of general intelligence.

Shearer, B. (2004). **Multiple intelligences theory after 20 years.** *Teachers College Record, 106,* **2–16.** This is the organizing paper in a special issue of the *Teachers College Record* that devotes 10 articles to reviewing aspects of Gardner's theory of multiple intelligences and its application to education. Most authors are staunch supporters of the theory, but several of the articles provide critical evaluation.

Sternberg, R. J., & the Rainbow Project Collaborators. (2006). **The Rainbow Project: Enhancing the SAT through assessments of analytical, practical, and creative skills.** *Intelligence, 34,* **321–350.** This article reviews Sternberg's triarchic theory of successful intelligence and presents the results of a study using the theory to develop an assessment device that improves prediction of success in college.

Reading for Personal Interest

Nisbett, R. E. (2009). *Intelligence and how to get it: Why schools and cultures count.* **New York: Norton.** In this highly readable book, social psychologist Richard Nisbett explores the roles of genes, family, schools, and culture on the development of intelligence. He explores many of the issues that we examine in the final three chapters of this book, including the effects of schooling on intelligence, why children from different cultures often seem smarter than children from other cultures, and the Flynn effect, among others.

13 ORIGINS, MODIFICATION, AND STABILITY OF INTELLECTUAL DIFFERENCES

IN THIS CHAPTER

Emily and Alexandra were cousins, born the same month and had attended the same school since kindergarten. As often as not, they were in the same class. Although they shared many friends and some interests (Emily was more into sports than Alexandra, and beginning in sixth grade, Alexandra was more interested in fashion and boys than Emily was), they differed consistently in their academic performance. Alexandra was usually near the top of her class and, in fact, became upset when she received grades below a B. Emily had always been a bit more laid-back about school. She did well in most of her courses but was generally in the middle of her class in terms of grades, and she rarely got upset when she received a poor grade. (In fact, in third grade, Emily tried to soothe a distressed Alexandra, who had received a C on a major math test, by telling her, "That's OK, a C's not so bad. I get Ds and Fs a lot, and nothing really bad ever happens.") Both teachers' assessments and scores on standardized tests indicated that Alexandra was gifted, whereas Emily was average in intelligence. Differences in the girls' intellectual performance and academic abilities had been apparent since they started school, if not before, and remained relatively constant through high school.

Everyone knows that, at any age, some children are smarter than others. The last chapter focused on how such individual differences can be conceptualized and measured. Although the measurement of individual differences in intelligence has fascinated researchers and educators for years, an even more basic question is "What are the origins of individual differences in children's thinking?" Why, for example, does Alexandra seem smarter than Emily? As with many things in psychology, there are two extreme camps. On one side—the *nature* side—individual differences in intelligence are viewed as part of our biological heritage, with experience playing only a minor role. That is, people are born smart or not so smart, and this is a stable characteristic across the life span (A. R. Jensen, 1998). On the other side—the *nurture* side—individual differences in intelligence are viewed as being highly influenced by experience. That is, our environments make us smart or not so smart, we can increase (or decrease) our intelligence through experience, and intelligence is

not even stable across situations, let alone years (Ceci, 1996). These are socially and educationally important issues. How we view intelligence in terms of its origins (what are the seeds of intelligence?) and its modifiability (can intelligence be enhanced through education and, if so, how much?) affects real-world decisions, particularly as they relate to education and one's occupation.

As we mentioned in Chapter 1, developmental psychologists long ago abandoned models that pitted nature against nurture in explaining the course of the life span in favor of models that describe development as resulting from the continuous and bidirectional interaction of multiple factors, from the genetic through the cultural, over time (Goldhaber, 2012; Sameroff, 2010). The proper question here is not *how much* of intelligence is attributable to nature (genes, biology) and *how much* to nurture (experience, environment) but, rather, *how do nature and nurture interact to produce a particular pattern of development or of intelligence?* This can best be accomplished by using models that seriously consider the transaction between biological and environmental factors. We introduced two of those models in Chapter 2 (the developmental systems approach and Scarr and McCartney's genotype → environment theory). Basically, these models propose that a bidirectional interaction occurs between organismic factors (for example, genes and hormones) and environmental factors (for example, physical and social environments) and that the two are intricately entwined, making it impossible to evaluate one without considering the other (that is, a contextualist perspective). Yet even within these transactional models, there is considerable latitude for interpretation of which factors (genotype versus social environment, for example) play the major role in shaping development and intellect.

In this chapter, we examine some of the research relating to these issues. We first introduce a transactional approach to intelligence, a variant of the developmental systems approach introduced in Chapter 2. We then look at recent work in behavioral genetics that supports a strong role for genetics in intelligence. We follow this with research focusing on the role of environmental factors in influencing intelligence—in the establishment as well as the modification and maintenance of intelligence. Finally, we include a section on the stability of intelligence from infancy to young adulthood. There is no definitive conclusion at the end of this chapter—no bold statement saying what the origin of intelligence is or is not. But we hope the chapter will provide enough theory and data for students to appreciate better what is perhaps the most magnificent quality of our species—our intelligence.

TRANSACTIONAL APPROACH TO THE STUDY OF INTELLIGENCE

Chapters 1 and 2 introduced a general approach to studying development. This approach emphasized the bidirectionality of structure and function. Bidirectionality can be studied at many levels, of course, from the function of a firing neuron affecting its subsequent growth to the actions of a child influencing how significant others respond to him or her. We want to focus on this latter level now, examining the transaction between a child and people in that child's immediate environment and how this transaction might affect a developing intellect.

It has long been recognized that children play a critical role in their own development. Jean Piaget clearly recognized this, placing the child's mental and physical actions at the center of his theory. Yet throughout most of the 20th century, theorists who looked at the development of intelligence tended to view children as passive beings who are either constrained by their biology to develop in a certain way or are shaped and molded by their environment (usually their early environment). Theorists in neither of these camps gave much emphasis to children themselves.

This began to change in the 1960s, with Richard Bell (1968) emphasizing the idea that parent and child have equal abilities to contribute to a social exchange and that each affects the other. This viewpoint holds that cognitive influences are transactional (Blair & Raver, 2012; Sameroff, 2009): Not only do parents act to produce behavior in their children, children also modify their parents' behaviors.

The transactional model as proposed by Arnold Sameroff views the child's biological constitution (genotype in Figure 13.1) as having an organizing effect on the development of the child (phenotype in Figure 13.1). However, the child's environment (environtype in Figure 13.1) also has an organizing effect on the child. What is critical in the transactional model are the *bidirectional* effects between the multiple levels of organization (compare this with the developmental systems approach described in Chapter 2 and Figure 2.2). The environment and child have reciprocating effects, which influence that child's biology, and these factors continue to transact during development. From this viewpoint, then, *development is seen as the continuous and bidirectional interaction between an active organism with a unique biological constitution and a changing environment.*

FIGURE 13.1 **The transactional model of development, reflecting the continuous interaction of the child's constitution and the environment over time.**

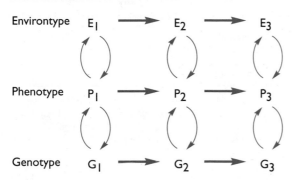

Source: Sameroff, A. (2009). The transactional model. In A. Sameroff (Ed.), *The transactional model of development: How children and contexts shape each other* (p. 15). Washington, DC: American Psychological Association.

The transactional model has been used to understand the nature of differences in intelligence among children as a function of SES, which is customarily defined in terms of level of family income, parents' occupational status, and years of parental education. Research has consistently shown that a significant portion of the differences in IQ, basic cognitive abilities such as working memory, and academic achievement among children can be attributed to SES factors (Ackerman & Brown, 2006; Hackman et al., 2015; NICHD Early Child Care Research Network, 2005; see Nisbett et al., 2012), with children from low-income homes faring worse in school than children from more advantaged homes.

Variables such as SES do not influence children independently of other factors. Thus, a high correlation exists between SES and home environment, friend selection, neighborhood, academic expectation, and academic opportunities, among other factors. In pioneering research, Arnold Sameroff and Michael Chandler (1975) proposed that

some caretaking environments (middle-income homes) are more likely to produce intellectually and socially competent children than are others (lower-income homes). Furthermore, children who experience perinatal trauma (trauma at or around the time of birth) were proposed to be especially susceptible to nonsupportive caretaking, so the negative consequences of early biological impairment are exacerbated in such environments. That is, Sameroff and Chandler (1975) proposed a transaction between infants' biological constitutions and their environment, as reflected by differences in SES.

Support for Sameroff and Chandler's model was provided by an examination of the outcomes of children experiencing stress at birth (oxygen deprivation, or anoxia) as a function of their SES level. Although differences in developmental level between typical and biologically impaired infants are obvious at birth in both lower- and middle-income groups, these differences are diminished, or often even eliminated, by age 6 or 7 years in middle-income homes. In contrast, these differences are either maintained or increase with age in lower-income homes. Sameroff and Chandler speculated that distressed infants—characterized by more aversive cries; slower attainment of social-developmental milestones, such as smiling and vocalization; and a sickly appearance—receive different types of treatment in different environments. In reasonably affluent and well-educated families, these distressed children might receive lavish attention and stimulation, facilitating the amelioration of their impaired condition. In deprived, stressed, and poorly educated families, these same infant characteristics result in a pattern of reduced attention and stimulation and, thus, continued cognitive and social deficits. That is, there is a transaction between parent and child, with the particular characteristics of the child interacting with the particular characteristics of the parents, yielding distinct patterns of development.

In other early research, Philip Sanford Zeskind and Craig Ramey (1978, 1981) experimentally assessed the effects of different caretaking environments as a function of infants' biological status in a series of studies. Infants from poor, rural environments who had been classified as at high risk for intellectual impairment were assigned to one of two caregiving environments. Infants in one group received medical care and nutritional supplements, and they participated in an educationally oriented day-care program beginning at approximately 3 months of age (experimental group). Infants in a control group received the medical care and nutritional supplements but did not participate in the day-care program. Within each group, approximately half of the infants were classified as fetally malnourished at birth, whereas the remaining infants were described as biologically typical. Fetal malnourishment typically produces infants who are developmentally delayed and lethargic and have aversive cries.

At 3 months of age, fetally malnourished infants in both the control and experimental groups had lower developmental scores on the Bayley Mental Developmental Index than the nonmalnourished (typical) infants did. However, Stanford-Binet IQ scores at 24 and 36 months demonstrated (a) higher IQ scores overall for the experimental than for the control children, (b) no difference in IQ scores between the typical and fetally malnourished infants in the experimental group, and (c) higher IQ scores for the typical than for the fetally malnourished infants in the control group. IQ scores at 36 months are shown for the four groups of this experiment in Table 13.1. In general, the pattern of IQ change observed in this experiment is similar to what Sameroff and Chandler (1975) observed, with the effects of a nonsupportive environment (the

TABLE 13.1 **Mean Stanford-Binet scores at 36 months for children in the Zeskind and Ramey (1981) study.**

	Biologically normal	Fetally malnourished
Experimental (day care) group	98.1	96.4
Control group	84.7	70.6

Source: Adapted from Zeskind, P. S., & Ramey, C. T. (1981). Sequelae of fetal malnutrition: A longitudinal, transactional, and synergistic approach. *Child Development, 52,* 213–218. Copyright 1981 The Society for Research in Child Development, Inc.

control group) being especially deleterious for the biologically distressed children.

Zeskind and Ramey (1978) also measured the degree of mother-child interaction in the home. They reported no difference in the amount of maternal attention received by fetally malnourished and normal infants in the experimental group. In the control group, however, fetally malnourished infants received less maternal attention by age 24 months than the typical children did. Consistent with Sameroff's transactional interpretation, Zeskind and Ramey proposed that the improved responsivity of fetally malnourished infants receiving the educational day care resulted in increased attention from their mothers and a generally positive developmental outcome. In contrast, the withdrawn and sickly behavior of the fetally malnourished infants in the control group resulted in less maternal attention, exaggerating the injurious effects of their biological impairment.

Although the patterns reported while children were still participating in the enrichment program are impressive and demonstrate the transaction of children's biology and environment in development, they do not mean that the effects of fetal malnutrition have necessarily disappeared. When environments change (as when children leave the enrichment program), patterns of interaction can also change, and the residual effects of fetal malnutrition might return (Zeskind, 1996). But the pattern demonstrated by Zeskind and Ramey (1978, 1981) provides an elegant demonstration of the dynamic relation between children's biology and their environment over time, and it indicates that any simple interpretations of biological causes or environmental causes are likely wrong.

Most of the research we examine in the remainder of this chapter does not fit together as nicely as the Zeskind and Ramey study. Some examine genetic factors, and others examine detailed characteristics of the home environment. It is the unusual study that carefully measures biological and environmental characteristics and has good experimental controls while assessing intelligence in natural contexts. Nonetheless, all the research presented here can be viewed from the perspective of the transactional model. Although the next several sections are roughly divided into accounts of genetic factors and environmental factors, never lose sight of the fact that intelligence (or any other aspect of cognitive development) is always a transaction between an active organism with its own biological dispositions and a changing environment.

Section Review

Most contemporary theorists adopt some variant of a *transactional model* for studying the development of intelligence, emphasizing the interactive and bidirectional relations of children and their environments.

- The transactional model views development as the continuous and bidirectional interaction between an active organism with a unique biological constitution and a changing environment.

- Differences in parenting behaviors associated with SES transact with differences in infants' biological constitution to produce different patterns of development and thus different outcomes with respect to intelligence.

Ask Yourself . . .

1. How can we apply the transactional model of development to understanding individual differences in intelligence?

BEHAVIORAL GENETICS AND THE HERITABILITY OF INTELLIGENCE

Behavioral genetics examines patterns of individual differences in often-complex behaviors as a function of the genetic relationship between individuals. Stated simply, derived statistics provide estimates of the percentage of variance, or differences in a trait, that can be accounted for by genetics, environment, and their interaction.

According to some, we have entered the age of *genomics*, a period when the entire human genome will be known and connections between genotypes and phenotypes will be elucidated (Venter et al., 2001). This is, indeed, an exciting time for biological science, and relationships between genes and behavior are continually being discovered (Mandelman & Girgorenko, 2011; Plomin & Schalkwyk, 2007), making anyone who claims that genetics are unimportant for explaining individual differences in complex behavior such as intelligence very much out of touch with contemporary science. However, one must be careful not to let this "genomicophelia" cause us to lose track of the fact that genes are only part (albeit a critical part) of a complex developmental system and that their expressions are governed by events surrounding them during development (Gottlieb, 2007; Meaney, 2010; see Chapter 2). Genes must be seen as interacting with their local environments; thus, genotype-phenotype relations should vary at different points in development and under different environmental conditions. Moreover, the search for genes for intelligence has not been as productive as scientists had originally hoped. In general, many genes are involved in determining general intelligence (in interaction with the environment, of course), but so far, the quest to isolate specific genes has been elusive, likely because the effect of any single gene on general intelligence is very small in magnitude (Butcher et al., 2008; Nisbett et al., 2012). Moreover, when individual genes associated with intelligence have been found, their effect is usually mediated by the environment, as in the version of one gene associated with higher IQ, but only when children were breast-fed (Caspi et al., 2007), which was discussed in Chapter 2.

Concept of Heritability

Before we delve too deeply into the data of behavioral genetics, some explanation concerning what is meant by the term heritability is appropriate here. Heritability is the extent to which differences in any trait within a population can be attributed to inheritance. Heritability is expressed as a statistic that ranges from 0 (none of the differences in a trait are attributed to inheritance) to 1.0 (100% of the differences in a trait are attributed to inheritance). It reflects the proportion of variance in an observed trait that results from genetic variability.

Heritability is a population statistic, in that it describes average differences among people within a population. It does not refer to how much of any one person's intelligence (or height, or personality characteristics) can be attributed to inherited/genetic factors, only to what percentage of the difference in a trait within a specific population can be attributed to inheritance, on average.

For the purpose of illustration, assume that individual differences in height are the result of only two factors: genes and diet. On an isolated island, every person receives 100% of his or her nutritional needs (no one receives less or more). The average height of men on the island is 6 feet. If you were to meet two men from this island, one being 6 feet 1 inch tall and the other being 5 feet 11 inches tall, 100% of the 2-inch difference in their height would be attributable to genes—in other words, heritability would be 1.0. The reason for this is that their environments (diets, in this case) are homogeneous (no differences in environments exist). Thus, any difference in height between people must be attributable to genes.

What would happen if a famine hit the island, changing the diet of the people and, thus, the average height (from 6 feet to 5 feet 10 inches, say)? If the change were uniform (if, for example, everyone was getting 75% of his or her nutritional needs), the heritability would still be 1.0. Although the environment would have changed drastically, it would have changed equally for everyone. If the effects of the famine were not uniform, however, the heritability picture would change. If some people still received 100% of their nutritional needs, others 75%, and still others only 50%, now when you meet two men from the island who differed by 2 inches in height you would know that, on average, some proportion of this difference must be attributable to differences in diet—that is, heritability in this latter case would be something less than

1.0. The more heterogeneous, or variable, the environments are, the lower the heritability will be. Heritability is thus relative, varying with the environmental conditions in which people within the population live.

The concept of heritability is the same regardless of whether we are studying height or intelligence. One difference between concepts such as height and intelligence, however, is that of measurement. When we express height in inches or meters, we can be confident that the measure accurately reflects the underlying concept. There is less confidence with intelligence. In most studies examining the heritability of intelligence, IQ or other psychometric tests are used to measure intelligence. Thus, the findings of these studies more accurately pertain to the heritability of IQ (and usually g), with IQ being one (popular) index of intelligence.

Most of the research in behavioral genetics (and in the studies to follow examining the effects of home environment) are correlational, not experimental, in nature. Given the reliance on correlations for interpreting the findings of these studies, let us say a few words about correlations as they are used in the remainder of this chapter. Correlations measure the degree to which two factors vary with respect to one another. Correlations range from 1.0 (a perfect positive relation) to -1.0 (a perfect negative relation), with 0 being chance (no systematic relation). For example, we would expect a positive correlation between height and weight. Taller people, on average, are heavier than shorter people. There are many exceptions, of course, so the correlation will not be perfect. But we would expect a correlation in the magnitude of 0.60 or 0.70. The correlation between weight and some measure of intelligence, however, should be close to 0. Among a group of adults, we would not expect heavy people to be more or less smart, on average, than light people.

In familial studies of intelligence, the IQs of people with a known genetic relationship are correlated. For example, the IQs of sets of monozygotic twins might be obtained, and the score of each twin paired with his or her mate's. These scores can be contrasted with the IQs of randomly chosen, genetically unrelated people. In the latter case, the IQ of one person is paired at random with the IQ of another, and the correlation is computed. In the former case, a high correlation is expected, because the twins are genetically identical and grew up in the same home at the same time. In fact, the strong genetic position would predict a correlation of 1.0 even for monozygotic twins reared apart. In the case of the unrelated people, the correlation should be 0; knowing the IQ of one person does not help predict the IQ of another randomly selected person. Thus, the higher the correlation, the greater the relationship. These statistics are then used to infer the degree to which a characteristic is heritable.

The statistical models underlying heritability are complicated and beyond the scope of this chapter. (See Appendix B of Plomin et al., 2012, for a discussion of the statistical models underlying estimates of heritability.) Contemporary models consider not only genetic and environmental effects but also the interaction of these effects (G × E) (Moffitt, Caspi, & Rutter, 2006). For example, a certain characteristic, like aggression, might be more strongly expressed in one environment than in another.

These models also consider the covariation of genetic and environmental effects, or genotype-environment correlations. In fact, Sandra Scarr and Kathleen McCartney's (1983) genotype → environment model, discussed in Chapter 2, reflects such correlations. Thus, although it is not trivial to interpret results from behavioral genetics research in terms of the transactional model discussed earlier (and patterns of correlations might not tell the entire story of genetic and environmental effects), most contemporary behavioral geneticists would agree with the basic tenets of the transactional model presented earlier. This is not to say that behavioral geneticists view the developing nature of intelligence the same way as do people such as Sameroff, discussed in the previous section. However, both groups of scientists see intelligence as developing through a dynamic relationship between one's biological constitution and a changing environment and this relationship as varying during development.

We should comment here that variance associated with genetic and environmental effects cannot be truly identified as if each contributes something unique to the phenotype. As we've argued in earlier chapters, all development should be viewed as the product of the continuous, bidirectional interaction of factors at multiple levels of organization, from the genetic through the cultural. Thus, attributing a certain proportion of differences in IQ to genetics and another proportion to environment has serious limitations (see D. S. Moore, 2001). Nonetheless, we believe that this general approach of behavioral genetics provides an estimate of how a particular trait is apt to vary as a function of genetic relatedness in known environments and, thus, provides useful information about the source of individual differences in a trait, including intelligence.

Elementary Cognitive Tasks and Intelligence

Elementary cognitive tasks (ECTs), or basic-level processes, are simple laboratory tests designed to measure people's response times as they make presumably simple decisions. These include short-term memory scanning, retrieval of familiar words from the long-term store, and simple categorization tasks (A. R. Jensen, 1998). Some of these tasks were described in Chapter 12 in the discussion of information-processing approaches to individual differences. The basic processes measured by ECTs are presumed to be closely related to physiological functioning and, thus, primarily under the influence of endogenous (and inherited) factors.

Arthur Jensen, among others, has presented evidence that response times for several ECTs are significantly related to g-factor scores obtained from conventional psychometric tests (see A. R. Jensen, 1993, 1998; see also Sheppard & Vernon, 2008). As noted in Chapter 12, significant relations have been found between basic-level processes and verbal ability for both adults (Hunt, Davidson, & Lansman, 1981) and children (Fry & Hale, 2000). Following Jensen's argument, variations in these basic cognitive processes are probably inherited and are the basis for individual differences in intelligence. To bolster this contention, several researchers have demonstrated significant relationships between aspects of evoked brain potentials measured via EEG apparatus and psychometrically measured intelligence (see A. R. Jensen, 1998).

Stephen Petrill, Lee Ann Thompson, and Douglas Detterman (1995) assessed the genetic basis of performance on ECTs by administering a series of timed cognitive tasks to 287 monozygotic (genetically identical) and dizygotic (genetically nonidentical) twin pairs 6 to 13 years of age. The correlation between decision times on the information-processing tasks and psychometrically measured intelligence had previously been found to be significant (correlation = −.42). Decision times also proved to be highly heritable. The correlation of decision times for the identical twins was 0.61, but the correlation was only 0.39 for the nonidentical twins. This resulted in a heritability of about 45% (see also McGue et al., 1984). Heritability for other cognitive tasks was lower, with the heritability of simple reaction times being zero. Nevertheless, the findings clearly reflect a strong genetic basis for overall speed of processing (decision time) on experimental cognitive tasks, and this speed component was strongly related to a general intellectual factor (that is, *g*).

Even if speed of information processing is highly heritable, why should it correlate so strongly with psychometric measures of intelligence? A. R. Jensen (1993) states the dilemma: "It seems almost incredible that individual differences in reaction time (RT) in simple tasks that involve no intellectual content and are so easy as to be performed by most persons in less than 1 second should be correlated with scores on nonspeeded, complex tests of reasoning ability, vocabulary, and general knowledge—the kinds of content that compose IQ tests" (p. 53). A. R. Jensen (1993) proposed three possible brain-based reasons for the high correlations of reaction times with measures of *g*. First, speed of information processing might reflect speed of nerve transmission. Speed is important because of the brain's limited capacity to process information. Only so much can be done at once; faster processing will permit more to be done, and this will be true across domains (Neubauer & Fink, 2009). Second, evidence suggests that people whose reaction times are more variable across trials have lower psychometrically measured intelligence (Eysenck, 1987). Third, the longer neurally encoded information can be maintained in immediate consciousness, the more efficient cognition will be. Thus, more durable memory traces, with information being retained longer in short-term memory, result in more effective information processing. Jensen acknowledged that the neurological aspects of his theory remain

speculative, but he stated that the theory is consistent with the empirical evidence showing a strong relation between speed of information processing and *g*.

Although the findings and theories regarding ECTs are intriguing and applauded by many, not all researchers are ready to accept them as conclusive or as representative of functioning on higher-level cognitive tasks. For example, Stephen Ceci (1996) argued that other important cognitive skills, such as strategic and metacognitive processes, are ignored in this research. Also, it is well established that response times on simple cognitive tasks can vary greatly as a function of a person's knowledge base. Response times are fast when decisions are made concerning very familiar information but are slower when dealing with less familiar information (Case, Kurland, & Goldberg, 1982; Chi, 1977). Differences in knowledge base might be indirectly responsible for many of the group and individual differences observed in some of these experiments, and such differences might well be more a function of education and general experience than they are of genetics (see Ceci, 1996; see also Chapter 11 for a compelling argument of this).

Familial Studies of Intelligence

Most researchers in behavioral genetics take the position that the primary influence of genes on intelligence is indirect. Genes do not necessarily make someone intelligent but, rather, influence the behavior and the experiences an individual will have. For example, the genes of a child's parents influence how those parents behave toward the child, affecting a substantial part of that child's experiences, especially early in life. And children's own genotypes determine which situations they find comfortable and pleasing, which causes them to seek out some environments and to avoid others (Bouchard et al., 1990; Sameroff, 2009; Scarr, 1993). Thus, although genes surely influence things such as the rate of neural transmission or the durability of memory traces, which might have a direct effect on cognitive functioning (A. R. Jensen, 1998), their *indirect* effect, through the behavior of parents and of the children themselves, can have even greater consequences for the development of intellect. (Review Scarr and McCartney's genotype → environment theory in Chapter 2.)

The preponderance of research examining the heritability of intelligence has dealt with comparisons of IQ scores among people of varying genetic relationships (or **familial studies of intelligence**). If one holds a genetic theory of intelligence, then the greater the genetic similarity between two groups of individuals, the higher the correlations of their IQs should be. One of two general approaches has usually been taken: *adoption studies*, in which the parents who rear the children are genetically unrelated to them (Plomin, Fulker, et al., 1997; Weinberg, Scarr, & Waldman, 1992), and *twin studies*, in which monozygotic twins separated early in life are contrasted with dizygotic (nonidentical) twins and with people of varying genetic relationships (Bouchard et al., 1990).

Many large-scale and tightly controlled adoption and twin studies have been conducted over the past half century, and their findings are relatively consistent. Thomas Bouchard and Matt McGue (1981) reviewed 111 familial studies of intelligence,

FIGURE 13.2 Average correlations of familial studies of intelligence.

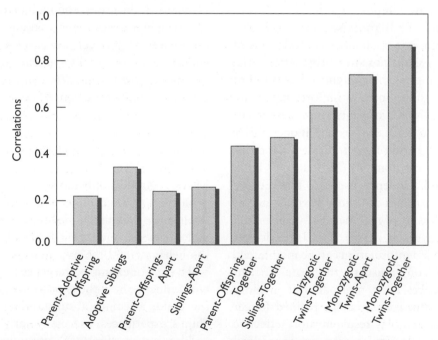

Source: Adapted from data published by Bouchard, T. J., Jr., & McGue, M. (1981). Familial studies of intelligence: A review. *Science, 212,* 1055–1059.

including only studies that met strict methodological and statistical criteria. Some of the average correlations from this investigation are summarized in Figure 13.2. The results of several dozen additional studies during the past several decades have not altered the patterns shown in this figure (Plomin et al., 2012; Plomin & Petrill, 1997).

Generally, the correlations increase as genetic similarity increases, implying a significant role for genetics in patterns of individual differences in intelligence. From these correlations, heritability estimates are derived. The easiest way to compute a heritability coefficient (H) is by using data from twin studies. The correlation (denoted as r) based on data from nonidentical twins is subtracted from the correlation based on data from identical twins, and the difference is doubled; that is,

H = (r identical twins − r nonidentical twins) × 2

If you take the correlations for the IQs of identical twins reared together shown in Figure 13.2 (0.86) and those of nonidentical twins reared together (0.60), the resulting computation is $H = (0.86 − 0.60) × 2 = 0.52$. This means that the heritability of intelligence (at least based on this data set) is 0.52, or that 52% of the differences in intelligence between people is attributed to genetics.

Based on the dozens of studies conducted during the past 30 years or so, most research provides estimates of the heritability of IQ from about 0.4 to 0.8 (Nisbett et al., 2012). A somewhat conservative conclusion would be that the heritability of IQ is approximately 0.50, meaning that, on average, 50% of the difference in intelligence between people in a population can be attributed to genetics (Plomin et al., 2012; Plomin & Petrill, 1997). However, recall that heritability is a population statistic and, thus, is subject to change across time and populations. So, for example, research has indicated that IQ has a higher heritability in middle childhood than in early childhood (O. S. Davis, Haworth, & Plomin, 2009), is higher in North American Whites than in North American Blacks, and is higher in Whites living in Great Britain than in Whites living in America (see Ceci, 1993).

Role of the Environment in Behavioral Genetics Analyses

If we accept the 0.50 heritability figure, this means that about 50% of the differences in IQ between people are attributable to *nongenetic* effects—namely, environment (Plomin et al., 2012; Plomin & Petrill, 1997). In family comparisons, behavioral geneticists typically consider the environmental effects of shared and nonshared environments. A **shared environment** is a home environment shared by different family members. A **nonshared environment** is an environment unique to an individual (not shared by a sibling, for instance). Thus, twins growing up in the same home at the same time would share the same family environment. Nontwin siblings growing up in the same family at different times would not share the same environment to the extent that twins do. As noted in Chapter 2, research has consistently shown that siblings become less alike the older they get and that this reflects the contribution of nonshared environments (McCartney, Harris, & Bernieri, 1990). Following the arguments of Scarr and McCartney (1983; Scarr, 1992, 1993), with increasing age, children's genotypes influence them to select their own environments, and the experiences they have in those environments affect their intelligence. Thus, some portion of the nonshared environmental effects can likely be attributed to indirect genetic effects (active genotype → environment effects in Scarr and McCartney's model). In addition, estimates of the heritability of IQ (that is, genetic effects) increase from childhood into adolescence and adulthood (Plomin et al., 1997), although this varies with the overall level of a child's IQ. Children with exceptionally high IQs are slower to display the adult pattern (that is, increased genetic effects, similar to adults) than are children with average IQs (Brant et al., 2013). One hypothesis for this effect is that children with superior intelligence have an extended sensitive period that results in an extended period of cortical thickness followed by more rapid pruning of neurons and synapses (Shaw et al., 2006; see Chapter 2).

In contrast to genetic and nonshared environment effects, research has consistently found that the effects of shared environment on IQ are modest (McCartney et al., 1990; Turkheimer & Waldron, 2000). Nancy Segal (2000) developed the *virtual twin* method to illustrate this. Segal defined virtual twins as unrelated siblings of about the same age who grew up in the same family from early infancy. For example, two adopted siblings, or a biological child and an adopted child, separated by fewer than 9 months in age, would be virtual twins. In such cases, they share the same family environment, similar to that shared by monozygotic or dizygotic twins, but they are not genetically related. Segal reported a significant correlation between the IQs of the virtual twins (0.26), but consistent with the argument that shared environments have only small effects on intellectual development, this correlation was substantially less than that found between monozygotic twins (0.86), dizygotic twins (0.60), or full siblings (0.50).

It is too early to conclude, however, that shared environments have little impact on the development of intelligence. For example, Mike Stoolmiller (1999) proposed that the lack of effects of shared environment in adoption studies can be attributed to statistical anomalies, associated with the restricted range of family environmental qualities in such studies. Adoptive parents are a select group, and although they may differ in measures such as SES, few provide inadequate environments for their children. In fact, the SES of the birth parents of most adoptive children is lower than that of the adoptive parents, and this is associated with an IQ score for the adoptive children that is, on average, 12 to 18 points higher than for similar children not adopted (Duyme, Dumaret, & Tomkiewicz, 1999; van IJzendoorn, Juffer, & Poelhuis, 2005). As a result, these studies greatly underestimate the degree of shared-family environment, and when this is taken into consideration, the amount of variance accounted for by shared-family environment increases substantially.

The behavioral genetics research we've reported here looks at correlations of IQs (or other tests of cognitive ability) as a function of the degree of genetic similarity, and the conclusion is clear: The more similar two groups of people are genetically, the higher the correlation. But remember that correlations are independent of means—in this case, average levels of IQ scores. When looking at average levels of IQ, environment (as reflected, for example, by the average level of IQ in the parental home) can have a greater effect than biology. How can this be? How can there be such an overpowering genetic relation when looking at correlations and a strong environmental effect when looking at means?

Sandra Scarr and Richard Weinberg (1976; Weinberg et al., 1992) illustrated the combined impact of environment and genetics on intelligence in a transracial adoption study, mentioned briefly in Chapter 12. Black children, born primarily of parents from lower-income homes, were adopted as infants by White, primarily upper-middle-class families. The average IQ of the adopted children was found to be 110, or 20 points higher than the average IQ of comparable children being reared in the local Black community and comparable with the estimated IQs of their adopted parents. This effect demonstrates the potent influence of environment on IQ. However, the correlation between the children's IQs and their biological mothers' educational level (IQ scores were not available for the biological mothers) was significantly higher (0.43) than was a similar correlation with the educational level of the children's adoptive parents (0.29).

The findings of this study appear paradoxical at first. How could the level of the children's IQs be more similar to that of their adopted parents yet the correlation of their IQs be higher with the educational level of their biological mothers? To help understand this difference, keep in mind that correlations in this type of research reflect the degree to which knowing a parent's IQ (or equivalent) score will predict where a child's IQ will fall relative to other children in his or her particular group. Correlations are independent of level of IQ; that is, correlations predict rank order and not IQ scores. In fact, the 20-point IQ difference between the children and their biological mothers could, theoretically, have been accompanied by a perfect correlation (1.0). In such a hypothetical situation, the child with the highest IQ of all the children (125, let's say) would have the biological mother with the highest IQ of all the mothers (105, let's say), and the child with the next highest IQ (119, for instance) would have the biological mother with the next highest IQ (101, for example), and so on, until the child with the lowest IQ (82, say), who would have the biological mother with the lowest IQ (65, perhaps). The correlation would be perfect, yet there would be, on average, a 20-point IQ difference between the children and their biological mothers.

In Scarr and Weinberg's study (1976), the adopted children had all been placed in intellectually stimulating homes and had received similar treatment at the hands of their academically accelerating, adoptive parents. Such stimulation was responsible for their relatively high levels of IQ in comparison with those of their biological mothers. Furthermore, given the similar patterns of experience that these children had, individual differences among the children were best predicted by genetics. When environmental conditions are relatively homogeneous, as they presumably were for the adopted children in Scarr and Weinberg's study, the best predictor of individual differences in intelligence is genetics. Again, prediction refers to knowing a child's relative rank in a specified group of children (that is, where the child stands compared with his or her peers); it does not refer to the actual level of IQ. When environments vary considerably (that is, are heterogeneous), differences in environments will play a more substantial role in affecting individual differences in intelligence (see later discussion). Thus, had the environments of the adopted families been more varied, chances are the correlations between the IQs of the children and the educational level (and IQ, presumably) of their adoptive parents would have been greater. In other words, the heritability of intelligence is not constant but varies as a function of the similarity of environments among the people under study. As we noted earlier, however, nonshared environmental factors increase in influence as children get older, and these factors serve, essentially, to make the environments experienced by children more dissimilar to one another. Because these nonshared environments are influenced by their genetics (active genotype → environment effects), however, one would still expect the correlations of children's IQs with their biological parents to be high relative to those of adoptive parents during adolescence.

Several studies have explicitly assessed the interaction of genetics and environment on IQ using patterns of correlations derived from sets of siblings (Hanscombe et al., 2012; D. C. Rowe, Jacobson, & van der Oord, 1999; Turkheimer et al., 2003). For example, David Rowe and his colleagues (1999) obtained verbal IQ scores from 3,139 sibling pairs, including sets of monozygotic and dizygotic twins as well as adopted siblings. The siblings, all adolescents, were White, African American, and Hispanic, and they came from economically diverse backgrounds. Of particular interest to D. C. Rowe and his colleagues (1999) was the relation between education level of the children's parents and the heritability of IQ. The range of education of the parents was from no school to graduate or professional training. Rowe and his colleagues first computed correlations of IQs between siblings as a function of genetic relationship and found, similar to other research, that correlations increased as the degree of genetic similarity increased. For example, the correlation of the monozygotic twins was 0.73, the correlation of full siblings was 0.39, and the correlation of unrelated siblings was 0.07. The researchers next computed estimates of genetic and shared environmental effects as a function of parental education. For the overall sample, the researchers reported a genetic effect of 0.57 and an effect of shared environment of 0.13, which is similar to results reported by others. The patterns differed, however, when education level of the parents was considered (see Figure 13.3). For adolescents in the low-education group (parents had high school education or less), D. C. Rowe and his colleagues (1999) reported a genetic effect of 0.26 and an effect of shared environment of 0.23. In other words, both genetics and shared environment accounted for about one quarter of

the variability of differences in verbal IQ for the low-education group. In contrast, for the high-education group (parents had greater than high school education), the researchers reported a genetic effect of 0.74 and an effect of shared environment of 0. In related research, Eric Turkheimer and his colleagues (2003) reported that approximately 60% of individual differences in IQ for children living in poverty was accounted for by shared environment, with the contribution of genetics being close to zero. In general, shared environmental experiences have a greater impact on the heritability of IQ for low-SES children than for higher-SES children.

FIGURE 13.3 **Genetic and shared-environment effects of IQ for adolescents for the overall sample and for the low-education and the high-education families.** Genetic and shared-environment effects changed substantially when education of the parents was considered, illustrating the important role that environment has on estimates of the heritability of IQ.

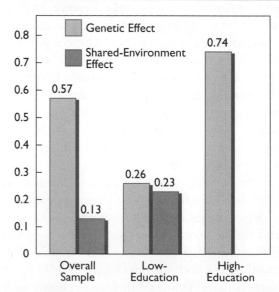

Source: Adapted from Rowe, D. C., Jacobson, K. C., & van der Oord, E. J. C. G. (1999). Genetic and environmental influences on vocabulary IQ: Parental education level as a moderator. *Child Development, 70*, 1151–1162.

In other research, Elliot Tucker-Drob and his colleagues (2011) administered a version of the Bayley Scales of Infant Development to 750 pairs of twins, initially at 10 months of age and again at 2 years. They reported a negligible genetic effect on mental functioning at 10 months, irrespective of the SES level of the infants' parents. The picture was different, however at 2 years: The genetic effect increased for children from higher-SES homes, accounting for nearly 50% of the individual differences in mental performance, whereas the genetic effect remained near zero for children from low-SES homes.

These findings indicate, consistent with the theorizing of others (Bronfenbrenner & Ceci, 1994; Scarr, 1992), that heritability increases with improved environmental conditions and that children living in poverty rarely have the opportunity to develop to their full genetic potential (Nisbett et al., 2012). This is because harmful environments might have a particularly strong influence on the development of certain traits, whereas according to Scarr (1992), average or above-average environments will have little impact beyond that contributed by genetics. The findings presented clearly indicate that environment and genetics do, indeed, interact and that these interactions can be found by using the methods of behavioral genetics.

Section Review

Behavioral genetics examines patterns of individual differences in often-complex behaviors as a function of the genetic relationship between individuals.

Concept of Heritability

- *Heritability* is a statistic that refers to the extent to which differences in a trait within a population are the result of inheritance.
- Heritability is a population statistic, and the greater the variation in environments among people in a population, the lower the heritability of any trait (including intelligence) will be.

Elementary Cognitive Tasks and Intelligence

- *Elementary cognitive tasks* are simple laboratory tests designed to measure people's response times as they make presumably simple decisions and are related to intelligence.
- The heritability of basic-level processes is relatively high, suggesting that some aspects of physiological functioning, such as speed of nerve transmission, may be the basis of intelligence (or *g*).

Familial Studies of Intelligence

- *Familial studies of intelligence*, comparing the IQs of people with varying degrees of genetic relations (monozygotic twins, adopted siblings), have been a major tool for assessing the heritability of intelligence.
- Studies show that the correlations of IQ between groups of people increase as genetic similarity increases. The current estimate for the heritability of IQ is about 0.50, meaning that, on average, 50% of the difference in IQ scores among people in a population can be attributed to inheritance.

Role of the Environment in Behavioral Genetics Analyses

- Behavioral geneticists distinguish between genetic, *shared environment*, and *nonshared environment* effects.
- The heritability of IQ for children from low-SES homes is more influenced by shared environments than the heritability of IQ for children from higher-SES homes.

Ask Yourself ...

2. How is the heritability of a trait determined?
3. Conceptually, how is speed of processing and reaction time related to intelligence?
4. What have familial studies taught us about the heritability of intelligence?
5. What do we know about the genetic and environmental influences on intelligence? How do these influences vary with SES?

EXPERIENCE AND INTELLIGENCE

The research on the impact of SES level on the heritability estimates of IQ make it clear that environment, broadly defined, contributes to individual differences in intelligence. But, as we mentioned earlier, this research is primarily concerned with *correlations*—patterns of IQ scores between people of different degrees of genetic relatedness. Other researchers have examined how different types of childhood experiences contribute to the *level* of intellectual functioning that a child achieves.

In discussing experience and intelligence, it is useful to distinguish among the establishment, the modification, and the maintenance of intelligence. What factors are responsible for establishing intellectual competence? Once a certain level of intellectual functioning has been achieved, what is necessary to maintain that level? Finally, to what extent can an established level of intelligence be modified, either positively or negatively? Factors that influence the establishment of intelligence most certainly also exert an influence on its maintenance and modification. But it is important to recognize that these three aspects of the intelligence-experience relationship can be distinct. Once intellectual competence is established, the child will not necessarily maintain that same relative level of intelligence independent of his or her surroundings. That is, establishing some level of intellectual ability does not guarantee that it will be maintained or that it cannot be modified.

Establishing Intellectual Competence

Extremes in environments can have drastic effects on intelligence. Studies with laboratory animals clearly show that social, emotional, and intellectual functioning are greatly impaired when animals are raised in restricted environments (Bogart et al., 2014; Greenough, Black, & Wallace, 1987). Although these lab experiments cannot be done with children, some naturalistic studies have been done in institutions and homes to assess the consequences of growing up in impoverished environments.

Institutionalization Studies

In the early decades of the 20th century, there were numerous institutions in Europe and North America for infants and children who could not be cared for by their parents. These institutions tended to be understaffed, with children getting little in the way of social stimulation (W. Dennis, 1973; Spitz, 1945). The results of such early living conditions were increased susceptibility to illness; delayed physical, mental, and social development (Provence & Lipton, 1962; Skeels, 1966); and in some cases, death (Spitz, 1945).

For example, Wayne Dennis (1973) contrasted the outcomes of children reared in an orphanage in Beirut, Lebanon, called the Crèche, with those of infants placed in adoptive homes. The Crèche was a charity-run institution for illegitimate children. Infants received little direct stimulation in the form of play or other social interactions. The infants spent much of their day in small cribs without toys and with sheets covering the sides, limiting substantially what they could see. Life was more varied for older children, but opportunities for intellectual stimulation and the development of normal patterns of adult-child interaction were minimal. Furthermore, many of the primary caretakers were "graduates" of the Crèche themselves and were characterized by low IQ scores and a general unresponsiveness toward their young wards. Dennis reported that infants who remained institutionalized displayed signs of severe intellectual impairment within their first year and that their average IQs by age 16 ranged from 50 to 80. In contrast, infants leaving the Crèche for adoptive homes before the age of 2 years regained normal intellectual functioning, having average IQ scores by age 16 of about 100. Children adopted following their second birthday also demonstrated gains in intellectual performance, but they typically performed several years below their age level on all subsequent testings.

The effects of social deprivation appear early, within the first 2 or 3 months of life, and are reflected in infants' responses to simply being held. For example, Sally Provence and Rose Lipton (1962) describe 2- and 3-month-old institutionalized infants as feeling "something like sawdust dolls; they moved, they bent easily at the proper joints, but they felt stiff or wooden" (p. 56). Signs of intellectual impairment and inappropriate social reactions to adults increased during the first 2 years, although these signs declined somewhat as children became able to move around on their own and were moved from

nurseries to wards for older children (Provence & Lipton, 1962; Skeels, 1966).

The influence of spending their early years in institutions persisted years after children were removed from the foundling homes and placed in adoptive or foster homes. For example, Provence and Lipton (1962) followed into the preschool years a small group of institutionalized infants who had been placed in foster homes, most from 18 to 24 months of age. Provence and Lipton commented on the considerable resilience and capacity for improvement that these children showed but also noted that early institutionalization still caused long-term problems. These children, although relating to other toddlers, did not form strong personal attachments, either to other children or to adults. Their emotional behavior was described as "increasingly impoverished and predominantly bland. . . . One gained the impression on watching them that they had largely given up on their efforts to initiate a contact with the adult" (Provence & Lipton, 1962, p. 145). These children continued to improve, socially and intellectually, during the preschool years so that many looked, on casual observation, like normal children. Closer examination, however, revealed problems in forming emotional relationships, controlling impulses, developing language, and solving problems flexibly. In testing situations with adults, the children rarely sought assistance from their mothers and only infrequently turned to their mothers for comfort when distressed.

Although we would like to think that such institutions are a thing of the past, they are not. Many children in some poorer countries today are abandoned and spend significant parts of their lives as wards of the state, sometimes receiving care not much better than institutionalized children early in the last century. With the fall of communism in Eastern Europe in the 1990s, one heart-wrenching discovery was institutions in Romania for infants and young children that were at least as horrendous as any that existed during the Great Depression. (The Romanian government encouraged its citizens to have many children as a way to increase economic production. In fact, families with fewer than five children were punished with increased taxes. As a result, many parents could not support all of their children, and the state developed a network of institutions to handle the increase in abandoned children [C. A. Nelson et al., 2009].) UNICEF estimates that approximately 1.5 million children in Central and Eastern Europe live in public institutions, and many children in parts of Asia, South America, and Africa are abandoned, orphaned, or living in abject poverty (C. A. Nelson, 2007).

The effect on cognition of children living in these modern-day institutions was similar to that found for children growing up in orphanages earlier in the last century. Children who spend their first 2 years in such institutions display impaired levels of basic cognitive abilities, such as visual memory, attention, inhibitory control, and executive function (Beckett et al., 2010; Merz et al., 2016; Pollak et al., 2010); have difficulty processing emotional facial expressions (Moulson et al., 2015); and have lower IQs, often within the intellectually disabled range, than similar children who are adopted or placed in foster care (Doom, Georgieff, & Gunnar, 2015; van IJzendoorn & Juffer, 2005).

Modern researchers examining the effects of institutionalization have some tools that researchers of earlier generations did not. Brain-imaging techniques can provide scientists with a look at how early deprivation can affect the structure and functioning of children's brains (Chugani et al., 2001; Eluvathingal et al., 2006; Tottenham et al., 2010). For example, in one study, researchers compared the PET scans of 10 adopted children who had formerly lived in a Romanian institution from birth for an average of 38 months of age with a group of age-matched children having epilepsy (Chugani et al., 2001). The adopted orphans were from 7 to 11 years old when tested and had an average Wechsler IQ of 81. Some of the greatest differences in glucose metabolism between the Romanian orphan group and the control children were in the prefrontal cortex and the temporal lobe, both of which are associated with higher cognitive functions. The hippocampus and amygdala, areas involved in memory and emotion, also showed differences. Subsequent research showed that former Romanian orphans had less white matter (mainly myelinated axons) in parts of the brain that serve as pathways between the amygdala and frontal lobes (Eluvathingal et al., 2006) and displayed less cortical activity (using EEG recordings) than noninstitutionalized control children (Moulson, Fox, et al., 2009; Moulson, Westerlund, et al., 2009).

The negative consequences of institutionalization on brain development are substantial, if not surprising. According to Charles Nelson (2007), "Institutionalization appears to lead to a reduction in cortical brain activity (both metabolically and electrophysiologically) and to dysregulation of neuroendocrine systems that mediate social behavior" (p. 16). Nelson proposed that such children do not receive the stimulation that developing brains have evolved to expect, thus hampering brain development. As C. A. Nelson (2007) writes, "Many forms of institutional rearing lack most elements of a mental-health-promoting environment. As a result, the young nervous system, which actively awaits and seeks out environmental input, is robbed of such input" (p. 16). Looking at data from Romanian institutionalized children, Nelson proposes that too many neurons and synapses are lost in the deprived children, most of which can never be replaced, suggesting a sensitive period from which these children cannot fully recover.

Institutionalization studies are natural experiments and demonstrate how extremes in early environment can affect children's intellectual development. But such studies, although informative, lack the experimental rigor that psychologists like. Furthermore, such early deprived environments probably represent an extreme of child-rearing and might not apply to the vast majority of parent-child interaction styles.

Home Environment: Naturalistic Studies of Parent-Child Interaction

Many studies have examined aspects of children's home environments and related them to IQ and other measures of intellectual performance (Melhuish et al., 2008; NICHD Early Child Care Research Network, 2005). One of the more impressive longitudinal projects evaluating the quality of parent-child interactions and later intelligence was begun in the 1970s by Betty Caldwell, Richard Bradley, and their colleagues. They developed an inventory for assessing the quality of the home environment, called the Home Observation for Measurement of the Environment (HOME) scale (R. H. Bradley, Caldwell, & Elardo, 1977; Caldwell & Bradley, 1978). The HOME scale is divided into six subscales and is used to code aspects of a child's home environment that relate to intellectual development. Following are some sample items from the six subscales:

1. Emotional and Verbal Responsivity of the Mother
   a. Mother spontaneously vocalizes to child at least twice during visit (excluding scolding).
   b. Mother responds to child's vocalizations with a vocal or verbal response.
   c. Mother caresses or kisses child at least once during visit.

2. Avoidance of Restriction and Punishment
   a. Mother does not shout at child during visit.
   b. Mother neither slaps nor spanks child during visit.
   c. Mother does not interfere with child's actions or restrict child's movement more than three times during visit.

3. Organization of Physical and Temporal Environment
   a. Someone takes the child to the grocery store at least once a week.
   b. When Mother is away, care is provided by one of three regular substitutes.
   c. The child's environment appears safe and free of hazards.

4. Provision of Appropriate Play Materials
   a. Child has a pull or push toy.
   b. Mother provides toys or interesting activities for child during interview.
   c. Mother provides toys involving literature and music (books, records).

5. Maternal Involvement With Child
   a. Mother tends to keep child within visual range and to look at him or her often.
   b. Mother talks to child while doing her work.
   c. Mother structures child's play period.

6. Opportunities for Variety in Daily Stimulation
   a. Father provides some caregiving every day.
   b. Mother reads stories to child at least three times a week.
   c. Child has at least three or more books of his or her own.

Subsequent studies revealed moderate correlations (0.30 to 0.60) between HOME scores and IQ measures (R. H. Bradley & Caldwell, 1976; R. H. Bradley et al., 1989; Espy, Molfese, & DiLalla, 2001). More specifically, mothers who were emotionally and verbally responsive

to their infants, who provided more play materials for their children, and who were generally more involved with their children during observations when infants were 6 and 24 months of age had children with higher Stanford-Binet IQ scores at 54 months of age than did mothers who provided less stimulation for their youngsters (R. H. Bradley & Caldwell, 1976). Table 13.2 presents the correlations between 6- and 24-month HOME scores and 54-month IQ scores for children in this study. Subsequent research using the HOME scale demonstrated that descriptions of the home environment during the first 2 years of life predicted academic performance at age 11 reasonably well (B. S. Bradley, 1989).

More recent research has essentially confirmed the findings of Caldwell, Bradley, and their colleagues and given more consideration to the role that fathers play in the quality of the home environment: Children who grow up in emotionally supportive homes and receive cognitively rich experiences tend to have higher IQs than children who grow up in homes with less intellectual stimulation (Brooks-Gunn, Linver, & Fauth, 2005; Nettle, 2008; NICHD Early Child Care Research Network, 2002; Yogman, Kindlon, & Earls, 1995). However, the picture is complicated. A beneficial early environment, for example, is not apt to have long-term consequences if later environments are less supportive. That is, when the childhood environment is stable, patterns of development are usually stable, but when the childhood environment is constantly changing, patterns of intellectual development are also apt to change (B. S. Bradley, 1989). Thus, not only is a beneficial early environment important for sound intellectual development, but so is its stability—the beneficial environment needs to be continuous.

TABLE 13.2 **Correlations between 54-month Stanford-Binet performance and scores on the HOME scale at 6 and 24 months.**

HOME subscale	Correlations	
	6 months	24 months
1. Emotional and Verbal Responsivity of Mother	.27	.50**
2. Avoidance of Restriction and Punishment	.10	.28**
3. Organization of Physical and Temporal Environment	.31*	.33*
4. Provision of Appropriate Play Materials	.44**	.56**
5. Maternal Involvement With Child	.28*	.55**
6. Opportunities for Variety in Daily Stimulation	.30*	.39**
Total score	.44**	.57**
Multiple correlation[a]	.50*	.63**

Source: Bradley, R. H., & Caldwell, B. M. (1976). The relation of infants' home environment to mental test performance at fifty-four months: A follow-up study. *Child Development, 47,* 1172–1174. Copyright © 1976 The Society for Research in Child Development, Inc. Adapted with permission.

a. This represents the correlation of all HOME subscales with Binet scores.

* p < .05.

** p < .01.

Children at Risk

The adverse effects of a nonstimulating environment are often exaggerated for children with early health problems (Caughy, 1996; Zeskind & Ramey, 1978). Early biological risk makes infants especially susceptible to the effects of poor parenting. Unfortunately, their biological impairments contribute to their problems by causing their often highly stressed parents to be less responsive to them. This in turn results in their slower intellectual development, which may further promote less intellectual stimulation from their parents. The result is a transaction that is less than conducive to good intellectual functioning.

Biological risks are only some of the factors that can adversely affect a child's intellectual development. Although far from the deprivation experienced by institutionalized children mentioned previously, children in many homes receive little direct attention, are talked to only minimally, and live in environments that are not conducive to developing intellectual skills suited for academic learning. For example, Betty Hart and Todd Risley (1995) documented that children's IQs are related to how much their parents talk to them and that by the age of 4 children from welfare families have heard approximately 30 million fewer words than children from professional families (see Chapter 9). Few children live in perfect homes, but as the risk factors mount, so do the negative effects on intelligence. This is known as the **cumulative deficit effect**. Multiple risks persisting over many years add up, and as a result, children who do not receive intervention display deficits in social, emotional, and cognitive functioning (G. W. Evans & Cassells, 2014).

The cumulative effects of multiple risk factors were illustrated in a longitudinal study conducted by Arnold Sameroff and his colleagues (1993). Children from mainly lower-SES homes were administered IQ tests at 4 and 13 years of age. Children's home environments were also evaluated for risk factors (for example, family size, father absence, maternal education, maternal stress, maternal anxiety). First, Sameroff and his colleagues reported that a composite score of risk factors associated with each child's home life accounted for 34% of the variance in IQ scores at 4 years of age and for 37% at 13 years of age. (This percentage increased to 50% at both ages when researchers used a more liberal measure of risk factors.) This relation is clearly seen in Figure 13.4, which shows IQ scores of 4-year-old children as a function of number of risk factors. Thus, environmental risk contributed significantly to children's IQ; this remained true even after SES and mothers' IQ scores were taken into consideration. Second, the researchers reported that children's IQ scores at age 4 were significantly related with their IQ scores at age 13 (correlation = 0.72). However, environmental risk scores were also highly correlated from 4 to 13 years (correlation = 0.76). Thus, children living in nonsupportive and high-risk environments at age 4 were likely to be living in similar environments at age 13. It is exactly under such conditions that high correlations in IQs over time are expected. It is also worth remembering that cumulated risks affect the whole child and not just intelligence. For example, in one study, cumulative risk exposure over childhood associated with poverty (for example, substandard housing, family turmoil) was associated with dysregulated cardiovascular responses and elevated cortisol levels (a measure of stress) during the teen years (G. W. Evans & Kim, 2007; 2012). Findings such as these provide support for *cascade models* of development (Masten & Cicchetti, 2010), which propose that early effects in one domain can spill over to other domains. For instance, Marc Bornstein and his colleagues have shown that infants who were more active and explored more at 5 months of age had higher levels of academic achievement in adolescence (Bornstein, Hahn, & Suwalsky, 2013).

FIGURE 13.4 **Cumulative effect, from Sameroff et al., 1993.** The relationship between the number of risk factors and IQ for a group of 4-year-old children. The greater the number of risk factors, such as low family income and father absence, the lower children's IQs tended to be.

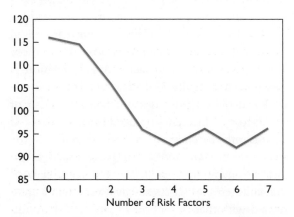

Source: Sameroff, A. J., Seifer, R., Baldwin, A., & Baldwin, C. (1993). Stability of intelligence from preschool to adolescence: The influence of social risk factors. *Child Development, 64,* 80–97.

A number of other longitudinal studies have examined the effects of combined biological and environmental risk on children's intellectual performance (Caughy, 1996; Landry et al., 1997). For example, Margaret Caughy (1996) examined the relation between several biological risk factors (low birth weight, length of hospitalization, rehospitalization during first year), environmental risk factors (low income, low maternal education, quality of the home environment as measured by a version of HOME scale), and tests of mathematical and reading readiness in a group of 867 children (ages 5 and 6 years). Caughy reported a strong relation between maternal education and HOME scores with both reading and mathematics performance. Not surprisingly, children from more intellectually supportive homes performed better on these tests. Also, biological risks (for example, low birth weight) adversely affected children's academic scores, although the impact of biological risk was not as great overall as that of environmental risk. And importantly, the children who were most adversely affected were those who experienced early health problems *and* who lived in intellectually nonstimulating environments, as reflected primarily by low HOME scores. For example, children who were rehospitalized during their first year of life and came from homes with low HOME scores (indicating a nonsupportive intellectual environment) had significantly lower mathematics scores than did children who came from similar homes (that is, also having low HOME scores) but who were not rehospitalized. In contrast, rehospitalization did not affect academic scores for those children who came from homes with higher HOME scores (that is, a supportive intellectual environment). These findings are consistent with the transactional model described earlier, and they indicate that children living in nonsupportive homes are especially affected by biological risk. A similar pattern between biological impairment at birth and quality of parents has been reported for measures of executive control at ages 6 and 9 years (C. A. C. Clark & Woodward, 2015).

Experience Counts

More than 40 years of research makes it clear that experiences during the preschool years set the stage for later intellectual accomplishments. Supportive and responsive environments tend to produce intelligent and competent children. Other research has extended beyond the family and shown that the quality of early child care outside the home predicts subsequent intellectual attainment (Li et al., 2013; Vandell et al., 2010).

For example, a study of more than 1,300 children examined the relationship between quality of nonrelative preschool child care and functioning at age 15 (Vandell et al., 2010). The researchers reported that quality child care was associated with greater cognitive-academic achievement in adolescence as well as with better emotional functioning (less externalizing behavior).

It is impossible to specify when, during childhood, these experiences are most important. Rather, from the available literature one can conclude that early experience is important, but so is later experience. From a transactional perspective, we cannot put any numbers or percentages on how much of intellectual growth is influenced by nature versus nurture. From the current perspective, in fact, *how much* is the wrong question. The better question concerns how nature and nurture interact to yield a particular pattern of development.

Modification and Maintenance of Intellectual Functioning

It seems clear from the preceding discussion that individual differences in intelligence can be influenced by a child's early environment. A related series of questions concerns the modification of intelligence. Will the elevated or depressed IQ levels found in some populations still be present decades later, or can people's level of intellectual functioning be modified by subsequent experiences? In this section, the modification and maintenance of intellectual functioning are considered for two related sets of conditions. First, to what extent are the intellectual deficits resulting from an impoverished early environment permanent? That is, can the deleterious effects of deprivation be ameliorated? And second, to what extent are the intellectual benefits resulting

from enriched early environments permanent? In other words, are intellectual skills acquired during the preschool years maintained into later childhood?

Modification of Intellectual Impairment Caused by Early Experience

As we noted earlier, an impoverished environment often results in reduced mental functioning. Based on the results of institutionalization studies of the type described earlier (W. Dennis, 1973; Spitz, 1945), it was once assumed that the deleterious effects of stimulus and social deprivation were permanent. Nevertheless, evidence suggesting the reversibility of the negative consequences of early deprivation has surfaced from time to time. Observations of children reared in relative isolation, for example, have indicated some plasticity of intellectual functioning with rehabilitation.

One of the best-documented studies concerning the mental growth of isolated children is that of Jarmila Koluchova (1976). A set of monozygotic twins who were physically and psychologically normal at 11 months experienced abuse, neglect, and malnutrition until discovered at 7 years 2 months of age. The children had no language and an estimated mental age of about 3 years. They were placed in foster care and provided with an educational program in the hope that they would attain some semblance of intellectual normalcy. The program was far more successful than originally expected; the twins had WISC scores of 93 and 95 by 11 years of age and 101 and 100 by 14 years. Several other studies have similarly reported normal intellectual or language functioning following educational intervention for children initially classified as intellectually impaired because of neglect or isolation during the preschool years (see Clarke & Clarke, 1976). Related to these findings are reports of drastic changes in the intellectual performance of children from war-torn Southeast Asia in the 1970s who were adopted into American homes (E. A. Clark & Hanisee, 1982; Winick, Meyer, & Harris, 1975), which we discussed briefly in Chapter 2. It must be noted, however, that these are exceptions. Not all children who experience severe deprivation early in life show such reversibility as a result of later education (Curtiss, 1977).

Harold Skeels (1966) reported one controversial study concerning the reversibility of the negative effects of early experience, which we discussed briefly in Chapter 1. He studied infants who were wards of an orphanage. The orphanage was similar to many other Depression-era institutions, overcrowded and understaffed, and it was the type of institution that had been associated with reduced mental functioning by as early as 4 months of age (Spitz, 1945). During the course of several years, 13 children (10 girls and 3 boys) were transferred to a school for the intellectually impaired and placed on the wards of the brighter women inmates. These infants all showed signs of intellectual impairment at the time of placement. Their IQ scores ranged from 35 to 89, with an average of 64.3. The average age at placement was 19 months, with a range from 7 to 36 months. These 13 children made up the experimental group. A contrast group (eight boys and four girls) was chosen from children who remained in the orphanage until at least the age of 4. The mean IQ score of the children in this group was 86.7 when first tested (mean age at first test = 16 months), with a range from 50 to 101.

The children in the experimental group received loving attention from the intellectually impaired women. There was competition between wards to see who would have the first baby to walk or to talk. The attendants also spent much time with the youngsters. In almost every case, a single adult (inmate or attendant) became closely attached to a child, resulting in an intense, one-to-one relationship that was supplemented by other adults. The experimental children remained in the institution for an average of 19 months and were then returned to the orphanage, with most being subsequently placed in adoptive homes. On their removal from the school for the intellectually impaired, each child was administered an IQ test; the average score was 91.8, an increase of 27.5 points. The children in the contrast group were tested at approximately 4 years of age and had an average IQ score of 60.5 points, a decline of 26.2 points. Both groups of children were retested approximately 2.5 years later, with the experimental group having an average score of 95.9 and the contrast group an average of 66.1 (see Figure 1.4 in Chapter 1).

The results of this study are very impressive, and they demonstrate that toddlers characterized as severely impaired can realize significant gains in intelligence when placed in certain environments. Skeels extended his study by following these people into adulthood when they were 25 to 35 years old. IQ tests were not given, but information was obtained concerning the occupational and educational levels of the participants, as was information pertaining to their social adjustment. All 13 people in the experimental group had married, whereas only 2 of the 11 surviving members of the contrast group had married. The median number of years of formal education completed by the experimental group was 12 (that is, high school education), whereas the contrast group had completed a median of only 2.75 years. Most experimental participants or their spouses were employed in skilled or semiskilled jobs. The range of SES, based on income and occupation, was comparable with regional norms. In comparison, people in the contrast group were in the lowest two socioeconomic levels. Four of the people in the contrast group remained institutional inmates; five held menial jobs, such as dishwashers or cafeteria help; and only one had a skilled occupation (compositor and typesetter). IQ scores were available for some of the 28 children of the experimental participants and ranged from 86 to 125, with an average of 103.9. In general, people in the experimental group, who started life with a severe disadvantage, were normal by a variety of intellectual, occupational, and social standards.

The Skeels study (1966) demonstrates the potential plasticity of human intelligence. However, the study is not without its detractors. As an experiment, it leaves much to be desired. Skeels took advantage of a naturally occurring situation and assessed the effects of early environments within the constraints imposed on him by ethical and institutional considerations. As a result, there is much to fault with the methodology of the study, and although the study has been widely praised, its serious shortcomings have also been noted (see Longstreth, 1981).

One interpretation of Skeels's study, consistent with the transactional view of development, is that the cognitive immaturity of the intellectually impaired women might actually have facilitated social interaction with the children, providing those children with stimulation they would not normally have received in the orphanage. In most situations, the characteristics of the severely impaired children in the experimental group would not produce lavish attention from adults. Most well-intending adults who direct their attention to a child expect some response in return. Children who are nonresponsive and generally lethargic tend not to elicit continued stimulation from adults, particularly adults from highly stressed homes (Sameroff & Chandler, 1975). This presumably would be especially true of overburdened members of an institution's staff. Because of the limited mental capacity of the inmates, however, their attention might have been repeatedly directed to the children even in the absence of appropriate responses. After prolonged stimulation, the children might have become more responsive and begun the climb back to normal intellectual functioning. That is, the intellectual immaturity of the institutionalized women in the Skeels study may have matched the needs of the children.

Of course, highly responsive people of normal or above-normal intelligence could also have served as appropriate "therapists" for these children, as was apparently the case in the Asian adoption studies cited earlier (E. A. Clark & Hanisee, 1982). But this is not the type of experience that these children could have expected from the orphanage staff. Moreover, had the children remained in the institution for the intellectually impaired for considerably longer, their intellectual gains would surely have been lost. As their intelligence increased, so would their needs for intellectual stimulation, quickly exceeding the boundaries of what the intellectually impaired women could have provided.

As we noted earlier, deprived environments for young children are not ancient history. Such environments were prevalent in Romania and other countries in the 1990s and are still found in parts of Eastern Europe, Asia, and Africa today. Many infants discovered in these orphanages were adopted into advantaged homes across the globe. Some were adopted very early in life (0 to 6 months), whereas others were not adopted until after 2 or 3 years of age (Beckett et al., 2006; Rutter & the English and Romanian Adoptees (ERA) Study Team, 1998; Rutter,

O'Connor, & the ERA Study Team, 2004). What happened to these children, all of whom were suffering from the effects of malnutrition and emotional neglect when adopted? Were they able to catch up, and if so, by how much? What effect did age of adoption (or, stated another way, time spent institutionalized) have on their eventual recovery? Research examining the course of development for Romanian children adopted in the United Kingdom (UK) provides some preliminary answers to these questions (Beckett et al., 2006; T. G. O'Connor et al., 2000). Romanian children left their institutions for adoptive UK homes at ages ranging from a few months to 42 months of age. For comparison purposes, they were classified into one of three groups: (1) those adopted from 0 to 6 months, (2) those adopted from 6 to 24 months, and (3) those adopted at more than 24 months. These children were compared with a group of infants born in the United Kingdom and adopted by other UK parents. All the UK-born children were adopted from 0 to 6 months of age. All children were administered the McCarthy scale at 6 and 11 years of age; this scale produces a global cognitive index (GCI) that has a population mean of 100 (like an IQ test).

Figure 13.5 shows the average IQs of adopted Romanian children at ages 6 and 11 years as a function of their age of placement in UK homes. As you can see, despite the early deprivation experienced by these children, those who were adopted within their first 6 months of life showed no long-term effects of their deprivation, having IQ scores comparable to those of the UK sample. IQs were lower for children adopted at later ages, particularly those adopted after 24 months. However, note that the 11-year IQs were higher than the 6-year IQs for these late-adopted children, suggesting a catch-up effect for the children who experienced the longest deprivation.

FIGURE 13.5 **IQ scores for adopted Romanian children at 6 and 11 years of age as a function of their age of placement in adoptive homes.** Also shown are the IQs for a group of UK adopted children.

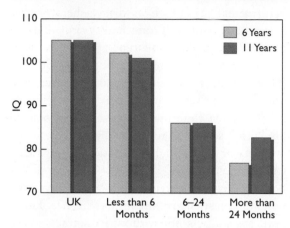

Source: Beckett, C., Maughan, B., Rutter, M., Castle, J., Colvert, E., Groothues, C., . . . Sonuga-Barke, E. J. S. (2006). Do the effects of early severe deprivation on cognition persist into early adolescence? Findings from the English and Romanian Adoptee Study. *Child Development, 77,* 696–711.

As we mentioned previously, there are methodological problems with these studies. For instance, children from these institutions who are adopted or selected for foster care may be brighter or more maturationally advanced than children who remain institutionalized. One study was able to overcome this problem by randomly assigning Romanian infants who had been abandoned at birth to either foster care or continued institutional care. These infants were then tested at 54 months of age and compared to a group of never-institutionalized infants being reared by their biological families in Bucharest, Romania (C. A. Nelson et al., 2007). (To conduct such a random-assignment study raises certain ethical issues, which the authors of this study considered carefully and discussed in some detail.)

The effects of institutionalization on IQ were significant, with the institutionalized group having an average IQ of 73 at 54 months, compared to average IQs of 81 for the foster care group and of 109 for the never-institutionalized group. Perhaps of greater interest were differences in the IQs of children in the foster care group as a function of their age at placement (see Figure 13.6). Children who were placed in foster care by 2 years of age had significantly higher IQs than children who were placed in foster care after age 2. In fact, as you can see from the figure, children placed in foster care after 30 months of age had IQs similar to those of children in the institutionalized group (72 vs. 73). A similar pattern of results was found for language development, with children who were placed in foster care earlier showing greater subsequent language development than children placed in foster care at a later age. In fact, children placed in foster

care after 24 months of age displayed the same severe language delays as children who remained institutionalized (Windsor et al., 2011).

These findings indicate not only the remarkable resilience of children to the effects of early deprivation but also the long-term consequences of prolonged nutritional, social, and emotional neglect. One should not be surprised that children who experienced more than 2 years of extreme deprivation demonstrated some long-term effects. However, that many of these children were functioning above normal at 6 years of age is impressive, and we must wait for future research before we know if this group will show any subsequent gains.

Compensatory Education Programs

Along similar lines, the short-term effectiveness of **compensatory education programs** has been well documented by several projects designed to provide preschool children from low-income homes with the intellectual skills necessary to do well in school. It has long been recognized that poverty is associated with lower academic and educational attainment. Parents from poor families typically fail to provide the type of child-rearing environments associated with academic attainment, and as a result, children from impoverished homes start school behind their middle-class peers, usually stay behind, and often lose even more ground the longer they stay in school (Ackerman, & Brown, 2006; NICHD Early Child Care Research Network, 2005). Beginning in the 1960s, compensatory education programs were established in the United States that aimed to provide preschool children at high risk for intellectual impairment and academic failure with the intellectual skills to do well in school (Klaus & Gray, 1968; Ramey, Campbell, &

FIGURE 13.6 **IQs at 54 months for children in the foster care group by age of placement in the study by Nelson and colleagues (2007).** Children placed in foster care before 2 years of age had significantly higher IQs than children placed in foster care after 2 years of age.

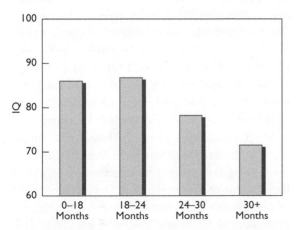

Source: Nelson, C. A., III, Zeanah, C. H., Fox, N. A., Marshall, P. J., Smuke, A. T., & Guthrie, D. (2007). Cognitive recovery in socially deprived young children: The Bucharest Early Intervention Program. *Science, 318,* 1937–1940.

Finkelstein, 1984). Such programs have raised the IQ scores of high-risk children by 10 to 15 points during the program.

Generally, children in the more rigorous, highly structured programs demonstrated the greatest gains. In some studies, large gains in IQ level were noted relative to control children and to the children's performance before they entered the programs (see Barnett, 1995). In others, intervention began shortly after birth, with children demonstrating high IQ scores relative to control children at every age tested, thus never needing compensation for below-average intellectual achievement (Garber, 1988; Ramey et al., 1984).

Many studies have attempted to increase children's intellectual functioning using a variety of methods, from nutritional supplements to training in executive function. John Protzko, Joshua Aronson, and Clancy Blair (2013) performed a series of meta-analyses on studies that purported to enhance young children's intellectual functioning and concluded that intelligence can, indeed, be increased. The factors they found to significantly increase young children's intellectual functioning were dietary supplements for infants (especially those containing long-chain polyunsaturated fatty acids), enrolling children in intense early educational intervention programs, reading to children in an interactive manner (see "Reading and Talking to Children" in Chapter 3), and attending preschool.

Before we move on, let us consider a final question relating to the reversibility of deleterious effects of early experience: At what age is plasticity lost? Unfortunately, we are not able to answer this question. We do know from animal research that plasticity is reduced with age and that we are most malleable as infants (see Chapter 2). Human development has been proposed to be highly *canalized* during the first 18 or 24 months of life, meaning that all children follow the species-typical path "under a wide range of diverse environments and exhibit strong self-righting tendencies following exposure to severely atypical environments" (McCall, 1981, p. 5). In other words, although early maladaptive environments might adversely affect infants, there is a strong tendency to return to a course of normalcy given an appropriate environment. This plasticity is progressively reduced later in life, beginning as early as 18 or 24 months of age. In general, the earlier intervention is begun, the greater its chance of reversing an established behavior pattern, if for no other reason than older children and adults are more reluctant than younger children to accept the imposition of a drastically changed environment.

Maintenance of the Beneficial Effects of Early Experience on Intelligence

If the effects of a negative early environment can be reversed, what about the effects of a beneficial early environment? If intelligence can be modified for the better by experiences later in childhood, can a later-childhood environment also modify a child's intellectual functioning for the worse? For the most part, evidence of the long-term effects of positive early environments comes from follow-up studies of preschool compensatory education programs. Although the initial reports of these programs were favorable, doubts concerning their long-term effectiveness began to surface shortly thereafter. The initial gains in IQ and academic performance shown by program graduates were slowly lost, and by the end of the fourth grade, levels of intellectual attainment were comparable between children who had participated in the programs and those who had not

(R. H. Bradley, Burchinal, & Casey, 2001; Klaus & Gray, 1968). Figure 13.7 shows the typical pattern of IQ changes for graduates of preschool intervention programs.

Despite these findings, researchers were not ready to dismiss the influence of early compensatory education on the later intellectual functioning of high-risk children, and several investigators inquired into the long-term (middle school and beyond) consequences of the preschool experience. Two of the more comprehensive investigations of the long-term effects of preschool compensatory education programs were reported by Irving Lazar and his colleagues (1982), who evaluated the effects of 11 experimental programs, and by W. Steven Barnett (1995), who examined the effects of 36 model demonstration projects and large-scale public programs, such as Head Start. The findings of the two studies were similar. Compensatory preschool programs had minimal long-term effects on IQ and academic achievement. Although the

FIGURE 13.7 **Typical pattern of IQ changes for experimental and control children during preschool program (2 to 6 years) and after.**

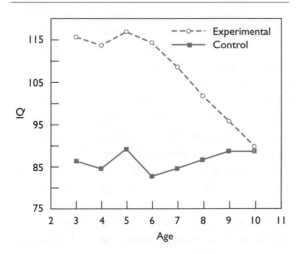

programs had an initial impact on children's IQ scores, few reliable differences were found between experimental and control participants by 10 years of age. Preschool graduates did score higher on some achievement tests than control children did, but this effect was not widespread.

More encouraging findings were found for school competence. For example, Lazar and his colleagues (1982) reported the median rate of assignment to special education classes was 13.8% for children who had participated in preschool programs and 28.6% for control children. Although less dramatic, there were also significant group differences in the percentage of children who were held back in grade. The median grade-retention rate was 30.5% for children in the control group and 25.8% for children who had participated in the preschool programs. Differences were also found in children's attitudes toward achievement. Program graduates were more likely to give achievement-related reasons for being proud of themselves, and the mothers of the experimental children felt more positively about their children and their likelihood of success than did the mothers of the control subjects.

There have been some important exceptions to this general pattern, including the North Carolina Abecedarian Program (Campbell & Ramey, 1994; Campbell et al., 2001, 2002; Ramey et al., 2000). Children from rural North Carolina who were identified as at risk for intellectual impairment attended an educationally oriented day-care program beginning shortly after birth and continuing until they entered first grade. When tested at age 12, children who had attended the preschool program had significantly higher IQ scores (94) than did control children (88). Also, children in the preschool group scored consistently higher on a battery of academic tests (Woodcock-Johnson Psychoeducational Battery; see Figure 13.8). Many of these differences were maintained when participants were tested at age 21 (Campbell et al., 2002), although the effects were greater for women than for men. As adults, members of the experimental group continued to score higher on measures of math and reading, were more likely to attend college (36% versus 14%), were more likely to have a skilled job (47% versus 27%), were less likely to have had their first child at age 18 or younger (36% versus 45%), and were less likely to smoke (39% versus 55%) or to use marijuana (18% versus 39%) than were members of the control group (T. Zimmerman, 2007). Similar effects of greater sixth-grade reading and math achievement for high-risk children who attended an urban preschool program relative to control

FIGURE 13.8 **Mean scores on Woodcock-Johnson Psychoeducational Battery at age 12 for children who participated in the Abecedarian preschool program and control children.**

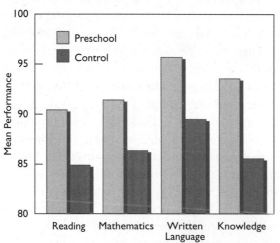

Source: Adapted from data presented in Campbell, F.A., & Ramey, C. T. (1994). Effects of early intervention on intellectual and academic achievement: A follow-up study of children from low-income families. *Child Development, 65,* 684–698.

children have also been reported (Reynolds et al., 1996). There were also some noncognitive benefits for children who attended the Abecedarian Program; graduates of the Abecedarian Program had significantly lower risk factors associated with cardiovascular and metabolic diseases than control children when evaluated in their mid-30s (Campbell et al., 2014).

Head Start, a nationwide, publicly funded program, was not set up as an experiment, making it difficult to evaluate the long-term benefits in a scientific way. However, research has shown positive effects of Head Start attendance on children's early math and literacy skills (E. B. Miller et al., 2014), and several studies have shown that children who attended Head Start were more likely to complete high school (Ludwig & Miller, 2007) and, for African Americans, were less likely to be charged with or convicted of a crime (Graces, Thomas, & Currie, 2002). This has caused some analysts to conclude that the Head Start Program, as it is currently operated, is worth the public expense from a strictly economic perspective (Ludwig & Phillips, 2008).

The findings of the long-term benefits of preschool intervention are somewhat mixed. On the one hand, most (but not all) studies found that the intellectual benefits realized during the preschool years were lost when the program responsible for those gains was discontinued. Once intellectual competence is attained, it must be maintained. Apparently, the intellectual environment for most of the low-income children was not sufficiently supportive after leaving the program to maintain the level of intelligence established during the preschool years. On the other hand, several studies have reported long-term intellectual effects, and taken together, several significant and important noncognitive benefits of compensatory education have been found. The difference in assignment to special education classes alone represents a significant savings in tax dollars, justifying the cost of the preschool programs (Karoly et al., 1998). Furthermore, differences in grade retention (and presumably the probability of completing high school) and in personal and maternal attitudes suggest that program graduates will be more likely to succeed economically in the years to come than will children in the control conditions. In an extensive review of the literature, economist Flavio Cunha and his colleagues (2006) reported that early interventions have long-term effects on motivation, which in turn affects achievement-test scores, school participation, delinquency, and teenage pregnancy rates, and concluded that "early interventions have a substantial effect on adult performance and have a high economic return" (p. 801).

How Modifiable Is Human Intelligence?

In general, the results of the studies reviewed in the previous sections indicate that the negative effects of early experience can be reversed and that the beneficial effects of an early stimulating environment can be altered by experiences that follow. Human intelligence is modifiable in both positive and negative directions. Intelligence is not something that, once gotten, is necessarily kept. Intelligence, as measured by IQ tests, reflects a person's intellectual functioning at a given time. Once established, intelligence (or any other complex behavior, for that matter) must be maintained. If the environmental supports responsible for establishing cognitive competence are removed, we should not be surprised that intelligence suffers.

The results of these studies reflect a flexible cognitive system that can be greatly modified by changes in the environment during childhood.

However, the research cited can be criticized for not being representative of the way the world is structured for most children. Fortunately, few children spend their early years restricted to stultifying institutions, and most children who are provided stimulating environments as preschoolers can expect comparably stimulating environments in the years to come. These studies indicate what *can* happen to levels of intelligence during childhood, not necessarily what actually *does* happen. Children's environments do change normally over time, such as the transition from home to school and a related shift from a family-centered to a peer-centered lifestyle. To the extent that these changes in environments do not represent major shifts in intellectual emphasis, levels of intelligence can be expected to be maintained. The more diverse the changing environments are, the greater the change in level of intelligence that can be expected.

Section Review

Researchers have examined how different types of childhood experiences contribute to the level of intellectual functioning that a child achieves.

Establishing Intellectual Competence

- Early approaches to assessing the effects of experience on intelligence examined the effects of institutionalization on children's IQs, demonstrating that intellectual functioning can be seriously impaired under conditions of physical and social deprivation.
- Naturalistic studies of parent-child interaction, often assessing the quality of the environment using the *HOME scale*, generally find that parents who provide their children with a variety of objects to play with and who are responsive have brighter

children than do parents who provide less intellectual stimulation.

- The effects of a nonstimulating environment tend to be especially detrimental for children with early medical problems.
- The *cumulative deficit effect* refers to multiple risks that persist over many years adding up and contributing to deficits in social, emotional, and cognitive functioning.

Modification and Maintenance of Intellectual Functioning

- Early environmentally induced intellectual impairment can be reversed under certain conditions.
- Children from intellectually impoverished, low-income homes who receive cognitively enriched early experience through intensive *compensatory education programs* display immediate gains in IQ scores.
- Follow-up data indicate that many of the gains manifested by these children in compensatory education programs are lost after the program ends.

How Modifiable Is Human Intelligence?

- Once intellectual accomplishments are established, they must be maintained by subsequent environments. If the contexts of early, middle, and later childhood are highly similar, the relative level of intelligence is likely to be comparable across these years.

Ask Yourself . . .

6. What is an example of the cumulative deficit effect? How does this relate to the cascade effect?
7. What types of early environments support intellectual functioning and development? What types are detrimental? What evidence is there that the effects of these early experiences are stable over time versus open to modification?

STABILITY OF INTELLIGENCE

We like to believe that the world we live in is relatively stable and predictable. This predilection includes some implicit beliefs concerning the stability of mental functioning. To what extent is intellectual functioning, as measured by IQ or other general assessments of intelligence, stable over time? Will a bright 5-year-old turn out to be an intelligent teenager, or is a prediction of adolescent and adult intelligence from early childhood intelligence no more reliable than tossing a coin? And what about infancy? Is there any way that we can predict what level of intellectual functioning a child will attain from assessments during infancy? And on a different level, has the average intelligence of people stayed the same over decades? Are we perhaps getting smarter (or dumber) as a culture or a species?

Defining Stability

Before looking at any evidence, let us define again what is meant by stability. Obviously, stability does not mean that intelligence stays the same over time. Of course, children get smarter as they get older. Rather, stability refers to the relative constancy of individual differences—the extent to which different children maintain their rank order over time in comparison with their peers. Is the valedictorian of her kindergarten class likely to be among the top students when her high school class graduates? Is the highly attentive 4-month-old likely to be a better reader than his less attentive peer? Stability in this sense is measured by correlations of rank order. If a group of children is given IQ tests at age 5, for example, they can be ranked in IQ score from highest to lowest. If that same group is tested again at age 10, we can compare the rankings of the children's IQ scores at the two ages. If the rankings are similar, the correlation will be positive and high. If there is no stability of individual differences in IQ scores between ages 5 and 10, the correlation will be close to 0. It is also possible, although unlikely, that the brightest children at age 5 will be, on the average, the least bright children at age 10, resulting in a negative correlation. Note that the correlations used to assess stability are unrelated to the actual level of performance. Correlations may be high, implying stability, even though the average level of performance might have systematically increased (or decreased) for most members of the sample.

In the following sections we examine research on the stability of individual differences in intelligence over time. For the most part, IQ data are used as a measure of intellectual functioning, although several studies that used other measures of cognition are also reported. In addition to investigating stability of intelligence via cross-age correlations, we also examine patterns of change. That is, although there might be high correlations between measures of intelligence at two ages, it does not mean that intelligence has not changed during that period. In other words, the relationship between developmental function—patterns of change that characterize the species—and the stability of individual differences will be evaluated.

Predicting Later Intelligence From Tests in Infancy

One research topic in cognitive development that received much attention in the recent past has been that of predicting childhood IQ from measures taken in infancy. Before presenting this research, let us provide a little necessary history.

Psychometricians have generally believed that intelligence is stable across time, including from infancy into childhood. In part, this prediction is based on the assumption that human intelligence can be described most accurately as a unitary construct that varies in a continuous fashion over time. From a psychometric perspective, this is best described as a single general factor of intelligence, g. When developmental function is continuous and quantitative in nature, there is every reason to expect that individual differences will be stable (**continuity with stability**).

Testing this hypothesis is relatively straightforward: Tests given in infancy are correlated with IQ tests given in childhood. The problem, of course, is developing tests that assess intelligence in infancy. Such tests have been around for nearly 70 years in the form of infant psychometric scales that produce a DQ (developmental quotient) with the same psychometric properties as IQ tests. Examples from one of these tests, the Bayley Scales of Infant Development, were presented in Chapter 12. However, when babies who were given the Bayley or other scales are later administered IQ tests in early childhood, the correlations are disappointingly low. Prediction is only slightly greater for high-risk infants. Table 13.3 summarizes the results of studies examining the relationship between infant tests of development and later IQ scores for both typically developing and high-risk samples as a function of age at testing (both in infancy and in childhood). As can be seen, the correlations are uniformly low; the average correlation between infant tests and IQ scores at 6 years of age is only 0.11 for typically developing infants. Prediction is often considerably higher for infants scoring very low on the tests (for example, below 80), suggesting some power of these tests to predict pathology in limited situations (see McCall, Hogarty, & Hurlburt, 1972).

TABLE 13.3 **Median correlations between DQ test scores and later IQ test scores for normal and high-risk samples.**

Infant test (months)	Normal sample					High-risk sample			
	Age at follow-up test (years)					Age at follow-up test (years)			
	3	4–5	6+	Mean		3	4–5	6+	Mean
3–4	.04	.06	.07	.06		.14	.08	.07	.10
	(4)*	(2)	(3)			(2)	(4)	(2)	
5–7	.25	.20	.06	.15		.27	.24	.28	.26
	(14)	(5)	(6)			(5)	(13)	(3)	
8–11	.20	.23	.21	.21		.29	.23	.29	.27
	(8)	(5)	(3)			(6)	(10)	(6)	
Mean	.16	.16	.11			.23	.18	.21	

Source: Fagan, J. F., III, & Singer, J. T. (1983). Infant recognition memory as a measure of intelligence. In L. P. Lipsitt & C. K. Rovee-Collier (Eds.), *Advances in infancy research* (Vol. 2, pp. 32–78). Norwood, NJ: Ablex. Reprinted with permission.

* Numbers in parentheses represent number of studies in each median correlation.

This should be very discouraging for people who believe the continuity-with-stability theory of intelligence, yet there is always the argument that the infant DQ tests are not sensitive enough and that new tests will eventually find the relationship. Others have looked at these data, however, and are not surprised. The reason for the low correlations is that development varies in a discontinuous way between infancy and childhood, with *qualitative* differences in the nature of intelligence. When developmental function is discontinuous (that is, relatively abrupt and qualitative in nature), there is no reason to expect stability. Using Piaget's account of cognitive development, the bright sensorimotor child might become a bright preoperational child, for example, but because of the substantial difference in the nature of cognition between the infant and the preschool child, such stability should not be expected.

This discontinuity-with-instability position was best articulated by Robert McCall and his colleagues (McCall, Eichorn, & Hogarty, 1977), who demonstrated, using longitudinal data, little stability of individual differences in cognitive performance even across different stages in infancy, to say nothing of between infancy and later childhood. For example, McCall and his associates were able to identify five stages in cognitive development between birth and 3 years of age using data from DQ tests: (1) birth to 2 months, (2) 2 to 8 months, (3) 8 to 13 months, (4) 13 to 21 months, and (5) 21 to between 31 and 36 months. These stages correspond roughly and Piaget's stages of sensorimotor development, as outlined in Chapter 5. McCall and his colleagues found substantial stability of individual differences (that is, high cross-age correlations) when comparing performance *within* a stage (for example, from 8 to 12 months) but much less stability (that is, low cross-age correlations) when comparisons were made *between* stages (for example, from 10 to 14 months). These data very nicely demonstrate continuity with stability for contrasts *within* a cognitive stage and discontinuity with instability for contrasts *between* cognitive stages.

This, basically, is where the argument stood until the 1980s, when new research reported evidence for stability of intelligence from infancy to childhood. The evidence came from what to many was an unlikely source—measures of infant memory and attention. Recall the habituation/dishabituation paradigm from our discussions of infant perception and attention in Chapter 4. Infants are presented a stimulus (a picture, for example), and their attention to that stimulus is noted (in this case, looking time). The same stimulus is presented repeatedly, with the typical finding that infant attention to the stimulus decreases. When attention to the stimulus decreases sufficiently (usually to 50% of what it was on the initial trials), the infant is said to have habituated to the stimulus.

This same technique has been used to assess recognition memory. Sometime after habituation (minutes, hours, or even days), the infant is shown two stimuli, usually simultaneously. One stimulus is the same picture the infant had been habituated to earlier. The other stimulus is a new one. Memory is indicated if infants look at the novel stimulus more than at the habituated stimulus. They remember the old stimulus and are still tired of looking at it. This *preference-for-novelty* measure has been used extensively and has revealed much about infant memory capacity. (See further discussion in Chapter 8.)

Psychologists began to look for relationships between individual differences in measures of infant attention/memory and childhood IQ.

Joseph Fagan was the first person to systematically examine this relationship, which is fitting, given that he was a pioneer of the preference-for-novelty technique in assessing infant recognition memory.

In an early review, Fagan and Lynn Singer (1983) examined the results of previously published experiments concerning the prediction of childhood intelligence from infants' preferences for novelty by means of visual recognition, and they also reported the results of their own longitudinal study. The ages of the infants assessed ranged from 3 to 7 months, and assessments of later childhood IQ for 12 sets of data ranged from 2 to 7.5 years. The range of correlations between infants' preferences for novelty and later IQ was 0.33 to 0.66, with a mean value of 0.44. That is, the stronger an infant's preference for novelty was (the more they looked at the novel versus the familiar stimulus), the higher their IQ during early childhood was apt to be. Compare this with the values given in Table 13.3, where average correlations between sensorimotor tests and IQ scores for normal infants ranged from 0.16 (for IQ tests given from the ages of 3 to 5 years) to 0.11 (for IQ tests given at age 6 and beyond). Similar results were later reported using habituation measures, with infants who habituate faster having higher childhood IQs (see Bornstein, 1989; Bornstein et al., 2006; Bornstein & Sigman, 1986).

Habituation and preference-for-novelty tasks have been used with hearing and touch as well as vision, and researchers have reported comparable correlations with childhood IQ when infants are tested in these other modalities (for hearing, see J. J. O'Connor, Cohen, & Parmelee, 1984; for touch, see Rose et al., 1991). Results are found both for full-term infants (Rose, Feldman, & Wallace, 1992) and for preterm infants (Rose et al., 1989). Subsequent reviews of the literature demonstrated the reliability of these findings (Bornstein et al., 2006; McCall & Carriger, 1993). Average correlations between infant measures of habituation or preference for novelty and childhood IQ are about 0.40 or higher. This compares with correlations of about 0.15 between tests like the Bayley scales and later IQ. (The latest version of the Bayley [2005] scales includes items to assess some of the basic cognitive abilities believed to underlie infant intelligence. To our knowledge, no published studies have assessed the new Bayley scales' ability to predict childhood IQ.)

The evidence just cited indicates a moderate degree of continuity of developmental function and stability of individual differences from infancy to early childhood. Given these findings, how might continuity of developmental function be interpreted? Marc Bornstein and Marian Sigman (1986) examined several possibilities and concluded that the high correlations can best be explained by the continuity of an underlying process. This model proposes that a constant process underlies individual differences in both the allocation of infant attention and later performance on tests of intelligence. The question is, what might that process be?

Most researchers have assumed that habituation and preference for novelty involve information-processing mechanisms that are stable in form during infancy and into childhood (Bornstein & Sigman, 1986; Fagan, 1992, 2011; McCall & Carriger, 1993). Recall from our discussion of executive function in Chapter 7 that there are age-related differences in memory span, working memory, speed of processing, ability to inhibit thoughts and behaviors, ability to resist interference, and cognitive flexibility. Individual differences in these basic-level abilities are first seen in infancy and may be at the core of intelligence (Reznick, 2009). For

example, habituation and recognition memory involve encoding a stimulus, storing it, categorizing it, comparing a present stimulus with a memory representation, and discriminating the old from the new stimulus. McCall and Carriger (1993) further suggested that the information-processing mechanisms underlying performance might be "the disposition to inhibit responding to familiar stimuli and to stimuli of minor prominence (e.g., low energy, static, etc.)" (p. 77). Such a position is consistent with the evidence presented in Chapter 7 of age-related differences in sensitivity to interference and the ability to inhibit prepotent responses.

Another related aspect of information processing that might underlie both infant and childhood measures is the ability to process novelty. In particular, the preference-for-novelty paradigm used for assessing recognition memory involves the handling of novel information. Unlike many of the sensorimotor skills assessed on infant scales of intelligence, these abilities are also characteristic of cognition in later life and, thus, might serve as a basis for the continuity of intelligence. Along similar lines, Robert Sternberg (1985) argues that response to novelty is a major element of individual differences in intelligence that is constant across the life span (recall Sternberg's theory of successful intelligence from Chapter 12). He proposes that how people react to novel situations is central to most definitions of intelligence. Even what Piaget called assimilation and accommodation, for example, are essentially means for dealing with novel environmental events. In a similar vein, Harriet Rheingold (1985) stressed the importance of novelty in development. She asserted that the development of behavior, including mental processes, can be viewed as a process of becoming familiar with our world (both internal and external). The child's task in development is essentially to render the novel familiar. Thus, like Sternberg, Rheingold sees the process of acquiring new knowledge—that is, of rendering the novel familiar—to be a central aspect of development that is continuous throughout life.

Does this new evidence of continuity with stability from infancy to childhood mean that there is a general factor of intelligence, or *g*? The data certainly seem to point in that direction. Fagan (1992) believes that the origins of intelligence can be found in the infant's ability to process information and that such processing is tapped by habituation and recognition memory procedures. These basic-level information-processing abilities have a high heritability. This all suggests that there is a strong biological (genetic and possibly prenatal) basis for individual differences in intelligence. Fagan (1992) proposes that what underlies intelligence is best thought of as information-processing mechanisms rather than as a mental factor; nevertheless, the relatively high prediction of later intelligence from infant measures is consistent with the continuity-with-stability position advocated by *g* theorists.

Some evidence supports the idea of the stability of information-processing mechanisms that underlie tests in both infancy and childhood. For example, Susan Rose and Judith Feldman (1995) reported that visual-recognition memory tests given at 7 months correlated significantly at age 11 years not only with IQ scores (correlation = 0.41) but also with perceptual speed (correlation = 0.38). In other work, Thomas Dougherty and Marshall Haith (1997) found infant visual reaction time (the time it took infants to begin an eye movement toward a picture after it appeared) measured at 3.5 months of age correlated significantly both with childhood IQ (correlation = 0.44) and with childhood (age 4) visual reaction times (measured similarly as they were in infancy; correlation = 0.51). These studies argue

for cognitive continuity from infancy through childhood and for speed of processing as a likely component that underlies intellectual performance and that is responsible, at least in part, for the stability observed.

Yet the correlations, although substantially higher than those found with infant DQ tests, are far from perfect, and Fagan and others point out that individual differences in infant information processing do not constitute the whole picture. For example, reliable differences in IQ scores are found between children of different races and different parental educational backgrounds in the United States. But no differences are found between children of different races or with different parental educational backgrounds on measures of recognition memory (Fagan, 1984). This suggests that experiential factors play a separate role in the establishment of intelligence.

Catherine Tamis-LeMonda and Marc Bornstein (1989; see also Bornstein, 1989) nicely illustrated the combined influence of basic information-processing abilities and environmental factors. They demonstrated that the quality of mother-child interaction predicted childhood intelligence at age 4 independent of infant habituation rates. In other words, how parents interact with their babies has an important influence on their children's intelligence beyond that measured by habituation rate. This means that intelligence is a multifaceted thing, and we must interpret any global pronouncements concerning its development very cautiously.

Intelligence is not a single, well-defined dimension. If a *g* factor does exist, it reflects only part of the picture. The work of Fagan, Bornstein, and others suggests that at least some aspects of intelligence vary continuously during infancy and childhood and are stable over time. Yet the earlier claim by McCall and his colleagues—that intelligence during infancy changes in a discontinuous manner and is unstable over time—is also likely true. The difference is that the various investigators are measuring different aspects of infant intelligence, with some aspects changing continuously and showing stability and others changing discontinuously and showing instability.

Stability of IQ Scores During Childhood

Although infant psychometric measures do not predict later IQ scores well, the stability of individual differences in intelligence as measured by IQ tests increases dramatically by age 2. Table 13.4 summarizes the findings of longitudinal studies by Bayley (1949) and by Honzik, MacFarlane, and Allen (1948), and it presents the correlations between scores on IQ tests given at various times during childhood and IQ scores as young adults (17 or 18 years of age). Whereas the correlations between intelligence tests given at 12 months and at 18 years are approximately 0, the correlations rise quickly by the beginning

TABLE 13.4 **Cross-age correlations between IQ tests given in childhood and adult IQ scores.**

Age of tesing	Honzik, MacFarlane, and Allen (1948)	Bayley (1949)
1 year	—	−.14
2–3 years	.33	.40
4–5 years	.42	.52
6–7 years	.67	.68
8 9 years	.71	.80
10–11 years	.73	.87
12–13 years	.79	—
14–15 years	.76	.84

Sources: Bayley, N. (1949). Consistency and variability in the growth of intelligence from birth to eighteen years. *Journal of Genetic Psychology, 75,* 165–196; Honzik, M. P., MacFarlane, J. W., & Allen, L. (1948). Stability of mental test performance between 2 and 18 years. *Journal of Experimental Education, 17,* 309–324.

of the third year and are relatively stable from age 8 or so on. Correlations of IQs measured in adolescence or young adulthood continue to persist into old age (Deary, 2014; Deary, Pattie, & Starr, 2013; Schalke et al., 2012). Claire Kopp and Robert McCall (1982) stated, "Following age 5, IQ is perhaps the most stable, important behavioral characteristic yet measured" (p. 39).

Why should there be such a high degree of stability in IQ scores during childhood, especially when predictions from infant psychometric tests are so poor? In all likelihood, the reason for the increased stability of IQ scores beginning around age 2 is the increasing similarity both of the test items and of the nature of intelligence for children 2 years of age and beyond. Following Piaget, a qualitative change in intelligence occurs sometime from 18 to 30 months of age. Children become adept symbol users during this period, and they will remain symbol users throughout their lives. IQ tests are constructed to reflect meaningful dimensions of intelligence for people of a given age, and accordingly, the ability to retrieve and manipulate symbols is a central aspect of most (if not all) intelligence tests from the 2-year level onward. There is thus a continuity of developmental function to the extent that symbolic functioning is involved in measuring intelligence at all ages. Although continuity of developmental function does not necessitate stability of individual differences, it can be seen from the earlier discussion of IQ prediction based on infancy data that such a relationship probably exists.

Patterns of IQ Change During Childhood

Despite the impressive stability of the rank order of IQ scores from the early school years, there is still room for change, particularly change in the level of IQ. Recall that correlations of rank order are statistically independent of average values. So, for example, the average level of IQ scores could vary substantially for a particular sample of children and affect the correlations of rank order only minimally.

Robert McCall, Mark Appelbaum, and Pamela Hogarty (1973) examined patterns of IQ change during childhood based on data from the Fels Longitudinal Study. In their study, the data of 80 people (38 males and 42 females) who had been administered a Stanford-Binet IQ test at 17 points in development (ages 2.5, 3, 3.5, 4, 4.5, 5, 5.5, 6, 7, 8, 9, 10, 11, 12, 14, 15, and 17 years) were examined for changes in level and pattern of IQ scores over time.

First, how much change, in IQ points, was observed? The range of IQ scores for a given child was obtained, and the difference between a child's highest score during the 17 testing sessions and his or her lowest score was computed. Note that this is not the difference between a child's IQ score at 17 years and his or her score at 2.5 years but the difference between the highest and lowest scores a child received, independent of age. The average shift in IQ score for children in this sample was 28.5 points. The range for 21% of the children in this sample was 20 points or less, and 43% of the children shifted from 21 to 30 points sometime from 2.5 to 17 years of age. Slightly more than one third of the sample (36%) showed shifts of more than 30 points, with one child displaying an amazing increase of 74 points! Although such a drastic change is rare, other researchers have reported shifts of more than 50 points (Honzik et al., 1948; T. Moore, 1967). In general, it's fair to say that, on average, IQ scores changed substantially during the 15-year period.

One potential problem with longitudinal studies is that children can become "test wise" because of repeated testings. It is possible that the large shifts in IQ scores observed in this study were the result of practice effects, with the children getting better at taking the tests with experience, and that this resulted in elevated levels of performance as they grew older. This explanation, although reasonable, was not supported by the data. McCall and his colleagues (1973) subjected the IQ scores to cluster analysis, a statistical technique that discerns common patterns among sets of data. Thus, children showing similar patterns of IQ change over time would be grouped together in a single cluster. The cluster analysis yielded five distinct patterns of IQ change, graphed in Figure 13.9. The first thing to note is that the general trend is *not* consistently increasing IQ scores with each subsequent testing, making unlikely the hypothesis that the large IQ shifts observed for this sample were caused by practice effects.

The largest group was Cluster 1 (45% of the sample), with children displaying minimal systematic variation from a slightly rising pattern during childhood. Cluster 2 (11%) showed a sharp decline in IQ from ages 4 to 6 years, with a slight recovery in middle childhood, followed by a decrease in adolescence. Cluster 3 (13%) also showed a decline in IQ scores during the preschool years, followed by relatively stable performance from 6 to 14 years and an increase to age 17. Cluster 4 (9%) demonstrated a rapid rise in IQ scores, peaking from 8 to 10 years, followed by a comparably sharp decline. Cluster 5 (6%) showed a steady rise in IQ scores until age 8 or 10 years, much like the pattern for children in Cluster 4, but displayed less of a subsequent drop in scores. The data for 16% of the sample followed no consistent pattern.

Note in Figure 13.9 that the children having the highest IQ scores (Cluster 4) also displayed

FIGURE 13.9 **Mean IQ scores over time for five clusters of children in the study by McCall and colleagues (1973).**

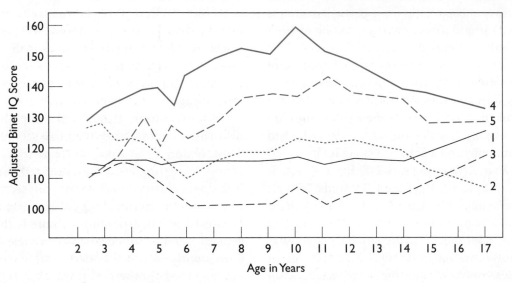

Source: McCall, R. B., Appelbaum, M. I., & Hogarty, P. S. (1973). Developmental changes in mental performance. *Monographs of the Society for Research in Child Development, 38*(Serial No. 150). Copyright © 1973 The Society for Research in Child Development, Inc. Reprinted with permission.

the greatest amount of IQ change. This result is consistent with the findings of other investigators, who have similarly reported that very bright children tend to change more in test scores over time than do children with lower scores (Terman & Merrill, 1937). Along these same lines, it is interesting to observe that for the two groups of children showing the overall highest levels of IQ (Clusters 4 and 5), scores increased until 8 or 10 years of age and then declined. One speculative interpretation of this pattern is that a transition in cognitive functioning (concrete to formal operations, for example) occurs at 8 to 10 years and that bright concrete operational thinkers, although making the transition to formal operations sooner than less bright children, do not maintain their

high level of performance for this qualitatively different style of thought. McCall and his colleagues (1973) also suggested that children's intellectual performance during the early school years is under the direct influence of their parents, who emphasize acquiring basic skills in math and reading. As children grow older and develop interests outside the home, parents' influence on their intellectual functioning wanes, and IQ scores drop accordingly (compare with Scarr & McCartney, 1983).

McCall and his colleagues (1973) obtained some support for this latter position. As part of the Fels Longitudinal Study, children and their parents were evaluated on a variety of behavioral and attitudinal factors. McCall and his associates examined aspects of parents' child-rearing, including their attitudes toward discipline and academic achievement. The children having the highest overall IQ scores and showing the most change in test scores during childhood (Clusters 4 and 5) were characterized by having parents who were classified as accelerating, in that they strove to increase their children's mental or motor development. These parents also tended to have clear household policies, were rewarding, and had medium to severe penalties for children's transgressions. The researchers described these parents as providing an encouraging and rewarding environment with some structure and enforcement of the rules. These findings are consistent with the researchers' view that the children's increase in IQ scores during the early school years resulted from the influence of their academically oriented parents. Children in the two clusters showing decreasing preschool IQ scores (Clusters 2 and 3) tended to have parents who were minimally accelerating. Children in Cluster 2 were the least severely penalized, whereas children in Cluster 3 were the most severely punished of any group. The parents of children in Cluster 1 showed a wide range of attitudes and behaviors.

This study by McCall and his colleagues (1973) indicates that substantial changes in IQ scores occur during childhood for some children. These findings should be considered relative to the very high stability of individual differences reported in the literature. How can rank order of individual differences be so high yet actual levels of IQ vary so drastically for some children? One clue to this paradox can be found by again examining Figure 13.9. Note that the lines depicting IQ change for the five clusters remain relatively distinct during the 15-year period. After age 7, there are only two points at which any line crosses another. Thus, despite the substantial variability in IQ scores that these lines

reflect, the rank order of the various clusters remained essentially unchanged for most testings. Moreover, recall again that the children who showed the greatest amount of change were high-IQ children. Because of the way IQ tests are constructed, a change in IQ score from 130 to 160 is not the same as a 30-point shift from 75 to 105. In the former case, a child's relative rank order changes from approximately the 97th to the 99th+ percentile. In both cases, a child would be brighter than all but a small minority of his or her agemates. In contrast, a change in IQ from 75 to 105 represents a change in relative rank order from about the 5th to the 63rd percentile, a change from borderline intellectually impaired to slightly above normal! As the data indicate, changes of the former type are more common than are changes of the latter type, leaving the impression, both statistically and intuitively, that intelligence is relatively stable over time (McCall et al., 1973).

Are People Getting Smarter? The Flynn Effect

In discussing the stability and consistency of IQ scores over time, we have necessarily made use of longitudinal data, in which the same people are tested at different points in their development. But a related question about changes in IQ over time can be asked: Has the absolute level of intelligence, as measured by IQ, changed during the past century? And if so, are we getting smarter or dumber?

As we mentioned in Chapter 12, IQ tests are routinely restandardized. One reason for this is to keep the tests relevant for contemporary populations. Questions that might have been appropriate for people in 1930 can be meaningless for people in 2017. Perhaps more critically, however, tests are restandardized so that the average remains at or about 100. If people start scoring higher or lower, on average, than 100, the test loses some of the statistical properties that make it such a valuable assessment tool. So there are several ways of evaluating whether average IQ scores have changed over historical time. One is to examine the scores of many people who take the same test at different times (for example, in 1960 versus in 1980). Another is to give people today versions of earlier IQ tests, standardized on samples decades before.

What prediction would you make? On the one hand, scores on standardized tests, such as the SAT, have reportedly declined during the past 40 years, and there has been much lament in the popular press about the "dumbing of America." Perhaps, then, IQ scores have gone down through the decades. On the other hand, more people are receiving both primary and secondary education than in decades past, and public health has improved considerably since the early years of the 20th century. So perhaps we're getting smarter.

The answer is that we're getting smarter and that this phenomenon is not limited to the United States but is worldwide. The average increase in IQ is about 3 to 15 points per decade, depending on what measure of IQ is used, which corresponds to more than a full standard deviation since 1940 (Trahan et al., 2014). This has been termed the **Flynn effect**, after James Flynn (1987, 2007, 2012), the first person to describe the phenomenon systematically. The increase appears to be larger for people on the low end of the IQ range, at least in most countries (Teasdale & Owen, 1989), and the effect seems to be slowing down or to have stopped (or even reversed) in recent decades in some countries (Teasdale & Owen,

2008). Moreover, the effect is not limited to the developed world but has been observed in rural areas of Kenya as well (T. C. Daley et al., 2003). Interestingly, a similar gain in Piagetian formal operational abilities among adolescents was also observed from the late 1960s to the mid-1990s (Flieller, 1999).

Figure 13.10 shows the gains in IQ from 1948 to 2002 for various IQ tests and subtests that would have occurred if the tests had not been periodically adjusted. The largest gains are for the Raven's Progressive Matrices test and the Similarities subtest of the WISC, both of which assess fluid intelligence. (In the Similarities subtest, children must tell how two things, such as radio and television—both forms of communication—or shark and butterfly—both animals—are alike.) The gain was much less for the Information, Arithmetic, and Vocabulary subtests of the WISC, each of which is proposed to assess crystalized intelligence.

How can this be explained? One possibility concerns more education for more people, which surely is a contributor to the change (Blair et al., 2005). However, the largest changes in performance are for *fluid abilities*, which are supposedly less influenced by education and cultural differences than are crystalized abilities, such as vocabulary (see Chapter 12). That is, the type of cognitions that have changed the most are those *least* influenced by education and culture. Another explanation relates to better nutrition and health care (T. C. Daley et al., 2003; see Neisser, 1998). More people are healthy; thus, fewer people score very low on IQ tests. A third speculation is that life has gotten more complex. Today, we are constantly bombarded with visual messages not only from television but also from photographs and billboards (Greenfield, 1998). The 20th century also saw the advent of movies,

FIGURE 13.10 **Examples of gains in intelligence test scores.** Shown here are IQ gains from 1948 to 2002, in the United States, as measured by Raven's Progressive Matrices, by the Wechsler Intelligence Scale for Children (Full Scale), and by several subtests of the Wechsler Intelligence Scale for Children (for brief descriptions of the subtests, see Table 12.1). These are the gains that would have occurred if the tests were not made more difficult and the scoring systems were not adjusted at each test revision.

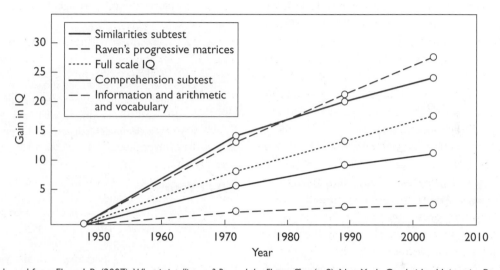

Source: Adapted from Flynn, J. R. (2007). *What is intelligence? Beyond the Flynn effect* (p. 8). New York: Cambridge University Press.

VCRs, DVDs, computers, video games, and smartphones. Children grow up inundated with visual information that must be organized and comprehended, and the argument goes, these experiences may directly affect fluid intelligence. James Flynn (2007, 2012) argues that improvements in education, greater use of technology, and more people being engaged in intellectually demanding work have led to a greater number of people dealing with abstract concepts than was the case in decades past, which in turn is responsible for elevated IQ scores.

The flexibility of fluid intelligence is demonstrated in studies examining cognitive abilities in 4- to 14-year-old Greek and Chinese children (Demetriou et al., 2005; Kazi et al., 2012). Although no differences were found in measures of general intelligence between the two groups, the Chinese children outperformed the Greek children on all measures involving visual/spatial processing. The researchers attributed these substantial differences to the Chinese children's extensive practice with their logographic (pictorial symbols) writing system, in contrast to the phonetic system used by Greek children.

If these gains reflect true increases in intelligence, they would indicate cultural changes of enormous magnitude. J. R. Flynn (1987, 2007, 2012), however, thinks otherwise. Surely some aspects of intellectual functioning have changed. But the absurdity of a 30-point or more IQ increase since 1900 must cause one to ponder what the IQ test is actually measuring. The IQ test is a good measure of intelligence and permits us to know where a person stands relative to other people in his or her cohort. But the fact that IQ can change so substantially over historical time emphasizes the relative nature of the measure. This does not diminish its usefulness, but it does suggest that an IQ score is not *the* measure of a permanent and stable intelligence.

Section Review

Stability of intelligence is the degree to which the rank order of individual differences remains constant over time.

Defining Stability and Predicting Later Intelligence From Tests in Infancy

- Stability is evaluated by cross-age correlations, with high correlations reflecting stability of individual differences.
- Evidence from the psychometric literature indicates that the correlation between scores on sensorimotor tests given in infancy and IQ scores later in childhood is low.
- Other research has shown significant correlations between measures of infants' preference for novelty and rate of habituation and later IQ scores.
- The findings suggest that infant intelligence is multifaceted, with some aspects presumably developing in a continuous fashion (*continuity with stability*) and others developing in a discontinuous fashion (*discontinuity with instability*).

Stability of IQ Scores During Childhood and Patterns of IQ Change During Childhood

- Stability of individual differences in intelligence over the course of childhood increases with age.

- These changes are attributed to age-related increases in the similarity of cognitive functioning between children and adults.
- Despite the high cross-age correlations, there are significant changes in the level and pattern of IQ over age.

Are People Getting Smarter? The Flynn Effect

- The *Flynn effect* refers to the systematic increase in IQ scores during the 20th century.
- Although speculative, changes in nutrition, health, and education, as well as a generally more complex visual environment, have been hypothesized to account for this effect.

Ask Yourself . . .

8. How are various aspects of infant cognition and behavior related to later IQ?
9. What is meant by IQ stability? Imagine a child whose IQ increases with age, yet the child's rank among peers remains the same. Is this child's IQ considered stable? What about a child whose IQ doesn't change significantly with age, yet her rank among her peers drops. Is this child's IQ considered stable?
10. What is the Flynn effect, and how might we explain it? Consider how many times a day the average person searches for answers to a question on Google or looks up a recipe online, as opposed to retrieving it from memory. Now think about how much we use computers for shopping, getting directions, correspondence, and booking travel, to name a few, compared to the average person in the 1970s or 1980s. How might you expect this to affect the Flynn effect post-2007, after the introduction of the first iPhone? Which aspects of intelligence would you predict to increase or decrease, and why?

KEY TERMS AND CONCEPTS

behavioral genetics
compensatory education
    programs
continuity with stability
cumulative deficit effect
discontinuity with instability

elementary cognitive tasks
    (ECTs)
familial studies of
    intelligence
Flynn effect
heritability

HOME scale
nonshared environment
shared environment
stability
transactional model

SUGGESTED READINGS

Scholarly Works

Flynn, J. R. (2007). *What is intelligence? Beyond the Flynn effect.* New York: Cambridge University Press. In this book, the discoverer of the Flynn effect speculates about the rising IQ over the past century and presents the view that intelligence is a dynamic phenomenon, involving the interaction of genetics, neurology, and experience at multiple levels.

Nelson, C. A., III, Zeanah, C. H., Fox, N. A., Marshall, P. J., Smuke, A. T., & Guthrie, D. (2007). Cognitive recovery in socially deprived young children: The Bucharest Early Intervention Program. *Science, 318,* 1937–1940. This study examines the effect on IQ of social deprivation and its reversal in a group of abandoned Romanian children who were randomly assigned either to foster care or to an institution. Not only are the findings of great interest, the study raises and addresses the ethical issues of doing this type of research.

Sameroff, A. (Ed.). (2009). *The transactional model of development: How children and contexts shape each other.* Washington, DC: American Psychological Association. This edited volume includes chapters written by experts in various areas of developmental psychology, showing how the transactional model can be applied to understanding children and their development. Of particular interest for issues of cognitive development is the opening chapter by Sameroff himself ("The Transactional Model") and the chapter by Mary Gauvain ("Social and Cultural Transactions in Cognitive Development: A Cross-Generational View").

Reading for Personal Interest

Nelson, C. A., Furtado, E. A., Fox, N. A., & Zeanah, C. H., Jr. (2009, May–June). The deprived human brain. *American Scientist, 97,* 222–229. In this article, Charles Nelson and his colleagues describe the many effects of institutionalization as well as children's ability to recover from such effects, as illustrated in the Bucharest Early Intervention Project.

Rutter, M. (2006). *Genes and behavior: Nature-nurture interplay explained.* Malden, MA: Blackwell. This book provides a highly readable and up-to-date account of research in behavioral genetics, written by one of the leaders of the field who also knows a thing or two about development. We were tempted to include this in the category *Scholarly Works* because it is so thorough, but it is written so that it can be understood by the educated layperson.

GLOSSARY

accommodation In Piaget's theory, the process of changing a mental structure to incorporate new information; contrast with *assimilation*. (Chapter 5)

accommodation (of the lens) In vision, the process of adjusting the lens of the eye to focus on objects at different distances. (Chapter 4)

active intermodal mapping In Meltzoff and Moore's account of neonatal cognitive abilities, the ability to integrate information from two senses. (Chapter 10)

active rehearsal See *cumulative rehearsal.*

adaptation In Piaget's theory, the process of adjusting one's cognitive structures to meet environmental demands; includes the complementary processes of assimilation and accommodation. (Chapter 5)

adaptive strategy choice model Siegler's model to describe how strategies change over time; the view that multiple strategies exist within a child's cognitive repertoire at any one time, with these strategies competing with one another for use. (Chapter 7)

analogical reasoning Reasoning that involves using something one already knows to help reason about something not known yet. (Chapter 7)

animism Attributing human properties, like hopes, feelings, and thoughts, to inanimate things. (Chapter 6)

A-not-B object permanence task Object permanence task in which the infant has to retrieve a hidden object at one location (B) after having retrieved it several times previously from another one (A). (Chapter 4)

anthropomorphism A bias to attribute human characteristics to an object, god, or other entity. (Chapter 6)

appearance/reality distinction The knowledge that the appearance of an object does not necessarily correspond to its reality. (Chapter 5)

approximate number system (ANS) An intuitive, nonsymbolic system for thinking about quantities. (Chapter 11)

architectural constraints Ways in which the architecture of the brain is organized at birth; the type and manner in which information can be processed by the brain. (Chapter 2)

articulatory loop In Baddeley and Hitch's model of the short-term store, a system that stores phonological information. (Chapter 7)

artificialism The belief that everything that exists was constructed by people (or God) for specific purposes, much as artifacts (for example, tools, tables, automobiles) are constructed. (Chapter 6)

assimilation In Piaget's theory, the process of incorporating information into already existing cognitive structures; contrast with *accommodation*. (Chapter 5)

attention deficit hyperactivity disorder (ADHD) An inability to sustain attention, believed to be caused by deficits in behavioral inhibition. People with ADHD display hyperactivity, exhibit impulsiveness, show great difficulty sustaining attention, and are at high risk for academic difficulties. (Chapter 7)

autobiographical memory Personal and long-lasting memories that are the basis for one's personal life history. (Chapter 8)

automatic processes Cognitive processes that require no mental effort (or mental space) for their execution and are hypothesized (a) to occur without intention and without conscious awareness, (b) not to interfere with the execution of other processes, (c) not to improve with practice, and (d) not to be influenced by individual differences in intelligence, motivation, or education; contrast with *effortful processes*. (Chapter 7)

axon The long fiber of a neuron that carries messages from that cell to another. (Chapter 2)

Bayesian statistical inference A mathematical probability theory that accounts for learning as a process by which prior knowledge is compared to currently observed evidence. (Chapter 4)

behavioral genetics The study of genetic effects on behavior and on complex psychological characteristics such as intelligence and personality. (Chapters 2, 13)

belief-desire reasoning The process whereby we explain and predict what people do based on what we understand their desires and beliefs to be. (Chapter 6)

bidirectionality of structure and function (or structure function) The reciprocal interaction of structure and function to produce a pattern of development. (Chapter 1)

bilingualism Speaking two languages proficiently. (Chapter 9)

biologically primary abilities Cognitive abilities that have been selected for in evolution and are acquired universally; children typically have high motivation to perform tasks, such as language, involving them. (Chapter 2)

biologically secondary abilities Cognitive abilities, such as reading, that build on biologically primary abilities but are principally cultural inventions that often require tedious repetition and external motivation for their mastery. (Chapter 2)

Black English A dialect of American English, characterized by some special rules of pronunciation and syntax, used mostly (but not exclusively) by members of the African American community. (Chapter 9)

bottom-up processing Processing that begins with sensory input or is stimulus driven, as opposed to top-down processing. (Chapter 7)

bound morphemes Morphemes that cannot stand alone but are attached to free morphemes, such as the word endings *ed* and *ing* in English. (Chapter 9)

Broca's area An area of the frontal region of the brain, typically in the left hemisphere, associated with speech production. (Chapter 9)

causal perception The understanding of temporal sequencing, that earlier events have effects on later events. More generally, an understanding of cause and effect relationships. (Chapter 6)

centration In Piaget's theory, the tendency of preoperational children to attend to one aspect of a situation to the exclusion of others; contrast with *decentration*. (Chapter 5)

cerebral cortex See *neocortex*.

child-directed speech The specialized register of speech adults and older children use when talking to infants and young children. (Chapter 9)

chronotopic constraints Neural limitations on the developmental timing of events. (Chapter 2)

cognition The processes or faculties by which knowledge is acquired and manipulated. (Chapter 1)

cognitive flexibility The ability to shift between sets of tasks or rules. (Chapter 7)

cognitive self-guidance system In Vygotsky's theory, the use of private speech to guide problem-solving behavior. (Chapter 9)

collective monologues Egocentric exchanges between two or more children with participants talking *with* one another but not necessarily *to* one another, such that what one child says has little to do with the comments of the other. (Chapter 9)

communicative competence Mastery of five aspects of language: semantics, syntax, morphology, phonology, and pragmatics. (Chapter 9)

compensatory education programs Programs designed to provide preschool children from low-income homes with the intellectual skills necessary to do well in school. (Chapter 13)

componential subtheory (or analytic intelligence) In Sternberg's theory of successful intelligence, an information-processing model of intelligence that includes three types of components: knowledge acquisition, performance, and metacomponents. (Chapter 12)

concrete operations In Piaget's theory, the third major stage of cognitive development, in which children can decenter their perception, are less egocentric, and can think logically about concrete objects. (Chapter 5) conjugate-reinforcement procedure Conditioning procedure used in memory research with infants in which children's behaviors control aspects of a visual display. (Chapter 8)

conservation In Piaget's theory, the knowledge that the quantity of a substance remains the same despite changes in its form. (Chapter 5)

conservation of number In Piaget's theory, the knowledge that the number of items in an array remains the same despite changes in the form of the array. (Chapter 11)

contextual subtheory (or practical intelligence) In Sternberg's theory of successful intelligence, the idea that intelligence must be viewed in terms of the context in which it occurs. (Chapter 12)

continuity with stability The expectation and research finding that there is stability of individual differences in cognitive performance over time when the developmental function underlying performance is continuous and quantitative in nature; see also *stability*; contrast with *discontinuity with instability*. (Chapter 13)

convergence (of the eyes) Both eyes looking at the same object. (Chapter 4)

coordination (of the eyes) Both eyes following a moving stimulus in a coordinated fashion. (Chapter 4)

core knowledge Expression used by some infant researchers to refer to the set of knowledge that young infants possess in certain domains, including objects, people and social relations, numbers and quantities, and geometry. (Chapter 4)

corpus callosum A thick mass of nerves that connects the right and left hemispheres of the neocortex. (Chapter 2)

creoles Languages that develop when children transform the pidgin of their parents to a grammatically more complex "true" language. (Chapter 9)

critical period See *sensitive period*.

cross-modal matching See *intersensory matching*.

crystallized abilities In Cattell's theory of intelligence, intellectual abilities that develop from cultural context and learning experience; contrast with *fluid abilities*. (Chapter 12)

cultural relativism The idea that intellectual skills critical for survival in one's culture may not be important in another. (Chapter 12)

cumulative (active) rehearsal In memory research, type of rehearsal in which a person repeats the most recently presented word and then rehearses it with as many other different words as possible; contrast with *passive rehearsal*. (Chapter 7)

cumulative deficit effect The phenomenon by which multiple risks persisting over many years add up, resulting in children who display deficits in social, emotional, and cognitive functioning. (Chapter 13)

decentration In Piaget's theory, the ability of concrete operational children to consider multiple aspects of a stimulus or situation; contrast with *centration*. (Chapter 5)

declarative memory Facts and events stored in the long-term memory, which come in two types: episodic and semantic memory; see also *explicit memory*; contrast with *nondeclarative memory*. (Chapter 8)

declarative metacognition The explicit, conscious, and factual knowledge a person has about the characteristics of the task he or she is performing, one's own weak and strong points with respect to performing the task, and the possible strategies that could be used on the task; contrast with *procedural metacognition*. (Chapter 7)

decomposition An arithmetic strategy in which children transform the original problem into two or more simpler problems. (Chapter 11)

deep structure In Chomsky's theory, the grammatical organization and meaning that underlie all language; contrast with *surface structure*. (Chapter 9)

deferred imitation Imitation of a modeled act sometime after viewing the behavior. (Chapter 8)

dendrites The numerous fibers of a neuron that receive messages from other neurons. (Chapter 2)

dentate gyrus Part of the hippocampus that continues to develop after birth and plays an important role in memory. (Chapter 8)

design stance The assumption that tools are designed for an intended function. (Chapter 6)

development (or ontogeny) Predictable changes that occur in structure or function over the life span. (Chapter 1)

developmental cognitive neuroscience The perspective that takes data from a variety of sources—molecular biology, cell biology, artificial intelligence, evolutionary theory, as well as conventional cognitive development—to create a picture of how the mind/brain develops. (Chapter 2)

developmental contextual model Model proposing that all parts of the organism (such as genes, cells, tissues, and organs), as well as the whole organism itself, interact dynamically with the contexts within which the organism is embedded. See also *developmental systems approach*. (Chapter 1)

developmental function The form that development takes over time. (Chapter 1)

developmental quotient (DQ) tests A test of infant abilities, such as the Bayley Scales of Infant Development. (Chapter 12)

developmental systems approach (or developmental contextual model) Perspective that views development as the result of bidirectional interaction between all levels of biological and experiential variables. (Chapter 2)

developmentally appropriate programs Preschool programs that take children's natural propensities for play and activity into consideration. (Chapter 11)

deviation IQ Method of constructing IQ scores that compares a child's performance to that of other children the same age; contrast with *mental age*. (Chapter 12)

differential approach See *psychometric approach*.

differentiation (of neurons) The final stage of neuronal development, in which neurons gain in size, produce more dendrites, and extend their axons farther away from the cell body. (Chapter 2)

differentiation theory Eleanor Gibson's theory that infants develop the ability to perceive increasingly specific differences between stimuli as the result of experience and exploration. In part, as they learn about the world, the sense of familiarity allows them to distinguish old stimuli from novel ones. (Chapter 4)

direct-instruction programs Preschool programs that stress formal instruction. (Chapter 11)

discontinuity with instability The expectation and research finding that there is instability of individual differences in cognitive performance over time when the developmental function underlying performance is discontinuous and qualitative in nature; see also *stability*; contrast with *continuity with stability*. (Chapter 13)

dishabituation The tendency to show renewed interest in a stimulus when some features of it have been changed; contrast with *habituation*. (Chapter 4)

domain-general abilities General underlying cognitive abilities that influence performance over a wide range of situations (or domains); contrast with *domain-specific abilities*. (Chapter 1)

domain-specific abilities Cognitive abilities specific to one cognitive domain under control of a specific mind/brain function; contrast with *domain-general abilities*. (Chapter 1)

dual representation (or dual encoding, dual orientation) The ability to represent an object simultaneously as the object itself and as a representation of something else. (Chapter 5)

dyslexia Reading disability, such that a person has difficulty in learning to read despite an average intelligence. (Chapter 11)

effortful processes Cognitive processes that consume some of the information-processing system's limited capacity and are hypothesized to (a) be available to conscious awareness, (b) interfere with the execution of other processes, (c) improve with practice, and (d) be influenced by individual differences in intelligence, motivation, or education; contrast with *automatic processes*. (Chapter 7)

egocentric (or private) speech Children's speech that is apparently produced for the self and not directed to others. (Chapter 9)

egocentricity In Piaget's theory, the tendency to interpret objects and events from one's own perspective. (Chapter 5)

elementary cognitive tasks (ECTs) Simple laboratory tests designed to measure subjects' response times as they make presumably simple decisions; the low-level, or basic, processes measured by ECTs are presumed to be closely related to physiological functioning and thus primarily under the influence of endogenous (and inherited) factors. (Chapter 13)

emergent literacy The skills, knowledge, and attitudes that are presumed to be developmental precursors to conventional forms of reading and writing and the environments that support these developments. (Chapter 11)

empiricism Philosophical perspective that nature provides only species-general learning mechanisms, with cognition arising as a result of experience. (Chapter 1)

emulation A form of social learning that refers to understanding the goal of a model and engaging in similar behavior to achieve that goal, without necessarily reproducing the exact actions of the model. (Chapter 10)

epigenesis The emergence of new structures and functions during the course of development. (Chapter 2)

episodic memory Long-term memory of events or episodes; contrast with *semantic memory*; see also *autobiographical memory*, *event memory*. (Chapter 8)

equilibration In Piaget's theory, the process by which balance is restored to the cognitive structures through assimilation and accommodation. (Chapter 5)

event memory Memory for everyday events, a form of episodic memory. (Chapter 8)

evolution The process of change in gene frequencies in populations over many generations that in time produces new species. (Chapter 2)

evolutionary developmental psychology The application of the principles of modern evolutionary biology to explain human development. (Chapter 2)

evolutionary educational psychology Principles of evolution applied to educational psychology. (Chapter 11)

evolved probabilistic cognitive mechanisms Information-processing mechanisms that have evolved to solve recurrent problems faced by ancestral populations that are expressed in a probabilistic fashion in each individual in a generation. These mechanisms

are universal in that they will develop in a species-typical manner when an individual experiences a species-typical environment over the course of ontogeny. (Chapter 2)

executive function The processes involved in regulating attention and in determining what to do with information just gathered or retrieved from long-term memory. (Chapters 1, 7)

experience-dependent processes (or experience-dependent synaptogenesis) Processes whereby synapses are formed and maintained as a result of the unique experiences of an individual; contrast with *experience-expectant processes*. (Chapter 2)

experience-expectant processes (or experience-expectant synaptogenesis) Processes whereby synapses are formed and maintained when an organism has species-typical experiences; as a result, functions (such as vision) will develop for all members of a species, given a species-typical environment; contrast with *experience-dependent processes*. (Chapter 2)

experiential subtheory (or creative intelligence) In Sternberg's theory of successful intelligence, the subtheory concerned with how prior knowledge influences performance, specifically with the individual's ability to deal with novelty and the degree to which processing is automatized. (Chapter 12)

explicit measures Measures of cognition that require the participant to report on the contents of his or her cognition or behave in observable ways that are directly related to the task at hand. (Chapter 4)

explicit memory See *declarative memory*.

externality effect The tendency of young infants (1-month-olds) to direct their attention primarily to the outside of a figure and to spend little time inspecting internal features. (Chapter 4)

fact retrieval In information-processing approaches to cognition, the retrieval of a fact directly from long-term memory without using effortful procedures. (Chapter 11)

factor analysis A statistical technique used to define mental factors by analyzing results from intelligence tests. (Chapter 12)

factors In psychometric approaches to intelligence, a set of related mental skills (such as verbal or spatial skills) that underlies intellectual functioning. (Chapter 12)

false-belief task A type of task used in theory-of-mind studies, in which the child must infer that another person does not possess knowledge that he or she possesses (that is, that other person holds a belief that is false). (Chapter 6)

familial studies of intelligence Studies in which some measure or measures of intelligence among people of a known genetic relationship are correlated; the extent to which performance varies as a function of genetic similarity is used as an indication of the heritability of that measure; see also *heritability*. (Chapter 13)

fast mapping The ability to learn new words based on very little input. (Chapter 9)

finalism Young children's tendency to attribute human causes to natural events. (Chapter 6)

fixed-action patterns See *innate releasing mechanisms*.

fluid abilities In Cattell's theory of intelligence, intellectual abilities that are biologically determined and reflected in tests of memory span and spatial thinking; contrast with *crystallized abilities*. (Chapter 12)

Flynn effect The systematic increase in IQ scores (from 5 to 9 points per decade) observed over the 20th century. (Chapter 13)

folk biology How people naturally come to understand the biological world. (Chapter 6)

folk knowledge How people naturally come to understand aspects of their world. Folk knowledge is differentiated from scientific knowledge. (Chapter 6)

folk physics How people naturally come to understand aspects of the physical world. (Chapter 6)

folk psychology How people naturally come to understand the psychological world. (Chapter 6)

forethought In Bandura's social cognitive theory, the ability to anticipate the consequences of one's actions and the actions of others. (Chapter 10)

formal operations In Piaget's theory, the final stage of cognitive development, in which children are able to apply abstract logical rules. (Chapter 5)

free morphemes Morphemes that can stand alone as a word, such as *dog*, *chase*, or *happy*. (Chapter 9)

function In developmental psychology, action related to a structure, such as movement of a muscle, firing of a nerve, or activation of a mental representation; contrast with *structure*; see also *bidirectionality of structure and function*. (Chapter 1)

functional fixedness A cognitive bias that involves a tendency to limit one's use and perception of an object as only working in the way it is typically used. The inability to realize that something known to have a particular use could have other functions. (Chapter 6)

functional invariants In Piaget's theory, the processes of organization and adaptation that characterize all biological systems and operate throughout the life span. (Chapter 5)

fuzzy-trace theory Brainerd and Reyna's theory proposing that information is encoded on a continuum from verbatim to fuzzy, gistlike traces and that developmental differences in many aspects of cognition can be attributed to age differences in encoding and in differences in sensitivity to output interference. (Chapter 5)

fuzzy traces In fuzzy-trace theory, imprecise memory representations that are more easily accessed, generally require less effort to use, and are less susceptible to interference and forgetting than verbatim traces. (Chapter 5)

g (or Spearman's g, general intelligence) In psychometric theory, the idea that intelligence can be expressed in terms of a single factor, general intelligence, or *g*, first formulated by Spearman in the early 1900s. (Chapter 12)

Gardner's theory of multiple intelligences See *theory of multiple intelligences*.

gender consistency The concept that gender remains the same despite changes in behavior. (Chapter 10)

gender constancy The concept that gender remains the same despite changes in physical appearance, time, and behavior; includes gender identity, gender stability, and gender consistency. (Chapter 10)

gender identification The process of identifying oneself as male or female and adopting the roles and values of that gender. (Chapter 10)

gender identity The ability of children to identify themselves as either boys or girls. (Chapter 10)

gender schema A mentalistic structure consisting of a set of expectations and associations that guide processing with respect to gender. (Chapter 10)

gender stability The concept that gender remains the same over time. (Chapter 10)

general genetic law of cultural development The idea that cognition occurs on two planes, first the social, between individuals, and later the psychological, as it is internalized by the child. (Chapter 3)

general intelligence See *g*.

genetic determinism The idea that one's genes determine one's behavior. (Chapter 1)

genotype → environment theory In Scarr and McCartney's theory, the proposal that one's genotype (genetic constitution) influences which environments one encounters and the type of experiences one has, or that genes drive experience. Three types of genotype → environment effects are proposed: passive, evocative, and active. (Chapter 2)

goal-directed behavior Means-end problem solving, seen first in the latter part of the first year. (Chapters 5, 7)

Goldilocks effect The phenomenon whereby infants take an active role in sampling their environment, looking longer at stimuli that are neither too simple nor too complex. (Chapter 4)

grammar center An area in the frontal lobe that is specifically related to processing grammatical information. (Chapter 9)

guided participation Adult-child interactions, not only during explicit instruction but also during the more routine activities and communication of everyday life; the process and system of involvement of individuals with others as they communicate and engage in shared activities; contrast with *zone of proximal development*; see also *sociocultural perspective*. (Chapter 3)

habituation The tendency to decrease responding to a stimulus that has been presented repeatedly; contrast with *dishabituation*. (Chapter 4)

heritability The extent to which differences in any trait within a population can be attributed to inheritance. (Chapter 13)

hierarchical model of cognitive abilities Model proposing that intelligence is composed of specific cognitive abilities (for example, verbal, spatial, speed of processing, memory) that are intercorrelated and influenced by a higher-order general intellectual factor, *g*. (Chapter 12)

holophrases (holophrastic speech) Children's use of one-word sentences. (Chapter 9)

HOME scale The Home Observation for Measurement of the Environment scale, a scale developed by Bradley, Caldwell, and Elardo that provides a detailed analysis of parental behavior and characteristics of the home environment that are hypothesized to be associated with intelligence. (Chapter 13)

hypothetico-deductive reasoning In Piaget's theory, a formal operational ability to think hypothetically. (Chapter 5)

imaginary audience Expression of adolescent egocentrism, with adolescents feeling that they are constantly "onstage," or playing to an imaginary audience. (Chapter 5)

imaginary friends Make-believe friends. (Chapter 5)

imitative learning Reproduction of observed behavior to achieve a specific goal. May require an understanding of the goal that the model had in mind, as well as the reproduction of important components of the observed behavior. (Chapter 10)

implicit association test (IAT) A test that uses the speed with which people make decisions about words or concepts (for example, *good* and *bad*) when they are associated with different social groups (for example, boys and girls) to assess implicit attitudes. (Chapter 10)

implicit measures Measures thought to capture aspects of cognition that are unconscious and cannot be expressed directly or verbally. (Chapter 4)

implicit memory See *nondeclarative memory*.

individual differences Differences in patterns of intellectual aptitudes among people of a given age. (Chapter 1)

inductive reasoning The type of thinking that goes from specific observations to broad generalizations and, in Piaget's theory, is characteristic of formal operational thought. (Chapter 5)

infant-directed speech The specialized register of speech adults and older children use when talking specifically to infants. (Chapter 9)

infantile amnesia The inability to remember events from infancy and early childhood. (Chapter 8)

inhibition The ability to prevent one from making some cognitive or behavioral response. (Chapter 7)

innate releasing mechanisms Inherited sets of behaviors elicited by specific sets of stimuli without the need of prior environmental experience. (Chapter 10)

inner speech In Vygotsky's theory, the covert language used to guide thought. (Chapter 9)

integrative theory of numerical development Siegler and Lortie-Forgues's theory proposing that mathematical development can be explained by the continuing growth of understanding of numerical magnitudes. (Chapter 11)

intelligence Acting or thinking in ways that are goal directed and adaptive. (Chapter 12)

intelligence quotient (IQ) tests Aptitude tests, such as the Stanford-Binet and Wechsler scales, intended to measure aspects of intellectual functioning. (Chapter 12)

intentional agents Beings whose behavior is based on what they know and what they want and who act deliberately to achieve their goals. (Chapter 6)

interactive specialization Models proposing that specialization and localization in the adult brain are the result of self-organizing, domain-general mechanisms operating on experience during development. (Chapter 2)

intersensory integration The coordination of information from two or more sensory modalities. (Chapter 4)

intersensory matching (cross-modal matching) The ability to recognize an object initially inspected in one modality (touch, for example) via another modality (vision, for example). (Chapter 4)

knowledge base The general background knowledge a person possesses, which influences most cognitive task performance. (Chapter 7)

language acquisition device (LAD) In Chomsky's theory, the hypothetical construct possessed by all humans at birth enabling them to acquire language. (Chapter 9)

language acquisition support system (LASS) The idea proposed by Bruner that adults and older children have learning devices that interact with children's language acquisition devices (LAD). (Chapter 9)

legitimate peripheral participation From sociocultural theory, the idea that children acquire mature, culturally appropriate behaviors simply by observation of skilled members of their community. (Chapter 3)

less-is-more hypothesis Newport's hypothesis that the cognitive limitations of infants and young children may serve to simplify the body of language they process, thus making it easier to learn the complicated syntactical system of any human language. (Chapter 9)

lexical constraints Constraints that facilitate word learning in young children by limiting the possible interpretations that an utterance is likely to have. See also *whole-object assumption, taxonomic assumption*, and *mutual exclusivity assumption*. (Chapter 9)

lexicon The words that a child knows, or vocabulary. (Chapter 9)

limited resource capacity The concept that one's information-processing ability is restricted (that people can only do so many things at any single time). Metaphors for capacity include mental space, mental energy or effort, and time. (Chapter 7)

local enhancement (or stimulus enhancement) An individual notices activity at a particular location, moves to that location, and, in a process of trial and error, discovers a useful behavior. (Chapter 10)

long-term memory In information-processing approaches to cognition, the large and presumably permanent repository of information in the brain. (Chapter 7)

Matthew effect With respect to reading, the phenomenon in which the difference between good and poor readers increases over time. (Chapter 11)

mean length of utterance (MLU) A measure of language development defined by the average number of meaningful language units (root words and endings) a child uses at any one time. (Chapter 9)

memory span The number of items a person can hold in the short-term store, assessed by testing the number of (usually) unrelated items that can be recalled in exact order. (Chapter 7)

memory strategies See *mnemonics.*

mental age Level of mental functioning (in years) as measured by the number of items passed on an intelligence test, formerly used in determining IQ scores; contrast with *deviation IQ*. (Chapter 12)

mental rotation Form of spatial visualization in which a person must mentally rotate a visual stimulus to determine if it matches another stimulus. (Chapter 6)

meta-analysis A statistical technique that allows an investigator to evaluate the magnitude of a significant effect across a large number of studies by providing an estimate of effect size, expressed in terms of how large average differences between targeted groups are across the various studies, taking into consideration the overall amount of variability. (Chapter 11)

meta-attention Knowledge of factors that influence one's attention. (Chapter 7)

metacognition Knowledge about one's own thoughts and the factors that influence thinking. (Chapter 7)

metacommunication Knowledge of the adequacy of one's own communication abilities. (Chapter 9)

metamemory Knowledge of one's own memory abilities and the factors that influence memory. (Chapter 7)

microgenetic development In Vygotsky's sociocultural theory, changes that occur over relatively brief periods of time, in seconds, minutes, or days, as opposed to larger-scale changes, as conventionally studied in ontogenetic development. (Chapter 3)

migration (of neurons) The movement of neurons to their permanent positions in the brain, most of which is completed during the prenatal period. (Chapter 2)

mimicry A form of social learning that involves the duplication of a behavior without any understanding of the goal of that behavior. (Chapter 10)

min strategy An arithmetic strategy in which children faced with an addition problem start with the largest addend and count up from there. (Chapter 11)

mindblindness A deficit in theory of mind, characteristic of people with autism, in which a person cannot read the minds of others. (Chapter 6)

mirror neurons Neurons in the brain that become active both when the individual makes a particular motion and when the individual sees another individual making that same motion. These neurons are believed to facilitate observational learning. (Chapter 10)

mnemonics (or memory strategies) Effortful techniques used to improve memory, including rehearsal, organization, and elaboration. (Chapter 7)

modularity Concept that certain areas of the brain are dedicated to performing specific cognitive tasks. (Chapter 1)

morphemes Meaningful language units. See also *bound morphemes, free morphemes.* (Chapter 9)

morphology In the study of language development, the knowledge of word formation. (Chapter 9)

motherese See *child-directed speech, infant-directed speech.*

multiple intelligences See *theory of multiple intelligences.*

mutual exclusivity assumption A type of lexical constraint in which children believe that different words refer to different things. (Chapter 9)

mutual imitation Imitative-like behavior in which the adult imitates a behavior that is first emitted by the baby, which in turn activates the baby to continue that behavior. (Chapter 10)

myelin A sheet of fatty substance that develops around the neurons to promote faster transmission of electrical signals through the nervous system. (Chapter 2)

myelination The development of myelin around neurons, which proceeds at different rates in different areas of the brain. (Chapter 2)

nativism Philosophical perspective that human intellectual abilities are innate. (Chapter 1)

nativist theories (of language acquisition) Theories that propose that children are born with a broad theory of language that they modify in accordance with the speech they hear growing up; contrast with *social-interactionist theories*. (Chapter 9)

natural selection In Darwin's theory of evolution, the idea that more individuals are produced in a generation than can usually survive and that variations in individuals make some members of a species more fit than others and thus more likely to survive to reproduce; according to Darwin, natural selection is the primary mechanism for evolution. (Chapter 2)

neocortex The outer layer of the brain, which gives humans their highly developed intelligence. (Chapter 2)

neonatal imitation The ability of newborns to reproduce some behavior, such as a facial expression, that they have seen in others. (Chapter 10)

neuroconstructivism The view that inherited and evolved learning abilities interact with a structured environment to produce species-typical patterns of cognitive growth. (Chapter 2)

neurogenesis (or proliferation) The process of nerve-cell division by mitosis. (Chapter 2)

neuroimaging techniques New technologies that permit imaging of brain activities, including high-density event-related potentials, positron emission tomography (PET), and functional magnetic resonance imaging (fMRI). (Chapter 2)

neuron Nervous system cell through which electrical and chemical signals are transmitted. (Chapter 2)

neurotransmitters Chemicals in synapses that serve to transmit electrical impulses between neurons. (Chapter 2)

nondeclarative (or procedural or implicit) memory Knowledge in the long-term store of procedures that is unconscious; contrast with *declarative memory*. (Chapter 8)

nonshared environment A home environment that is unique to an individual, not shared by a sibling, for instance. (Chapter 13)

numerosity The ability to determine quickly the number of items in a set without counting. (Chapter 4)

object and location memory A form of spatial cognition that involves locating and remembering objects in arrays. Unlike other forms of spatial cognition, object and location memory tends to be better in females than in males and shows relatively little improvement over development. (Chapter 6)

object cohesion and continuity The knowledge that individual objects are seen as cohesive wholes with distinct boundaries. (Chapter 4)

object constancy The knowledge that an object remains the same despite changes in how it is viewed. (Chapter 4)

object permanence The knowledge that objects have an existence in time and space independent of one's own perception or action on those objects. (Chapter 4)

object-oriented play (or object play) Play that involves manipulation or exploration of objects and using objects as tools (to build something, for instance). (Chapter 6)

observational learning The ability to learn about the world simply by watching, central to Bandura's social cognitive theory; according to Bandura, observational learning includes four subprocesses: attentional processes, retention processes, production processes, and motivational processes. (Chapter 10)

ontogenetic adaptations Behaviors that play a specific role in survival for an individual at one time only and then disappear when they are no longer needed. (Chapter 10)

ontogenetic development Development of the individual over his or her lifetime. (Chapter 3)

operations In Piaget's theory, particular types of cognitive schemes that are mental (that is, require symbols), derive from action, exist in organized systems (structures of the whole), and follow a set of logical rules, most importantly that of reversibility. (Chapter 5)

ordinality A basic understanding of *more than* and *less than* relationships. (Chapter 4)

organization (in memory research) The structure discovered or imposed upon a set of items that is used to guide memory performance. (Chapter 7)

organization (in Piaget's theory) The idea that every intellectual operation is related to all other acts of intelligence. (Chapter 5)

other-race effect The phenomenon whereby people develop an increasing ability to discriminate between faces of their own race relative to those of other races. (Chapter 4)

overextensions In the study of language development, the stretching of a familiar word beyond its correct meaning; for example, calling all four-legged mammals *doggie*. (Chapter 9)

overimitation Copying all actions of a model, even those that are irrelevant to achieving a task goal. (Chapter 10)

overregularization In the study of language development, the tendency to apply rules to words when they are not appropriate, for example, *runned*, *foots*, *mices*. (Chapter 9)

passive rehearsal Style of rehearsing in which a person includes few (usually one) unique items per rehearsal set; contrast with *cumulative rehearsal*. (Chapter 7)

perceptual centration See *centration*.

perceptual decentration See *decentration*.

perceptual narrowing A process by which infants become tuned to sociocultural relevant information as a result of experiences during the first year of life. Infants' ability to make discriminations among frequently experienced stimuli, such as faces from their own race, increase, whereas they become relatively less effective discriminating among infrequently experienced stimuli, such as faces from other races. (Chapter 4)

personal fable A belief in one's uniqueness and invulnerability, which is an expression of adolescent egocentrism. (Chapter 5)

phonemes Individual sounds that are used to make up words. (Chapter 4)

phonemic awareness The knowledge that words consist of separable sounds; contrast with *phonological recoding*. (Chapters 9, 11)

phonological recoding Reading skills used to translate written symbols into sounds and words; contrast with *phonemic awareness*. (Chapter 11)

phonology In language acquisition, the knowledge of how words are pronounced. (Chapter 9)

phylogenetic development Development over evolutionary time. (Chapter 3)

pidgins Structurally simple communication systems that arise when people who share no common language come into constant contact. (Chapter 9)

plasticity The extent to which behavior or brain functioning can be changed. (Chapters 1, 2)

positive manifold In psychometric approaches to intelligence, the high correlations among scores on sets of cognitive tests that have little in common with one another in terms of content or types of strategies used. (Chapter 12)

pragmatics In the study of language development, knowledge about how language can be adjusted to fit different circumstances. (Chapter 9)

preference-for-novelty paradigms Tasks in which an infant's preference, usually measured in looking time, for a novel as opposed to a familiar stimulus is used as an indication of memory for the familiar stimulus. (Chapter 8)

preoperations In Piaget's theory, the second major stage of cognitive development (approximately ages 2 to 7), characterized by prelogical, intuitive thought. (Chapter 5)

principle of persistence The knowledge that objects remain cohesive and cannot undergo a spontaneous or uncaused change in the course of an event. (Chapter 4)

private (egocentric) speech Children's speech apparently for self and not directed to others. (Chapter 9)

problem solving Process in which someone has a specific goal in mind that cannot be attained immediately because of the presence of one or more obstacles; problem solving involves a goal, obstacles to that goal, strategies for overcoming the obstacles, and an evaluation of the results. (Chapter 7)

procedural memory See *nondeclarative memory*.

procedural metacognition The knowledge about when strategies are necessary as well as monitoring how well one is performing on a task; contrast with *declarative metacognition*. (Chapter 7)

production deficiency Children's tendency not to use spontaneously a strategy that they are capable of using when instructed; contrast with *utilization deficiency*. (Chapter 7)

productive vocabulary The language a child can actually produce, or speak; contrast with *receptive vocabulary*. (Chapter 9)

proliferation (of neurons; neurogenesis) The process of nerve-cell division by mitosis. (Chapter 2)

promiscuous teleology Children's tendency to reason about events and objects in terms of purpose. (Chapter 6)

prospective memory Remembering to do something in the future. (Chapter 8)

psychometric (differential) approach The theory that intelligence can be described in terms of mental factors and that tests can be constructed that reveal individual differences in the factors underlying mental performance. (Chapter 12)

Pygmalion effect A form of self-fulfilling prophecy, in which a person internalizes the expectations of an authority figure. (Chapter 12)

rapid automatized naming (RAN) The ability to rapidly name as many familiar items (words, numbers, colors, digits) as possible. (Chapter 11)

reasoning A particular type of problem solving that involves making inferences. (Chapter 7)

receptive vocabulary The language that a child can understand; contrast with *productive vocabulary*. (Chapter 9)

reflective abstraction In Piaget's theory, the ability to reflect upon knowledge one already possesses, and without the need of additional information from the external environment, to arrive at new knowledge; characteristic of adolescent thought. (Chapter 5)

rehearsal A memory strategy in which target information is repeated; see also *cumulative rehearsal, passive rehearsal*. (Chapter 7)

relational mapping The application of what one knows about one set of elements (the relation of A to B) to relations about different elements (the relation of C to D). (Chapter 7)

relational shift In analogical reasoning, the proposal that there is in development a shift from focusing on perceptual similarity to relational similarity to solve problems. (Chapter 7)

representation The mental encoding of information. (Chapters 1, 5)

representational constraints Representations that are hard-wired into the brain so that some types of knowledge are innate. (Chapter 2)

representational insight The knowledge that an entity can stand for something other than itself. (Chapter 5)

resistance to interference The ability to ignore irrelevant information so that it does not impede task performance; its inverse is interference sensitivity. (Chapter 7)

reversibility In Piaget's theory, the knowledge that an operation can be reversed, characteristic of the concrete operational period. (Chapter 5)

scaffolding An expert, when instructing a novice, responding contingently to the novice's responses in a learning situation, so that the novice gradually increases his or her understanding of a problem. (Chapter 3)

scale errors Errors that occur when children attempt to use a miniature object as if it were a real one. These errors are a symptom of children's difficulty with *dual representation*. (Chapter 5)

schema An abstract representation of an object or event. (Chapter 4)

scheme An abstract representation of an object or event. (Chapter 5)

scientific reasoning A type of reasoning that involves the generation of hypotheses and the systematic testing of those hypotheses. (Chapter 7)

scripts A form of schematic organization, with real-world events organized in terms of temporal and causal relations between component acts. (Chapter 8)

selective attention Concentration on chosen stimuli without distraction by nontarget stimuli. (Chapter 7)

selective cell death (or apoptosis) Early developmental process in which neurons that are not activated by sensory and motor experience die. (Chapter 2)

self-concept The way a person defines himself or herself. (Chapter 10)

self-efficacy The belief that one can influence one's own thoughts and behavior. (Chapter 10)

self-reflection In Bandura's social cognitive theory, the ability to analyze one's thoughts and actions. (Chapter 10)

self-regulation The process of adopting standards of acceptable behavior, including aspirational standards (hoped-for levels of accomplishment) as well as social and moral standards. (Chapter 10)

semantic memory Long-term memory representation of definitions and relations among language terms; contrast with *episodic memory*. (Chapter 8)

semantics In language acquisition, knowledge of the meaning of words and sentences. (Chapter 9)

semilingualism Underdeveloped language, typically when one has acquired two or more languages and there are deficiencies in both languages. (Chapter 9)

sensitive period The time in development (usually early in life) when a certain skill or ability is most easily acquired. (Chapter 2)

sensorimotor stage In Piaget's theory, the first major stage of cognitive development (birth to approximately 2 years), in which children understand their world through sensory and motor experiences. (Chapter 5)

sequential bilingualism A situation in which children learn a second language after mastering the first. (Chapter 9)

shared attention (or joint attention) Two people both attending to the same thing or event and sharing that experience. (Chapter 6)

shared environment A home environment shared by different family members. (Chapter 13)

short-term/working memory (STWM) Memory store that can hold a limited amount of information for a matter of seconds; cognitive operations are executed in the short-term store and information can be maintained indefinitely in the short-term store through operations such as rehearsal; see also *working memory*. (Chapter 7)

simultaneous bilingualism A situation in which children are exposed from birth to two languages. (Chapter 9)

social cognition Thinking about the self, other people, and social relationships. (Chapter 10)

social cognitive theory Bandura's theory of how individuals operate cognitively on their social experiences and how these cognitive operations influence behavior and development. (Chapter 10)

social information processing As exemplified by Dodge's theory, the view that social information must be encoded, compared with other pertinent information, and retrieved so that social interactions run smoothly. (Chapter 10)

social learning The acquisition of social information and behavior; situations in which one individual comes to behave similarly to others. (Chapter 10)

social learning theory An earlier version of Bandura's social cognitive theory. (Chapter 10)

social-interactionist theories (of language acquisition) The position that children's domain-general social-cognitive abilities and the social environment play a central role in language development; contrast with *nativist perspective*. (Chapter 9)

sociocultural perspective A perspective of cognitive development emphasizing that development is guided by adults interacting with children, with the cultural context determining to a large extent how, where, and when these interactions take place; see also *guided participation*, *zone of proximal development*. (Chapters 1, 3)

sociodramatic play A social form of symbolic play in which children take on different roles and follow a story line as if they were in a theatrical performance. (Chapter 5)

sociohistorical development Changes that have occurred in one's culture and the values, norms, and technologies such a history has generated. (Chapter 3)

source monitoring The awareness of the origins of one's memories, knowledge, or beliefs. (Chapters 5, 8)

span of apprehension The number of items that people can keep in mind at any one time, or the amount of information that people can attend to at a single time. (Chapter 7)

spatial cognition The type of cognition that involves processing visual information in terms of spatial relationships, including spatial orientation, spatial visualization, and object and location memory. (Chapter 6)

spatial orientation How people understand the placement of objects in space with themselves as the reference point. (Chapter 6)

spatial visualization An aspect of spatial cognition that involves the mental manipulations of visual stimuli, such as performing mental rotation or solving embedded-figures problems. (Chapter 6)

Spearman's g See *g* (*general intelligence*).

speech register A distinct style of speaking used only in specific contexts (for example, when talking to children or when talking in school). (Chapter 9)

stability In developmental psychology, the degree to which a person maintains over time the same rank order in comparison with peers for a particular characteristic. (Chapters 1, 13)

Stanford-Binet An individually administered IQ test. (Chapter 12)

statistical learning In language learning, a domain-general mechanism in which infants essentially keep track of how often different syllables follow one another and use this information to determine which sound sequences are meaningful (that is, are words) and which are not. (Chapter 9)

stereotype threat Phenomenon in which minority members perform worse on IQ or other tests after being reminded of the negative stereotype concerning their group's performance on such tests. (Chapters 11, 12)

Sternberg's triarchic theory See *theory of successful intelligence.*

strategies Goal-directed and deliberately implemented mental operations used to facilitate task performance; see also *mnemonics*. (Chapters 1, 7)

structure In developmental psychology, a substrate of the organism that develops, such as muscle, nervous tissue, or mental knowledge; contrast with *function*; see *bidirectionality of structure and function.* (Chapter 1)

sum strategy A simple addition strategy used by young children that involves counting together the two addends of a problem. (Chapter 11)

surface structure In Chomsky's theory, the actual words of a sentence, derived from the deep structure. (Chapter 9)

symbolic play (also called *fantasy, pretend,* or *make-believe play*) A type of play that includes an "as if" orientation to objects, actions, and other people and increases during early childhood as a result of children's growing abilities to use symbols to represent something other than itself. (Chapter 5)

symbolization In Bandura's social cognitive theory, the ability to think about one's social behavior in terms of words and images. (Chapter 10)

synapse The tiny space between the dendrite of one neuron and the axon of another through which chemical messages are passed. (Chapter 2)

synaptogenesis The process of synapse formation. (Chapter 2)

syntactic bootstrapping In learning the meaning of words, the idea that the grammatical form of speech may give children important clues for guessing what a word means. (Chapter 9)

syntax In language acquisition, the knowledge of how words are put together to form grammatical sentences. (Chapter 9)

taxonomic assumption A type of lexical constraint in which children assume that words refer to things that are similar. (Chapter 9)

teaching (or instructed learning) A form of social learning in which a more accomplished person intentionally conveys his or her knowledge and/or skills to a less accomplished person. (Chapter 10)

telegraphic speech Children's economical use of words, including only high-information words that are most important in conveying meaning. (Chapter 9)

theory of mind A person's concepts of mental activity; used to refer to how children conceptualize mental activity and how they attribute intention to and predict the behavior of others; see also *belief-desire reasoning.* (Chapter 6)

theory of multiple intelligences Gardner's theory postulating eight (possibly nine) components, or modules, of intelligence: (1) linguistic, (2) logical-mathematical, (3) musical, (4) spatial, (5) bodily-kinesthetic, (6) interpersonal, (7) intrapersonal, and (8) naturalistic. (Chapter 12)

theory of successful intelligence (or theory of triarchic intelligence) Sternberg's theory that describes intelligence in terms of three subtheories: contextual, experiential, and componential. (Chapter 12) theory theories Theories of cognitive development that combine neonativism and constructivism, proposing that cognitive development progresses by children generating, testing, and changing theories about the physical and social world. (Chapter 6)

thirty million word gap Difference in the number of words children from high-income versus low-income families hear by age 3. (Chapter 9)

tools of intellectual adaptation Vygotsky's term for methods of thinking and problem-solving strategies that children internalize from their interactions with more competent members of society. (Chapter 3)

top-down processing Processing that is conceptually driven, as opposed to bottom-up or data-driven processing. (Chapter 7)

transactional model A framework that views development as the continuous and bidirectional interchange between an active organism with a unique biological constitution and a changing environment. (Chapter 13)

transgender children Children whose natal, or birth, sex is inconsistent with their gender identity. (Chapter 10)

underextensions Incorrectly restricting the use of a term (for example, believing that only one's pet, Fido, deserves the label *dog*). (Chapter 9)

universal grammar In nativist theories of language acquisition, the innate grammar that characterizes all human languages. (Chapter 9)

utilization deficiency The inability of children to benefit from strategies they are able to implement; contrast with *production deficiency*. (Chapter 7)

verbatim traces In fuzzy-trace theory, precise, literal memory representations that are less easily accessed, generally require more effort to use, and are more susceptible to interference and forgetting than fuzzy traces. (Chapter 5)

vicarious learning In Bandura's social cognitive theory, learning without the need to receive specific reinforcement for one's behavior; rather, learning by observing others. (Chapter 10)

video deficit The phenomenon whereby children much younger than 2 years of age learn and remember information better when they view or interact with a live model rather than via video. (Chapter 11)

violation-of-expectation method Based on habituation/dishabituation procedures, techniques in which increases in infants' looking time are interpreted as reflecting a violation of an expected outcome. (Chapter 4)

visual preference paradigm In research with infants, observing the amount of time infants spend looking at different visual stimuli to determine which one they prefer (that is, look at more often); such preferences indicate an ability to discriminate between stimuli. (Chapter 4)

visuospatial scratch pad In Baddeley and Hitch's model of the short-term store, a system that stores visual information. (Chapter 7)

Wechsler scales Individually administered IQ tests, including the WPPSI, WISC, and WAIS. (Chapter 12)

WEIRD societies Acronym for Western, educated, industrialized, rich, and democratic, the type of societies in which most psychological research is done. Much of the world, and our species for most of our history, lives under very different conditions, thus limiting what can be said about cognitive universals. (Chapter 3)

Wernicke's area A region of the brain located in the cortex of the temporal lobe, typically in the left hemisphere, associated with comprehension of language. (Chapter 9)

whole-object assumption A type of lexical constraint in which children assume when hearing a word that it refers to the whole object and not to some part of that object. (Chapter 9)

wishful thinking A characteristic of preschool thought such that children often do not differentiate between their wishes and their expectations. (Chapter 10)

word spurt The rapid increase in word (mostly nouns) learning that occurs at about 18 months of age. (Chapter 9)

working memory The capacity to store and transform information being held in the short-term system. See also *short-term/working memory*. (Chapter 7)

zone of proximal development In Vygotsky's theory, the difference between a child's actual level of ability and the level of ability that he or she can achieve when working under the guidance of an instructor; contrast with *guided participation*; see also *sociocultural perspective*. (Chapter 3)

REFERENCES

Abravanel, E., & Sigafoos, A. D. (1984). Explaining the presence of imitation during early infancy. *Child Development, 55*, 381–392.

Ackerman, B. P., & Brown, E. D. (2006). Income poverty, poverty co-factors, and the adjustment of children in school. In R. V. Kail (Ed.), *Advances in child development and behavior* (Vol. 34, pp. 91–129). Oxford, UK: Elsevier.

Ackil, J. K., Van Abbema, D. L., & Bauer, P. J. (2003). After the storm: Enduring differences in mother-child recollections of traumatic and nontraumatic events. *Journal of Experimental Child Psychology, 84*, 286–309.

Ackil, J. K., & Zaragoza, M. S. (1995). Developmental differences in eyewitness suggestibility and memory for source. *Journal of Experimental Child Psychology, 60*, 57–83.

Adams, J. W., & Hitch, G. J. (1997). Working memory and children's mental addition. *Journal of Experimental Child Psychology, 67*, 21–38.

Adams, M. J., Treiman, R., & Pressley, M. (1998). Reading, writing, and literacy. In W. Damon (Series Ed.) & K. A. Renninger & I. E. Sigel (Vol. Eds.), *Handbook of child psychology: Vol. 4. Child psychology in practice* (5th ed., pp. 275–355). New York: Wiley.

Adams, R. J., & Courage, M. L. (1998). Human newborn color vision: Measurement with chromatic stimuli varying in excitation purity. *Journal of Experimental Child Psychology, 68*, 22–34.

Adams, R. J., Courage, M. L., & Mercer, M. E. (1994). Systematic measurement of human neonatal color vision. *Vision Research, 34*, 1691–1701.

Adey, P. S., & Shayer, M. (1992). Accelerating the development of formal thinking in middle and high school students: II. Postproject effects on science achievement. *Journal of Research in Science Teaching, 29*, 81–92.

Adler, S. (1990). Multicultural clients: Implications for the SLP. *Language, Speech, and Hearing in the Schools, 21*, 135–139.

Aguiar, A., & Baillargeon, R. (1998). Eight-and-a-half-month-old infants' reasoning about containment events. *Child Development, 69*, 636–653.

Aguiar, A., & Baillargeon, R. (1999). 2.5-month-old infants' reasoning about when objects should and should not be occluded. *Cognitive Psychology, 39*, 116–157.

Aimone, J. B., & Gage, F. H. (2011). Modeling new neuron function: A history of using computational neuroscience to study adult neurogenesis. *European Journal of Neuroscience, 33*(6), 1160–1169.

Ainsworth, M. D. S., Blehar, M. C., Waters, E., & Wall, S. (1978). *Patterns of attachment: A psychological study of the strange situation.* Hillsdale, NJ: Erlbaum.

Aitchinson, J. (1994). *Words in the mind: An introduction to the mental lexicon* (2nd ed.). Oxford, UK: Blackwell.

Akers, K. G., Martinez-Canabal, A., Restivo, L., Yiu, A. P., De Cristofaro, A., Hsiang, H. L. L., . . . Ohira, K. (2014). Hippocampal neurogenesis regulates forgetting during adulthood and infancy. *Science, 344*(6184), 598–602.

Akhtar, N. (1999). Acquiring basic word order: Evidence for data-driven learning of syntactic structure. *Journal of Child Language, 26*, 339–356.

Alderson-Day, B., & Fernyhough, C. (2015). Inner speech: Development, cognitive functions, phenomenology, and neurobiology. *Psychological Bulletin, 141*, 931–965.

Alexander, J. M., Schwanenflugel, P. J., & Carr, M. (1995). Development of metacognition in gifted children: Directions for future research. *Developmental Review, 15*, 1–37.

Alexander, R. D. (1989). Evolution of the human psyche. In P. Mellers & C. Stringer (Eds.), *The human revolution: Behavioral and biological perspectives on the origins of modern humans* (pp. 455–513). Princeton, NJ: Princeton University Press.

Alibali, M. W. (1999). How children change their minds: Strategy change can be gradual or abrupt. *Developmental Psychology, 35*, 127–145.

Allen, D., Banks, M. S., & Schefrin, B. (1988). Chromatic discrimination in human infants. *Investigative Ophthalmology and Visual Science, 29*(Suppl.), 25.

Allix, N. M. (2000). The theory of multiple intelligences: A case of missing cognitive matter. *Australian Journal of Education, 44*, 272–288.

Alloway, T. P., & Alloway, R. G. (2010). Investigating the predictive roles of working memory and IQ in academic attainment. *Journal of Experimental Child Psychology, 106*, 20–29.

Als, H. (1995). The preterm infant: A model for the study of fetal brain expectation. In J.-P. Lecanuet, W. Fifer, N. Krasnegor, & W. Smotherman (Eds.), *Fetal development: A psychobiological perspective* (pp. 439–471). Hillsdale, NJ: Erlbaum.

Ambady, N., Shih, M., Kim, A., & Pittinsky, T. L. (2001). Stereotype susceptibility in children: Effects of identity activation on quantitative performance. *Psychological Science, 12*, 385–390.

American Academy of Pediatrics. (2011). Media use by children younger than 2 years. *Pediatrics, 128*, 1040–1045.

American Academy of Pediatrics. (2014). *Literacy promotion: An essential component of primary care pediatric practice.* Elk Grove, IL: American Academy of Pediatrics.

Anastasi, A. (1988). *Psychological testing* (6th ed.). New York: Macmillan.

Anderson, V., Morse, S., Catroppa, C., Haritou, F., & Rosenfeld, J. (2004). Thirty-month outcome from early childhood head injury: A prospective analysis of neurobehavioral recovery. *Brain, 127*, 2608–2620.

Anderson, V., Spencer-Smith, M., Leventer, R., Coleman, L., Anderson, P., Williams, J., . . . Jacobs, R. (2009). Childhood brain insult: Can age at insult help us predict outcome? *Brain, 132*, 45–56.

Anderson, V., Spencer-Smith, M., & Wood, A. (2011). Do children really recover better? Neurobehavioural plasticity after early brain insult. *Brain, 134*, 2197–2221.

Anisfeld, M., Turkewitz, G., Rose, S. A., Rosenberg, F. R., Sheiber, F. J., Couturier-Fagan, D. A., . . . Sommer, I. (2001). No compelling evidence that newborns imitate oral gestures. *Infancy, 2*, 111–122.

Annett, M. (1973). Laterality of childhood hemiplegia and the growth of speech and intelligence. *Cortex, 9*, 4–33.

Anooshian, L. J., & Young, D. (1981). Developmental changes in cognitive maps of a familiar neighborhood. *Child Development, 52*, 341–348.

Anzures, G., Quinn, P. C., Pascalis, O., Slater, A. M., Ranaka, J. W., & Lee, K. (2013). Developmental origins of the other-race effect. *Current Directions in Psychological Science, 22*, 173–178.

Anzures, G., Wheeler, A., Quinn, P. C., Pascalis, O., Slater, A. M., Heron-Delaney, M., . . . Lee, K. (2012). Brief daily exposure to Asian females reverses perceptual narrowing for Asian faces in Caucasian infants. *Journal of Experimental Child Psychology, 112*, 484–495.

Arden, R., & Plomin, R. (2006). Sex differences in variance of intelligence across childhood. *Personality and Individual Differences, 41*, 39–48.

Arffa, S. (2007). The relationship of intelligence to executive function and nonexecutive function measures in a sample of average, above average, and gifted youth. *Archives of Clinical Neuropsychology, 22*, 969–978.

Argynbayev, A., Kabylbekova, D., & Yaylaci, Y. (2014). Exploiting films in detecting semilingualism among multilingual speakers in Kazakhstan. *Procedia-Social and Behavioral Sciences, 122*, 2–7.

Ashcraft, M. H. (1990). Strategic processing in children's mental arithmetic: A review and proposal. In D. F. Bjorklund (Ed.), *Children's strategies: Contemporary views of cognitive development* (pp. 185–211). Hillsdale, NJ: Erlbaum.

Asher, S. R., & Markel, R. A. (1974). Sex differences in comprehension of high- and low-interest reading material. *Journal of Educational Psychology, 66*, 680–687.

Aslin, R. N. (2007). What's in a look? *Developmental Science, 10*, 48–53.

Aslin, R. N. (2014). Infant learning: Historical, conceptual, and methodological challenges. *Infancy, 19*(1), 2–27.

Aslin, R. N., & Jackson, R. W. (1979). Accommodative-convergence in young infants: Development of a synergistic sensory-motor system. *Canadian Journal of Psychology, 33*, 222–231.

Aslin, R. N., Jusczyk, P. W., & Pisoni, D. B. (1998). Speech and auditory processing during infancy. In W. Damon (Series Ed.) & D. Kuhn & R. S. Siegler (Vol. Eds.), *Handbook of child psychology: Vol 2. Cognition, perception, and language* (5th ed., pp. 147–198). New York: Wiley.

Aslin, R. N., Saffran, J. R., & Newport, E. L. (1998). Computation of conditional probability statistics by 8-month-old infants. *Psychological Science, 9*, 321–324.

Astington, J. W., & Jenkins, J. M. (1995). Theory of mind development and social understanding. *Cognition and Emotion, 9*, 151–165.

Astuti, R. (2001). Are we all natural dualists? A cognitive developmental approach. The 2000 Malinowski Memorial Lecture. *Journal of the Royal Anthropological Institute, 7*, 429–447.

Astuti, R., Solomon, G. E. A., & Carey, S. (2004). Constraints on conceptual development: A case study of the acquisition of folk biological and folk sociological knowledge in Madagascar. *Monographs of the Society for Research in Child Development, 69*(3, Serial No. 277).

Atance, C. M. (2015). Young children's thinking about the future. *Child Development Perspectives, 9*, 178–182.

Atkinson, R. C., & Shiffrin, R. M. (1968). Human memory: A proposed system and its control processes. In K. W. Spence & J. T. Spence (Eds.), *The psychology of learning and motivation: Advances in research and theory* (Vol. 2, pp. 89–195). New York: Academic.

Atran, S., & Henrich, J. (2010). The evolution of religion: How cognitive by-products, adaptive learning heuristics, ritual displays, and group competition generate deep commitments to prosocial religions. *Biological Theory, 5*(1), 18–30.

August, G. J. (1987). Production deficiencies in free recall: A comparison of hyperactive, learning-disabled, and normal children. *Journal of Abnormal Child Psychology, 15,* 429–440.

Avis, J., & Harris, P. L. (1991). Belief-desire reasoning among Baka children: Evidence for a universal conception of mind. *Child Development, 62*(3), 460–467.

Ayduk, O., Mendoza-Denton, R., Mischel, W., Downey, G., Peake, P., & Rodriguez, M. L. (2000). Regulating the interpersonal self: Strategic self-regulation for coping with rejection sensitivity. *Journal of Personality and Social Psychology, 79,* 776–792.

Ayduk, O., Zayas, V., Downey, G., Cole, A. B., Shoda, Y., & Mischel, W. (2008). Rejection sensitivity and executive control: Joint predictors of borderline personality features. *Journal of Research in Personality, 42,* 151–168.

Aylward, G. P. (1997). *Infant and early childhood neuropsychology.* New York: Plenum.

Azevedo, F. A., Carvalho, L. R., Grinberg, L. T., Farfel, J. M., Ferretti, R. E., Leite, R. E., . . . Herculano-Houzel, S. (2009). Equal numbers of neuronal and nonneuronal cells make the human brain an isometrically scaled-up primate brain. *Journal of Comparative Neurology, 513,* 532–541.

Babai, R., Sekal, R., & Stavy, R. (2010). Persistence of the intuitive conception of living things in adolescence. *Journal of Science Education and Technology, 19*(1), 20–26.

Bachevalier, J. (2014). The development of memory from a neurocognitive and comparative perspective. In P. J. Bauer & R. Fivush (Eds.), *The Wiley handbook on the development of children's memory* (Vol. 1, pp. 109–125). Chichester, UK: Wiley-Blackwell.

Baddeley, A. D. (1986). *Working memory.* Oxford, UK: Clarendon.

Baddeley, A. D., & Hitch, G. J. (1974). Working memory. In G. Bower (Ed.), *The psychology of learning and motivation: Advances in research and theory* (Vol. 8, pp. 47–89). New York: Academic.

Badian, N. A. (1983). Dyscalculia and nonverbal disorders of learning. In H. R. Myklebust (Ed.), *Progress in learning disabilities* (pp. 235–264). New York: Stratton.

Bahrick, L. E. (1995). Intermodal origins of self-perception. In P. Rochat (Ed.), *The self in infancy: Theory and research* (pp. 349–373). New York: Elsevier Science.

Bahrick, L. E. (2002). Generalization of learning in three-and-a-half-month-old infants on the basis of amodal relations. *Child Development, 73,* 667–681.

Bahrick, L. E., Hernandez-Reif, M., & Pickens, J. N. (1997). The effect of retrieval cues on visual preferences and memory in infancy: Evidence for a four-phase attention function. *Journal of Experimental Child Psychology, 67,* 1–20.

Bahrick, L. E., Lickliter, R., & Flom, R. (2004). Intersensory redundancy guides the development of selective attention, perception, and cognition in infancy. *Current Directions in Psychological Science, 13,* 99–102.

Bahrick, L. E., Parker, J. F., Fivush, R., & Levitt, M. (1998). The effects of stress on young children's memory for a natural disaster. *Journal of Experimental Psychology: Applied, 4,* 308–331.

Bahrick, L. E., & Pickens, J. N. (1995). Infant memory for object motion across a period of three months: Implications for a four-phase attention function. *Journal of Experimental Child Psychology, 59,* 343–371.

Bahrick, L. E., & Watson, J. S. (1985). Detection of intermodal proprioceptive-visual contingency as a potential basis of self-perception in infancy. *Developmental Psychology, 21,* 963–973.

Bailey, D. H., Zhou, X., Zhang, Y., Cui, J., Fuchs, L. S., Jordan, B. C., . . . Siegler, R. S. (2015). Development of fraction concepts and procedures in U.S. and Chinese children. *Journal of Experimental Child Psychology, 129,* 68–83.

Baillargeon, R. (1987). Object permanence in 3½- and 4½-month-old infants. *Developmental Psychology, 23,* 655–664.

Baillargeon, R. (2004). Infants' reasoning about hidden objects: Evidence for event-general and event-specific expectations. *Developmental Science, 7,* 391–424.

Baillargeon, R. (2008). Innate ideas revisited: For a principle of persistence in infants' physical reasoning. *Perspectives on Psychological Science, 3,* 2–13.

Baillargeon, R., & DeVos, J. (1991). Object permanence in young infants: Further evidence. *Child Development, 62,* 1227–1246.

Baillargeon, R., Kotovsky, L., & Needham, A. (1995). The acquisition of physical knowledge in infancy. In G. Lewis, D. Premack, & D. Sperber (Eds.), *Casual understandings in cognition and culture* (pp. 79–116). Oxford, UK: Oxford University Press.

Baillargeon, R., Scott, R., & Bian, L. (2016). Psychological reasoning in infancy. *Annual Review of Psychology, 67,* 159–186.

Baird, A. A., Kagan, J., Gaudette, T., Walz, K. A., Hershlag, N., & Boas, D. A. (2002). Frontal lobe activation during object permanence: Data from near-infrared spectroscopy. *Neurolmage, 16,* 120–126.

Bakeman, R., Adamson, L. B., Konner, M., & Barr, R. G. (1990). !Kung infancy: The social context of object exploration. *Child Development, 61,* 794–809.

Baker, S. T., Friedman, O., & Leslie, A. M. (2010). The opposites task: Using general rules to test cognitive flexibility in preschoolers. *Journal of Cognition and Development, 11,* 240–254.

Baker Palmer, S., Fais, L., Golinkoff, R. M., & Werker, J. F. (2012). Perceptual narrowing of linguistic sign occurs in the 1st year of life. *Child Development, 83,* 543–553.

Baker-Ward, L., Gordon, B. N., Ornstein, P. A., Larus, D. M., & Clubb, P. A. (1993). Young children's long-term retention of a pediatric visit. *Child Development, 64,* 1519–1533.

Baker-Ward, L., & Ornstein, P. A. (1988). Age differences in visual-spatial memory performance: Do children really out-perform adults when playing Concentration? *Bulletin of the Psychonomic Society, 26,* 331–332.

Baldwin, D. A. (1993). Infants' ability to consult the speaker for clues to word reference. *Journal of Child Language, 20,* 395–418.

Bandura, A. (1986). *Social foundations of thought and action: A social cognitive theory.* Englewood Cliffs, NJ: Prentice Hall.

Bandura, A. (1989). Social cognitive theory. In R. Vasta (Ed.), *Annals of child development: Six theories of child development* (Vol. 6, pp. 1–60). Greenwich, CT: JAI Press.

Bandura, A. (1997). *Self-efficacy: The exercise of control.* New York: Freeman.

Bandura, A. (2006). Toward a psychology of human agency. *Perspectives on Psychological Science, 1,* 164–180.

Bandura, A., Barbaranelli, C., Caprara, G. V., & Pastorelli, C. (1996). Multifaceted impact of self-efficacy beliefs on academic functioning. *Child Development, 67,* 1206–1222.

Banerjee, S. C., Greene, K., Yanovistzky, I., Bagdasarov, Z., Choi, S. Y., & Magsamen-Conrad, K. (2015). Adolescent egocentrism and indoor tanning: Is the relationship direct or mediated? *Journal of Youth Studies, 18*(3), 357–375.

Barbaresi, W. J., Colligan, R. C., Weaver, A. L., Voigt, R. G., Killian, J. M., & Katusic, S. K. (2013). Mortality, ADHD, and psychosocial adversity in adults with childhood ADHD: A prospective study. *Pediatrics, 131*(4), 637–644.

Bard, K. (2007). Neonatal imitation in chimpanzees (*Pan troglodytes*). *Animal Cognition, 10,* 233–242.

Bardi, L., Regolin, L., & Simion, F. (2011). Biological motion preference in humans at birth: Role of dynamic and configural properties. *Developmental Science, 14,* 353–359.

Bardi, L., Regolin, L., & Simion, F. (2014). The first time ever I saw your feet: Inversion effect in newborns' sensitivity to biological motion. *Developmental Psychology, 50,* 986–993.

Barkley, R. A. (1990). Attention deficit disorders: History, definition, and diagnosis. In M. Lewis & S. M. Lewis (Eds.), *Handbook of developmental psychopathology: Perspectives in developmental psychology* (pp. 3–14). New York: Plenum.

Barkley, R. A. (1997). Behavioral inhibition, sustained attention, and executive functions. Constructing a unifying theory of ADHD. *Psychological Bulletin, 121,* 65–94.

Barkley, R. A. (Ed.). (2014). *Attention-deficit hyperactivity disorder: A handbook for diagnosis and treatment.* New York: Guilford Press.

Barnes, M. A., Dennis, M., & Haefele-Kalvaitis, J. (1996). The effects of knowledge availability and knowledge accessibility on coherence and elaborative inferencing in children six to fifteen years of age. *Journal of Experimental Child Psychology, 61,* 216–241.

Barnett, W. S. (1995). Long-term effects of early childhood programs on cognitive and school outcomes. *The Future of Children, 5*(3), 25–50.

Baron-Cohen, S. (1995). *Mindblindness: An essay on autism and theory of mind.* Cambridge, MA: MIT Press.

Baron-Cohen, S. (2005). The empathizing system: A revision of the 1994 model of the mindreading system. In B. J. Ellis & D. F. Bjorklund (Eds.), *Origins of the social mind: Evolutionary psychology and child development* (pp. 468–492). New York: Guilford Press.

Baron-Cohen, S., Allen, J., & Gillberg, C. (1992). Can autism be detected at 18 months? The needle, the haystack, and the CHAT. *British Journal of Psychiatry, 161,* 839–843.

Baron-Cohen, S., Leslie, A. M., & Frith, U. (1985). Does the autistic child have a "theory of mind"? *Cognition, 21,* 37–46.

Barr, R. (2010). Transfer of learning between 2D and 3D sources during infancy: Informing theory and practice. *Developmental Review, 30,* 128–154.

Barr, R. (2013). Memory constraints on infant learning from picture books, television, and touchscreens. *Child Development Perspectives, 4,* 205–210.

Barr, R., & Hayne, H. (2003). It's not what you know, it's who you know: Older siblings facilitate imitation during infancy. *International Journal of Early Years Education, 11,* 7–21.

Barr, R., Muentener, P., Garcia, A., Fujimoto, M., & Chavez, V. (2007). Age-related changes in deferred imitation from television by 6- to 18-month-olds. *Developmental Science, 10,* 910–921.

Barrett, H. C. (2004). Descent versus design in Shuar children's reasoning about animals. *Journal of Cognition and Culture, 4,* 25–50.

Barrett, H. C. (2005). Cognitive development and the understanding of animal behavior. In B. J. Ellis & D. F. Bjorklund (Eds.), *Origins of the social mind: Evolutionary psychology and child development* (pp. 438–467). New York: Guilford Press.

Barrett, H. C., & Behne, T. (2005). Children's understanding of death as the cessation of agency: A test using sleep vs. death. *Cognition, 96*, 93–108.

Barrett, T. M., Davis, E. F., & Needham, A. (2007). Learning about tools in infancy. *Developmental Psychology, 43*, 352–368.

Barrouillet, P. (2011). Dual-process theories and cognitive development: Advances and challenges. *Developmental Review, 31*, 79–85.

Barrouillet, P. (2015). Theories of cognitive development: From Piaget to today. *Developmental Review, 38*, 1–12.

Bartlett, F. C. (1932). *Remembering: A study in experimental and social psychology*. Cambridge, UK: Cambridge University Press.

Basne, R., Gawronski, B., Rebetez, C., Gutt, H., & Morton, B. (2010). The development of spontaneous gender stereotyping in childhood: Relations to stereotype knowledge and stereotype flexibility. *Developmental Science, 13*, 298–306.

Bates, E., Carlson-Luden, V., & Bretherton, I. (1980). Perceptual aspects of tool using in infancy. *Infant Behavior and Development, 3*, 127–140.

Bateson, P. (2002). The corpse of a wearisome debate. *Science, 297*, 2212–2213.

Batki, A., Baron-Cohen, S., Wheelwright, S., Connellan, J., & Ahluwalia, J. (2000). Is there an innate gaze module? Evidence from human neonates. *Infant Behavior and Development, 23*, 223–229.

Batty, G. D., Der, G., Macintyre, S., & Deary, I. J. (2006). Does IQ explain socioeconomic inequalities in health? Evidence from a population based cohort study in the west of Scotland. *British Medical Journal, 332*, 580–584.

Bauer, P. J. (1993). Memory for gender-consistent and gender-inconsistent event sequences by twenty-five-month-old children. *Child Development, 64*, 285–297.

Bauer, P. J. (2002). Long-term recall memory: Behavioral and neuro-developmental changes in the first 2 years of life. *Current Directions in Psychological Science, 11*, 137–141.

Bauer, P. J. (2007). *Remembering the times of our lives: Memory in infancy and beyond*. Mahwah, NJ: Erlbaum.

Bauer, P. J. (2009). The cognitive neuroscience of the development of memory. In M. L. Courage & N. Cowan (Eds.), *The development of memory in infancy and childhood* (pp. 115–144). New York: Psychology Press.

Bauer, P. J. (2014). The development of forgetting: Childhood amnesia. In P. J. Bauer & R. Fivush (Eds.), *The Wiley*

handbook on the development of children's memory (Vol. 2, pp. 519–544). Chichester, UK: Wiley-Blackwell.

Bauer, P. J., Larkina, M., & Deocampo, J. (2011). Early memory development. In U. Goswami (Ed.), *The Blackwell-Wiley handbook of childhood cognitive development* (2nd ed., pp. 153–179). London: Wiley-Blackwell.

Bauer, P. J., & Mandler, J. M. (1989). One thing follows another: Effects of temporal structure on 1- to 2-year-olds' recall of events. *Developmental Psychology, 25*, 197–206.

Bauer, P. J., & Mandler, J. M. (1992). Putting the horse before the cart: The use of temporal order in recall of events by one-year-old children. *Developmental Psychology, 28*, 441–452.

Bauer, P. J., Wenner, J. A., Dropik, P. L., & Wewerka, S. S. (2000). Parameters of remembering and forgetting in the transition from infancy to early childhood. *Monographs of the Society for Research in Child Development, 65*(4, Serial No. 263).

Bauer, P. J., Wiebe, S. A., Waters, J. M., & Bangston, S. K. (2001). Re-exposure breeds recall: Effects of experience on 9-month-olds' ordered recall. *Journal of Experimental Child Psychology, 80*, 174–200.

Bauer, R. H. (1979). Memory, acquisition, and category clustering in learning-disabled children. *Journal of Experimental Child Psychology, 27*, 365–383.

Baumeister, R. F., Bratslavsky, E., Muraven, M., & Tice, D. M. (1998). Ego depletion: Is the active self a limited resource? *Journal of Personality and Social Psychology, 74*(5), 1252.

Bayley, N. (1949). Consistency and variability in the growth of intelligence from birth to eighteen years. *Journal of Genetic Psychology, 75*, 165–196.

Bayley, N. (2005). *Bayley Scales of Infant and Toddler Development* (3rd ed.). San Antonio, TX: Harcourt Assessment.

Beal, C. R., & Flavell, J. H. (1982). Effects of increasing salience of message ambiguities on kindergarteners' evaluations of communicative success and message adequacy. *Developmental Psychology, 10*, 43–48.

Beck, S. R., Apperly, I. A., Chappell, C., Guthrie, C., & Cutting, N. (2011). Making tools isn't child's play. *Cognition, 119*, 301–306.

Becker, W. C., & Gersten, R. (1982). A follow-up of Follow Through: The later effects of the direct instruction model for children in fifth and sixth grades. *American Educational Research Journal, 19*, 75–92.

Beckett, C., Castle, J., Rutter, M., & Sonuga-Barke, E. J. (2010). Institutional deprivation, specific cognitive functions, and scholastic achievement: English and

Romanian adoptees (ERA) study findings. In M. Rutter, E. J. Sonuga-Barke, C. Beckett, J. Castle, J. Kreppner, R. Kumsta, . . . & C. A. Bell (Eds.), Deprivation-specific psychological patterns: Effects of institutional deprivation. *Monographs of the Society for Research in Child Development, 75*(1), 125–142.

Beckett, C., Maughan, B., Rutter, M., Castle, J., Colvert, E., Groothues, C., . . . Sonuga-Barke, E. J. S. (2006). Do the effects of early severe deprivation on cognition persist into early adolescence? Findings from the English and Romanian Adoptee Study. *Child Development, 77,* 696–711.

Behrend, D. A., Rosengren, K., & Perlmutter, M. (1989). A new look at children's private speech: The effects of age, task difficulty, and parent presence. *International Journal of Behavioral Development, 12,* 305–320.

Beilin, H. (1992). Piaget's enduring contribution to developmental psychology. *Developmental Psychology, 28,* 191–204.

Beilock, S. L., Gunderson, E. A., Ramirez, G., & Levine, S. C. (2010). Female teachers' math anxiety impacts girls' math achievement. *Proceedings of the National Academy of Sciences, 107,* 1860–1863.

Bell, M. A., & Fox, N. A. (1992). The relations between frontal brain electrical activity and cognitive development during infancy. *Child Development, 63,* 1142–1163.

Bell, M. A., Wolfe, C. D., & Adkins, D. R. (2007). Frontal lobe development during infancy and childhood: Contributions of brain electrical activity temperament, and language to individual differences in working memory and inhibition control. In D. Coch, K. W. Fischer, & G. Dawson (Eds.), *Human behavior, learning, and the developing brain: Typical development* (pp. 247–276). New York: Guilford Press.

Bell, R. Q. (1968). A reinterpretation of the direction of effects in studies of socialization. *Psychological Review, 75,* 81–95.

Belsky, J., & Most, R. K. (1981). From exploration to play: A cross-sectional study of infant free play behavior. *Developmental Psychology, 17,* 630–639.

Bem, S. (1981). Gender schema theory: A cognitive account of sex-typing. *Psychological Review, 88,* 354–364.

Benbow, C. P., & Stanley J. C. (1983). Sex differences in mathematical reasoning: More facts. *Science, 222,* 1029–1031.

Benedict, H. (1979). Early lexical development: Comprehension and production. *Journal of Child Language, 6,* 183–200.

Berenbaum, S. A., & Hines, M. (1992). Early androgens are related to childhood sex-typed toy preferences. *Psychological Science, 3,* 203–206.

Berg, D. H. (2008). Working memory and arithmetic calculation in children: The contributory roles of processing speed, short-term memory, and reading. *Journal of Experimental Child Psychology, 99,* 288–308.

Bergman, L. R., Ferrer-Wreder, L., & Žukauskien , R. (2015). Career outcomes of adolescents with below average IQ: Who succeeded against the odds? *Intelligence, 52,* 9–17.

Bering, J. M. (2012). *The belief instinct: The psychology of souls, destiny, and the meaning of life.* New York: Norton.

Bering, J. M., & Bjorklund, D. F. (2004). The natural emergence of afterlife reasoning as a developmental regularity. *Developmental Psychology, 40,* 217–233.

Bering, J. M., Hernández Blasi, C., & Bjorklund, D. F. (2005). The development of "afterlife" beliefs in religiously and secularly schooled children. *British Journal of Developmental Psychology, 23,* 587–607.

Bering, J. M., & Parker, B. D. (2006). Children's attributions of intentions to an invisible agent. *Developmental Psychology, 42,* 253–262.

Berk, L. E. (1986). Relationship of elementary school children's private speech to behavioral accompaniment to task, attention, and task performance. *Developmental Psychology, 22,* 671–680.

Berk, L. E. (1992). Children's private speech: An overview of theory and the status of research. In R. M. Diaz & L. E. Berk (Eds.), *Private speech: From social interaction to self-regulation* (pp. 17–53). Hillsdale, NJ: Erlbaum.

Berk, L. E., & Landau, S. (1993). Private speech of learning disabled and normally achieving children in classroom academic and laboratory contexts. *Child Development, 64,* 556–571.

Berk, L. E., Mann, T., & Ogan, A. (2006). Make-believe play: Wellspring for development of self-regulation. In D. G. Singer, R. M. Golinkoff, & K. Hirsh-Pasek (Eds.), *Play = learning: How play motivates and enhances children's cognitive and social-emotional growth* (pp. 74–100). New York: Oxford University Press.

Berk, L. E., & Meyers, A. B. (2013). The role of make-believe and the development of executive functions: Status of research and future directions. *American Journal of Play, 6,* 98–110.

Berk, L. E., & Spuhl, S. T. (1995). Maternal intervention, private speech, and task performance in preschool children. *Early Childhood Research Quarterly, 10,* 145–169.

Berko, J. (1958). The child's learning of English morphology. *Word, 14,* 150–177.

Bernstein, A. C. (1978). *Flight of the stork.* New York: Delacorte Press.

Bernstein, A. C., & Cowan, P. A. (1975). Children's concepts of how people get babies. *Child Development, 46,* 77–91.

Bernstein, B. (1971). *Class codes and control* (Vol. 1). London: Routledge & Kegan Paul.

Bertenthal, B. I. (1996). Origins and early development of perception, action, and representation. *Annual Review of Psychology, 47*, 431–435.

Bertenthal, B. I., & Campos, J. J. (1987). New directions in the study of early experience. *Child Development, 58*, 560–567.

Bertenthal, B. I., Proffitt, D. R., & Cutting, J. E. (1984). Infant sensitivity to figural coherence in bio-mechanical motions. *Journal of Experimental Child Psychology, 37*, 213–230.

Berthier, N. E., DeBois, S., Poirier, C. R., Novak, M. A., & Clifton, R. K. (2000). Where's the ball? Two- and three-year-olds reason about unseen events. *Developmental Psychology, 36*, 384–401.

Best, D. L. (1993). Inducing children to generate mnemonic organizational strategies: An examination of long-term retention and materials. *Developmental Psychology, 29*, 324–336.

Best, D. L., & Ornstein, P. A. (1986). Children's generation and communication of mnemonic organizational strategies. *Developmental Psychology, 22*, 845–853.

Best, J. R., & Miller, P. H. (2010). A developmental perspective on executive function. *Child development, 81*(6), 1641–1660.

Bhatt, R. S., Bertin, E., Hayden, A., & Reed, A. (2005). Face processing in infancy: Developmental changes in the use of different kinds of relational information. *Child Development, 76*, 169–181.

Bhatt, R. S., Rovee-Collier, C., & Shyi, C.-W. G. (1994). Perception and 24-hour retention of feature relations in infancy. *Developmental Psychology, 30*, 142–150.

Bialystok, E. (2011). Coordination of executive functions in monolingual and bilingual children. *Journal of Experimental Child Psychology, 110*(3), 461–468.

Bialystok, E., & Craik, F. I. M. (2010). Cognitive and linguistic processing in the bilingual mind. *Current Directions in Psychological Science, 19*, 19–23.

Bialystok, E., Craik, F. I., Binns, M. A., Ossher, L., & Freedman, M. (2014). Effects of bilingualism on the age of onset and progression of MCI and AD: Evidence from executive function tests. *Neuropsychology, 28*(2), 290–304.

Bialystok, E., Craik, F., & Luk, G. (2008). Cognitive control and lexical access in younger and older individuals. *Journal of Experimental Psychology: Learning, Memory, and Cognition, 34*, 859–873.

Bialystok, E., Craik, F., & Luk, G. (2012). Bilingualism: Consequences for mind and brain. *Trends in Cognitive Sciences, 16*(4), 240–250.

Bialystok, E., & Feng, X. (2011). Language proficiency and its implications for monolingual and bilingual children. In A. Y. Durgunoglu & C. Goldenberg (Eds.), *Language and Literacy Development in Bilingual Settings* (pp. 121–139). New York: Guilford Press.

Bialystok, E., & Hakuta, K. (1994). *In other words.* New York: Basic Books.

Bickerton, D. (1990). *Language and species.* Chicago: University of Chicago Press.

Bisanz, J., Morrison, F. J., & Dunn, M. (1995). The effects of age and schooling on the acquisition of elementary quantitative skills. *Developmental Psychology, 31*, 221–236.

Bivens, J. A., & Berk, L. E. (1990). A longitudinal study of the development of elementary school children's private speech. *Merrill-Palmer Quarterly, 36*, 443–463.

Bjorklund, D. F. (1980). Developmental differences in the timing of children's awareness of category relations in free recall. *International Journal of Behavioral Development, 3*, 61–70.

Bjorklund, D. F. (1987a). A note on neonatal imitation. *Developmental Review, 7*, 86–92.

Bjorklund, D. F. (1987b). How age changes in knowledge base contribute to the development of children's memory: An interpretive review. *Developmental Review, 7*, 93–130.

Bjorklund, D. F. (1997a). In search of a metatheory for cognitive development (or, Piaget is dead and I don't feel so good myself). *Child Development, 68*, 142–146.

Bjorklund, D. F. (1997b). The role of immaturity in human development. *Psychological Bulletin, 122*, 153–169.

Bjorklund, D. F. (2003). Evolutionary psychology from a developmental systems perspective: Comment on Lickliter and Honeycutt. *Psychological Bulletin, 129*, 836–841.

Bjorklund, D. F. (2007a). The most educable of species. In J. S. Carlson & J. R. Levin (Eds.), *Psychological perspectives on contemporary educational issues* (pp. 119–129). Greenwich, CT: Information Age.

Bjorklund, D. F. (2007b). *Why youth is not wasted on the young: Immaturity in human development.* Oxford, UK: Blackwell.

Bjorklund, D. F. (2013). Cognitive development: An overview. In P. D. Zelazo (Ed.), *The Oxford handbook of developmental psychology: Vol. 1. Body and mind* (pp. 447–476). Oxford, UK: Oxford University Press.

Bjorklund, D. F. (2015). Developing adaptations. *Developmental Review, 38*, 13–35.

Bjorklund, D. F., & Beers, C. (2016). The adaptive value of cognitive immaturity: Applications of evolutionary developmental psychology to early education. In D. C. Geary & D. B. Berch (Eds.), *Evolutionary perspectives on education and child development* (pp. 3–32). New York: Springer.

Bjorklund, D. F., & Bering, J. M. (2003). Big brains, slow development, and social complexity: The developmental and evolutionary origins of social cognition. In M. Brüne, H. Ribbert, & W. Schiefenhövel (Eds.), *The social brain: Evolutionary aspects of development and pathology* (pp. 133–151). Wiley: New York.

Bjorklund, D. F., & Bernholtz, J. F. (1986). The role of knowledge base in the memory performance of good and poor readers. *Journal of Experimental Child Psychology, 41*, 367–373.

Bjorklund, D. F., & Bjorklund, B. R. (1992). *Looking at children: An introduction to child development*. Belmont, CA: Wadsworth.

Bjorklund, D. F., Bjorklund, B. R., Brown, R. D., & Cassel, W. S. (1998). Children's susceptibility to repeated questions: How misinformation changes children's answers and their minds. *Applied Developmental Science, 2*, 99–111.

Bjorklund, D. F., Brown, R. D., & Bjorklund, B. R. (2002). Children's eyewitness memory: Changing reports and changing representations. In P. Graf & N. Ohta (Eds.), *Lifespan memory development* (pp. 101–126). Cambridge, MA: MIT Press.

Bjorklund, D. F., Causey, K., & Periss, V. (2010). The evolution and development of human social cognition. In P. Kappeler & J. Silk (Eds.), *Mind the gap: Tracing the origins of human universals* (pp. 351–371). Berlin: Springer-Verlag.

Bjorklund, D. F., Coyle, T. R., & Gaultney, J. F. (1992). Developmental differences in the acquisition of an organizational strategy: Evidence for the utilization deficiency hypothesis. *Journal of Experimental Child Psychology, 54*, 434–448.

Bjorklund, D. F., Dukes, C., & Brown, R. D. (2009). The development of memory strategies. In M. L. Courage & N. Cowan (Eds.), *The development of memory in infancy and childhood* (pp. 145–175). New York: Psychology Press.

Bjorklund, D. F., & Ellis, B. J. (2014). Children, childhood, and development in evolutionary perspective. *Developmental Review, 34*, 225–264.

Bjorklund, D. F., Ellis, B. J., & Rosenberg, J. S. (2007). Evolved probabilistic cognitive mechanisms. In R. V. Kail (Ed.), *Advances in child development and behavior* (Vol. 35, pp. 1–39). Oxford, UK: Elsevier.

Bjorklund, D. F., & Gardiner, A. K. (2011). Object play and tool use: Developmental and evolutionary perspectives. In A. D. Pellegrini (Ed.), *The Oxford handbook of the development of play* (pp. 153–171). Oxford, UK: Oxford University Press.

Bjorklund, D. F., Gaultney, J. F., & Green, B. L. (1993). "I watch, therefore I can do": The development of meta-imitation over the preschool years and the advantage of optimism in one's imitative skills. In R. Pasnak & M. L. Howe (Eds.), *Emerging themes in cognitive development* (Vol. 1, pp. 79–102). New York: Springer-Verlag.

Bjorklund, D. F., & Green, B. L. (1992). The adaptive nature of cognitive immaturity. *American Psychologist, 47*, 46–54.

Bjorklund, D. F., & Harnishfeger, K. K. (1987). Developmental differences in the mental effort requirements for the use of an organizational strategy in free recall. *Journal of Experimental Child Psychology, 44*, 109–125.

Bjorklund, D. F., & Harnishfeger, K. K. (1995). The role of inhibition mechanisms in the evolution of human cognition and behavior. In F. N. Dempster & C. J. Brainerd (Eds.), *New perspectives on interference and inhibition in cognition* (pp. 141–173). New York: Academic.

Bjorklund, D. F., & Hernández Blasi, C. (2012). *Child and adolescent development: An integrative approach*. Belmont, CA: Wadsworth.

Bjorklund, D. F., Hernández Blasi, C., & Ellis, B. J. (2016). Evolutionary developmental psychology. In D. Buss (Ed.), *Evolutionary psychology handbook* (Vol. 2, pp. 904–925). New York: Wiley.

Bjorklund, D. F., Hubertz, M. J., & Reubens, A. C. (2004). Young children's arithmetic strategies in social context: How parents contribute to children's strategy development while playing games. *International Journal of Behavioral Development, 28*, 347–357.

Bjorklund, D. F., & Jacobs, J. W. (1985). Associative and categorical processes in children's memory: The role of automaticity in the development of organization in free recall. *Journal of Experimental Child Psychology, 39*, 599–617.

Bjorklund, D. F., & Kipp, K. (2002). Social cognition, inhibition, and theory of mind: The evolution of human intelligence. In R. J. Sternberg & J. C. Kaufman (Eds.), *The evolution of intelligence* (pp. 27–53). Mahwah, NJ: Erlbaum.

Bjorklund, D. F., Miller, P. H., Coyle, T. R., & Slawinski, J. L. (1997). Instructing children to use memory strategies: Evidence of utilization deficiencies in memory training studies. *Developmental Review, 17*, 411–442.

Bjorklund, D. F., & Pellegrini, A. D. (2002). *The origins of human nature: Evolutionary developmental psychology*. Washington, DC: American Psychological Association.

Bjorklund, D. F., Periss, V., & Causey, K. (2009). The benefits of youth. *European Journal of Developmental Psychology, 6*, 120–137.

Bjorklund, D. F., & Rosenblum, K. E. (2002). Context effects in children's selection and use of simple arithmetic strategies. *Journal of Cognition and Development, 3,* 225–242.

Bjorklund, D. F., & Schwartz, R. (1996). The adaptive nature of developmental immaturity: Implications for language acquisition and language disabilities. In M. Smith & J. D'amico (Eds.), *Childhood language disorders* (pp. 17–40). New York: Thieme Medical.

Bjorklund, D. F., & Sellers, P. D., II. (2014). Memory development in evolutionary perspective. In P. Bauer & R. Fivush (Eds.), *The Wiley handbook on the development of children's memory* (pp. 126–150). Chichester, UK: Wiley-Blackwell.

Bjorklund, D. F., & Zeman, B. R. (1982). Children's organization and metamemory awareness in the recall of familiar information. *Child Development, 53,* 799–810.

Black, J. E., Jones, T. A., Nelson, C. A., & Greenough, W. T. (1998). Neuronal plasticity and the developing brain. In N. E. Alessi, J. T. Coyle, S. I. Harrison, & S. Eth (Eds.), *Handbook of child and adolescent psychiatry* (Vol. 6, pp. 31–53). New York: Wiley.

Blair, C. (2006). How similar are fluid cognition and general intelligence? A developmental neuroscience perspective on fluid cognition as an aspect of human cognitive ability. *Behavioral and Brain Sciences, 29,* 109–160.

Blair, C., & Diamond, A. (2008). Biological processes in prevention and intervention: The promotion of self-regulation as a means of preventing school failure. *Development and Psychopathology, 20,* 899–911.

Blair, C., Gamson, D., Thorne, S., & Bak, D. (2005). Rising mean IQ: Cognitive demand of mathematics education for young children, population exposure to formal schooling, and the neurobiology of the prefrontal cortex. *Intelligence, 33,* 93–106.

Blair, C., & Raver, C. C. (2012). Child development in the context of adversity: Experiential canalization of brain and behavior. *American Psychologist, 67,* 309–318.

Blakemore, C., & Van Sluyters, R. C. (1975). Innate and environmental factors in the development of the kitten's visual cortex. *Journal of Physiology, 248,* 663–716.

Bloom, L. (1993). *Language development form two to three.* Cambridge, UK: Cambridge University Press.

Bloom, L. (1998). Language acquisition in developmental contexts. In W. Damon (Series Ed.) & D. Kuhn & R. S. Siegler (Vol. Eds.), *Handbook of child psychology: Vol 2. Cognition, perception, and language* (5th ed., pp. 309–371). New York: Wiley.

Bloom, L., Hood, L., & Lightbown, P. (1974). Imitation in language development: If, when and why. *Cognitive Psychology, 6,* 380–420.

Bloom, L., Lightbown, P., & Hood, L. (1975). Structure and variation in child language. *Monographs of the Society for Research in Child Development, 40*(2, Serial No. 160).

Bloom, P. (2000). *How children learn the meanings of words.* Cambridge, MA: MIT Press.

Bloom, P. (2004). *Descartes' baby: How the science of child development explains what makes us human.* New York: Basic Books.

Blumberg, F. C., & Torenberg, M. (2005). The effects of spatial configuration on preschoolers' attention strategies, selective attention, and incidental learning. *Infant and Child Development, 14,* 243–258.

Blumberg, F. C., Torenberg, M., & Randall, J. D. (2005). The relationship between preschoolers' selective attention and memory for location strategies. *Cognitive Development, 20,* 242–255.

Bock, J. (2005). Farming, foraging, and children's play in the Okavango Delta, Botswana. In A. D. Pellegrini & P. K. Smith (Eds.), *The nature of play: Great apes and humans* (pp. 254–281). New York: Guilford Press.

Boesch, C., & Tomasello, M. (1998). Chimpanzee and human culture. *Current Anthropology, 39,* 591–604.

Bogart, S. L., Bennett, A. J., Schapiro, S. J., Reamer, L. A., & Hopkins, W. D. (2014). Different early rearing experiences have long-term effects on cortical organization in captive chimpanzees (*Pan troglodytes*). *Developmental Science, 17,* 161–174.

Bogartz, R. S., & Shinskey, J. L. (1998). On perception of a partially occluded object in 6-month-olds. *Cognitive Development, 13,* 141–163.

Bogartz, R. S., Shinskey, J. L., & Speaker, C. (1997). Interpreting infant looking: The event set x event set design. *Developmental Psychology, 33,* 408–422.

Bogdan, R. J. (2010). *Our own minds: Sociocultural grounds for self-consciousness.* Cambridge, MA: MIT Press.

Bonawitz, E., Shafto, P., Gweon, H., Goodman, N. D., Spelke, E., & Schulz, L. (2011). The double-edged sword of pedagogy: Instruction limits spontaneous exploration and discover. *Cognition, 120,* 322–330.

Booth, J. L., & Siegler, R. S. (2008). Numerical magnitude representations influence arithmetic learning. *Child Development, 79,* 1016–1031.

Borke, H. (1975). Piaget's mountains revisited: Changes in the egocentric landscape. *Developmental Psychology, 11,* 240–243.

Borkowski, J. G., & Peck, V. A. (1986). Causes and consequences of metamemory in gifted children. In R. J. Sternberg & J. C. Davidson (Eds.), *Conceptions of giftedness* (pp. 182–200). Cambridge, UK: Cambridge University Press.

Borkowski, J. G., Peck, V. A., Reid, M. K., & Kurtz, B. (1983). Impulsivity and strategy transfer: Metamemory as mediator. *Child Development, 54,* 459–473.

Borkowski, J. G., Reid, M. K., & Kurtz, B. E. (1984). Metacognition and retardation: Pragmatic, theoretical and applied perspectives. In P. H. Brooks, R. Sperber, & C. McCauley (Eds.), *Learning and cognition in the mentally retarded* (pp. 55–75). Hillsdale, NJ: Erlbaum.

Bornstein, M. H. (1989). Stability in early mental development: From attention and information processing in infancy to language and cognition in childhood. In M. H. Bornstein & N. A. Krasnegor (Eds.), *Stability and continuity in mental development: Behavioral and biological perspectives* (pp. 147–170). Hillsdale, NJ: Erlbaum.

Bornstein, M. H., & Bradley, R. H. (Eds.). (2014). *Socioeconomic status, parenting, and child development.* London: Routledge.

Bornstein, M. H., Ferdinandsen, K., & Gross, C. G. (1981). Perception of symmetry in infancy. *Developmental Psychology, 17,* 82–86.

Bornstein, M. H., Hahn, C.-S., Bell, C., Haynes, O. M., Slater, A., Golding, J., . . . the ALSPAC Study Team. (2006). Stability in cognition across childhood. *Psychological Science, 17,* 151–158.

Bornstein, M. H., Hahn, C.-S., & Suwalsky, J. T. D. (2013). Physically developed and exploratory young infants contribute to their own long-term academic achievement. *Psychological Science, 24,* 1906–1917.

Bornstein, M. H., Haynes, O. M., O'Reilly, A. W., & Painter, K. M. (1996). Solitary and collaborative pretense play in early childhood: Sources of individual variation in the development of representational competence. *Child Development, 67,* 2910–2929.

Bornstein, M. H., & Sigman, M. D. (1986). Continuity in mental development from infancy. *Child Development, 57,* 251–274.

Bosch, L., & Sebastian-Galles. (2001). Evidence of early language discrimination abilities in infants from bilingual environments. *Infancy, 2,* 29–49.

Bouchard, T. J., Jr., Lykken, D. T., McGue, M., Segal, N. L., & Tellegen, A. (1990). Sources of human psychological differences: The Minnesota study of twins reared apart. *Science, 250,* 223–228.

Bouchard, T. J., Jr., & McGue, M. (1981). Familial studies of intelligence: A review. *Science, 212,* 1055–1059.

Bowyer-Crane, C., Snowling, M. J., Duff, F. J., Fieldsend, E., Carroll, J. M., Miles, J., . . . Hulme, C. (2008). Improving early language and literacy skills: Differential effects of an oral language versus a phonology with reading intervention. *Journal of Child Psychology and Psychiatry, 49,* 422–432.

Bradley, B. S. (1989). *Visions of infancy. A critical introduction to child psychology.* Oxford, UK: Basil Blackwell.

Bradley, R. H., Burchinal, M. R., & Casey, P. H. (2001). Early intervention: The moderating role of the home environment. *Applied Developmental Science, 5,* 2–8.

Bradley, R. H., & Caldwell, B. M. (1976). The relation of infants' home environment to mental test performance at fifty-four months: A follow-up study. *Child Development, 47,* 1172–1174.

Bradley, R. H., Caldwell, B. M., & Elardo, R. (1977). Home environment, social status, and mental test performance. *Journal of Educational Psychology, 69,* 697–701.

Bradley, R. H., Caldwell, B. M., Rock, S. L., Ramey, C. T., Barnard, K. E., Gray C., . . . Johnson, D. L. (1989). Home environments and cognitive development in the first 3 years of life: A collaborative study including six sites and three ethnic groups in North America. *Developmental Psychology, 25,* 217–235.

Brainerd, C. J. (1978). *Piaget's theory of intelligence.* Englewood Cliffs, NJ: Prentice Hall.

Brainerd, C. J. (1996). Piaget: A centennial celebration. *Psychological Science, 7,* 191–195.

Brainerd, C. J., & Allen, T. W. (1971). Training and generalization of density conservation: Effects of feedback and consecutive similar stimuli. *Child Development, 42,* 693–704.

Brainerd, C. J., & Brainerd, S. H. (1972). Order of acquisition of number and liquid quantity conservation. *Child Development, 43,* 1401–1405.

Brainerd, C. J., & Gordon, L. L. (1994). Development of verbatim and gist memory for numbers. *Developmental Psychology, 30,* 163–177.

Brainerd, C. J., & Mojardin, A. H. (1999). Children's and adults' spontaneous false memories for sentences: Long-term persistence and mere-testing effects. *Child Development, 69,* 1361–1377.

Brainerd, C. J., & Reyna, V. F. (1990). Gist is the grist: Fuzzy-trace theory and the new intuitionism. *Developmental Review, 10,* 3–17.

Brainerd, C. J., & Reyna, V. F. (1993). Domains of fuzzy trace theory. In M. L. Howe & R. Pasnak (Eds.), *Emerging themes in cognitive development* (Vol. 1, pp. 50–93). New York: Springer-Verlag.

Brainerd, C. J., & Reyna, V. F. (1996). Mere memory testing creates false memories in children. *Developmental Psychology, 32,* 467–478.

Brainerd, C. J., & Reyna, V. F. (2012). Reliability of children's testimony in an era of developmental reversals. *Developmental Review, 32,* 224–267.

Brainerd, C. J., & Reyna, V. F. (2014). Dual processes in memory development: Fuzzy-trace theory. In P. J. Bauer & R. Fivush (Eds.), *The Wiley handbook on the development of children's memory* (Vol. 1, pp. 480–512). Chichester, UK: Wiley-Blackwell.

Brainerd, C. J., & Reyna, V. F. (2015). Fuzzy-trace theory and lifespan cognitive development. *Developmental Review, 38,* 89–121.

Brainerd, C. J., Reyna, V. F., & Ceci, S. J. (2008). Developmental reversals in false memory: A review of data and theory. *Psychological Review, 134,* 343–382.

Brainerd, C. J., Reyna, V. F., & Zember, E. (2011). Theoretical and forensic implications of developmental studies of the DRM illusion. *Memory & Cognition, 39*(3), 365–380.

Brannon, D., Dauksa, L., Coleman, N., Israelson, L., & Williams, T. (2013). Measuring the effect that the partners' dialogic reading program has on preschool children's expressive language. *Creative Education, 4,* 14–19.

Brant, A. M., Munakata, Y., Boomsma, D. I., DeFries, J. C., Haworth, C. M. A., Keller, M. C., . . . Hewitt, J. K. (2013). The nature and nurture of high IQ: An extended sensitive period for intellectual development. *Psychological Science, 24,* 1487–1495.

Brazelton, T. B. (1973). *Neonatal Behavioral Assessment Scale* (Clinics in Developmental Medicine, No. 50). Philadelphia: Lippincott.

Bremner, A. J., & Mareschal, D. (2004). Reasoning . . . what reasoning? *Developmental Science, 7,* 419–421.

Briars, D., & Siegler, R. S. (1984). A featural analysis of preschoolers' counting knowledge. *Developmental Psychology, 20,* 607–618.

Broesch, T. L., & Bryant, G. A. (2015). Prosody in infant-directed speech is similar across Western and traditional cultures. *Journal of Cognition and Development, 16,* 31–43.

Bronfenbrenner, U., & Ceci, S. J. (1994). Nature-nurture reconceptualized in developmental perspective: A bio-ecological model. *Psychological Review, 101,* 568–586.

Bronfenbrenner, U., & Morris, P. A. (2006). The bioecological model of human development. In W. Damon & R. M. Lerner (Series Eds.) & R. M. Lerner (Vol. Ed.), *Handbook of child psychology: Vol. 1. Theoretical models of human development* (6th ed., pp. 793–828). New York: Wiley.

Bronner, M., & Hatten, M. E. (2012). Neurogenesis and migration. In L. R. Squire, D. Berg, F. E. Bloom, S. du Lac, A. Ghosh, & N. C. Spitzer (Eds.), *Fundamental neuro science* (4th ed., pp. 339–361). New York: Elsevier.

Bronson, G. W. (1990). Changes in infants' visual scanning across the 2–14-week age period. *Journal of Experimental Child Psychology, 49,* 101–125.

Brooks, R., & Meltzoff, A. N. (2002). The importance of eyes: How infants interpret adult looking behavior. *Developmental Psychology, 38,* 958–966.

Brooks-Gunn, J., & Lewis, M. (1984). The development of early self-recognition. *Developmental Review, 4,* 215–239.

Brooks-Gunn, J., Linver, M. R., & Fauth, R. C. (2005). *Children's competence and socioeconomic status in the family and neighborhood.* New York: Guilford Press.

Brown, A. L., & Kane, M. J. (1988). Preschool children can learn to transfer: Learning to learn and learning by example. *Cognitive Psychology, 20,* 493–523.

Brown, A. L., Kane, M. J., & Long, C. (1989). Analogical transfer in young children: Analogies as tools for communication and exposition. *Applied Cognitive Psychology, 3,* 275–293.

Brown, D. A., & Lamb, M. E. (2015). Can children be useful witnesses? It depends how they are questioned. *Child Development Perspectives, 9,* 250–255.

Brown, R. (1973). *A first language: The early stages.* Cambridge, MA: Harvard University Press.

Brown, R., & Hanlon, C. (1970). Derivational complexity and the order of acquisition in child speech. In J. R. Hayes (Ed.), *Cognition and the development of language* (pp. 11–53). New York: Wiley.

Bruck, M., Ceci, S. J., Francoeur, E., & Barr, R. (1995). "I hardly cried when I got my shot!" Influencing children's reports about a visit to their pediatrician. *Child Development, 66,* 193–208.

Bruck, M., Ceci, S. J., & Principe, G. F. (2006). The child and the law. In W. Damon & R. M. Lerner (Series Eds.) & K. A. Renninger & I. E. Sigel (Vol. Eds.), *Handbook of child psychology: Vol. 4. Child psychology in practice* (6th ed., pp. 776–816). New York: Wiley.

Bruner, J. S. (1966). On cognitive growth. In J. S. Bruner, R. R. Olver, & P. M. Greenfield (Eds.), *Studies in cognitive growth* (pp. 225–256). New York: Wiley.

Bruner, J. S. (1972). The nature and uses of immaturity. *American Psychologist, 27,* 687–708.

Bruner, J. S. (1983). *Child's talk: Learning to use language.* New York: Norton.

Brunswick, N., Martin, G. N., & Rippon, G. (2012). Early cognitive profiles of emergent readers: A longitudinal study. *Journal of Experimental Child Psychology, 111,* 268–285.

Bryant, P. E., MacLean, M., Bradley, L. L., & Crossland, J. (1990). Rhyme and alliteration, phoneme detection, and learning to read. *Developmental Psychology, 26,* 429–438.

Buccino, G., Vogt, G. S., Ritzl, A., Fink, G. R., Zilles, K., Freund, H.-J., & Rizzolatti, G. (2004). Neural circuits underlying imitation learning of hand actions: An event-related fMRI study. *Neuron, 42,* 323–334.

Buchsbaum, D., Bridgers, S., Weisberg, D. S., & Gopnik, A. (2012). The power of possibility: Causal learning, counterfactual reasoning, and pretend play. *Philosophical Transactions of the Royal Society B: Biological Sciences, 367,* 2202–2212.

Budgwig, N. (1990). The linguistic marking of nonprototypical agency: An exploration into children's use of passives. *Linguistics, 28,* 1221–1252.

Bullock, M., & Lutkenhaus, P. (1988). The development of volitional behavior in the toddler years. *Child Development, 59,* 664–674.

Bullock, M., Sodian, B., & Koerber, S. (2009). Doing experiments and understanding science: Development of scientific reasoning from childhood to adulthood. In W. Schneider & M. Bullock (Eds.), *Human development from early childhood to early adulthood: Findings from a 20-year longitudinal study* (pp. 173–197). New York: Psychology Press.

Burts, D. C., Hart, C. H., Charlesworth, R., DeWolf, D. M., Ray, J., Manuel, K., & Fleege, P. O. (1993). Developmental appropriateness of kindergarten programs and academic outcomes in first grade. *Journal of Research in Childhood Education, 8,* 23–31.

Bush, E. B., Quas, J. A., Yim, I. S., Nikolayev, M., Clark, S. E., & Larson, R. P. (2014). Stress, interviewer support, and children's eyewitness identification. *Child Development, 85,* 1292–1305.

Bushnell, I. W. R., Sai, F., & Mullin, J. T. (1989). Neonatal recognition of the mother's face. *British Journal of Developmental Psychology, 7,* 3–15.

Buss, D. M. (2009). The great struggles of life: Darwin and the emergence of evolutionary psychology. *American Psychologist, 64,* 140–148.

Butcher, L. M., Davis, O. S. P., Craig, I. W., & Plomin, R. (2008). Genome-wide quantitative trait locus association scan of general cognitive ability using pooled DNA and 500K single nucleotide polymorphism microarrays. *Genes, Brains and Behavior, 7,* 435–446.

Buttelmann, D., Carpenter, M., Call, J., & Tomasello, M. (2008). Rational tool use and tool choice in human infants and great apes. *Child Development, 79,* 609–626.

Buttelmann, D., Zmyj, N., Daum, M. M., & Carpenter, M. (2013). Selective imitation of in-group over out-group members in 14-month-olds. *Child Development, 84,* 422–428.

Byne, W., Bradley, S. J., Coleman, E., Eyler, A. E., Green, R., Menvielle, E. J., . . . Tompkins, D. A. (2012). Report of the American Psychiatric Association Task Force on treatment of gender identity disorder. *Archives of Sexual Behavior, 41,* 759–796.

Byrne, R. W. (2005). Social cognition: Imitation, imitation, imitation. *Current Biology, 15,* R489–R500.

Byrne, R. W., & Whiten, A. (Eds.). (1988). *Machiavellian intelligence: Social expertise and the evolution of intellect in monkeys, apes, and humans.* Oxford, UK: Clarendon.

Byrnes, J. P., & Fox, N. A. (1998). The educational relevance of research in cognitive neuroscience. *Educational Psychology Review, 10,* 297–342.

Cacchione, T., Schaub, S., & Rakoczy, H. (2013). Fourteen-month-old infants infer the continuous identity of objects on the basis of nonvisible causal properties. *Developmental Psychology, 49*(7), 1325–1329.

Cahan, S., & Cohen, N. (1989). Age versus schooling effects on intelligence development. *Child Development, 60,* 1239–1249.

Cain, K., Oakhill, J., & Bryant, P. (2004). Children's reading comprehension ability: Concurrent prediction by working memory, verbal ability, and component skills. *Journal of Educational Psychology, 96,* 31–42.

Cairns, R. B. (1979). *Social development: The origins and plasticity of interchanges.* San Francisco: W. H. Freeman.

Caldera, Y. M., O'Brien, M., Truglio, R. T., Alvarez, M., & Huston, A. C. (1999). Children's play preferences, construction play with blocks, and visual-spatial skills: Are they related? *International Journal of Behavioral Development, 23,* 855–872.

Caldwell, B. M., & Bradley, R. H. (1978). *Home observation for measurement of the environment.* Little Rock: University of Arkansas at Little Rock.

Callaghan, T., & Corbit, J. (2015). The development of symbolic representation. In R. Lerner (Series Ed.) & L. Liben & U. Muller (Vol. Eds.), *Handbook of child psychology and developmental science: Vol. 2. Cognitive processes* (7th ed., pp. 250–295). New York: Wiley.

Calvin, W. H., & Bickerton, D. (2000). *Lingua ex Machina: Reconciling Darwin and Chomsky with the human brain.* Cambridge, MA: MIT Press.

Cameron-Faulkner, T., Lieven, T., & Tomasello, M. (2003). A construction-based analysis of child-directed speech. *Cognitive Science, 27,* 843–873.

Campbell, F. A., Conti, G., Heckman, J. J., Hyeok Moon, S., Pinto, R., Pungello, E., & Pan, Y. (2014). Early childhood investments substantially boost adult health. *Science, 343,* 1478–1485.

Campbell, F. A., Pungello, E. P., Miller-Johnson, S., Burchinal, M., & Ramey, C. T. (2001). The development of cognitive and academic abilities: Growth curves from an early childhood educational experiment. *Developmental Psychology, 37,* 231–242.

Campbell, F. A., & Ramey, C. T. (1994). Effects of early intervention on intellectual and academic achievement: A follow-up study of children from low-income families. *Child Development, 65,* 684–698.

Campbell, F. A., Ramey, C. T., Pungello, E., Sparlfng, J., & Miller-Johnson, S. (2002). Early childhood education:

Young adult outcomes from the Abecedarian project. *Applied Developmental Science, 6,* 42–57.

Capon, N., & Kuhn, D. (1979). Logical reasoning in the supermarket: Adult females' use of a proportional reasoning strategy in an everyday context. *Developmental Psychology, 15,* 450–452.

Caravolas, M., Lervåg, A., Mousikou, P., Efrim, C., Litavsky, M., Onochie-Quintanilla, E., . . . Hulme, C. (2012). Common patterns of prediction of literacy development in different alphabetic orthographies. *Psychological Science, 23,* 678–686.

Carey, S. (1985). Are children fundamentally different kinds of thinkers and learners than adults? In S. F. Chapman, J. W. Segal, & R. Glaser (Eds.), *Thinking and learning skills* (Vol. 2, pp. 485–517). Hillsdale, NJ: Erlbaum.

Carey, S. (1999). Sources of conceptual change. In E. K. Scholnick, K. Nelson, S. A. Gelman, & P. Miller (Eds.), *Conceptual development: Piaget's legacy* (pp. 293–326). Hillsdale, NJ: Erlbaum.

Carey, S. (2009). *The origin of concepts.* New York: Oxford University Press.

Carey, S. (2010). Beyond fast mapping. *Language Learning and Development, 6*(3), 184–205.

Carey, S., & Bartlett, E. (1978). *Acquiring a single new word.* Proceedings of the Stanford Child Language Conference. (Republished in *Papers and Reports on Child Language Development, 15,* 17–29.)

Carlson, S. M., Claxton, L. J., & Moses, L. J. (2015). The relation between executive function and theory of mind is more than skin deep. *Journal of Cognition and Development, 16,* 186–197.

Carlson, S. M., Moses, L. J., & Hix, H. R. (1998). The role of inhibitory processes in young children's difficulties with deception and false belief. *Child Development, 69,* 672–691.

Carlson, S. M., & White, R. E. (2013). Executive function, pretend play, and imagination. In M. Taylor (Ed.), *The Oxford handbook of the development of imagination* (pp. 161–174). New York: Oxford University Press.

Carlson, S. M., White, R. E., & Davis-Unger, A. C. (2014). Evidence for a relationship between executive function and pretense representation in preschool children. *Cognitive Development, 29,* 1–16.

Carlson, S. M., Zelazo, P. D., & Faja, S. (2013). Executive function. An overview. In P. D. Zelazo (Ed.), *The Oxford handbook of developmental psychology: Vol. 1. Body and mind* (pp. 706–743). Oxford, UK: Oxford University Press.

Caron, A. J. (2009). Comprehension of the representational mind in infancy. *Developmental Review, 29,* 69–95.

Caron, S. L., & Ahlgrim, C. J. (2012). Children's understanding and knowledge of conception and birth: Comparing children from England, the Netherlands, Sweden, and the United States. *American Journal of Sexuality Education, 7*(1), 16–36.

Carpenter, M., Akhtar, N., & Tomasello, M. (1998). Fourteen- through 18-month-old infants differentially imitate intentional and accidental actions. *Infant Behavior and Development, 21*(2), 315–330.

Carpenter, M., Call, J., & Tomasello, M. (2005). Twelve- and 18-month-olds copy actions in terms of goals. *Developmental Science, 8,* F13–F20.

Carpenter, M., Nagell, K., & Tomasello, M. (1998). Social cognition, joint attention, and communicative competence from 9 to 15 months of age. *Monographs of the Society for Research in Child Development, 63*(4, Serial No. 255).

Carpenter, T. P., & Moser, J. M. (1982). The development of addition and subtraction problem-solving skills. In T. P. Carpenter, J. M. Moser, & T. A. Romberg (Eds.), *Addition and subtraction: A cognitive perspective* (pp. 9–24). Hillsdale, NJ: Erlbaum.

Carr, M., Borkowski, J. G., & Maxwell, S. E. (1991). Motivational components of under-achievement. *Developmental Psychology, 27,* 108–118.

Carr, M., Kurtz, B. E., Schneider, W., Turner, L. A., & Borkowski, J. G. (1989). Strategy acquisition and transfer among American and German children: Environmental influences on metacognitive development. *Developmental Psychology, 25,* 765–771.

Carraher, T. N., Carraher, D., & Schliemann, A. D. (1985). Mathematics in the streets and in the schools. *British Journal of Developmental Psychology, 3,* 21–29.

Carrol, J. B. (1993). *Human cognitive abilities.* New York: Cambridge University Press.

Case, R. (1985). *Intellectual development: Birth to adulthood.* New York: Academic.

Case, R. (1991). Stages in the development of the young child's first sense of self. *Developmental Review, 11,* 210–230.

Case, R. (1992). *The mind's staircase: Exploring the conceptual underpinnings of children's thought and knowledge.* Hillsdale, NJ: Erlbaum.

Case, R., Kurland, M., & Goldberg, J. (1982). Operational efficiency and the growth of short-term memory span. *Journal of Experimental Child Psychology, 33,* 386–404.

Caselli, M. C., Bates, E., Casadio, P., Fenson, J., Fenson, L., Sanders, L., & Weir, J. (1995). A cross-linguistic study of early lexical development. *Cognitive Development, 10,* 159–199.

Casler, K., Eshleman, A., Greene, K., & Terziyan, T. (2011). Children's scale errors with tools. *Developmental Psychology, 47*(3), 857–866.

Casler, K., & Kelemen, D. (2005). Young children's rapid learning about artifacts. *Developmental Science, 8,* 472–480.

Caspi, A., Williams, B., Kim-Cohen, J., Craig, I. W., Milne, B. J., Poulton, R., . . . Moffitt, T. E. (2007). Moderation of breastfeeding effects on the IQ by genetic variation in fatty acid metabolism. *Proceeding of the National Academy of Sciences, 104,* 18860–18865.

Cassel, W. S., & Bjorklund, D. F. (1995). Developmental patterns of eyewitness memory and suggestibility: An ecologically based short-term longitudinal study. *Law & Human Behavior, 19,* 507–532.

Cassel, W. S., Roebers, C. E. M., & Bjorklund, D. F. (1996). Developmental patterns of eyewitness responses to increasingly suggestive questions. *Journal of Experimental Child Psychology, 61,* 116–133.

Castellanos, F. X., Sonuga-Barke, E. J., Scheres, A., Di Martino, A., Hyde, C., & Walters, J. R. (2005). Varieties of attention-deficit/hyperactivity disorder-related intra-individual variability. *Biological Psychiatry, 57,* 1416–1423.

Cattell, R. B. (1971). *Abilities: Their structure, growth and action.* Boston: Houghton Mifflin.

Caughy, M. O. (1996). Health and environmental effects on the academic readiness of school-age children. *Developmental Psychology, 32,* 515–522.

Causey, K. B. (2010). *Remembering the future: Individual differences in metacognitive representation predict prospective memory performance on time-based and event-based tasks in early childhood.* Doctoral dissertation, Florida Atlantic University.

Causey, K. B., & Bjorklund, D. F. (2011). The evolution of cognition. In V. Swami (Ed.), *Evolutionary psychology: A critical reader* (pp. 32–71). London: British Psychological Society.

Causey, K. B., & Bjorklund, D. F. (2014). Prospective memory in preschool children: Influences of agency, incentive, and underlying cognitive mechanisms. *Journal of Experimental Child Psychology, 127,* 36–51.

Ceci, S. J. (1983). Automatic and purposive semantic processing characteristics of normal and language/learning disabled (L/LD) children. *Developmental Psychology, 19,* 427–439.

Ceci, S. J. (1991). How much does schooling influence general intelligence and its cognitive components? A reassessment of the evidence. *Developmental Psychology, 27,* 703–722.

Ceci, S. J. (1993). Contextual trends in intellectual development. *Developmental Review, 13,* 403–435.

Ceci, S. J. (1996). *On intelligence: A bio-ecological treatise on intellectual development* (2nd ed.). Cambridge, MA: Harvard University Press.

Ceci, S. J., & Bruck, M. (1993). Suggestibility of the child witness: A historical review and synthesis. *Psychological Bulletin, 113,* 403–439.

Ceci, S. J., & Bruck, M. (1995). *Jeopardy in the courtroom: A scientific analysis of children's testimony.* Washington, DC: American Psychological Association.

Ceci, S. J., Bruck, M., & Battin, D. (2000). The suggestibility of children's testimony. In D. F. Bjorklund (Ed.), *False-memory creation in children and adults: Theory, research, and implications* (pp. 169–201). Mahwah, NJ: Erlbaum.

Ceci, S. J., Hritz, A., & Royer, C. (2016). Understanding suggestibility. In W. T. O'Donohue & M. Fanetti (Eds.), *Forensic interviews regarding child sexual abuse: A guide to best practices* (pp. 141–153). New York: Springer.

Ceci, S. J., Loftus, E. F., Leichtman, M., & Bruck, M. (1994). The role of source misattributions in the creation of false beliefs among preschoolers. *International Journal of Clinical and Experimental Hypnosis, 62,* 304–320.

Ceci, S. J., Ross, D. F., & Toglia, M. P. (1987). Age differences in suggestibility: Psycholegal implications. *Journal of Experimental Psychology: General, 117,* 38–49.

Ceci, S. J., & Williams, W. M. (1997). Schooling, intelligence, and income. *American Psychologist, 52,* 1051–1058.

Cervantes, C. A., & Callanan, M. A. (1998). Labels and explanations in mother-child emotion talk: Age and gender differentiation. *Developmental Psychology, 34,* 88–98.

Chae, Y., Goodman, G. S., Larson, R. P., Augusti, E. M., Alley, D., VanMeenen, K. M., . . . Coulter, K. P. (2014). Children's memory and suggestibility about a distressing event: The role of children's and parents' attachment. *Journal of Experimental Child Psychology, 123,* 90–111.

Chall, J. S. (1979). The great debate: Ten years later, with a modest proposal for reading stages. In L. B. Resmck & P. A. Weaver (Eds.), *Theory and practice of early reading* (Vol. 1, pp. 29–55). Hillsdale, NJ: Erlbaum.

Chandler, M., Fritz, A. S., & Hala, S. (1989). Small-scale deceit: Deception as a marker of two-, three-, and four-year-olds' early theories of mind. *Child Development, 60,* 1263–1277.

Chappell, J., Cutting, N., Apperly, I. A., & Beck, S. R. (2013). The development of tool manufacture in humans: What helps young children make innovative tools? *Philosophical Transactions of the Royal Society B: Biological Sciences, 368,* 1630.

Charity, A. H., Scarborough, H. S., & Griffin, D. M. (2004). Familiarity with school English in African American children and its relation to early reading achievement. *Child Development, 75,* 1340–1356.

Chechile, R. A., & Richman, C. L. (1982). The interaction of semantic memory with storage and retrieval processes. *Developmental Review, 2,* 237–250.

Chelune, G. J., & Baer, R. A. (1986). Developmental norms for the Wisconsin Card Sorting Test. *Journal of Clinical and Experimental Neuropsychology, 8*, 219–228.

Chen, C., & Stevenson, H. W. (1988). Cross-linguistic differences in digit span of preschool children. *Journal of Experimental Child Psychology, 46*, 150–158.

Chen, C., & Stevenson, H. W. (1995). Motivation and mathematics achievement: A comparative study of Asian-American, Caucasian-American, and East Asian high school students. *Child Development, 66*, 1215–1234.

Chen, J.-Q. (2004). Theory of multiple intelligences: Is it a scientific theory? *Teachers College Record, 106*, 17–23.

Chen, J.-Q., Moran, S., & Gardner, H. (Eds.). (2009). *Multiple intelligences around the world.* San Francisco: Jossey-Bass.

Chen, Z., & Klahr, D. (1999). All other things being equal: Acquisition and transfer of the control of variables strategy. *Child Development, 70*, 1098–1120.

Chen, Z., Sanchez, R. P., & Campbell, T. (1997). From beyond to within their grasp: The rudiments of analogical problem solving in 10- and 13-month olds. *Developmental Psychology, 33*, 790–801.

Chen, Z., & Siegler, R. S. (2000). Across the great divide: Bridging the gap between understanding of toddlers' and older children's thinking. *Monographs of the Society for Research in Child Development, 65*(2, Serial No. 261).

Cheyne, J. A., & Rubin, K. H. (1983). Playful precursors of problem solving in preschoolers. *Developmental Psychology, 19*, 577–584.

Chi, M. T. H. (1977). Age differences in memory span. *Journal of Experimental Child Psychology, 23*, 266–281.

Chi, M. T. H. (1978). Knowledge structure and memory development. In R. Siegler (Ed.), *Children's thinking: What develops?* (pp. 73–96). Hillsdale, NJ: Erlbaum.

Chi, M. T. H., Feltovich, P. J., & Glaser, R. (1981). Categorization and representation of physics problems by experts and novices. *Cognitive Science, 5*, 121–152.

Chomsky, N. (1957). *Syntactic structures.* The Hague: Mouton.

Chomsky, N. (1959). Review of B. F. Skinner's *Verbal Behavior: Language, 35*, 26–129.

Christian, K., Morrison, F. J., Frazier, J. A., & Massetti, G. (2000). Specificity in the nature and timing of cognitive growth in kindergarten and first grade. *Journal of Cognition and Development, 1*, 429–448.

Chu, F. C., vanMarle, K., & Geary, D. C. (2015). Early numerical foundations of young children's mathematical development. *Journal of Experimental Child Psychology, 132*, 205–212.

Chuah, Y. M. L., & Maybery, M. T. (1999). Verbal and spatial short-term memory: Common sources of developmental change? *Journal of Experimental Child Psychology, 73*, 7–44.

Chudek, M., Baron, A. S., & Birch, S. (2016). Unselective overimitators: The evolutionary implications of children's indiscriminate copying of successful and prestigious models. *Child Development, 87*, 782–794.

Chugani, H. T., Behen, M. E., Muzik, O., Juhasz, C., Nagy, F., & Chugani, D. C. (2001). Local brain functional activity following early deprivation: A study of postinstitutionalized Romanian orphans. *NeuroImage, 117*, 1290–1301.

Chugani, H. T., Phelps, M. E., & Mazziotta, J. C. (1987). Positron emission tomography study of human brain functional development. *Annals of Neurology, 22*, 487–497.

Church, R. B., & Goldin-Meadow, S. (1986). The mismatch between gesture and speech as an index of transitional knowledge. *Cognition, 23*, 43–71.

Cicchetti, D. (1989). How research on child maltreatment has informed the study of child development: Perspectives from developmental psychopathology. In D. Cicchetti & V. Carlson (Eds.), *Child maltreatment: Theory and research on causes and consequences of child abuse and neglect* (pp. 579–619). New York: Cambridge University Press.

Clark, C. A. C., & Woodward, L. J. (2015). Relation of perinatal risk and early parenting to executive control at the transition to school. *Developmental Science, 18*, 525–542.

Clark, E. A., & Hanisee, J. (1982). Intellectual and adaptive performance of Asian children in adoptive American settings. *Developmental Psychology, 18*, 595–599.

Clarke, A. D. B., & Clarke, A. M. (1976). Formerly isolated children. In A. M. Clarke & A. D. B. Clarke (Eds.), *Early experience: Myth and evidence* (pp. 27–34). London: Open Books.

Clearfield, M. W., & Westfahl, S. M.-C. (2006). Familiarization in infants' perception of addition problems. *Journal of Cognition and Development, 7*, 27–43.

Clements, W. A., & Perner, J. (1994). Implicit understanding of belief. *Cognitive Development, 9*, 377–395.

Clements, W. A., Rustin, C. L., & McCallum, S. (2000). Promoting the transition from implicit to explicit understanding: A training study of false belief. *Developmental Science, 3*, 81–92.

Clerc, J., Miller, P. H., & Cosnefroy, L. (2014). Young children's transfer of strategies: Utilization deficiencies, executive function, and metacognition. *Developmental Review, 34*(4), 378–393.

Clubb, P. A., Nida, R. E., Merritt, K., & Ornstein, P. A. (1993). Visiting the doctor: Children's knowledge and memory. *Cognitive Development, 8*, 361–372.

Coffman, J. L., Ornstein, P. A., McCall, L. E., & Curran, P. J. (2008). Linking teachers' memory-relevant language and the development of children's memory skills. *Developmental Psychology, 44*, 1640–1654.

Cohen, L. B. (1972). Attention-getting and attention-holding processes of infant visual preferences. *Child Development, 43*, 869–879.

Cohen, L. B., & Cashon, C. H. (2006). Infant cognition. In W. Damon & R. M. Lerner (Series Eds.) & D. Kuhn & R. S. Siegler (Vol. Eds.), *Handbook of child psychology: Vol. 2. Cognition, perception, and language* (6th ed., pp. 214–251). New York: Wiley.

Cohen, L. B., & Strauss, M. S. (1979). Concept acquisition in the human infant. *Child Development, 50*, 419–424.

Cohen, M. (1996). Preschoolers' practical thinking and problem solving: The acquisition of an optimal solution. *Cognitive Development, 11*, 357–373.

Coie, J. D., & Dodge, K. A. (1998). Aggression and antisocial behavior. In W. Damon (Series Ed.) & N. Eisenberg (Vol. Ed.), *Handbook of child psychology: Vol. 3. Social, emotional, and personality development* (5th ed., pp. 779–862). New York: Wiley.

Cole, M. (1990). Cognitive development and formal schooling: The evidence from cross-cultural research. In L. C. Moll (Ed.), *Vygotsky and education* (pp. 319–348). New York: Cambridge University Press.

Cole, M. (2006). Culture and cognitive development in phylogenetic, historical, and ontogenetic perspective. In W. Damon & R. M. Lerner (Series Eds.) & D. Kuhn & R. S. Siegler (Vol. Eds.), *Handbook of child psychology: Vol. 2. Cognition, perception, and language* (6th ed., pp. 636–683). New York: Wiley.

Cole, M., & Scribner, S. (1977). Cross-cultural studies of memory and cognition. In R. V. Kail, Jr., & J. W. Hagen (Eds.), *Perspectives on the development of memory and cognition* (pp. 239–271). Hillsdale, NJ: Erlbaum.

College Board. (2013). *2013 College-Bound Seniors: Total group profile report.* Retrieved from http://media .collegeboard.com/digitalServices/pdf/research/2013/ TotalGroup-2013.pdf

Collie, R., & Hayne, R. (1999). Deferred imitation by 6- and 9-month-old infants: More evidence for declarative memory. *Developmental Psychobiology, 35*, 83–90.

Colombo, J. (2002). Infant attention grows up: The emergence of a developmental cognitive neuroscience perspective. *Current Directions in Psychological Science, 11*(6), 196–200.

Connor, J. M., & Serbin, L. A. (1977). Behaviorally based masculine and feminine activity-preference scales for preschoolers: Correlates with other classroom behaviors and cognitive tests. *Child Development, 48*, 1411–1416.

Cony-Murray, C., & Turiel, E. (2012). Jimmy's baby doll and Jenny's truck: Young children's reasoning about gender norms. *Child Development, 83*, 146–158.

Cook, M., & Mineka, S. (1989). Observational conditioning of fear to fear-relevant versus fear-irrelevant stimuli in rhesus monkeys. *Journal of Abnormal Psychology, 98*, 448–459.

Cooley, C. H. (1902). *Human nature and the social order.* New York: Scribner's.

Cooper, R. P., & Aslin, R. N. (1990). Preference for infant-directed speech in the first month after birth. *Child Development, 61*, 1584–1595.

Cooper, R. P., & Aslin, R. N. (1994). Developmental differences in infant attention to the spectral properties of infant-directed speech. *Child Development, 65*, 1663–1677.

Cordes, S., & Brannon, E. M. (2009). Crossing the divide: Infants discriminate small from large numerosities. *Developmental Psychology, 45*, 1583–1594.

Cosmides, L., & Tooby, J. (1987). From evolution to behavior: Evolutionary psychology as the missing link. In J. Dupre (Ed.), *The latest and the best essays on evolution and optimality* (pp. 276–306). Cambridge, MA: MIT Press.

Cosmides, L., & Tooby, J. (1992). Cognitive adaptations for social exchange. In J. H. Barkow, L. Cosmides, & J. Tooby (Eds.), *The adapted mind: Evolutionary psychology and the generation of culture* (pp. 163–228). New York: Oxford University Press.

Cosmides, L., Tooby, J., & Barkow, J. H. (1992). Introduction: Evolutionary psychology and conceptual integration. In J. H. Barkow, L. Cosmides, & J. Tooby (Eds.), *The adapted mind: Evolutionary psychology and the generation of culture* (pp. 3–15). New York: Oxford University Press.

Costa-Giomi, E., & Ilari, B. (2014). Infants' preferential attention to sung and spoken stimuli. *Journal of Research in Music Education, 62*, 188–194.

Courage, M. L., & Howe, M. L. (1998). The ebb and flow of infant attentional preferences: Evidence for long-term recognition memory in 3-month-olds. *Journal of Experimental Child Psychology, 70*, 26–53.

Courage, M. L., & Howe, M. L. (2001). Long-term retention in 3.5-month-olds: Familiarization time and individual differences in attentional style. *Journal of Experimental Child Psychology, 79*, 271–293.

Courage, M. L., Murphy, A. N., Goulding, S., & Setliff, A. E. (2010). When television is on: The impact of infant-directed video on 6- and 18-month-olds' toy play and on parent-infant interaction. *Infant Behavior and Development, 33*, 176–188.

Courage, M. L., & Setliff, A. E. (2010). When babies watch television: Attention-getting, attention holding, and the implications for learning from video material. *Developmental Review, 30,* 220–238.

Cowan, N. (2014). Working memory underpins cognitive development, learning, and education. *Educational Psychology Review, 26*(2), 197–223.

Cowan, N. (2016). Working memory maturation: Can we get at the essence of cognitive growth? *Perspectives on Psychological Science, 11*(2), 239–264.

Cowan, N., & Alloway, T. (2009). Development of working memory in childhood. In M. L. Courage & N. Cowan (Eds.), *The development of memory in infancy and childhood* (pp. 304–342). New York: Psychology Press.

Cowan, N., Nugent, L. D., Elliott, E. M., Ponomarev, I., & Saults, J. S. (1999). The role of attention in the development of short-term memory: Age differences in the verbal span of apprehension. *Child Development, 70,* 1082–1097.

Cox, B. C., Ornstein, P. A., Naus, M. J., Maxfield, D., & Zimler, J. (1989). Children's concurrent use of rehearsal and organizational strategies. *Developmental Psychology, 25,* 619–627.

Cox, D., & Waters, H. S. (1986). Sex differences in the use of organization strategies: A developmental analysis. *Journal of Experimental Child Psychology, 41,* 18–37.

Coyle, T. R., & Bjorklund, D. F. (1997). Age differences in, and consequences of, multiple- and variable strategy use on a multitrial sort-recall task. *Developmental Psychology, 33,* 372–380.

Coyle, T. R., Pillow, D. R., Snyder, A. C., & Kochunov, P. (2011). Processing speed mediates the development of general intelligence (g) in adolescence. *Psychological Science, 22,* 1265–1269.

Coyle, T. R., Read, L. E., Gaultney, J. F., & Bjorklund, D. F. (1998). Giftedness and variability in strategic processing on a multitrial memory task: Evidence for stability in gifted cognition. *Learning and Individual Differences, 10,* 273–290.

Crabtree, J. W., & Riesen, A. H. (1979). Effects of the duration of dark rearing on visually guided behavior in the kitten. *Developmental Psychobiology, 12,* 291–303.

Cragg, L., & Gilmore, C. (2014). Skills underlying mathematics: The role of executive function in the development of mathematics proficiency. *Trends in Neuroscience and Education, 3,* 63–68.

Crick, N. R., & Dodge, K. A. (1994). A review and reformulation of social information-processing mechanisms in children's social adjustment. *Psychological Bulletin, 115,* 74–101.

Crivello, C., Kuzyk, O., Rodrigues, M., Friend, M., Zesiger, P., & Poulin-Dubois, D. (2016). The effects of bilingual growth on toddlers' executive function. *Journal of Experimental Child Psychology, 141,* 121–132.

Croker, S., & Buchanan, H. (2011). Scientific reasoning in a real-world context: The effect of prior belief and outcome on children's hypothesis-testing strategies. *British Journal of Developmental Psychology, 29*(3), 409–424.

Csibra, G., Bíró, S., Koós, O., & Gergely, G. (2003). One-year-old infants use teleological representations of actions productively. *Cognitive Science, 27,* 111–133.

Csibra, G., & Gergely, G. (2011). Natural pedagogy as evolutionary adaptation. *Philosophical Transactions of the Royal Society of London, Biological Sciences, 366,* 1149–1157.

Cuban, L. (2004). Assessing the 20-year impact of multiple intelligences on schooling. *Teachers College Record, 106,* 140–146.

Cummins, D. D. (1996). Evidence of deontic reasoning in 3- and 4-year-old children. *Memory and Cognition, 24,* 823–829.

Cummins, D. D. (1998). Social norms and other minds: The evolutionary roots of higher cognition. In D. D. Cummins & C. Allen (Eds.), *The evolution of mind* (pp. 30–50). New York: Oxford University Press.

Cummins, D. D. (2013). Deontic and epistemic reasoning in children revisited: Comment on Dack and Astington. *Journal of Experimental Child Psychology, 116,* 762–769.

Cunha, F., Heckman, J. J., Lochner, L. J., & Masterov, D. V. (2006). Interpreting the evidence on life cycle skill formation. In E. A. Hanushek & F. Welch (Eds.), *Handbook of the economics of education* (pp. 607–812). Amsterdam: North-Holland.

Cunningham, A. E. (1990). Explicit versus implicit instruction in phonemic awareness. *Journal of Experimental Child Psychology, 50,* 429–444.

Curtiss, S. (1977). *Genie: A psycholinguistic study of a modern day "wild child."* New York: Academic.

Cutting, N., Apperly, I. A., Chappell, C., & Beck, S. R. (2014). The puzzling difficulty of tool innovation: Why can't children piece their knowledge together? *Journal of Experimental Child Psychology, 125,* 110–117.

Cynader, M., Berman, N. M., & Hein, A. (1976). Recovery of function in cat visual cortex following prolonged deprivation. *Experimental Brain Research, 25,* 139–156.

Dack, L. A., & Astington, J. W. (2011). Deontic and epistemic reasoning in children. *Journal of Experimental Child Psychology, 110,* 94–114.

Daehler, M. W., Lonardo, R., & Bukatko, D. (1979). Matching and equivalence judgments in very young children. *Child Development, 50,* 170–179.

Daley, C. E., & Onwuebuzie, A. J. (2011). Race and intelligence. In R. J. Sternberg & S. B. Kaufman (Eds.), *The Cambridge handbook of intelligence* (pp. 293–306). Cambridge, UK: Cambridge University Press.

Daley, T. C., Whaley, S. E., Sigman, M. D., Espenosa, M. P., & Neumann, C. (2003). IQ on the rise: The Flynn effect in rural Kenyan children. *Psychological Science, 14*, 215–219.

Daly, M., Delany, L., Egan, M., & Baumeister, R. F. (2015). Childhood self-control and unemployment throughout the life span: Evidence from two British cohort studies. *Psychological Science, 26*, 709–723.

Damast, A. M., Tamis-LeMonda, C. S., & Bornstein, M. H. (1996). Mother-child play: Sequential interactions and the relation between maternal beliefs and behaviors. *Child Development, 67*, 1752–1766.

Daneman, M., & Blennerhassett, A. (1984). How to assess the listening comprehension skills of prereaders. *Journal of Educational Psychology, 76*, 1372–1381.

Daneman, M., & Green, I. (1986). Individual differences in comprehending and producing words in context. *Journal of Memory and Language, 25*, 1–18.

Dapretto, M., Davies, M. S., Pfeifer, J. H., Scott, A. A., Sigman, M., Bookheimer, S. Y., & Iacoboni, M. (2006). Understanding emotions in others: Mirror neuron dysfunction in children with autism spectrum disorders. *Nature Neuroscience, 9*, 28–30.

Darwin, C. (1859). *On the origin of species*. New York: Modern Library.

Darwin, C. (1871). *The descent of man, and selection in relation to sex*. London: John Murray.

Das, J. P. (1984). Cognitive deficits in mental retardation. A process approach. In P. H. Brooks, R. Sperber, & C. McCauley (Eds.), *Learning and cognition in the mentally retarded* (pp. 115–128). Hillsdale, NJ: Erlbaum.

Dasen, P. R. (Ed.). (1977). *Piagetian psychology: Cross cultural contributions*. New York: Gardner.

Davis, C. L., Tomporowski, P. D., McDowell, J. E., Austin, B. P., Miller, P. H., Yanasak, N. E., . . . Naglieri, J. A. (2011). Exercise improves executive function and achievement and alters brain activation in overweight children: A randomized, controlled trial. *Health Psychology, 30*(1), 91–98.

Davis, K., Christodoulou, J., Seider, S., & Gardner, H. (2011). The theory of multiple intelligences. In R. J. Sternberg & B. Kaufman (Eds.), *The Cambridge handbook of intelligence* (pp. 485–503). Cambridge, UK: Cambridge University Press.

Davis, O. S., Haworth, C. M., & Plomin, R. (2009). Dramatic increase in heritability of cognitive development from early to middle childhood: An 8-year longitudinal study of 8,700 pairs of twins. *Psychological Science, 20*, 1301–1308.

Dawson, G., Toth, K., Abbott, R., Osterling, J., Munson, J., Estes, A., & Liaw, J. (2004). Early social attention impairments in autism: Social orienting, joint attention, and attention to distress. *Developmental Psychology, 40*, 271–283.

de Haan, M. (2015). Neuroscientific methods with children. In R. Lerner (Series Ed.) & W. F. Overton & P. C. M. Molenaar (Vol. Eds.), *Handbook of child psychology and developmental science: Vol. 1. Theory and method* (7th ed., pp. 683–712). New York: Wiley.

de Haan, M., Bauer, P. J., Georgieff, M. K., & Nelson, C. A. (2000). Explicit memory in low-risk infants aged 19 months born between 27 and 42 weeks gestation. *Developmental Medicine and Child Neurology, 42*, 304–312.

de Haan, M., Oliver, A., & Johnson, M. H. (1998). Electrophysiological correlates of face processing by adults and 6-month-old infants. *Journal of Cognitive Neuroscience* (Annual Meeting Supplement), *36*.

De Houwer, A. (1995). Bilingual language acquisition. In P. Fletcher & B. MacWhinney (Eds.), *The handbook of child language* (pp. 219–250). Oxford, UK: Blackwell.

De Lisi, R., & Staudt, J. (1980). Individual differences in college students' performance on formal operations tasks. *Journal of Applied Developmental Psychology, 1*, 163–174.

De Smedt, B., Noël, M.-P., Gilmore, C., & Ansari, D. (2013). How do symbolic and non-symbolic numerical magnitude processing relate to individual differences in children's mathematical skills? A review of evidence from brain and behavior. *Trends in Neuroscience and Education, 2*, 48–55.

de Villiers, J. G., & de Villiers, P. A. (1973). A cross sectional study of the acquisition of grammatical morphemes in child speech. *Journal of Psychosomatic Research, 2*, 267–278.

de Villiers, J. G., & de Villiers, P. A. (1978). *Language acquisition*. Cambridge, MA: Harvard University Press.

De Vries, R. (1969). Constancy of generic identity in the years three to six. *Monographs of the Society for Research in Child Development, 34*(3, Serial No. 127).

Deák, G. O. (2006). Do children really confuse appearance and reality? *Trends in Cognitive Sciences, 10*(12), 546–550.

Deák, G. O., Ray, S. D., & Brenneman, K. (2003). Children's perseverative appearance/reality errors are related to emerging language skills. *Child Development, 74*, 944–964.

Deary, I. J. (2008). Why do intelligent people live longer? *Nature, 456*, 175–176.

Deary, I. J. (2012). Intelligence. *Annual Review of Psychology, 63*, 453–482.

Deary, I. J. (2013). Intelligence. *Current Biology, 23,* R673–R676.

Deary, I. J. (2014). The stability of intelligence from childhood to old age. *Current Directions in Psychological Science, 23,* 239–245.

Deary, I. J., Batty, G. D., Pattie, A., & Gale, C. R. (2008). More intelligent, more dependable children live longer: A 55-year longitudinal study of a representative sample of the Scottish nation. *Psychological Science, 19,* 874–880.

Deary, I. J., & Der, G. (2005). Reaction time explains IQ's association with death. *Psychological Science, 16,* 64–69.

Deary, I. J., Egan, V., Gibson, G. J., Austin, E. J., Brand, C. R., & Kellaghan, T. (1996). Intelligence and the differentiation hypothesis. *Intelligence, 23,* 105–132.

Deary, I. J., Pattie, A., & Starr, J. M. (2013). The stability of intelligence from age 11 to age 90 years: The Lotian Birth Cohort of 1921. *Psychological Science, 24,* 2361–2368.

Deary, I. J., Weiss, A., & Batty, G. D. (2010). Intelligence and personality as predictors of illness and death: How researchers in differential psychology and chronic disease epidemiology are collaborating to understand and address health inequalities. *Psychological Science in the Public Interest, 11,* 53–79.

DeCasper, A. J., & Fifer, W. P. (1980). Of human bonding: Newborns prefer their mother's voice. *Science, 208,* 1174–1176.

DeCasper, A. J., Lecanuet, J.-P., Busnel, M.-C., Granier-Deferre, C., & Maugeais, R. (1994). Fetal reactions to recurrent maternal speech. *Infant Behavior and Development, 17,* 159–164.

DeCasper, A. J., & Spence, M. J. (1986). Prenatal maternal speech influences newborns' perception of speech sounds. *Infant Behavior and Development, 9,* 133–150.

Decety, J., & Cacioppo, J. T. (Eds.). (2010). *Handbook of social neuroscience.* New York: Oxford University Press.

Delevati, N. M., & Bergamasco, N. H. P. (1999). Pain in the neonate: An analysis of facial movements and crying in response to nociceptive stimuli. *Infant Behavior and Development, 22,* 137–143.

DeLoache, J. S. (1987). Rapid change in the symbolic functioning of very young children. *Science, 238,* 1556–1557.

DeLoache, J. S. (1991). Symbolic functioning in very young children: Understanding of pictures and models. *Child Development, 62,* 736–752.

DeLoache, J. S. (2010). Early development of the understanding and use of symbolic artifacts. In U. Goswami (Ed.), *The Wiley-Blackwell handbook of childhood cognitive development* (2nd ed., pp. 312–336). West Sussex, UK: Blackwell.

DeLoache, J. S., & Brown, A. L. (1983). Very young children's memory for the location of objects in a large scale environment. *Child Development, 54,* 888–897.

DeLoache, J. S., Cassidy, D. J., & Brown, A. L. (1985). Precursors of mnemonic strategies in very young children's memory for the location of hidden objects. *Child Development, 56,* 125–137.

DeLoache, J. S., Chiong, C., Sherman, K., Islam, N., Vanderborght, M., Troseth, G. L., . . . O'Doherty, K. (2010). Do babies learn from baby media? *Psychological Science, 21,* 1570–1574.

DeLoache, J. S., & DeMendoza, O. A. P. (1987). Joint picturebook reading of mothers and one-year-old children. *British Journal of Developmental Psychology, 5,* 111–123.

DeLoache, J. S., & LoBue, V. (2009). The narrow fellow in the grass: Human infants associate snakes and fear. *Developmental Science, 12,* 201–207.

DeLoache, J. S., LoBue, V., Vanderborght, M., & Chiong, C. (2013). On the validity and robustness of the scale error phenomenon in early childhood. *Infant Behavior and Development, 36*(1), 63–70.

DeLoache, J. S., & Marzolf, D. P. (1992). When a picture is not worth a thousand words: Young children's understanding of pictures and models. *Cognitive Development, 7,* 317–329.

DeLoache, J. S., Miller, K. F., & Pierroutsakos, S. L. (1998). Reasoning and problem solving. In W. Damon (Series Ed.) & D. Kuhn & R. S. Siegler (Vol. Eds.), *Handbook of child psychology: Vol 2. Cognition, perception, and language* (5th ed., pp. 801–850). New York: Wiley.

DeLoache, J. S., Miller, K. F., & Rosengren, K. S. (1997). The credible shrinking room: Very young children's performance with symbolic and nonsymbolic relations. *Psychological Science, 8,* 308–313.

DeLoache, J. S., Uttal, D. H., & Rosengren, K. S. (2004). Scale errors offer evidence for a perception-action dissociation early in life. *Science, 304,* 1027–1029.

Deloitte. (2009). *Deloitte's State of the Media Democracy Survey, third edition: Rethink what you know.* Retrieved from https://www2.deloitte.com/content/dam/Deloitte/global/Documents/Technology-Media-Telecommunications/gx-tmt-deloitte-democracy-survey.pdf

Delpit, L. D. (1990). Language diversity and learning. In S. Hynd & D. L. Rubin (Eds.), *Perspectives on talk and learning* (pp. 247–266). Urbana, IL: National Council of Teachers of English.

Delpit, L. D., & Dowdy, J. K. (2002). *The skin that we speak: Thoughts on language and culture in the classroom.* New York: New Press.

DeMarie, D., & Ferron, J. (2003). Capacity, strategies, and metamemory: Tests of a three-factor model of memory development. *Journal of Experimental Child Psychology, 84*, 167–193.

DeMarie, D., Miller, P. H., Ferron, J., & Cunningham, W. R. (2004). Path analysis tests for theoretical models of children's memory performance. *Journal of Cognition and Development, 5*, 461–492.

DeMarie-Dreblow, D., & Miller, P. H. (1988). The development of children's strategies for selective attention: Evidence for a transitional period. *Child Development, 59*, 1504–1513.

Demetriou, A., Xiang Kui, Z., Spanoudis, G., Christou, C., Kyriakides, L., & Platsidou, M. (2005). The architecture, dynamics, and development of mental processing: Greek, Chinese, or universal? *Intelligence, 33*, 109–141.

Dempster, F. N. (1981). Memory span: Sources of individual and developmental differences. *Psychological Bulletin, 89*, 63–100.

Dempster, F. N. (1993). Resistance to interference: Developmental changes in a basic processing mechanism. In M. L. Howe & R. Pasnak (Eds.), *Emerging themes in cognitive development: Vol. 1. Foundations* (pp. 3–27). New York: Springer-Verlag.

Denison, S., Reed, C., & Xu, F. (2013). The emergence of probabilistic reasoning in very young infants: Evidence from 4.5 and 6-month-olds. *Developmental Psychology, 49*(2), 243–249.

Denison, S., & Xu, F. (2010). Integrating physical constraints in statistical inference by 11-month-old infants. *Cognitive Science, 34*(5), 885–908.

Dennett, D. (1990). The interpretation of texts, people, and other artifacts. *Philosophy and Phenomenological Quarterly, 1*(Suppl.), 177–194.

Dennis, E. L., Jahanshad, N., McMahon, K. L., de Zubicaray, G. I., Martin, N. G., Hickie, I. B., . . . Thompson, P. M. (2013). Development of brain structural connectivity between ages 12 and 30: A 4-Tesladiffusion imaging study in 439 adolescents and adults. *NeuroImage, 64*, 671–684.

Dennis, M. (1989). Language and the young damaged brain. In T. Boll & B. K. Bryant (Eds.), *Clinical neuropsychology and brain function: Research, measurement and practice* (pp. 85–124). Washington, DC: American Psychological Association.

Dennis, W. (1973). *Children of the Creche.* New York: Appleton-Century-Crofts.

DeStefano, J. (1972). Social variation in language: Implications for teaching reading to black ghetto children. In J. A. Figurel (Ed.), *Better reading in urban schools* (pp. 18–24). Newark, DE: International Reading Association.

Detterman, D. K. (1987). What does reaction time tell us about intelligence? In P. E. Vernon (Ed.), *Speed of information processing and intelligence* (pp. 177–200). Norwood, NJ: Ablex.

Detterman, D. K., & Daniel, M. H. (1989). Correlations of mental tests with each other and with cognitive variables are highest for low IQ groups. *Intelligence, 13*, 340–359.

Detterman, D. K., & Thompson, L. A. (1997). What is so special about special education? *American Psychologist, 52*, 1082–1090.

Devine, A., Soltész, F., Nobes, A., Goswami, U., & Szűcs, D. (2013). Gender differences in developmental dyscalculia depend on diagnostic criteria. *Journal of Learning and Instruction, 27*, 31–39.

Devine, R. T., & Hughes, C. (2014). Relations between false belief understanding and executive function in early childhood: A meta-analysis. *Child Development, 85*(5), 1777–1794.

Devine, R. T., White, N., Ensor, R., & Hughes, C. (2016). Theory of mind in middle childhood: Longitudinal associations with executive function and social competence. *Developmental Psychology, 52*, 758–771.

DeWolf, M. N., Grounds, M. A., Bassok, M., & Holyoak, K. J. (2014). Magnitude comparison with different types of rational numbers. *Journal of Experimental Psychology: Human Perception and Performance, 40*, 71–82.

Di Giorgio, E., Turati, C., Altoè, G., & Simion, F. (2012). Face detection in complex visual displays: An eye-tracking study with 3- and 6-month-old infants and adults. *Journal of Experimental Child Psychology, 113*(1), 66–77.

Diamond, A. (1985). Development of the ability to use recall to guide action as indicated by infants' performance on AB. *Child Development, 56*, 868–883.

Diamond, A. (1991). Frontal lobe involvement in cognitive changes during the first year of life. In K. R. Gibson & A. C. Petersen (Eds.), *Brain maturation and cognitive development: Comparative and cross-cultural perspectives* (pp. 127–180). New York: Aldine de Gruyter.

Diamond, A. (2013). Executive functions. *Annual Review of Psychology, 64*, 135–168.

Diamond, A., Cruttenden, L., & Neiderman, D. (1994). AB with multiple wells: 1. Why are multiple wells sometimes easier than two wells? 2. Memory or memory + inhibition? *Developmental Psychology, 30*, 192–205.

Diamond, A., Kirkham, N., & Amso, D. (2002). Conditions under which young children can hold two rules in mind and inhibit a prepotent response. *Developmental Psychology, 38*, 352–362.

Diamond, A., & Lee, K. (2011). Interventions shown to aid executive function development in children 4 to 12 years old. *Science, 333*(6045), 959–964.

Diamond, A., & Taylor, C. (1996). Development of an aspect of executive control: Development of the abilities to remember what I said and to "Do as I say, not as I do." *Developmental Psychobiology, 29*, 315–324.

Díaz, R. M. (1983). Thought and two languages: The impact of bilingualism on cognitive development. *Review of Research in Education, 10*, 23–54.

Díaz, R. M., & Berk, L. E. (2014). *Private speech: From social interaction to self-regulation.* New York: Psychology Press.

Diesendruck, G., & Markson, L. (2001). Children's avoidance of lexical overlap: A pragmatic account. *Developmental Psychology, 37*, 630–641.

Dirix, C. E. H., Nijhuis, J. G., Jongsma, H. W., & Hornstra, C. (2009). Aspects of fetal learning and memory. *Child Development, 80*, 1251–1258.

Dobzhansky, T. (1964). Biology, molecular and organismic. *American Zoologist, 4*, 443–452.

Dodge, K. A. (1986). A social information processing model of social competence in children. In M. Perlmutter (Ed.), *Minnesota symposium on child psychology* (Vol. 18, pp. 77–125). Hillsdale, NJ: Erlbaum.

Dodge, K. A., Coie, J. D., & Lynam, D. (2006). Aggression and antisocial behavior in youth. In W. Damon & R. M. Lerner (Series Eds.) & N. Eisenberg (Vol. Ed.), *Handbook of child psychology: Vol. 3. Social, emotional, and personality development* (6th ed., pp. 719–788). New York: Wiley.

Dodge, K. A., Pettit, G. S., Bates, J. E., & Valente, E. (1995). Social information processing patterns partially mediate the effect of early physical abuse on later conduct problems. *Journal of Abnormal Psychology, 104*, 632–643.

Dodge, K. A., Pettit, G. S., McClaskey, C. L., & Brown, M. M. (1986). Social competence in children. *Monographs of the Society for Research in Child Development, 51*(2, Serial No. 213).

Dodge, K. A., & Price, J. M. (1994). On the relation between social information processing and socially competent behavior in early school-age children. *Child Development, 65*, 1385–1397.

Doman, G. (1984). *How to multiply your baby's intelligence.* Garden City, NY: Doubleday.

Doom, J. R., Georgieff, M. K., & Gunnar, M. R. (2015). Institutional care and iron deficiency increase ADHD symptomology and lower IQ 2.5–5 years post-adoption. *Developmental Science, 18*, 484–494.

Dore, F. Y., & Dumas, C. (1987). Psychology of animal cognition: Piagetian studies. *Psychological Bulletin, 102*, 219–233.

Dougherty, T. M., & Haith, M. M. (1997). Infant expectations and reaction time as predictors of childhood speed of processing and IQ. *Developmental Psychology, 33*, 146–155.

Drachman, D. B., & Coulombre, A. J. (1962). Experimental clubfoot and arthrogryposis multiplex congenita. *Lancet, 7255*, 523–526.

Droit-Volet, S. (2013). Time perception in children: A neurodevelopmental approach. *Neuropsychologia, 51*(2), 220–234.

Duckworth, A. L., & Seligman, M. E. P. (2005). Self-discipline outdoes IQ in predicting academic performance of adolescence. *Psychological Science, 16*, 939–944.

Duckworth, A. L., & Steinberg, L. (2015). Unpacking self-control. *Child Development Perspectives, 9*, 32–37.

Duffy, S., Huttenlocher, J., & Levine, S. (2005). It's all relative: How young children encode extent. *Journal of Cognition and Development, 6*, 51–63.

Duffy, S., & Kitayama, S. (2007). Mnemonic context effect in two cultures: An examination of culturally contingent attention strategies. *Cognitive Science, 31*, 1009–1020.

Duffy, S., Toriyama, R., Itakura, S., & Kitayama, S. (2009). Development of cultural strategies of attention in North American and Japanese children. *Journal of Experimental Child Psychology, 102*, 351–359.

Dunbar, R. I. M. (1992). Neocortex size as a constraint on group size in primates. *Journal of Human Evolution, 20*, 469–493.

Dunbar, R. I. M. (2014). The social brain: Psychological underpinnings and implications for the structure of organization. *Psychological Science, 23*, 109–114.

Duncan, J., Seitz, R. J., Kolodny, J., Bor, D., Herzog, H., Ahmed, A., . . . Emslie, H. (2000). A neural basis for general intelligence. *Science, 289*, 457–460.

Duncan, R., & Tarulli, D. (2009). On the persistence of private speech: Empirical and theoretical considerations. In A. Winsler, C. Fernyhough, & I. Montero (Eds.), *Private speech, executive functioning, and the development of verbal self-regulation* (pp. 176–187). Cambridge, UK: Cambridge University Press.

Duyme, M., Dumaret, A., & Tomkiewicz, S. (1999). How can we boost IQs of "dull" children? A late adoption study. *Proceedings of the National Academy of Sciences, 96*, 8790–8794.

Eagan, S. K., & Perry, D. G. (2001). Gender identity: A multidimensional analysis with implications for psychological adjustment. *Developmental Psychology, 37*, 451–463.

Easterbrook, M. A., Kisilevsky, B. S., Hains, S. M. J., & Muir, D. W. (1999). Faceness or complexity: Evidence from newborn visual tracking of facelike stimuli. *Infant Behavior and Development, 22*, 17–35.

Eaton, W. O., & Von Bargen, D. (1981). Asynchronous development of gender understanding in preschool children. *Child Development, 52*, 1020–1027.

Eigsti, I.-M., Zayas, V., Mischel, W., Shoda, Y., Ayduk, O., Dadlani, M. B., . . . Casey, B. J. (2006). Predicting cognitive control from preschool to late adolescence and young adulthood. *Psychological Science, 17*, 478–484.

Eilers, R. W., Gavin, W. J., & Wilson, W. R. (1979). Linguistic experience and phonemic perception in infancy: A cross-linguistic study. *Child Development, 50*, 14–18.

Eimas, P. D., & Quinn, P. C. (1994). Studies on the formation of perceptually based basic-level categories in young infants. *Child Development, 65*, 903–917.

Eimas, P. D., Siqueland, E. R., Jusczyk, P., & Vigorito, J. (1971). Speech perception in infants. *Science, 71*, 303–306.

Einstein, G. O., & McDaniel, M. A. (2005). Prospective memory: Multiple retrieval processes. *Current Directions in Psychological Science, 14*, 286–290.

Eizenman, D. R., & Bertenthal, B. I. (1998). Infants' perception of object unity in translating and rotating displays. *Developmental Psychology, 34*, 426–434.

Elischberger, H. B. (2005). The effects of prior knowledge on children's memory and suggestibility. *Journal of Experimental Child Psychology, 92*, 247–275.

Elkind, D. (1967). Egocentrism in adolescence. *Child Development, 38*, 1025–1033.

Elkind, D. (1987). *Miseducation: Preschoolers at risk*. New York: Knopf.

Elkind, D., & Bowen, R. (1979). Imaginary audience behavior in children and adolescents. *Developmental Psychology, 15*, 38–44.

Ellis, H. (1894). *Man and woman: A study of human secondary sexual characters*. London: Walter Scott.

Ellis, N. C., & Hennelley, R. A. (1980). A bilingual word-length effect: Implications for intelligence testing and the relative ease of mental calculation in Welsh and English. *British Journal of Psychology, 71*, 43–52.

Elman, J. L. (1994). Implicit learning in neural networks: The importance of starting small. In C. Umilta & M. Moscovitch (Eds.), *Attention and performance XV: Conscious and nonconscious information processing* (Vol. 15, pp. 861–888). Cambridge, MA: MIT Press.

Elman, J. L., Bates, E. A., Johnson, M. H., Karmiloff-Smith, A., Parisi, D., & Plunket, K. (1996). *Rethinking innateness: A connectionist perspective on development*. Cambridge, MA: MIT Press.

Else-Quest, N. M., Hyde, J. S., & Linn, M. C. (2010). Cross-national patterns of gender differences in mathematics: A meta-analysis. *Psychological Bulletin, 136*, 103–127.

Eluvathingal, T. J., Chugani, H. T., Behen, M. E., JuhAsz, C., Muzik, O., Maqbool, M., . . . Makki, M. (2006). Abnormal brain connectivity in children after early severe socioemotional deprivation: A diffusion tensor imaging study. *Pediatrics, 117*, 2093–2100.

Emmons, N. A., & Kelemen, D. A. (2014). The development of children's prelife reasoning: Evidence from two cultures. *Child Development, 85*(4), 1617–1633.

Emmons, N. A., & Keleman, D. A. (2015). I've got a feeling: Urban and rural indigenous children's beliefs about early life mentality. *Journal of Experimental Child Psychology, 138*, 106–125.

Erdelyi, M. (1994). Hypnotic hypermnesia: The empty set of hypermnesia. *International Journal of Clinical and Experimental Hypnosis, 42*, 379–390.

Eriksson, M., Marschik, P. B., Tulviste, T., Almgren, M., Pérez Pereira, M., Wehberg, S., . . . Gallego, C. (2012). Differences between girls and boys in emerging language skills: Evidence from 10 language communities. *British Journal of Developmental Psychology, 30*(2), 326–343.

Eriksson, P. S., Perfilieva, E., Bjoerk-Eriksson, T., Alborn, A.-M., Nordborg, C., Peterson, D. A., & Gage, F. H. (1998). Neurogenesis in the adult human hippocampus. *Nature Medicine, 4*, 1313–1317.

Espy, K. A., Molfese, V. J., & DiLalla, L. F. (2001). Effects of environmental measures on intelligence in young children: Growth curve modeling of longitudinal data. *Merrill-Palmer Quarterly, 47*, 42–73.

Evans, E. M. (2001). Cognitive and contextual factors in the emergence of diverse belief systems: Creation versus evolution. *Cognitive Psychology, 42*, 217–266.

Evans, G. W., & Cassells, R. C. (2014). Childhood poverty, cumulative risk exposure, and mental health in emerging adults. *Clinical Psychological Science, 2*, 287–296.

Evans, G. W., & Kim, P. (2007). Childhood poverty and health: Cumulative risk exposure and stress dysregulation. *Psychological Science, 18*, 953–957.

Evans, G. W., & Kim, P. (2012). Childhood poverty and young adults' allostatic load: The mediating role of childhood cumulative risk. *Psychological Science, 23*, 979–983.

Evans, J. St. B. T. (2012). Dual-process theories of deductive reasoning: Facts and fallacies. In K. J. Holyoak & R. G. Morrison, *The Oxford handbook of thinking and reasoning* (pp. 115–133). New York: Oxford University Press.

Evans, M. A. (1985). Self-initiated speech repairs: A reflection of communicative monitoring in young children. *Developmental Psychology, 21*, 365–371.

Evans, N., & Levinson, S. (2009). The myth of language universals: Language diversity and its importance for cognitive science. *Behavioral and Brain Science, 32*, 429–492.

Eysenck, H. J. (1987). Speed of information processing, reaction time, and the theory of intelligence. In P. E. Vernon (Ed.), *Speed of information processing and intelligence* (pp. 21–67). Norwood, NJ: Ablex.

Fagan, J. F., III. (1973). Infants' delayed recognition memory and forgetting. *Journal of Experimental Child Psychology, 16,* 424–450.

Fagan, J. F., III. (1974). Infant recognition memory: The effects of length of familiarization and type of discrimination task. *Child Development, 45,* 351–356.

Fagan, J. F., III. (1984). The relationship of novelty preferences during infancy to later intelligence and recognition memory. *Intelligence, 8,* 339–346.

Fagan, J. F., III. (1992). Intelligence: A theoretical viewpoint. *Current Directions in Psychological Science, 1,* 82–86.

Fagan, J. F., III. (2011). Intelligence in infancy. In R. J. Sternberg & S. B. Kaufman (Eds.), *The Cambridge handbook of intelligence* (pp. 130–143). Cambridge, UK: Cambridge University Press.

Fagan, J. F., III., & Singer, J. T. (1983). Infant recognition memory as a measure of intelligence. In L. P. Lipsitt & C. K. Rovee-Collier (Eds.), *Advances in infancy research* (Vol. 2, pp. 31–78). Norwood, NJ: Ablex.

Fagen, J., Prigot, J., Carroll, M., Pioli, L., Stein, A., & Franco, A. (1997). Auditory context and memory retrieval in young infants. *Child Development, 68,* 1057–1066.

Fagot, B. I., Leinbach, M. D., & Hagan, R. (1986). Gender labeling and the adoption of sex-typed behaviors. *Developmental Psychology, 22,* 440–443.

Fair, J., Flom, R., Jones, J., & Martin, J. (2012). Perceptual learning: 12-month-olds' discrimination of monkey faces. *Child Development, 83,* 1996–2006.

Fantz, R. L. (1958). Pattern vision in young infants. *Psychological Record, 8,* 43–47.

Fantz, R. L. (1961). The origin of form perception. *Scientific American, 204,* 66–72.

Fantz, R. L., & Miranda, S. B. (1975). Newborn attention to form of contour. *Child Development, 46,* 224–228.

Farroni, T., Csibra, G., Simion, F., & Johnson, M. H. (2002). Eye contact detection in humans from birth. *Proceedings of the National Academy of Sciences, 99,* 9602–9605.

Fay-Stammbach, T., Hawes, D. J., & Meredith, P. (2014). Parenting influences on executive function in early childhood: A review. *Child Development Perspectives, 8,* 258–264.

Fecteau, S., Carmant, L., Tremblay, C., Robert, M., Bouthillier, A., & Theoret, H. (2004). A motor resonance mechanism in children? Evidence from subdural electrodes in a 36-month-old child. *Neuroreport, 15,* 2625–2627.

Feigenson, L., Carey, S., & Hauser, M. (2002). The representations underlying infants' choice of more: Object-files versus analog magnitudes. *Psychological Science, 13,* 150–156.

Feigenson, L., Dehaene, S., & Spelke, E. S. (2004). Core systems of number. *Trends in Cognitive Sciences, 8*(7), 307–314.

Feigenson, L., Libertus, M. E., & Halberda, J. (2013). Links between the intuitive sense of number and formal mathematics ability. *Child Development Perspectives, 7,* 74–79.

Fein, G. (1981). Pretend play: An integrative review. *Child Development, 52,* 1095–1118.

Feinberg, I. (1982–1983). Schizophrenia: Caused by a fault in programmed synaptic elimination during adolescence? *Journal of Psychiatric Research, 4,* 319–334.

Feingold, A. (1988). Cognitive gender differences are disappearing. *American Psychologist, 43,* 95–103.

Feingold, A. (1992). Sex differences in variability in intellectual abilities: A new look at an old controversy. *Review of Educational Research, 62,* 61–84.

Feldman, R., & Eidelman, A. I. (2004). Parent-infant synchrony and the social-emotional development of triplets. *Developmental Psychology, 40,* 1133–1147.

Fernald, A. (1992). Human maternal vocalizations to infants as biologically relevant signals: An evolutionary perspective. In J. H. Barkow, L. Cosmides, & J. Tooby (Eds.), *The adaptive mind: Evolutionary psychology and the generation of culture* (pp. 391–428). New York: Oxford University Press.

Fernald, A., Marchman, V. A., & Weisleder, A. (2013). SES differences in language processing skill and vocabulary are evident at 18 months. *Developmental Science, 16*(2), 234–248.

Fernald, A., & Mazzie, C. (1991). Prosody and focus in speech to infants and adults. *Developmental Psychology, 27,* 209–221.

Fernald, A., Pinto, J. P., Swingley, D., Weinberg, A., & McRoberts, G. W. (1998). Rapid gains in speed of verbal processing by infants in the 2nd year. *Psychological Science, 9,* 228–231.

Fernald, A., Taeschner, T., Dunn, J., Papousek, M., Fukui, I., & Boysson-Bardies, B. de. (1989). A cross-language study of prosodic modifications in mothers' and fathers' speech to infants. *Journal of Child Language, 16,* 477–501.

Ferrari, P. F., Visalberghi, E., Paukner, A., Fogassi, L., Ruggiero, A., & Suomi, S. J. (2006). Neonatal imitation in rhesus macaques. *PLOS Biology, 4*(9), e302.

Ferreira, F., & Morrison, F. J. (1994). Children's knowledge of syntactic constituents: Effects of age and schooling. *Developmental Psychology, 30,* 663–678.

Ferry, A. L., Hespos, S. J., & Waxman, S. R. (2010). Categorization in 3- and 4-month-old infants: An advantage of words over tones. *Child Development, 81,* 472–479.

Ferry, A. L., Hespos, S. J., & Waxman, S. R. (2013). Nonhuman primate vocalizations support categorization in very young human infants. *Proceedings of the National Academy of Sciences, 110,* 15231–15235.

Field, T. M., Guy, L., & Umbel, V. (1985). Infants' responses to mothers' imitative behaviors. *Infant Mental Health Journal, 6*, 40–44.

Field, T. M., Woodson, R., Greenberg, R., & Cohen, D. (1982). Discrimination and imitation of facial expression by neonates. *Science, 218*, 179–181.

Finkelstein, N. W., & Ramey, C. T. (1977). Learning to control the environment in infancy. *Child Development, 48*, 806–819.

Finn, A. S., Kalra, P. B., Goetz, C., Leonard, J. A., Sheridan, M. A., & Gabriel, J. D. E. (2016). Developmental dissociation between the maturation of procedural memory and declarative memory. *Journal of Experimental Child Psychology, 142*, 212–220.

Fischer, K. W., & Bidell, T. (1991). Constraining nativist inferences about cognitive capacities. In S. Carey & R. Gelman (Eds.), *The epigenesis of mind: Essays on biology and cognition* (pp. 199–235). Hillsdale, NJ: Erlbaum.

Fisher, A. V., Godwin, K. E., & Seltman, H. (2014). Visual environment, attention allocation, and learning in young children: When too much of a good thing may be bad. *Psychological Sciences, 25*, 1362–1370.

Fisher, C., & Tokura, H. (1996). Acoustic cues to grammatical structure in infant-directed speech: Cross-linguistic evidence. *Child Development, 67*, 3192–3218.

Fivush, R. (2008). Remembering and reminiscing: How individual lives are constructed in family narratives. *Memory Studies, 1*, 49–58.

Fivush, R. (2011). The development of autobiographical memory. *Annual Review of Psychology, 62*, 559–582.

Fivush, R. (2014). Maternal reminiscing style: The sociocultural construction of autobiographical memory across childhood and adolescence. In P. J. Bauer & R. Fivush (Eds.), *The Wiley handbook on the development of children's memory* (Vol. 2, pp. 568–585). Chichester, UK: Wiley-Blackwell.

Fivush, R., Haden, C. A., & Reese, E. (2006). Elaborating on elaborations: Role of maternal reminiscing style in cognitive and socioemotional development. *Child Development, 77*, 1568–1588.

Fivush, R., & Hamond, N. R. (1990). Autobiographical memory across the preschool years: Toward reconceptualizing childhood amnesia. In R. Fivush & J. A. Hudson (Eds.), *Knowing and remembering in young children* (pp. 223–248). Cambridge, UK: Cambridge University Press.

Fivush, R., & Hudson, J. A. (Eds.). (1990). *Knowing and remembering in young children*. Cambridge, UK: Cambridge University Press.

Fivush, R., Kuebli, J., & Clubb, P. A. (1992). The structure of events and event representations: A developmental analysis. *Child Development, 63*, 188–201.

Fivush, R., & Zaman, W. (2014). Gender, subjective perspective, and autobiographical consciousness. In P. J. Bauer & R. Fivush (Eds.), *The Wiley handbook on the development of children's memory* (Vol. 2, pp. 586–604). Chichester, UK: Wiley-Blackwell.

Flannagan, D., Baker-Ward, L., & Graham, L. (1995). Talk about preschool: Patterns of topic discussion and elaboration related to gender and ethnicity. *Sex Roles, 32*, 1–15.

Flavell, J. H. (1970). Developmental studies of mediated memory. In H. W. Reese & L. P. Lipsitt (Eds.), *Advances in child development and child behavior* (Vol. 5, pp. 181–211). New York: Academic.

Flavell, J. H. (1978). Developmental stage: Explanans or explanandum? *Behavioral and Brain Sciences, 2*, 187.

Flavell, J. H., Beach, D. R., & Chinsky, J. H. (1966). Spontaneous verbal rehearsal in a memory task as a function of age. *Child Development, 37*, 283–299.

Flavell, J. H., Green, F. L., & Flavell, E. R. (1986). Development of knowledge about the appearance-reality distinction. *Monographs of the Society for Research in Child Development, 51*(1, Serial No. 212).

Flavell, J. H., Green, F. L., & Flavell, E. R. (1995). The development of children's knowledge about attentional focus. *Developmental Psychology, 31*, 706–712.

Flavell, J. H., Green, F. L., Flavell, E. R., & Grossman, J. B. (1997). The development of children's knowledge about inner speech. *Developmental Psychology, 68*, 39–47.

Flavell, J. H., & Miller, P. H. (1998). Social cognition. In W. Damon (Series Ed.) & D. Kuhn & R. S. Siegler (Vol. Eds.), *Handbook of child psychology: Vol 2. Cognition, perception, and language* (5th ed., pp. 851–898). New York: Wiley.

Flieller, A. (1999). Comparison of the development of formal thought in adolescent cohorts aged 10 to 15 years (1967–1996 and 1972–1993). *Developmental Psychology, 35*, 1048–1058.

Flin, R., Boon, J., Knox, A., & Bull, R. (1992). The effect of a five-month delay on children's and adults' eyewitness memory. *British Journal of Psychology, 83*, 323–336.

Flinn, M., & Ward, C. (2005). Evolution of the human child. In B. J. Ellis & D. F. Bjorklund (Eds.), *Origins of the social mind: Evolutionary psychology and child development* (pp. 19–44). New York: Guilford Press.

Flynn, E., O'Malley, C., & Wood, D. (2004). A longitudinal, microgenetic study of the emergence of false belief understanding and inhibition skills. *Developmental Science, 7*, 103–115.

Flynn, J. R. (1987). Massive IQ gains in 14 nations: What IQ tests really measure. *Psychological Bulletin, 101*, 171–191.

Flynn, J. R. (2007). *What is intelligence? Beyond the Flynn effect*. New York: Cambridge University Press.

Flynn, J. R. (2012). *Are we getting smarter? Rising IQ in the twenty-first century*. New York: Cambridge University Press.

Flynn, J. R., & Blair, C. (2013). The history of intelligence: New spectacles for developmental psychology. In P. D. Zelazo (Ed.), *The Oxford handbook of developmental psychology: Vol. 1. Body and mind* (pp. 765–790). Oxford, UK: Oxford University Press.

Folds, T. H., Footo, M., Gottentag, R. E., & Ornstein, P. A. (1990). When children mean to remember: Issues of context specificity, strategy effectiveness, and intentionality in the development of memory. In D. F. Bjorklund (Ed.), *Children's strategies: Contemporary views of cognitive development* (pp. 67–91). Hillsdale, NJ: Erlbaum.

Foley, M. A., & Ratner, H. H. (1998). Distinguishing between memories for thoughts and deeds: The role of prospective processing in children's source monitoring. *British Journal of Developmental Psychology, 16*, 465–184.

Foley, M. A., Ratner, H. H., & Gentes, E. (2010). Helping children enter into another's experiences: The look and feel of it. *Journal of Cognition and Development, 11*, 217–239.

Foley, M. A., Santini, C., & Sopasakis, M. (1989). Discriminating between memories: Evidence for children's spontaneous elaborations. *Journal of Experimental Child Psychology, 48*, 146–169.

Fontaine, R. G. (2006). Applying systems principles to models of social information processing and aggressive behavior in youth. *Aggression and Violent Behavior, 11*, 64–76.

Ford, R. M., Driscoll, T., Shum, D., & Macaulay, C. E. (2012). Executive and theory-of-mind contributions to event-based prospective memory in children: Exploring the self-projection hypothesis. *Journal of Experimental Child Psychology, 111*(3), 468–489.

Foss, J., & Hakes, D. (1978). *Psycholinguistics: An introduction to the study of language*. Englewood Cliffs, NJ: Prentice Hall.

Fox, S. E., Levitt, P., & Nelson, C. A., III. (2010). How timing and quality of early experience influence the development of brain architecture. *Child Development, 81*, 28–40.

Fraga, M. F., Ballestar, E., Paz, M. F., Ropero, S., Setien, F., Ballestar, M. L., . . . Esteller, M. (2005). Epigenetic differences arise during the lifetime of monozygotic twins. *Proceedings of the National Academy of Sciences, 102*(30), 10604–10609.

Franchak, J., Kretch, K., Soska, K., & Adolph, K. (2011). Head-mounted eye tracking: A new method to describe infant looking. *Child Development, 82*(6), 1738–1750.

Frank, M. C., Amso, D., & Johnson, S. (2014). Visual search and attention to faces during early infancy. *Journal of Experimental Child Psychology, 118*, 13–26.

Frank, M. C., Vul, E., & Johnson, S. (2009). Development of infants' attention to faces during the first year. *Cognition, 110*, 160–170.

Franklin, A., Pilling, M., & Davies, I. (2005). The nature of infant color categorization: Evidence from eye movements on a target detection task. *Journal of Experimental Child Psychology, 91*, 227–248.

Frazier, J. A., & Morrison, F. J. (1998). The influence of extended-year schooling on growth of achievement and perceived competence in early elementary school. *Child Development, 69*, 495–517.

Freud, S. (1963). Three essays on the theory of sexuality. In J. Strachey (Ed. and Trans.), *The standard edition of the complete psychological works of Sigmund Freud* (Vol. 7, pp. 7–122). London: Hogarth.

Frick, A., & Newcombe, N. S. (2012). Getting the big picture: Development of spatial scaling abilities. *Cognitive Development, 27*(3), 270–282.

Friedman, S. (1972). Habituation and recovery of visual response in the alert human newborn. *Journal of Experimental Child Psychology, 13*, 339–349.

Friedman, W. J. (1986). The development of children's knowledge of temporal structure. *Child Development, 57*, 1386–1400.

Friedman, W. J. (1991). The development of children's memory for the time of past events. *Child Development, 62*, 139–155.

Friedman, W. J. (2000). The development of children's knowledge of the times of future events. *Child Development, 71*, 913–932.

Friedman, W. J. (2008). Developmental perspectives on the psychology of time. In S. Grondin (Ed.), *The psychology of time* (pp. 345–366). Bingley, UK: Emerald.

Friedman, W. J., Gardner, A. G., & Zubin, N. R. E. (1995). Children's comparisons of the recency of two events from the past year. *Child Development, 66*, 44–66.

Frisby, C. L., & Beaujean, A. A. (2015). Testing Spearman's hypotheses using a bi-factor model with WAIS-IV/WMS-IV standardization data. *Intelligence, 51*, 79–97.

Froese, T., & Leavens, D. A. (2014). The direct perception hypothesis: Perceiving the intention of another's action hinders its precise imitation. *Frontiers in Psychology, 5*, 1–15.

Fry, A., & Hale, S. (2000). Relationships among processing speed, working memory and fluid intelligence in children. *Biological Psychology, 54*, 1–34.

Fuligni, A. J., & Stevenson, H. W. (1995). Time use and mathematics achievement among American, Chinese, and Japanese high school students. *Child Development, 66*, 830–842.

Furman, L. N., & Walden, T. A. (1990). Effects of script knowledge on preschool children's communicative interactions. *Developmental Psychology, 26,* 227–233.

Furth, H. G. (1964). Research with the deaf: Implications for language and cognition. *Psychological Bulletin, 62,* 251–267.

Fuson, K. C. (1988). *Children's counting and concepts of number.* New York: Springer-Verlag.

Fuson, K. C., Pergament, G. G., Lyons, B. G., & Hall, J. W. (1985). Children's conformity to the cardinality rule as a function of set size and counting accuracy. *Child Development, 56,* 1429–1436.

Fuster, J. M. (1989). *The prefrontal cortex: Anatomy, physiology, and neuropsychology of the frontal lobe.* New York: Raven.

Galanaki, E. P. (2012). The imaginary audience and the personal fable: A test of Elkind's theory of adolescent egocentrism. *Psychology, 3*(6), 457–466.

Gallup, G. G., Jr. (1979). Self-recognition in chimpanzees and man: A developmental and comparative perspective. In M. Lewis & L. A. Rosenblum (Eds.), *Genesis of behavior: The child and its family* (Vol. 2, pp. 107–126). New York: Plenum.

Galsworthy, M. J., Dionne, G., Dale, P. S., & Plomin, R. (2000). Sex differences in early verbal and nonverbal cognitive development. *Developmental Science, 3,* 206–215.

Ganea, P. A., Allen, M. L., Butler, L., Carey, S., & DeLoache, J. S. (2009). Toddlers' referential understanding of pictures. *Journal of Experimental Child Psychology, 104,* 283–295.

Ganea, P. A., Bloom Pickard, M., & DeLoache, J. S. (2008). Transfer between picture books and the real world by very young children. *Journal of Cognition and Development, 9,* 46–66.

Ganger, J., & Brent, M. R. (2004). Reexamining the vocabulary spurt. *Developmental Psychology, 40,* 621–632.

Gangestad, S. W., & Thornhill, R. (1997). Human sexual selection and developmental stability. In J. A. Simpson & D. T. Kenrick (Eds.), *Evolutionary social psychology* (pp. 169–195). Mahwah, NJ: Erlbaum.

Ganley, C. M., Vasilyeva, M., & Dulaney, A. (2014). Spatial ability mediates the gender difference in middle school students' science performance. *Child Development, 85,* 1419–1432.

Garber, H. L. (1988). *The Milwaukee Project: Preventing mental retardation in children at risk.* Washington, DC: American Association on Mental Retardation.

Gardiner, A. K. (2014). Beyond irrelevant actions: Understanding the role of intentionality in children's imitation of relevant actions. *Journal of Experimental Child Psychology, 119,* 54–72.

Gardiner, A. K., Bjorklund, D. F., Greif, M. L., & Gray, S. K. (2012). Choosing and using tools: Prior experience and task difficulty influence preschoolers' tool-use strategies. *Cognitive Development, 27,* 240–254.

Gardiner, A. K., & Causey, K. B. (2015, March). *Preschoolers independently discern causal structure when observing an unknowledgeable demonstrator.* Paper presented at meeting of the Society for Research in Child Development, Philadelphia, PA.

Gardiner, A. K., Greif, M., & Bjorklund, D. F. (2011). Guided by intention: Preschoolers' imitation reflects inferences of causation. *Journal of Cognition and Development, 12*(3), 355–373.

Gardner, H. (1983). *Frames of mind: The theory of multiple intelligences.* New York: Basic Books.

Gardner, H. (Ed.). (1993). *Multiple intelligences: The theory in practice.* New York: Basic Books.

Gardner, H. (1999). Are there additional intelligences? The case for naturalist, spiritual, and existential intelligences. In J. Kane (Ed.), *Education, information and transformation* (pp. 111–131). Englewood Cliffs, NJ: Prentice Hall.

Gardner, H. (2006). *Multiple intelligences: New horizons in theory and practice.* New York: Basic Books.

Gardner, H. (2014). Howard's response to Jeanne Bamberger. In M. L. Kornhaber & E. Winner (Eds.), *Mind, work, and life: A Festschrift on the occasion of Howard Gardner's 70th birthday* (pp. 54–57). Cambridge, MA: Offices of Howard Gardner.

Gardner, H., & Moran, S. (2006). The science of multiple intelligences theory: A response to Lynn Waterhouse. *Educational Psychologist, 41,* 227–232.

Garnham, W. A., & Ruffman, T. (2001). Doesn't see, doesn't know: Is anticipatory looking really related to understanding belief? *Developmental Science, 4,* 94–100.

Garon, N., Smith, I. M., & Bryson, S. E. (2014). A novel executive function battery for preschoolers: Sensitivity to age differences. *Child Neuropsychology, 20*(6), 713–736.

Gaskins, S., Haight, W., & Lancy, D. F. (2007). The cultural construction of play. In A. Göncü & S. Gaskins (Eds.), *Play and development: Evolutionary, sociocultural, and functional perspectives* (pp. 179–202). Mahwah, NJ: Erlbaum.

Gathercole, S. E., Alloway, T. P., Willis, C., & Adams, A.-M. (2006). Working memory in children with reading disabilities. *Journal of Experimental Child Psychology, 93,* 265–281.

Gathercole, V. C. M. (2013). *Issues in the assessment of bilinguals.* Bristol, UK: Multilingual Matters.

Gaultney, J. F. (1995). The effect of prior knowledge and metacognition on the acquisition of a reading comprehension strategy. *Journal of Experimental Child Psychology, 59,* 142–163.

Gaultney, J. F. (1998). Utilization deficiencies among children with learning disabilities. *Learning and Individual Differences, 10*, 13–28.

Gaultney, J. F., Bjorklund, D. F., & Goldstein, D. (1996). To be young, gifted, and strategic: Advantages for memory performance. *Journal of Experimental Child Psychology, 61*, 43–66.

Gauvain, M. (2001). *The social context of cognitive development.* New York: Guilford Press.

Gauvain, M. (2013). Sociocultural contexts of development. In P. D. Zelazo (Ed.), *The Oxford handbook of developmental psychology: Vol. 1. Body and mind* (pp. 425–451). Oxford, UK: Oxford University Press.

Gauvain, M., & Munroe, R. L. (2009). Contributions of societal modernity to cognitive development: A comparison of four cultures. *Child Development, 80*, 1628–1642.

Gauvain, M., & Perez, S. (2015). Cognitive development in cultural context. In R. Lerner (Series Ed.) & L. Liben & U. Muller (Vol. Eds.), *Handbook of child psychology and developmental science: Vol. 2. Cognitive processes* (7th ed., pp. 854–896). New York: Wiley.

Gava, L., Valenza, E., Turati, C., & de Schonen, S. (2008). Effect of partial occlusion on newborns' face preference and recognition. *Developmental Science, 11*, 563–574.

Geary, D. C. (1993). Mathematical disabilities: Cognitive, neuropsychological, and genetic components. *Psychological Bulletin, 114*, 345–362.

Geary, D. C. (1994). *Children's mathematical development: Research and practical applications.* Washington, DC: American Psychological Association.

Geary, D. C. (1995). Reflections of evolution and culture in children's cognition: Implications for mathematical development and instruction. *American Psychologist, 50*, 24–37.

Geary, D. C. (2005). *The origin of mind: Evolution of brain, cognition, and general intelligence.* Washington, DC: American Psychological Association.

Geary, D. C. (2006). Development of mathematical understanding. In W. Damon & R. M. Lerner (Series Eds.) & D. Kuhn & R. S. Siegler (Vol. Eds.), *Handbook of child psychology: Vol. 2. Cognition, perception, and language* (6th ed., pp. 777–810). New York: Wiley.

Geary, D. C. (2007). Educating the evolved mind: Conceptual foundations for an evolutionary educational psychology. In J. S. Carlson & J. R. Levin (Eds.), *Educating the evolved mind: Conceptual foundations for an evolutionary educational psychology* (pp. 1–99). Charlotte, NC: Information Age.

Geary, D. C. (2010a). Evolution and education. *Psicothema, 22*, 35–40.

Geary, D. C. (2010b). *Male, female: The evolution of human sex differences* (2nd ed.). Washington, DC: American Psychological Association.

Geary, D. C. (2011). Cognitive predictors of achievement growth in mathematics: A five year longitudinal study. *Developmental Psychology, 47*, 1539–1552.

Geary, D. C., & Berch, D. B. (2016). Evolution and children's cognitive and academic development. In D. C. Geary & D. B. Berch (Eds.), *Evolutionary perspectives on education and child development* (pp. 217–249). New York: Springer.

Geary, D. C., Bow-Thomas, C. C., Fan, L., & Siegler, R. S. (1993). Even before formal instructions, Chinese children outperform American children in mental arithmetic. *Cognitive Development, 8*, 517–529.

Geary, D. C., Bow-Thomas, C. C., Liu, F., & Siegler, R. S. (1996). Development of arithmetic competencies in Chinese and American children: Influence of age, language, and schooling. *Child Development, 67*, 2022–2044.

Geary, D. C, & Brown, S. C. (1991). Cognitive addition: Strategy choice and speed-of-processing differences in gifted, normal and mathematically disabled children. *Developmental Psychology, 27*, 398–406.

Geary, D. C., Brown, S. C., & Samaranayake, V. A. (1991). Cognitive addition: A short longitudinal study of strategy choice and speed of processing differences in normal and mathematically disabled children. *Developmental Psychology, 27*, 787–797.

Geary, D. C., Fan, L., & Bow-Thomas, C. C. (1992). Numerical cognition: Loci of ability differences comparing children from China and the United States. *Psychological Science, 3*, 180–185.

Geary, D. C., Hoard, M. K., & Bailey, D. H. (2012). Fact retrieval deficits in low achieving children and children with mathematical learning disability. *Journal of Learning Disabilities, 45*, 291–307.

Geerdts, M. S., Van de Walle, G. A., & LoBue, V. (2015). Daily animal exposure and children's biological concepts. *Journal of Experimental Child Psychology, 130*, 132–146.

Gelman, R. (1969). Conservation acquisition: A problem of learning to attend to relevant attributes. *Journal of Experimental Child Psychology, 7*, 167–187.

Gelman, R., & Gallistel, C. R. (1978). *The child's understanding of number.* Cambridge, MA: Harvard University Press.

Gelman, R., & Williams, F. M. (1998). Enabling constraints for cognitive development and learning: Domain-specificity and epigenesis. In W. Damon (Series Ed.) & D. Kuhn & R. S. Siegler (Vol. Eds.), *Handbook of child psychology: Vol 2. Cognition, perception, and language* (5th ed., pp. 575–630). New York: Wiley.

Gelman, S. A., & Kremer, K. E. (1991). Understanding natural cause: Children's explanations of how objects and their properties originate. *Child Development, 62,* 396–414.

Genesee, F. (2003). Rethinking bilingual acquisition. In J. M. deWaele (Ed.), *Bilingualism: Challenges and directions for future research* (pp. 158–182). Clevedon, UK: Multilingual Matters.

Gentner, D. (1989). The mechanisms of analogical learning. In S. Vosniadou & A. Ortony (Eds.), *Similarity and analogical reasoning* (pp. 199–241). London: Cambridge University Press.

Georgiou, G. K., Parrila, R., Cui, Y., & Papadopoulos, T. C. (2013). Why is rapid automatized naming related to reading? *Journal of Experimental Child Psychology, 115,* 218–225.

Gergely, G., Bekkering, H., & Kiraly, I. (2002). Rational imitation in pre-verbal infants. *Nature, 415,* 755.

Gergely, G., & Csibra, G. (2005). The social construction of the cultural mind: Imitative learning as a mechanism of human pedagogy. *Interaction Studies, 6,* 463–481.

Gergely, G., Nádasdy, Z., Csibra, G., & Bíró, S. (1995). Taking the intentional stance. *Cognition, 56,* 165–193.

Gerken, L., Balcomb, F. K., & Minton, J. L. (2011). Infants avoid "labouring in vain" by attending more to learnable than unlearnable linguistic patterns. *Developmental Science, 14,* 972–979.

German, T., & Johnson, S. (2002). Function and the origins of the design stance. *Journal of Cognition and Development, 3,* 279–300.

Gervais, W. M. (2013). Perceiving minds and gods: How mind perception enables, constrains, and is triggered by belief in gods. *Perspectives on Psychological Science, 8,* 380–394.

Gesell, A., & Amatruda, C. (1954). *Developmental diagnosis.* New York: Paul B. Holber.

Ghatala, E. S. (1984). Developmental changes in incidental memory as a function of meaningfulness and encoding condition. *Developmental Psychology, 20,* 208–211.

Ghatala, E. S., Levm, J. R., Pressley, M., & Goodwin, D. (1986). A componential analysis of the effects of derived and supplied strategy-utility information on children's strategy selection. *Journal of Experimental Child Psychology, 41,* 76–92.

Gibson, E. (1991). *An odyssey in learning and perception.* Cambridge, MA: MIT Press.

Giedd, J. N. (2012). The digital revolution and adolescent brain development. *Journal of Adolescent Health, 51,* 101–105.

Giedd, J. N. (2015). The amazing teen brain. *American Scientist, 312,* 33–37.

Giedd, J. N., Bluenthal, J., Jeffries, N. O., Castellanos, F. X., Lrj, H., Zijdenbos, A., . . . Rapoport, J. L. (1999). Brain development during childhood and adolescence: A longitudinal MRI study. *Nature Neuroscience, 2,* 861–863.

Gignac, G. E. (2014). Fluid intelligence shares closer to 60% of its variance with working memory capacity and is a better indicator of general intelligence. *Intelligence, 47,* 122–133.

Gladwell, M. (2008). *Outliers: The story of success.* New York: Little, Brown.

Gleitman, L. R. (1990). The structural sources of verb meanings. *Language Acquisition, 1,* 3–55.

Gliga, T., Elsabbagh, M., Andravizou, A., & Johnson, M. (2009). Faces attract infants' attention in complex displays. *Infancy, 14,* 550–562.

Gluckman, M., & Johnson, S. P. (2013). Attentional capture by social stimuli in young infants. *Frontiers in Psychology, 4,* 527.

Göbel, S. M., Moeller, K., Pixner, S., Kaufman, L., & Nuerk, H.-C. (2014). Language affects symbolic arithmetic in children: The case of number word inversion. *Journal of Experimental Child Psychology, 119,* 17–25.

Goldberg, R. F., & Thompson-Schill, S. L. (2009). Developmental "roots" in mature biological knowledge. *Psychological Science, 20,* 480–487.

Goldberg, S., & Lewis, M. (1969). Play behavior in the year-old infant: Early sex differences. *Child Development, 40,* 21–32.

Goldfield, B. A., & Reznick, J. S. (1990). Early lexical acquisition: Rate, content, and the vocabulary spurt. *Journal of Child Language, 17,* 171–184.

Goldhaber, D. (2012). *The nature-nurture debates: Bridging the gaps.* Cambridge, UK: Cambridge University Press.

Goldin-Meadow, S. (2009). How gesture promotes learning throughout childhood. *Child Development Perspectives, 3,* 106–111.

Goldin-Meadow, S. (2015). From action to abstraction: Gesture as a mechanism of change. *Developmental Review, 38,* 167–184.

Goldin-Meadow, S., & Cook, S. W. (2012). Gesture in thought. In K. J. Holyoak & R. G. Morrison (Eds.), *The Oxford handbook of thinking and reasoning* (pp. 631–649). New York: Oxford University Press.

Goldin-Meadow, S., Cook, S. W., & Mitchell, Z. A. (2009). Gesturing gives children new ideas about math. *Psychological Science, 20,* 267–272.

Goldin-Meadow, S., Levine, S. C., Hedges, L. V., Huttenlocher, J., Raudenbush, S. W., & Small, S. L. (2014). New evidence about language and cognitive development based on a longitudinal study: Hypotheses for intervention. *American Psychologist, 69*(6), 588.

Goldman, R., & Goldman, J. (1982). *Children's sexual thinking: A comparative study of children aged 5 to 15 years in Australia, North America, Britain, and Sweden.* London: Routledge & Kegan Paul.

Goldstein, D., Hasher, L., & Stein, D. K. (1983). Processing of occurrence-rate and item information by children of different ages and abilities. *American Journal of Psychology, 96*, 220–241.

Goldstein, S., & Barkley, R. A. (1998). ADHD, hunting, and evolution: "Just so stories." *ADHD Report, 6*(5), 1–4.

Golinkoff, R. M., Can, D. D., Soderstrom, M., & Hirsh-Pasek, K. (2015). (Baby) talk to me: The social context of infant-directed speech and its effects on early language acquisition. *Current Directions in Psychological Science, 24*, 339–344.

Golombok, S., Rust, J., Zervoulis, K., Croudace, T., Golding, J., & Hines, M. (2008). Developmental trajectories of sex-typed behavior in boys and girls: A longitudinal general population study of children aged 2.5–8 years. *Child Development, 79*, 1583–1593.

Goodman, G. S., Aman, C. J., & Hirschman, J. (1987). Child sexual and physical abuse: Children's testimony. In C. J. Ceci, M. P. Toglia, & D. F. Ross (Eds.), *Children's eyewitness memory* (pp. 1–23). New York: Springer-Verlag.

Goodman, G. S., & Clarke-Stewart, A. (1991). Suggestibility in children's testimony: Implications for sexual abuse investigations. In J. Doris (Ed.), *The suggestibility of children's recollections: Implications for eyewitness testimony* (pp. 77–82). Washington, DC: American Psychological Association.

Goodman, G. S., Quas, J. A., Batterman-Faunce, J. M., Riddlesberger, M. M., & Kuhn, J. (1994). Predictors of accurate and inaccurate memories of traumatic events experienced in childhood. *Consciousness and Cognition, 3*, 269–294.

Goodman, G. S., Quas, J. A., Batterman-Faunce, J. M., Riddlesberger, M. M., & Kuhn, J. (1997). Children's reactions to and memory for a stressful event: Influences of age, anatomical dolls, knowledge, and parental attachment. *Applied Developmental Science, 1*, 54–75.

Goodman, J. F. (1992). *When slow is fast enough: Educating the delayed preschool child.* New York: Guilford Press.

Goodz, N. S. (1982). Is before really easier to understand than after? *Child Development, 53*, 822–825.

Gopnik, A. (2009). *The philosophical baby: What children's minds tell us about truth, love, and the meaning of life.* New York: Farber, Straus, and Giroux.

Gopnik, A. (2011). The theory theory 2.0: Probabilistic models and cognitive development. *Child Development Perspectives, 5*(3), 161–163.

Gopnik, A., & Astington, J. W. (1988). Children's understanding of representational change and its relation to the understanding of false belief and the appearance-reality distinction. *Child Development, 59*, 26–37.

Gopnik, A., Glymour, C., Sobel, D. M., Shulz, L. E., Kushnir, T., & Danks, D. (2004). A theory of causal learning in children: Causal maps and Bayes nets. *Psychological Review, 111*(1), 3–32.

Gopnik, A., Griffiths, T. L., & Lucas, C. G. (2015). When younger learners can be better (or at least more open-minded) than older ones. *Current Directions in Psychological Science, 24*, 87–92.

Gopnik, A., & Slaughter, V. (1991). Young children's understanding of changes in their mental states. *Child Development, 62*, 98–110.

Gopnik, A., Sobel, D. M., Schulz, L., & Glymour, C. (2001). Causal learning mechanisms in very young children: Two, three, and four-year-olds infer causal relations from patterns of variation and covariation. *Developmental Psychology, 37*, 620–629.

Gopnik, A., & Wellman, H. M. (2012). Reconstructing constructivism: Causal models, Bayesian learning mechanisms, and the theory theory. *Psychological Bulletin, 138*(6), 1085–1108.

Gopnik, M., & Crago, M. D. (1991). Familial aggregation of a developmental language disorder. *Cognition, 39*, 1–50.

Gordon, P. (2004). Numerical cognition without words: Evidence from Amazonia. *Science, 306*, 496–499.

Gosso, Y., Otta, E., de Lima Salum e Morais, M., Leite Ribeiro, F. J., & Raad Bussab, V. S. (2005). Play in hunter-gatherer society. In A. D. Pellegrini & P. K. Smith (Eds.), *Play in humans and great apes* (pp. 213–253). Mahwah, NJ: Erlbaum.

Goswami, U. (1995). Transitive relational mapping in three- and four-year-olds: The analogy of Goldilocks and the Three Bears. *Child Development, 66*, 877–892.

Goswami, U. (1996). Analogical reasoning and cognitive development. In H. W. Reese (Ed.), *Advances in child development and behavior* (Vol. 26, pp. 92–138). San Diego, CA: Academic.

Goswami, U., & Brown, A. L. (1990). Higher-order structure and relational reasoning: Contrasting analogical and thematic relations. *Cognition, 36*, 207–226.

Gottfredson, L. S. (1997). Mainstream science on intelligence: An editorial with 52 signatories, history, and bibliography. *Intelligence, 24*(1), 13–23.

Gottfredson, L. S., & Deary, I. J. (2004). Intelligence predicts health and longevity, but why? *Current Directions in Psychological Science, 13*, 1–4.

Gottlieb, G. (1971). Ontogenesis of sensory functioning in birds and mammals. In E. Tobach, L. R. Aronson, & E. Shaw (Eds.), *The biopsychology of development* (pp. 67–128). New York: Academic.

Gottlieb, G. (1991a). Experiential canalization of behavioral development: Theory. *Developmental Psychology, 27,* 4–13.

Gottlieb, G. (1991b). Experiential canalization of behavioral development: Results. *Developmental Psychology, 27,* 35–39.

Gottlieb, G. (1992). *Individual development and evolution: The genesis of novel behavior.* New York: Oxford University Press.

Gottlieb, G. (2000). Environmental and behavioral influences on gene activity. *Current Directions in Psychological Science, 9,* 93–102.

Gottlieb, G. (2007). Probabilistic epigenesis. *Developmental Science, 10,* 1–11.

Gottlieb, G., Wahlsten, D., & Lickliter, R. (2006). The significance of biology for human development: A developmental psychobiological systems view. In W. Damon & R. M. Lerner (Series Eds.) & R. M. Lerner (Vol. Ed.), *Handbook of child psychology: Vol. 1. Theoretical models of human development* (6th ed., pp. 210–257). New York: Wiley.

Gould, E., Beylfn, A., Tanapat, P., Reeves, A., & Shors, T. J. (1999). Learning enhances adult neurogenesis in the hippocampal formation. *Nature Neuroscience, 2,* 260–265.

Gould, S. J. (1992). Mozart and modularity. *Natural History, 101,* 8–14.

Gould, S. J. (2002). *The structure of evolutionary theory.* Cambridge, MA: Harvard University Press.

Gouze, K. R. (1987). Attention and social problem-solving as correlates of aggression in preschool males. *Journal of Abnormal Child Psychology, 15,* 181–197.

Graces, E., Thomas, D., & Currie, J. (2002). Longer term effects of Head Start. *American Economic Review, 92,* 999–1012.

Graham, S., & Hudley, C. (1994). Attributions of aggressive and nonaggressive African-American early adolescent boys: A study of construct accessibility. *Developmental Psychology, 30,* 365–373.

Grammer, J. K., Purtell, K. M., Coffman, J. L., & Ornstein, P. A. (2011). Relations between children's metamemory and strategic performance: Time-varying covariates in early elementary school. *Journal of Experimental Child Psychology, 108*(1), 139–155.

Gray, P. (2013). *Free to learn: Why unleashing the instinct to play will make our children happier, more self-reliant, and better students for life.* New York: Basic Books.

Gray, P. (2016). Children's natural ways of educating themselves still works: Even for the three Rs. In D. C. Geary & D. B. Berch (Eds.), *Evolutionary perspectives on education and child development* (pp. 66–94). New York: Springer.

Gredlein, J. M., & Bjorklund, D. F. (2005). Sex differences in young children's use of tools in a problem-solving task: The role of object-oriented play. *Human Nature, 16,* 211–232.

Green, L. J. (2002). *African American English: A linguistic introduction.* Cambridge, UK: Cambridge University Press.

Greenfield, P. M. (1998). The cultural evolution of IQ. In U. Neisser (Ed.), *The rising cure: Long-term gains in IQ and related measures* (pp. 81–123). Washington, DC: American Psychological Association.

Greenfield, P. M. (2009). Linking social change and developmental change: Shifting pathways of human development. *Developmental Psychology, 45,* 401–418.

Greenough, W. T., Black, J. E., & Wallace, C. S. (1987). Experience and brain development. *Child Development, 58,* 539–559.

Greenough, W. T., McDonald, J., Parnisari, R., & Camel, J. E. (1986). Environmental conditions modulate degeneration and new dendrite growth in cerebellum of senescent rats. *Brain Research, 380,* 136–143.

Greenwald, A. G., McGhee, D. E., & Schwartz, J. K. L. (1998). Measuring individual differences in implicit cognition: The implicit association test. *Journal of Personality and Social Psychology, 74,* 1464–1480.

Greif, M. L., Kemler Nelson, D., Keil, F., & Gutierrez, F. (2006). What do children want to know about animals and artifacts? *Psychological Science, 17,* 455–459.

Grice, H. P. (1975). Logic and conversation. In P. Cole & J. Morgan (Eds.), *Speech acts: Syntax and semantics* (Vol. 3, pp. 41–58). New York: Academic.

Griffey, J. A. F., & Little, A. C. (2014). Infants' visual preferences for facial traits associated with adult attractiveness judgments: Data from eye-tracking. *Infant Behavior & Development, 37,* 268–275.

Groen, G. J., & Resnick, L. B. (1977). Can preschool children invent addition algorithms? *Journal of Educational Psychology, 69,* 645–652.

Gross, L. (2006). Evolution of neonatal imitation. *PLOS Biology, 4*(9), e311.

Grunau, R. E. (2013). Neonatal pain in very preterm infants: Long-term effects on brain, neurodevelopment and pain reactivity. *Rambam Maimonides Medical Journal, 4*(4), e0025.

Grunau, R. E., Oberlander, T. F., Whitfield, M. F., Fitzgerald, C., Morison, S. J., & Saul, J. P. (2001). Pain reactivity in former extremely low birth weight infants at corrected age 8 months compared with term born controls. *Infant Behavior and Development, 24,* 41–55.

Guberman, S. R. (1996). The development of everyday mathematics in Brazilian children with limited formal education. *Child Development, 67,* 1609–1623.

Guerra, N. G., Huesmann, L. R., & Hanish, L. (1995). The role of normative beliefs in children's social behavior. In N. Eisenberg (Ed.), *Review of personality and social psychology: Social development* (Vol. 15, pp. 140–158). Thousand Oaks, CA: Sage.

Guilford, J. P. (1988). Some changes in the structure-of-the-intellect model. *Educational and Psychological Measurement, 48,* 1–4.

Güler, O. E., Larkina, M., Kleinknecht, E. E., & Bauer, P. J. (2010). Memory strategies and retrieval success in preschool children: Relations to maternal behavior over time. *Journal of Cognition and Development, 11,* 159–184.

Gunderson, E. A., Spaepen, E., Gibson, D., Goldin-Meadow, S., & Levine, S. C. (2015). Gesture as a window onto children's number knowledge. *Cognition, 144,* 14–28.

Guttentag, R. E. (1984). The mental effort requirement of cumulative rehearsal: A developmental study. *Journal of Experimental Child Psychology, 37,* 92–106.

Habermas, T., & Bluck, S. (2000). Getting a life: The emergence of the life story in adolescence. *Psychological Bulletin, 126,* 748–769.

Habermas, T., & de Silveira, C. (2008). The development of global coherence in life narratives across adolescence: Temporal, causal and thematic aspects. *Developmental Psychology, 44,* 707–721.

Hackman, D. A., Betancourt, L. M., Gallop, R., Romer, D., Brodsky, N. L., Hurt, H., & Farah, M. J. (2015). Mapping the trajectory of socioeconomic disparity in working memory: Prenatal and neighborhood factors. *Child Development, 85,* 1433–1445.

Haden, C. A., Haine, R. A., & Fivush, R. (1997). Developing narrative structure in parent–child reminiscing across the preschool years. *Developmental Psychology, 33*(2), 295–307.

Haden, C. A., & Ornstein, P. A. (2009). Research on talking about the past: The past, present, and future. *Journal of Cognition and Development, 10,* 135–142.

Haden, C. A., Ornstein, P. A., Eckerman, C. O., & Didow, S. M. (2001). Mother-child conversational interactions as events unfold: Linkages to subsequent remembering. *Child Development, 72,* 1016–1031.

Haier, R. J., Siegel, B. V., Nuechterlein, K. H., Hazlett, E., Wu, J. C., Paek, J., . . . Buchsbaum, M. S. (1988). Cortical glucose metabolic rate correlates of abstract reasoning and attention studies with positron emission tomography. *Intelligence, 12,* 199–217.

Haight, W. L., & Miller, P. J. (1993). *Pretending at home: Early development in a sociocultural context.* Albany: State University of New York Press.

Haith, M. M. (1966). The response of the human newborn to visual movement. *Journal of Experimental Child Psychology, 3,* 235–243.

Haith, M. M. (1993). Preparing for the 21st century: Some goals and challenges for studies of infant sensory and perceptual development. *Developmental Review, 13,* 354–371.

Hakuta, K., Bialystok, E., & Wiley, E. (2003). Critical evidence: A test of the critical period hypothesis for second-language acquisition. *Psychological Science, 14,* 31–38.

Hakuta, K., & Garcia, E. E. (1989). Bilingualism and education. *American Psychologist, 44,* 374–379.

Hala, S., & Chandler, M. (1996). The role of strategic planning in accessing false-belief understanding. *Child Development, 67,* 2948–2966.

Hala, S., Chandler, M., & Fritz, A. S. (1991). Fledgling theories of mind: Deception as a marker of three-year-olds' understanding of false belief. *Child Development, 62,* 83–97.

Haley, M. H. (2004). Learner-centered instruction and the theory of multiple intelligences with second language learners. *Teachers College Record, 106,* 163–180.

Halford, G. S. (1993). *Children's understanding: The development of mental models.* Hillsdale, NJ: Erlbaum.

Halim, M. L., Ruble, D. N., Tamis-LeMonde, C. S., Zosuls, K. M., Lurye, L. E., & Greulich, F. K. (2014). Pink frilly dresses and the avoidance of all things "girly": Children's appearance rigidity and cognitive theories of gender development. *Developmental Psychology, 50,* 1091–1101.

Halit, H., de Haan, M., & Johnson, M. H. (2003). Cortical specialisation for face processing: Face-sensitive event-related potential components in 3 and 12 month-old infants. *NeuroImage, 1*(9), 1180–1193.

Halliday, M. A. K. (1973). *Explorations in the functions of language.* London: Edward Arnold.

Halpern, D. F. (1992). *Sex differences in cognitive abilities* (2nd ed.). Hillsdale, NJ: Erlbaum.

Halpern, D. F. (1997). Sex differences in intelligence. *American Psychologist, 52,* 1091–1102.

Halpern, D. F. (2004). A cognitive-process taxonomy for sex differences in cognitive abilities. *Current Directions in Psychological Science, 13,* 135–139.

Halpern, D. F. (2012). *Sex differences in cognitive abilities* (4th ed.). New York: Psychology Press.

Halpern, D. F., Benbow, C. P., Geary, D. C., Gur, R. C., Hyde, J. S., & Gernsbacher, M. A. (2007). The science of sex differences in science and mathematics. *Psychological Science in the Public Interest, 8,* 1–51.

Hamlin, J. K., Hallinan, E. V., & Woodward, A. L. (2008). Do as I do: 7-month-old infants selectively reproduce others' goals. *Developmental Science, 11,* 487–494.

Hamond, N. R., & Fivush, R. (1991). Memories of Mickey Mouse: Young children recount their trip to Disneyworld. *Cognitive Development, 6,* 433–448.

Han, J. J., Leitchman, M. D., & Wang, Q. (1998). Autobiographical memory in Korean, Chinese, and American children. *Developmental Psychology, 34,* 701–713.

Hanania, R., & Smith, L. B. (2010). Selective attention and attention switching: Towards a unified developmental approach. *Developmental Science, 13*(4), 622–635.

Hanscombe, K. B., Trzaskowski, M., Haworth, C. M. A., Davis, O. S. P., Dale, P. S., & Plomin, R. (2012, February 1). Socioeconomic status (SES) and children's intelligence (IQ): In a UK-representative sample SES moderates the environmental, not genetic, effect on IQ. *PLOS One.*

Hargrave, A. C., & Sénéchal, M. (2000). A book reading intervention with preschool children who have limited vocabularies: The benefits of regular reading and dialogic reading. *Early Childhood Research Quarterly, 15,* 75–90.

Harlow, H. F. (1959). The development of learning in the rhesus monkey. *American Scientist, 47,* 459–479.

Harlow, H. F., Dodsworth, R. O., & Harlow, M. K. (1965). Total isolation in monkeys. *Proceedings of the National Academy of Sciences, 54,* 90–97.

Harnishfeger, K. K. (1995). The development of cognitive inhibition: Theories, definitions, and research evidence. In F. Dempster & C. Brainerd (Eds.), *New perspectives on interference and inhibition in cognition* (pp. 175–204). New York: Academic.

Harnishfeger, K. K., & Bjorklund, D. F. (1990a). Children's strategies: A brief history. In D. F. Bjorklund (Ed.), *Children's strategies: Contemporary views of cognitive development* (pp. 1–22). Hillsdale, NJ: Erlbaum.

Harnishfeger, K. K., & Bjorklund, D. F. (1990b). Memory functioning of gifted and nongifted middle school children. *Contemporary Educational Psychology, 15,* 346–363.

Harnishfeger, K. K., & Pope, R. S. (1996). Intending to forget: The development of cognitive inhibition in directed forgetting. *Journal of Experimental Child Psychology, 62,* 292–315.

Harris, P. L. (2012). *Trusting what you're told: How children learn from others.* Cambridge, MA: Harvard University Press.

Harris, P. L., Brown, E., Marriott, C., Whittall, S., & Harmer, S. (1991). Monsters, ghosts and witches: Testing the limits of fantasy-reality distinction in young children. *British Journal of Developmental Psychology, 9,* 105–123.

Harris, P. L., & Nunez, M. (1996). Understanding of permission rules by preschool children. *Child Development, 67,* 1572–1591.

Hart, B., & Risley, T. R. (1995). *Meaningful differences in the everyday experience of young American children.* Baltimore: Brookes.

Hart, B., & Risley, T. R. (2003, Spring). The early catastrophe: The 30 million word gap by age 3. *American Educator,* 4–9.

Hart, C. L., Taylor, M. D., Smith, G. D., Whalley, L. J., Starr, J. M., Hole, D. J., . . . Deary, I. J. (2005). Childhood IQ and all-cause mortality before and after age 65: Prospective observational study linking the Scottish Mental Survey 1932 and the Midspan studies. *British Journal of Health Psychology, 10,* 153–165.

Harter, S., Waters, P., & Whitesell, N. R. (1998). Relational self-worth: Differences in perceived worth as a person across interpersonal contexts among adolescents. *Child Development, 69,* 756–766.

Hasher, L., & Zacks, R. T. (1979). Automatic and effortful processes in memory. *Journal of Experimental Psychology: General, 108,* 356–388.

Hashimoto, R., & Sakai, K. L. (2002). Specialization in the left prefrontal cortex for sentence comprehension. *Neuron, 35,* 589–597.

Hasselhorn, M. (1992). Task dependency and the role of category typicality and metamemory in the development of an organizational strategy. *Child Development, 63,* 202–214.

Hatano, G., & Inagaki, K. (2013). *Young children's thinking about the biological world.* Psychology Press.

Haun, D. B., Jordan, F. M., Vallortigara, G., & Clayton, N. S. (2010). Origins of spatial, temporal and numerical cognition: Insights from comparative psychology. *Trends in Cognitive Sciences, 14*(12), 552–560.

Hauser, M. D., Carey, S., & Hauser, L. B. (2000). Spontaneous number representation in semi-free-ranging rhesus monkeys. *Proceedings of the Royal Society of London, Series B, 267,* 829–833.

Hayes, B. K., & Hennessy, R. (1996). The nature and development of nonverbal implicit memory. *Journal of Experimental Child Psychology, 63,* 22–43.

Hayne, H. (2007). Infant memory development: New questions, new answers. In L. M. Oakes & P. J. Bauer (Eds.), *Short- and long-term memory in infancy and early childhood: Taking the first steps towards remembering* (pp. 209–239). New York: Oxford University Press.

Hayne, H., & Simcock, G. (2009). Memory development in toddlers. In M. L. Courage & N. Cowan (Eds.), *The development of memory in infancy and childhood* (pp. 43–68). New York: Psychology Press.

Heath, S. B. (1989). Oral and literate traditions among Black Americans living in poverty. *American Psychologist, 44,* 367–373.

Hebb, D. O. (1949). *The organization of behavior.* New York: Wiley.

Heckman, J. J. (2006). Skill formation and the economics of investing in disadvantaged children. *Science, 312,* 1900–1902.

Hedges, L. V., & Nowell, A. (1995). Sex differences in mental test scores, variability, and numbers of high scoring individuals. *Science, 269,* 41–45.

Hedrick, A. M., San Souci, P., Haden, C. A., & Ornstein, P. A. (2009). Mother-child joint conversational exchanges during events: Linkages to children's memory reports over time. *Journal of Cognition and Development, 10,* 143–161.

Heimann, M. (1989). Neonatal imitation gaze aversion and mother-infant interaction. *Infant Behavior and Development, 12,* 495–505.

Henrich, J., Heine, S. J., & Norenzayan, A. (2010). The weirdest people in the world. *Behavioral and Brain Sciences, 33,* 61–135.

Henry, L. A., & MacLean, M. (2003). Relationships between working memory, expressive vocabulary and arithmetic reasoning in children with and without intellectual disabilities. *Educational and Child Psychology, 20,* 51–63.

Herculano-Houze, S. (2012). The remarkable, yet not extraordinary, human brain as a scaled-up primate brain and its associated cost. *Proceedings of the National Academy of Sciences, 109,* 10661–10668.

Herman, J. F., Shiraki, J. H., & Miller, B. S. (1985). Young children's ability to infer spatial relationships: Evidence from a large, familiar environment. *Child Development, 36,* 1195–1203.

Herman, J. F., & Siegel, A. W. (1978). The development of cognitive mapping of the large-scale environment. *Journal of Experimental Child Psychology, 26,* 389–406.

Hernandez, D. J. (2011). *Double jeopardy: How third-grade reading skills and poverty influence high school graduation.* New York: Annie E. Casey Foundation.

Hernández Blasi, C. (1996). Vygotsky y la escuela sociohistorica. In R. A. Clemente & C. Hernández Blasi (Eds.), *Contextos de desarrollo psicoilogico y educacion* (pp. 51–67). Malaga, Spain: Aljibe.

Herrnstein, R. J., & Murray, C. (1994). *The bell curve: Intelligence and class structure in American life.* New York: Simon & Schuster.

Hespos, S. J., & Baillargeon, R. (2001). Reasoning about containment events in very young infants. *Cognition, 78,* 207–245.

Hickling, A. K., & Gelman, S. A. (1994). How does your garden grow? Early conceptualization of seeds and their place in the plant growth cycle. *Child Development, 66,* 856–876.

Hill, P., Duggan, P., & Lapsley, D. (2012). Subjective invulnerability, risk behavior, and adjustment in early adolescence. *Journal of Early Adolescence, 32*(4), 489–501.

Hill, P., & Lapsley, D. (2011). Adaptive and maladaptive narcissism in adolescent development. In C. T. Barry, P. K. Kerig, K. K. Stellwagen, & B. D. Tammy (Eds.), *Narcissism and Machiavellianism in youth: Implications for the development of adaptive and maladaptive behavior* (pp. 89–105). Washington, DC: American Psychological Association.

Hillman, C. H., Buck, S. M., Themanson, J. R., Pontifex, M. B., & Castelli, D. M. (2009). Aerobic fitness and cognitive development: Event-related brain potential and task performance indices of executive control in preadolescent children. *Developmental Psychology, 45,* 114–129.

Hirsh, P. L., & Sandberg, E. H. (2013). Development of map construction skills in childhood. *Journal of Cognition and Development, 14,* 397–423.

Hirsh-Pasek, K., Hyson, M. C., & Rescorla, L. (1990). Academic environments in preschool: Challenge or pressure? *Early Education and Development, 1,* 401–423.

Hobson, R. P., Chidambi, G., Lee, A., & Meyer, J. (2006). Foundations for self-awareness: An exploration through autism. *Monographs of the Society for Research in Child Development, 71*(2, Serial No. 284).

Hoehl, S., Zettersten, M., Schleihauf, H., Grätz, S., & Pauen, S. (2014). The role of social interaction and pedagogical cues for eliciting and reducing overimitation in preschoolers. *Journal of Experimental Child Psychology, 122,* 122–133.

Hoerr, T. R. (2004). How MI informs teaching at New City School. *Teachers College Record, 106,* 40–48.

Hoerr, T. R. (2014). Howard Gardner: Making a difference for students. In M. L. Kornhaber & E. Winner (Eds.), *Mind, work, and life: A Festschrift on the occasion of Howard Gardner's 70th birthday* (pp. 525–536). Cambridge, MA: Offices of Howard Gardner.

Hoff, E. (2000). Soziale umwelt und sprachlernen [The social environment and language learning]. In H. Grimm (Ed.), *Enzyklopadie der Psychologie: Vol. C3/3. Sprachentwicklung* [*Encyclopedia: Vol. 3. Language Development*] (pp. 463–494). Gottingen: Hogrefe.

Hoff, E. (2006). How social contexts support and shape language development. *Developmental Review, 26,* 55–88.

Hoff, E. (2013). Interpreting the early language trajectories of children from low-SES and language minority homes:

Implications for closing achievement gaps. *Developmental Psychology, 49*, 4–14.

Hoff, E. (2014). *Language development* (5th ed.). Belmont, CA: Wadsworth.

Hoff, E., & Naigles, L. (2002). How children use input to acquire a lexicon. *Child Development, 73*, 418–433.

Hoff-Ginsburg, E. (1985). Some contributions of mothers' speech to their children's syntactic growth. *Journal of Child Language, 12*, 367–385.

Hoffman, M. L. (1975). Altruistic behavior and the parent-child relationship. *Journal of Personality and Social Psychology, 31*, 937–943.

Hofstede, G. H., & Hofstede, G. (2001). *Culture's consequences: Comparing values, behaviors, institutions and organizations across nations.* Thousand Oaks, CA: Sage.

Hogrefe, G.-J., Wimmer, H., & Perner, J. (1986). Ignorance versus false belief: A developmental lag in attribution of epistemic states. *Child Development, 57*, 567–582.

Hollebrandse, B., van Hout, A., & Hendriks, P. (2011). First and second-order false-belief reasoning: Does language support reasoning about the beliefs of others? In *Proceedings of the workshop on reasoning about other minds: Logical and cognitive perspectives* (pp. 93–107). Barcelona, Spain: CEUR Workshop Proceedings.

Hollich, G., Hirsh-Pasek, K., & Golinkoff, R. M. (2000). Breaking the language barrier: An emergentist coalition model of word learning. *Monographs of the Society for Research in Child Development, 65*(3, Serial No. 262).

Holmboe, K., Pasco Fearon, R. M., Csibra, G., Tucker, L., & Johnson, M. H. (2008). "Freeze-frame": A new infant inhibition task and its relation to frontal cortex tasks in infancy and early childhood. *Journal of Experimental Child Psychology, 100*, 89–114.

Holyoak, K. J., Junn, E. N., & Billman, D. O. (1984). Development of analogical problem-solving skills. *Child Development, 55*, 2042–2055.

Honda, N., Ohgi, S., Wada, N., Loo, K. K., Higashimoto, Y., & Fukuda, K. (2013). Effect of therapeutic touch on brain activation of preterm infants in response to sensory punctate stimulus: A near-infrared spectroscopy-based study. *Archives of Disease in Childhood. Fetal and Neonatal Edition, 98*, F244–F248.

Honzik, M. P., MacFarlane, J. W., & Allen, L. (1948). Stability of mental test performance between 2 and 18 years. *Journal of Experimental Education, 17*, 309–324.

Hood, B. M. (2004). Is looking good enough or does it beggar belief? *Developmental Science, 7*, 415–417.

Hood, B. M., Carey, S., & Prasada, S. (2000). Predicting the outcomes of physical events: Two-year-olds fail to reveal knowledge of solidity and support. *Child Development, 71*, 1540–1554.

Hooper, L. M., Flynn, E. G., Wood, L. A. N., & Whiten, A. (2010). Observational learning of tool use in children: Investigating cultural spread through diffusion chains and learning mechanisms through ghost displays. *Journal of Experimental Child Psychology, 106*, 82–97.

Hopkins, E. J., Smith, E. D., & Lillard, A. S. (2013, April). *The development of substitute object pretense: The role of executive function and theory of mind.* Paper presented at the Biennial Meeting of the Society for Research in Child Development, Seattle.

Horner, V., & Whiten, A. (2005). Causal knowledge and imitation/emulation switching in chimpanzees (*Pan troglodytes*) and children (*Homo Sapiens*). *Animal Cognition, 8*, 164–181.

Horner, V., Whiten, A., Flynn, E., & de Waal, F. B. M. (2006). Faithful replication of foraging techniques along cultural transmission chains by chimpanzees and children. *Proceedings of the National Academy of Sciences, 103*, 13878–13883.

Howard, L. H., Henderson, A. M. E., Carrazza, C., & Woodward, A. L. (2015). Infants' and young children's imitation of linguistic in-group and out-group informants. *Child Development, 86*, 259–275.

Howe, M. L. (2000). *The fate of early memories: Developmental science and the retention of childhood experiences.* Washington, DC: American Psychological Press.

Howe, M. L. (2013). Memory development: Implications for adults recalling childhood experiences in the courtroom. *Nature Reviews Neuroscience, 14*(12), 869–876.

Howe, M. L. (2014). The co-emergence of the self and autobiographical memory: An adaptive view of early memory. In P. J. Bauer & R. Fivush (Eds.), *The Wiley handbook on the development of children's memory* (Vol. 2, pp. 545–567). Chichester, UK: Wiley-Blackwell.

Howe, M. L., & Courage, M. L. (1993). On resolving the enigma of infantile amnesia. *Psychological Bulletin, 113*, 305–326.

Howe, M. L., Courage, M. L., & Rooksby, M. (2009). The genesis and development of autobiographical memory. In M. L. Courage & N. Cowan (Eds.), *The development of memory in infancy and childhood* (pp. 178–196). New York: Psychology Press.

Howe, M. L., Wimmer, M. C., Gagnon, N., & Plumpton, S. (2009). An associative-activation theory of children's and adults' memory illusions. *Journal of Memory and Language, 60*, 229–251.

Hudson, J. A. (1990). The emergence of autobiographical memory in mother-child conversation. In R. Fivush & J. A. Hudson (Eds.), *Knowing and remembering in young children* (pp. 166–196). Cambridge, UK: Cambridge University Press.

Hudson, J. A., & Mayhew, E. M. (2009). The development of memory for recurring events. In M. L. Courage & N. Cowan (Eds.), *The development of memory in infancy and childhood* (pp. 69–91). New York: Psychology Press.

Hughes, C., Ensor, R., Wilson, A., & Graham, A. (2010). Tracking executive function across the transition to school: A latent variable approach. *Developmental Neuropsychology, 35*, 20–36.

Hulme, C., & Snowling, M. J. (2009). *Developmental disorders of language learning and cognition*. Chichester, UK: Wiley.

Hulme, C., & Snowling, M. J. (2013). Learning to read: What we know and what we need to understand better. *Child Development Perspectives, 7*, 1–5.

Hulme, C., Thomson, N., Muir, C., & Lawrence, A. (1984). Speech rate and the development of spoken words: The role of rehearsal and item identification processes. *Journal of Experimental Child Psychology, 38*, 241–253.

Humphrey, N. K. (1976). The social function of intellect. In P. P. G. Bateson & R. A. Hinde (Eds.), *Growing points in ethology* (pp. 303–317). Cambridge, UK: Cambridge University Press.

Hunt, E. (2012). What makes nations intelligent? *Perspectives on Psychological Science, 7*, 284–306.

Hunt, E., Davidson, J., & Lansman, M. (1981). Individual difference in long-term memory access. *Memory and Cognition, 9*, 599–608.

Huntsinger, C. S., Jose, P. E., & Larson, S. L. (1998). Do parent practices to encourage academic competence influence the social adjustment of young European American and Chinese American children? *Developmental Psychology, 34*, 747–756.

Huttenlocher, J., & Vasileya, M. (2003). How toddlers represent enclosed spaces. *Cognitive Sciences, 27*, 749–766.

Huttenlocher, J., Vasilyeva, M., Newcombe, N. S., & Duffy, S. (2008). Developing symbolic capacity one step at a time. *Cognition, 16*, 1–12.

Huttenlocher, J., Waterfall, H., Vasilyeva, M., Vevea, J., & Hedges, L. V. (2010). Sources of variability in children's language growth. *Cognitive Psychology, 61*(4), 343–365.

Huttenlocher, P. R. (1979). Synaptic density in human frontal cortex: Developmental changes and effects of aging. *Brain Research, 163*, 195–205.

Huttenlocher, P. R. (1994). Synapto-genesis, synapse elimination, and neural plasticity in human cerebral cortex. In C. A. Nelson (Ed.), Threats to optimal development. *The Minnesota symposium on child psychology* (Vol. 27, pp. 35–54). Hillsdale, NJ: Erlbaum.

Huttenlocher, P. R., & Dabholkar, A. S. (1997). Regional differences in synaptogenesis in human cerebral cortex. *Journal of Comparative Neurology, 387*, 167–178.

Hutton, J. S., Horowitz-Kraus, T., Mendelsohn, A. L., DeWitt, T., Holland, S. K., & the C-MIND Authorship Consortium. (2015). Home reading environment and brain activation in preschool children listening to stories. *Pediatrics, 136*, 466–478.

Hyde, J. S. (1981). How large are cognitive gender differences? A meta-analysis using w^2 and d. *American Psychologist, 36*, 892–901.

Hyde, J. S. (2005). Gender similarity hypothesis. *American Psychologist, 60*, 581–592.

Hyde, J. S., Fennema, E., & Lamon, S. J. (1990). Gender differences in mathematics performance: A meta-analysis. *Psychological Bulletin, 107*, 139–155.

Hyde, J. S., Lindberg, S. M., Linn, M. C., Ellis, A. B., & Williams, C. C. (2008). Gender similarities characterize math performance. *Science, 321*, 494–495.

Hyde, J. S., & Linn, M. C. (1988). Gender differences in verbal ability: A meta-analysis. *Psychological Bulletin, 194*, 53–69.

Hymes, D. (1972). On communicative competence. In J. B. Pride & J. Holmes (Eds.), *Sociolinguistics* (pp. 269–293). Harmondsworth, UK: Penguin.

Hymovitch, B. (1952). The effects of experimental variations on problem solving in the rat. *Journal of Comparative and Physiological Psychology, 45*, 313–321.

Hyson, M. C., Hirsh-Pasek, K., & Rescorla, L. (1990). Academic environments in preschool: Challenge or pressure? *Early Education and Development, 1*, 401–423.

Iida, Y., Miyazaki, M., & Uchida, S. (2010). Developmental changes in cognitive reaction time of children aged 6–12 years. *European Journal of Sport Science, 10*(3), 151–158.

Inagaki, K., & Hatano, G. (1991). Constrained person analogy in young children's biological inference. *Cognitive Development, 6*, 219–231.

Inagaki, K., & Hatano, G. (1993). Young children's understanding of the mind-body distinction. *Child Development, 64*, 1534–1549.

Inagaki, K., & Hatano, G. (2002). *Young children's naive thinking about the biological world*. New York: Psychology Press.

Inagaki, K., & Hatano, G. (2006). Young children's conception of the biological world. *Current Directions in Psychological Science, 15*, 177–181.

Inhelder, B., & Piaget, J. (1958). *The growth of logical thinking from childhood to adolescence*. New York: Basic Books.

Istomina, Z. M. (1975). The development of voluntary memory in preschool-age children. *Soviet Psychology, 13*, 5–64.

Iverson, J. M., & Goldin-Meadow, S. (2005). Gesture paves the way for language development. *Psychological Science, 16*, 368–371.

Jack, F., MacDonald, S., Reese, E., & Hayne, H. (2009). Maternal reminiscing style during early childhood predicts the age of adolescents' earliest memories. *Child Development, 80*, 496–505.

Jacobson, S. W. (1979). Matching behavior in the young infant. *Child Development, 50*, 425–430.

Jacoby, L. L. (1991). A process dissociation framework: Separating automatic from intentional uses of memory. *Journal of Memory and Language, 30*, 513–541.

Jenkins, J. M., & Astington, J. W. (1996). Cognitive factors and family structure associated with theory of mind development in young children. *Developmental Psychology, 32*, 70–78.

Jensen, A. R. (1993). Why is reaction time correlated with psychometric *g*? *Current Directions in Psychological Science, 2*, 53–56.

Jensen, A. R. (1998). *The g factor: The science of mental ability*. Westport, CT: Praeger.

Jensen, P. S., Mrazek, D., Knapp, P. K., Steinberg, L., Pfeffer, C., Schwalter, J., & Shapiro, T. (1997). Evolution and revolution in child psychiatry: ADHD as a disorder of adaptation. *Journal of the American Academy of Child & Adolescent Psychiatry, 36*, 1672–1681.

Joffe, T. H. (1997). Social pressures have selected for an extended juvenile period in primates. *Journal of Human Evolution, 32*, 593–605.

Johnson, E. K., & Jusczyk, P. W. (2003). Exploring statistical learning by 8-month-olds: The role of complexity and variation. In D. Houston, A. Seidl, G. Hollich, E. Johnson, & A. Jusczyk (Eds.), *Jusczyk Lab Final Report* Retrieved from http://hincapie.psych.purdue.edu/Jusczyk

Johnson, J. S., & Newport, E. L. (1989). Critical period effects in second language learning: The influence of maturational state on the acquisition of English as a second language. *Cognitive Psychology, 21*, 60–99.

Johnson, M. H. (1998). The neural basis of cognitive development. In W. Damon (Series Ed.) & D. Kuhn & R. S. Siegler (Vol. Eds.), *Handbook of child psychology: Vol 2. Cognition, perception, and language* (5th ed., pp. 631–678). New York: Wiley.

Johnson, M. H. (2000). Functional brain development in infants: Elements of an interactive specialization framework. *Child Development, 71*, 75–81.

Johnson, M. H. (2010). Understanding the social world: A developmental neuroscience approach. In M. H. Johnson (Ed.), *Child development at the intersection of emotion and cognition* (pp. 153–174). Washington, DC: American Psychological Association.

Johnson, M. H., & de Haan, M. (2011). *Developmental cognitive neuroscience: An introduction* (3rd ed.). Malden, MA: Wiley-Blackwell.

Johnson, M. H., Dziurawiec, S., Ellis, H. D., & Morton, J. (1991). Newborns' preferential tracking of faces and its subsequent decline. *Cognition, 40*, 1–19.

Johnson, M. H., Posner, M. I., & Rothbart, M. K. (1991). Components of visual orienting in early infancy: Contingency learning, anticipatory looking, and disengaging. *Journal of Cognitive Neuroscience, 3*, 335–344.

Johnson, S. P. (Ed.). (2010). *Neoconstructivism: The new science of cognitive development*. New York: Oxford University Press.

Johnson, S. P., & Aslin, R. N. (1995). Perception of object unity in 2-month-old infants. *Developmental Psychology, 31*, 739–745.

Johnson, S. P., & Aslin, R. N. (1996). Perception of object unity in young infants: The roles of motion, depth, and orientation. *Cognitive Development, 11*, 161–180.

Johnson, S. P., & Hannon, E. E. (2015). Perceptual development. In R. Lerner (Series Ed.) & L. Liben & U. Muller (Vol. Eds.), *Handbook of child psychology and developmental science: Vol. 2. Cognitive processes* (7th ed., pp. 63–112). Hoboken, NJ: Wiley.

Johnson, S. P., Hannon, E. E., & Amso, D. (2005). Perceptual development. In B. Hopkins (Ed.), *Cambridge encyclopedia of child development* (pp. 210–216). Cambridge, UK: Cambridge University Press.

Johnston, C., Campbell-Yeo, M., Fernandes, A., Inglis, D., Streiner, D., & Zee, R. (2014). Skin-to-skin care for procedural pain in neonates. *Cochrane Database of Systematic Reviews, 1*. Art. No.: CD008435.

Jones, S. S. (1996). Imitation or exploration? Young infants' matching of adults' oral gestures. *Child Development, 67*, 1952–1969.

Jones, S. S. (2006). Exploration or imitation? The effect of music on 4-week-old infants' tongue protrusions. *Infant Behavior and Development, 29*, 126–130.

Jones, S. S. (2007). Imitation in infancy: The development of mimicry. *Psychological Science, 18*, 593–599.

Jones, S. S. (2009). The development of imitation in infancy. *Philosophical Transactions of the Royal Society B, 346*, 2325–2335.

Jordan, N. C., Hansen, N., Fuch, L. S., Siegler, R. C., Gersten, R., & Micklos, D. (2013). Developmental predictors of fraction concepts and procedures. *Journal of Experimental Child Psychology, 116*, 45–58.

Jowkar-Baniani, G., & Schmuckler, M. (2011). Picture perception in infants: Generalization from two-dimensional to three-dimensional displays. *Infancy, 16*(2), 211–226.

Jowkar-Baniani, G., & Schmuckler, M. (2013). The role of perceptual similarity of the task environments in children's perseverative responding. *Journal of Experimental Child Psychology, 116*(3), 640–658.

Jusczyk, P. W. (1997). *The discovery of spoken language.* Cambridge, MA: MIT Press.

Justice, E. M., Baker-Ward, L., Gupta, S., & Jannings, L. R. (1997). Means to the goal of remembering: Developmental changes in awareness of strategy use–performance relations. *Journal of Experimental Child Psychology, 65,* 293–314.

Kagan, J. (1971). *Change and continuity in infancy.* New York: Wiley.

Kagan, J. (1976). New views on cognitive development. *Journal of Youth and Adolescence, 5,* 113–129.

Kail, R. V. (1991). Development of processing speed in childhood and adolescence. In H. W. Reese (Ed.), *Advances in child development and behavior* (Vol. 23, pp. 151–187). San Diego, CA: Academic Press.

Kail, R. V. (1997). Processing time, imagery, and spatial memory. *Journal of Experimental Child Psychology, 64,* 67–78.

Kail, R. V., & Ferrer, E. (2008). Processing speed in childhood and adolescence: Longitudinal models for examining developmental change. *Child Development, 78,* 1760–1770.

Kail, R. V., & Salthouse, T. A. (1994). Processing speed as a mental capacity. *Acta Psychologica, 86,* 199–225.

Kalichman, S. C. (1988). Individual differences in water-level task performance: A component-skill analysis. *Developmental Review, 8,* 273–295.

Kalish, C. W., & Lawson, C. A. (2008). Development of social category representation: Early appreciation of roles and deontic relations. *Child Development, 79,* 577–593.

Kamawar, D., LeFevre, J.-A., Bisanz, J., Fast, L., Skwarchuk, S.-L., Smith-Chant, B., & Penner-Wilger, M. (2010). Knowledge of counting principles: How relevant is order irrelevance? *Journal of Experimental Child Psychology, 105,* 138–145.

Kanazawa, S. (2004). General intelligence as a domain-specific adaptation. *Psychological Review, 111,* 512–523.

Kannass, K. N., Colombo, J., & Wyss, N. (2010). Now, pay attention! The effects of instruction on children's attention. *Journal of Cognition and Development, 11*(4), 509–532.

Kaplan, H., Hill, K., Lancaster, J., & Hurtado, A. M. (2000). A theory of human life history evolution: Diet, intelligence, and longevity. *Evolutionary Anthropology, 9,* 156–185.

Karama, S., Ad-Dab'bagh, Y., Haier, R. J., Deary, I. J., Lyttelton, O. C., Lepage, C., . . . the Brain Development Cooperative Group. (2009). Positive association between cognitive ability and cortical thickness in a representative U.S. sample of healthy 6- to 18-year-olds. *Intelligence, 37,* 145–155.

Karg, K., Schmelz, M., Call, J., & Tomasello, M. (2014). All great ape species (*Gorilla gorilla, Pan paniscus, Pan troglodytes, Pongo abelii*) and two-and-a-half-year-old children (*Homo sapiens*) discriminate appearance from reality. *Journal of Comparative Psychology, 128,* 431–439.

Karmiloff-Smith, A. (1992). *Beyond modularity: A developmental perspective on cognitive science.* Cambridge, MA: MIT Press.

Karoly, L. A., Greenwood, P. W., Everingham, S. S., Hoube, J., Kilburn, M. R., Rydell, C. P., . . . Chiesa, J. (1998). *Investing in our children: What we know and don't know about the costs and benefits of early childhood interventions.* Santa Monica, CA: RAND.

Karzon, R. G. (1985). Discrimination of polysyllabic sequences by one- to four-month-old infants. *Journal of Experimental Child Psychology, 39,* 326–342.

Kaye, K. (1982). *The mental and social life of babies: How parents create persons.* Chicago: University of Chicago Press.

Kaye, K., & Marcus, J. (1981). Infant imitation: The sensory-motor agenda. *Developmental Psychology, 17,* 258–265.

Kazi, S., Demetriou, A., Spanoudis, G., Xiang Kui Zhang, X. K., & Wang, Y. (2012). Mind–culture interactions: How writing molds mental fluidity in early development. *Intelligence, 40,* 622–637.

Kee, D. W. (1994). Developmental differences in associative memory: Strategy use, mental effort, and knowledge-access interactions. In H. W. Reese (Ed.), *Advances in child development and behavior* (Vol. 25, pp. 7–32). New York: Academic.

Keen, R. (2003). Representation of objects and events: Why do infants look so smart and toddlers look so dumb? *Current Directions in Psychological Science, 12,* 79–83.

Kelemen, D. (1999a). The scope of teleological thinking in preschool children. *Cognition, 70,* 241–272.

Kelemen, D. (1999b). Why are rocks pointy? Children's preferences for teleological explanations of the natural world. *Developmental Psychology, 35,* 1440–1453.

Kelemen, D. (2004). Are children "intuitive theists"? Reasoning about purpose and design in nature. *Psychological Science, 15,* 295–301.

Keller, H. (2012). Autonomy and relatedness revisited: Cultural manifestations of universal human needs. *Child Development Perspectives, 6,* 12–18.

Keller, H., Lohaus, A., Kuensemueller, P., Abels, M., Yovsi, R., Voelker, S., . . . Mohite, P. (2004). The bio-culture of parenting: Evidence from five cultural communities. *Parenting: Science and Practice, 4,* 25–50.

Kellman, P. J., & Banks, M. S. (1998). Infant visual perception. In W. Damon (Series Ed.) & D. Kuhn & R. S. Siegler (Vol. Eds.), *Handbook of child psychology: Vol 2. Cognition, perception, and language* (5th ed., pp. 103–146). New York: Wiley.

Kellman, P. J., & Spelke, E. S. (1983). Perception of partly occluded objects in infancy. *Cognitive Development, 15*, 483–524.

Kelly, D. J., Liu, S., Lee, K., Quinn, P. C., Pascalis, O., Slater, A. M., & Ge, L. (2009). Development of the other-race effect in infancy: Evidence toward universality? *Journal of Experimental Child Psychology, 104*, 105–114.

Kelly, D. J., Quinn, P. C., Slater, A. M., Lee, K., Ge, L., & Pascalis, O. (2007). The other-race effect develops during infancy. *Psychological Science, 18*, 1084–1089.

Kelly, R., Hammond, S., Dissanayake, C., & Ihsen, E. (2011). The relationship between symbolic play and executive function in young children. *Australian Journal of Early Childhood, 36*, 21–27.

Kenney-Benson, G. A., Pomerantz, E. M., Ryan, A. M., & Patrick, H. (2006). Sex differences in math performance: The role of children's approach to schoolwork. *Developmental Psychology, 42*, 11–26.

Kent, R. (2005). Speech development. In B. Hopkins (Ed.), *The Cambridge encyclopedia of child development* (pp. 257–264). New York: Cambridge University Press.

Kenward, B. (2012). Over-imitating preschoolers believe unnecessary actions are normative and enforce their performance by a third party. *Journal of Experimental Child Psychology, 112*, 195–207.

Kerns, K. A. (2000). The CyberCruiser: An investigation of development of prospective memory in children. *Journal of the International Neuropsychological Society, 6*, 62–70.

Kersten, A. W., & Earles, J. L. (2001). Less really is more for adults learning a miniature artificial language. *Journal of Memory and Language, 44*, 250–273.

Keupp, S., Behne, T., & Rakoczy, H. (2013). Why do children overimitate? Normativity is crucial. *Journal of Experimental Child Psychology, 116*, 392–406.

Keuup, S., Behne, T., Zachow, J., Kasbohm, A., & Rakoczy, H. (2015). Over-imitation is not automatic: Context sensitivity in children's overimitation and action interpretation of causally irrelevant actions. *Journal of Experimental Child Psychology, 130*, 163–175.

Kidd, C., Piantadosi, S. T., & Aslin, R. N. (2012). The Goldilocks effect: Human infants allocate attention to visual sequences that are neither too simple nor too complex. *PlOS One, 7*(5), e36399.

Kidd, C., Piantadosi, S. T., & Aslin, R. N. (2014). The Goldilocks effect in infant auditory attention. *Child Development, 85*(5), 1795–1804.

Kikuchi, Y., Senju, A., Tojo, Y., Osanai, H., & Hasegawa, T. (2009). Faces do not capture special attention in children with autism spectrum disorder: A change blindness study. *Child Development, 80*, 1421–1433.

Kim, K. H. S., Relkin, N. R., Lee, K.-M., & Hirsch, J. (1997). Distinct cortical areas associated with native and second languages. *Nature, 388*, 171–174.

Kipp, K., & Pope, S. (1997). The development of cognitive inhibition in stream-of-consciousness and directed speech. *Cognitive Development, 12*, 239–260.

Kirby, J. R., Georgiou, G. K., Martinussen, R., & Parrila, R. (2010). Naming speed and reading: From prediction to instruction. *Reading Research Quarterly, 45*, 341–362.

Kirschner, S., & Tomasello, M. (2009). Joint drumming: Social context facilitates synchronization in preschool children. *Journal of Experimental Child Psychology, 102*, 299–314.

Kitamura, C., Thanavishuth, C., Burnham, D., & Luksaneeyanawin, S. (2002). Universality and specificity in infant-directed speech: Pitch modifications as a function of infant age and sex in a tonal and nontonal language. *Infant Behavior and Development, 24*, 372–392.

Kitayama, S., Duffy, S., Kawamura, T., & Larsen, J. T. (2003). Perceiving an object and its context in different cultures: A cultural look at new look. *Psychological Science, 14*, 201–206.

Kittler, P. M., Krinsky-McHale, S. J., & Devenny, D. A. (2008). Dual-task processing as a measure of executive function: A comparison between adults with Williams and Down syndromes. *American Journal on Mental Retardation, 113*, 117–132.

Klaczynski, P. A. (2000). Motivated scientific reasoning biases, epistemological beliefs, and theory polarization: A two-process approach to adolescent cognition. *Child Development, 71*, 1347–1366.

Klaczynski, P. A. (2009). Cognitive and social cognitive development: Dual-process research and theory. In J. Evans & K. Frankish (Eds.), *In two minds: Dual processes and beyond* (pp. 265–292). Oxford, UK: Oxford University Press.

Klaczynski, P. A., & Narasimham, G. (1998). Development of scientific reasoning biases: Cognitive versus ego-protective explanations. *Developmental Psychology, 34*, 175–187.

Klaus, R. A., & Gray, S. (1968). The early training project for disadvantaged children: A report after five years. *Monographs of the Society for Research in Child Development, 33*(4, Serial No. 120).

Klibanoff, R. S., Levine, C., Huttenlocher, J., Vasilyeve, M., & Hedges, L. V. (2006). Preschool children's mathematical knowledge: The effect of teacher "math talk." *Developmental Psychology, 32*, 59–69.

Kliegel, M., & Jager, T. (2007). The effects of age and cue-action reminders on event-based prospective memory performance in preschoolers. *Cognitive Development, 22*, 33–46.

Kohlberg, L. (1966). A cognitive-developmental analysis of children's sex-role concepts and attitudes. In E. E. Maccoby (Ed.), *The development of sex differences* (pp. 82–173). Stanford, CA: Stanford University Press.

Kohlberg, L., Yaeger, J., & Hjertholm, E. (1968). Private speech: Four studies and a review of theories. *Child Development, 39*, 691–736.

Köhler, W. (1925). Intelligence of apes. *Journal of Genetic Psychology, 32*, 674–690.

Kolb, B. (1989). Brain development, plasticity and behavior. In M. Johnson (Ed.), *Brain development and cognition* (pp. 338–357). Oxford, UK: Blackwell.

Kolb, B., Mychasiuk, R., Muhammad, A., Li, Y., Frost, D. O., & Gibb, R. (2012). Experience and the developing prefrontal cortex. *Proceedings of the National Academy of Sciences, 109*(Supplement 2), 17186–17193.

Kolb, B., & Whishaw, I. Q. (1981). Neonatal frontal lesions in the rat: Sparing of learned but not species-typical behavior in the presence of reduced brain weight and critical thickness. *Journal of Comparative and Physiological Psychology, 95*, 235–276.

Kolb, B., & Whishaw, I. Q. (1990). *Fundamentals of human neuropsychology* (3rd ed.). San Francisco: W. H. Freeman.

Koluchova, J. (1976). A report on the further development of twins after severe and prolonged deprivation. In A. M. Clarke & A. D. B. Clarke (Eds.), *Early experience: Myth and evidence* (pp. 56–66). London: Open Books.

Konner, M. (2010). *The evolution of childhood: Relationships, emotions, mind.* Cambridge, MA: Belknap Press.

Kopp, C. B., & McCall, R. B. (1982). Predicting later mental performance for normal, at-risk, and handicapped infants. In P. Bakes & O. G. Brim (Eds.), *Life-span development and behavior* (Vol. 4, pp. 33–60). New York: Academic.

Kopp, C. B., Sigman, M., & Parmelee, A. H. (1974). Longitudinal study of sensorimotor development. *Developmental Psychology, 10*, 687–695.

Kornhuber, H. H., Bechfnger, D., Jung, H., & Sauer, E. (1985). A quantitative relationship between the extent of localized cerebral lesions and the intellectual and behavioral deficiency in children. *European Archives of Psychiatry and Neurological Science, 235*, 125–133.

Koshmider, J. W., & Ashcraft, M. H. (1991). The development of children's mental multiplication skills. *Journal of Experimental Child Psychology, 51*, 53–89.

Kotovsky, L., & Baillargeon, R. (1994). Calibration-based reasoning about collision events in 11-month-old infants. *Cognition, 51*, 107–129.

Kotovsky, L., & Baillargeon, R. (2000). Reasoning about collisions involving inert objects in 7.5-month-old infants. *Developmental Science, 3*, 344–359.

Kovács, A. M. (2009). Early bilingualism enhances mechanisms of false-belief reasoning. *Developmental Science, 12*, 48–54.

Kovács, A. M., & Mehler, J. (2009). Cognitive gains in 7-month-old bilingual infants. *Proceedings of the National Academy of Sciences, 106*, 6556–6560.

Krehm, M., Onishi, K. H., & Vouloumanos, A. (2014). I see your point: Infants under 12 months understand that pointing is communicative. *Journal of Cognition and Development, 15*(4), 527–538.

Kreutzer, M. A., Leonard, C., & Flavell, J. H. (1975). An interview study of children's knowledge about memory. *Monographs of the Society for Research in Child Development, 40*(1, Serial No. 159).

Krizman, J., Marian, V., Shook, A., Skoe, E., & Kraus, N. (2012). Subcortical encoding of sound is enhanced in bilinguals and relates to executive function advantages. *Proceedings of the National Academy of Sciences, 109*(20), 7877–7881.

Kroupina, M. G., Bauer, P. J., Gunnar, M. R., & Johnson, D. E. (2010). Institutional care as a risk for declarative memory development. In P. J. Bauer (Ed.), Varieties of early experience: Implications for the development of declarative memory in infancy. *Advances in Child Development and Behavior* (Vol. 38, pp. 138–160). London: Elsevier.

Krumhansl, C. L., & Jusczyk, P. W. (1990). Infants' perception of phrase structure in music. *Psychological Science, 1*, 70–73.

Kuhl, P. K. (2007, April). *Language and the infant brain: How children learn.* Plenary talk presented at meeting of the Cognitive Development Society, Santa Fe, NM.

Kuhl, P. K., Andruski, J. E., Christovich, I. A., Christovich, L. A., Kozhevnikova, E. V., Ryskfna, V. L., . . . Lacerda, F. (1997). Cross-language analysis of phonetic units in language addressed to infants. *Science, 277*, 684–686.

Kuhl, P. K., & Meltzoff, A. N. (1982). The bimodal perception of speech in infancy. *Science, 218*, 1138–1141.

Kuhl, P. K., Stevens, E., Hayashi, A., Deguchi, T., Kiritani, S., & Iverson, P. (2006). Infants show a facilitation effect for native language phonetic perception between 6 and 12 months. *Developmental Science, 9*, F13–F21.

Kuhl, P. K., Williams, K. A., Lacerda, F., Stevens, K. N., & Lindblom, B. (1992). Linguistic experience alters phonetic perception in infants by 6 months of age. *Science, 255*, 606–608.

Kuhn, D. (1989). Children and adults as intuitive scientists. *Psychological Review, 96*, 674–689.

Kuhn, D., Amsel, E., & O'Loughlin, M. (1988). *The development of scientific thinking skills*. San Diego, CA: Academic.

Kuhn, D., Pease, M., & Wirkala, C. (2009). Coordinating the effects of multiple variables: A skill fundamental to scientific thinking. *Journal of Experimental Child Psychology, 103*, 268–284.

Kurtz, B. E. (1990). Cultural differences in children's cognitive and meta-cognitive development. In W. Schneider & F. E. Weinert (Eds.), *Interactions among aptitudes, strategies, and knowledge in cognitive performance* (pp. 177–199). New York: Springer-Verlag.

Kurtz, B. E., Schneider, W., Carr, M., Borkowski, J. G., & Rellinger, E. (1990). Strategy instruction and attributional beliefs in West Germany and the United States: Do teachers foster metacognitive development? *Contemporary Educational Psychology, 15*, 268–283.

Kurtz, B. E., & Weinert, F. E. (1989). Metamemory, memory performance, and causal attributions in gifted and average children. *Journal of Experimental Child Psychology, 48*, 45–61.

Laboratory of Comparative Human Cognition. (1983). Culture and cognitive development. In P. H. Mussen (Series Ed.) & W. Kessen (Vol. Ed.), *Handbook of child psychology: Vol. 1. History, theory, and methods* (4th ed., pp. 295–356). New York: Wiley.

LaFreniere, P., & MacDonald, K. (2013). A post-genomic view of behavioral development and adaptation to the environment. *Developmental Review, 33*, 89–109.

Lamb, M. E., Sternberg, K. J., & Esplin, P. W. (1998). Conducting investigative interviews of alleged sexual abuse victims. *Child Abuse & Neglect, 22*, 813–823.

Lancy, D. F. (2015). *The anthropology of childhood* (2nd ed.). Cambridge, UK: Cambridge University Press.

Lancy, D. F. (2016). Teaching: Natural or cultural? In D. C. Geary & D. B. Berch (Eds.), *Evolutionary perspectives on education and child development* (pp. 33–66). New York: Springer.

Lancy, D. F., & Grove, M. A. (2010). The role of adults in children's learning. In D. F. Lancy, J. Bock, & S. Gaskins (Eds.), *The anthropology of learning childhood* (pp. 145–179). New York: AltaMira Press.

Landry, S. H., Smith, K. E., Miller-Loncar, C. L., & Swank, P. R. (1997). Predicting cognitive-language and social growth curves from early maternal behaviors in children at varying degrees of biological risk. *Developmental Psychology, 33*, 1040–1053.

Lane, D. M., & Pearson, D. A. (1982). The development of selective attention. *Merrill-Palmer Quarterly, 28*, 317–337.

Lange, G., & Jackson, P. (1974). Personal organization in children's free recall. *Child Development, 45*, 1060–1067.

Lange, G., & Pierce, S. H. (1992). Memory-strategy learning and maintenance in preschool children. *Developmental Psychology, 28*, 453–462.

Langlois, J. H., Ritter, J. M., Roggman, L. A., & Vaughn, L. S. (1991). Facial diversity and infant preferences for attractive faces. *Developmental Psychology, 27*, 79–84.

Langlois, J. H., Roggman, L. A., Casey, R. J., Ritter, J. M., Rieser-Danner, L. A., & Jenkins, V. Y. (1987). Infant preferences for attractive faces: Rudiments of a stereotype? *Developmental Psychology, 23*, 363–369.

Larkpna, M., Güler, O. E., Kleinknecht, E. E., & Bauer, P. J. (2008). Maternal provision of structure in a deliberate memory task in relation to their preschool children's recall. *Journal of Experimental Child Psychology, 100*, 235–251.

Lave, J., & Wenger, E. (1991). *Situated learning: Legitimate peripheral participation*. Cambridge, UK: Cambridge University Press.

Lazar, I., Darlington, R., Murray, H., Royce, J., & Snipper, A. (1982). Lasting effects of early education: A report from the Consortium for Longitudinal Studies. *Monographs of the Society for Research in Child Development, 47*(2–3, Serial No. 195).

Leaper, C. (2013). Gender development during childhood. In P. D. Zelazo (Ed.), *The Oxford handbook of developmental psychology: Vol. 2. Self and other* (pp. 326–377). Oxford, UK: Oxford University Press.

Leaper, C., Anderson, K. J., & Sanders, P. (1998). Moderators of gender effects on parents' talk to their children: A meta-analysis. *Developmental Psychology, 34*, 3–27.

Lee, K., Bull, R., & Ho, R. M. H. (2013). Developmental changes in executive functioning. *Child Development, 84*, 1933–1953.

Lee, K., Quinn, P. C., Pascalis, O., & Slater, A. (2013). Development of face-processing ability in childhood. In P. D. Zelazo (Ed.), *The Oxford handbook of developmental psychology: Vol. 1. Body and mind* (pp. 338–370). Oxford, UK: Oxford University Press.

Lee, P. C. (2013). The human child's nature orientation. *Child Development Perspectives, 6*, 193–198.

LeFevre, J.-A., Skwarchuk, S.-L., Smith-Chant, B. L., Fast, L., Kamawar, D., & Bisanz, J. (2009). Home numeracy experiences and children's math performance in the early school years. *Canadian Journal of Behavioural Science, 41*, 55–66.

Legerstee, M. (1991). The role of person and object in eliciting early imitation. *Journal of Experimental Child Psychology, 51*, 423–433.

Legerstee, M., Anderson, D., & Schaffer, A. (1998). Five- and eight-month-old infants recognize their faces and voices as familiar social stimuli. *Child Development, 69*, 37–50.

Le Grand, R., Mondloch, C. J., Maurer, D., & Brent, H. P. (2001). Early visual experience and face processing. *Nature, 410*, 890.

Lehmann, M., & Hasselhorn, M. (2007). Variable memory strategy use in children's adaptive intratask learning behavior: Developmental changes and working memory influences in free recall. *Child Development, 78*, 1068–1082.

Lehmann, M., & Hasselhorn, M. (2012). Rehearsal dynamics in elementary school children. *Journal of Experimental Child Psychology, 111*(3), 552–560.

Leichtman, M. D., & Ceci, S. J. (1993). The problem of infantile amnesia: Lessons from fuzzy-trace theory. In M. L. Howe & R. Pasnak (Eds.), *Emerging themes in cognitive development: Foundations* (Vol. 1, pp. 195–213). New York: Springer-Verlag.

Leichtman, M. D., & Ceci, S. J. (1995). The effect of stereotypes and suggestion on preschoolers' reports. *Developmental Psychology, 31*, 568–578.

Lemaire, P., & Callies, S. (2009). Children's strategies in complex arithmetic. *Journal of Experimental Child Psychology, 103*, 49–65.

Lenhart, A., Kahne, J., Middaugh, E., Macgill, A. R., Evans, C., & Vitak, J. (2008, September 18). *Teens, video games and civics: Teens' gaming experiences are diverse and include significant social interaction and civic engagement.* Pew Internet and American Life Project. Retrieved from http://www.pewinternet.org/PPF/r/263/report_display .asp.

Lenneberg, E. H. (1967). *Biological foundations of language.* New York: Wiley.

Lenroot, R. K., & Giedd, J. N. (2007). The structural development of the human brain as measured longitudinally with magnetic resonance imaging. In D. Coch, K. W. Fischer, & G. Dawson (Eds.), *Human behavior, learning, and the developing brain: Typical development* (pp. 50–73). New York: Guilford Press.

Leon, D. A., Lawlor, D. A., Clark, H., Batty, G. D., & Macintyre, S. (2009). The association of childhood intelligence with mortality risk from adolescence to middle age: Findings from the Aberdeen children of the 1950s cohort study. *Intelligence, 37*, 520–528.

Lepage, J. F., & Theoret, H. (2006). EEG evidence for the presence of an action observation-execution matching system in children. *European Journal of Neuroscience, 23*, 2505–2510.

Lepage, J. F., & Theoret, H. (2007). The mirror neuron system: Grasping others' actions from birth? *Developmental Science, 10*, 513–529.

Lerner, R. M. (1991). Changing organism-context relations as the basic process of development: A developmental contextual perspective. *Developmental Psychology, 27*, 27–32.

Lerner, R. M. (2006). Developmental science, developmental systems, and contemporary theories of human development. In W. Damon & R. M. Lerner (Series Eds.) & R. M. Lerner (Vol. Ed.), *Handbook of child psychology: Vol. 1. Theoretical models of human development* (6th ed., pp. 1–17). New York: Wiley.

Lervåg, A., Bråten, I., & Hulme, C. (2009). The cognitive and linguistic foundations of early reading development: A Norwegian latent variable longitudinal study. *Developmental Psychology, 45*, 764.

Leslie, A. M. (1994). ToMM, ToBy, and agency: Core architecture and domain specificity. In L. Hirschfeld & S. Gelman (Eds.), *Mapping the mind: Domain specificity in cognition and culture* (pp. 119–148). Cambridge, UK: Cambridge University Press.

Leslie, A. M., & Keeble, S. (1987). Do six-month-old infants perceive causality? *Cognition, 25*, 265–288.

Levine, S. C., Huttenlocher, J., Taylor, A., & Langrock, A. (1999). Early sex differences in spatial skills. *Developmental Psychology, 35*, 940–949.

Levitt, P. (2003). Structural and functional maturation of the developing primate brain. *Journal of Pediatrics, 143*, S35–S45.

Lewis, C., Freeman, N. H., Kyriakidou, C., Maridaki-Kassotaki, K., & Berridge, D. M. (1996). Social influence on fasle belief access: Specific sibling influences or general apprenticeship? *Child Devleopment, 67*, 2930–2947.

Lewis, C., Koyasu, M., Oh, S., Ogawa, A., Short, B., & Huang, Z. (2009, Spring). Culture, executive function, and social understanding. *New Directions in Child and Adolescent Development, 123*, 69–85.

Lewis, K. D. (1999). Maternal style in reminiscing: Relations to child individual differences. *Cognitive Development, 14*, 381–399.

Lewis, M. (1969). Infants' responses to facial stimuli during the first year of life. *Developmental Psychology, 1*, 75–86.

Lewis, M. (1991). Ways of knowing: Objective self-awareness of consciousness? *Developmental Review, 11*, 231–243.

Lewis, M. (1993). The emergence of human emotions. In M. Lewis & J. M. Haviland (Eds.), *Handbook of emotions* (pp. 223–235). New York: Guilford Press.

Lewis, M., & Brooks-Gunn, J. (1979). *Social cognition and the acquisition of self.* New York: Plenum.

Lewis, M., & Carmody, D. P. (2008). Self-representation and brain development. *Developmental Psychology, 44,* 1329–1334.

Lewis, M., & Freedle, R. O. (1973). Mother-infant dyad: The cradle of meaning. In P. Pilner, L. Krames, & T. Alloway (Eds.), *Communication and affect: Language and thought* (pp. 127–155). New York: Academic.

Lewis, M., & Ramsay, D. (2004). Development of self-recognition, personal pronoun use, and pretend play during the 2nd year. *Child Development, 75,* 1821–1831.

Lewis, M., Sullivan, M. W., Stanger, C., & Weiss, M. (1989). Self development and self-conscious emotions. *Child Development, 60,* 146–156.

Lewkowicz, D. J. (2004). Perception of serial order in infants. *Developmental Science, 7,* 175–184.

Lewkowicz, D. J., & Ghazanfar, A. A. (2006). The decline of cross-species intersensory perception in human infants. *Proceedings of the National Academy of Sciences, 103,* 6771–6774.

Lewkowicz, D. J., & Ghazanfar, A. A. (2009). The emergence of multisensory systems through perceptual narrowing. *Trends in Cognitive Sciences, 13,* 470–478.

Lewkowicz, D. J., Leo, I., & Simion, F. (2010). Intersensory perception at birth: Newborns match nonhuman primate faces and voices. *Infancy, 15,* 46–60.

Lewkowicz, D. J., & Lickliter, R. (Eds.). (2013). *The development of intersensory perception: Comparative perspectives.* New York: Psychology Press.

Lewkowicz, D. J., & Turkewitz, G. (1980). Cross-modal equivalence in early infancy: Auditory-visual intensity matching. *Developmental Psychology, 16,* 597–607.

Li, W., Frakas, G., Duncan, G. J., Burchinal, M. R., & Vandell, D. L. (2013). Timing of high-quality child care and cognitive, language, and preacademic development. *Developmental Psychology, 49,* 1440–1451.

Liben, L. S. (2009). The road to understanding maps. *Current Directions in Psychological Science, 18,* 310–315.

Liben, L. S., & Signorella, M. L. (1993). Gender-schematic processing in children: The role of initial interpretations of stimuli. *Developmental Psychology, 29,* 141–149.

Liben, L. S., & Yekel, C. A. (1996). Preschoolers understanding of plan and oblique maps: The role of geometric and representational correspondence. *Child Development, 67,* 2780–2796.

Liberman, I. Y., Shankweiler, D., Fischer, R. N., & Carter, B. (1974). Explicit syllable and phoneme segmentation in the young child. *Journal of Experimental Child Psychology, 18,* 201–212.

Libertus, M., Feigenson, L., & Halberda, J. (2011). Preschool acuity of the approximate number system correlates with school math ability. *Developmental Science, 14,* 1292–1300.

Lickliter, R. (1990). Premature visual stimulation accelerates intersensory functioning in bobwhite quail neonates. *Developmental Psychobiology, 23,* 15–27.

Lickliter, R. (2000). The role of sensory stimulation in perinatal development: Insights from comparative research for care of the high-risk infant. *Developmental and Behavioral Pediatrics, 21,* 437–447.

Lickliter, R. (2013). Biological development: Theoretical approaches, techniques, and key findings. In P. D. Zelazo (Ed.), *The Oxford handbook of developmental psychology: Vol. 1. Body and mind* (pp. 65–90). Oxford, UK: Oxford University Press.

Lickliter, R., & Honeycutt, H. (2015). Biology, development, and human systems. In R. Lerner (Series Ed.) & W. F. Overton & P. C. M. Molenaar (Vol. Eds.), *Handbook of child psychology and developmental science: Vol. 1. Theory and method* (7th ed., pp. 162–207). Wiley: New York.

Lidstone, J. S., Meins, E., & Fernyhough, C. (2010). The roles of private speech and inner speech in planning during middle childhood: Evidence from a dual task paradigm. *Journal of Experimental Child Psychology, 107*(4), 438–451.

Lidstone, J. S., Meins, E., & Fernyhough, C. (2011). Individual differences in children's private speech: Consistency across tasks, timepoints, and contexts. *Cognitive Development, 26*(3), 203–213.

Lieberman, P. (1967). *Intonations, perception, and language.* Cambridge, MA: MIT Press.

Lietz, P. (2006). A meta-analysis of gender differences in reading achievement at the secondary school level. *Studies in Educational Evaluation, 32,* 317–344.

Lillard, A. S. (2011). Mother-child fantasy play. In A. Pellegrini (Ed.), *The Oxford handbook of the development of play* (pp. 284–295). New York: Oxford University Press.

Lillard, A. S. (2015). The development of play. In R. Lerner (Series Ed.) & L. Liben & U. Muller (Vol. Eds.), *Handbook of child psychology and developmental science: Vol. 2. Cognitive processes* (7th ed., pp. 425–468). New York: Wiley.

Lillard, A. S., Drell, M. B., Richey, E., Boguszewski, K., & Smith, E. D. (2015). Further examination of the immediate impact of television on children's executive function. *Developmental Psychology, 51,* 92–805.

Lillard, A. S., & Erisir, A. (2011). Old dogs learning new tricks: Neuroplasticity beyond the juvenile period. *Developmental Review, 31*, 207–239.

Lillard, A. S., & Kavanaugh, R. D. (2014). The contribution of symbolic skills to the development of an explicit theory of mind. *Child Development, 85*, 1535–1551.

Lillard, A. S., Lerner, M. D., Hopkins, E. J., Dore, R. A., Smith, E. D., & Palmquist, C. M. (2013). The impact of pretend play on children's development: A review of the evidence. *Psychological Bulletin, 139*, 1–34.

Lillard, A. S., Li, H., & Boguszewski, K. (2015). Television and children's executive function. In J. B. Benson (Ed.), *Advances in child development and behavior, 48*, 219–247.

Lillard, A. S., & Peterson, J. (2011). The immediate impact of different types of television on young children's executive function. *Pediatrics, 128*, 644–649.

Lin, C.-Y. C., & Fu, V. R. (1990). A comparison of child-rearing practices among Chinese, immigrant Chinese, and Caucasian-American parents. *Child Development, 61*, 429–433.

Lindberg, M. A. (1980). The role of knowledge structures in the ontogeny of learning. *Journal of Experimental Child Psychology, 30*, 401–410.

Lindberg, M. A. (1991). An interactive approach to assessing the suggestibility and testimony of eyewitnesses. In J. Doris (Ed.), *The suggestibility of children's recollections: Implications for eyewitness testimony* (pp. 47–55). Washington, DC: American Psychological Association.

Lindberg, M. A., Keiffer, J., & Thomas, S. W. (2000). Eyewitness testimony for physical abuse as a function of personal experience, development, and focus of study. *Journal of Applied Developmental Psychology, 21*, 555–591.

Linebarger, D. L., & Vaala, S. E. (2010). Screen media and language development in infants and toddlers: An ecological perspective. *Developmental Review, 30*, 176–202.

Linn, M. C., & Petersen, A. C. (1985). Emergence and characterization of sex differences in spatial ability: A meta-analysis. *Child Development, 56*, 1479–1498.

Lipko, A. R., Dunlosky, J., & Merriman, W. E. (2009). Persistent overconfidence despite practice: The roles of task experience in preschoolers' recall predications. *Journal of Experimental Child Psychology, 103*, 152–166.

Lipton, J. S., & Spelke, E. (2000). Origins of number sense: Large-number discrimination in human infants. *Psychological Science, 15*, 396–401.

Liston, C., & Kagan, J. (2002). Brain development: Memory enhancement in early childhood. *Nature, 419*, 896.

Liston, C., Watts, R., Tottenham, N., Davidson, M. C., Niogi, S., Ulug, A. M., . . . Casey, B. J. (2006). Frontostriatal microstructure modulates efficient recruitment of cognitive control. *Cerebral Cortex, 16*, 553–560.

Liszkowski, U., Carpenter, M., & Tomasello, M. (2007). Pointing out new news, old news, and absent referents at 12 months of age. *Developmental Science, 10*, F1–F7.

Liszkowski, U., Schafer, M., Carpenter, M., & Tomasello, M. (2009). Pre-linguistic infants, not chimpanzees, communicate about absent entities. *Psychological Science, 20*, 654–660.

Liu, D., Sabbagh, M. A., Gehring, W. J., & Wellman, H. M. (2009). Neural correlates of children's theory of mind development. *Child Development, 80*, 318–326.

Liu, S., Xia, W. S., Xia, N. G., Quinn, P. C., Zhjang, Y., Chen, H., . . . Lee, K. (2015). Development of visual preference for own- versus other-race faces in infancy. *Developmental Psychology, 51*, 500–511.

Lloyd, M. E., & Miller, J. K. (2014). Implicit memory. In P. J. Bauer & R. Fivush (Eds.), *The Wiley handbook on the development of children's memory* (Vol. 1, pp. 336–366). Chichester, UK: Wiley-Blackwell.

LoBue, V., & DeLoache, J. S. (2008). Detecting the snake in the grass: Attention to fear-relevant stimuli by adults and young children. *Psychological Science, 19*, 284–289.

LoBue, V., & DeLoache, J. S. (2010). Superior detection of threat-relevant stimuli in infancy. *Developmental Science, 13*, 221–228.

Locke, J. L. (1993). *The child's path to spoken language.* Cambridge, MA: Harvard University Press.

Locke, J. L. (1994). Phases in the child's development of language. *American Scientist, 82*, 436–445.

Locke, J. L. (2009). Evolutionary developmental linguistics: Naturalization of the faculty of language. *Language Sciences, 31*, 33–59.

Locke, J. L., & Bogin, B. (2006). Language and life history: A new perspective on the development and evolution of human language. *Behavioral and Brain Sciences, 29*, 259–280.

Lockman, J. J. (2000). A perception-action perspective on tool use development. *Child Development, 71*, 137–144.

Loftus, E. F., & Pickrell, J. E. (1995). The formation of false memories. *Psychiatric Annals, 25*, 720–725.

Longstreth, L. E. (1981). Revisiting Skeels' final study: A critique. *Developmental Psychology, 17*, 620–625.

Lonigan, C. J., Burgess, S. R., & Anthony, J. L. (2000). Development of emergent literacy and early reading skills in preschool children: Evidence from a latent-variable longitudinal study. *Developmental Psychology, 36*, 596–613.

Lonigan, C. J., Purpura, D. J., Wilson, S. B., Walker, P. M., & Clancy-Menchetti, J. (2013). Evaluating the components of an emergent literacy intervention for preschool children at risk for reading difficulties. *Journal of Experimental Child Psychology, 114,* 1111–1130.

Looft, W. R., & Bartz, W. H. (1969). Animism revived. *Psychological Bulletin, 71,* 1–19.

Lopez, D. F., Little, T. D., Oetitngen, G., & Baltes, P. B. (1998). Self-regulation and school performance: Is there optimal level of action-control? *Journal of Experimental Child Psychology, 70,* 54–74.

Lourenco, S. F., & Frick, A. (2014). Remembering where: The origins and early development of spatial memory. In P. J. Bauer & R. Fivush (Eds.), *The Wiley handbook on the development of children's memory* (Vol. 1, pp. 367–393). Chichester, UK: Wiley-Blackwell.

Ludwig, J., & Miller, D. L. (2007). Does Head Start improve children's life chances? Evidence from a regression discontinuity design. *Quarterly Journal of Economics, 122,* 159–208.

Ludwig, J., & Phillips, D. A. (2008). Long-term effects of Head Start on low-income children. *Annals of the New York Academy of Science, 113,* 257–286.

Luecke-Aleska, D., Anderson, D. R., Collins, P. A., & Schmitt, K. L. (1995). Gender constancy and television viewing. *Developmental Psychology, 31,* 773–780.

Lukowski, A. F., & Bauer, P. J. (2014). Long-term memory in infancy and early childhood. In P. J. Bauer & R. Fivush (Eds.), *The Wiley handbook on the development of children's memory* (Vol. 1, pp. 230–254). Chichester, UK: Wiley-Blackwell.

Luna, B., Thulborn, K. R., Monoz, D. P., Merriam, E. P., Garver, K. E., Minshew, N. J., . . . Sweeney, J. A. (2001). Maturation of widely distributed brain function subserves cognitive development. *NeuroImage, 13,* 786–793.

Lundy, B. L. (2013). Paternal and maternal mind-mindedness and preschoolers' theory of mind: The mediating role of interactional attunement. *Social Development, 22,* 58–74.

Luria, A. R. (1973). *The working brain.* New York: Basic Books.

Luria, A. R. (1976). *Cognitive development: Its cultural and social foundations.* Cambridge, MA: Harvard University Press.

Lutchmaya, S., Baron-Cohen, S., & Raggatt, P. (2002). Foetal testosterone and vocabulary size in 18- and 24-month-old infants. *Infant Behavior and Development, 24,* 418–424.

Lyn, H., & Savage-Rumbaugh, S. (2013). The use of emotional symbols in language-using apes. In S. Watanabe & S. Kuczaj (Eds.), *The science of the mind* (pp. 113–127). Tokyo: Springer Japan.

Lynch, M. P., Eilers, R. E., Oller, K., & Urbano, R. C. (1990). Innateness, experience, and music perception. *Psychological Science, 1,* 272–276.

Lyons, D. E., Young, A. G., & Keil, F. C. (2007). The hidden structure of overimitation. *Proceedings of the National Academy of Sciences, 104,* 19751–19756.

Lyytinen, H., Ahonen, T., Eklund, K., Guttorm, T. K., Laakso, M. L., Leinonen, S., . . . Viholainen, H. (2001). Developmental pathways of children with and without familial risk for dyslexia during the first years of life. *Developmental Neuropsychology, 20,* 535–554.

Macchi Cassia, V., Turati, C., & Simion, F. (2004). Can a nonspecific bias toward top-heavy patterns explain newborns' face preference? *Psychological Science, 15*(6), 379–383.

Maccoby, E. E., & Jacklin, C. N. (1974). *The psychology of sex differences.* Stanford, CA: Stanford University Press.

Macfarlane, A. (1975). Olfaction in the development of social preferences in the humane neonate. *CIBA Foundation Symposium 33: Parent-infant interaction.* Amsterdam, Netherlands: Elsevier.

Machluf, K., & Bjorklund, D. F. (2015). Social cognitive development from an evolutionary perspective. In V. Zeigler-Hill, L. Welling, & T. Shackelford (Eds.), *Evolutionary perspectives on social psychology* (pp. 27–38). New York: Springer.

MacLean, P. D. (1990). *The triune brain in evolution: Role in paleocerebral functions.* New York: Plenum.

MacWhinney, B. (2015). Language development. In R. Lerner (Series Ed.) & L. Liben & U. Muller (Vol. Eds.), *Handbook of child psychology and developmental science: Vol. 2. Cognitive processes* (7th ed., pp. 296–338). New York: Wiley.

Magno, C. (2010). The role of metacognitive skills in developing critical thinking. *Metacognition and Learning, 5*(2), 137–156.

Mahy, C. E., & Moses, L. J. (2011). Executive functioning and prospective memory in young children. *Cognitive Development, 26*(3), 269–281.

Mahy, C. E., Moses, L. J., & Kliegel, M. (2014). The development of prospective memory in children: An executive framework. *Developmental Review, 34,* 305–326.

Makin, J. W., & Porter, R. H. (1989). Attractiveness of lactating females' breast odors to neonates. *Child Development, 60,* 803–810.

Malloy, P. (1987). Frontal lobe dysfunction in obsessive-compulsive disorder. In E. Perecman (Ed.), *The frontal lobes revisited* (pp. 211–218). New York: IRBN.

Mandel, D. R., Jusczyk, P. W., & Pisoni, D. B. (1995). Infants' recognition of sound patterns of their own names. *Psychological Science, 5,* 314–317.

Mandel, D. R., Kemler Nelson, D. G., & Jusczyk, P. W. (1996). Infants remember the order of words in a spoken sentence. *Cognitive Development, 11*, 181–196.

Mandelman, D. D., & Girgorenko, E. L. (2011). Intelligence: Genes, environments, and their interactions. In R. J. Sternberg & S. B. Kaufman (Eds.), *The Cambridge handbook of intelligence* (pp. 85–106). Cambridge, UK: Cambridge University Press.

Mandler, J. M. (2000). Perceptual and conceptual processes in infancy. *Journal of Cognition and Development, 1*, 3–36.

Marcon, R. A. (1999). Differential impact of preschool models on development and early learning of inner-city children: A three cohort study. *Developmental Psychology, 35*, 358–375.

Marcovtich, S., Zelazo, P. D., & Schmuckler, M. A. (2002). The effect of the number of A trials on performance on the A-not-B task. *Infancy, 3*, 519–529.

Marcus, G. F. (1995). Children's over-regularization of English plurals: A quantitative analysis. *Journal of Child Language, 22*, 447–460.

Marcus, G. F., Pinker, S., Ullman, M., Hollander, M., Rosen, T. J., & Xu, F. (1992). Overregularization in language acquisition. *Monographs of the Society for Research in Child Development, 57*(4, Serial No. 228).

Marean, G. C., Werner, L. A., & Kuhl, P. K. (1992). Vowel categorization by very young infants. *Developmental Psychology, 28*, 396–405.

Mares, M., & Sivakumar, G. (2014). "Vámonos means go, but that's made up for the show": Reality confusions and learning from educational TV. *Developmental Psychology, 50*(11), 2498–2511.

Margolis, R. L., Chuang, D.-M., & Post, R. M. (1994). Programmed cell death: Implications for neuropsychiatric disorders. *Biological Psychiatry, 35*, 946–956.

Markant, J. C., & Thomas, K. M. (2013). Postnatal brain development. In P. D. Zelazo (Ed.), *The Oxford handbook of developmental psychology: Vol. 1. Body and mind* (pp. 129–163). Oxford, UK: Oxford University Press.

Markman, E. M. (2014). Constraints on word learning: Speculations about their nature, origins, and domain specificity. In M. R. Gunnar & M. Maratsos (Eds.), *Modularity and constraints in language and cognition* (pp. 59–102). New York: Psychology Press.

Markman, E. M., & Wachtel, G. A. (1988). Children's use of mutual exclusivity to constrain the meaning of words. *Cognitive Psychology, 20*, 121–157.

Marlier, L., Schaal, B., & Soussignan, R. (1998). Neonatal responsiveness to the odor of amniotic and lacteal fluids: A test of perinatal chemosensory continuity. *Child Development, 69*, 611–623.

Marsh, H. W. (1989). Sex differences in the development of verbal and mathematics constructs: The High School and Beyond Study. *American Educational Research Journal, 26*, 191–225.

Marshall, P. J. (2015). Neuroscience, embodiment, and development. In R. Lerner (Series Ed.) & W. F. Overton & P. C. M. Molenaar (Vol. Eds.), *Handbook of child psychology and developmental science: Vol. 1. Theory and method* (7th ed., pp. 244–283). Wiley: New York.

Marshall, P. J., & Meltzoff, A. N. (2014). Neural mirroring mechanisms and imitation in human infants. *Philosophical Transactions of the Royal Society B, 369*, 659–669.

Martarelli, C. S., & Mast, F. W. (2013). Is it real or is it fiction? Children's bias toward reality. *Journal of Cognition and Development, 14*, 141–153.

Martin, C. L., & Halverson, C. F. (1981). A schematic processing model of sex-typing and stereotyping in children. *Child Development, 49*, 1119–1134.

Martin, C. L., & Halverson, C. F. (1987). The roles of cognition in sex role acquisition. In D. B. Carter (Ed.), *Current conceptions of sex roles and sex typing: Theory and research* (pp. 123–137). New York: Praeger.

Martin, C. L., & Ruble, D. N. (2004). Children's search for gender cues. *Current Directions in Psychological Science, 13*, 67–70.

Martin, C. L., Ruble, D. N., & Szkrybalo, J. (2002). Cognitive theories of early gender development. *Psychological Bulletin, 128*, 903–933.

Martinussen, R., Hayden, J., Hogg-Johnson, S., & Tannock, R. (2005). A meta-analysis of working memory impairments in children with attention-deficit/hyperactivity disorder. *Journal of the American Academy of Child & Adolescent Psychiatry, 44*(4), 377–384.

Masataka, N. (1996). Perception of motherese in a signed language by 6-month-old deaf infants. *Developmental Psychology, 32*, 874–879.

Masataka, N. (1998). Perception of motherese in Japanese sign language by 6-month-old hearing infants. *Developmental Psychology, 34*, 241–246.

Masataka, N. (1999). Preferences for infant-directed singing in 2-day old hearing infants of deaf parents. *Developmental Psychology, 35*, 1001–1005.

Masten, A. S., & Cicchetti, D. (2010). Developmental cascades. *Development and Psychopathology, 22*, 491–495.

Masters, S., & Soares, M. (1993). Is the gender difference in mental rotation disappearing? *Behavioral Genetics, 23*, 337–341.

Mastropieri, M. A., & Scruggs, T. E. (1991). *Teaching students ways to remember: Strategies for learning mnemonically.* Cambridge, MA: Brookline Books.

Masur, E. F., & Rodemaker, J. E. (1999). Mothers' and infants' spontaneous vocal, verbal, and action imitation during the second year. *Merrill-Palmer Quarterly, 45,* 392–412.

Matheny, A. P., Jr., Wilson, R. S., Dolan, A. B., & Krantz, J. Z. (1981). Behavioral contrasts in twinships: Stability and patterns of differences in childhood. *Child Development, 52,* 579–598.

Maurer, D., & Lewis, T. L. (2013). Sensitive periods in visual development. In P. D. Zelazo (Ed.), *The Oxford handbook of developmental psychology: Vol. 1. Body and mind* (pp. 202–234). Oxford, UK: Oxford University Press.

Maurer, D., Mondloch, C. J., & Lewis, T. L. (2007). Effects of early visual deprivation on perceptual and cognitive development. *Progress in Brain Research, 164,* 87–104.

Maurer, D., & Salapatek, P. (1976). Developmental changes in the scanning of faces by young infants. *Child Development, 47,* 523–527.

Mayer, A., & Träuble, B. E. (2013). Synchrony in the onset of mental state understanding across cultures? A study among children in Samoa. *International Journal of Behavioral Development, 37*(1), 21–28.

Mazzoni, G. (1998). Memory suggestibility and meta-cognition in child eyewitness testimony: The roles of source monitoring and self-efficacy. *European Journal of Psychology of Education, 13,* 43–60.

McBride-Chang, C., & Wang, Y. (2015). Learning to read Chinese: Universal and unique cognitive cores. *Child Development Perspectives, 9,* 196–200.

McCall, R. B. (1981). Nature-nurture and the two realms of development: A proposed integration with respect to mental development. *Child Development, 52,* 1–12.

McCall, R. B., Appelbaum, M. I., & Hogarty, P. S. (1973). Developmental changes in mental performance. *Monographs of the Society for Research in Child Development, 38*(3, Serial No. 150).

McCall, R. B., & Carriger, M. S. (1993). A meta-analysis of infant habituation and recognition memory performance as predictors of later IQ. *Child Development, 64,* 57–79.

McCall, R. B., Eichorn, D. H., & Hogarty, P. S. (1977). Transitions in early mental development. *Monographs of the Society for Research in Child Development, 42*(3, Serial No. 171).

McCall, R. B., Hogarty, P. S., & Hurlburt, N. (1972). Transitions in infant sensori-motor development and the prediction of childhood IQ. *American Psychologist, 27,* 728–748.

McCall, R. B., Kennedy, C. B., & Appelbaum, M. I. (1977). Magnitude of discrepancy and the distribution of attention in infants. *Child Development, 48,* 772–785.

McCarthy, D. (1954). Language development in children. In L. Carmichael (Ed.), *A manual of child psychology* (2nd ed., pp. 492–630). New York: Wiley.

McCartney, K., Harris, M. J., & Bernieri, F. (1990). Growing up and growing apart: A development meta-analysis of twin studies. *Psychological Bulletin, 107,* 226–237.

McCormack, T. (2015). The development of temporal cognition. In R. Lerner (Series Ed.) & L. Liben & U. Muller (Vol. Eds.), *Handbook of child psychology and developmental science: Vol. 2. Cognitive processes* (7th ed., pp. 624–670). New York: Wiley.

McDonnell, C. G., Valentino, K., Comas, M., & Nuttall, A. K. (2016). Mother-child reminiscing at risk: Maternal attachment, elaboration, and child autobiographical memory specificity. *Journal of Experimental Child Psychology, 143,* 75–84.

McDonough, L., Mandler, J. M., McKee, R. D., & Squire, L. R. (1995). The deferred imitation task as a nonverbal measure of declarative memory. *Proceedings of the National Academy of Sciences, 92,* 7580–7584.

McGilly, K., & Siegler, R. S. (1990). The influence of encoding strategic knowledge on children's choices among serial recall strategies. *Developmental Psychology, 26,* 931–941.

McGown, C., Gregory, A., & Weinstein, R. S. (2010). Expectations, stereotypes, and self-fulfilling prophecies in classroom and school life. In J. L. Meece & J. S. Eccles (Eds.), *Handbook of research on schools, schooling, and human development* (pp. 256–274). New York: Routledge.

McGue, M., Bouchard, T. J., Jr., Lykken, D. T., & Feuer, D. (1984). Information processing abilities in twins reared apart. *Intelligence, 8,* 239–258.

McGuigan, N. (2013). The influence of model status on the tendency of young children to over-imitate. *Journal of Experimental Child Psychology, 116,* 962–969.

McGuigan, N., Makinson J., & Whiten, A. (2011). From over-imitation to super-copying: Adults imitate causally irrelevant aspects of tool use with higher fidelity than young children. *British Journal of Psychology, 102,* 1–18.

McGuigan, N., & Whiten, A. (2009). Emulation and "over-emulation" in the social learning of causally opaque versus causally transparent tool use by 23 and 30-month-old children. *Journal of Experimental Child Psychology, 104,* 367–381.

Meaney, M. J. (2010). Epigenetics and the biological definition of gene x environment interactions. *Child Development, 81,* 41–79.

Meaney, M. J. (2013). Epigenetics and the environmental regulation of the genome and its function. In D. Narvaez, J. Panksepp, A. N. Schore, & T. R. Gleason (Eds.), *Evolution, early experience and human development: From research to practice and policy* (pp. 99–128). Oxford: Oxford University Press.

Medin, D., Waxman, S., Woodring, J., & Washinawatok, K. (2010). Human-centeredness is not a universal feature of young children's reasoning: Culture and experience matter when reasoning about biological entities. *Cognitive Development, 25*(3), 197–207.

Mejia-Arauz, R., Rogoff, B., & Paradise, R. (2005). Cultural variation in children's observation during a demonstration. *International Journal of Behavioral Development, 29*, 282–291.

Melby-Lervåg, M., Lyster, S.-A. H., & Hulme, C. (2012). Phonological skills and their role in learning to read: A meta-analytic review. *Psychological Bulletin, 138*, 322–352.

Melhuish, E. C., Sylva, K., Sammons, P., Siraj-Blatchford, I., Taggart, B., Phan, M. B., & Malin, A. (2008). Preschool influences on mathematics achievement. *Science, 321*, 1161–1162.

Melinder, A. M., Kristen, W., Alexander, K. W., Cho, Y., Goodman, G. S., Thoresen, C., . . . Magnussen, S. (2010). Children's eyewitness memory: A comparison of two interviewing strategies. *Journal of Experimental Child Psychology, 105*, 155–177.

Melot, A.-M. (1998). The relationship between metacognitive knowledge and metacognitive experiences: Acquisition and re-elaboration. *European Journal of Psychology of Education, 13*, 75–89.

Meltzoff, A. N. (1988). Infant imitation after a 1-week delay: Long-term memory for novel acts and multiple stimuli. *Developmental Psychology, 24*, 470–476.

Meltzoff, A. N. (1995). Understanding the intentions of others: Reenactment of intended acts by 18-month-old children. *Developmental Psychology, 31*, 838–850.

Meltzoff, A. N., Kuhl, P. K., Movellan, J., & Sejnowski, T. J. (2009). Foundations for a new science of learning. *Science, 325*, 284–288.

Meltzoff, A. N., & Moore, M. K. (1977). Imitation of facial and manual gestures by human neonates. *Science, 198*, 75–78.

Meltzoff, A. N., & Moore, M. K. (1985). Cognitive foundations and social functions of imitation and intermodal representation in infancy. In J. Mehler & R. Fox (Eds.), *Neonate cognition: Beyond the booming buzzing confusion* (pp. 139–156). Hillsdale, NJ: Erlbaum.

Meltzoff, A. N., & Moore, M. K. (1992). Early imitation within a functional framework: The importance of person identity, movement, and development. *Infant Behavior and Development, 15*, 479–505.

Mendelson, M. J., & Haith, M. M. (1976). The relation between audition and vision in the human newborn. *Monographs of the Society for Research in Child Development, 41*(4, Serial No. 167).

Mervis, C. B., & Bertrand, J. (1994). Acquisition of the novel name-nameless category (N3C) principle. *Child Development, 65*, 1646–1662.

Merz, E. C., Harlé, K. M., Noble, K. G., & McCall, R. B. (2016). Executive function in previously institutionalized children. *Child Development Perspectives, 10*, 105–110.

Michotte, A. (1963). *The perception of causality*. London: Methuen.

Miller, D. I., & Halpern, D. F. (2014). The new science of cognitive sex differences. *Trends in cognitive sciences, 18*(1), 37–45.

Miller, E. B., Farkas, G., Lowe, D., Vandell, D. L., & Duncan, G. J. (2014). Do the effects of Head Start vary by parental preacademic stimulation? *Child Development, 85*, 1385–1400.

Miller, J. G., & Kinsbourne, M. (2012). Culture and neuroscience in developmental psychology: Contributions and challenges. *Child Development Perspectives, 6*, 35–41.

Miller, K. F., Smith, C. M., Zhu, J., & Zhang, H. (1995). Preschool origins of cross-national differences in mathematical competence. *Psychological Science, 6*, 56–60.

Miller, L. C., Lechner, R. E., & Rugs, D. (1985). Development of conversational responsiveness: Preschoolers' use of responsive listener cues and relevant comments. *Developmental Psychology, 21*, 473–480.

Miller, L. T., & Vernon, P. A. (1996). Intelligence, reaction time, and working memory in 4- to 6-year-old children. *Intelligence, 22*, 155–190.

Miller, P. H. (1990). The development of strategies of selective attention. In D. F. Bjorklund (Ed.), *Children's strategies: Contemporary views of cognitive development* (pp. 157–184). Hillsdale, NJ: Erlbaum.

Miller, P. H. (2014). The history of memory development research: Remembering our roots. In P. J. Bauer & R. Fivush (Eds.), *The Wiley handbook on the development of children's memory* (Vol. 1, pp. 19–40). Chichester, UK: Wiley-Blackwell.

Miller, P. H., Haynes, V. F., DeMarie-Dreblow, D., & Woody-Ramsey, J. (1986). Children's strategies for gathering information in three tasks. *Child Development, 57*, 1429–1439.

Miller, P. H., & Seier, W. L. (1994). Strategy utilization deficiencies in children: When, where, and why. In H. W. Reese (Ed.), *Advances in child development and behavior* (Vol. 25, pp. 107–156). New York: Academic.

Miller, P. H., Seier, W. L., Probert, J. S., & Aloise, P. A. (1991). Age differences in the capacity demands of a strategy among spontaneously strategic children. *Journal of Experimental Child Psychology, 52*, 149–165.

Miller, P. H., & Weiss, M. G. (1982). Children's and adults' knowledge about what variables affect selective attention. *Child Development, 53,* 543–549.

Miller, S. A. (2009). Children's understanding of second-order mental states. *Psychological Bulletin, 135,* 749–773.

Miller-Jones, D. (1989). Culture and testing. *American Psychologist, 44,* 360–366.

Milligan, K., Astington, J. W., & Dack, L. A. (2007). Language and theory of mind: Meta-analysis of the relationship between language ability and false-belief understanding. *Child Development, 78,* 622–646.

Mills, K. L., Goddings, A. L., Clasen, L. S., Giedd, J. N., & Blakemore, S. J. (2014). The developmental mismatch in structural brain maturation during adolescence. *Developmental Neuroscience, 36,* 147–160.

Milner, B. (1964). Some effects of frontal lobectomy in man. In J. M. Warren & K. Akert (Eds.), *The frontal granular cortex and behavior* (pp. 313–334). New York: McGraw-Hill.

Mischel, W., Ebbesen, E. B., & Raskoff Zeiss, A. (1972). Cognitive and attentional mechanisms in delay of gratification. *Journal of Personality and Social Psychology, 21,* 204–218.

Mistry, J. (1997). The development of remembering in cultural context. In N. Cowan (Ed.), *The development of memory in childhood* (pp. 343–386). Hove, UK: Psychology Press.

Mix, K. S., Huttenlocher, J., & Levine, S. C. (2002). Multiple cues for quantification in infancy: Is number one of them? *Psychological Bulletin, 128,* 278–294.

Miyake, A., & Friedman, N. P. (2012). The nature and organization of individual differences in executive: Four general conclusions. *Current Directions in Psychological Sciences, 21,* 8–14.

Moely, B. E., Hart, S. S., Leal, L., Santulli, K. A., Rao, N., Johnson, T., & Hamilton, L. B. (1992). The teacher's role in facilitating memory and study strategy development in the elementary school classroom. *Child Development, 63,* 653–672.

Moely, B. E., Santulli, K. A., & Obach, M. S. (1995). Strategy instruction, metacognition, and motivation in the elementary school classroom. In F. Weinert & W. Schneider (Eds.), *Memory performance and competencies: Issues in growth and development* (pp. 301–321). Hillsdale, NJ: Erlbaum.

Moffitt, T. E., Arseneault, L., Belsky, D., Dickson, N., Hancox, R. J., Harrington, H., . . . Caspi, A. (2011, February 15). A gradient of childhood self-control predicts health, wealth, and public safety. *Proceedings of the National Academy of Sciences, 108,* 2693–2698.

Moffitt, T. E., Caspi, A., & Rutter, M. (2006). Measured gene-environment interactions in psychology: Concepts, research strategies, and implications for research, intervention, and public understanding of genetics. *Perspective on Psychological Science, 1,* 5–27.

Mol, S. E., & Neuman, S. B. (2014). Sharing information books with kindergartners: The role of parents' extratextual talk and socioeconomic status. *Early Childhood Research Quarterly, 29,* 399–410.

Molfese, D. L., & Molfese, V. J. (1980). Cortical responses of preterm infants to phonetic and nonphonetic speech stimuli. *Developmental Psychology, 16,* 574–581.

Molfese, D. L., & Molfese, V. J. (1985). Electrophysiological indices of auditory discrimination in newborn infants: The bases for predicting later language development? *Infant Behavior and Development, 8,* 197–211.

Moll, H., & Tomasello, M. (2012). Three-year-olds understand appearance and reality—just not about the same object at the same time. *Developmental Psychology, 48,* 1124–1132.

Monastersky, R. (2005). Women and science: The debate goes on. *Chronicle of Higher Education, 51.* Retrieved from http://chronicle.com/free/v51/i26/26a00102.htm

Mondloch, C. J., Lewis, T. L., Budreau, D. R., Maurer, D., Dannemiller, J. L., Stephens, B. R., & Kleiner-Gathercoal, K. A. (1999). Face perception during early infancy. *Psychological Science, 10,* 419–422.

Monette, S., Bigras, M., & Lafrenière, M.-A. (2015). Structure of executive functions in typically developing kindergarteners. *Journal of Experimental Child Psychology, 140,* 120–139.

Monk, C. S., Webb, S. J., & Nelson, C. A. (2001). Prenatal neurobiological development: Molecular mechanisms and anatomical change. *Developmental Neuropsychology, 19,* 211–236.

Montag, J. L., Jones, M. N., & Smith, L. S. (2015). The words children hear: Picture books and the statistics for language learning. *Psychological Science, 26*(9), 1–8.

Moore, D. S. (2001). *The dependent gene: The fallacy of "nature vs. nurture."* New York: Freeman Books.

Moore, D. S. (2013). Behavioral genetics, genetics, and epigenetic. In P. D. Zelazo (Ed.), *The Oxford handbook of developmental psychology: Vol. 1. Body and mind* (pp. 91–128). Oxford, UK: Oxford University Press.

Moore, D. S. (2015). *The developing genome: An introduction to behavioral epigenetics.* New York: Oxford University Press.

Moore, D. S., & Cocas, L. A. (2006). Perception precedes computation: Can familiarity preferences explain apparent calculation by human babies? *Developmental Psychology, 42,* 666–678.

Moore, D. S., & Johnson, S. P. (2009). Mental rotation in human infants: A sex difference. *Psychological Science, 19*, 1063–1066.

Moore, D. S., Spence, M. J., & Katz, G. S. (1997). Six-month-olds' categorization of natural infant-directed utterances. *Developmental Psychology, 33*, 980–989.

Moore, K. L., & Persaud, T. V. N. (2003). *The developing human: Clinically oriented embryology* (7th ed.). Philadelphia: Saunders.

Moore, T. (1967). Language and intelligence: A longitudinal study of the first eight years. Part I. Patterns of development in boys and girls. *Human Development, 10*, 88–106.

Morelli, G. A., Rogoff, B., & Angelillo, C. (2003). Cultural variation in young children's access to work or involvement in specialized child-focused activities. *International Journal of Behavioral Development, 27*, 264–274.

Morgante, J. D., & Keen, R. (2008). Vision and action: The effect of visual feedback on infants' exploratory behaviors. *Infant Behavior & Development, 31*, 729–733.

Morisset, C. E., Barnard, K. E., & Booth, C. L. (1995). Toddlers' language development: Sex differences within social risk. *Developmental Psychology, 31*, 851–865.

Morrison, F. J., Griffith, E. M., & Alberts, D. M. (1997). Nature-nurture in the classroom: Entrance age, school readiness, and learning in children. *Developmental Psychology, 33*, 254–262.

Morrison, F. J., Griffith, E. M., & Frazier, J. A. (1996). Schooling and the 5–7 shift: A natural experiment. In A. Sameroff & M. M. Haith (Eds.), *Reason and responsibility: The passage through childhood* (pp. 161–186). Chicago: University of Chicago Press.

Morrongiello, B. A., Fenwich, K. D., Hillier, L., & Chance, G. (1994). Sound localization in newborn human infants. *Developmental Psychobiology, 27*, 519–538.

Mortensen, E. L., Michaelsen, K. F., Sanders, S. A., & Refnisch, J. M. (2002). The association between duration of breastfeeding and adult intelligence. *Journal of the American Medical Association, 287*, 2365–2371.

Morton, J., & Johnson, M. H. (1991). CONSPEC and CONLEARN: A two-process theory of infant face recognition. *Psychological Review, 98*, 164–181.

Moser, A., Zimmerman, L., Dickerson, K., Grenell, A., Barr, R., & Gerhardstein, P. (2015). They can interact, but can they learn? Toddlers' transfer learning from touchscreens and television. *Journal of Experimental Child Psychology, 137*, 137–153.

Moskowitz, B. A. (1978). The acquisition of language. *Scientific American, 239*, 92–108.

Mou, Y., & VanMarle, K. (2014). Two core systems of numerical representation in infants. *Developmental Review, 34*(1), 1–25.

Moulson, M. C., Fox, N. A., Zeanah, C. H., & Nelson, C. A. (2009). Early adverse experiences and the neurobiology of facial processing. *Developmental Psychology, 45*, 17–30.

Moulson, M. C., Shutts, K., Fox, N. A., Zeanah, C. H., Spelke, E. S., & Nelson, C. A. (2015). Effects of early institutionalization on the development of emotion processing: A case for relative sparing? *Developmental Science, 18*, 298–313.

Moulson, M. C., Westerlund, A., Fox, N. A., Zeanah, C. H., & Nelson, C. A. (2009). The effects of early experience on face recognition: An event-related potential study of institutionalized children in Romania. *Child Development, 80*, 1039–1056.

Muir-Broaddus, J. E. (1995). Gifted underachievers: Insights from the characteristics of strategic functioning associated with giftedness and achievement. *Learning and Individual Differences, 7*, 189–206.

Mullen, M. K. (1994). Earliest recollections of childhood: A demographic analysis. *Cognition, 52*, 55–79.

Mullen, M. K., & Yi, S. (1995). The cultural context of talk about the past: Implications for the development of autobiographical memory. *Cognitive Development, 10*, 407–419.

Müller, G. B. (2003). Embryonic motility: Environmental influences and evolutionary innovation. *Evolution & Development, 5*, 56–60.

Mullis, I. V. S., Martin, M. O., Foy, P., & Arora, A. (2012). *TIMSS 2011 international results in mathematics*. Chestnut Hill, MA: Boston College.

Mullis, I. V. S., Martin, M. O., Gonzalez, E. J., & Kennedy, A. M. (2003). *PIRLS 2001 international report: IEA's study of reading literacy achievement in primary schools*. Chestnut Hill, MA: Boston College. Retrieved from http://timss.bc.edu/pirls2001.html

Munroe, R. H., Shimmin, H. S., & Munroe, R. L. (1984). Gender understanding and sex role preference in four cultures. *Developmental Psychology, 20*, 673–682.

Murray, R., & Ramstetter, C. (2013). The crucial role of recess in school. *Pediatrics, 131*, 183–188.

Mussolin, C., Nys, J., Leybaert, J., & Content, A. (2016). How approximate and exact number skills are related to each other across development: A review. *Developmental Review, 39*, 1–15.

Muter, V., Hulme, C., Snowling, M. J., & Stevenson, J. (2004). Phonemes, rimes and language skills as foundations of early reading development: Evidence from a longitudinal study. *Developmental Psychology, 40*, 663–681.

Muter, V., Hulme, C., Snowling, M. J., & Taylor, S. (1998). Segmentation, not rhyming, predicts early progress in learning to read. *Journal of Experimental Child Psychology, 71*, 3–27.

Muzzatti, B., & Agnoli, F. (2007). Gender and mathematics: Attitudes and stereotype threat susceptibility in Italian children. *Developmental Psychology, 43*, 747–759.

Myowa-Yamakoshi, M., & Tomonaga, M. (2001). Development of face recognition in an infant gibbon (*Hylobates agilis*). *Infant Behavior and Development, 24*, 215–227.

Myowa-Yamakoshi, M., Tomonaga, M., Tanaka, M., & Matsuzawa, T. (2004). Imitation in neonatal chimpanzees (*Pan troglodytes*). *Developmental Science, 7*, 437–442.

Nadig, A. S., & Sedivy, J. C. (2002). Evidence of perspective-taking constraints in children's on-line reference resolution. *Psychological Science, 13*, 329–336.

Nagell, K., Olguin, K., & Tomasello, M. (1993). Processes of social learning in the tool use of chimpanzees (*Pan troglodytes*) and human children (*Homo sapiens*). *Journal of Comparative Psychology, 107*, 174–186.

Nagy, E. (2006). From imitation to conversation: The first dialogues with human neonates. *Infant and Child Development, 15*, 223–232.

Nagy, E., & Molnar, P. (2004). Homo imitans or homo provocans? Human imprinting model of neonatal imitation. *Infant Behavior and Development, 27*, 54–63.

Nagy, E., Pal, A., & Orvos, H. (2014). Learning to imitate individual finger movements by the human neonate. *Developmental Science, 17*, 841–857.

Naito, M., & Miura, H. (2001). Japanese children's numerical competencies: Age- and schooling-related influences in the development of number concepts and addition skills. *Developmental Psychology, 37*, 217–230.

Nash, M. R. (1987). What, if anything, is age regressed about hypnotic age regression? A review of the empirical literature. *Psychological Bulletin, 102*, 42–52.

Nash, M. R., Drake, M., Wiley, R., Khalsa, S., & Lynn, S. J. (1986). The accuracy of recall of hypnotically age regressed subjects. *Journal of Abnormal Psychology, 95*, 298–300.

Nathanson, A. I., Aladé, F., Sharp, M. L., Rasmusse, E. E., & Christy, K. (2014). The relation between television exposure and executive function among preschoolers. *Developmental Psychology, 50*, 1497–1506.

Neisser, U. (Ed.). (1998). *The rising curve: Long-term gains in IQ and related measures*. Washington, DC: American Psychological Association.

Neisser, U., Boodoo, G., Bouchard, T. J., Boykin, A. W., Brody, N., Ceci, S. J., . . . Urbina, S. (1996). Intelligence: Knowns and unknowns. *American Psychologist, 51*, 77–101.

Nelson, C. A. (2001). Neural plasticity and human development: The role of experience in sculpting memory systems. *Developmental Science, 3*, 115–130.

Nelson, C. A. (2007). A neurobiological perspective on early human deprivation. *Child Development Perspectives, 1*, 13–18.

Nelson, C. A., Furtado, E. A., Fox, N. A., & Zeanah, C. H., Jr. (2009). The deprived human brain. *American Scientist, 97*, 222–229.

Nelson, C. A., Thomas, K. M., & de Haan, M. (2006). Neural bases of cognitive development. In W. Damon & R. M. Lerner (Series Eds.) & D. Kuhn & R. S. Siegler (Vol. Eds.), *Handbook of child psychology: Vol. 2. Cognition, perception, and language* (6th ed., pp. 3–57). New York: Wiley.

Nelson, C. A., III, Zeanah, C. H., Fox, N. A., Marshall, P. J., Smuke, A. T., & Guthrie, D. (2007). Cognitive recovery in socially deprived young children: The Bucharest Early Intervention Program. *Science, 318*, 1937–1940.

Nelson, K. (1973). Structure and strategy in learning to talk. *Monographs of the Society for Research in Child Development, 38*(1–2, Serial No. 149).

Nelson, K. (1974). Variations in children's concepts by age and category. *Child Development, 45*, 577–584.

Nelson, K. (1993). The psychological and social origins of autobiographical memory. *Psychological Science, 4*, 7–14.

Nelson, K. (1996). *Language in cognitive development: The emergence of the mediated mind*. New York: Cambridge University Press.

Nelson, K. (2005). Evolution and development of human memory systems. In B. J. Ellis & D. F. Bjorklund (Eds.), *Origins of the social mind: Evolutionary psychology and child development* (pp. 354–382). New York: Guilford Press.

Nelson, K. (2014). Sociocultural theories of memory development. In P. J. Bauer & R. Fivush (Eds.), *The Wiley handbook on the development of children's memory* (Vol. 1, pp. 87–108). Chichester, UK: Wiley-Blackwell.

Nesse, R. M., & Williams, G. C. (1994). *Why we get sick: The new science of Darwinian medicine*. New York: Times Books.

Nettelbeck, T. (2011). Basic processes of intelligence. In R. J. Sternberg & S. B. Kaufman (Eds.), *The Cambridge handbook of intelligence* (pp. 371–393). Cambridge, UK: Cambridge University Press.

Nettelbeck, T., & Burns, N. R. (2010). Processing speed, working memory and reasoning ability from childhood to old age. *Personality and Individual Differences, 48*(4), 379–384.

Nettle, D. (2008). Why do some dads get more involved than others? Evidence from a large British cohort. *Evolution and Human Behavior, 29*(6), 416–423.

Neubauer, A., & Fink, A. (2009). Intelligence and neural efficiency: Measures of brain activity versus measures of functional connectivity in the brain. *Intelligence, 37,* 223–229.

Neuenschwander, R., Röthlisberger, M., Cimeli, P., & Roebers, C. M. (2012). How do different aspects of self-regulation predict successful adaptation to school? *Journal of Experimental Child Psychology, 113,* 353–371.

Neville, H. J. (1991). Neurobiology of cognitive and language processing: Effects of early experience. In K. R. Gibson & A. C. Petersen (Eds.), *Brain maturation and cognitive development: Comparative and cross-cultural perspectives* (pp. 355–380). New York: Adaline de Gruyter Press.

Newcombe, N. S. (2002). The nativist-empiricist controversy in the context of recent research on spatial and quantitative development. *Psychological Science, 13,* 395–401.

Newcombe, N. S. (2010). What is neoconstructivism? In S. P. Johnson (Ed.), *Neoconstructivism: The new science of cognitive development* (pp. v–viii). New York: Oxford University Press.

Newcombe, N. S. (2011). What is neuroconstructivism? *Child Development Perspectives, 5,* 157–160.

Newcombe, N. S., Bandura, M. M., & Taylor, D. C. (1983). Sex differences in spatial ability and spatial activities. *Sex Roles, 9,* 377–386.

Newcombe, N. S., Drummey, A. B., Fox, N. A., Lie, E., & Ottinger-Alberts, W. (2000). Remembering early childhood: How much, how, and why (or why not). *Current Directions in Psychological Science, 9,* 55–58.

Newcombe, N. S., & Fox, N. A. (1994). Infantile amnesia: Through a glass darkly. *Child Development, 65,* 31–40.

Newcombe, N. S., & Huttenlocher, J. (2006). Development of spatial cognition. In W. Damon & R. M. Lerner (Series Eds.) & D. Kuhn & R. S. Siegler (Vol. Eds.), *Handbook of child psychology: Vol. 2. Cognition, perception, and language* (6th ed., pp. 734–776). New York: Wiley.

Newcombe, N. S., Huttenlocher, J., Drummey, A. B., & Wiley, J. (1998). The development of spatial location coding: Use of external frames of reference and dead reckoning. *Cognitive Development, 13,* 185–200.

Newcombe, N. S., Huttenlocher, J., & Learmonth, A. (1999). Infants' coding of location in continuous space. *Infant Behavior and Development, 22,* 483–510.

Newport, E. L. (1990). Maturational constraints on language learning. *Cognitive Science, 14,* 11–28.

Newport, E. L. (1991). Contrasting concepts of the critical period for language. In S. Carey & R. Gelman (Eds.), *Epigenesis of mind: Essays in biology and knowledge* (pp. 111–130). Hillsdale, NJ: Erlbaum.

Ng, F. F.-Y., Pomerantz, E. M., & Lam, S.-F. (2007). European American and Chinese parents' responses to children's success and failure: Implications for children's responses. *Developmental Psychology, 43,* 1239–1255.

Nicely, P., Tamis-LeMonda, C. S., & Bornstein, M. H. (1999). Mothers' attuned responses to infant affect expressivity promote earlier achievement of language milestones. *Infant Behavior and Development, 22,* 557–568.

NICHD Early Child Care Research Network. (2002). Child-care structure → process → outcome: Direct and indirect effects of child-care quality on young children's development. *Psychological Science, 13,* 199–206.

NICHD Early Child Care Research Network. (2005). Duration and developmental timing of poverty and children's cognitive and social development from birth through third grade. *Child Development, 76,* 795–810.

Nielsen, M. (2006). Copying actions and copying outcomes: Social learning through the second year. *Developmental Psychology, 42,* 555–565.

Nielsen, M. (2012). Imitation, pretend play, and childhood: Essential elements in the evolution of human culture? *Journal of Comparative Psychology, 126,* 170–181.

Nielsen, M., Moore, C., & Mohamedally, J. (2015). Young children overimitate in third-party contexts. *Journal of Experimental Child Psychology, 112,* 73–83.

Nielsen, M., Mushin, I., Tomaselli, K., & Whiten, A. (2014). Where culture takes hold: "Overimitation" and its flexible deployment in Western, Aboriginal, and Bushmen children. *Child Development, 85,* 2169–2184.

Nielsen, M., Simcock, G., & Jenkins, L. (2008). The effect of social engagement on 24-month-olds' imitation from live and televised models. *Developmental Science, 11,* 722–731.

Nielsen, M., Suddendorf, T., & Slaughter, V. (2006). Mirror self-recognition beyond the face. *Child Development, 77,* 176–185.

Nielsen, M., & Tomaselli, K. (2010). Overimitation in Kalahari Bushman children and the origins of human cultural cognition. *Psychological Science, 21,* 729–736.

Nielsen, M., Tomaselli, K., Mushin, I., & Whiten, A. (2014). Exploring tool innovation: A comparison of Western and Bushman children. *Journal of Experimental Child Psychology, 126,* 384–394.

Nigro, G., Brandimonte, M. A., Cicogna, P., & Cosenza, M. (2014). Episodic future thinking as a predictor of children's prospective memory. *Journal of Experimental Child Psychology, 127,* 82–94.

Nisbett, R. E., Aronson, J., Blair, C., Dickens, W., Flynn, J., Halpern, D. F., & Turkheimer, E. (2012). Intelligence: New findings and theoretical development. *American Psychologist, 67,* 130–159.

Nisbett, R. E., Peng, K., Choi, I., & Norenzayan, A. (2001). Culture and systems of thought: Holistic vs. analytic cognition. *Psychological Review, 108,* 291–310.

Norton, E. S., & Wolf, M. (2012). Rapid automatized naming (RAN) and reading fluency: Implications for understanding and treatment of reading disabilities. *Annual Review of Psychology, 63,* 427–452.

Nunes, T., & Bryant, P. (2015). The development of mathematical reasoning. In R. M. Lerner (Series Ed.) & L. Liben & U. M. Müller (Vol. Eds.), *Handbook of child psychology and developmental science: Vol. 2. Cognitive Processes* (7th ed., pp. 715–762). New York: Wiley.

Nyiti, R. M. (1982). The validity of "cultural differences explanation" in the rate of Piagetian cognitive development. In D. A. Wagner & H. W. Stevenson (Eds.), *Cultural perspectives on child development* (pp. 146–165). San Francisco: W. H. Freeman.

Oakes, L. M. (1994). Development of infants' use of continuity cues in their perception of causality. *Developmental Psychology, 30,* 869–879.

Oberman, L. M., Hubbard, E. M., McCleery, J. P., Altschuler, E. L., Pineda, J. A., & Ramachandran, V. S. (2005). EEG evidence for mirror neuron dysfunction in autism spectrum disorder. *Cognitive Brain Research, 24,* 190–198.

O'Brien, M., & Huston, A. C. (1985). Development of sex-typed play behavior in toddlers. *Developmental Psychology, 21,* 866–871.

O'Connor, J. J., Cohen, S., & Parmelee, A. H. (1984). Infant auditory discrimination in preterm and full-term infants as a predictor of 5 year intelligence. The effects of global severe privation on cognitive competence: Extension and longitudinal follow-up. *Developmental Psychology, 20,* 159–165.

O'Connor, T. G., Rutter, M., Beckett, C., Keaveney, L., Kreppner, J. M., & the English and Romanian Adoptees Study Team. (2000). The effects of global severe privation on cognitive competence: Extension and longitudinal follow-up. *Child Development, 71,* 376–390.

Odegard, T. M., Cooper, C. M., Lampinen, J. M., Reyna, V. F., & Brainerd, C. J. (2009). Children's eyewitness memory for multiple real-life events. *Child Development, 80,* 1877–1890.

Ogbu, J. U. (1986). The consequences of the American caste system. In U. Neisser (Ed.), *The school achievement of minority children: New perspectives* (pp. 19–56). Hillsdale, NJ: Erlbaum.

Ogbu, J. U., & Stern, P. (2001). Caste status and intellectual development. In R. J. Sternberg & E. L. Grigorenko (Eds.), *Environmental effects on cognitive abilities* (pp. 3–37). Mahwah, NJ: Erlbaum.

Öhman, A., Flykt, A., & Esteves, F. (2001). Emotion drives attention: Detecting the snake in the grass. *Journal of Experimental Psychology: General, 130,* 466–478.

Oliver, B. R., Dale, P. S., & Plomin, R. (2005). Predicting literacy at age 7 from preliteracy at age 4: A longitudinal genetic analysis. *Psychological Science, 16,* 861–865.

Olson, K. R., & Dweck, C. S. (2009). Social cognitive development: A new look. *Child Development Perspectives, 3,* 60–65.

Olson, K. R., Key, A. C., & Eaton, N. R. (2015). Gender cognition in transgender children. *Psychological Science, 26,* 467–474.

O'Neill, M., Bard, K. A., Linnell, M., & Fluck, M. (2005). Maternal gestures with 20-month-old infants in two contexts. *Developmental Science, 8,* 352–359.

Onishi, K. H., & Baillargeon, R. (2005). Do 15-month-old infants understand false belief? *Science, 308,* 255–258.

Oostenbroek, J., Suddendorf, T., Nielsen, M., Redshaw, J., Kennedy-Costantini, S., Davis, J., . . . Slaughter, V. (2016). Comprehensive longitudinal study challenges the existence of neonatal imitation in humans. *Current Biology, 26,* 1–5.

Opfer, J. E., & Gelman, S. A. (2001). Children's and adults' models for predicting teleological action: The development of a biology-based model. *Child Development, 72,* 1367–1381.

Oppenheim, R. W. (1981). Ontogenetic adaptations and retrogressive processes in the development of the nervous system and behavior. In K. J. Connolly & H. F. R. Prechtl (Eds.), *Maturation and development: Biological and psychological perspectives* (pp. 73–108). Philadelphia: International Medical.

Oppenheim, R. W., Milligan, C. E., & von Bartheld, C. S. (2012). Programed cell death and neurotrophic factors. In L. R. Squire, D. Berg, F. E. Bloom, S. du Lac, A. Ghosh, & N. C. Spitzer (Eds.), *Fundamental neuroscience* (4th ed., pp. 405–435). New York: Elsevier.

Organisation for Economic Co-operation and Development. (2014). *PISA 2012 results in focus: What 15 year olds know and what they can do with what they know.* Retrieved from https://www.oecd.org/pisa/keyfindings/pisa-2012-results-overview.pdf

Ornstein, P. A., Baker-Ward, L., Gordon, B. N., Pelphrey, K. A., Tyler, C. S., & Gramzow, E. (2006). The influence of prior knowledge and repeated questioning on children's long-term retention of the details of a pediatric examination. *Developmental Psychology, 42,* 332–344.

Ornstein, P. A., Baker-Ward, L., & Naus, M. J. (1988). The development of mnemonic skill. In M. Weinert & M. Perlmutter (Eds.), *Memory development* (pp. 31–50). Hillsdale, NJ: Erlbaum.

Ornstein, P. A., Coffman, J., Grammar, J., San Souci, P., & McCall, L. (2010). Linking the classroom context and the development of children's memory skills. In J. L. Meece & J. S. Eccles (Eds.), *Handbook of research on schools, schooling, and human development* (pp. 42–59). New York: Routledge.

Ornstein, P. A., Gordon, B. N., & Larus, D. M. (1992). Children's memory for a personally experienced event: Implications for testimony. *Applied Developmental Psychology, 6,* 49–60.

Ornstein, P. A., Grammar, J. K., & Coffman, J. L. (2009). Teachers' "mnemonic style" and the development of skilled memory. In H. S. Waters & W. Schneider (Eds.), *Metacognition, strategy use, and instruction* (pp. 23–53). New York: Guilford Press.

Ornstein, P. A., & Greenhoot, A. F. (2000). Remembering the distant past: Implications of research on children's memory for the recovered memory debate. In D. F. Bjorklund (Ed.), *False-memory creation in children and adults: Theory, research, and implications* (pp. 203–237). Mahwah, NJ: Erlbaum.

Ornstein, P. A., Hale, G. A., & Morgan, J. S. (1977). Developmental differences in recall and output organization. *Bulletin of the Psychonomic Society, 9,* 29–32.

Ornstein, P. A., & Light, L. L. (2010). Memory development across the lifespan. In R. M. Lerner (Series Ed.) & W. F. Overton (Vol. Ed.), *Handbook of life-span development: Vol. 1. Biology, cognition and methods across the life-span* (pp. 259–305). Hoboken, NJ: Wiley.

Ornstein, P. A., Merritt, K. A., Baker-Ward, L., Furtado, E., Gordon, B. N., & Principe, G. F. (1998). Children's knowledge, expectation, and long-term retention. *Applied Cognitive Psychology, 12,* 387–405.

Ornstein, P. A., & Naus, M. J. (1978). Rehearsal processes in children's memory. In P. A. Ornstein (Ed.), *Memory development in children* (pp. 69–99). Hillsdale, NJ: Erlbaum.

Ornstein, P. A., Naus, M. J., & Liberty, C. (1975). Rehearsal and organizational processes in children's memory. *Child Development, 46,* 818–830.

Ornstein, P. A., Naus, M. J., & Stone, B. P. (1977). Rehearsal training and developmental differences in memory. *Developmental Psychology, 13,* 15–24.

Oshima-Takane, Y., Goodz, E., & Derevensky, J. L. (1996). Birth order effects on early language development: Do secondborn children learn from overheard speech? *Child Development, 67,* 621–634.

Oshima-Takane, Y., & Robbins, M. (2003). Linguistic environment of secondborn children. *First Language, 23,* 21–40.

O'Sullivan, J. T., Howe, M. L., & Marche, T. A. (1996). Children's beliefs about long-term retention. *Child Development, 67,* 2989–3009.

Otgaar, H., Candel, I., Scoboria, A., & Merckelbach, H. (2010). Script knowledge enhances the development of children's false memories. *Acta psychologica, 133*(1), 57–63.

Otgaar, H., Verschuere, B., Meijer, E. H., & van Oorsouw, K. (2012). The origin of children's implanted false memories: Memory traces or compliance? *Acta Psychologica, 139*(3), 397–403.

Ovando, C. J. (2003). Bilingual education in the United States: Historical development and current issues. *Bilingual Research Journal, 27*(1), 1–24.

Over, H., & Carpenter, M. (2013). The social side of imitation. *Child Development Perspectives, 7,* 6–11.

Ozturk, O., Shayan, S., Liszkowski, U., & Mijad, A. (2013). Language is not necessary for color categories. *Developmental Science, 16,* 111–115.

Paap, K. R., Johnson, H. A., & Sawi, O. (2015). Bilingual advantages in executive functioning either do not exist or are restricted to very specific and undetermined circumstances. *Cortex, 69,* 265–278.

Panksepp, J. (1998). Attention deficit hyperactivity disorders, psychostimulants, and intolerance of childhood playfulness: A tragedy in the making? *Current Directions in Psychological Science, 7,* 91–98.

Papaeliou, C. F., Maniadaki, K., & Kakouros, E. (2012). Association between story recall and other language abilities in schoolchildren with ADHD. *Journal of Attention Disorders, 19*(1), 53–62.

Papousek, H. (1977). Entwicklung der Lernfahigkeit lm Saughngsalter [The development of learning ability in infancy]. In G. Nissen (Ed.), *Intelhgenz, Lernen und Lernstorungen* [*Intelligence, learning, and learning disabilities*] (pp. 75–93). Berlin: Springer-Verlag.

Pascalis, O., de Haan, M., & Nelson, C. A. (2002). Is face processing species-specific during the first year of life? *Science, 296,* 1321–1323.

Pascalis, O., & Kelly, D. J. (2009). The origins of face processing in humans. *Perspectives on Psychological Science, 4,* 200–209.

Pascalis, O., Loevenbruck, H., Quinn, P. C., Kandel, S., Tanaka, J. W., & Lee, K. (2014). On the links among face processing, language processing, and narrowing during development. *Child Development Perspectives, 8,* 65–70.

Pascalis, O., Scott, L. S., Kelly, D. J., Shannon, R. W., Nicholson, E., Coleman, M., & Nelson, C. A. (2005). Plasticity of face processing in infancy. *Proceedings of the National Academy of Sciences, 102*, 5297–5300.

Patterson, M. L., & Werker, J. F. (2003). Two-month-old infants match phonetic information in lips and voice. *Developmental Science, 6*, 191–196.

Paulesu, E., Demonet, J.-F., Fazio, F., McCrory, E., Chanoine, V., Brunswick, N., . . . Frith, U. (2001). Dyslexia: Cultural diversity and biological unity. *Science, 291*, 2165–2167.

Pavarini, G., de Hollanda Souza, D., & Hawk, C. K. (2013). Parental practices and theory of mind development. *Journal of Child and Family Studies, 22*(6), 844–853.

Paz-Alonso, P. M., Larson, R. P., Castelli, P., Alley, D., & Goodman, G. S. (2009). Memory development: Emotion, stress, and trauma. In M. L. Courage & N. Cowan (Eds.), *The development of memory in infancy and childhood* (pp. 197–239). Hove, UK: Psychology Press.

Pearson, B. Z., Fernandez, S. C., Lewedag, V., & Oller, D. K. (1997). The relation of input factors to lexical learning by bilingual infants (ages 10 to 30 months). *Applied Psycholinguistics, 18*, 41–58.

Pellegrini, A. D. (2013a). Object use in childhood: Development and possible functions. *Behaviour, 150*, 813–843.

Pellegrini, A. D. (2013b). Play. In P. Zelazo (Ed.), *The Oxford handbook of developmental psychology: Vol. 2. Self and other* (pp. 276–299). Oxford, UK: Oxford University Press.

Pellegrini, A. D. (2016). Object use in childhood: Development of possible functions. In D. C. Geary & D. B. Berch (Eds.), *Evolutionary perspectives on education and child development* (pp. 95–115). New York: Springer.

Pellegrini, A. D., & Bjorklund, D. F. (2004). The ontogeny and phylogeny of children's object and fantasy play. *Human Nature, 15*, 23–43.

Pellegrini, A. D., & Dupuis, D. (2010). Developmental and educational role of recess in school. In J. L. Meece & J. S. Eccles (Eds.), *Handbook of research on schools, schooling, and human development* (pp. 356–365). New York: Routledge.

Pellegrini, A. D., & Glada, L. (1991). Longitudinal relations among preschoolers' symbolic play, metalinguistic verbs, and emergent literacy. In J. Christie (Ed.), *Play and early literacy development* (pp. 47–68). Albany: SUNY Press.

Pellegrini, A. D., & Gustafson, K. (2005). Boys' and girls' uses of objects for exploration, play, and tools in early childhood. In A. Pellegrini & P. Smith (Eds.), *The nature of play: Great apes and humans* (pp. 113–138). New York: Guilford Press.

Pellegrini, A. D., Huberty, P. D., & Jones, I. (1995). The effects of play deprivation on children's recess and classroom behaviors. *American Educational Research Journal, 32*, 845–864.

Pennington, B. F. (2015). A typical cognitive development. In R. Lerner (Series Ed.) & L. Liben & U. Muller (Vol. Eds.), *Handbook of child psychology and developmental science: Vol. 2. Cognitive processes* (7th ed., pp. 995–1042). New York: Wiley.

Perani, D., Saccuman, M. C., Scifo, P., Spada, D., Andreolli, G., Rovelli, R., . . . Koelsch, S. (2010). Functional specializations for music processing in the human newborn brain. *Proceedings of the National Academy of Sciences, 107*(10), 4758–4763.

Perez, B. (2004). *Becoming biliterate: A study of two-way bilingual immersion education.* Mahwah, NJ: Erlbaum.

Perner, J. (1991). *Understanding the representational mind.* Cambridge, MA: MIT Press.

Perner, J., & Lang, B. (2000). Theory of mind and executive function: Is there a developmental relationship? In S. Baron-Cohen, H. Tager-Flusberg, & D. Cohen (Eds.), *Understanding other minds: Perspectives from autism and developmental cognitive neuroscience* (2nd ed., pp. 150–181). Oxford, UK: Oxford University Press.

Perner, J., Ruffman, T., & Leekam, S. R. (1994). Theory of mind is contagious: You catch it from your sibs. *Child Development, 67*, 1228–1238.

Perner, J., & Wimmer, H. (1985). "John thinks that Mary thinks that. . . ." Attribution of second order beliefs by 5- to 10-year-old children. *Journal of Experimental Child Psychology, 39*, 437–471.

Perry, D. G., Perry, L. C., & Rasmussen, P. (1986). Cognitive learning mediators of aggression. *Child Development, 57*, 700–711.

Peskin, J. (1992). Ruse and representations: On children's ability to conceal information. *Developmental Psychology, 28*, 84–89.

Peterson, C. (2012). Children's autobiographical memories across the years: Forensic implications of childhood amnesia and eyewitness memory for stressful events. *Developmental Review, 32*(3), 287–306.

Peterson, C., Grant, V., & Boland, L. (2005). Childhood amnesia in children and adolescents: Their earliest memories. *Memory, 13*(6), 622–637.

Peterson, C., Morris, G., Baker-Ward, L., & Flynn, S. (2014). Predicting which childhood memories persist: Contributions of memory characteristics. *Developmental Psychology, 50*, 439–448.

Peterson, C., Wang, Q., & Hou, Y. (2009). "When I was little": Childhood recollections in Chinese and European

Canadian grade school children. *Child Development, 80,* 506–518.

Peterson, C., Warren, K. L., & Short, M. M. (2011). Infantile amnesia across the years: A 2-year follow-up of children's earliest memories. *Child Development, 82*(4), 1092–1105.

Petitto, L. A. (2000). On the biological foundations of human language. In K. Emmorey & H. Lane (Eds.), *The signs of language revisited: An anthology in honor of Ursula Bellugi and Edward Klima* (pp. 447–471). Mahwah, NJ: Erlbaum.

Petrill, S. A. (1997). Molarity versus modularity of cognitive functioning? A behavioral genetic perspective. *Current Directions in Psychological Science, 6,* 96–99.

Petrill, S. A., Thompson, L. A., & Detterman, D. K. (1995). The genetic and environmental variance underlying elementary cognitive tasks. *Behavioral Genetics, 25,* 199–209.

Pfeifer, J. H., Iacoboni, M., Mazziotta, J. C., & Dapretto, M. (2008). Mirroring others' emotions relates to empathy and interpersonal competence in children. *NeuroImage, 39,* 2076–2085.

Phillips, S., King, S., & DuBois, L. C. (1978). Spontaneous activity of female versus male newborns. *Child Development, 49,* 590–597.

Piaget, J. (1930). *The child's conception of physical causality.* London: Routledge & Kegan Paul.

Piaget, J. (1946). *Le développement de la notion de temps chez l'enfant.* Paris: PUF.

Piaget, J. (1952). *The origins of intelligence in children.* New York: Norton.

Piaget, J. (1954). *The construction of reality in the child.* New York: Basic Books.

Piaget, J. (1955). *The language and thought of the child.* New York: World.

Piaget, J. (1962). *Play, dreams, and imitation in childhood.* New York: Norton.

Piaget, J. (1965). *The moral judgment of the child.* New York: Free Press. (Original work published 1932)

Piaget, J. (1969). *The child's conception of the world.* Lanham, MD: Rowman & Littlefield. (Original work published 1929)

Piaget, J. (1971). *Biology and knowledge.* Chicago: University of Chicago Press.

Piaget, J., & Inhelder, B. (1967). *The child's conception of space.* New York: Norton.

Piaget, J., & Inhelder, B. (1969). *The psychology of the child.* New York: Basic Books.

Piaget, J., & Inhelder, B. (1973). *Memory and intelligence.* New York: Basic Books.

Piasta, S. B., Justice, L. M., McGinty, A. S., & Kaderavek, J. N. (2012). Increasing young children's contact with print during shared reading: Longitudinal effects on literacy achievement. *Child Development, 83,* 810–820.

Piazza, M., Facoetti, A., Trussardi, A. N., Berteletti, I., Conte, S., & Lucangeli, D. (2010). Developmental trajectory of number acuity reveals a severe impairment in developmental dyscalculia. *Cognition, 116,* 33–41.

Pica, P., Lemer, C., Izard, V., & Dehaene, S. (2004). Exact and approximate arithmetic in an Amazonian indigene group. *Science, 306,* 499–503.

Pickering, S. J. (2006). Assessment of working memory in children. In S. J. Pickering (Ed.), *Working memory and education* (pp. 242–273). East Sussex, UK: Psychology Press.

Pierucci, J. M., O'Brien, C. T., McInnis, M. A., Gilpin, A. T., & Barber, A. B. (2014). Fantasy orientation constructs and related executive function development in preschool: Developmental benefits to executive functions by being a fantasy-oriented child. *International Journal of Behavioral Development, 38,* 62–69.

Pillemer, D. B., & White, S. H. (1989). Childhood events recalled by children and adults. In H. W. Reese (Ed.), *Advances in child development and behavior* (Vol. 21, pp. 297–340). New York: Academic.

Pillow, B. H. (1988). Young children's understanding of attentional limits. *Child Development, 59,* 31–46.

Pinker, S. (1994). *The language instinct: How the mind creates language.* New York: Morrow.

Pinker, S. (1997). *How the mind works.* New York: Norton.

Pipe, M.-E., & Salmon, K. (2009). Memory development and the forensic context. In M. L. Courage & N. Cowan (Eds.), *The development of memory in infancy and childhood* (pp. 241–282). Hove, UK: Psychology Press.

Plomin, R., DeFries, J. C., Knopik, V. S., & Niederhiser, J. M. (2012). *Behavioral genetics* (6th ed.). New York: Worth.

Plomin, R., Fulker, D. W., Corley, R., & DeFries, J. C. (1997). Nature, nurture, and cognitive development from 1 to 6 years: A parent-offspring adoption study. *Psychological Science, 8,* 442–447.

Plomin, R., & Petrill, S. A. (1997). Genetics and intelligence: What's new? *Intelligence, 24,* 53–77.

Plomin, R., & Schalkwyk, L. C. (2007). Microarrays. *Developmental Science, 10,* 19–23.

Plotkin, H. (2001). Some elements of a science of culture. In E. Whitehouse (Ed.), *The debated mind: Evolutionary psychology versus ethnography* (pp. 91–109). New York: Berg.

Plotnik, J. M., de Waal, F. B. M., & Reiss, D. (2006). Self-recognition in an Asian elephant. *Proceedings of the National Academy of Sciences, 103,* 17053–17057.

Plumert, J. M. (1995). Relation between children's overestimation of their physical abilities and accident proneness. *Developmental Psychology, 31*, 866–876.

Plumert, J. M., & Hund, A. M. (2001). The development of memory for location: What role do spatial prototypes play? *Child Development, 72*, 370–384.

Plumert, J. M., Kearney, J. K., & Cremer, J. F. (2004). Children's perception of gap avoidances: Bicycling across traffic-filled intersections in an immersive virtual environment. *Child Development, 75*, 1243–1253.

Plumert, J. M., Kearney, J. K., & Cremer, J. F. (2007). Children's road crossing: A window into perceptual-motor development. *Current Directions in Psychological Science, 16*, 255–258.

Plumert, J. M., & Schwebel, D. C. (1997). Social and temperamental influences on children's overestimation of their physical abilities: Links to accidental injuries. *Journal of Experimental Child Psychology, 67*, 317–337.

Pollak, S. D., Nelson, C. A., Schlaak, M. F., Roeber, B. J., Wewerka, S. S., Wiik, K. L., . . . Gunnar, M. R. (2010). Neurodevelopmental effects of early deprivation in postinstitutionalized children. *Child Development, 81*, 224–236.

Pons, F., Lewkowicz, D. J., Soto-Faraco, S., & Sebastian-Galles, N. (2009). Narrowing of intersensory speech perception in infancy. *Proceedings of the National Academy of Sciences, 106*, 10598–10602.

Poole, D. A. (1995). Strolling fuzzy-trace theory through eyewitness testimony (or vice versa). *Learning and Individual Differences, 7*, 87–93.

Poole, D. A., & Bruck, M. (2012). Divining testimony? The impact of interviewing props on children's reports of touching. *Developmental Review, 32*, 165–180.

Poole, D. A., & Lamb, M. E. (1998). *Investigative interviews of children: A guide for helping professionals.* Washington, DC: American Psychological Association.

Poole, D. A., & Lindsay, D. S. (2002). Reducing child witnesses' false reports of misinformation from parents. *Journal of Experimental Child Psychology, 81*, 117–140.

Poole, D. A., & White, L. (1995). Tell me again and again: Stability and change in the repeated testimonies of children and adults. In. M. S. Zaragoza, J. R. Graham, C. N. Gordon, R. Hirschman, & Y. S. Ben Porath (Eds.), *Memory and testimony in the child witness* (pp. 24–43). Newbury Park, CA: Sage.

Poulin-Dubois, D., & Forbes, J. N. (2002). Toddlers' attention to intentions-in-action in learning novel action words. *Developmental Psychology, 38*, 104–114.

Poulin-Dubois, D., Serbin, L. A., Kenyon, B., & Derbyshire, A. (1994). Infants' intermodal knowledge about gender. *Developmental Psychology, 30*, 436–442.

Povinelli, D. J., Landau, K. R., & Perilloux, H. K. (1996). Self-recognition in young children using delayed versus live feedback: Evidence of a developmental asynchrony. *Child Development, 67*, 1540–1554.

Povinelli, D. J., & Simon, B. B. (1998). Young children's understanding of briefly versus extremely delayed images of the self: Emergence of the autobiographical stance. *Developmental Psychology, 34*, 188–194.

Powell, M. B., Roberts, K. P., Ceci, S. J., & Hembrooke, H. (1999). The effects of repeated experience on children's suggestibility. *Developmental Psychology, 35*, 1462–1477.

Power, T. G. (2000). *Play and exploration in children and animals.* Hillsdale, NJ: Erlbaum.

Preissler, M. A., & Bloom, P. (2007). Two-year-olds appreciate the dual nature of pictures. *Psychological Science, 18*, 1–2.

Premack, D., & Woodruff, G. (1978). Does the chimpanzee have a theory of mind? *Behavioral and Brain Sciences, 1*, 515–526.

Prencipe, A., Kesek, A., Cohen, J., Lamm, C., Lewis, M. D., & Zelazo, P. D. (2011). Development of hot and cool executive function during the transition to adolescence. *Journal of Experimental Child Psychology, 108*(3), 621–637.

Pressley, M. (1982). Elaboration and memory development. *Child Development, 53*, 296–309.

Pressley, M., Borkowski, J. G., & Schneider, W. (1989). Good information processing: What is it and what education can do to promote it. *International Journal of Educational Research, 13*, 857–867.

Pressley, M., & Hilden, K. R. (2006). Cognitive strategies. In W. Damon & R. M. Lerner (Series Eds.) & D. Kuhn & R. S. Siegler (Vol. Eds.), *Handbook of child psychology: Vol. 2. Cognition, perception, and language* (6th ed., pp. 511–556). New York: Wiley.

Pressley, M., & Woloshyn, V. (1995). *Cognitive strategy instruction that really improves children's academic performance* (2nd ed.). Cambridge, MA: Brookline Books.

Price, T. S., Eleu, T. C., Dale, P. S., Stevenson, J., Saudfno, K., & Plomin, R. (2000). Genetic and environmental covariation between verbal and nonverbal cognitive development in infancy. *Child Development, 71*, 948–959.

Principe, G. F., Ceci, S. J., & Bruck, M. (2014). *Children's memory: Psychology and the law.* New York: Wiley.

Principe, G. F., Cherson, M., DiPuppo, J., & Schindewolf, E. (2012). Children's natural conversations following exposure to a rumor: Linkages to later false reports. *Journal of Experimental Child Psychology, 113*, 383–400.

Principe, G. F., Hafnes, B., Adkins, A., & Guiliano, S. (2010). False rumors and true belief: Memory processes underlying children's errant reports of rumored events. *Journal of Experimental Child Psychology, 107*, 407–422.

Principe, G. F., Kanaya, T., Ceci, S. J., & Singh, M. (2006). Believing is seeing: How rumors can engender false memories in preschoolers. *Psychological Science, 17*, 243–248.

Principe, G. F., & Smith, E. (2008). Seeing things unseen: Fantasy beliefs and false reports. *Journal of Cognition and Development, 9*, 89–111.

Prior, A., & MacWhinney, B. (2010). A bilingual advantage in task switching. *Bilingualism: Language and Cognition, 13*, 253–262.

Prior, H., Schwarz, A., & Gunturkun, O. (2008). Mirror-induced behavior in the magpie (*Pica pica*): Evidence of self-recognition. *PLOS Biology, 6*(8), e202.

Protzko, J., Aronson, J., & Blair, C. (2013). How to make a young child smarter: Evidence from the Database of Rising Intelligence. *Perspectives on Psychological Science, 8*, 25–40.

Provence, S., & Lipton, R. C. (1962). *Infants in institutions: A comparison of their development with family-reared infants during the first year of life.* New York: International Universities Press.

Qawasmi, A., Landeros-Weisenberger, A., & Bloch, M. H. (2013). Meta-analysis of LCPUFA supplementation of infant formula and visual acuity. *Pediatrics, 131*, e262–e272.

Quartier, V., Zimmermann, G., & Nashat, S. (2010). Sense of time in children with attention-deficit/hyperactivity disorder (ADHD). *Swiss Journal of Psychology, 69*, 7–15.

Quas, J. A., Bauer, A., & Boyce, W. T. (2004). Physiological reactivity, social support, and memory in early childhood. *Child Development, 75*, 797–814.

Quinn, P. C., Kelly, D. J., Lee, K., Pascalis, O., & Slater, A. M. (2008). Preference for attractive faces in human infants extends beyond conspecifics. *Developmental Science, 11*, 76–83.

Quinn, P. C., Yahr, J., Kuhn, A., Slater, A. M., & Pascalis, O. (2002). Representation of the gender of human faces by infants: A preference for female. *Perception, 31*, 1109–1121.

Quon, E., & Atance, C. M. (2010). A comparison of preschoolers' memory, knowledge, and anticipation of events. *Journal of Cognition and Development, 11*, 37–60.

Radesky, J. S., Silverstein, M., Zuckerman, B., & Christakis, D. A. (2014). Infant self-regulation and early childhood media exposure. *Pediatrics, 133*, e1172–e1178.

Radvansky, G. A., & Ashcraft, M. H. (2016). *Cognition* (6th ed.). Boston: Pearson.

Ramachandran, V. S. (2000). *Mirror neurons and imitation learning as the driving force behind "the great leap forward" in human evolution.* The Third Culture. Retrieved from http://www.edge.org/3rd_culture/ramachandran/ramachandran_index.html

Ramachandran, V. S., & Oberman, L. M. (2006). Broken mirrors: A theory of autism. *Scientific American, 295*, 62–69.

Raman, L., & Gelman, S. A. (2008). Do children endorse psychosocial factors in the transmission of illness and disgust? *Developmental Psychology, 44*, 801–813.

Ramani, G. B., & Siegler, R. S. (2008). Promoting broad and stable improvements in low-income children's numerical knowledge through playing number board games. *Child Development, 79*, 375–394.

Ramey, C. T., Campbell, F. A., Burchinal, M., Skinner, M. L., Gardner, D. M., & Ramey, S. L. (2000). Persistent effects of early childhood education on high-risk children and their mothers. *Applied Developmental Science, 4*, 2–14.

Ramey, C. T., Campbell, F. A., & Finkelstein, N. W. (1984). Course and structure of intellectual development in children at risk for developmental retardation. In P. H. Brooks, R. Sperber, & C. McCauley (Eds.), *Learning and cognition in the mentally retarded* (pp. 341–403). Hillsdale, NJ: Erlbaum.

Ramsey-Rennels, J. L., & Langlois, J. H. (2006). Infants' differential processing of female and male faces. *Current Directions in Psychological Science, 15*, 59–62.

Ratner, H. H. (1984). Memory demands and the development of young children's memory. *Child Development, 55*, 2173–2191.

Raven, J. C., Court, J. H., & Raven, J. H. (1975). *Manual for Raven's Progressive Matrices and Vocabulary Scales.* London: Lewis.

Raven, J. C., Raven, J. C., & Court, J. H. (2003). *Manual for Raven's Progressive Matrices and Vocabulary Scales. Section 1: General overview.* San Antonio, TX: Harcourt Assessment.

Raymond, C. L., & Benbow, C. P. (1986). Gender differences in mathematics: A function of parental support and student sex typing? *Developmental Psychology, 22*, 808–819.

Recht, D. R., & Leslie, L. (1988). Effect of prior knowledge on good and poor readers' memory of text. *Journal of Educational Psychology, 80*, 16–20.

Redcay, E., Haist, F., & Courchesne, E. (2008). Functional neuroimaging of speech perception during a pivotal period in language acquisition. *Developmental Science, 11*, 237–252.

Reed, J., Hirsh-Pasek, K., & Golinkoff, R. M. (2012). A tale of two schools: The promise of playful learning. In B. Falk (Ed.), *Defending childhood: Keeping the promise of early education* (pp. 24–47). New York: Teachers College Press.

Reeder, K. (1981). How young children learn to do things with words. In P. S. Dale & D. Ingram (Eds.), *Child language—An international perspective* (pp. 135–150). Baltimore: University Park.

Reese, E. (1995). Predicting children's literacy from mother-child conversations. *Cognitive Development, 10,* 381–405.

Reese, E. (2014). Taking the long way: Longitudinal approaches to autobiographical memory development. In P. J. Bauer & R. Fivush (Eds.), *The Wiley handbook on the development of children's memory* (Vol. 2, pp. 972–995). Chichester, UK: Wiley-Blackwell.

Reese, E., Haden, C. A., & Fivush, R. (1996). Mothers, fathers, daughters and sons: Gender differences in autobiographical reminiscing. *Research on Language and Social Interaction, 29,* 27–56.

Reese, E., Yan, C., Jack, F., & Hayne, H. (2010). Emerging identities: Narrative and self from early childhood to early adolescence. In K. C. McLean & M. Pasupathi (Eds.), *Narrative development in adolescence: Creating the storied self* (pp. 23–44). New York: Springer-Verlag.

Reiss, D., & Marino, L. (2001). Mirror self-recognition in the bottlenose dolphin: A case of cognitive convergence. *Proceedings of the National Academy of Sciences, 98,* 5937–5942.

Rennels, J. L., Kayl, A. J., Langlois, J. H., Davis, R. E., & Orlewicz, M. (2016). Asymmetries in infants' attention toward and categorization of male faces: The potential role of experience. *Journal of Experimental Child Psychology, 142,* 137–157.

Renninger, K. A. (1992). Individual interest and development: Implications for theory and practice. In K. A. Renninger, S. Hidi, & A. Krapp (Eds.), *The role of interest in learning and development* (pp. 361–398). Hillsdale, NJ: Erlbaum.

Rescorla, L., Hyson, M. C., & Hirsh-Pasek, K. (Eds.). (1991). *Academic instruction in early childhood: Challenge or pressure?* San Francisco: Jossey-Bass.

Reynolds, A. J., Mavrogenes, N. A., Bezuczko, N., & Hagemann, M. (1996). Cognitive and family-support mediators of preschool effectiveness: A confirmatory analysis. *Child Development, 67,* 1119–1140.

Reznick, J. S. (2009). Working memory in infants and toddlers. In M. L. Courage & N. Cowan (Eds.), *The development of memory in infancy and childhood* (pp. 343–365). New York: Psychology Press.

Rheingold, H. L. (1985). Development as the acquisition of familiarity. *Annual Review of Psychology, 36,* 1–17.

Richert, R., Robb, M. B., Fender, J. G., & Wartella, E. (2010). Word learning from baby videos. *Archives of Pediatric and Adolescent Medicine, 164,* 432–437.

Richland, L. E., & Burchinal, M. R. (2013). Early executive function predicts reasoning development. *Psychological Science, 24*(1), 87–92.

Richland, L. E., Chan, T.-K., Morrison, R. G., & Au, T. (2010). Young children's analogical reasoning across cultures: Similarities and differences. *Journal of Experimental Child Psychology, 105,* 146–153.

Richland, L. E., Morrison, R. G., & Holyoke, K. J. (2006). Children's development of analogical reasoning: Insights from scene analogy problems. *Journal of Experimental Child Psychology, 94,* 249–273.

Richmond, J., & Nelson, C. A. (2007). Accounting for changes in declarative memory: A cognitive neuroscience perspective. *Developmental Review, 27,* 349–373.

Rickford, J. R. (1999). *African American vernacular English.* Malden, MA: Blackwell.

Ridderinkhof, K. R., & van der Molen, M. (1995). A psychophysiological analysis of developmental differences in the ability to resist interference. *Child Development, 66,* 1040–1056.

Ridderinkhof, K. R., van der Molen, M., & Band, G. P. H. (1997). Sources of interference from irrelevant information: A developmental study. *Journal of Experimental Child Psychology, 65,* 315–341.

Rindermann, H., & Ceci, S. J. (2010). Educational policy and country outcomes in international cognitive competence studies. *Perspectives on Psychological Science, 4,* 551–577.

Ringel, B. A., & Springer, C. J. (1980). On knowing how well one is remembering: The persistence of strategy use during transfer. *Journal of Experimental Child Psychology, 29,* 322–333.

Ritchie, S. J., & Bates, T. C. (2013). Enduring links from childhood mathematics and reading achievement to adult socioeconomic status. *Psychological Science, 24,* 1301–1308.

Ritchie, S. J., Bates, T. C., & Plomin, R. (2015). Does learning to read improve intelligence? A longitudinal multivariate analysis in identical twins from age 7 to 16. *Child Development, 86,* 23–36.

Rittle-Johnson, B. (2006) Promoting transfer: Effects of self-explanation and direct instruction. *Child Development, 77,* 1–29.

Rittle-Johnson, B., & Siegler, R. S. (1999). Learning to spell: Variability, choice, and change in children's strategy use. *Child Development, 70,* 332–348.

Riva, D., & Cazzaniga, L. (1986). Late effects of unilateral brain lesions sustained before and after age one. *Neuropsychology, 24,* 423–428.

Rizzolatti, G., & Craighero, L. (2004). The mirror neuron system. *Annual Review of Neuroscience, 27,* 169–192.

Rizzolatti, G., Fadiga, L., Fogassi, L., & Gallese, V. (1996). Premotor cortex and the recognition of motor actions. *Cognitive Brain Research, 3*, 131–141.

Rizzolatti, G., Fogassi, L., & Gallese, V. (2005). Mirrors in the mind. *Scientific American, 295*, 54–61.

Robb, M. B., Richert, R., & Wartella, E. (2009). Just a talking book? Word learning from watching baby videos. *British Journal of Developmental Psychology, 27*, 27–45.

Rochat, P. (2009). *Other minds: Social origins of self-consciousness.* New York: Cambridge University Press.

Rochat, P., & Morgan, R. (1995). Spatial determinants in the perception of self-produced leg movements by 3- to 5-month-old infants. *Developmental Psychology, 31*, 626–636.

Rochat, P., & Striano, T. (2002). Who's in the mirror? Self-other discrimination in specular images by four- and nine-month-old infants. *Child Development, 73*, 35–46.

Rodríguez, P., Lago, M. O., Enesco, I., & Guerrero, S. (2013). Children's understanding of counting: Detection of errors and pseudoerrors by kindergarten and primary school children. *Journal of Experimental Child Psychology, 114*, 35–46.

Roe, K. V., Drivas, A., Karagellis, A., & Roe, A. (1985). Sex differences in vocal interaction with mother and stranger in Greek infants: Some cognitive implications. *Developmental Psychology, 21*, 372–377.

Roebers, C. M. (2002). Confidence judgments in children's and adults' event recall and suggestibility. *Developmental Psychology, 38*, 1052–1067.

Roebers, C. M., Moga, N., & Schneider, W. (2001). The role of accuracy motivation on children's and adults' event recall. *Journal of Experimental Child Psychology, 78*, 313–329.

Roebers, C. M., & Schneider, W. (2001). Individual differences in children's eyewitness recall: The influence of intelligence and shyness. *Applied Developmental Science, 5*, 9–20.

Rogoff, B. (1990). *Apprenticeship in thinking: Cognitive development in social context.* New York: Oxford University Press.

Rogoff, B. (1998). Cognition as a collaborative process. In W. Damon (Series Ed.) & D. Kuhn & R. S. Siegler (Vol. Eds.), *Handbook of child psychology: Vol 2. Cognition, perception, and language* (5th ed., pp. 679–744). New York: Wiley.

Rogoff, B. (2003). *The cultural nature of human development.* New York: Oxford University Press.

Rogoff, B., Mistry, J., Goncu, A., & Mosier, C. (1993). Guided participation in cultural activity by toddlers and caregivers. *Monographs of the Society for Research in Child Development, 58*(8, Serial No. 236).

Rogoff, B., & Waddell, K. J. (1982). Memory for information organized in a scene by children from two cultures. *Child Development, 53*, 1224–1228.

Rohwer, W. D., Jr., & Litrowink, J. (1983). Age and individual differences in the learning of a memorization procedure. *Journal of Educational Psychology, 75*, 799–810.

Roid, G. (2003). *Stanford-Binet Intelligence Scales* (5th ed.). Scarborough, Canada: Nelson Education.

Rose, S. A., & Feldman, J. F. (1995). Prediction of IQ and specific cognitive abilities at 11 years from infancy measures. *Developmental Psychology, 31*, 685–696.

Rose, S. A., Feldman, J. F., Jankowski, J. J., & Caro, D. M. (2002). A longitudinal study of visual expectation and reaction time in the first year of life. *Child Development, 73*, 47–61.

Rose, S. A., Feldman, J. F., & Wallace, I. F. (1992). Infant information processing in relation to six-year cognitive outcomes. *Child Development, 63*, 1126–1141.

Rose, S. A., Feldman, J. F., Wallace, I. F., & McCarton, C. (1989). Infant visual attention: Relation to birth status and developmental outcome during the first 5 years. *Developmental Psychology, 25*, 560–576.

Rose, S. A., Feldman, J. F., Wallace, I. F., & McCarton, C. (1991). Information processing at 1 year: Relation to birth status and developmental outcome during the first 5 years. *Developmental Psychology, 27*, 723–737.

Rose, S. A., Gottfried, A. W., & Bridger, W. H. (1981). Cross-modal transfer in 6-month-old infants. *Developmental Psychology, 17*, 661–669.

Rose, S. A., Gottfried, A. W., Melloy-Carminar, P., & Bridger, W. H. (1982). Familiarity and novelty preferences in infant recognition memory: Implications for information processing. *Developmental Psychology, 18*, 704–713.

Rosenthal, R., & Jacobson, L. (1968). *Pygmalion in the classroom: Teacher expectation and pupils' intellectual development.* New York: Rinehart and Winston.

Rosenthal, R., & Rubin, D. B. (1982). Further meta-analytic procedures for assessing cognitive gender differences. *Journal of Educational Psychology, 74*, 708–712.

Ross, J., Anderson, J. R., & Campbell, R. N. (2011). I remember me: Mnemonic self-reference effects in preschool children. *Monographs of the Society for Research in Child Development, 76*(3, Serial No. 300).

Röthlisberger, M., Neuenschwander, R., Cimeli, P., Michel, E., & Roebers, C. M. (2012). Improving executive functions in 5- and 6-year-olds: Evaluation of a small group intervention in prekindergarten and kindergarten children. *Infant and Child Development, 21*(4), 411–429.

Rothmayr, C., Sodian, B., Hajak, G., Döhnel, K., Meinhardt, J., & Sommer, M. (2011). Common and distinct neural networks for false-belief reasoning and inhibitory control. *Neuroimage, 56*(3), 1705–1713.

Rovee-Collier, C., & Cuevas, K. (2009). The development of infant memory. In M. L. Courage & N. Cowan (Eds.), *The development of memory in infancy and childhood* (pp. 11–41). New York: Psychology Press.

Rovee-Collier, C., & Giles, A. (2010). Why a neuromaturational model of memory fails: Exuberant learning in early infancy. *Behavioural Processes, 83*(2), 197–206.

Rovee-Collier, C., Schechter, A., Shyi, C.-W. G., & Shields, P. (1992). Perceptual identification of contextual attributes and infant memory retrieval. *Developmental Psychology, 28*, 307–318.

Rovee-Collier, C., & Shyi, C.-W. G. (1992). A functional and cognitive analysis of infant long-term retention. In M. L. Howe, C. J. Brainerd, & V. F. Reyna (Eds.), *Development of long-term retention* (pp. 3–55). New York: Springer-Verlag.

Rowe, D. C., Jacobson, K. C., & van der Oord, E. J. C. G. (1999). Genetic and environmental influences on vocabulary IQ: Parental education level as a moderator. *Child Development, 70*, 1151–1162.

Rowe, M. L., & Goldin-Meadow, S. (2009). Differences in early gesture explain SES disparities in child vocabulary size at school entry. *Science, 323*, 951–953.

Rubin, K. H., Fein, G., & Vandenberg, B. (1983). Play. In P. H. Mussen (Series Ed.) & E. M. Hetherington (Vol. Ed.), *Handbook of child psychology: Vol. 4. Socialization, personality, and social development* (4th ed., pp. 693–774). New York: Wiley.

Rubin, K. H., & Krasnor, L. R. (1986). Social cognitive and social behavior perspectives on problem solving. In M. Perlmutter (Ed.), *Minnesota Symposium on Child Psychology* (Vol. 18, pp. 1–68). Hillsdale, NJ: Erlbaum.

Rubinsten, O., & Henik, A. (2009). Developmental dyscalculia: Heterogeneity might not mean different mechanisms. *Trends in Cognitive Sciences, 13*, 92–99.

Rubio-Fernández, P., & Geurts, B. (2012). How to pass the false-belief task before your fourth birthday. *Psychological Science, 24*(1), 27–33.

Ruble, D. N., Balaban, T., & Cooper, J. (1981). Gender constancy and the effects of sex-typed televised toy commercials. *Child Development, 52*, 667–673.

Ruble, D. N., & Martin, C. L. (1998). Gender development. In W. Damon (Series Ed.) & N. Eisenberg (Vol. Ed.), *Handbook of child psychology: Vol. 3. Social, emotional, and personality development* (5th ed., pp. 933–1016). New York: Wiley.

Ruble, D. N., Martin, C. L., & Berenbaum, S. A. (2006). Gender development. In W. Damon & R. M. Lerner (Series Eds.) & N. Eisenberg (Vol. Ed.), *Handbook of child psychology: Vol. 3. Social, emotional, and personality development* (6th ed. pp. 858–932). Hoboken, NJ: Wiley.

Ruble, D. N., Taylor, L. J., Cyphers, L., Greulich, F. K., Lurye, L. E., & Shrout, P. E. (2007). The role of gender constancy in early gender development. *Child Development, 78*, 1121–1136.

Ruff, H. A., & Birch, H. G. (1974). Infant visual fixation: The effect of concentricity, curvilinearity, and number of directions. *Journal of Experimental Child Psychology, 17*, 460–473.

Ruffman, T. (2014). To belief or not belief: Children's theory of mind. *Developmental Review, 34*, 265–293.

Ruffman, T., Perner, J., Naito, M., Parkin, L., & Clements, W. A. (1998). Older (but not younger) siblings facilitate false belief understanding. *Developmental Psychology, 34*, 161–174.

Ruffman, T., Rustin, C., Garnham, W., & Parked, A. (2001). Source monitoring and false memories in children: Relation to certainty and executive functioning. *Journal of Experimental Child Psychology, 80*, 95–111.

Rugani, R., Fontanari, L., Simoni, E., Regolin, L., & Vallortigara, G. (2009). Arithmetic in newborn chicks. *Proceedings of the Royal Society of London, Series B, 276*, 2451–2460.

Ruiz, A. M., & Santos, L. R. (2013). Understanding differences in the way human and non-human primates represent tools: The role of teleological-intentional information. In C. M. Sanz, J. Call, & C. Boesch (Eds.), *Tool use in animals: Cognition and ecology* (pp. 119–133). Cambridge, UK: Cambridge University Press.

Russell, J., Mauthner, N., Sharpe, S., & Tidswell, T. (1991). The "windows tasks" as a measure of strategic deception in preschoolers and autistic subjects. *British Journal of Developmental Psychology, 9*, 331–349.

Russo, R., Nichelli, P., Gibertoni, M., & Cornia, C. (1995). Developmental trends in implicit and explicit memory: A picture completion study. *Journal of Experimental Child Psychology, 59*, 566–578.

Rutter, M. (2006). *Genes and behavior: Nature-nurture interplay explained.* Malden, MA: Blackwell.

Rutter, M., & the English and Romanian Adoptees Study Team. (1998). Developmental catch-up and deficit following adoptions after severe global and early deprivation. *Journal of Child Psychology and Psychiatry, 39*, 465–476.

Rutter, M., O'Connor, T. G., and the English and Romanian Adoptees (ERA) Study Team. (2004). Are there biological programming effects for psychological development? Findings from a study of Romanian adoptees. *Developmental Psychology, 40*, 81–94.

Ryan, C. (2013). *Language use in the United States: 2011: American community survey reports.* U.S. Census Bureau. Retrieved from https://www.census.gov/prod/2013pubs/acs-22.pdf

Sabbagh, M. A., Xu, F., Carlson, S. M., Moses, L. J., & Lee, K. (2006). The development of executive functioning and theory of mind. *Psychological Science, 17*, 74–81.

Sabin, E. J., Clemmer, E. J., O'Connell, D. C., & Kowal, S. (1979). A pausological approach to speech development. In A. W. Siegman & S. Feldstein (Eds.), *Of speech and time: Temporal speech patterns in interpersonal contexts* (pp. 35–55). Hillsdale, NJ: Erlbaum.

Saccuzzo, D. P., Johnson, N. E., & Guertin, T. L. (1994). Information processing in gifted versus non-gifted African American, Latino, Filipino, and white children: Speeded versus nonspeeded paradigms. *Intelligence, 19*, 219–243.

Sachs, J. (1977). The adaptive significance of linguistic input to prelinguistic infants. In C. E. Snow & C. A. Ferguson (Eds.), *Talking to children: Language input and acquisition* (pp. 51–61). Cambridge, UK: Cambridge University Press.

Sackett, P. R., Hardison, C. M., & Cullen, M. J. (2004). On interpreting stereotype threat as accounting for African American–white differences on cognitive tests. *American Psychologist, 59*, 7–13.

Sacks, O. (1985). *The man who mistook his wife for a hat.* New York: Touchstone Books.

Sacks, O. (1989). *Seeing voices: A journey into the world of the deaf.* New York: Harper Perennial.

Saffran, J. R., Aslin, R. N., & Newport, E. L. (1996). Statistical learning by 8-month-old infants. *Science, 274*, 1926–1928.

Saffran, J. R., Johnson, E. K., Aslin, R. N., & Newport, E. L. (1999). Statistical learning of tone sequences by human infants and adults. *Cognition, 70*, 27–52.

Saffran, J. R., Werker, J., & Werner, L. A. (2006). The infant's auditory world: Hearing, speech and the beginnings of language. In W. Damon & R. M. Lerner (Series Eds.) & D. Kuhn & R. S. Siegler (Vol. Eds.), *Handbook of child psychology: Vol. 2. Cognition, perception, and language* (6th ed., pp. 58–106). New York: Wiley.

Sakai, K. L. (2005). Language acquisition and brain development. *Science, 310*, 815–919.

Salapatek, P. (1975). Pattern perception in early infancy. In L. B. Cohen & P. Salapatek (Eds.), *Infant perception: From sensation to cognition* (Vol. 1, pp. 133–248). New York: Academic.

Salapatek, P., & Kessen, W. (1966). Visual scanning of triangles by the human newborn. *Journal of Experimental Child Psychology, 3*, 155–167.

Salatas, H., & Flavell, J. H. (1976). Behavioral and metamnemonic indicators of strategic behaviors under remember instructions in first grade. *Child Development, 47*, 81–89.

Salmon, K., Champion, F., Pipe, M., Mewton, L., & McDonald, S. (2008). The child in time: The influence of parent-child discussion about a future experience on how it is remembered. *Memory, 16*, 485–499.

Salmon, K., & Pipe, M.-E. (1997). Props and children's event reports: The impact of a 1-year delay. *Journal of Experimental Child Psychology, 65*, 261–292.

Sameroff, A. J. (2009). The transactional model. In A. Sameroff (Ed.), *The transactional model of development: How children and contexts shape each other* (pp. 23–32). Washington, DC: American Psychological Association.

Sameroff, A. J. (2010). A unified theory of development: A dialectic integration of nature and nurture. *Child Development, 81*, 6–22.

Sameroff, A. J., & Chandler, M. J. (1975). Reproductive risk and the continuum of caretaking causality. In F. D. Horowitz (Ed.), *Review of child development research* (Vol. 4, pp. 187–244). Chicago: University of Chicago Press.

Sameroff, A. J., Seifer, R., Baldwin, A., & Baldwin, C. (1993). Stability of intelligence from preschool to adolescence: The influence of social risk factors. *Child Development, 64*, 80–97.

Sandman, C. A., Washwa, P., Hetrick, W., Porto, M., & Peeke, H. V. S. (1997). Human fetal heart rate dishabituation between thirty and thirty-two weeks gestation. *Developmental Psychology, 68*, 1031–1040.

Sarsour, K., Sheridan, M., Jutte, D., Nuru-Jeter, A., Hinshaw, S., & Boyce, W. T. (2011). Family socioeconomic status and child executive functions: The roles of language, home environment, and single parenthood. *Journal of the International Neuropsychological Society, 17*(1), 120–132.

Savage-Rumbaugh, E. S., Murphy, J., Sevcik, R. A., Brakke, K. E., Williams, S. L., & Rumbaugh, D. M. (1993). Language comprehension in ape and child. *Monographs of the Society for Research in Child Development, 58*(3–4, Serial No. 233).

Sawyer, A. C. P., Miller-Lewis, L. R., Searle, A. K., Sawyer, M. G., & Lunch, A. W. (2015). Is greater improvement in early self-regulation associated with fewer behavioral problems later in childhood? *Developmental Psychology, 51*, 1740–1755.

Scammon, R. E. (1930). The measurement of the body in childhood. In J. A. Harris, C. M. Jackson, D. G. Paterson, & R. E. Scammon (Eds.), *The measurement of man* (pp. 173–215). Minneapolis: University of Minnesota Press.

Scarf, D., Gross, J., Colombo, M., & Hayne, H. (2013). To have and to hold: Episodic memory in 3- and 4-year-old children. *Developmental Psychobiology, 55*, 125–132.

Scarr, S. (1992). Developmental theories for the 1990s: Development and individual differences. *Child Development, 63*, 1–19.

Scarr, S. (1993). Biological and cultural diversity: The legacy of Darwin for development. *Child Development, 64*, 1333–1353.

Scarr, S., & McCartney, K. (1983). How people make their own environments: A theory of genotype-environment effects. *Child Development, 54*, 424–435.

Scarr, S., & Weinberg, R. A. (1976). IQ test performance of black children adopted by white families. *American Psychologist, 31*, 726–739.

Scarr, S., & Weinberg, R. A. (1978). The influence of "family background" on intellectual attainment. *American Sociological Review, 43*, 674–692.

Schaal, B., Marlier, L., & Soussignan, R. (2000). Human fetuses learn odors from their pregnant mother's diet. *Chemical Senses, 25*, 729–737.

Schacter, D. L. (1992). Understanding implicit memory. *American Psychologist, 47*, 559–569.

Schacter, D. L., Norman, K. A., & Koutstaal, W. (2000). The cognitive neuroscience of constructive memory. In D. F. Bjorklund (Ed.), *False-memory creation in children and adults: Theory, research, and implications* (pp. 129–168). Mahwah, NJ: Erlbaum.

Schafer, G., & Plunkett, K. (1998). Rapid word learning by fifteen-month-olds under tightly controlled conditions. *Child Development, 69*, 309–320.

Schalke, D., Brunner, M., Geiser, C., Preckel, F., Keller, U., Spengler, M., & Martin, R. (2012). Stability and change in intelligence from age 12 to age 52: Results from the Luxembourg MAGRIP Study. *Developmental Psychology, 49*, 1529–1543.

Schanberg, S. M., & Field, T. M. (1987). Sensory deprivation stress and supplemental stimulation in the rat pup and preterm human. *Child Development, 58*, 1431–1447.

Schauble, L. (1990). Belief revision in children: The role of prior knowledge and strategies for generating evidence. *Journal of Experimental Child Psychology, 49*, 31–57.

Schauble, L. (1996). The development of scientific reasoning in knowledge-rich context. *Developmental Psychology, 32*, 102–119.

Schellenberg, E. G., & Trehub, S. E. (1996). Natural musical intervals: Evidence from infant listeners. *Psychological Science, 5*, 272–277.

Schellenberg, E. G., & Trehub, S. E. (1999). Culture-general and culture-specific factors in the discrimination of melodies. *Journal of Experimental Child Psychology, 74*, 107–127.

Schirduan, V., & Case, K. S. (2004). Mindful curriculum leadership for students with attention deficit hyperactivity disorder: Leading in elementary schools by using Multiple Intelligences Theory (SUMIT). *Teachers College Record, 106*, 87–95.

Schlagmuller, M., & Schneider, W. (2002). The development of organizational strategies in children: Evidence from a microgenetic longitudinal study. *Journal of Experimental Child Psychology, 81*, 298–319.

Schlam, T. R., Wilson, N. L., Shoda, Y., Mischel, W., & Ayduk, O. (2013). Preschoolers' delay of gratification predicts their body mass 30 years later. *Journal of Pediatrics, 162*, 90–93.

Schliemann, A. D. (1992). Mathematical concepts in and out of school in Brazil: From developmental psychology to better teaching. *Newsletter of the International Society for the Study of Behavioural Development* (2, Serial No. 22), 1–3.

Schlottmann, A., & Ray, E. (2010). Goal attribution to schematic animals: Do 6-month-olds perceive biological motion as animate? *Developmental Science, 13*, 1–10.

Schmidt, F. L., & Hunter, J. (2004). General mental ability in the world of work: Occupational attainment and job performance. *Journal of Personality and Social Psychology, 86*, 162–173.

Schneider, W. (1986). The role of conceptual knowledge and metamemory in the development of organizational processes in memory. *Journal of Experimental Child Psychology, 42*, 218–236.

Schneider, W. (2015). *Memory development from early childhood to early adulthood.* New York: Springer.

Schneider, W., & Artelt, C. (2010). Metacognition and mathematics education. *ZDM Mathematics Education, 42*(2), 149–161.

Schneider, W., & Bjorklund, D. F. (1992). Expertise, aptitude, and strategic remembering. *Child Development, 63*, 461–473.

Schneider, W., & Bjorklund, D. F. (1998). Memory. In W. Damon (Series Ed.) & D. Kuhn & R. S. Siegler (Vol. Eds.), *Handbook of child psychology: Vol 2. Cognition, perception, and language* (5th ed., pp. 467–521). New York: Wiley.

Schneider, W., Bjorklund, D. F., & Maier-Brückner, W. (1996). The effects of expertise and IQ on children's memory: When knowledge is, and when it is not enough. *International Journal of Behavioral Development, 19*, 773–796.

Schneider, W., & Bullock, M. (Eds.). (2009). *Human development from early childhood to early adulthood: Findings from a 20-year longitudinal study.* New York: Psychology Press.

Schneider, W., Gruber, H., Gold, A., & Opwis, K. (1993). Chess expertise and memory for chess positions in children and adults. *Journal of Experimental Child Psychology, 56,* 328–349.

Schneider, W., Knopf, M., & Sodian, B. (2009). Verbal memory development from early childhood to early adulthood. In W. Schneider & M. Bullock (Eds.), *Human development from early childhood to early adulthood: Findings from a 20-year longitudinal study* (pp. 63–90). New York: Psychology Press.

Schneider, W., Körkel, J., & Weinert, F. E. (1989). Domain-specific knowledge and memory performance: A comparison of high- and low-aptitude children. *Journal of Educational Psychology, 81,* 306–312.

Schneider, W., Kron, V., Hunnerkopf, M., & Krajewski, K. (2004). The development of young children's memory strategies: Findings from the Wurzburg Longitudinal Memory Study. *Journal of Experimental Child Psychology, 88,* 193–209.

Schneider, W., Kron-Sperl, V., & Hunnerkopf, M. (2009). The development of young children's memory strategies: Evidence from the Wurzburg Longitudinal Memory Study. *European Journal of Developmental Psychology, 6,* 70–99.

Schneider, W., & Lockl, K. (2002). The development of metacognitive knowledge in children and adolescents. In T. Perfect & B. Schwartz (Eds.), *Applied metacognition* (pp. 224–257). Cambridge, UK: Cambridge University Press.

Schneider, W., Schlagmuller, M., & Vise, M. (1998). The impact of metamemory and domain-specific knowledge on memory performance. *European Journal of Psychology of Education, 13,* 91–103.

Schröder, L., Keller, H., Kärtner, J., Kleis, A., Abels, M., Yovsi, R. D., . . . Papaligoura, A. (2013). Early reminiscing in cultural contexts: Cultural models, maternal reminiscing styles, and children's memories. *Journal of Cognition and Development, 14,* 10–34.

Schroeder, M., Graham, S. A., McKeough, A., Stock, H., & Palmer, J. (2010). Gender differences in preschoolers' understanding of the concept of life. *Journal of Early Childhood Research, 8*(3), 227–238.

Schulman, A. H., & Kaplowitz, C. (1977). Mirror-image response during the first two years of life. *Developmental Psychobiology, 10,* 133–142.

Schumann-Hengsteler, R. (1992). The development of visuospatial memory: How to remember location. *International Journal of Behavioral Development, 15,* 445–471.

Schwanenflugel, P. J., Hamilton, C. E., Neutharth-Pritchard, S., Restrepo, A. A., Bradley, B. A., & Webb, M.-Y. (2010). Paved for Success: An evaluation of a comprehensive preliteracy program for four-year-old children. *Journal of Literacy Research, 42*(3), 227–275.

Schwanenflugel, P. J., & Knapp, N. F. (2016). *The psychology of reading: Theory and applications.* New York: Guilford Press.

Schwenck, C., Bjorklund, D. F., & Schneider, W. (2007). Factors influencing the incidence of utilization deficiencies and other patterns of recall/strategy-use relations in a strategic memory task. *Child Development, 78,* 1771–1787.

Schwenck, C., Bjorklund, D. F., & Schneider, W. (2009). Developmental and individual differences in young children's use and maintenance of a selective memory strategy. *Developmental Psychology, 45,* 1034–1050.

Sclafani, V., Paukner, A., Suomi, S. J., & Ferari, P. F. (2015). Imitation promotes affiliation in infant macaques at risk for impaired social behaviors. *Developmental Science, 18,* 614–621.

Searle, J. R. (1992). *The rediscovery of the mind.* Cambridge, MA: MIT Press.

Seed, A., & Byrne, R. (2010). Animal tool-use. *Current biology, 20*(23), R1032–R1039.

Segal, N. (2000). Virtual twins: New findings on within-family environmental influences on intelligence. *Journal of Educational Psychology, 92,* 442–448.

Senden, M. von (1960). *Space and sight: The perception of space and shape in the congenitally blind before and after operation.* Glencoe, IL: Free Press.

Sénéchal, M., & LeFevre, J.-A. (2002). Parental involvement in the development of children's reading skills: A 50-year longitudinal study. *Child Development, 73,* 445–460.

Sénéchal, M., & LeFevre, J.-A. (2014). Continuity and change in the home literacy environment as predictors of growth in vocabulary and reading. *Child Development, 85,* 1552–1568.

Senghas, A., & Coppola, M. (2001). Children creating language: How Nicaraguan Sign Language acquired a spatial grammar. *Psychological Science, 12,* 323–326.

Senghas, A., Kita, S., & Ozyurek, A. (2004). Children creating core properties of language: Evidence from an emerging sign language in Nicaragua. *Science, 305,* 1179–1782.

Serbin, L. A., & Sprafkin, C. (1986). The saliency of gender and the process of sex typing in three- to seven-year-old children. *Child Development, 57,* 1188–1199.

Sercombe, H. (2014). Risk, adaptation and the functional teenage brain. *Brain and Cognition, 89,* 61–69.

Seress, L. (2001). Morphological changes of the human hippocampal formation from midgestation to early childhood. In C. A. Nelson & M. Luciana (Eds.), *Handbook of developmental cognitive neuroscience* (pp. 45–58). Cambridge, MA: MIT Press.

Seymour, P. H. K., Aro, M., & Erskine, J. M. (2003). Foundations of literacy acquisition in European orthographies. *British Journal of Psychology, 94,* 143–174.

Shackelford, T. K., & Larsen, R. J. (1997). Facial asymmetry as an indicator of psychological, emotional, and physiological distress. *Journal of Personality and Social Psychology, 72,* 456–466.

Shahaeian, A., Peterson, C. C., Slaughter, V., & Wellman, H. M. (2011). Culture and the sequence of steps in theory of mind development. *Developmental Psychology, 47*(5), 1239.

Shatz, M. (1983). Communication. In P. H. Mussen (Series Ed.) & J. H. Flavell & E. M. Markman (Vol. Eds.), *Handbook of child psychology: Vol. 3. Cognitive development* (4th ed., pp. 495–555). New York: Wiley.

Shatz, M., & Gelman, R. (1973). The development of communication skills. *Monographs of the Society for Research in Child Development, 38*(5, Serial No. 152).

Shaw, P., Eckstrand, K., Sharp, W., Blumenthal, J., Lerch, J. P., Greenstein, D., . . . Rapoport, J. L. (2007). Attention-deficit/hyperactivity disorder is characterized by a delay in cortical maturation. *Proceedings of the National Academy of Sciences, 104,* 19649–19654.

Shaw, P., Greenstein, D., Lerch, J., Clasen, L., Lenroot, R., Gogtay, N., . . . Giedd, J. (2006). Intellectual ability and cortical development in children and adolescents. *Nature, 440,* 676–679.

Shaywitz, S. E., Mody, M., & Shaywitz, B. A. (2006). Neural mechanisms in dyslexia. *Current Directions in Psychological Science, 15,* 278–281.

Shaywitz, S. E., Shaywitz, B. A., Pugh, K. R., Fulbright, R. K., Constable, R. T., Mencl, W. E., . . . Gore, J. C. (1998). Functional disruption in the organization of the brain for reading in dyslexia. *Proceedings of the National Academy of Sciences, 95,* 2636–2641.

Sheppard, L. D., & Vernon, P. A. (2008). Intelligence and speed of information-processing: A review of 50 years of research. *Personality and Individual Differences, 44,* 535–551.

Shin, H.-E., Bjorklund, D. F., & Beck, E. F. (2007). The adaptive nature of children's overestimation in a strategic memory task. *Cognitive Development, 22,* 197–212.

Shinskey, J. L., & Munakata, Y. (2005). Familiarity breeds searching: Infants reverse their novelty preferences when reaching for hidden objects. *Psychological Science, 16,* 596–600.

Shoda, Y., Mischel, W., & Peake, P. K. (1990). Predicting adolescent cognitive and social competence from preschool delay of gratification: Identifying diagnostic conditions. *Developmental Psychology, 26,* 978–986.

Shore, J. R. (2004). Teacher education and multiple intelligences: A case study of multiple intelligences and teacher efficacy in two teacher preparation courses. *Teachers College Record, 106,* 112–139.

Shore, T. J. (2014). The adult brain makes new neurons, and effortful learning keeps them alive. *Current Directions in Psychological Science, 23,* 311–318.

Shtulman, A., & Valcarcel, J. (2012). Scientific knowledge suppresses but does not supplant earlier intuitions. *Cognition, 124*(2), 209–215.

Shusterman, A., Lee, S. A., & Spelke, E. S. (2008). Young children's spontaneous use of geometry in maps. *Developmental Science, 11,* F1–F7.

Shutts, K., Banaji, M. R., & Spelke, E. S. (2010). Social categories guide young children's preferences for novel objects. *Developmental Science, 13,* 599–610.

Shwe, H. I., & Markman, E. M. (1997). Young children's appreciation of the mental impact of their communicative signals. *Developmental Psychology, 33,* 630–636.

Siegal, M. (1997). *Knowing children: Experiments in conversation and cognition.* Hove, UK: Psychology Press.

Siegal, M. (2008). *Marvelous minds: The discovery of what children know.* Oxford, UK: Oxford University Press.

Siegal, M., & Share, D. L. (1990). Contamination sensitivity in young children. *Developmental Psychology, 26,* 455–458.

Siegel, L. S. (1993). The cognitive basis of dyslexia. In R. Pasnak & M. L. Howe (Eds.), *Emerging themes in cognitive development: Competencies* (Vol. 2, pp. 33–52). New York: Springer-Verlag.

Siegel, L. S., & Ryan, E. B. (1988). Development of grammatical-sensitivity, phonological, and short-term memory skills in normally achieving and learning disabled children. *Developmental Psychology, 24,* 28–37.

Siegel, L. S., & Ryan, E. B. (1989). The development of working memory in normally achieving and subtypes of learning disabled children. *Child Development, 60,* 973–980.

Siegler, R. S. (1996). *Emerging minds: The process of change in children's thinking.* New York: Oxford University Press.

Siegler, R. S. (2000). The rebirth of children's learning. *Child Development, 71,* 26–35.

Siegler, R. S. (2002). Microgenetic studies of self-explanation. In N. Garnott & J. Parziale (Eds.), *Microdevelopment: A process-oriented perspective for studying development and learning* (pp. 31–58). Cambridge, MA: Cambridge University Press.

Siegler, R. S. (2006). Microgenetic analyses of learning. In W. Damon & R. M. Lerner (Series Eds.) & D. Kuhn & R. S. Siegler (Vol. Eds.), *Handbook of child psychology:*

Vol. 2. Cognition, perception, and language (6th ed., pp. 464–510). New York: Wiley.

Siegler, R. S., & Jenkins, E. (1989). *How children discover strategies*. Hillsdale, NJ: Erlbaum.

Siegler, R. S., & Lortie-Forgues, H. (2014). An integrative theory of numerical development. *Child Development Perspectives, 8,* 144–150.

Siegler, R. S., & Mu, Y. (2008). Chinese children excel on novel mathematics problems even before elementary school. *Psychological Science, 19,* 759–763.

Siegler, R. S., & Opfer, J. (2003). The development of numerical estimation: Evidence for multiple representations of numerical quantity. *Psychological Science, 14,* 237–243.

Siegler, R. S., & Ramani, G. B. (2009). Playing linear number board games—but not circular ones—improves low-income preschoolers' numerical understanding. *Journal of Educational Psychology, 101,* 545–560.

Siegler, R. S., & Shrager, J. (1984). Strategy choices in addition and subtraction: How do children know what to do? In C. Sophian (Ed.), *Origins of cognitive skills* (pp. 229–260). Hillsdale, NJ: Erlbaum.

Siegler, R. S., Thompson, C. A., & Schneider, M. (2011). An integrated theory of whole number and fractions development. *Cognitive Psychology, 62,* 273–296.

Signorella, M. L., Bigler, R. S., & Liben, L. S. (1993). Developmental differences in children's gender schemata about others: A meta-analytic review. *Developmental Review, 13,* 147–183.

Silverman, I., & Eals, M. (1992). Sex differences in spatial abilities: Evolutionary theory and data. In J. H. Barkow, L. Cosmides, & J. Tooby (Eds.), *The adapted mind: Evolutionary psychology and the generation of culture* (pp. 229–293). New York: Oxford University Press.

Simcock, G., & DeLoache, J. (2006). Get the picture? The effects of iconicity on toddlers' reenactment from picture books. *Developmental Psychology, 42,* 1352–1357.

Simcock, G., & Hayne, H. (2002). Breaking the barrier? Children fail to translate their preverbal memories into language. *Psychological Science, 13,* 225–231.

Simon, T. J., Hespos, S. J., & Rochat, P. (1995). Do infants understand simple arithmetic? A replication of Wynn (1992). *Cognitive Development, 10,* 253–269.

Simpson, E. A., Murray, L., Paukner, A., & Ferrar, P. F. (2014). The mirror neuron system as revealed through neonatal imitation: Presence from birth, predictive power and evidence of plasticity. *Philosophical Transactions of the Royal Society B, 369,* 1–12.

Singh, A., Uijtdewilligen, L., Twisk, J. W. R., van Mechelen, W., Mai, J. M., & Chinapaw, M. J. M. (2012). Physical activity and performance at school: A systematic review of the literature including a methodological quality assessment. *Archives of Pediatric Adolescent Medicine, 166,* 49–55.

Singh, L., Fu, C. S., Rahman, A. A., Hameed, W. B., Sanmugam, S., Agarwal, P., . . . & Rifkin-Graboi, A. (2015). Back to basics: A bilingual advantage in infant visual habituation. *Child Development, 86*(1), 294–302.

Sjöwall, D., Roth, L., Lindqvist, S., & Thorell, L. B. (2013). Multiple deficits in ADHD: Executive dysfunction, delay aversion, reaction time variability, and emotional deficits. *Journal of Child Psychology and Psychiatry, 54*(6), 619–627.

Skeels, H. M. (1966). Adult status of children with contrasting early life experiences. *Monographs of the Society for Research in Child Development, 31*(3, Serial No. 105).

Skinner, B. F. (1957). *Verbal behavior.* New York: Appleton-Century-Crofts.

Skoczenski, A. M., & Norcia, A. M. (2002). Late maturation of visual hyperacuity. *Psychological Science, 13,* 537–541.

Skolnick, D., & Bloom, P. (2006). What does Batman think about SpongeBob? Children's understanding of the fantasy/fantasy distinction. *Cognition, 101*(1), B9–B18.

Skolnick Weisberg, D., & Bloom, P. (2009). Young children separate multiple pretend worlds. *Developmental Science, 12*(5), 699–705.

Skouteris, H., Spataro, J., & Lazaridis, M. (2006). Young children's use of a delayed video representation to solve a retrieval problem pertaining to self. *Developmental Science, 9,* 505–517.

Skwarchuk, S.-L., Sowinski, C., & LeFevre, J.-A. (2014). Formal and informal home learning activities in relation to children's early numeracy and literacy skills: The development of a home numeracy model. *Journal of Experimental Child Psychology, 121,* 63–84.

Slaby, R. G., & Frey, K. S. (1975). Development of gender constancy and selective attention to same-sex models. *Child Development, 46,* 849–856.

Slaby, R. G., & Guerra, N. G. (1988). Cognitive mediators of aggression in adolescent offenders: 1. Assessment. *Developmental Psychology, 24,* 580–588.

Slater, A. M. (1995). Visual perception and memory at birth. In C. Rovee-Collier & L. P. Lipsitt (Eds.), *Advances in infancy research* (Vol. 9, pp. 107–162). Norwood, NJ: Ablex.

Slater, A. M., Mattock, A., & Brown, E. (1990). Size constancy at birth: Newborn infants' responses to retinal and real size. *Journal of Experimental Child Psychology, 49,* 314–322.

Slater, A. M., Mattock, A., Brown, E., & Bremner, G. J. (1991). Form perception at birth: Cohen and Younger (1984) revisited. *Journal of Experimental Child Psychology, 51,* 395–406.

Slater, A. M., Quinn, P. C., Hayes, R., & Brown, E. (2000). The role of facial orientation in newborn infants' preference for attractive faces. *Developmental Science, 3,* 181–185.

Slater, A. M., Von der Schulenburgb, C., Brown, E., Badenochb, M., Butterworth, G., & Parsons, S. (1998). Newborn infants prefer attractive faces. *Infant Behavior and Development, 21,* 345–354.

Slaughter, V., Jaakkola, K., & Carey, S. (1999). Constructing a coherent theory: Children's biological understanding of life and death. In M. Siegel & C. Peterson (Eds.), *Children's understanding of biology and health* (pp. 71–98). Cambridge, UK: Cambridge University Press.

Slaughter, V., & Perez-Zapata, D. (2014). Cultural variation in the development of mind reading. *Child Development Perspectives, 8,* 237–241.

Slobin, D. I. (1970). Universals of grammatical development in children. In G. B. Flores, J. Arcais, & W. J. M. Levelt (Eds.), *Advances in psycholinguistics* (pp. 174–186). Amsterdam, Netherlands: North-Holland.

Smith, E. D., & Lillard, A. S. (2012). Play on: Retrospective evidence for the persistence of pretend play into middle childhood. *Journal of Cognition and Development, 13*(4), 524–549.

Smith, P. K. (1982). Does play matter? Functional and evolutionary aspects of animal and human play. *Behavioral and Brain Sciences, 5,* 139–184.

Smith, P. K. (2005). Social and pretend play in children. In A. D. Pellegrini & P. K. Smith (Eds.), *Play in humans and great apes* (pp. 173–209). Mahwah, NJ: Erlbaum.

Smith, P. K., & Dutton, S. (1979). Play and training in direct and innovative problem solving. *Child Development, 50,* 830–836.

Smith, R. E., Bayen, U. J., & Martin, C. (2010). The cognitive processes underlying event-based prospective memory in school age children and young adults: A formal model-based study. *Developmental Psychology, 46,* 230–244.

Snedecker, J., Geren, J., & Shafto, C. L. (2007). Starting over: International adoption as a natural experiment in language development. *Psychological Science, 18,* 79–87.

Snow, C. E. (1972). Mother's speech to children learning language. *Child Development, 43,* 549–565.

Snow, C. E., Arlman-Rupp, A., Hassing, Y., Jobse, J., Joosten, J., & Vorster, J. (1976). Mothers' speech in three social classes. *Journal of Psycholinguistic Research, 5,* 1–20.

Snow, C. E., & Ferguson C. A. (Eds.). (1977). *Talking to children: Language input and acquisition.* Cambridge, UK: Cambridge University Press.

Snow, C. E., & Yusun Kang, J. (2006). Becoming bilingual, biliterate, and bicultural. In W. Damon (Series Ed.) &

K. A. Renninger & I. E. Sigel (Vol. Eds.), *Handbook of child psychology: Vol. 4. Child psychology in practice* (6th ed., pp. 75–102). New York: Wiley.

Sodian, B., Kristen, S. E., & Licata, M. (2015). *The longitudinal relation of implicit and explicit false belief understanding.* Presented at Bienniel Meeting of the Society for Research in Child Development, Philadelphia, PA.

Sodian, B., & Kristen-Antonow, S. (2015). Declarative joint attention as a foundation of theory of mind. *Developmental Psychology, 51,* 1190–1200.

Sodian, B., & Schneider, W. (1999). Memory strategy development: Gradual increase, sudden insight, or roller coaster? In F. E. Weinert & W. Schneider (Eds.), *Individual development from 3 to 12: Findings from the Munich longitudinal study* (pp. 61–77). Cambridge, UK: Cambridge University Press.

Sodian, B., Schneider, W., & Perlmutter, M. (1986). Recall, clustering, and metamemory in young children. *Journal of Experimental Child Psychology, 41,* 395–410.

Sodian, B., Taylor, C., Harris, P. L., & Perner, J. (1991). Early deception and the child's theory of mind: False trails and genuine markers. *Child Development, 62,* 468–483.

Soley, G., & Hannon, E. E. (2010). Infants prefer the musical meter of their own culture: A cross-cultural comparison. *Developmental Psychology, 46,* 286–292.

Somerville, S. C., Wellman, H. M., & Cultice, J. C. (1983). Young children's deliberate reminding. *Journal of Genetic Psychology, 143,* 87–96.

Sonuga-Barke, E. J. S. (2002). Psychological heterogeneity in ADHD—A dual pathway model of behaviour and cognition. *Behavioural Brain Research, 130,* 29–36.

Southgate, V., Johnson, M. H., Osborne, T., & Csibra, G. (2009). Predictive motor activation during action observation in human infants. *Biology Letters, 5,* 769–772.

Southgate, V., & Vernetti A. (2014). Belief-based action prediction in preverbal infants. *Cognition, 130,* 1–10.

Sowell, E. R., Trauner, D. A., Gamst, A., & Jernigan, T. L. (2002). Development of cortical and subcortical brain structures in childhood and adolescence: A structural MRI study. *Developmental Medicine & Child Neurology, 44,* 4–16.

Spear, L. P. (2000). Neurobehavioral changes in adolescence. *Current Directions in Psychological Science, 9,* 111–114.

Spear, L. P. (2007). Brain development and adolescent behavior. In D. Coch, K. W. Fischer, & G. Dawson (Eds.), *Human behavior, learning, and the developing brain: Typical development* (pp. 362–396). New York: Guilford Press.

Spearman, C. (1927). *The abilities of man.* New York: Macmillan.

Spelke, E. S. (1976). Infants' intermodal perception of events. *Cognitive Psychology, 5*, 553–560.

Spelke, E. S. (1985). Perception of unity, persistence and identity: Thoughts on infants' conceptions of objects. In J. Mehler & R. Fox (Eds.), *Neonate cognition* (pp. 89–113). Hillsdale, NJ: Erlbaum.

Spelke, E. S. (2000). Core knowledge. *American Psychologist, 55*, 1233–1243.

Spelke, E. S., & Cortelyou, A. (1981). Perceptual aspects of social knowing: Looking and listening in infancy. In M. E. Lamb & L. R. Sherrod (Eds.), *Infant social cognition: Empirical and theoretical considerations* (pp. 61–84). Hillsdale, NJ: Erlbaum.

Spelke, E. S., & Kinzler, K. D. (2007). Core knowledge. *Developmental Science, 10*, 89–96.

Spelke, E. S., & Newport, E. L. (1998). Nativism, empiricism, and the development of knowledge. In W. Damon (Series Ed.) & R. Learner (Vol. Ed.), *Handbook of child psychology: Vol. 1. Theories of theoretical models of human development* (5th ed., pp. 275–340). New York: Wiley.

Spence, M. J. (1996). Young infants' long-term auditory memory: Evidence for changes in preference as a function of delay. *Developmental Psychobiology, 29*, 685–695.

Spencer, J. P., Blumberg, M. S., McMurray, B., Robinson, S. R., Samuelson, L. K., & Tomblin, J. B. (2009). Short arms and talking legs: Why we should no longer abide the nativist-empincist debate. *Child Development Perspectives, 3*, 79–87.

Spinath, B., Pinath, F. M., Harlaar, N., & Plomin, R. (2006). Predicting school achievement from general cognitive ability, self-perceived ability, and intrinsic value. *Intelligence, 34*, 363–374.

Spitz, R. (1945). Hospitalism: An inquiry into the genesis of psychiatric conditions in early childhood. *Psychoanalytic Study of the Child, 1*, 53–74.

Springer, K. (1999). How a naive theory of biology is acquired. In M. Siegal & C. C. Peterson (Eds.), *Children's understanding of biology and health* (pp. 45–70). Cambridge, UK: Cambridge University Press.

Stake, J. E., & Nickens, S. D. (2005). Adolescent girls' and boys' science peer relationship and perceptions of the possible self as scientist. *Sex Roles, 52*, 1–12.

Stanley, J. C., Benbow, C. P., Brody, L. E., Dauber, S., & Lupkowski, A. E. (1992). Gender differences on eighty-six nationally standardized aptitude and achievement tests. In N. Coangelo, S. G. Assouline, & D. L. Ambroson (Eds.), *Talent development* (pp. 42–65). Unionville, NY: Trillium.

Stanovich, K. E. (1986). Matthew effects in reading: Some consequences of individual differences in the acquisition of literacy. *Reading Research Quarterly, 21*, 360–406.

Steele, C. M. (1997). A threat in the air: How stereotypes shape intellectual identity and performance. *American Psychologist, 52*, 613–629.

Steele, C. M., & Aronson, J. (1995). Stereotype threat and the intellectual test performance of African Americans. *Journal of Social and Personality Psychology, 69*, 797–811.

Steiner, J. E. (1979). Human facial expressions in response to taste and smell stimulation. In H. W. Reese & L. P. Lipsitt (Eds.), *Advances in child development and behavior* (Vol. 13, pp. 257–295). New York: Academic.

Stern, D. N., Spieker, S., Barnett, R. K., & MacKain, K. (1983). The prosody of maternal speech: Infant age and context related changes. *Journal of Child Language, 10*, 1–15.

Sternberg, R. J. (1985). *Beyond IQ: A triarchic theory of human intelligence*. Cambridge, UK: Cambridge University Press.

Sternberg, R. J. (1988). *The triarchic mind: A new theory of human intelligence*. New York: Viking.

Sternberg, R. J. (2004). Culture and intelligence. *American Psychologist, 59*, 325–338.

Sternberg, R. J. (2005). The theory of successful intelligence. *Interamerican Journal of Psychology, 39*, 189–202.

Sternberg, R. J. (2011). The theory of successful intelligence. In R. J. Sternberg & S. B. Kaufman (Eds.), *The Cambridge handbook of intelligence* (pp. 504–527). Cambridge, UK: Cambridge University Press.

Sternberg, R. J. (2014). The development of adaptive competence: Why cultural psychology is necessary and not just nice. *Developmental Review, 34*, 208–224.

Sternberg, R. J., Ferrari, M., & Clinkenbeard, P. (1996). Identification, instruction, and assessment of gifted children: A construct validation of a triarchic model. *Gifted Child Quarterly, 40*, 129–137.

Sternberg, R. J., & the Rainbow Project Collaborators. (2006). The Rainbow Project: Enhancing the SAT through assessments of analytical, practical, and creative skills. *Intelligence, 34*, 321–350.

Sternberg, R. J., Torff, B., & Grigorenko, E. L. (1998). Teaching triachically improves school achievement. *Journal of Educational Psychology, 90*, 374–384.

Stevenson, H. W., & Lee, S. Y. (1990). Context of achievement. *Monographs of the Society for Research in Child Development, 55*(1–2, Serial No. 221).

Stiles, J. (2009). On genes, brains, and behavior: Why should developmental psychologists care about brain development? *Child Development Perspectives, 3*, 196–202.

Stiles, J., Brown, T. T., Haist, F., & Jernigan, T. L. (2015). Brain and cognitive development. In R. Lerner (Series Ed.) & L. Liben & U. Muller (Vol. Eds.), *Handbook of child psychology and developmental science: Vol. 2. Cognitive processes* (7th ed., pp. 9–62). Wiley: New York.

Stiles, J., Reilly, J. S., Levine, S. C., Trauner, D. A., & Nass, R. (2012). Neural plasticity and cognitive development: Insights from children with perinatal brain injury. New York: Oxford University Press.

Stipek, D. (1984). Young children's performance expectations: Logical analysis or wishful thinking? In J. G. Nicholls (Ed.), *Advances in motivation and achievement: The development of achievement motivation* (Vol. 3, pp. 33–56). Greenwich, CT: JAI.

Stipek, D., & Daniels, D. (1988). Declining perceptions of competence: A consequence of changes in the child or the educational environment? *Journal of Educational Psychology, 80,* 352–356.

Stipek, D., Feiler, R., Blyer, P., Ryan, R., Milburn, S., & Salmon, J. M. (1998). Good beginnings: What difference does the program make in preparing children for school. *Journal of Applied Developmental Psychology, 19,* 41–46.

Stipek, D., Feiler, R., Daniels, D., & Milburn, S. (1995). Effects of different instructional approaches on young children's achievement and motivation. *Child Development, 66,* 209–223.

Stock, R., Desoete, A., & Roeyers, H. (2009). Mastery of the counting principles in toddlers: A crucial step in the development of budding arithmetic abilities? *Learning and Individual Differences, 19,* 419–422.

Stoddart, T., & Turiel, E. (1985). Children's concepts of cross-gender activities. *Child Development, 56,* 1241–1252.

Stoel-Gammon, C., & Menn, L. (1997). Phonological development: Learning sounds and sound patterns. In J. Berko Gleason (Ed.), *The development of language* (4th ed., 69–121). Boston: Allyn & Bacon.

Stone, C. A., & Day, M. C. (1978). Levels of availability of a formal operational strategy. *Child Development, 49,* 1054–1065.

Stone, L. J., & Church, J. (1973). *Childhood and adolescence: A psychology of the growing person.* New York: Random House.

Stoolmiller, M. (1999). Implications of the restricted range of family environments for estimates of heritability and nonshared environment in behavior genetic adoption studies. *Psychological Bulletin, 125,* 393–407.

Storch, S. A., & Whitehurst, G. J. (2002). Oral language and code-related precursors to reading: Evidence from a longitudinal structural model. *Developmental Psychology, 38,* 934–947.

Strenze, T. (2007). Intelligence and socioeconomic success: A meta-analytic review of longitudinal research. *Intelligence, 35,* 401–426.

Streri, A., Lhote, M., & Dutilleul, S. (2000). Haptic perception in newborns. *Developmental Science, 3,* 319–327.

Streri, A., & Spelke, E. S. (1989). Effects of motion and figural goodness on haptic object perception in infancy. *Child Development, 60,* 1111–1125.

Striano, T., Tomasello, M., & Rochat, P. (2001). Social and object support for early symbolic play. *Developmental Science, 4,* 442–455.

Subbotsky, E., & Slater, E. (2011). Children's discrimination of fantastic vs realistic visual displays after watching a film with magical content. *Perceptual and Motor Skills, 112*(2), 603–609.

Subiaul, F., Winters, K., Krumpak, K., & Core, C. (2016). Vocal overimitation in preschool-age children. *Journal of Experimental Child Psychology, 141,* 145–160.

Suddendorf, T., & Corballis, M. C. (2007). The evolution of foresight: What is mental time travel, and is it unique to humans? *Behavioral and Brain Sciences, 30,* 299–313.

Sullivan, K., & Winner, E. (1993). Three-year-olds' understanding of mental states: The influence of trickery. *Journal of Experimental Child Psychology, 56,* 135–148.

Sullivan, M. W., Rovee-Collier, C. K., & Tynes, D. M. (1979). A conditioning analysis of infant long-term memory. *Child Development, 50,* 152–162.

Sundet, J. M., Eriksen, W., & Tambs, K. (2008). Intelligence correlations between brothers decrease with increasing age differences: Evidence for shared environmental effects in young adults. *Psychological Science, 19,* 843–847.

Suomi, S., & Harlow, H. (1972). Social rehabilitation of isolate-reared monkeys. *Developmental Psychology, 6,* 487–496.

Sussman, A. L. (2001). Reality monitoring of performed and imagined interactive events: Developmental and contextual effects. *Journal of Experimental Child Psychology, 79,* 115–138.

Suzuki, L. A., & Valencia, R. R. (1997). Race-ethnicity and measured intelligence: Educational implications. *American Psychologist, 52,* 1103–1114.

Swanson, H. L. (2011). Working memory, attention, and mathematical problem solving: A longitudinal study of elementary school children. *Journal of Educational Psychology, 103*(4), 821–837.

Swanson, H. L., & Jerman, O. (2007). The influence of working-memory on reading growth in subgroups of children with reading disabilities. *Journal of Experimental Child Psychology, 96,* 249–283.

Symons, D. K., Peterson, C. C., Slaughter, V., Roche, J., & Doyle, E. (2005). Theory of mind and mental state discourse during book reading and story-telling tasks. *British Journal of Developmental Psychology, 23,* 81–102.

Szkrybalo, J., & Ruble, D. N. (1999). "God made me a girl": Sex-category constancy judgments and explanations revisited. *Developmental Psychology, 35,* 393–402.

Szűcs, D., & Goswami, U. (2013). Developmental dyscalculia: Fresh perspectives. *Trends in Neuroscience and Education, 2*, 33–37.

Talwar, V., & Crossman, A. (2011). From little white lies to filthy liars: The evolution of honesty and deception in young children. *Advances in Child Development and Behaviour, 40*(140), 139–179.

Tamis-LeMonda, C. S., & Bornstein, M. H. (1989). Habituation and maternal encouragement of attention in infancy as predictors of toddler language, play, and representational competence. *Child Development, 60*, 738–751.

Tanner, J. M. (1978). *Fetus into man: Physical growth from conception to maturity.* Cambridge, MA: Harvard University Press.

Tapia, J. C., & Lichtman, J. W. (2012). Synapse elimination. In L. R. Squire, D. Berg, F. E. Bloom, S. du Lac, A. Ghosh, & N. C. Spitzer (Eds.), *Fundamental neuroscience* (4th ed., pp. 437–455). New York: Elsevier.

Tardif, T., & Wellman, H. M. (2000). Acquisition of mental state language in Mandarin- and Cantonese-speaking children. *Developmental Psychology, 36*, 25–43.

Taumoepeau, M., & Ruffman, T. (2008). Stepping stones to others' minds: Maternal talk relates to child mental state language and emotion understanding at 15, 24 and 33 months. *Child Development, 19*, 284–302.

Taylor, M. J. (1999). *Imaginary companions and the children who create them.* New York: Oxford University Press.

Taylor, M. J., Batty, M., & Itier, R. J. (2004). The faces of development: A review of early face processing over childhood. *Journal of Cognitive Neuroscience, 16*, 1426–1442.

Teasdale, T. W., & Owen, D. R. (1989). Continuing secular increases in intelligence and a stable prevalence of high intelligence levels. *Intelligence, 13*, 255–262.

Teasdale, T. W., & Owen, D. R. (2008). Secular declines in cognitive test scores: A reversal of the Flynn effect. *Intelligence, 36*, 121–126.

Téglás, E., Vul, E., Girotto, V., Gonzalez, M., Tenenbaum, J., & Bonatti, L. L. (2011). Pure reasoning in 12-month-old infants as probabilistic inference. *Science, 332*(6033), 1054–1059.

Terman, L. M., & Merrill, M. A. (1937). *Measuring intelligence.* Boston: Houghton Mifflin.

Thaler, N. S., & Jones-Forrester, S. (2012). IQ testing and the Hispanic client. In L. T. Benuto (Ed.), *Guide to psychological assessment with Hispanics* (pp. 81–98). New York: Springer.

Thibaut, J.-P., French, R. M., & Vezneva, M. (2010). The development of analogy-making in children: Cognitive load and executive function. *Journal of Experimental Child Psychology, 106*, 1–19.

Thibodeau, R. B., Gilpin, A. T., Brown, M. M., & Myers, B. A. (2016). The effects of fantastical pretend-play on the development of executive functions: An intervention study. *Journal of Experimental Child Psychology, 145*, 120–138.

Thierry, K. L., & Spence, M. J. (2002). Source-monitoring training facilitates preschoolers' eyewitness memory performance. *Developmental Psychology, 38*, 428–437.

Thomas, L. (1993). *The fragile species.* New York: Charles Scribner's Sons.

Thomas, S. C., & Johnson, M. H. (2008). New advances in understanding sensitive periods in brain development. *Current Directions in Psychology Science, 17*, 1–5.

Thompson, J. R., & Chapman, R. S. (1977). Who is "Daddy" revisited? The status of two-year-olds' overextended words in use and comprehension. *Journal of Child Language, 4*, 359–375.

Timney, B., Mitchell, D. E., & Cynader, M. (1980). Behavioral evidence for prolonged sensitivity to effects of monocular deprivation in dark-reared cats. *Journal of Neurophysiology, 43*, 1041–1054.

Tinbergen, N. (1951). *The study of instinct.* New York: Oxford University Press.

Tomasello, M. (1999). *The cultural origins of human cognition.* Cambridge, MA: Harvard University Press.

Tomasello, M. (2000). Culture and cognitive development. *Current Directions in Psychological Science, 9*, 37–40.

Tomasello, M. (2005). *Constructing a language: A usage-based theory of language acquisition.* Cambridge, MA: Harvard University Press.

Tomasello, M. (2006). Acquiring linguistic constructions. In W. Damon & R. M. Lerner (Series Eds.) & D. Kuhn & R. S. Siegler (Vol. Eds.), *Handbook of child psychology: Vol. 2. Cognition, perception, and language* (6th ed., pp. 255–298). New York: Wiley.

Tomasello, M. (2009). *Why we cooperate.* New York: Bradford.

Tomasello, M. (2014). *A natural history of human thinking.* Cambridge, MA: Harvard University Press.

Tomasello, M. (2016). Cultural learning redux. *Child Development, 87*, 643–653.

Tomasello, M., & Carpenter, M. (2007). Shared intentionality. *Developmental Science, 10*, 121–125.

Tomasello, M., Carpenter, M., & Liszkowski, U. (2007). A new look at infant pointing. *Child Development, 78*(3), 705–722.

Tomasello, M., Kruger, A. C., & Ratner, H. H. (1993). Cultural learning. *Behavioral and Brain Sciences, 16*, 495–511.

Tommasi, M., Pezzuti, L., Colomb, R., Francisco J., Abad, F. J., Saggino, A., & Orsini, A. (2015). Increased educational level is related with higher IQ scores but lower g-variance: Evidence from the standardization of the WAIS-R for Italy. *Intelligence, 50,* 68–74.

Tondel, G. M., & Candy, T. R. (2008). Accommodation and vergence latencies in human infants. *Vision Research, 48,* 564–576.

Tonkova-Yompol'skaya, R. V. (1969). Development of speech intonation in infants during the first two years of life. *Soviet Psychology, 7,* 48–54.

Tooby, J., & Cosmides, L. (1992). The psychological foundations of culture. In J. H. Barkow, L. Cosmides, & J. Tooby (Eds.), *The adapted mind: Evolutionary psychology and the generation of culture* (pp. 19–136). New York: Oxford University Press.

Tooby, J., & Cosmides, L. (2005). Conceptual foundations of evolutionary psychology. In D. M. Buss (Ed.), *Handbook of evolutionary psychology* (pp. 5–67). Hoboken, NJ: Wiley.

Toth, J. P. (2000). Nonconscious forms of human memory. In E. Tulving & F. I. M. Craik (Eds.), *The Oxford handbook of memory* (pp. 245–261). New York: Oxford University Press.

Tottenham, N., Hare, T. A., Quinn, B. T., McCarry, T. W., Nurse, M., Gilhooly, T., . . . Casey, B. J. (2010). Prolonged institutional rearing is associated with atypically large amygdala volume and difficulties in emotional regulation. *Developmental Science, 13,* 46–61.

Toub, T. S., Rajan, V., Golinkoff, R. M., & Hirsh-Pasek, K. (2016). Guide play: A solution to the play versus discovery learning dichotomy. In D. C. Geary & D. B. Berch (Eds.), *Evolutionary perspectives on education and child development* (pp. 117–141). New York: Springer.

Trahan, L. H., Stuebing, K. K., Fletcher, J. M., & Hiscock, M. (2014). The Flynn effect: A meta-analysis. *Psychological Bulletin, 140,* 1332–1360.

Trainor, L. J. (1996). Infant preferences for infant-directed versus noninfant-directed playsongs and lullabies. *Infant Behavior and Development, 19,* 83–92.

Trainor, L. J., Austin, C. M., & Desjardins, R. N. (2000). Is infant-directed speech prosody a result of the vocal expression of emotion? *Psychological Science, 11,* 188–195.

Trehub, S. E. (1976). The discrimination of foreign speech contrasts by infants and adults. *Child Development, 47,* 466–472.

Trehub, S. E. (2003). The developmental origins of musicality. *Nature Neuroscience, 6,* 669–673.

Trehub, S. E., & Nakata, T. (2001–2002). Emotion and music in infancy [Special issue]. *Musicae Scientiae, 5*(1), 37–61.

Trehub, S. E., & Schellenberg, E. G. (1995). Music: Its relevance to infants. *Annals of Child Development, 11,* 1–24.

Trehub, S. E., Trainor, L. J., & Unyk, A. M. (1993). Music and speech processing in the first year of life. In H. W. Reese (Ed.), *Advances in child development and behavior* (Vol. 24, pp. 2–35). San Diego, CA: Academic.

Trieman, R., Cohen, J., Mulqueeny, K., Kessler, B., & Schechtman, S. (2007). Young children's knowledge about printed names. *Child Development, 78,* 1458–1471.

Trionfi, G., & Reese, E. (2009). A good story: Children with imaginary companions create richer narratives. *Child Development, 80,* 1301–1313.

Tsao, F.-M., Liu, H.-M., & Kuhl, P. K. (2004). Speech perception in infancy predicts language development in the second year of life: A longitudinal study. *Child Development, 75,* 1067–1084.

Tucker-Drob, E. M., Rhemtulla, M., Harden, K. P., Turkheimer, E., & Fisk, D. (2011). Emergence of a gene x socioeconomic status interaction on infant mental ability between 10 months and 2 years. *Psychological Science, 22,* 125–133.

Tudge, J., Putnam, S., & Valsiner, J. (1996). Culture and cognition in developmental perspective. In R. B. Cairns, G. H. Elder Jr., & E. J. Costello (Eds.), *Developmental science* (pp. 190–222). New York: Cambridge University Press.

Tulkin, S. R., & Konner, M. J. (1973). Alternative conceptions of intellectual functioning. *Human Development, 16*(1–2), 33–52.

Tulving, E. (1987). Multiple memory systems and consciousness. *Human Neurobiology, 6,* 67–80.

Tulving, E. (2005). Episodic memory and autonoesis: Uniquely human? In H. S. Terrace & J. Metcalfe (Eds.), *The missing link in cognition: Origins of self-reflective consciousness* (pp. 3–56). New York: Oxford University Press.

Turati, C. (2004). Why faces are not special to newborns: An alternative account of the face preference. *Current Directions in Psychological Science, 13,* 5–8.

Turati, C., Simion, F., Milani, I., & Umiltà, C. (2002). Newborns' preference for faces: What is crucial? *Developmental Psychology, 38*(6), 875–882.

Turkewitz, G., & Kenny, P. (1982). Limitations on input as a basis for neural organization and perceptual development: A preliminary theoretical statement. *Developmental Psychobiology, 15,* 357–368.

Turkheimer, E., Haley, A., Waldron, M., D'onofrio, B., & Gottesman, I. I. (2003). Sociometric status modifies heritability of IQ in young children. *Psychological Science, 14,* 623–628.

Turkheimer, E., & Waldron, M. (2000). Nonshared environment: A theoretical, methodological, and quantitative review. *Psychological Bulletin, 126,* 78–108.

Turnbull, M., Hart, D., & Lapkin, S. (2003). Grade 6 French immersion students' performance on large-scale literacy and mathematics: Exploring two hypotheses. *Alberta Journal of Educational Research, 49*, 6–23.

Turner, A. M., & Greenough, W. T. (1985). Differential rearing effects on rat visual cortex synapses. I. Synaptic and neuronal density and synapses per neuron. *Brain Research, 329*, 195–203.

Tustin, K., & Hayne, H. (2010). Defining the boundary: Age-related changes in childhood amnesia. *Developmental Psychology, 46*, 1049–1061.

Tversky, A., & Kahneman, D. (1973). Availability—heuristic for judging frequency and probability. *Cognitive Psychology, 5*, 207–232.

Tzourio-Mazoyer, N., De Schonen, S., Crivello, F., Reutter, B., Aujard, Y., & Mazoyer, B. (2002). Neural correlates of woman face processing by 2-month-old infants. *NeuroImage, 15*, 454–461.

Ungerer, J. A., Zelazo, P. R., Kearsley, R. B., & O'Leary, K. (1981). Developmental changes in the representation of objects in symbolic play from 18 to 34 months of age. *Child Development, 52*, 186–195.

U.S. Census Bureau. (2014). *Measuring America: Computer and Internet trends in America*. Retrieved from https://www.census.gov/hhes/computer/files/2012/Computer_Use_Infographic_FINAL

Usher, J. A., & Neisser, U. (1993). Childhood amnesia and the beginnings of memory for four early life events. *Journal of Experimental Psychology: General, 122*, 155–165.

Uttal, D. H. (2000). Seeing the big picture: Map use and the development of spatial cognition. *Developmental Science, 3*, 247–286.

Uttal, D. H., Fisher, J. A., & Taylor, H. A. (2006). Words and maps: Developmental changes in mental models of spatial information acquired from descriptions and depictions. *Developmental Science, 9*, 221–235.

Uttal, D. H., Meadow, N., Tipton, E., Hand, L., Alden, A., & Warren, C. (2013). The malleability of spatial skills: A meta-analysis of training studies. *Psychological Bulletin, 139*(2), 352–402.

Uttal, D. H., & Wellman, H. M. (1989). Young children's representation of spatial information acquired from maps. *Developmental Psychology, 25*, 128–138.

Uzgiris, I. C. (1964). Situational generality of conservation. *Child Development, 35*, 831–841.

Uzgiris, I. C., & Hunt, J. McV. (1975). *Assessment in infancy: Ordinal scales of psychological development*. Urbana, IL: University of Illinois Press.

Vaden, V. C., & Woolley, J. D. (2011). Does God make it real? Children's belief in religious stories from the Judeo-Christian tradition. *Child Development, 82*, 1120–1135.

Valdez-Menchaca, M. C., & Whitehurst, G. J. (1992). Accelerating language development through picture book reading: A systematic extension to Mexican day care. *Developmental Psychology, 28*, 1106–1114.

Valenza, E., & Bulf, H. (2011). Early development of object unity: Evidence for perceptual completion in newborns. *Developmental Science, 14*, 799–808.

Vandell, D. L., Belsky, J., Burchinal, M., Steinberg, L., Vandergrift, N., & and the NICHD Early Child Care Research Network. (2010). Do effects of early child care extend to age 15 years? Results from the NICHD Study of Early Child Care and Youth Development. *Child Development, 81*, 737–756.

Vander Linde, E., Morrongiello, B. A., & Rovee-Collier, C. (1985). Determinants of retention in 8-week-old infants. *Developmental Psychology, 21*, 601–613.

Vandermaas-Peeler, M., Boomgarden, E., Finn, L., & Pittard, C. (2012). Parental support of numeracy during a cooking activity with four-year-olds. *International Journal of Early Years Education, 20*, 78–93.

van der Ven, S. H. G., Boom, J., Kroesnergen, E. H. J., & Leseman, P. M. (2012). Microgenetic patterns of children's multiplication learning: Confirming the overlapping wave model by latent growth modeling. *Journal of Experimental Child Psychology, 113*, 1–19.

van IJzendoorn, M. H., & Juffer, F. (2005). Adoption is a successful natural intervention enhancing adopted children's IQ and school performance. *Current Directions in Psychological Science, 14*, 326–330.

van IJzendoorn, M. H., Juffer, F., & Poelhuis, C. W. K. (2005). Adoption and cognitive development: A meta-analytic comparison of adopted and nonadopted children's IQ and school performance. *Psychological Bulletin, 131*, 301–316.

Van Loosbroek, E., & Smitsman, A. W. (1990). Visual perception of numerosity in infancy. *Developmental Psychology, 26*, 916–922.

Van Valin, R. D. (2002). The development of subject-auxiliary inversion in English wh-questions: An alternative analysis. *Journal of Child Language, 29*, 161–175.

Varnhagen, C. K., Morrison, F. J., & Everall, R. (1994). Age and schooling effects in story recall and story production. *Developmental Psychology, 30*, 969–979.

Varnum, M. E., Grossmann, I., Kltayama, S., & Nisbett, R. E. (2010). The origin of cultural differences in cognition: The social orientation hypothesis. *Current Directions in Psychological Science, 19*, 9–13.

Vartanian, L. R. (2000). Revisiting the imaginary audience and personal fable constructs of adolescent egocentrism: A conceptual review. *Adolescence, 35*, 639–661.

Vasilyeva, M., Duffy, S., & Huttenlocher, J. (2007). Developmental changes in the use of absolute and relative information: The case of spatial extent. *Journal of Cognition and Development, 8,* 455–471.

Vasilyeva, M., Laski, E. V., Ermakova, A., Lai, W.-F., Jeong, Y., & Hachigian, A. (2015). Re-examining the language account of cross-national differences in base-10 number representations. *Journal of Experimental Child Psychology, 129,* 12–25.

Vasilyeva, M., & Lourenco, S. F. (2012). Development of spatial cognition. *Wiley Interdisciplinary Reviews: Cognitive Science, 3*(3), 349–362.

Vasta, R., & Liben, L. S. (1996). The water-level task: An intriguing puzzle. *Current Directions in Psychological Science, 5,* 171–177.

Vellutino, F. R., & Scanlon, D. M. (1985). Free recall of concrete and abstract words in poor and normal readers. *Journal of Experimental Child Psychology, 39,* 363–380.

Venter, J. C., Adams, M. D., Myers, E. W., Li, P. W., Mural, R. J., Sutton, G. G., . . . Zhu, X. (2001). The sequence of the human genome. *Science, 291,* 1304–1351.

Verdine, B. N., Irwin, C. M., Golinkoff, R. M., & Hirsh-Pasel, K. (2014). Contributions of executive function and spatial skills to preschool mathemtics achievement. *Journal of Experimental Child Psychology, 126,* 37–51.

Vernon, P. E., & Kantor, L. (1986). Reaction time correlations with intelligence test scores obtained under either timed or untimed conditions. *Intelligence, 10,* 315–330.

Vernon-Feagans, L., Willoughby, M., Garrett-Pewters, P., & The Family Life Project Key Investigators. (2016). Predictors of behavioral regulation in kindergarten: Household chaos, parenting, and early executive functions. *Developmental Psychology, 52,* 430–441.

Vinter, A. (1986). The role of movement in eliciting early imitations. *Child Development, 57,* 66–71.

Virtala, P., Huotilainen, M., Partanen, E., Fellman, V., & Tervaniemi, M. (2013). Newborn infants' auditory system is sensitive to Western music chord categories. *Frontiers in Psychology, 4,* 492–501.

Voigt, B., Aberle, I., Schönfeld, J., & Kliegel, M. (2015). Time-based prospective memory in schoolchildren. *Zeitschrift für Psychologie, 38,* 162–174.

Volbert, R. (2000). Sexual knowledge of preschool children. *Journal of Psychology and Human Sexuality, 12,* 22–48.

Volkow, N. (2007, April). *Drug addiction: A brain developmental disorder: Adolescence-typical alcohol sensitivities and intake.* Invited address presented at meeting of the Society for Research in Child Development, Boston.

Volpe, J. J. (2000). Overview: Normal and abnormal human brain development. *Mental Retardation and Developmental Disabilities Research Reviews, 6,* 1–5.

von Stumm, S., & Plomin, R. (2015). Socioeconomic status and the growth of intelligence from infancy through adolescence. *Intelligence, 48,* 30–36.

Vouloumanos, A., & Curtin, S. (2014). Foundational tuning: How infants' attention to speech predicts language development. *Cognitive Science, 38*(8), 1675–1686.

Vouloumanos, A., Hauser, M., Werker, J., & Martin, A. (2010). The tuning of human neonates preference for speech. *Child Development, 81*(2), 517–527.

Vouloumanos, A., & Waxman, S. (2014). Listen up! Speech is for thinking during infancy. *Trends in Cognitive Sciences, 18*(12), 642–646.

Vouloumanos, A., & Werker, J. F. (2007). Listening to language at birth: Evidence for a bias for speech in neonates. *Developmental Science, 10,* 159–171.

Voyer, D., & Voyer, S. D. (2014). Gender differences in scholastic achievement: A meta-analysis. *Psychological Bulletin, 140,* 1174–2104.

Vukovic, R. V., Fuchs, L. S., Geary, D. C., Jordan, N. C., Gersten, R., & Siegler, R. S. (2014). Sources of individual differences in children's understanding of fractions. *Child Development, 85,* 1461–1476.

Vygotsky, L. S. (1962). *Thought and language.* Cambridge, MA: MIT Press.

Vygotsky, L. S. (1978). *Mind in society: The development of higher psychological processes.* Cambridge, MA: Harvard University Press.

Vygotsky, L. S. (1981). The genesis of higher mental functions. In J. V. Wertsch (Ed.), *The concept of activity in Soviet psychology* (pp. 144–188). Armonk, NY: Sharpe.

Wagner, R. K., Torgesen, J. K., Rashotte, C. A., Hecht, S. A., Barker, T. A., Burgess, S. R., . . . Garon, T. (1997). Changing relations between phonological processing abilities and word level reading as children develop from beginning to skilled readers: A 5-year longitudinal study. *Developmental Psychology, 33,* 468–479.

Walker, T. (2014). How Finland keeps kids focused through free play. *The Atlantic.* Retrieved from http://www.theatlantic.com/education/archive/2014/06/how-finland-keeps-kids-focused/373544

Walsh, M. (2014, June 3). This poor child is confused, not "transgendered." Retrieved from http://themattwalshblog.com/2014/06/03/this-poor-child-is-confused-not-transgendered/

Walton, G. E., Bower, N. J. A., & Bower, T. G. R. (1992). Recognition of familiar faces by newborns. *Infant Behavior and Development, 15,* 265–269.

Wang, Q. (2001). Culture effects on adults' earliest childhood recollection and self-description: Implications for the relation between memory and the self. *Journal of Personality and Social Psychology, 81,* 220–233.

Wang, Q. (2006). Earliest recollections of self and others in European American and Taiwanese young adults. *Psychological Science, 17*, 708–714.

Wang, Q. (2014). The cultured self and remembering. In P. J. Bauer & R. Fivush (Eds.), *The Wiley handbook on the development of children's memory* (Vol. 2, pp. 605–625). Chichester, UK: Wiley-Blackwell.

Wang, S., Baillargeon, R., & Paterson, S. (2005). Detecting continuity violations in infancy: A new account and new evidence from covering and tube events. *Cognition, 95*, 129–173.

Wang, S., & Gathercole, S. (2013). Working memory deficits in children with reading difficulties: Memory span and dual task coordination. *Journal of Experimental Child Psychology, 115*, 188–197.

Wang, S., Kaufman, L., & Baillargeon, R. (2003). Should all stationary objects move when hit? Developments in infants' causal and statistical expectations about collision events. *Infant Behavior and Development, 26*, 529–567.

Want, S. C., & Harris, P. L. (2001). Learning from other peoples' mistakes: Causal understanding in learning to use a tool. *Child Development, 72*, 431–443.

Ward, J. (2015). *The student's guide to cognitive neuroscience* (3rd ed.). New York: Psychology Press.

Warneken, F., & Tomasello, M. (2006). Altruistic helping in human infants and young chimpanzees. *Science, 311*, 1301–1303.

Warren, A. R., & McCloskey, L. A. (1997). Language in social contexts. In J. Berko Gleason (Ed.), *The development of language* (4th ed., pp. 210–258). Boston: Allyn & Bacon.

Warren, A. R., & Tate, C. S. (1992). Egocentrism in children's telephone conversations: Recent evidence regarding Piaget's position. In R. Diaz & L. Berk (Eds.), *From social interaction to self-regulation* (pp. 245–264). Hillsdale, NJ: Erlbaum.

Warren-Leubecker, A., & Bohannon, J. N. (1989). Pragmatics: Language in social context. In J. B. Berko Gleason (Ed.), *The development of language* (2nd ed., pp. 327–368). Columbus, OH: Charles E. Merrill.

Wartenburger, I., Heekereb, H. R., Abutalebi, J., Cappa, S. F., Villringer, A., & Perani, D. (2003). Early setting of grammatical processing in the bilingual brain. *Neuron, 37*, 159–170.

Wason, P., & Johnson-Laird, P. (1972). *Psychology of reasoning: Structure and content.* Cambridge, MA: Harvard University Press.

Waterhouse, L. (2006). Inadequate evidence for multiple intelligences, Mozart effect, and emotional intelligence theories. *Educational Psychologist, 41*(4), 247–255.

Waters, H. S., & Kunnman, T. W. (2009). Metacognition and strategy discovery in early childhood. In H. S. Waters & W. Schneider (Eds.), *Metacognition, strategy use, and instruction* (pp. 3–22). New York: Guilford Press.

Watkins, M. W., Lei, P., & Canivez, G. L. (2007). Psychometric intelligence and achievement: A cross-lagged panel analysis. *Intelligence, 35*, 59–68.

Webb, S. J., & Nelson, C. A. (2001). Perceptual priming of upright and inverted faces in children and adults. *Journal of Experimental Child Psychology, 79*, 1–22.

Wechsler, D. (2004). *The Wechsler intelligence scale for children—fourth edition.* London: Pearson Assessment.

Weikum, W. M., Vouloumanos, A., Navarra, J., Soto-Faraco, S., Sebastian-Galles, N., & Werker, J. F. (2007). Visual language discrimination in infancy. *Science, 316*, 1159.

Weinberg, R. A., Scarr, S., & Waldman, I. D. (1992). The Minnesota Transracial Adoption Study: A follow-up of IQ test performance at adolescence. *Intelligence, 16*, 117–135.

Weinert, F. E., & Schneider, W. (1992). *The Munich Longitudinal Study on the Genesis of Individual Competencies (LOGIC).* Munich, Germany: Max Planck Institute for Psychological Research.

Welch, M. K. (1999). Preschoolers' understanding of mind: Implications for suggestibility. *Cognitive Development, 14*, 101–131.

Wellman, H. M. (1988). The early development of memory strategies. In F. Weinert & M. Perlmutter (Eds.), *Memory development: Universal changes and individual differences* (pp. 3–29). Hillsdale, NJ: Erlbaum.

Wellman, H. M. (1990). *The child's theory of mind.* Cambridge, MA: MIT Press.

Wellman, H. M. (2011). Reinvigorating explanations for the study of early cognitive development. *Child Development Perspectives, 5*, 33–38.

Wellman, H. M., Cross, D., & Watson, J. (2001). Meta-analysis of theory-of-mind development: The truth about false belief. *Child Development, 72*, 655–684.

Wellman, H. M., & Lempers, J. D. (1977). The naturalistic communication abilities of two-year-olds. *Child Development, 48*, 1052–1057.

Wertsch, J. V., & Tulviste, P. (1992). L. S. Vygotsky and contemporary developmental psychology. *Developmental Psychology, 28*, 548–557.

Wexler-Sherman, C., Gardner, H., & Feldman, D. H. (1988). A pluralistic view of early assessment: The Project Spectrum approach. *Theory Into Practice, 27*, 77–83.

Wheldall, K., & Joseph, R. (1986). Young black children's sentence comprehension skills: A comparison of performance in standard English and Jamaican Creole. *First Language, 6*, 149–154.

White, S., Milne, E., Rosen, S., Hansen, P., Swettenham, J., Frith, U., & Ramus, F. (2006). The role of sensorimotor impairments in dyslexia: A multiple case study of dyslexic children. *Developmental Science, 9,* 237–269.

White, S. H. (2000). Conceptual foundations of IQ testing. *Psychology, Public Policy, and Law, 6,* 33–43.

Whitehurst, G. J., Falco, F., Lonigan, C. J., Fischal, J. E., DeBaryshe, B. D., Valdez-Manchaca, M. C., & Caufield, M. (1988). Accelerating language development through picture book reading. *Developmental Psychology, 24,* 552–559.

Whitehurst, G. J., & Lonigan, C. J. (1998). Child development and emergent literacy. *Child Development, 69,* 848–872.

Whitehurst, G. J., & Sonnenschein, S. (1985). The development of communication: A functional analysis. In G. J. Whitehurst (Ed.), *Annals of child development* (Vol. 2, pp. 1–48). Greenwich, CT: JAI.

Whiten, A., & Flynn, E. G. (2010). The transmission and evolution of experimental "microcultures" in groups of young children. *Developmental Psychology, 46,* 1694–1709.

Whiten, A., McGuigan, N., Marshall-Pescini, S., & Hopper, L. M. (2009). Emulation, imitation, over-imitation and the scope of culture for child and chimpanzee. *Philosophical Transactions of the Royal Society of London: Biological Sciences, 364,* 2417–2428.

Whitham, J. C., Gerald, M. S., Santiago, C., & Maestripieri, D. (2007). Intended receivers and functional significance of grunt and girney vocalizations in free-ranging female rhesus macaques. *Ethology, 113,* 862–874.

Wickelgren, L. (1967). Convergence in the human newborn. *Journal of Experimental Child Psychology, 5,* 74–85.

Wiebe, S. A., Sheffield, T., Nelson, J. M., Clark, C. A., Chevalier, N., & Espy, K. A. (2011). The structure of executive function in 3-year-olds. *Journal of Experimental Child Psychology, 108*(3), 436–452.

Wilcox, J., & Webster, E. (1980). Early discourse behavior: An analysis of children's responses to listener feedback. *Child Development, 51,* 1120–1125.

Wilcox, T., & Chapa, C. (2004). Priming infants to use color and pattern information in an individuation task. *Cognition, 90,* 265–302.

Willatts, P. (1990). Development of problem-solving strategies in infancy. In D. F. Bjorklund (Ed.), *Children's strategies: Contemporary views of cognitive development* (pp. 23–66). Hillsdale, NJ: Erlbaum.

Williams, J. H., Whiten, A., Suddendorf, T., & Perrett, D. I. (2001). Imitation, mirror neurons and autism. *Neuroscience & Bio-behavioral Review, 25,* 287–295.

Williamson, R. A., & Markman, E. M. (2006). Precision of imitation as a function of preschoolers' understanding of the goal of the demonstration. *Developmental Psychology, 42,* 723–731.

Wilson, S. P., & Kipp, K. (1998). The development of efficient inhibition: Evidence from directed-forgetting tasks. *Developmental Review, 18,* 86–123.

Wimmer, H., & Perner, J. (1983). Beliefs about beliefs: Representation and constraining function of wrong beliefs in young children's understanding of deception. *Cognition, 13,* 103–128.

Wimmer, M. C., & Howe, M. L. (2010). Are children's memory illusions created differently than adults'? Evidence from levels-of-processing and divided attention paradigms. *Journal of Experimental Child Psychology, 107,* 31–49.

Windsor, J., Benigno, J. P., Wing, C. A., Carroll, P. J., Koga, S. F., Nelson, C. A., . . . Zeanah, C. H. (2011). Effect of foster care on young children's language learning. *Child Development, 82,* 1040–1046.

Winer, G. A. (1980). Class-inclusion reasoning in children: A review of the empirical literature. *Child Development, 51,* 309–328.

Winick, M., Meyer, K. K., & Harris, R. C. (1975). Malnutrition and environmental enrichment by early adoption. *Science, 190,* 1173–1175.

Winsler, A. (2003). Overt and covert verbal problem-solving strategies: Developmental trends in use, awareness, and relations with task performance in children age 5 to 17. *Child Development, 74,* 659–678.

Winsler, A., Fernyhough, C., & Montero, I. (Eds.). (2009). *Private speech, executive functioning, and the development of verbal self-regulation.* Cambridge, UK: Cambridge University Press.

Witelson, S. F. (1985). On hemisphere specialization and cerebral plasticity from birth: Mark II. In C. Best (Ed.), *Hemispheric function and collaboration in the child* (pp. 33–85). New York: Academic.

Witelson, S. F. (1987). Neurobiological aspects of language in children. *Child Development, 58,* 653–688.

Wood, D., Bruner, J. S., & Ross, G. (1976). The role of tutoring in problem-solving. *Journal of Child Psychology and Psychiatry, 17,* 89–100.

Wood, J. N., & Spelke, E. S. (2005). Infants' enumeration of actions: Numerical discrimination and its signature limits. *Developmental Science, 8,* 173–181.

Woods, B. T., & Carey, S. (1979). Language deficits after apparent clinical recovery from childhood aphasia. *Annals of Neurology, 6,* 405–409.

Woody-Dorning, J., & Miller, P. H. (2001). Children's individual differences in capacity: Effects on strategy production and utilization. *British Journal of Developmental Psychology, 19,* 543–557.

Woolley, J. D. (1997). Thinking about fantasy: Are children fundamentally different thinkers and believers from adults? *Child Development, 68,* 991–1011.

Woolley, J. D., & Boerger, E. A. (2002). Development of beliefs about the origins of controllability of dreams. *Developmental Psychology, 38,* 24–41.

Woolley, J. D., Boerger, E. A., & Markman, A. B. (2004). A visit from the Candy Witch: Factors influencing young children's belief in a novel fantastical being. *Developmental Science, 7,* 456–468.

Woolley, J. D., & Ghossainy, M. E. (2013). Revisiting the fantasy-reality distinction: Children as naive skeptics. *Child Development, 84*(5), 1496–1510.

Woolley, J. D., & Wellman, H. M. (1992). Children's conceptions of dreams. *Cognitive Development, 7,* 365–380.

Woumans, E., Santens, P., Sieben, A., & Duyck, W. (2015). Bilingualism delays clinical manifestation of Alzheimer's disease. *Bilingualism: Language and Cognition, 18,* 568–574.

Wynn, K. (1992). Addition and subtraction by human infants. *Nature, 358,* 749–750.

Xu, F., Spelke, E. S., & Goddad, S. (2005). Number sense in infants. *Developmental Science, 8,* 88–101.

Yang, T. X., Chan, R. C., & Shum, D. (2011). The development of prospective memory in typically developing children. *Neuropsychology, 25*(3), 342–352.

Yeats, K. O., & Taylor, G. H. (2005). Neurobehavioral outcomes of mild head injury in children and adolescents. *Pediatric Rehabilitation, 8,* 5–16.

Yogman, M. W., Kindlon, D., & Earls, F. (1995). Father involvement and cognitive/behavioral outcomes of preterm infants. *Journal of the American Academy of Child and Adolescent Psychiatry, 34,* 58–66.

Yoon, J. M., & Johnson, S. C. (2009). Biological motion displays elicit social behavior in 12-month-olds. *Child Development, 80,* 1069–1975.

Youngblade, L. M., & Dunn, J. (1995). Individual differences in young children's pretend play with mother and sibling: Links to relationships and understanding of other people's feelings and beliefs. *Child Development, 66,* 1472–1492.

Younger, B., & Gottlieb, S. (1988). Development of categorization skills: Changes in the nature or structure of infant form categories? *Developmental Psychology, 24,* 611–619.

Zack, E., Barr, R., Gerhardstein, P., Dickerson, K., & Meltzoff, A. N. (2009). Infant imitation from television using novel touch-screen technology. *British Journal of Developmental Psychology, 27,* 13–16.

Žebec, M. S., Demetriou, A., & Kotrla-Topić, M. (2015). Changing expressions of general intelligence in development: A 2-wave longitudinal study from 7 to 18 years of age. *Intelligence, 49,* 94–109.

Zelazo, P. D. (2006). The Dimensional Change Card Sort (DCCS): A method of assessing executive function in children. *Nature Protocols–Electronic Edition, 1*(1), 297–301.

Zelazo, P. D. (2015). Executive function: Reflection, iterative reprocessing, complexity, and the developing brain. *Developmental Review, 38,* 55–68.

Zelazo, P. D., & Boseovski, J. J. (2001). Video reminders in a representational change task: Memory for cues but not beliefs or statements. *Journal of Experimental Child Psychology, 78,* 107–129.

Zelazo, P. D., & Carlson, S. M. (2012). Hot and cool executive function in childhood and adolescence: Development and plasticity. *Child Development Perspectives, 6*(4), 354–360.

Zelazo, P. D., Frye, D., & Rapus, T. (1996). An age-related dissociation between knowing rules and using them. *Cognitive Development, 11,* 37–63.

Zelazo, P. D., Kearsley, R. B., & Stack, D. M. (1995). Mental representation for visual sequences: Increased speed of central processing from 22 to 32 months. *Intelligence, 20,* 41–63.

Zelazo, P. D., Müller, U., Frye, D., & Marcovitch, S. (2003). The development of executive function in early childhood: VI. The development of executive function: Cognitive complexity and control—revised. *Monographs of the Society for Research in Child Development, 68*(3, Serial No. 274).

Zeskind, P. S. (1996, April). *Infant crying: A biobehavioral synchrony between infants and caregivers.* Paper presented at the Conference on Human Development, Birmingham, AL.

Zeskind, P. S., & Ramey, C. T. (1978). Fetal malnutrition: An experimental study of its consequences on infant development in two caregiver environments. *Child Development, 49,* 1155–1162.

Zeskind, P. S., & Ramey, C. T. (1981). Sequelae of fetal malnutrition: A longitudinal, transactional, and synergistic approach. *Child Development, 52,* 213–218.

Zheng, X., Swanson, H. L., & Marcoulides, G. A. (2011). Working memory components as predictors of children's mathematical word problem solving. *Journal of Experimental Child Psychology, 110,* 481–498.

Zhou, X., Huang, J., Wang, B., Zhao, Z., Yang, L., & Zhengzheng, Y. (2006). Parent-child interaction and children's number learning. *Early Child Development and Care, 176,* 763–775.

Ziegler, J. C., & Goswami, U. (2005). Reading acquisition, developmental dyslexia, and skilled reading across languages: A psycholinguistic grain size theory. *Psychological Bulletin, 131,* 3–29.

Zimmerman, F. J., Christakis, D. A., & Meltzoff, A. N. (2007). Associations between media viewing and language development in children under age 2 years. *Journal of Pediatrics, 151,* 364–368.

Zimmerman, T. (Ed.). (2007). *Poverty and early childhood intervention.* Chapel Hill, NC: The Carolina Abecedarian Program.

Zisenwine, T., Kaplan, M., Kushnir, J., & Sadeh, A. (2013). Nighttime fears and fantasy-reality differentiation in preschool children. *Child Psychiatry and Human Development, 44,* 186–199.

Zmyj, N., & Bischof-Köhler, D. (2015). The development of gender constancy in early childhood and its relation to time comprehension and false-belief understanding. *Journal of Cognitive Development, 16,* 455–470.

Zuber, J., Pixner, S., Moeller, K., & Nuerk, H.-C. (2009). On the language-specificity of basic number processing: Transcoding in a language with inversion and its relation to working memory capacity. *Journal of Experimental Child Psychology, 102,* 60–77.

Zucker, K. J., Bradley, S. J., Kuksis, M., Pecore, K., Birkenfeld-Adams, A., Doering, R. W., . . . Wild, J. (1999). Gender constancy judgments in children with gender identity disorder: Evidence for a developmental lag. *Archives of Sexual Behavior, 28,* 475–502.

Zwicker, S., Moore, C., & Povinelli, D. (2012). The development of body representations: The integration of visual-proprioceptive information. In V. Slaughter and C. A. Ironwell (Eds.), *Early development of body representations* (pp. 19–36). Cambridge, MA: Cambridge University Press.

INDEX